I CHING

周易

I CHING

*The Classic Chinese
Oracle of Change*

*The First Complete
Translation With
Concordance*

TRANSLATED BY

RUDOLF RITSEMA

AND

STEPHEN KARCHER

ELEMENT

Shaftesbury, Dorset ∗ Rockport, Massachusetts ∗ Brisbane, Queensland

© Stephen Karcher and Rudolf Ritsema 1994

First published in Great Britain in 1994 by
ELEMENT BOOKS LIMITED
Shaftesbury, Dorset SP7 8BP

Published in the USA in 1994 by
ELEMENT BOOKS INC.
42 Broadway, Rockport, MA 01966

Published in Australia in 1994 by
ELEMENT BOOKS LIMITED
for Jacaranda Wiley Limited
33 Park Road, Milton, Brisbane, 4064

First paperback edition 1995

Designed and created by
THE BRIDGEWATER BOOK COMPANY

Rudolf Ritsema is an orientalist and President of the
Eranos Foundation, famed for it's seminars on Jungian psychology.
Stephen Karcher PhD is Co-Director of the Eranos *I Ching* Project.

Printed and bound in Great Britain by
REDWOOD BOOKS LTD

British Library Cataloguing in
Publication data available

Library of Congress Cataloguing in
Publication data available

ISBN 1-85230-669-6

The authors wish to thank the Eranos Foundation for its continuing support in memory of Olga Fröbe-Kapteyn and Alwina von Keller, who
inspired the Foundation's involvement with the *I Ching*. We also wish to
thank the many participants and friends in the conferences and seminars,
group and individual consultations, who gave of their insight, experience
and spirit in the shaping of this work.
Special thanks go to Ian Fenton for his editorial assistance and Element
Books for their care and sensitivity in this presentation.
The publishers wish to thank Valerie Hylton for drawing this project to
their attention.

One thousand copies of this book have been specially printed and bound
for distribution as the *Eranos Yearbook 62–1993* through *64–1995*

CONTENTS

PART ONE

周易

INTRODUCTION

WHAT IS THE *I CHING*?

The *I Ching* offers a way to see into difficult situations, particularly those emotionally charged ones where rational knowledge fails us yet we are called upon to decide and act. It gives voice to a spirit concerned with how we can best live as individuals in contact with both inner and outer worlds.

The *I Ching* is able to do this because it is an oracle. It is a particular kind of imaginative space set off for a dialogue with the gods or spirits, the creative basis of experience now called the unconscious. An oracle translates a problem or question brought to it into an image language like that of dreams. It changes the way you experience the situation in order to connect you with the inner forces that are shaping it. The oracle's images dissolve what is blocking the connection, making the spirits available.

This procedure is made for situations when you feel gripped by something behind the ordinary events of life. The *I Ching* portrays various sorts of crossroads. Its symbols make up a dictionary of the forces that move and change the soul. Working with these images dissolves your view of your situation and reforms awareness of these forces. The goal of this process is an intuitive clarity traditionally called *shen ming* or the *light of the gods*. It is a bright spirit that is creative, clear-seeing and connected.

Consulting an oracle and seeing yourself in terms of the symbols or magic spells it presents is a way of contacting what has been repressed in the creation of the modern world. It puts you back into what the ancients called the sea of soul by giving advice on attitudes and actions that lead to the experience of imaginative meaning. Oracular consultation insists on the importance of imagination. It is the heart of magic through which the living world speaks to you. The modern interest in alternative cultures and the old ways is a reflection of our need to recover this heart of magic, for it is the way our inner being speaks, thinks and acts.

The *I Ching* or *I* (pronounced "ee") was the fundamental text of traditional Chinese culture. It is a divinatory system with 3000 year old roots in the traditions of magic and shamanism. Nearly all that was significant in traditional China – philosophy, science, politics and popular culture – was founded on interpretations and adaptations of the *I*. The core of the book is the oldest and most complex divinatory system to survive into modern times.

This divinatory core is a set of 64 six-line figures or *kua*, usually called hexagrams, and a way to consult them. The figures represent all the possible combinations of six *opened* — — and *whole* —— lines. Each figure has a name and a group of short phrases associated with it. These combinations of texts and figures act like mirrors for the unconscious forces shaping any given moment, problem or situation. In traditional terms, the book provides symbols which comprehend the light of the gods, the unconscious forces that are creating what you experience. In itself still and unmoving, when stimulated by consultation the book produces an echo which can reach the depths, grasp the seeds, and penetrate the wills of all the beings under heaven.

The act of consultation is based upon chance, the random division of a set of 50 yarrow stalks or throwing and counting three coins six times. This chance event empowers a spirit beyond conscious control. It gives the forces behind your situation the chance to speak by singling out one or more of the book's symbols. Through this procedure, what you see as a problem to be mastered becomes a *sign* or *symbolic occurrence* that links you with another world. Like a shaman's drum and dance, these symbols can speak to you on many levels, beginning a creative process which, in traditional terms, completes the ceaseless activity of heaven. This is religion at its fundamental level. It reflects a sense of spirit that unites the great and the small, a spirit that moves in each individual.

These oracular texts only really come to life in the context of a particular situation. They refer to unique events that evade scientific laws and rules. Your question, your life, your problem provide the necessary catalyst that creates meaning. The magic occurs when, in a particular situation and through your particular experience, you ask the spirit for an image to guide you.

● *The Name of the Book*

The central concern of the *I Ching* is expressed by the key term in its name, *I*. Traditionally the book is simply called *I*. The second term, *ching*, denotes a classic or fundamental text. It means standard, channel through which something passes, loom. The *I Ching* is the classic, channel or loom of *I*. Though often translated as change or changes, *I* is neither orderly change – the change of the seasons, for example – nor the change of one thing into another, like water changing to ice or a caterpillar to a butterfly. Unpredictable and, as the tradition says, unfathomable, *I* originates in and

is a way of dealing with trouble. It articulates possible responses to fate, necessity or calamity – that which "crosses" your path.

The term *I* emphasizes imagination, openness and fluidity. It suggests the ability to change direction quickly and the use of a variety of imaginative stances to mirror the variety of being. The most adequate English translation of this is *versatility*, the ability to remain available to and be moved by the unforeseen demands of time, fate and psyche. This term interweaves the *I* of the cosmos, the *I* of the book, and your own *I*, if you use it.

I in the human world is understood in terms of three other themes, *tao*, *te*, and *chün tzu*. *Tao*, literally way, is the flow or stream of creative energy that makes life possible, the way *in which* everything happens and the way *on which* everything happens. *Te*, often translated as power or virtue, refers to the power to realize *tao* in action, to become what you are meant to be. A *chün tzu* is someone who seeks to acquire *te* through divination, to live connected with *tao*. The *I Ching*'s statements are invitations to a dialogue with the way, its power and its virtue. What the *chün tzu* finds through this dialogue is significance, the experience of spirit, meaning and connection.

The oldest name of this oracle was *Chou I*, for it was first developed as the *I* or versatility-book of the *Chou* kings (1100–400 BCE). Intrinsically, however, the term *chou* means universal, encompassing everything, moving in a circle. When stimulated by consultation, the *Chou I* describes the circle of events that connects the spirit world and the human heart. Using this book of magic spells is a way to encompass the ever-changing movement of *tao*. It is *Chou I, Encompassing Versatility*.

• *What is Divination?*

Antique civilization, both East and West, used divination and oracle to keep in contact with unseen powers. Sacrifices offered to the spirits and Gods were not just bribes or pleas. They opened communication between humans and spirits so a dialogue could take place.

The idea that words, things and events can become omens that open communication with a spirit-world is based on an insight into the way the psyche works – that in every symptom, conflict or problem we experience there is a spirit trying to communicate with us. Each encounter with trouble is an opening to this spirit, usually opposed by the ego because it wants to enforce its will on the world. Divination gives a voice to what the ego has rejected. It brings up the hidden complement or shadow of the situation in order to link you with the myths and spirits behind it. This changes the way you see yourself, your situation and the world around you.

Studies of divinatory systems in tribal cultures show that this process was and is consistently used to give information about individual questions, problems and choices for which rational knowledge or common social rules are not enough. It is the dark mirror that gives true answers, the place where the spirit of an individual can speak with all the other spirits in the world. These systems are often sponsored by an animal magician whose mysterious symbols offer an alternative to public laws and regulations. Some type of procedure using chance provides a gap through which this spirit expresses itself by picking out one of the available symbols. A final diagnosis and plan of action come out of the creative interaction between the symbol, the inquirer and the diviner, over which the spirit presides. This interaction breaks down the old stories you are telling yourself in order to make up more effective ones. It produces advice on how to act in harmony with the "spirit of the time."

Thus divination is not an ideology or a belief but a creative way of contacting the spirit. It is imagination perceiving forces and inventing ways to deal with them. This involves a combination of analysis and intuition that normal thinking usually keeps apart. This process values imagination and creativity. It shifts the way you make decisions.

Opening this space, where identity becomes fluid and the spirits involve themselves in your life, is the purpose of divination. Using a divinatory system is an exploration of the unconscious side of a situation. The symbols evoked adjust the balance between you and the unknown forces behind it.

The language is the key to the contact. The words are, as the Chinese say, "fish-traps" for spirit or *tao*.

● *Origin, History and Development
of the Classic of I*

The *I Ching* is the oldest and most complex divinatory system to survive the disenchantment of the ancient world. It represents a way of knowing common to both magical or pre-technological cultures and to the world we contact each night in dreams. Central to both is the idea that life requires a proper relation to the spirit-world.

The traditional story of the origin of the *I Ching* reflects this concern. In this account, the *I Ching* was created by three sage-kings who founded Chinese culture: Fu Hsi, King Wen and the Duke of Chou, his son.

Fu Hsi was the legendary First Emperor, a shaman, diviner, and magician. His rule represents the first Golden Age, when humans and spirits communicated freely. Fu Hsi contemplated the shapes of heaven, the patterns of the earth, bird and animal markings and the movements of his body and soul. Then he spontaneously brought forth the trigram figures of the *I Ching*. They were a way to organize the world and communicate with its spirits. Through this magical communication a constant influx of spirit kept the human world in order.

The second part of this story occurs in a declining era full of troubles, anxiety and sorrow. It centers on the conflict between Chou the Tyrant, the last king of the Shang Dynasty (1520–1030 BCE), and King Wen, a spiritual reformer and founder of the Chou Dynasty (1100–480 BCE). King Wen, literally King Writing or King Pattern, spent several years in Shang prisons. As a prisoner, he meditated on the distance between the Golden Age of Fu Hsi and the complicated world which had developed since. He sought to understand how the Golden Age might be recovered.

King Wen first re-arranged the eight trigram figures to reflect the complexity of the human world. He then combined them to create 64 hexagrams and added writing to the figures, giving each hexagram a name and a divinatory message. This was the new magic. His son, the Duke of Chou, added a commentary to the lines. The trigrams, hexagrams and texts became the *Chou I*, the Oracle Book of the Kings of Chou. The Chou nobles used this magic in their struggle to restore the Golden Age of Fu Hsi, and, once in power, to stay in contact with the spirits and the Way of Heaven.

This story, popularized in the Han Dynasty (200 BCE–220 CE), reflects the importance of the *I Ching*'s power to connect humans and spiritual forces, making "spirit power" and knowledge available. As such, it is mythically true. But modern scholarship has shown that the factual origins of the book are the reverse of this account. The oldest part of the book is words, not diagrams and systems. It is made up of omens, images and magic spells from an oral shamanistic, divinatory tradition. These phrases were assembled between 1000 and 750 BCE, probably first written down in connection with a simple system of whole and opened lines. At some point in this process the next level of symbolization emerged. This was the formation of the hexagrams, the six-line figures that display and organize the divinatory texts. Wu Hsien, literally the Conjoining Shaman, discovered a numerical system of organizing the texts and the yarrow-stalk method of consultation. The development of the trigrams as a means of correlating magical systems developed in the later Han Period.

One of the meanings of the term *I* relates to this practise. Among other things, *I* means easy. The Yarrow-stalk Oracle with its texts and figures was much easier to use than Ancient China's other oracle system, consulting the cracks a heated bronze rod produced in specially prepared tortoise shells or ox bones. It was this easy quality that led to the most important development in the history of the *I Ching*: its imaginative use by individuals outside the ruling family.

A gap of five to seven hundred years occurs between the oldest parts of the *I Ching* and the next layer of the text. During this time the personal use of the Oracle developed. The Warring States Period (500–200 BCE) was a golden age of imaginative thought, the most creative period in Chinese culture. The creative thinking sprang up, however, against a background of political fragmentation and violence.

The personal use of the Yarrow-stalk Oracle grew out of this period, when being in accord with the time and the spirits was often a matter of life and death. So, too, did the sense that the use of the book opened a way or path through the chaos of a crumbling social order. Most probably, a group of diviners and magicians assembled the texts and developed the hexagrams to make this more powerful spirit available. It created a faith in the individual connection to the images of the psyche and a hope that this connection could heal the time.

The political chaos finally ended with the emergence of the Han Dynasty (206 BCE–220 CE), which was the beginning of Imperial China. During the Han, culture was consolidated and re-defined. This process included the codification of writing and the establishment of the *Ching* or Classics of antiquity. The *Chou I* became the *I Ching* or *Classic of I*.

Cosmologists of the Han discovered the perfect symbolism for the numerical structure of both the cosmos and the human mind in the trigrams and hexagrams of the *I Ching*. Confucian thinkers, developing an imperial philosophy, created a social hierarchy for the lines and fixed interpretations of the texts. The system of the trigrams was expanded in this period to explain the hexagram structure and to link it with other image systems in the natural sciences and medicine.

However, in codifying the *Classic of I* the Han editors were in a strange position. They felt that the texts contained the magic of a Golden Age when people were nearer to the Gods and that such a time might be repeated through using them. The oldest texts, however, were not immediately understandable, for the divinatory tradition that explained their use had been lost. So the Han editors gathered and transcribed various oral traditions dealing with the use of the Yarrow-stalk Oracle that originated in the Warring States Period and added them to the older texts.

These treatises, called the *Ten Wings*, contain both oracular texts and interpretive strategies. One in particular, the *Hsi tz'u chuan* (*Commentary on the Attached Evidences*) or *Ta chuan* (*The Great Commentary*) defines an imaginative stance to be taken toward the book which preserves the core of the old shamanic tradition as it was developed for personal use.

According to this tradition, the function of the *I* is to provide symbols (*hsiang*). The text came into existence through a mysterious mode of imaginative induction, also called *hsiang,* which endows things with symbolic significance. Acted upon simultaneously by figures in heaven, patterns on earth and events in the psyche, the old shamans and magicians spontaneously *hsiang*-ed or symbolized to form the texts and figures as links to important spirits and energies.

The *chün tzu*, the ideal user of the book, can take advantage of this fundamental spirit power. He or she observes the figure obtained through divination and takes joy in its words, turning and rolling them in the heart. These words translate or symbolize (*hsiang*) the situation, connecting it with the level of reality from which the symbols flow. Through this action, the *chün tzu* becomes *hsiang* or symbolizing, linking the divinatory tools and the spirits connected with *I* directly to the ruling power of the personality. To do this is called *shen,* which refers to whatever is numinous, spiritually potent.

Like the shamans and sages of old, this tradition maintains, the person who uses these symbols to connect with *I* will have access to the numinous world and acquire a helping-spirit, a *shen*. The *I Ching* is more than a spirit, it channels or connects you to spirit. It puts its users in a position to create and experience their own spirit as a point of connection with the forces that govern the world. It is this imaginative power that was elaborated, re-interpreted and defined throughout later Chinese history as the basis of philosophy, morals and ethics. It is a way to connect with the creative imagination that underlies all systems and creeds.

■

USING THE *I*

● *This Translation*

The *I Ching* is a diviner's manual or active sourcebook for what
C. G. Jung called the archetypal forces. It organizes the play of these
forces into images so that an individual reading becomes possible. Using it
begins with a problem and a question. But there is a general question
behind each specific demand: "How can I act in creative relation with the
spirits or forces shaping this moment of time?" These forces represent the
flow of life and the experience of its meaning, its way or *tao*.

The *I Ching*'s response to this question comes through the texts of one
of the hexagrams. These texts present open-ended clusters of images and
ideas that mirror structures of the psyche, a quality they share with dreams
and spontaneous fantasies. They act as corrections or interventions from
an implicit order, the *tao*. Each opens a field of potential meaning that
will support a series of stories, while eliminating others. Spirit or energy
moves through individual, creative interaction with the images. To use the
I Ching as an oracle, we have to use this creative potential.

This book is an attempt to present the oracular core of the *I Ching* as a
psychological tool. The purpose is to recover oracular language and the
use of divination as a connection between the individual and the unseen –
the world of images described by myth, dream, shamanic journey or
mystery cult. Researched for over 40 years, the final form of the
translation grew out of several years of seminars, conferences, individual
and group consultations that included artists, thinkers and scholars from
all over the world.

The fundamental concern is to give people the means to live and
choose in a meaningful way by making them aware of imaginative value.
For the *I Ching* fills an important gap in the modern approach to the
psyche. Its oracular texts connect the study of what C. G. Jung called the
archetypes, and what the ancient world called the Gods, directly to
individual experience. The present translation is an attempt to go behind
historical, philological and philosophical analysis to revive the divinatory
core, the psychological root of the book as a living practise.

We go to ancient China to find this way of seeing things because Old Chinese permitted the development of a special oracular language. It is made up of symbols with no rigid subject-verb, noun-adjective, pronoun or person distinctions. They combine and interact the way dream-images do. The *I Ching* is both an epitome of this language and of the divinatory world-view. It is a tool used in the care of the soul, a tool through which hidden parts of modern culture, East and West, might be re-activated.

The basic text used for the translation is the *Chou-i-chê-chung*, the *Kang Hsi* or Palace Edition of 1715. It is the last of the classic versions of the text, and is used today throughout the East when someone consults the Oracle. This text served as the basis for Richard Wilhelm's translation and for the modern standard text, the *Harvard Yenching Edition*.

The Palace Edition is inclusive and represents the end of a long textual tradition. It systematically reproduces all the layers of the text and a great number of commentaries that seek to explain the images. We have left these commentaries, based on Confucian moral philosophy and imperial political thought, aside. We have assembled and translated all the parts of the book that contain oracular texts. This is the core of the book, the images from which interpretations are made.

The translation of these images is an attempt to make their imaginative power available to the modern user. Here no *a priori* meaning is assumed or imposed. The possible meanings are gathered together with no presumption that they must conform to one single interpretation. The terms are seen as the centers of force-fields in the imagination that have gathered meanings over time. They are translated as functions, all of which can exist in any individual. They do not literally apply to a particular gender or social position. Bringing out this multivalence makes the individual quality of the encounter with the Oracle available for the first time in a western language. It presents the imaginative field from which interpretations are made.

There are four basic principles used in this approach. All of them represent a different way of using words than in ordinary language.

–Each Chinese character is translated throughout by the same English core-word. This one-to-one translation emphasizes a nuclear meaning of the term and makes possible the first Concordance in a western language. Whenever possible these core-words are gerunds (-ing verb forms) to show that the terms are fields of action which include all a verb's persons, voices and forms as well as the verbal noun and adjective.

–Each of these terms is provided with a group of possible meanings that resonate in the original. They provide an imaginative network that relates the terms to individual situations. These meanings are not limited to a single period or level of culture but are drawn from the history of the language. They include recent archeological findings as well as the traditional analysis of the ideogram.

–The word-order of the original statements is strictly preserved. Except for articles (a, an, the) each word in the translation represents one and only one Chinese character in the exact order of the original. No prepositions, connectives, verb forms or explanatory words are added in an attempt to make things make sense by explaining beforehand what they mean.

–The structural elements of the hexagrams are connected to the system of magic images from which traditional science developed. Words that have acquired special meanings in the *I Ching* itself are also explored.

This way of looking at the *I Ching* is both very old and radically new. It is based on a psychological re-creation of ancient divinatory practises. The focus is on the development of the divinatory tradition as it passed out of the hands of professionals associated with the Chinese Court and into the hands of private individuals, but before it was made to serve a particular moral philosophy. This development began in a time of social breakdown and creative activity that offers many parallels to our own, a time when people needed to connect with the spirits outside of normal social structures. It feeds the development of the individual personality.

The circles of reference for the words and images revolve around you, the user. They are meant to eliminate the *a priori* interpretation a translation usually imposes, allowing you to position yourself within the dynamic field – the spirit – each term implies. Turning and rolling the words in your heart, the tradition suggests, is the key to contacting the numinous world opened by the Oracle. Like the sudden insight in a dream interpretation, intuitive meaning and a connection to the spirits is the result.

Questioning the Oracle

The *I Ching* is a guide to decision making in situations when the flow of life is troubled. It helps you see what forces are at work, how they may develop, and how you can relate to them. It takes the way you are looking at things apart and opens up new insights.

The urge to consult the Oracle arises when you feel entangled with something that evades the usual methods of problem–solving. Resistance, reluctance, anxiety, strong desire, the sense of something hidden or confusing, the need for more information, the sense of an important opportunity, the need to feel in contact with something larger than yourself all indicate that you need to see-behind or see-through the situation. The Oracle can open this deeper perspective; the responsibility and decision remain yours.

The first step is making the question. The question is important, because it is the point of contact that focuses the divinatory images and connects them to your personal situation. It clarifies a moment of time and draws it out of the flux of experience to act as a link to fundamental energies.

Making a question has two parts. The first part is soul-searching. Search out the feelings, images and experiences that lie behind the immediate situation – what you feel, remember, are afraid of, what you think the effects of the problem might be, what it symbolizes for you, what relations and issues it involves, what is at stake, why you are uncertain or anxious about making a decision. This establishes the subjective field. The answer will focus on these concerns. Talking to someone about the situation can often help you bring these things out and clarify them.

This leads to the second step – a clear formulation of the question based on what you want to do in the situation. Be precise. Examine what you want to do with as much honesty and awareness as you can. And, if possible, come to a conclusion, presenting it as a question: "What about doing this?" "What will happen if I...?" "What should my attitude be toward ...?" The Oracle will connect you with an archetypal image through this question. This clarifies the dynamic forces at work in your psyche, the seeds of future events.

This process allows you to break through the wall that usually separates you from the spirit world beyond your immediate control. The response will not be a simple yes-or-no answer, though it will include specific advice so be open to a surprise. What you are really asking for is an understanding in depth upon which you can base your decisions and actions. The question is the precise point of contact with the unknown, and it enables you to open and focus the divinatory space. It is part of a process of expansion and contraction that leads from an unconscious relation with a disturbing force to specific advice on how to handle the situation.

• *Getting an Answer*

The *I Ching* is organized through a set of 64 six-line figures or hexagrams. These hexagrams are the link between your question and the divinatory texts that answer it. Usually, you select a hexagram through one of two different methods. Both methods generate six numbers, each number being either 6, 7, 8, or 9. These numbers indicate the types of lines that make up your *Primary Hexagram*. This hexagram then keys the texts that answer your question.

Each hexagram is made up of six *opened* — — and/or *whole* —— lines. The lines have specific qualities, called *supple* and *solid*, which link them with the two primary agents in Eastern thought, *yin* and *yang*. Each hexagram can be thought of as a set of six empty places through which energy moves and changes. Energy comes into the hexagram from below and leaves at the top. The places are numbered accordingly. The lowest is the first and the highest the sixth. These hexagrams represent possible modes of change in the world, the dynamic qualities of time.

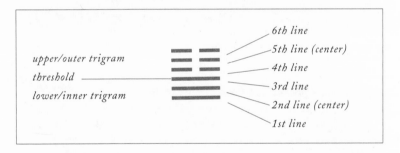

Each hexagram is also thought of as being composed of two *trigrams* or three-line figures. They represent basic elements or processes – wind and wood, fire and light, earth, heaven, mountain, marsh, running water, thunder – and have a wide range of associations. From this perspective each hexagram portrays the dynamic relation between a lower or *inner* element and an upper or *outer* element. This makes the division between the third and fourth lines particularly important as an interface between the inner and outer worlds. It also assigns a special value to the 2nd and 5th lines as centers of the inner and outer realms.

Each place in a hexagram, moving from below to above, can be occupied by one of four kinds of lines. These lines correspond to the four

possible numbers that come from the consultation procedure: 6, 7, 8 or 9. The *yin* or *opened* lines correspond to the even numbers 6 and 8, the *yang* or *whole* lines to the odd numbers 7 and 9.

The central numbers (7 and 8) constellate a *young* or *growing* line:

8 ━━ ━━   *young yin (does not change)*

7 ━━━━   *young yang (does not change)*

The extreme numbers (6 and 9) constellate an *old* line which is *transforming* (PIEN) into its opposite:

9 ━━○━━   *old yang changes into* ━━ ━━ *young yin*

6 ━X━   *old yin changes into* ━━━━ *young yang*

These *Transforming Lines* have special significance. They represent precise points of change in the psyche and emphasize particular hexagram texts.

You get the numbers which produce these lines in two ways. The simplest is by tossing three coins six times. Heads are yin and have the value 2; tails are yang and have the value 3. Traditionally you would use copper *cash*, Chinese coins with a square hole in the center which are inscribed on one side (value 2) and empty (or with Manchu characters) on the other (value 3). Adding the results of each toss produces 6, 7, 8 or 9:

heads(2)heads(2)+heads(2)= 6 = ━━X━━ *old or changing yin*

heads(2)+heads(2)+tails(3)= 7 = ━━━━━ *young yang*

heads(2)+tails(3)+tails(3)= 8 = ━━ ━━ *young yin*

tails(3)+tails(3)+tails(3)= 9 = ━━○━━ *old or changing yang*

Throwing the coins six times gives you six numbers. Arranged from the bottom up, and translated into lines, this produces the *Primary Hexagram*. When any of these lines are *Transforming Lines,* indicated by a 6 or a 9, they will change into their opposite. When they do this they generate a second hexagram, the *Related Hexagram,* which indicates the way the situation described in the *Primary Hexagram* may develop. Use the table on page 814 to find out which hexagram you have obtained. First identify the two trigrams, then look up the hexagram number. If there are *Transforming Lines,* indicated by a 6 or 9 in the consultation procedure, generate the new *Related Hexagram* which is produced when they change. Find that number in the same way.

The coin-oracle was popularized in the Southern Sung period (1127–1279) and has been used for several hundred years. It yields quick results. However it has a particular bias, for the mathematical odds involved are symmetrical. The probability that a *yin* line will transform is equal to that of a *yang* line, as is the proportion of stable *yin* and stable *yang.* This reflects binary choice and does not penetrate as deeply into the situation as the other, older and more complicated way of consulting the Oracle. This method, the yarrow-stalk method, uses a set of 50 thin sticks or batons about 12–18 inches long, traditionally yarrow-stalks (*achillea millefolium*) taken from the tips of the plant.

Using the yarrow-stalks reflects the nature of *yin* and *yang* as they were perceived in traditional Chinese science and allows time for reflection during the consultation process. The mathematical odds using yarrow-stalks are asymmetrical. These asymmetrical ratios reflect a *qualitative* difference, the intrinsic tendency of *yin* towards stability and of *yang* towards transformation.

The basic unit of this process of consultation is dividing and counting out the bunch of yarrow-stalks three times. Each time this is done a number, and thus a line of the *Primary Hexagram,* is produced.

Clear an open space on a table and quiet your mind. While thinking of your question and your plan of action, open yourself to whatever may come. You should note whatever emotions, images or memories come up, or whatever occurs around you during the process.

- Put the bunch of yarrow-stalks on the table in front of you. Make sure that you have 50. Take one stalk from the bunch and put it aside. This is the observer or witness, also called the center of the world. It will remain unused throughout the entire procedure of forming a hexagram.

- Divide the remaining bunch of 49 stalks into two random portions.

- Take one stalk from the pile on the left and put it between the 4th and 5th fingers of your left hand.

- Pick up the pile on the right and count it out in groups of 4, laying the groups out on the table in front of you, until you have a remainder of 1, 2, 3, or 4 stalks. Put this remainder between the 3rd and 4th fingers of your left hand.

- Take up the remaining pile and count it out in groups of 4, laying them out in front of you, until you have a remainder of 1, 2, 3, or 4 stalks. Put this remainder between the 2nd and 3rd fingers of your left hand.

- Take all the stalks between fingers of your left hand and put them aside. They are out for this line.

- Make one bunch of the remaining groups of stalks. Repeat the entire procedure, again putting the stalks between your fingers aside.

- Repeat the procedure a third time. This time count the number of groups of 4 on the table in front of you. You will have either 6, 7, 8, or 9 groups. The number of groups gives you the first or bottom line of your hexagram.

- Go through this procedure 5 more times to form the complete hexagram, making the lines from the bottom up. At the end of the process gather the stalks together and return them to their wrapping or container. As in the coin method look up the numbers and names of the hexagrams you have formed.

You are now ready to read the answer to your question.

Reading the Response

The Oracle's response to the question you have asked comes through the texts of one of the 64 hexagrams. Turn to the hexagram texts indicated by your consultation. Read *all the basic texts in the Primary Hexagram* plus the texts of the *specific Transforming Lines* that are indicated by your consultation. Read *only the Image of the Related Hexagram*.

These texts describe energy fields and can generate many meanings. The confusion you feel when you begin to work with them is a necessary part of the process. Through it your sense of yourself and the situation becomes fluid, opened to new ways of seeing things.

This initial confusion triggers a sort of landslide of potential meaning. Being imaginatively open or versatile is the key to the interaction. The texts speak directly to your unconscious. When they touch a meaningful complex, *shen* or awareness of spirit is excited. Like key images in the remembering of a dream, certain definitions will emerge from the field. For the tradition insists that these words do not conform to a rule. Rather, as you walk around them, allowing them to act on your imagination, spontaneously the rules arrive. This is a living process. The images interact with, re-form and clarify the situation in your psyche.

Each reading begins with the *Image* of the *Primary Hexagram*. This is the basic context in which the Oracle sees both your question and its answer.

● *The* Image of the Situation *describes an archetypal situation. It is each hexagram's central oracular statement, the ground in which all other parts of the hexagram are embedded. The name of the hexagram, the first word of the* Image, *provides both a description of your situation and advice as to the most effective way to deal with it. The text places it in the dynamic of time, indicating key qualities and actions associated with it.*

The *Image* is the fundamental divinatory text. The first word of this text forms the name or title of your hexagram. Together they are the hexagram's central oracular statement. The *Image* comes from the T'UAN, the oldest section of the text. The ideogram T'UAN consists of the graphs for swine and for a hog or boar's head. In China, pigs were a symbol of riches and intelligence, an essential sign of good fortune, and the boar's head was offered on sacrificial occasions. The *Image* suggests that knowing the image of the time, and basing your action upon it, is a key to realizing the riches and intelligence inherent in the situation.

All of the terms in the *Image,* and in the other sections that follow, are presented with their *Associated Contexts*. These are possible meanings of the terms, usually including the traditional analysis of the ideogram. These *Associated Contexts* are given the first time a term appears in a hexagram; if the term is repeated you should refer back to the first occurrence. Hyphens (-) indicate that two English words together translate one Chinese character. Punctuation marks give you a sense of the implicit pauses or emphases in the original text. Divinatory formulas such as **significant, pitfall, adversity, without fault, Harvesting Trial, Growing, without not Harvesting** or **repentance extinguished**, give

specific advice on whether the action you are contemplating leads toward or away from the experience of spirit and meaning.

As you read through the texts, certain terms will offer themselves as keys to your situation. Examine the meanings and let them suggest ways of understanding your situation. Use these meanings, even if they are contradictory, as you read through the other sections of your hexagram. The ultimate interpretation accumulates as the possible meanings interact.

The next section comments on the dynamic relation between the inner and the outer aspects of your situation. It describes the tension between your inner process and the outer world you are confronting.

- Outer and Inner Aspects *analyses the matter under consideration in terms of the dynamic relation of its outer and inner elements. This is described through the relation between the outer and inner trigrams and their nets of associated qualities.*

This section acts as a shorthand reference to the supplementary material on the *Universal Compass* dealing with traditional systems of correlative thinking. It gathers material from the 8th Wing and a Han Dynasty text central to the system of correlative thinking, *The Comprehensive Discussions in the White Tiger Hall.*

The next section of your hexagram indicates what you should *not* do in the situation, not because it is wrong, but because it goes counter to the spirit of the time.

- Counter Indications *describes an opposite to your situation. It indicates what is not effective at the present time.*

This section stems from the traditional view that the four inner lines of each hexagram form two overlapping Nuclear Trigrams, which thus form a Nuclear Hexagram. It focuses your understanding of the central *Image* by showing a contrary, the shadow that is split off as the *Image* comes into light.

The texts entitled *Contrasted Definitions, Sequence, Attached Evidences* (in certain hexagrams), *Symbol Tradition* and *Image Tradition* were composed later than the *Image*. They are interpretive strategies which come from the Ten Wings, each commenting on or amplifying the *Image* from a particular perspective.

The *Sequence* explains what led up to your present situation, thus suggesting why you are asking your question.

● *The* Sequence *puts the* Image *in a series with the hexagram that precedes it in terms of a completed action which calls up a following action. It suggests that activating the energy of this hexagram depends upon understanding it as a part of a necessary succession of events.*

The *Sequence*, from the 9th Wing, represents a transitional area. It always contains the statement: "Anterior acquiescence has the use-of ...". This indicates that activating your hexagram's energies depends upon understanding and accepting as valid the succession of events the *Sequence* describes. The action of the preceding hexagram is conceived of as the point of departure for your present situation.

The *Contrasted Definitions* accent a particular quality of your hexagram as a clue to understanding how it works.

● *The* Contrasted Definitions *offer a key to your situation by picking out a central feature and contrasting it with a central feature of an adjoining hexagram.*

The pairs of *Contrasted Definitions* are taken from the 10th Wing and are given with the hexagrams they describe.

In certain hexagrams there is a section called *Attached Evidences*. This indicates that the actions and attitudes described in the hexagram were felt to be particularly important in developing and deepening individual character, the ability to be independent and in touch with *tao*.

● *The* Attached Evidences *indicate the action of this hexagram is particularly relevant to actualizing-tao and describe how it can aid the process of realizing tao in action.*

These texts occur at only ten of the hexagrams and are drawn from the Eighth Wing.

The section called *Symbol Tradition* uses the Symbols of the trigrams to derive a particular attitude. They are linked with the *chün tzu*, the ideal user of the *I Ching*, or the *Earlier Kings*, who suggest a model from the Golden Age. This implies that part of being a *chün tzu* is being able to see things as symbols. It connects you with the way the *tao* is moving.

● *The* Symbol Tradition *describes the* Image *in terms of the relation between the Symbols of its two trigrams. It derives a specific action from this relation which*

gives access to the ideal of the chün tzu in this situation: a person who uses divination to order their life according to tao rather than personal desires.

The trigrams and their attributes are described in the Reference Material. What is particularly relevant is that the *Symbol Tradition* derives a specific action from the relation of the trigrams. This action is said to typify the behavior of the *chün tzu* in conforming to and furthering the moment described.

The last interpretive section is called the *Image Tradition*. It repeats specific phrases from the *Image* and comments on them. It is probably the latest section, and has a distinct analytical quality.

● *The* Image Tradition *amplifies key terms and qualities of the* Image. *It also analyses the* Image *in terms of: the correspondence of pairs of lines; the actions and relations of supple and solid, assigned to the opened and whole lines; and the appropriateness of the lines to their places, particularly the center lines of the trigrams.*

The *Image Tradition* paraphrases the *Image* and analyses the actions described by the trigram symbols. It offers analogies to the central image and examines:

the resonance or *correspondence* of pairs of lines: 1 and 4, 2 and 5, 3 and 6;

the dynamic relation of *supple* and *solid*, qualities assigned to the opened and whole lines, and how they move in the situation;

the appropriateness of the lines to their places in the hierarchical structure of the hexagram, particularly in relation to the center lines of the trigrams: opened lines are considered appropriate to even-numbered spaces, and whole lines appropriate to odd-numbered spaces.

The nature of this commentary is suggested by its characteristic term: *indeed,* YEH. It is an intensifier which means: in truth, in actual fact, as a matter of fact, sometimes translated as the verb "to be." This section of the Ten Wings sponsored an extensive commentary tradition called *i-li* or moral-principle analysis which developed a view of the social value and function of the various line-positions.

The texts of the *Transforming Lines* are qualitatively different from the texts which surround and amplify the *Image* of your *Primary Hexagram*.

These texts reflect the precise points of connection with the psychic forces involved in your question, "hot spots" where they cross and mix. They reveal the potential significance of individual action within the situation described by the *Primary Hexagram* as a whole, suggesting what your plan might lead to and how it might get there.

• *The* Transforming Lines *represent precise points of connection with the psychic forces involved in your question. They are activated by a 6 or a 9 in the consultation procedure. They give you advice on the direction of specific actions and the potential consequences. As the activated lines change into their opposites they generate a second hexagram, the* Related Hexagram, *which is an image of overall future potential.*

The texts of the *Transforming Lines* come from the T'UAN and from the commentaries on the lines in the 3rd and 4th Wings. These texts are constellated when a specific line is *transforming* (PIEN) into its contrary and thus *transforms* the hexagram in question, the *Primary Hexagram,* into a new one, the *Related Hexagram.* The *Related Hexagram* indicates the direction in which your situation may evolve if you choose to act in the way described. You should read only those *Transforming Lines* constellated in the response to your question. The *a)* text is the oldest text, while the *b)* text is a clarifying comment on it. Like the *Image Tradition,* the *b)* text is characterized by the intensifier *indeed,* YEH, which means: in truth, in actual fact.

The *Image* of the *Related Hexagram* generated when the *Transforming Lines* change into their opposites gives an indication of how your situation may develop. This can be a goal, an image of desire, reassurance or warning. It is not an immutable future, but an indication of the potential contained in your present situation. Changing the way you act or perceive things can change this potential.

• *Keywords: Traps for Tao*

Certain terms have a special significance in the *I Ching,* in addition to their ordinary meanings. These keywords evolved as the *I* became a tool used by private individuals. They reflect a troubled time, like our own, when people could not necessarily count on social structures to support them, but had to find their own path. Together, these keywords give a

picture of the world of the *I Ching* and how it seeks to help you.

The most fundamental term is:

> **Tao**: way or path; ongoing process of being and course it traces for each specific being or thing; keyword. The ideogram: go and head, leading and the path it creates.

The term **tao** has no equivalent in English. The literal meaning is way or path, and the term describes both the movement on this way and the way itself. **Tao** is the ongoing, self-renewing and purposive energy of life, continually creating as it moves. It traces a way or path which is, potentially, reflected in each individual being. To be "in" **tao** or connected to **tao** is to experience meaning and move with the energy of life. This is fundamental value. It is experienced as meaning, joy, freedom, connection, compassion, creativity, insight.

Tao is not limited by any system or morality, and it continually undermines rational definitions. It is not predictable, but **versatile**.

> **Versatility**, I: sudden and unpredictable change; mental mobility and openness; easy and light, not difficult and heavy.

Versatility describes the way **tao** moves, a sudden substitution of one thing or image for another. This often appears as trouble or difficulty, for it challenges the fixity of things. **Versatility** also indicates the imaginative fluidity necessary to adapt to the movement of **tao**. It connects the way, the Book of *I* and the imagination, the continual flow of images in what the tradition calls the heart-mind, the heart of magic.

This connection occurs through **symbols** and **symbolizing**.

> **Symbol**, HSIANG: image invested with intrinsic power to connect visible and invisible; magic spell; figure, form, shape, likeness; pattern, model; create an image, imitate; act, play; writing.

The *I* – the "way" of the *I Ching* – provides **symbols**, direct analogies to the movement of energy in the invisible world. The **symbols** are **versatile**. They act like weirs or fishtraps in the flow of **tao**, accumulating the quality of mind it represents. You connect with the energy by imagining yourself through the **symbols**, a process which indicates what is and what is not in harmony with time and **tao**. The term **symbol** is connected with two other terms:

- **Trial**, CHEN: test by ordeal; inquiry by divination and its result; righteous, firm; separating wheat from chaff; the kernel, the proven core; fourth stage of the Time Cycle. The ideogram: pearl and divination.

- **Vessel/holding**, TING: bronze cauldron with three feet and two ears, sacred vessel used to cook food for sacrifice to gods and ancestors; founding symbol of family or dynasty; melting pot, receptacle; hold, contain, transform; establish, secure; precious, respectable.

The **symbols** produced by the *I* through divination try or test an action by submitting it to the spirits and revealing its hidden roots. When you use these **symbols** in a **versatile** way, as imaginative models, they act like a sacred **vessel**, enacting a process of containment, sacrifice and transformation.

By doing this you acquire **te**, the virtue and power that comes through reflecting **tao** in the events of your life.

- **Actualize-tao**, TE: realize tao in action; power, virtue; ability to follow the course traced by the ongoing process of the cosmos; keyword. The ideogram: to go, straight, and heart. Linked with TE, acquire: acquiring that which makes a being become what it is meant to be.

The movement of **tao** constantly offers **symbols** which the heart may respond to. Using these **symbols** to adapt to the movement of **tao** clarifies and deepens the heart, opening it to the spirit-power called *shen ming* or the *light of the gods*. **Actualizing-tao** suggests that the continual process of straightening, clarifying and deepening the heart enables you to become what you are meant to be, correcting and straightening movement on the path or way of life. Someone who seeks to acquire this virtue, and thus to live their life as a manifestation of **tao**, is a **chün tzu**.

- **Chün tzu**: ideal of a person who uses divination to order his/her life in accordance with tao rather than wilful intention.

The term **chün tzu**, literally chief son, has no real equivalent in English. It first described a lower order of nobility. As these orders fell apart, it evolved into the ideal of a person who uses *I* divination and its **versatile symbols** to live life in connection with **tao**, acquiring the power and virtue of the spirits. You are a **chün tzu** when you use the oracle to

understand what is in harmony with **tao** in any given situation in your life, to help and protect yourself through **tao** rather than seeking control by imposing your will. **Versatility** is the tool, an imaginative way of understanding and acting that opens the **tao** or way. The oracle is meant for those who strive for the ideal of **chün tzu**. It only makes sense from this perspective.

The **chün tzu** lives in **Heaven[and]Earth**, a world of continual change, of mixtures and movement, energies and spirits.

- **Heaven[and]Earth**, T'IEN TI: dynamic relation between the primal powers and the world it produces; cosmos, natural or human world; keyword.

This world is nowhere absolute. It results from the interaction of the two primal powers as they mix or **intertwine** to form a variegated cosmos. **Heaven[and]Earth** is the world of the myriad beings, humans, animals and spirits, where nothing is fixed. The *I* reflects this world; it is effective there. Through it the **chün tzu** seeks to lead a meaningful and enjoyable human life, connected to the spirits, the **tao** and the living world. Part of this is a continual recognition of imperfection and change, and a careful dis-identification with the primal powers.

- **Heaven**, T'IEN: highest; sky, firmament, heavens; power above the human as opposed to earth, TI, below; the Symbol of the trigram Force, CH'IEN. The ideogram: great and the one above.

- **Earth**, TI: ground on which the human world rests; basis of all things, nourishes all things; the Symbol of the trigram Field, K'UN.

Seeking neither purity nor immortality, the **chün tzu** lives in the stream of time that flows through **Heaven[and]Earth** as an image of the way. Two basic terms describe this flow.

- **Come**, LAI, and **Go**, WANG, describe the stream of time as it flows from the future through the present into the past; come, LAI, indicates what is approaching; move toward, arrive at; go, WANG, indicates what is departing; proceed, move on.

This time flows from and returns to a source. **Coming** events have an objective reality, and they cast images which may be seen through divination. **Come** and **go** also refer to the hexagrams as images of time. Lines enter a hexagram from below and within, **coming**, and leave above and outside, **going**. The stream of time, and the way or **tao**, originates within and flows through each individual. Thus this **coming** and **going** contrasts with the sense of personal history in which life moves from the past into the future. It means that letting **go** of the places where you are bound to the past and paying attention to what is **coming** on the stream of time is part of being **versatile**. Through it you acquire **te**.

There are two basic orientations of the will used as the **chün tzu** seeks to adapt to the events that **come** on the stream of time. Between them, they implement imaginative **versatility**.

- **Great**, TA: big, noble, important, very; orient the will toward a self-imposed goal, impose direction; ability to lead or guide your life; contrasts to small, HSIAO, flexible adaptation to what crosses your path.

   Great People, TA JEN: important, noble, influential; those who impose a ruling principle on their lives; effect of the great within an individual.

- **Small**, HSIAO: little, common, unimportant; adapting to what crosses your path; ability to move in harmony with the vicissitudes of life; contrasts with great, TA, self-imposed theme or goal.

   Small People, HSIAO JEN: lowly, common, humble; those who adjust to circumstances with the flexibility of the small; effect of the small within an individual.

Though these terms include the ordinary meanings of noble and humble, exceptional and common, powerful and ,weak their significance lies in the direction they give to the will. The **chün tzu** seeks the freedom to move between these attitudes, picking them up and putting them down as the time demands. **Great** and **Great People**, the effect of the **great** on an individual, means imposing an idea on things, independent of what that idea might be. Only when it is connected to **actualizing-tao** is it valued in itself. **Small** and **Small People**, the effect of the **small** in an individual, is not simply the shadow of the **great**, but points at the ability to let go of self-importance, quickly and humbly adapting to what crosses your path. The **chün tzu** is not only a **Great Person** or only a **Small Person**, but seeks the capacity to act quickly and fluidly as both.

Divination with the *I* helps and supports connection with **tao** and the acquisition of **te**, the experience of meaning and the pleasure and benefit that comes with the connection. The basic divinatory terms of the *I* reflect this. Events are valued according to whether they lead towards or away from this experience.

- **Significant**, CHI: leads to the experience of meaning; favorable, propitious, advantageous, appropriate. The ideogram: scholar and mouth, wise words of a sage.

- **Pitfall**, HSIUNG: leads away from the experience of meaning; stuck and exposed to danger, unable to take in the situation; flow of life and spirit is blocked; unfortunate, baleful.

These terms emphasize that within the constant movement of things it is possible to choose. You may take advantage of the insight given by the *I* and its **symbols** to move with this flow. Implicit in this is the idea that through these **symbols** you not only acquire meaning and benefit, but that you can help the world around you by being in accord with **tao**.

Encounters with the Oracle

The *I Ching* is meant to be used when you are troubled and you seek a meaning in the disturbance. It offers insight into the question you pose and practical advice on how to deal with it. Its images act as a guide to personal transformation, leading to a deeper knowledge of yourself and your actions. It is a way of thinking and imagining that gives you the tools to make changes.

The *I Ching*'s words and images have been called "magic spells" because of their uncanny ability to connect you with unseen forces. This opens a liminal space in which you can contact what is moving the soul. Inside this circle, your sense of yourself and your situation dissolves and re-forms. You receive information about what is possible and effective in a given situation. It shows your way or *tao* at work.

Because they are open symbols, the divinatory terms do not force you into the mold of a specific morality. All of the terms can refer to any person, regardless of age, gender or social position. They foster an imaginative process that both protects you and helps your spirit emerge. Your dialogue with them weaves a new story or context for your experience of yourself and your situation.

Using the *I* in this way is like working with dreams. The images do not offer standard predictions of an unalterable future. They describe the way energy is moving to create possible futures. This presents you with an opportunity to interact with the energy clusters or complexes of the psyche. Changing your relation to these forces can change what will happen to you.

You learn this "way" by doing it, by continually moving between the images and their connection to the events of your life. By involving yourself in these clusters of meaning, by trying out the stories they suggest, you open yourself to *I* and its function: to make conscious the imaginative background and the goal of the situation in which you find yourself, giving you the information necessary to make choices.

In a traditional culture, where myth is alive, people take a step back into the imagination before they start on any significant action. They encounter an image there and move into the action through the image that they have found. This oracular image carries them, keeping them connected with the imaginative ground. It acts as a sign and a talisman, gathering energy, warning, offering hope and direction. Similarly, these images answer the basic question that appears today in a moving or disturbing experience – What is going on? What will happen to me? What should I do? – in order to connect you with the creative ground beneath it.

The following series of Encounters with the Oracle gives you a sense of the ways the *I Ching* can be used and the sorts of situations in which people turn to it. Look at the hexagrams involved as you read through the consultations.

Perhaps the most fundamental quality of the Oracle is to recognize and act as a witness to your situation. This grounds you in an image that is larger than your personal awareness. Such recognition is the basic connection to the symbolic world.

● EXAMPLE 1

● *A Voice in the Wilderness*

He first encountered the I Ching *25 years ago. Like other people at the time, he was searching for a better way to live his life. He had made a moral and political decision that put him into exile, and felt lost in a forest of conflicting emotions, thoughts, philosophies and possibilities, with no real sense of how to*

look at them. *It was a dangerous time, full of sudden change and violence, and his life was in flux. Wandering in the wilderness of the time, he encountered the* I Ching *and asked this question.*

Question: Who are you? How should I use you?

Answer: Hexagram 50, no *Transforming Lines*

The answer was Hexagram 50, **The Vessel/Holding**, with no *Transforming Lines*.

Here, the book described itself and his relation to it:

> ... in terms of the imaginative capacity of a sacred vessel. It emphasizes that securing and imaginatively transforming the material at hand is the adequate way to handle it. To be in accord with the time, you are told to: **hold** and transform things in the **vessel!**
>
> **Vessel/holding**, TING: bronze cauldron with three feet and two ears, sacred vessel used to cook food for sacrifice to gods and ancestors; founding symbol of family or dynasty; melting pot, receptacle; hold, contain, transform; establish, secure; precious, respectable.

The book presented itself as a process of imaginative transformation that could contain the fragmented pieces of his life. He should put what he needed to cook into the **Vessel** through posing it as a question. It would respond. His problem would be held, contained, transformed, centered in another imaginative dimension. Through this process he could establish and secure himself.

He was amazed at the feeling of being talked to directly. The voice cut into his dislocation and loneliness, offering a way to understand and evaluate the things he was going through. Particularly, the *Contrasted Definitions* told him that he should understand the painful events leading to his present situation as **skinning**:

> **Skin,** KO: take off the covering, skin or hide; change, renew, molt; remove, peel off; revolt, overthrow, degrade from office; leather armor, protection.

This linked his personal feeling of being without protection to a kind of molting, an *objective* change. **Skinning** connects political revolt and personal vulnerability. It could open him to the imaginative practise of the **Vessel**, through which he could **grasp renewal**:

Grasp, CH'Ü: lay hold of, take and use, seize, appropriate; grasp the meaning, understand. The ideogram: ear and hand, hear and grasp.

What was **anterior**, the bitter quarrels, old sorrows, previous causes, grievances and broken relationships that brought him to this situation, could simply **depart**.

Anterior, KU: come before as cause; formerly, ancient; reason, purpose, intention; grievance, quarrel, dissatisfaction, sorrow, mourning resulting from previous causes and intentions; situation leading to a divination.

Depart, CH'O: leave, quit, remove; repudiate, reject, dismiss.

Inner and Outer Aspects told him that this imaginative process could establish an inner **Ground**. It could bring disconnected things together to feed a spreading **Radiance**, a warm clarity of spirit. The *Counter Indication* told him he should not separate things, **parting** his energy into different streams. He should put all the disparate pieces of his life into the **Vessel** to be **cooked**. In this way, the *Symbol Tradition* told him, he could correct his situation.

Correct, CHENG rectify deviation or one-sidedness; proper, straight, exact, regular; constant, rule, model. The ideogram: stop and one, hold to one thing.

He could become aware of and live out his own destiny, giving a form to **fate**:

Fate, MING: individual destiny; birth and death as limits of life; issue orders with authority; consult the gods. The ideogram: mouth and order, words with heavenly authority.

For, in the words of the *Image Tradition*, the **Vessel** was a **symbol indeed**:

Symbol, HSIANG: image invested with intrinsic power to connect visible and invisible; magic spell; figure, form, shape, likeness; pattern; model; create an image, imitate; act, play; writing.

The *I Ching* offered itself to him personally as an imaginative process. This was like putting on a new fate, entering an imaginal world. The goal of the advice it gave was **significance**, the personal experience of meaning. Now, 25 years later, he realized that this is true in a much broader way. The feeling of being in touch with the hidden spirit of the time that the

book offers is a counter to the alienation and fragmentation spreading throughout our world – the purpose for which the *I Ching* was originally assembled.

● EXAMPLE 2

The Invisible Woman

She asked the question because she felt cornered, frightened and desperate. The one thing she had to hang on to was her writing. She had staked almost everything on it. She had abandoned a professional training program, given up her house and friends. She was working at a menial job and took care of a sick old man in exchange for room and board. She was cut off from the man she was in love with. She wanted to write a book. She had thought she could do it quickly and well and the book would open a new life. Now she couldn't write. She blamed her impossible situation. She could see no way out. Panicked, shaky and heading for a breakdown, she decided to consult the I Ching.

Question: What can I do about my living and working situation?

Answer: Hexagram 47, no *Transforming Lines*

The answer was Hexagram 47, **Confining**, with no *Transforming Lines.*

The *Image* of this hexagram took hold of her desperation and loneliness and re-defined it:

> This hexagram describes your situation in terms of restriction and distress. It emphasizes that turning inward through accepting enclosure is the adequate way to handle it. To be in accord with the time, you are told to: **confine!**
>
> **Confine,** K'UN: enclose, restrict, limit; oppressed; impoverish, distress; afflicted, exhausted, disheartened, weary. The ideogram: an enclosed tree.

The emotional connection was immediate. She was **confined,** and the *Image* validated her feelings of being disheartened and weary, at the end of her rope. The image of the tree imprisoned in this distress – the Tree of Life, for her – was particularly vivid. It was the fundamental quality of this moment of her life.

At the same time, the *Image* advised her to go deeper into the situation, to accept and *internalize* it as part of her **fate**. The affirmation that **confining** had an objective quality brought a great sense of relief. She was not obliged to fight against it. The situation was, in the words of the *Image*, **without fault**, without personal error that leads to harm.

Outer and Inner Aspects gave her an image for the conflict she felt between her desires and her experience, a conflict that was pulling her apart. She was seeing the outer world through the **Open** and **stimulating words**: meeting with others, cheering and inspiring speech, widening acquaintance, working for mutual profit. She felt this *should* be happening. Her real situation was an empty caricature of what she wanted.

The *Inner Aspect* explained this emptiness. It showed the stream of psychic energy falling into danger and toiling through a dark passage, the **Gorge.** This was dissolving the inner forms she normally used to think about herself and her world. The possibility of contact in the outer world was being undermined and drawn in. The map was changing; it no longer fit the territory.

The *Counter Indication* contrasted her **confining** isolation with the cooperation of **people** living or working together in a **dwelling.** **Confining** had cut the links to family, friends and the cooperation of the workplace. It was drawing energy *in* and *down*. She felt this as oppression, affliction and isolation.

The "why" of this experience – and it was very important to find a purpose – emerged through the *Attached Evidences*. These texts relate the action of certain hexagrams to **actualizing-tao**, the struggle to acquire the power and the virtue to become an individual. **Confining** is characterized as **actualizing-tao's marking-off.**

> **Mark-off**, PIEN: distinguish by dividing; mark off a plot of land; frame which divides a bed from its stand; discuss and dispute. The ideogram: knife and acrid, biting division.

Her isolation, however it had been produced, had the deeper goal of clearly distinguishing her from others. Its acrid quality surrounded her, setting her off from teachers, friends, family, and lover.

Terms from the *Attached Evidences* and the *Contrasted Definitions* suggested that this bitter **confining** was also a time of **exhausting**.

> **Exhaust**, CH'IUNG: bring to an end; limit, extremity; destitute; investigate exhaustively; end without a new beginning. The ideogram: cave and naked person, bent with disease or old age.

This connected to the inner dissolving and toil associated with **Gorge**, the night-sea journey. She was surrounded by the dying forms of things. **Confining** was challenging her to dis-identify with them, to become her own new person.

The *Image*, the central divinatory statement, linked **confining** and **Growing**.

> **Grow**, HENG: success through a sacrifice; pervade, persevere; bring to full growth; enjoy; vigorous, effective; second stage of the Time Cycle.

Confining was a sacrifice offered to her spirit. The key to **growing** was accepting the inwardness of being confined, allowing it to stimulate *inner* growth and independence. Such acceptance was **without fault**.

Two things in the *Image* were of central importance. First was **Great People**:

> **Great People**, TA JEN: important, noble, influential; those who impose a ruling principle on their lives; effect of the great within an individual; keyword.

Great People are not simply the important or influential people from whom she wanted approval. They are those who are able to impose a direction on their lives from within. The inner meaning of this term was very important. She was invited to develop the capacity to be **great** rather than continually searching for recognition and approval in other people's eyes. The inner **growth** of **confining** could produce the insight and courage to do so.

This was particularly important because at this crossroads of her life **possessing words** was not **trustworthy**.

> **Possess**, YU: in possession of, have, own; opposite of lack, WU.

> **Trustworthy**, HSIN: truthful, faithful, consistent over time; integrity; confide in, follow; credentials; contrasts with conforming, FU, connection in a specific moment. The ideogram: person and word, true speech.

Normally she was very facile with words, even glib. She never **lacked** them, but always had them in her **possession**. She had begun to write with this attitude, **trusting** her ability to impress people with **words**. But here, her **words** were not to be **trusted**. They would not endure. They were unconnected. They lacked integrity. This was the moment of truth, no way to escape. Her writer's block was part of **confining**.

The *Image Tradition* moved the deadlock. Here **confining** was described as a situation in which the **solid** – what is firm, strong and purposive, a focus she desperately needed – is **enshrouded**, shadowed and hidden from view.

> **Enshroud**, YEN: screen, shade from view, hide, cover. The ideogram: hand and cover.

As we looked at this image, the hand suddenly turned over. Her whole presence changed, relaxed and deepened. She admitted that she had begun to paint. The painting was a secret. No one knew about it. It expressed a separate, secret world, infusing images from her daily life with an intense feeling tone she could not explain with her usual facility. It was where the underground stream was moving, disconnected from ambition and approval. Staying in the situation, staying with her concerns and feelings, but abandoning the glib and **untrustworthy** relation to **words**, allowed the deepening process to work.

This process **reaches-to her very chün tzu**, the possibility of becoming an individual rather than a random assemblage of collective desires. **Honoring the mouth** and its glib facility was being **exhausted**. Inner **stimulating** was **opening** new possibilities for living and, eventually, writing, that were not directly connected to **honoring the mouth**.

The reading ended with the *Symbol Tradition* and the **chün tzu** who **uses involving fate to release purpose**. At present she was completely **involved** in her problems.

> **Involve**, CHIH: include, entangle, implicate; induce, cause. The ideogram: person walking, induced to follow.

But by seeing and accepting this entanglement as **fate** and letting it induce inner movement, a **purpose** could be **released** that would, in turn, **release** her.

> **Purpose**, CHIH: focus of mind and heart; will, inclination, resolve. The ideogram: heart and scholar, high inner resolve, or heart and go, inner determination.

> **Release**, SUI: loose, let go, free; unhindered, in accord; follow, spread out, progress; penetrate, invade. The ideogram: go and follow your wishes, unimpeded movement.

> **Involving fate** implied that the events of her life that were confusing her were given by creative forces beyond her direct control. This is how

fate speaks. Confronting **fate's involvement** imaginatively puts you on the way to the **chün tzu**. Conscious **purpose** is **released** from **confinement** in unconscious drives, a transformation of ambition that connects it to the heart and to the **great**. This sense of **purpose** could **release** her. It was the reality of this moment of her life. As she let herself flow into this image, her panic dissolved. She was ready to discover the **purpose** in the dark moment where she was presently **confined**.

This reading shifted what seemed a practical concern into the area of inner development which shadowed it. **Confining** was offered as a talisman, a guiding image through a dark passage. The converse can also be true. A reading can also warn you of practical danger in the most direct way.

● EXAMPLE 3

● *Burning your Bridges*

He was a writer and businessman. He posed this question because he wanted to act but felt uncertain about the consequences. His desire conflicted with a sense of danger lurking just under the surface. He had been involved in this relationship for several years and his daily life was bound up in it. But the tension had become intolerable. His partner's jealousy and volatile instability had contributed to two heart attacks. Recently, he had fallen in love with another, younger woman. His attempts to speak about this brought on a suicide attempt. He wanted to get out. Now. He was willing to act decisively, felt emotionally and morally entitled to do so, but wanted to know if his underlying fear was justified.

Question: What about ending my relationship with X?

Answer: Hexagram 56, 9/6, Hexagram 62

The answer was Hexagram 56, **Sojourning**, with a *Transforming Line* at the top, leading to Hexagram 62, **Small Exceeding**.

The *Image* of the *Primary Hexagram* was a clear warning. It told him succinctly that if he ended this relationship at this time he would become a **sojourner**:

This hexagram describes your situation in terms of wandering journeys and living in exile ...

Sojourn, LÜ: travel; stay in places other than your home; itinerant troops, temporary residents; visitor, guest, lodger. Ideogram: banner and people around it, loyal to a symbol rather than their temporary residence.

The *Sequence* stated that his current life, his **residing**, would **necessarily** be **let-go**, slipping through his hands.

Reside(-in), CHÜ: dwell, live in, stay; sit down, fill an office; settled parts of a country. The ideogram: body and seat.

Let-go, SHIH: lose, omit, miss, fail, let slip; out of control. The ideogram: drop from the hand.

Ending the relationship would uproot him. Once a **sojourner**, he would find himself becoming **exceedingly small**, the *Image* of the *Related Hexagram*.

This hexagram describes your situation in terms of an overwhelming variety of encounters and details. It emphasizes that an excessive concern with adapting yourself to these inner and outer events is the adequate way to handle it. To be in accord with the time, you are told to: be **excessively small**!

Small, HSIAO: little, common, unimportant; adapting to what crosses your path; ability to move in harmonious relation to the vicissitudes of life; contrasts with great, TA, self-imposed theme or goal; keyword.

Exceed, KU: go beyond, pass by, pass over; excessive, transgress; error, fault.

He would be wandering in a maze, forced to adapt to an **excessive** variety of things while losing the **great**, the ability to impose an idea on them. This was very important. He drew much of his identity from the place where he lived and had a major project in hand. Both would suffer from **sojourning**, the loss of his **residing** and the necessary **excessive** concern with the **small**.

For there was a lurking danger here, fiery and explosive. The *Transforming Line* described it.

a) **A bird burning its nest.**
Sojourning people beforehand laughing,
**   afterwards crying-out sobbing.**
Losing the cattle, tending-towards versatility.
Pitfall.

b) **Using Sojourning to locate-in the above.**
One's righteousness burning indeed.
Losing the cattle, tending-towards versatility.
Completing absolutely-nothing: having hearing indeed.

He was playing with fire. It was no **laughing** matter. By acting in this way, at this time, he would **burn** up everything familiar. His literal and emotional **nest** would be consumed in the blaze of rage and conflict his action would set off. It was a **pitfall**, a trap where he would be cut off from meaning and exposed to attack.

> **Pitfall**, HSIUNG: leads away from the experience of meaning; stuck and exposed to danger, unable to take in the situation; flow of life and spirit is blocked; unfortunate, baleful; keyword.

There was a suggestion of self-righteousness here too, of taking things too lightly, not realizing the extent of his own dependence and involvement. This **righteousness** and desire for independence could easily set the blaze off. It would be consumed along with everything else.

> **Righteous**, YI: proper and just, meets the standards; things in their proper place; the heart that rules itself; upright, moral rule; contrasts with Harvest, LI, advantage or profit.

So he should keep the contrary, **Harvest** and the work at hand, firmly in mind, letting it yield insight into the situation over time.

> **Harvest**, LI: advantageous, profitable; acute, insightful; benefit, nourish; third stage of Time Cycle.

If he would only hear this, he would **complete absolutely-nothing**, carry nothing of this plan through. At this time, such a move would be a disaster for all concerned. In the end all he would hear would be the ominous sounds of **crying** and **sobbing**.

A hexagram can suggest the quality that permeates a moment of time, one that you should reflect and reflect on, or it can warn of dangers that can cut you off from the flow of life and meaning. A reading can also suggest a limit beyond which effort is futile, releasing you from the burden of an illusary responsibility.

● EXAMPLE 4

● *A Shrine to Darkness*

The woman had suddenly called to begin analysis. She was professionally successful, happily married with children, and had no obvious symptoms. But in the first encounter it came out that she had been born in a small village in eastern Europe, father unknown, and that she and her mother were taken into the Displaced Person camps at the end of the war. During a transport they were separated. She never saw her mother again. When she spoke of these events her voice became flat and expressionless, as if they had happened to someone else. She had no recollection of them, in fact no memories before adolescence. She had learned of these events from others. She also said that she never dreamed.

Immediately a dream came that was so vivid she was forced to recount it. It put her back into her lost childhood, at a Christmas party in the village where she was born. There were candles on the evergreen tree, a joyful gathering. There was a gift waiting for her.

The situation seemed fairly clear. There was a whole complex of events and memories, possibly containing traumatic material, split off from consciousness. The strategy was to bring about contact with this material – a light in the darkness – and to offer a vessel for assimilating it.

But nothing worked. The woman became hostile and aggressive, releasing a poisonous black cloud of negativity. He saw this at first as resistance to the very dark material, and offered to work with it. Everything was ridiculed. They were completely blocked. His impulse was to ask, angrily, why she was wasting both of their time. But he knew this could also be a test, to see if he would repeat an old rejection pattern. It went on week after week. Baffled and emotionally entangled, he asked for more information.

Question: Please give me an image of this analytical relationship. What should my attitude toward it be?

Answer: Hexagram 36, no *Transforming Lines*

The answer was Hexagram 36, **Brightness Hiding**, with no *Transforming Lines*.

The *Image* of the hexagram described the situation in terms of **brightness** conscious intelligence **hidden** or harmed.

Brightness, MING: light-giving aspect of burning, heavenly bodies and consciousness; with fire, a Symbol of the trigram Radiance, LI.

Hide, YI: keep out of sight; remote, distant from the center; equalize by lowering; squat, level, make ordinary; pacified, colorless; cut, wound, destroy, exterminate.

This hexagram is the inverse of the one preceeding it, Hexagram 35, **Prospering**. There the light and warmth of **Radiance** – and the ability to see and become aware – emerge into the daylight. Here they are hidden beneath the earth. **Brightness** emphasizes consciousness, discrimination, spreading awareness. Here it is lowered, leveled, **proscribed, both injured and injuring**.

Injure, SHANG: hurt, wound, grieve, distress; mourn, sad at heart, humiliated.

Proscribe, CHU: exclude, reject by proclamation; denounce, forbid; reprove, seek as a criminal; condemn to death; clear away.

The *Counter Indication* to this situation is the analytical action *par excellence*, Hexagram 40, **Taking-apart**:

This hexagram describes your situation in terms of reflection, understanding and release from tension. It emphasizes that analysing things in order to be delivered from compulsion is the adequate way to handle it. To be in accord with the time, you are told to: **take** things **apart**!

Take-apart, HSIEH: loosen, disjoin, untie, sever, scatter; analyse, explain, understand; release, dispel sorrow; eliminate effects, solve problems; resolution, deliverance. The ideogram: horns and knife, cutting into forward thrust.

The question was posed about the *analytical relationship*, not the people involved. Everything in the *Image* and the qualities related to it states that analysis is powerless in this situation, in fact, the particular quality of analytic consciousness is both harmed and harmful.

There are no *Transforming Lines* which would give indications of ways to act or react in the situation. It is simply so. The light of the dream twinkling in the darkness, **Radiance** in the **earth**, stays there. Counter indicated, **taking** things **apart** and analysing their motivations cannot get at it.

However, this *Image* gave the analyst a way to reflect on the situation. It stated this was an objective situation, not a matter of blame or praise. This freed him from the necessity to act out his own angry feelings, to assume responsibility, or to blame the woman involved. It **brightened** and honored the **hidden**, gave it a place by grounding it in an objective reality, like the shrine to the Furies in classical Athens. For it showed a shadow **hidden** in analysing that falls between its general truth and the individual. *Not* all situations can or should be **brightened**, and the analyst does *not* always have the power to bring the light out of the darkness.

The ideal of the **chün tzu** here involved the ability to watch over the **crowds**, what is held in common with others, the common ground. The **chün tzu** must be able to choose, to **brighten** or to **darken. Brightness** is not a good in itself. The analyst speculated on many possibilities. Perhaps her psyche had deliberately chosen this encounter to seal off the experience. Perhaps his own **dark** experience was interacting with hers in a harmful way. Perhaps they were simply incompatibile. Though none of these things could be known, he could free both of them from a circle of blame and recrimination. As a **chün tzu**, he could choose to leave it in **darkness**, recognizing in this **darkness** a limit of analysing, a little shrine at the edge of the night.

- EXAMPLE 5

The King and I

This question was posed by a teacher, writer, psychologist and musician who had become involved with the fate of the Australian koala, considered by Aboriginal tribes as the secret knower and trickster. As he became acquainted with these remarkable animals, he found out that they were dying as a species. From a population of over 10 million in 1930, they had been reduced to fewer than 30,000. They seldom mated and most matings were non-productive. At the time of this reading, drought and severe bush fires were destroying the habitat of the remaining koalas. With no government support, he helped to build what is now the only hospital and study center in the world devoted to koalas. Volunteer crews with mechanical "cherry-pickers" were dispatched to rescue the koalas from burning trees where they were trapped and dying. He developed a burn treatment protocol for use in the intensive care unit which proved highly successful. Treatment, however, was very expensive.

Surprisingly the koalas, who had never seen a human being before and are

quite capable of inflicting serious bites, knew they were being helped and cooperated with the sometimes painful treatment. An intense bonding resulted for both humans and animals.

When the time came for him to leave the hospital and return home, he became deeply upset. He was completely enervated and disoriented at the prospect of leaving before the results of the treatment on Terry Glen, an animal he had rescued, were known. He knew that his own depression and concern could very quickly prove contagious, affecting the animals and undermining the morale of the team of volunteers. He knew he must do something. So he posed the question to the I Ching.

Question: What is going on? How should I relate to the people who are working here with me?

Answer: Hexagram 55, no *Transforming Lines*

The answer was Hexagram 55, **Abounding**, with no *Transforming Lines*.

The ***Image*** of this hexagram described his situation:

> ... in terms of profusion and abundance reaching culmination. It emphasizes that exuberantly increasing things to their fullest is the adequate way to handle it. To be in accord with the time, you are told to: **abound!**
>
> **Abound**, FENG: abundant, plentiful, copious; grow wealthy; at the point of overflowing; exuberant, fertile, prolific; rich in talents, property, friends; fullness, culmination; ripe, sumptuous, fat.

The situation was described as something full to the brim, culminating, spilling over and thus moving to an end. The emotional tone, however, was exuberant, prolific, sumptuous, fertile, joyful.

The *Image* brought an immediate connection, focusing his emotions. His experience as a counselor had taught him that when an **abundance** of powerful psychic material overflows into the personal it can cause panic and dysfunction. His contact with the koalas had activated deep feelings. Their overflow signalled that his consciousness was drawn too thin to handle it. It was spilling over into a whole range of symptoms, from panic to enervation. This had to be grounded by an image, a guideline for personal action.

The fundamental divinatory instruction was:

Abounding, Growing.
The king imagining it.
No grief. Properly sun centering.

Immersed in this very powerful emotional field, he was told he must not grieve over the fact it was culminating. The term described not only his confusion and anxious melancholy, but the hidden careworn quality that was enervating him.

> **Grieve(-over),** YU: sorrow, melancholy; mourn; anxious, careworn; hidden sorrow. The ideogram: heart, head, and limp, heart-sick and anxious.

But he should not hide away. He must be like the sun as it reaches zenith, the **center** of the heavens, shedding its brightest rays as it begins to set. The *Outer and Inner Aspects* amplified the image of the **sun centering**. He was to convert his inner sadness into positive **Radiance**, and let this **radiance** permeate and fertilize the outer world, **stirring-up** action, germinating and inspiring. He was to increase the **Radiance** of everything, **abounding** but not entangled in grief or anxiety.

The *Sequence* suggested that he had been profoundly changed, **converted**, by coming to this **place**. The behavior of the koalas, who are among the oldest animals still living on earth, showed that something from the distant past, his totemic spirit, had found him. Working with the koalas, he had acquired something **great**, something that organized his life.

> **Convert,** KUEI: change to another form, persuade; return to yourself or the place where you belong; restore, revert, become loyal; turn into; give a young girl in marriage. The ideogram: arrive and wife, become mistress of a household.

> **Great,** TA: big, noble, important, very; orient the will toward a self-imposed goal, impose direction; ability to lead or guide your life; contrasts with small, HSIAO, flexible adaptation to what crosses your path; keyword.

What he should *not* do, the *Counter Indication*, was to be **exceedingly great** – exclusively focused on one thing - and be isolated by it. **Exceeding** was quite different from **abounding**.

Exceed, KU: go beyond, pass by, pass over; excessive, transgress; error, fault.

The *Contrasted Definitions* showed the present situation contrasted with **sojourning**, an important image throughout his life:

Sojourn, LÜ: travel, stay in places other than your home; itinerant troops, temporary residents; visitor, guest, lodger. The ideogram: banner and people around it, loyal to a symbol rather than their temporary residence.

The **numerous anteriority**, the many people who, each for his or her own reason, had come together here, was modulating once again into **connecting the few**, seeking out the others in the world who could also be connected to what was happening here. He could **sojourn** under this banner. He has recently published a significant book on these animals and the myths around them, *Koala: Australia's Ancient Ones*, (New York: MacMillan, 1994).

The *Symbol Tradition* reinforced the sense that everything in the situation was **culminating**.

Culminate, CHIH: bring to the highest degree; arrive at the end or summit; superlative.

It also connected to the other thing that was holding him. He was scheduled to be an expert witness for the defense in an upcoming trial. Here **severing litigating** spoke about cutting the connection to the litigation, allowing the **punishing** to occur.

Sever, CHE: break off, separate, sunder, cut in two; discriminate, judge the true and false.

It later proved that his testimony would have been useless, and that he would have become embroiled in an endless series of legal complications.

Finally the *Image* spoke to his deepest concern in the situation: how he could relate to the people and the extremely sensitive animals in the situation who could easily be infected by **grieving**. The way to deal with it was to **imagine it** as if he were a **king**. This was the sacrifice to the spirit that would ensure **growing**.

King(hood), WANG: effective ruler, by authority of the Emperor, from whom others derive their power.

Imagine, CHIA: create in the mind; fantasize, suppose, pretend, imitate; fiction; illusory, unreal; costume. The ideogram: person and borrow.

He was invited to **imagine** himself as the **king**, the one from whom blessings flow and others derive their **power**. The **king**'s function was not to focus on a specific goal, but to stay in contact with **tao** or the way and pass the power on through a generosity that rivals the **sun** at midday. He was invited to put on the **king's** costume, to **radiate** its **abounding** and generous power with neither care nor sadness. This image would carry him through.

The last days in the hospital went well. Dressing himself in the costume of the **king**, he was able to encourage people at their work and remain **abundant** and joyful. Playing this role on the last day, he saw Terry Glen, the koala he had personally saved. These animals, whom the tribes consider to be clever and tricky as well as knowing, do not usually bond to humans. But this one had established a deep bond. When he approached, the koala put the soft, vulnerable part of his hand on his cheek, patted him knowingly and affectionately, then deliberately pushed him away. **No grieving**. It was time to go.

The hexagrams can give you images that carry you through dangerous situations. They can also reflect on your basic drives and attitudes, particularly when they are changing or they bring you into conflict with the world. Such reflection can save you from compulsive action and being trapped in a conflict that no one can win.

EXAMPLE 6

Growing Pains

He was a young doctor completing training in psychiatry. His drive was bringing him into a real conflict with some of his supervisors. He engaged in dangerous sports and held amateur records. He was interested in several spiritual disciplines and alternative approaches to medicine. He was convinced that he could only really help people by giving them a sense of spiritual meaning. Because of his passionate convictions, and the force with which they were expressed, his training was troubled. He was indignant about its narrow approach to problems of personal meaning. His supervisors told him, however,

that his views on spirituality were a personal matter, that it was dangerous to all concerned to introduce his views in a psychoanalytical setting, and that he was being "unscientific." This conflict was threatening to explode, and he sought reflection on his drive through posing the question to the I Ching.

Question: What about my *drive* to bring spiritual practises into psychoanalytic therapy?

Answer: Hexagram 4, 6/6, Hexagram 7

The answer was Hexagram 4, **Enveloping,** with a *Transforming Line* at the top, leading to Hexagram 7, **Legions/Leading.**

The *Image* of the *Primary Hexagram* shifted his sense of championing a cause like a Zen master shocking a disciple. It saw him and his drive:

> ... in terms of concealment and clouded awareness. It emphasizes that actively accepting this concealment in order to nurture growth is the adequate way to handle it. To be in accord with the time, you are told to: **envelop!**
>
> **Envelop**, MENG: cover, pull over, hide, conceal; lid or cover; clouded awareness, dull; ignorance, immaturity; unseen beginnings. The ideogram: plant and covered, hidden growth.

The *Image* has two aspects: concealment and immaturity, unseen beginnings and ignorance. The first shock was: your desire is immature and your awareness confused. Because the terms extend to all the components in the situation, it also implies: the situation is immature, your idea "ahead of its time." So the second shock was: revealing your idea too soon will destroy its hidden growth. He was told: Keep it to yourself until you are ready. You are not ready yet.

The *Outer and Inner Aspects* revealed that the firm limit he was encountering in the outer world was there to *protect* his development. The defining top line of the outer trigram, **Bound**, was transforming. This would eventually transform his overabundant yang energy – his drive toward confrontation – into the primal receptive and structuring power of **Field**.

The inner world was characterized by **Gorge**, the night sea journey through toil and danger that dissolves the old forms of experience. This deep psychic process was what the outer limit was protecting. He had to do what was for him the most difficult thing possible: accept the limitation and wait, **enveloped**, trusting the inner breakdown and change.

This was not going back to the starting point. The *Counter Indication*, **returning**, emphasized that the situation was **enveloped** precisely to *further* growth. The *Related Hexagram*, **Legions/Leading**, had the same *Counter Indication*. The message was trust in an unconscious process, not trying again and again.

The *Image* and *Image Tradition* brought out several things about the drive. This was a favorable divination – **Harvesting Trial** – and bringing the situation to full **growth** involved a sacrifice to the spirit. The question was what sacrifice was involved. The use of the pronoun **I/me/my** in these texts was unusual. It put the focus on his subjective experience, what he thought and felt, not what was being done to him. Other terms in the *Image* elicited the fact that he had asked this question before in many different ways, in fact he was constantly asking it. This going back again and again was **obscuring** the real problem.

> **Obscure**, TU: confuse, muddy, agitate; muddled, cloudy, turbid; agitated water; annoy through repetition.

But the *Image Tradition* indicated that this compulsive repetition could be focused on **correcting** the situation.

> **Correct**, CHENG: rectify deviation or one-sidedness; proper, straight, exact, regular; constant, rule, model. The ideogram: stop and one, hold to one thing.

By seeing the hostile response to his compulsive striving as a compensation of one-sidedness within himself, he could **achieve** a real degree of intuitive **wisdom**.

> **Achieve**, KUNG: work done, results; real accomplishment, praise, worth, merit. The ideogram: workman's square and forearm, combining craft and strength.

Understanding this one-sidedness was the center of the reading, the key to his desire. It gave access to the **all-wise**, the spiritual gift he sought to give to others.

> **All-wise**, SHENG: intuitive universal wisdom; mythical sages; holy, sacred; mark of highest distinction. The ideogram: ear and inform, one who knows all from a single sound.

Here several terms emerged. From the *Sequence* came **immaturity**.

Immature, CHIH: small, tender, young, delicate; undeveloped; conceited, haughty; late grain.

Accepting that the drive was real but **immature** cautioned him against arrogance and protected the vulnerability of his idealism.

From the *Contrasted Definitions* came a conscious and public acceptance of a *lack* of clarity. He was to be **motley and-also conspicuous**, emphasizing vulnerability and incompletion rather than fixed purpose.

The *Symbol Tradition* reinforced the move toward images of organic growth rather than spiritual drive, **using fruiting movement to nurture actualizing-tao.**

> **Fruit**, KUO: plants' annual produce; tree fruits; come to fruition, fruits of actions; produce, results, effects; reliable; conclude, surpass. The ideogram: tree topped by a round fruit.

> **Nurture**, YÜ: bring up, support, rear, raise; increase.

This is the long term process of **nurturing** and bearing **fruit**. It acts indirectly over time, not directly and immediately.

All these things formed a context for the *Transforming Line*. This line defined his "drive" – not the purpose behind it – as an attempt to **smite** what was **enveloping** him.

> **Smite**, CHI: hit, beat, attack; hurl against, rush a position; rouse to action. The ideogram: hand and hit, fist punching.

Such an attack, hurling himself against what was actually *protecting* his **immaturity**, transformed the quality of the **enveloping**. It became **smiting** in its turn, attacking him. In this adversarial situation one or the other party ends by having recourse to **outlawry**.

> **Outlawry**, K'OU: break the laws; violent people, outcasts, bandits.

The only way to take advantage of this situation was to **resist** this **outlawry**.

> **Resist**, YÜ: withstand, oppose; bring to an end; prevent. The ideogram: rule and worship, imposing ethical or religious limits.

This implies ceasing to **smite** what was **enveloping**, ceasing to impose his will, break rules, or antagonize his superiors. The **enveloping** was not their fault. The only possibility of **achieving** something comes not through **smiting**, but through **yielding**.

Yield(-to), SHUN: give way and bear produce; comply, agree, follow, obey; unresisting, docile, flexible; nourish, provide; the Action of the trigram Field, K'UN. The ideogram: head and current, water flowing from the head of a river, yielding to the banks.

This was the only action that could connect **above** and **below**. He had a choice. He could accept this and **yield** or continue to **smite** the **envelopment** and be turned into an **outlaw**. This was the key to his inner process.

This choice could result in a new way of acting. The *Image* of the *Related Hexagram* described the beginning of this new focus:

... in terms of unorganized crowds or bunches of things. It emphasizes that organizing these things into functional units is the adequate way to handle it. To be in accord with the time, you are told to: **lead**!

Legions/leading, SHIH: troops; an organized unit, a metropolis; leader, general, model, master; organize, make functional; take as a model, imitate. The ideogram: heap and whole, organize confusion into functional units.

The ideal of the **legions** represents a different way to organize drive and energy. They exist to **yield** and **serve.** They are seen not as an instrument of offensive war, **smiting** what opposes them, but as an instrument of culture. The **leader**, master or teacher − what he wished to become − provides a model, a pattern to be imitated. By **yielding** and **serving**, the potential **outlaws** can become the **legions**. The **leader**, at the moment **enveloped** in confusion and **immaturity**, is potentially the **all-wise**, a model or pattern of intuitive wisdom.

The final answer to his real and sincere drive to bring spirit into people's lives was first to bring order out of his own confusion. The **enveloping** was a gift; it was there to help him. Through **yielding** to it comes inner organization and the possibility to serve rather than impose his will. He could himself become a model, with an indirect yet deep effect on his surroundings. Then who he was rather than what he wanted would lead others to the spirit.

This reading gave insight into a basic drive, and how it might be developed. Questioning the Oracle can also bring out an unconscious "shadow" complex. It shows the underside of an attitude toward the world that has become automatic, at the moment it begins to generate uneasiness and conflict.

EXAMPLE 7

The Man Who Wasn't There

At first, you hardly noticed that there was something unusual about him. He was quiet, gentle, withdrawn yet not cold, intelligent and sympathetic. His habitual pose was "standing back, on the edge of things." But just beneath the surface you felt something stirring.

    He lived a quiet life, and had never traveled. He worked with a small group that had little outside contact. But the "mushrooming therapy industry," as he called it, had created a series of powerful "schools" in his area. The growing hostility between them profoundly disturbed him, though he did not know exactly why. He wondered if he "should sit back, taking my usual observer position, or break in, take a stand, come out and be seen?" The question itself was the tip of an iceberg; beneath it something was knocking at the door.

Question: Should I remain insular, an observer?

Answer: Hexagram 5, 9/5, Hexagram 11

    The answer was Hexagram 5, **Attending**, with a *Transforming Line* in the fifth place, leading to Hexagram 11, **Pervading**.

    The *Image* of the *Primary Hexagram* immediately shifted his sense of the problem. It was not a question of choosing between "insularity" and the aggression involved in championing a cause.

    This hexagram describes your situation in terms of being compelled to wait for and serve something. It emphasizes that fixing your attention on what is required while waiting carefully for the right moment to act is the adequate way to handle it. To be in accord with the time, you are told to: **attend**!

    Attend, HSÜ: take care of, look out for, serve; turn your mind to what is necessary; wait, await, wait on; hesitate, doubt; obstinate, fixed. The ideogram: rain and stop, compelled to wait, or rain and origin, providing what is needed.

    Attending has two interconnected qualities: to take care of, serve, provide what is necessary, i.e. to wait *on* something, and to expect, to wait *for* something. One waits *for* the right moment, or the right occasions, to wait *on*, to provide what is needed. It has a public face, yet is not aggressive or imposing. It combines flexibility and the idea of serving, helping, **attending** on. This is the stance of the courtier, the mediator, the facilitator.

The *Counter Indication* is **polarizing**.

> **Polarize**, K'UEI: separate, oppose; contrary, mutually exclusive; distant from, absent, remote; animosity, anger; astronomical or polar opposition: the ends of an axis, 180 degrees apart.

He was specifically enjoined *not* to polarize his situation further by setting things in opposition to each other. His immediate association was to an intellectual attitude that produced the anger and animosity he saw characterizing the professional situation around him. **Attending** was *not* this intellectuality. It could also suggest an attitude toward something inside himself.

The *Contrasted Definitions* further characterized **attending** as **not advancing**.

> **Advance**, CHIN: exert yourself, make progress, climb; be promoted; further the development of, augment; adopt a religion or conviction; offer, introduce.

Thus promoting the growth of a particular sect or opinion, including his own, was counter indicated.

The *Sequence* and the *Symbol Tradition* supplied more information. There was something **immature** in the situation and he was obliged to **nourish** it. This must be accepted and understood. This **nourishing** proceeded through the way or **tao** of **drinking[and]taking-in**.

> **Drinking[and]taking-in**, YIN SHIH: comprehensive term for eating, drinking and breathing; a meal, eating together.

> **Tao**: way or path; ongoing process of being and the course it traces for each specific person or thing; keyword. The ideogram: go and head, leading and the path it creates.

In this situation, the **chün tzu** would use **tao** and its potent virtue to **repose delighting**.

> **Repose**, YEN: rest, leisure, peace of mind; banquet, feast. The ideogram: shelter and rest, a wayside inn.

> **Delight**, LO: take joy or pleasure in; pleasant, relaxed; also: music as harmony, elegance and pleasure.

The *Transforming Line* further focused the action of **attending** as tending-towards liquor taken-in:

> **Liquor,** CHIU: alcoholic beverages, distilled spirits; spirit which perfects the good and evil in human nature. The ideogram: liquid above fermenting must, separating the spirits.

> **Take-in,** SHIH: eat, ingest, swallow, devour; incorporate.

Repose, delight, liquor, banquets, feasts, music, leisure, peace of mind, pleasure, relaxation, harmony, elegance, shelter and rest imply something quite different than either official battles or insular withdrawal. They imply socializing in unofficial ways and **taking-in** the spirit of life. This puts people at their ease, defuses oppositions, and undermines rigid intellectual oppositions through pleasure and personal contact. **Taking-in liquor** was an important part of this, literally and symbolically. It made the spirits bright. In old China, **attendants** on the gods were expected to **take-in** large amounts of this sacred sort of spirit on social and ceremonial occasions. It was an offering to the spirit that brought people together.

On the most pragmatic level this told him to **attend** at those occasions and times when **liquor** was **taken-in**, when spirit was available. The injunction was: you can have a non-polarizing effect on your situation by **attending** on occasions where there is social contact instead of academic warfare. This could **indeed** correct the center of things. Putting the emphasis here where it belonged redressed an imbalance.

> **Correct,** CHENG: rectify deviation or one-sidedness; proper, straight, exact, regular; constant, rule, model. The ideogram: stop and one, hold to one thing.

> **Center,** CHUNG: inner, central; put in the center; middle, stable point enabling you to face inner and outer changes; middle line of trigram. The ideogram: field divided in two equal parts.

This **attends** to the growing maturity of the situation and furthers a **pervading** spirit, the *Image* of the *Related Hexagram*.

He became very uneasy. This complex of terms touched a hidden center in himself that was in **polar** opposition to his normal attitude. We could feel the Man Who Wasn't There moving. "I don't usually circulate, I don't usually drink, social occasions frighten me. In fact, there is something both exciting and very frightening in this. It reaches a part of me that is very inhibited." The **immaturity** in the situation extended to something in him. **Attending tending-towards liquor taken-in corrected** something one-sided and out of balance. It was through delight, pleasure, expansion, mutual enjoyment and social contact that it could be **nourished**.

The *Image* of the *Primary Hexagram* states that **growing** comes through **shining**, making one's light and one's capacity to illuminate things available. It would make him stand out and be seen.

> **Shine**, KUANG: illuminate; give off brilliant, bright light; honor, glory, éclat; result of action, contrasts with brightness, MING, light of heavenly bodies. The ideogram: fire above person, lifting the light.

Attending and **shining** connected the inner and the outer so the spirit could flow. It **possessed conformity**.

> **Possessing conformity**, YU FU: inner and outer are in accord; confidence of the spirits has been captured; sincere, truthful; proper to take action.

At such a time it was fitting to enter the stream of life with a purpose.

> **Wading the Great River**, SHE TA CH'UAN: consciously moving into the flow of time; enter the stream of life with a goal or purpose; embark on a significant enterprise.

What emerged from the hidden center was that he longed to "shine" and to travel. Both were part of the "attractive and frightening" complex exemplified by **taking-in liquor** and the **chün tzu** who could **repose delighting**.

The *Image Tradition* indicated that connecting with this hidden desire was **actually** his own **righteousness**. It compensated one-sidedness and through that connection linked his situation to the **heavenly situation** and the flow of the spirit. The *Image* of the *Related Hexagram* indicated that this correcting could open a **pervading** stream of energy flowing through him into the world. But he must make the effort to communicate and spread it.

> This hexagram describes your situation in terms of prospering and expanding. It emphasizes that continually spreading this prosperity through communicating is the adequate way to handle it. To be in accord with the time, you are told to: **pervade!**

Pervade, T'AI: spread and reach everywhere, permeate, diffuse; communicate; great, extensive, abundant, prosperous; smooth, slippery; extreme, extravagant, prodigal. Mount T'AI in eastern China was a sacred mountain connecting heaven and earth. The emperor made offerings there to establish harmony between humans and the great spirits. The ideogram: person in water, connected to the universal medium.

Behind the frightening complex was a time of real creative connection, not only for himself, but for the things and people he **attended** on. Though there was a danger of being carried away as he embarked on the **pervading** stream, he was asked to move out of his insularity by moving into and through its shadow. This imbued the events of his life with **significance**. It challenged him to **attend** on the frightening and attractive complex without **polarizing** his relation to it. Spreading this spirit was meaningful, for by doing so he could further **tao**.

Each answer the Oracle gives is an attempt to provide you with the information you need in order to make a choice at a difficult moment in your life. It can also be used to explore the options open to you at these crossroads, helping you to see farther into the choices to be made.

● *EXAMPLE 8*

● *The Dark Forest*

She was about to take responsibility – financial, administrative and artistic – for a large training program. She wanted the responsibility and scope and felt a drive to succeed. But as the time to begin grew near, fears, anxieties and uncertainties which she couldn't understand would periodically overwhelm her. She felt something strange behind them, something dark in the ambition itself. So to find out what was lurking there, she posed a question to the I *Ching.*

First Question: What about wholeheartedly taking responsibility for this Program?

First Answer: Hexagram 26, no *Transforming Lines*

The answer was Hexagram 26, **Great Accumulating**, with no *Transforming Lines.*

The *Image* of this hexagram described her situation:

... in terms of an overriding concern that defines what is valuable. It emphasizes that bringing the variety of things under the control of this central idea is the adequate way to handle it. To be in accord with the time, you are told to: **accumulate** the **great!**

Great, TA: big, noble, important, very; orient the will toward a self-imposed goal, impose direction; ability to lead or guide your life; contrasts to small, HSIAO, flexible adaptation to what crosses your path; keyword.

Accumulate, CH'U: hoard, gather, retain, herd together; control, restrain; domesticate, tame, train; raise, feed, sustain, bring up. The ideogram: field and black, fertile black soil good for pastures, accumulated through retaining silt.

This seemed a very fortunate answer. It spoke of the necessity to subordinate everything to the one **great** concern, **accumulating** the people, things, ideas, contacts, experience to make it manifest. The time was right to **Wade the Great River**, to enter the stream of life with a goal or embark on a significant enterprise.

The fact that there were no *Transforming Lines* indicated the process of **accumulating** could take a long time and would permeate every part of her life. With this her fears suddenly appeared.

What came out was that she was very much afraid of losing herself in this **great** enterprise. She had been consumed by her work up till now, and deeply identified with her employer and teacher. Her personal life had been reduced to virtually nothing. So the reading suddenly focused on the opposite of **accumulating,** on what was being *lost*.

It was **not dwelling**.

Dwell, CHI: home, house, household, family; domestic, within doors; live in. The ideogram: roof and pig or dog, the most valued domestic animals.

What should and would *not* happen, the *Counter Indication*, was **Converting** the **Maiden**:

Convert, KUEI: change to another form, persuade; return to yourself or the place where you belong; restore, revert, become loyal; turn into; give a young girl in marriage. The ideogram: arrive and wife, become mistress of a household.

Maiden(hood), MEI: girl not yet nubile; younger sister, daughter of a

secondary wife. The ideogram: woman and not-yet.

What would be lost was **dwelling** – home, household, family – and the **conversion** of a **maiden**. It suggested something fundamentally feminine would remain untouched.

The answer said it was possible to go ahead with the program if she was willing to submit everything to the rule of the **great**. She had already been put in this position for several years and suffered from the loss of a personal life. Lurking in her family history was a major business failure through badly timed ambition, the shadow of **great accumulating**. Her fears intensified rather than diminished with this favorable answer. So she asked for an image of the other fork in the road.

Second Question: What about *not* assuming responsibility for this Program?

Second Answer: Hexagram 41, 9/2, 6/3, 6/4, Hexagram 30

The answer to the second question, about *not* taking responsibility for the program, was Hexagram 41, **Diminishing**, with *Transforming Lines* in the second, third and fourth places, leading to Hexagram 30, **Radiance**.

The *Image* of the *Primary Hexagram* indicated that giving up the direction of the program would be a sacrifice. She would feel it as a real loss and would be made smaller by it.

> This hexagram describes your situation in terms of sacrifice and loss. It emphasizes that lessening yourself and decreasing your involvements is the adequate way to handle it. To be in accord with the time, you are told to: **diminish**!
>
> **Diminish**, SUN: lessen, make smaller; take away from; lose, damage, spoil, wound; bad luck; blame, criticize; offer up, give away. The ideogram: hand and ceremonial vessel, offering sacrifice.

Unlike the fear that emerged from the first reading, this image of loss and sacrifice attracted her, drew her on to know more.

The *Image* revealed that **diminishing**, through **possessing conformity**, could bring her inner and outer life into accord.

> **Possessing conformity**, YU FU: inner and outer are in accord; confidence of the spirits has been captured; sincere, truthful; proper to take action.

It was **without fault**, without error or harm, and could be a source or

spring of **significance** and growth. In this situation, it was advantageous to **possess a direction**, a goal or purpose. Finding out what this purpose was involved **asking-why**.

Ask-why, HO: interjection: why? how? why not?; interrupt with questions; intimidate, heckle. The ideogram: speak and beg, demanding an answer.

This involves questioning your concerns, demanding answers, cutting into things, breaking into patterns of behavior, the things one does unquestioningly.

The *Contrasted Definitions* show that **diminishing** and **augmenting**, the following hexagram, form a pair. **Diminishing** is the hidden **beginning** of **increase** and **augmenting**. If you want to **augment** something, you must first **decrease** it.

Decrease, SHUAI: grow or make smaller; fade, decline, decay, diminish, cut off; grow old; adversity, misfortune.

Decreasing makes energy available for the **beginning** of a new cycle. It is *not* going back to start over. The *Counter Indication* is **returning**. **Diminishing** begins something new. Its **inner stimulation begins** a new formative process, and **diminishing** involvement makes this energy available. But you must have a sacrificial utensil, a method or tool here described as **two platters**, to **avail-of** this power and apply it to your own situation.

The *Image Tradition* explains that these **two platters**, the sacrificial method or utensil, are **diminishing** the **solid** and **augmenting** the **supple**.

Solid, KANG: quality of the whole lines; firm, strong, unyielding, persisting.

Supple, JOU: quality of the opened lines; flexible, pliant, tender, adaptible.

You use **asking-why** to **diminish** what was formerly **solid**, firm, purposeful, strong. This emptying out of former purposes enables you to **associate-with** the spiritual quality of the time.

Associate(-with), YÜ: consort with, combine; companions; group, band, company; agree with, comply, help. The ideogram: pair of hands reaching downward meets a pair of hands reaching upward, helpful association.

The *Attached Evidences* indicated that the action she was asking about – **diminishing** her commitment – was connected with **actualizing-tao**, acquiring the virtue and power to become an individual. **Diminishing** is **actualizing-tao's adjusting**.

Adjust, HSIU: regulate, repair, clean up, renovate.

This is at first **heavy** and hard to bear. She would suffer from it, feeling the loss, the decrease, growing personally smaller, held down and unable to fly.

Heavy, NAN: arduous, grievous, difficult; hardship, distress; harass; contrasts with versatile, I, deal lightly with. The ideogram: domestic bird with clipped tail and drying sticky earth.

But what comes out of this heavy work is **versatility**, imaginative mobility and the capacity to adjust to the movement of **tao**.

Because **tao** is **moving** in what is **above** in this situation, the **chün tzu curbs anger** in order to **block appetites**.

Curb, CH'ENG: reprimand, reprove, repress; warn, caution; corrective punishment. The ideogram: heart and action, the heart acting on itself.

Curbing anger, forcing **anger** to act on itself, **blocks** or obstructs the unconscious drive of the **appetites** in order to make you aware of them.

Appetites, YÜ: drives, instinctive craving; wishes, passions, desires, aspirations; long for, seek ardently; covet.

Through **diminishing** you are made aware that what you are seeking in others is actually part of yourself. **Asking-why, diminishing** the **solid** and **blocking** the **appetites** frees you from the stuck quality of unconscious involvements. This makes energy available to what was excluded or repressed in the former situation.

With this, she found herself in the center of a net of compulsions fighting their way to the surface through her fears. Even if the time was propitious for launching her program, what was at stake in **diminishing** it was her own life and her ability to live it, her **actualizing-tao**.

The *Transforming Lines* gave each of her fears a face. They indicated that each could be resolved through the **diminishing** implied by her question, giving up direction of this new program. The **transforming** lines suggested the possibility of **transformation**.

Transform, PIEN: abrupt, radical, fundamental mutation from one state of being to another; transformation of lines in hexagrams; contrasts with change, HUA, gradual metamorphosis.

The *Transforming Line* at the second place indicated that what she had asked about was a **Harvesting Trial**, an advantageous divination. It would **nowhere diminish** her but **augment** her. Its **purpose activated** from her own **center**. In this situation, the act of **chastising** was a trap or **pitfall**.

Chastise, CHENG: punish, subjugate, discipline; reduce to order; punishing expedition. The ideogram: step and correct, a rectifying move.

This line separated her from a particular role she had created for herself, a combination of bearing responsibility, enforcing order and isolation that she called "the Policewoman." The late childhood fears were lurking here. Because she was afraid that this program was her only chance for financial security, she found herself constantly **chastising** others in order to make her place secure.

The *Transforming Line* in the third place addressed a deep fear of isolation and loneliness. It affirmed that where there were **three people moving** they would be **diminished** by **one**. **The-one** person, herself, was separating from a group. But she should not fear. Through the **diminishing** of walking alone, this **one person** would join hands with a **friend**.

Friend, YU: companion, associate; of the same mind; attached, fraternal, in pairs. The ideogram: two hands joined.

The *Transforming Line* in the fourth place showed her **affliction diminished** by this action.

Afflict, CHI: sickness, disorder, defect, calamity; injurious; pressure and consequent anger, hate or dislike. The ideogram: sickness and dart, a sudden affliction.

This described the panic, fear and disorientation that would suddenly grip her, as well as the explosive anger of **chastising** and the continual pressure to succeed. **Diminishing** what created this, and doing it **swiftly**, would permit **rejoicing**, returning joy to **afflicted** parts of her life.

Rejoice, HSI: feel and give joy; delight, exult; cheerful, merry. The ideogram: joy (music) and mouth, expressing joy.

The result of this **diminishing**, shown by the *Related Hexagram*, was Hexagram 30, **Radiance**.

The *Image* of this hexagram described the evolution of her situation:

> ... in terms of expanding light, warmth and awareness. It emphasizes that joining with and depending on what spreads this light, the action of **Radiance**, is the adequate way to handle it. To be in accord with the time, you are told to: **congregate**!

> **Radiance**, LI: glowing light, spreading in all directions; light-giving, discriminating, articulating; divide and arrange in order; the power of consciousness. The ideogram: bird and weird, the magical fire-bird with brilliant plumage.

> **Congregate**, LI: cling together; depend on, attached to, rely on; couple, pair, herd. The ideogram: deer flocking together.

Here the dark forest was illuminated, and the way was clear. Behind **diminishing** and growing smaller was not isolation, loneliness and **affliction** but the potential for awareness. It pointed at another, warmer and more conscious connection, **congregating** with **people**. Both forks in this road were possible, the decision was hers. But this reading indicated that one of them was the way of **transformation**. **Heavy** at first with a sense of loss and sacrifice, it led to **joy** and companionship. It would free her from the dark forest, the **afflicting** drives and fears of compulsion.

THE GLOBAL SYSTEM *THE UNIVERSAL COMPASS*

● *Divination and Traditional Science*

Much of traditional Chinese science began in the *I Ching*. The system behind it, first codified in the Han dynasty, grew out of imagistic, correlative or magical thinking. It connects to terms and figures used in the *I Ching*, and can extend and amplify the oracular images. This system describes the way psychic energy moves in the world and in the individual in a precise yet imaginative way. It formed the basic categories of traditional Chinese thought and perception, providing a way to navigate the world by pointing out what would develop from a particular moment or experience.

This system is organic and complicated. You should not expect to remember or master it all in one reading. Use it as reference material. The section of the Hexagrams called *Outer and Inner Aspects* gives you a concentrated version of these systems as they relate to individual hexagrams. From there you can refer back to the full system. Let it gradually penetrate the way you think about things as you use it.

This system uses three categories – the Time Cycle, Yin-Yang Dynamics, and the Correspondance of Qualities – to describe the quality and direction of moving energy. It is expressed in a fundamental chart called the *Universal Compass*. It portrays a constantly moving world made up of organically interdependent forces.

The *Universal Compass* consists of a set of concentric circles that represent interlocking cycles:

● *1* The Time Cycle

● *2* The Yin and Yang Hemicycles

● *3* The Eight Phases of Yin-Yang Dynamics

● *4* The Five Transformative Moments

These cycles connect with:

● 5 The Cycle of the Eight Trigrams

The cycle of trigrams connects in turn with the hexagrams of the *I Ching*. Thus the hexagrams are linked to the interaction of all these qualities in a dynamic and systematic way.

The basic premise of the *Universal Compass* is that it describes energetic processes of the world-organism or world-soul. Through this system your question and your situation are linked with an organic, constantly moving world.

● *The Time Cycle*

The basic connection between *I Ching* divination and the system of the *Universal Compass* is the quality of time. This connection is expressed in the four fundamental terms of the Time Cycle: **Spring**, YÜAN; **Growing, Growth**, HENG; **Harvest, Harvesting**, LI; and **Trial**, CHEN. These terms have divinatory meanings that come from the oldest layers of the *I Ching*'s texts. They developed into the model of a dynamic process used to describe all units or spans of time.

● **Spring**, YÜAN, as a divinatory term, refers to the power to originate something. It is an adjective meaning great, excellent, very much, very potent and indicates that you are connected to the source or origin of things. As the first phase of the Time Cycle it refers to: the vernal season, the East, sunrise; issue forth, begin to appear, arise; rising or issuing from the ground, thus source or origin; the first sign of day, the beginning, the first cause or generating power of the cosmos; the eldest, the head, original, primary; the head of a river, the source of thoughts in the individual, the source of authority in the social field. It is the primal originating power itself and the place in space or time where it appears.

● **Grow, Growing**, HENG, as a divinatory term, indicates that something can be successful, vigorous and effective if a sacrifice is offered to the proper spirits at the proper time. As the second phase of the Time Cycle it refers to: summer, the South, midday; any manifestation of vigorous life; all-pervading; increase gradually, become by degrees, pervade, spread; influence throughout as heaven influences, penetrates and increases all things; prosperous, successful, effectual, carried to completion. It is the power that gives full-grown form to what is initiated or sprouted in **Spring**, YÜAN. The ideogram suggests success through offering a gift to a superior.

●   **Harvest, Harvesting**, LI, as a divinatory term, indicates what is advantageous, profitable, of great benefit and full of insight. As the third phase of the Time Cycle it refers to: autumn, the West, sunset; the season's yield of natural produce; the product of an action or effort, gains, profit, interest on money; reaping and gathering in; benefit, nourish; the edge or point of a knife; sharp, acute. It stands for both the sharpness of the blade that reaps and for the profit gathered. The ideogram suggests a knife and ripe grain standing in the field.

●   **Trial**, CHEN, refers to the act of divination itself, trying or proving something by submitting it to the judgement of the spirits. As the fourth and final phase of the Time Cycle it refers to: winter, the North, midnight; test, ordeal, proof; separating wheat from chaff, the valuable from the useless; the test-withstanding, resistent part of something, the kernel; undefiled, uncorrupted and uncorruptable, pure, virtuous, righteous, firm. It stands for testing by ordeal and the lasting solid core that emerges from it. The ideogram suggests a pearl and divination.

The core that emerges from **Trial** or Winter is the seed of **Spring**, beginning the cycle anew.

●   *Yin and Yang: Struction and Action*

Yin and *yang* are the fundamental categories of this system, but translating these terms is difficult. We can call *yang* **Action**, but then are left with words like passive or static for *yin*. **Struction**, derived from Latin *struere*, to erect or construct, suggests that each of these powers exists in its own right.

The categories *yin* and *yang* grew from a wide range of shifting qualities:

YIN	YANG
Yin / **struction** applies to:	*Yang* / **action** applies to:
the shady, cool Southern ▌	▌ *the bright, warm Northern*
bank of a river	*bank of a river*
the shady, cool Northern ▌	▌ *the bright, warm Southern*
slope of a mountain	*slope of a mountain*
Water ▌	▌ *Fire*
Moon ▌	▌ *Sun*
Lower ▌	▌ *Upper*
Interior ▌	▌ *Exterior*
Dark ▌	▌ *Bright*
Moist ▌	▌ *Dry*
Soft ▌	▌ *Hard*
Obscure ▌	▌ *Manifest*
Contracting ▌	▌ *Expanding*
Reaction ▌	▌ *Stimulus*
Incoming ▌	▌ *Outgoing*
Completing ▌	▌ *Beginning*
Response ▌	▌ *Move*
Receptive ▌	▌ *Initiating*
To be ▌	▌ *To do*
The ideogram *yin* suggests hillshadows and clouds	The ideogram *yang* suggests sunrise and a sunlit flag.

The terms evolved into dynamic categories through which all phenomena could be analysed:

- Yang, **action**, is the light, active aspect of all phenomena. It refers to: movement, dynamic development, thrust, stimulus, drive; focusing on a goal, giving direction to something. By creating the future, yang destroys the present, negating anything that exists in a positive or consolidated sense. The yang aspect of phenomena is their dynamic mode of becoming: arousal, transformation and dissolution. It is united, continuous, uni-directional, a closed system where all things are categorically equal.

● Yin, **struction**, is the shadowy, structive aspect of phenomena. It refers to: build, make concrete, establish; limited, bound, given specific being; consolidating, conserving, structuring something. By consolidating the present, yin stops forward motion, drive or purpose. The yin aspect of phenomena is the result of contraction and concentration; it is their positive (from *ponere*, to place, to put) mode of existence. It is diverse, adaptible extension in space, an open system where all things are categorically discontinuous.

However, with one exception, the actual terms *yin* and *yang* do not occur in the oldest layers of the *I Ching*. What does occur is the pair of **opened** — — and **whole** ——— lines. These lines and the qualities associated with them are the divinatory basis underlying the categories *yin* and *yang*.

● **Opened**, P'I, refers to: open up, disclose, burst forth; develop through germinating each thing. The ideogram suggests a double door, toil, and the body: the literal womb and the separateness of each physical being. The corresponding quality in a person or a situation is **supple**, JOU: flexible, pliant, tender, adaptable. This term advises adapting to what is given, developing each thing in its turn through yielding to it.

● **Whole**, HO, refers to: all, unite all; together. The ideogram suggests a double door and a cover, an image of uniting everything for one purpose. The corresponding quality in a person or situation is **solid**, KANG: firm, strong, unyielding, persisting. This term advises taking the initiative, acting in a spirited, focused way to impose an idea on things.

The *Universal Compass* is divided into two basic hemicyles which reflect these primary categories. All things in the world, inner or outer, female or male, human or non-human are made up of a mixture of these two powers. In a divinatory sense they represent two fundamental ways of acting or being in the world, stances each person can take at different times to connect with the flow of *tao* or energy.

Yin and Yang: Choice and Change

The oldest form of the *I* oracle was a series of phrases connected to single lines which indicated the choice made by a spirit. These lines may have been related to cracks that appeared in the bones used in ritual pyromancy. There were four kinds of lines associated with the oracle, even in its oldest form. Two of these indicated relatively stable conditions; the other two indicated changing conditions that were open to surprise and intervention. These lines and numbers are still used to build a hexagram.

8 = an unvarying opened line   ▬▬ ▬▬

6 = a transforming opened line   ▬X▬

7 = an unvarying whole line   ▬▬▬

9 = a transforming whole line   ▬O▬

The extreme quality of the transforming lines indicated gaps or openings in the fabric of the world. As the hexagrams were assembled, this transformative quality evolved into the process through which one hexagram could change into another, showing the direction the original situation may evolve through the intervention of a spirit.

The transformation of lines was also used to show the way *yin* and *yang* interact. It evolved into a description of how each of these primal

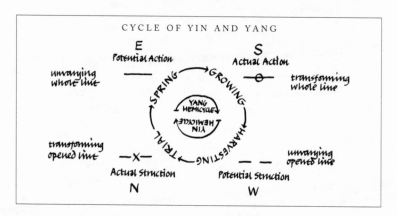

spirits enter a situation, come to predominate, and leave, calling up its contrary or complement. This kind of thinking was joined to the Time Cycle by identifying each kind of line with a season.

The yin and yang hemicycles were then elaborated around a central axis or *Pivot of Equalization* by articulating each of them into three analogous phases:

- The *Pivoting Phase* is the first move out of the center. The qualities emerge as hidden germs, interior or *in potentia*.

    Pivot, SHU, refers to: hinge, axis, center; starting point, fundamental.

    The *Pivoting Phase* produces *youngest yin* and *youngest yang, Potential Struction* or *Potential Action*.

- The *Phase of Wholeness* is a threshold. The qualities are full-grown but still contained or **whole**.

    Whole, HO, refers to: all, unite all; uniting everything within.

    The *Phase of Wholeness* produces *contracted yin*, the opaque, concentrated inwardness of Struction, and *bright yang*, the clear outward essence of Action.

- The *Disclosing Phase* breaks the boundaries. The qualities expand and exhaust themselves. This leads back to the neutral center from which the opposite hemicycle begins.

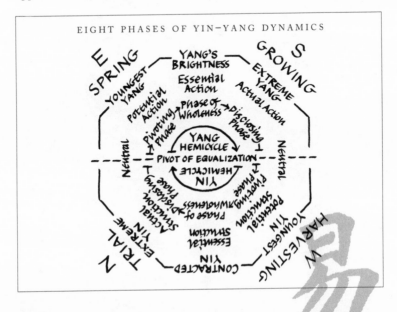

EIGHT PHASES OF YIN–YANG DYNAMICS

Disclose, K'AI, refers to: open, reveal, unfold; enact rites, clear land. The ideogram suggests a house bursting open through rising inner pressure.

The *Disclosing Phase* produces *extreme yin* and *extreme yang, Actual Struction* and *Actual Action, flooding below* and *flaming above.*

The central Pivot of Equalization is a gate through which the two primary agencies pass. It is common to both hemicycles and acts as the transition between them. The agencies either cancel each other out at the end of a complete cycle or come into an active balance at its midpoint.

● *The Five Transformative Moments*

In the middle Han Dynasty, a large convention of scholars was gathered by Imperial Edict to standardize and systematize the *Ching* or Classics. The official report of this convention, PO HU T'UNG, *The Comprehensive Discussions in the White Tiger Hall,* combined the other systems of correspondance which had evolved with a cycle of five processes or *Transformative Moments,* the WU HSING.

These five processes are not substances, but stages of transformation. They are translated as adjectives: **Woody, Fiery, Earthy, Metallic, Streaming**. The term *Moment* expresses their function as both points of

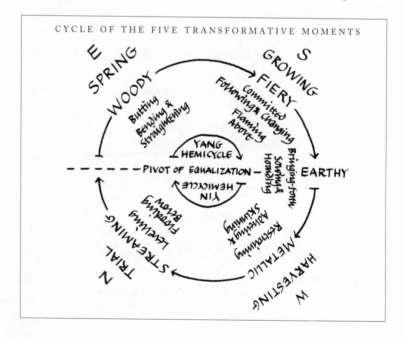

CYCLE OF THE FIVE TRANSFORMATIVE MOMENTS

time and qualities of transformation. These *Transformative Moments* evoke each other in a particular order. They form a cycle which was combined with the Time Cycle and the Cycle of Yin-Yang Interaction and linked to the trigrams of the *I Ching*. To make the systems interlock, the Earthy Moment was made into an axis corresponding to the *Pivot of Equalization*. This allowed the Seasons and the Moments to coincide.

- **Woody**, MU, describes organic growth or development. It refers to: origins, beginnings; break open, burst forth; Spring, East, daybreak. It is associated with youngest yang and Potential Action, which arise after the Yin Hemicycle is exhausted. Its Action is **butt**, CHU: to push against something with the horns. It manifests as the *bending* and *straightening* of sprouting plants pushing their way through the surface of the earth. This germinating thrust inaugurates the Yang Hemicycle of the *Universal Compass*.

- **Fiery**, HUO, describes combustion, heat, and light. It refers to: fire, flame; flame up, blaze, glow; burning and consuming; upward motion; Summer, South, midday. It is associated with extreme yang and Actual Action flaring up, blazing out and spreading. Its Actions are **committed following**, WEI SUI, and **changing**, HUA. They manifest as *flaming above*. The Fiery Moment consumes Wood and changes it to ashes or Earth. It brings the Yang Hemicycle of the *Universal Compass* to a close.

- **Earthy**, T'U, describes soil, ground, dust, clay, ashes. It is the point around which the seasons, the cardinal points, and the alternation of day and night revolve. It represents the *Pivot of Equalization* where yin and yang, Action and Struction, are in balance, neutralizing each other or creatively interacting. Its Action is **bringing-forth**, T'U. It manifests as *sowing* and *hoarding* a crop. The Earthy Moment connects the hemicycles. It is the moment of balance and transition.

- **Metallic**, CHIN, describes metals, and particularly gold as their quintessence. It refers to: ore; smelting, crystalization, concentration, coagulation; the hard forms of cast metal resulting from those processes; Autumn, West, sunset. It is associated with youngest yin and Potential Struction. Its Action is **restraining**, CHIN, holding something in a

specific form. It manifests as *adhering*, casting molten metal in molds, and *skinning*, stripping the molds away. The Metallic Moment casts Earth into fixed forms. It begins the Yin Hemicycle of the *Universal Compass*.

Streaming, SHUI, describes fluids and flowing. It refers to: floods, tides; dissolving, liquefying; flowing water, streams, rivers; downward motion; Winter, North, midnight. It is associated with extreme yin and Actual Struction overflowing and spreading out. Its Action is **leveling**, CHUN, equalizing and evening out differences. It manifests as *flooding below*, which disappears into the neutral Pivot of Equalization. The Streaming Moment dissolves the fixed forms of Metal. It brings the Yin Hemicycle of the *Universal Compass* to a close.

The Trigram Cycle

The most important connection between *I* divination and the Universal Compass is the Cyclic Order of the Eight Trigrams. The arrangement of these trigrams and their attributes in a cyclic order enabled scholars, magicians and diviners to correlate hundreds of different systems of magical correspondence with the divinatory practise of the *I Ching*. All of these systems could then be entered simultaneously by manipulating the yarrow-stalks, the mysterious pointers of *yin* and *yang*.

The Eight Trigrams and Their Attributes

The eight trigrams represent all the possible combinations of three opened and whole lines. Each of the hexagrams in the *I Ching* is seen as the dynamic relation between two of these trigrams. The bottom trigram with all its associated qualities represents the inner aspect of the situation, the upper trigram with its net of associations represents the outer aspect. The hexagram itself is thus a dynamic relation between the inner and the outer, the individual and the cosmos. The integration of the trigrams into the *Universal Compass* means that the other systems of association can be used to describe the way energy is moving in a particular divinatory situation.

EIGHT TRIGRAMS AND THEIR ATTRIBUTES			
TRIGRAM	*IMAGE*	*ACTION*	*SYMBOL*
☰	FORCE CH'IEN	PERSISTING	HEAVEN
☷	FIELD K'UN	YIELDING	EARTH
☳	SHAKE CHEN	STIRRING-UP	THUNDER
☵	GORGE K'AN	VENTURING FALLING	STREAM
☶	BOUND KEN	STOPPING	MOUNTAIN
☴	GROUND SUN	ENTERING	WOOD WIND
☲	RADIANCE LI	CONGREGATING	FIRE BRIGHTNESS
☱	OPEN TUI	STIMULATING	MARSH

The trigrams and their attributes are arranged in three different systems or orders: a conceptual order, a family order and, most significant, the cyclic order.

● *Trigrams in Pairs: the Conceptual Order*

In the simplest order the trigrams form pairs, which polarizes their qualities. These pairs of opposites are called the arrangement according to Fu Hsi.

THE CONCEPTUAL ORDER ACCORDING TO FU HSI			
FORCE/FIELD	SHAKE/GROUND	GORGE/RADIANCE	BOUND/OPEN
☰ ☷	☳ ☴	☵ ☲	☶ ☱

● *The Trigrams as a Family*

In this arrangement the trigrams articulate an ideal family which was thought to reflect the organization of the cosmos. The trigrams are grouped as parents, sons and daughters.

THE TRIGRAMS AS A FAMILY		
FATHER ≡ FORCE	MOTHER ≡≡ FIELD	
	SONS	
ELDEST SHAKE	MIDDLE GORGE	YOUNGEST BOUND
	DAUGHTERS	
ELDEST GROUND	MIDDLE RADIANCE	YOUNGEST OPEN

Father and Mother, **Force**, CH'IEN, and **Field**, K'UN, represent pure cosmic principles. They intermingle to produce the six variegated trigrams through **twining**, SO, twisting together. The variegated trigrams signify the different ages of **womanhood**, NÜ, and **manhood**, NAN: the **long-lived** or senior, CHANG; the **central** or middle, CHUNG; and the **junior** or youngest, SHAO.

● *The Cycle of Trigrams*

In the cyclic order the trigrams are seen as phases of a continuing process. Their meaning in the 64 hexagrams of the *I Ching* refers mainly to their place in this order of evocation. This order is called the arrangement according to King Wen. In it each trigram has an *Image*, an *Action* and a *Symbol*, as well as a location within the *Family* of trigrams. Other specific actions are thought to connect one trigram with the next.

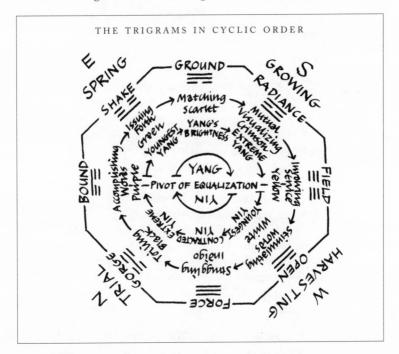

THE TRIGRAMS IN CYCLIC ORDER

● **Shake,** CHEN ☳

Shake, CHEN, begins the cyclic order. A stirring whole line emerges below two watery opened lines, causing things to *issue-forth-from* the concealing Earth.

   Shake, CHEN: arouse, excite, inspire; thunder rising from below; awe, alarm, trembling; fertilizing intrusion. The ideogram: excite and rain.

Symbol: **Thunder**, LEI: rising, arousing power.

Actions: **Stir-up**, TUNG: excite, influence, move, affect; work, take action; come out of the egg or the bud. The ideogram: strength and heavy, able to move weighty things.

Family: the first or eldest son, **long-lived manhood**, CHANG NAN, energetic and inspiring.

In the *Universal Compass*, **Shake**, CHEN, is related to the beginning of the Woody Moment and belongs to the East, where seeds break open and development originates. Its color is green, the color of spring, nature and beginnings.

- **Ground**, SUN ☴

After the issuing-forth of **Shake**, CHEN, things *match* and *couple*, giving birth to new generations. **Ground**, SUN, brings *matching* and *coupling*. An opened line, supple yin, subtly penetrates from below.

Ground, SUN: base on which things rest; support, foundation; mild, subtly penetrating; nourishing. The ideogram: stand and things arranged on it, the subtle influence of the ground.

Symbols: **Wood/tree**, MU: all things woody or wooden, alive or constructed from wood; associated with the Woody Moment. The ideogram: a tree with roots and branches.

Wind, FENG: moving air, breeze, gust; weather and its influence on mood and humor; fashion, usage.

Action: **Enter**, JU: penetrate, go into, enter on, progress; put into, encroach on; contrary of issue-forth, CH'U.

Family: eldest or first daughter, **long-lived womanhood**, CHANG NÜ, influencing and nourishing.

In the *Universal Compass*, **Ground**, SUN, is related to the culmination of the Woody Moment. Its color is scarlet, a vivid red connoting luck, honor, marriage and riches.

- **Radiance**, LI ☲

Through the *matching* and *coupling* of **Ground**, SUN, things give birth to new generations. Together they *mutually visualize* new possibilities. **Radiance**, LI, brings *mutual visualizing*, envisioning common goals. It is represented by the single opened line which holds two whole lines together.

Radiance, LI: glowing light, spreading in all directions; light-giving, discriminating, articulating; divide and arrange in order; the power of consciousness. The ideogram: bird and weird, the magical fire-bird with brilliant plumage.

Symbols: **Brightness**, MING: light-giving aspect of burning, heavenly bodies and consciousness. The ideogram: sun and moon.

Fire, HUO: warming and consuming aspect of burning.

Action: **Congregate**, LI: cling together; depend on, attached to, rely on; couple, pair, herd. The ideogram: deer flocking together.

Family: middle or second daughter, **central womanhood**, CHUNG NÜ, mature and supportive.

In the *Universal Compass* **Radiance**, LI, relates to the Fiery Moment and belongs to the South, the realm of change through combustion. Its color is crimson, which connotes fire, burning, stripping and denuding.

- **Field**, K'UN ☷

After the *mutual visualizing* of **Radiance**, LI, comes the common labor of serving, sowing and hoarding the produce of the Earth. **Field**, K'UN brings involving service, difficult labor undertaken together.

Field, K'UN, surface of the world; concrete extension; basis of all existence, where Force or heaven exerts its power; all-involving service; earth; moon, wife, mother; courtiers, servants. The ideogram: terrestrial globe and stretch out, stability and extension.

Symbol: **Earth**, TI: ground on which the human world rests; basis of all things, nourishes all things form.

Action: **Yield(-to)**, SHUN: give way and bear produce; comply, agree, follow, obey; unresisting, docile, flexible; nourish, provide. The ideogram: head and current, water flowing from the head of a river, yielding to the banks.

Family: mother as the essence of yin, origin of the opened lines in the six variegated trigrams.

In the *Universal Compass,* **Field**, K'UN, is related to the Earthy Moment and belongs to the South-West, where things are reduced to dust and fertile soil. Its color is yellow, the color of the middle, the soil of central China and the Emperor.

● **Open,** TUI ☱

After the common labor of **Field,** K'UN, the joy of Harvest breaks forth in *stimulating words.* **Open,** TUI, brings stimulating words that cheer and inspire. It is represented by the single opened line leading two whole lines.

Open, TUI: an open surface, promoting interaction and interpenetration; responsive, free, unhindered, pleasing; opening, passage; the mouth; exchange, barter; straight, direct; meet, gather; place where water accumulates. The ideogram: person, mouth and vapor, speaking with others.

Symbol: **Marsh,** TSE: open surface of a flat body of water and the vapors rising from it; fertilize, enrich; kindness, favor.

Action: **Stimulate,** SHUO: rouse to action and good feeling; stir up, urge on; persuade; set out in words; free from constraint, cheer, delight. The ideogram: words and exchange.

Family: youngest or third daughter, **junior womanhood,** SHAO NÜ, light-hearted, whimsical and magical.

In the *Universal Compass,* **Open,** TUI, relates to the beginning of the Metallic Moment and belongs to the West, the realm of restraining to essential form. Its color is white, the color of mourning, which connotes clear, pure, immaculate, plain.

● **Force,** CH'IEN ☰

After the *stimulation* of **Open,** TUI, comes a *struggle* for survival, giving form to each being and feeling. **Force,** CH'IEN, brings *struggling,* lonely single grappling with primary forces.

Force, CH'IEN: spirit power, creative and destructive; unceasing forward motion; dynamic, enduring, untiring; firm, stable; heaven, sovereign, father; also: dry up, parched, exhausted, cleared away. The ideogram: sprouts or vapors rising from the ground and sunlight, both fecundating moisture and scorching drought.

Symbol: **Heaven,** T'IEN: highest; sky, firmament, heavens; power above the human as opposed to earth, TI, below. The ideogram: great and the one above.

Action: **Persist,** CHIEN: strong, robust, dynamic, tenacious; continuous; unwearied heavenly bodies in their orbits.

Family: father as the essence of yang, ancestor of the whole lines in the six variegated trigrams.

In the *Universal Compass,* **Force,** CH'IEN, relates to the culmination of the Metallic Moment. Its color is indigo, the color of the sky's depths, the venerability of gods and spiritual agencies.

● **Gorge,** K'AN ☵

With the *struggle* of **Force,** CH'IEN, comes heavy labor and isolation. **Gorge,** K'AN, brings toiling, difficult but worthy labor. It is represented by the whole line venturing on between two opened lines.

    Gorge, K'AN: dangerous place; hole, cavity, hollow; pit, snare, trap, grave, precipice; critical time, test; risky. The ideogram: earth and pit.

    Symbol: **Stream,** SHUI: flowing water; fluid, dissolving; river, tide, flood. The ideogram: rippling water.

    Action: **Venture falling,** HSIEN HSIEN: risk falling until a bottom is reached, filling and overcoming the danger of the Gorge.

    Fall, HSIEN: fall down or into, sink, drop, descend; falling water; be captured.

    Venture, HSIEN: risk without reserve; key point, point of danger; difficulty, obstruction that must be confronted; water falling and filling the holes on its way. The ideogram: mound and all or whole, everything engaged at one point.

    Family: middle or second son, **central manhood,** CHUNG NAN, courageous and venturesome.

In the *Universal Compass,* **Gorge,** K'AN, relates to the Streaming Moment and belongs to the North where direction and shape are dissolved. Its color is black, suggesting dark obscure toiling.

● **Bound,** KEN ☶

Venturing, falling and filling all obstacles, the toiling of **Gorge,** K'AN, streams out and encounters the limits. **Bound,** KEN, brings accomplishing words that articulate the end of a cycle. It is represented by the whole line capping two opened lines.

    Bound, KEN: limit, boundary; encounter an obstacle, stop; still, quiet, motionless; confine, enclose, mark off; turn around to look behind; hard, adamant, obstinate; perverse. The ideogram: eye and person turning round to compare and group what is behind.

    Symbol: **Mountain,** SHAN: limit, boundary. The ideogram: three peaks, a mountain range.

Action: **Stop,** CHIH: bring or come to a standstill. The ideogram: a foot stops walking.

Family: youngest or third son, **junior manhood,** SHAO NAN, the limit or bound.

In the *Universal Compass,* **Bound,** KEN, relates to the neutral end point between Yin and Yang Hemicycles, where the primary agencies cancel each other out. Its color is purple, suggesting a dark weather-beaten face and the Heavenly Palace of the Immortals. The immobility of the Mountain prepares the *issuing-forth* of a new cycle.

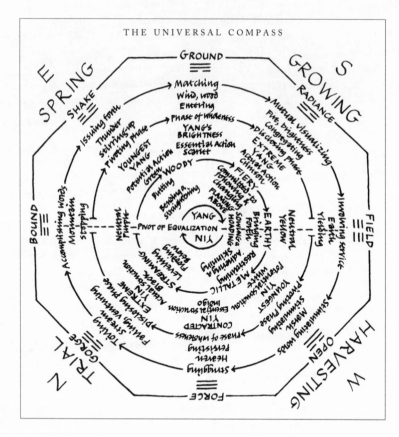

THE UNIVERSAL COMPASS

● *Using the Universal Compass*

The diagram opposite connects the Time Cycle, the phases of Yin and Yang, the Five Transformative Moments and the Cyclic Order of the Trigrams. Through these interconnections, the trigrams of a given hexagram are related to a web of qualities that give you insight into how psychic energy is moving and transforming the dynamics of your situation.

The *Universal Compass* represents a fluid, changing world whose ground is imaginative energy. It can be applied to any kind of situation. It particularly helps to place you in the image of your situation by describing the relation between its inner and outer aspects and the direction of their probable development. Use it along with the *Image of the Situation* to open the imaginative background to a question you pose to the *I Ching*.

PART TWO

周易

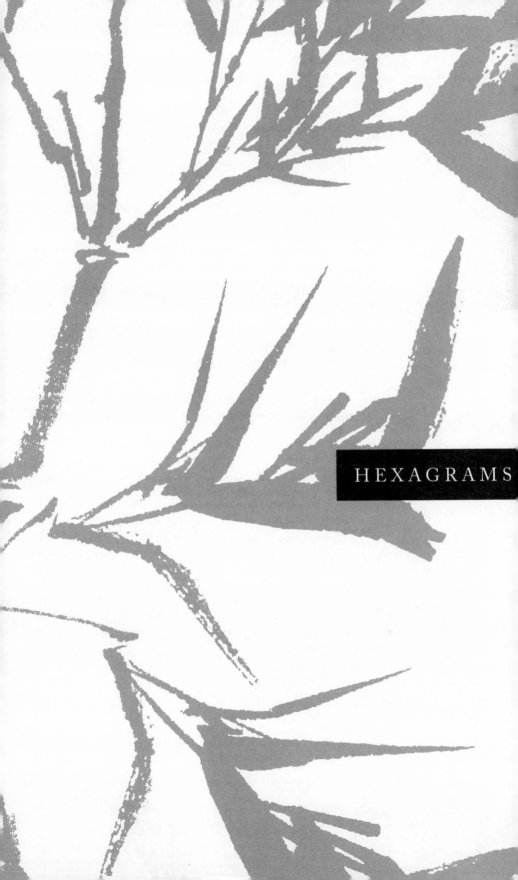

HEXAGRAMS

A QUICK GUIDE TO THE ORACLE

This procedure for asking a question and reading the response summarizes the information in Using the I.

- *1* Find your question. Make your anxieties and your desires clear. What is it you really want to ask? Decide on what you would *like to do* and use it to focus your question: "What about ...?" See page 18–19 for more information.

- *2* Decide which method you want to use to get an answer, coins or yarrow-stalks. See page 20–23 for the procedure. Each method gives one of four numbers – 6, 7, 8 or 9 – six times. Each number indicates a line of your *Primary Hexagram,* starting from the bottom up. If there are *Transforming Lines,* shown by a 6 or a 9, change them into their opposite to generate the *Related Hexagram.*

- *3* Find the number of your *Primary Hexagram,* and of the *Related Hexagram* if there are *Transforming Lines,* in the *Key* on page 814. Locate the lower trigram (the lower three lines) on the left side of the chart and the upper trigram (the upper three lines) on the top.

- *4* Turn to the Hexagram Texts indicated by these numbers (pages 94–672). You can use all the basic texts of the *Primary Hexagram,* the *Transforming Lines* indicated by a 6 or 9 in your reading, and the *Image* of the *Related Hexagram,* the one generated when your *Transforming Lines* change. These sections are described briefly on the next page.

- *5* Read the *Image of the Situation* at the beginning of the *Primary Hexagram.* This is the *I Ching*'s basic advice. Then read through the other sections. Don't worry if you are confused at first, it is part of the process. See which terms and definitions connect with your problem, your feelings and your state of mind. Then focus on the *Transforming Lines,* if there are any, and the *Image* of the *Related Hexagram.*

● *6* The *Primary Hexagram* gives you a picture of what is happening now, the *Transforming Line* shows how the situation is likely to change if you go ahead with the action you asked about, and the *Related Hexagram* gives an image of future potential. Guidance in your situation comes from the interaction of the divinatory terms with your imagination. Take the time to let the terms that have struck you make stories about the way you should act. This is a real, living process and there is a spirit behind it. The section *Encounters with the Oracle* on pages 33–64 gives examples of questions, answers and the process of interpretation.

● *Hexagram Texts and their Functions*

The Image of the Situation *describes an archetypal situation. It is each hexagram's central oracular statement, the ground in which all other parts of the hexagram are embedded. The name of the hexagram, the first word of the* Image, *provides both a description of your situation and advice as to the most effective way to deal with it. The text places it in the dynamic of time, indicating key qualities and actions associated with it.*

● Outer and Inner Aspects *analyses the matter under consideration in terms of your dynamic relation to its outer and inner elements. This is described through the relation between the outer and inner trigrams and their nets of associated qualities. This section acts as a shorthand reference to the supplementary material on the* Universal Compass *dealing with traditional systems of correlative thinking.*

● Counter Indications *describes an opposite to your situation. It indicates what is* not *effective at the present time.*

● *The* Sequence *puts the* Image *in a series with the hexagram that precedes it in terms of a completed action which calls up a following action. It suggests that activating the energy of this hexagram depends upon understanding it as a part of a necessary succession of events.*

● *The* Contrasted Definitions *offer a key to your situation by picking out a central feature and contrasting it with a central feature of an adjoining hexagram.*

- *The* Attached Evidences *see the action of this hexagram as particularly relevant to* actualizing-tao *and describe how it can aid the process of realizing tao in action.*

- *The* Symbol Tradition *describes the* Image *in terms of the relation between the Symbols of its two trigrams. It derives a specific action from this relation which gives access to the ideal of the* chün tzu *in this situation: a person who uses divination to order their life according to* tao *rather than personal desires.*

- *The* Image Tradition *amplifies key terms and qualities of the* Image. *It also analyses the Image in terms of: the* correspondence *of pairs of lines; the actions and relations of* supple *and* solid, *assigned to the opened and whole lines; and the* appropriateness *of the lines to their places, particularly the center lines of the trigrams.*

- *The* Transforming Lines *represent precise points of connection with the psychic forces involved in your question. They are activated by a 6 or a 9 in the consultation procedure. They give you advice on the direction of specific actions and the potential consequences. As the activated lines change into their opposites they produce a new hexagram, the* Related Hexagram, *which is an image of overall future potential.*

- *The* Image *of the* Related Hexagram *produced when the* Transforming Lines *change into their opposites gives an indication of how your situation may develop. This can be a goal, an image of desire, reassurance or warning. It is not an immutable future, but an indication of the potential contained in your present situation. Changing the way you act or perceive things can change this potential.*

● *Orthography and Punctuation*

Punctuation, orthographic signs and the use of **bold**, *italic* and SMALL CAPITALS are consistent throughout the translation and have specific meanings:

Bold in the Hexagram texts always indicates a **core-word**, the particular English word used to translate one single Chinese ideogram, for example: **Force**.

SMALL CAPITALS, usually following a **bold core-word**, indicate the transliteration of the Chinese word (according to the Wade-Giles system), for example: **Force**, CH'IEN.

The use of a hyphen (-) indicates that two or more English words are joined together to translate one single Chinese ideogram and should be thought of as one unit, for example: **Go-to-meet**, YA, or **Issue-forth-from**, CH'U.

With the exception of articles (a, an, the) each **core-word** consistently represents one and only one Chinese ideogram throughout the texts. They occur in the exact order of the original text.

Italics indicates the title of a major section of a Hexagram, such as *Image of the Situation, Sequence*, or *Transforming Lines*, or the *Associated Contexts*, the circles of definitions given with each Chinese term. Remember that the *Associated Contexts* for a term are only given *the first time a term appears in a hexagram* or *when it only appears in a* Transforming Line.

A full stop (.) indicates the end of a line or internal punctuation in the Chinese text. Such punctuation is rare. We have used the *colon* (:) and *comma* (,) to indicate implicit pauses and emphases in the lines that show the relation between terms. The *colon* should be read as an equal sign, the *comma* as indicating a series of connected things.

Indentation of a line in the *Associated Contexts* corresponds to the beginning of a line in the Chinese text. Definitions for the first term in a line *that has not already appeared* are given there. A space between sections in the *Associated Contexts* corresponds to the beginning of a new subsection of the text. In the section *Image Tradition*, the longest section in each hexagram, these subsections are indicated by Roman Numerals (I, II, III, IV, V). *Transforming Lines a)* and *b)* indicate different kinds of texts: the oldest is the Line text *a)*, the commentary is Line text *b)*.

HEXAGRAM				HEXAGRAM		
1		FORCE CH'IEN *page 94*		17		FOLLOWING SUI *page 242*
2		FIELD K'UN *page 103*		18		CORRUPTING KUI *page 251*
3		SPROUTING CHUN *page 114*		19		NEARING LIN *page 260*
4		ENVELOPING MENG *page 124*		20		VIEWING KUAN *page 268*
5		ATTENDING HSÜ *page 133*		21		GNAWING BITE SHIH HO *page 276*
6		ARGUING SUNG *page 142*		22		ADORNING PI *page 284*
7		LEGIONS/LEADING SHIH *page 151*		23		STRIPPING PO *page 293*
8		GROUPING PI *page 160*		24		RETURNING FU *page 301*
9		SMALL ACCUMULATING HSIAO CH'U *page 168*		25		WITHOUT EMBROILING WU WANG *page 311*
10		TREADING LÜ *page 177*		26		GREAT ACCUMULATING TA CH'U *page 319*
11		PREVADING T'AI *page 186*		27		JAWS/SWALLOWING YI *page 327*
12		OBSTRUCTION PI *page 197*		28		GREAT EXCEEDING TA KUO *page 336*
13		CONCORDING PEOPLE T'UNG JEN *page 206*		29		GORGE K'AN *page 344*
14		GREAT POSSESSING TA YU *page 215*		30		RADIANCE LI *page 353*
15		HUMBLING CH'IEN *page 223*		31		CONJOINING HSIEN *page 362*
16		PROVIDING-FOR/PROVISION YÜ *page 232*		32		PERSEVERING HENG *page 371*

● A list
to the
Hexagrams

HEXAGRAM	HEXAGRAM
33 RETIRING TUN *page 381*	**49** SKINNING KO *page 530*
34 GREAT INVIGORATING TA CHUANG *page 389*	**50** THE VESSEL/HOLDING TING *page 540*
35 PROSPERING CHIN *page 397*	**51** SHAKE CHEN *page 550*
36 BRIGHTNESS HIDING MING YI *page 406*	**52** BOUND KEN *page 559*
37 DWELLING PEOPLE CHIA JEN *page 415*	**53** INFILTRATING CHIEN *page 567*
38 POLARIZING K'UEI *page 424*	**54** CONVERTING MAIDENHOOD KUEI MEI *page 577*
39 LIMPING CHIEN *page 435*	**55** ABOUNDING FENG *page 586*
40 TAKING-APART HSIEH *page 444*	**56** SOJOURNING LÜ *page 596*
41 DIMINISHING SUN *page 453*	**57** GROUND SUN *page 605*
42 AUGMENTING YI *page 462*	**58** OPEN TUI *page 614*
43 PARTING KUAI *page 473*	**59** DISPERSING HUAN *page 622*
44 COUPLING KOU *page 483*	**60** ARTICULATING CHIEH *page 630*
45 CLUSTERING TS'UI *page 492*	**61** CENTER CONFIRMING CHUNG FU *page 638*
46 ASCENDING SHENG *page 502*	**62** SMALL EXCEEDING HSIAO KUO *page 647*
47 CONFINING K'UN *page 510*	**63** ALREADY FORDING CHI CHI *page 656*
48 THE WELL/WELLING CHING *page 521*	**64** NOT-YET FORDING WEI CHI *page 665*

• **The Sections of the Hexagrams**

The following table compares the names and the locations of the various texts that make up a hexagram in the present translation with the Chinese original and the Wilhem/Baynes translation.

Chinese terms are romanized according to the Wade-Giles system, used in most references to classical Chinese literature in the last hundred years. Other publications using the Pin yin method will include conversion tables between the two systems.

THIS TRANSLATION	K'ANG HSI EDITION	WILHELM/BAYNES
• *Image of the Situation*	1st & 2nd Wings, T'UAN CHUAN	The Name The Judgement
• *Outer and Inner Aspects*	From 8th Wing, SHUO KUA; amplified by PO HU T'UNG, The Comprehensive Discussions in the White Tiger Hall	Discussion of the Trigrams
• *Counter Indications*	HO KUA or Nuclear Trigrams	HO KUA or Nuclear Trigrams
• *Contrasted Definitions*	10th Wing, TSA KUA	Miscellaneous Notes
• *Attached Evidences*	Extracts from 8th Wing, HSI TZ'U CHUAN	Appended Judgements
• *Sequence*	9th Wing, HSÜ KUA	The Sequence
• *Symbol Tradition*	3rd & 4th Wing, HSIANG CHUAN	The Image
• *Image Tradition*	1st & 2nd Wings, T'UAN CHUAN	Commentary on the Decision
• *Transforming Lines a)*	1st & 2nd Wing, T'UAN CHUAN	The Lines a)
• *Transforming Lines b)*	3rd & 4th Wing, HSIANG CHUAN	The Lines b)

易

FORCE ■ CH'IEN

This hexagram describes your situation in terms of the primal spirit power that both creates and destroys. It emphasizes that dynamic, unwearied persisting, the action of **Force**, is the adequate way to handle it. To be in accord with the time, you are told to: **persist!**

● *Image of the Situation*

Force: Spring Growing Harvesting Trial.

Associated Contexts **Force**, CH'IEN: spirit power, creative and destructive; unceasing forward motion; dynamic, enduring, untiring; firm, stable; heaven, sovereign, father; also: dry up, parched, exhausted, cleared away. The ideogram: sprouts or vapors rising from the ground and sunlight, both fecundating moisture and scorching drought. **Force** is the Heaven trigram doubled and includes that trigram's attributes: *Symbol*: Heaven, T'IEN: highest; sky, firmament, heavens; power above the human as opposed to earth, TI, below. The ideogram: great and the one above. *Action*: **Persist**, CHIEN: strong, robust, dynamic, tenacious; continuous; unwearied heavenly bodies in their orbits. **Spring Growing Harvesting Trial: Spring**, YÜAN; **Grow**, HENG; **Harvest**, LI; and **Trial**, CHEN, are the four stages of the Time Cycle, the model for all dynamic processes. They indicate that your question is connected to the cycle as a whole rather than a part of it, and that the origin (Spring) of a favorable result (Harvesting Trial) is an offering to the spirits (Growing).

● *Outer and Inner Aspects*

☰ **Force**: The force of heaven struggles on, persistent and unwearied; heavenly bodies persist in their orbits. **Force** is the center of the yin hemicycle, completing the formative process.

Connection to both inner and outer: struggling forces are bound together in dynamic tension, the Metallic Moment culminating. Force brings elements to grips, creating enduring relations.

The first two hexagrams represent the extreme modes of the interplay of yin and yang. Force is the extreme yang mode, where differentiation and tension are at their peak.

As the whole and opened lines, these extremes twine or twist together to produce the 62 composite hexagrams, the web of possible human situations. When one of the composite hexagrams is obtained as an oracle, you should imagine yourself through its Image and texts.

On the contrary, do not identify with **Force**, for such identification leads to parching exhaustion without the ability to realize anything. Your situation contains enormous creative potential, but it is threatened by this fundamental one-sidedness.

● *Contrasted Definitions*

Force: solid.
Field: supple.

Associated Contexts **Solid**, KANG: quality of the whole lines; firm, strong, unyielding, persisting.

Field, K'UN: surface of the world; concrete extension; basis of all existence, where Force or heaven exerts its power; all-involving service; earth; moon, wife, mother; courtiers, servants. The ideogram: terrestrial globe and stretch out, stability and extension. Image of Hexagram 2.

Supple, JOU: quality of the opened lines; flexible, pliant, tender, adaptable.

● *Symbol Tradition*

Heaven moves persistingly.
A chün tzu uses originating strength not to pause.

Associated Contexts **Move**, HSING: move or move something; motivate, emotionally moving; walk, act, do. The ideogram: stepping left then right.

Chün tzu: ideal of a person who uses divination to order his/her life in accordance with tao rather than wilful intention; keyword. **Use(-of)**, YI: make use of, by means of, owing to; employ, make functional. **Origin**, TZU: source, beginning, ground; cause, reason, motive; line of descent; path to the origin; yourself, intrinsic. **Strengthen**, CH'IANG: invigorate, test; compel, rely on force; determined, sturdy; overcome a desire.

Not, PU: simple negative. **Pause,** HSI: stop and rest, repose; breathe, a breathing-spell; suspended.

● *Image Tradition*

> The great Force, Spring in-fact. [I]
> The myriad beings's own beginning.
>
> Thereupon primary heaven. [II]
> Clouds moving, rain spreading-out.
> The kinds: being diffusing forms.
>
> Great brightening completing beginning. [III]
> The six situations: the season accomplishing.
> The season riding six dragons used going-to-meet heaven.
>
> Force: tao transforming changes. [IV]
> Each-one correcting innate fate.
> Protection uniting the great harmony.
>
> Thereupon Harvesting Trial. [V]
> Heads issuing-forth-from the multitudinous beings.
> Myriad cities, conjoining, soothing.

Associated Contexts [I] **Great,** TA: big, noble, important, very; orient the will toward a self-imposed goal, impose direction; ability to lead or guide your life; contrasts with small, HSIAO, flexible adaptation to what crosses your path; keyword. Image of Hexagrams 14, 26, 28, 34. **Spring,** YÜAN: source, origin, head; great, excellent; arise, begin, generating power; first stage of the Time Cycle. **In-fact,** TSAI: in actual fact, currently.

Myriad, WAN: countless; many, everyone; lit.: ten thousand. The ideogram: swarm of insects. **Being(s),** WU: creature, thing, any single being; matter, substance, essence; nature of things. **'s/have(-it)/it/them,** CHIH: expresses possession, directly or as an object pronoun. **Own,** TZU: possession and the things possessed; avail of, depend on; property, riches. **Begin,** SHIH: commence, start, open; earliest, first; beginning of a time-span, ended by completion, CHUNG. The ideogram: woman and eminent, beginning new life.

[II] **Thereupon,** NAI: on that ground, because of. **Primary,** T'UNG: origin, beginning; first of a class; clue, hint; whole, general.

Clouds, YÜN: fog, mist, water vapor; connects to the Streaming Moment and Stream, the Symbol of the trigram Gorge, K'AN. **Rain**, YÜ: all precipitation; sudden showers, fast and furious; associated with the trigram Gorge, K'AN and the Streaming Moment. **Spread-out**, SHIH: expand, diffuse, distribute, arrange, exhibit; add to, aid. The ideogram: flag and indeed, claiming new country.

Kinds, P'IN: species and their essential qualities; sorts, classes; classify, select. **Diffuse**, LIU: flow out, spread, permeate. **Form**, HSING: shape; body, bodily; material appearance.

[III] **Brightness**, MING: light-giving aspect of burning, heavenly bodies and consciousness; with fire, the Symbol of the trigram Radiance, LI. **Complete**, CHUNG: end of a cycle that begins the next; last, whole, all; contrasts with exhaust, CH'IUNG, final end. The ideogram: silk cocoons, follow and ice, winter linking one year with the next.

Six, LU: transforming opened line; six lines or places of a hexagram; sixth. **Situation**, WEI: place or seat according to rank; post, position, command; right, proper; established, arranged. The ideogram: person and stand, servants in their places. **Season**, SHIH: quality of the time; the right time, opportune, in harmony; planning in accord with the time; seasons of the year. The ideogram: sun and temple, time as sacred. **Accomplish**, CH'ENG: complete, finish, bring about; perfect, full, whole; play your part, do your duty; mature. The ideogram: weapon and man, able to bear arms, thus fully developed.

Ride, CH'ENG: ride an animal or a chariot; have the upper hand, seize the right time; control strong power; overcome the nature of the other; supple opened line above a solid whole line. **Dragon**, LUNG: powerful spirit-energy emerging from waters below; mythical shape-changer with supreme power; connected with heaven, T'IEN, and the trigram Force, CH'IEN. **Go-to-meet**, YA: advance to encounter and receive; invoke; anticipate, face, provide for; govern; drive or tame a horse; extending everywhere, as the imperial power.

[IV] **Tao**: way or path; ongoing process of being and the course it traces for each specific person or thing; keyword. The ideogram: go and head, leading and the path it creates. **Transform**, PIEN: abrupt, radical, fundamental mutation from one state of being to another; transformation of lines in hexagrams; contrasts with change, HUA, gradual metamorphosis. **Change**, HUA: gradual, continuous metamorphosis; influence someone; contrasts with transform, PIEN, sudden mutation. The ideogram: person alive and dead, the life-process.

Each-one, KO: every, all, wherever; each separate thing. **Correct**, CHENG: rectify deviation or one-sidedness; proper, straight, exact, regular; constant, rule, model. The ideogram: stop and one, hold to one thing. **Innate**, HSING: inborn character; spirit, quality, ability; naturally, without constraint. The ideogram: heart and produce, spontaneous feeling. **Fate**, MING: individual destiny; birth and death as limits of life; issue orders with authority; consult the gods. The ideogram: mouth and order, words with heavenly authority.

Protect, PAO: guard, defend, keep safe; secure. **Unite**, HO: join, match, correspond, agree, collect, reply; unison, harmony; also: close, shut the mouth. The ideogram: mouth and assemble. **Harmony**, HO: concord, union; conciliate; at peace, mild; fit, tune, adjust.

[V] **Harvesting Trial**, LI CHIEN: advantageous divination; putting the action in question to the test is beneficial.

Head, SHOU: literal head; leader, foremost; subject headings; beginning, model; superior, upper, front. **Issue-forth(-from)**, CH'U: emerge from, come out of, proceed from, spring from; the Action of the trigram Shake, CHEN; contrary of enter, JU. The ideogram: stem with branches and leaves emerging. **Multitude**, SHU: the people; mass, herd; all, the whole.

City, KUO: area of only human constructions; political unit, polis. First of the territorial zones: city, suburbs, countryside, forests. **Conjoin**, HSIEN: come into contact with, influence; reach, join together; put together as parts of a previously separated whole; come into conjunction, as the celestial bodies; totally, completely; lit.: broken piece of pottery, the halves of which join to identify partners. Image of Hexagram 31. **Soothe**, NING: calm, pacify; create peace of mind; tranquil, quiet. The ideogram: shelter above heart, dish and breath, physical and spiritual comfort.

● *Transforming Lines*

Initial nine

a) **Immersed dragon, no availing-of.**

b) **Immersed dragon, no availing-of.**
Yang located below indeed.

Associated Contexts a) **Immerse**, CH'IEN: submerge, hide in water; make away with; secret, reserved; carefully. **No**, WU: simple negative; un-, dis-. **Avail-of**, YUNG: take advantage of; benefit from, profit by; use for a specific purpose; apply to advantage. The ideogram: to divine and center, applying divination to central concerns.

b) **Yang**: Action; dynamic and light aspect of phenomena: arouses, transforms, dissolves existing structures; linear thrust; stimulus, drive, focus; direct or orient something. **Locate(-in)**, TSAI: live in, dwell, reside; belong to, involved with, depend on; within. The ideogram: earth and persevere, place on the earth. **Below**, HSIA: anything below, in all senses; lower, inner; lower trigram; opposite of above, SHANG. **Indeed**, YEH: intensifier; indicates comment on previous statement.

Nine at-second

a) **Visualizing dragon located-in the fields.**
Harvesting: visualizing Great People.

b) **Visualizing dragon located-in the fields.**
Actualizing-tao spreading-out throughout indeed.

Associated Contexts a) **Visualize**, CH'IEN: seeing in all its aspects: vision, being visible, forming mental images; visit, call on, consult. The ideogram: eye above person, active and receptive sight. **Locate(-in)**, TSAI: live in, dwell, reside; belong to, involved with, depend on; within. The ideogram: earth and persevere, place on the earth. **Fields**, T'IEN: cultivated land, plantation; also: hunting, game in the fields cannot escape the hunt. The ideogram: square divided into four sections, delineating fields.

Harvest, LI: advantageous, profitable; acute, insightful; benefit, nourish; third stage of the Time Cycle. **Great People**, TA JEN: important, noble, influential; those who impose a ruling principle on their lives; effect of the great within an individual; keyword.

b) **Actualize-tao**, TE: realize tao in action; power, virtue; ability to follow the course traced by the ongoing process of the cosmos; keyword. The ideogram: to go, straight, and heart. Linked with acquire, TE: acquiring that which makes a being become what it is meant to be. **Throughout**, P'U: universal, all; great, pervading light. The ideogram: sun and equal, equal to the sun. **Indeed**, YEH: intensifier; indicates comment on previous statement.

Nine at-third

a) A chün tzu completing the day: Force, Force.
Nightfall, awe, like adversity.
Without fault.

b) Completing the day: Force, Force.
Reversing returning tao indeed.

Associated Contexts a) **Day/sun,** JIH: actual sun and the time of a sun-cycle, a day. **Force,** CH'IEN: the doubled character intensifies this quality.

Nightfall, HSI: day's end, dusk; late; last day of month or year. **Awe,** T'I: alarmed and cautious; respect, regard, fear; stand in awe of. The ideogram: heart and versatile, the heart aware of sudden change. **Like,** JO: same as; just as, similar to. **Adversity,** LI: danger; threatening, malevolent demon. This has two aspects: grind, sharpen, improve, perfect, stimulate; and: poisonous, sinister, cruel, contrary. It indicates a spirit or ghost that seeks revenge by inflicting suffering upon the living. Pacifying or exorcizing such a spirit can have a healing effect. The ideogram: sheltering cliff and stinging insect.

Without fault, WU CHIU: no error or harm in the situation.

b) **Reverse,** FAN: turn and move in the opposite direction; turn around or upside down (180 degrees); change to the opposite position; contrary. **Return,** FU: go back, turn back to the starting point; recur, reappear, come again; restore, recover, retrace; an earlier time or place. The ideogram: step and retrace a path. Image of Hexagram 24. **Indeed,** YEH: intensifier; indicates comment on previous statement.

Nine at-fourth

a) Maybe capering located-in the abyss.
Without fault.

b) Maybe capering located-in the abyss.
Advancing, without fault indeed.

Associated Contexts a) **Maybe,** HUO: possible but not certain, perhaps. **Caper,** YO: play, frolic, dance and leap for joy, frisk, gambol. The ideogram: foot and feather, light-footed. **Locate(-in),** TSAI: live in, dwell, reside; belong to, involved with, depend on; within. The ideogram:

earth and persevere, place on the earth. **Abyss**, YÜAN: deep hole or gulf, where backwaters eddy and accumulate; whirlpool; deep water.

Without fault, WU CHIN: no error or harm in the situation.

b) **Advance**, CHIN: exert yourself, make progress, climb; be promoted; further the development of, augment; adopt a religion or conviction; offer, introduce. **Indeed**, YEH: intensifier; indicates comment on previous statement.

Nine at-fifth

a) **Flying dragon located-in heaven.**
Harvesting: visualizing Great People.

b) **Flying dragon located-in heaven.**
Great People creating indeed.

Associated   Contexts *a)* **Fly**, FEI: spread your wings, fly away; let free; swift. **Locate(-in)**, TSAI: live in, dwell, reside; belong to, involved with, depend on; within. The ideogram: earth and persevere, place on the earth.

Harvest, LI: advantageous, profitable; acute, insightful; benefit, nourish; third stage of the Time Cycle. **Visualize**, CH'IEN: seeing in all its aspects: vision, being visible, forming mental images; visit, call on, consult. The ideogram: eye above person, active and receptive sight. **Great People**, TA JEN: important, noble, influential; those who impose a ruling principle on their lives; effect of the great within an individual; keyword.

b) **Create**, TSAO: make, construct, build, form, establish. **Indeed**, YEH: intensifier; indicates comment on previous statement.

Nine above

a) **Overbearing dragon possesses repenting.**

b) **Overbearing dragon possesses repenting.**
Overfilling, not permitting lasting indeed.

Associated   Contexts *a)* **Overbearing**, K'ANG: excessive, over-powering authority; disparage; rigid, unbending; excessive display of force. **Possess**, YU: in possession of, have, own; opposite of lack, WU. **Repent**, HUI: dissatisfaction with past conduct causing a change of heart; proceeds from abashment, LIN, shame and confusion at having lost the right way.

b) **Overfill,** YING: at the point of overflowing; more than wanted, stretch beyond; replenished, full; arrogant. The ideogram: vessel and too much. **Not permitting,** PU K'O: not possible; contradicts an inherent principle. The ideogram: mouth and breath, silent consent. **Last,** CHIU: long, protracted; enduring. **Indeed,** YEH: intensifier; indicates comment on previous statement.

Availing-of Nines (all lines are transforming)

a) **Visualizing flocking dragons without a head.**
Significant.

b) **Availing-of nines.**
Heavenly actualizing-tao not permitting
activating the head indeed.

Associated Contexts a) **Visualize,** CH'IEN: seeing in all its aspects: vision, being visible, forming mental images; visit, call on, consult. The ideogram: eye above person, active and receptive sight. **Flock,** CH'ÜN: herd, group; people of same kind, friends, equals; all, entire; move in unison, flock together. The ideogram: chief and sheep, flock around a leader. **Without,** WU: devoid of; -less as suffix.

Significant, CHI: leads to the experience of meaning; favorable, propitious, advantageous, appropriate; keyword. The ideogram: scholar and mouth, wise words of a sage.

b) **Avail-of,** YUNG: take advantage of; benefit from, profit by; use for a specific purpose; apply to advantage. The ideogram: to divine and center, applying divination to central concerns. **Nine,** CHIU: number of a transforming whole line; superlative: best, perfect; ninth.

Actualize-tao, TE: realize tao in action; power, virtue; ability to follow the course traced by the ongoing process of the cosmos; keyword. The ideogram: to go, straight, and heart. Linked with acquire, TE: acquiring that which makes a being become what it is meant to be. **Not permitting,** PU K'O: not possible; contradicts an inherent principle. The ideogram: mouth and breath, silent consent. **Activate,** WEI: act or cause to act; do, make, manage; make active; attend to, help; because of. **Indeed,** YEH: intensifier; indicates comment on previous statement.

FIELD ▌ *K'UN*

This hexagram describes your situation in terms of the primal structuring power confronted with many forces and obstacles. It emphasizes that giving way in order to serve and yield results, the action of **Field**, is the adequate way to handle it. To be in accord with the time, you are told to: **yield!**

●   *Image of the Situation*

> **Field: Spring Growing Harvesting, female horse's Trial.**
> **A chün tzu possesses directed going.**
> **Beforehand delusion, afterwards acquiring.**
> **A lord Harvesting.**
> **Western South: acquiring partnering.**
> **Eastern North: losing partnering.**
> **Quiet Trial significant.**

Associated Contexts **Field**, K'UN: surface of the world; concrete extension; basis of all existence, where Force or heaven exerts its power; all-involving service; earth; moon, wife, mother; courtiers, servants. The ideogram: terrestrial globe and stretch out, stability and extension. **Field**, K'UN, is the earth trigram doubled and includes that trigram's attributes: *Symbol*: **Earth**, TI: ground on which the human world rests; basis of all things, nourishes all things. *Action*: **Yield(-to)**, SHUN: give way and bear produce; comply, agree, follow, obey; unresisting, docile, flexible; nourish, provide. The ideogram: head and current, water flowing from the head of a river, yielding to the banks. **Spring Growing Harvesting Trial**: **Spring**, YÜAN: **Grow**, HENG; **Harvest**, LI; and **Trial**, CHEN, are the four stages of the Time Cycle, the model for all dynamic processes. They indicate that your question is connected to the cycle as a whole rather than a part of it, and that the origin (Spring) of a favorable result (Harvesting Trial) is an offering to the spirits (Growing). **Female**, P'IN: female sexual organs, particularly of farm animals; concave, hollow. The ideogram: cattle and ladle, a hollow reproductive organ. **Horse**, MA: symbol of spirited strength in the natural world, counterpart of dragon, LUNG;

associated with the trigram Force, CH'IEN, heaven, T'IEN, and high noon. **'s/have(-it)/it/them**, CHIH: expresses possession, directly or as an object pronoun. **Trial**, CHEN: test by ordeal; inquiry by divination and its result; righteous, firm; separating wheat from chaff; the kernel, the proven core; fourth stage of the Time Cycle. The ideogram: pearl and divination.

Chün tzu: ideal of a person who uses divination to order his/her life in accordance with tao rather than wilful intention; keyword. **Possessing directed going**, YU YU WANG: imposing a direction on the flow of time from present to past; have a specific goal or purpose.

Before(hand)/earlier, HSIEN: come before in time; first, at first; formerly, past, previous; begin, go ahead of. **Delude**, MI: confused, stupefied, infatuated; blinded by vice; bewitch, fascinate, deceive. **After(wards)/later**, HOU: come after in time, subsequent; put oneself after; the second; attendants, heirs, successors, posterity. **Acquire**, TE: obtain the desired object; wish for, desire covetously; gains, possessions. The ideogram: go and obstacle, going through obstacles to the goal.

Lord, CHU: ruler, master, chief; authority. The ideogram: lamp and flame, giving light. **Harvest**, LI: advantageous, profitable; acute, insightful; benefit, nourish; third stage of the Time Cycle.

Western South: the neutral Earthy Moment between the yang and yin hemicycles; bring forth concrete results, ripe fruits of late summer. **Partner**, P'ENG: associate for mutual benefit; two equal or similar things; companions, friends, peers; join in; commercial ventures. The ideogram: linked strings of cowries or coins.

Eastern North: border, limit, completion; boundary between cycles: Mountain; accomplishing words, summing up before new germination; dark, cold, lonely winter night. **Lose**, SANG: fail to obtain, cease, become obscure; forgotten, destroyed; lament, mourn; funeral. The ideogram: weep and the dead.

Quiet, AN: peaceful, still, settled; calm, tranquilize. The ideogram: woman under a roof, a tranquil home. **Significant**, CHI: leads to the experience of meaning; favorable, propitious, advantageous, appropriate; keyword. The ideogram: scholar and mouth, wise words of a sage.

● *Outer and Inner Aspects*

☷ **Field**: The field of earth yields and sustains, serving in order to produce. **Field** is the equalizing point between yin and yang where things labor and serve.

Connection to both inner and outer: the common labor of sowing and hoarding, the Earthy Moment. **Field** produces concrete results through serving.

The first two hexagrams represent extreme modes of the interplay of yin and yang. **Field** is the extreme yin mode, where the two agencies equalize and cancel each other out.

As the whole and opened lines, these extremes twine or twist together to produce the 62 composite hexagrams, the web of possible human situations. When one of the composite hexagrams is obtained as an oracle, you should imagine yourself through its Image and texts.

On the contrary, do not identify with **Field**, for such identification leads to complete stagnation without the ability to initiate action. Your situation contains enormous formative potential, but it is threatened by this fundamental one-sidedness.

● *Contrasted Definitions*

> **Force: solid.**
> **Field: supple.**

Associated Contexts **Force**, CH'IEN: spirit power, creative and destructive; unceasing forward motion; dynamic, enduring, untiring; firm, stable; heaven, sovereign, father; also: dry up, parched, exhausted, cleared away. The ideogram: sprouts or vapors rising from the ground and sunlight, both fecundating moisture and scorching drought. Image of Hexagram 1. **Solid**, KANG: quality of the whole lines; firm, strong, unyielding, persisting.

Supple, JOU: quality of the opened lines; flexible, pliant, tender, adaptable.

- *Symbol Tradition*

Earth potency: Field.
A chün tzu uses munificent actualizing-tao to carry the beings.

Associated Contexts **Potency**, SHIH: power, influence, strength; authority, dignity; virility. The ideogram: strength and skill.

Use(-of), YI: make use of, by means of, owing to; employ, make functional. **Munificence**, HOU: liberal, kind, generous; create abundance; thick, large. The ideogram: gift of a superior to an inferior. **Actualize-tao**, TE: realize tao in action; power, virtue; ability to follow the course traced by the ongoing process of the cosmos; keyword. The ideogram: to go, straight, and heart. Linked with acquire, TE: acquiring that which makes a being become what it is meant to be. **Carry**, TSAI: bear, carry with you; contain, sustain; load a ship or cart, cargo; fill in, complete. **Being(s)**, WU: creature, thing, any single being; matter, substance, essence; nature of things.

- *Image Tradition*

Culminating Field, Spring in-fact. [I]
The myriad beings's own birth.
Thereupon yielding receiving heaven.
Field: munificence carrying the beings.

Actualizing-tao uniting without delimiting. [II]
Containing generosity, the shining great.
The kinds: being conjoining Growing.
The female horse: earth sorting.
Moving, the earth without delimiting.

Supple yielding, Harvesting Trial. [III]
A chün tzu directing moving.
Beforehand delusion letting-go tao.
Afterwards yielding acquiring rules.

Western South: acquiring partnering. [IV]
Thereupon associating sorting movement.
Eastern North: losing partnering.
Thereupon completing possesses reward.

Quiet Trial's significance. [V]
Corresponding earth without delimiting.

Associated Contexts **[I] Culminate**, CHIH: bring to the highest
degree; arrive at the end or summit; superlative. **Spring**, YÜAN: source,
origin, head; great, excellent; arise, begin, generating power; first stage of
the Time Cycle. **In-fact**, TSAI: in actual fact, currently.

Myriad, WAN: countless; many, everyone; lit.: ten thousand. The
ideogram: swarm of insects. **Own**, TZU: possession and the things
possessed; avail of, depend on; property, riches. **Birth/give-birth-to**,
SHENG: produce, beget, grow, bear, arise; life, vitality. The ideogram:
earth and sprout.

Thereupon, NAI: on that ground, because of. **Receive**, CH'ENG:
receive gifts or commands from superiors or customers; take in hand;
catch falling water. The ideogram: accepting a seal of office. **Heaven**,
T'IEN: highest; sky, firmament, heavens; power above the human as
opposed to earth, TI, below; the Symbol of the trigram Force, CH'IEN.
The ideogram: great and the one above.

[II] Unite, HO: join, match, correspond, agree, collect, reply; unison,
harmony; also: close, shut the mouth. The ideogram: mouth and
assemble. **Without**, WU: devoid of; -less as suffix. **Delimit**, CHIANG:
define frontiers, draw limits; boundary, border.

Contain, HAN: retain, embody, cherish; withold, tolerate; lit.: contain
in the mouth, put a coin in a corpse's mouth. **Generous**, HUNG: liberal,
large; vast, expanded; give or share willingly, munificent; develop fully.
Shine, KUANG: illuminate; give off brilliant, bright light; honor, glory,
éclat; result of action, contrasts with brightness, MING, light of heavenly
bodies. The ideogram: fire above person, lifting the light. **Great**, TA: big,
noble, important, very; orient the will toward a self-imposed goal, impose
direction; ability to lead or guide your life; contrasts with small, HSIAO,
flexible adaptation to what crosses your path; keyword. Image of
Hexagrams 14, 26, 28, 34.

Kinds, P'IN: species and their essential qualities; sorts, classes; classify,
select. **Conjoin**, HSIEN: come into contact with, influence; reach, join

together; put together as parts of a previously separated whole; come into conjunction, as the celestial bodies; totally, completely; lit.: broken piece of pottery, the halves of which join to identify partners. Image of Hexagram 31. **Grow**, HENG: success through a sacrifice; pervade, persevere; bring to full growth; enjoy; vigorous, effective; second stage of the Time Cycle.

Sort, LEI: group according to kind, class with; like nature or purpose; species, class, genus.

Move, HSING: move or move something; motivate, emotionally moving; walk, act, do. The ideogram: stepping left then right.

[III] Harvesting Trial, LI CHEN: advantageous divination; putting the action in question to the test is beneficial.

Let-go, SHIH: lose, omit, miss, fail, let slip; out of control. The ideogram: drop from the hand. **Tao**: way or path; ongoing process of being and the course it traces for each specific person or thing; keyword. The ideogram: go and head, leading and the path it creates.

Rules, CH'ANG: unchanging principles; regular, constant, habitual; maintain laws and customs.

[IV] Associate(-with), YÜ: consort with, combine; companions; group, band, company; agree with, comply, help. The ideogram: pair of hands reaching downward meets a pair of hands reaching upward, helpful association.

Complete, CHUNG: end of a cycle that begins the next; last, whole, all; contrasts with exhaust, CH'IUNG, final end. The ideogram: silk cocoons, follow and ice, winter linking one year with the next. **Reward**, CH'ING: gift given from gratitude or benevolence; favor from heaven; congratulate with gifts. The ideogram: heart, follow and deer (wealth), the heart expressed through gifts.

[V] Correspond, YING: be in agreement or harmony; resonate together, invoke and fulfill each other; answer to, suitable; relation between the lines (1:4, 2:5, 3:6) when they form the pair opened and whole, supple and solid. The ideogram: heart and obey.

● *Transforming Lines*

Initial six

a) **Treading frost, hardening ice culminating.**

b) **Treading frost hardening the ice:**
   Yin begins solidifying indeed.
   Docilely involving one's tao:
   Culminating hardening the ice indeed.

Associated Contexts a) **Tread**, LÜ: step, path, track; footsteps; walk a path or way; course of the stars; act, practise; conduct; salary, means of subsistence. The ideogram: body and repeating steps, following a trail. Image of Hexagram 10. **Frost**, SHUANG: frozen dew, hoar-frost, rime; crystallized; severe, frigid. **Harden**, CHIEN: make or become hard; establish, strengthen; durable, resolute. **Ice**, PING: frozen water; icy, freezing; clear, pure.

b) **Yin**: Struction: consolidating, shadowy aspect of phenomena: conserves, substantializes, creates structures; spacial extension; limited, bound, given specific being; build, make something concrete. **Begin**, SHIH: commence, start, open; earliest, first; beginning of a time-span, ended by completion, CHUNG. The ideogram: woman and eminent, beginning new life. **Solidify**, NING: congeal, freeze, curdle, stiffen; coagulate, make solid or firm. **Indeed**, YEH: intensifier; indicates comment on previous statement.
   Docile, HSÜN: amiable, mild, yielding; tame; gradually attained. **Involve**, CHIH: include, entangle, implicate; induce, cause. The ideogram: person walking, induced to follow. **One's/one**, CH'I: third person pronoun; also: it/its, he/his, she/hers, they/theirs.

Six at-second

a) **Straightening on-all-sides, great.**
   Not repeating: without not Harvesting.

b) **Six at-second's stirring-up.**
   Straightening used on-all-sides indeed.
   Not repeating: without not Harvesting.
   Earthly tao shining indeed.

Associated Contexts a) **Straighten**, CHIH: correct the crooked, reform, repay injustice; proceed directly; sincere, upright, just; blunt, outspoken. **Sides(on-all-sides)**, FANG: limits, boundaries; square, surface of the earth extending to the four cardinal points; everywhere.
   Not, PU: simple negative. **Repeat**, HSI: series of similar acts; practise, rehearse; familiar with, skilled. The ideogram: two wings and a cap,

thought carried by repeated movements. **Without not Harvesting**, WU PU LI: nothing for which this will not be beneficial; advantageous potential, borderline where the balance is swinging from not Harvesting to actually Harvesting.

b) **Stir-up**, TUNG: excite, influence, move, affect; work, take action; come out of the egg or the bud; the Action of the trigram Shake, CHEN. The ideogram: strength and heavy, move weighty things.

Indeed, YEH: intensifier; indicates comment on previous statement.

Six at-third

a) Containing composition permitting Trial.
Maybe adhering-to kingly affairs:
Without accomplishing possessing completion.

b) Containing composition permitting Trial.
Using the season: shooting-forth indeed.
Maybe adhering-to kingly affairs:
Knowing the shining great indeed.

Associated Contexts *a)* **Composition**, CHANG: a well-composed whole and its structure; beautiful creations; elegant, clear, brilliant; contrasts with pattern, WEN, beauty of intrinsic design. **Permit**, K'O: possible because in harmony with an inherent principle. The ideogram: mouth and breath, silent consent.

Maybe, HUO: possible but not certain, perhaps. **Adhere(-to)**, TS'UNG: follow a way, hold to a doctrine, school, or person; hear and comply with, agree to; forced to follow, follower. The ideogram: two men walking, one following the other. **King(hood)**, WANG: effective ruler, by authority of the Emperor, from whom others derive their power. **Affairs**, SHIH: all kinds of personal activity; matters at hand; business, occupation; manage a business, case in court.

Without, WU: devoid of; -less as suffix. **Accomplish**, CH'ENG: complete, finish, bring about; perfect, full, whole; play your part, do your duty; mature. The ideogram: weapon and man, able to bear arms, thus fully developed.

b) **Season**, SHIH: quality of the time; the right time, opportune, in harmony; planning in accord with the time; seasons of the year. The ideogram: sun and temple, time as sacred. **Shoot-forth**, FA: expand, send out; shoot an arrow; ferment, rise; be displayed. The ideogram: stance, bow and arrow, shooting from a solid base. **Indeed**, YEH: intensifier; indicates comment on previous statement.

Know, CHIH: understand, perceive, remember; informed, aware, wise. The ideogram: arrow and mouth, words focused and swift.

Six at-fourth

a) **Bundled-in the bag.**
   Without fault, without praise.

b) **Bundled-in the bag, without fault.**
   Consideration not harmful indeed.

Associated Contexts a) **Bundle-in**, KUA: enclose, envelop, tie up; embrace, include. **Bag,** NANG: sack, purse; put in a bag; property, salary.

Without fault, WU CHIU: no error or harm in the situation. **Praise,** YÜ: admire and approve; magnify, eulogize; flatter. The ideogram: words and give, offering words.

b) **Consider,** SHEN: act carefully, seriously; cautious, attentive, circumspect; still, quiet, sincere. The ideogram: heart and true. **Not,** PU: simple negative. **Harm,** HAI: damage, injure, offend; suffer; hurtful, hindrance; fearful, anxious. **Indeed,** YEH: intensifier; indicates comment on previous statement.

Six at-fifth

a) **A yellow apron. Spring significant.**

b) **A yellow apron, Spring significant.**
   Pattern located-in the center indeed.

Associated Contexts a) **Yellow,** HUANG: color of the productive middle; associated with the Earthy Moment between yang and yin hemicycles; color of soil in central China; emblematic and imperial color of China since the Yellow Emperor (2500 BCE). **Apron,** SHANG: ceremonial garment; skirt, clothes; curtains of a carriage. The ideogram: garment and manifest, clothing as display.

b) **Pattern,** WEN: intrinsic or natural design and its beauty; stylish, elegant; noble; contrasts with composition, CHANG, a conscious creation.

Locate(-in), TSAI: live in, dwell, reside; belong to, involved with, depend on; within. The ideogram: earth and persevere, place on the earth. **Center**, CHUNG: inner, central; put in the center; middle, stable point enabling you to face inner and outer changes; middle line of trigram. The ideogram: field divided in two equal parts. Image of Hexagram 61. **Indeed**, YEH: intensifier; indicates comment on previous statement.

Six above

a) **Dragons struggling tending-towards the countryside. Their blood: indigo, yellow.**

b) **Dragons struggling tending-towards the countryside. Their tao exhausted indeed.**

Associated Contexts *a)* **Dragon**, LUNG: powerful spirit-energy emerging from waters below; mythical shape-changer with supreme power; connected with heaven, T'IEN and the trigram Force, CH'IEN. **Struggle**, CHAN: fight with, combat; make war, join battle; hostilities; alarmed, terrified. **Tend-towards**, YÜ: move toward but not reach, in the direction of; contrasts with reach(-to), HU, actually arriving. **Countryside**, YEH: cultivated fields and grassland, where nature and human construction interact; third of the territorial zones: city, suburbs, countryside, forests.

Their/they, CH'I: third person pronoun; also: one/one's, it/its, he/his, she/hers. **Blood**, HSÜEH: yin fluid that maintains life; money, property. **Indigo**, HSÜAN: color associated with the Metallic Moment; deep blue-black, color of the sky's depths; profound, subtle, deep; veneration of the gods and spirits. **Yellow**, HUANG: color of the productive middle; associated with the Earthy Moment between the yang and yin hemicycles; color of soil in central China; emblematic and imperial color of China since the Yellow Emperor (2500 BCE).

b) **Exhaust**, CH'IUNG: bring to an end; limit, extremity; destitute; investigate exhaustively; end without a new beginning. The ideogram: cave and naked person, bent with disease or old age. **Indeed**, YEH: intensifier; indicates comment on previous statement.

Availing-of Sixes (all lines are transforming)

a) **Harvesting: perpetual Trial.**

b) **Availing-of the sixes, perpetual Trial.**
Using the great to complete indeed.

Associated Contexts *a)* **Perpetual**, YUNG: continuing; everlasting, ever-flowing. The ideogram: flowing water.

b) **Avail-of**, YUNG: take advantage of; benefit from, profit by; use for a specific purpose; apply to advantage. The ideogram: to divine and center, applying divination to central concerns. **Six**, LU: transforming opened line; six lines or places of a hexagram; sixth.

Indeed, YEH: intensifier; indicates comment on previous statement.

SPROUTING ▪ *CHUN*

This hexagram describes your situation in terms of beginning growth. It emphasizes that collecting potential in preparation for arduous labor is the adequate way to handle it. To be in accord with the time, you are told to: **sprout!**

- *Image of the Situation*

  Sprouting.
  Spring Growing Harvesting Trial.
  No availing-of possessing directed going.
  Harvesting: installing feudatories.

  Associated Contexts **Sprout**, CHUN: begin or cause to grow; assemble, accumulate, bring under control; hoard possessions; establish a military camp; difficult, arduous. The ideogram: sprout piercing hard soil.
  Spring Growing Harvesting Trial: **Spring**, YÜAN; **Grow**, HENG; **Harvest**, LI; and **Trial**, CHEN, are the four stages of the Time Cycle, the model for all dynamic processes. They indicate that your question is connected to the cycle as a whole rather than a part of it, and that the origin (Spring) of a favorable result (Harvesting Trial) is an offering to the spirits (Growing).
  No, WU: simple negative; un-, dis-. **Avail-of**, YUNG: take advantage of; benefit from, profit by; use for a specific purpose; apply to advantage. The ideogram: to divine and center, applying divination to central concerns. **Possessing directed going**, YU YU WANG: imposing a direction on the flow of time from present to past; have a specific goal or purpose.
  Harvest, LI: advantageous, profitable; acute, insightful; benefit, nourish; third stage of the Time Cycle. **Install**, CHIEN: set up, establish; confirm a position or law. **Feudatory**, HOU: nobles entrusted with governing the provinces; active in daily life rather than governing from the center; contrasts with prince, KUNG, executives at the court.

• *Outer and Inner Aspects*

☵ **Gorge**: Stream ventures and falls into the gorge, flowing on through toil and danger. **Gorge** ends the yin hemicycle by leveling and dissolving forms.

Connection to the outer: flooding and leveling dissolve direction and shape, the Streaming Moment. **Gorge** ventures, falls, toils and flows on.

☳ **Shake**: Thunder rises from below, shaking and stirring things up. **Shake** begins the yang hemicycle by germinating new action.

Connection to the inner: sprouting energies thrusting from below, the Woody Moment beginning. **Shake** stirs things up to issue-forth.

The outer trigram completes a cycle, the inner begins a new one. Inner stirring-up is **sprouting**, pushing through the leveling stream.

• *Counter Indications*

Nuclear trigrams **Bound**, KEN, and **Field**, K'UN, result in Counter Hexagram 23, **Stripping**, PO. **Sprouting**'s abundant new energy is contrasted with **stripping** things and reducing them to the essential.

• *Sequence*

> Possessing Heaven[and]Earth.
> Therefore afterwards the myriad beings giving-birth in-truth.
> Overfilling Heaven[and]Earth's interspace
>   implies verily the myriad beings.
> Anterior acquiescence has the use-of Sprouting.
> Sprouting implies overfilling indeed.
> Sprouting implies beings's beginning giving-birth indeed.

Associated Contexts **Possess**, YU: in possession of, have, own; opposite of lack, WU. **Heaven[and]Earth**, T'IEN TI: dynamic relation between the primal powers and the world it produces; cosmos, natural or human world; keyword.

Therefore afterwards, JAN HOU: logical consequence of, necessarily follows in time. **Myriad**, WAN: countless; many, everyone; lit.: ten thousand. The ideogram: swarm of insects. **Being(s)**, WU: creature, thing,

any single being; matter, substance, essence; nature of things. **Birth/give-birth-to**, SHENG: produce, beget, grow, bear, arise; life, vitality. The ideogram: earth and sprout. **In-truth**, YEN: statement is complete and correct.

    Overfill, YING: at the point of overflowing; more than wanted, stretch beyond; replenished, full; arrogant. The ideogram: vessel and too much. **'s/have(-it)/it/them**, CHIH: expresses possession, directly or as an object pronoun. **Interspace**, HSIEN: space between, interval, crevice; vacant, empty. **Imply**, CHE: further signify; additional meaning. **Verily**, WEI: the epitome of; in truth, the only; very important. **Indeed**, YEH: intensifier; indicates comment on previous statement.

    Anterior ... the use-of: activating this hexagram depends on understanding and accepting the previous statement.

    Begin, SHIH: commence, start, open; earliest, first; beginning of a time-span, ended by completion, CHUNG. The ideogram: woman and eminent, beginning new life.

• *Contrasted Definitions*

> **Sprouting: visualizing and-also not letting-go one's residing.**
> **Enveloping: motley and-also conspicuous.**

Associated Contexts **Visualize**, CHIEN: seeing in all its aspects: vision, being visible, forming mental images; visit, call on, consult. The ideogram: eye above person, active and receptive sight. **And-also**, ERH: joins and contrasts two terms. **Not**, PU: simple negative. **Let-go**, SHIH: lose, omit, miss, fail, let slip; out of control. The ideogram: drop from the hand. **One's/one**, CH'I third person pronoun; also: it/its, he/his, she/hers, they/theirs. **Reside(-in)**, CHÜ: dwell, live in, stay; sit down, fill an office; settled parts of a country. The ideogram: body and seat.

    Envelop, MENG: cover, pull over, hide, conceal; lid or cover; clouded awareness, dull; ignorance, immaturity; unseen beginnings. The ideogram: plant and covered, hidden growth. Image of Hexagram 4. **Motley**, TSA: mingled, variegated, mixed; disorder. **Conspicuous**, CHU: manifest, obvious, clear.

● *Symbol Tradition*

Clouds, Thunder, Sprouting.
A chün tzu uses the canons to coordinate.

Associated Contexts **Clouds**, YÜN: fog, mist, water vapor; connects to the Streaming Moment and Stream, the Symbol of the trigram Gorge, K'AN. **Thunder**, LEI: rising, arousing power; the Symbol of the trigram Shake, CHEN.

Chün tzu: ideal of a person who uses divination to order his/her life in accordance with tao rather than wilful intention; keyword. **Use(-of)**, YI: make use of, by means of, owing to; employ, make functional. **Canons**, CHING: standards, laws; regular, regulate; the Five Classics. The ideogram: warp-threads in a loom. **Coordinate**, LUN: classify, bind, adjust; weave together; lit.: unravel and twist silk together into threads.

● *Image Tradition*

Sprouting. [I]
Solid[and]Supple beginning mingling and-also
                              heaviness giving-birth indeed.

Stirring-up reaching-to venturing center. [II]
Great Growing: Trial.
Thunder[and]Rain's stirring-up, fullness overfilling.
Heaven creating grass, duskiness.
Proper to instal feudatories and-also not to soothe.

Associated Contexts **[I] Solid[and]Supple**, KANG JOU: field of creative tension between the whole and opened lines and their qualities; field of psychic movement. **Mingle**, CHIAO: blend with, communicate, join, exchange; trade, business; copulation; friendship. **Heavy**, NAN: arduous, grievous, difficult; hardship, distress; harass; contrasts with versatile, I, deal lightly with. The ideogram: domestic bird with clipped tail and drying sticky earth.

[II] Stir-up, TUNG: excite, influence, move, affect; work, take action; come out of the egg or the bud; the Action of the trigram Shake, CHEN. The ideogram: strength and heavy, move weighty things. **Reach(-to)**, HU: arrive at a goal; reach towards and achieve; connect; contrasts with tend-

towards, YU. **Venture**, HSIEN: risk without reserve; key point, point of danger; difficulty, obstruction that must be confronted; water falling and filling the holes on its way; the Action of the trigram Gorge, K'AN. The ideogram: mound and all or whole, everything engaged at one point. **Center**, CHUNG: inner, central; put in the center; middle, stable point enabling you to face inner and outer changes; middle line of trigram. The ideogram: field divided in two equal parts. Image of Hexagram 61.

Great, TA: big, noble, important, very; orient the will toward a self-imposed goal, impose direction; ability to lead or guide your life; contrasts with small, HSIAO, flexible adaptation to what crosses your path; keyword. Image of Hexagrams 14, 26, 28, 34. **Grow**, HENG: success through a sacrifice; pervade, persevere; bring to full growth; enjoy; vigorous, effective; second stage of the Time Cycle. **Trial**, CHEN: test by ordeal; inquiry by divination and its result; righteous, firm; separating wheat from chaff; the kernel, the proven core; fourth stage of the Time Cycle. The ideogram: pearl and divination.

Thunder[and]Rain, LEI YÜ: fertilizing shock of storms; associated with the trigrams Shake, CHEN, and Gorge, K'AN. **Full**, MAN: as much as possible; replete, bulging, stuffed, abounding; complete; proud.

Heaven, T'IEN: highest; sky, firmament, heavens; power above the human as opposed to earth, TI, below; the Symbol of the trigram Force, CH'IEN. The ideogram: great and the one above. **Create**, TSAO: make, construct, build, form, establish. **Grass**, TS'AO: all grassy plants and herbs; young, tender plants; rough draft; hastily. **Duskiness**, MAI: obscure, indistinct; insufficient light; times of day when it is not fully light. The ideogram: day and not-yet.

Proper, YI: reasonable of itself; fit and right, harmonious; ought, should. **Soothe**, NING: calm, pacify; create peace of mind; tranquil, quiet. The ideogram: shelter above heart, dish and breath, physical and spiritual comfort.

• *Transforming Lines*

Initial nine

a) **Stone pillar.**
Harvesting: residing-in Trial.
Harvesting: installing feudatories.

b) **Although a stone pillar, purpose moving correctly indeed.**
Using valuing the mean below.
The great acquiring the commoners indeed.

Associated Contexts *a)* **Stone**, P'AN: large conspicuous rock, foundation stone; stable, immovable. **Pillar**, HUAN: post or tablet marking a grave.

b) **Although**, SUI: even though, supposing that, if, even if. **Purpose**, CHIH: focus of mind and heart; will, inclination, resolve. The ideogram: heart and scholar, high inner resolve, or heart and go, inner determination. **Move**, HSING: move or move something; motivate, emotionally moving; walk, act, do. The ideogram: stepping left then right. **Correct**, CHENG: rectify deviation or one-sidedness; proper, straight, exact, regular; constant, rule, model. The ideogram: stop and one, hold to one thing.

Value, KUEI: regard as valuable, give worth and dignity to; precious, high priced; honorable, exalted, illustrious. The ideogram: cowries (coins) and basket. **Mean**, CHIEN: low, poor, cheap; depreciate, undervalue; opposite of value, KUEI. **Below**, HSIA: anything below, in all senses; lower, inner; lower trigram; opposite of above, SHANG.

Acquire, TE: obtain the desired object; wish for, desire covetously; gains, possessions. The ideogram: go and obstacle, going through obstacles to the goal. **Commoners**, MIN: class of workers the state draws on to sustain the social hierarchy; undeveloped potential outside the organized personality.

Six at-second

a) **Sprouting thus, quitting thus.**
Riding a horse, arraying thus.
In-no-way outlawry, matrimonial allying.
Woman[and]Son, Trial: not nursing.
Ten years-revolved, thereupon nursing.

b) **Six at-second's heaviness.**
Riding a solid indeed.
Ten years-revolved, thereupon nursing.
Reversing rules indeed.

Associated Contexts a) **Thus ... thus**, JU...JU: when there is one thing, then there must be the second thing. **Quit**, CHAN: stop, change because unsuccessful; unable to advance.

Ride, CH'ENG: ride an animal or a chariot; have the upper hand, seize the right time; control strong power; overcome the nature of the other; supple opened line above a solid whole line. **Horse**, MA: symbol of spirited strength in the natural world, counterpart of dragon, LUNG; associated with the trigram Force, CH'IEN, heaven, T'IEN, and high noon. **Array**, PAN: classify and display; arrange according to rank; assign to a group, as soldiers to their units. The ideogram: knife between two gems, separating values.

In-no-way, FEI: strong negative; not so. The ideogram: a box filled with opposition. **Outlawry**, K'OU: break the laws; violent people, outcasts, bandits. **Matrimonial allying**, HUN KOU: legal institution of marriage; make alliances through marriage rather than force.

Woman[and]Son, NÜ TZU: particular relation between a woman and her child. **Nurse**, TZU: love, care for and shelter; act as a mother. The ideogram: child and shelter.

Ten, SHIH: goal and end of reckoning; whole, complete, all; entire, perfected, the full amount; reach everywhere, receive everything. The ideogram: East–West line crosses North–South line, a grid that contains all. **Years-revolved**, NIEN: number of years elapsed; a person's age; contrasts with year's-time, SUI, length of time in a year. **Thereupon**, NAI: on that ground, because of.

b) **Solid**, KANG: quality of the whole lines; firm, strong, unyielding, persisting.

Reverse, FAN: turn and move in the opposite direction; turn around or upside down (180 degrees); change to the opposite position; contrary. **Rules**, CH'ANG: unchanging principles; regular, constant, habitual; maintain laws and customs.

Six at-third

a) Approaching stag, lacking precaution.
Namely, entering tending-towards the forest center.
A chün tzu almost not thus stowing-away.
Going abashed.

b) **Approaching stag, without precaution.**
Using adhering-to wildfowl indeed.
A chün tzu stowing it:
Going abashment exhausted indeed.

Associated Contexts a) **Approach,** CHI: come near to, advance toward; about to do; soon. **Stag,** LU: mature male deer with horns. **Lacking,** WU: strong negative; does not possess. **Precaution,** YÜ: provide against, preventive measures; anxious, vigilant, ready; preoccupied with, think about, expect; mishap, accident.

Namely, WEI: precisely, only that. **Enter,** JU: penetrate, go into, enter on, progress; put into, encroach on; Action of the trigram Ground, SUN, contrary of issue-forth, CH'U. **Tend-towards,** YÜ: move toward but not reach, in the direction of; contrasts with reach(-to), HU, actually arriving. **Forest,** LIN: area with no mark of human construction; woods, wild luxuriance; wilderness; last of the territorial zones: city, suburbs, countryside, forests.

Almost, CHI: nearly, about to; subtle, almost imperceptible; the first sign. **Thus,** JU: as, in this way. **Stow (-away),** SHE: set aside, put away, store; halt, rest in; temporary lodgings, breathing-spell.

Go, WANG, and come, LAI, describe the stream of time as it flows from future through present to past; go, WANG, indicates what is departing from present to past; proceed, move on; keyword. **Abashment,** LIN: distress, shame, regret, humiliation; aware of having lost the right track; leads to repenting, HUI, correcting the direction of mind and life.

b) **Without,** WU: devoid of; -less as suffix.

Adhere(-to), TS'UNG: follow a way, hold to a doctrine, school, or person; hear and comply with, agree to; forced to follow, follower. The ideogram: two men walking, one following the other. **Wildfowl,** CH'IN: all wild and game birds; untamed.

It/them/have(-it)/'s, CHIH: expresses possession, directly or as an object pronoun.

Exhaust, CH'IUNG: bring to an end; limit, extremity; destitute; investigate exhaustively; end without a new beginning. The ideogram: cave and naked person, bent with disease or old age.

Six at-fourth

a) **Riding a horse, arraying thus.**
Seeking matrimonial allying.
Going significant.
Without not Harvesting.

b) **Seeking and-also going.**
   Brightness indeed.

Associated Contexts a) **Ride,** CH'ENG: ride an animal or a chariot; have the upper hand, seize the right time; control strong power; overcome the nature of the other; supple opened line above a solid whole line. **Horse,** MA: symbol of spirited strength in the natural world, counterpart of dragon, LUNG; associated with the trigram Force, CH'IEN, heaven, T'IEN, and high noon. **Array,** PAN: classify and display; arrange according to rank; assign to a group, as soldiers to their units. The ideogram: knife between two gems, separating values. **Thus,** JU: as, in this way.

   Seek, CH'IU: search for, aim at, wish for, desire; implore, supplicate; covetous. **Matrimonial allying,** HUN KOU: legal institution of marriage; make alliances through marriage rather than force.

   Go, WANG, and come, LAI, describe the stream of time as it flows from future through present to past; go, WANG, indicates what is departing from present to past; proceed, move on; keyword. **Significant,** CHI: leads to the experience of meaning; favorable, propitious, advantageous, appropriate; keyword. The ideogram: scholar and mouth, wise words of a sage.

   Without not Harvesting, WU PU LI: nothing for which this will not be beneficial; advantageous potential, borderline where the balance is swinging from not Harvesting to actually Harvesting.

b) **Brightness,** MING: light-giving aspect of burning, heavenly bodies and consciousness; with fire, the Symbol of the trigram Radiance, LI.

   Nine at-fifth

a) **Sprouting: one's juice.**
   The small, Trial: significant.
   The great, Trial: pitfall.

b) **Sprouting: one's juice.**
   Spreading-out not-yet shining indeed.

Associated Contexts a) **Juice,** KAO: active principle, essence; oil, grease, ointment; fertilizing, rich; genius.

   Small, HSIAO: little, common, unimportant; adapting to what crosses your path; ability to move in harmony with the vicissitudes of life; contrasts with great, TA, self-imposed theme or goal; keyword. Image of

Hexagrams 9 and 62. **Significant**, CHI: leads to the experience of meaning; favorable, propitious, advantageous, appropriate; keyword. The ideogram: scholar and mouth, wise words of a sage.

Pitfall, HSIUNG: leads away from the experience of meaning; stuck and exposed to danger, unable to take in the situation; flow of life and spirit is blocked; unfortunate, baleful; keyword.

b) **Spread-out**, SHIH: expand, diffuse, distribute, arrange, exhibit; add to, aid. The ideogram: flag and indeed, claiming new country. **Not-yet**, WEI: temporal negative; something will but has not yet occurred; contrary of already, CHI. Image of Hexagram 64. **Shine**, KUANG: illuminate; give off brilliant, bright light; honor, glory, éclat; result of action, contrasts with brightness, MING, light of heavenly bodies. The ideogram: fire above person, lifting the light.

Six above

a) **Riding a horse, arraying thus.**
Weeping blood, coursing thus.

b) **Weeping blood, coursing thus.**
Wherefore permitting long-living indeed?

Associated Contexts *a)* **Ride**, CH'ENG: ride an animal or a chariot; have the upper hand, seize the right time; control strong power; overcome the nature of the other; supple opened line above a solid whole line. **Horse**, MA: symbol of spirited strength in the natural world, counterpart of dragon, LUNG; associated with the trigram Force, CH'IEN, heaven, T'IEN, and high noon. **Array**, PAN: classify and display; arrange according to rank; assign to a group, as soldiers to their units. The ideogram: knife between two gems, separating values. **Thus**, JU: as, in this way.

Weep, CH'I: lament wordlessly; grieved, heart-broken. **Blood**, HSÜEH: yin fluid that maintains life; money, property. **Course**, LIEN: move, flow like ripples spreading on water; unceasing.

b) **Wherefore**, HO: interrogative: why? for what reason? what is? and affirmation: therefore, for that reason. **Permit**, K'O: possible because in harmony with an inherent principle. The ideogram: mouth and breath, silent consent. **Long-living**, CHANG: enduring, constant; senior, superior, greater; increase, prosper; respect, elevate.

ENVELOPING ■ *MENG*

This hexagram describes your situation in terms of concealment and clouded awareness. It emphasizes that actively accepting this concealment in order to nurture growth is the adequate way to handle it. To be in accord with the time, you are told to: **envelop**!

● *Image of the Situation*

> Enveloping, Growing.
> In-no-way me seeking youthful Enveloping.
> Youthful Enveloping seeking me.
> The initial oracle-consulting notifying.
> Twice, three-times: obscuring.
> Obscuring, by-consequence not notifying.
> Harvesting Trial.

Associated Contexts **Envelop**, MENG: cover, pull over, hide, conceal; lid or cover; clouded awareness, dull; ignorance, immaturity; unseen beginnings. The ideogram: plant and covered, hidden growth. **Grow**, HENG: success through a sacrifice; pervade, persevere; bring to full growth; enjoy; vigorous, effective; second stage of the Time Cycle.

In-no-way, FEI: strong negative; not so. The ideogram: a box filled with opposition. **Me/I/my**, WO: first person pronoun; indicates an unusually strong emphasis on your own subjective experience. **Seek**, CH'IU: search for, aim at, wish for, desire; implore, supplicate; covetous. **Youthful**, T'UNG: young person between eight and fifteen; young animals and plants.

Initial, CH'U: first step or part; beginning, incipient; bottom line of hexagram. The ideogram: knife and garment, cutting out the pattern. **Oracle-consulting**, SHIH: yarrow stalk divination; find your allotted destiny. **Notify**, KAO: proclaim, order, decree; advise, inform, tell. The ideogram: mouth and ox head, imposing speech.

Twice, three-times, TSAI SAN: serial repetition. **Obscure**, TU: confuse, muddy, agitate; muddled, cloudy, turbid; agitated water; annoy through repetition.

124

By-consequence(-of), TSE: very strong connection; reason, cause, result; rule, law, pattern, standard; therefore. **Not**, PU: simple negative.

Harvesting Trial, LI CHEN: advantageous divination; putting the action in question to the test is beneficial.

● *Outer and Inner Aspects*

☶ **Bound**: Mountains bound, limit and set a place off, stopping forward movement. **Bound** completes a full yin-yang cycle.

Connection to the outer: accomplishing words, which express things fully. **Bound** articulates what is complete and suggests what is beginning.

☵ **Gorge**: Stream ventures and falls into the gorge, flowing on through toil and danger. **Gorge** ends the yin hemicycle by leveling and dissolving forms.

Connection to the inner: flooding and leveling dissolve direction and shape, the Streaming Moment. **Gorge** ventures, falls, toils and flows on.

An outer limit hides and shields inner venturing; inner growth is **enveloped** and awareness of new growth is clouded.

● *Counter Indications*

Nuclear trigrams **Field**, K'UN, and **Shake**, CHEN, result in Counter Hexagram 24, **Returning**, FU. **Enveloping**'s preparation for moving on is contrasted with **returning** to the starting point to begin again.

● *Sequence*

Beings giving-birth necessarily Enveloping.
Anterior acquiescence has the use-of Enveloping.
Enveloping implies envelopment indeed.
Beings's immaturity indeed.

Associated Contexts **Being(s)**, WU: creature, thing, any single being; matter, substance, essence; nature of things. **Birth/give-birth-to**, SHENG: produce, beget, grow, bear, arise; life, vitality. The ideogram: earth and sprout. **Necessarily**, PI: unavoidably, indispensably, certainly.

Anterior ... the use-of: activating this hexagram depends on understanding and accepting the previous statement.

Imply, CHE: further signify; additional meaning.

's/have(-it)/it/them, CHIH: expresses possession, directly or as an object pronoun. **Indeed**, YEH: intensifier; indicates comment on previous statement. **Immature**, CHIH: small, tender, young, delicate; undeveloped; conceited, haughty; late grain.

● *Contrasted Definitions*

**Sprouting: visualizing and-also not letting-go one's residing.
Enveloping: motley and-also conspicuous.**

Associated Contexts **Sprout**, CHUN: begin or cause to grow; assemble, accumulate, bring under control; hoard possessions; gather soldiers in a military camp; difficult, arduous. The ideogram: sprout piercing hard soil. Image of Hexagram 3. **Visualize**, CHIEN: seeing in all its aspects: vision, being visible, forming mental images; visit, call on, consult. The ideogram: eye above person, active and receptive sight. **And-also**, ERH: joins and contrasts two terms. **Let-go**, SHIH: lose, omit, miss, fail, let slip; out of control. The ideogram: drop from the hand. **One's/one**, CH'I: third person pronoun; also: it/its, he/his, she/hers, they/theirs. **Reside(-in)**, CHÜ: dwell, live in, stay; sit down, fill an office; settled parts of a country. The ideogram: body and seat.

Motley, TSA: mingled, variegated, mixed; disorder. **Conspicuous**, CHU: manifest, obvious, clear.

Symbol Tradition

**Below mountain issuing-forth springwater. Enveloping.
A chün tzu uses fruiting movement to nurture actualizing-tao.**

Associated Contexts **Below**, HSIA: anything below, in all senses; lower, inner; lower trigram; opposite of above, SHANG. **Mountain**, SHAN: limit, boundary; the Symbol of the trigram Bound, KEN. The ideogram: three peaks, a mountain range. **Issue-forth(-from)**, CH'U: emerge from, come out of, proceed from, spring from; the Action of the trigram Shake, CHEN; contrary of enter, JU. The ideogram: stem with branches and leaves emerging. **Springwater**, CH'ÜAN: headwaters of a river; pure water. The ideogram: water and white, pure water at the source.

Chün tzu: ideal of a person who uses divination to order his/her life in accordance with tao rather than willful intention; keyword. **Use(-of)**, YI: make use of, by means of, owing to; employ, make functional. **Fruit**, KUO: plant's annual produce; tree fruits; come to fruition, fruits of actions; produce, results, effects; reliable; conclude, surpass. The ideogram: tree topped by a round fruit. **Move**, HSING: move or move something; motivate, emotionally moving; walk, act, do. The ideogram: stepping left then right. **Nurture**, YÜ: bring up, support, rear, raise; increase. **Actualize-tao**, TE: realize tao in action; power, virtue; ability to follow the course traced by the ongoing process of the cosmos; keyword. The ideogram: to go, straight, and heart. Linked with acquire, TE: acquiring that which makes a being become what it is meant to be.

● *Image Tradition*

> **Enveloping. Below mountain possessing venturing. [I]**
> **Venturing and-also stopping. Enveloping.**
>
> **Enveloping, Growing. [II]**
> **Using Growing movement.**
> **Season centering indeed.**
>
> **In-no-way me seeking youthful Enveloping. [III]**
> **Youthful Enveloping seeking me.**
> **Purpose corresponding indeed.**
>
> **The initial oracle-consulting notifying. [IV]**
> **Using solid centering indeed.**
> **Twice, three-times: obscuring.**
> **Obscuring, by-consequence not notifying.**
> **Obscuring Enveloping indeed.**
> **Enveloping used to nourish correcting:**
> **The all-wise achieving indeed.**

Associated Contexts **[I] Possess**, YU: in possession of, have, own; opposite of lack, WU. **Venture**, HSIEN: risk without reserve; key point, point of danger; difficulty, obstruction that must be confronted; water falling and filling the holes on its way; the Action of the trigram Gorge,

K'AN. The ideogram: mound and all or whole, everything engaged at one point.

Stop, CHIH: bring or come to a standstill; the Action of the trigram Bound, KEN. The ideogram: a foot stops walking.

[II] Season, SHIH: quality of the time; the right time, opportune, in harmony; planning in accord with the time; seasons of the year. The ideogram: sun and temple, time as sacred. **Center**, CHUNG: inner, central; put in the center; middle, stable point enabling you to face inner and outer changes; middle line of trigram. The ideogram: field divided in two equal parts. Image of Hexagram 61.

[III] Purpose, CHIH: focus of mind and heart; will, inclination, resolve. The ideogram: heart and scholar, high inner resolve, or heart and go, inner determination. **Correspond**, YING: be in agreement or harmony; resonate together, invoke and fulfill each other; answer to, suitable; relation between the lines (1:4, 2:5, 3:6) when they form the pair opened and whole, supple and solid. The ideogram: heart and obey.

[IV] Solid, KANG: quality of the whole lines; firm, strong, unyielding, persisting.

Nourish, YANG: feed, sustain, support; provide, care for; bring up, improve, grow, develop. **Correct**, CHENG: rectify deviation or one-sidedness; proper, straight, exact, regular; constant, rule, model. The ideogram: stop and one, hold to one thing.

All-wise, SHENG: intuitive universal wisdom; mythical sages; holy, sacred; mark of highest distinction. The ideogram: ear and inform, one who knows all from a single sound. **Achieve**, KUNG: work done, results; real accomplishment, praise, worth, merit. The ideogram: workman's square and forearm, combining craft and strength.

● *Transforming Lines*

Initial six

a) **Shooting-forth Enveloping.**
   Harvesting: availing-of punishing people.
   Availing-of stimulating fettering shackles.
   Using going abashed.

b) Harvesting: availing-of punishing people.
Using correcting laws indeed.

Associated Contexts a) **Shoot-forth**, FA: expand, send out; shoot an arrow; ferment, rise; be displayed. The ideogram: stance, bow and arrow, shooting from a solid base.

Harvest, LI: advantageous, profitable; acute, insightful; benefit, nourish; third stage of the Time Cycle. **Avail-of**, YUNG: take advantage of; benefit from, profit by; use for a specific purpose; apply to advantage. The ideogram: to divine and center, applying divination to central concerns. **Punish**, HSING: legal punishment; physical penalties for severe criminal offenses; whip, torture, behead. **People, person**, JEN: humans individually and collectively; an individual; humankind. Image of Hexagrams 13 and 37.

Stimulate, SHUO: rouse to action and good feeling; free from constraint, stir up, urge on; persuade, cheer, delight; set out in words; the Action of the trigram Open, TUI. The ideogram: words and exchange. **Fetter**, CHIH: tie, manacle; restrain and hinder movement, clog wheels; impede. **Shackles**, KU: chains used to secure prisoners; restrain freedom of action; self-restraint, good principles.

Go, WANG, and come, LAI, describe the stream of time as it flows from future through present to past; go, WANG, indicates what is departing from present to past; proceed, move on; keyword. **Abashment**, LIN: distress, shame, regret, humiliation; aware of having lost the right track; leads to repenting, HUI, correcting the direction of mind and life.

b) **Laws**, FA: rules, statutes, model, method.

Nine at-second

a) **Enwrapping Enveloping. Significant.**
Letting-in the wife. Significant.
The son controlling the dwelling.

b) **The son controlling the dwelling.**
Solid[and]Supple articulating indeed.

Associated Contexts a) **Enwrap**, PAO: envelop, hold, contain; patient; take on responsibility, engaged. The ideogram: enfold and self, a fetus in the womb. **Significant**, CHI: leads to the experience of meaning; favorable, propitious, advantageous, appropriate; keyword. The ideogram: scholar and mouth, wise words of a sage.

Let-in, NA: allow to enter; take in, grow smaller; insert; collect. The ideogram: silk and enter, shrinking silk threads. **Wife**, FU: responsible position of married woman within the household; contrasts with consort, CH'I, her legal position and concubine, CH'IEH, secondary wives. The ideogram: woman, hand and broom, household duties.

Son(hood), TZU: living up to ideal of ancestors as highest human development; act with concern and reverence; male child; offspring, posterity; seed, kernel, egg; sage, teacher; nadir, deepest point, midnight, mid-winter. **Control**, K'O: command; check, impede, prevail, obstruct, repress; adequate, able. The ideogram: roof beams support a house, controlling the structure. **Dwell**, CHI: home, house, household, family; domestic, within doors; live in. The ideogram: roof and pig or dog, the most valued domestic animals. Image of Hexagram 37.

b) **Solid[and]Supple**, KANG JOU: field of creative tension between the whole and opened lines and their qualities; field of psychic movement. **Articulate**, CHIEH: separate and distinguish, as well as join, different things; express thought through speech; joint, section, chapter, interval, unit of time; zodiacal sign; moderate, regulate; lit.: nodes on bamboo stalks. Image of Hexagram 60.

Six at-third

a) **No availing-of grasping womanhood.**
Visualizing a metallic husband.
Not possessing the body.
Without direction: Harvesting.

b) **No availing-of grasping womanhood.**
Movement not yielding indeed.

Associated Contexts *a)* **No**, WU: simple negative; un-, dis-. **Avail-of**, YUNG: take advantage of; benefit from, profit by; use for a specific purpose; apply to advantage. The ideogram: to divine and center, applying divination to central concerns. **Grasp**, CH'Ü: lay hold of, take and use, seize, appropriate; grasp the meaning, understand. The ideogram: ear and hand, hear and grasp. **Woman(hood)**, NÜ: a woman; what is inherently female.

Metallic, CHIN: smelting and casting; all things pertaining to metal, particularly gold; autumn, West, sunset; one of the Five Moments. **Husband**, FU: household manager; administer with thrift and prudence;

responsible for; sustain with your earnings; old enough to assume responsibility; married man.

Body, KUNG: physical being, power and self expression; contrasts with individuality, SHEN, the total personality.

Without direction: Harvesting, WU YU LI: no plan or direction is advantageous; in order to take advantage of the situation, do not impose a direction on events.

b) **Yield(-to)**, SHUN: give way and bear produce; comply, agree, follow, obey; unresisting, docile, flexible; nourish, provide; the Action of the trigram Field, K'UN. The ideogram: head and current, water flowing from the head of a river, yielding to the banks.

Six at-fourth

a) **Confining Enveloping. Abashment.**

b) **Confining Enveloping's abashment.**
Solitariness distancing substance indeed.

Associated Contexts a) **Confine**, K'UN: enclose, restrict, limit; oppressed; impoverish, distress; afflicted, exhausted, disheartened, weary. The ideogram: an enclosed tree. Image of Hexagram 47. **Abashment**, LIN: distress, shame, regret, humiliation; aware of having lost the right track; leads to repenting, HUI, correcting the direction of mind and life.

b) **Solitary**, TI: alone, single; isolated, abandoned. **Distance**, YÜAN: far off, remote; keep at a distance; alienated. The ideogram: go and a long way. **Substance**, SHIH: real, solid, full; results, fruits, possessions; essence; honest, sincere. The ideogram: string of coins under a roof, riches in the house.

Six at-fifth

a) **Youthful Enveloping. Significant.**

b) **Youthful Enveloping's significance.**
Yielding uses Ground indeed.

Associated Contexts a) **Significant**, CHI: leads to the experience of meaning; favorable, propitious, advantageous, appropriate; keyword. The ideogram: scholar and mouth, wise words of a sage.

b) **Yield(-to)**, SHUN: give way and bear produce; comply, agree, follow, obey; unresisting, docile, flexible; nourish, provide; the Action of the trigram Field, K'UN. The ideogram: head and current, water flowing from the head of a river, yielding to the banks. **Ground**, SUN: base on which things rest; support, foundation; mild, subtly penetrating; nourishing. The ideogram: stand and things arranged on it, the subtle influence of the ground. Image of Hexagram 57.

Nine above

a) **Smiting Enveloping.**
Not Harvesting: activating outlawry.
Harvesting: resisting outlawry.

b) **Harvesting: availing-of resisting outlawry.**
Above[and]Below yielding indeed.

Associated Contexts *a)* **Smite**, CHI: hit, beat, attack; hurl against, rush a position; rouse to action. The ideogram: hand and hit, fist punching.

Harvest, LI: advantageous, profitable; acute, insightful; benefit, nourish; third stage of the Time Cycle. **Activate**, WEI: act or cause to act; do, make, manage; make active; attend to, help; because of. **Outlawry**, K'OU: break the laws; violent people, outcasts, bandits.

Resist, YÜ: withstand, oppose; bring to an end; prevent. The ideogram: rule and worship, imposing ethical or religious limits.

b) **Avail-of**, YUNG: take advantage of; benefit from, profit by; use for a specific purpose; apply to advantage. The ideogram: to divine and center, applying divination to central concerns.

Above[and]Below, SHANG HSIA: realm of dynamic interaction between the upper and the lower; the vertical dimension. **Yield(-to)**, SHUN: give way and bear produce; comply, agree, follow, obey; unresisting, docile, flexible; nourish, provide; the Action of the trigram Field, K'UN. The ideogram: head and current, water flowing from the head of a river, yielding to the banks.

5

ATTENDING ▪ *HSÜ*

This hexagram describes your situation in terms of being compelled to wait for and serve something. It emphasizes that fixing your attention on what is required while waiting carefully for the right moment to act is the adequate way to handle it. To be in accord with the time, you are told to: **attend!**

● *Image of the Situation*

> **Attending, possessing conformity.**
> **Shining Growing, Trial: significant.**
> **Harvesting: wading the Great River.**

Associated Contexts **Attend**, HSÜ: take care of, look out for, serve; turn your mind to what is necessary; wait, await, wait on; hesitate, doubt; obstinate, fixed. The ideogram: rain and stop, compelled to wait, or rain and origin, providing what is needed. **Possessing conformity**, YU FU: inner and outer are in accord; confidence of the spirits has been captured; sincere, truthful; proper to take action.

   Shine, KUANG: illuminate; give off brilliant, bright light; honor, glory, éclat; result of action, contrasts with brightness, MING, light of heavenly bodies. The ideogram: fire above person, lifting the light. **Grow**, HENG: success through a sacrifice; pervade, persevere; bring to full growth; enjoy; vigorous, effective; second stage of the Time Cycle. **Trial**, CHEN: test by ordeal; inquiry by divination and its result; righteous, firm; separating wheat from chaff; the kernel, the proven core; fourth stage of the Time Cycle. The ideogram: pearl and divination. **Significant**, CHI: leads to the experience of meaning; favorable, propitious, advantageous, appropriate; keyword. The ideogram: scholar and mouth, wise words of a sage.

   Harvest, LI: advantageous, profitable; acute, insightful; benefit, nourish; third stage of the Time Cycle. **Wading the Great River**, SHE TA CH'UAN: consciously moving into the flow of time; enter the stream of life with a goal or purpose; embark on a significant enterprise.

- ## Outer and Inner Aspects

⚏ **Gorge**: Stream ventures and falls into the gorge, flowing on through toil and danger. **Gorge** ends the yin hemicycle by leveling and dissolving forms.

Connection to the outer: flooding and leveling dissolve direction and shape, the Streaming Moment. **Gorge** ventures, falls, toils and flows on.

☰ **Force**: The force of heaven struggles on, persistent and unwearied; heavenly bodies persist in their orbits. **Force** is the center of the yin hemicycle, completing the formative process.

Connection to the inner: struggling forces are bound together in dynamic tension, the Metallic Moment culminating. **Force** brings elements to grips, creating enduring relations.

Persistent inner concentration confronts outer danger by careful **attending** on events.

- ## Counter Indications

Nuclear trigrams **Radiance**, LI, and **Open**, TUI, result in Counter Hexagram 38, **Polarizing**, K'UEI. **Attending** to the needs at hand is contrasted with creating distance and tension through **polarizing**.

- ## Sequence

> **Being immature not permitting not nourishing indeed.**
> **Anterior acquiescence has the use-of Attending.**
> **Attending implies drinking[and]taking-in's tao indeed.**

Associated Contexts **Being(s)**, WU: creature, thing, any single being; matter, substance, essence; nature of things. **Immature**, CHIH: small, tender, young, delicate; undeveloped; conceited, haughty; late grain. **Not permitting**, PU K'O: not possible; contradicts an inherent principle. The ideogram: mouth and breath, silent consent. **Not**, PU: simple negative. **Nourish**, YANG: feed, sustain, support; provide, care for; bring up, improve, grow, develop. **Indeed**, YEH: intensifier; indicates comment on previous statement.

Anterior ... the use-of: activating this hexagram depends on understanding and accepting the previous statement.

Imply, CHE: further signify; additional meaning. **Drinking[and] taking-in**, YIN SHIH: comprehensive term for eating, drinking and breathing; a meal, eating together. **'s/have(-it)/it/them**, CHIH: expresses possession, directly or as an object pronoun. **Tao**: way or path; ongoing process of being and the course it traces for each specific person or thing; keyword. The ideogram: go and head, leading and the path it creates.

● *Contrasted Definitions*

Attending: not advancing indeed.
Arguing: not connecting indeed.

Associated Contexts **Advance**, CHIN: exert yourself, make progress, climb; be promoted; further the development of, augment; adopt a religion or conviction; offer, introduce.

Argue, SUNG: dispute, plead in court, contend before a ruler, demand justice; wrangles, quarrels, litigation. The ideogram: words and public, public disputation. Image of Hexagram 6. **Connect**, CH'IN: attach to, approach, come near; cherish, help, favor; intimate; relatives, kin.

● *Symbol Tradition*

Above clouds with-respect-to heaven. Attending.
A chün tzu uses drinking[and]taking-in to repose delighting.

Associated Contexts **Above**, SHANG: anything above, in all senses; higher, upper, outer; upper trigram; opposite of below, HSIA. **Clouds**, YÜN: fog, mist, water vapor; connects to the Streaming Moment and Stream, the Symbol of the trigram Gorge, K'AN. **With-respect-to**, YÜ: relates to, refers to; hold a position in. **Heaven**, T'IEN: highest; sky, firmament, heavens; power above the human as opposed to earth, TI, below; the Symbol of the trigram Force, CH'IEN. The ideogram: great and the one above.

Chün tzu: ideal of a person who uses divination to order his/her life in accordance with tao rather than wilful intention; keyword. **Use(-of)**, YI: make use of, by means of, owing to; employ, make functional. **Repose**, YEN: rest, leisure, peace of mind; banquet, feast. The ideogram: shelter and rest, a wayside inn. **Delight**, LO: take joy or pleasure in; pleasant, relaxed; also: music as harmony, elegance and pleasure.

- *Image Tradition*

Attending: hair-growing indeed. [I]
Venturing located-in precedence indeed.
Solid persisting and-also not falling.
Actually one's righteousness, not confining exhaustion.

Attending, possessing conformity. [II]
Shining Growing, Trial: significant.
Situation reaching-to the heavenly situation.
Using correcting centering indeed.

Harvesting: wading the Great River. [III]
Going possesses achievement indeed.

Associated Contexts [I] **Hair-growing**, HSÜ: beard, hair; patience symbolized as waiting for hair to grow; hold back, wait for; slow; necessary.

Venture, HSIEN: risk without reserve; key point, point of danger; difficulty, obstruction that must be confronted; water falling and filling the holes on its way; the Action of the trigram Gorge, K'AN. The ideogram: mound and all or whole, everything engaged at one point. **Locate(-in)**, TSAI: live in, dwell, reside; belong to, involved with, depend on; within. The ideogram: earth and persevere, place on the earth. **Precede**, CH'IEN: come before in time and thus in value; anterior, former, ancient; lead forward.

Solid, KANG: quality of the whole lines; firm, strong, unyielding, persisting. **Persist**, CHIEN: strong, robust, dynamic, tenacious; continuous; unwearied heavenly bodies in their orbits; the Action of the trigram Force, CH'IEN. **And-also**, ERH: joins and contrasts two terms. **Fall**, HSIEN: fall down or into, sink, drop, descend; falling water; the Action of the trigram Gorge, K'AN.

Actually, YI: truly, really, at present. The ideogram: a dart and done, strong intention fully expressed. **One's/one**, CH'I: third person pronoun; also: it/its, he/his, she/hers, they/theirs. **Righteous**, YI: proper and just, meets the standards; things in their proper place; the heart that rules itself; upright, moral rule; contrasts with Harvest, LI, advantage or profit. **Confine**, K'UN: enclose, restrict, limit; oppressed; impoverish, distress; afflicted, exhausted, disheartened, weary. The ideogram: an enclosed tree. Image of Hexagram 47. **Exhaust**, CH'IUNG: bring to an end; limit, extremity; destitute; investigate exhaustively; end without a new beginning. The ideogram: cave and naked person, bent with disease or old age.

[II] Situation, WEI: place or seat according to rank; post, position, command; right, proper; established, arranged. The ideogram: person and stand, servants in their places. **Reach(-to)**, HU: arrive at a goal; reach towards and achieve; connect; contrasts with tend-toward, YU.

Correct, CHENG: rectify deviation or one-sidedness; proper, straight, exact, regular; constant, rule, model. The ideogram: stop and one, hold to one thing. **Center**, CHUNG: inner, central; put in the center; middle, stable point enabling you to face inner and outer changes; middle line of trigram. The ideogram: field divided in two equal parts. Image of Hexagram 61.

[III] Go, WANG, and come, LAI, describe the stream of time as it flows from future through present to past; go, WANG, indicates what is departing from present to past; proceed, move on; keyword. **Possess**, YU: in possession of, have, own; opposite of lack, WU. **Achieve**, KUNG: work done, results; real accomplishment, praise, worth, merit. The ideogram: workman's square and forearm, combining craft and strength.

- *Transforming Lines*

    Initial nine

    a) **Attending tending-towards the suburbs.**
    Harvesting: availing-of persevering.
    Without fault.

    b) **Attending tending-towards the suburbs.**
    Not opposing heavy moving indeed.
    Harvesting: availing-of persevering, without fault.
    Not-yet letting-go rules indeed.

Associated Contexts a) **Tend-towards**, YÜ: move toward but not reach, in the direction of; contrasts with reach(-to), HU, actually arriving. **Suburbs**, CHIAO: area adjoining a city where human constructions and nature interpenetrate; second of the territorial zones: city, suburbs, countryside, forests.

Avail-of, YUNG: take advantage of; benefit from, profit by; use for a specific purpose; apply to advantage. The ideogram: to divine and center, applying divination to central concerns. **Persevere,** HENG: continue in the same way or spirit; constant, perpetual, regular; self-renewing; extend everywhere. Image of Hexagram 32.

Without fault, WU CHIU: no error or harm in the situation.

b) **Oppose,** FAN: resist; violate, offend, attack; possessed by an evil spirit; criminal. The ideogram: violate and dog, brutal offense. **Heavy,** NAN: arduous, grievous, difficult; hardship, distress; harass; contrasts with versatile, I, deal lightly with. The ideogram: domestic bird with clipped tail and drying sticky earth. **Move,** HSING: move or move something; motivate, emotionally moving; walk, act, do. The ideogram: stepping left then right.

Not-yet, WEI: temporal negative; something will but has not yet occurred; contrary of already, CHI. Image of Hexagram 64. **Let-go,** SHIH: lose, omit, miss, fail, let slip; out of control. The ideogram: drop from the hand. **Rules,** CH'ANG: unchanging principles; regular, constant, habitual; maintain laws and customs.

Nine at-second

a) Attending tending-towards sands.
　The small possesses words.
　Completing significant.

b) Attending tending-towards sands.
　Overflowing located-in the center indeed.
　Although the small possesses words,
　　　　　　　using completing significant indeed.

Associated Contexts a) **Tend-towards,** YÜ: move toward but not reach, in the direction of; contrasts with reach(-to), HU, actually arriving. **Sands,** SHA: beach, sandbanks, shingle; gravel, pebbles; granulated. The ideogram: water and few, areas laid bare by receding water.

Small, HSIAO: little, common, unimportant; adapting to what crosses your path; ability to move in harmony with the vicissitudes of life; contrasts with great, TA, self-imposed theme or goal; keyword. Image of Hexagrams 9 and 62. **Word,** YEN: speech, spoken words, sayings; talk, discuss, address. The ideogram: mouth and rising vapor, words as speech.

Complete, CHUNG: end of a cycle that begins the next; last, whole, all; contrasts with exhaust, CH'IUNG, final end. The ideogram: silk cocoons, follow and ice, winter linking one year with the next.

b) **Overflow**, YEN: flow over the top; inundate, spread out; abundant, rich.
　　Although, SUI: even though, supposing that, if, even if.

Nine at-third

a) **Attending tending-towards bogs.**
　　Involving outlawry culminating.

b) **Attending tending-towards bogs.**
　　Calamity located outside indeed.
　　Originating-from my involving outlawry.
　　Respectful consideration, not destroying indeed.

Associated Contexts a) **Tend-towards**, YÜ: move toward but not reach, in the direction of; contrasts with reach(-to), HU, actually arriving. **Bog**, NI: wet spongy soil; mire, slush, quicksand; unable to move.
　　Involve, CHIH: include, entangle, implicate; induce, cause. The ideogram: person walking, induced to follow. **Outlawry**, K'OU: break the laws; violent people, outcasts, bandits. **Culminate**, CHIH: bring to the highest degree; arrive at the end or summit; superlative.

b) **Calamity**, TSAI: disaster from outside; flood, plague, drought, blight, ruin; contrasts with blunder, SHENG, indicating personal fault. The ideogram: water and fire, elemental powers. **Outside**, WAI: outer, exterior, external; people working in places other than their home; unfamiliar, foreign; the upper trigram, as opposed to inside, NEI, the lower.
　　Origin, TZU: source, beginning, ground; cause, reason, motive; line of descent; path to the origin; yourself, intrinsic. **My/me/I**, WO: first person pronoun; indicates an unusually strong emphasis on your own subjective experience.
　　Respect(ful), CHING: reverent, attentive; stand in awe of, honor; inner respect; contrasts with courtesy, KUNG, good manners. The ideogram: teacher's rod taming speech and attitude. **Consider**, SHEN: act carefully, seriously; cautious, attentive, circumspect; still, quiet, sincere. The ideogram: heart and true. **Destroy**, PAI: ruin, defeat, violate, subvert, break.

Six at-fourth

a) **Attending tending-towards blood.**
 Issuing-forth originates-from the cave.

b) **Attending tending-towards blood.**
 Yielding uses hearkening indeed.

Associated Contexts a) **Tend-towards**, YÜ: move toward but not reach, in the direction of; contrasts with reach(-to), HU, actually arriving. **Blood**, HSÜEH: yin fluid that maintains life; money, property.

 Issue-forth(-from), CH'U: emerge from, come out of, proceed from, spring from; the Action of the trigram Shake, CHEN; contrary of enter, JU. The ideogram: stem with branches and leaves emerging. **Origin**, TZU: source, beginning, ground; cause, reason, motive; line of descent; path to the origin; your self, intrinsic. **Cave**, HSÜEH: hole used for dwelling; cavern, den, pit; open grave.

b) **Yield(-to)**, SHUN: give way and bear produce; comply, agree, follow, obey; unresisting, docile, flexible; nourish, provide; the Action of the trigram Field, K'UN. The ideogram: head and current, water flowing from the head of a river, yielding to the banks. **Hearken**, T'ING: listen to, obey, accept, acknowledge; examine, judge, decide. The ideogram: ear and actualizing-tao, hear and obey.

Nine at-fifth

a) **Attending tending-towards liquor taken-in.**
 Trial: significant.

b) **Liquor taken-in, Trial: significant.**
 Using centering correcting indeed.

Associated Contexts a) **Tend-towards**, YÜ: move toward but not reach, in the direction of; contrasts with reach(-to), HU, actually arriving. **Liquor**, CHIU: alcoholic beverages, distilled spirits; spirit which perfects the good and evil in human nature. The ideogram: liquid above fermenting must, separating the spirits. **Take-in**, SHIH: eat, ingest, swallow, devour; incorporate.

b) **Centering correcting**, CHUNG CHENG: central and correct; make rectifying one-sidedness and error your central concern; reaching a stable center in yourself can correct the situation.

Six above

a) **Entering tending-towards the cave.**
Possessing not urging's visitors.
Three people coming.
Respecting them: completing significant.

b) **Not urging's visitors coming.**
Respecting them: completing significant.
Although not an appropriate situation,
not-yet the great let-go indeed.

Associated Contexts a) **Enter,** JU: penetrate, go into, enter on, progress; put into, encroach on; the Action of the trigram Ground, SUN, contrary of issue-forth, CH'U. **Tend-towards,** YÜ: move toward but not reach, in the direction of; contrasts with reach-to, HU, actually arriving. **Cave,** HSÜEH: hole used for dwelling; cavern, den, pit; open grave.

Urge, SU: strong specific desire; quick, hurried; call, invite. **Visitor,** K'O: guest; stranger, foreign, from afar; squatter.

Three, SAN: number three, third time or place; active phases of a cycle; superlative; beginning of repetition. **People, person,** JEN: humans individually and collectively; an individual; humankind. Image of Hexagrams 13 and 37. **Come,** LAI, and go, WANG, describe the stream of time as it flows from future through present to past; come, LAI, indicates what is approaching; move toward, arrive at; keyword.

Respect(ful), CHING: reverent, attentive; stand in awe of, honor; inner respect; contrasts with courtesy, KUNG, good manners. The ideogram: teacher's rod taming speech and attitude. **Them/it, have(-it)/'s,** CHIH: expresses possession, directly or as an object pronoun. **Complete,** CHUNG: end of a cycle that begins the next; last, whole, all; contrasts with exhaust, CH'IUNG, final end. The ideogram: silk cocoons, follow and ice, winter linking one year with the next.

b) **Although,** SUI: even though, supposing that, if, even if. **Appropriate,** TANG: suitable; opportune, convenient; adequate, competent; equal to; whole lines in uneven places and opened lines in even places. **Not-yet,** WEI: temporal negative; something will but has not yet occurred; contrary of already, CHI. Image of Hexagram 64. **Great,** TA: big, noble, important, very; orient the will toward a self-imposed goal, impose direction; ability to lead or guide your life; contrasts with small, HSIAO, flexible adaptation to what crosses your path; keyword. Image of Hexagrams 14, 26, 28, 34. **Let-go,** SHIH: lose, omit, miss, fail, let slip; out of control. The ideogram: drop from the hand.

6

ARGUING ▪ *SUNG*

This hexagram describes your situation in terms of a dispute. It emphasizes that actively expressing your claims and objections is the adequate way to handle it. To be in accord with the time, you are told to: **argue!**

● *Image of the Situation*

> **Arguing, possessing conformity. Blocking awe.**
> **Centering significant. Completing: pitfall.**
> **Harvesting: visualizing Great People.**
> **Not Harvesting: wading the Great River.**

Associated Contexts **Argue**, SUNG: dispute, plead in court, contend before a ruler, demand justice; wrangles, quarrels, litigation. The ideogram: words and public, public disputation. **Possessing conformity**, YU FU: inner and outer are in accord; confidence of the spirits has been captured; sincere, truthful; proper to take action. **Block**, CHIH: obstruct, stop up, close, restrain, fill up. **Awe**, T'I: alarmed and cautious; respect, regard, fear; stand in awe of. The ideogram: heart and versatile, the heart aware of sudden change.

Center, CHUNG: inner, central; put in the center; middle, stable point enabling you to face inner and outer changes; middle line of trigram. The ideogram: field divided in two equal parts. Image of Hexagram 61. **Significant**, CHI: leads to the experience of meaning; favorable, propitious, advantageous, appropriate; keyword. The ideogram: scholar and mouth, wise words of a sage. **Complete**, CHUNG: end of a cycle that begins the next; last, whole, all; contrasts with exhaust, CH'IUNG, final end. The ideogram: silk cocoons, follow and ice, winter linking one year with the next. **Pitfall**, HSIUNG: leads away from the experience of meaning; stuck and exposed to danger, unable to take in the situation; flow of life and spirit is blocked; unfortunate, baleful; keyword.

Harvest, LI: advantageous, profitable; acute, insightful; benefit, nourish; third stage of the Time Cycle. **Visualize**, CHIEN: seeing in all its aspects: vision, being visible, forming mental images; visit, call on, consult. The ideogram: eye above person, active and receptive sight. **Great People**, TA JEN: important, noble, influential; those who impose a ruling principle on their lives; effect of the great within an individual; keyword.

Not, PU: simple negative. **Wading the Great River**, SHE TA CH'UAN: consciously moving into the flow of time; enter the stream of life with a goal or purpose; embark on a significant enterprise.

• *Outer and Inner Aspects*

☰ **Force**: The force of heaven struggles on, persistent and unwearied; heavenly bodies persist in their orbits. **Force** is the center of the yin hemicycle, completing the formative process.

Connection to the outer: struggling forces are bound together in dynamic tension, the Metallic Moment culminating. **Force** brings elements to grips, creating enduring relations.

☵ **Gorge**: Stream ventures and falls into the gorge, flowing on through toil and danger. **Gorge** ends the yin hemicycle by leveling and dissolving forms.

Connection to the inner: flooding and leveling dissolve direction and shape, the Streaming Moment. **Gorge** ventures, falls, toils and flows on.

Without a solid inner base for action, outer struggle must express itself as verbal **arguing**.

• *Counter Indications*

Nuclear trigrams **Ground**, SUN, and **Radiance**, LI, result in Counter Hexagram 37, **Dwelling People**, CHIA JEN. The opposition and contradiction in **arguing** is contrasted with the fellow feeling of **people dwelling** and living together.

- *Sequence*

Drinking[and]taking-in necessarily possesses Arguing.
Anterior acquiescence has the use-of Arguing.

Associated Contexts Drinking[and]taking-in, YIN SHIH: comprehensive term for eating, drinking and breathing; a meal, eating together. **Necessarily**, PI: unavoidably, indispensably, certainly. **Possess**, YU: in possession of, have, own; opposite of lack, WU.

Anterior ... the use-of: activating this hexagram depends on understanding and accepting the previous statement.

- *Contrasted Definitions*

Attending: not advancing indeed.
Arguing: not connecting indeed.

Associated Contexts **Attend**, HSÜ: take care of, look out for, care or service of; turn your mind to; needs; obstinate, fixed on; wait, await, wait on; hesitate, doubt. The ideogram: rain and stopped, compelled to wait, or rain and origin, providing what is needed. Image of Hexagram 5. **Advance**, CHIN: exert yourself, make progress, climb; be promoted; further the development of, augment; adopt a religion or conviction; offer, introduce. **Indeed**, YEH: intensifier; indicates comment on previous statement.

Connect, CH'IN: attach to, approach, come near; cherish, help, favor; intimate; relatives, kin.

- *Symbol Tradition*

Heaven associating-with stream,
contradicting movements. Arguing.
A chün tzu uses arousing affairs to plan beginning.

Associated Contexts **Heaven**, T'IEN: highest; sky, firmament, heavens; power above the human as opposed to earth, TI, below; the Symbol of the trigram Force, CH'IEN. The ideogram: great and the one above. **Associate(-with)**, YÜ: consort with, combine; companions; group, band, company; agree with, comply, help. The ideogram: pair of hands reaching downward meets a pair of hands reaching upward, helpful association. **Stream**, SHUI: flowing water; fluid, dissolving; river, tide, flood; the Symbol of the trigram Gorge, K'AN. The ideogram: rippling water. **Contradict**, WEI: oppose, disregard, disobey; seditious, perverse. **Move**, HSING: move or move something; motivate, emotionally moving; walk, act, do. The ideogram: stepping left then right.

Chün tzu: ideal of a person who uses divination to order his/her life in accordance with tao rather than wilful intention; keyword. **Use(-of)**, YI: make use of, by means of, owing to; employ, make functional. **Arouse**, TSO: stir up, stimulate, rouse from inactivity; generate; appear, arise. The ideogram: person and beginning. **Affairs**, SHIH: all kinds of personal activity; matters at hand; business, occupation; manage a business, case in court. **Plan**, MOU: plot, ponder, deliberate; project, device, stratagem. **Begin**, SHIH: commence, start, open; earliest, first; beginning of a time-span, ended by completion, CHUNG. The ideogram: woman and eminent, beginning new life.

● *Image Tradition*

Arguing. Solid above, venture below. [I]
Venturing and-also persisting. Arguing.

Arguing, possessing conformity. [II]
Blocking awe, centering significant.
Solid coming and-also acquiring the center indeed.

Completing: pitfall. [III]
Arguing not permitting accomplishment indeed.

Harvesting: visualizing Great People. [IV]
Honoring centering correcting indeed.

Not Harvesting: wading the Great River. [V]
Entering tending-towards the abyss indeed.

Associated Contexts **[I] Solid**, KANG: quality of the whole lines; firm, strong, unyielding, persisting. **Above**, SHANG: anything above, in all senses; higher, upper, outer; upper trigram; opposite of below, HSIA. **Venture**, HSIEN: risk without reserve; key point, point of danger; difficulty, obstruction that must be confronted; water falling and filling the holes on its way; the Action of the trigram Gorge, K'AN. The ideogram: mound and all or whole, everything engaged at one point. **Below**, HSIA: anything below, in all senses; lower, inner; lower trigram; opposite of above, SHANG.

And-also, ERH: joins and contrasts two terms. **Persist**, CHIEN: strong, robust, dynamic, tenacious; continuous; unwearied heavenly bodies in their orbits; the Action of the trigram Force, CH'IEN.

[II] **Come**, LAI, and go, WANG, describe the stream of time as it flows from future through present to past; come, LAI, indicates what is approaching; move toward, arrive at; keyword. **Acquire**, TE: obtain the desired object; wish for, desire covetously; gains, possessions. The ideogram: go and obstacle, going through obstacles to the goal.

[III] **Not permitting**, PU K'O: not possible; contradicts an inherent principle. The ideogram: mouth and breath, silent consent. **Accomplish**, CH'ENG: complete, finish, bring about; perfect, full, whole; play your part, do your duty; mature. The ideogram: weapon and man, able to bear arms, thus fully developed.

[IV] **Honor**, SHANG: esteem, give high rank to; eminent; put one thing on top of another. **Centering correcting**, CHUNG CHENG: central and correct; make rectifying one-sidedness and error your central concern; reaching a stable center in yourself can correct the situation.

[V] **Enter**, JU: penetrate, go into, enter on, progress; put into, encroach on; the Action of the trigram Ground, SUN, contrary of issue-forth, CH'U. **Tend-towards**, YÜ: move toward but not reach, in the direction of; contrasts with reach(-to), HU, actually arriving. **Abyss**, YÜAN: deep hole or gulf, where backwaters eddy and accumulate; whirlpool; deep water.

● *Transforming Lines*

Initial six

a) **Not a perpetual place, affairs.**
The small possesses words, completing significant.

b) **Not a perpetual place, affairs.**
Arguing not permitting long-living indeed.
Although the small possesses words,
                              one's differentiation brightening indeed.

Associated Contexts a) **Perpetual,** YUNG: continuing; everlasting, ever-flowing. The ideogram: flowing water. **Place,** SO: where something belongs or comes from; residence, dwelling; habitual focus or object.

Small, HSIAO: little, common, unimportant; adapting to what crosses your path; ability to move in harmony with the vicissitudes of life; contrasts with great, TA, self-imposed theme or goal; keyword. Image of Hexagrams 9 and 62. **Word,** YEN: speech, spoken words, sayings; talk, discuss, address. The ideogram: mouth and rising vapor, words as speech.

b) **Long-living,** CHANG: enduring, constant; senior, superior, greater; increase, prosper; respect, elevate.

Although, SUI: even though, supposing that, if, even if. **One's/one,** CH'I: third person pronoun; also: it/its, he/his, she/hers, they/theirs. **Differentiate,** PIEN: argue, dispute, criticize; sophisticated, artful. The ideogram: words and sharp or pungent. **Brightness,** MING: light-giving aspect of burning, heavenly bodies and consciousness; with fire, the Symbol of the trigram Radiance, LI.

Nine at-second

a) **Not controlling Arguing.**
Converting and-also escaping one's capital.
People, three hundred doors.
Without blunder.

b) **Not controlling Arguing.**
Converting escaping, skulking indeed.
Below origin, above Arguing.
Distress culminating, reaping indeed.

Associated Contexts a) **Control,** K'O: command; check, impede, prevail, obstruct, repress; adequate, able. The ideogram: roof beams support a house, controlling the structure.

Convert, KUEI: change to another form, persuade; return to yourself or the place where you belong; restore, revert, become loyal; turn into; give a young girl in marriage. The ideogram: arrive and wife, become

mistress of a household. Image of Hexagram 54. **Escape**, P'U: flee, run away, turn tail; deserter, fugitive. The ideogram: go and first, precipitous flight. **One's/one**, CH'I: third person pronoun; also: it/its, he/his, she/hers, they/theirs. **Capital**, YI: populous fortified city, center and symbol of the domain it rules. The ideogram: enclosure and official seal.

People, person, JEN: humans individually and collectively; an individual; humankind. Image of Hexagrams 13 and 37. **Three**, SAN: number three, third time or place; active phases of a cycle; superlative; beginning of repetition. **Hundred**, PO: numerous, many, all; a whole class or type. **Door**, HU: inner door, chamber door; a household; contrasts with gate, MEN, the outer door.

Without, WU: devoid of; -less as suffix. **Blunder**, SHENG: mistake due to ignorance or fault; contrasts with calamity, TSAI, disaster from without. The ideogram: eye and grow, a film clouding sight.

b) **Skulk**, TS'UAN: sneak away and hide; furtive, stealthy; seduce into evil. The ideogram: cave and rat, rat lurking in its hole.

Origin, TZU: source, beginning, ground; cause, reason, motive; line of descent; path to the origin; yourself, intrinsic.

Distress, HUAN: tribulation, grief, affliction. The ideogram: heart and clamour, the heart distressed. **Culminate**, CHIH: bring to the highest degree; arrive at the end or summit; superlative. **Reap**, TO: harvest, collect, gather up, pick; arrange. The ideogram: hand and join, taking in both hands.

Six at-third

a) Taking-in ancient actualizing-tao. Trial.
Adversity, completing significant.
Maybe adhering-to kingly affairs:
Without accomplishment.

b) Taking-in ancient actualizing-tao.
Adhering-to the above significant indeed.

Associated Contexts a) **Take-in**, SHIH: eat, ingest, swallow, devour; incorporate. **Ancient**, CHIU: of old, long before; worn out, spoiled; defunct. **Actualize-tao**, TE: realize tao in action; power, virtue; ability to follow the course traced by the ongoing process of the cosmos; keyword. The ideogram: to go, straight, and heart. Linked with acquire, TE: acquiring that which makes a being become what it is meant to be. **Trial**, CHEN: test by ordeal; inquiry by divination and its result; righteous, firm; separating wheat from chaff; the kernel, the proven core; fourth stage of the Time Cycle. The ideogram: pearl and divination.

Adversity, LI: danger; threatening, malevolent demon. This has two aspects: grind, sharpen, improve, perfect, stimulate; and: poisonous, sinister, cruel, contrary. It indicates a spirit or ghost that seeks revenge by inflicting suffering upon the living. Pacifying or exorcizing such a spirit can have a healing effect. The ideogram: sheltering cliff and stinging insect.

Maybe, HUO: possible but not certain, perhaps. **Adhere(-to)**, TS'UNG: follow a way, hold to a doctrine, school, or person; hear and comply with, agree to; forced to follow, follower. The ideogram: two men walking, one following the other. **King(hood)**, WANG: effective ruler, by authority of the Emperor, from whom others derive their power.

Without, WU: devoid of; -less as suffix.

Nine at-fourth

a) **Not controlling Arguing.**
   Returning, approaching fate.
   Denying quiet Trial. Significant.

b) **Returning, approaching fate.**
   Denying quiet Trial.
   Not letting-go indeed.

Associated Contexts a) **Control**, K'O: command; check, impede, prevail, obstruct, repress; adequate, able. The ideogram: roof beams support a house, controlling the structure.

Return, FU: go back, turn back to the starting point; recur, reappear, come again; restore, recover, retrace; an earlier time or place. The ideogram: step and retrace a path. Image of Hexagram 24. **Approach**, CHI: come near to, advance toward; about to do; soon. **Fate**, MING: individual destiny; birth and death as limits of life; issue orders with authority; consult the gods. The ideogram: mouth and order, words with heavenly authority.

Deny, YÜ: retract, repudiate; deterioration, regress. **Quiet**, AN: peaceful, still, settled; calm, tranquilize. The ideogram: woman under a roof, a tranquil home. **Trial**, CHEN: test by ordeal; inquiry by divination and its result; righteous, firm; separating wheat from chaff; the kernel, the

proven core; fourth stage of the Time Cycle. The ideogram: pearl and divination.

b) **Let-go**, SHIH: lose, omit, miss, fail, let slip; out of control. The ideogram: drop from the hand.

Nine at-fifth

a) **Arguing. Spring significant.**

b) **Arguing, Spring significant.**
Using centering correcting indeed.

Associated Contexts a) **Spring**, YÜAN: source, origin, head; great, excellent; arise, begin, generating power; first stage of the Time Cycle.

Nine above

a) **Maybe bestowing's pouched belt.**
Completing dawn three-times depriving it.

b) **Using Arguing acquiesces-in submitting.**
Truly not standing respectfully indeed.

Associated Contexts a) **Maybe**, HUO: possible but not certain, perhaps. **Bestow**, HSI: grant, confer upon; reward, gift. The ideogram: metal used in coins and insignia. **'s/have(-it)/it/them**, CHIH: expresses possession, directly or as an object pronoun. **Pouched belt**, P'AN TAI: sash that serves as a purse; money-belt.

Dawn, CHAO: early morning, before daybreak; opposite of nightfall, HSI. **Three-times**, SAN: serial repetition. **Deprive**, CH'IH: strip (of rank), take away; undress; put an end to. **It/them/have(-it)/'s**, CHIH: expresses possession, directly or as an objectpronoun.

b) **Acquiesce(-in)**, SHOU: accept, make peace with, agree to; at rest, satisfied; patient. **Submit**, FU: yield to, serve; undergo.

Truly, YI: statement is true and precise. **Stand**, TSU: base, foot, leg; rest on, support; stance. The ideogram: foot and calf resting. **Respect(ful)**, CHING: reverent, attentive; stand in awe of, honor; inner respect; contrasts with courtesy, KUNG: good manners. The ideogram: teacher's rod taming speech and attitude.

L E G I O N S / L E A D I N G ▮ *SHIH*

This hexagram describes your situation in terms of unorganized crowds or bunches of things. It emphasizes that organizing these things into functional units is the adequate way to handle it. To be in accord with the time, you are told to: **lead**!

● *Image of the Situation*

Legions: Trial.
Respectable people significant.
Without fault.

Associated Contexts **Legions/leading**, SHIH: troops; an organized unit, a metropolis; leader, general, model, master; organize, make functional; take as a model, imitate. The ideogram: heap and whole, organize confusion into functional units. **Trial**, CHEN: test by ordeal; inquiry by divination and its result; righteous, firm; separating wheat from chaff; the kernel, the proven core; fourth stage of the Time Cycle. The ideogram: pearl and divination.

　　　Respectable, CHANG: worthy of respect; standard by which others are measured. **People, person**, JEN: humans individually and collectively; an individual; humankind. Image of Hexagrams 13 and 37. **Significant**, CHI: leads to the experience of meaning; favorable, propitious, advantageous, appropriate; keyword. The ideogram: scholar and mouth, wise words of a sage.

　　　Without fault, WU CHIU: no error or harm in the situation.

● *Outer and Inner Aspects*

☷ **Field**: The field of earth yields and sustains, serving in order to produce. **Field** is the equalizing point between yin and yang where things labor and serve.

　　　Connection to the outer: the common labor of sowing and hoarding, the Earthy Moment. **Field** produces concrete results through serving.

☵ **Gorge**: Stream ventures and falls into the gorge, flowing on through toil and danger. **Gorge** ends the yin hemicycle by leveling and dissolving forms.

Connection to the inner: flooding and leveling dissolve direction and shape, the Streaming Moment. **Gorge** ventures, falls, toils and flows on.

An inner willingness for work and danger sustains the involving service of the **legions** and their **leaders.**

• *Counter Indications*

Nuclear trigrams **Field**, K'UN, and **Shake**, CHEN, result in Counter Hexagram 24, **Returning**, FU. **Legions**' constant forward thrust is contrasted with **returning** to the starting point to begin again.

• *Sequence*

> **Arguing necessarily possesses crowds rising-up.**
> **Anterior acquiescence has the use-of Legions.**
> **Legions imply crowds indeed.**

Associated Contexts **Argue**, SUNG: dispute, plead in court, contend before a ruler, demand justice; wrangles, quarrels, litigation. The ideogram: words and public, public disputation. Image of Hexagram 6. **Necessarily**, PI: unavoidably, indispensably, certainly. **Possess**, YU: in possession of, have, own; opposite of lack, WU. **Crowds**, CHUNG: many people, large group; majority; in common. **Rise-up**, CH'I: stand up, lift; undertake, begin, originate.

Anterior ... the use-of: activating this hexagram depends on understanding and accepting the previous statement.

Imply, CHE: further signify; additional meaning. **Indeed**, YEH: intensifier; indicates comment on previous statement.

• *Contrasted Definitions*

> **Grouping: delighting.**
> **Legions: grieving.**

Associated Contexts **Group**, PI: compare and select, order things and put them in classes; find what you belong with; sort, examine correspondences; choose and harmonize; unite. The ideogram: person who stops walking, looking around to examine and compare. Image of Hexagram 8. **Delight,** LO: take joy or pleasure in; pleasant, relaxed; also: music as harmony, elegance and pleasure.

Grieve(-over), YU: sorrow, melancholy; mourn; anxious, careworn; hidden sorrow. The ideogram: heart, head, and limp, heart-sick and anxious.

● *Symbol Tradition*

> **Earth center possessing stream. Legions.**
> **A chün tzu uses tolerating commoners to accumulate crowds.**

Associated Contexts **Earth,** TI: ground on which the human world rests; basis of all things, nourishes all things; the Symbol of the trigram Field, K'UN: **Center,** CHUNG: inner, central; put in the center; middle, stable point enabling you to face inner and outer changes; middle line of trigram. The ideogram: field divided in two equal parts. Image of Hexagram 61. **Stream,** SHUI: flowing water; fluid, dissolving; river, tide, flood; the Symbol of the trigram Gorge, K'AN. The ideogram: rippling water.

Chün tzu: ideal of a person who uses divination to order his/her life in accordance with tao rather than wilful intention; keyword. **Use(-of),** YI: make use of, by means of, owing to; employ, make functional. **Tolerate,** JUNG: allow, contain, endure, bear with; accept graciously. The ideogram: full stream bed, tolerating and containing. **Commoners,** MIN: class of workers the state draws on to sustain the social hierarchy; undeveloped potential outside the organized personality. **Accumulate,** CH'U: retain, hoard, gather, herd together; control, restrain; domesticate, tame, train; raise, feed, sustain, bring up. The ideogram: field and black, fertile black soil good for pastures, accumulated through retaining silt. Image of Hexagrams 9 and 26.

● *Image Tradition*

> **Legions: crowds indeed. [I]**
> **Trial: correcting indeed.**
> **Able to use the crowds correcting:**

Actually permitting using kinghood. [II]
Solid centering and-also corresponding.

Movement venturing and-also yielding. [III]
Using the latter poisons Below Heaven and-also
         the commoners adhering-to it.
Actually significant, furthermore wherefore faulty?

Associated Contexts [I] **Correct,** CHENG: rectify deviation or one-sidedness; proper, straight, exact, regular; constant, rule, model. The ideogram: stop and one, hold to one thing.

 Able, NENG: enable; ability, power, skill, art; competent, talented; duty, function, capacity. The ideogram: an animal with strong hooves and bones, able to carry and defend.

[II] **Actually,** YI: truly, really, at present. The ideogram: a dart and done, strong intention fully expressed. **Permit,** K'O: possible because in harmony with an inherent principle. The ideogram: mouth and breath, silent consent. **King(hood),** WANG: effective ruler, by authority of the Emperor, from whom others derive their power.

 Solid, KANG: quality of the whole lines; firm, strong, unyielding, persisting. **And-also,** ERH: joins and contrasts two terms. **Correspond,** YING: be in agreement or harmony; resonate together, invoke and fulfill each other; answer to, suitable; relation between the lines (1:4, 2:5, 3:6) when they form the pair opened and whole, supple and solid. The ideogram: heart and obey.

[III] **Move,** HSING: move or move something; motivate, emotionally moving; walk, act, do. The ideogram: stepping left then right. **Venture,** HSIEN: risk without reserve; key point, point of danger; difficulty, obstruction that must be confronted; water falling and filling the holes on its way; the Action of the trigram Gorge, K'AN. The ideogram: mound and all or whole, everything engaged at one point. **Yield(-to),** SHUN: give way and bear produce; comply, agree, follow, obey; unresisting, docile, flexible; nourish, provide; the Action of the trigram Field, K'UN. The ideogram: head and current, water flowing from the head of a river, yielding to the banks.

 Latter, TZ'U: what was last spoken of. **Poison,** TU: noxious, malignant, hurtful, destructive; despise. **Below Heaven,** T'IEN HSIA: the human world, between heaven and earth. **Adhere(-to),** TS'UNG: follow a way, hold to a doctrine, school, or person; hear and comply with, agree to; forced to follow, follower. The ideogram: two men walking, one following the other. **It/them/have(-it)/'s,** CHIH: expresses possession, directly or as an object pronoun.

Furthermore, YU: in addition to; higher degree of. **Wherefore,** HO: interrogative: why? for what reason? what is? and affirmation: therefore, for that reason. **Fault,** CHIU: unworthy conduct that leads to harm, illness, misfortune. The ideogram: person and differ, differ from what you should be.

● *Transforming Lines*

Initial six

a) **Legions issuing-forth using ordinance.**
Obstructing virtue: pitfall.

b) **Legions issuing-forth using ordinance.**
Letting-go ordinance: pitfall indeed.

Associated Contexts a) **Issue-forth(-from),** CH'U: emerge from, come out of, proceed from, spring from; the Action of the trigram Shake, CHEN; contrary of enter, JU. The ideogram: stem with branches and leaves emerging. **Ordinance,** LÜ: law, fixed regulation; regulate by law, divide into right and wrong. The ideogram: writing and move, codes that govern action.

Obstruct, P'I: closed, stopped; bar the way; obstacle; unfortunate, wicked; refuse, disapprove, deny. The ideogram: mouth and not, blocked communication. Image of Hexagram 12. **Virtue,** TSANG: essential force or quality; generous, good, dexterous. **Pitfall,** HSIUNG: leads away from the experience of meaning; stuck and exposed to danger, unable to take in the situation; flow of life and spirit is blocked; unfortunate, baleful; keyword.

b) **Let-go,** SHIH: lose, omit, miss, fail, let slip; out of control. The ideogram: drop from the hand.

Nine at-second

a) **Locating Legions, centering significant.**
Without fault.
The king three-times bestowing fate.

b) Locating Legions, centering significant.
Receiving heavenly favor indeed.
The king three-times bestowing fate.
Cherishing the myriad fiefdoms indeed.

Associated Contexts a) **Locate(-in)**, TSAI: live in, dwell, reside; belong to, involved with, depend on; within. The ideogram: earth and persevere, place on the earth.

Three-times, SAN: serial repetition. **Bestow**, HSI: grant, confer upon; reward, gift. The ideogram: metal used in coins and insignia. **Fate**, MING: individual destiny; birth and death as limits of life; issue orders with authority; consult the gods. The ideogram: mouth and order, words with heavenly authority.

b) **Receive**, CH'ENG: receive gifts or commands from superiors or customers; take in hand; catch falling water. The ideogram: accepting a seal of office. **Heaven**, T'IEN: highest; sky, firmament, heavens; power above the human as opposed to earth, TI, below; the Symbol of the trigram Force, CH'IEN. The ideogram: great and the one above. **Favor**, CH'UNG: receive or confer gifts, obtain grace, win favor; dote on a woman; gifted for.

Cherish, HUAI: dwell on, think of; carry in the heart or womb; cling to. The ideogram: heart and hide, cherish in the heart. **Myriad**, WAN: countless; many, everyone; lit.: ten thousand. The ideogram: swarm of insects. **Fiefdom**, PANG: region governed by a feudatory, an order of nobility.

Six at-third

a) Legions maybe carting corpses.
Pitfall.

b) Legions maybe carting corpses.
The great without achievement indeed.

Associated Contexts a) **Maybe**, HUO: possible but not certain, perhaps. **Cart**, YÜ: carrying capacity of a vehicle; contain, hold, sustain. **Corpse**, SHIH: dead human body; effigy, statue; inefficient, useless; impersonate.

Pitfall, HSIUNG: leads away from the experience of meaning; stuck and exposed to danger, unable to take in the situation; flow of life and spirit is blocked; unfortunate, baleful; keyword.

b) **Great**, TA: big, noble, important, very; orient the will toward a self-imposed goal, impose direction; ability to lead or guide your life; contrasts with small, HSIAO, flexible adaptation to what crosses your path; keyword. Image of Hexagrams 14, 26, 28, 34. **Without,** WU: devoid of; -less as suffix. **Achieve**, KUNG: work done, results; real accomplishment, praise, worth, merit. The ideogram: workman's square and forearm, combining craft and strength.

Six at-fourth

a) **Legions: the left resting.**
Without fault.

b) **The left resting, without fault.**
Not-yet letting-go the rules indeed.

Associated Contexts a) **Left**, TSO: left side, left hand; secondary; deputy, assistant; inferior. **Rest(ing-place)**, TZ'U: camp, inn, shed; halting-place, breathing-spell; put in consecutive order. The ideogram: two and breath, pausing to breath.

b) **Not-yet**, WEI: temporal negative; something will but has not yet occurred; contrary of already, CHI. Image of Hexagram 64. **Let-go**, SHIH: lose, omit, miss, fail, let slip; out of control. The ideogram: drop from the hand. **Rules**, CH'ANG: unchanging principles; regular, constant, habitual; maintain laws and customs.

Six at-fifth

a) **The fields possess wild-fowl.**
Harvesting: holding-on-to words.
Without fault.
The long-living son conducting Legions.
The junior son carting corpses.
Trial: pitfall.

b) The long-living son conducting Legions.
Using centering movement indeed.
The junior son carting corpses.
Commissioning not appropriate indeed.

Associated Contexts a) **Fields**, T'IEN: cultivated land, plantation; also: hunting, game in the fields cannot escape the hunt. The ideogram: square divided into four sections, delineating fields. **Wildfowl**, CH'IN: all wild and game birds; untamed.

Harvest, LI: advantageous, profitable; acute, insightful; benefit, nourish; third stage of the Time Cycle. **Hold-on(-to)**, CHIH: lay hold of, seize, take in hand; keep, maintain, look after. The ideogram: criminal and seize. **Word**, YEN: speech, spoken words, sayings; talk, discuss, address. The ideogram: mouth and rising vapor, words as speech.

Long-living, CHANG: enduring, constant; senior, superior, greater; increase, prosper; respect, elevate. **Son(hood)**, TZU: living up to ideal of ancestors as highest human development; act with concern and reverence; male child; offspring, posterity; seed, kernel, egg; sage, teacher; nadir, deepest point, midnight, mid-winter. **Conduct**, SHUAI: lead; leader, chief, commander; follow, follower.

Junior, TI: younger relatives who owe respect to their elders. **Cart**, YÜ: carrying capacity of a vehicle; contain, hold, sustain. **Corpse**, SHIH: dead human body; effigy, statue; inefficient, useless; impersonate.

Pitfall, HSIUNG: leads away from the experience of meaning; stuck and exposed to danger, unable to take in the situation; flow of life and spirit is blocked; unfortunate, baleful; keyword.

b) **Commission**, SHIH: employ for a task; command, order; messenger, agent. The ideogram: person and office. **Not**, PU: simple negative. **Appropriate**, TANG: suitable; opportune, convenient; adequate, competent; equal to; whole lines in uneven places and opened lines in even places.

Six above

a) The Great Chief possesses fate.
Disclosing the city, receiving a dwelling.
Small People, no availing-of.

b) **The Great Chief possesses fate.**
Using correcting achieving indeed.
Small People, no availing-of.
Necessarily disarraying the fiefdoms indeed.

Associated Contexts a) **Great,** TA: big, noble, important, very; orient the will toward a self-imposed goal, impose direction; ability to lead or guide your life; contrasts with small, HSIAO, flexible adaptation to what crosses your path; keyword. Image of Hexagrams 14, 26, 28, 34. **Chief,** CHÜN: effective ruler; preside over, take the lead; influence others; term of respect. The ideogram: mouth and director, giving orders. **Fate,** MING: individual destiny; birth and death as limits of life; issue orders with authority; consult the gods. The ideogram: mouth and order, words with heavenly authority.

Disclose, K'AI: open, reveal, unfold, display; enact rites, clear land; final phase of both hemicycles in the Universal Compass. The ideogram: house doors bursting open. **City,** KUO: area of only human constructions; political unit, polis. First of the territorial zones: city, suburbs, countryside, forests. **Receive,** CH'ENG: receive gifts or commands from superiors or customers; take in hand; catch falling water. The ideogram: accepting a seal of office. **Dwell,** CHI: home, house, household, family; domestic, within doors; live in. The ideogram: roof and pig or dog, the most valued domestic animals. Image of Hexagram 37.

Small People, HSIAO JEN: lowly, common, humble; those who adjust to circumstances with the flexibility of the small; effect of the small within an individual; keyword. **No,** WU: simple negative; un-, dis-. **Avail-of,** YUNG: take advantage of; benefit from, profit by; use for a specific purpose; apply to advantage. The ideogram: to divine and center, applying divination to central concerns.

b) **Achieve,** KUNG: work done, results; real accomplishment, praise, worth, merit. The ideogram: workman's square and forearm, combining craft and strength.

Disarray, LUAN: throw into disorder, mislay, confuse; out of place; discord, insurrection, anarchy. **Fiefdom,** PANG: region governed by a feudatory, an order of nobility.

8

GROUPING ▪ *PI*

This hexagram describes your situation in terms of how you categorize people and things and how you relate to these categories. It emphasizes that joining people and things through recognizing their essential qualities is the adequate way to handle it. To be in accord with the time, you are told to: **group**!

● *Image of the Situation*

> **Grouping, significant.**
> **Retracing the oracle-consulting: Spring, perpetual Trial.**
> **Without fault.**
> **Not soothing, on-all-sides coming.**
> **Afterwards, husbanding: pitfall.**

Associated Contexts **Group**, PI: order things and put them in classes, compare and select; find what you belong with; compare, sort, examine correspondences; select and harmonize; unite. The ideogram: person who stops walking, looking around to examine and compare. **Significant**, CHI: leads to the experience of meaning; favorable, propitious, advantageous, appropriate; keyword. The ideogram: scholar and mouth, wise words of a sage.

Retrace, YÜAN: repeat, another; trace to the source. The ideogram: pure water at its source. **Oracle-consulting**, SHIH: yarrow stalk divination; find your allotted destiny. **Spring**, YÜAN: source, origin, head; great, excellent; arise, begin, generating power; first stage of the Time Cycle. **Perpetual**, YUNG: continuing; everlasting, ever-flowing. The ideogram: flowing water. **Trial**, CHEN: test by ordeal; inquiry by divination and its result; righteous, firm; separating wheat from chaff; the kernel, the proven core; fourth stage of the Time Cycle. The ideogram: pearl and divination.

Without fault, WU CHIU: no error or harm in the situation.

Not, PU: simple negative. **Soothe**, NING: calm, pacify; create peace of mind; tranquil, quiet. The ideogram: shelter above heart, dish and breath, physical and spiritual comfort. **Sides (on-all-sides)**, FANG: limits, boundaries; square, surface of the earth extending to the four cardinal points; everywhere. **Come**, LAI, and go, WANG, describe the stream of time as it flows from future through present to past; come, LAI, indicates what is approaching; move toward, arrive at; keyword.

After(wards)/later, HOU: come after in time, subsequent; put oneself after; the second; attendants, heirs, successors, posterity. **Husband**, FU: household manager; administer with thrift and prudence; responsible for; sustain with your earnings; old enough to assume responsibility; married man. **Pitfall**, HSIUNG: leads away from the experience of meaning; stuck and exposed to danger, unable to take in the situation; flow of life and spirit is blocked; unfortunate, baleful; keyword.

- ## *Outer and Inner Aspects*

☵ **Gorge**: Stream ventures and falls into the gorge, flowing on through toil and danger. **Gorge** ends the yin hemicycle by leveling and dissolving forms.

Connection to the outer: flooding and leveling dissolve direction and shape, the Streaming Moment. **Gorge** ventures, falls, toils and flows on.

☷ **Field**: The field of earth yields and sustains, serving in order to produce. **Field** is the equalizing point between yin and yang where things labor and serve.

Connection to the inner: the common labor of sowing and hoarding, the Earthy Moment. **Field** produces concrete results through serving.

The relation to the outer world dissolves and changes. New ways to **group** people and things appear on the inner field.

- ## *Counter Indications*

Nuclear trigrams **Bound**, KEN, and **Field**, KUN, result in Counter Hexagram 23, **Stripping**, PO. Finding new ways to **group** people and things is contrasted with **stripping** forms away and eliminating them.

- ## *Sequence*

> **Crowds necessarily possess a place to Group.**
> **Anterior acquiescence has the use-of Grouping.**
> **Grouping implies Groups.**

Associated Contexts **Crowds,** CHUNG: many people, large group; majority; in common. **Necessarily,** PI: unavoidably, indispensably, certainly. **Possess,** YU: in possession of, have, own; opposite of lack, WU. **Place,** SO: where something belongs or comes from; residence, dwelling; habitual focus or object.

Anterior ... the use-of: activating this hexagram depends on understanding and accepting the previous statement.

Imply, CHE: further signify; additional meaning.

- *Contrasted Definitions*

Grouping: delighting.
Legions: grieving.

Associated Contexts **Delight,** LO: take joy or pleasure in; pleasant, relaxed; also: music as harmony, elegance and pleasure.

Legions/leading, SHIH: troops; an organized unit, a metropolis; leader, general, model, master; organize, make functional; take as a model, imitate. The ideogram: heap and whole, organize confusion into functional units. Image of Hexagram 7. **Grieve,** YU: sorrow, melancholy; mourn; anxious, careworn; hidden sorrow. The ideogram: heart, head, and limp, heart-sick and anxious.

- *Symbol Tradition*

Above earth possessing stream. Grouping.
The Earlier Kings used installing myriad cities
to connect the connoted feudatories.

Associated Contexts **Above,** SHANG: anything above, in all senses; higher, upper, outer; upper trigram; opposite of below, HSIA. **Earth,** TI: ground on which the human world rests; basis of all things, nourishes all things; the Symbol of the trigram Field, K'UN. **Stream,** SHUI: flowing water; fluid, dissolving; river, tide, flood; the Symbol of the trigram Gorge, K'AN. The ideogram: rippling water.

Earlier Kings, HSIEN WANG: ideal rulers of old; the golden age; primal time, power in harmony with nature; model for the chün tzu. **Use(-of),** YI: make use of, by means of, owing to; employ, make functional. **Install,** CHIEN: set up, establish; confirm a position or law.

Myriad, WAN: countless; many, everyone; lit.: ten thousand. The ideogram: swarm of insects. **City**, KUO: area of only human constructions; political unit, polis. First of the territorial zones: city, suburbs, countryside, forests. **Connect**, CH'IN: attach to, approach, come near; cherish, help, favor; intimate; relatives, kin. **Connote**, CHU: imply the meaning; signify. The ideogram: words and imply. **Feudatory**, HOU: nobles entrusted with governing the provinces; active in daily life rather than governing from the center; contrasts with prince, KUNG, executives at the court.

- *Image Tradition*

> Grouping significant indeed. [I]
> Grouping bracing indeed.
> Yielding adhering-to the below indeed.
>
> Retracing the oracle-consulting: Spring, perpetual Trial. [II]
> Without fault.
> Using solid centering indeed.
>
> Not soothing, on-all-sides coming. [III]
> Above[and]Below corresponding indeed.
> Afterwards, husbanding: pitfall.
> One's tao exhausted indeed.

Associated Contexts **[I] Indeed**, YEH: intensifier; indicates comment on previous statement.

Brace/jawbones, FU: support, consolidate, reinforce, strengthen, stiffen, prop up, fix; steady, firm, rigid; help, rescue; support the speaking mouth. The ideogram: cart and great.

Yield(-to), SHUN: give way and bear produce; comply, agree, follow, obey; unresisting, docile, flexible; nourish, provide; the Action of the trigram Field, K'UN. The ideogram: head and current, water flowing from the head of a river, yielding to the banks. **Adhere(-to)**, TS'UNG: follow a way, hold to a doctrine, school, or person; hear and comply with, agree to; forced to follow, follower. The ideogram: two men walking, one following the other. **Below**, HSIA: anything below, in all senses; lower, inner; lower trigram; opposite of above, SHANG.

[II] **Solid**, KANG: quality of the whole lines; firm, strong, unyielding, persisting. **Center**, CHUNG: inner, central; put in the center; middle, stable point enabling you to face inner and outer changes; middle line of trigram. The ideogram: field divided in two equal parts. Image of Hexagram 61.

[III] **Above[and]Below**, SHANG HSIA: realm of dynamic interaction between the upper and the lower; the vertical dimension. **Correspond**, YING: be in agreement or harmony; resonate together, invoke and fulfill each other; answer to, suitable; relation between the lines (1:4, 2:5, 3:6) when they form the pair opened and whole, supple and solid. The ideogram: heart and obey.

One's/one, CH'I: third person pronoun; also: it/its, he/his, she/hers, they/theirs. **Tao**: way or path; ongoing process of being and the course it traces for each specific person or thing; keyword. The ideogram: go and head, leading and the path it creates. **Exhaust**, CH'IUNG: bring to an end; limit, extremity; destitute; investigate exhaustively; end without a new beginning. The ideogram: cave and naked person, bent with disease or old age.

- *Transforming Lines*

    Initial six

    a) **Possessing conformity, Grouping it.**
    Without fault.
    Possessing conformity, overfilling the jar.
    Completing coming possesses more significance.

    b) **Grouping's initial six.**
    Possessing more significance indeed.

Associated Contexts *a)* **Possessing conformity**, YU FU: inner and outer are in accord; confidence of the spirits has been captured; sincere, truthful; proper to take action. **It/them/have(-it)/'s**, CHIH: expresses possession, directly or as an object pronoun.

Overfill, YING: at the point of overflowing; more than wanted, stretch beyond; replenished, full; arrogant. The ideogram: vessel and too much. **Jar**, FOU: earthenware vessels; wine-jars and drums. The ideogram: jar containing liquor.

Complete, CHUNG: end of a cycle that begins the next; last, whole, all; contrasts with exhaust, CH'IUNG, final end. The ideogram: silk cocoons, follow and ice, winter linking one year with the next. **More**, T'O: another; add to.

b) **'s/have(-it)/it/them**, CHIH: expresses possession, directly or as an object pronoun.

Six at-second

a) **Grouping's origin inside.**
 Trial: significant.

b) **Grouping's origin inside.**
 Not originating letting-go indeed.

Associated Contexts *a)* **'s/have(-it)/it/them**, CHIH: expresses possession, directly or as an object pronoun. **Origin**, TZU: source, beginning, ground; cause, reason, motive; line of descent; path to the origin; yourself, intrinsic. **Inside**, NEI: within, inner, interior; inside of the house and those who work there, particularly women; the lower trigram, as opposed to outside, WAI, the upper. The ideogram: border and enter, cross a border.

b) **Let-go**, SHIH: lose, omit, miss, fail, let slip; out of control. The ideogram: drop from the hand.

Six at-third

a) **Grouping's in-no-way people.**

b) **Grouping's in-no-way people.**
 Reaching-to not truly injuring.

Associated Contexts *a)* **'s/have(-it)/it/them**, CHIH: expresses possession, directly or as an object pronoun. **In-no-way people**, FEI JEN: there are no people, no people are involved; also: worthless people; barbarians, rebels, foreign slaves, captives.

b) **Reach(-to)**, HU: arrive at a goal; reach toward and achieve; connect; contrasts with tend-towards, YU. **Truly**, YI: statement is true and precise. **Injure**, SHANG: hurt, wound, grieve, distress; mourn, sad at heart, humiliated.

Six at-fourth

a) **Outside Grouping it.**
   Trial: significant.

b) **Outside Grouping with-respect-to eminence.**
   Using adhering-to the above indeed.

Associated Contexts a) **Outside**, WAI: outer, exterior, external; people working in places other than their home; unfamiliar, foreign; the upper trigram, as opposed to inside, NEI, the lower. **It/them/have(-it)/'s,** CHIH: expresses possession, directly or as an object pronoun.

b) **With-respect-to,** YÜ: relates to, refers to; hold a position in. **Eminent,** HSIEN: moral and intellectual power; worthy, excellent, virtuous; sage second to the all-wise, SHENG.

Nine at-fifth

a) **Manifest Grouping.**
   The king avails-of three beaters.
   Letting-go the preceding wildfowl.
   Capital people not admonished. Significant.

b) **Manifest Grouping's significance.**
   Situation correctly centered indeed.
   Stowing-away countering, grasping yielding.
   Letting-go the preceding wildfowl indeed.
   Capital people not admonished.
   Commissioning centering above indeed.

Associated Contexts a) **Manifest**, HSIEN: apparent, conspicuous; illustrious; make clear.
   King(hood), WANG: effective ruler, by authority of the Emperor, from whom others derive their power. **Avail-of,** YUNG: take advantage of; benefit from, profit by; use for a specific purpose; apply to advantage. The ideogram: to divine and center, applying divination to central concerns. **Three,** SAN: number three, third time or place; active phases of a cycle; superlative; beginning of repetition. **Beater,** CH'U: servants who drive animals toward hunters; order people to their places; drive on, whip up, animate, exhort.

Let-go, SHIH: lose, omit, miss, fail, let slip; out of control. The ideogram: drop from the hand. **Precede**, CH'IEN: come before in time and thus in value; anterior, former, ancient; lead forward. **Wildfowl**, CH'IN: all wild and game birds; untamed.

Capital, YI: populous fortified city, center and symbol of the domain it rules. The ideogram: enclosure and official seal. **People, person**, JEN: humans individually and collectively; an individual; humankind. Image of Hexagrams 13 and 37. **Admonish**, CHIEH: make someone obey; rule of conduct, precept, warning. The ideogram: words and warning.

b) **'s/have(-it)/it/them**, CHIH: expresses possession, directly or as an object pronoun.

Situation, WEI: place or seat according to rank; post, position, command; right, proper; established, arranged. The ideogram: person and stand, servants in their places. **Correct**, CHENG: rectify deviation or one-sidedness; proper, straight, exact, regular; constant, rule, model. The ideogram: stop and one, hold to one thing.

Stow(-away), SHE: set aside, put away, store; halt, rest in; temporary lodgings, breathing-spell. **Counter**, NI: oppose, resist, seek out; contrary, rebellious, refractory. The ideogram: go and rise against, active revolt. **Grasp**, CH'Ü: lay hold of, take and use, seize, appropriate; grasp the meaning, understand. The ideogram: ear and hand, hear and grasp.

Commission, SHIH: employ for a task; command, order; messenger, agent. The ideogram: person and office.

Six above

a) **Without a head, Grouping it.**
Pitfall.

b) **Without a head, Grouping it.**
Without a place to complete indeed.

Associated Contexts a) **Without**, WU: devoid of; -less as suffix. **Head**, SHOU: literal head; leader, foremost; subject headings; beginning, model; superior, upper, front. **It/them/have(-it)/'s**, CHIH: expresses possession, directly or as an object pronoun.

b) **Complete**, CHUNG: end of a cycle that begins the next; last, whole, all; contrasts with exhaust, CH'IUNG, final end. The ideogram: silk cocoons, follow and ice, winter linking one year with the next.

9

SMALL ACCUMULATING ▪
HSIAO CH'U

This hexagram describes your situation in terms of a variety of seemingly unconnected events and impulses. It emphasizes that retaining and hoarding these experiences through adapting to them is the adequate way to handle it. To be in accord with the time, you are told to: **accumulate the small!**

● *Image of the Situation*

> **Small Accumulating, Growing.**
> **Shrouding clouds, not raining.**
> **Originating-from my Western suburbs.**

Associated Contexts **Small**, HSIAO: little, common, unimportant; adapting to what crosses your path; ability to move in harmonious relation to the vicissitudes of life; contrasts with great, TA, self-imposed theme or goal; keyword. **Accumulate**, CH'U: hoard, gather, retain, herd together; control, restrain; domesticate, tame, train; raise, feed, sustain, bring up. The ideogram: field and black, fertile black soil good for pastures, accumulated through retaining silt. **Grow**, HENG: success through a sacrifice; pervade, persevere; bring to full growth; enjoy; vigorous, effective; second stage of the Time Cycle.

 Shroud, MI: dense, close together, thick, tight; hidden, secret; retired, intimate. **Clouds**, YÜN: fog, mist, water vapor; connects to the Streaming Moment and Stream, the Symbol of the trigram Gorge, K'AN. **Not**, PU: simple negative. **Rain**, YÜ: all precipitation; sudden showers, fast and furious; associated with the trigram Gorge, K'AN, and the Streaming Moment.

 Origin, TZU: source, beginning, ground; cause, reason, motive; line of descent; path to the origin; yourself, intrinsic. **My/me/I**, WO: first person pronoun; indicates an unusually strong emphasis on your own subjective experience. **West**, HSI: corresponds to autumn, Harvest and the Streaming Moment; begins the yin hemicycle of the Universal Compass. **Suburbs**, CHIAO: area adjoining a city where human constructions and nature interpenetrate; second of the territorial zones: city, suburbs, countryside, forests.

- *Outer and Inner Aspects*

☴ **Ground**: Wind and wood subtly enter from the ground, penetrating and pervading. **Ground** is the center of the yang hemicycle, spreading pervasive action.

Connection to the outer: penetrating and bringing together, the Woody Moment culminating. **Ground** pervades, matches and couples, seeding a new generation.

☰ **Force**: The force of heaven struggles on, persistent and unwearied; heavenly bodies persist in their orbits. **Force** is the center of the yin hemicycle, completing the formative process.

Connection to the inner: struggling forces bound together in dynamic tension, the Metallic Moment culminating. **Force** brings elements to grips, creating enduring relations.

An enduring force **accumulates** within through penetrating and matching the **small**.

- *Counter Indications*

Nuclear trigrams **Radiance**, LI, and **Open**, TUI, result in Counter Hexagram 38, **Polarizing**, K'UEI. **Accumulating small** things through flexible adaptation is contrasted with **polarizing** them into opposing groups.

- *Sequence*

Grouping necessarily possesses a place to Accumulate.
Anterior acquiescence has the use-of Small Accumulating.

Associated Contexts **Group**, PI: compare and select, order things and put them in classes; find what you belong with; sort, examine correspondences; choose and harmonize; unite. The ideogram: person who stops walking, looking around to examine and compare. **Necessarily**, PI: unavoidably, indispensably, certainly. **Possess**, YU: in possession of,

have, own; opposite of lack, WU. **Place**, SO: where something belongs or comes from; residence, dwelling; habitual focus or object.

Anterior ... the use-of: activating this hexagram depends on understanding and accepting the previous statement.

● *Contrasted Definitions*

> **Small Accumulating: few indeed.**
> **Treading: not abiding indeed.**

Associated Contexts **Few**, KUA: small number; seldom, rarely; unusual, solitary. **Indeed**, YEH: intensifier; indicates comment on previous statement.

Tread, LÜ: step, path, track; footsteps; walk a path or way; course of the stars; act, practise; conduct; salary, means of subsistence. The ideogram: body and repeating steps, following a trail. Image of Hexagram 10. **Abide**, CH'U: rest in, dwell; stop yourself; arrive at a place or condition; distinguish, decide; do what is proper. The ideogram: tiger, stop and seat, powerful movement coming to rest.

● *Symbol Tradition*

> **Wind moving above heaven. Small Accumulating.**
> **A chün tzu uses highlighting the pattern to actualize-tao.**

Associated Contexts **Wind**, FENG: moving air, breeze, gust; weather and its influence on mood and humor; fashion, usage; wind and wood are the Symbols of the trigram Ground, SUN. **Move**, HSING: move or move something; motivate, emotionally moving; walk, act, do. The ideogram: stepping left then right. **Above**, SHANG: anything above, in all senses; higher, upper, outer; upper trigram; opposite of below, HSIA. **Heaven**, T'IEN: highest; sky, firmament, heavens; power above the human as opposed to earth, TI, below; the Symbol of the trigram Force, CH'IEN. The ideogram: great and the one above.

Chün tzu: ideal of a person who uses divination to order his/her life in accordance with tao rather than wilful intention; keyword. **Use(-of)**, YI: make use of, by means of, owing to; employ, make functional. **Highlight**, YI: emphasize what is inherently good; concentrate, focus on; virtuous, worthy; an accomplished, graceful woman. **Pattern**, WEN: intrinsic or natural design and its beauty; stylish, elegant; noble; contrasts with composition, CHANG, a conscious creation. **Actualize-tao**, TE: realize tao in action; power, virtue; ability to follow the course traced by the ongoing process of the cosmos; keyword. The ideogram: to go, straight, and heart. Linked with acquire, TE: acquiring that which makes a being become what it is meant to be.

● *Image Tradition*

> **Small Accumulating. [I]**
> **Supple acquiring the situation and-also**
> > **Above[and]Below corresponding-to it.**
> **Spoken-thus: Small Accumulating.**
>
> **Persisting and-also Ground. [II]**
> **Solid centering and-also purpose moving.**
> **Thereupon Growing.**
>
> **Shrouding clouds, not raining: [III]**
> **Honoring going indeed.**
> **Originating-from my Western suburbs:**
> **Spreading-out, not-yet moving indeed.**

Associated Contexts **[I] Supple**, JOU: quality of the opened lines; flexible, pliant, tender, adaptable. **Acquire**, TE: obtain the desired object; wish for, desire covetously; gains, possessions. The ideogram: go and obstacle, going through obstacles to the goal. **Situation**, WEI: place or seat according to rank; post, position, command; right, proper; established, arranged. The ideogram: person and stand, servants in their places. **And-also**, ERH: joins and contrasts two terms. **Above[and]Below**, SHANG HSIA: realm of dynamic interaction between the upper and the lower; the vertical dimension. **Correspond(-to)**, YING: be in agreement or harmony; resonate together, invoke and fulfill each other; answer to, suitable; relation between the lines (1:4, 2:5, 3:6) when they form the pair opened and whole, supple and solid. The ideogram: heart and obey. **It/them/have(-it)/'s**, CHIH: expresses possession, directly or as an object pronoun.

    Spoken-thus, YÜEH: designated, termed, called. The ideogram: open mouth and tongue.

[II] Persist, CHIEN: strong, robust, dynamic, tenacious; continuous; unwearied heavenly bodies in their orbits; the Action of the trigram Force, CH'IEN. **Ground**, SUN: base on which things rest; support, foundation; mild, subtly penetrating; nourishing. The ideogram: stand and things arranged on it, the subtle influence of the ground. Image of Hexagram 57.

Solid, KANG: quality of the whole lines; firm, strong, unyielding, persisting. **Center**, CHUNG: inner, central; put in the center; middle, stable point enabling you to face inner and outer changes; middle line of trigram. The ideogram: field divided in two equal parts. Image of Hexagram 61. **Purpose**, CHIH: focus of mind and heart; will, inclination, resolve. The ideogram: heart and scholar, high inner resolve, or heart and go, inner determination.

Thereupon, NAI: on that ground, because of.

[III] Honor, SHANG: esteem, give high rank to; eminent; put one thing on top of another. **Go**, WANG, and come, LAI, describe the stream of time as it flows from future through present to past; go, WANG, indicates what is departing from present to past; proceed, move on; keyword.

Spread-out, SHIH: expand, diffuse, distribute, arrange, exhibit; add to, aid. The ideogram: flag and indeed, claiming new country. **Not-yet**, WEI: temporal negative; something will but has not yet occurred; contrary of already, CHI. Image of Hexagram 64.

● *Transforming Lines*

Initial nine

a) Returning originating-from tao.
Wherefore one's fault? Significant.

b) Returning originating-from tao.
One's righteousness significant indeed.

Associated Contexts a) **Return**, FU: go back, turn back to the starting point; recur, reappear, come again; restore, recover, retrace; an earlier time or place. The ideogram: step and retrace a path. Image of Hexagram 24. **Tao**: way or path; ongoing process of being and the course it traces for each specific person or thing; keyword. The ideogram: go and head, leading and the path it creates.

Wherefore, HO: interrogative: why? for what reason? what is? and affirmation: therefore, for that reason. **One's/one**, CH'I: third person pronoun; also: it/its, he/his, she/hers, they/theirs. **Fault**, CHIU: unworthy conduct that leads to harm, illness, misfortune. The ideogram: person and differ, differ from what you should be. **Significant**, CHI: leads to the experience of meaning; favorable, propitious, advantageous, appropriate; keyword. The ideogram: scholar and mouth, wise words of a sage.

b) **Righteous**, YI: proper and just, meets the standards; things in their proper place; the heart that rules itself; upright, moral rule; contrasts with Harvest, LI, advantage or profit.

Nine at-second

a) **Hauling-along, returning. Significant.**

b) **Hauling-along, returning, locating-in the center.**
Truly not originating-from letting-go indeed.

Associated Contexts a) **Haul-along**, CH'IEN: haul or pull, drag behind; pull an animal on a rope; pull toward. The ideogram: ox and halter. **Return**, FU: go back, turn back to the starting point; recur, reappear, come again; restore, recover, retrace; an earlier time or place. The ideogram: step and retrace a path. Image of Hexagram 24. **Significant**, CHI: leads to the experience of meaning; favorable, propitious, advantageous, appropriate; keyword. The ideogram: scholar and mouth, wise words of a sage.

b) **Locate(-in)**, TSAI: live in, dwell, reside; belong to, involved with, depend on; within. The ideogram: earth and persevere, place on the earth.
    Truly, YI: statement is true and precise. **Let-go**, SHIH: lose, omit, miss, fail, let slip; out of control. The ideogram: drop from the hand.

Nine at-third

a) **Carting stimulating the spokes.**
Husband, consort, reversing eyes.

b) **Husband, consort, reversing eyes.**
Not able to correct the home indeed.

Associated Contexts a) **Cart**, YÜ: carrying capacity of a vehicle; contain, hold, sustain. **Stimulate**, SHUO: rouse to action and good feeling; free from constraint, stir up, urge on; persuade, cheer, delight; set out in

words; the Action of the trigram Open, TUI. The ideogram: words and exchange. **Spokes,** FU: braces that connect hub and rim of wheel; tributaries.

Husband, FU: household manager; administer with thrift and prudence; responsible for; sustain with your earnings; old enough to assume responsibility; married man. **Consort,** CH'I: single official partner; legal status of married woman (first wife); contrasts with function of wife, FU, head of household, and concubine, CH'IEH, secondary wives. **Reverse,** FAN: turn and move in the opposite direction; turn around or upside down (180 degrees); change to the opposite position; contrary. **Eye,** MU: eye and its functions: look, see, glance, observe.

b) **Able,** NENG: enable; ability, power, skill, art; competent, talented; duty, function, capacity. The ideogram: an animal with strong hooves and bones, able to carry and defend. **Correct,** CHENG: rectify deviation or one-sidedness; proper, straight, exact, regular; constant, rule, model. The ideogram: stop and one, hold to one thing. **Home,** SHIH: place of rest, dwelling, family; the grave.

Six at-fourth

a) **Possessing conformity.**
Blood departing, awe issuing-forth.
Without fault.

b) **Possessing conformity, awe issuing-forth.**
Uniting purposes above indeed.

Associated Contexts a) **Possessing conformity,** YU FU: inner and outer are in accord; confidence of the spirits has been captured; sincere, truthful; proper to take action.

Blood, HSÜEH: yin fluid that maintains life; money, property. **Depart,** CH'Ü: leave, quit, remove; repudiate, reject, dismiss. **Awe,** T'I: alarmed and cautious; respect, regard, fear; stand in awe of. The ideogram: heart and versatile, the heart aware of sudden change. **Issue-forth(-from),** CH'U: emerge from, come out of, proceed from, spring from; the Action of the trigram Shake, CHEN; contrary of enter, JU. The ideogram: stem with branches and leaves emerging.

Without fault, WU CHIU: no error or harm in the situation.

b) **Unite**, HO: join, match, correspond, agree, collect, reply; unison, harmony; also: close, shut the mouth. The ideogram: mouth and assemble.

Nine at-fifth

a) Possessing conformity, binding thus.
Affluence: using one's neighbor.

b) Possessing conformity, binding thus.
Not solitary affluence indeed.

Associated Contexts a) **Possessing conformity**, YU FU: inner and outer are in accord; confidence of the spirits has been captured; sincere, truthful; proper to take action. **Bind**, LÜAN: tie, connect, take hold of; bent, contracted. The ideogram: hand and connect, binding things. **Thus**, JU: as, in this way.

Affluence, FU: rich, abundant; wealth; enrich, provide for; flow toward, accrue. **One's/one**, CH'I: third person pronoun; also: it/its, he/his, she/hers, they/theirs. **Neighbor**, LIN: person living nearby; extended family; assist, support.

b) **Solitary**, TI: alone, single; isolated, abandoned.

Nine above

a) Already rain, already abiding.
Honoring actualizing-tao carrying.
The wife, Trial: adversity.
The moon almost facing.
A chün tzu chastising: pitfall.

b) Already rain, already abiding.
Actualizing-tao amassing carrying indeed.
A chün tzu chastising: pitfall.
Possessing a place to doubt indeed.

Associated Contexts a) **Already**, CHI: completed, done, has occurred; past tense, contrary of not-yet, WEI. Image of Hexagram 63.

Carry, TSAI: bear, carry with you; contain, sustain; load a ship or cart, cargo; fill in, complete.

Wife, FU: responsible position of married woman within the household; contrasts with consort, CH'I, her legal position and concubine, CH'IEH, secondary wives. The ideogram: woman, hand and broom, household duties. **Trial**, CHEN: test by ordeal; inquiry by divination and its result; righteous, firm; separating wheat from chaff; the kernel, the proven core; fourth stage of the Time Cycle. The ideogram: pearl and divination. **Adversity**, LI: danger; threatening, malevolent demon. This has two aspects: grind, sharpen, improve, perfect, stimulate; and: poisonous, sinister, cruel, contrary. It indicates a spirit or ghost that seeks revenge by inflicting suffering upon the living. Pacifying or exorcizing such a spirit can have a healing effect. The ideogram: sheltering cliff and stinging insect.

Moon, YÜEH: actual moon and moon-month; yin, the sun being yang. **Almost**, CHI: nearly, about to; subtle, almost imperceptible; the first sign. **Face**, WANG: full moon; moon directly facing the sun; 15th day of the moon-month; look at hopefully.

Chastise, CHENG: punish, subjugate, discipline; reduce to order; punishing expedition. The ideogram: step and correct, a rectifying move. **Pitfall**, HSIUNG: leads away from the experience of meaning; stuck and exposed to danger, unable to take in the situation; flow of life and spirit is blocked; unfortunate, baleful; keyword.

b) **Amass**, CHI: hoard, accumulate, pile up, store up, add up, increase.

Doubt, YI: suspect, distrust; dubious; surmise, conjecture.

10

TREADING ▮ LÜ

This hexagram describes your situation in terms of finding and making your way. It emphasizes that doing this step by step is the adequate way to handle it. To be in accord with the time, you are told to: **tread**!

● *Image of the Situation*

> **Treading a tiger tail.**
> **Not snapping-at people. Growing.**

Associated Contexts **Tread**, LÜ: step, path, track; footsteps; walk a path or way; course of the stars; act, practise; conduct; salary, means of subsistance. The ideogram: body and repeating steps, following a trail. **Tiger**, HU: fierce king of animals; extreme yang; opposed to and protects against demoniacs on North–South axis of Universal Compass. **Tail**, WEI: animal's tail; last, extreme; remnants, unimportant.

Not, PU: simple negative. **Snap-at**, TIEH: bite, seize with the teeth, maul; sneering laughter, rebuke. The ideogram: mouth and reach. **People**, **person**, JEN: humans individually and collectively; an individual; humankind. Image of Hexagrams 13 and 37. **Grow**, HENG: success through a sacrifice; pervade, persevere; bring to full growth; enjoy; vigorous, effective; second stage of the Time Cycle.

● *Outer and Inner Aspects*

☰ **Force**: The force of heaven struggles on, persistent and unwearied; heavenly bodies persist in their orbits. **Force** is the center of the yin hemicycle, completing the formative process.

Connection to the outer: struggling forces are bound together in dynamic tension, the Metallic Moment culminating. **Force** brings elements to grips, creating enduring relations.

☱ **Open**: vapor rising from the marsh's open surface stimulates and fertilizes; stimulating words cheer and inspire. **Open** begins the yin hemicycle by initiating the formative process.

Connection to the inner: liquifying, casting, skinning off the mold, the Metallic Moment beginning. **Open** stimulates, cheers and reveals innate form.

Inner stimulation alternates with outer struggle, **treading** a path step by step.

- ## Counter Indications

Nuclear trigrams **Ground**, SUN, and **Radiance**, LI, result in Counter Hexagram 37, **Dwelling People**, CHIA JEN. **Treading** and moving along a path is contrasted with staying with **people** in their **dwelling**.

- ## Sequence

**Beings Accumulating, therefore afterwards possessing codes.
Anterior acquiescence has the use-of Treading.**

Associated Contexts **Being(s)**, WU: creature, thing, any single being; matter, substance, essence; nature of things. **Accumulate**, CH'U: retain, hoard, gather, herd together; control, restrain; domesticate, tame, train; raise, feed, sustain, bring up. The ideogram: field and black, fertile black soil good for pastures, accumulated through retaining silt. Image of Hexagrams 9 and 26. **Therefore afterwards**, JAN HOU: logical consequence of, necessarily follows in time. **Possess**, YU: in possession of, have, own; opposite of lack, WU. **Codes**, LI: rites, rules, ritual; usage, manners; worship, ceremony, observance. The ideogram: worship and sacrificial vase, handling a sacred vessel.
Anterior ... the use-of: activating this hexagram depends on understanding and accepting the previous statement.

- ## Contrasted Definitions

**Small Accumulating: few indeed.
Treading: not abiding indeed.**

Associated Contexts **Small**, HSIAO: little, common, unimportant; adapting to what crosses your path; ability to move in harmony with the vicissitudes of life; contrasts with great, TA, self-imposed theme or goal;

keyword. **Small Accumulating**, HSIAO CH'U, is the Image of Hexagram 9.
Few, KUA: small number; seldom, rarely; unusual, solitary. **Indeed**, YEH:
intensifier; indicates comment on previous statement.

    Abide, CH'U: rest in, dwell; stop yourself; arrive at a place or
condition; distinguish, decide; do what is proper. The ideogram: tiger,
stop and seat, powerful movement coming to rest.

● *Attached Evidences*

> **Treading: actualizing-tao's foundation indeed.**
> **Treading: harmonizing and-also culminating.**
> **Treading: using harmonizing movement.**

Associated Contexts **Actualize-tao**, TE: realize tao in action; power,
virtue; ability to follow the course traced by the ongoing process of the
cosmos; keyword. The ideogram: to go, straight, and heart. Linked with
acquire, TE: acquiring that which makes a being become what it is meant
to be. **'s/have(-it)/it/them**, CHIH: expresses possession, directly or as an
object pronoun. **Foundation**, CHI: base of wall or building; basis, starting
point; found, establish.

    Harmony, HO: concord, union; conciliate; at peace, mild; fit, tune,
adjust. **And-also**, ERH: joins and contrasts two terms. **Culminate**, CHIH:
bring to the highest degree; arrive at the end or summit; superlative.

    Use(-of), YI: make use of, by means of, owing to; employ, make
functional. **Move**, HSING: move or move something; motivate,
emotionally moving; walk, act, do. The ideogram: stepping left then right.

● *Symbol Tradition*

> **Heaven above, marsh below. Treading.**
> **A chün tzu uses differentiating Above[and]Below.**
> **[A chün tzu uses] setting-right the commoners, the purpose.**

Associated Contexts **Heaven**, T'IEN: highest; sky, firmament,
heavens; power above the human as opposed to earth, TI, below; the
Symbol of the trigram Force, CH'IEN. The ideogram: great and the one
above. **Above**, SHANG: anything above, in all senses; higher, upper, outer;
upper trigram; opposite of below, HSIA. **Marsh**, TSE: open surface of a
flat body of water and the vapors rising from it; fertilize, enrich; kindness,

favor; the Symbol of the trigram Open, TUI. **Below**, HSIA: anything below, in all senses; lower, inner; lower trigram; opposite of above, SHANG.

Chün tzu: ideal of a person who uses divination to order his/her life in accordance with tao rather than wilful intention; keyword. **Differentiate**, PIEN: argue, dispute, criticize; sophisticated, artful. The ideogram: words and sharp or pungent. **Above[and]Below**, SHANG HSIA: realm of dynamic interaction between the upper and the lower; the vertical dimension.

Set-right, TING: settle, fix, put in place; at rest, repose. **Commoners**, MIN: class of workers the state draws on to sustain the social hierarchy; undeveloped potential outside the organized personality. **Purpose**, CHIH: focus of mind and heart; will, inclination, resolve. The ideogram: heart and scholar, high inner resolve, or heart and go, inner determination.

- *Image Tradition*

> **Treading. Supple Treading solid indeed. [I]**
> **Stimulating and-also corresponding reaching-to Force.**
> **That uses Treading a tiger tail.**
>
> **Not snapping-at people. Growing. [II]**
> **Solid centering correctly.**
> **Treading the supreme situation and-also not ailing.**
> **Shining brightness indeed.**

Associated Contexts **[I] Supple**, JOU: quality of the opened lines; flexible, pliant, tender, adaptable. **Solid**, KANG: quality of the whole lines; firm, strong, unyielding, persisting.

Stimulate, SHUO: rouse to action and good feeling; free from constraint, stir up, urge on; persuade, cheer, delight; set out in words; the Action of the trigram Open, TUI. The ideogram: words and exchange. **Correspond(-to)**, YING: be in agreement or harmony; resonate together, invoke and fulfill each other; answer to, suitable; relation between the lines (1:4, 2:5, 3:6) when they form the pair opened and whole, supple and solid. The ideogram: heart and obey. **Reach(-to)**, HU: arrive at a goal; reach toward and achieve; connect; contrasts with tend-towards, YU. **Force**, CH'IEN: spirit power, creative and destructive; unceasing forward motion; dynamic, enduring, untiring; firm, stable; heaven, sovereign, father; also: dry up, parched, exhausted, cleared away. The ideogram:

sprouts or vapors rising from the ground and sunlight, both fecundating moisture and scorching drought. Image of Hexagram 1. **That uses**, SHIH YI: involves and is involved by.

[II] Centering correcting, CHUNG CHENG: central and correct; make rectifying one-sidedness and error your central concern; reaching a stable center in yourself can correct the situation.

Supreme, TI: highest, above all on earth; sovereign lord, source of power; emperor. **Situation**, WEI: place or seat according to rank; post, position, command; right, proper; established, arranged. The ideogram: person and stand, servants in their places. **Ail**, CHIU: chronic disease; disheartened, distressed by.

Shine, KUANG: illuminate; give off brilliant, bright light; honor, glory, éclat; result of action, contrasts with brightness, MING, light of heavenly bodies. The ideogram: fire above person, lifting the light. **Brightness**, MING: light-giving aspect of burning, heavenly bodies and consciousness; with fire, the Symbol of the trigram Radiance, LI.

● *Transforming Lines*

Initial nine

a) **Sheer Treading going.**
Without fault.

b) **Sheer Treading's going.**
Solitarily moving desire indeed.

Associated Contexts *a)* **Sheer**, SU: plain, unadorned; original color or state; clean, pure. The ideogram: white silk, symbol of mourning. **Go**, WANG, and come, LAI, describe the stream of time as it flows from future through present to past; go, WANG, indicates what is departing from present to past; proceed, move on; keyword.
Without fault, WU CHIU: no error or harm in the situation.

b) **Solitary**, TI: alone, single; isolated, abandoned. **Desire**, YÜAN: wish, hope or long for; covet; desired object.

Nine at-second

a) **Treading tao, smoothing, smoothing.**
Shade people, Trial: significant.

b) Shade people, Trial: significant.
Centering, not originating-from disarray indeed.

Associated Contexts a) **Tao**: way or path; ongoing process of being and the course it traces for each specific person or thing; keyword. The ideogram: go and head, leading and the path it creates. **Smooth**, T'AN: plain, leveled; even, make smooth; tranquil, composed, at ease. The doubled character intensifies this quality.

Shade, YU: hidden from view; retired, solitary, secret; dark, obscure, occult, mysterious; ignorant. The ideogram: small within hill, a cave or grotto. **Trial**, CHEN: test by ordeal; inquiry by divination and its result; righteous, firm; separating wheat from chaff; the kernel, the proven core; fourth stage of the Time Cycle. The ideogram: pearl and divination. **Significant**, CHI: leads to the experience of meaning; favorable, propitious, advantageous, appropriate; keyword. The ideogram: scholar and mouth, wise words of a sage.

b) **Center**, CHUNG: inner, central; put in the center; middle, stable point enabling you to face inner and outer changes; middle line of trigram. The ideogram: field divided in two equal parts. Image of Hexagram 61. **Origin**, TZU: source, beginning, ground; cause, reason, motive; line of descent; path to the origin; yourself, intrinsic. **Disarray**, LUAN: throw into disorder, mislay, confuse; out of place; discord, insurrection, anarchy.

Six at-third

a) Squinting enabling observing.
Halting enabling Treading.
Treading a tiger tail.
Snapping-at people: pitfall.
Martial people activating: tending-towards a Great Chief.

b) Squinting enabling observing.
Not the stand to use possessing brightness indeed.
Halting enabling Treading.
Not the stand to use associating-with moving indeed.
Snapping-at people's pitfall.
Situation not appropriate indeed.
Martial people activating: tending-towards a Great Chief.
Purpose solid indeed.

Associated Contexts a) **Squint**, MIAO: look at with one eye, glance at; obstructed vision. **Able**, NENG: enable; ability, power, skill, art; competent, talented; duty, function, capacity. The ideogram: an animal with strong hooves and bones, able to carry and defend. **Observe**, SHIH: see and inspect carefully; gain knowledge of; compare and imitate. The ideogram: see and omen, taking account of what you see.

   Halt, P'O: limp; lame, crippled; indecorous.

   Pitfall, HSIUNG: leads away from the experience of meaning; stuck and exposed to danger, unable to take in the situation; flow of life and spirit is blocked; unfortunate, baleful; keyword.

   Martial, WU: military, warlike; strong, stern; power to make war. The ideogram: fight and stop, force deterring aggression. **Activate**, WEI: act or cause to act; do, make, manage; make active; attend to, help; because of. **Tend-towards**, YÜ: move toward but not reach, in the direction of; contrasts with reach(-to), HU, actually arriving. **Great**, TA: big, noble, important, very; orient the will toward a self-imposed goal, impose direction; ability to lead or guide your life; contrasts with small, HSIAO, flexible adaptation to what crosses your path; keyword. Image of Hexagrams 14, 26, 28, 34. **Chief**, CHÜN: effective ruler; preside over, take the lead; influence others; term of respect. The ideogram: mouth and director, giving orders.

b) **Stand**, TSU: base, foot, leg; rest on, support; stance. The ideogram: foot and calf resting.

   Associate(-with), YÜ: consort with, combine; companions; group, band, company; agree with, comply, help. The ideogram: pair of hands reaching downward meets a pair of hands reaching upward, helpful association.

   Appropriate, TANG: suitable; opportune, convenient; adequate, competent; equal to; whole lines in uneven places and opened lines in even places.

   Nine at-fourth

   a) **Treading a tiger tail.**
      Pleading, pleading: completing significant.

b) Pleading, pleading: completing significant.
Purpose moving indeed.

Associated Contexts a) **Plead,** SU: defend or prosecute a case in court; enter a plea; statement of grievance. The doubled character intensifies this quality. **Complete,** CHUNG: end of a cycle that begins the next; last, whole, all; contrasts with exhaust, CH'IUNG: final end. The ideogram: silk cocoons, follow and ice, winter linking one year with the next. **Significant,** CHI: leads to the experience of meaning; favorable, propitious, advantageous, appropriate; keyword. The ideogram: scholar and mouth, wise words of a sage.

Nine at-fifth

a) Parting Treading. Trial: adversity.

b) Parting Treading, Trial: adversity.
Situation correcting appropriate indeed.

Associated Contexts a) **Part,** KUAI: separate, fork, cut off, decide; pull or flow in different directions; certain, settled; prompt, decisive, stern. Image of Hexagram 43. **Trial,** CHEN: test by ordeal; inquiry by divination and its result; righteous, firm; separating wheat from chaff; the kernel, the proven core; fourth stage of the Time Cycle. The ideogram: pearl and divination. **Adversity,** LI: danger; threatening, malevolent demon. This has two aspects: grind, sharpen, improve, perfect, stimulate; and: poisonous, sinister, cruel, contrary. It indicates a spirit or ghost that seeks revenge by inflicting suffering upon the living. Pacifying or exorcizing such a spirit can have a healing effect. The ideogram: sheltering cliff and stinging insect.

b) **Correct,** CHENG: rectify deviation or one-sidedness; proper, straight, exact, regular; constant, rule, model. The ideogram: stop and one, hold to one thing. **Appropriate,** TANG: suitable; opportune, convenient; adequate, competent; equal to; whole lines in uneven places and opened lines in even places.

Nine above

a) Observing Treading, predecessors auspicious.
One's recurring Spring significant.

b) **Spring significant located above.**
The great possesses reward indeed.

Associated Contexts a) **Observe**, SHIH: see and inspect carefully;
gain knowledge of; compare and imitate. The ideogram: see and omen,
taking account of what you see. **Predecessor**, K'AO: deceased ancestor,
especially the grandfather; the ancients; aged, long-lived; consult, verify.
The ideogram: old and ingenious, the old wise man. **Auspicious**,
HSIANG: omen of good luck and prosperity; sign, auspices.

One's/one, CH'I: third person pronoun; also: it/its, he/his, she/hers,
they/theirs. **Recur**, HSÜAN: return to the same point; orbit, revolve; spiral.
Spring, YÜAN: source, origin, head; great, excellent; arise, begin,
generating power; first stage of the Time Cycle. **Significant**, CHI: leads to
the experience of meaning; favorable, propitious, advantageous,
appropriate; keyword. The ideogram: scholar and mouth, wise words of a
sage.

b) **Locate(-in)**, TSAI: live in, dwell, reside; belong to, involved with,
depend on; within. The ideogram: earth and persevere, place on the earth.

Great, TA: big, noble, important, very; orient the will toward a self-
imposed goal, impose direction; ability to lead or guide your life; contrasts
with small, HSIAO, flexible adaptation to what crosses your path;
keyword. Image of Hexagrams 14, 26, 28, 34. **Reward**, CH'ING: gift given
from gratitude or benevolence; favor from heaven; congratulate with gifts.
The ideogram: heart, follow and deer (wealth), the heart expressed
through gifts.

PERVADING ▪ *T'AI*

This hexagram describes your situation in terms of prospering and expanding. It emphasizes that continually spreading this prosperity through communicating is the adequate way to handle it. To be in accord with the time, you are told to: **pervade!**

● *Image of the Situation*

> **Pervading.**
> **The small going, the great coming.**
> **Significance Growing.**

Associated Contexts **Pervade**, T'AI: spread and reach everywhere, permeate, diffuse; communicate; great, extensive, abundant, prosperous; smooth, slippery; extreme, extravagant, prodigal. Mount T'AI in eastern China was a sacred mountain connecting heaven and earth. The emperor made offerings there to establish harmony between humans and the great spirits. The ideogram: person in water, connected to the universal medium.

　　Small, HSIAO: little, common, unimportant; adapting to what crosses your path; ability to move in harmony with the vicissitudes of life; contrasts with great, TA, self-imposed theme or goal; keyword. Image of Hexagrams 9 and 62. **Go**, WANG, and **Come**, LAI, describe the stream of time as it flows from future through present to past. Go, WANG, indicates what is departing; proceed, move on; come, LAI, indicates what is approaching; move toward, arrive at; keywords. **Great**, TA: big, noble, important, very; orient the will toward a self-imposed goal, impose direction; ability to lead or guide your life; contrasts with small, HSIAO, flexible adaptation to what crosses your path; keyword. Image of Hexagrams 14, 26, 28, 34.

　　Significant, CHI: leads to the experience of meaning; favorable, propitious, advantageous, appropriate; keyword. The ideogram: scholar and mouth, wise words of a sage. **Grow**, HENG: success through a sacrifice; pervade, persevere; bring to full growth; enjoy; vigorous, effective; second stage of the Time Cycle.

● *Outer and Inner Aspects*

☷ **Field**: The field of earth yields and sustains, serving in order to produce. **Field** is the equalizing point between yin and yang where things labor and serve.

Connection to the outer: the common labor of sowing and hoarding, the Earthy Moment. **Field** produces concrete results through serving.

☰ **Force**: The force of heaven struggles on, persistent and unwearied; heavenly bodies persist in their orbits. **Force** is the center of the yin hemicycle, completing the formative process.

Connection to the inner: struggling forces are bound together in dynamic tension, the Metallic Moment culminating. **Force** brings elements to grips, creating enduring relations.

An enduring force spreads from within, **pervading** the earth which yields and brings-forth. This is a time of creative abundance.

● *Counter Indications*

Nuclear trigrams **Shake**, CHEN, and **Open**, TUI, result in Counter Hexagram 54, **Converting Maidenhood**, KUEI MEI. **Pervading** and spreading in all directions is contrasted with turning toward a specific place where one belongs through **converting maidenhood**.

● *Sequence*

> **Treading and-also Pervading.**
> **Therefore afterwards quieting.**
> **Anterior acquiescence has the use-of Pervading.**
> **Pervading implies interpenetrating indeed.**

Associated Contexts **Tread**, LÜ: step, path, track; footsteps; walk a path or way; course of the stars; act, practise; conduct; salary, means of subsistence. The ideogram: body and repeating steps, following a trail. Image of Hexagram 10. **And-also**, ERH: joins and contrasts two terms.

Therefore afterwards, JAN HOU: logical consequence of, necessarily follows in time. **Quiet**, AN: peaceful, still, settled; calm, tranquilize. The ideogram: woman under a roof, a tranquil home.

Anterior ... the use-of: activating this hexagram depends on understanding and accepting the previous statement.

Imply, CHE: further signify; additional meaning. **Interpenetrate**, T'UNG: mutually penetrate; permeate, flow through, reach everywhere; see clearly, communicate with. **Indeed**, YEH: intensifier; indicates comment on previous statement.

● *Contrasting Definitions*

Obstructing, Pervading: reversing one's sorting indeed.

Associated Contexts **Obstruct**, P'I: closed, stopped; bar the way; obstacle; unfortunate, wicked; refuse, disapprove, deny. The ideogram: mouth and not, blocked communication. Image of Hexagram 12. **Reverse**, FAN: turn and move in the opposite direction; turn around or upside down (180 degrees); change to the opposite position; contrary. **One's/one**, CH'I: third person pronoun; also: it/its, he/his, she/hers, they/theirs. **Sort**, LEI: group according to kind, class with; like nature or purpose; species, class, genus.

● *Symbol Tradition*

Heaven[and]Earth mingling. Pervading.
The crown-prince uses property
to accomplish Heaven[and]Earth's tao.
[The crown-prince uses] bracing
to mutualize Heaven[and]Earth's propriety.
[The crown-prince] uses the left to right the commoners.

Associated Contexts **Heaven[and]Earth**, T'IEN TI: dynamic relation between the primal powers and the world it produces; cosmos, natural or human world; keyword. **Mingle**, CHIAO: blend with, communicate, join, exchange; trade, business; copulation; friendship.

Crown-prince, HOU: successor to the sovereign. The ideogram: one, mouth and shelter, one with the sovereign's orders. **Use(-of)**, YI: make use of, by means of, owing to; employ, make functional. **Property**, TS'AI: possessions, goods, substance, wealth. The ideogram: pearl and value. **Accomplish**, CH'ENG: complete, finish, bring about; perfect, full, whole; play your part, do your duty; mature. The ideogram: weapon and man, able to bear arms, thus fully developed. **'s/have(-it)/it/them**, CHIH: expresses possession, directly or as an object pronoun. **Tao**: way or path; ongoing process of being and the course it traces for each specific person or thing; keyword. The ideogram: go and head, leading and the path it creates.

Brace/jawbones, FU: support, consolidate, reinforce, strengthen, stiffen, prop up, fix; steady, firm, rigid; help, rescue; support the speaking mouth. The ideogram: cart and great. **Mutual**, HSIANG: reciprocal assistance, encourage, help; bring together, blend with; examine, inspect; by turns. **Proper**, YI: reasonable of itself; fit and right, harmonious; ought, should.

Left, TSO: left side, left hand; secondary; deputy, assistant; inferior. **Right**, YU: right side, right hand; noble, honorable; make things right. **Commoners**, MIN: class of workers the state draws on to sustain the social hierarchy; undeveloped potential outside the organized personality.

● *Image Tradition*

> The small going, the great coming: significance Growing. [I]
> By-consequence-of that Heaven[and]Earth mingling
> and-also the myriad beings interpenetrating indeed.
> Above[and]Below mingling and-also
> one's purpose concording indeed.
>
> Inside yang and-also outside yin. [II]
> Inside persisting and-also outside yielding.
> Inside chün tzu and-also outside Small People.
> A chün tzu: tao long-living.
> Small People: tao dissolving indeed.

Associated Contexts [I] **By-consequence(-of)**, TSE: very strong connection; reason, cause, result; rule, law, pattern, standard; therefore. **That**, SHIH: preceding statement. **Myriad**, WAN: countless; many, everyone; lit.: ten thousand. The ideogram: swarm of insects. **Being(s)**, WU: creature, thing, any single being; matter, substance, essence; nature of things.

Above[and]Below, SHANG HSIA: realm of dynamic interaction between the upper and the lower; the vertical dimension. **Purpose,** CHIH: focus of mind and heart; will, inclination, resolve. The ideogram: heart and scholar, high inner resolve, or heart and go, inner determination. **Concord**, T'UNG: harmonize, unite, equalize, assemble; agree, share in; together, at once, same time and place. The ideogram: cover and mouth, silent understanding and perfect fit. Image of Hexagram 13.

[II] **Inside**, NEI: within, inner, interior; inside of the house and those who work there, particularly women; the lower trigram, as opposed to outside, WAI, the upper. The ideogram: border and enter, cross a border. **Yang:** Action; dynamic and light aspect of phenomena: arouses, transforms, dissolves existing structures; linear thrust; stimulus, drive, focus; direct or orient something. **Outside**, WAI: outer, exterior, external; people working in places other than their home; unfamiliar, foreign; the upper trigram, as opposed to inside, NEI, the lower. **Yin**: Struction; consolidating, shadowy aspect of phenomena: conserves, substantializes, creates structures; spacial extension; limited, bound, given specific being; build, make something concrete.

Persist, CHIEN: strong, robust, dynamic, tenacious; continuous; unwearied heavenly bodies in their orbits; the Action of the trigram Force, CH'IEN. **Yield(-to)**,SHUN: give way and bear produce; comply, agree, follow, obey; unresisting, docile, flexible; nourish, provide; the Action of the trigram Field, K'UN. The ideogram: head and current, water flowing from the head of a river, yielding to the banks.

Chün tzu: ideal of a person who uses divination to order his/her life in accordance with tao rather than wilful intention; keyword. **Small People**, HSIAO JEN: lowly, common, humble; those who adjust to circumstances with the flexibility of the small; effect of the small within an individual; keyword.

Long-living, CHANG: enduring, constant; senior, superior, greater; increase, prosper; respect, elevate. **Dissolve**, HSIAO: liquify, melt, thaw; diminish, disperse; eliminate, exhaust. The ideogram: water dissolving differences.

• *Transforming Lines*

Initial Nine

a) **Eradicating thatch-grass intertwisted.**
Using one's classification.
Chastising significant.

b) **Eradicating thatch-grass, chastising significant.**
Purpose located outside indeed.

Associated Contexts a) **Eradicate**, PA: pull up, root out, extirpate; extricate from difficulties; elevate, promote. **Thatch-grass**, MAO: thick grass used for the roofs of humble houses. **Intertwist**, JU: interlaced; entangled roots.

Classification, HUI: class, collection, series; same kind; put or group together. **Chastise**, CHENG: punish, subjugate, discipline; reduce to order; punishing expedition. The ideogram: step and correct, a rectifying move.

b) **Locate(-in)**, TSAI: live in, dwell, reside; belong to, involved with, depend on; within. The ideogram: earth and persevere, place on the earth.

Nine at-second

a) **Enwrapping wasteland.**
Availing-of crossing the channel.
Not putting-off abandoning.
Partnering extinguished.
Acquiring honor, tending-towards centering moving.

b) **Enwrapping wasteland, acquiring honor,**
tending-towards centering moving.
Using the shining great indeed.

Associated Contexts a) **Enwrap**, PAO: envelop, hold, contain; patient; take on responsibility, engaged. The ideogram: enfold and self, a fetus in the womb. **Wasteland**, HUANG: wild, barren, deserted, unproductive; jungle, moor, heath; reckless, neglectful.

Avail-of, YUNG: take advantage of; benefit from, profit by; use for a specific purpose; apply to advantage. The ideogram: to divine and center, applying divination to central concerns. **Cross**, P'ING: cross a river without a boat; cross a dry or frozen river. The ideogram: horse and ice. **Channel**, HO: bed of river or stream; running water.

Not, PU: simple negative. **Put-off**, HSIA: delay; put at a distance; far away, remote in time. **Abandon**, YI: leave behind, forget; die; lose through unawareness. The ideogram: go and value, value is gone.

Partner, P'ENG: associate for mutual benefit; two equal or similar things; companions, friends, peers; join in; commercial ventures. The ideogram: linked strings of cowries or coins. **Extinguish**, WANG: ruin, destroy; gone, dead, lost without trace; extinct, forgotten, out of mind. The ideogram: person concealed by a wall, out of sight.

Acquire, TE: obtain the desired object; wish for, desire covetously; gains, possessions. The ideogram: go and obstacle, going through obstacles to the goal. **Honor**, SHANG: esteem, give high rank to; eminent; put one thing on top of another. **Tend-towards**, YÜ: move toward but not reach, in the direction of; contrasts with reach(-to), HU, actually arriving. **Center**, CHUNG: inner, central; put in the center; middle, stable point enabling you to face inner and outer changes; middle line of trigram. The ideogram: field divided in two equal parts. Image of Hexagram 61. **Move**, HSING: move or move something; motivate, emotionally moving; walk, act, do. The ideogram: stepping left then right.

b) **Shine**, KUANG: illuminate; give off brilliant, bright light; honor, glory, éclat; result of action, contrasts with brightness, MING, light of heavenly bodies. The ideogram: fire above person, lifting the light.

Nine at-third

a) Without evening, not unevening.
Without going, not returning.
Drudgery, Trial: without fault.
No cares: one's conforming.
Tending-towards taking-in possesses blessing.

b) Without going, not returning.
Heaven[and]Earth, the border indeed.

Associated Contexts a) **Without**, WU: devoid of; -less as suffix. **Even**, P'ING: level, make even or equal; uniform, peaceful, tranquil; restore quiet, harmonize. **Not**, PU: simple negative. **Uneven**, PEI: any difference in level; inclined, falling down, tipped over, delapidated; also: rising; bank, shore, dam, dikes.

Return, FU: go back, turn back to the starting point; recur, reappear, come again; restore, recover, retrace; an earlier time or place. The ideogram: step and retrace a path. Image of Hexagram 24.

Drudgery, CHIEN: difficult, hard, repetitive work; hard to cultivate; distressing, sorrowful. The ideogram: sticky earth and a person looking around, hard work in comparison to others. **Trial**, CHEN: test by ordeal; inquiry by divination and its result; righteous, firm; separating wheat from chaff; the kernel, the proven core; fourth stage of the Time Cycle. The ideogram: pearl and divination. **Without fault**, WU CHIU: no error or harm in the situation.

No, WU: simple negative; un-, dis-. **Care**, HSÜ: fear, doubt, concern; heartfelt attachment; relieve, soothe, aid; sympathy, compassion, consolation. The ideogram: heart and blood, the heart's blood affected. **Conforming**, FU: accord between inner and outer in a particular moment; sincere, truthful, verified, reliable, in accord with the spirits; capture; prisoners, spoils; contrasts with trustworthy, HSIN, consistent over time. The ideogram: bird's claw enclosing young animals, possessive grip. Image of Hexagram 61.

Tend-towards, YÜ: move toward but not reach, in the direction of; contrasts with reach(-to), HU, actually arriving. **Take-in**, SHIH: eat, ingest, swallow, devour; incorporate. **Possess**, YU: in possession of, have, own; opposite of lack, WU. **Bless**, FU: heavenly gifts; make happy; spiritual power and goodwill. The ideogram: spirit and plenty, heavenly gifts in abundance.

b) **Border**, CHI: limit, frontier, line which joins and divides. The ideogram: place and sacrifice, border between human and spirit.

Six at-fourth

a) **Fluttering, fluttering.**
Not affluence: using one's neighbor.
Not warning: using conforming.

b) **Fluttering, fluttering: not affluence.**
Altogether letting-go substance indeed.
Not warning: using conforming.
Centering the heart desiring indeed.

Associated Contexts a) **Flutter**, P'IEN: fly or run about; bustle, fussy. The ideogram: young bird leaving the nest. The doubled character intensifies this quality.

Not, PU: simple negative. **Affluence**, FU: rich, abundant; wealth; enrich, provide for; flow towards, accrue. **Neighbor**, LIN: person living nearby; extended family; assist, support.

Warn, CHIEH: alert, alarm, put on guard; caution, inform; guard against, refrain from (as in a diet). The ideogram: spear held in both hands, warning enemies and alerting friends. **Conforming**, FU: accord between inner and outer in a particular moment; sincere, truthful, verified, reliable, in accord with the spirits; capture; prisoners, spoils; contrasts with trustworthy, HSIN, consistent over time. The ideogram: bird's claw enclosing young animals, possessive grip. Image of Hexagram 61.

b) **Altogether**, CHIEH: all, the whole; the same sort, all alike; entirely. **Let-go**, SHIH: lose, omit, miss, fail, let slip; out of control. The ideogram: drop from the hand. **Substance**, SHIH: real, solid, full; results, fruits, possessions; essence; honest, sincere. The ideogram: string of coins under a roof, riches in the house.

Center, CHUNG: inner, central; put in the center; middle, stable point enabling you to face inner and outer changes; middle line of trigram. The ideogram: field divided in two equal parts. Image of Hexagram 61. **Heart**, HSIN: heart as center of being; seat of mind's images and affections; moral nature; source of desires, intentions, will. **Desire**, YÜAN: wish, hope or long for; covet; desired object.

Six at-fifth

a) The supreme burgeoning, converting maidenhood.
Using satisfaction, Spring significant.

b) Using satisfaction, Spring significant.
Center uses moving desire indeed.

Associated Contexts a) **Supreme**, TI: highest, above all on earth; sovereign lord, source of power; emperor. **Burgeon**, YI: beginning of growth after seedburst, CHIA; early spring; associated with the Woody Moment. **Supreme Burgeoning**, TI YI, refers to the great Shang emperor (1191–1151 BCE) who took a wife from the family of King Wen's ancestors in order to assure an heir. This ennobled the line from which the Chou Dynasty would come. It is an omen of great happiness and good fortune in the future. **Convert**, KUEI: change to another form, persuade; return to yourself or the place where you belong; restore, revert, become loyal; turn into; give a young girl in marriage. The ideogram: arrive and wife, become mistress of a household. **Maiden(hood)**, MEI: girl not yet nubile, virgin; younger sister; daughter of a secondary wife. The ideogram: woman and not-yet. **Converting Maidenhood** is the Image of Hexagram 54.

Satisfaction, CHIH: fulfilment, gratification, happy in realizing your aim; take pleasure in, fulfil a need. **Spring**, YÜAN: source, origin, head; great, excellent; arise, begin, generating power; first stage of the Time Cycle.

b) **Center**, CHUNG: inner, central; put in the center; middle, stable point enabling you to face inner and outer changes; middle line of trigram. The ideogram: field divided in two equal parts. Image of Hexagram 61. **Move**, HSING: move or move something; motivate, emotionally moving; walk, act, do. The ideogram: stepping left then right. **Desire**, YÜAN: wish, hope or long for; covet; desired object.

Six above

a) **The bulwark returned tending-towards the moat.**
No availing-of legions.
Originating-from the capital, notifying fate.
Trial: abashment.

b) **The bulwark returned tending-towards the moat.**
One's fate disarrayed indeed.

Associated Contexts **a) Bulwark**, CH'ENG: city wall, citadel, place walled for defence. **Return**, FU: go back, turn back to the starting point; recur, reappear, come again; restore, recover, retrace; an earlier time or place. The ideogram: step and retrace a path. Image of Hexagram 24. **Tend-towards**, YÜ: move toward but not reach, in the direction of; contrasts with reach(-to), HU, actually arriving. **Moat**, HUANG: ditch around city or fort.

No, WU: simple negative; un-, dis-. **Avail-of**, YUNG: take advantage of; benefit from, profit by; use for a specific purpose; apply to advantage. The ideogram: to divine and center, applying divination to central concerns. **Legions/leading**, SHIH: troops; an organized unit, a metropolis; leader, general, model, master; organize, make functional; take as a model, imitate. The ideogram: heap and whole, organize confusion into functional units. Image of Hexagram 7.

Origin, TZU: source, beginning, ground; cause, reason, motive; line of descent; path to the origin; yourself, intrinsic. **Capital**, YI: populous fortified city, center and symbol of the domain it rules. The ideogram:

enclosure and official seal. **Notify**, KAO: proclaim, order, decree; advise, inform, tell. The ideogram: mouth and ox head, imposing speech. **Fate**, MING: individual destiny; birth and death as limits of life; issue orders with authority; consult the gods. The ideogram: mouth and order, words with heavenly authority.

Trial, CHEN: test by ordeal; inquiry by divination and its result; righteous, firm; separating wheat from chaff; the kernel, the proven core; fourth stage of the Time Cycle. The ideogram: pearl and divination. **Abashment**, LIN: distress, shame, regret, humiliation; aware of having lost the right track; leads to repenting, HUI, correcting the direction of mind and life.

b) **Disarray**, LUAN: throw into disorder, mislay, confuse; out of place; discord, insurrection, anarchy.

OBSTRUCTION ▪ *PI*

This hexagram describes your situation in terms of being blocked or interfered with. It emphasizes that accepting the hindrances that temporarily interrupt the flow of life and thwart communication is the adequate way to handle it. To be in accord with the time, you are told to: accept **obstruction**!

● *Image of the Situation*

> **Obstructing it, in-no-way people.**
> **Not Harvesting: chün tzu, Trial.**
> **The great going, the small coming.**

Associated Contexts **Obstruct**, P'I: closed, stopped; bar the way; obstacle; unfortunate, wicked; refuse, disapprove, deny. The ideogram: mouth and not, blocked communication. **It/them/have(-it)/'s**, CHIH: expresses possession, directly or as an object pronoun. **In-no-way people**, FEI JEN: there are no people, no people are involved; also: worthless people; barbarians, rebels, foreign slaves, captives.

Not, PU: simple negative. **Harvest**, LI: advantageous, profitable; acute, insightful; benefit, nourish; third stage of the Time Cycle. **Chün tzu**: ideal of a person who uses divination to order his/her life in accordance with tao rather than wilful intention; keyword. **Trial**, CHEN: test by ordeal; inquiry by divination and its result; righteous, firm; separating wheat from chaff; the kernel, the proven core; fourth stage of the Time Cycle. The ideogram: pearl and divination.

Great, TA: big, noble, important, very; orient the will toward a self-imposed goal, impose direction; ability to lead or guide your life; contrasts with small, HSIAO, flexible adaptation to what crosses your path; keyword. Image of Hexagrams 14, 26, 28, 34. **Go**, WANG, and **Come**, LAI, describe the stream of time as it flows from future through present to past. Go, WANG, indicates what is departing; proceed, move on; come, LAI, indicates what is approaching; move toward, arrive at; keywords. **Small**, HSIAO, little, common, unimportant; adapting to what crosses your path; ability to move in harmony with the vicissitudes of life;

contrasts with great, TA, self-imposed theme or goal; keyword. Image of Hexagrams 9 and 62.

● *Outer and Inner Aspects*

☰ **Force**: The force of heaven struggles on, persistent and unwearied; heavenly bodies persist in their orbits. **Force** is the center of the yin hemicycle, completing the formative process.

Connection to the outer: struggling forces are bound together in dynamic tension, the Metallic Moment culminating. **Force** brings elements to grips, creating enduring relations.

☷ **Field**: The field of earth yields and sustains, serving in order to produce. **Field** is the equalizing point between yin and yang where things labor and serve.

Connection to the inner: the common labor of sowing and hoarding, the Earthy Moment. **Field** produces concrete results through serving.

An outer struggle blocks bringing-forth; the productivity of the field is **obstructed** and confined within.

● *Counter Indications*

Nuclear trigrams **Ground**, SUN, and **Bound**, KEN, result in Counter Hexagram 53, **Infiltrating**, CHIEN. **Obstructed** communication is contrasted with **infiltrating**'s subtle and continual outward penetration.

● *Sequence*

**Beings not permitted to use completing interpenetrating.
Anterior acquiescence has the use-of Obstruction.**

Associated Contexts **Beings not permitted to use ...** : no one is allowed to make use of; nothing can exist by means of. **Complete**, CHUNG: end of a cycle that begins the next; last, whole, all; contrasts with exhaust, CH'IUNG, final end. The ideogram: silk cocoons, follow and ice, winter linking one year with the next. **Interpenetrate**, T'UNG: mutually penetrate; permeate, flow through, reach everywhere; see clearly, communicate with.

Anterior ... the use-of: activating this hexagram depends on understanding and accepting the previous statement.

- *Contrasted Definitions*

  Obstruction, Pervading: reversing one's sorting indeed.

  Associated Contexts **Pervade**, T'AI: spread and reach everywhere, permeate, diffuse; communicate; extensive, abundant, prosperous; smooth, slippery; extreme, extravagant, prodigal. The ideogram: person in water, connected to the universal medium. Image of Hexagram 11. **Reverse**, FAN: turn and move in the opposite direction; turn around or upside down (180 degrees); change to the opposite position; contrary. **One's/one**, CH'I: third person pronoun; also: it/its, he/his, she/hers, they/theirs. **Sort**, LEI: group according to kind, class with; like nature or purpose; species, class, genus. **Indeed**, YEH: intensifier; indicates comment on previous statement.

- *Symbol Tradition*

  Heaven, earth, not mingling. Obstruction.
  A chün tzu uses parsimonious actualizing-tao to cast-out heaviness.
  [A chün tzu uses] not permitting splendor to use benefits.

  Associated Contexts **Heaven**, T'IEN: highest; sky, firmament, heavens; power above the human as opposed to earth, TI, below; the Symbol of the trigram Force, CH'IEN. The ideogram: great and the one above. **Earth**, TI: ground on which the human world rests; basis of all things, nourishes all things; the Symbol of the trigram Field, K'UN. **Mingle**, CHIAO: blend with, communicate, join, exchange; trade, business; copulation; friendship.
  Use(-of), YI: make use of, by means of, owing to; employ, make functional. **Parsimonious**, CHIEN: thrifty; moderate, temperate; stingy, scanty. **Actualize-tao**, TE: realize tao in action; power, virtue; ability to follow the course traced by the ongoing process of the cosmos; keyword. The ideogram: to go, straight, and heart. Linked with acquire, TE: acquiring that which makes a being become what it is meant to be. **Cast-out**, P'I: expel, repress, exclude, punish; exclusionary laws and their enforcement. The ideogram: punish, authority and mouth, give orders to

expel. **Heavy,** NAN: arduous, grievous, difficult; hardship, distress; harass; contrasts with versatile, I, deal lightly with. The ideogram: domestic bird with clipped tail and drying sticky earth.

Not permitting, PI K'O: not possible; contradicts an inherent principle. The ideogram: mouth and breath, silent consent. **Splendor,** JUNG: glory, elegance, honor, beauty; flowering; elaborate carved corners of a temple roof. **Benefits,** LU: pay, salary, income; have the use of; goods received, revenues; offical recognition.

● *Image Tradition*

> **Obstructing it, in-no-way people. [I]**
> **Not Harvesting: chün tzu, Trial.**
> **The great going, the small coming.**
> **By-consequence-of that Heaven[and]Earth not mingling**
> **and-also the myriad beings not interpenetrating indeed.**
> **Above[and]Below not mingling and-also**
> **Below Heaven without fiefdoms indeed.**
>
> **Inside yin and-also outside yang. [II]**
> **Inside supple and-also outside solid.**
> **Inside Small People and-also outside chün tzu.**
> **Small People: tao long-living.**
> **A chün tzu: tao dissolving indeed.**

Associated Contexts **[I] By-consequence(-of),** TSE: very strong connection; reason, cause, result; rule, law, pattern, standard; therefore. **That,** SHIH: preceding statement. **And-also,** ERH: joins and contrasts two terms. **Myriad,** WAN: countless; many, everyone; lit.: ten thousand. The ideogram: swarm of insects. **Being(s),** WU: creature, thing, any single being; matter, substance, essence; nature of things.

Above[and]Below, SHANG HSIA: realm of dynamic interaction between the upper and the lower; the vertical dimension. **Below Heaven,** T'IEN HSIA: the human world, between heaven and earth. **Without,** WU: devoid of; -less as suffix. **Fiefdom,** PANG: region governed by a feudatory, an order of nobility.

[II] Inside, NEI: within, inner, interior; inside of the house and those who work there, particularly women; the lower trigram, as opposed to outside, WAI, the upper. The ideogram: border and enter, cross a border.

Yin: Struction; consolidating, shadowy aspect of phenomena: conserves, substantializes, creates structures; spacial extension; limited, bound, given specific being; build, make something concrete. **Outside**, WAI: outer, exterior, external; people working in places other than their home; unfamiliar, foreign; the upper trigram, as opposed to inside, NEI, the lower. **Yang:** Action; dynamic and light aspect of phenomena: arouses, transforms, dissolves existing structures; linear thrust; stimulus, drive, focus; direct or orient something.

Supple, JOU: quality of the opened lines; flexible, pliant, tender, adaptable. **Solid**, KANG: quality of the whole lines; firm, strong, unyielding, persisting.

Small People, HSIAO JEN: lowly, common, humble; those who adjust to circumstances with the flexibility of the small; effect of the small within an individual; keyword.

Tao: way or path; ongoing process of being and the course it traces for each specific person or thing; keyword. The ideogram: go and head, leading and the path it creates. **Long-living**, CHANG: enduring, constant; senior, superior, greater; increase, prosper; respect, elevate. **Dissolve**, HSIAO: liquify, melt, thaw; diminish, disperse; eliminate, exhaust. The ideogram: water dissolving differences.

● *Transforming Lines*

Initial six

a) **Eradicating thatch-grass intertwisted.**
Using one's classification.
Trial: significant. Growing.

b) **Eradicating thatch-grass, Trial: significant.**
Purpose located-in a chief indeed.

Associated Contexts a) **Eradicate**, PA: pull up, root out, extirpate; extricate from difficulties; elevate, promote. **Thatch-grass**, MAO: thick grass used for the roofs of humble houses. **Intertwist**, JU: interlaced; entangled roots.

Classification, HUI: class, collection, series; same kind; put or group together.

Significant, CHI: leads to the experience of meaning; favorable, propitious, advantageous, appropriate; keyword. The ideogram: scholar

and mouth, wise words of a sage. **Grow**, HENG: success through a sacrifice; pervade, persevere; bring to full growth; enjoy; vigorous, effective; second stage of the Time Cycle.

b) **Purpose**, CHIH: focus of mind and heart; will, inclination, resolve. The ideogram: heart and scholar, high inner resolve, or heart and go, inner determination. **Locate(-in)**, TSAI: live in, dwell, reside; belong to, involved with, depend on; within. The ideogram: earth and persevere, place on the earth. **Chief**, CHÜN: effective ruler; preside over, take the lead; influence others; term of respect. The ideogram: mouth and director, giving orders.

Six at-second

a) **Enwrapping receiving.**
Small People significant.
Great People Obstructed. Growing.

b) **Great People Obstructed. Growing.**
Not disarraying the flock indeed.

Associated Contexts a) **Enwrap**, PAO: envelop, hold, contain; patient; take on responsibility, engaged. The ideogram: enfold and self, a fetus in the womb. **Receive**, CH'ENG: receive gifts or commands from superiors or customers; take in hand; catch falling water. The ideogram: accepting a seal of office.

Great People, TA JEN: important, noble, influential; those who impose a ruling principle on their lives; effect of the great within an individual; keyword. **Grow**, HENG: success through a sacrifice; pervade, persevere; bring to full growth; enjoy; vigorous, effective; second stage of the Time Cycle.

b) **Disarray**, LUAN: throw into disorder, mislay, confuse; out of place; discord, insurrection, anarchy. **Flock**, CH'ÜN: herd, group; people of same kind, friends, equals; all, entire; move in unison, flock together. The ideogram: chief and sheep, flock around a leader.

Six at-third

a) **Enwrapping embarrassing.**

b) **Enwrapping embarrassing.**
Situation not appropriate indeed.

Associated Contexts a) **Enwrap**, PAO: envelop, hold, contain; patient; take on responsibility, engaged. The ideogram: enfold and self, a fetus in the womb. **Embarrassed**, HSIU: conscious of guilt or fault; unworthy; ashamed, confused; shy, blushing. The ideogram: sheep, sheepish feeling.

b) **Situation**, WEI: place or seat according to rank; post, position, command; right, proper; established, arranged. The ideogram: person and stand, servants in their places. **Appropriate**, TANG: suitable; opportune, convenient; adequate, competent; equal to; whole lines in uneven places and opened lines in even places.

Nine at-fourth

a) **Possessing fate, without fault.**
Cultivating radiant satisfaction.

b) **Possessing fate, without fault.**
Purpose moving indeed.

Associated Contexts a) **Possess**, YU: in possession of, have, own; opposite of lack, WU. **Fate**, MING: individual destiny; birth and death as limits of life; issue orders with authority; consult the gods. The ideogram: mouth and order, words with heavenly authority. **Without fault**, WU CHIU: no error or harm in the situation.

Cultivate, CHOU: till fields or gardens; continue successively, like annual plowing. The ideogram: fields and long life. **Radiance**, LI: glowing light, spreading in all directions; light-giving, discriminating, articulating; divide and arrange in order; the power of consciousness. The ideogram: bird and weird, the magical fire-bird with brilliant plumage. Image of Hexagram 30. **Satisfaction**, CHIH: fulfilment, gratification, happy in realizing your aim; take pleasure in, fulfil a need.

b) **Purpose**, CHIH: focus of mind and heart; will, inclination, resolve. The ideogram: heart and scholar, high inner resolve, or heart and go, inner determination. **Move**, HSING: move or move something; motivate, emotionally moving; walk, act, do. The ideogram: stepping left then right.

Nine at-fifth

a) **Relinquishing Obstruction.**
   Great People significant.
   Its extinction, its extinction.
   Attaching tending-towards bushy mulberry-trees.

b) **Great People's significance.**
   Situation correcting appropriate indeed.

Associated Contexts a) **Relinquish**, HSIU: let go of, stop temporarily, rest; resign, release; act gently, enjoy; relaxed. The ideogram: person leaning on a tree.

Great People, TA JEN: important, noble, influential; those who impose a ruling principle on their lives; effect of the great within an individual; keyword. **Significant**, CHI: leads to the experience of meaning; favorable, propitious, advantageous, appropriate; keyword. The ideogram: scholar and mouth, wise words of a sage.

Its/it, CH'I: third person pronoun; also: one/one's, he/his, she/hers, they/theirs. **Extinguish**, WANG: ruin, destroy; gone, dead, lost without trace; extinct, forgotten, out of mind. The ideogram: person concealed by a wall, out of sight. The doubled character intensifies this quality.

Attach, HSI: fasten to, bind, tie; retain, continue; keep in mind, emotionally attached. **Tend-towards**, YÜ: move toward but not reach, in the direction of; contrasts with reach(-to), HU, actually arriving. **Bushy**, PAO: luxuriant growth, dense thicket; conceal, screen; sleeping-mats; wrap as a gift. The ideogram: wrap and bushes. **Mulberry-tree**, SANG: literal tree and silk production; tranquility; retired, rural place.

b) **'s/have(-it)/it/them**, CHIH: expresses possession, directly or as an object pronoun.

Situation, WEI: place or seat according to rank; post, position, command; right, proper; established, arranged. The ideogram: person and stand, servants in their places. **Correct**, CHENG: rectify deviation or one-sidedness; proper, straight, exact, regular; constant, rule, model. The ideogram: stop and one, hold to one thing. **Appropriate**, TANG: suitable; opportune, convenient; adequate, competent; equal to; whole lines in uneven places and opened lines in even places.

Nine above

a) **Subverting Obstruction.**
Beforehand Obstruction, afterwards rejoicing.

b) **Obstruction completed, by-consequence subverting.**
Wherefore permitting long-living indeed?

Associated Contexts *a)* **Subvert**, CHING: undermine, overturn, overthrow; falling; pour out, empty; waste, squander. The ideogram: man, head and ladle, emptying out old ideas.

Before(hand)/earlier, HSIEN: come before in time; first, at first; formerly, past, previous; begin, go ahead of. **After(wards)/later**, HOU: come after in time, subsequent; put oneself after; the second; attendants, heirs, successors, posterity. **Rejoice(-in)**, HSI: feel and give joy; delight, exult; cheerful, merry. The ideogram: joy (music) and mouth, expressing joy.

b) **Wherefore**, HO: interrogative: why? for what reason? what is? and affirmation: therefore, for that reason. **Permit**, K'O: possible because in harmony with an inherent principle. The ideogram: mouth and breath, silent consent.

CONCORDING PEOPLE ∎
T'UNG JEN

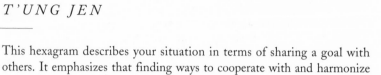

This hexagram describes your situation in terms of sharing a goal with others. It emphasizes that finding ways to cooperate with and harmonize people's efforts is the adequate way to handle it. To be in accord with the time, you are told to: **concord people!**

● *Image of the Situation*

> **Concording People, tending-towards the countryside. Growing.**
> **Harvesting: wading the Great River.**
> **Harvesting: chün tzu, Trial.**

Associated Contexts **Concord**, T'UNG: harmonize, unite, equalize, assemble; agree, share in; together, at once, same time and place. The ideogram: cover and mouth, silent understanding and perfect fit. **People, person**, JEN: humans individually and collectively; an individual; humankind. **Tend-towards**, YÜ: move toward but not reach, in the direction of; contrasts with reach(-to), HU, actually arriving. **Countryside**, YEH: cultivated fields and grassland, where nature and human construction interact; third of the territorial zones: city, suburbs, countryside, forests. **Grow**, HENG: success through a sacrifice; pervade, persevere; bring to full growth; enjoy; vigorous, effective; second stage of the Time Cycle.

Harvest, LI: advantageous, profitable; acute, insightful; benefit, nourish; third stage of the Time Cycle. **Wading the Great River**, SHE TA CH'UAN: consciously moving into the flow of time; enter the stream of life with a goal or purpose; embark on a significant enterprise.

Chün tzu: ideal of a person who uses divination to order his/her life in accordance with tao rather than wilful intention; keyword. **Trial**, CHEN: test by ordeal; inquiry by divination and its result; righteous, firm; separating wheat from chaff; the kernel, the proven core; fourth stage of the Time Cycle. The ideogram: pearl and divination.

● *Outer and Inner Aspects*

☰ **Force**: The force of heaven struggles on, persistent and unwearied; heavenly bodies persist in their orbits. **Force** is the center of the yin hemicycle, completing the formative process.

Connection to the outer: struggling forces are bound together in dynamic tension, the Metallic Moment culminating. **Force** brings elements to grips, creating enduring relations.

☲ **Radiance**: Fire and brightness radiate light and warmth, attached to their support; congregating people see and become aware. **Radiance** ends the yang hemicycle, consuming action in awareness.

Connection to the inner: light, heat, consciousness bring about continual change, the Fiery Moment. **Radiance** spreads outward, congregating, becoming aware and changing.

Warmth and brightness radiate outward through **people**'s enduring struggle to find ways to **concord**.

● *Counter Indications*

Nuclear trigrams **Force**, CH'IEN, and **Ground**, SUN, result in Counter Hexagram 44, **Coupling**, KOU. **Concording people**'s conscious attempt to create enduring forms of union is contrasted with spontaneous **coupling**.

● *Sequence*

> **Beings not permitted to use completing Obstruction.**
> **Anterior acquiescence has the use-of Concording People.**

Associated Contexts **Beings not permitted to use ...** : no one is allowed to make use of; nothing can exist by means of. **Complete,** CHUNG: end of a cycle that begins the next; last, whole, all; contrasts with exhaust, CH'IUNG: final end. The ideogram: silk cocoons, follow and ice, winter linking one year with the next. **Obstruct,** P'I: closed, stopped; bar the way; obstacle; unfortunate, wicked; refuse, disapprove, deny. The ideogram: mouth and not, blocked communication. Image of Hexagram 12.

Anterior ... the use-of: activating this hexagram depends on understanding and accepting the previous statement.

Contrasted Definitions

Great Possessing: crowds indeed.
Concording People: connecting indeed.

Associated Contexts **Great**, TA: big, noble, important, very; orient the will toward a self-imposed goal, impose direction; ability to lead or guide your life; contrasts with small, HSIAO, flexible adaptation to what crosses your path; keyword. Image of Hexagrams 14, 26, 28, 34. **Possess**, YU: in possession of, have, own; opposite of lack, WU. **Great Possessing** is the Image of Hexagram 14. **Crowds**, CHUNG: many people, large group; majority; in common. **Indeed**, YEH: intensifier; indicates comment on previous statement.

Connect, CH'IN: attach to, approach, come near; cherish, help, favor; intimate; relatives, kin.

Symbol Tradition

Heaven associating-with fire. Concording People.
A chün tzu uses sorting the clans to mark-off the beings.

Associated Contexts **Heaven**, T'IEN: highest; sky, firmament, heavens; power above the human as opposed to earth, TI, below; the Symbol of the trigram Force, CH'IEN. The ideogram: great and the one above. **Associate(-with)**, YÜ: consort with, combine; companions; group, band, company; agree with, comply, help. The ideogram: pair of hands reaching downward meets a pair of hands reaching upward, helpful association. **Fire**, HUO: warming and consuming aspect of burning; fire and brightness are the Symbols of Radiance, LI.

Use(-of), YI: make use of, by means of, owing to; employ, make functional. **Sort**, LEI: group according to kind, class with; like nature or purpose; species, class, genus. **Clan**, TSU: extended family with same ancester and surname; kin, relatives; tribe, class, kind. The ideogram: flag and spear, a rallying point. **Mark-off**, PIEN: distinguish by dividing; mark off a plot of land; frame which divides a bed from its stand; discuss and dispute. The ideogram: knife and acrid, biting division.

Being(s), WU: creature, thing, any single being; matter, substance, essence; nature of things.

● *Image Tradition*

> Concording People. [I]
> Supple acquiring the situation.
> Acquiring centering and-also corresponding reaching-to Force.
> Spoken-thus: Concording People.
>
> Concording People: spoken-thus. [II]
> Concording People, tending-towards the countryside. Growing.
> Harvesting: wading the Great River.
> Force moving indeed.
>
> Pattern brightening uses persisting. [III]
> Centering correcting and-also corresponding.
> A chün tzu, correcting indeed.
> Verily a chün tzu activating enables
>   interpenetrating Below Heaven's purpose.

Associated Contexts **[I] Supple**, JOU: quality of the opened lines; flexible, pliant, tender, adaptable. **Acquire**, TE: obtain the desired object; wish for, desire covetously; gains, possessions. The ideogram: go and obstacle, going through obstacles to the goal. **Situation**, WEI: place or seat according to rank; post, position, command; right, proper; established, arranged. The ideogram: person and stand, servants in their places.

    Center, CHUNG: inner, central; put in the center; middle, stable point enabling you to face inner and outer changes; middle line of trigram. The ideogram: field divided in two equal parts. Image of Hexagram 61. **And-also**, ERH: joins and contrasts two terms. **Correspond(-to)**, YING: be in agreement or harmony; resonate together, invoke and fulfill each other; answer to, suitable; relation between the lines (1:4, 2:5, 3:6) when they form the pair opened and whole, supple and solid. The ideogram: heart and obey. **Reach(-to)**, HU: arrive at a goal; reach towards and achieve; connect; contrasts with tend-towards, YU. **Force**, CH'IEN: spirit power, creative and destructive; unceasing forward motion; dynamic, enduring, untiring; firm, stable; heaven, sovereign, father; also: dry up, parched,

exhausted, cleared away. The ideogram: sprouts or vapors rising from the ground and sunlight, both fecundating moisture and scorching drought. Image of Hexagram 1.

Spoken-thus, YÜEH: designated, termed, called. The ideogram: open mouth and tongue.

[II] Move, HSING: move or move something; motivate, emotionally moving; walk, act, do. The ideogram: stepping left then right.

[III] Pattern, WEN: intrinsic or natural design and its beauty; stylish, elegant; noble; contrasts with composition, CHANG, a conscious creation. **Brightness**, MING: light-giving aspect of burning, heavenly bodies and consciousness; with fire, the Symbol of the trigram Radiance, LI. **Persist**, CHIEN: strong, robust, dynamic, tenacious; continuous; unwearied heavenly bodies in their orbits; the Action of the trigram Force, CH'IEN.

Centering correcting, CHUNG CHENG: central and correct; make rectifying one-sidedness and error your central concern; reaching a stable center in yourself can correct the situation.

Verily, WEI: the epitome of; in truth, the only; very important. **Activate**, WEI: act or cause to act; do, make, manage; make active; attend to, help; because of. **Able**, NENG: enable; ability, power, skill, art; competent, talented; duty, function, capacity. The ideogram: an animal with strong hooves and bones, able to carry and defend. **Interpenetrate**, T'UNG: mutually penetrate; permeate, flow through, reach everywhere; see clearly, communicate with. **Below Heaven**, T'IEN HSIA: the human world, between heaven and earth. **'s/have(-it)/it/them**, CHIH: expresses possession, directly or as an object pronoun. **Purpose**, CHIH: focus of mind and heart; will, inclination, resolve. The ideogram: heart and scholar, high inner resolve, or heart and go, inner determination.

- *Transforming Lines*

    Initial nine

    a) **Concording People tending-towards the gate.**
    Without fault.

    b) **Issuing-forth-from the gate Concording People.**
    Furthermore whose fault indeed?

Associated Contexts a) **Gate**, MEN: outer door, between court-yard and street; a text or master as gate to a school of thought.

Without fault, WU CHIU: no error or harm in the situation.

b) **Issue-forth(-from)**, CH'U: emerge from, come out of, proceed from, spring from; the Action of the trigram Shake, CHEN; contrary of enter, JU. The ideogram: stem with branches and leaves emerging.

Furthermore, YU: in addition to; higher degree of. **Whose**, SHUI: relative and interrogative pronoun; also: whose? **Fault**, CHIU: unworthy conduct that leads to harm, illness, misfortune. The ideogram: person and differ, differ from what you should be.

Six at-second

a) **Concording People tending-towards ancestry.**
   Abashment.

b) **Concording People tending-towards ancestry.**
   Abashment: tao indeed.

Associated Contexts a) **Ancestry**, TSUNG: clan, kin, origin; those who bear the same surname; ancestral hall and tablets; honor, revere; a doctrine; contrasts with predecessor, K'AO: individual ancestors.

Abashment, LIN: distress, shame, regret, humiliation; aware of having lost the right track; leads to repenting, HUI, correcting the direction of mind and life.

b) **Tao**: way or path; ongoing process of being and the course it traces for each specific person or thing; keyword. The ideogram: go and head, leading and the path it creates.

Nine at-third

a) **Hiding-away arms, tending-towards the thickets.**
   Ascending one's high mound.
   Three year's-time not rising.

b) **Hiding-away arms, tending-towards the thickets.**
   Antagonistic solid indeed.
   Three year's-time not rising.
   Quieting movement indeed.

Associated Contexts a) **Hide-away**, FU: conceal, place in ambush; secretly, silently; prostrate, fall on your face; humble. The ideogram: man and dog, man crouching. **Arms**, JUNG: weapons; armed people, soldiers; military, violent. The ideogram: spear and armor, offensive and defensive weapons. **Thicket**, MANG: underbrush, tangled vegetation, thick grass, jungle; rustic, rude, socially inept.

Ascend, SHENG: go up; climb step by step; rise in office; advance through effort; accumulate; bring out and fulfill; lit.: a measure for fermented liquor, ascension as distillation. Image of Hexagram 46. **One's/one**, CH'I: third person pronoun; also: it/its, he/his, she/hers, they/theirs. **High(-ness)**, KAO: high, elevated, lofty, eminent; excellent, advanced. **Mound**, LING: grave-mound, barrow; small hill.

Three, SAN: number three, third time or place; active phases of a cycle; superlative; beginning of repetition. **Year's-time**, SUI: actual length of time in a year; contrasts with years-revolved, NIEN, number of years elapsed. **Not**, PU: simple negative. **Rise**, HSING: get up, grow, lift; begin, give rise to, construct; be promoted; flourishing, fashionable. The ideogram: lift, two hands and unite, lift with both hands.

b) **Antagonistic**, TI: opposed and equal; competitor, enemy; a contest between equals. **Solid**, KANG: quality of the whole lines; firm, strong, unyielding, persisting.

Quiet, AN: peaceful, still, settled; calm, tranquilize. The ideogram: woman under a roof, a tranquil home.

Nine at-fourth

a) **Riding one's rampart.**
Nothing controlling attacking.
Significant.

b) **Riding one's rampart.**
Righteously nothing controlling indeed.
One's significance.
By-consequence confining and-also
       reversing by-consequence indeed.

Associated Contexts a) **Ride**, CH'ENG: ride an animal or a chariot; have the upper hand, seize the right time; control strong power; overcome the nature of the other; supple opened line above a solid whole line. **One's/one**, CH'I: third person pronoun; also: it/its, he/his, she/hers, they/theirs. **Rampart**, YUNG: defensive wall; bulwark, redoubt.

Nothing/nowhere, FU: strong negative; not a single thing/place. **Control**, K'O: command; check, impede, prevail, obstruct, repress; adequate, able. The ideogram: roof beams support a house, controlling the structure. **Attack**, KUNG: fight with; aggression; go to work, apply to; rouse by criticizing, put in order; stimulate vital power; urgent desire. The ideogram: toil and strike.

Significant, CHI: leads to the experience of meaning; favorable, propitious, advantageous, appropriate; keyword. The ideogram: scholar and mouth, wise words of a sage.

b) **Righteous**, YI: proper and just, meets the standards; things in their proper place; the heart that rules itself; upright, moral rule; contrasts with Harvest, LI, advantage or profit.

By-consequence(-of), TSE: very strong connection; reason, cause, result; rule, law, pattern, standard; therefore. **Confine**, K'UN: enclose, restrict, limit; oppressed; impoverish, distress; afflicted, exhausted, disheartened, weary. The ideogram: an enclosed tree. Image of Hexagram 47. **Reverse**, FAN: turn and move in the opposite direction; turn around or upside down (180 degrees); change to the opposite position; contrary.

Nine at-fifth

a) Concording People beforehand crying-out sobbing
                                        and-also afterwards laughing.
  Great legions controlling mutual meeting.

b) Beforehand Concording People have-it.
  Using centering straightening indeed.
  Great legions controlling mutual meeting.
  Words mutualize controlling indeed.

Associated Contexts a) **Before(hand)/earlier**, HSIEN: come before in time; first, at first; formerly, past, previous; begin, go ahead of. **Cry-out/outcry**, HAO: call out, proclaim; signal, order, command; mark, label, sign. **Sob**, T'AO: cry, weep aloud; wailing children. The ideogram: mouth and omen, ominous sounds. **After(wards)/later**, HOU: come after in time, subsequent; put oneself after; the second; attendant, heirs, successors, posterity. **Laugh**, HSIAO: manifest joy or mirth; giggle, laugh at, ridicule; pleased, merry; associated with the Fiery Moment.

Legions/leading, SHIH: troops; an organized unit, a metropolis; leader, general, model, master; organize, make functional; take as a model,

imitate. The ideogram: heap and whole, organize confusion into functional units. Image of Hexagram 7. **Control**, K'O: command; check, impede, prevail, obstruct, repress; adequate, able. The ideogram: roof beams support a house, controlling the structure. **Mutual**, HSIANG: reciprocal assistance, encourage, help; bring together, blend with; examine, inspect; by turns. **Meet**, YÜ: come on unexpectedly, encounter; occur, happen; pleasant meeting, lucky coincidence; agree.

b) **Have(-it)/it/them/'s**, CHIH: expresses possession, directly or as an object pronoun.

Straighten, CHIH: correct the crooked, reform, repay injustice; proceed directly; sincere, upright, just; blunt, outspoken.

Word, YEN: speech, spoken words, sayings; talk, discuss, address. The ideogram: mouth and rising vapor, words as speech.

Nine above

a) Concording People tending-towards the suburbs.
   Without repenting.

b) Concording People tending-towards the suburbs.
   Purpose not-yet acquired indeed.

Associated Contexts a) **Suburbs**, CHIAO: area adjoining a city where human constructions and nature interpenetrate; second of the territorial zones: city, suburbs, countryside, forests. **Without repenting**, WU HUI: devoid of the sort of trouble that leads to sorrow, regret and the necessity to change your attitude.

b) **Not-yet**, WEI: temporal negative; something will but has not yet occurred; contrary of already, CHI. Image of Hexagram 64.

14

GREAT POSSESSING ▮ *TA YU*

This hexagram describes your situation in terms of your relation to an overriding concern or central idea. It emphasizes that organizing all your efforts around this idea is the adequate way to handle it. To be in accord with the time, you are told to: **possess** the **great**!

● *Image of the Situation*

Great Possessing, Spring Growing.

Associated Contexts **Great**, TA: big, noble, important, very; orient the will toward a self-imposed goal, impose direction; ability to lead or guide your life; contrasts to small, HSIAO: flexible adaptation to what crosses your path; keyword. **Possess**, YU: be in possession of, have, own; possessions; opposite of lack, WU. **Spring**, YÜAN: source, origin, head; great, excellent; arise, begin, generating power; first stage of the Time Cycle. **Grow**, HENG: success through a sacrifice; pervade, persevere; bring to full growth; enjoy; vigorous, effective; second stage of the Time Cycle.

● *Outer and Inner Aspects*

☲ **Radiance**: Fire and brightness radiate light and warmth, attached to their support; congregating people see and become aware. **Radiance** ends the yang hemicycle, consuming action in awareness.
　Connection to the outer: light, heat, consciousness bring continual change, the Fiery Moment. **Radiance** spreads outward, congregating, becoming aware and changing.

☰ **Force**: The force of heaven struggles on, persistent and unwearied; heavenly bodies persist in their orbits. **Force** is the center of the yin hemicycle, completing the formative process.
　Connection to the inner: struggling forces are bound together in dynamic tension, the Metallic Moment culminating. **Force** brings elements to grips, creating enduring relations.

Great force within **possesses** and spreads brightness and warmth, congregating with people and being seen. This is a time of abundance.

- *Counter Indications*

Nuclear trigrams **Open**, TUI, and **Force**, CH'IEN, result in Counter Hexagram 43, **Parting**, KUAI. Being **possessed** by a single **great** idea is contrasted with **parting** energy into diverging streams.

- *Sequence*

Associating-with People Concording implies
> beings necessarily converting in-truth.

Anterior acquiescence has the use-of Great Possessing.

Associated Contexts **Associate(-with)**, YÜ: consort with, combine; companions; group, band, company; agree with, comply, help. The ideogram: pair of hands reaching downward meets a pair of hands reaching upward, helpful association. **People, person**, JEN: humans individually and collectively; an individual; humankind. **Concord**, T'UNG: harmonize, unite, equalize, assemble; agree, share in; together, at once, same time and place. The ideogram: cover and mouth, silent understanding and perfect fit. **Concording People** is the Image of Hexagram 13. **Imply**, CHE: further signify; additional meaning. **Being(s)**, WU: creature, thing, any single being; matter, substance, essence; nature of things. **Necessarily**, PI: unavoidably, indispensably, certainly. **Convert**, KUEI: change to another form, persuade; return to yourself or the place where you belong; restore, revert, become loyal; turn into; give a young girl in marriage. The ideogram: arrive and wife, become mistress of a household. Image of Hexagram 54. **In-truth**, YEN: statement is complete and correct.

Anterior ... the use-of: activating this hexagram depends on understanding and accepting the previous statement.

- *Contrasted Definitions*

Great Possessing: crowds indeed.
Concording People: connecting indeed.

Associated Contexts **Crowds**, CHUNG: many people, large group; majority; in common. **Indeed**, YEH: intensifier; indicates comment on previous statement.

Connect, CH'IN: attach to, approach, come near; cherish, help, favor; intimate; relatives, kin.

● *Symbol Tradition*

> **Fire located above heaven. Great Possessing.**
> **A chün tzu uses terminating hate to display improvement.**
> **[A chün tzu uses] yielding-to heaven to relinquish fate.**

Associated Contexts **Fire**, HUO: warming and consuming aspect of burning; fire and brightness are the Symbols of the trigram Radiance, LI. **Locate(-in)**, TSAI: live in, dwell, reside; belong to, involved with, depend on; within. The ideogram: earth and persevere, place on the earth. **Above**, SHANG: anything above, in all senses; higher, upper, outer; upper trigram; opposite of below, HSIA. **Heaven**, T'IEN: highest; sky, firmament, heavens; power above the human as opposed to earth, TI, below; the Symbol of the trigram Force, CH'IEN. The ideogram: great and the one above.

Chün tzu: ideal of a person who uses divination to order his/her life in accordance with tao rather than wilful intention; keyword. **Use(-of)**, YI: make use of, by means of, owing to; employ, make functional. **Terminate**, O: cut off, check, extinguish, bring to a standstill. The ideogram: go and why, no reason to move. **Hate**, WU: dislike, dread; averse to, ashamed of; repulsive, vicious, vile, ugly, wicked. The ideogram: twisted bowels and heart, heart entangled in emotion. **Display**, YANG: spread, extend, scatter, divulge; publish abroad, make famous. The ideogram: hand and expand, spreading a message. **Improve**, SHAN: make better, reform, perfect, repair; virtuous, wise; mild, docile; clever, skillful, handy. The ideogram: mouth and sheep, gentle speech.

Yield(-to), SHUN: give way and bear produce; comply, agree, follow, obey; unresisting, docile, flexible; nourish, provide; the Action of the trigram Field, K'UN. The ideogram: head and current, water flowing from the head of a river, yielding to the banks. **Relinquish**, HSIU: let go of, stop temporarily, rest; resign, release; act gently, enjoy; relaxed. The ideogram: person leaning on a tree. **Fate**, MING: individual destiny; birth and death as limits of life; issue orders with authority; consult the gods. The ideogram: mouth and order, words with heavenly authority.

• *Image Tradition*

> **Great Possessing. [I]**
> **Supple acquiring the dignifying situation, the great centering.**
> **And-also Above[and]Below corresponding-to it.**
> **Spoken-thus: Great Possessing.**
>
> **One's actualizing-tao: solid persisting and-also**
> **pattern brightening. [II]**
> **Corresponding reaching-to heaven and-also the season moving.**
> **That uses Spring Growing.**

Associated Contexts **[I] Supple**, JOU: quality of the opened lines; flexible, pliant, tender, adaptable. **Acquire**, TE: obtain the desired object; wish for, desire covetously; gains, possessions. The ideogram: go and obstacle, going through obstacles to the goal. **Dignify**, TSUN: honor, make eminent; noble, respected. The ideogram: presenting wine to a guest. **Situation**, WEI: place or seat according to rank; post, position, command; right, proper; established, arranged. The ideogram: person and stand, servants in their places. **Center**, CHUNG: inner, central; put in the center; middle, stable point enabling you to face inner and outer changes; middle line of trigram. The ideogram: field divided in two equal parts. Image of Hexagram 61.

    And-also, ERH: joins and contrasts two terms. **Above[and]Below**, SHANG HSIA: realm of dynamic interaction between the upper and the lower; the vertical dimension. **Correspond(-to)**, YING: be in agreement or harmony; resonate together, invoke and fulfill each other; answer to, suitable; relation between the lines (1:4, 2:5, 3:6) when they form the pair opened and whole, supple and solid. The ideogram: heart and obey. **It/them/have(-it)/'s**, CHIH: expresses possession, directly or as an object pronoun.

    Spoken-thus, YÜEH: designated, termed, called. The ideogram: open mouth and tongue.

[II] One's/one, CH'I: third person pronoun; also: it/its, he/his, she/hers, they/theirs. **Actualize-tao**, TE: realize tao in action; power, virtue; ability to follow the course traced by the ongoing process of the cosmos; keyword. The ideogram: to go, straight, and heart. Linked with acquire, TE: acquiring that which makes a being become what it is meant to be. **Solid**, KANG: quality of the whole lines; firm, strong, unyielding, persisting. **Persist**, CHIEN: strong, robust, dynamic, tenacious; continuous; unwearied heavenly bodies in their orbits; the Action of the trigram Force, CH'IEN: **Pattern**, WEN: intrinsic or natural design and its beauty; stylish, elegant; noble; contrasts with composition, CHANG, a conscious creation. **Brightness**, MING: lightgiving aspect of burning, heavenly bodies and consciousness; with fire, the Symbol of the trigram Radiance, LI.

Reach(-to), HU: arrive at a goal; reach toward and achieve; connect; contrasts with tend-towards, YU. **Season**, SHIH: quality of the time; the right time, opportune, in harmony; planning in accord with the time; seasons of the year. The ideogram: sun and temple, time as sacred. **Move**, HSING: move or move something; motivate, emotionally moving; walk, act, do. The ideogram: stepping left then right.

That uses, SHIH YI: involves and is involved by.

- *Transforming Lines*

Initial nine

a) **Without mingling harm.**
In-no-way faulty.
Drudgery by-consequence without fault.

b) **Great Possessing, the initial nine.**
Without mingling harm indeed.

Associated Contexts *a)* **Without**, WU: devoid of; -less as suffix. **Mingle**, CHIAO: blend with, communicate, join, exchange; trade, business; copulation; friendship. **Harm**, HAI: damage, injure, offend; suffer; hurtful, hindrance; fearful, anxious.

In-no-way, FEI: strong negative; not so. The ideogram: a box filled with opposition. **Fault**, CHIU: unworthy conduct that leads to harm, illness, misfortune. The ideogram: person and differ, differ from what you should be.

Drudgery, CHIEN: difficult, hard, repetitive work; hard to cultivate; distressing, sorrowful. The ideogram: sticky earth and a person looking around, hard work in comparison to others. **By-consequence(-of)**, TSE: very strong connection; reason, cause, result; rule, law, pattern, standard; therefore. **Without fault**, WU CHIU: no error or harm in the situation.

Nine at-second

a) The great chariot used to carry.
Possessing directed going. Without fault.

b) The great chariot used to carry.
Amassing centering, not destroying indeed.

Associated Contexts a) **Chariot**, CH'E: wheeled travelling vehicle; contrasts with cart, YÜ, which carries. **Carry**, TSAI: bear, carry with you; contain, sustain; load a ship or cart, cargo; fill in, complete.

Possessing directed going, YU YU WANG: imposing a direction on the flow of time from present to past; have a specific goal or purpose. **Without fault**, WU CHIU: no error or harm in the situation.

b) **Amass**, CHI: hoard, accumulate, pile up, store up, add up, increase. **Not**, PU: simple negative. **Destroy**, PAI: ruin, defeat, violate, subvert, break.

Nine at-third

a) A prince availing-of Growing,
tending-towards heavenly sonhood.
Small People nowhere controlling.

b) A prince availing-of Growing,
tending-towards heavenly sonhood.
Small People harmful indeed.

Associated Contexts a) **Prince**, KUNG: nobles acting as ministers of state in the capital; governing from the center rather than active in daily life; contrasts with feudatory, HOU, governors of the provinces. **Avail-of**, YUNG: take advantage of; benefit from, profit by; use for a specific purpose; apply to advantage. The ideogram: to divine and center, applying divination to central concerns. **Tend-towards**, YÜ: move toward but not reach, in the direction of; contrasts with reach(-to), HU, actually arriving. **Son(hood)**, TZU: living up to ideal of ancestors as highest human development; act with concern and reverence; male child; offspring, posterity; seed, kernel, egg; sage, teacher; nadir, deepest point, midnight, mid-winter.

Small People, HSIAO JEN: lowly, common, humble; those who adjust to circumstances with the flexibility of the small; effect of the small within an individual; keyword. **Nothing/nowhere**, FU: strong negative; not a single thing/place. **Control**, K'O: command; check, impede, prevail, obstruct, repress; adequate, able. The ideogram: roof beams support a house, controlling the structure.

b) **Harm**, HAI: damage, injure, offend; suffer; hurtful, hindrance; fearful, anxious.

Nine at-fourth

a) **In-no-way one's preponderance.**
Without fault.

b) **In-no-way one's preponderance. Without fault.**
Brightness differentiating clearly indeed.

Associated Contexts a) **In-no-way**, FEI: strong negative; not so. The ideogram: a box filled with opposition. **Preponderance**, P'ENG: forceful, dominant; overbearing, encroaching. The ideogram: drum beats, dominating sound.
Without fault, WU CHIU: no error or harm in the situation.

b) **Differentiate**, PIEN: argue, dispute, criticize; sophisticated, artful. The ideogram: words and sharp or pungent. **Clearly**, CHE: make clear, illuminate; shine, emit light; starlight.

Six at-fifth

a) **Your conforming: mingling thus, impressing thus. Significant.**

b) **Your conforming, mingling thus.**
Trustworthiness uses shooting-forth purpose indeed.
Impressing thus, having significance.
Versatility and-also without preparing indeed.

Associated Contexts a) **Your**, CHÜEH: intensifying personal pronoun, specifically you! your!; intensify, concentrate, tense, contract; lit.: muscle spasms. **Conforming**, FU: accord between inner and outer in a particular moment; sincere, truthful, verified, reliable, in accord with the spirits; capture; prisoners, spoils; contrasts with trustworthy, HSIN,

consistent over time. The ideogram: bird's claw enclosing young animals, possessive grip. Image of Hexagram 61. **Mingle**, CHIAO: blend with, communicate, join, exchange; trade, business; copulation; friendship. **Thus**, JU: as, in this way. **Impress**, WEI: impose on, intimidate; august, solemn; pomp, majesty. **Significant**, CHI: leads to the experience of meaning; favorable, propitious, advantageous, appropriate; keyword. The ideogram: scholar and mouth, wise words of a sage.

b) **Trustworthy**, HSIN: truthful, faithful, consistent over time; integrity; confide in, follow; credentials; contrasts with conforming, FU, connection in a specific moment. The ideogram: person and word, true speech. **Shoot-forth**, FA: expand, send out; shoot an arrow; ferment, rise; be displayed. The ideogram: stance, bow and arrow, shooting from a solid base. **Purpose**, CHIH: focus of mind and heart; will, inclination, resolve. The ideogram: heart and scholar, high inner resolve, or heart and go, inner determination.

   Versatility, I: sudden and unpredictable change; mental mobility and openness; easy and light, not difficult and heavy; occurs in name of the I CHING. **Without**, WU: devoid of; -less as suffix. **Prepare**, PEI: make ready, provide for; sufficient.

   Nine above

   a) **Originating-from heaven shielding it.**
   Significant, without not Harvesting.

   b) **Great Possessing the above: significant.**
   Originating-from heaven shielding indeed.

Associated Contexts a) **Origin**, TZU: source, beginning, ground; cause, reason, motive; line of descent; path to the origin; yourself, intrinsic. **Shield**, YU: protect; defended by spirits; heavenly kindness and protection. The ideogram: numinous and right hand, spirit power.

   Significant, CHI: leads to the experience of meaning; favorable, propitious, advantageous, appropriate; keyword. The ideogram: scholar and mouth, wise words of a sage. **Without not Harvesting**, WU PU LI: nothing for which this will not be beneficial; advantageous potential, borderline where the balance is swinging from not Harvesting to actually Harvesting.

HUMBLING ▪ *CH'IEN*

This hexagram describes your situation in terms of the necessity to cut through pride and complication. It emphasizes that keeping close to fundamental things through keeping your words unpretentious is the adequate way to handle it. To be in accord with the time, you are told to: be **humble**!

• *Image of the Situation*

> **Humbling, Growing.**
> **A chün tzu possesses completing.**

Associated Contexts **Humble**, CH'IEN: think and speak of yourself in a modest way; respectful, unassuming, retiring, unobtrusive; yielding, compliant, reverent, lowly. The ideogram: words and unite, keeping words close to underlying facts. **Grow**, HENG: success through a sacrifice; pervade, persevere; bring to full growth; enjoy; vigorous, effective; second stage of the Time Cycle.

  Chün tzu: ideal of a person who uses divination to order his/her life in accordance with tao rather than wilful intention; keyword. **Possess**, YU: in possession of, have, own; opposite of lack, WU. **Complete**, CHUNG: end of a cycle that begins the next; last, whole, all; contrasts with exhaust, CH'IUNG, final end. The ideogram: silk cocoons, follow and ice, winter linking one year with the next.

• *Outer and Inner Aspects*

⚏ **Field**: The field of earth yields and sustains, serving in order to produce. **Field** is the equalizing point between yin and yang where things labor and serve.

  Connection to the outer: the common labor of sowing and hoarding, the Earthy Moment. **Field** produces concrete results through serving.

⚏ **Bound**: Mountains bound, limit and set a place off, stopping forward movement. **Bound** completes a full yin-yang cycle.

Connection to the inner: accomplishing words, which express things. **Bound** articulates what is complete to suggest what is beginning.

Articulating inner limits sustains **humble** service on the wide field of earth. These trigrams form the Pivot of Equalization, where yin and yang come into creative balance.

Counter Indications

Nuclear trigrams **Shake**, CHEN, and **Gorge**, K'AN, result in Counter Hexagram 40, **Taking-apart**, HSIEH. Keeping words and actions together through **humbling** is contrasted with **taking** them **apart** to analyse their motivation.

Sequence

Possessing the Great implies not permitting using overfilling.
Anterior acquiescence has the use-of Humbling.

Associated Contexts **Great**, TA: big, noble, important, very; orient the will toward a self-imposed goal, impose direction; ability to lead or guide your life; contrasts with small, HSIAO, flexible adaptation to what crosses your path; keyword. **Great Possessing** is the Image of Hexagram 14. **Imply**, CHE: further signify; additional meaning. **Not permitting**, PU K'O: not possible; contradicts an inherent principle. The ideogram: mouth and breath, silent consent. **Use(-of)**, YI: make use of, by means of, owing to; employ, make functional. **Overfill**, YING: at the point of overflowing; more than wanted, stretch beyond; replenished, full; arrogant. The ideogram: vessel and too much.

    Anterior ... the use-of: activating this hexagram depends on understanding and accepting the previous statement.

Contrasted Definitions

Humbling: levity indeed.
Provision: indolence indeed.

Associated Contexts **Levity**, CH'ING: frivolous, think lightly of, unimportant; alert, agile; gentle. The ideogram: cart and stream, empty cart floating downstream. **Indeed**, YEH: intensifier; indicates comment on previous statement.

Provide-for/provision, YÜ: ready, prepared for; pre-arrange, take precaution, think beforehand; satisfied, contented, at ease. The ideogram: sonhood and elephant, careful, reverent and very strong. Image of Hexagram 16. **Indolence**, TAI: idle, inattentive, careless; self-indulgent; disdainful, contemptuous.

● *Attached Evidences*

> **Humbling: actualizing-tao's handle indeed.**
> **Humbling: dignifying and-also shining.**
> **Humbling: using paring the codes.**

Associated Contexts **Actualize-tao**, TE: realize tao in action; power, virtue; ability to follow the course traced by the ongoing process of the cosmos; keyword. The ideogram: to go, straight, and heart. Linked with acquire, TE: acquiring that which makes a being become what it is meant to be. **'s/have(-it)/it/them**, CHIH: expresses possession, directly or as an object pronoun. **Handle**, PING: haft; control of, power to.

Dignify, TSUN: honor, make eminent; noble, respected. The ideogram: presenting wine to a guest. **And-also**, ERH: joins and contrasts two terms. **Shine**, KUANG: illuminate; give off brilliant, bright light; honor, glory, éclat; result of action, contrasts with brightness, MING: light of heavenly bodies. The ideogram: fire above person, lifting the light.

Pare, CHIH: cut away; form, tailor, carve; invent; limit, prevent. The ideogram: knife and incomplete. **Codes**, LI: rites, rules, ritual; usage, manners; worship, ceremony, observance. The ideogram: worship and sacrificial vase, handling a sacred vessel.

● *Symbol Tradition*

> **Earth center possessing mountain. Humbling.**
> **A chün tzu uses reducing the numerous to augment the few.**
> **[A chün tzu uses] evaluating beings to even spreading-out.**

Associated Contexts **Earth**, TI: ground on which the human world rests; basis of all things, nourishes all things; the Symbol of the trigram Field, K'UN. **Center**, CHUNG: inner, central; put in the center; middle, stable point enabling you to face inner and outer changes; middle line of trigram. The ideogram: field divided in two equal parts. Image of Hexagram 61. **Mountain**, SHAN: limit, boundary; the Symbol of the trigram Bound, KEN. The ideogram: three peaks, a mountain range.

Reduce, P'OU: diminish in number; collect in fewer, larger groups. **Numerous**, TO: great number, many; often. **Augment**, YI: increase, advance, promote, benefit, strengthen; pour in more; full, superabundant; restorative. The ideogram: water and vessel, pouring in more. Image of Hexagram 42. **Few**, KUA: small number; seldom, rarely; unusual, solitary.

Evaluate, CH'ENG: assess, appraise; weigh, estimate, reckon; designate, name. The ideogram: weigh and grain, attributing value. **Being(s)**, WU: creature, thing, any single being; matter, substance, essence; nature of things. **Even**, P'ING: level, make even or equal; uniform, peaceful, tranquil; restore quiet, harmonize. **Spread-out**, SHIH: expand, diffuse, distribute, arrange, exhibit; add to, aid. The ideogram: flag and indeed, claiming new country.

● *Image Tradition*

> **Humbling, Growing. [I]**
> **Heavenly tao fording below and-also shining brightness.**
> **Earthly tao lowly and-also moving above.**
>
> **Heavenly tao lessening overfilling**
> **   and-also augmenting Humbling. [II]**
> **Earthly tao transforming overfilling and-also diffusing Humbling.**
>
> **Souls[and]Spirits harming overfilling**
> **   and-also blessing Humbling. [III]**
> **People tao hating overfilling and-also loving Humbling.**
>
> **Humbling dignifying and-also shining. [IV]**
> **Lowliness and-also not permitting passing-beyond.**
> **A chün tzu's completing indeed.**

Associated Contexts **[I] Heaven**, T'IEN highest; sky, firmament, heavens; power above the human as opposed to earth, TI, below; the Symbol of the trigram Force, CH'IEN. The ideogram: great and the one above. **Tao**: way or path; ongoing process of being and the course it traces for each specific person or thing; keyword. The ideogram: go and head, leading and the path it creates. **Ford**, CHI: cross a river at a ford or shallow place; overcome an obstacle, embark on a course of action; help, relieve; cease. The ideogram: water and level, running smooth over a flat bottom. Image of Hexagrams 63 and 64. **Below**, HSIA: anything below, in all senses; lower, inner; lower trigram; opposite of above, SHANG. **Brightness**, MING: light-giving aspect of burning, heavenly bodies and consciousness; with fire, the Symbol of the trigram Radiance, LI.

　　Lowly, PEI: speak and think of yourself humbly; modest, yielding; base, mean, contemptible. **Move**, HSING: move or move something; motivate, emotionally moving; walk, act, do. The ideogram: stepping left then right. **Above**, SHANG: anything above, in all senses; higher, upper, outer; upper trigram; opposite of below, HSIA.

[II] **Heaven**, T'IEN: highest; sky, firmament, heavens; power above the human as opposed to earth, TI, below. The symbol of the trigram Force, CH'IEN. The ideogram: great and the one above. **Lessen**, K'UEI: diminish, injure, wane; lack, defect, failure.

　　Transform, PIEN: abrupt, radical, fundamental mutation from one state of being to another; transformation of lines in hexagrams; contrasts with change, HUA, gradual metamorphosis. **Diffuse**, LIU: flow out, spread, permeate.

[III] **Souls[and]Spirits**, KUEI SHEN: the whole range of imaginal beings both inside and outside the individual; spiritual powers, gods, demons, ghosts, powers, faculties. **Harm**, HAI: damage, injure, offend; suffer; hurtful, hindrance; fearful, anxious. **Bless**, FU: heavenly gifts; make happy; spiritual power and goodwill. The ideogram: spirit and plenty, heavenly gifts in abundance.

　　People, person, JEN: humans individually and collectively; an individual; humankind. Image of Hexagrams 13 and 37. **Hate**, WU: dislike, dread; averse to, ashamed of; repulsive, vicious, vile, ugly, wicked. The ideogram: twisted bowels and heart, heart entangled in emotion. **Love**, HAO: affection; fond of, take pleasure in; fine, graceful.

[IV] **Pass-beyond**, YÜ: go beyond set time or limits; get over a wall or obstacle; pass to the other side.

• *Transforming Lines*

Initial six

a) **Humbling, Humbling: chün tzu.**
Availing-of wading the Great River. Significant.

b) **Humbling, Humbling: chün tzu.**
Lowliness uses originating-from herding indeed.

Associated Contexts a) **Humbling**, CH'IEN: The doubled character intensifies this quality.
Avail-of, YUNG: take advantage of; benefit from, profit by; use for a specific purpose; apply to advantage. The ideogram: to divine and center, applying divination to central concerns. **Wading the Great River**, SHE TA CH'UAN: consciously moving into the flow of time; enter the stream of life with a goal or purpose; embark on a significant enterprise. **Significant**, CHI: leads to the experience of meaning; favorable, propitious, advantageous, appropriate; keyword. The ideogram: scholar and mouth, wise words of a sage.

b) **Origin**, TZU: source, beginning, ground; cause, reason, motive; line of descent; path to the origin; yourself, intrinsic. **Herd**, MU: tend cattle; watch over, superintend; ruler, teacher.

Six at-second

a) **Calling Humbling. Trial: significant.**

b) **Calling Humbling, Trial: significant.**
Centering the heart acquiring indeed.

Associated Contexts a) **Call**, MING: bird and animal cries, through which they recognize each other; distinctive sound, song, statement. The ideogram: bird and mouth, a distinguishing call. **Trial**, CHEN: test by ordeal; inquiry by divination and its result; righteous, firm; separating wheat from chaff; the kernel, the proven core; fourth stage of the Time Cycle. The ideogram: pearl and divination. **Significant**, CHI: leads to the experience of meaning; favorable, propitious, advantageous, appropriate; keyword. The ideogram: scholar and mouth, wise words of a sage.

b) **Heart**, HSIN: heart as center of being; seat of mind's images and affections; moral nature; source of desires, intentions, will. **Acquire**, TE: obtain the desired object; wish for, desire covetously; gains, possessions. The ideogram: go and obstacle, going through obstacles to the goal.

Nine at-third

a) **Toiling Humbling: chün tzu.**
Possessing completing significant.

b) **Toiling Humbling: chün tzu.**
The myriad commoners submitting indeed.

Associated Contexts a) **Toil**, LAO: labor, take pains, exert yourself; burdened, careworn; worthy actions. The ideogram: strength and fire, producing heat.
Significant, CHI: leads to the experience of meaning; favorable, propitious, advantageous, appropriate; keyword. The ideogram: scholar and mouth, wise words of a sage.

b) **Myriad**, WAN: countless; many, everyone; lit.: ten thousand. The ideogram: swarm of insects. **Commoners**, MIN: class of workers the state draws on to sustain the social hierarchy; undeveloped potential outside the organized personality. **Submit**, FU: yield to, serve; undergo.

Six at-fourth

a) **Without not Harvesting, demonstrating Humbling.**

b) **Without not Harvesting, demonstrating Humbling.**
Not contradicting by-consequence indeed.

Associated Contexts a) **Without not Harvesting**, WU PU LI: nothing for which this will not be beneficial; advantageous potential, borderline where the balance is swinging from not Harvesting to actually Harvesting. **Demonstrate**, HUI: show, signal, point out. The ideogram: hand and act, giving signals.

b) **Not**, PU: simple negative. **Contradict**, WEI: oppose, disregard, disobey; seditious, perverse. **By-consequence(-of)**, TSE: very strong connection; reason, cause, result; rule, law, pattern, standard; therefore.

Six at-fifth

a) **Not affluence: using one's neighbor.**
  Harvesting: availing-of encroaching subjugating.
  Without not Harvesting.

b) **Harvesting: availing-of encroaching subjugating.**
  Chastising, not submitting indeed.

Associated Contexts a) **Not**, PU: simple negative. **Affluence**, FU: rich, abundant; wealth; enrich, provide for; flow toward, accrue. **One's/one**, CH'I: third person pronoun; also: it/its, he/his, she/hers, they/theirs. **Neighbor**, LIN: person living nearby; extended family; assist, support.

Harvest, LI: advantageous, profitable; acute, insightful; benefit, nourish; third stage of the Time Cycle. **Avail-of**, YUNG: take advantage of; benefit from, profit by; use for a specific purpose; apply to advantage. The ideogram: to divine and center, applying divination to central concerns. **Encroach**, CH'IN: invade, usurp, appropriate; advance stealthily, enter secretly; possessed by a spirit. **Subjugate**, FA: chastise rebels, make dependent; cut down, subject to rule. The ideogram: man and lance, armed soldiers.

Without not Harvesting, WU PU LI: nothing for which this will not be beneficial; advantageous potential, borderline where the balance is swinging from not Harvesting to actually Harvesting.

b) **Chastise**, CHENG: punish, subjugate, discipline; reduce to order; punishing expedition. The ideogram: step and correct, a rectifying move. **Submit**, FU: yield to, serve; undergo.

Six above

a) **Calling Humbling.**
  Harvesting: availing-of moving legions.
  Chastising the capital city.

b) **Calling Humbling.**
  Purpose not-yet acquired indeed.
  Permitting availing-of moving legions.
  Chastising the capital city indeed.

Associated Contexts a) **Call,** MING: bird and animal cries, through which they recognize each other; distinctive sound, song, statement. The ideogram: bird and mouth, a distinguishing call.

Harvest, LI: advantageous, profitable; acute, insightful; benefit, nourish; third stage of the Time Cycle. **Avail-of,** YUNG: take advantage of; benefit from, profit by; use for a specific purpose; apply to advantage. The ideogram: to divine and center, applying divination to central concerns. **Legions/leading,** SHIH: troops; an organized unit, a metropolis; leader, general, model, master; organize, make functional; take as a model, imitate. The ideogram: heap and whole, organize confusion into functional units. Image of Hexagram 7.

Chastise, CHENG: punish, subjugate, discipline; reduce to order; punishing expedition. The ideogram: step and correct, a rectifying move. **Capital,** YI: populous fortified city, center and symbol of the domain it rules. The ideogram: enclosure and official seal. **City,** KUO: area of only human constructions; political unit, polis. First of the territorial zones: city, suburbs, countryside, forests.

b) **Purpose,** CHIH: focus of mind and heart; will, inclination, resolve. The ideogram: heart and scholar, high inner resolve, or heart and go, inner determination. **Not-yet,** WEI: temporal negative; something will but has not yet occurred; contrary of already, CHI. Image of Hexagram 64. **Acquire,** TE: obtain the desired object; wish for, desire covetously; gains, possessions. The ideogram: go and obstacle, going through obstacles to the goal.

Permit, K'O: possible because in harmony with an inherent principle. The ideogram: mouth and breath, silent consent.

16

PROVIDING-FOR/PROVISION ▪
YÜ

This hexagram describes your situation in terms of what is needed to meet the future. It emphasizes that accumulating strength through foresight and prudence so things can be fully enjoyed is the adequate way to handle it. To be in accord with the time, you are told to: **provide-for!**

● *Image of the Situation*

Providing-for, Harvesting: installing feudatories to move legions.

Associated Contexts **Provide(-for)/provision**, YÜ: ready, prepared for; prearrange, take precaution, think beforehand; satisfied, contented, at ease. The ideogram: son and elephant, careful, reverent and very strong. **Harvest**, LI: advantageous, profitable; acute, insightful; benefit, nourish; third stage of the Time Cycle. **Install**, CHIEN: set up, establish; confirm a position or law. **Feudatory**, HOU: nobles entrusted with governing the provinces; active in daily life rather than governing from the center; contrasts with prince, KUNG, executives at the court. **Move**, HSING: move or move something; motivate, emotionally moving; walk, act, do. The ideogram: stepping left then right. **Legions/leading**, SHIH: troops; an organized unit, a metropolis; leader, general, model, master; organize, make functional; take as a model, imitate. The ideogram: heap and whole, organize confusion into functional units. Image of Hexagram 7.

● *Outer and Inner Aspects*

☳ **Shake**: Thunder rises from below, shaking and stirring things up. **Shake** begins the yang hemicycle by germinating new action.

　　Connection to the outer: sprouting energies thrusting from below, the Woody Moment beginning. **Shake** stirs things up to issue-forth.

☷ **Field**: The field of earth yields and sustains, serving in order to produce. **Field** is the equalizing point between yin and yang where things labor and serve.

Connection to the inner: the common labor of sowing and hoarding, the Earthy Moment. **Field** produces concrete results through serving.

Inner sowing and hoarding **provides-for** a rousing summons to action that comes from outside

●   *Counter Indications*

Nuclear trigrams **Gorge**, K'AN, and **Bound**, KEN, result in Counter Hexagram 39, **Limping**, CHIEN. Building up reserves to **provide-for** the future is contrasted with **limping** forward even though hampered.

●   *Sequence*

> **Possessing the Great and-also enabling Humbling**
> > **necessarily Provides-for.**
> **Anterior acquiescence has the use-of Providing-for.**

Associated Contexts **Possess**, YU: in possession of, have, own; opposite of lack, WU. **Great**, TA: big, noble, important, very; orient the will toward a self-imposed goal, impose direction; ability to lead or guide your life; contrasts with small, HSIAO, flexible adaptation to what crosses your path; keyword. **Great Possessing** is the Image of Hexagram 14. **And-also**, ERH: joins and contrasts two terms. **Able**, NENG: enable; ability, power, skill, art; competent, talented; duty, function, capacity. The ideogram: an animal with strong hooves and bones, able to carry and defend. **Humble**, CH'IEN: think and speak of yourself in a modest way; respectful, unassuming, retiring, unobtrusive; yielding, compliant, reverent, lowly. The ideogram: words and unite, keeping words close to underlying facts. Image of Hexagram 15. **Necessarily**, PI: unavoidably, indispensably, certainly.

   Anterior ... the use-of: activating this hexagram depends on understanding and accepting the previous statement.

●   *Contrasted Definitions*

> **Humbling: levity indeed.**
> **Provision: indolence indeed.**

Associated Contexts **Levity**, CH'ING: frivolous, think lightly of, unimportant; alert, agile; gentle. The ideogram: cart and stream, empty cart floating downstream. **Indeed**, YEH: intensifier; indicates comment on previous statement.

Indolence, TAI: idle, inattentive, careless; self-indulgent; disdainful, contemptuous.

● *Attached Evidences*

Redoubling gates, smiting clappers.
Used to await violent visitors.
Surely, grasping connotes Providing-for.

Associated Contexts **Redouble**, CH'UNG: repeat, reiterate, add to; build up by layers. **Gate**, MEN: outer door, between court-yard and street; a text or master as gate to a school of thought. **Smite**, CHI: hit, beat, attack; hurl against, rush a position; rouse to action. The ideogram: hand and hit, fist punching. **Clapper**, T'O: board used by watchmen to strike the hours.

Use(-of), YI: make use of, by means of, owing to; employ, make functional. **Await**, TAI: expect, wait for, welcome (friendly or hostile), provide against. **Violent**, PAO: fierce, oppressive, cruel; strike hard. **Visitor**, K'O: guest; stranger, foreign, from afar; squatter.

Surely, KAI: preceding statement is undoubtedly true. **Grasp**, CH'U: lay hold of, take and use, seize, appropriate; grasp the meaning, understand. The ideogram: ear and hand, hear and grasp. **Connote**, CHU: imply the meaning; signify. The ideogram: words and imply.

● *Symbol Tradition*

Thunder issuing-forth-from earth impetuously. Providing-for.
The Earlier Kings used arousing delight to extol actualizing-tao.
Exalting worship's Supreme Above.
Using equaling the grandfather predecessors.

Associated Contexts **Thunder**, LEI: rising, arousing power; the Symbol of the trigram Shake, CHEN. **Issue-forth(-from)**, CH'U: emerge from, come out of, proceed from, spring from; the Action of the trigram Shake, CHEN; contrary of enter. JU. The ideogram: stem with branches and leaves emerging. **Earth**, TI: ground on which the human world rests; basis of all things, nourishes all things; the Symbol of the trigram Field, K'UN. **Impetuous**, FEN: sudden energy; lively, spirited, impulsive; excite, arouse; press on.

Earlier Kings, HSIEN WANG: ideal rulers of old; the golden age, primal time, power in harmony with nature; model for the chün tzu. **Arouse**, TSO: stir up, stimulate, rouse from inactivity; generate; appear, arise. The ideogram: person and beginning. **Delight**, LO: take joy or pleasure in; pleasant, relaxed; also: music as harmony, elegance and pleasure. **Extol**, CH'UNG: praise, honor, magnify, revere; eminent, lofty; worthy of worship. **Actualize-tao**, TE: realize tao in action; power, virtue; ability to follow the course traced by the ongoing process of the cosmos; keyword. The ideogram: to go, straight, and heart. Linked with acquire, TE: acquiring that which makes a being become what it is meant to be.

Exalting worship, YIN CHIEN: superlative of worship; glorify; intensify feelings of praise and awe. **'s/have(-it)/it/them**, CHIH: expresses possession, directly or as an object pronoun. **Supreme Above**, SHANG TI: highest power in universe, lord of all.

Equal, P'EI: on the same level; pair, husband or wife; together. **Grandfather**, TSU: second ancestor generation; deceased grandfather, honored more than actual father. **Predecessor**, K'AO: deceased ancestor, especially the grandfather; the ancients; aged, long-lived; consult, verify. The ideogram: old and ingenious, the old wise man.

● *Image Tradition*

> **Providing-for. Solid corresponding and-also purpose moving. [I]**
> **Yielding uses stirring-up. Providing-for.**
>
> **Providing-for: yielding uses stirring-up. [II]**
> **Anterior Heaven[and]Earth thus having-it.**
> **And-also even-more installing feudatories to move legions reached.**
>
> **Heaven[and]Earth uses yielding stirring-up. [III]**
> **Anterior Sun[and]Moon not exceeding.**
> **And-also the four seasons not straying.**

The all-wise person uses yielding stirring-up. [IV]
By-consequence punishing flogging purifies
and-also the commoners submit.
Actually Provision's season righteously great in-fact.

Associated Contexts [I] **Solid**, KANG: quality of the whole lines; firm, strong, unyielding, persisting. **Correspond(-to)**, YING: be in agreement or harmony; resonate together, invoke and fulfill each other; answer to, suitable; relation between the lines (1:4, 2:5, 3:6) when they form the pair opened and whole, supple and solid. The ideogram: heart and obey. **Purpose**, CHIH: focus of mind and heart; will, inclination, resolve. The ideogram: heart and scholar, high inner resolve, or heart and go, inner determination.

Yield(-to), SHUN: give way and bear produce; comply, agree, follow, obey; unresisting, docile, flexible; nourish, provide; the Action of the trigram Field, K'UN. The ideogram: head and current, water flowing from the head of a river, yielding to the banks. **Stir-up**, TUNG: excite, influence, move, affect; work, take action; come out of the egg or the bud; the Action of the trigram Shake, CHEN. The ideogram: strength and heavy, move weighty things.

[II] **Anterior**, KU: come before as cause; formerly, ancient; reason, purpose, intention; grievance, quarrel, dissatisfaction, sorrow, mourning resulting from previous causes and intentions; situation leading to a divination. **Heaven[and]Earth**, T'IEN TI: dynamic relation between the primal powers and the world it produces; cosmos, natural or human world; keyword. **Thus**, JU: as, in this way.

Even-more, K'UANG: even more so, all the more. **Reach(-to)**, HU: arrive at a goal; reach towards and achieve; connect; contrasts with tend-towards, YU.

[III] **Sun[and]Moon**, JIH YÜEH: the two dimensions of calendar time that define any specific moment; time as interlocking cycles. **Not**, PU: simple negative. **Exceed**, KU: go beyond, pass by, pass over; excessive, transgress; error, fault. Image of Hexagrams 28 and 62.

Four seasons, SSU SHIH: the four dynamic qualities of time that make up the year and the Time Cycle; the right time, in accord with the time; time as sacred; all-encompassing. **Stray**, T'E: wander blindly; deviate, err, alter, doubt; excess.

[IV] All-wise, SHENG: intuitive universal wisdom; mythical sages; holy, sacred; mark of highest distinction. The ideogram: ear and inform, one who knows all from a single sound. **People, person**, JEN: humans individually and collectively; an individual; humankind. Image of Hexagrams 13 and 37.

By-consequence(-of), TSE: very strong connection; reason, cause, result; rule, law, pattern, standard; therefore. **Punish**, HSING: legal punishment; physical penalties for severe criminal offenses; whip, torture, behead. **Flog**, FA: punish with blows, beat, whip; used to find out the truth. **Purify**, CH'ING: clean a water course; limpid, unsullied; right principles. **Commoners**, MIN: class of workers the state draws on to sustain the social hierarchy; undeveloped potential outside the organized personality. **Submit**, FU: yield to, serve; undergo.

Actually ... in-fact, YI TSAI: stresses the importance of a statement. The ideogram: a dart and done, strong intention fully expressed. **Righteous**, YI: proper and just, meets the standards; things in their proper place; the heart that rules itself; upright, moral rule; contrasts with Harvest, LI, advantage or profit.

● *Transforming Lines*

Initial six

a) **Calling Provision.**
   Pitfall.

b) **Initial six, calling Provision.**
   Purpose exhausted, pitfall indeed.

Associated Contexts a) **Call**, MING: bird and animal cries, through which they recognize each other; distinctive sound, song, statement. The ideogram: bird and mouth, a distinguishing call.

Pitfall, HSIUNG: leads away from the experience of meaning; stuck and exposed to danger, unable to take in the situation; flow of life and spirit is blocked; unfortunate, baleful; keyword.

b) **Exhaust**, CH'IUNG: bring to an end; limit, extremity; destitute; investigate exhaustively; end without a new beginning. The ideogram: cave and naked person, bent with disease or old age.

Six at-second

a) **Chain-mail tending-towards petrification:**
   Not completing the day.
   Trial: significant.

b) **Not completing the day, Trial: significant.**
   Using centering correcting indeed.

Associated Contexts a) **Chain-mail**, CHIEH: chain-armor; tortoise or crab shell; protective covering; border, limit; protection, support. **Tend-towards**, YÜ: move toward but not reach, in the direction of; contrasts with reach(-to), HU, actually arriving. **Petrify**, SHIH: become stone or stony; rocks, stony land; objects made of stone; firm, decided; a barren womb.

   Complete, CHUNG: end of a cycle that begins the next; last, whole, all; contrasts with exhaust, CH'IUNG, final end. The ideogram: silk cocoons, follow and ice, winter linking one year with the next. **Day/sun**, JIH: actual sun and the time of a sun-cycle, a day.

   Trial, CHEN: test by ordeal; inquiry by divination and its result; righteous, firm; separating wheat from chaff; the kernel, the proven core; fourth stage of the Time Cycle. The ideogram: pearl and divination. **Significant**, CHI: leads to the experience of meaning; favorable, propitious, advantageous, appropriate; keyword. The ideogram: scholar and mouth, wise words of a sage.

b) **Centering correcting**, CHUNG CHENG: central and correct; make rectifying one-sidedness and error your central concern; reaching a stable center in yourself can correct the situation.

Six at-third

a) **Skeptical Providing-for, repenting.**
   Procrastinating possesses repenting.

b) **Skeptical Providing-for possesses repenting.**
   Situation not appropriate indeed.

Associated Contexts a) **Skeptical**, YÜ: doubtful, cynical; wonder at, wide-eyed suprise. **Repent**, HUI: dissatisfaction with past conduct causing a change of heart; proceeds from abashment, LIN, shame and confusion at having lost the right way.

   Procrastinate, CH'IH: delay, act at leisure, retard; slow, late.

b) **Situation**, WEI: place or seat according to rank; post, position, command; right, proper; established, arranged. The ideogram: person and stand, servants in their places. **Appropriate**, TANG: suitable; opportune, convenient; adequate, competent; equal to; whole lines in uneven places and opened lines in even places.

Nine at-fourth

a) **Antecedent Provision.**
The great possesses acquiring.
No doubting.
Partners join-together suddenly.

b) **Antecedent Provision, the great possesses acquiring.**
Purpose: the great moving indeed.

Associated Contexts a) **Antecedent**, YU: come before as origin and cause; through, by, from; depend on; permit, enter by way of.

Acquire, TE: obtain the desired object; wish for, desire covetously; gains, possessions. The ideogram: go and obstacle, going through obstacles to the goal.

No, WU: simple negative; un-, dis-. **Doubt**, YI: suspect, distrust; dubious; surmise, conjecture.

Partner, P'ENG: associate for mutual benefit; two equal or similar things; companions, friends, peers; join in; commercial ventures. The ideogram: linked strings of cowries or coins. **Join-together**, HO: unite for a purpose; assemble friends for a specific aim. **Suddenly**, TSAN: quick, prompt, abrupt action; collect together. The ideogram: clasp used to gather the hair.

Six at-fifth

a) **Trial: affliction.**
Persevering, not dying.

b) **Six at-fifth, Trial: affliction.**
Riding a solid indeed.
Persevering, not dying.
Center not-yet extinguished indeed.

Associated Contexts a) **Trial**, CHEN: test by ordeal; inquiry by divination and its result; righteous, firm; separating wheat from chaff; the kernel, the proven core; fourth stage of the Time Cycle. The ideogram: pearl and divination. **Afflict**, CHI: sickness, disorder, defect, calamity; injurious; pressure and consequent anger, hate or dislike. The ideogram: sickness and dart, a sudden affliction.

Persevere, HENG: continue in the same way or spirit; constant, perpetual, regular; self-renewing; extend everywhere. Image of Hexagram 32. **Die**, SSU: sudden or untimely death; run out of energy; immobile, fixed.

b) **Ride**, CH'ENG: ride an animal or a chariot; have the upper hand, seize the right time; control strong power; overcome the nature of the other; supple opened line above a solid whole line. **Solid**, KANG: quality of the whole lines; firm, strong, unyielding, persisting.

Center, CHUNG: inner, central; put in the center; middle, stable point enabling you to face inner and outer changes; middle line of trigram. The ideogram: field divided in two equal parts. Image of Hexagram 61. **Not-yet**, WEI: temporal negative; something will but has not yet occurred; contrary of already, CHI. Image of Hexagram 64. **Extinguish**, WANG: ruin, destroy; gone, dead, lost without trace; extinct, forgotten, out of mind. The ideogram: person concealed by a wall, out of sight.

Six above

a) **Dim Providing-for.**
   Accomplishment: possessing denial.
   Without fault.

b) **Dim Providing-for located above.**
   Wherefore permitting long-living indeed?

Associated Contexts a) **Dim**, MING: dark, obscure; misinformed, immature, cavern, the underworld. The ideogram: 16th day of moon-month, when the moon begins to dim.

Accomplish, CHENG: complete, finish, bring about; perfect, full, whole; play your part, do your duty; mature. The ideogram: weapon and man, able to bear arms thus fully developed. **Deny**, YÜ: retract, repudiate; deterioration, regress.

Without fault, WU CHIU: no error or harm in the situation.

b) **Locate(-in)**, TSAI: live in, dwell, reside; belong to, involved with, depend on; within. The ideogram: earth and persevere, place on the earth. **Above**, SHANG: anything above, in all senses; higher, upper, outer; upper trigram; opposite of below, HSIA.

   Wherefore, HO: interrogative: why? for what reason? what is? and affirmation: therefore, for that reason. **Permit**, K'O: possible because in harmony with an inherent principle. The ideogram: mouth and breath, silent consent. **Long-living**, CHANG: enduring, constant; senior, superior, greater; increase, prosper; respect, elevate.

FOLLOWING ▪ SUI

This hexagram describes your situation in terms of being impelled or drawn into moving forward. It emphasizes that yielding to the impulse by accepting guidance is the adequate way to handle it. To be in accord with the time, you are told to: **follow**!

● *Image of the Situation*

> **Following.**
> **Spring Growing Harvesting Trial.**
> **Without fault.**

Associated Contexts **Follow**, SUI: come or go after; pursue, impelled to move; come after in inevitable sequence; move in the same direction, comply with what is ahead; follow a way or religion; according to, next, subsequent. The ideogram: go and fall, unavoidable movement.

Spring Growing Harvesting Trial: Spring, YÜAN: **Grow**, HENG: **Harvest**, LI; and **Trial**, CHEN, are the four stages of the Time Cycle, the model for all dynamic processes. They indicate that your question is connected to the cycle as a whole rather than a part of it, and that the origin (Spring) of a favorable result (Harvesting Trial) is an offering to the spirits (Growing).

Without fault, WU CHIU: no error or harm in the situation.

● *Outer and Inner Aspects*

☱ **Open**: vapor rising from the marsh's open surface stimulates and fertilizes; stimulating words cheer and inspire. **Open** begins the yin hemicycle by initiating the formative process.

Connection to the outer: liquifying, casting, skinning off the mold, the Metallic Moment beginning. **Open** stimulates, cheers and reveals innate form.

☳ **Shake**: Thunder rises from below, shaking and stirring things up. **Shake** begins the yang hemicycle by germinating new action.

Connection to the inner: sprouting energies thrusting from below, the Woody Moment beginning. **Shake** stirs things up to issue-forth.

Stimulating words in the outer world stir-up **following** within. These trigrams emphasize the Pivoting Phase, initiating new actions.

● *Counter Indications*

Nuclear trigrams **Ground**, SUN, and **Bound**, KEN, result in Counter Hexagram 53, **Infiltrating**, CHIEN. Actively **following** a specific model is contrasted with **infiltrating** through diffuse penetration.

● *Sequence*

> **Providing-for necessarily possesses Following.**
> **Anterior acquiescence has the use-of Following.**

Associated Contexts **Provide-for/provision**, YÜ: ready, prepared for; pre-arrange, take precaution, think beforehand; satisfied, contented, at ease. The ideogram: sonhood and elephant, careful, reverent and very strong. Image of Hexagram 16. **Necessarily**, PI: unavoidably, indispensably, certainly. **Possess**, YU: in possession of, have, own; opposite of lack, WU.

   Anterior ... the use-of: activating this hexagram depends on understanding and accepting the previous statement.

● *Contrasted Definitions*

> **Following: without anteriority indeed.**
> **Corrupting: by-consequence stability indeed.**

Associated Contexts **Without**, WU: devoid of; -less as suffix. **Anterior**, KU: come before as cause; formerly, ancient; reason, purpose, intention; grievance, quarrel, dissatisfaction, sorrow, mourning resulting from previous causes and intentions; situation leading to a divination. **Indeed**, YEH: intensifier; indicates comment on previous statement.

   Corrupt, KU: rotting, poisonous; intestinal worms, venomous insects; evil magic; disorder, error; pervert by seduction, flattery; unquiet ghost. The ideogram: dish and worms, putrefaction and poisonous decay. Image of Hexagram 18. **By-consequence(-of)**, TSE: very strong connection; reason, cause, result; rule, law, pattern, standard; therefore. **Stability**, CH'IH: firm, prepared for; careful, respectful.

● *Symbol Tradition*

> **Marsh center possessing thunder. Following.**
> **A chün tzu uses turning-to darkening to enter a reposing pause.**

Associated Contexts **Marsh**, TSE: open surface of a flat body of water and the vapors rising from it; fertilize, enrich; kindness, favor; the Symbol of the trigram Open, TUI. **Center**, CHUNG: inner, central; put in the center; middle, stable point enabling you to face inner and outer changes; middle line of trigram. The ideogram: field divided in two equal parts. Image of Hexagram 61. **Thunder**, LEI: rising, arousing power; the Symbol of the trigram Shake, CHEN.

Chün tzu: ideal of a person who uses divination to order his/her life in accordance with tao rather than wilful intention; keyword. **Use(-of)**, YI: make use of, by means of, owing to; employ, make functional. **Turn-to**, HSIANG: direct your mind toward, seek. **Darken**, HUI: make or become dark; last day of the moon; obscure, night, mist. **Enter**, JU: penetrate, go into, enter on, progress; put into, encroach on; the Action of the trigram Ground, SUN, contrary of issue-forth, CH'U. **Repose**, YEN: rest, leisure, peace of mind; banquet, feast. The ideogram: shelter and rest, a wayside inn. **Pause**, HSI: stop and rest, repose; breathe, a breathing-spell; suspended.

● *Image Tradition*

> **Following. Solid coming and-also supple below. [I]**
> **Stirring-up and-also stimulating. Following.**
>
> **Great Growing, Trial: without fault. [II]**
> **And-also Below Heaven Following the season.**
> **Actually Following the season's righteous great in-fact.**

Associated Contexts **[I] Solid**, KANG: quality of the whole lines; firm, strong, unyielding, persisting. **Come**, LAI, and go, WANG, describe the stream of time as it flows from future through present to past; come,

LAI, indicates what is approaching; move toward, arrive at; keyword. **And-also**, ERH: joins and contrasts two terms. **Supple**, JOU: quality of the opened lines; flexible, pliant, tender, adaptable. **Below**, HSIA: anything below, in all senses; lower, inner; lower trigram; opposite of above, SHANG.

Stir-up, TUNG: excite, influence, move, affect; work, take action; come out of the egg or the bud; the Action of the trigram Shake, CHEN. The ideogram: strength and heavy, move weighty things. **Stimulate**, SHUO: rouse to action and good feeling; free from constraint, stir up, urge on; persuade, cheer, delight; set out in words; the Action of the trigram Open, TUI. The ideogram: words and exchange.

[II] **Great**, TA: big, noble, important, very; orient the will toward a self-imposed goal, impose direction; ability to lead or guide your life; contrasts with small, HSIAO, flexible adaptation to what crosses your path; keyword. Image of Hexagrams 14, 26, 28, 34. **Grow**, HENG: success through a sacrifice; pervade, persevere; bring to full growth; enjoy; vigorous, effective; second stage of the Time Cycle. **Trial**, CHEN: test by ordeal; inquiry by divination and its result; righteous, firm; separating wheat from chaff; the kernel, the proven core; fourth stage of the Time Cycle. The ideogram: pearl and divination.

Below Heaven, T'IEN HSIA: the human world, between heaven and earth. **Season**, SHIH: quality of the time; the right time, opportune, in harmony; planning in accord with the time; seasons of the year. The ideogram: sun and temple, time as sacred.

Actually ... in-fact, YI TSAI: stresses the importance of a statement. The ideogram: a dart and done, strong intention fully expressed. **'s/have(-it)/it/them**, CHIH: expresses possession, directly or as an object pronoun. **Righteous**, YI: proper and just, meets the standards; things in their proper place; the heart that rules itself; upright, moral rule; contrasts with Harvest, LI, advantage or profit.

● *Transforming Lines*

Initial nine

a) **An office: possessing denial. Trial: significant.**
  Issuing-forth-from the gate, mingling possesses achievement.

b) **An office: possessing denial.**
Adhering-to correcting significant indeed.
Issuing-forth-from the gate, mingling possesses achievement.
Not letting-go indeed.

Associated Contexts a) **Office**, KUAN: government officials, magistrates, dignitaries. **Deny**, YÜ: retract, repudiate; deterioration, regress. **Significant**, CHI: leads to the experience of meaning; favorable, propitious, advantageous, appropriate; keyword. The ideogram: scholar and mouth, wise words of a sage.

Issue-forth(-from), CH'U: emerge from, come out of, proceed from, spring from; the Action of the trigram Shake, CHEN; contrary of enter, JU. The ideogram: stem with branches and leaves emerging. **Gate**, MEN: outer door, between court-yard and street; a text or master as gate to a school of thought. **Mingle**, CHIAO: blend with, communicate, join, exchange; trade, business; copulation; friendship. **Achieve**, KUNG: work done, results; real accomplishment, praise, worth, merit. The ideogram: workman's square and forearm, combining craft and strength.

b) **Adhere(-to)**, TS'UNG: follow a way, hold to a doctrine, school, or person; hear and comply with, agree to; forced to follow, follower. The ideogram: two men walking, one following the other. **Correct**, CHENG: rectify deviation or one-sidedness; proper, straight, exact, regular; constant, rule, model. The ideogram: stop and one, hold to one thing.

Not, PU: simple negative. **Let-go**, SHIH: lose, omit, miss, fail, let slip; out of control. The ideogram: drop from the hand.

Six at-second

a) **Tied-to the small son.**
Letting-go the respectable husband.

b) **Tied-to the small son.**
Nowhere joining associating indeed.

Associated Contexts a) **Tie(-to)**, HSI: connect, attach to, bind; devoted to; relatives. The ideogram: person and connect, ties between humans. **Small**, HSIAO: little, common, unimportant; adapting to what crosses your path; ability to move in harmony with the vicissitudes of life; contrasts with great, TA, self-imposed theme or goal; keyword. Image of Hexagrams 9 and 62. **Son(hood)**, TZU: living up to ideal of ancestors as highest human development; act with concern and reverence; male child; offspring, posterity; seed, kernel, egg; sage, teacher; nadir, deepest point, midnight, mid-winter.

Let-go, SHIH: lose, omit, miss, fail, let slip; out of control. The ideogram: drop from the hand. **Respectable**, CHANG: worthy of respect; standard by which others are measured. **Husband**, FU: household manager; administer with thrift and prudence; responsible for; sustain with your earnings; old enough to assume responsibility; married man.

b) **Nothing/nowhere**, FU: strong negative; not a single thing/place. **Join**, CHIEN: add or bring together; unite, absorb; attend to many things. The ideogram: hand grasps two grain stalks, two things at once. **Associate (-with)**, YÜ: consort with, combine; companions; group, band, company; agree with, comply, help. The ideogram: pair of hands reaching downward meets a pair of hands reaching upward, helpful association.

Six at-third

a) **Tied-to the respectable husband.**
Letting-go the small son.
Following possessing seeking, acquiring.
Harvesting: residing-in Trial.

b) **Tied-to the respectable husband.**
Below, purpose stowed-away indeed.

Associated Contexts a) **Tie(-to)**, HSI: connect, attach to, bind; devoted to; relatives. The ideogram: person and connect, ties between humans. **Respectable**, CHANG: worthy of respect; standard by which others are measured. **Husband**, FU: household manager; administer with thrift and prudence; responsible for; sustain with your earnings; old enough to assume responsibility; married man.

Let-go, SHIH: lose, omit, miss, fail, let slip; out of control. The ideogram: drop from the hand. **Small**, HSIAO: little, common, unimportant; adapting to what crosses your path; ability to move in harmony with the vicissitudes of life; contrasts with great, TA, self-imposed theme or goal; keyword. Image of Hexagrams 9 and 62. **Son(hood)**, TZU: living up to ideal of ancestors as highest human development; act with concern and reverence; male child; offspring, posterity; seed, kernel, egg; sage, teacher; nadir, deepest point, midnight, mid-winter.

Seek, CH'IU: search for, aim at, wish for, desire; implore, supplicate; covetous. **Acquire,** TE: obtain the desired object; wish for, desire covetously; gains, possessions. The ideogram: go and obstacle, going through obstacles to the goal.

Harvest, LI: advantageous, profitable; acute, insightful; benefit, nourish; third stage of the Time Cycle. **Reside(-in),** CHÜ: dwell, live in, stay; sit down, fill an office; settled parts of a country. The ideogram: body and seat.

b) **Purpose,** CHIH: focus of mind and heart; will, inclination, resolve. The ideogram: heart and scholar, high inner resolve, or heart and go, inner determination. **Stow(-away),** SHE: set aside, put away, store; halt, rest in; temporary lodgings, breathing-spell.

Nine at-fourth

a) Following possessing catching. Trial: pitfall.
Possessing conformity, locating-in tao uses brightening.
Wherefore faulty?

b) Following possessing catching.
One's righteousness: pitfall indeed.
Possessing conformity located-in tao.
Brightening achieving indeed.

Associated Contexts a) **Catch,** HUO: take in hunt; catch a thief; obtain, seize; hit the mark, opportune moment; prisoner, spoils, prey; slave, servant. **Pitfall,** HSIUNG: leads away from the experience of meaning; stuck and exposed to danger, unable to take in the situation; flow of life and spirit is blocked; unfortunate, baleful; keyword.

Possessing conformity, YU FU: inner and outer are in accord; confidence of the spirits has been captured; sincere, truthful; proper to take action. **Locate(-in),** TSAI: live in, dwell, reside; belong to, involved with, depend on; within. The ideogram: earth and persevere, place on the earth. **Tao:** way or path; ongoing process of being and the course it traces for each specific person or thing; keyword. The ideogram: go and head, leading and the path it creates. **Brightness,** MING: light-giving aspect of burning, heavenly bodies and consciousness; with fire, the Symbol of the trigram Radiance, LI.

Wherefore, HO: interrogative: why? for what reason? what is? and affirmation: therefore, for that reason. **Fault,** CHIU: unworthy conduct that leads to harm, illness, misfortune. The ideogram: person and differ, differ from what you should be.

b) **One's/one**, CH'I: third person pronoun; also: it/its, he/his, she/hers, they/theirs. **Achieve**, KUNG: work done, results; real accomplishment, praise, worth, merit. The ideogram: workman's square and forearm, combining craft and strength.

Nine at-fifth

a) **Conformity tending-towards excellence. Significant.**

b) **Conformity tending-towards excellence significant.**
   Situation correctly centering indeed.

Associated Contexts a) **Conforming**, FU: accord between inner and outer in a particular moment; sincere, truthful, verified, reliable, in accord with the spirits; capture; prisoners, spoils; contrasts with trustworthy, HSIN, consistent over time. The ideogram: bird's claw enclosing young animals, possessive grip. **Tend-towards**, YÜ: move toward but not reach, in the direction of; contrasts with reach(-to), HU, actually arriving. **Excellence**, CHIA: superior quality; fine, delicious, glorious; happy, pleased; rejoice in, praise. The ideogram: increasing goodness, pleasure and happiness. **Significant**, CHI: leads to the experience of meaning; favorable, propitious, advantageous, appropriate; keyword. The ideogram: scholar and mouth, wise words of a sage.

b) **Situation**, WEI: place or seat according to rank; post, position, command; right, proper; established, arranged. The ideogram: person and stand, servants in their places. **Correct**, CHENG: rectify deviation or one-sidedness; proper, straight, exact, regular; constant, rule, model. The ideogram: stop and one, hold to one thing.

Six above

a) **Grappling, tying-to it.**
   Thereupon adhering holding-fast-to it.
   The king availing-of Growing tending-towards
                        the Western mountain.

b) **Grappling, tying-to it.**
Exhausting the above indeed.

Associated Contexts a) **Grapple,** CHÜ: grasp and detain; restrain, attach to, hook. **Tie(-to),** HSI: connect, attach to, bind; devoted to; relatives. The ideogram: person and connect, ties between humans. **It/them/have(-it)/'s,** CHIH: expresses possession, directly or as an object pronoun.

Thereupon, NAI: on that ground, because of. **Adhere(-to),** TS'UNG: follow a way, hold to a doctrine, school, or person; hear and comply with, agree to; forced to follow, follower. The ideogram: two men walking, one following the other. **Hold-fast(-to),** WEI: hold together; tie to, connect; reins, net.

King(hood), WANG: effective ruler, by authority of the Emperor, from whom others derive their power. **Avail-of,** YUNG: take advantage of; benefit from, profit by; use for a specific purpose; apply to advantage. The ideogram: to divine and center, applying divination to central concerns. **Tend-towards,** YÜ: move toward but not reach, in the direction of; contrasts with reach(-to), HU, actually arriving. **West,** HSI: corresponds to autumn, Harvest and the Streaming Moment; begins yin hemicycle of Universal Compass. **Mountain,** SHAN: limit, boundary; the Symbol of the trigram Bound, KEN. The ideogram: three peaks, a mountain range.

b) **Exhaust,** CH'IUNG: bring to an end; limit, extremity; destitute; investigate exhaustively; end without a new beginning. The ideogram: cave and naked person, bent with disease or old age. **Above,** SHANG: anything above, in all senses; higher, upper, outer; upper trigram; opposite of below, HSIA.

CORRUPTING ▪ *KU*

This hexagram describes your situation in terms of disorder, perversion and putrefaction. It emphasizes that letting things rot away so they become obsolete is the adequate way to handle it. To be in accord with the time, you are told to: accept **corrupting**!

● *Image of the Situation*

> **Corrrupting, Spring Growing.**
> **Harvesting: wading the Great River.**
> **Before seedburst three days, after seedburst three days.**

Associated Contexts **Corrupt**, KU: rotting, poisonous; intestinal worms, venomous insects; evil magic; disorder, error; pervert by seduction, flattery; unquiet ghost. The ideogram: dish and worms, putrefaction and poisonous decay. **Spring**, YÜAN: source, origin, head; great, excellent; arise, begin, generating power; first stage of the Time Cycle. **Grow**, HENG: success through a sacrifice; pervade, persevere; bring to full growth; enjoy; vigorous, effective; second stage of the Time Cycle.

Harvest, LI: advantageous, profitable; acute, insightful; benefit, nourish; third stage of the Time Cycle. **Wading the Great River**, SHE TA CH'UAN: consciously moving into the flow of time; enter the stream of life with a goal or purpose; embark on a significant enterprise.

Before(hand)/earlier, HSIEN: come before in time; first, at first; formerly, past, previous; begin, go ahead of. **Seedburst**, CHIA: seeds bursting forth in spring; first of the Ten Heavenly Barriers in calendar system; begin, first, number one; associated with the Woody Moment. **Three**, SAN: number three, third time or place; active phases of a cycle; superlative; beginning of repetition. **Day/sun**, JIH: actual sun and the time of a sun-cycle, a day. **After(wards)/later**, HOU: come after in time, subsequent; put oneself after; the second; attendants, heirs, successors, posterity.

● *Outer and Inner Aspects*

⚎ **Bound**: Mountains bound, limit and set a place off, stopping forward movement. **Bound** completes a full yin-yang cycle.

Connection to the outer: accomplishing words, which express things fully. **Bound** articulates what is complete and suggests what is beginning.

⚏ **Ground**: Wind and wood subtly enter from the ground, penetrating and pervading. **Ground** is the center of the yang hemicycle, spreading pervasive action.

Connection to the inner: penetrating and bringing together, the Woody Moment culminating. **Ground** pervades, matches and couples, seeding a new generation.

The outer limit blocks penetration and matching, turning growth in on itself and **corrupting** it.

● *Counter Indications*

Nuclear trigrams **Shake**, CHEN, and **Open**, TUI, result in Counter Hexagram 54, **Converting Maidenhood**, KUEI MEI. Stagnation and rotting away through **corrupting** are contrasted with finding a new field of activity in **converting maidenhood**.

● *Sequence*

> **Using rejoicing Following people implies necessarily**
> > > **possessing affairs.**
> **Anterior acquiescence has the use-of Corrupting.**
> **Corrupting implies affairs indeed.**

Associated Contexts **Use(-of)**, YI: make use of, by means of, owing to; employ, make functional. **Rejoice(-in)**, HSI: feel and give joy; delight, exult; cheerful, merry. The ideogram: joy (music) and mouth, expressing joy. **Follow**, SUI: come or go after; pursue, impelled to move; come after in inevitable sequence; move in the same direction, comply with what is ahead; follow a way or religion; according to, next, subsequent. The ideogram: go and fall, unavoidable movement. Image of Hexagram 17. **People, person**, JEN: humans individually and collectively; an individual;

humankind. Image of Hexagrams 13 and 37. **Imply**, CHE: further signify; additional meaning. **Necessarily**, PI: unavoidably, indispensably, certainly. **Possess**, YU: in possession of, have, own; opposite of lack, WU. **Affairs**, SHIH: all kinds of personal activity; matters at hand; business, occupation; manage a business, case in court.

Anterior ... the use-of: activating this hexagram depends on understanding and accepting the previous statement. **Indeed**, YEH: intensifier; indicates comment on previous statement.

● *Contrasted Definitions*

> **Following: without anteriority indeed.**
> **Corrupting: by-consequence stability indeed.**

Associated Contexts **Without**, WU: devoid of; -less as suffix. **Anterior**, KU: come before as cause; formerly, ancient; reason, purpose, intention; grievance, quarrel, dissatisfaction, sorrow, mourning resulting from previous causes and intentions; situation leading to a divination.

By-consequence(-of), TSE: very strong connection; reason, cause, result; rule, law, pattern, standard; therefore. **Stability**, CH'IH: firm, prepared for; careful, respectful.

● *Symbol Tradition*

> **Below mountain possessing wind. Corrupting.**
> **A chün tzu uses rousing the commoners to nurture actualizing-tao.**

Associated Contexts **Below**, HSIA: anything below, in all senses; lower, inner; lower trigram; opposite of above, SHANG. **Mountain**, SHAN: limit, boundary; the Symbol of the trigram Bound, KEN. The ideogram: three peaks, a mountain range. **Wind**, FENG: moving air, breeze, gust; weather and its influence on mood and humor; fashion, usage; wind and wood are the Symbols of the trigram Ground, SUN.

Chün tzu: ideal of a person who uses divination to order his/her life in accordance with tao rather than wilful intention; keyword. **Rouse**, CHEN: stir up, excite, stimulate; issue forth; put in order. The ideogram: hand and shake, shaking things up. **Commoners**, MIN: class of workers the state draws on to sustain the social hierarchy; undeveloped potential outside the organized personality. **Nurture**, YÜ: bring up, support, rear, raise; increase. **Actualize-tao**, TE: realize tao in action; power, virtue; ability to follow the course traced by the ongoing process of the cosmos; keyword. The ideogram: to go, straight, and heart. Linked with acquire, TE: acquiring that which makes a being become what it is meant to be.

Image Tradition

> Corrupting. Above solid and-also below supple. [I]
> Ground and-also stopping. Corrupting.
>
> Corrupting, Spring Growing. [II]
> And-also Below Heaven regulated indeed.
>
> Harvesting: wading the Great River. [III]
> Going possesses affairs indeed.
>
> Before seedburst three days, after seedburst three days. [IV]
> Completing, by-consequence possessing the beginning.
> Heaven moving indeed.

Associated Contexts **[I] Above**, SHANG: anything above, in all senses; higher, upper, outer; upper trigram; opposite of below, HSIA. **Solid**, KANG: quality of the whole lines; firm, strong, unyielding, persisting. **And-also**, ERH: joins and contrasts two terms. **Supple**, JOU: quality of the opened lines; flexible, pliant, tender, adaptable.

Ground, SUN: base on which things rest; support, foundation; mild, subtly penetrating; nourishing. The ideogram: stand and things arranged on it, the subtle influence of the ground. Image of Hexagram 57. **Stop**, CHIH: bring or come to a standstill; the Action of the trigram Bound, KEN. The ideogram: a foot stops walking.

[II] Below Heaven, T'IEN HSIA: the human world, between heaven and earth. **Regulate**, CHIH: govern well, ensure prosperity; remedy disorder, heal; someone fit to govern land, house and heart.

[III] Go, WANG, and come, LAI, describe the stream of time as it flows from future through present to past; go, WANG, indicates what is departing from present to past; proceed, move on; keyword.

[IV] Complete, CHUNG: end of a cycle that begins the next; last, whole, all; contrasts with exhaust, CH'IUNG, final end. The ideogram: silk cocoons, follow and ice, winter linking one year with the next. **Begin**, SHIH: commence, start, open; earliest, first; beginning of a time-span, ended by completion, CHUNG. The ideogram: woman and eminent, beginning new life.

    Heaven, T'IEN: highest; sky, firmament, heavens; power above the human as opposed to earth, TI, below; the Symbol of the trigram Force, CH'IEN. The ideogram: great and the one above. **Move**, HSING: move or move something; motivate, emotionally moving; walk, act, do. The ideogram: stepping left then right.

• *Transforming Lines*

Initial six

a) **Managing the father's Corrupting.**
Possessing sonhood.
Predecessors without fault.
Adversity, completing significant.

b) **Managing the father's Corrupting.**
Intention receiving the predecessors indeed.

Associated Contexts a) **Manage**, KAN: cope with, deal with, able; undertake, attend to business; trunk, stem, spine, skeleton. **Father(hood)**, FU: ruler of the family; act as a father, paternal, patriarchal; authoritative rule. The ideogram: hand and rod, the chastising father. **'s/have(-it)/it/them**, CHIH: expresses possession, directly or as an object pronoun.

    Son(hood), TZU: living up to ideal of ancestors as highest human development; act with concern and reverence; male child; offspring, posterity; seed, kernel, egg; sage, teacher; nadir, deepest point, midnight, mid-winter.

    Predecessor, K'AO: deceased ancestor, especially the grandfather; the ancients; aged, long-lived; consult, verify. The ideogram: old and ingenious, the old wise man. **Without fault**, WU CHIU: no error or harm in the situation.

    Adversity, LI: danger; threatening, malevolent demon. This has two aspects: grind, sharpen, improve, perfect, stimulate; and: poisonous,

sinister, cruel, contrary. It indicates a spirit or ghost that seeks revenge by inflicting suffering upon the living. Pacifying or exorcizing such a spirit can have a healing effect. The ideogram: sheltering cliff and stinging insect. **Significant**, CHI: leads to the experience of meaning; favorable, propitious, advantageous, appropriate; keyword. The ideogram: scholar and mouth, wise words of a sage.

b) **Intention**, YI: thought, meaning, idea, will, motive; what gives words their significance. The ideogram: heart and sound, heartfelt expression. **Receive**, CH'ENG: receive gifts or commands from superiors or customers; take in hand; catch falling water. The ideogram: accepting a seal of office.

Nine at-second

a) **Managing the mother's Corrupting.**
   Not permitting Trial.

b) **Managing the mother's Corrupting.**
   Acquiring centering tao indeed.

Associated Contexts a) **Manage**, KAN: cope with, deal with, able; undertake, attend to business; trunk, stem, spine, skeleton. **Mother(hood)**, MU: child-bearing and nourishing. The ideogram: two breasts. **'s/have(-it)/it/them**, CHIH: expresses possession, directly or as an object pronoun.

   Not permitting, PU K'O: not possible; contradicts an inherent principle. The ideogram: mouth and breath, silent consent. **Trial**, CHEN: test by ordeal; inquiry by divination and its result; righteous, firm; separating wheat from chaff; the kernel, the proven core; fourth stage of the Time Cycle. The ideogram: pearl and divination.

b) **Acquire**, TE: obtain the desired object; wish for, desire covetously; gains, possessions. The ideogram: go and obstacle, going through obstacles to the goal. **Center**, CHUNG: inner, central; put in the center; middle, stable point enabling you to face inner and outer changes; middle line of trigram. The ideogram: field divided in two equal parts. Image of Hexagram 61. **Tao**: way or path; ongoing process of being and the course it traces for each specific person or thing; keyword. The ideogram: go and head, leading and the path it creates.

Nine at-third

a) **Managing the father's Corrupting.**
The small possesses repenting.
Without the great: fault.

b) **Managing the father's Corrupting.**
Completing without fault indeed.

Associated Contexts a) **Manage**, KAN: cope with, deal with, able; undertake, attend to business; trunk, stem, spine, skeleton. **Father(hood)**, FU: ruler of the family; act as a father, paternal, patriarchal; authoritative rule. The ideogram: hand and rod, the chastising father. **'s/have(-it)/it/them**, CHIH: expresses possession, directly or as an object pronoun.

Small, HSIAO: little, common, unimportant; adapting to what crosses your path; ability to move in harmony with the vicissitudes of life; contrasts with great, TA, self-imposed theme or goal; keyword. Image of Hexagrams 9 and 62. **Repent**, HUI: dissatisfaction with past conduct causing a change of heart; proceeds from abashment, LIN, shame and confusion at having lost the right way.

Great, TA: big, noble, important, very; orient the will toward a self-imposed goal, impose direction; ability to lead or guide your life; contrasts with small, HSIAO, flexible adaptation to what crosses your path; keyword. Image of Hexagrams 14, 26, 28, 34. **Fault**, CHIU: unworthy conduct that leads to harm, illness, misfortune. The ideogram: person and differ, differ from what you should be.

b) **Without fault**, WU CHIU: no error or harm in the situation.

Six at-fourth

a) **Enriching the father's Corrupting.**
Going: visualizing abashment.

b) **Enriching the father's Corrupting.**
Going: not-yet acquiring indeed.

Associated Contexts a) **Enrich**, YÜ: make richer (excluding land); material, mental or spiritual wealth; bequeath; generous, abundant. The ideogram: garments, portable riches. **Father(hood)**, FU: ruler of the family; act as a father, paternal, patriarchal; authoritative rule. The ideogram: hand and rod, the chastising father. **'s/have(-it)/it/them/'s,** CHIH: expresses possession, directly or as an object pronoun.

Visualize, CHIEN: seeing in all its aspects: vision, being visible, forming mental images; visit, call on, consult. The ideogram: eye above person, active and receptive sight. **Abashment,** LIN: distress, shame, regret, humiliation; aware of having lost the right track; leads to repenting, HUI, correcting the direction of mind and life.

b) **Not-yet,** WEI: temporal negative; something will but has not yet occurred; contrary of already, CHI. Image of Hexagram 64. **Acquire,** TE: obtain the desired object; wish for, desire covetously; gains, possessions. The ideogram: go and obstacle, going through obstacles to the goal.

Six at-fifth

a) **Managing the father's Corrupting.**
    Availing-of praise.

b) **Managing the father availing-of praise.**
    Receiving uses actualizing-tao indeed.

Associated Contexts a) **Manage,** KAN: cope with, deal with, able; undertake, attend to business; trunk, stem, spine, skeleton. **Father(hood),** FU: ruler of the family; act as a father, paternal, patriarchal; authoritative rule. The ideogram: hand and rod, the chastising father. **'s/have(-it)/it/them,** CHIH: expresses possession, directly or as an object pronoun.

Avail-of, YUNG: take advantage of; benefit from, profit by; use for a specific purpose; apply to advantage. The ideogram: to divine and center, applying divination to central concerns. **Praise,** YÜ: admire and approve; magnify, eulogize; flatter. The ideogram: words and give, offering words.

b) **Receive,** CH'ENG: receive gifts or commands from superiors or customers; take in hand; catch falling water. The ideogram: accepting a seal of office.

Nine above

a) **Not affairs, kingly feudatories.**
  Honoring highness: one's affair.

b) **Not affairs, kingly feudatories.**
  Purpose permitted by-consequence indeed.

Associated Contexts a) **Not**, PU: simple negative. **King(hood)**, WANG: effective ruler, by authority of the Emperor, from whom others derive their power. **Feudatory**, HOU: nobles entrusted with governing the provinces; active in daily life rather than governing from the center; contrasts with prince, KUNG, executives at the court.

Honor, SHANG: esteem, give high rank to; eminent; put one thing on top of another. **High(-ness)**, KAO: high, elevated, lofty, eminent; excellent, advanced. **One's/one**, CH'I: third person pronoun; also: it/its, he/his, she/hers, they/theirs.

b) **Purpose**, CHIH: focus of mind and heart; will, inclination, resolve. The ideogram: heart and scholar, high inner resolve, or heart and go, inner determination. **Permit**, K'O: possible because in harmony with an inherent principle. The ideogram: mouth and breath, silent consent.

NEARING ▪ *LIN*

This hexagram describes your situation in terms of approaching and being approached. It emphasizes that acting without immediately expecting to attain what you desire is the adequate way to handle it. To be in accord with the time, you are told to: **near**!

● *Image of the Situation*

> **Nearing, Spring Growing Harvesting Trial.**
> **Culminating tending-towards the eighth moon: possessing a pitfall.**

Associated Contexts **Near**, LIN: approach, behold with care, look down on sympathetically; condescend; bless or curse by coming nearer; a superior visiting an inferior. **Spring Growing Harvesting Trial: Spring**, YÜAN: **Grow**, HENG; **Harvest**, LI; and **Trial**, CHEN, are the four stages of the Time Cycle, the model for all dynamic processes. They indicate that your question is connected to the cycle as a whole rather than a part of it, and that the origin (Spring) of a favorable result (Harvesting Trial) is an offering to the spirits (Growing).

Culminate, CHIH: bring to the highest degree; arrive at the end or summit; superlative. **Tend-towards**, YÜ: move toward but not reach, in the direction of; contrasts with reach(-to), HU, actually arriving. **Eight**, PA: number of highly valued essentials: eight trigrams, eight immortals, eight compass points; eighth. **Moon**, YÜEH: actual moon and moon-month; yin, the sun being yang. **Possess**, YU: in possession of, have, own; opposite of lack, WU. **Pitfall**, HSIUNG: leads away from the experience of meaning; stuck and exposed to danger, unable to take in the situation; flow of life and spirit is blocked; unfortunate, baleful; keyword.

● *Outer and Inner Aspects*

☷ **Field**: The field of earth yields and sustains, serving in order to produce. **Field** is the equalizing point between yin and yang where things labor and serve.

Connection to the outer: the common labor of sowing and hoarding, the Earthy Moment. **Field** produces concrete results through serving.

☱ **Open:** vapor rising from the marsh's open surface stimulates and fertilizes; stimulating words cheer and inspire. **Open** begins the yin hemicycle by initiating the formative process.
Connection to the inner: liquifying, casting, skinning off the mold, the Metallic Moment beginning. **Open** stimulates, cheers and reveals innate form.

Inner stimulation combined with an outer willingness to serve invites **nearing**.

● *Counter Indications*

Nuclear trigrams **Field**, K'UN and **Shake**, CHEN, result in Counter Hexagram 24, **Returning**, FU. Coming **nearer** is contrasted with **returning** to a starting point to begin again.

● *Sequence*

> **Possessing affairs and-also afterwards permitting the great.**
> **Anterior acquiescence has the use-of Nearing.**
> **Nearing implies the great indeed.**

Associated Contexts **Affairs**, SHIH: all kinds of personal activity; matters at hand; business, occupation; manage a business, case in court. **And-also**, ERH: joins and contrasts two terms. **After(wards)/later**, HOU: come after in time, subsequent; put oneself after; the second; attendants, heirs, successors, posterity. **Permit**, K'O: possible because in harmony with an inherent principle. The ideogram: mouth and breath, silent consent. **Great**, TA: big, noble, important, very; orient the will toward a self-imposed goal, impose direction; ability to lead or guide your life; contrasts with small, HSIAO, flexible adaptation to what crosses your path; keyword. Image of Hexagrams 14, 26, 28, 34.
  Anterior ... the use-of: activating this hexagram depends on understanding and accepting the previous statement.
  Imply, CHE: further signify; additional meaning. **Indeed**, YEH: intensifier; indicates comment on previous statement.

● *Contrasted Definitions*

> **Nearing Viewing's righteousness.**
> **Maybe associating-with, maybe seeking.**

Associated Contexts **View**, KUAN: contemplate, observe from a distance; look at carefully, gaze at; also: a monastery, an observatory; scry, divine through liquid in a cup. The ideogram: see and waterbird, observe through air or water. Image of Hexagram 20. **'s/have(-it)/it/them**, CHIH: expresses possession, directly or as an object pronoun. **Righteous**, YI: proper and just, meets the standards; things in their proper place; the heart that rules itself; upright, moral rule; contrasts with Harvest, LI, advantage or profit.

 Maybe, HUO: possible but not certain, perhaps. **Associate(-with)**, YÜ: consort with, combine; companions; group, band, company; agree with, comply, help. The ideogram: pair of hands reaching downward meets a pair of hands reaching upward, helpful association. **Seek**, CH'IU: search for, aim at, wish for, desire; implore, supplicate; covetous.

● *Symbol Tradition*

> **Above marsh possessing earth. Nearing.**
> **A chün tzu uses teaching to ponder without exhausting.**
> **[A chün tzu uses] tolerating**
>   **to protect the commoners without delimiting.**

Associated Contexts **Above**, SHANG: anything above, in all senses; higher, upper, outer; upper trigram; opposite of below, HSIA. **Marsh**, TSE: open surface of a flat body of water and the vapors rising from it; fertilize, enrich; kindness, favor; the Symbol of the trigram Open, TUI. **Earth**, TI: ground on which the human world rests; basis of all things, nourishes all things; the Symbol of the trigram Field, K'UN.

 Chün tzu: ideal of a person who uses divination to order his/her life in accordance with tao rather than wilful intention; keyword. **Use(-of)**, YI: make use of, by means of, owing to; employ, make functional. **Teach**, CHIAO: instruct, show; precept, doctrine. **Ponder**, SSU: reflect, consider, remember; deep thought; desire, wish. The ideogram: heart and field, the heart's concerns. **Without**, WU: devoid of; -less as suffix. **Exhaust**, CH'IUNG: bring to an end; limit, extremity; destitute; investigate exhaustively; end without a new beginning. The ideogram: cave and naked person, bent with disease or old age.

Tolerate, JUNG: allow, contain, endure, bear with; accept graciously. The ideogram: full stream bed, tolerating and containing. **Protect**, PAO: guard, defend, keep safe; secure. **Commoners**, MIN: class of workers the state draws on to sustain the social hierarchy; undeveloped potential outside the organized personality. **Delimit**, CHIANG: define frontiers, draw limits; boundary, border.

● *Image Tradition*

> **Nearing. [I]**
> **Solid drenched and-also long-living.**
> **Stimulating and-also yielding.**
> **Solid centering and-also corresponding.**
>
> **Great Growing uses correcting. [II]**
> **Heavenly tao indeed.**
>
> **Culminating tending-towards the eighth moon:**
> **possessing a pitfall. [III]**
> **Dissolving, not lasting indeed.**

Associated Contexts **Solid**, KANG: quality of the whole lines; firm, strong, unyielding, persisting. **Drench**, CH'IN: soak, penetrate, immerse, steep in; imbued with. **Long-living**, CHANG: enduring, constant; senior, superior, greater; increase, prosper; respect, elevate.

Stimulate, SHUO: rouse to action and good feeling; free from constraint, stir up, urge on; persuade, cheer, delight; set out in words; the Action of the trigram Open, TUI. The ideogram: words and exchange. **Yield(-to)**, SHUN: give way and bear produce; comply, agree, follow, obey; unresisting, docile, flexible; nourish, provide; the Action of the trigram Field, K'UN. The ideogram: head and current, water flowing from the head of a river, yielding to the banks.

Center, CHUNG: inner, central; put in the center; middle, stable point enabling you to face inner and outer changes; middle line of trigram. The ideogram: field divided in two equal parts. Image of Hexagram 61. **Correspond(-to)**, YING: be in agreement or harmony; resonate together, invoke and fulfill each other; answer to, suitable; relation between the lines (1:4, 2:5, 3:6) when they form the pair opened and whole, supple and solid. The ideogram: heart and obey.

[II] **Grow**, HENG: success through a sacrifice; pervade, persevere; bring to full growth; enjoy; vigorous, effective; second stage of the Time Cycle. **Correct**, CHENG: rectify deviation or one-sidedness; proper, straight, exact, regular; constant, rule, model. The ideogram: stop and one, hold to one thing.

Heaven, T'IEN: highest; sky, firmament, heavens; power above the human as opposed to earth, TI, below; the Symbol of the trigram Force, CH'IEN. The ideogram: great and the one above. **Tao**: way or path; ongoing process of being and the course it traces for each specific person or thing; keyword. The ideogram: go and head, leading and the path it creates.

[III] **Dissolve**, HSIAO: liquify, melt, thaw; diminish, disperse; eliminate, exhaust. The ideogram: water dissolving differences. **Not**, PU: simple negative. **Last**, CHIU: long, protracted; enduring.

- *Transforming Lines*

   Initial nine

   a) **Conjunction Nearing, Trial: significant.**

   b) **Conjunction Nearing, Trial: significant.**
   Purpose moving, correcting indeed.

Associated Contexts a) **Conjoin**, HSIEN: come into contact with, influence; reach, join together; put together as parts of a previously separated whole; come into conjunction, as the celestial bodies; totally, completely; lit.: broken piece of pottery, the halves of which join to identify partners. Image of Hexagram 31. **Trial**, CHEN: test by ordeal; inquiry by divination and its result; righteous, firm; separating wheat from chaff; the kernel, the proven core; fourth stage of the Time Cycle. The ideogram: pearl and divination. **Significant**, CHI: leads to the experience of meaning; favorable, propitious, advantageous, appropriate; keyword. The ideogram: scholar and mouth, wise words of a sage.

b) **Purpose**, CHIH: focus of mind and heart; will, inclination, resolve. The ideogram: heart and scholar, high inner resolve, or heart and go, inner determination. **Move**, HSING: move or move something; motivate, emotionally moving; walk, act, do. The ideogram: stepping left then right.

Nine at-second

a) **Conjunction Nearing: significant.**
  Without not Harvesting.

b) **Conjunction Nearing: significant.**
  Without not Harvesting.
  Not-yet yielding-to fate indeed.

Associated Contexts a) **Conjoin**, HSIEN: come into contact with, influence; reach, join together; put together as parts of a previously separated whole; come into conjunction, as the celestial bodies; totally, completely; lit.: broken piece of pottery, the halves of which join to identify partners. Image of Hexagram 31. **Significant**, CHI: leads to the experience of meaning; favorable, propitious, advantageous, appropriate; keyword. The ideogram: scholar and mouth, wise words of a sage.

  Without not Harvesting, WU PU LI: nothing for which this will not be beneficial; advantageous potential, borderline where the balance is swinging from not Harvesting to actually Harvesting.

b) **Not-yet**, WEI: temporal negative; something will but has not yet occurred; contrary of already, CHI. Image of Hexagram 64. **Fate**, MING: individual destiny; birth and death as limits of life; issue orders with authority; consult the gods. The ideogram: mouth and order, words with heavenly authority.

Six at-third

a) **Sweetness Nearing.**
  Without direction: Harvesting.
  Already grieving-over it:
  Without fault.

b) **Sweetness Nearing.**
  Situation not appropriate indeed.
  Already grieving-over it:
  Fault not long-living indeed.

Associated Contexts a) **Sweet**, KAN: taste corresponding to the Earthy Moment; agreeable, happy, delightful, refreshing; grateful.

Without direction: Harvesting, WU YU LI: no plan or direction is advantageous; in order to take advantage of the situation, do not impose a direction on events.

Already, CHI: completed, done, has occurred; past tense, contrary of not-yet, WEI. Image of Hexagram 63. **Grieve(-over)**, YU: sorrow, melancholy; mourn; anxious, careworn; hidden sorrow. The ideogram: heart, head, and limp, heart-sick and anxious. **It/them/have(-it)/'s**, CHIH: expresses possession, directly or as an object pronoun.

Without fault, WU CHIU: no error or harm in the situation.

b) **Situation**, WEI: place or seat according to rank; post, position, command; right, proper; established, arranged. The ideogram: person and stand, servants in their places. **Appropriate**, TANG: suitable; opportune, convenient; adequate, competent; equal to; whole lines in uneven places and opened lines in even places.

Fault, CHIU: unworthy conduct that leads to harm, illness, misfortune. The ideogram: person and differ, differ from what you should be.

Six at-fourth

a) **Culminating Nearing.**
Without fault.

b) **Culminating Nearing, without fault.**
Situation appropriate indeed.

Associated Contexts a) **Without fault**, WU CHIU: no error or harm in the situation.

b) **Situation**, WEI: place or seat according to rank; post, position, command; right, proper; established, arranged. The ideogram: person and stand, servants in their places. **Appropriate**, TANG: suitable; opportune, convenient; adequate, competent; equal to; whole lines in uneven places and opened lines in even places.

Six at-fifth

a) **Knowledge Nearing.**
A Great Chief's propriety.
Significant.

b) **A Great Chief's propriety.**
Moving the center's designating indeed.

Associated Contexts a) **Know**, CHIH: understand, perceive, remember; informed, aware, wise. The ideogram: arrow and mouth, words focused and swift.

Chief, CHÜN: effective ruler; preside over, take the lead; influence others; term of respect. The ideogram: mouth and director, giving orders. **Proper**, YI: reasonable of itself; fit and right, harmonious; ought, should.

Significant, CHI: leads to the experience of meaning; favorable, propitious, advantageous, appropriate; keyword. The ideogram: scholar and mouth, wise words of a sage.

b) **Move**, HSING: move or move something; motivate, emotionally moving; walk, act, do. The ideogram: stepping left then right. **Designate**, WEI: represent in words, assign a name or meaning; report on, talk about. The ideogram: words and belly, describing the essential.

Six above

a) **Magnanimity Nearing.**
Significant. Without fault.

b) **Magnanimity Nearing's significance.**
Purpose located inside indeed.

Associated Contexts a) **Magnanimous**, TUN: generous; honest, substantial, important, wealthy; honor, increase; firm, solid. The ideogram: strike and accept, warrior magnanimous in attack and defense.

Significant, CHI: leads to the experience of meaning; favorable, propitious, advantageous, appropriate; keyword. The ideogram: scholar and mouth, wise words of a sage. **Without fault**, WU CHIU: no error or harm in the situation.

b) **Purpose**, CHIH: focus of mind and heart; will, inclination, resolve. The ideogram: heart and scholar, high inner resolve, or heart and go, inner determination. **Locate(-in)**, TSAI: live in, dwell, reside; belong to, involved with, depend on; within. The ideogram: earth and persevere, place on the earth. **Inside**, NEI: within, inner, interior; inside of the house and those who work there, particularly women; the lower trigram, as opposed to outside, WAI, the upper. The ideogram: border and enter, cross a border.

20

VIEWING ▪ *KUAN*

This hexagram describes your situation in terms of something seen from a distance, out of immediate reach. It emphasizes that carefully observing and divining the meaning is the adequate way to handle it. To be in accord with the time, you are told to: **view!**

● *Image of the Situation*

> **Viewing: hand-washing and-also not worshipping.**
> **Possessing conformity, like a presence.**

Associated Contexts **View**, KUAN: contemplate, observe from a distance; look at carefully, gaze at; also: a monastery, an observatory; scry, divine through liquid in a cup. The ideogram: see and waterbird, observe through air or water. **Hand-washing**, KUAN: wash the hands before a sacramental act; ablutions, a basin. **And-also**, ERH: joins and contrasts two terms. **Not**, PU: simple negative. **Worship**, CHIEN: honor the gods and ancestors; make sacrifice; recommend or introduce yourself. The ideogram: leading animals to green pastures.

Possessing conformity, YU FU: inner and outer are in accord; confidence of the spirits has been captured; sincere, truthful; proper to take action. **Like**, JO: same as; just as, similar to. **Presence**, YUNG: noble bearing; prestige, dignity; imposing; haughty, conceited; lit.: a large head.

● *Outer and Inner Aspects*

☴ **Ground**: Wind and wood subtly enter from the ground, penetrating and pervading. **Ground** is the center of the yang hemicycle, spreading pervasive action.

Connection to the outer: penetrating and bringing together, the Woody Moment culminating. **Ground** pervades, matches and couples, seeding a new generation.

☷ **Field**: The field of earth yields and sustains, serving in order to produce. **Field** is the equalizing point between yin and yang where things labor and serve.

Connection to the inner: the common labor of sowing and hoarding, the Earthy Moment. **Field** produces concrete results through serving.

Entering and penetrating the inner field, images of distant actions come into **view**.

● *Count. r Indications*

Nuclear trigrams **Bound**, KEN, and **Field**, K'UN, result in Counter Hexagram 23, **Stripping**, PO. **Viewing** the entire field of action is contrasted with actively **stripping** away aims and objects.

● *Sequence*

> **Being great therefore afterwards permitting Viewing.**
> **Anterior acquiescence has the use-of Viewing.**

Associated Contexts **Being(s)**, WU: creature, thing, any single being; matter, substance, essence; nature of things. **Great**, TA: big, noble, important, very; orient the will toward a self-imposed goal, impose direction; ability to lead or guide your life; contrasts with small, HSIAO, flexible adaptation to what crosses your path; keyword. Image of Hexagrams 14, 26, 28, 34. **Therefore afterwards**, JAN HOU: logical consequence of, necessarily follows in time. **Permit**, K'O: possible because in harmony with an inherent principle. The ideogram: mouth and breath, silent consent.
   Anterior ... the use-of: activating this hexagram depends on understanding and accepting the previous statement.

● *Contrasted Definitions*

> **Nearing Viewing's righteousness.**
> **Maybe associating-with, maybe seeking.**

Associated Contexts **Near**, LIN: approach or be approached: behold with care, look on sympathetically; condescend; bless or curse by coming nearer; a superior visits an inferior. Image of Hexagram 19. **'s/have(-it)/it/them**, CHIH: expresses possession, directly or as an object pronoun. **Righteous**, YI: proper and just, meets the standards; things in

their proper place; the heart that rules itself; upright, moral rule; contrasts with Harvest, LI, advantage or profit.

Maybe, HUO: possible but not certain, perhaps. **Associate(-with),** YÜ: consort with, combine; companions; group, band, company; agree with, comply, help. The ideogram: pair of hands reaching downward meets a pair of hands reaching upward, helpful association. **Seek,** CH'IU: search for, aim at, wish for, desire; implore, supplicate; covetous.

● *Symbol Tradition*

> **Wind moving above earth. Viewing.**
> **The Earlier Kings used inspecting on-all-sides,**
> **Viewing the commoners to set-up teaching.**

Associated Contexts **Wind,** FENG: moving air, breeze, gust; weather and its influence on mood and humor; fashion, usage; wind and wood are the Symbols of the trigram Ground, SUN. **Move,** HSING: move or move something; motivate, emotionally moving; walk, act, do. The ideogram: stepping left then right. **Above,** SHANG: anything above, in all senses; higher, upper, outer; upper trigram; opposite of below, HSIA. **Earth,** TI: ground on which the human world rests; basis of all things, nourishes all things; the Symbol of the trigram Field, K'UN.

Earlier Kings, HSIEN WANG: ideal rulers of old; the golden age, primal time, power in harmony with nature; model for the chün tzu. **Use(-of),** YI: make use of, by means of, owing to; employ, make functional. **Inspect,** HSING: examine on all sides, careful inquiry; watchful. **Sides (on-all-sides),** FANG: limits, boundaries; square, surface of the earth extending to the four cardinal points; everywhere. **Commoners,** MIN: class of workers the state draws on to sustain the social hierarchy; undeveloped potential outside the organized personality. **Set-up,** SHE: establish, institute; arrange, set in order; spread a net. The ideogram: words and impel, establish with words. **Teach,** CHIAO: instruct, show; precept, doctrine.

● *Image Tradition*

> **The great: Viewing located above. [I]**
> **Yielding and-also Ground.**
> **Centering correcting uses Viewing Below Heaven.**

Viewing: hand-washing and-also not worshipping. [II]
Possessing conformity, like a presence.
Viewing below and-also changing indeed.

Viewing heaven's spirit tao. [III]
And-also the four seasons not straying.
The all-wise person uses spirit tao to set-up teaching.
And-also actually Below Heaven submitting.

Associated Contexts [I] **Locate(-in)**, TSAI: live in, dwell, reside;
belong to, involved with, depend on; within. The ideogram: earth and
persevere, place on the earth.

Yield(-to), SHUN: give way and bear produce; comply, agree, follow,
obey; unresisting, docile, flexible; nourish, provide; the Action of the
trigram Field, K'UN. The ideogram: head and current, water flowing from
the head of a river, yielding to the banks. **Ground**, SUN: base on which
things rest; support, foundation; mild, subtly penetrating; nourishing. The
ideogram: stand and things arranged on it, the subtle influence of the
ground. Image of Hexagram 57.

Centering correcting, CHUNG CHENG: central and correct; make
rectifying one-sidedness and error your central concern; reaching a stable
center in yourself can correct the situation. **Below Heaven**, T'IEN HSIA:
the human world, between heaven and earth.

[II] **Below**, HSIA: anything below, in all senses; lower, inner; lower
trigram; opposite of above, SHANG. **Change**, HUA: gradual, continuous
metamorphosis; influence someone; contrasts with transform, PIEN,
sudden mutation. The ideogram: person alive and dead, the life-process.
Indeed, YEH: intensifier; indicates comment on previous statement.

[III] **Heaven**, T'IEN: highest; sky, firmament, heavens; power above the
human as opposed to earth, TI, below; the Symbol of the trigram Force,
CH'IEN. The ideogram: great and the one above. **Spirit(s)**, SHEN:
independent spiritual powers that confer intensity on heart and mind by
acting on the soul, KUEI; gods, daimons. **Tao**: way or path; ongoing
process of being and the course it traces for each specific person or thing;
keyword. The ideogram: go and head, leading and the path it creates.

Four seasons, SSU SHIH: the four dynamic qualities of time that make
up the year and the Time Cycle; the right time, in accord with the time;
time as sacred; all-encompassing. **Stray**, T'E: wander blindly; deviate, err,
alter, doubt; excess.

All-wise, SHENG: intuitive universal wisdom; mythical sages; holy, sacred; mark of highest distinction. The ideogram: ear and inform, one who knows all from a single sound. **People, person**, JEN: humans individually and collectively; an individual; humankind. Image of Hexagrams 13 and 37.

Actually, YI: truly, really, at present. The ideogram: a dart and done, strong intention fully expressed. **Submit**, FU: yield to, serve; undergo.

● *Transforming Lines*

Initial six

a) **Youthful Viewing.**
Small People: without fault.
Chün tzu: abashment.

b) **Initial six, youthful Viewing.**
Small People: tao indeed.

Associated Contexts a) **Youthful**, T'UNG: young person between eight and fifteen; young animals and plants.

Small People, HSIAO JEN: lowly, common, humble; those who adjust to circumstances with the flexibility of the small; effect of the small within an individual; keyword. **Without fault**, WU CHIU: no error or harm in the situation.

Chün tzu: ideal of a person who uses divination to order his/her life in accordance with tao rather than wilful intention; keyword. **Abashment**, LIN: distress, shame, regret, humiliation; aware of having lost the right track; leads to repenting, HUI, correcting the direction of mind and life.

Six at-second

a) **Peeping-through Viewing.**
Harvesting: woman Trial.

b) **Peeping-through Viewing: woman Trial.**
Truly permitting the demoniac indeed.

Associated Contexts a) **Peep-through**, K'UEI: observe from hiding; stealthily, furtive.

Harvest, LI: advantageous, profitable; acute, insightful; benefit, nourish; third stage of the Time Cycle. **Woman(hood)**, NÜ: a woman; what is inherently female. **Trial**, CHEN: test by ordeal; inquiry by divination and its result; righteous, firm; separating wheat from chaff; the kernel, the proven core; fourth stage of the Time Cycle. The ideogram: pearl and divination.

b) **Truly**, YI: statement is true and precise. **Demon(iac)**, CH'OU: possessed by a malignant genius; ugly, physically or morally deformed; vile, disgraceful, shameful; drunken. The ideogram: fermenting liquor and soul. Demoniac and tiger are opposed on the Universal Compass North–South axis; the tiger (Extreme Yang) scares away and protects against demoniacs (Extreme Yin).

Six at-third

a) **Viewing my birth, advancing, withdrawing.**

b) **Viewing my birth, advancing, withdrawing.**
　　Not-yet letting-go tao indeed.

Associated Contexts *a)* **My/me/I**, WO: first person pronoun; indicates an unusually strong emphasis on your own subjective experience. **Birth/give-birth-to**, SHENG: produce, beget, grow, bear, arise; life, vitality. The ideogram: earth and sprout. **Advance**, CHIN: exert yourself, make progress, climb; be promoted; further the development of, augment; adopt a religion or conviction; offer, introduce. **Withdraw(-from)**, T'UI: draw back, retreat, recede; decline, refuse.

　b) **Not-yet**, WEI: temporal negative; something will but has not yet occurred; contrary of already, CHI. Image of Hexagram 64. **Let-go**, SHIH: lose, omit, miss, fail, let slip; out of control. The ideogram: drop from the hand.

Six at-fourth

a) **Viewing the city's shining.**
　　Harvesting: availing-of guesting tending-towards kinghood.

b) **Viewing the city's shining.**
　　Honoring guesting indeed.

Associated Contexts a) **City**, KUO: area of only human constructions; political unit, polis. First of the territorial zones: city, suburbs, countryside, forests. **Shine**, KUANG: illuminate; give off brilliant, bright light; honor, glory, éclat; result of action, contrasts with brightness, MING, light of heavenly bodies. The ideogram: fire above person, lifting the light.

Harvest, LI: advantageous, profitable; acute, insightful; benefit, nourish; third stage of the Time Cycle. **Avail-of**, YUNG: take advantage of; benefit from, profit by; use for a specific purpose; apply to advantage. The ideogram: to divine and center, applying divination to central concerns. **Guest**, PIN: entertain a guest; visit someone, enjoy hospitality; receive a stranger. **Tend-towards**, YÜ: move toward but not reach, in the direction of; contrasts with reach(-to), HU, actually arriving. **King(hood)**, WANG: effective ruler, by authority of the Emperor, from whom others derive their power.

b) **Honor**, SHANG: esteem, give high rank to; eminent; put one thing on top of another.

Nine at-fifth

a) **Viewing my birth.**
A chün tzu: without fault.

b) **Viewing my birth.**
Viewing the commoners indeed.

Associated Contexts a) **My/me/I**, WO: first person pronoun; indicates an unusually strong emphasis on your own subjective experience. **Birth/give-birth-to**, SHENG: produce, beget, grow, bear, arise; life, vitality. The ideogram: earth and sprout.

Chün tzu: ideal of a person who uses divination to order his/her life in accordance with tao rather than wilful intention; keyword. **Without fault**, WU CHIU: no error or harm in the situation.

Nine above

a) **Viewing one's birth.**
A chün tzu: without fault.

b) **Viewing one's birth.**
   Purpose not-yet evened indeed.

Associated Contexts a) **One's/one**, CH'I: third person pronoun; also: it/its, he/his, she/hers, they/theirs. **Birth/give-birth-to**, SHENG: produce, beget, grow, bear, arise; life, vitality. The ideogram: earth and sprout.

    Chün tzu: ideal of a person who uses divination to order his/her life in accordance with tao rather than wilful intention; keyword. **Without fault,** WU CHIU: no error or harm in the situation.

b) **Purpose**, CHIH: focus of mind and heart; will, inclination, resolve. The ideogram: heart and scholar, high inner resolve, or heart and go, inner determination. **Not-yet**, WEI: temporal negative; something will but has not yet occurred; contrary of already, CHI. Image of Hexagram 64. **Even**, P'ING: level, make even or equal; uniform, peaceful, tranquil; restore quiet, harmonize.

21

GNAWING BITE ▪ *SHIH HO*

This hexagram describes your situation in terms of confronting a tenacious obstacle. It emphasizes that biting through and picking things clean until the essential is revealed is the adequate way to handle it. To be in accord with the time, you are told to: **gnaw** and **bite** through!

● *Image of the Situation*

> **Gnawing Bite, Growing.**
> **Harvesting: availing-of litigating.**

Associated Contexts **Gnaw**, SHIH: bite away, chew; bite persistently and remove; snap at, nibble; reach the essential by removing the unnecessary. The ideogram: mouth and divination, revealing the essential. **Bite**, HO: close the jaws, bite through, crush between the teeth. The ideogram: mouth and cover, jaws fit together as a lid fits a vessel. **Grow**, HENG: success through a sacrifice; pervade, persevere; bring to full growth; enjoy; vigorous, effective; second stage of the Time Cycle.

Harvest, LI: advantageous, profitable; acute, insightful; benefit, nourish; third stage of the Time Cycle. **Avail-of**, YUNG: take advantage of; benefit from, profit by; use for a specific purpose; apply to advantage. The ideogram: to divine and center, applying divination to central concerns. **Litigate**, YÜ: legal proceedings; take a case to court. The ideogram: two dogs and words, barking arguments at each other.

● *Outer and Inner Aspects*

☲ **Radiance**: Fire and brightness radiate light and warmth, attached to their support; congregating people see and become aware. **Radiance** ends the yang hemicycle, consuming action in awareness.

Connection to the outer: light, heat, consciousness bring continual change, the Fiery Moment. **Radiance** spreads outward, congregating, becoming aware and changing.

☳ **Shake**: Thunder rises from below, shaking and stirring things up. **Shake** begins the yang hemicycle by germinating new action.

Connection to the inner: sprouting energies thrusting from below, the Woody Moment beginning. **Shake** stirs things up to issue-forth.

Inner stirring-up spreads outer awareness, **gnawing** through obstacles with thunder's incisive **bite**. These trigrams begin and end the yang hemicycle; they emphasize taking action.

● *Counter Indications*

Nuclear trigrams **Gorge**, K'AN, and **Bound**, KEN, result in Counter Hexagram 39, **Limping**, CHIEN. The resolute action necessary to **gnaw** and **bite** through is contrasted with **limping's** hampered movement.

● *Sequence*

> **Permitting Viewing and-also afterwards**
>
> > **possessing a place to unite.**
> **Anterior acquiescence has the use-of Gnawing Bite.**
> **Gnawing Bite implies uniting indeed.**

Associated Contexts **Permit**, K'O: possible because in harmony with an inherent principle. The ideogram: mouth and breath, silent consent. **View**, KUAN: contemplate, observe from a distance; look at carefully, gaze at; also: a monastery, an observatory; scry, divine through liquid in a cup. The ideogram: see and waterbird, observe through air or water. Image of Hexagram 20. **And-also**, ERH: joins and contrasts two terms. **After(wards)/later**, HOU: come after in time, subsequent; put oneself after; the second; attendant, heirs, successors, posterity. **Possess**, YU: in possession of, have, own; opposite of lack, WU. **Place**, SO: where something belongs or comes from; residence, dwelling; habitual focus or object. **Unite**, HO: join, match, correspond, agree, collect, reply; unison, harmony; also: close, shut the mouth. The ideogram: mouth and assemble.

Anterior ... the use-of: activating this hexagram depends on understanding and accepting the previous statement.

Imply, CHE: further signify; additional meaning. **Indeed**, YEH: intensifier; indicates comment on previous statement.

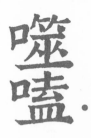

• *Contrasted Definitions*

Gnawing Bite: taking-in indeed.
Adorning: without complexion indeed.

Associated Contexts **Take-in,** SHIH: eat, ingest, swallow, devour; incorporate.

Adorn, PI: embellish, ornament, deck out, beautify; variegated (flowers); elegant, brilliant; also: energetic, passionate, eager, intrepid; capable of great effort; brave. The ideogram: cowrie shells (money) and flowers, linking ornaments and value. Image of Hexagram 22. **Without,** WU: devoid of; -less as suffix. **Complexion,** SE: appearance, expression; color, hue; air, manner, deportment; beautiful.

• *Symbol Tradition*

Thunder, lightning. Gnawing Bite.
The Earlier Kings used brightening flogging to enforce the laws.

Associated Contexts **Thunder,** LEI: rising, arousing power; the Symbol of the trigram Shake, CHEN. **Lightning,** TIEN: lighting flash, electric discharge; sudden clarity; look attentively.

Earlier Kings, HSIEN WANG: ideal rulers of old; the golden age, primal time, power in harmony with nature; model for the chün tzu. **Use(-of),** YI: make use of, by means of, owing to; employ, make functional. **Brightness,** MING: light-giving aspect of burning, heavenly bodies and consciousness; with fire, the Symbol of the trigram Radiance, LI. **Flog,** FA: punish with blows, beat, whip; used to find out the truth. **Enforce,** LAI: compel obedience; have charge of; imposed by highest authority; arrest, deliver for punishment. **Laws,** FA: rules, statutes, model, method.

• *Image Tradition*

Jaws center possesses being. Spoken-thus: Gnawing Bite. [I]
Gnawing Bite and-also Growing.
Solid[and]Supple apportioning.

Stirring-up and-also brightening. [II]
Thunder, lightning, uniting and-also composing.

Supple acquiring the center and-also moving above. [III]
Although not an appropriate situation,
Harvesting: availing-of litigating indeed.

Associated Contexts [I] **Jaws/swallow**, YI: mouth, jaws, cheeks, chin; take in, ingest; feed, nourish, sustain, rear; furnish what is necessary. The ideogram: open jaws. Image of Hexagram 27. **Center**, CHUNG: inner, central; put in the center; middle, stable point enabling you to face inner and outer changes; middle line of trigram. The ideogram: field divided in two equal parts. Image of Hexagram 61. **Being(s)**, WU: creature, thing, any single being; matter, substance, essence; nature of things. **Spoken-thus**, YÜEH: designated, termed, called. The ideogram: open mouth and tongue.

    Solid[and]Supple, KANG JOU: field of creative tension between the whole and opened lines and their qualities; field of psychic movement. **Apportion**, FEN: divide for distribution; sort out; allot to.

[II] **Stir-up**, TUNG: excite, influence, move, affect; work, take action; come out of the egg or the bud; the Action of the trigram Shake, CHEN. The ideogram: strength and heavy, move weighty things.

    Composition, CHANG: a well-composed whole and its structure; beautiful creations; elegant, clear, brilliant; contrasts with pattern, WEN, beauty of intrinsic design.

[III] **Supple**, JOU: quality of the opened lines; flexible, pliant, tender, adaptable. **Acquire**, TE: obtain the desired object; wish for, desire covetously; gains, possessions. The ideogram: go and obstacle, going through obstacles to the goal. **Move**, HSING: move or move something; motivate, emotionally moving; walk, act, do. The ideogram: stepping left then right. **Above**, SHANG: anything above, in all senses; higher, upper, outer; upper trigram; opposite of below, HSIA.

    Although, SUI: even though, supposing that, if, even if. **Not**, PU: simple negative. **Appropriate**, TANG: suitable; opportune, convenient; adequate, competent; equal to; whole lines in uneven places and opened lines in even places. **Situation**, WEI: place or seat according to rank; post, position, command; right, proper; established, arranged. The ideogram: person and stand, servants in their places.

Transforming Lines

Initial nine

a) **Shoes locked-up, submerging the feet.
Without fault.**

b) **Shoes locked-up, submerging the feet.
Not moving indeed.**

Associated Contexts a) **Shoes**, CHÜ: footwear, sandals. **Lock-up**, CHIAO: imprison, lock up the feet; prison, pen. **Submerge**, MIEH: plunge under water, put out a fire; exterminate, finish, cut off. The ideogram: water and destroy. **Foot**, CHIH: literal foot; foundation, base.

Without fault, WU CHIU: no error or harm in the situation.

Six at-second

a) **Gnawing flesh, submerging the nose.
Without fault.**

b) **Gnawing flesh, submerging the nose.
Riding a solid indeed.**

Associated Contexts a) **Flesh**, FU: muscles, organs, skin, in contrast to bones. **Submerge**, MIEH: plunge under water, put out a fire; exterminate, finish, cut off. The ideogram: water and destroy. **Nose**, PI: literal nose; the first, original.

Without fault, WU CHIU: no error or harm in the situation.

b) **Ride**, CH'ENG: ride an animal or a chariot; have the upper hand, seize the right time; control strong power; overcome the nature of the other; supple opened line above a solid whole line. **Solid**, KANG: quality of the whole lines; firm, strong, unyielding, persisting.

Six at-third

a) **Gnawing seasoned meat. Meeting poison.
The small abashed.
Without fault.**

b) **Meeting poison.**
   Situation not appropriate indeed.

Associated Contexts a) **Seasoned**, HSI: dried meat, prepared for a journey. **Meat**, JU: flesh of animals, pulp of fruit. **Meet**, YÜ: come on unexpectedly, encounter; occur, happen; pleasant meeting, lucky coincidence; agree. **Poison**, TU: noxious, malignant, hurtful, destructive; despise.

   Small, HSIAO: little, common, unimportant; adapting to what crosses your path; ability to move in harmony with the vicissitudes of life; contrasts with great, TA, self-imposed theme or goal; keyword. Image of Hexagrams 9 and 62. **Abashment**, LIN: distress, shame, regret, humiliation; aware of having lost the right track; leads to repenting, HUI, correcting the direction of mind and life.

   Without fault, WU CHIU: no error or harm in the situation.

Nine at-fourth

a) **Gnawing parched meat-bones.**
   Acquiring a metallic arrow.
   Harvesting: drudgery, Trial.
   Significant.

b) **Harvesting: drudgery, Trial significant.**
   Not-yet shining indeed.

Associated Contexts a) **Parch**, KAN: dry up; dried, exhausted, dessicated; cleaned away, gone. **Meat-bones**, TZU: meat with bones; bones left after a meal.

   Metallic, CHIN: smelting and casting; all things pertaining to metal, particularly gold; autumn, West, sunset; one of the Five Moments. **Arrow**, SHIH: arrow, javelin, dart; swift, direct as an arrow; marshal together.

   Drudgery, CHIEN: difficult, hard, repetitive work; hard to cultivate; distressing, sorrowful. The ideogram: sticky earth and a person looking around, hard work in comparison to others. **Trial**, CHEN: test by ordeal; inquiry by divination and its result; righteous, firm; separating wheat from chaff; the kernel, the proven core; fourth stage of the Time Cycle. The ideogram: pearl and divination.

Significant, CHI: leads to the experience of meaning; favorable, propitious, advantageous, appropriate; keyword. The ideogram: scholar and mouth, wise words of a sage.

b) **Not-yet**, WEI: temporal negative; something will but has not yet occurred; contrary of already, CHI. Image of Hexagram 64. **Shine**, KUANG: illuminate; give off brilliant, bright light; honor, glory, éclat; result of action, contrasts with brightness, MING, light of heavenly bodies. The ideogram: fire above person, lifting the light.

Six at-fifth

a) **Gnawing parched meat. Acquiring yellow metal.**
   Trial: adversity.
   Without fault.

b) **Trial: adversity, without fault.**
   Acquiring the appropriate indeed.

Associated Contexts a) **Parch**, KAN: dry up; dried, exhausted, dessicated; cleaned away, gone. **Meat**, JU: flesh of animals, pulp of fruit. **Yellow**, HUANG: color of the productive middle; associated with the Earthy Moment between the yang and yin hemicycles; color of soil in central China; emblematic and imperial color of China since the Yellow Emperor (2500 BCE). **Metallic**, CHIN: smelting and casting; all things pertaining to metal, particularly gold; autumn, West, sunset; one of the Five Moments.
   Trial, CHEN: test by ordeal; inquiry by divination and its result; righteous, firm; separating wheat from chaff; the kernel, the proven core; fourth stage of the Time Cycle. The ideogram: pearl and divination.
   Adversity, LI: danger; threatening, malevolent demon. This has two aspects: grind, sharpen, improve, perfect, stimulate; and: poisonous, sinister, cruel, contrary. It indicates a spirit or ghost that seeks revenge by inflicting suffering upon the living. Pacifying or exorcizing such a spirit can have a healing effect. The ideogram: sheltering cliff and stinging insect.
   Without fault, WU CHIU: no error or harm in the situation.

Nine above

a) **Wherefore locking-up submerging the ears?**
Pitfall.

b) **Wherefore locking-up submerging the ears?**
Understanding not brightened indeed.

Associated Contexts a) **Wherefore**, HO: interrogative: why? for what reason? what is? and affirmation: therefore, for that reason. **Lock-up**, CHIAO: imprison, lock up the feet; prison, pen. **Submerge**, MIEH: plunge under water, put out a fire; exterminate, finish, cut off. The ideogram: water and destroy. **Ear**, ERH: organ of hearing; handle, sides.

Pitfall, HSIUNG: leads away from the experience of meaning; stuck and exposed to danger, unable to take in the situation; flow of life and spirit is blocked; unfortunate, baleful; keyword.

b) **Understand**, TS'UNG: perceive quickly, astute, sharp; discriminate intelligently. The ideogram: ear and quick.

ADORNING ▮ *PI*

This hexagram describes your situation in terms of its outward presentation. It emphasizes that building intrinsic value by embellishing appearance and displaying valor is the adequate way to handle it. To be in accord with the time, you are told to: **adorn!**

● *Image of the Situation*

Adorning, Growing.
The small, Harvesting: possessing directed going.

Associated Contexts **Adorn**, PI: embellish, ornament, deck out, beautify; variegated (flowers); elegant, brilliant; also: energetic, passionate, eager, intrepid; capable of great effort; brave. The ideogram: cowrie shells (money) and flowers, linking ornaments and value. **Grow**, HENG: success through a sacrifice; pervade, persevere; bring to full growth; enjoy; vigorous, effective; second stage of the Time Cycle.

Small, HSIAO: little, common, unimportant; adapting to what crosses your path; ability to move in harmony with the vicissitudes of life; contrasts with great, TA, self-imposed theme or goal; keyword. Image of Hexagrams 9 and 62. **Harvest**, LI: advantageous, profitable; acute, insightful; benefit, nourish; third stage of the Time Cycle. **Possessing directed going**, YU YU WANG: imposing a direction on the flow of time from present to past; have a specific goal or purpose.

● *Outer and Inner Aspects*

☶ **Bound**: Mountains bound, limit and set a place off, stopping forward movement. **Bound** completes a full yin-yang cycle.

Connection to the outer: accomplishing words, which express things fully. **Bound** articulates what is complete and suggests what is beginning.

☲ **Radiance**: Fire and brightness radiate light and warmth, attached to their support; congregating people see and become aware. **Radiance** ends the yang hemicycle, consuming action in awareness.

Connection to the inner: light, heat, consciousness bring about continual change, the Fiery Moment. **Radiance** spreads outward, congregating, becoming aware and changing.

The outer boundary limits spreading brightness to **adorning** what can be seen.

● *Counter Indications*

Nuclear trigrams **Shake**, CHEN, and **Gorge**, K'AN, result in Counter Hexagram 40, **Taking-apart**, HSIEH. **Adorning** the outward appearance is contrasted with **taking** things **apart** to find their inner motivation.

● *Sequence*

> **Beings not permitted to use unconsidered uniting**
> **and-also climaxing.**
> **Anterior acquiescence has the use-of Adorning.**
> **Adorning implies embellishing indeed.**

Associated Contexts **Beings not permitted to use …**: no one is allowed to make use of; nothing can exist by means of. **Unconsidered**, KOU: offhand, impromptu, improvised; careless, improper; illicit. **Unite**, HO: join, match, correspond, agree, collect, reply; unison, harmony; also: close, shut the mouth. The ideogram: mouth and assemble. **And-also**, ERH: joins and contrasts two terms. **Climax**, YI: come to a high point and stop, bring to an end; use up, lay aside; decline, reject.

Anterior … the use-of: activating this hexagram depends on understanding and accepting the previous statement.

Imply, CHE: further signify; additional meaning. **Embellish**, SHIH: ornament, paint, brighten, patch up the appearance; apply cosmetics; pretend, make believe. **Indeed**, YEH: intensifier; indicates comment on previous statement.

● *Contrasted Definitions*

> **Gnawing Bite: taking-in indeed.**
> **Adorning: without complexion indeed.**

Associated Contexts **Gnaw**, SHIH: bite away, chew; bite persistently and remove; snap at, nibble; reach the essential by removing the unnecessary. The ideogram: mouth and divination, revealing the essential. **Bite**, HO: close the jaws, bite through, crush between the teeth. The ideogram: mouth and cover, jaws fit together as a lid fits a vessel. **Gnawing Bite** is the Image of Hexagram 21. **Take-in**, SHIH: eat, ingest, swallow, devour; incorporate.

Without, WU: devoid of; -less as suffix. **Complexion**, SE: appearance, expression; color, hue; air, manner, deportment; beautiful.

● *Symbol Tradition*

> **Below mountain possessing fire. Adorning.**
> **A chün tzu uses brightening the multitudinous standards**
> > **without daring to sever litigating.**

Associated Contexts **Below**, HSIA: anything below, in all senses; lower, inner; lower trigram; opposite of above, SHANG. **Mountain**, SHAN: limit, boundary; the Symbol of the trigram Bound, KEN. The ideogram: three peaks, a mountain range. **Possess**, YU: in possession of, have, own; opposite of lack, WU. **Fire**, HUO: warming and consuming aspect of burning; fire and brightness are the Symbols of the trigram Radiance, LI.

Chün tzu: ideal of a person who uses divination to order his/her life in accordance with tao rather than wilful intention; keyword. **Use(-of)**, YI: make use of, by means of, owing to; employ, make functional. **Brightness**, MING: light-giving aspect of burning, heavenly bodies and consciousness; with fire, the Symbol of the trigram Radiance, LI. **Multitude**, SHU: the people; mass, herd; all, the whole. **Standard**, CHENG: measure, test, limit, rule; musical interval; subjugate, regulate; capacity, endurance. **Dare**, KAN: have the courage to, try, permit yourself: bold, intrepid; rash, offensive. **Sever**, CHE: break off, separate, sunder, cut in two; discriminate, judge the true and false. **Litigate**, YÜ: legal proceedings; take a case to court. The ideogram: two dogs and words, barking arguments at each other.

● *Image Tradition*

Adorning, Growing. [I]
Supple coming and-also patterning solid.
Anterior Growth.
Above apportioning solid and-also patterning supple.

The anterior small, Harvesting: possessing directed going. [II]
Heavenly pattern indeed.
Pattern brightening, stopping:
People pattern indeed.

Viewing reaching-to the heavenly pattern. [III]
Using scrutinizing the seasons transforming.
Viewing reaching-to the people pattern.
Using changes accomplishing Below Heaven.

Associated Contexts **[I] Supple**, JOU: quality of the opened lines; flexible, pliant, tender, adaptable. **Come**, LAI, and go, WANG: describe the stream of time as it flows from future through present to past; come, LAI, indicates what is approaching; move toward, arrive at; keyword. **Pattern**, WEN: intrinsic or natural design and its beauty; stylish, elegant; noble; contrasts with composition, CHANG, a conscious creation. **Solid**, KANG: quality of the whole lines; firm, strong, unyielding, persisting.

 Anterior, KU: come before as cause; formerly, ancient; reason, purpose, intention; grievance, quarrel, dissatisfaction, sorrow, mourning resulting from previous causes and intentions; situation leading to a divination.

 Above, SHANG: anything above, in all senses; higher, upper, outer; upper trigram; opposite of below, HSIA. **Apportion**, FEN: divide for distribution; sort out; allot to.

[II] Heaven, T'IEN: highest; sky, firmament, heavens; power above the human as opposed to earth, TI, below; the Symbol of the trigram Force, CH'IEN. The ideogram: great and the one above.

 Stop, CHIH: bring or come to a standstill; the Action of the trigram Bound, KEN. The ideogram: a foot stops walking.

 People, person, JEN: humans individually and collectively; an individual; humankind. Image of Hexagrams 13 and 37.

[III] **View**, KUAN: contemplate, observe from a distance; look at carefully, gaze at; also: a monastery, an observatory; scry, divine through liquid in a cup. The ideogram: see and waterbird, observe through air or water. Image of Hexagram 20. **Reach(-to)**, HU: arrive at a goal; reach towards and achieve; connect; contrasts with tend-towards, YU.

Scrutinize, CH'A: investigate, observe carefully, learn the particulars, get at the truth. The ideogram: sacrifice as central to understanding. **Season**, SHIH: quality of the time; the right time, opportune, in harmony; planning in accord with the time; seasons of the year. The ideogram: sun and temple, time as sacred. **Transform**, PIEN: abrupt, radical, fundamental mutation from one state of being to another; transformation of lines in hexagrams; contrasts with change, HUA, gradual metamorphosis.

Change, HUA: gradual, continuous metamorphosis; influence someone; contrasts with transform, PIEN, sudden mutation. The ideogram: person alive and dead, the life-process. **Accomplish**, CH'ENG: complete, finish, bring about; perfect, full, whole; play your part, do your duty; mature. The ideogram: weapon and man, able to bear arms, thus fully developed. **Below Heaven**, T'IEN HSIA: the human world, between heaven and earth.

● *Transforming Lines*

Initial nine

a) **Adorning one's feet.**
Stowing-away the chariot and-also afoot.

b) **Stowing-away the chariot and-also afoot.**
Righteously nothing to ride indeed.

Associated Contexts a) **One's/one**, CH'I: third person pronoun; also: it/its, he/his, she/hers, they/theirs. **Foot**, CHIH: literal foot; foundation, base.

Stow(-away), SHE: set aside, put away, store; halt, rest in; temporary lodgings, breathing-spell. **Chariot**, CH'E: wheeled travelling vehicle; contrasts with cart, YÜ, which carries. **Afoot**, T'U: travel on foot; footman, foot-soldier; follower, disciple; ruffian, bond-servant.

b) **Righteous**, YI: proper and just, meets the standards; things in their proper place; the heart that rules itself; upright, moral rule; contrasts with Harvest, LI, advantage or profit. **Nothing/nowhere**, FU: strong negative; not a single thing/place. **Ride**, CH'ENG: ride an animal or a chariot; have the upper hand, seize the right time; control strong power; overcome the nature of the other; supple opened line above a solid whole line.

Six at-second

a) **Adorning: one's hair-growing.**

b) **Adorning: one's hair-growing.**
   Associating-with the above, rising indeed.

Associated Contexts a) **One's/one**, CH'I: third person pronoun; also: it/its, he/his, she/hers, they/theirs. **Hair-growing**, HSÜ: beard, hair; patience symbolized as waiting for hair to grow; hold back, wait for; slow; necessary.
   b) **Associate(-with)**, YÜ: consort with, combine; companions; group, band, company; agree with, comply, help. The ideogram: pair of hands reaching downward meets a pair of hands reaching upward, helpful association. **Rise**, HSING: get up, grow, lift; begin, give rise to, construct; be promoted; flourishing, fashionable. The ideogram: lift, two hands and unite, lift with both hands.

Nine at-third

a) **Adorning thus, soaking thus.**
   Perpetual Trial significant.

b) **Perpetual Trial's significance.**
   Completing absolutely-nothing: having a mound indeed.

Associated Contexts a) **Thus … thus**, JU … JU: when there is one thing, then there must be the second thing. **Soak**, JU: immerse, steep; damp, wet; stain, pollute, blemish; urinate on.
   Perpetual, YUNG: continuing; everlasting, ever-flowing. The ideogram: flowing water. **Trial**, CHEN: test by ordeal; inquiry by divination and its result; righteous, firm; separating wheat from chaff; the kernel, the proven core; fourth stage of the Time Cycle. The ideogram: pearl and divination. **Significant**, CHI: leads to the experience of

meaning; favorable, propitious, advantageous, appropriate; keyword. The ideogram: scholar and mouth, wise words of a sage.

b) **'s/have(-it)/it/them**, CHIH: expresses possession, directly or as an object pronoun.
    Complete, CHUNG: end of a cycle that begins the next; last, whole, all; contrasts with exhaust, CH'IUNG, final end. The ideogram: silk cocoons, follow and ice, winter linking one year with the next. **Absolutely-no(thing)**, MO: complete elimination; not any, by no means. **Mound**, LING: grave-mound, barrow; small hill.

Six at-fourth

    a) **Adorning thus, hoary thus.**
      A white horse, soaring thus.
      In-no-way outlawry, matrimonial allying.

    b) **Six at-fourth. Appropriate situation to doubt indeed.**
      In-no-way outlawry, matrimonial allying.
      Completing without surpassing indeed.

Associated Contexts a) **Thus ... thus**, JU ... JU: when there is one thing, then there must be the second thing. **Hoary**, PO: silvery grey hair; old and venerable, aging.
    White, PO: associated with autumn, Harvest and the Metallic Moment; clear, immaculate; plain, pure, essential; explicit; color of death and mourning. **Horse**, MA: symbol of spirited strength in the natural world, counterpart of dragon, LUNG; associated with the trigram Force, CH'IEN, heaven, T'IEN, and high noon. **Soar**, HAN: fly high; rising sun, the firebird with red plumage; trunk or stem of a plant; vertical support. The ideogram: feathers and dawn. **Thus**, JU: as, in this way.
    In-no-way, FEI: strong negative; not so. The ideogram: a box filled with opposition. **Outlawry**, K'OU: break the laws; violent people, outcasts, bandits. **Matrimonial allying**, HUN KOU: legal institution of marriage; make alliances through marriage rather than force.

b) **Appropriate**, TANG: suitable; opportune, convenient; adequate, competent; equal to; whole lines in uneven places and opened lines in even places. **Situation**, WEI: place or seat according to rank; post, position, command; right, proper; established, arranged. The ideogram: person and stand, servants in their places. **Doubt**, YI: suspect, distrust; dubious; surmise, conjecture.

Complete, CHUNG: end of a cycle that begins the next; last, whole, all; contrasts with exhaust, CH'IUNG: final end. The ideogram: silk cocoons, follow and ice, winter linking one year with the next. **Surpass**, YU: exceed; beyond measure, excessive; extraordinary; transgress, blame.

Six at-fifth

a) Adorning tending-towards a hill-top garden.
  Rolled plain-silk: little, little.
  Abashment. Completing significant.

b) Six at-fifth's significance.
  Possessing rejoicing indeed.

Associated Contexts a) **Tend-towards**, YÜ: move toward but not reach, in the direction of; contrasts with reach(-to), HU, actually arriving. **Hill-top**, CH'IU: hill with hollow top used for worship and as grave-site; knoll, hillock. **Garden**, YÜAN: enclosed garden; park, yard; imperial tombs.

   Roll, SHU: gather into a bundle, bind together; restrain. **Plain-silk**, PAI: unbleached, undyed silk. **Little**, CHIEN: small, narrow, insignificant, petty; diminish, contract. The doubled character intensifies this quality.

   Abashment, LIN: distress, shame, regret, humiliation; aware of having lost the right track; leads to repenting, HUI, correcting the direction of mind and life. **Complete**, CHUNG: end of a cycle that begins the next; last, whole, all; contrasts with exhaust, CH'IUNG, final end. The ideogram: silk cocoons, follow and ice, winter linking one year with the next. **Significant**, CHI: leads to the experience of meaning; favorable, propitious, advantageous, appropriate; keyword. The ideogram: scholar and mouth, wise words of a sage.

b) **'s/have(-it)/it/them**, CHIH: expresses possession, directly or as an object pronoun.
   Rejoice(-in), HSI: feel and give joy; delight, exult; cheerful, merry. The ideogram: joy (music) and mouth, expressing joy.

Nine above

a) White Adorning.
  Without fault.

b) White Adorning, without fault.
  Acquiring purpose above indeed.

Associated Contexts a) **White**, PO: associated with autumn, Harvest and the Metallic Moment; clear, immaculate; plain, pure, essential; explicit; color of death, and mourning.

Without fault, WU CHIU: no error or harm in the situation.

b) **Acquire**, TE: obtain the desired object; wish for, desire covetously; gains, possessions. The ideogram: go and obstacle, going through obstacles to the goal. **Purpose**, CHIH: focus of mind and heart; will, inclination, resolve. The ideogram: heart and scholar, high inner resolve, or heart and go, inner determination.

23

STRIPPING ▪ *PO*

This hexagram describes your situation in terms of something outmoded or worn out. It emphasizes that eliminating what has become unusable is the adequate way to handle it. To be in accord with the time, you are told to: **strip!**

- *Image of the Situation*

   Stripping not Harvesting: possessing directed going.

   Associated Contexts **Strip**, PO: flay, peel, skin; remove, uncover, degrade; split, slice; reduce to essentials; slaughter an animal. The ideogram: knife and carve, trenchant action. **Not**, PU: simple negative. **Harvest**, LI: advantageous, profitable; acute, insightful; benefit, nourish; third stage of the Time Cycle. **Possessing directed going**, YU YU WANG: imposing a direction on the flow of time from present to past; have a specific goal or purpose.

- *Outer and Inner Aspects*

   ☶ **Bound**: Mountains bound, limit and set a place off, stopping forward movement. **Bound** completes a full yin-yang cycle.

   Connection to the outer: accomplishing words, which express things fully. **Bound** articulates what is complete and suggests what is beginning.

   ☷ **Field**: The field of earth yields and sustains, serving in order to produce. **Field** is the equalizing point between yin and yang where things labor and serve.

   Connection to the inner: the common labor of sowing and hoarding, the Earthy Moment. **Field** produces concrete results through serving.

   Outer accomplishing **strips** away the previous cycle, while inner bringing-forth prepares the new. These trigrams form the Pivot of Equalization, where yin and yang come into creative balance.

● *Counter Indications*

The doubled nuclear trigram **Field**, K'UN, results in Counter Hexagram 2, **Field**, K'UN. The need for trenchant action in **stripping** is contrasted with the quiet yielding of **field**.

● *Sequence*

> **Actually involving embellishing, therefore**
> > **afterwards Growing by-consequence used-up.**
> **Anterior acquiescence has the use-of Stripping.**
> **Stripping implies a Stripper indeed.**

Associated Contexts **Actually**, YI: truly, really, at present. The ideogram: a dart and done, strong intention fully expressed. **Involve**, CHIH: include, entangle, implicate; induce, cause. The ideogram: person walking, induced to follow. **Embellish**, SHIH: ornament, paint, brighten, patch up the appearance; apply cosmetics; pretend, make believe. **Therefore afterwards**, JAN HOU: logical consequence of, necessarily follows in time. **Grow**, HENG: success through a sacrifice; pervade, persevere; bring to full growth; enjoy; vigorous, effective; second stage of the Time Cycle. **By-consequence(-of)**, TSE: very strong connection; reason, cause, result; rule, law, pattern, standard; therefore. **Use-up**, CHIN: exhaust, use all; ended, an empty vessel.

　　Anterior ... the use-of: activating this hexagram depends on understanding and accepting the previous statement.

　　Imply, CHE: further signify; additional meaning. **Indeed**, YEH: intensifier; indicates comment on previous statement.

● *Contrasted Definitions*

> **Stripping: rotten indeed.**
> **Returning: reversing indeed.**

Associated Contexts **Rotten**, LAN: corrupt, putrid, antiquated, worn out, dirty; a running sore; boil over. **Return**, FU: go back, turn back to the starting point; recur, reappear, come again; restore, recover, retrace; an earlier time or place. The ideogram: step and retrace a path. Image of Hexagram 24. **Reverse**, FAN: turn and move in the opposite direction;

turn around or upside down (180 degrees); change to the opposite position; contrary.

● *Symbol Tradition*

Mountain adjoining with-respect-to earth. Stripping.
Using munificence above to quiet the position below.

Associated Contexts **Mountain**, SHAN: limit, boundary; the Symbol of the trigram Bound, KEN. The ideogram: three peaks, a mountain range. **Adjoin**, FU: next to, lean on; join; near, approaching. **With-respect-to**, YÜ: relates to, refers to; hold a position in. **Earth**, TI: ground on which the human world rests; basis of all things, nourishes all things; the Symbol of the trigram Field, K'UN.

Use(-of), YI: make use of, by means of, owing to; employ, make functional. **Munificence**, HOU: liberal, kind, generous; create abundance; thick, large. The ideogram: gift of a superior to an inferior. **Above**, SHANG: anything above, in all senses; higher, upper, outer; upper trigram; opposite of below, HSIA. **Quiet**, AN: peaceful, still, settled; calm, tranquilize. The ideogram: woman under a roof, a tranquil home. **Position**, CHAI: dwelling site, good situation in life; consolidate, reside, fill an office. **Below**, HSIA: anything below, in all senses; lower, inner; lower trigram; opposite of above, SHANG.

● *Image Tradition*

Stripping. A Stripper indeed. [I]
Supple transforming solid indeed.

Not Harvesting: possessing directed going. [II]
Small People long-living indeed.

Yielding and-also stopping it. [III]
Viewing symbols indeed.

A chün tzu honors the dissolving pause to overfill emptiness. [IV]
Heaven moving indeed.

Associated Contexts **[I] Supple**, JOU: quality of the opened lines; flexible, pliant, tender, adaptable. **Transform**, PIEN: abrupt, radical, fundamental mutation from one state of being to another; transformation of lines in hexagrams; contrasts with change, HUA, gradual metamorphosis. **Solid**, KANG: quality of the whole lines; firm, strong, unyielding, persisting.

[II] Small People, HSIAO JEN: lowly, common, humble; those who adjust to circumstances with the flexibility of the small; effect of the small within an individual; keyword. **Long-living**, CHANG: enduring, constant; senior, superior, greater; increase, prosper; respect, elevate.

[III] Yield(-to), SHUN: give way and bear produce; comply, agree, follow, obey; unresisting, docile, flexible; nourish, provide; the Action of the trigram Field, K'UN. The ideogram: head and current, water flowing from the head of a river, yielding to the banks. **And-also**, ERH: joins and contrasts two terms. **Stop**, CHIH: bring or come to a standstill; the Action of the trigram Bound, KEN. The ideogram: a foot stops walking. **It/them/have(-it)/'s**, CHIH: expresses possession, directly or as an object pronoun.

    View, KUAN: contemplate, observe from a distance; look at carefully, gaze at; also: a monastery, an observatory; scry, divine through liquid in a cup. The ideogram: see and waterbird, observe through air or water. Image of Hexagram 20. **Symbol**, HSIANG: image invested with intrinsic power to connect visible and invisible; magic spell; figure, form, shape, likeness; pattern, model; create an image, imitate; act, play; writing.

[IV] Chün tzu: ideal of a person who uses divination to order his/her life in accordance with tao rather than wilful intention; keyword. **Honor**, SHANG: esteem, give high rank to; eminent; put one thing on top of another. **Dissolving pause**, HSIAO HSI: yin or structure dissolves so that yang or action may emerge; transitional phase of Universal Compass. **Overfill**, YING: at the point of overflowing; more than wanted, stretch beyond; replenished, full; arrogant. The ideogram: vessel and too much. **Empty**, HSÜ: no images or concepts; vacant, unsubstantial; empty yet fertile space.

    Heaven, T'IEN: highest; sky, firmament, heavens; power above the human as opposed to earth, TI, below; the Symbol of the trigram Force, CH'IEN. The ideogram: great and the one above. **Move**, HSING: move or move something; motivate, emotionally moving; walk, act, do. The ideogram: stepping left then right.

● *Transforming Lines*

Initial six

a) **Stripping the bed, using the stand.**
   Discarding the Trial: pitfall.

b) **Stripping the bed, using the stand.**
   Below using submerging indeed.

Associated Contexts a) **Bed**, CH'UANG: sleeping place; couch, sofa, lounge; bench around a well. **Stand**, TSU: base, foot, leg; rest on, support; stance. The ideogram: foot and calf resting.
   Discard, MIEH: disregard, ignore; petty, worthless, insignificant; trash. **Trial**, CHEN: test by ordeal; inquiry by divination and its result; righteous, firm; separating wheat from chaff; the kernel, the proven core; fourth stage of the Time Cycle. The ideogram: pearl and divination. **Pitfall**, HSIUNG: leads away from the experience of meaning; stuck and exposed to danger, unable to take in the situation; flow of life and spirit is blocked; unfortunate, baleful; keyword.

b) **Submerge**, MIEH: plunge under water, put out a fire; exterminate, finish, cut off. The ideogram: water and destroy.

Six at-second

a) **Stripping the bed, using marking-off.**
   Discarding the Trial: pitfall.

b) **Stripping the bed, using marking-off.**
   Not-yet possessing associating indeed.

Associated Contexts a) **Bed**, CH'UANG: sleeping place; couch, sofa, lounge; bench around a well. **Mark-off**, PIEN: distinguish by dividing; mark off a plot of land; frame which divides a bed from its stand; discuss and dispute. The ideogram: knife and acrid, biting division.
   Discard, MIEH: disregard, ignore; petty, worthless, insignificant; trash. **Trial**, CHEN: test by ordeal; inquiry by divination and its result; righteous, firm; separating wheat from chaff; the kernel, the proven core; fourth stage of the Time Cycle. The ideogram: pearl and divination. **Pitfall**, HSIUNG: leads away from the experience of meaning; stuck and exposed to danger, unable to take in the situation; flow of life and spirit is blocked; unfortunate, baleful; keyword.

b) **Not-yet**, WEI: temporal negative; something will but has not yet occurred; contrary of already, CHI. Image of Hexagram 64. **Possess**, YU: in possession of, have, own; opposite of lack, WU. **Associate(-with)**, YU: consort with, combine; com,panions; group, band, company; agree with, comply, help. The ideogram: pair of hands reaching downward meets a pair of hands reaching upward, helpful association.

Six at-third

a) **Stripping it, without fault.**

b) **Stripping it, without fault.**
   Letting-go Above[and]Below indeed.

Associated Contexts a) **Without fault**, WU CHIU: no error or harm in the situation.

b) **Let-go**, SHIH: lose, omit, miss, fail, let slip; out of control. The ideogram: drop from the hand. **Above[and]Below**, SHANG HSIA: realm of dynamic interaction between the upper and the lower; the vertical dimension.

Six at-fourth

a) **Stripping the bed, using flesh.**
   Pitfall.

b) **Stripping the bed, using flesh.**
   Slicing close-to calamity indeed.

Associated Contexts a) **Bed**, CH'UANG: sleeping place; couch, sofa, lounge; bench around a well. **Flesh**, FU: muscles, organs, skin, in contrast to bones.
   Pitfall, HSIUNG: leads away from the experience of meaning; stuck and exposed to danger, unable to take in the situation; flow of life and spirit is blocked; unfortunate, baleful; keyword.

b) **Slice**, CH'IEH: cut, carve, mince; urge, press; a resumé. **Close-to**, CHIN: near in time or place, next to; approach; recently, lately; familiar. **Calamity**, TSAI: disaster from outside; flood, plague, drought, blight, ruin; contrasts with blunder, SHENG, indicating personal fault. The ideogram: water and fire, elemental powers.

Six at-fifth

a) Threading fish.
　Using housing people, favor.
　Without not Harvesting.

b) Using housing people, favor.
　Completing without surpassing indeed.

Associated Contexts a) **Thread**, KUAN: string together; string of a thousand coins. **Fish**, YÜ: scaly, aquatic beings hidden in the water; symbol of abundance; connected with the Streaming Moment.

House, KUNG: residence, mansion; surround; fence, walls, roof. **People, person**, JEN: humans individually and collectively; an individual; humankind. Image of Hexagrams 13 and 37. **Favor**, CH'UNG: receive or confer gifts, obtain grace, win favor; dote on a woman; gifted for.

Without not Harvesting, WU PU LI: nothing for which this will not be beneficial; advantageous potential, borderline where the balance is swinging from not Harvesting to actually Harvesting.

b) **Complete**, CHUNG: end of a cycle that begins the next; last, whole, all; contrasts with exhaust, CH'IUNG, final end. The ideogram: silk cocoons, follow and ice, winter linking one year with the next. **Without**, WU: devoid of; -less as suffix. **Surpass**, YU: exceed; beyond measure, excessive; extraordinary; transgress, blame.

Nine above

a) The ripe fruit not taken-in.
　A chün tzu acquiring a cart.
　Small People Stripping the hut.

b) A chün tzu acquiring a cart.
　Commoners: the place to carry indeed.
　Small People Stripping the hut.
　Completing, not permitting availing-of indeed.

Associated Contexts a) **Ripe**, SHIH: mature, full-grown; great, eminent. **Fruit**, KUO: plants' annual produce; tree fruits; come to fruition, fruits of actions; produce, results, effects; reliable; conclude, surpass. The ideogram: tree topped by a round fruit. **Take-in**, SHIH: eat, ingest, swallow, devour; incorporate.

Acquire, TE: obtain the desired object; wish for, desire covetously; gains, possessions. The ideogram: go and obstacle, going through obstacles to the goal. **Cart**, YÜ: carrying capacity of a vehicle; contain, hold, sustain.

Hut, LU: thatched hut, cottage, roadside lodge, hovel; house as personal shelter.

b) **Commoners**, MIN: class of workers the state draws on to sustain the social hierarchy; undeveloped potential outside the organized personality. **Place**, SO: where something belongs or comes from; residence, dwelling; habitual focus or object. **Carry**, TSAI: bear, carry with you; contain, sustain; load a ship or cart, cargo; fill in, complete.

Complete, CHUNG: end of a cycle that begins the next; last, whole, all; contrasts with exhaust, CH'IUNG, final end. The ideogram: silk cocoons, follow and ice, winter linking one year with the next. **Not permitting**, PU K'O: not possible; contradicts an inherent principle. The ideogram: mouth and breath, silent consent. **Avail-of**, YUNG: take advantage of; benefit from, profit by; use for a specific purpose; apply to advantage. The ideogram: to divine and center, applying divination to central concerns.

RETURNING ▪ *FU*

This hexagram describes your situation in terms of something that is re-emerging. It emphasizes that going back to this starting point in order to begin anew is the adequate way to handle it. To be in accord with the time, you are told to: **return**!

● *Image of the Situation*

> **Returning, Growing.**
> **Issuing-forth, entering, without affliction.**
> **Partnering coming, without fault.**
> **Reversing Returning one's tao.**
> **The seventh day coming: Returning.**
> **Harvesting: possessing directed going.**

Associated Contexts **Return**, FU: go back, turn back to the starting point; recur, reappear, come again; restore, recover, retrace; an earlier time or place. The ideogram: step and retrace a path. **Grow**, HENG: success through a sacrifice; pervade, persevere; bring to full growth; enjoy; vigorous, effective; second stage of the Time Cycle.

Issue-forth(-from), CH'U: emerge from, come out of, proceed from, spring from; the Action of the trigram Shake, CHEN; contrary of enter, JU. The ideogram: stem with branches and leaves emerging. **Enter**, JU: penetrate, go into, enter on, progress; put into, encroach on; the Action of the trigram Ground, SUN, contrary of issue-forth, CH'U. **Without**, WU: devoid of; -less as suffix. **Afflict**, CHI: sickness, disorder, defect, calamity; injurious; pressure and consequent anger, hate or dislike. The ideogram: sickness and dart, a sudden affliction.

Partner, P'ENG: associate for mutual benefit; two equal or similar things; companions, friends, peers; join in; commercial ventures. The ideogram: linked strings of cowries or coins. **Come**, LAI, and go, WANG, describe the stream of time as it flows from future through present to past; come, LAI, indicates what is approaching; move toward, arrive at; keyword. **Without fault**, WU CHIU: no error or harm in the situation.

Reverse, FAN: turn and move in the opposite direction; turn around or upside down (180 degrees); change to the opposite position; contrary. **One's/one**, CH'I: third person pronoun; also: it/its, he/his, she/hers, they/theirs. **Tao**: way or path; ongoing process of being and the course it traces for each specific person or thing; keyword. The ideogram: go and head, leading and the path it creates.

Seven, CH'I: number seven, seventh; seven planets; seventh day when moon changes from crescent to waxing; the Tangram game makes pictures of all phenomena from seven basic shapes. **Day/sun**, JIH: actual sun and the time of a sun-cycle, a day.

Harvest, LI: advantageous, profitable; acute, insightful; benefit, nourish; third stage of the Time Cycle. **Possessing directed going**, YU YU WANG: imposing a direction on the flow of time from present to past; have a specific goal or purpose.

● *Outer and Inner Aspects*

☷ **Field**: The field of earth yields and sustains, serving in order to produce. **Field** is the equalizing point between yin and yang where things labor and serve.

Connection to the outer: the common labor of sowing and hoarding, the Earthy Moment. **Field** produces concrete results through serving.

☳ **Shake**: Thunder rises from below, shaking and stirring things up. **Shake** begins the yang hemicycle by germinating new action.

Connection to the inner: sprouting energies thrusting from below, the Woody Moment beginning. **Shake** stirs things up to issue-forth.

Returning to the energy germinating within prepares and opens a new field of activity.

● *Counter Indications*

The doubled nuclear trigram **Field**, K'UN, results in Counter Hexagram 2, **Field**, K'UN. Actively **returning** to the starting point is contrasted with the quiet receptivity of **field**.

- *Sequence*

> **Beings not permitted to use completing using-up.**
> **Above Stripping exhausted, below reversing.**
> **Anterior acquiescence has the use-of Returning.**

Associated Contexts **Beings not permitted to use ...:** no one is allowed to make use of; nothing can exist by means of. **Complete,** CHUNG: end of a cycle that begins the next; last, whole, all; contrasts with exhaust, CH'IUNG, final end. The ideogram: silk cocoons, follow and ice, winter linking one year with the next. **Use-up,** CHIN: exhaust, use all; ended, an empty vessel.

Above, SHANG: anything above, in all senses; higher, upper, outer; upper trigram; opposite of below, HSIA. **Strip,** PO: flay, peel, skin; remove, uncover, degrade; split, slice; reduce to essentials; slaughter an animal. The ideogram: knife and carve, trenchant action. Image of Hexagram 23. **Exhaust,** CH'IUNG: bring to an end; limit, extremity; destitute; investigate exhaustively; end without a new beginning. The ideogram: cave and naked person, bent with disease or old age. **Below,** HSIA: anything below, in all senses; lower, inner; lower trigram; opposite of above, SHANG.

Anterior ... the use-of: activating this hexagram depends on understanding and accepting the previous statement.

- *Contrasted Definitions*

> **Stripping: rotten indeed.**
> **Returning: reversing indeed.**

Associated Contexts **Rotten,** LAN: corrupt, putrid, antiquated, worn out, dirty; a running sore; boil over. **Indeed,** YEH: intensifier; indicates comment on previous statement.

- *Attached Evidences*

> **Returning: actualizing-tao's root indeed.**
> **Returning: the small and-also marking-off with-respect-to beings.**
> **Returning: using originating knowledge.**

Associated Contexts **Actualize-tao,** TE: realize tao in action; power, virtue; ability to follow the course traced by the ongoing process of the cosmos; keyword. The ideogram: to go, straight, and heart. Linked with acquire, TE: acquiring that which makes a being become what it is meant to be. **'s/have(-it)/it/them,** CHIH: expresses possession, directly or as an object pronoun. **Root,** PEN: origin, cause, source of nourishment; essential. The ideogram: tree with roots in earth.

Small, HSIAO: little, common, unimportant; adapting to what crosses your path; ability to move in harmony with the vicissitudes of life; contrasts with great, TA, self-imposed theme or goal; keyword. Image of Hexagrams 9 and 62. **And-also,** ERH: joins and contrasts two terms. **Mark-off,** PIEN: distinguish by dividing; mark off a plot of land; frame which divides a bed from its stand; discuss and dispute. The ideogram: knife and acrid, biting division. **With-respect-to,** YÜ: relates to, refers to; hold a position in. **Being(s),** WU: creature, thing, any single being; matter, substance, essence; nature of things.

Use(-of), YI: make use of, by means of, owing to; employ, make functional. **Origin,** TZU: source, beginning, ground; cause, reason, motive; line of descent; path to the origin; yourself, intrinsic. **Know,** CHIH: understand, perceive, remember; informed, aware, wise. The ideogram: arrow and mouth, words focused and swift.

● *Symbol Tradition*

> **Thunder located-in earth center. Returning.**
> **The Earlier Kings used culminating sun to bar the passages.**
> **Bargaining sojourners [used culminating sun] not to move.**
> **The crown-prince [used culminating sun]**
> > **not to inspect on-all-sides.**

Associated Contexts **Thunder,** LEI: rising, arousing power; the Symbol of the trigram Shake, CHEN. **Locate(-in),** TSAI: live in, dwell, reside; belong to, involved with, depend on; within. The ideogram: earth and persevere, place on the earth. **Earth,** TI: ground on which the human world rests; basis of all things, nourishes all things; the Symbol of the trigram Field, K'UN. **Center,** CHUNG: inner, central; put in the center; middle, stable point enabling you to face inner and outer changes; middle line of trigram. The ideogram: field divided in two equal parts. Image of Hexagram 61.

Earlier Kings, HSIEN WANG: ideal rulers of old; the golden age, primal time, power in harmony with nature; model for the chün tzu. **Culminating sun**, CHIH JIH: acme of any time period; midday, summer solstice; midpoint of life. **Bar**, PI: close a door, stop up a hole; obstruct, exclude, screen. The ideogram: door and hand, closing the door. **Passage**, KUAN: market gate, customs house, frontier post; limit, crisis, important point.

Bargain, SHANG: argue over prices; consult, deliberate, do business; dealers, travelling merchants; hour before sunrise and sunset. The ideogram: stutter and sentences, repetitive speaking. **Sojourn**, LÜ: travel, stay in places other than your home; itinerant troops, temporary residents; visitor, guest, lodger. The ideogram: banner and people around it, loyal to a symbol rather than their temporary residence. Image of Hexagram 56. **Not**, PU: simple negative. **Move**, HSING: move or move something; motivate, emotionally moving; walk, act, do. The ideogram: stepping left then right.

Crown-prince, HOU: successor to the sovereign. The ideogram: one, mouth and shelter, one with the sovereign's orders. **Inspect**, HSING: examine on all sides, careful inquiry; watchful. **Sides(on-all-sides)**, FANG: limits, boundaries; square, surface of the earth extending to the four cardinal points; everywhere.

● *Image Tradition*

Returning, Growing. Solid reversing. [I]
Stirring-up and-also using yielding movement.
That uses issuing-forth, entering, without affliction.

Partnering coming, without fault. [II]
Reversing Returning one's tao.
The seventh day coming: Returning.
Heaven moving indeed.

Harvesting: possessing directed going. [III]
Solid long-living indeed.
Reaching-to Returning one's visualizing Heaven[and]Earth's heart.

Associated Contexts **[I] Solid**, KANG: quality of the whole lines; firm, strong, unyielding, persisting.

Stir-up, TUNG: excite, influence, move, affect; work, take action; come out of the egg or the bud; the Action of the trigram Shake, CHEN. The ideogram: strength and heavy, move weighty things. **Yield(-to)**, SHUN: give way and bear produce; comply, agree, follow, obey; unresisting, docile, flexible; nourish, provide; the Action of the trigram Field, K'UN. The ideogram: head and current, water flowing from the head of a river, yielding to the banks.

That uses, SHIH YI: involves and is involved by.

[II] Heaven, T'IEN: highest; sky, firmament, heavens; power above the human as opposed to earth, TI, below; the Symbol of the trigram Force, CH'IEN. The ideogram: great and the one above.

[III] Long-living, CHANG: enduring, constant; senior, superior, greater; increase, prosper; respect, elevate.

Reach(-to), HU: arrive at a goal; reach toward and achieve; connect; contrasts with tend-towards, YU. **Visualize**, CHIEN: seeing in all its aspects: vision, being visible, forming mental images; visit, call on, consult. The ideogram: eye above person, active and receptive sight. **Heaven[and]Earth**, T'IEN TI: dynamic relation between the primal powers and the world it produces; cosmos, natural or human world; keyword. **Heart**, HSIN: heart as center of being; seat of mind's images and affections; moral nature; source of desires, intentions, will.

- *Transforming Lines*

Initial nine

a) **Not distancing Returning.**
   Without merely repenting.
   Spring significant.

b) **Not distancing's Returning.**
   Using adjusting individuality indeed.

Associated Contexts a) **Distance**, YÜAN: far off, remote; keep at a distance; alienated. The ideogram: go and a long way.

Merely, CHIH: nothing more than. **Repent**, HUI: dissatisfaction with past conduct causing a change of heart; proceeds from abashment, LIN, shame and confusion at having lost the right way.

Spring, YÜAN: source, origin, head; great, excellent; arise, begin, generating power; first stage of the Time Cycle. **Significant**, CHI: leads to the experience of meaning; favorable, propitious, advantageous, appropriate; keyword. The ideogram: scholar and mouth, wise words of a sage.

b) **Adjust**, HSIU: regulate, repair, clean up, renovate. **Individuality**, SHEN: total person: psyche, body and lifespan; character, virtue, duty; contrasts with body, KUNG, physical being.

Six at-second

a) **Relinquishing Returning.**
   Significant.

b) **Relinquishing Returning's significance.**
   Using humanity below indeed.

Associated Contexts a) **Relinquish**, HSIU: let go of, stop temporarily, rest; resign, release; act gently, enjoy; relaxed. The ideogram: person leaning on a tree.
   Significant, CHI: leads to the experience of meaning; favorable, propitious, advantageous, appropriate; keyword. The ideogram: scholar and mouth, wise words of a sage.

b) **Humanity**, JEN: fellow-feeling, regard for others; benevolence, fulfil social duties; unselfish, kind, merciful.

Six at-third

a) **Imminent Returning. Adversity.**
   Without fault.

b) **Imminent Returning's adversity.**
   Righteous, without fault indeed.

Associated Contexts a) **Imminent**, P'IN: on the brink of; pressing, urgent. **Adversity**, LI: danger; threatening, malevolent demon. This has two aspects: grind, sharpen, improve, perfect, stimulate; and: poisonous, sinister, cruel, contrary. It indicates a spirit or ghost that seeks revenge by inflicting suffering upon the living. Pacifying or exorcizing such a spirit can have a healing effect. The ideogram: sheltering cliff and stinging insect.

b) **Righteous**, YI: proper and just, meets the standards; things in their proper place; the heart that rules itself; upright, moral rule; contrasts with Harvest, LI, advantage or profit.

Six at-fourth

a) **Centering movement, solitary Returning.**

b) **Centering movement, solitary Returning.**
Using adhering-to tao indeed.

Associated Contexts a) **Solitary**, TI: alone, single; isolated, abandoned.

b) **Adhere(-to)**, TS'UNG: follow a way, hold to a doctrine, school, or person; hear and comply with, agree to; forced to follow, follower. The ideogram: two men walking, one following the other.

Six at-fifth

a) **Magnanimous Returning.**
Without repenting.

b) **Magnanimous Returning, without repenting.**
Centering originating-from the predecessor indeed.

Associated Contexts a) **Magnanimous**, TUN: generous; honest, substantial, important, wealthy; honor, increase; firm, solid. The ideogram: strike and accept, warrior magnanimous in attack and defense.

Without repenting, WU HUI: devoid of the sort of trouble that leads to sorrow, regret and the necessity to change your attitude.

b) **Predecessor**, K'AO: deceased ancestor, especially the grandfather; the ancients; aged, long-lived; consult, verify. The ideogram: old and ingenious, the old wise man.

Six above

a) **Deluding Returning. Pitfall.**
    Possessing Calamity[and]Blunder.
    Availing-of moving legions:
    Completing possesses great destroying.
    Using one's city chief: pitfall.
    Culminating tending-towards ten years-revolved not
                              controlling chastisement.

b) **Deluding Returning's pitfall.**
    Reversing the chief: tao indeed.

Associated Contexts a) **Delude**, MI: confused, stupified, infatuated; blinded by vice; bewitch, fascinate, deceive. **Pitfall**, HSIUNG: leads away from the experience of meaning; stuck and exposed to danger, unable to take in the situation; flow of life and spirit is blocked; unfortunate, baleful; keyword.

    Possess, YU: in possession of, have, own; opposite of lack, WU. **Calamity[and]Blunder**, TSAI SHENG: disaster from without and within; natural disaster combined with misfortune due to ignorance or fault; ruin, defeat, rout, collapse.

    Avail-of, YUNG: take advantage of; benefit from, profit by; use for a specific purpose; apply to advantage. The ideogram: to divine and center, applying divination to central concerns. **Legions/leading**, SHIH: troops; an organized unit, a metropolis; leader, general, model, master; organize, make functional; take as a model, imitate. The ideogram: heap and whole, organize confusion into functional units. Image of Hexagram 7.

    Great, TA: big, noble, important, very; orient the will toward a self-imposed goal, impose direction; ability to lead or guide your life; contrasts with small, HSIAO, flexible adaptation to what crosses your path; keyword. Image of Hexagrams 14, 26, 28, 34. **Destroy**, PAI: ruin, defeat, violate, subvert, break.

    City, KUO: area of only human constructions; political unit, polis. First of the territorial zones: city, suburbs, countryside, forests. **Chief**, CHÜN: effective ruler; preside over, take the lead; influence others; term of respect. The ideogram: mouth and director, giving orders.

    Culminate, CHIH: bring to the highest degree; arrive at the end or summit; superlative. **Tend-towards**, YÜ: move toward but not reach, in the direction of; contrasts with reach(-to), HU, actually arriving.

Ten, SHIH: goal and end of reckoning; whole, complete, all; entire, perfected, the full amount; reach everywhere, receive everything. The ideogram: East–West line crosses North–South line, a grid that contains all. **Years-revolved**, NIEN: number of years elapsed; a person's age; contrasts with year's-time, SUI, length of time in a year. **Control**, K'O: command; check, impede, prevail, obstruct, repress; adequate, able. The ideogram: roof beams support a house, controlling the structure. **Chastise**, CHENG: punish, subjugate, discipline; reduce to order; punishing expedition. The ideogram: step and correct, a rectifying move.

25

WITHOUT EMBROILING ▮

WU WANG

This hexagram describes your situation as being without confusion or fault. It emphasizes that acting while remaining free from entangling, vanity or recklessness is the adequate way to handle it. To be in accord with the time, you are told: act **without** becoming **embroiled**!

● *Image of the Situation*

> **Without Embroiling.**
> **Spring Growing Harvesting Trial.**
> **One in-no-way correcting: possessing blunder.**
> **Not Harvesting: possessing directed going.**

Associated Contexts **Without**, WU: devoid of; -less as suffix. **Embroil**, WANG: caught up in, entangled, involved; disorder, incoherence; foolish, wild, reckless; false, brutish behaviour; vain, idle, futile.

Spring Growing Harvesting Trial: **Spring**, YÜAN: **Grow**, HENG; **Harvest**, LI; and **Trial**, CHEN, are the four stages of the Time Cycle, the model for all dynamic processes. They indicate that your question is connected to the cycle as a whole rather than a part of it, and that the origin (Spring) of a favorable result (Harvesting Trial) is an offering to the spirits (Growing).

One's/one, CH'I: third person pronoun; also: he/his, she/hers, they/theirs, it/its. **In-no-way**, FEI: strong negative; not so. The ideogram: a box filled with opposition. **Correct**, CHENG: rectify deviation or one-sidedness; proper, straight, exact, regular; constant, rule, model. The ideogram: stop and one, hold to one thing. **Possess**, YU: in possession of, have, own; opposite of lack, WU. **Blunder**, SHENG: mistake due to ignorance or fault; contrasts with calamity, TSAI, disaster from without. The ideogram: eye and grow, a film clouding sight.

Not, PU: simple negative. **Harvest**, LI: advantageous, profitable; acute, insightful; benefit, nourish; third stage of the Time Cycle. **Possessing directed going**, YU YU WANG: imposing a direction on the flow of time from present to past; have a specific goal or purpose.

- ## Outer and Inner Aspects

☰ **Force**: The force of heaven struggles on, persistent and unwearied; heavenly bodies persist in their orbits. **Force** is the center of the yin hemicycle, completing the formative process.

Connection to the outer: struggling forces are bound together in dynamic tension, the Metallic Moment culminating. **Force** brings elements to grips, creating enduring relations.

☳ **Shake**: Thunder rises from below, shaking and stirring things up. **Shake** begins the yang hemicycle by germinating new action.

Connection to the inner: sprouting energies thrusting from below, the Woody Moment beginning. **Shake** stirs things up to issue-forth.

Germinating inner growth remains **without embroiling** through its connection to heaven's persistent struggle.

- ## Counter Indications

Nuclear trigrams **Ground**, SUN, and **Bound**, KEN, result in Counter Hexagram 53, **Infiltrating**, CHIEN. Remaining **without embroiling** is contrasted with actively **infiltrating** the world's confusion.

- ## Sequence

**Actually Returning, by-consequence not Embroiling.
Anterior acquiescence has the use-of Without Embroiling.**

Associated Contexts **Actually**, YI: truly, really, at present. The ideogram: a dart and done, strong intention fully expressed. **Return**, FU: go back, turn back to the starting point; recur, reappear, come again; restore, recover, retrace; an earlier time or place. The ideogram: step and retrace a path. Image of Hexagram 24. **By-consequence(-of)**, TSE: very strong connection; reason, cause, result; rule, law, pattern, standard; therefore.

Anterior ... the use-of: activating this hexagram depends on understanding and accepting the previous statement.

● *Contrasted Definitions*

> **Great Accumulating: the season indeed.**
> **Without Embroiling: calamity indeed.**

Associated Contexts **Great**, TA: big, noble, important, very; orient the will toward a self-imposed goal, impose direction; ability to lead or guide your life; contrasts with small, HSIAO, flexible adaptation to what crosses your path; keyword. **Accumulate**, CH'U: retain, hoard, gather, herd together; control, restrain; domesticate, tame, train; raise, feed, sustain, bring up. The ideogram: field and black, fertile black soil good for pastures, accumulated through retaining silt. **Great Accumulating** is the Image of Hexagram 26. **Season**, SHIH: quality of the time; the right time, opportune, in harmony; planning in accord with the time; seasons of the year. The ideogram: sun and temple, time as sacred. **Indeed**, YEH: intensifier; indicates comment on previous statement.

   Calamity, TSAI: disaster from outside; flood, plague, drought, blight, ruin; contrasts with blunder, SHENG, indicating personal fault. The ideogram: water and fire, elemental powers.

● *Symbol Tradition*

> **Below heaven thunder moving. Beings associating**
> **Without Embroiling.**
> **The Earlier Kings used luxuriance suiting the season**
> **to nurture the myriad beings.**

Associated Contexts **Below**, HSIA: anything below, in all senses; lower, inner; lower trigram; opposite of above, SHANG. **Heaven**, T'IEN: highest; sky, firmament, heavens; power above the human as opposed to earth, TI, below; the Symbol of the trigram Force, CH'IEN. The ideogram: great and the one above. **Thunder**, LEI: rising, arousing power; the Symbol of the trigram Shake, CHEN. **Move**, HSING: move or move something; motivate, emotionally moving; walk, act, do. The ideogram: stepping left then right. **Being(s)**, WU: creature, thing, any single being; matter, substance, essence; nature of things. **Associate(-with)**, YÜ: consort with, combine; companions; group, band, company; agree with, comply, help. The ideogram: pair of hands reaching downward meets a pair of hands reaching upward, helpful association.

Earlier Kings, HSIEN WANG: ideal rulers of old; the golden age, primal time, power in harmony with nature; model for the chün tzu. **Use(-of)**, YI: make use of, by means of, owing to; employ, make functional. **Luxuriance**, MAO: thriving, flourishing, vigorous; highly developed, elegant. The ideogram: plants and flourish. **Suiting**, TUI: correspond to, agree with, consistent; pair; parallel sentences in poetic language. **Nurture**, YÜ: bring up, support, rear, raise; increase. **Myriad**, WAN: countless; many, everyone; lit.: ten thousand. The ideogram: swarm of insects.

- *Image Tradition*

> **Without Embroiling. [I]**
> Solid originating-from the outside coming and-also
> activating a lord with-respect-to the inside.
> Stirring-up and-also persisting.
>
> Solid centering and-also corresponding. [II]
> Great Growing using correcting.
> Heaven's fate indeed.
>
> One in-no-way correcting: possessing blunder. [III]
> Not Harvesting: possessing directed going.
> Without Embroiling's going.
> Actually wherefore having-it?
> Heavenly fate not shielding.
> Actually moving in-fact.

Associated Contexts [I] **Solid**, KANG: quality of the whole lines; firm, strong, unyielding, persisting. **Origin**, TZU: source, beginning, ground; cause, reason, motive; line of descent; path to the origin; yourself, intrinsic. **Outside**, WAI: outer, exterior, external; people working in places other than their home; unfamiliar, foreign; the upper trigram, as opposed to inside, NEI, the lower. **Come**, LAI, and go, WANG, describe the stream of time as it flows from future through present to past. Come, LAI, indicates what is approaching; move toward, arrive at; keyword. **And-also**, ERH: joins and contrasts two terms. **Activate**, WEI: act or cause to act; do, make, manage; make active; attend to, help; because of. **Lord**, CHU: ruler, master, chief; authority. The ideogram: lamp and flame, giving light. **With-respect-to**, YÜ: relates to, refers to; hold a position in.

Inside, NEI: within, inner, interior; inside of the house and those who work there, particularly women; the lower trigram, as opposed to outside, WAI, the upper. The ideogram: border and enter, cross a border.

Stir-up, TUNG: excite, influence, move, affect; work, take action; come out of the egg or the bud; the Action of the trigram Shake, CHEN. The ideogram: strength and heavy, move weighty things. **Persist**, CHIEN: strong, robust, dynamic, tenacious; continuous; unwearied heavenly bodies in their orbits; the Action of the trigram Force, CH'IEN.

[II] Center, CHUNG: inner, central; put in the center; middle, stable point enabling you to face inner and outer changes; middle line of trigram. The ideogram: field divided in two equal parts. Image of Hexagram 61. **Correspond(-to)**, YING: be in agreement or harmony; resonate together, invoke and fulfill each other; answer to, suitable; relation between the lines (1:4, 2:5, 3:6) when they form the pair opened and whole, supple and solid. The ideogram: heart and obey.

Grow, HENG: success through a sacrifice; pervade, persevere; bring to full growth; enjoy; vigorous, effective; second stage of the Time Cycle.

's/have(-it)/it/them, CHIH: expresses possession, directly or as an object pronoun. **Fate**, MING: individual destiny; birth and death as limits of life; issue orders with authority; consult the gods. The ideogram: mouth and order, words with heavenly authority.

[III] Actually, YI: truly, really, at present. The ideogram: a dart and done, strong intention fully expressed. **Wherefore**, HO: interrogative: why? for what reason? what is? and affirmation: therefore, for that reason. **Have(-it)/it/them/'s**, CHIH: expresses possession, directly or as an object pronoun.

Shield, YU: protect; defended by spirits; heavenly kindness and protection. The ideogram: numinous and right hand, spirit power.

Actually ... in-fact, YI TSAI: stresses the importance of a statement. The ideogram: a dart and done, strong intention fully expressed.

● *Transforming Lines*

Initial nine

a) **Without Embroiling. Going significant.**

b) **Without Embroiling's going.
Acquiring purpose indeed.**

Associated Contexts a) **Significant**, CHI: leads to the experience of meaning; favorable, propitious, advantageous, appropriate; keyword. The ideogram: scholar and mouth, wise words of a sage.

b) **Acquire**, TE: obtain the desired object; wish for, desire covetously; gains, possessions. The ideogram: go and obstacle, going through obstacles to the goal. **Purpose**, CHIH: focus of mind and heart; will, inclination, resolve. The ideogram: heart and scholar, high inner resolve, or heart and go, inner determination.

Six at-second

a) Not tilling the crop. Not clearing the plow-land.
　By-consequence, Harvesting: possessing directed going.

b) Not tilling the crop.
　Not-yet affluence indeed.

Associated Contexts a) **Till**, KENG: plow; labor at, cultivate. **Crop**, HUO: grain gathered in autumn; reap, harvest. **Clear**, TZU: cultivate wild or overgrown land; reclaim. **Plow-land**, YÜ: newly opened fields, after two or three years plowing.

b) **Not-yet**, WEI: temporal negative; something will but has not yet occurred; contrary of already, CHI. Image of Hexagram 64. **Affluence**, FU: rich, abundant; wealth; enrich, provide for; flow towards, accrue.

Six at-third

a) Without Embroiling's calamity.
　Maybe attaching's cattle.
　Moving people's acquiring:
　Capital people's calamity.

b) Moving people acquiring cattle.
　Capital people, calamity indeed.

Associated Contexts a) **Maybe**, HUO: possible but not certain, perhaps. **Attach**, HSI: fasten to, bind, tie; retain, continue; keep in mind, emotionally attached. **Cattle**, NIU: ox, bull, cow, calf; kine; power and strength of work animals.

People, person, JEN: humans individually and collectively; an individual; humankind. Image of Hexagrams 13 and 37. **Acquire**, TE: obtain the desired object; wish for, desire covetously; gains, possessions. The ideogram: go and obstacle, going through obstacles to the goal.

Capital, YI: populous fortified city, center and symbol of the domain it rules. The ideogram: enclosure and official seal.

Nine at-fourth

a) **Permitting Trial.**
   Without fault.

b) **Permitting Trial, without fault.**
   Firmly possessing it indeed.

Associated Contexts a) **Permit**, K'O: possible because in harmony with an inherent principle. The ideogram: mouth and breath, silent consent. **Trial**, CHEN: test by ordeal; inquiry by divination and its result; righteous, firm; separating wheat from chaff; the kernel, the proven core; fourth stage of the Time Cycle. The ideogram: pearl and divination.

Without fault, WU CHIU: no error or harm in the situation.

b) **Firm**, KU: constant, fixed, steady; chronic, recurrent. The ideogram: old and enclosure, long preserved. **It/them/have(-it)/'s**, CHIH: expresses possession, directly or as an object pronoun.

Nine at-fifth

a) **Without Embroiling's affliction.**
   No medicinal-herbs, possessing rejoicing.

b) **Without Embroiling's medicinal-herbs.**
   Not permitting testing indeed.

Associated Contexts a) **Afflict**, CHI: sickness, disorder, defect, calamity; injurious; pressure and consequent anger, hate or dislike. The ideogram: sickness and dart, a sudden affliction.

No, WU: simple negative; un-, dis-. **Medicinal-herbs**, YAO: plants used as remedies; medical as opposed to other ways of healing. **Rejoice(-in)**, HSI: feel and give joy; delight, exult; cheerful, merry. The ideogram: joy (music) and mouth, expressing joy.

b) **Not permitting**, PU K'O: not possible; contradicts an inherent principle. The ideogram: mouth and breath, silent consent. **Test**, SHIH: compare, try, experiment; tempt.

Nine above

a) Without Embroiling. Moving possessing blunder.
Without direction: Harvesting.

b) Without Embroiling's moving:
Exhaustion's calamity indeed.

Associated Contexts a) **Without direction: Harvesting**, WU YU LI: no plan or direction is advantageous; in order to take advantage of the situation, do not impose a direction on events.

b) **Exhaust**, CH'IUNG: bring to an end; limit, extremity; destitute; investigate exhaustively; end without a new beginning. The ideogram: cave and naked person, bent with disease or old age.

26

GREAT ACCUMULATING ▮
TA CH'U

This hexagram describes your situation in terms of an overriding concern that defines what is valuable. It emphasizes that bringing the variety of things under the control of this central idea is the adequate way to handle it. To be in accord with the time, you are told to: **accumulate** the **great**!

● *Image of the Situation*

> **Great Accumulating.**
> **Harvesting Trial.**
> **Not dwelling, taking-in. Significant.**
> **Harvesting: wading the Great River.**

Associated Contexts **Great**, TA: big, noble, important, very; orient the will toward a self-imposed goal, impose direction; ability to lead or guide your life; contrasts to small, HSIAO, flexible adaptation to what crosses your path; keyword. **Accumulate**, CH'U: hoard, gather, retain, herd together; control, restrain; domesticate, tame, train; raise, feed, sustain, bring up. The ideogram: field and black, fertile black soil good for pastures, accumulated through retaining silt.

Harvesting Trial, LI CHEN: advantageous divination; putting the action in question to the test is beneficial.

Not, PU: simple negative. **Dwell**, CHI: home, house, household, family; domestic, within doors; live in. The ideogram: roof and pig or dog, the most valued domestic animals. Image of Hexagram 37. **Take-in**, SHIH: eat, ingest, swallow, devour; incorporate. **Significant**, CHI: leads to the experience of meaning; favorable, propitious, advantageous, appropriate; keyword. The ideogram: scholar and mouth, wise words of a sage.

Harvest, LI: advantageous, profitable; acute, insightful; benefit, nourish; third stage of the Time Cycle. **Wading the Great River**, SHE TA CH'UAN: consciously moving into the flow of time; enter the stream of life with a goal or purpose; embark on a significant enterprise.

Outer and Inner Aspects

☶ **Bound**: Mountains bound, limit and set a place off, stopping forward movement. **Bound** completes a full yin-yang cycle.

Connection to the outer: accomplishing words, which express things fully. **Bound** articulates what is complete and suggests what is beginning.

☰ **Force**: The force of heaven struggles on, persistent and unwearied; heavenly bodies persist in their orbits. **Force** is the center of the yin hemicycle, completing the formative process.

Connection to the inner: struggling forces are bound together in dynamic tension, the Metallic Moment culminating. **Force** brings elements to grips, creating enduring relations.

The outer limit retains and **accumulates** heaven's **great** inner force, bringing it to expression. This is a time of abundance.

Counter Indications

Nuclear trigrams **Shake**, CHEN, and **Open**, TUI, result in Counter Hexagram 54, **Converting Maidenhood**, KUEI MEI. The will and power that grows from **great accumulating** is contrasted with the submissive attitude of the **converting maiden.**

Sequence

> Possessing Without Embroiling therefore afterwards
> permitting Accumulating.
> Anterior acquiescence has the use-of Great Accumulating.

Associated Contexts **Possess**, YU: in possession of, have, own; opposite of lack, WU. **Without**, WU: devoid of; -less as suffix. **Embroil**, WANG: caught up in, entangled, involved; disorder, incoherence; foolish, wild, reckless; false, brutish behaviour; vain, idle, futile. **Without Embroiling** is the Image of Hexagram 25. **Therefore afterwards**, JAN HOU: logical consequence of, necessarily follows in time. **Permit**, K'O: possible because in harmony with an inherent principle. The ideogram: mouth and breath, silent consent.

Anterior ... the use-of: activating this hexagram depends on understanding and accepting the previous statement.

● *Contrasted Definitions*

> **Great Accumulating: the season indeed.**
> **Without Embroiling: calamity indeed.**

Associated Contexts **Season**, SHIH: quality of the time; the right time, opportune, in harmony; planning in accord with the time; seasons of the year. The ideogram: sun and temple, time as sacred. **Indeed**, YEH: intensifier; indicates comment on previous statement.

Calamity, TSAI: disaster from outside; flood, plague, drought, blight, ruin; contrasts with blunder, SHENG, indicating personal fault. The ideogram: water and fire, elemental powers.

● *Symbol Tradition*

> **Heaven located-in mountain center. Great Accumulating.**
> **A chün tzu uses**
> > **the numerous recorded preceding words going to move.**
> **[A chün tzu] uses accumulating one's actualizing-tao.**

Associated Contexts **Heaven**, T'IEN: highest; sky, firmament, heavens; power above the human as opposed to earth, TI. below; the Symbol of the trigram Force, CH'IEN. The ideogram: great and the one above. **Locate(-in)**, TSAI: live in, dwell, reside; belong to, involved with, depend on; within. The ideogram: earth and persevere, place on the earth. **Mountain**, SHAN: limit, boundary; the Symbol of the trigram Bound, KEN. The ideogram: three peaks, a mountain range. **Center**, CHUNG: inner, central; put in the center; middle, stable point enabling you to face inner and outer changes; middle line of trigram. The ideogram: field divided in two equal parts. Image of Hexagram 61.

Chün tzu: ideal of a person who uses divination to order his/her life in accordance with tao rather than wilful intention; keyword. **Use(-of)**, YI: make use of, by means of, owing to; employ, make functional. **Numerous**, TO: great number, many; often. **Record**, SHIH: write down, inscribe; memorize, learn; recognize; annals, momuments. **Precede**, CH'IEN: come before in time and thus in value; anterior, former, ancient; lead forward.

Word, YEN: speech, spoken words, sayings; talk, discuss, address. The ideogram: mouth and rising vapor, words as speech. **Go**, WANG, and come, LAI, describe the stream of time as it flows from future through present to past; go, WANG, indicates what is departing from present to past; proceed, move on; keyword. **Move**, HSING: move or move something; motivate, emotionally moving; walk, act, do. The ideogram: stepping left then right.

One/one's, CH'I: third person pronoun; also: it/its, he/his, she/hers, they/theirs. **Actualize-tao**, TE: realize tao in action; power, virtue; ability to follow the course traced by the ongoing process of the cosmos; keyword. The ideogram: to go, straight, and heart. Linked with acquire, TE: acquiring that which makes a being become what it is meant to be.

● *Image Tradition*

> Great Accumulating. [I]
> Solid persisting: staunch substance, resplendent shining.
> A day renewing one's actualizing-tao.
> Above solid and-also honoring eminence.
>
> Ability to stop persisting. [II]
> The great correcting indeed.
>
> Not dwelling, taking-in significant. [III]
> Nourishing eminence indeed.
> Harvesting: wading the Great River.
> Corresponding reaching-to heaven indeed.

Associated Contexts [I] **Solid**, KANG: quality of the whole lines; firm, strong, unyielding, persisting. **Persist**, CHIEN: strong, robust, dynamic, tenacious; continuous; unwearied heavenly bodies in their orbits; the Action of the trigram Force, CH'IEN. **Staunch**, TU: firm, solid, reliable; pure; consolidate, establish; sincere, honest. **Substance**, SHIH: real, solid, full; results, fruits, possessions; essence; honest, sincere. The ideogram: string of coins under a roof, riches in the house. **Resplendent**, HUI: glorious, sun-like, refulgent; brighten. **Shine**, KUANG: illuminate; give off brilliant, bright light; honor, glory, éclat; result of action, contrasts with brightness, MING, light of heavenly bodies. The ideogram: fire above person, lifting the light.

Day/sun, JIH: actual sun and the time of a sun-cycle, a day. **Renew,** HSIN: restore, improve, make or get better; new, fresh; the best, the latest.

Above, SHANG: anything above, in all senses; higher, upper, outer; upper trigram; opposite of below, HSIA. **And-also,** ERH: joins and contrasts two terms. **Honor,** SHANG: esteem, give high rank to; eminent; put one thing on top of another. **Eminent,** HSIEN: moral and intellectual power; worthy, excellent, virtuous; sage second to the all-wise, SHENG.

[II] Able, NENG: enable; ability, power, skill, art; competent, talented; duty, function, capacity. The ideogram: an animal with strong hooves and bones, able to carry and defend. **Stop,** CHIH: bring or come to a standstill; the Action of the trigram Bound, KEN. The ideogram: a foot stops walking.

Correct, CHENG: rectify deviation or one-sidedness; proper, straight, exact, regular; constant, rule, model. The ideogram: stop and one, hold to one thing.

[III] Nourish, YANG: feed, sustain, support; provide, care for; bring up, improve, grow, develop.

Correspond(-to), YING: be in agreement or harmony; resonate together, invoke and fulfill each other; answer to, suitable; relation between the lines (1:4, 2:5, 3:6) when they form the pair opened and whole, supple and solid. The ideogram: heart and obey. **Reach(-to),** HU: arrive at a goal; reach towards and achieve; connect; contrasts with tend-towards, YU.

● *Transforming Lines*

Initial nine

a) **Possessing adversity.**
Harvesting: climaxing.

b) **Possessing adversity, Harvesting: climaxing.**
Not opposing calamity indeed.

Associated Contexts a) **Adversity,** LI: danger; threatening, malevolent demon. This has two aspects: grind, sharpen, improve, perfect, stimulate; and: poisonous, sinister, cruel, contrary. It indicates a spirit or ghost that seeks revenge by inflicting suffering upon the living. Pacifying

or exorcizing such a spirit can have a healing effect. The ideogram: sheltering cliff and stinging insect.

Climax, YI: come to a high point and stop, bring to an end; use up, lay aside; decline, reject.

b) **Oppose**, FAN: resist; violate, offend, attack; possessed by an evil spirit; criminal. The ideogram: violate and dog, brutal offense.

Nine at-second

a) **Carting, stimulating the axle-strap.**

b) **Carting, stimulating the axle-strap.**
Centering without surpassing indeed.

Associated Contexts a) **Cart**, YÜ: carrying capacity of a vehicle; contain, hold, sustain. **Stimulate**, SHUO: rouse to action and good feeling; free from constraint, stir up, urge on; persuade, cheer, delight; set out in words; the Action of the trigram Open, TUI. The ideogram: words and exchange. **Axle-strap**, FU: fastens the body of a cart to axle and wheels.

b) **Surpass**, YU: exceed; beyond measure, excessive; extraordinary; transgress, blame.

Nine at-third

a) **A fine horse, pursuing.**
Harvesting: drudgery, Trial.
Spoken-thus: an enclosed cart, escorting.
Harvesting: possessing directed going.

b) **Harvesting: possessing directed going.**
Uniting purposes above indeed.

Associated Contexts a) **Fine**, LIANG: excellent, refined, valuable; gentle, considerate, kind; natural. **Horse**, MA: symbol of spirited strength in the natural world, counterpart of dragon, LUNG; associated with Force, CH'IEN, heaven, T'IEN, and high noon. **Pursue**, CHU: chase, follow closely, press hard; expel, drive out. The ideogram: pig (wealth) and go, chasing fortune.

Drudgery, CHIEN: difficult, hard, repetitive work; hard to cultivate; distressing, sorrowful. The ideogram: sticky earth and a person looking around, hard work in comparison to others. **Trial**, CHEN: test by ordeal; inquiry by divination and its result; righteous, firm; separating wheat from chaff; the kernel, the proven core; fourth stage of the Time Cycle. The ideogram: pearl and divination.

Spoken-thus, YÜEH: designated, termed, called. The ideogram: open mouth and tongue. **Enclose**, HSIEN: put inside a fence or barrier; restrain, obstruct, forbid; pen, corral. **Cart**, YÜ: carrying capacity of a vehicle; contain, hold, sustain. **Escort**, WEI: accompany, protect, guard, defend, honor; restrain; military outpost.

Possessing directed going, YU YU WANG: imposing a direction on the flow of time from present to past; have a specific goal or purpose.

b) **Unite**, HO: join, match, correspond, agree, collect, reply; unison, harmony; also: close, shut the mouth. The ideogram: mouth and assemble. **Purpose**, CHIH: focus of mind and heart; will, inclination, resolve. The ideogram: heart and scholar, high inner resolve, or heart and go, inner determination.

Six at-fourth

a) **Youthful cattle's stable.**
Spring significant.

b) **Six at-fourth, Spring significant.**
Possessing rejoicing indeed.

Associated Contexts a) **Youthful**, T'UNG: young person between eight and fifteen; young animals and plants. **Cattle**, NIU: ox, bull, cow, calf; kine; power and strength of work animals. **'s/have(-it)/it/them**, CHIH: expresses possession, directly or as an object pronoun. **Stable**, KU: shed or pen for cattle and horses.

Spring, YÜAN: source, origin, head; great, excellent; arise, begin, generating power; first stage of the Time Cycle.

b) **Rejoice(-in)**, HSI: feel and give joy; delight, exult; cheerful, merry. The ideogram: joy (music) and mouth, expressing joy.

Six at-fifth

a) **A gelded pig's tusks.**
Significant.

b) **Six at-fifth's significance.**
Possessing reward indeed.

Associated Contexts a) **Geld,** FEN: castrate a pig; deprive, take out.
Pig, SHIH: all swine; sign of wealth and good fortune; associated with the
Streaming Moment. **'s/have(-it)/it/them,** CHIH: expresses possession,
directly or as an object pronoun. **Tusk,** YA: teeth of animals; toothlike,
jagged, gnaw; ivory; a tax collector.

b) **Reward,** CH'ING: gift given from gratitude or benevolence; favour from
heaven; congratulate with gifts. The ideogram: heart, follow and deer
(wealth), the heart expressed through gifts.

Nine above

a) **Wherefore heaven's highway? Growing.**

b) **Wherefore heaven's highway?**
Tao: the great moving indeed.

Associated Contexts a) **Wherefore,** HO: interrogative: why? for
what reason? what is? and affirmation: therefore, for that reason.
's/have(-it)/it/them, CHIH: expresses possession, directly or as an object
pronoun. **Highway,** CH'Ü: main road, thoroughfare; where many ways meet.
　　Grow, HENG: success through a sacrifice; pervade, persevere; bring to
full growth; enjoy; vigorous, effective; second stage of the Time Cycle.

b) **Tao:** way or path; ongoing process of being and the course it traces for
each specific person or thing; keyword. The ideogram: go and head,
leading and the path it creates.

27

JAWS/SWALLOWING ▮ *YI*

This hexagram describes your situation in terms of nourishing and being nourished. It emphasizes that opening in order to take things in as well as providing nourishment to others is the adequate way to handle it. To be in accord with the time, you are told to: open your **jaws** and **swallow**!

● *Image of the Situation*

> **Jaws, Trial: significant.**
> **Viewing Jaws.**
> **Originating-from seeking mouth substance.**

Associated Contexts **Jaws/swallow**, YI: mouth, jaws, cheeks, chin; take in, ingest; feed, nourish, sustain, rear; furnish what is necessary. The ideogram: open jaws. **Trial**, CHEN: test by ordeal; inquiry by divination and its result; righteous, firm; separating wheat from chaff; the kernel, the proven core; fourth stage of the Time Cycle. The ideogram: pearl and divination. **Significant**, CHI: leads to the experience of meaning; favorable, propitious, advantageous, appropriate; keyword. The ideogram: scholar and mouth, wise words of a sage.

View, KUAN: contemplate, observe from a distance; look at carefully, gaze at; also: a monastery, an observatory; scry, divine through liquid in a cup. The ideogram: see and waterbird, observe through air or water. Image of Hexagram 20.

Origin, TZU: source, beginning, ground; cause, reason, motive; line of descent; path to the origin; yourself, intrinsic. **Seek**, CH'IU: search for, aim at, wish for, desire; implore, supplicate; covetous. **Mouth**, K'OU: literal mouth, words going out and food coming in; entrance, hole. **Substance**, SHIH: real, solid, full; results, fruits, possessions; essence; honest, sincere. The ideogram: string of coins under a roof, riches in the house.

● *Outer and Inner Aspects*

☶ **Bound**: Mountains bound, limit and set a place off, stopping forward movement. **Bound** completes a full yin-yang cycle.

Connection to the outer: accomplishing words, which express things fully. **Bound** articulates what is complete and suggests what is beginning.

☲ **Shake**: Thunder rises from below, shaking and stirring things up. **Shake** begins the yang hemicycle by germinating new action.

Connection to the inner: sprouting energies thrusting from below, the Woody Moment beginning. **Shake** stirs things up to issue-forth.

Previous accomplishments are **swallowed** in order to nourish germinating new energies.

- *Counter Indications*

The doubled nuclear trigram **Field**, K'UN, results in Counter Hexagram 2, **Field**, K'UN. Actively **swallowing** and taking things in contrasted with the passive receptivity of **field.**

- *Sequence*

> **Beings accumulating therefore afterwards permitting nourishing.**
> **Anterior acquiescence has the use-of Jaws.**
> **Jaws imply nourishing indeed.**

Associated Contexts **Being(s)**, WU: creature, thing, any single being; matter, substance, essence; nature of things. **Accumulate**, CH'U: retain, hoard, gather, herd together; control, restrain; domesticate, tame, train; raise, feed, sustain, bring up. The ideogram: field and black, fertile black soil good for pastures, accumulated through retaining silt. Image of Hexagrams 9 and 26. **Therefore afterwards**, JAN HOU: logical consequence of, necessarily follows in time. **Permit**, K'O: possible because in harmony with an inherent principle. The ideogram: mouth and breath, silent consent. **Nourish**, YANG: feed, sustain, support; provide, care for; bring up, improve, grow, develop.

Anterior ... the use-of: activating this hexagram depends on understanding and accepting the previous statement.

Imply, CHE: further signify; additional meaning. **Indeed**, YEH: intensifier; indicates comment on previous statement.

● *Contrasted Definitions*

> **Great Exceeding: toppling indeed.**
> **Jaws: nourishing correcting indeed.**

Associated Contexts **Great**, TA: big, noble, important, very; orient the will toward a self-imposed goal, impose direction; ability to lead or guide your life; contrasts with small, HSIAO, flexible adaptation to what crosses your path; keyword. **Exceed**, KU: go beyond, pass by, pass over; excessive, transgress; error, fault. **Great Exceeding** is the Image of Hexagram 28. **Topple**, TIEN: fall over because top-heavy; overthrow, subvert; top, summit.

Correct, CHENG: rectify deviation or one-sidedness; proper, straight, exact, regular; constant, rule, model. The ideogram: stop and one, hold to one thing.

● *Symbol Tradition*

> **Below mountain possessing thunder. Jaws.**
> **A chün tzu uses considering words to inform.**
> **[A chün tzu uses] articulating to drink[and]take-in.**

Associated Contexts **Below**, HSIA: anything below, in all senses; lower, inner; lower trigram; opposite of above, SHANG. **Mountain**, SHAN: limit, boundary; the Symbol of the trigram Bound, KEN. The ideogram: three peaks, a mountain range. **Possess**, YU: in possession of, have, own; opposite of lack, WU. **Thunder**, LEI: rising, arousing power; the Symbol of the trigram Shake, CHEN.

Chün tzu: ideal of a person who uses divination to order his/her life in accordance with tao rather than wilful intention; keyword. **Use(-of)**, YI: make use of, by means of, owing to; employ, make functional. **Consider**, SHEN: act carefully, seriously; cautious, attentive, circumspect; still, quiet, sincere. The ideogram: heart and true. **Word**, YEN: speech, spoken words, sayings; talk, discuss, address. The ideogram: mouth and rising vapor, words as speech. **Inform**, YÜ: tell, warn; talk with, converse, exchange ideas.

Articulate, CHIEH: separate and distinguish, as well as join, different things; express thought through speech; joint, section, chapter, interval, unit of time; zodiacal sign; moderate, regulate; lit.: nodes on bamboo stalks. Image of Hexagram 60. **Drinking[and]taking-in**, YIN SHIH: comprehensive term for eating, drinking and breathing; a meal, eating together.

- *Image Tradition*

> **Jaws. Trial: significant. [I]**
> **Nourishing correcting, by-consequence significant indeed.**
>
> **Viewing Jaws. [II]**
> **Viewing one's place to nourish indeed.**
> **Originating-from seeking mouth substance.**
> **Viewing one's origin: nourishing indeed.**
>
> **Heaven[and]Earth nourishes the myriad beings. [III]**
> **The all-wise person nourishes eminence**
>   **used to extend-to the myriad commoners.**
> **Actually Jaws's season great in-fact.**

Associated Contexts **[I] By-consequence(-of)**, TSE: very strong connection; reason, cause, result; rule, law, pattern, standard; therefore.

[II] One's/one, CH'I: third person pronoun; also: it/its, he/his, she/hers, they/theirs. **Place**, SO: where something belongs or comes from; residence, dwelling; habitual focus or object.

[III] Heaven[and]Earth, T'IEN TI: dynamic relation between the primal powers and the world it produces; cosmos, natural or human world; keyword. **Myriad**, WAN: countless; many, everyone; lit.: ten thousand. The ideogram: swarm of insects.
    All-wise, SHENG: intuitive universal wisdom; mythical sages; holy, sacred; mark of highest distinction. The ideogram: ear and inform, one who knows all from a single sound. **People, person**, JEN: humans individually and collectively; an individual; humankind. Image of Hexagrams 13 and 37. **Eminent**, HSIEN: moral and intellectual power; worthy, excellent, virtuous; sage second to the all-wise, SHENG. **Extend(-to)**, CHI: reach to, draw out, prolong; continuous, enduring. **Commoners**, MIN: class of workers the state draws on to sustain the social hierarchy; undeveloped potential outside the organized personality.

Actually ... in-fact, YI TSAI: stresses the importance of a statement. The ideogram: a dart and done, strong intention fully expressed. **'s/have(-it)/it/them,** CHIH: expresses possession, directly or as an object pronoun. **Season,** SHIH: quality of the time; the right time, opportune, in harmony; planning in accord with the time; seasons of the year. The ideogram: sun and temple, time as sacred.

● *Transforming Lines*

Initial nine

a) **Stowing-away simply the psyche tortoise.**
   Viewing my pendent Jaws.
   Pitfall.

b) **Viewing my pendent Jaws.**
   Truly not the stand to value indeed.

Associated Contexts a) **Stow(-away),** SHE: set aside, put away, store; halt, rest in; temporary lodgings, breathing-spell. **Simply,** ERH: just so, only. **Psyche,** LING: life force, vital energy; spirit of a being; magical action or influence. **Tortoise,** KUEI: turtles; armored animals, shells and shields; long-living; oracle-consulting by tortoise shell; image of the macrocosm: heaven and earth, between them the soft flesh of humans.

My/me/I, WO: first person pronoun; indicates an unusually strong emphasis on your own subjective experience. **Pendent,** TO: hanging; flowering branch, date or grape clusters.

Pitfall, HSIUNG: leads away from the experience of meaning; stuck and exposed to danger, unable to take in the situation; flow of life and spirit is blocked; unfortunate, baleful; keyword.

b) **Truly,** YI: statement is true and precise. **Not,** PU: simple negative. **Stand,** TSU: base, foot, leg; rest on; support; stance. The ideogram: foot and calf resting. **Value,** KUEI: regard as valuable, give worth and dignity to; precious, high priced; honorable, exalted, illustrious. The ideogram: cowries (coins) and basket.

Six at-second

a) Toppling Jaws.
 Rejecting the canons, tending-towards the hill-top.
 Jaws chastising: pitfall.

b) Six at-second, chastising: pitfall.
 Movement letting-go sorting indeed.

Associated Contexts a) **Reject**, FU: push away, expel, brush off; oppose, contradict; perverse, proud. The ideogram: hand and do not, pushing something away. **Canons**, CHING: standards, laws; regular, regulate; the Five Classics. The ideogram: warp-threads in a loom. **Tend-towards**, YÜ: move toward but not reach, in the direction of; contrasts with reach(-to), HU, actually arriving. **Hill-top**, CH'IU: hill with hollow top used for worship and as grave-site; knoll, hillock.

Chastise, CHENG: punish, subjugate, discipline; reduce to order; punishing expedition. The ideogram: step and correct, a rectifying move. **Pitfall**, HSIUNG: leads away from the experience of meaning; stuck and exposed to danger, unable to take in the situation; flow of life and spirit is blocked; unfortunate, baleful; keyword.

b) **Move**, HSING: move or move something; motivate, emotionally moving; walk, act, do. The ideogram: stepping left then right. **Let-go**, SHIH: lose, omit, miss, fail, let slip; out of control. The ideogram: drop from the hand. **Sort**, LEI: group according to kind, class with; like nature or purpose; species, class, genus.

Six at-third

a) Rejecting Jaws. Trial: pitfall.
 Ten years-revolved, no availing-of.
 Without direction: Harvesting.

b) Ten years-revolved, no availing-of.
 Tao, the great rebelling indeed.

Associated Contexts a) **Reject**, FU: push away, expel, brush off; oppose, contradict; perverse, proud. The ideogram: hand and do not, pushing something away. **Pitfall**, HSIUNG: leads away from the experience of meaning; stuck and exposed to danger, unable to take in the situation; flow of life and spirit is blocked; unfortunate, baleful; keyword.

Ten, SHIH: goal and end of reckoning; whole, complete, all; entire, perfected, the full amount; reach everywhere, receive everything. The ideogram: East–West line crosses North–South line, a grid that contains all. **Years-revolved**, NIEN: number of years elapsed; a person's age; contrasts with year's-time, SUI, length of time in a year. **No**, WU: simple negative; un-, dis-. **Avail-of**, YUNG: take advantage of; benefit from, profit by; use for a specific purpose; apply to advantage. The ideogram: to divine and center, applying divination to central concerns.

Without direction: Harvesting, WU YU LI: no plan or direction is advantageous; in order to take advantage of the situation, do not impose a direction on events.

b) **Tao**: way or path; ongoing process of being and the course it traces for each specific person or thing; keyword. The ideogram: go and head, leading and the path it creates. **Rebel**, PEI: go against nature or usage; insubordinate; perverse, unreasonable.

Six at-fourth

a) **Toppling Jaws. Significant.**
Tiger observing: glaring, glaring.
His appetites: pursuing, pursuing.
Without fault.

b) **Toppling Jaws' significance.**
Spreading-out shining above indeed.

Associated Contexts a) **Tiger**, HU: fierce king of animals; extreme yang; opposed to and protects against demoniacs on North–South axis of Universal Compass. **Observe**, SHIH: see and inspect carefully; gain knowledge of; compare and imitate. The ideogram: see and omen, taking account of what you see. **Glare**, TAN: stare intensely; obstruct, prevent. The ideogram: look and hesitate, staring without acting. The doubled character intensifies this quality.

His/he, CH'I: third person pronoun; also: one/one's, it/its, she/hers, they/theirs. **Appetites**, YÜ: drives, instinctive craving; wishes, passions, desires, aspirations; long for, seek ardently; covet. **Pursue**, CHU: chase, follow closely, press hard; expel, drive out. The ideogram: pig (wealth) and go, chasing fortune. The doubled character intensifies this quality.

Without fault, WU CHIU: no error or harm in the situation.

b) **Spread-out,** SHIH: expand, diffuse, distribute, arrange, exhibit; add to, aid. The ideogram: flag and indeed, claiming new country. **Shine,** KUANG: illuminate; give off brilliant, bright light; honor, glory, éclat; result of action, contrasts with brightness, MING, light of heavenly bodies. The ideogram: fire above person, lifting the light. **Above,** SHANG: anything above, in all senses; higher, upper, outer; upper trigram; opposite of below, HSIA.

Six at-fifth

a) **Rejecting the canons.**
   Residing-in Trial significant.
   Not permitting wading the Great River.

b) **Residing-in Trial's significance.**
   Yielding uses adhering-to the above indeed.

Associated Contexts a) **Reject,** FU: push away, expel, brush off; oppose, contradict; perverse, proud. The ideogram: hand and do not, pushing something away. **Canons,** CHING: standards, laws; regular, regulate; the Five Classics. The ideogram: warp-threads in a loom.

   Reside(-in), CHÜ: dwell, live in, stay; sit down, fill an office; settled parts of a country. The ideogram: body and seat.

   Not permitting, PU K'O: not possible; contradicts an inherent principle. The ideogram: mouth and breath, silent consent. **Wading the Great River,** SHE TA CH'UAN: consciously moving into the flow of time; enter the stream of life with a goal or purpose; embark on a significant enterprise.

b) **Yield(-to),** SHUN: give way and bear produce; comply, agree, follow, obey; unresisting, docile, flexible; nourish, provide; the Action of the trigram Field, K'UN: The ideogram: head and current, water flowing from the head of a river, yielding to the banks. **Adhere(-to),** TS'UNG: follow a way, hold to a doctrine, school, or person; hear and comply with, agree to; forced to follow, follower. The ideogram: two men walking, one following the other. **Above,** SHANG: anything above, in all senses; higher, upper, outer; upper trigram; opposite of below, HSIA.

Nine above

  a) **Antecedent Jaws. Adversity significant.**
   Harvesting: wading the Great River.

  b) **Antecedent Jaws, adversity significant.**
   The great possessing reward indeed.

Associated Contexts a) **Antecedent**, YU: come before as origin and cause; through, by, from; depend on; permit, enter by way of. **Adversity**, LI: danger; threatening, malevolent demon. This has two aspects: grind, sharpen, improve, perfect, stimulate; and: poisonous, sinister, cruel, contrary. It indicates a spirit or ghost that seeks revenge by inflicting suffering upon the living. Pacifying or exorcizing such a spirit can have a healing effect. The ideogram: sheltering cliff and stinging insect.

   Harvest, LI: advantageous, profitable; acute, insightful; benefit, nourish; third stage of the Time Cycle. **Wading the Great River**, SHE TA CH'UAN: consciously moving into the flow of time; entering the stream of life with a goal or purpose; keyword.

b) **Reward**, CH'ING: gift given from gratitude or benevolence; favor from heaven; congratulate with gifts. The ideogram: heart, follow and deer (wealth), the heart expressed through gifts.

28

GREAT EXCEEDING ▮ *TA KUO*

This hexagram describes your situation in terms of your connection to a ruling principle. It emphasizes that pushing the guiding idea beyond ordinary limits and accepting the results is the adequate way to handle it. To be in accord with the time, you are told to: **greatly exceed!**

● *Image of the Situation*

> **Great Exceeding, the ridgepole sagging.**
> **Harvesting: possessing directed going.**
> **Growing.**

Associated Contexts **Great**, TA: big, noble, important, very; orient the will toward a self-imposed goal, impose direction; ability to lead or guide your life; contrasts to small, HSIAO, flexible adaptation to what crosses your path; keyword. **Exceed**, KU: go beyond, pass by, pass over; excessive, transgress; error, fault. **Ridgepole**, TUNG: highest and key beam in a house; summit, crest. **Sag**, NAO: yield, bend, distort, twist; disturbed, confused.

Harvest, LI: advantageous, profitable; acute, insightful; benefit, nourish; third stage of the Time Cycle. **Possessing directed going**, YU YU WANG: imposing a direction on the flow of time from present to past; have a specific goal or purpose.

Grow, HENG: success through a sacrifice; pervade, persevere; bring to full growth; enjoy; vigorous, effective; second stage of the Time Cycle.

● *Outer and Inner Aspects*

☱ **Open**: vapor rising from the marsh's open surface stimulates and fertilizes; stimulating words cheer and inspire. **Open** begins the yin hemicycle by initiating the formative process.

Connection to the outer: liquifying, casting, skinning off the mold, the Metallic Moment beginning. **Open** stimulates, cheers and reveals innate form.

☴ **Ground**: Wind and wood subtly enter from the ground, penetrating and pervading. **Ground** is the center of the yang hemicycle, spreading pervasive action.

Connection to the inner: penetrating and bringing together, the Woody Moment culminating. **Ground** pervades, matches and couples, seeding a new generation.

Great inner penetration, stimulated in the outer world, **exceeds** all normal forms and relations.

● *Counter Indications*

The doubled nuclear trigram **Force**, CH'IEN, results in Counter Hexagram 1, **Force**, CH'IEN. The exclusive creative drive of **great exceeding** is contrasted with the simultaneous creation and destruction of the **force**.

● *Sequence*

> **Not nourishing, by-consequence not permitting stirring-up.**
> **Anterior acquiescence has the use-of Great Exceeding.**

Associated Contexts **Not**, PU: simple negative. **Nourish**, YANG: feed, sustain, support; provide, care for; bring up, improve, grow, develop. **By-consequence(-of)**, TSE: very strong connection; reason, cause, result; rule, law, pattern, standard; therefore. **Not permitting**, PU K'O: not possible; contradicts an inherent principle. The ideogram: mouth and breath, silent consent. **Stir-up**, TUNG: excite, influence, move, affect; work, take action; come out of the egg or the bud; the Action of the trigram Shake, CHEN. The ideogram: strength and heavy, move weighty things.

Anterior ... the use-of: activating this hexagram depends on understanding and accepting the previous statement.

● *Contrasted Definitions*

> **Great Exceeding: toppling indeed.**
> **Jaws: nourishing correcting indeed.**

Associated Contexts **Topple**, TIEN: fall over because top-heavy; overthrow, subvert; top, summit. **Indeed**, YEH: intensifier; indicates comment on previous statement.

Jaws/swallow, YI: mouth, jaws, cheeks, chin; take in, ingest; feed, nourish, sustain, rear; furnish what is necessary. The ideogram: open jaws. Image of Hexagram 27. **Correct**, CHENG: rectify deviation or one-sidedness; proper, straight, exact, regular; constant, rule, model. The ideogram: stop and one, hold to one thing.

• *Symbol Tradition*

> **Marsh submerging wood. Great Exceeding.**
> **A chün tzu uses solitary establishing not to fear.**
> **[A chün tzu uses] retiring-from the age without melancholy.**

Associated Contexts **Marsh**, TSE: open surface of a flat body of water and the vapors rising from it; fertilize, enrich; kindness, favor; the Symbol of the trigram Open, TUI. **Submerge**, MIEH: plunge under water, put out a fire; exterminate, finish, cut off. The ideogram: water and destroy. **Wood/tree**, MU: all things woody or wooden, alive or constructed from wood; associated with the Woody Moment; wood and wind are the Symbols of the trigram Ground, SUN. The ideogram: a tree with roots and branches.

Chün tzu: ideal of a person who uses divination to order his/her life in accordance with tao rather than wilful intention; keyword. **Use(-of)**, YI: make use of, by means of, owing to; employ, make functional. **Solitary**, TI: alone, single; isolated, abandoned. **Establish**, LI: set up, institute, order, arrange; stand erect; settled principles. **Fear**, CHÜ: afraid, intimidated, apprehensive; stand in awe of.

Retire, TUN: withdraw; run away, flee; conceal yourself, become obscure, invisible; secluded, non-social. The ideogram: walk and swine (wealth and luck), satisfaction through walking away. Image of Hexagram 33. **Age**, SHIH: an age, an epoch, a generation; the world, mankind; the time, as "in the time of." **Without**, WU: devoid of; -less as suffix. **Melancholy**, MEN: sad, unhappy, chagrined, heavy-hearted. The ideogram: gate and heart, the heart confined.

● *Image Tradition*

Great Exceeding. [I]
Great implies Exceeding indeed.
The ridgepole sagging.
Roots, tips, fading indeed.

Solid Exceeding and-also centering. [II]
Ground and-also stimulating movement.
Harvesting: possessing directed going.

Thereupon Growing. [III]
Actually Great Exceeding's season great in-fact.

Associated Contexts **[I] Imply**, CHE: further signify; additional meaning.

Root, PEN: origin, cause, source of nourishment; essential. The ideogram: tree with roots in earth. **Tips**, MO: growing ends, outermost twigs; last, most distant. **Fade**, JO: lose strength or freshness, wither, wane; fragile, feeble, weak; decayed, ruined; infirm purpose.

[II] Solid, KANG: quality of the whole lines; firm, strong, unyielding, persisting. **And-also**, ERH: joins and contrasts two terms. **Center**, CHUNG: inner, central; put in the center; middle, stable point enabling you to face inner and outer changes; middle line of trigram. The ideogram: field divided in two equal parts. Image of Hexagram 61.

Ground, SUN: base on which things rest; support, foundation; mild, subtly penetrating; nourishing. The ideogram: stand and things arranged on it, the subtle influence of the ground. Image of Hexagram 57. **Stimulate**, SHUO: rouse to action and good feeling; free from constraint, stir up, urge on; persuade, cheer, delight; set out in words; the Action of the trigram Open, TUI. The ideogram: words and exchange. **Move**, HSING: move or move something; motivate, emotionally moving; walk, act, do. The ideogram: stepping left then right.

[III] Thereupon, NAI: on that ground, because of.

Actually ... in-fact, YI TSAI: stresses the importance of a statement. The ideogram: a dart and done, strong intention fully expressed. **'s/have(-it)/it/them**, CHIH: expresses possession, directly or as an object pronoun. **Season**, SHIH: quality of the time; the right time, opportune, in

harmony; planning in accord with the time; seasons of the year. The ideogram: sun and temple, time as sacred.

● *Transforming Lines*

Initial six

a) **A sacrifice availing-of white thatch-grass.
Without fault.**

b) **A sacrifice availing-of white thatch-grass.
Supple located below indeed.**

Associated Contexts a) **Sacrifice**, CHIEH: make offerings to gods and the dead; depend on, call on, borrow; lit.: straw mat used to hold offerings. **Avail-of**, YUNG: take advantage of; benefit from, profit by; use for a specific purpose; apply to advantage. The ideogram: to divine and center, applying divination to central concerns. **White**, PO: associated with autumn, Harvest and the Metallic Moment; clear, immaculate; plain, pure, essential; explicit; color of death and mourning. **Thatch-grass**, MAO: thick grass used for the roofs of humble houses.

Without fault, WU CHIU: no error or harm in the situation.

b) **Supple**, JOU: quality of the opened lines; flexible, pliant, tender, adaptable. **Locate(-in)**, TSAI: live in, dwell, reside; belong to, involved with, depend on; within. The ideogram: earth and persevere, place on the earth. **Below**, HSIA: anything below, in all senses; lower, inner; lower trigram; opposite of above, SHANG.

Nine at-second

a) **A withered willow giving-birth-to a sprig.
A venerable husband acquiring his woman consort.
Without not Harvesting.**

b) **A venerable husband, a woman consort.
Exceeding uses mutual associating indeed.**

Associated Contexts a) **Withered**, K'U: dry up; dry wood, dried up bogs; decayed, rotten. The ideogram: tree and old. **Willow**, YANG: all thriving, fast growing trees; willow, poplar, tamarisk, aspen. The ideogram: tree and expand. **Birth/give-birth-to**, SHENG: produce, beget, grow, bear, arise; life, vitality. The ideogram: earth and sprout. **Sprig**, T'I: tender new shoot of a tree, twig, new branch.

Venerable, LAO: term of respect due to old age. **Husband**, FU: household manager; administer with thrift and prudence; responsible for; sustain with your earnings; old enough to assume responsibility; married man. **Acquire**, TE: obtain the desired object; wish for, desire covetously; gains, possessions. The ideogram: go and obstacle, going through obstacles to the goal. **His/he**, CH'I: third person pronoun; also: one/one's, it/its, she/hers, they/theirs. **Woman(hood)**, NÜ: a woman; what is inherently female. **Consort**, CH'I: single official partner; legal status of married woman (first wife); contrasts with function of wife, FU, head of household, and concubine, CH'IEH, secondary wives.

Without not Harvesting, WU PU LI: nothing for which this will not be beneficial; advantageous potential, borderline where the balance is swinging from not Harvesting to actually Harvesting.

b) **Mutual**, HSIANG: reciprocal assistance, encourage, help; bring together, blend with; examine, inspect; by turns. **Associate(-with)**, YÜ: consort with, combine; companions; group, band, company; agree with, comply, help. The ideogram: pair of hands reaching downward meets a pair of hands reaching upward, helpful association.

Nine at-third

a) **The ridgepole buckling. Pitfall.**

b) **The ridgepole buckling's pitfall.**
Not permitted to use possessing bracing indeed.

Associated Contexts a) **Buckle**, JAO: distort, wrench out of shape, collapse, break; weak; flexible, lithe. **Pitfall**, HSIUNG: leads away from the experience of meaning; stuck and exposed to danger, unable to take in the situation; flow of life and spirit is blocked; unfortunate, baleful; keyword.

b) **Possess**, YU: in possession of, have, own; opposite of lack, WU. **Brace/jawbones**, FU: support, consolidate, reinforce, strengthen, stiffen, prop up, fix; steady, firm, rigid; help, rescue; support the speaking mouth. The ideogram: cart and great.

Nine at-fourth

a) **The ridgepole crowning. Significant.**
Possessing more: abashment.

b) **The ridgepole crowning's significance.**
Not sagging, reaching-to the below indeed.

Associated Contexts a) **Crown**, LUNG: place above all others; peak; high, surpassing. **Significant**, CHI: leads to the experience of meaning; favorable, propitious, advantageous, appropriate; keyword. The ideogram: scholar and mouth, wise words of a sage.

Possess, YU: in possession of, have, own; opposite of lack, WU. **More**, T'O: another; add to. **Abashment**, LIN: distress, shame, regret, humiliation; aware of having lost the right track; leads to repenting, HUI, correcting the direction of mind and life.

b) **Reach(-to)**, HU: arrive at a goal; reach toward and achieve; connect; contrasts with tend-towards, YU. **Below**, HSIA. anything below, in all senses; lower, inner; lower trigram; opposite of above, SHANG.

Nine at-fifth

a) **A withered willow giving-birth-to flowers.**
A venerable wife acquiring her notable husband.
Without fault, without praise.

b) **A withered willow giving-birth-to flowers.**
Wherefore permitting lasting indeed?
A venerable wife, a notable husband.
Truly permitting the demoniac indeed.

Associated Contexts a) **Withered**, K'U: dry up; dry wood, dried up bogs; decayed, rotten. The ideogram: tree and old. **Willow**, YANG: all thriving, fast growing trees; willow, poplar, tamarisk, aspen. The ideogram: tree and expand. **Birth/give-birth-to**, SHENG: produce, beget, grow, bear, arise; life, vitality. The ideogram: earth and sprout. **Flower**, HUA: beauty, abundance; variegated, elegant, blooming, garden-like; symbol of culture and literature.

Venerable, LAO: term of respect due to old age. **Wife**, FU: responsible position of married woman within the household; contrasts with consort,

CH'I, her legal position and concubine, CH'IEH, secondary wives. The ideogram: woman, hand and broom, household duties. **Acquire**, TE: obtain the desired object; wish for, desire covetously; gains, possessions. The ideogram: go and obstacle, going through obstacles to the goal. **Hers/she**, CH'I: third person pronoun; also: one/one's, it/its, he/his, they/their. **Notable**, SHIH: learned, upright, important man; scholar, gentleman. **Husband**, FU: household manager; administer with thrift and prudence; responsible for; sustain with your earnings; old enough to assume responsibility; married man.

Without fault, WU CHIU: no error or harm in the situation. **Praise**, YÜ: admire and approve; magnify, eulogize; flatter. The ideogram: words and give, offering words.

b) **Wherefore**, HO: interrogative: why? for what reason? what is? and affirmation: therefore, for that reason. **Permit**, K'O: possible because in harmony with an inherent principle. The ideogram: mouth and breath, silent consent. **Last**, CHIU: long, protracted; enduring.

Truly, YI: statement is true and precise. **Demon(iac)**, CH'OU: possessed by a malignant genius; ugly, physically or morally deformed; vile, disgraceful, shameful; drunken. The ideogram: fermenting liquor and soul. Demoniac and tiger are opposed on the Universal Compass North–South axis; the tiger (Extreme Yang) scares away and protects against demoniacs (Extreme Yin).

Six above

a) Exceeding wading submerges the peak. Pitfall.
Without fault.

b) Exceeding wading's pitfall.
Not permitting fault indeed.

Associated Contexts a) **Wade**, SHE: walk in or through the water; spend time on something; contrasts with ford, CHI, to cross. The ideogram: step and water. **Peak**, TING: top, summit, crown; carry on the head; superior. **Pitfall**, HSIUNG: leads away from the experience of meaning; stuck and exposed to danger, unable to take in the situation; flow of life and spirit is blocked; unfortunate, baleful; keyword.

Without fault, WU CHIU: no error or harm in the situation.

b) **Fault**, CHIU: unworthy conduct that leads to harm, illness, misfortune. The ideogram: person and differ, differ from what you should be.

29

GORGE ▮ *K'AN*

This hexagram describes your situation in terms of a dangerous situation you cannot avoid. It emphasizes that taking the risk without reserve, the action of **Gorge**, is the adequate way to handle it. To be in accord with the time, you are told to: **venture** and **fall!**

- *Image of the Situation*

> **Repeating Gorge.**
> **Possessing conformity.**
> **Holding-fast the heart Growing.**
> **Movement possesses honor.**

Associated Contexts **Repeat,** HSI: series of similar acts; practice, rehearse; familiar with, skilled. The ideogram: two wings and a cap, thought carried by repeated movements. **Gorge,** K'AN: dangerous place; hole, cavity, hollow; pit, snare, trap, grave, precipice; critical time, test; risky. The ideogram: earth and pit.

Gorge is the stream trigram doubled and includes that trigram's attributes: *Symbol:* **Stream,** SHUI: flowing water; fluid, dissolving; river, tide, flood. The ideogram: rippling water. *Action:* **Venture falling,** HSIEN HSIEN: risk falling until a bottom is reached, filling and overcoming the danger of the Gorge. **Fall,** HSIEN: fall down or into, sink, drop, descend; falling water; be captured. **Venture,** HSIEN: risk without reserve; key point, point of danger; difficulty, obstruction that must be confronted; water falling and filling the holes on its way. The ideogram: mound and all or whole, everything engaged at one point.

Possessing conformity, YU FU: inner and outer are in accord; confidence of the spirits has been captured; sincere, truthful; proper to take action.

Hold-fast, WEI: hold together; tie to, connect; reins, net. **Heart,** HSIN: heart as center of being; seat of mind's images and affections; moral nature; source of desires, intentions, will. **Grow,** HENG: success through a sacrifice; pervade, persevere; bring to full growth; enjoy; vigorous, effective; second stage of the Time Cycle.

Move, HSING: move or move something; motivate, emotionally moving; walk, act, do. The ideogram: stepping left then right. **Possess**, YU: in possession of, have, own; opposite of lack, WU. **Honor**, SHANG: esteem, give high rank to; eminent; put one thing on top of another.

• *Outer and Inner Aspects*

☵ **Gorge**: Stream ventures and falls into the gorge, flowing on through toil and danger. **Gorge** ends the yin hemicycle by leveling and dissolving forms.

Connection to both inner and outer: flooding and leveling dissolve direction and shape, the Streaming Moment. **Gorge** ventures, falls, toils and flows on.

• *Counter Indications*

Nuclear trigrams **Bound**, KEN, and **Shake**, CHEN, result in Counter Hexagram 27, **Jaws/Swallowing**, YI. Wholehearted outer venturing into the danger of the **gorge** is contrasted with taking things in through **swallowing**.

• *Sequence*

> **Beings not permitted to use completing Exceeding.**
> **Anterior acquiescence has the use-of Gorge.**
> **Gorge implies falling indeed.**

Associated Contexts **Beings not permitted to use ...** : no one is allowed to make use of; nothing can exist by means of. **Complete**, CHUNG: end of a cycle that begins the next; last, whole, all; contrasts with exhaust, CH'IUNG: final end. The ideogram: silk cocoons, follow and ice, winter linking one year with the next. **Exceed**, KU: go beyond, pass by, pass over; excessive, transgress; error, fault. Image of Hexagrams 28 and 62.

Anterior ... the use-of: activating this hexagram depends on understanding and accepting the previous statement.

Imply, CHE: further signify; additional meaning. **Indeed**, YEH: intensifier; indicates comment on previous statement.

- ### Contrasted Definitions

  Above Radiance and-also below Gorge indeed.

  Associated Contexts **Above**, SHANG: anything above, in all senses; higher, upper, outer; upper trigram; opposite of below, HSIA. **Radiance**, LI: glowing light, spreading in all directions; light-giving, discriminating, articulating; divide and arrange in order; the power of consciousness. The ideogram: bird and weird, the magical fire-bird with brilliant plumage. Image of Hexagram 30. **And-also**, ERH: joins and contrasts two terms. **Below**, HSIA: anything below, in all senses; lower, inner; lower trigram; opposite of above, SHANG.

- ### Symbol Tradition

  Streams reiterating culminating. Repeating Gorge.
  A chün tzu uses rules actualizing-tao to move.
  [A chün tzu uses] repeating to teach affairs.

  Associated Contexts **Reiterate**, CHIEN: repeat, duplicate; successive. **Culminate**, CHIH: bring to the highest degree; arrive at the end or summit; superlative.

  Chün tzu: ideal of a person who uses divination to order his/her life in accordance with tao rather than wilful intention; keyword. **Use(-of)**, YI: make use of, by means of, owing to; employ, make functional. **Rules**, CH'ANG: unchanging principles; regular, constant, habitual; maintain laws and customs. **Actualize-tao**, TE: realize tao in action; power, virtue; ability to follow the course traced by the ongoing process of the cosmos; keyword. The ideogram: to go, straight, and heart. Linked with acquire, TE: acquiring that which makes a being become what it is meant to be.

  Teach, CHIAO: instruct, show; precept, doctrine. **Affairs**, SHIH: all kinds of personal activity; matters at hand; business, occupation; manage a business, case in court.

● *Image Tradition*

> **Repeating Gorge. [I]**
> **Redoubling venturing indeed.**
> **Stream diffusing and-also not overfilling.**
> **Movement venturing and-also not letting-go one's trustworthiness.**
>
> **Holding-fast the heart's Growing,**
>   **thereupon using solid centering indeed. [II]**
> **Movement possesses honor. Going possesses achievement indeed.**
> **Heaven venturing, not permitting ascending indeed.**
> **Earth venturing, mountains, rivers, hill-tops, mounds indeed.**
>
> **The kingly prince sets-up venturing used to guard his city. [III]**
> **Actually venturing's season availing-of the great in-fact.**

Associated Contexts **[I] Redouble**, CH'UNG: repeat, reiterate, add to; build up by layers.

Diffuse, LIU: flow out, spread, permeate. **Not**, PU: simple negative. **Overfill**, YING: at the point of overflowing; more than wanted, stretch beyond; replenished, full; arrogant. The ideogram: vessel and too much.

Let-go, SHIH: lose, omit, miss, fail, let slip; out of control. The ideogram: drop from the hand. **One's/one, his/he**, CH'I: third person pronoun; also: it/its, she/hers, they/theirs. **Trustworthy**, HSIN: truthful, faithful, consistent over time; integrity; confide in, follow; credentials; contrasts with conforming, FU, connection in a specific moment. The ideogram: person and word, true speech.

[II] 's/have(-it)/it/them, CHIH: expresses possession, directly or as an object pronoun. **Thereupon**, NAI: on that ground, because of. **Solid**, KANG: quality of the whole lines; firm, strong, unyielding, persisting. **Center**, CHUNG: inner, central; put in the center; middle, stable point enabling you to face inner and outer changes; middle line of trigram. The ideogram: field divided in two equal parts. Image of Hexagram 61.

Go, WANG, and come, LAI, describe the stream of time as it flows from future through present to past; go, WANG, indicates what is departing from present to past; proceed, move on; keyword. **Achieve**, KUNG: work done, results; real accomplishment, praise, worth, merit. The ideogram: workman's square and forearm, combining craft and strength.

Heaven, T'IEN: highest; sky, firmament, heavens; power above the human as opposed to earth, TI, below; the Symbol of the trigram Force, CH'IEN. The ideogram: great and the one above. **Not permitting**, PU K'O: not possible; contradicts an inherent principle. The ideogram: mouth and breath, silent consent. **Ascend**, SHENG: go up; climb step by step; rise in office; advance through effort; accumulate; bring out and fulfill; lit.: a measure for fermented liquor, ascension as distillation. Image of Hexagram 46.

Earth, TI: ground on which the human world rests; basis of all things, nourishes all things; the Symbol of the trigram Field, K'UN. **Mountain**, SHAN: limit, boundary; the Symbol of the trigram Bound, KEN. The ideogram: three peaks, a mountain range. **River**, CH'UAN: water flowing between banks; current, channel; associated with the Streaming Moment and the trigram Gorge, K'AN. **Hill-top**, CH'IU: hill with hollow top used for worship and as grave-site; knoll, hillock. **Mound**, LING: grave-mound, barrow; small hill.

[III] **King(hood)**, WANG: effective ruler, by authority of the Emperor, from whom others derive their power. **Prince**, KUNG: nobles acting as ministers of state in the capital; governing from the center rather than active in daily life; contrasts with feudatory, HOU, governors of the provinces. **Set-up**, SHE: establish, institute; arrange, set in order; spread a net. The ideogram: words and impel, establish with words. **Guard**, SHOU: keep in custody; protect, ward off harm, attend to, supervise. **City**, KUO: area of only human constructions; political unit, polis. First of the territorial zones: city, suburbs, countryside, forests.

Actually ... in-fact, YI TSAI: stresses the importance of a statement. The ideogram: a dart and done, strong intention fully expressed. **Season**, SHIH: quality of the time; the right time, opportune, in harmony; planning in accord with the time; seasons of the year. The ideogram: sun and temple, time as sacred. **Avail-of**, YUNG: take advantage of; benefit from, profit by; use for a specific purpose; apply to advantage. The ideogram: to divine and center, applying divination to central concerns. **Great**, TA: big, noble, important, very; orient the will toward a self-imposed goal, impose direction; ability to lead or guide your life; contrasts with small, HSIAO, flexible adaptation to what crosses your path; keyword. Image of Hexagrams 14, 26, 28, 34.

- *Transforming Lines*

    Initial six

    a) **Repeating Gorge.**
    Entering tending-towards the Gorge, the recess.
    Pitfall.

    b) **Repeating Gorge, entering Gorge.**
    Letting-go tao: pitfall indeed.

Associated Contexts a) **Enter,** JU: penetrate, go into, enter on, progress; put into, encroach on; the Action of the trigram Ground, SUN, contrary of issue-forth, CH'U. **Tend-towards,** YÜ: move toward but not reach, in the direction of; contrasts with reach(-to), HU, actually arriving. **Recess,** TAN: pit within a large cave, entered from the side.

   Pitfall, HSIUNG: leads away from the experience of meaning; stuck and exposed to danger, unable to take in the situation; flow of life and spirit is blocked; unfortunate, baleful; keyword.

b) **Tao**: way or path; ongoing process of being and the course it traces for each specific person or thing; keyword. The ideogram: go and head, leading and the path it creates.

    Nine at-second

    a) **Gorge possessing venturing.**
    Seeking, the small acquiring.

    b) **Seeking, the small acquiring.**
    Not-yet issuing-forth-from the center indeed.

Associated Contexts a) **Seek,** CH'IU: search for, aim at, wish for, desire; implore, supplicate; covetous. **Small,** HSIAO: little, common, unimportant; adapting to what crosses your path; ability to move in harmony with the vicissitudes of life; contrasts with great, TA, self-imposed theme or goal; keyword. Image of Hexagrams 9 and 62. **Acquire,** TE: obtain the desired object; wish for, desire covetously; gains, possessions. The ideogram: go and obstacle, going through obstacles to the goal.

b) **Not-yet**, WEI: temporal negative; something will but has not yet occurred; contrary of already, CHI. Image of Hexagram 64. **Issue-forth(-from)**, CH'U: emerge from, come out of, proceed from, spring from; the Action of the trigram Shake, CHEN; contrary of enter, JU. The ideogram: stem with branches and leaves emerging.

Six at-third

a) **Coming's Gorge, the Gorge.**
Venturing moreover reclining.
Entering tending-towards the Gorge, the recess. No availing-of.

b) **Coming's Gorge, the Gorge.**
Completing without achieving indeed.

Associated Contexts a) **Come**, LAI, and go, WANG, describe the stream of time as it flows from future through present to past; come, LAI, indicates what is approaching; move toward, arrive at; keyword.

Moreover, CH'IEH: further, and also. **Recline**, CHEN: lean back or on; soften, relax; head rest, back support; stake to tie cattle.

Enter, JU: penetrate, go into, enter on, progress; put into, encroach on; the Action of the trigram Ground, SUN, contrary of issue-forth, CH'U. **Tend-towards**, YÜ: move toward but not reach, in the direction of; contrasts with reach(-to), HU, actually arriving. **Recess**, TAN: pit within a large cave, entered from the side. **No**, WU: simple negative; un-, dis-.

b) **Without**, WU: devoid of; -less as suffix. **Achieve**, KUNG: work done, results; real accomplishment, praise, worth, merit. The ideogram: workman's square and forearm, combining craft and strength.

Six at-fourth

a) **A cup, liquor, a platter added.**
Availing-of a jar.
Letting-in bonds originating-from the window.
Completing, without fault.

b) **A cup, liquor, a platter added.**
Solid[and]Supple, the border indeed.

Associated Contexts a) **Cup**, TSUN: quantity a libation vessel contains; glass, decanter, bottle. **Liquor**, CHIU: alcoholic beverages, distilled spirits; spirit which perfects the good and evil in human nature. The ideogram: liquid above fermenting must, separating the spirits. **Platter**, KUEI: wood or bamboo plate; sacrificial utensil. **Add**, ERH: join to something previous; reiterate, repeat; second, double; assistant.

Jar, FOU: earthenware vessels; wine-jars and drums. The ideogram: jar containing liquor.

Let-in, NA: allow to enter; take in, grow smaller; insert; collect. The ideogram: silk and enter, shrinking silk threads. **Bonds**, YO: cords, ropes; contracts, treaties, legal and moral obligations; moderate, restrain, restrict. **Origin**, TZU: source, beginning, ground; cause, reason, motive; line of descent; path to the origin; yourself, intrinsic. **Window**, YU: opening in wall or roof to let in light; open, instruct, enlighten.

Without fault, WU CHIU: no error or harm in the situation.

b) **Solid[and]Supple**, KANG JOU: field of creative tension between the whole and opened lines and their qualities; field of psychic movement. **Border**, CHI: limit, frontier, line which joins and divides. The ideogram: place and sacrifice, border between human and spirit.

Nine at-fifth

a) **Gorge not overfilled.**
Merely already evened.
Without fault.

b) **Gorge not overfilled.**
Centering, not-yet great indeed.

Associated Contexts a) **Merely**, CHIH: nothing more than. **Already**, CHI: completed, done, has occurred; past tense, contrary of not-yet, WEI. Image of Hexagram 63. **Even**, P'ING: level, make even or equal; uniform, peaceful, tranquil; restore quiet, harmonize.

Without fault, WU CHIU: no error or harm in the situation.

b) **Not-yet**, WEI: temporal negative; something will but has not yet occurred; contrary of already, CHI. Image of Hexagram 64.

Six above

a) **Tying availing-of stranded ropes.**
Dismissing tending-towards dense jujube-trees.
Three year's-time, not acquiring. Pitfall.

b) **Six above, letting-go tao.**
Pitfall: three year's-time indeed.

Associated Contexts a) **Tie(-to)**, HSI: connect, attach to, bind; devoted to; relatives. The ideogram: person and connect, ties between humans. **Stranded ropes**, HUI MO: three stranded ropes; royal garments; beautiful, honorable.

Dismiss, CHIH: put aside; judge and find wanting. **Tend-towards**, YÜ: move toward but not reach, in the direction of; contrasts with reach(-to), HU, actually arriving. **Dense**, TS'UNG: close-set, bushy, crowded; a grove. **Jujube-tree**, CHI: thorny bush or tree; sign of a court of justice or site of official literary examinations.

Three, SAN: number three, third time or place; active phases of a cycle; superlative; beginning of repetition. **Year's-time**, SUI: actual length of time in a year; contrasts with years-revolved, NIEN, number of years elapsed. **Acquire**, TE: obtain the desired object; wish for, desire covetously; gains, possessions. The ideogram: go and obstacle, going through obstacles to the goal. **Pitfall**, HSIUNG: leads away from the experience of meaning; stuck and exposed to danger, unable to take in the situation; flow of life and spirit is blocked; unfortunate, baleful; keyword.

b) **Tao**: way or path; ongoing process of being and the course it traces for each specific person or thing; keyword. The ideogram: go and head, leading and the path it creates.

30

RADIANCE ▪ LI

This hexagram describes your situation in terms of expanding light, warmth and awareness. It emphasizes that joining with and depending on what spreads this light, the action of **Radiance,** is the adequate way to handle it. To be in accord with the time, you are told to: **congregate!**

● *Image of the Situation*

> **Radiance, Harvesting Trial.**
> **Growing. Accumulating female cattle. Significant.**

Associated Contexts **Radiance,** LI: glowing light, spreading in all directions; light-giving, discriminating, articulating; divide and arrange in order; the power of consciousness. The ideogram: bird and weird, the magical fire-bird with brilliant plumage. **Radiance** is the brightness and fire trigram doubled and includes that trigram's attributes: *Symbols:* **Brightness,** MING: light-giving aspect of burning, heavenly bodies and consciousness. The ideogram: sun and moon. **Fire,** HUO: warming and consuming aspect of burning. *Action:* **Congregate,** LI: cling together; depend on, attached to, rely on; couple, pair, herd. The ideogram: deer flocking together. **Harvesting Trial,** LI CHEN: advantageous divination; putting the action in question to the test is beneficial.

Grow, HENG: success through a sacrifice; pervade, persevere; bring to full growth; enjoy; vigorous, effective; second stage of the Time Cycle. **Accumulate,** CH'U: retain, hoard, gather, herd together; control, restrain; domesticate, tame, train; raise, feed, sustain, bring up. The ideogram: field and black, fertile black soil good for pastures, accumulated through retaining silt. Image of Hexagrams 9 and 26. **Female,** P'IN: female sexual organs, particularly of farm animals; concave, hollow. The ideogram: cattle and ladle, a hollow reproductive organ. **Cattle,** NIU: ox, bull, cow, calf; kine; power and strength of work animals. **Significant,** CHI: leads to the experience of meaning; favorable, propitious, advantageous, appropriate; keyword. The ideogram: scholar and mouth, wise words of a sage.

- *Outer and Inner Aspects*

☲ **Radiance**: Fire and brightness radiate light and warmth, attached to their support; congregating people see and become aware. **Radiance** ends the yang hemicycle, consuming action in awareness.

Connection to both inner and outer: light, heat, consciousness bring continual change, the Fiery Moment. **Radiance** spreads outward, congregating, becoming aware and changing.

- *Counter Indications*

Nuclear trigrams **Open**, TUI, and **Ground**, SUN, result in Counter Hexagram 28, **Great Exceeding**, TA KUO. **Radiance** spreading in all directions is contrasted with the single sharp focus of **great exceeding**.

- *Sequence*

Falling necessarily possesses a place to congregate.
Anterior acquiescence has the use-of Radiance.
Radiance implies congregating indeed.

Associated Contexts **Fall**, HSIEN: fall down or into, sink, drop, descend; falling water; the Action of the trigram Gorge, K'AN: **Necessarily**, PI: unavoidably, indispensably, certainly. **Possess**, YU: in possession of, have, own; opposite of lack, WU: **Place**, SO: where something belongs or comes from; residence, dwelling; habitual focus or object.

Anterior ... the use-of: activating this hexagram depends on understanding and accepting the previous statement.

Imply, CHE: further signify; additional meaning. **Indeed**, YEH: intensifier; indicates comment on previous statement.

- *Contrasted Definitions*

  Above Radiance and-also below Gorge indeed.

  Associated Contexts **Above**, SHANG: anything above, in all senses; higher, upper, outer; upper trigram; opposite of below, HSIA. **And-also**, ERH: joins and contrasts two terms. **Below**, HSIA: anything below, in all senses; lower, inner; lower trigram; opposite of above, SHANG. **Gorge**, K'AN: dangerous place; hole, cavity, hollow; pit, snare, trap, grave, precipice; critical time, test; risky. The ideogram: earth and pit. Image of Hexagram 29.

- *Symbol Tradition*

  Brightness doubled arousing Radiance.
  Great People use consecutive brightening
  **   to illuminate tending-towards the four sides.**

  Associated Contexts **Doubled**, LIANG: twice, both, again, dual, a pair. **Arouse**, TSO: stir up, stimulate, rouse from inactivity; generate; appear, arise. The ideogram: person and beginning.
      Great People, TA JEN: important, noble, influential; those who impose a ruling principle on their lives; effect of the great within an individual; keyword. **Use(-of)**, YI: make use of, by means of, owing to; employ, make functional. **Consecutive**, CHI: follow after, continue; take another's place; line of succession, adopt an heir. The ideogram: silk thread and continuous. **Illuminate**, CHAO: shine light on; enlighten, reflect: care for, supervise. The ideogram: fire and brightness. **Tend-towards**, YÜ: move toward but not reach, in the direction of; contrasts with reach(-to), HU, actually arriving. **Four sides**, SSU FANG: the cardinal points; the limits or boundaries of the earth; everywhere, all around.

- *Image Tradition*

  Radiance. Congregating indeed. [I]
  Sun[and]Moon congregating reach-to heaven.
  The hundred grains, grasses, trees congregating reach-to earth.
  Redoubling brightness uses congregating to reach-to correcting.
  Thereupon changes accomplishing Below Heaven.

Supple congregating reaches-to centering correcting. [II]
Anterior Growing.
That uses accumulating female cattle, significant indeed.

Associated Contexts [I] Sun[and]Moon, JIH YÜEH: the two
dimensions of calendar time that define any specific moment; time as
interlocking cycles. **Reach(-to)**, HU: arrive at a goal; reach towards and
achieve; connect; contrasts with tend-towards, YU. **Heaven**, T'IEN:
highest; sky, firmament, heavens; power above the human as opposed to
earth, TI, below; the Symbol of the trigram Force, CH'IEN: The
ideogram: great and the one above.

Hundred, PO: numerous, many, all; a whole class or type. **Grains**, KU:
cereal crops, corn; substantial, well-off; income; bless with plenty. **Grass**,
TS'AO: all grassy plants and herbs; young, tender plants; rough draft;
hastily. **Tree/wood**, MU: all things woody or wooden, alive or constructed
from wood; associated with the Woody Moment; wood and wind are the
Symbols of the trigram Ground, SUN. The ideogram: a tree striking its
roots down and sending up branches. **Earth**, TI: ground on which the
human world rests; basis of all things, nourishes all things; the Symbol of
the trigram Field, K'UN.

Redouble, CH'UNG: repeat, reiterate, add to; build up by layers.
Correct, CHENG: rectify deviation or one-sidedness; proper, straight,
exact, regular; constant, rule, model. The ideogram: stop and one, hold to
one thing.

Thereupon, NAI: on that ground, because of. **Change**, HUA: gradual,
continuous metamorphosis; influence someone; contrasts with transform,
PIEN, sudden mutation. The ideogram: person alive and dead, the life-
process. **Accomplish**, CH'ENG: complete, finish, bring about; perfect, full,
whole; play your part, do your duty; mature. The ideogram: weapon and
man, able to bear arms, thus fully developed. **Below Heaven**, T'IEN HSIA:
the human world, between heaven and earth.

[II] **Supple**, JOU: quality of the opened lines; flexible, pliant, tender,
adaptable. **Centering correcting**, CHUNG CHENG: central and correct;
make rectifying one-sidedness and error your central concern; reaching a
stable center in yourself can correct the situation.

Anterior, KU: come before as cause; formerly, ancient; reason,
purpose, intention; grievance, quarrel, dissatisfaction, sorrow, mourning
resulting from previous causes and intentions; situation leading to
a divination.

That uses, SHIH YI: involves and is involved by.

● *Transforming Lines*

Initial nine

a) Treading, polishing therefore.
Respecting it.
Without fault.

b) Treading, polishing it respectfully.
Using casting-out fault indeed.

Associated Contexts a) **Tread**, LÜ: step, path, track; footsteps; walk a path or way; course of the stars; act, practise; conduct; salary, means of subsistence. The ideogram: body and repeating steps, following a trail. Image of Hexagram 10. **Polish**, TS'O: file away imperfections; wash or plate with gold; confused, in disorder, mixed. The ideogram: metal and old, clearing away accumulated disorder. **Therefore**, JAN: follows logically, thus.

Respect(ful), CHING: reverent, attentive; stand in awe of, honor; inner respect; contrasts with courtesy, KUNG, good manners. The ideogram: teacher's rod taming speech and attitude. **It/them/have(-it)/'s**, CHIH: expresses possession, directly or as an object pronoun.

Without fault, WU CHIU: no error or harm in the situation.

b) **Cast-out**, P'I: expel, repress, exclude, punish; exclusionary laws and their enforcement. The ideogram: punish, authority and mouth, give orders to expel. **Fault**, CHIU: unworthy conduct that leads to harm, illness, misfortune. The ideogram: person and differ, differ from what you should be.

Six at-second

a) Yellow Radiance. Spring significant.

b) Yellow Radiance, Spring significant.
Acquiring centering tao indeed.

Associated Contexts a) **Yellow**, HUANG: color of the productive middle; associated with the Earthy Moment between the yang and yin hemicycles; color of soil in central China; emblematic and imperial color of China since the Yellow Emperor (2500 BCE). **Spring**, YÜAN: source,

origin, head; great, excellent; arise, begin, generating power; first stage of the Time Cycle.

b) **Acquire**, TE: obtain the desired object; wish for, desire covetously; gains, possessions. The ideogram: go and obstacle, going through obstacles to the goal. **Center**, CHUNG: inner, central; put in the center; middle, stable point enabling you to face inner and outer changes; middle line of trigram. The ideogram: field divided in two equal parts. Image of Hexagram 61. **Tao**: way or path; ongoing process of being and the course it traces for each specific person or thing; keyword. The ideogram: go and head, leading and the path it creates.

Nine at-third

a) **Sun going-down's Radiance.**
Not drumbeating a jar and-also singing.
By-consequence great old-age's lamenting. Pitfall.

b) **Sun going-down's Radiance.**
Wherefore permitting lasting indeed?

Associated Contexts a) **Sun/day**, JIH: actual sun and the time of a sun-cycle, a day. **Go-down**, TSE: sun setting, afternoon; waning moon; decline. **'s/have(-it)/it/them**, CHIH: expresses possession, directly or as an object pronoun.

Not, PU: simple negative. **Drumbeating**, KU: skin or earthenware drums; play a drum; excite, arouse, encourage; joyous, happy. **Jar**, FOU: earthenware vessels; wine-jars and drums. The ideogram: jar containing liquor. **Sing**, KO: chant, sing elegies, sad or mournful songs; associated with the Earthy Moment, turning from yang to yin.

By-consequence(-of), TSE: very strong connection; reason, cause, result; rule, law, pattern, standard; therefore. **Great**, TA: big, noble, important, very; orient the will toward a self-imposed goal, impose direction; ability to lead or guide your life; contrasts with small, HSIAO, flexible adaptation to what crosses your path; keyword. Image of Hexagrams 14, 26, 28, 34. **Old-age**, TIEH: seventy or older; aged, no longer active. **Lament**, CHÜEH: express intense regret or sorrow; mourn over; painful recollections. **Pitfall**, HSIUNG: leads away from the experience of meaning; stuck and exposed to danger, unable to take in the situation; flow of life and spirit is blocked; unfortunate, baleful; keyword.

b) **Wherefore**, HO: interrogative: why? for what reason? what is? and affirmation: therefore, for that reason. **Permit**, K'O: possible because in harmony with an inherent principle. The ideogram: mouth and breath, silent consent. **Last**, CHIU: long, protracted; enduring.

Nine at-fourth

a) **Assailing thus, its coming thus.**
    Burning thus. Dying thus. Thrown-out thus.

b) **Assailing thus, its coming thus.**
    Without a place to tolerate indeed.

Associated Contexts a) **Assail**, T'U: rush against; abrupt attack; suddenly stricken; insolent, offensive. **Thus**, JU: as, in this way. **Its/it**, CH'I: third person pronoun; also: one/one's, he/his, she/hers, they/theirs. **Come**, LAI, and go, WANG, describe the stream of time as it flows from future through present to past; come, LAI, indicates what is approaching; move toward, arrive at; keyword.

 Burn, FEN: set fire to, destroy completely. **Die**, SSU: sudden or untimely death; run out of energy; immobile, fixed. **Throw-out**, CH'I: reject, discard, abandon, push aside, break off: renounce, forget.

b) **Without**, WU: devoid of; -less as suffix. **Tolerate**, JUNG: allow, contain, endure, bear with; accept graciously. The ideogram: full stream bed, tolerating and containing.

Six at-fifth

a) **Issuing-forth tears like gushing. Sadness like lamenting.**
    Significant.

b) **Six at-fifth's significance.**
    Radiance: the kingly prince indeed.

Associated Contexts a) **Issue-forth(-from)**, CH'U: emerge from, come out of, proceed from, spring from; the Action of the trigram Shake, CHEN; contrary of enter, JU. The ideogram: stem with branches and leaves emerging. **Tears**, T'I: weep, cry; water from the eyes. **Like**, JO: same as; just as, similar to. **Gush**, T'O: water surging in streams; falling tears; heavy rain. **Sad**, CH'I: unhappy, low in spirits, distressed; mourn, sorrow over; commiserate with. **Lament**, CHÜEH: express intense regret or sorrow; mourn over; painful recollections.

b) **'s/have(-it)/it/them**, CHIH: expresses possession, directly or as an object pronoun. **King(hood)**, WANG: effective ruler, by authority of the Emperor, from whom others derive their power. **Prince**, KUNG: nobles acting as ministers of state in the capital; governing from the center rather than active in daily life; contrasts with feudatory, HOU, governors of the provinces.

Nine above

a) **Kinghood availing-of issuing-forth chastising.**
Possessing excellence.
Severing the head. Catching in-no-way its demons.
Without fault.

b) **Kinghood availing-of issuing-forth chastising.**
Using correcting the fiefdoms indeed.

Associated Contexts a) **King(hood)**, WANG: effective ruler, by authority of the Emperor, from whom others derive their power. **Avail-of**, YUNG: take advantage of; benefit from, profit by; use for a specific purpose; apply to advantage. The ideogram: to divine and center, applying divination to central concerns. **Issue-forth(-from)**, CH'U: emerge from, come out of, proceed from, spring from; the Action of the trigram Shake, CHEN; contrary of enter, JU. The ideogram: stem with branches and leaves emerging. **Chastise**, CHENG: punish, subjugate, discipline; reduce to order; punishing expedition. The ideogram: step and correct, a rectifying move.

Excellence, CHIA: superior quality; fine, delicious, glorious; happy, pleased; rejoice in, praise. The ideogram: increasing goodness, pleasure and happiness.

Sever, CHE: break off, separate, sunder, cut in two; discriminate, judge the true and false. **Head**, SHOU: literal head; leader, foremost; subject headings; beginning, model; superior, upper, front. **Catch**, HUO: take in hunt; catch a thief; obtain, seize; hit the mark, opportune moment; prisoner, spoils, prey; slave, servant. **In-no-way**, FEI: strong negative; not so. The ideogram: a box filled with opposition. **Its/it**, CH'I: third person pronoun; also: one/one's, he/his, she/hers, they/theirs. **Demon(iac)**, CH'OU: possessed by a malignant genius; ugly, physically or morally deformed; vile, disgraceful, shameful; drunken. The ideogram: fermenting liquor and soul. Demoniac and tiger are opposed on the Universal

Compass North–South axis; the tiger (Extreme Yang) scares away and protects against demoniacs (Extreme Yin).

Without fault, WU CHIU: no error or harm in the situation.

b) **Fiefdom,** PANG: region governed by a feudatory, an order of nobility.

CONJOINING ▪ *HSIEN*

This hexagram describes your situation in terms of the influence that separated parts of an intrinsic whole have on each other. It emphasizes that bringing these parts into contact is the adequate way to handle the situation. To be in accord with the time, you are told to: **conjoin**!

● *Image of the Situation*

> **Conjoining, Growing.**
> **Harvesting Trial.**
> **Grasping womanhood significant.**

Associated Contexts **Conjoin**, HSIEN: come into contact with, influence; reach, join together; put together as parts of a previously separated whole; come into conjunction, as the celestial bodies; totally, completely; lit.: broken piece of pottery, the halves of which join to identify partners. **Grow**, HENG: success through a sacrifice; pervade, persevere; bring to full growth; enjoy; vigorous, effective; second stage of the Time Cycle.

    Harvesting Trial, LI CHEN: advantageous divination; putting the action in question to the test is beneficial.

    Grasp, CH'Ü: lay hold of, take and use, seize, appropriate; grasp the meaning, understand. The ideogram: ear and hand, hear and grasp. **Woman(hood)**, NÜ: a woman; what is inherently female. **Significant**, CHI: leads to the experience of meaning; favorable, propitious, advantageous, appropriate; keyword. The ideogram: scholar and mouth, wise words of a sage.

● *Outer and Inner Aspects*

    ☱ **Open**: vapor rising from the marsh's open surface stimulates and fertilizes; stimulating words cheer and inspire. **Open** begins the yin hemicycle by initiating the formative process.

    Connection to the outer: liquifying, casting, skinning off the mold, the Metallic Moment beginning. **Open** stimulates, cheers and reveals innate form.

362

☰☰ (5) **Bound**: Mountains bound, limit and set a place off, stopping forward movement. **Bound** completes a full yin-yang cycle.

Connection to the inner: accomplishing words, which express things. **Bound** articulates what is complete to suggest what is beginning.

Inner accomplishment provides the foundation for **conjoining** through outer stimulation and cheer.

- *Counter Indications*

Nuclear trigrams **Force**, CH'IEN, and **Ground**, SUN, result in Counter Hexagram 44, **Coupling**, KOU. **Conjoining**'s active drive to restore an intrinsic whole is contrasted with the spontaneous meeting of **coupling**.

- *Sequence*

> **Possessing Heaven[and]Earth:**
> **Therefore afterwards possessing the myriad beings.**
> **Possessing the myriad beings:**
> **Therefore afterwards possessing Man[and]Woman.**
> **Possessing Man[and]Woman:**
> **Therefore afterwards possessing Husband[and]Wife.**
> **Possessing Husband[and]Wife:**
> **Therefore afterwards possessing Father[and]Son.**
> **Possessing Father[and]Son:**
> **Therefore afterwards possessing Chief[and]Servant.**
> **Possessing Chief[and]Servant:**
> **Therefore afterwards possessing Above[and]Below.**
> **Possessing Above[and]Below:**
> **Therefore afterwards the codes**
> > **righteously possessing a place to polish.**

Associated Contexts **Possess**, YU: in possession of, have, own; opposite of lack, WU. **Heaven[and]Earth**, T'IEN TI: dynamic relation between the primal powers and the world it produces; cosmos, natural or human world; keyword.

Therefore afterwards, JAN HOU: logical consequence of, necessarily follows in time. **Myriad**, WAN: countless; many, everyone; lit.: ten thousand. The ideogram: swarm of insects. **Being(s)**, WU: creature, thing, any single being; matter, substance, essence; nature of things.

Man[and]Woman, NAN NÜ: creative relation between what is inherently male and what is inherently female.

Husband[and]Wife, FU FU: the cooperative effort of man and woman in establishing and maintaining a home.

Father[and]Son, FU TZU: proper relation between generations serving and living up to the ideal of the ancestors, carrying on a tradition.

Chief[and]Servant, CHÜN CH'EN: cooperative relation between those who give orders and those who carry them out.

Above[and]Below, SHANG HSIA: realm of dynamic interaction between the upper and the lower; the vertical dimension.

Codes, LI: rites, rules, ritual; usage, manners; worship, ceremony, observance. The ideogram: worship and sacrificial vase, handling a sacred vessel. **Righteous**, YI: proper and just, meets the standards; things in their proper place; the heart that rules itself; upright, moral rule; contrasts with Harvest, LI, advantage or profit. **Place**, SO: where something belongs or comes from; residence, dwelling; habitual focus or object. **Polish**, TS'O: file away imperfections; wash or plate with gold; confused, in disorder, mixed. The ideogram: metal and old, clearing away accumulated disorder.

● *Contrasted Definitions*

Conjoining: urging indeed.
Persevering: lasting indeed.

Associated Contexts **Urge**, SU: strong specific desire; quick, hurried; call, invite. **Indeed**, YEH: intensifier; indicates comment on previous statement.

Persevere, HENG: continue in the same way or spirit; constant, perpetual, regular; self-renewing; extend everywhere. Image of Hexagram 32. **Last**, CHIU: long, protracted; enduring.

● *Symbol Tradition*

Above mountain possessing marsh. Conjoining.
A chün tzu uses emptiness to acquiesce people.

Associated Contexts **Above**, SHANG: anything above, in all senses; higher, upper, outer; upper trigram; opposite of below, HSIA. **Mountain**, SHAN: limit, boundary; the Symbol of the trigram Bound, KEN. The ideogram: three peaks, a mountain range. **Marsh**, TSE: open surface of a flat body of water and the vapors rising from it; fertilize, enrich; kindness, favor; the Symbol of the trigram Open, TUI.

Chün tzu: ideal of a person who uses divination to order his/her life in accordance with tao rather than wilful intention; keyword. **Use(-of)**, YI: make use of, by means of, owing to; employ, make functional. **Empty**, HSÜ: no images or concepts; vacant, unsubstantial; empty yet fertile space. **Acquiesce(-in)**, SHOU: accept, make peace with, agree to; at rest, satisfied; patient. **People, person**, JEN: humans individually and collectively; an individual; humankind. Image of Hexagrams 13 and 37.

- *Image Tradition*

> **Conjoining. Influencing indeed. [I]**
> **Above supple and-also below solid.**
> **The two agencies influencing correspondence**
> > **use mutual associating.**
>
> **Stopping and-also stimulating. [II]**
> **Below manhood, womanhood.**
> **That uses Growth Harvesting Trial,**
> > **grasping womanhood significant.**
>
> **Heaven[and]Earth influencing and-also**
> > **the myriad beings changing give-birth. [III]**
> **The all-wise person influencing the people at-heart**
> > **and-also Below Heaven harmony evening.**
>
> **Viewing one's place to influence. [IV]**
> **And-also actually Heaven[and]Earth,**
> > **the myriad beings's motives permitting visualizing.**

Associated Contexts [I] **Influence**, KAN: excite, act on, touch; affect someone's feelings, move the heart. The ideogram: heart and all, pervasive influence.

Supple, JOU: quality of the opened lines; flexible, pliant, tender, adaptable. **And-also**, ERH: joins and contrasts two terms. **Below**, HSIA: anything below, in all senses; lower, inner; lower trigram; opposite of above, SHANG. **Solid**, KANG: quality of the whole lines; firm, strong, unyielding, persisting.

Two, ERH: pair, even numbers, binary, duplicate. **Agencies**, CH'I: fluid energy, configurative power, vital force; interacts with essence, CHING, to produce things and beings. The ideogram: vapor and rice, heat and moisture producing substance. **Correspond(-to)**, YING: be in agreement or harmony; resonate together, invoke and fulfill each other; answer to, suitable; relation between the lines (1:4, 2:5, 3:6) when they form the pair opened and whole, supple and solid. The ideogram: heart and obey. **Mutual**, HSIANG: reciprocal assistance, encourage, help; bring together, blend with; examine, inspect; by turns. **Associate(-with)**, YÜ: consort with, combine; companions; group, band, company; agree with, comply, help. The ideogram: pair of hands reaching downward meets a pair of hands reaching upward, helpful association.

[II] Stop, CHIH: bring or come to a standstill; the Action of the trigram Bound, KEN. The ideogram: a foot stops walking. **Stimulate**, SHUO: rouse to action and good feeling; free from constraint, stir up, urge on; persuade, cheer, delight; set out in words; the Action of the trigram Open, TUI. The ideogram: words and exchange.

Man(hood), NAN: a man; what is inherently male. The ideogram: fields and strength, hard labor in the fields.

That uses, SHIH YI: involves and is involved by.

[III] Change, HUA: gradual, continuous metamorphosis; influence someone; contrasts with transform, PIEN, sudden mutation. The ideogram: person alive and dead, the life-process. **Birth/give-birth-to**, SHENG: produce, beget, grow, bear, arise; life, vitality. The ideogram: earth and sprout.

All-wise, SHENG: intuitive universal wisdom; mythical sages; holy, sacred; mark of highest distinction. The ideogram: ear and inform, one who knows all from a single sound. **Heart**, HSIN: heart as center of being; seat of mind's images and affections; moral nature; source of desires, intentions, will. **Below Heaven**, T'IEN HSIA: the human world, between heaven and earth. **Harmony**, HO: concord, union; conciliate; at peace, mild; fit, tune, adjust. **Even**, P'ING: level, make even or equal; uniform, peaceful, tranquil; restore quiet, harmonize.

[IV] View, KUAN: contemplate, observe from a distance; look at carefully, gaze at; also: a monastery, an observatory; scry, divine through liquid in a cup. The ideogram: see and waterbird, observe through air or water. Image of Hexagram 20. **One's/one**, CH'I: third person pronoun; also: it/its, he/his, she/hers, they/theirs.

Actually, YI: truly, really, at present. The ideogram: a dart and done, strong intention fully expressed. **'s/have(-it)/it/them**, CHIH: expresses possession, directly or as an object pronoun. **Motive**, CH'ING: true nature; feelings, desires, passions. The ideogram: heart and green, germinated in the heart. **Permit**, K'O: possible because in harmony with an inherent principle. The ideogram: mouth and breath, silent consent. **Visualize**, CHIEN: seeing in all its aspects: vision, being visible, forming mental images; visit, call on, consult. The ideogram: eye above person, active and receptive sight.

● *Transforming Lines*

Initial six

a) **Conjoining one's big-toes.**

b) **Conjoining one's big-toes.**
Purpose located outside indeed.

Associated Contexts a) **Big-toe/thumb**, MU: in lower trigram: big-toe; in upper trigram: thumb; the big-toe enables the foot to walk, the thumb enables the hand to grasp.

b) **Purpose**, CHIH: focus of mind and heart; will, inclination, resolve. The ideogram: heart and scholar, high inner resolve, or heart and go, inner determination. **Locate(-in)**, TSAI: live in, dwell, reside; belong to, involved with, depend on; within. The ideogram: earth and persevere, place on the earth. **Outside**, WAI: outer, exterior, external; people working in places other than their home; unfamiliar, foreign; the upper trigram, as opposed to inside, NEI, the lower.

Six at-second

a) **Conjoining one's calves.**
Pitfall. Residing significant.

b) **Although a pitfall, residing significant.**
Yielding, not harming indeed.

Associated Contexts a) **Calf**, FEI: muscle of lower leg; rely on; prop, rest.

Pitfall, HSIUNG: leads away from the experience of meaning; stuck and exposed to danger, unable to take in the situation; flow of life and spirit is blocked; unfortunate, baleful; keyword. **Reside(-in)**, CHÜ: dwell, live in, stay; sit down, fill an office; settled parts of a country. The ideogram: body and seat.

b) **Although**, SUI: even though, supposing that, if, even if.

Yield(-to), SHUN: give way and bear produce; comply, agree, follow, obey; unresisting, docile, flexible; nourish, provide; the Action of the trigram Field, K'UN: The ideogram: head and current, water flowing from the head of a river, yielding to the banks. **Not**, PU: simple negative. **Harm**, HAI: damage, injure, offend; suffer; hurtful, hindrance; fearful, anxious.

> **Nine at-third**
>
> *a)* **Conjoining one's thighs.**
> **Holding-on-to one's following.**
> **Going abashed.**
>
> *b)* **Conjoining one's thighs.**
> **Truly not abiding indeed.**
> **Purpose located-in following people.**
> **A place to hold-on-to the below indeed.**

Associated Contexts a) **Thigh**, KU: upper leg that provides power for walking; strands of a rope. **Hold-on(-to)**, CHIH: lay hold of, seize, take in hand; keep, maintain, look after. The ideogram: criminal and seize. **Follow**, SUI: come or go after; pursue, impelled to move; come after in inevitable sequence; move in the same direction, comply with what is ahead; follow a way or religion; according to, next, subsequent. The ideogram: go and fall, unavoidable movement. Image of Hexagram 17.

Go, WANG, and **come**, LAI, describe the stream of time as it flows from future through present to past; go, WANG, indicates what is departing from present to past; proceed, move on; keyword. **Abashment**, LIN: distress, shame, regret, humiliation; aware of having lost the right track; leads to repenting, HUI, correcting the direction of mind and life.

b) **Truly**, YI: statement is true and precise. **Not**, PU: simple negative. **Abide**, CH'U: rest in, dwell; stop yourself; arrive at a place or condition;

distinguish, decide; do what is proper. The ideogram: tiger, stop and seat, powerful movement coming to rest.

Purpose, CHIH: focus of mind and heart; will, inclination, resolve. The ideogram: heart and scholar, high inner resolve, or heart and go, inner determination. **Locate(-in)**, TSAI: live in, dwell, reside; belong to, involved with, depend on; within. The ideogram: earth and persevere, place on the earth.

Nine at-fourth

a) **Trial: significant, repenting extinguished.**
Wavering, wavering: going, coming.
Partnering adheres-to simply pondering.

b) **Trial: significant, repenting extinguished.**
Not-yet influencing harming indeed.
Wavering, wavering: going, coming.
Not-yet the shining great indeed.

Associated Contexts a) **Trial**, CHEN: test by ordeal; inquiry by divination and its result; righteous, firm; separating wheat from chaff; the kernel, the proven core; fourth stage of the Time Cycle. The ideogram: pearl and divination. **Repenting extinguished**, HUI WANG: previous troubles and consequent remorse will disappear.

Waver, CH'UNG: irresolute, hesitating; unsettled, disturbed; fluctuate, sway to and fro. The doubled character intensifies this quality. **Come**, LAI, and **Go**, WANG describe the stream of time as it flows from future through present to past. Come, LAI, indicates what is approaching; move toward, arrive at; go, WANG, indicates what is departing; proceed, move on; keywords.

Partner, P'ENG: associate for mutual benefit; two equal or similar things; companions, friends, peers; join in; commercial ventures. The ideogram: linked strings of cowries or coins. **Adhere(-to)**, TS'UNG: follow a way, hold to a doctrine, school, or person; hear and comply with, agree to; forced to follow, follower. The ideogram: two men walking, one following the other. **Simply**, ERH: just so, only. **Ponder**, SSU: reflect, consider, remember; deep thought; desire, wish. The ideogram: heart and field, the heart's concerns.

b) **Not-yet**, WEI: temporal negative; something will but has not yet occurred; contrary of already, CHI. Image of Hexagram 64. **Harm**, HAI: damage, injure, offend; suffer; hurtful, hindrance; fearful, anxious.

Shine, KUANG: illuminate; give off brilliant, bright light; honor, glory, éclat; result of action, contrasts with brightness, MING, light of heavenly bodies. The ideogram: fire above person, lifting the light. **Great**, TA: big, noble, important, very; orient the will toward a self-imposed goal, impose direction; ability to lead or guide your life; contrasts with small, HSIAO, flexible adaptation to what crosses your path; keyword. Image of Hexagrams 14, 26, 28, 34.

Nine at-fifth

a) **Conjoining one's neck.**
Without repenting.

b) **Conjoining one's neck.**
Purpose, the tips indeed.

Associated Contexts *a)* **Neck**, MEI: muscular base of neck, shoulders and arms; source of strength in arms and shoulders; persist.
Without repenting, WU HUI: devoid of the sort of trouble that leads to sorrow, regret and the necessity to change your attitude.

b) **Purpose**, CHIH: focus of mind and heart; will, inclination, resolve. The ideogram: heart and scholar, high inner resolve, or heart and go, inner determination. **Tips**, MO: growing ends, outermost twigs; last, most distant.

Six above

a) **Conjoining one's jawbones, cheeks, tongue.**

b) **Conjoining one's jawbones, cheeks, tongue.**
The spouting mouth stimulating indeed.

Associated Contexts *a)* **Jawbones/brace**, FU: support, consolidate, reinforce, strengthen, stiffen, prop up, fix; rigid, steady, firm; help, rescue; support the mouth that speaks. The ideogram: cart and great. **Cheeks**, CHIA: sides of the face; speak, articulate. **Tongue**, SHE: tongue in the mouth; clapper in a bell, valve in a pump, hook of a clasp; talkative, wordy.

b) **Spout**, T'ENG: spurt, burst forth; open mouth, loud talk. **Mouth**, K'OU: literal mouth, words going out and food coming in; entrance, hole.

PERSEVERING ▪ *HENG*

This hexagram describes your situation in terms of continuity and endurance. It emphasizes that continuing on and renewing the way you are following is the adequate way to handle the situation. To be in accord with the time, you are told to: **persevere!**

- *Image of the Situation*

   Persevering, Growing.
   Without fault.
   Harvesting Trial.
   Harvesting: possessing directed going.

   Associated Contexts **Persevere**, HENG: continue in the same way or spirit; constant, perpetual, regular; self-renewing; extend everywhere; the moon almost full. **Grow**, HENG: success through a sacrifice; pervade, persevere; bring to full growth; enjoy; vigorous, effective; second stage of the Time Cycle.
   Without fault, WU CHIU: no error or harm in the situation.
   Harvesting Trial, LI CHEN: advantageous divination; putting the action in question to the test is beneficial.
   Harvest, LI: advantageous, profitable; acute, insightful; benefit, nourish; third stage of the Time Cycle. **Possessing directed going**, YU YU WANG: imposing a direction on the flow of time from present to past; have a specific goal or purpose.

- *Outer and Inner Aspects*

   ☳ **Shake:** Thunder rises from below, shaking and stirring things up. **Shake** begins the yang hemicycle by germinating new action.
   Connection to the outer: sprouting energies thrusting from below, the Woody Moment beginning. **Shake** stirs things up to issue-forth.

☴ **Ground:** Wind and wood subtly enter from the ground, penetrating and pervading. **Ground** is the center of the yang hemicycle, spreading pervasive action.

Connection to the inner: penetrating and bringing together, the Woody Moment culminating. **Ground** pervades, matches and couples, seeding a new generation.

Inner penetration and coupling provide the basis for dynamic **persevering** in the outer world.

● *Counter Indications*

Nuclear trigrams **Open**, TUI, and **Force**, CH'IEN, result in Counter Hexagram 43, **Parting**, KUAI. Lasting cohesion through **persevering** is contrasted with splitting, separating and **parting**.

● *Sequence*

> **Husband[and]Wife's tao.**
> **Not permitting using not lasting indeed.**
> **Anterior acquiescence has the use-of Persevering.**
> **Persevering implies lasting indeed.**

Associated Contexts **Husband[and]Wife**, FU FU: the cooperative effort of man and woman in establishing and maintaining a home. **'s/have(-it)/it/them**, CHIH: expresses possession, directly or as an object pronoun. **Tao**: way or path; ongoing process of being and the course it traces for each specific person or thing; keyword. The ideogram: go and head, leading and the path it creates.

Not permitting, PU K'O: not possible; contradicts an inherent principle. The ideogram: mouth and breath, silent consent. **Use(-of)**, YI: make use of, by means of, owing to; employ, make functional. **Not**, PU: simple negative. **Last**, CHIU: long, protracted; enduring. **Indeed**, YEH: intensifier; indicates comment on previous statement.

Anterior ... the use-of: activating this hexagram depends on understanding and accepting the previous statement.

Imply, CHE: further signify; additional meaning.

● *Contrasted Definitions*

Conjoining: urging indeed.
Persevering: lasting indeed.

Associated Contexts **Conjoin**, HSIEN: come into contact with, influence; reach, join together; put together as parts of a previously separated whole; come into conjunction, as the celestial bodies; totally, completely; lit.: broken piece of pottery, the halves of which join to identify partners. Image of Hexagram 31. **Urge**, SU: strong specific desire; quick, hurried; call, invite.

● *Attached Evidences*

Persevering: actualizing-tao's firmness indeed.
Persevering: motley and-also not restricting.
Persevering: using the-one actualizing-tao.

Associated Contexts **Actualize-tao**, TE: realize tao in action; power, virtue; ability to follow the course traced by the ongoing process of the cosmos; keyword. The ideogram: to go, straight, and heart. Linked with acquire, TE: acquiring that which makes a being become what it is meant to be. **Firm**, KU: constant, fixed, steady; chronic, recurrent. The ideogram: old and enclosure, long preserved.

Motley, TSA: mingled, variegated, mixed; disorder. **And-also**, ERH: joins and contrasts two terms. **Restrict**, YEN: keep in order, maintain discipline; subjugate, repress; narrow, obedient.

One, the-one, YI: single unit; number one; undivided, simple, whole; any one of; first, the first.

● *Symbol Tradition*

Thunder, wind, Persevering.
A chün tzu uses establishing, not versatility on-all-sides.

Associated Contexts **Thunder**, LEI: rising, arousing power; the Symbol of the trigram Shake, CHEN. **Wind**, FENG: moving air, breeze, gust; weather and its influence on mood and humor; fashion, usage; wind and wood are the Symbols of the trigram Ground, SUN.

Chün tzu: ideal of a person who uses divination to order his/her life in accordance with tao rather than wilful intention; keyword. **Establish**, LI: set up, institute, order, arrange; stand erect; settled principles. **Versatility**, I: sudden and unpredictable change; mental mobility and openness; easy and light, not difficult and heavy; occurs in name of the I CHING. **Sides (on-all-sides)**, FANG: limits, boundaries; square, surface of the earth extending to the four cardinal points; everywhere.

- *Image Tradition*

> Persevering. Lasting indeed. [I]
> Above solid and-also below supple.
> Thunder, wind, mutually associating.
> Ground and-also stirring-up.
> Solid[and]Supple altogether corresponding. Persevering.
>
> Persevering Growing, without fault. [II]
> Harvesting Trial.
> Lasting with-respect-to one's tao indeed.
> Heaven[and]Earth's tao.
> Persevering lasting and-also not climaxing indeed.
> Harvesting: possessing directed going.
> Completing by-consequence possessing the beginning indeed.
>
> Sun[and]Moon acquiring heaven and-also
> enabling lasting illumination. [III]
> The four seasons transforming changes and-also
> enabling lasting accomplishment.
> The all-wise person lasting with-respect-to his tao
> and-also Below Heaven the changes accomplishing.
>
> Viewing one's place to Persevere. [IV]
> And-also actually Heaven[and]Earth,
> the myriad beings's motives permitting visualizing.

Associated Contexts **[I] Above**, SHANG: anything above, in all senses; higher, upper, outer; upper trigram; opposite of below, HSIA. **Solid**, KANG: quality of the whole lines; firm, strong, unyielding, persisting. **Below**, HSIA: anything below, in all senses; lower, inner; lower trigram; opposite of above, SHANG. **Supple**, JOU: quality of the opened lines; flexible, pliant, tender, adaptable.

Mutual, HSIANG: reciprocal assistance, encourage, help; bring together, blend with; examine, inspect; by turns. **Associate(-with)**, YÜ: consort with, combine; companions; group, band, company; agree with, comply, help. The ideogram: pair of hands reaching downward meets a pair of hands reaching upward, helpful association.

Ground, SUN: base on which things rest; support, foundation; mild, subtly penetrating; nourishing. The ideogram: stand and things arranged on it, the subtle influence of the ground. Image of Hexagram 57. **Stir-up**, TUNG: excite, influence, move, affect; work, take action; come out of the egg or the bud; the Action of the trigram Shake, CHEN. The ideogram: strength and heavy, move weighty things.

Solid[and]Supple, KANG JOU: field of creative tension between the whole and opened lines and their qualities; field of psychic movement. **Altogether**, CHIEH: all, the whole; the same sort, all alike; entirely. **Correspond(-to)**, YING: be in agreement or harmony; resonate together, invoke and fulfill each other; answer to, suitable; relation between the lines (1:4, 2:5, 3:6) when they form the pair opened and whole, supple and solid. The ideogram: heart and obey.

[II] **With-respect-to**, YÜ: relates to, refers to; hold a position in. **One's/one**, CH'I: third person pronoun; also: it/its, he/his, she/hers, they/theirs. **Heaven[and]Earth**, T'IEN TI: dynamic relation between the primal powers and the world it produces; cosmos, natural or human world; keyword. **Climax**, YI: come to a high point and stop, bring to an end; use up, lay aside; decline, reject.

Complete, CHUNG: end of a cycle that begins the next; last, whole, all; contrasts with exhaust, CH'IUNG: final end. The ideogram: silk cocoons, follow and ice, winter linking one year with the next. **By-consequence(-of)**, TSE: very strong connection; reason, cause, result; rule, law, pattern, standard; therefore. **Possess**, YU: in possession of, have, own; opposite of lack, WU. **Begin**, SHIH: commence, start, open; earliest, first; beginning of a time-span, ended by completion, CHUNG. The ideogram: woman and eminent, beginning new life.

[III] **Sun[and]Moon**, YIH YÜEH: the two dimensions of calendar time that define any specific moment; time as interlocking cycles. **Acquire**, TE: obtain the desired object; wish for, desire covetously; gains, possessions. The ideogram: go and obstacle, going through obstacles to the goal. **Heaven**, T'IEN: highest; sky, firmament, heavens; power above the human as opposed to earth, TI, below; the Symbol of the trigram Force,

CH'IEN. The ideogram: great and the one above. **Able**, NENG: enable; ability, power, skill, art; competent, talented; duty, function, capacity. The ideogram: an animal with strong hooves and bones, able to carry and defend. **Illuminate**, CHAO: shine light on; enlighten, reflect: care for, supervise. The ideogram: fire and brightness.

Four seasons, SSU SHIH: the four dynamic qualities of time that make up the year and the Time Cycle; the right time, in accord with the time; time as sacred; all-encompassing. **Transform**, PIEN: abrupt, radical, fundamental mutation from one state of being to another; transformation of lines in hexagrams; contrasts with change, HUA, gradual metamorphosis. **Change**, HUA: gradual, continuous metamorphosis; influence someone; contrasts with transform, PIEN, sudden mutation. The ideogram: person alive and dead, the life-process. **Accomplish**, CH'ENG: complete, finish, bring about; perfect, full, whole; play your part, do your duty; mature. The ideogram: weapon and man, able to bear arms, thus fully developed.

All-wise, SHENG: intuitive universal wisdom; mythical sages; holy, sacred; mark of highest distinction. The ideogram: ear and inform, one who knows all from a single sound. **People, person**, JEN: humans individually and collectively; an individual; humankind. Image of Hexagrams 13 and 37. **Below Heaven**, T'IEN HSIA: the human world, between heaven and earth.

[IV] View, KUAN: contemplate, observe from a distance; look at carefully, gaze at; also: a monastery, an observatory; scry, divine through liquid in a cup. The ideogram: see and waterbird, observe through air or water. Image of Hexagram 20. **Place**, SO: where something belongs or comes from; residence, dwelling; habitual focus or object.

Actually, YI: truly, really, at present. The ideogram: a dart and done, strong intention fully expressed. **Myriad**, WAN: countless; many, everyone; lit.: ten thousand. The ideogram: swarm of insects. **Being(s)**, WU: creature, thing, any single being; matter, substance, essence; nature of things. **Motive**, CH'ING: true nature; feelings, desires, passions. The ideogram: heart and green, germinated in the heart. **Permit**, K'O: possible because in harmony with an inherent principle. The ideogram: mouth and breath, silent consent. **Visualize**, CHIEN: seeing in all its aspects: vision, being visible, forming mental images; visit, call on, consult. The ideogram: eye above person, active and receptive sight.

● *Transforming Lines*

Initial six

a) **Diving Persevering, Trial: pitfall.
Without direction: Harvesting.**

b) **Diving Persevering's pitfall.
Beginning seeking depth indeed.**

Associated Contexts a) **Dive**, CHÜN: jump into deep water; deepen; serious, abstruse. **Trial**, CHEN: test by ordeal; inquiry by divination and its result; righteous, firm; separating wheat from chaff; the kernel, the proven core; fourth stage of the Time Cycle. The ideogram: pearl and divination. **Pitfall**, HSIUNG: leads away from the experience of meaning; stuck and exposed to danger, unable to take in the situation; flow of life and spirit is blocked; unfortunate, baleful; keyword.

Without direction: Harvesting, WU YU LI: no plan or direction is advantageous; in order to take advantage of the situation, do not impose a direction on events.

b) **Seek**, CH'IU: search for, aim at, wish for, desire; implore, supplicate; covetous. **Depth**, SHEN: deep water; profound, abstruse; ardent, strong, intense, inner; sound the depths.

Nine at-second

a) **Repenting extinguished.**

b) **Nine at-second, repenting extinguished.
Ability lasting, centering indeed.**

Associated Contexts a) **Repenting extinguished**, HUI WANG: previous troubles and consequent remorse will disappear.

b) **Center**, CHUNG: inner, central; put in the center; middle, stable point enabling you to face inner and outer changes; middle line of trigram. The ideogram: field divided in two equal parts. Image of Hexagram 61.

Nine at-third

a) **Not Persevering one's actualizing-tao.
Maybe receiving's embarrassing.
Trial: abashment.**

b) **Not Persevering one's actualizing-tao.
Without a place to tolerate indeed.**

Associated Contexts a) **Maybe**, HUO: possible but not certain, perhaps. **Receive**, CH'ENG: receive gifts or commands from superiors or customers; take in hand; catch falling water. The ideogram: accepting a seal of office. **Embarrassed**, HSIU: conscious of guilt or fault; unworthy; ashamed, confused; shy, blushing. The ideogram: sheep, sheepish feeling.

Trial, CHEN: test by ordeal; inquiry by divination and its result; righteous, firm; separating wheat from chaff; the kernel, the proven core; fourth stage of the Time Cycle. The ideogram: pearl and divination. **Abashment**, LIN: distress, shame, regret, humiliation; aware of having lost the right track; leads to repenting, HUI, correcting the direction of mind and life.

b) **Without**, WU: devoid of; -less as suffix. **Tolerate**, JUNG: allow, contain, endure, bear with; accept graciously. The ideogram: full stream bed, tolerating and containing.

Nine at-fourth

a) **The fields without wildfowl.**

b) **No lasting whatever: one's situation.
Quietly acquiring the wildfowl indeed.**

Associated Contexts a) **Fields**, T'IEN: cultivated land, plantation; also: hunting, game in the fields cannot escape the hunt. The ideogram: square divided into four sections, delineating fields. **Without**, WU: devoid of; -less as suffix. **Wildfowl**, CH'IN: all wild and game birds; untamed.

b) **No ... whatever**, FEI: strongest negative; not at all! **Situation**, WEI: place or seat according to rank; post, position, command; right, proper; established, arranged. The ideogram: person and stand, servants in their places.

Quiet, AN: peaceful, still, settled; calm, tranquilize. The ideogram: woman under a roof, a tranquil home.

Six at-fifth

a) **Persevering one's actualizing-tao: Trial.**
  Wife people: significant.
  The husband, the son: pitfall.

b) **Wife people, Trial: significant.**
  Adhering-to the-one and-also completing indeed.
  The husband, the son: paring righteously.
  Adhering-to the wife: pitfall indeed.

Associated Contexts *a)* **Trial**, CHEN: test by ordeal; inquiry by divination and its result; righteous, firm; separating wheat from chaff; the kernel, the proven core; fourth stage of the Time Cycle. The ideogram: pearl and divination.

Wife, FU: responsible position of married woman within the household; contrasts with consort, CH'I, her legal position and concubine, CH'IEH, secondary wives. The ideogram: woman, hand and broom, household duties. **Significant**, CHI: leads to the experience of meaning; favorable, propitious, advantageous, appropriate; keyword. The ideogram: scholar and mouth, wise words of a sage.

Husband, FU: household manager; administer with thrift and prudence; responsible for; sustain with your earnings; old enough to assume responsibility; married man. **Son(hood)**, TZU: living up to ideal of ancestors as highest human development; act with concern and reverence; male child; offspring, posterity; seed, kernel, egg; sage, teacher; nadir, deepest point, midnight, mid-winter. **Pitfall**, HSIUNG: leads away from the experience of meaning; stuck and exposed to danger, unable to take in the situation; flow of life and spirit is blocked; unfortunate, baleful; keyword.

b) **Adhere(-to)**, TS'UNG: follow a way, hold to a doctrine, school, or person; hear and comply with, agree to; forced to follow, follower. The ideogram: two men walking, one following the other.

Pare, CHIH: cut away; form, tailor, carve; invent; limit, prevent. The ideogram: knife and incomplete. **Righteous**, TI: proper and just, meets the standards; things in their proper place; the heart that rules itself; upright, moral rule; contrasts with Harvest, LI, advantage or profit.

Six above

a) **Rousing Persevering: pitfall.**

b) **Rousing Persevering located-in the above.**
The great without achievement indeed.

Associated Contexts a) **Rouse**, CHEN: stir up, excite, stimulate; issue forth; put in order. The ideogram: hand and shake, shaking things up. **Pitfall**, HSIUNG: leads away from the experience of meaning; stuck and exposed to danger, unable to take in the situation; flow of life and spirit is blocked; unfortunate, baleful; keyword.

b) **Locate(-in)**, TSAI: live in, dwell, reside; belong to, involved with, depend on; within. The ideogram: earth and persevere, place on the earth.

Great, TA: big, noble, important, very; orient the will toward a self-imposed goal, impose direction; ability to lead or guide your life; contrasts with small, HSIAO, flexible adaptation to what crosses your path; keyword. Image of Hexagrams 14, 26, 28, 34. **Without**, WU: devoid of; -less as suffix. **Achieve**, KUNG: work done, results; real accomplishment, praise, worth, merit. The ideogram: workman's square and forearm, combining craft and strength.

RETIRING ▪ *TUN*

This hexagram describes your situation in terms of conflict and consequent seclusion. It emphasizes that withdrawing from the affairs at hand to conceal youself in obscurity is the adequate way to handle it. To be in accord with the time, you are told to: **retire**!

● *Image of the Situation*

> **Retiring, Growing.**
> **The small: Harvesting Trial.**

Associated Contexts **Retire**, TUN: withdraw; run away, flee; conceal yourself, become obscure, invisible; secluded, non-social. The ideogram: walk and swine (wealth and luck), satisfaction through walking away. **Grow**, HENG: success through a sacrifice; pervade, persevere; bring to full growth; enjoy; vigorous, effective; second stage of the Time Cycle.

Small, HSIAO: little, common, unimportant; adapting to what crosses your path; ability to move in harmony with the vicissitudes of life; contrasts with great, TA, self-imposed theme or goal; keyword. Image of Hexagrams 9 and 62. **Harvesting Trial**, LI CHEN: advantageous divination; putting the action in question to the test is beneficial.

● *Outer and Inner Aspects*

☰ **Force**: The force of heaven struggles on, persistent and unwearied; heavenly bodies persist in their orbits. **Force** is the center of the yin hemicycle, completing the formative process.

Connection to the outer: struggling forces are bound together in dynamic tension, the Metallic Moment culminating. **Force** brings elements to grips, creating enduring relations.

☶ **Bound**: Mountains bound, limit and set a place off, stopping forward movement. **Bound** completes a full yin-yang cycle.

Connection to the inner: accomplishing words, which express things. **Bound** articulates what is complete to suggest what is beginning.

Inner accomplishing draws heaven's creative force into **retiring** from the world.

- *Counter Indications*

Nuclear trigrams **Force**, CH'IEN, and **Ground**, SUN, result in Counter Hexagram 44, **Coupling**, KOU. **Retiring** from active involvements is contrasted with spontaneous attraction and **coupling**.

- *Sequence*

> **Beings not permitted to use lasting residing-in their place.**
> **Anterior acquiescence has the use-of Retiring.**
> **Retiring implies withdrawing indeed.**

Associated Contexts **Beings not permitted to use ...** : no one is allowed to make use of; nothing can exist by means of. **Last,** CHIU: long, protracted; enduring. **Reside(-in),** CHÜ: dwell, live in, stay; sit down, fill an office; settled parts of a country. The ideogram: body and seat. **Their,** CH'I: third person pronoun; also: one/one's, he/his, she/hers, they/theirs, it/its. **Place,** SO: where something belongs or comes from; residence, dwelling; habitual focus or object.

Anterior ... the use-of: activating this hexagràm depends on understanding and accepting the previous statement.

Imply, CHE: further signify; additional meaning. **Withdraw(-from),** T'UI: draw back, retreat, recede; decline, refuse. **Indeed,** YEH: intensifier; indicates comment on previous statement.

- *Contrasted Definitions*

> **Great Invigorating: by-consequence stopping.**
> **Retiring: by-consequence withdrawing indeed.**

Associated Contexts **Great,** TA: big, noble, important, very; orient the will toward a self-imposed goal, impose direction; ability to lead or guide your life; contrasts with small, HSIAO, flexible adaptation to what crosses your path; keyword. **Invigorate,** CHUANG: inspirit, animate; strong, robust; full grown, flourishing, abundant; attain manhood (at 30);

damage through unrestrained strength. The ideogram: strength and scholar, intellectual impact. **Great Invigorating** is the Image of Hexagram 34. **By-consequence(-of)**, TSE: very strong connection; reason, cause, result; rule, law, pattern, standard; therefore. **Stop**, CHIH: bring or come to a standstill; the Action of the trigram Bound, KEN. The ideogram: a foot stops walking.

● *Symbol Tradition*

> **Below heaven possessing mountain. Retiring.**
> **A chün tzu uses distancing Small People.**
> **[A chün tzu uses] not hating and-also intimidating.**

Associated Contexts **Below**, HSIA: anything below, in all senses; lower, inner; lower trigram; opposite of above, SHANG. **Heaven**, T'IEN: highest; sky, firmament, heavens; power above the human as opposed to earth, TI, below; the Symbol of the trigram **Force**, CH'IEN. The ideogram: great and the one above. **Possess**, YU: in possession of, have, own; opposite of lack, WU. **Mountain**, SHAN: limit, boundary; the Symbol of the trigram Bound, KEN. The ideogram: three peaks, a mountain range.

Chün tzu: ideal of a person who uses divination to order his/her life in accordance with tao rather than wilful intention; keyword. **Use(-of)**, YI: make use of, by means of, owing to; employ, make functional. **Distance**, YÜAN: far off, remote; keep at a distance; alienated. The ideogram: go and a long way. **Small people**, HSIAO JEN: lowly, common, humble; those who adjust to circumstances with the flexibility of the small; effect of the small within an individual; keyword.

Not, PU: simple negative. **Hate**, WU: dislike, dread; averse to; ashamed of; repulsive, vicious, vile, ugly, wicked. The ideogram: twisted bowels and heart, heart entangled in emotion. **And-also**, ERH: joins and contrasts two terms. **Intimidate**, YEN: inspire with fear or awe; severe, rigid, strict, austere, demanding; a severe father; tight, a closed door.

● *Image Tradition*

> **Retiring, Growing. [I]**
> **Retiring and-also Growing indeed.**
> **Solid: appropriate situation and-also corresponding.**
> **Associating-with the season moving indeed.**

The small: Harvesting Trial. [II]
Drenched and-also long-living indeed.
Actually Retiring's season righteously great in-fact.

Associated Contexts **[I] Solid**, KANG: quality of the whole lines; firm, strong, unyielding, persisting. **Appropriate**, TANG: suitable; opportune, convenient; adequate, competent; equal to; whole lines in uneven places and opened lines in even places. **Situation**, WEI: place or seat according to rank; post, position, command; right, proper; established, arranged. The ideogram: person and stand, servants in their places. **Correspond(-to)**, YING: be in agreement or harmony; resonate together, invoke and fulfill each other; answer to, suitable; relation between the lines (1:4, 2:5, 3:6) when they form the pair opened and whole, supple and solid. The ideogram: heart and obey.

Associate(-with), YÜ: consort with, combine; companions; group, band, company; agree with, comply, help. The ideogram: pair of hands reaching downward meets a pair of hands reaching upward, helpful association. **Season**, SHIH: quality of the time; the right time, opportune, in harmony; planning in accord with the time; seasons of the year. The ideogram: sun and temple, time as sacred. **Move**, HSING: move or move something; motivate, emotionally moving; walk, act, do. The ideogram: stepping left then right.

[II] Drench, CH'IN: soak, penetrate, immerse, steep in; imbued with. **Long-living**, CHANG: enduring, constant; senior, superior, greater; increase, prosper; respect, elevate.

Actually ... in-fact, YI TSAI: stresses the importance of a statement. The ideogram: a dart and done, strong intention fully expressed. **'s/have(-it)/it/them**, CHIH: expresses possession, directly or as an object pronoun. **Righteous**, YI: proper and just, meets the standards; things in their proper place; the heart that rules itself; upright, moral rule; contrasts with Harvest, LI, advantage or profit.

● *Transforming Lines*

Initial six

a) **Retiring tail, adversity.**
   No availing-of possessing directed going.

b) **Retiring tail's adversity.**
   Not going, wherefore calamity indeed.

Associated Contexts a) **Tail**, WEI: animal's tail; last, extreme; remnants, unimportant. **Adversity**, LI: danger; threatening, malevolent demon. This has two aspects: grind, sharpen, improve, perfect, stimulate; and: poisonous, sinister, cruel, contrary. It indicates a spirit or ghost that seeks revenge by inflicting suffering upon the living. Pacifying or exorcizing such a spirit can have a healing effect. The ideogram: sheltering cliff and stinging insect.

   No, WU: simple negative; un-, dis-. **Avail-of**, YUNG: take advantage of; benefit from, profit by; use for a specific purpose; apply to advantage. The ideogram: to divine and center, applying divination to central concerns. **Possessing directed going**, YU YU WANG: imposing a direction on the flow of time from present to past; have a specific goal or purpose.

b) **Go**, WANG, and come, LAI, describe the stream of time as it flows from future through present to past; go, WANG, indicates what is departing from present to past; proceed, move on; keyword. **Wherefore**, HO: interrogative: why? for what reason? what is? and affirmation: therefore, for that reason. **Calamity**, TSAI: disaster from outside; flood, plague, drought, blight, ruin; contrasts with blunder, SHENG, indicating personal fault. The ideogram: water and fire, elemental powers.

   Six at-second

a) **Holding-on-to it: availing-of yellow cattle's skin.**
   Absolutely-nothing has mastering stimulating.

b) **Holding-on avails-of yellow cattle.**
   Firm purpose indeed.

Associated Contexts a) **Hold-on(-to)**, CHIH: lay hold of, seize, take in hand; keep, maintain, look after. The ideogram: criminal and seize. **Avail-of**, YUNG: take advantage of; benefit from, profit by; use for a specific purpose; apply to advantage. The ideogram: to divine and center, applying divination to central concerns. **Yellow**, HUANG: color of the productive middle; associated with the Earthy Moment between the yang and yin hemicycles; color of soil in central China; emblematic and imperial color of China since the Yellow Emperor (2500 BCE). **Cattle**, NIU: ox, bull, cow, calf; kine; power and strength of work animals. **Skin**,

KO: take off the covering, skin or hide; change, renew, molt; remove, peel off; revolt, overthrow, degrade from office; leather armor, protection. Image of Hexagram 49.

Absolutely-no(thing), MO: complete elimination; not any, by no means. **Master**, SHENG: have the upper hand, conquer; worthy of, able to; control, check, command. **Stimulate**, SHUO: rouse to action and good feeling; free from constraint, stir up, urge on; persuade, cheer, delight; set out in words; the Action of the trigram Open, TUI. The ideogram: words and exchange.

b) **Firm**, KU: constant, fixed, steady; chronic, recurrent. The ideogram: old and enclosure, long preserved. **Purpose**, CHIH: focus of mind and heart; will, inclination, resolve. The ideogram: heart and scholar, high inner resolve, or heart and go, inner determination.

Nine at-third

a) Tied Retiring. Possessing afflicting adversity.
   Accumulating servants, concubines, significant.

b) Tied Retiring's adversity.
   Possessing afflicting weariness indeed.
   Accumulating servants, concubines, significant.
   Not permitting Great Affairs indeed.

Associated Contexts a) **Tie(-to)**, HSI: connect, attach to, bind; devoted to; relatives. The ideogram: person and connect, ties between humans. **Afflict**, CHI: sickness, disorder, defect, calamity; injurious; pressure and consequent anger, hate or dislike. The ideogram: sickness and dart, a sudden affliction. **Adversity**, LI: danger; threatening, malevolent demon. This has two aspects: grind, sharpen, improve, perfect, stimulate; and: poisonous, sinister, cruel, contrary. It indicates a spirit or ghost that seeks revenge by inflicting suffering upon the living. Pacifying or exorcizing such a spirit can have a healing effect. The ideogram: sheltering cliff and stinging insect.

Accumulate, CH'U: retain, hoard, gather, herd together; control, restrain; domesticate, tame, train; raise, feed, sustain, bring up. The ideogram: field and black, fertile black soil good for pastures, accumulated through retaining silt. Image of Hexagrams 9 and 26. **Servant**, CH'EN: attendant, minister, vassal; courtier who can speak to the sovereign; wait on, serve in office. The ideogram: person bowing low.

Concubine, CH'IEH: secondary wife taken without ceremony to ensure a male descendant; handmaid. **Significant**, CHI: leads to the experience of meaning; favorable, propitious, advantageous, appropriate; keyword. The ideogram: scholar and mouth, wise words of a sage.

b) **Weariness**, PAI: fatigue; debilitated, exhausted, distressed; weak.

Not permitting, PU K'O: not possible; contradicts an inherent principle. The ideogram: mouth and breath, silent consent. **Affairs**, SHIH: all kinds of personal activity; matters at hand; business, occupation; manage a business, case in court.

Nine at-fourth

a) **Loving Retiring.**
A chün tzu significant.
Small People obstructing.

b) **A chün tzu lovingly Retiring.**
Small People obstructing indeed.

Associated Contexts a) **Love**, HAO: affection; fond of, take pleasure in; fine, graceful.

Significant, CHI: leads to the experience of meaning; favorable, propitious, advantageous, appropriate; keyword. The ideogram: scholar and mouth, wise words of a sage.

Obstruct, P'I: closed, stopped; bar the way; obstacle; unfortunate, wicked; refuse, disapprove, deny. The ideogram: mouth and not, blocked communication. Image of Hexagram 12.

Nine at-fifth

a) **Excellence Retiring, Trial: significant.**

b) **Excellence Retiring, Trial: significant.**
Using correcting the purpose indeed.

Associated Contexts a) **Excellence**, CHIA: superior quality; fine, delicious, glorious; happy, pleased; rejoice in, praise. The ideogram: increasing goodness, pleasure and happiness. **Trial**, CHEN: test by ordeal; inquiry by divination and its result; righteous, firm; separating wheat from chaff; the kernel, the proven core; fourth stage of the Time Cycle. The ideogram: pearl and divination. **Significant**, CHI: leads to the experience of meaning; favorable, propitious, advantageous, appropriate; keyword. The ideogram: scholar and mouth, wise words of a sage.

b) **Correct**, CHENG: rectify deviation or one-sidedness; proper, straight, exact, regular; constant, rule, model. The ideogram: stop and one, hold to one thing. **Purpose**, CHIH: focus of mind and heart; will, inclination, resolve. The ideogram: heart and scholar, high inner resolve, or heart and go, inner determination.

Nine above

a) **Rich Retiring, without not Harvesting.**

b) **Rich Retiring, without not Harvesting.**
Without a place to doubt indeed.

Associated Contexts a) **Rich**, FEI: fertile, abundant, fat; manure, fertilizer. **Without not Harvesting**, WU PU LI: nothing for which this will not be beneficial; advantageous potential, borderline where the balance is swinging from not Harvesting to actually Harvesting.

b) **Without**, WU: devoid of; -less as suffix. **Doubt**, YI: suspect, distrust; dubious; surmise, conjecture.

GREAT INVIGORATING ▪
TA CHUANG

This hexagram describes your situation in terms of the invigorating power of a central creative idea. It emphasizes that animating everything around you through this guiding motivation is the adequate way to handle it. To be in accord with the time, you are told to: **invigorate** through the **great**!

● *Image of the Situation*

Great Invigorating, Harvesting Trial.

Associated Contexts **Great**, TA: big, noble, important, very; orient the will toward a self-imposed goal; impose direction; ability to lead or guide your life; contrasts to small, HSIAO, flexible adaptation to what crosses your path; keyword. **Invigorate**, CHUANG: inspirit, animate; strong, robust; full grown, flourishing, abundant; attain manhood (at 30); damage through unrestrained strength. The ideogram: strength and scholar, intellectual impact. **Harvesting Trial**, LI CHEN: advantageous divination; putting the action in question to the test is beneficial.

● *Outer and Inner Aspects*

☳ **Shake**: Thunder rises from below, shaking and stirring things up. **Shake** begins the yang hemicycle by germinating new action.

　　Connection to the outer: sprouting energies thrusting from below, the Woody Moment beginning. **Shake** stirs things up to issue-forth.

☰ **Force**: The force of heaven struggles on, persistent and unwearied; heavenly bodies persist in their orbits. **Force** is the center of the yin hemicycle, completing the formative process.

　　Connection to the inner: struggling forces are bound together in dynamic tension, the Metallic Moment culminating. **Force** brings elements to grips, creating enduring relations.

Great inner force is directly expressed through the outward thrust of **invigorating** action.

- *Counter Indications*

Nuclear trigrams **Open**, TUI, and **Force**, CH'IEN, result in Counter Hexagram 43, **Parting**, KUAI. Concentrating effort through **invigorating** the **great** is contrasted with **parting** energy into diverse streams.

- *Sequence*

> **Beings not permitted to use completing Retiring.**
> **Anterior acquiescence has the use-of Great Invigorating.**

Associated Contexts **Beings not permitted to use ...** : no one is allowed to make use of; nothing can exist by means of. **Complete**, CHUNG: end of a cycle that begins the next; last, whole, all; contrasts with exhaust, CH'IUNG: final end. The ideogram: silk cocoons, follow and ice, winter linking one year with the next. **Retire**, TUN: withdraw; run away, flee; conceal yourself, become obscure, invisible; secluded, non-social. The ideogram: walk and swine (wealth and luck), satisfaction through walking away. Image of Hexagram 33.

Anterior ... the use-of: activating this hexagram depends on understanding and accepting the previous statement.

- *Contrasted Definitions*

> **Great Invigorating: by-consequence stopping.**
> **Retiring: by-consequence withdrawing indeed.**

Associated Contexts **By-consequence(-of)**, TSE: very strong connection; reason, cause, result; rule, law, pattern, standard; therefore. **Stop**, CHIH: bring or come to a standstill; the Action of the trigram Bound, KEN. The ideogram: a foot stops walking.

Withdraw(-from), T'UI: draw back, retreat, recede; decline, refuse. **Indeed**, YEH: intensifier; indicates comment on previous statement.

● *Symbol Tradition*

Thunder located above heaven. Great Invigorating.
A chün tzu uses no codes whatever, nowhere treading.

Associated Contexts **Thunder**, LEI: rising, arousing power; the
Symbol of the trigram Shake, CHEN. **Locate(-in)**, TSAI: live in, dwell,
reside; belong to, involved with, depend on; within. The ideogram: earth
and persevere, place on the earth. **Above**, SHANG: anything above, in all
senses; higher, upper, outer; upper trigram; opposite of below, HSIA.
Heaven, T'IEN: highest; sky, firmament, heavens; power above the
human as opposed to earth, TI, below; the Symbol of the trigram Force,
CH'IEN. The ideogram: great and the one above.

Chün tzu: ideal of a person who uses divination to order his/her life in
accordance with tao rather than wilful intention; keyword. **Use(-of)**, YI:
make use of, by means of, owing to; employ, make functional. **No ...
whatever**, FEI: strongest negative; not at all! **Codes**, LI: rites, rules, ritual;
usage, manners; worship, ceremony, observance. The ideogram: worship
and sacrificial vase, handling a sacred vessel. **Nothing/nowhere**, FU:
strong negative; not a single thing/place. **Tread**, LÜ: step, path, track;
footsteps; walk a path or way; course of the stars; act, practise; conduct;
salary, means of subsistance. The ideogram: body and repeating steps,
following a trail. Image of Hexagram 10.

● *Image Tradition*

Great Invigorating. The Great implies Invigorating indeed. [I]
Solid uses stirring-up. Anterior Invigorating.

Great Invigorating, Harvesting Trial. [II]
The Great implies correcting indeed.
Actually the correcting Great and-also
 Heaven[and]Earth's motives permitting visualizing.

Associated Contexts **[I] Imply**, CHE: further signify; additional
meaning.
 Solid, KANG: quality of the whole lines; firm, strong, unyielding,
persisting. **Stir-up**, TUNG: excite, influence, move, affect; work, take

action; come out of the egg or the bud; the Action of the trigram Shake, CHEN. The ideogram: strength and heavy, move weighty things. **Anterior**, KU: come before as cause; formerly, ancient; reason, purpose, intention; grievance, quarrel, dissatisfaction, sorrow, mourning resulting from previous causes and intentions; situation leading to a divination.

[II] Correct, CHENG: rectify deviation or one-sidedness; proper, straight, exact, regular; constant, rule, model. The ideogram: stop and one, hold to one thing.

Actually, YI: truly, really, at present. The ideogram: a dart and done, strong intention fully expressed. **And-also**, ERH: joins and contrasts two terms. **Heaven[and]Earth**, T'IEN TI: dynamic relation between the primal powers and the world it produces; cosmos, natural or human world; keyword. **'s/have(-it)/it/them**, CHIH: expresses possession, directly or as an object pronoun. **Motive**, CH'ING: true nature; feelings, desires, passions. The ideogram: heart and green, germinated in the heart. **Permit**, K'O: possible because in harmony with an inherent principle. The ideogram: mouth and breath, silent consent. **Visualize**, CHIEN: seeing in all its aspects: vision, being visible, forming mental images; visit, call on, consult. The ideogram: eye above person, active and receptive sight.

- *Transforming Lines*

  Initial nine

  a) **Invigorating tending-towards the feet.**
  Chastising: pitfall, possessing conformity.

  b) **Invigorating tending-towards the feet.**
  One's conforming exhausted indeed.

Associated Contexts *a)* **Tend-towards**, YÜ: move toward but not reach, in the direction of; contrasts with reach(-to), HU, actually arriving. **Foot**, CHIH: literal foot; foundation, base.

Chastise, CHENG: punish, subjugate, discipline; reduce to order; punishing expedition. The ideogram: step and correct, a rectifying move. **Pitfall**, HSIUNG: leads away from the experience of meaning; stuck and exposed to danger, unable to take in the situation; flow of life and spirit is blocked; unfortunate, baleful; keyword. **Possessing conformity**, YU FU: inner and outer are in accord; confidence of the spirits has been captured; sincere, truthful; proper to take action.

b) **One's/one**, CH'I: third person pronoun; also: it/its, he/his, she/hers, they/theirs. **Conforming**, FU: accord between inner and outer in a particular moment; sincere, truthful, verified, reliable, in accord with the spirits; capture; prisoners, spoils; contrasts with trustworthy, HSIN, consistent over time. The ideogram: bird's claw enclosing young animals, possessive grip. Image of Hexagram 61. **Exhaust**, CH'IUNG: bring to an end; limit, extremity; destitute; investigate exhaustively; end without a new beginning. The ideogram: cave and naked person, bent with disease or old age.

Nine at-second

a) **Trial: significant.**

b) **Nine at-second, Trial: significant.**
   Using centering indeed.

Associated Contexts a) **Trial**, CHEN: test by ordeal; inquiry by divination and its result; righteous, firm; separating wheat from chaff; the kernel, the proven core; fourth stage of the Time Cycle. The ideogram: pearl and divination. **Significant**, CHI: leads to the experience of meaning; favorable, propitious, advantageous, appropriate; keyword. The ideogram: scholar and mouth, wise words of a sage.

b) **Center**, CHUNG: inner, central; put in the center; middle, stable point enabling you to face inner and outer changes; middle line of trigram. The ideogram: field divided in two equal parts. Image of Hexagram 61.

Nine at-third

a) **Small People avail-of Invigorating.**
   A chün tzu avails-of absence.
   Trial: adversity.
   The he goat butts a hedge.
   Ruining his horns.

b) **Small People avail-of Invigorating.**
   A chün tzu: absence indeed.

Associated Contexts a) **Small People**, HSIAO JEN: lowly, common, humble; those who adjust to circumstances with the flexibility of the small; effect of the small within an individual; keyword. **Avail-of**, YUNG:

take advantage of; benefit from, profit by; use for a specific purpose; apply to advantage. The ideogram: to divine and center, applying divination to central concerns. **Absence**, WANG: emptiness, vacancy; lit.: a net, open spaces between threads; used as a negative. The ideogram: net and lost, empty spaces divide what is kept from what is lost.

Trial, CHEN: test by ordeal; inquiry by divination and its result; righteous, firm; separating wheat from chaff; the kernel, the proven core; fourth stage of the Time Cycle. The ideogram: pearl and divination. **Adversity**, LI: danger; threatening, malevolent demon. This has two aspects: grind, sharpen, improve, perfect, stimulate; and: poisonous, sinister, cruel, contrary. It indicates a spirit or ghost that seeks revenge by inflicting suffering upon the living. Pacifying or exorcizing such a spirit can have a healing effect. The ideogram: sheltering cliff and stinging insect.

He goat, TI YANG: ram or buck; three-year-old male at peak of strength. **Butt**, CHU: push or strike with the horns; attack, oppose, offend; stirred up, excited; obnoxious; associated with the Woody Moment. **Hedge**, FAN: row of bushes, fence, boundary; protect, fend off, enclose.

Ruin, LEI: destroy, break, overturn; debilitated, meager, emaciated; entangled. **His/he**, CH'I: third person pronoun; also: one/one's, it/its, she/hers, they/theirs. **Horns**, CHIO: strength and power; gore; dispute, test your strength; headland.

Nine at-fourth

a) **Trial: significant.**
Repenting extinguished.
The hedge broken-up, not ruined.
Invigorating tending-towards the Great: a cart's axle-straps.

b) **The hedge broken-up, not ruined.**
Honoring going indeed.

Associated Contexts a) **Trial**, CHEN: test by ordeal; inquiry by divination and its result; righteous, firm; separating wheat from chaff; the kernel, the proven core; fourth stage of the Time Cycle. The ideogram: pearl and divination. **Significant**, CHI: leads to the experience of meaning; favorable, propitious, advantageous, appropriate; keyword. The ideogram: scholar and mouth, wise words of a sage.

Repenting extinguished, HUI WANG: previous troubles and consequent remorse will disappear.

Hedge, FAN: row of bushes, fence, boundary; protect, fend off, enclose. **Break-up**, CHÜEH: streams diverging; break through an obstacle and scatter; separate, break into parts; cut or bite through; decide, pass sentence. The ideogram: water and parting. **Not**, PU: simple negative. **Ruin**, LEI: destroy, break, overturn; debilitated, meager, emaciated; entangled.

Tend-towards, YÜ: move toward but not reach, in the direction of; contrasts with reach(-to), HU, actually arriving. **Cart**, YÜ: carrying capacity of a vehicle; contain, hold, sustain. **Axle-strap**, FU: fastens the body of a cart to axle and wheels.

b) **Honor**, SHANG: esteem, give high rank to; eminent; put one thing on top of another. **Go**, WANG, and come, LAI, describe the stream of time as it flows from future through present to past; go, WANG, indicates what is departing from present to past; proceed, move on; keyword.

Six at-fifth

a) **Losing the goat, tending-towards versatility.**
   Without repenting.

b) **Losing the goat, tending-towards versatility.**
   Situation not appropriate indeed.

Associated Contexts a) **Lose**, SANG: fail to obtain, cease, become obscure; forgotten, destroyed; lament, mourn; funeral. The ideogram: weep and the dead. **Goat**, YANG: sheep and goats; direct thought and action. **Tend-towards**, YÜ: move toward but not reach, in the direction of; contrasts with reach(-to), HU, actually arriving. **Versatility**, I: sudden and unpredictable change; mental mobility and openness; easy and light, not difficult and heavy; occurs in name of the I CHING.

Without repenting, WU HUI: devoid of the sort of trouble that leads to sorrow, regret and the necessity to change your attitude.

b) **Situation**, WEI: place or seat according to rank; post, position, command; right, proper; established, arranged. The ideogram: person and stand, servants in their places. **Not**, PU: simple negative. **Appropriate**, TANG: suitable; opportune, convenient; adequate, competent; equal to; whole lines in uneven places and opened lines in even places.

Six above

a) **The he goat butts a hedge.**
   Not enabling withdrawing, not enabling releasing.
   Without direction: Harvesting.
   Drudgery by-consequence significant.

b) **Not enabling withdrawing, not enabling releasing.**
   Not ruminating indeed.
   Drudgery by-consequence significant.
   Fault not long-living indeed.

Associated Contexts a) **He goat,** TI YANG: ram or buck; three-year-old male at peak of strength. **Butt,** CHU: push or strike with the horns; attack, oppose, offend; stirred up, excited; obnoxious; associated with the Woody Moment. **Hedge,** FAN: row of bushes, fence, boundary; protect, fend off, enclose.

   Not, PU: simple negative. **Able,** NENG: enable; ability, power, skill, art; competent, talented; duty, function, capacity. The ideogram: an animal with strong hooves and bones, able to carry and defend. **Release,** SUI: loose, let go, free; unhindered, in accord; follow, spread out, progress; penetrate, invade. The ideogram: go and follow your wishes, unimpeded movement.

   Without direction: Harvesting, WU YU LI: no plan or direction is advantageous; in order to take advantage of the situation, do not impose a direction on events.

   Drudgery, CHIEN: difficult, hard, repetitive work; hard to cultivate; distressing, sorrowful. The ideogram: sticky earth and a person looking around, hard work in comparison to others. **Significant,** CHI: leads to the experience of meaning; favorable, propitious, advantageous, appropriate; keyword. The ideogram: scholar and mouth, wise words of a sage.

b) **Ruminate,** HSIANG: ponder and discuss; examine minutely, learn fully, watch over, pay attention to. The ideogram: word and sheep, ruminating on words.

   Fault, CHIU: unworthy conduct that leads to harm, illness, misfortune. The ideogram: person and differ, differ from what you should be. **Long-living,** CHANG: enduring, constant; senior, superior, greater; increase, prosper; respect, elevate.

P R O S P E R I N G ▪ *CHIN*

This hexagram describes your situation in terms of thriving in the full light of the sun. It emphasizes that contributing to this increase by helping things to flourish is the adequate way to handle it. To be in accord with the time, you are told to: **prosper**!

● *Image of the Situation*

> **Prospering, the calm feudatory avails-of bestowing horses**
> **to multiply the multitudes.**
> **Day-time sun three-times reflected.**

Associated Contexts **Prosper**, CHIN: grow and flourish, as young plants in the sun; increase, progress, permeate, impregnate; attached to. The ideogram: sun and reach, the daylight world. **Calm**, K'ANG: confident strength and poise; stability, peace, ease; joy, delight. **Feudatory**, HOU: nobles entrusted with governing the provinces; active in daily life rather than governing from the center; contrasts with prince, KUNG, executives at the court. **Avail-of**, YUNG: take advantage of; benefit from, profit by; use for a specific purpose; apply to advantage. The ideogram: to divine and center, applying divination to central concerns. **Bestow**, HSI: grant, confer upon; reward, gift. The ideogram: metal used in coins and insignia. **Horse**, MA: symbol of spirited strength in the natural world, counterpart of dragon, LUNG; associated with the trigram Force, CH'IEN, heaven, T'IEN, and high noon. **Multiply**, FAN: augment, enhance, increase; thriving, plentiful. **Multitude**, SHU: the people; mass, herd; all, the whole.

    Day-time, CHOU: daylight half of 24-hour cycle. **Sun/day**, JIH: actual sun and the time of a sun-cycle, a day. **Three-times**, SAN: serial repetition. **Reflect**, CHIEH: receive and pass on; follow in office; inherit, as father and son; associate with. The ideogram: hand and concubine, passed on through natural, not legal ways.

Outer and Inner Aspects

☲ **Radiance**: Fire and brightness radiate light and warmth, attached to their support; congregating people see and become aware. **Radiance** ends the yang hemicycle, consuming action in awareness.

Connection to the outer: light, heat, consciousness bring continual change, the Fiery Moment. **Radiance** spreads outward, congregating, becoming aware and changing.

☷ **Field**: The field of earth yields and sustains, serving in order to produce. **Field** is the equalizing point between yin and yang where things labor and serve.

Connection to the inner: the common labor of sowing and hoarding, the Earthy Moment. **Field** produces concrete results through serving.

Spreading outer light fertilizes the inner field, whose yielding service in turn spreads **prospering**.

• Counter Indications

Nuclear trigrams **Gorge**, K'AN, and **Bound**, KEN, result in Counter Hexagram 39, **Limping**, CHIEN. **Prospering**'s flourishing brightness is contrasted with the weak and hampered movement of **limping**.

• Sequence

> **Beings not permitted to use completing Invigorating.**
> **Anterior acquiescence has the use-of Prospering.**
> **Prospering implies advancing indeed.**

Associated Contexts **Beings not permitted to use ...** : no one is allowed to make use of; nothing can exist by means of. **Complete**, CHUNG: end of a cycle that begins the next; last, whole, all; contrasts with exhaust, CH'IUNG, final end. The ideogram: silk cocoons, follow and ice, winter linking one year with the next. **Invigorate**, CHUANG: inspirit, animate; strong, robust; full grown, flourishing, abundant; attain manhood (at 30); damage through unrestrained strength. The ideogram: strength and scholar, intellectual impact. Image of Hexagram 34.

Anterior ... the use-of: activating this hexagram depends on understanding and accepting the previous statement.

Imply, CHE: further signify; additional meaning. **Advance**, CHIN: exert yourself, make progress, climb; be promoted; further the development of, augment; adopt a religion or conviction; offer, introduce. **Indeed**, YEH: intensifier; indicates comment on previous statement.

- ## *Contrasted Definitions*

> **Prospering: day-time indeed.**
> **Brightness Hiding: proscribed indeed.**

Associated Contexts **Brightness**, MING: light-giving aspect of burning, heavenly bodies and consciousness; with fire, the Symbol of the trigram Radiance, LI. **Hide**, YI: keep out of sight; remote, distant from the center; equalize by lowering; squat, level, make ordinary; pacified, colorless; cut, wound, destroy, exterminate. **Brightness Hiding** is the Image of Hexagram 36. **Proscribe**, CHU: exclude, reject by proclamation; denounce, forbid; reprove, seek as a criminal; condemn to death; clear away.

- ## *Symbol Tradition*

> **Brightness issuing-forth above earth. Prospering.**
> **A chün tzu uses originating enlightening**
> **to brighten actualizing-tao.**

Associated Contexts **Issue-forth(-from)**, CH'U: emerge from, come out of, proceed from, spring from; the Action of the trigram Shake, CHEN; contrary of enter, JU. The ideogram: stem with branches and leaves emerging. **Above**, SHANG: anything above, in all senses; higher, upper, outer; upper trigram; opposite of below, HSIA. **Earth**, TI: ground on which the human world rests; basis of all things, nourishes all things; the Symbol of the trigram Field, K'UN.

Chün tzu: ideal of a person who uses divination to order his/her life in accordance with tao rather than wilful intention; keyword. **Use(-of)**, YI: make use of, by means of, owing to; employ, make functional. **Origin**, TZU: source, beginning, ground; cause, reason, motive; line of descent; path to the origin; yourself, intrinsic. **Enlighten**, CHAO: cast light on,

display, show; instruct, give knowlege; manifest, bright, splendid. The ideogram: sun and call, bring into the light. **Actualize-tao**, TE: realize tao in action; power, virtue; ability to follow the course traced by the ongoing process of the cosmos; keyword. The ideogram: to go, straight, and heart. Linked with acquire, TE: acquiring that which makes a being become what it is meant to be.

● *Image Tradition*

> **Prospering. Advancing indeed. [I]**
> **Brightness issuing-forth above earth.**
> **Yielding and-also congregating reaching-to great brightening.**
>
> **Supple advancing and-also moving above. [II]**
> **That uses the calm feudatory availing-of bestowing horses**
> **to multiply the multitudes.**
> **Day-time sun three-times reflected indeed.**

Associated Contexts **[I] Yield(-to)**, SHUN: give way and bear produce; comply, agree, follow, obey; unresisting, docile, flexible; nourish, provide; the Action of the trigram Field, K'UN. The ideogram: head and current, water flowing from the head of a river, yielding to the banks. **And-also**, ERH: joins and contrasts two terms. **Congregate**, LI: cling together; depend on, attached to, rely on; couple, pair, herd; the Action of the trigram Radiance, LI. The ideogram: deer flocking together. **Reach(-to)**, HU: arrive at a goal; reach towards and achieve; connect; contrasts with tend-towards, YU. **Great**, TA: big, noble, important, very; orient the will toward a self-imposed goal, impose direction; ability to lead or guide your life; contrasts with small, HSIAO, flexible adaptation to what crosses your path; keyword. Image of Hexagrams 14, 26, 28, 34.

[II] Supple, JOU: quality of the opened lines; flexible, pliant, tender, adaptable. **Move**, HSING: move or move something; motivate, emotionally moving; walk, act, do. The ideogram: stepping left then right.
   That uses, SHIH YI: involves and is involved by.

● *Transforming Lines*

Initial six

a) **Prospering thus, arresting thus.**
Trial: significant.
Absence: conforming.
Enriching, without fault.

b) **Prospering thus, arresting thus.**
Solitary moving correcting indeed.
Enriching, without fault.
Not-yet acquiescing-in fate indeed.

Associated Contexts a) **Thus ... thus,** JU ... JU: when there is one thing, then there must be the second thing. **Arrest,** TS'UI: stop, drive back, repress; force obedience, overpower, impel; scorn; destroy, break.

Trial, CHEN: test by ordeal; inquiry by divination and its result; righteous, firm; separating wheat from chaff; the kernel, the proven core; fourth stage of the Time Cycle. The ideogram: pearl and divination. **Significant,** CHI: leads to the experience of meaning; favorable, propitious, advantageous, appropriate; keyword. The ideogram: scholar and mouth, wise words of a sage.

Absence, WANG: emptiness, vacancy; lit.: a net, open spaces between threads; used as a negative. The ideogram: net and lost, empty spaces divide what is kept from what is lost. **Conforming,** FU: accord between inner and outer in a particular moment; sincere, truthful, verified, reliable, in accord with the spirits; capture; prisoners, spoils; contrasts with trustworthy, HSIN, consistent over time. The ideogram: bird's claw enclosing young animals, possessive grip. Image of Hexagram 61.

Enrich, YÜ: make richer (excluding land); material, mental or spiritual wealth; bequeath; generous, abundant. The ideogram: garments, portable riches. **Without fault,** WU CHIU: no error or harm in the situation.

b) **Solitary,** TI: alone, single; isolated, abandoned. **Correct,** CHENG: rectify deviation or one-sidedness; proper, straight, exact, regular; constant, rule, model. The ideogram: stop and one, hold to one thing.

Not-yet, WEI: temporal negative; something will but has not yet occurred; contrary of already, CHI. Image of Hexagram 64. **Acquiesce(-in),** SHOU: accept, make peace with, agree to; at rest, satisfied; patient. **Fate,** MING: individual destiny; birth and death as limits of life; issue orders with authority; consult the gods. The ideogram: mouth and order, words with heavenly authority.

Six at-second

a) **Prospering thus, apprehensive thus.**
Trial: significant.
Acquiescing-in closely-woven chain-mail: blessing.
Tending-towards one's kingly mother.

b) **Acquiescing-in closely-woven chain-mail: blessing.**
Using centering correcting indeed.

Associated Contexts a) **Thus ... thus,** JU ... JU: when there is one thing, then there must be the second thing. **Apprehensive,** CH'OU: anticipating adversity, afraid of what approaches; chagrined, grieved. The ideogram: heart and autumn, dreading the coming winter.

Trial, CHEN: test by ordeal; inquiry by divination and its result; righteous, firm; separating wheat from chaff; the kernel, the proven core; fourth stage of the Time Cycle. The ideogram: pearl and divination. **Significant,** CHI: leads to the experience of meaning; favorable, propitious, advantageous, appropriate; keyword. The ideogram: scholar and mouth, wise words of a sage.

Acquiesce(-in), SHOU: accept, make peace with, agree to; at rest, satisfied; patient. **Closely-woven,** TZU: compact, close textured, dense, solid, impenetrable. The ideogram: herbs and silk, dense fabric or foliage. **Chain-mail,** CHIEH: chain-armor; tortoise or crab shell; protective covering; border, limit; protection, support. **Bless,** FU: heavenly gifts; make happy; spiritual power and goodwill. The ideogram: spirit and plenty, heavenly gifts in abundance.

Tend-towards, YÜ: move toward but not reach, in the direction of; contrasts with reach(-to), HU, actually arriving. **One's/one,** CH'I: third person pronoun; also: it/its, he/his, she/hers, they/theirs. **King(hood),** WANG: effective ruler, by authority of the Emperor, from whom others derive their power. **Mother(hood),** MU: child-bearing and nourishing. The ideogram: two breasts.

b) **Centering correcting,** CHUNG CHENG: central and correct; make rectifying one-sidedness and error your central concern; reaching a stable center in yourself can correct the situation.

Six at-third

a) **Crowds, sincerity, repenting extinguished.**

b) **Crowds: sincerity's purpose.**
   Moving above indeed.

Associated Contexts a) **Crowds**, CHUNG: many people, large group; majority; in common. **Sincere**, YÜN: true, honest, loyal; according to the facts; have confidence in, permit, assent. The ideogram: vapor rising, words directed upwards. **Repenting extinguished**, HUI WANG: previous troubles and consequent remorse will disappear.

b) **'s/have(-it)/it/them**, CHIH: expresses possession, directly or as an object pronoun. **Purpose**, CHIH: focus of mind and heart; will, inclination, resolve. The ideogram: heart and scholar, high inner resolve, or heart and go, inner determination.

Nine at-fourth

a) **Prospering, thus bushy-tailed rodents.**
   Trial: adversity.

b) **Bushy-tailed rodents, Trial: adversity.**
   Situation not appropriate indeed.

Associated Contexts a) **Thus**, JU: as, in this way. **Bushy-tailed rodent**, SHIH SHU: animals which destroy stored grain; mean, thieving people; timid, skulking, mournful, brooding.

   Trial, CHEN: test by ordeal; inquiry by divination and its result; righteous, firm; separating wheat from chaff; the kernel, the proven core; fourth stage of the Time Cycle. The ideogram: pearl and divination. **Adversity**, LI: danger; threatening, malevolent demon. This has two aspects: grind, sharpen, improve, perfect, stimulate; and: poisonous, sinister, cruel, contrary. It indicates a spirit or ghost that seeks revenge by inflicting suffering upon the living. Pacifying or exorcizing such a spirit can have a healing effect. The ideogram: sheltering cliff and stinging insect.

b) **Situation**, WEI: place or seat according to rank; post, position, command; right, proper; established, arranged. The ideogram: person and stand, servants in their places. **Not**, PU: simple negative. **Appropriate**, TANG:

suitable; opportune, convenient; adequate, competent; equal to; whole lines in uneven places and opened lines in even places.

Six at-fifth

a) **Repenting extinguished.**
Letting-go, acquiring, no cares.
Going significant, without not Harvesting.

b) **Letting-go, acquiring, no cares.**
Going possessing reward indeed.

Associated Contexts a) **Repenting extinguished,** HUI WANG: previous troubles and consequent remorse will disappear.

Let-go, SHIH: lose, omit, miss, fail, let slip; out of control. The ideogram: drop from the hand. **Acquire,** TE: obtain the desired object; wish for, desire covetously; gains, possessions. The ideogram: go and obstacle, going through obstacles to the goal. **No,** WU: simple negative; un-, dis-. **Care,** HSÜ: fear, doubt, concern; heartfelt attachment; relieve, soothe, aid; sympathy, compassion, consolation. The ideogram: heart and blood, the heart's blood affected.

Go, WANG, and come, LAI, describe the stream of time as it flows from future through present to past; go, WANG, indicates what is departing from present to past; proceed, move on; keyword. **Significant,** CHI: leads to the experience of meaning; favorable, propitious, advantageous, appropriate; keyword. The ideogram: scholar and mouth, wise words of a sage. **Without not Harvesting,** WU PU LI: nothing for which this will not be beneficial; advantageous potential, borderline where the balance is swinging from not Harvesting to actually Harvesting.

b) **Possess,** YU: in possession of, have, own; opposite of lack, WU. **Reward,** CH'ING: gift given from gratitude or benevolence; favour from heaven; congratulate with gifts. The ideogram: heart, follow and deer (wealth), the heart expressed through gifts.

Nine above

a) **Prospering: one's horns.**
Holding-fast avails-of subjugating the capital.
Adversity significant, without fault.
Trial: abashment.

b) **Holding-fast avails-of subjugating the capital.**
Tao not-yet shining indeed.

Associated Contexts a) **One's/one**, CH'I: third person pronoun; also: it/its, he/his, she/hers, they/theirs. **Horns**, CHIO: strength and power; gore; dispute, test your strength; headland.

Hold-fast, WEI: hold together; tie to, connect; reins, net. **Subjugate**, FA: chastise rebels, make dependent; cut down, subject to rule. The ideogram: man and lance, armed soldiers. **Capital**, YI: populous fortified city, center and symbol of the domain it rules. The ideogram: enclosure and official seal.

Adversity, LI: danger; threatening, malevolent demon. This has two aspects: grind, sharpen, improve, perfect, stimulate; and: poisonous, sinister, cruel, contrary. It indicates a spirit or ghost that seeks revenge by inflicting suffering upon the living. Pacifying or exorcizing such a spirit can have a healing effect. The ideogram: sheltering cliff and stinging insect. **Significant**, CHI: leads to the experience of meaning; favorable, propitious, advantageous, appropriate; keyword. The ideogram: scholar and mouth, wise words of a sage. **Without fault**, WU CHIU: no error or harm in the situation.

Trial, CHEN: test by ordeal; inquiry by divination and its result; righteous, firm; separating wheat from chaff; the kernel, the proven core; fourth stage of the Time Cycle. The ideogram: pearl and divination. **Abashment**, LIN: : distress, shame, regret, humiliation; aware of having lost the right track; leads to repenting, HUI, correcting the direction of mind and life.

b) **Tao**: way or path; ongoing process of being and the course it traces for each specific person or thing; keyword. The ideogram: go and head, leading and the path it creates. **Not-yet**, WEI: temporal negative; something will but has not yet occurred; contrary of already, CHI. Image of Hexagram 64. **Shine**, KUANG: illuminate; give off brilliant, bright light; honor, glory, éclat; result of action, contrasts with brightness, MING, light of heavenly bodies. The ideogram: fire above person, lifting the light.

36

BRIGHTNESS HIDING ▪ *MING YI*

This hexagram describes your situation in terms of intelligence hidden or harmed. It emphasizes that deliberately concealing your light by entering what is beneath you is the adequate way to handle it. To be in accord with the time, you are told to: **hide** your **brightness**!

● *Image of the Situation*

Brightness Hiding, Harvesting: drudgery, Trial.

Associated Contexts **Brightness**, MING: light-giving aspect of burning, heavenly bodies and consciousness; with fire, the Symbol of the trigram Radiance, LI. **Hide**, YI: keep out of sight; remote, distant from the center; equalize by lowering; squat, level, make ordinary; pacified, colorless; cut, wound, destroy, exterminate. **Harvest**, LI: advantageous, profitable; acute, insightful; benefit, nourish; third stage of the Time Cycle. **Drudgery**, CHIEN: difficult, hard, repetitive work; hard to cultivate; distressing, sorrowful. The ideogram: sticky earth and a person looking around, hard work in comparison to others. **Trial**, CHEN: test by ordeal; inquiry by divination and its result; righteous, firm; separating wheat from chaff; the kernel, the proven core; fourth stage of the Time Cycle. The ideogram: pearl and divination.

● *Outer and Inner Aspects*

☷ **Field**: The field of earth yields and sustains, serving in order to produce. **Field** is the equalizing point between yin and yang where things labor and serve.

Connection to the outer: the common labor of sowing and hoarding, the Earthy Moment. **Field** produces concrete results through serving.

☲ **Radiance**: Fire and brightness radiate light and warmth, attached to their support; congregating people see and become aware. **Radiance** ends the yang hemicycle, consuming action in awareness.

Connection to the inner: light, heat, consciousness bring about continual change, the Fiery Moment. **Radiance** spreads outward, congregating, becoming aware and changing.

Congregating with what is below the common earth **hides brightness** and awareness.

● *Counter Indications*

Nuclear trigrams **Shake**, CHEN, and **Gorge**, K'AN, result in Counter Hexagram 40, **Taking-apart**, HSIEH. Dimming the intelligence when **brightness hides** is contrasted with the differentiating thought that **takes** things **apart** to analyse them.

● *Sequence*

> **Advancing necessarily possessing a place to injure.**
> **Anterior acquiescence has the use-of Brightness Hiding.**
> **Hiding implies injury.**

Associated Contexts **Advance,** CHIN: exert yourself, make progress, climb; be promoted; further the development of, augment; adopt a religion or conviction; offer, introduce. **Necessarily,** PI: unavoidably, indispensably, certainly. **Possess,** YU: in possession of, have, own; opposite of lack, WU. **Place,** SO: where something belongs or comes from; residence, dwelling; habitual focus or object. **Injure,** SHANG: hurt, wound, grieve, distress; mourn, sad at heart, humiliated.

Anterior ... the use-of: activating this hexagram depends on understanding and accepting the previous statement.

Imply, CHE: further signify; additional meaning.

● *Contrasted Definitions*

> **Prospering: day-time indeed.**
> **Brightness Hiding: proscribed indeed.**

Associated Contexts **Prospering,** CHIN: grow and flourish as young plants in the sun; increase, progress, permeate, impregnate; attached to. The ideogram: sun and reaching, the daylight world. Image of Hexagram 35.

Day-time, CHOU: daylight half of 24-hour cycle. **Indeed**, YEH: intensifier; indicates comment on previous statement.

Proscribe, CHU: exclude, reject by proclamation; denounce, forbid; reprove, seek as a criminal; condemn to death; clear away.

- ### Symbol Tradition

> **Brightness entering earth center. Brightness Hiding.**
> **A chün tzu uses supervising the crowds to avail-of**
> **darkening and-also Brightening.**

Associated Contexts **Enter**, JU: penetrate, go into, enter on, progress; put into, encroach on; the Action of the trigram Ground, SUN, contrary of issue-forth, CH'U. **Earth**, TI: ground on which the human world rests; basis of all things, nourishes all things; the Symbol of the trigram Field, K'UN. **Center**, CHUNG: inner, central; put in the center; middle, stable point enabling you to face inner and outer changes; middle line of trigram. The ideogram: field divided in two equal parts. Image of Hexagram 61.

Chün tzu: ideal of a person who uses divination to order his/her life in accordance with tao rather than wilful intention; keyword. **Use(-of)**, YI: make use of, by means of, owing to; employ, make functional. **Supervise**, LI: oversee, inspect, administer; visit subordinates; headquarters. **Crowds**, CHUNG: many people, large group; majority; in common. **Avail-of**, YUNG: take advantage of; benefit from, profit by; use for a specific purpose; apply to advantage. The ideogram: to divine and center, applying divination to central concerns. **Darken**, HUI: make or become dark; last day of the moon; obscure, night, mist. **And-also**, ERH: joins and contrasts two terms.

- ### Image Tradition

> **Brightness entering earth center. Brightness Hiding. [I]**
> **Inside pattern Brightening and-also outside supple yielding.**
>
> **Using the enveloped great: heaviness. [II]**
> **The pattern king uses it.**
> **Harvesting: drudgery, Trial.**
> **Darkening one's Brightness indeed.**

**Inside heaviness and-also enabling correcting one's purpose. [III]
The winnowing son uses it.**

Associated Contexts **[I] Inside**, NEI: within, inner, interior; inside
of the house and those who work there, particularly women; the lower
trigram, as opposed to outside, WAI, the upper. The ideogram: border
and enter, cross a border. **Pattern**, WEN: intrinsic or natural design and its
beauty; stylish, elegant; noble; contrasts with composition, CHANG, a
conscious creation. **Outside**, WAI: outer, exterior, external; people
working in places other than their home; unfamiliar, foreign; the upper
trigram, as opposed to inside, NEI, the lower. **Supple**, JOU: quality of the
opened lines; flexible, pliant, tender, adaptable. **Yield(-to)**, SHUN: give
way and bear produce; comply, agree, follow, obey; unresisting, docile,
flexible; nourish, provide; the Action of the trigram Field, K'UN, The
ideogram: head and current, water flowing from the head of a river,
yielding to the banks.

[II] Envelop, MENG: cover, pull over, hide, conceal; lid or cover; clouded
awareness, dull; ignorance, immaturity; unseen beginnings. The ideogram:
plant and covered, hidden growth. Image of Hexagram 4. **Great**, TA: big,
noble, important, very; orient the will toward a self-imposed goal, impose
direction; ability to lead or guide your life; contrasts with small, HSIAO,
flexible adaptation to what crosses your path; keyword. Image of
Hexagrams 14, 26, 28, 34. **Heavy**, NAN: arduous, grievous, difficult;
hardship, distress; harass; contrasts with versatile, I, deal lightly with. The
ideogram: domestic bird with clipped tail and drying sticky earth.

 King(hood), WANG: effective ruler, by authority of the Emperor,
from whom others derive their power. **It/them/have(-it)/'s**, CHIH:
expresses possession, directly or as an object pronoun.

 One's/one, CH'I: third person pronoun; also: it/its, he/his, she/hers,
they/theirs.

[III] Able, NENG: enable; ability, power, skill, art; competent, talented;
duty, function, capacity. The ideogram: an animal with strong hooves and
bones, able to carry and defend. **Correct**, CHENG: rectify deviation or
one-sidedness; proper, straight, exact, regular; constant, rule, model. The
ideogram: stop and one, hold to one thing. **Purpose**, CHIH: focus of mind
and heart; will, inclination, resolve. The ideogram: heart and scholar, high
inner resolve, or heart and go, inner determination.

 Winnow, CHI: separate grain from chaff by tossing it in the wind;

separate the valuable from the worthless, good from bad; sieve, winnowing-basket; fan out. **Son(hood)**, TZU: living up to ideal of ancestors as highest human development; act with concern and reverence; male child; offspring, posterity; seed, kernel, egg; sage, teacher; nadir, deepest point, midnight, mid-winter.

This text evokes the troubled time at the end of the Shang Dynasty (1100 BCE) when the figures who were to found the new Chou Dynasty were oppressed or held captive.

The Pattern King is King Wen, a pattern of justice and wisdom and a master diviner. He was the founding figure of the new Chou dynasty and was imprisoned by the last Shang tyrant for his outspoken rectitude.

The Winnowing Son is Prince Chi, a model of moral discrimination. As a diviner serving the last Shang tyrant, he shone like a light in the darkness. He refused to serve the new Dynasty, but passed on his wisdom and experience of ritual. He thus carefully discriminated between moral integrity and personal advantage.

Legend has it that Keng Wen and Prince Chi composed the fundamental texts of the I CHING.

- *Transforming Lines*

   Initial nine

   a) **Brightness Hiding tending-towards flying.**
   Drooping one's wings.
   A chün tzu tending-towards moving:
   Three days, not taking-in.
   Possessing directed going.
   A lord: people possessing words.

   b) **A chün tzu tending-towards moving:**
   Righteously not taking-in indeed.

Associated Contexts a) **Tend-towards**, YÜ: move toward but not reach, in the direction of; contrasts with reach(-to), HU, actually arriving. **Fly**, FEI: spread your wings, fly away; let free; swift.

   Droop, CH'UI: hang down, let fall; bow; condescend to inferiors; almost, near; suspended; hand down from past to future. **Wings**, YI: birds' wings; sails, flanks, side-rooms; brood over, shelter and defend.

   Move, HSING: move or move something; motivate, emotionally moving; walk, act, do. The ideogram: stepping left then right.

Three, SAN: number three, third time or place; active phases of a cycle; superlative; beginning of repetition. **Day/sun**, JIH: actual sun and the time of a sun-cycle, a day. **Not**, PU: simple negative. **Take-in**, SHIH: eat, ingest, swallow, devour; incorporate.

Possessing directed going, YU YU WANG: imposing a direction on the flow of time from present to past; have a specific goal or purpose.

Lord, CHU: ruler, master, chief; authority. The ideogram: lamp and flame, giving light. **People, person**, JEN: humans individually and collectively; an individual; humankind. Image of Hexagrams 13 and 37. **Word**, YEN: speech, spoken words, sayings; talk, discuss, address. The ideogram: mouth and rising vapor, words as speech.

b) **Righteous**, YI: proper and just, meets the standards; things in their proper place; the heart that rules itself; upright, moral rule; contrasts with Harvest, LI, advantage or profit.

Six at-second

a) **Brightness Hiding. Hiding tending-towards the left thigh. Availing-of a rescuing horse, invigorating significant.**

b) **Six at-second's significance. Yielding used by-consequence indeed.**

Associated Contexts a) **Tend-towards**, YÜ: move toward but not reach, in the direction of; contrasts with reach(-to), HU, actually arriving. **Left**, TSO: left side, left hand; secondary; deputy, assistant; inferior. **Thigh**, KU: upper leg that provides power for walking; strands of a rope.

Rescue, CHENG: aid, deliver from trouble; pull out, raise up, lift. The ideogram: hand and aid, a helping hand. **Horse**, MA: symbol of spirited strength in the natural world, counterpart of dragon, LUNG; associated with the trigram Force, CH'IEN, heaven, T'IEN, and high noon. **Invigorate**, CHUANG: inspirit, animate; strong, robust; full grown, flourishing, abundant; attain manhood (at 30); damage through unrestrained strength. The ideogram: strength and scholar, intellectual impact. Image of Hexagram 34. **Significant**, CHI: leads to the experience of meaning; favorable, propitious, advantageous, appropriate; keyword. The ideogram: scholar and mouth, wise words of a sage.

b) **'s/have(-it)/it/them**, CHIH: expresses possession, directly or as an

object pronoun. **By-consequence(-of)**, TSE: very strong connection; reason, cause, result; rule, law, pattern, standard; therefore.

Nine at-third

a) **Brightness Hiding tending-towards the South, hounding.**
   Acquiring its great, the head.
   Not permitting affliction: Trial.

b) **The South: hounding's purpose.**
   Thereupon acquiring the great indeed.

Associated Contexts a) **Tend-towards**, YÜ: move toward but not reach, in the direction of; contrasts with reach(-to), HU, actually arriving. **South**, NAN: corresponds to summer, ´ ʼrowing, and the Fiery Moment; end of the yang hemicycle; reference point of compass; rulers face South, thus true principles and correct decisions. **Hound**, SHOU: hunt with dogs; annual winter hunt; pursue closely, press hard; burn dry fields to drive game; inspect the frontiers.

   Acquire, TE: obtain the desired object; wish for, desire covetously; gains, possessions. The ideogram: go and obstacle, going through obstacles to the goal. **Its/it**, CH'I: third person pronoun; also: one/one's, he/his, she/hers, they/theirs. **Head**, SHOU: literal head; leader, foremost; subject headings; beginning, model; superior, upper, front.

   Not permitting, PU K'O: not possible; contradicts an inherent principle. The ideogram: mouth and breath, silent consent. **Afflict**, CHI: sickness, disorder, defect, calamity; injurious; pressure and consequent anger, hate or dislike. The ideogram: sickness and dart, a sudden affliction.

b) **Thereupon**, NAI: on that ground, because of.

Six at-fourth

a) **Entering tending-towards the left belly.**
   Catching Brightness Hiding's heart.
   Tending-towards issuing-forth-from the gate chambers.

b) **Entering tending-towards the left belly.**
Catching the heart, intention indeed.

Associated Contexts a) **Tend-towards**, YÜ: move toward but not
reach, in the direction of; contrasts with reach(-to), HU, actually arriving.
Left belly, TSO FU: the belly contains the internal organs; also: middle,
thick, substantial; intimate, dear; left belly holds the heart and spleen,
organs considered the seat of emotional drives.

   Catch, HUO: take in hunt; catch a thief; obtain, seize; hit the mark,
opportune moment; prisoner, spoils, prey; slave, servant. **Heart**, HSIN:
heart as center of being; seat of mind's images and affections; moral
nature; source of desires, intentions, will.

   Issue-forth(-from), CH'U: emerge from, come out of, proceed from,
spring from; the Action of the trigram Shake, CHEN; contrary of enter,
JU. The ideogram: stem with branches and leaves emerging. **Gate**, MEN:
outer door, between court-yard and street; text or master as gate to a
school of thought. **Chambers**, T'ING: family room, courtyard, hall;
domestic. The ideogram: shelter and hall, a secure place.

b) **Intention**, YI: thought, meaning, idea, will, motive; what gives words
their significance. The ideogram: heart and sound, heartfelt expression.

Six at-fifth

a) **The winnowing son's Brightness Hiding.**
Harvesting Trial.

b) **The winnowing son's Trial.**
Brightness not permitted to pause indeed.

Associated Contexts a) **'s/have(-it)/it/them**, CHIH: expresses
possession, directly or as an object pronoun.

   Harvesting Trial, LI CHEN: advantageous divination; fruit of an
action is a test or trial.

b) **Not permitting**, PU K'O: not possible; contradicts an inherent
principle. The ideogram: mouth and breath, silent consent. **Pause**, HSI:
stop and rest, repose; breathe, a breathing-spell; suspended.

Six above

a) **Not Brightening, darkening.**
Initially mounting tending-towards heaven.
Afterwards entering tending-towards earth.

b) **Initially mounting tending-towards heaven.**
Illuminating the four cities indeed.
Afterwards entering tending-towards earth.
Letting-go by-consequence indeed.

Associated Contexts a) **Not**, PU: simple negative. **Initial**, CH'U: first step or part; beginning, incipient; bottom line of hexagram. The ideogram: knife and garment, cutting out the pattern. **Mount**, TENG: ascend, step up; ripen, complete. **Tend-towards**, YÜ: move toward but not reach, in the direction of; contrasts with reach(-to), HU, actually arriving. **Heaven**, T'IEN: highest; sky, firmament, heavens; power above the human as opposed to earth, TI, below; the Symbol of the trigram Force, CH'IEN. The ideogram: great and the one above.

After(wards)/later, HOU: come after in time, subsequent; put oneself after; the second; attendants, heirs, successors, posterity.

b) **Illuminate**, CHAO: shine light on; enlighten, reflect: care for, supervise. The ideogram: fire and brightness. **Four**, SSU: number four, fourth; everywhere, all around; the earth with four sides, FANG. **City**, KUO: area of only human constructions; political unit, polis. First of the territorial zones: city, suburbs, countryside, forests.

Let-go, SHIH: lose, omit, miss, fail, let slip; out of control. The ideogram: drop from the hand. **By-consequence(-of)**, TSE: very strong connection; reason, cause, result; rule, law, pattern, standard; therefore.

37

DWELLING PEOPLE ▪ *CHIA JEN*

This hexagram describes your situation in terms of living and working with others in a common space. It emphasizes that caring for your relation with those who share this space and for the space itself is the adequate way to handle it. To be in accord with the time, you are told to: **dwell** with **people**!

- *Image of the Situation*

  Dwelling People, Harvesting: woman Trial.

  Associated Contexts **Dwell**, CHI: home, house, household, family; domestic, within doors; live in. The ideogram: roof and pig or dog, the most valued domestic animals. **People, person**, JEN: humans individually and collectively; an individual; humankind. **Harvest**, LI: advantageous, profitable; acute, insightful; benefit, nourish; third stage of the Time Cycle. **Woman(hood)**, NÜ: a woman; what is inherently female. **Trial**, CHEN: test by ordeal; inquiry by divination and its result; righteous, firm; separating wheat from chaff; the kernel, the proven core; fourth stage of the Time Cycle. The ideogram: pearl and divination.

- *Outer and Inner Aspects*

  ☴ **Ground**: Wind and wood subtly enter from the ground, penetrating and pervading. **Ground** is the center of the yang hemicycle, spreading pervasive action.

  Connection to the outer: penetrating and bringing together, the Woody Moment culminating. **Ground** pervades, matches and couples, seeding a new generation.

  ☲ **Radiance**: Fire and brightness radiate light and warmth, attached to their support; congregating people see and become aware. **Radiance** ends the yang hemicycle, consuming action in awareness.

  Connection to the inner: light, heat, consciousness bring about continual change, the Fiery Moment. **Radiance** spreads outward, congregating, becoming aware and changing.

Warm awareness inside the **dwelling** brings **people** together through gentle penetration.

- *Counter Indications*

Nuclear trigrams **Radiance**, LI, and **Gorge**, K'AN, result in Counter Hexagram 64, **Not-yet Fording**, WEI CHI. **People's** sense of being in the right place in their **dwelling** is contrasted with **not-yet fording** to an adequate situation.

- *Sequence*

> **Injury with-respect-to the outside implies**
> **necessarily reversing with-respect-to Dwelling.**
> **Anterior acquiescence has the use-of Dwelling People.**

Associated Contexts **Injure**, SHANG: hurt, wound, grieve, distress; mourn, sad at heart, humiliated. **With-respect-to**, YÜ: relates to, refers to; hold a position in. **Outside**, WAI: outer, exterior, external; people working in places other than their home; unfamiliar, foreign; the upper trigram, as opposed to inside, NEI, the lower. **Imply**, CHE: further signify; additional meaning. **Necessarily**, PI: unavoidably, indispensably, certainly. **Reverse**, FAN: turn and move in the opposite direction; turn around or upside down (180 degrees); change to the opposite position; contrary.

Anterior ... the use-of: activating this hexagram depends on understanding and accepting the previous statement.

- *Contrasted Definitions*

> **Polarizing: outside indeed.**
> **Dwelling People: inside indeed.**

Associated Contexts **Polarize**, K'UEI: separate, oppose; contrary, mutually exclusive; distant from, absent, remote; animosity, anger; astronomical or polar opposition: the ends of an axis, 180 degrees apart. Image of Hexagram 38. **Indeed**, YEH: intensifier; indicates comment on previous statement.

Inside, NEI: within, inner, interior; inside of the house and those who work there, particularly women; the lower trigram, as opposed to outside, WAI, the upper. The ideogram: border and enter, cross a border.

- *Symbol Tradition*

> **Wind originating-from fire issuing-forth. Dwelling People.**
> **A chün tzu uses words to possess beings and-also**
> > **movement to possess perseverance.**

Associated Contexts **Wind**, FENG: moving air, breeze, gust; weather and its influence on mood and humor; fashion, usage; wind and wood are the Symbols of the trigram Ground, SUN. **Origin**, TZU: source, beginning, ground; cause, reason, motive; line of descent; path to the origin; yourself, intrinsic. **Fire**, HUO: warming and consuming aspect of burning; fire and brightness are the Symbols of the trigram Radiance, LI. **Issue-forth(-from)**, CH'U: emerge from, come out of, proceed from, spring from; the Action of the trigram Shake, CHEN; contrary of enter, JU. The ideogram: stem with branches and leaves emerging.

Chün tzu: ideal of a person who uses divination to order his/her life in accordance with tao rather than wilful intention; keyword. **Use(-of)**, YI: make use of, by means of, owing to; employ, make functional. **Word**, YEN: speech, spoken words, sayings; talk, discuss, address. The ideogram: mouth and rising vapor, words as speech. **Possess**, YU: in possession of, have, own; opposite of lack, WU. **Being(s)**, WU: creature, thing, any single being; matter, substance, essence; nature of things. **And-also**, ERH: joins and contrasts two terms. **Move**, HSING: move or move something; motivate, emotionally moving; walk, act, do. The ideogram: stepping left then right. **Persevere**, HENG: continue in the same way or spirit; constant, perpetual, regular; self-renewing; extend everywhere. Image of Hexagram 32.

- *Image Tradition*

> **Dwelling People. [I]**
> **The woman correcting the situation reaching-to the inside.**
> **The man correcting the situation reaching-to the outside.**
> **Man[and]Woman correcting.**
> **Heaven[and]Earth's great righteousness indeed.**

Dwelling People possess an intimidating chief in-truth. [II]
Father[and]Mother's designating indeed.
The father, a father. The son, a son.
The senior, a senior. The junior, a junior.
The husband, a husband. The wife, a wife.
And-also Dwelling tao correcting.
Actually correcting Dwelling and-also Below Heaven set-right.

Associated Contexts [I] **Correct**, CHENG: rectify deviation or one-sidedness; proper, straight, exact, regular; constant, rule, model. The ideogram: stop and one, hold to one thing. **Situation**, WEI: place or seat according to rank; post, position, command; right, proper; established, arranged. The ideogram: person and stand, servants in their places. **Reach(-to)**, HU: arrive at a goal; reach towards and achieve; connect; contrasts with tend-towards, YU.

Man(hood), NAN: a man; what is inherently male. The ideogram: fields and strength, hard labor in the fields.

Man[and]Woman, NAN NÜ: creative relation between what is inherently male and what is inherently female.

Heaven[and]Earth, T'IEN TI: dynamic relation between the primal powers and the world it produces; cosmos, natural or human world; keyword. **'s/have(-it)/it/them**, CHIH: expresses possession, directly or as an object pronoun. **Great**, TA: big, noble, important, very; orient the will toward a self-imposed goal, impose direction; ability to lead or guide your life; contrasts with small, HSIAO, flexible adaptation to what crosses your path; keyword. Image of Hexagrams 14, 26, 28, 34. **Righteous**, YI: proper and just, meets the standards; things in their proper place; the heart that rules itself; upright, moral rule; contrasts with Harvest, LI, advantage or profit.

[II] **Intimidate**, YEN: inspire with fear or awe; severe, rigid, strict, austere, demanding; a severe father; tight, a closed door. **Chief**, CHÜN: effective ruler; preside over, take the lead; influence others; term of respect. The ideogram: mouth and director, giving orders. **In-truth**, YEN: statement is complete and correct.

Father[and]Mother, FU MU: cooperative relation between man and woman in ruling and caring for a family. **Designate**, WEI: represent in words, assign a name or meaning; report on, talk about. The ideogram: words and belly, describing the essential.

Father, FU: ruler of the family; act as a father, paternal, patriarchal; authoritative rule. The ideogram: hand and rod, the chastising father. **Son(hood)**, TZU: living up to ideal of ancestors as highest human development; act with concern and reverence; male child; offspring, posterity; seed, kernel, egg; sage, teacher; nadir, deepest point, midnight, mid-winter.

Senior, HSIUNG: elder; recognized as one to whom respect is due. **Junior**, TI: younger relatives who owe respect to their elders.

Husband, FU: household manager; administer with thrift and prudence; responsible for; sustain with your earnings; old enough to assume responsibility; married man. **Wife**, FU: responsible position of married woman within the household; contrasts with consort, CH'I, her legal position and concubine, CH'IEH, secondary wives. The ideogram: woman, hand and broom, household duties.

Tao: way or path; ongoing process of being and the course it traces for each specific person or thing; keyword. The ideogram: go and head, leading and the path it creates.

Actually, YI: truly, really, at present. The ideogram: a dart and done, strong intention fully expressed. **Below Heaven**, T'IEN HSIA: the human world, between heaven and earth. **Set-right**, TING: settle, fix, put in place; at rest, repose.

● *Transforming Lines*

Initial nine

a) **Enclosing: possessing Dwelling.**
Repenting extinguished.

b) **Enclosing: possessing Dwelling.**
Purpose not-yet transformed indeed.

Associated Contexts a) **Enclose**, HSIEN: put inside a fence or barrier; restrain, obstruct, forbid; pen, corral.

Repenting extinguished, HUI WANG: previous troubles and consequent remorse will disappear.

b) **Purpose**, CHIH: focus of mind and heart; will, inclination, resolve. The ideogram: heart and scholar, high inner resolve, or heart and go, inner determination. **Not-yet**, WEI: temporal negative; something will but has

not yet occurred; contrary of already, CHI. Image of Hexagram 64. **Transform**, PIEN: abrupt, radical, fundamental mutation from one state of being to another; transformation of lines in hexagrams; contrasts with change, HUA, gradual metamorphosis.

Six at-second

a) **Without direction, releasing.**
Locating the center, feeding.
Trial: significant.

b) **Six at-second's significance.**
Yielding uses Ground indeed.

Associated Contexts a) **Without**, WU: devoid of; -less as suffix. **Direct**, YU: move toward a specific place or goal; have a focus. The ideogram: person moving through or over water, direction without visible landmarks. **Release**, SUI: loose, let go, free; unhindered, in accord; follow, spread out, progress; penetrate, invade. The ideogram: go and follow your wishes, unimpeded movement.

Locate(-in), TSAI: live in, dwell, reside; belong to, involved with, depend on; within. The ideogram: earth and persevere, place on the earth. **Center**, CHUNG: inner, central; put in the center; middle, stable point enabling you to face inner and outer changes; middle line of trigram. The ideogram: field divided in two equal parts. Image of Hexagram 61. **Feed**, K'UEI: prepare and present food; provisions.

Significant, CHI: leads to the experience of meaning; favorable, propitious, advantageous, appropriate; keyword. The ideogram: scholar and mouth, wise words of a sage.

b) **Yield(-to)**, SHUN: give way and bear produce; comply, agree, follow, obey; unresisting, docile, flexible; nourish, provide; the Action of the trigram Field, K'UN. The ideogram: head and current, water flowing from the head of a river, yielding to the banks. **Ground**, SUN: base on which things rest; support, foundation; mild, subtly penetrating; nourishing. The ideogram: stand and things arranged on it, the subtle influence of the ground. Image of Hexagram 57.

Nine at-third

a) Dwelling People, scolding, scolding:
  Repenting, adversity significant.
  The wife, the son, giggling, giggling:
  Completing abashed.

b) Dwelling People, scolding, scolding:
  Not-yet letting-go indeed.
  The wife, the son, giggling, giggling:
  Letting-go Dwelling articulating indeed.

Associated Contexts a) **Scold**, HO: rebuke, blame, demand and enforce obedience; severe, stern. The doubled character intensifies this quality.

Repent, HUI: dissatisfaction with past conduct causing a change of heart; proceeds from abashment, LIN, shame and confusion at having lost the right way. **Adversity**, LI: danger; threatening, malevolent demon. This has two aspects: grind, sharpen, improve, perfect, stimulate; and: poisonous, sinister, cruel, contrary. It indicates a spirit or ghost that seeks revenge by inflicting suffering upon the living. Pacifying or exorcizing such a spirit can have a healing effect. The ideogram: sheltering cliff and stinging insect. **Significant**, CHI: leads to the experience of meaning; favorable, propitious, advantageous, appropriate; keyword. The ideogram: scholar and mouth, wise words of a sage.

Giggle, HSI: laugh or titter uncontrollably; merriment, delight, surprise; foolish.

Complete, CHUNG: end of a cycle that begins the next; last, whole, all; contrasts with exhaust, CH'IUNG: final end. The ideogram: silk cocoons, follow and ice, winter linking one year with the next. **Abashment**, LIN: distress, shame, regret, humiliation; aware of having lost the right track; leads to repenting, HUI, correcting the direction of mind and life.

b) **Not-yet**, WEI: temporal negative; something will but has not yet occurred; contrary of already, CHI. Image of Hexagram 64. **Let-go**, SHIH: lose, omit, miss, fail, let slip; out of control. The ideogram: drop from the hand.

Articulate, CHIEH: separate and distinguish, as well as join, different things; express thought through speech; joint, section, chapter, interval,

unit of time; zodiacal sign; moderate, regulate; lit.: nodes on bamboo stalks. Image of Hexagram 60.

Six at-fourth

a) **Affluence Dwelling, the great significant.**

b) **Affluence Dwelling, the great significant.**
Yielding located-in the situation indeed.

Associated Contexts a) **Affluence**, FU: rich, abundant; wealth; enrich, provide for; flow toward, accrue. **Significant**, CHI: leads to the experience of meaning; favorable, propitious, advantageous, appropriate; keyword. The ideogram: scholar and mouth, wise words of a sage.

b) **Yield(-to)**, SHUN: give way and bear produce; comply, agree, follow, obey; unresisting, docile, flexible; nourish, provide; the Action of the trigram Field, K'UN. The ideogram: head and current, water flowing from the head of a river, yielding to the banks. **Locate(-in)**, TSAI: live in, dwell, reside; belong to, involved with, depend on; within. The ideogram: earth and persevere, place on the earth.

Nine at-fifth

a) **The king imagines possessing a Dwelling.**
Beings: care significant.

b) **The king imagines possessing a Dwelling.**
Mingling mutual affection indeed.

Associated Contexts a) **King(hood)**, WANG: effective ruler, by authority of the Emperor, from whom others derive their power. **Imagine**, CHIA: create in the mind; fantasize, suppose, pretend, imitate; fiction; illusory, unreal; costume. The ideogram: person and borrow.
 Care, HSÜ: fear, doubt, concern; heartfelt attachment; relieve, soothe, aid; sympathy, compassion, consolation. The ideogram: heart and blood, the heart's blood affected. **Significant**, CHI: leads to the experience of meaning; favorable, propitious, advantageous, appropriate; keyword. The ideogram: scholar and mouth, wise words of a sage.

b) **Mingle**, CHIAO: blend with, communicate, join, exchange; trade, business; copulation; friendship. **Mutual**, HSIANG: reciprocal assistance, encourage, help; bring together, blend with; examine, inspect; by turns. **Affection**, AI: love, show affection; benevolent feelings; kindness, regard.

Nine above

a) **Possessing conformity, impressing thus.**
   Completing significant.

b) **Impressing thus: having significance.**
   Reversing individuality's designating indeed.

Associated Contexts a) **Possessing conformity**, YU FU: inner and outer are in accord; confidence of the spirits has been captured; sincere, truthful; proper to take action. **Impress**, WEI: impose on, intimidate; august, solemn; pomp, majesty. **Thus**, JU: as, in this way.

   Complete, CHUNG: end of a cycle that begins the next; last, whole, all; contrasts with exhaust, CH'IUNG, final end. The ideogram: silk cocoons, follow and ice, winter linking one year with the next. **Significant**, CHI: leads to the experience of meaning; favorable, propitious, advantageous, appropriate; keyword. The ideogram: scholar and mouth, wise words of a sage.

b) **Individuality**, SHEN: total person: psyche, body and lifespan; character, virtue, duty; contrasts with body, KUNG, physical being.

38

POLARIZING, ▪ *K'UEI*

This hexagram describes your situation in terms of things that are connected but should not join. It emphasizes that putting things in opposition while acknowledging their essential link is the adequate way to handle it. To be in accord with the time, you are told to: **polarize**!

- *Image of the Situation*

   Polarizing, Small Affairs significant.

   Associated Contexts **Polarize**, K'UEI: separate, oppose; contrary, mutually exclusive; distant from, absent, remote; animosity, anger; astronomical or polar opposition: the ends of an axis, 180 degrees apart. **Small**, HSIAO: little, common, unimportant; adapting to what crosses your path; ability to move in harmony with the vicissitudes of life; contrasts with great, TA, self-imposed theme or goal; keyword. Image of Hexagrams 9 and 62. **Affairs**, SHIH: all kinds of personal activity; matters at hand; business, occupation; manage a business, case in court. **Significant**, CHI: leads to the experience of meaning; favorable, propitious, advantageous, appropriate; keyword. The ideogram: scholar and mouth, wise words of a sage.

- *Outer and Inner Aspects*

   ☲ **Radiance**: Fire and brightness radiate light and warmth, attached to their support; congregating people see and become aware. **Radiance** ends the yang hemicycle, consuming action in awareness.
      Connection to the outer: light, heat, consciousness bring continual change, the Fiery Moment. **Radiance** spreads outward, congregating, becoming aware and changing.

   ☱ **Open**: vapor rising from the marsh's open surface stimulates and fertilizes; stimulating words cheer and inspire. **Open** begins the yin hemicycle by initiating the formative process.

Connection to the inner: liquifying, casting, skinning off the mold, the Metallic Moment beginning. **Open** stimulates, cheers and reveals innate form.

The conflict between inner form and outer radiance **polarizes** relationships.

● *Counter Indications*

Nuclear trigrams **Gorge**, K'AN, and **Radiance**, LI, result in Counter Hexagram 63, **Already Fording**, CHI CHI. The intense opposition in **polarizing** is contrasted with the resolved tensions of **already fording**.

● *Sequence*

> **Dwelling tao exhausted, necessarily turning-away.**
> **Anterior acquiescence has the use-of Polarizing.**
> **Polarizing implies turning-away indeed.**

Associated Contexts **Dwell**, CHI: home, house, household, family; domestic, within doors; live in. The ideogram: roof and pig or dog, the most valued domestic animals. Image of Hexagram 37. **Tao**: way or path; ongoing process of being and the course it traces for each specific person or thing; keyword. The ideogram: go and head, leading and the path it creates. **Exhaust**, CH'IUNG: bring to an end; limit, extremity; destitute; investigate exhaustively; end without a new beginning. The ideogram: cave and naked person, bent with disease or old age. **Necessarily**, PI: unavoidably, indispensably, certainly. **Turn-away**, KUAI: turn your back on something and focus on its opposite; contradict, cross purposes; cunning, crafty; perverse; contrasts with return, FU, going back to the start.

Anterior ... the use-of: activating this hexagram depends on understanding and accepting the previous statement.

Imply, CHE: further signify; additional meaning. **Indeed**, YEH: intensifier; indicates comment on previous statement.

- *Contrasted Definitions*

> **Polarizing: outside indeed.**
> **Dwelling People: inside indeed.**

Associated Contexts **Outside**, WAI: outer, exterior, external; people working in places other than their home; unfamiliar, foreign; the upper trigram, as opposed to inside, NEI, the lower.

People, person, JEN: humans individually and collectively; an individual; humankind. **Dwelling People** is the Image of Hexagram 37. **Inside**, NEI: within, inner, interior; inside of the house and those who work there, particularly women; the lower trigram, as opposed to outside, WAI, the upper. The ideogram: border and enter, cross a border.

- *Symbol Tradition*

> **Fire above, marsh below. Polarizing.**
> **A chün tzu uses concording and-also dividing.**

Associated Contexts **Fire**, HUO: warming and consuming aspect of burning; fire and brightness are the Symbols of the trigram Radiance, LI. **Above**, SHANG: anything above, in all senses; higher, upper, outer; upper trigram; opposite of below, HSIA. **Marsh**, TSE: open surface of a flat body of water and the vapors rising from it; fertilize, enrich; kindness, favor; the Symbol of the trigram Open, TUI. **Below**, HSIA: anything below, in all senses; lower, inner; lower trigram; opposite of above, SHANG.

Chün tzu: ideal of a person who uses divination to order his/her life in accordance with tao rather than wilful intention; keyword. **Use(-of)**, YI: make use of, by means of, owing to; employ, make functional. **Concord**, T'UNG: harmonize, unite, equalize, assemble; agree, share in; together, at once, same time and place. The ideogram: cover and mouth, silent understanding and perfect fit. Image of Hexagram 13. **And-also**, ERH: joins and contrasts two terms. **Divide**, YI: separate, break apart, sever; oppose; different, foreign, strange, unusual, rare.

● *Image Tradition*

Polarizing. [I]
Fire stirring-up and-also above.
Marsh stirring-up and-also below.

Two women concording: residing. [II]
Their purposes not concording: moving.
Stimulating and-also congregating reaching-to brightness.

Supple advancing and-also moving above. [III]
Acquiring the center and-also corresponding reaching the solid.
That uses Small Affairs significant.

Heaven, Earth, Polarizing and-also one's affairs
                                            concording indeed. [IV]
Man, Woman, Polarizing and-also
                            their purposes interpenetrating indeed.
The myriad beings Polarizing and-also their affairs sorted indeed.
Actually Polarizing's season availing-of the great in-fact.

Associated Contexts **[I] Stir-up**, TUNG: excite, influence, move, affect; work, take action; come out of the egg or the bud; the Action of the trigram Shake, CHEN. The ideogram: strength and heavy, move weighty things.

[II] Two, ERH: pair, even numbers, binary, duplicate. **Woman(hood)**, NÜ: a woman; what is inherently female. **Reside(-in)**, CHÜ: dwell, live in, stay; sit down, fill an office; settled parts of a country. The ideogram: body and seat.

   Their/they, CH'I: third person pronoun; also: one/one's, it/its, he/his, she/hers. **Purpose**, CHIH: focus of mind and heart; will, inclination, resolve. The ideogram: heart and scholar, high inner resolve, or heart and go, inner determination. **Not**, PU: simple negative. **Move**, HSING: move or move something; motivate, emotionally moving; walk, act, do. The ideogram: stepping left then right.

   Stimulate, SHUO: rouse to action and good feeling; free from constraint, stir up, urge on; persuade, cheer, delight; set out in words; the Action of the trigram Open, TUI. The ideogram: words and exchange. **Congregate**, LI: cling together; depend on, attached to, rely on; couple, pair, herd; the Action of the trigram Radiance, LI. The ideogram: deer

flocking together. **Reach(-to)**, HU: arrive at a goal; reach toward and achieve; connect; contrasts with tend-towards, YU. **Brightness**, MING: light-giving aspect of burning, heavenly bodies and consciousness; with fire, the Symbol of the trigram Radiance, LI.

[III] Supple, JOU: quality of the opened lines; flexible, pliant, tender, adaptable. **Advance**, CHIN: exert yourself, make progress, climb; be promoted; further the development of, augment; adopt a religion or conviction; offer, introduce.

    Acquire, TE: obtain the desired object; wish for, desire covetously; gains, possessions. The ideogram: go and obstacle, going through obstacles to the goal. **Center**, CHUNG: inner, central; put in the center; middle, stable point enabling you to face inner and outer changes; middle line of trigram. The ideogram: field divided in two equal parts. Image of Hexagram 61. **Correspond(-to)**, YING: be in agreement or harmony; resonate together, invoke and fulfill each other; answer to, suitable; relation between the lines (1:4, 2:5, 3:6) when they form the pair opened and whole, supple and solid. The ideogram: heart and obey. **Solid**, KANG: quality of the whole lines; firm, strong, unyielding, persisting.

    That uses, SHIH YI: involves and is involved by.

[IV] Heaven, T'IEN: highest; sky, firmament, heavens; power above the human as opposed to earth, TI, below; the Symbol of the trigram Force, CH'IEN. The ideogram: great and the one above. **Earth**, TI: ground on which the human world rests; basis of all things, nourishes all things; the Symbol of the trigram Field, K'UN. **One's/one**, CH'I: third person pronoun; also: it/its, he/his, she/hers, they/theirs. **Man(hood)**, NAN: a man; what is inherently male. The ideogram: fields and strength, hard labor in the fields. **Interpenetrate**, T'UNG: mutually penetrate; permeate, flow through, reach everywhere; see clearly, communicate with.

    Myriad, WAN: countless; many, everyone; lit.: ten thousand. The ideogram: swarm of insects. **Being(s)**, WU: creature, thing, any single being; matter, substance, essence; nature of things. **Sort**, LEI: group according to kind, class with; like nature or purpose; species, class, genus.

    Actually ... in-fact, YI TSAI: stresses the importance of a statement. The ideogram: a dart and done, strong intention fully expressed. **'s/have(-it)/it/them**, CHIH: expresses possession, directly or as an object pronoun. **Season**, SHIH: quality of the time; the right time, opportune, in harmony; planning in accord with the time; seasons of the year. The ideogram: sun and temple, time as sacred. **Avail-of**, YUNG: take advantage of; benefit from, profit by; use for a specific purpose; apply to advantage. The ideogram: to divine and center, applying divination to central concerns. **Great**, TA: big, noble, important, very; orient the will toward a self-imposed goal, impose direction; ability to lead or guide your life; contrasts with small, HSIAO, flexible adaptation to what crosses your path; keyword. Image of Hexagrams 14, 26, 28, 34.

- *Transforming Lines*

  Initial nine

  a) **Repenting extinguished.**
  Losing the horse, no pursuit, originating-from returning.
  Visualizing hateful people.
  Without fault.

  b) **Visualizing hateful people.**
  Using casting-out fault indeed.

  Associated Contexts a) **Repenting extinguished**, HUI WANG: previous troubles and consequent remorse will disappear.
  Lose, SANG: fail to obtain, cease, become obscure; forgotten, destroyed; lament, mourn; funeral. The ideogram: weep and the dead. **Horse**, MA: symbol of spirited strength in the natural world, counterpart of dragon, LUNG; associated with the trigram Force, CH'IEN, heaven, T'IEN, and high noon. **No**, WU: simple negative; un-, dis-. **Pursue**, CHU: chase, follow closely, press hard; expel, drive out. The ideogram: pig (wealth) and go, chasing fortune. **Origin**, TZU: source, beginning, ground; cause, reason, motive; line of descent; path to the origin; yourself, intrinsic. **Return**, FU: go back, turn back to the starting point; recur, reappear, come again; restore, recover, retrace; an earlier time or place. The ideogram: step and retrace a path. Image of Hexagram 24.
  Visualize, CHIEN: seeing in all its aspects: vision, being visible, forming mental images; visit, call on, consult. The ideogram: eye above person, active and receptive sight. **Hate**, WU: dislike, dread; averse to, ashamed of; repulsive, vicious, vile, ugly, wicked. The ideogram: twisted bowels and heart, heart entangled in emotion.
  Without fault, WU CHIU: no error or harm in the situation.

b) **Cast-out**, P'I: expel, repress, exclude, punish; exclusionary laws and their enforcement. The ideogram: punish, authority and mouth, give orders to expel. **Fault**, CHIU: unworthy conduct that leads to harm, illness, misfortune. The ideogram: person and differ, differ from what you should be.

Nine at-second

a) **Meeting a lord, tending-towards the street.**
   Without fault.

b) **Meeting a lord, tending-towards the street.**
   Not-yet letting-go tao indeed.

Associated Contexts *a)* **Meet**, YÜ: come on unexpectedly, encounter; occur, happen; pleasant meeting, lucky coincidence; agree. **Lord**, CHU: ruler, master, chief; authority. The ideogram: lamp and flame, giving light. **Tend-towards**, YÜ: move toward but not reach, in the direction of; contrasts with reach(-to), HU, actually arriving. **Street**, HSIANG: public space between dwellings, public square; side-street, alley, lane. The ideogram: place and public.
   Without fault, WU CHIU: no error or harm in the situation.

b) **Not-yet**, WEI: temporal negative; something will but has not yet occurred; contrary of already, CHI. Image of Hexagram 64. **Let-go**, SHIH: lose, omit, miss, fail, let slip; out of control. The ideogram: drop from the hand.

Six at-third

a) **Visualizing the cart pulled-back.**
   One's cattle hampered.
   One's person stricken, moreover nose-cut.
   Without initially possessing completion.

b) **Visualizing the cart pulled-back.**
   Situation not appropriate indeed.
   Without initially possessing completion.
   Meeting a solid indeed.

Associated Contexts a) **Visualize**, CHIEN: seeing in all its aspects: vision, being visible, forming mental images; visit, call on, consult. The ideogram: eye above person, active and receptive sight. **Cart**, YÜ: carrying capacity of a vehicle; contain, hold, sustain. **Pull-back**, YI: pull or drag something toward you; drag behind, take by the hand; leave traces.

One's/one, CH'I: third person pronoun; also: it/its, he/his, she/hers, they/theirs. **Cattle**, NIU: ox, bull, cow, calf; kine; power and strength of work animals. **Hamper**, CH'E: hinder, obstruct, hold or pull back; embarrass; select. The ideogram: hand and limit, grasp and control.

Stricken, YAO: afflicted by fate; untimely, premature death; tender, delicate, young; pleasing. The ideogram: great with a broken point, interrupted growth. **Moreover**, CH'IEH: further, and also. **Nose-cutting**, YI: punish through loss of public face or honor; contrasts with foot-cutting, YÜEH, crippling punishment for serious crime.

Without, WU: devoid of; -less as suffix. **Initial**, CH'U: first step or part; beginning, incipient; bottom line of hexagram. The ideogram: knife and garment, cutting out the pattern. **Possess**, YU: in possession of, have, own; opposite of lack, WU. **Complete**, CHUNG: end of a cycle that begins the next; last, whole, all; contrasts with exhaust, CH'IUNG, final end. The ideogram: silk cocoons, follow and ice, winter linking one year with the next.

b) **Situation**, WEI: place or seat according to rank; post, position, command; right, proper; established, arranged. The ideogram: person and stand, servants in their places. **Appropriate**, TANG: suitable; opportune, convenient; adequate, competent; equal to; whole lines in uneven places and opened lines in even places.

Meet, YÜ: come on unexpectedly, encounter; occur, happen; pleasant meeting, lucky coincidence; agree.

Nine at-fourth

a) Polarizing alone.
  Meeting Spring, husbanding.
  Mingling conforming.

b) Adversity, without fault.
  Mingling conforming, without fault.
  Purpose moving indeed.

Associated Contexts a) **Alone**, KU: solitary; without a protector; fatherless, orphan-like; as a title: the only, unequalled.

Meet, YÜ: come on unexpectedly, encounter; occur, happen; pleasant meeting, lucky coincidence; agree. **Spring**, YÜAN: source, origin, head; great, excellent; arise, begin, generating power; first stage of the Time Cycle. **Husband**, FU: household manager; administer with thrift and prudence; responsible for; sustain with your earnings; old enough to assume responsibility; married man.

Mingle, CHIAO: blend with, communicate, join, exchange; trade, business; copulation; friendship. **Conforming**, FU: accord between inner and outer in a particular moment; sincere, truthful, verified, reliable, in accord with the spirits; capture; prisoners, spoils; contrasts with trustworthy, HSIN, consistent over time. The ideogram: bird's claw enclosing young animals, possessive grip.

b) **Adversity**, LI: danger; threatening, malevolent demon. This has two aspects: grind, sharpen, improve, perfect, stimulate; and: poisonous, sinister, cruel, contrary. It indicates a spirit or ghost that seeks revenge by inflicting suffering upon the living. Pacifying or exorcizing such a spirit can have a healing effect. The ideogram: sheltering cliff and stinging insect. **Without fault**, WU CHIU: no error or harm in the situation.

Six at-fifth

a) **Repenting extinguished.**
   Your ancestor gnawing flesh.
   Going wherefore faulty?

b) **Your ancestor gnawing flesh.**
 — **Going possessing reward indeed.**

Associated Contexts a) **Repenting extinguished**, HUI WANG: previous troubles and consequent remorse will disappear.

Your, CHÜEH: intensifying personal pronoun, specifically you! your!; intensify, concentrate, tense, contract; lit.: muscle spasms. **Ancestry**, TSUNG: clan, kin, origin; those who bear the same surname; ancestral hall and tablets; honor, revere; a doctrine; contrasts with predecessor, K'AO, individual ancestors. **Gnaw**, SHIH: bite away, chew; bite persistently and remove; snap at, nibble; reach the essential by removing the unnecessary. The ideogram: mouth and divination, revealing the essential. Image of Hexagram 21. **Flesh**, FU: muscles, organs, skin, in contrast to bones.

Go, WANG, and come, LAI, describe the stream of time as it flows from future through present to past; go, WANG, indicates what is departing from present to past; proceed, move on; keyword. **Wherefore**, HO: interrogative: why? for what reason? what is? and affirmation: therefore, for that reason. **Fault**, CHIU: unworthy conduct that leads to harm, illness, misfortune. The ideogram: person and differ, differ from what you should be.

b) **Possess**, YU: in possession of, have, own; opposite of lack, WU. **Reward**, CH'ING: gift given from gratitude or benevolence; favor from heaven; congratulate with gifts. The ideogram: heart, follow and deer (wealth), the heart expressed through gifts.

Nine above

a) **Polarizing alone.**
  Visualizing pigs bearing mire.
  Carrying souls, the-one chariot.
  Beforehand stretching's bow.
  Afterwards stimulating's bow.
  In-no-way outlawry, matrimonial allying.
  Going meeting rain, by-consequence significant.

b) **Meeting rain's significance.**
  The flock, doubt extinguished indeed.

Associated Contexts a) **Alone**, KU: solitary; without a protector; fatherless, orphan-like; as a title: the only, unequalled.
  Visualize, CHIEN: seeing in all its aspects: vision, being visible, forming mental images; visit, call on, consult. The ideogram: eye above person, active and receptive sight. **Pig**, SHIH: all swine; sign of wealth and good fortune; associated with the Streaming Moment. **Bear**, FU: carry on your back; take on a responsibility; rely on, depend on; loaded down; burden, duty; math term for minus. **Mire**, T'U: mud, dirt, filth; besmear, blot out; stupid, pig-headed. The ideogram: earth and water.
  Carry, TSAI: bear, carry with you; contain, sustain; load a ship or cart, cargo; fill in, complete. **Soul**, KUEI: power that creates individual existence; union of volatile-soul, HUN, spiritual and intellectual power, and dense-soul, P'O, bodily strength and movement. The HUN rises after death, the P'O remains with the body and may communicate with the living. **One, the-one**, YI: single unit; number one; undivided, simple,

whole; any one of; first, the first. **Chariot**, CH'E: wheeled travelling vehicle; contrasts with cart, YÜ, which carries.

Before(hand)/earlier, HSIEN: come before in time; first, at first; formerly, past, previous; begin, go ahead of. **Stretch**, CHANG: draw a bow taut; open, extend, spread, display; make much of. **Bow**, HU: wooden bow; curved flag pole; curved, arched.

After(wards)/later, HOU: come after in time, subsequent; put oneself after; the second; attendant, heirs, successors, posterity.

In-no-way, FEI: strong negative; not so. The ideogram: a box filled with opposition. **Outlawry**, K'OU: break the laws; violent people, outcasts, bandits. **Matrimonial allying**, HUN KOU: legal institution of marriage; make alliances through marriage rather than force.

Go, WANG, and come, LAI, describe the stream of time as it flows from future through present to past; go, WANG, indicates what is departing from present to past; proceed, move on; keyword. **Meet**, YÜ: come on unexpectedly, encounter; occur, happen; pleasant meeting, lucky coincidence; agree. **Rain**, YÜ: all precipitation; sudden showers, fast and furious; associated with the trigram Gorge, K'AN, and the Streaming Moment. **By-consequence(-of)**, TSE: very strong connection; reason, cause, result; rule, law, pattern, standard; therefore.

b) **Flock**, CH'ÜN: herd, group; people of same kind, friends, equals; all, entire; move in unison, flock together. The ideogram: chief and sheep, flock around a leader. **Doubt**, YI: suspect, distrust; dubious; surmise, conjecture. **Extinguish**, WANG: ruin, destroy; gone, dead, lost without trace; extinct, forgotten, out of mind. The ideogram: person concealed by a wall, out of sight.

39

LIMPING ▪ *CHIEN*

This hexagram describes your situation in terms of being weak, afflicted or hampered. It emphasizes that going ahead even though haltingly is the adequate way to handle it. To be in accord with the time, you are told to: **limp!**

● *Image of the Situation*

> **Limping, Harvesting: Western South.**
> **Not Harvesting: Eastern North.**
> **Harvesting: visualizing Great People.**
> **Trial: significant.**

Associated Contexts **Limp**, CHIEN: walk lamely, proceed haltingly; weak-legged, afflicted, crooked; feeble, weak; unfortunate, difficult. The ideogram: foot and cold, impeded circulation in the feet. **Harvest**, LI: advantageous, profitable; acute, insightful; benefit, nourish; third stage of the Time Cycle. **Western South**: the neutral Earthy Moment between the yang and yin hemicycles; bring forth concrete results, ripe fruits of late summer.

Not, PU: simple negative. **Eastern North**: border, limit, completion; boundary between cycles: Mountain; accomplishing words, summing up before new germination; dark, cold, lonely winter night.

Visualize, CHIEN: seeing in all its aspects: vision, being visible, forming mental images; visit, call on, consult. The ideogram: eye above person, active and receptive sight. **Great People**, TA JEN: important, noble, influential; those who impose a ruling principle on their lives; effect of the great within an individual; keyword.

Trial, CHEN: test by ordeal; inquiry by divination and its result; righteous, firm; separating wheat from chaff; the kernel, the proven core; fourth stage of the Time Cycle. The ideogram: pearl and divination. **Significant**, CHI: leads to the experience of meaning; favorable, propitious, advantageous, appropriate; keyword. The ideogram: scholar and mouth, wise words of a sage.

Outer and Inner Aspects

⚏ **Gorge**: Stream ventures and falls into the gorge, flowing on through toil and danger. **Gorge** ends the yin hemicycle by leveling and dissolving forms.

Connection to the outer: flooding and leveling dissolve direction and shape, the Streaming Moment. **Gorge** ventures, falls, toils and flows on.

⚏ **Bound**: Mountains bound, limit and set a place off, stopping forward movement. **Bound** completes a full yin-yang cycle.

Connection to the inner: accomplishing words, which express things. **Bound** articulates what is complete to suggest what is beginning.

The inner limit intermittently blocks outer venturing, producing **limping**.

Counter Indications

Nuclear trigrams **Radiance**, LI, and **Gorge**, K'AN, result in Counter Hexagram 64, **Not-yet Fording**, WEI CHI. The need to **limp** forward, even if hampered, is contrasted with **not-yet** beginning to **ford** the stream of events.

Sequence

> **Turning-away necessarily possesses heaviness.**
> **Anterior acquiescence has the use-of Limping.**
> **Limping implies heaviness indeed.**

Associated Contexts **Turn-away**, KUAI: turn your back on something and focus on its opposite; contradict, cross purposes; cunning, crafty; perverse; contrasts with return, FU, going back to the start. **Necessarily**, PI: unavoidably, indispensably, certainly. **Possess**, YU: in possession of, have, own; opposite of lack, WU. **Heavy**, NAN: arduous, grievous, difficult; hardship, distress; harass; contrasts with versatile, I, deal lightly with. The ideogram: domestic bird with clipped tail and drying sticky earth.

Anterior ... the use-of: activating this hexagram depends on understanding and accepting the previous statement.

Imply, CHE: further signify; additional meaning. **Indeed**, YEH: intensifier; indicates comment on previous statement.

• *Contrasted Definitions*

Taking-apart: delay indeed.
Limping: heaviness indeed.

Associated Contexts **Take-apart**, HSIEH: loosen, disjoin, untie, sever, scatter; analyse, explain, understand; release, dispel sorrow; eliminate effects, solve problems; resolution, deliverance. The ideogram: horns and knife, cutting into forward thrust. Image of Hexagram 40. **Delay**, HUAN: retard, put off; let things take their course, tie loosely; gradually, leisurely; lax, tardy, negligent.

• *Symbol Tradition*

Above mountain possessing stream. Limping.
A chün tzu uses reversing individuality to renovate actualizing-tao.

Associated Contexts **Above**, SHANG: anything above, in all senses; higher, upper, outer; upper trigram; opposite of below, HSIA. **Mountain**, SHAN: limit, boundary; the Symbol of the trigram Bound, KEN. The ideogram: three peaks, a mountain range. **Stream**, SHUI: flowing water; fluid, dissolving; river, tide, flood; the Symbol of the trigram Gorge, K'AN. The ideogram: rippling water.

Chün tzu: ideal of a person who uses divination to order his/her life in accordance with tao rather than wilful intention; keyword. **Use(-of)**, YI: make use of, by means of, owing to; employ, make functional. **Reverse**, FAN: turn and move in the opposite direction; turn around or upside down (180 degrees); change to the opposite position; contrary. **Individuality**, SHEN: total person: psyche, body and lifespan; character, virtue, duty; contrasts with body, KUNG, physical being. **Renovate**, HSIU: repair, mend, clean, adorn; adjust, regulate; cultivate, practise, acquire skills. **Actualize-tao**, TE: realize tao in action; power, virtue; ability to follow the course traced by the ongoing process of the cosmos; keyword. The ideogram: to go, straight, and heart. Linked with acquire, TE, acquiring that which makes a being become what it is meant to be.

• *Image Tradition*

> **Limping. Heaviness indeed. [I]**
> **Venturing located-in precedence indeed.**
> **Visualizing venturing and-also enabling stopping.**
> **Actually knowing in-fact.**
>
> **Limping, Harvesting: Western South. [II]**
> **Going acquires the center indeed.**
> **Not Harvesting: Eastern North.**
> **One's tao exhausted indeed.**
>
> **Harvesting: visualizing Great People. [III]**
> **Going possesses achievement indeed.**
> **Appropriate situation, Trial: significant.**
> **Using correcting the fiefdoms indeed.**
> **Actually Limping's season availing-of the great in-fact.**

Associated Contexts **[I] Venture**, HSIEN: risk without reserve; key point, point of danger; difficulty, obstruction that must be confronted; water falling and filling the holes on its way; the Action of the trigram Gorge, K'AN. The ideogram: mound and all or whole, everything engaged at one point. **Locate(-in)**, TSAI: live in, dwell, reside; belong to, involved with, depend on; within. The ideogram: earth and persevere, place on the earth. **Precede**, CH'IEN: come before in time and thus in value; anterior, former, ancient; lead forward.

And-also, ERH: joins and contrasts two terms. **Able**, NENG: enable; ability, power, skill, art; competent, talented; duty, function, capacity. The ideogram: an animal with strong hooves and bones, able to carry and defend. **Stop**, CHIH: bring or come to a standstill; the Action of the trigram Bound, KEN. The ideogram: a foot stops walking.

Actually ... in-fact, YI TSAI: stresses the importance of a statement. The ideogram: a dart and done, strong intention fully expressed. **Know**, CHIH: understand, perceive, remember; informed, aware, wise. The ideogram: arrow and mouth, words focused and swift.

[II] Go, WANG, and come, LAI, describe the stream of time as it flows from future through present to past; go, WANG, indicates what is departing from present to past; proceed, move on; keyword. **Acquire**, TE: obtain the desired object; wish for, desire covetously; gains, possessions.

The ideogram: go and obstacle, going through obstacles to the goal. **Center**, CHUNG: inner, central; put in the center; middle, stable point enabling you to face inner and outer changes; middle line of trigram. The ideogram: field divided in two equal parts. Image of Hexagram 61.

One's/one, CH'I: third person pronoun; also: it/its, he/his, she/hers, they/theirs. **Tao:** way or path; ongoing process of being and the course it traces for each specific person or thing; keyword. The ideogram: go and head, leading and the path it creates. **Exhaust**, CH'IUNG: bring to an end; limit, extremity; destitute; investigate exhaustively; end without a new beginning. The ideogram: cave and naked person, bent with disease or old age.

[III] Achieve, KUNG: work done, results; real accomplishment, praise, worth, merit. The ideogram: workman's square and forearm, combining craft and strength.

Appropriate, TANG: suitable; opportune, convenient; adequate, competent; equal to; whole lines in uneven places and opened lines in even places. **Situation**, WEI: place or seat according to rank; post, position, command; right, proper; established, arranged. The ideogram: person and stand, servants in their places.

Correct, CHENG: rectify deviation or one-sidedness; proper, straight, exact, regular; constant, rule, model. The ideogram: stop and one, hold to one thing. **Fiefdom**, PANG: region governed by a feudatory, an order of nobility.

's/have(-it)/it/them, CHIH: expresses possession, directly or as an object pronoun. **Season**, SHIH: quality of the time; the right time, opportune, in harmony; planning in accord with the time; seasons of the year. The ideogram: sun and temple, time as sacred. **Avail-of**, YUNG: take advantage of; benefit from, profit by; use for a specific purpose; apply to advantage. The ideogram: to divine and center, applying divination to central concerns. **Great**, TA: big, noble, important, very; orient the will toward a self-imposed goal, impose direction; ability to lead or guide your life; contrasts with small, HSIAO, flexible adaptation to what crosses your path; keyword. Image of Hexagrams 14, 26, 28, 34.

• *Transforming Lines*

Initial six

a) **Going Limping, coming praise.**

b) **Going Limping, coming praise.**
Proper to await indeed.

Associated Contexts a) **Come**, LAI, and **Go**, WANG, describe the stream of time as it flows from future through present to past. Come, LAI, indicates what is approaching; move toward, arrive at; go, WANG, indicates what is departing; proceed, move on; keywords. **Praise**, YÜ: admire and approve; magnify, eulogize; flatter. The ideogram: words and give, offering words.

b) **Proper**, YI: reasonable of itself; fit and right, harmonious; ought, should. **Await**, TAI: expect, wait for, welcome (friendly or hostile), provide against.

Six at-second

a) **A king, a servant: Limping, Limping.**
In-no-way body's anteriority.

b) **A king, a servant: Limping, Limping.**
Completing without surpassing indeed.

Associated Contexts a) **King(hood)**, WANG: effective ruler, by authority of the Emperor, from whom others derive their power. **Servant**, CH'EN: attendant, minister, vassal; courtier who can speak to the sovereign; wait on, serve in office. The ideogram: person bowing low. **Limping**, CHIEN: the doubled character intensifies this quality.
 In-no-way, FEI: strong negative; not so. The ideogram: a box filled with opposition. **Body**, KUNG: physical being, power and self expression; contrasts with individuality, SHEN, the total personality. **Anterior**, KU: come before as cause; formerly, ancient; reason, purpose, intention; grievance, quarrel, dissatisfaction, sorrow, mourning resulting from previous causes and intentions; situation leading to a divination.

b) **Complete**, CHUNG: end of a cycle that begins the next; last, whole, all; contrasts with exhaust, CH'IUNG, final end. The ideogram: silk cocoons, follow and ice, winter linking one year with the next. **Without**, WU: devoid of; -less as suffix. **Surpass**, YU: exceed; beyond measure, excessive; extraordinary; transgress, blame.

Nine at-third

a) **Going Limping, coming reversing.**

b) **Going Limping, coming reversing.**
Inside rejoicing-in it indeed.

Associated Contexts a) **Come**, LAI, and **Go**, WANG, describe the stream of time as it flows from future through present to past. Come, LAI, indicates what is approaching; move toward, arrive at; go, WANG, indicates what is departing; proceed, move on; keywords.

b) **Inside**, NEI: within, inner, interior; inside of the house and those who work there, particularly women; the lower trigram, as opposed to outside, WAI, the upper. The ideogram: border and enter, cross a border. **Rejoice(-in)**, HSI: feel and give joy; delight, exult; cheerful, merry. The ideogram: joy (music) and mouth, expressing joy. **It/them/have(-it)/'s**, CHIH: expresses possession, directly or as an object pronoun.

Six at-fourth

a) **Going Limping, coming continuity.**

b) **Going Limping, coming continuity.**
Appropriate situation, substance indeed.

Associated Contexts a) **Come**, LAI, and **Go**, WANG, describe the stream of time as it flows from future through present to past. Come, LAI, indicates what is approaching; move toward, arrive at; go, WANG, indicates what is departing; proceed, move on; keywords. **Continuity**, LIEN: connected, continuous, attached, annexed, consistent; follow, reach, stick to, join; series.

b) **Substance**, SHIH: real, solid, full; results, fruits, possessions; essence; honest, sincere. The ideogram: string of coins under a roof, riches in the house.

Nine at-fifth

a) The great Limping, partnering coming.

b) The great Limping, partnering coming.
Using centering articulating indeed.

Associated Contexts a) **Partner,** P'ENG: associate for mutual benefit; two equal or similar things; companions, friends, peers; join in; commercial ventures. The ideogram: linked strings of cowries or coins. **Come,** LAI, and go, WANG, describe the stream of time as it flows from future through present to past; come, LAI, indicates what is approaching; move toward, arrive at; keyword.

b) **Articulate,** CHIEH: separate and distinguish, as well as join, different things; express thought through speech; joint, section, chapter, interval, unit of time; zodiacal sign; moderate, regulate; lit.: nodes on bamboo stalks. Image of Hexagram 60.

Six above

a) Going Limping, coming ripening.
Significant.
Harvesting: visualizing Great People.

b) Going Limping, coming ripening.
Purpose located inside indeed.
Harvesting: visualizing Great People.
Using adhering-to valuing indeed.

Associated Contexts a) **Come,** LAI, and **Go,** WANG. describe the stream of time as it flows from future through present to past. Come, LAI, indicates what is approaching; move toward, arrive at; go, WANG, indicates what is departing; proceed, move on; keywords. **Ripe,** SHIH: mature, full-grown; great, eminent.

b) **Purpose,** CHIH: focus of mind and heart; will, inclination, resolve. The ideogram: heart and scholar, high inner resolve, or heart and go, inner determination. **Inside,** NEI: within, inner, interior; inside of the house and those who work there, particularly women; the lower trigram, as opposed to outside, WAI, the upper. The ideogram: border and enter, cross a border.

Adhere(-to), TS'UNG: follow a way, hold to a doctrine, school, or person; hear and comply with, agree to; forced to follow, follower. The ideogram: two men walking, one following the other. **Value**, KUEI: regard as valuable, give worth and dignity to; precious, high priced; honorable, exalted, illustrious. The ideogram: cowries (coins) and basket.

TAKING-APART ▪ *HSIEH*

This hexagram describes your situation in terms of reflection and release from tension. It emphasizes that analysing and understanding things in order to be delivered from compulsion is the adequate way to handle it. To be in accord with the time, you are told to: **take** things **apart**!

● *Image of the Situation*

> **Taking-apart. Harvesting: Western South.**
> **Without a place to go:**
> **One's coming return significant.**
> **Possessing directed going:**
> **Daybreak significant.**

Associated Contexts **Take-apart**, HSIEH: loosen, disjoin, untie, sever, scatter; analyse, explain, understand; release, dispel sorrow; eliminate effects, solve problems; resolution, deliverance. The ideogram: horns and knife, cutting into forward thrust. **Harvest**, LI: advantageous, profitable; acute, insightful; benefit, nourish; third stage of the Time Cycle. **Western South**: the neutral Earthy Moment between the yang and yin hemicycles; bring forth concrete results, ripe fruits of late summer.

Without, WU: devoid of; -less as suffix. **Place**, SO: where something belongs or comes from; residence, dwelling; habitual focus or object. **Go**, WANG, and **Come**, LAI, describe the stream of time as it flows from future through present to past. Go, WANG, indicates what is departing; proceed, move on; come, LAI, indicates: what is approaching; move toward, arrive at; keywords.

One's/one, CH'I: third person pronoun; also: it/its, he/his, she/hers, they/theirs. **Return**, FU: go back, turn back to the starting point; recur, reappear, come again; restore, recover, retrace; an earlier time or place. The ideogram: step and retrace a path. Image of Hexagram 24. **Significant**, CHI: leads to the experience of meaning; favorable, propitious, advantageous, appropriate; keyword. The ideogram: scholar and mouth, wise words of a sage.

Possessing directed going, YU YU WANG: imposing a direction on the flow of time from present to past; have a specific goal or purpose. **Daybreak**, SU: first light, after dawn; early morning; early, careful attention.

● *Inner and Outer Aspects*

☳ **Shake**: Thunder rises from below, shaking and stirring things up.
Shake begins the yang hemicycle by germinating new action.

Connection to the outer: sprouting energies thrusting from below, the
Woody Moment beginning. **Shake** stirs things up to issue-forth.

☵ **Gorge**: Stream ventures and falls into the gorge, flowing on through
toil and danger. **Gorge** ends the yin hemicycle by leveling and dissolving
forms.

Connection to the inner: flooding and leveling dissolve direction and
shape, the Streaming Moment. **Gorge** ventures, falls, toils and flows on.

The outer trigram begins a new cycle while the inner completes the
previous one. Leveling inside **takes** outer stimuli **apart** and releases
blocked energy.

● *Counter Indications*

Nuclear trigrams **Gorge**, K'AN, and **Radiance**, LI, result in Counter
Hexagram 63, **Already Fording**, CHI CHI. **Taking** things **apart** to search
into motivations is contrasted with **already fording** the stream of events.

● *Sequence*

> **Beings not permitted to use completing heaviness.**
> **Anterior acquiescence has the use-of Taking-apart.**
> **Taking-apart implies delay indeed.**

Associated Contexts **Beings not permitted to use ...** : no one is
allowed to make use of; nothing can exist by means of. **Complete**,
CHUNG: end of a cycle that begins the next; last, whole, all; contrasts
with exhaust, CH'IUNG, final end. The ideogram: silk cocoons, follow and
ice, winter linking one year with the next. **Heavy**, NAN: arduous, grievous,
difficult; hardship, distress; harass; contrasts with versatile, I, deal lightly
with. The ideogram: domestic bird with clipped tail and drying sticky
earth.

Anterior ... the use-of: activating this hexagram depends on
understanding and accepting the previous statement.

Imply, CHE: further signify; additional meaning. **Delay**, HUAN: retard, put off; let things take their course, tie loosely; gradually, leisurely; lax, tardy, negligent. **Indeed**, YEH: intensifier; indicates comment on previous statement.

- *Contrasted Definitions*

> Taking-apart: delay indeed.
> Limping: heaviness indeed.

Associated Contexts **Limp**, CHIEN: walk lamely, proceed haltingly; weak-legged, afflicted, crooked; feeble, weak; unfortunate, difficult. The ideogram: foot and cold, impeded circulation in the feet. Image of Hexagram 39.

- *Symbol Tradition*

> Thunder, rain, arousing. Taking-apart.
> A chün tzu uses forgiving excess to pardon offenses.

Associated Contexts **Thunder**, LEI: rising, arousing power; the Symbol of the trigram Shake, CHEN. **Rain**, YÜ: all precipitation; sudden showers, fast and furious; associated with the trigram Gorge, K'AN, and the Streaming Moment. **Arouse**, TSO: stir up, stimulate, rouse from inactivity; generate; appear, arise. The ideogram: person and beginning.

Chün tzu: ideal of a person who uses divination to order his/her life in accordance with tao rather than wilful intention; keyword. **Use(-of)**, YI: make use of, by means of, owing to; employ, make functional. **Forgive,** SHE: excuse, pass over, set aside, reprieve. **Exceed**, KU: go beyond, pass by, pass over; excessive, transgress; error, fault. Image of Hexagrams 28 and 62. **Pardon**, YU: forgive, indulge, relax; lenient. **Offense**, TSUI: crime, sin, fault; violate laws or rules; incur blame, incriminated. The ideogram: net and wrong, entangled in guilt.

- *Image Tradition*

> Taking-apart. Venturing uses stirring-up. [I]
> Stirring-up and-also evading reaching-to venturing. Taking-apart.

Taking-apart, Harvesting: Western South. [II]
Going acquiring crowds indeed.
One's coming return significant.
Thereupon acquiring the center indeed.
Possessing directed going, daybreak significant.
Going possesses achievement indeed.

Heaven[and]Earth Taking-apart and-also
                              Thunder[and]Rain arousing. [III]
Thunder[and]Rain arousing and-also the hundred fruits,
                  grasses, trees, altogether seedburst boundary.
Actually Taking-apart's season great in-fact.

Associated Contexts **[I] Venture**, HSIEN: risk without reserve; key point, point of danger; difficulty, obstruction that must be confronted; water falling and filling the holes on its way; the Action of the trigram Gorge, K'AN. The ideogram: mound and all or whole, everything engaged at one point. **Stir-up**, TUNG: excite, influence, move, affect; work, take action; come out of the egg or the bud; the Action of the trigram Shake, CHEN. The ideogram: strength and heavy, move weighty things.

And-also, ERH: joins and contrasts two terms. **Evade**, MIEN: avoid, escape from, get away; be free of, dispense with; remove from office. The ideogram: a hare, known for its evasive skill. **Reach(-to)**, HU: arrive at a goal; reach towards and achieve; connect; contrasts with tend-towards, YU.

[II] Acquire, TE: obtain the desired object; wish for, desire covetously; gains, possessions. The ideogram: go and obstacle, going through obstacles to the goal. **Crowds**, CHUNG: many people, large group; majority; in common.

Thereupon, NAI: on that ground, because of. **Center**, CHUNG: inner, central; put in the center; middle, stable point enabling you to face inner and outer changes; middle line of trigram. The ideogram: field divided in two equal parts. Image of Hexagram 61.

Possess, YU: in possession of, have, own; opposite of lack, WU. **Achieve**, KUNG: work done, results; real accomplishment, praise, worth, merit. The ideogram: workman's square and forearm, combining craft and strength.

[III] **Heaven[and]Earth**, T'IEN TI: dynamic relation between the primal powers and the world it produces; cosmos, natural or human world; keyword. **Thunder[and]Rain**, LEI YÜ: fertilizing shock of storms; associated with the trigrams Shake, CHEN, and Gorge, K'AN.

Hundred, PO: numerous, many, all; a whole class or type. **Fruit**, KUO: plants' annual produce; tree fruits; come to fruition, fruits of actions; produce, results, effects; reliable; conclude, surpass. The ideogram: tree topped by a round fruit. **Grass**, TS'AO: all grassy plants and herbs; young, tender plants; rough draft; hastily. **Tree/wood**, MU: all things woody or wooden, alive or constructed from wood; associated with the Woody Moment; wood and wind are the Symbols of the trigram Ground, SUN. The ideogram: a tree striking its roots down and sending up branches. **Altogether**, CHIEH: all, the whole; the same sort, all alike; entirely. **Seedburst**, CHIA: seeds bursting forth in spring; first of the Ten Heavenly Barriers in calendar system; begin, first, number one; associated with the Woody Moment. **Boundary**, CHI: border, limit, frontier; confine.

Actually ... in-fact, YI TSAI: stresses the importance of a statement. The ideogram: a dart and done, strong intention fully expressed. **'s/have(-it)/it/them**, CHIH: expresses possession, directly or as an object pronoun. **Season**, SHIH: quality of the time; the right time, opportune, in harmony; planning in accord with the time; seasons of the year. The ideogram: sun and temple, time as sacred. **Great**, TA: big, noble, important, very; orient the will toward a self-imposed goal, impose direction; ability to lead or guide your life; contrasts with small, HSIAO, flexible adaptation to what crosses your path; keyword. Image of Hexagrams 14, 26, 28, 34.

• *Transforming Lines*

Initial six

a) **Without fault.**

b) **Solid[and]Supple's border.**
Righteous, without fault indeed.

Associated Contexts *a)* **Without fault**, WU CHIU: no error or harm in the situation.

b) **Solid[and]Supple**, KANG JOU: field of creative tension between the whole and opened lines and their qualities; field of psychic movement.

Border, CHI: limit, frontier, line which joins and divides. The ideogram: place and sacrifice, border between human and spirit.

Righteous, YI: proper and just, meets the standards; things in their proper place; the heart that rules itself; upright, moral rule; contrasts with Harvest, LI, advantage or profit.

Nine at-second

a) **The fields, catching three foxes.**
Acquiring a yellow arrow.
Trial: significant.

b) **Nine at-second, Trial: significant.**
Acquiring centering tao indeed.

Associated Contexts a) **Fields,** T'IEN: cultivated land, plantation; also: hunting, game in the fields cannot escape the hunt. The ideogram: square divided into four sections, delineating fields. **Catch,** HUO: take in hunt; catch a thief; obtain, seize; hit the mark, opportune moment; prisoner, spoils, prey; slave, servant. **Three,** SAN: number three, third time or place; active phases of a cycle; superlative; beginning of repetition. **Fox,** HU: crafty, shape-changing animal; used by spirits, often female; ambivalent night-spirit that can create havoc and bestow abundance.

Yellow, HUANG: color of the productive middle; associated with the Earthy Moment between yang and yin hemicycles; color of soil in central China; emblematic and imperial color of China since the Yellow Emperor (2500 BCE). **Arrow,** SHIH: arrow, javelin, dart; swift, direct as an arrow; marshal together.

Trial, CHEN: test by ordeal; inquiry by divination and its result; righteous, firm; separating wheat from chaff; the kernel, the proven core; fourth stage of the Time Cycle. The ideogram: pearl and divination.

b) **Tao:** way or path; ongoing process of being and the course it traces for each specific person or thing; keyword. The ideogram: go and head, leading and the path it creates.

Six at-third

a) **Bearing, moreover riding.**
Involving outlawry culminating.
Trial: abashment.

b) **Bearing, moreover riding.**
   Truly permitting the demoniac indeed.
   Originating-from my involving arms.
   Furthermore whose fault indeed.

Associated Contexts a) **Bear**, FU: carry on your back; take on a responsibility; rely on, depend on; loaded down; burden, duty; math term for minus. **Moreover**, CH'IEH: further, and also. **Ride**, CH'ENG: ride an animal or a chariot; have the upper hand, seize the right time; control strong power; overcome the nature of the other; supple opened line above a solid whole line.

   Involve, CHIH: include, entangle, implicate; induce, cause. The ideogram: person walking, induced to follow. **Outlawry**, K'OU: break the laws; violent people, outcasts, bandits. **Culminate**, CHIH: bring to the highest degree; arrive at the end or summit; superlative.

   Trial, CHEN: test by ordeal; inquiry by divination and its result; righteous, firm; separating wheat from chaff; the kernel, the proven core; fourth stage of the Time Cycle. The ideogram: pearl and divination. **Abashment**, LIN: distress, shame, regret, humiliation; aware of having lost the right track; leads to repenting, HUI, correcting the direction of mind and life.

b) **Truly**, YI: statement is true and precise. **Permit**, K'O: possible because in harmony with an inherent principle. The ideogram: mouth and breath, silent consent. **Demon(iac)**, CH'OU: possessed by a malignant genius; ugly, physically or morally deformed; vile, disgraceful, shameful; drunken. The ideogram: fermenting liquor and soul. Demoniac and tiger are opposed on the Universal Compass North–South axis; the tiger (Extreme Yang) scares away and protects against demoniacs (Extreme Yin).

   Origin, TZU: source, beginning, ground; cause, reason, motive; line of descent; path to the origin; yourself, intrinsic. **My/me/I**, WO: first person pronoun; indicates an unusually strong emphasis on your own subjective experience. **Arms**, JUNG: weapons; armed people, soldiers; military, violent. The ideogram: spear and armor, offensive and defensive weapons.

   Furthermore, YU: in addition to; higher degree of. **Whose**, SHUI: relative and interrogative pronoun; also: whose? **Fault**, CHIU: unworthy conduct that leads to harm, illness, misfortune. The ideogram: person and differ, differ from what you should be.

Nine at-fourth

a) Taking-apart and-also the thumbs.
Partnering culminating, splitting-off conforming.

b) Taking-apart and-also the thumbs.
Not-yet an appropriate situation indeed.

Associated Contexts a) **Thumb/big-toe**, MU: in lower trigram: big-toe; in upper trigram: thumb; the big-toe enables the foot to walk, the thumb enables the hand to grasp.

Partner, P'ENG: associate for mutual benefit; two equal or similar things; companions, friends, peers; join in; commercial ventures. The ideogram: linked strings of cowries or coins. **Culminate**, CHIH: bring to the highest degree; arrive at the end or summit; superlative. **Split-off**, SSU: lop off, split with an ax, rive; white (color eliminated). The ideogram: ax and possessive, splitting what belongs together. **Conforming**, FU: accord between inner and outer in a particular moment; sincere, truthful, verified, reliable, in accord with the spirits; capture; prisoners, spoils; contrasts with trustworthy, HSIN, consistent over time. The ideogram: bird's claw enclosing young animals, possessive grip. Image of Hexagram 61.

b) **Not-yet**, WEI: temporal negative; something will but has not yet occurred; contrary of already, CHI. Image of Hexagram 64. **Appropriate**, TANG: suitable; opportune, convenient; adequate, competent; equal to; whole lines in uneven places and opened lines in even places. **Situation**, WEI: place or seat according to rank; post, position, command; right, proper; established, arranged. The ideogram: person and stand, servants in their places.

Six at-fifth

a) A chün tzu holding-fast possesses Taking-apart.
Significant.
Possessing conformity, tending-towards Small People.

b) A chün tzu possessing Taking-apart.
Small People withdrawing indeed.

Associated Contexts a) **Hold-fast(-to)**, WEI: hold together; tie to, connect; reins, net. **Possessing conformity**, YU FU: inner and outer are in accord; confidence of the spirits has been captured; sincere, truthful;

proper to take action. **Tend-towards**, YÜ: move toward but not reach, in the direction of; contrasts with reach(-to), HU, actually arriving. **Small People**, HSIAO JEN: lowly, common, humble; those who adjust to circumstances with the flexibility of the small; effect of the small within an individual; keyword.

b) **Withdraw(-from)**, T'UI: draw back, retreat, recede; decline, refuse.

Six above

a) **A prince avails-of shooting a hawk,**
                                        tending-towards the high rampart's above.
   Without not Harvesting: catching it.

b) **A prince avails-of shooting a hawk.**
   Using Taking-apart rebelling indeed.

Associated Contexts a) **Prince**, KUNG: nobles acting as ministers of state in the capital; governing from the center rather than active in daily life; contrasts with feudatory, HOU, governors of the provinces. **Avail-of**, YUNG: take advantage of; benefit from, profit by; use for a specific purpose; apply to advantage. The ideogram: to divine and center, applying divination to central concerns. **Shoot**, SHE: shoot with a bow, point at and hit; project from, spurt, issue forth; glance at; scheme for. The ideogram: arrow and body. **Hawk**, SHUN: bird of prey used in hunting; falcon, kestrel. **Tend-towards**, YÜ: move toward but not reach, in the direction of; contrasts with reach(-to), HU, actually arriving. **High(-ness)**, KAO: high, elevated, lofty, eminent; excellent, advanced. **Rampart**, YUNG: defensive wall; bulwark, redoubt. **Above**, SHANG: anything above, in all senses; higher, upper, outer; upper trigram; opposite of below, HSIA.

Without not Harvesting, WU PU LI: nothing for which this will not be beneficial; advantageous potential, borderline where the balance is swinging from not Harvesting to actually Harvesting. **Catch**, HUO: take in hunt; catch a thief; obtain, seize; hit the mark, opportune moment; prisoner, spoils, prey; slave, servant. **It/them/have(-it)/'s**, CHIH: expresses possession, directly or as an object pronoun.

b) **Rebel**, PEI: go against nature or usage; insubordinate; perverse, unreasonable.

DIMINISHING ▪ *SUN*

This hexagram describes your situation in terms of sacrifice and loss. It emphasizes that lessening yourself and decreasing your involvements is the adequate way to handle it. To be in accord with the time, you are told to: **diminish!**

● *Image of the Situation*

> **Diminishing, possessing conformity.**
> **Spring significant.**
> **Without fault, permitting Trial.**
> **Harvesting: possessing directed going.**
> **Asking-why: having availing-of.**
> **Two platters permit availing-of presenting.**

Associated Contexts **Diminish**, SUN: lessen, make smaller; take away from; lose, damage, spoil, wound; bad luck; blame, criticize; offer up, give away. The ideogram: hand and ceremonial vessel, offering sacrifice. **Possessing conformity**, YU FU: inner and outer are in accord; confidence of the spirits has been captured; sincere, truthful; proper to take action.

Spring, YÜAN: source, origin, head; great, excellent; arise, begin, generating power; first stage of the Time Cycle. **Significant**, CHI: leads to the experience of meaning; favorable, propitious, advantageous, appropriate; keyword. The ideogram: scholar and mouth, wise words of a sage.

Without fault, WU CHIU: no error or harm in the situation. **Permit**, K'O: possible because in harmony with an inherent principle. The ideogram: mouth and breath, silent consent. **Trial**, CHEN: test by ordeal; inquiry by divination and its result; righteous, firm; separating wheat from chaff; the kernel, the proven core; fourth stage of the Time Cycle. The ideogram: pearl and divination.

Harvest, LI: advantageous, profitable; acute, insightful; benefit, nourish; third stage of the Time Cycle. **Possessing directed going**, YU YU WANG: imposing a direction on the flow of time from present to past;

have a specific goal or purpose. **Ask-why,** HO: interjection: why? how? why not?; interrupt with questions; intimidate, heckle. The ideogram: speak and beg, demanding an answer. **Have(-it)/it/them/'s,** CHIH: expresses possession, directly or as an object pronoun. **Avail-of,** YUNG: take advantage of; benefit from, profit by; use for a specific purpose; apply to advantage. The ideogram: to divine and center, applying divination to central concerns.

    Two, ERH: pair, even numbers, binary, duplicate. **Platter,** KUEI: wood or bamboo plate; sacrificial utensil. **Present(-to),** HSIANG: present in sacrifice, offer with thanks, give to the gods or a superior; confer dignity on.

- *Outer and Inner Aspects*

☶ **Bound**: Mountains bound, limit and set a place off, stopping forward movement. **Bound** completes a full yin-yang cycle.

    Connection to the outer: accomplishing words, which express things fully. **Bound** articulates what is complete and suggests what is beginning.

☱ **Open:** vapor rising from the marsh's open surface stimulates and fertilizes; stimulating words cheer and inspire. **Open** begins the yin hemicycle by initiating the formative process.

    Connection to the inner: liquifying, casting, skinning off the mold, the Metallic Moment beginning. **Open** stimulates, cheers and reveals innate form.

The outer limit **diminishes** involvement, stimulating new inner development.

- *Counter Indications*

Nuclear trigrams **Field**, K'UN, and **Shake**, CHEN, result in Counter Hexagram 24, **Returning**, FU. **Diminishing** and decreasing outer involvement are contrasted with **returning** to the beginning to start over again.

- *Sequence*

> **Delaying necessarily possesses a place to let-go.**
> **Anterior acquiescence has the use-of Diminishing.**

Associated Contexts **Delay**, HUAN: retard, put off; let things take their course, tie loosely; gradually; leisurely; lax, tardy, negligent. **Necessarily**, PI: unavoidably, indispensably, certainly. **Possess**, YU: in possession of, have, own; opposite of lack, WU. **Place**, SO: where something belongs or comes from; residence, dwelling; habitual focus or object. **Let-go**, SHIH: lose, omit, miss, fail, let slip; out of control. The ideogram: drop from the hand.

    Anterior ... the use-of: activating this hexagram depends on understanding and accepting the previous statement.

- *Contrasted Definitions*

> **Diminishing, Augmenting.**
> **Increasing, decreasing's beginning indeed.**

Associated Contexts **Augment**, YI: increase, advance, promote, benefit, strengthen; pour in more; full, superabundant; restorative. The ideogram: water and vessel, pouring in more. Image of Hexagram 42.

    Increase, SHENG: grow or make larger; flourishing, exuberant, full, abundant; heaped up; excellent, fine. **Decrease**, SHUAI: grow or make smaller; fade, decline, decay, diminish, cut off; grow old; adversity, misfortune. **'s/have(-it)/it/them**, CHIH: expresses possession, directly or as an object pronoun. **Begin**, SHIH: commence, start, open; earliest, first; beginning of a time-span, ended by completion, CHUNG. The ideogram: woman and eminent, beginning new life. **Indeed**, YEH: intensifier; indicates comment on previous statement.

- *Attached Evidences*

> **Diminishing: actualizing-tao's adjustment indeed.**
> **Diminishing: beforehand heaviness and-also afterwards versatility.**
> **Diminishing: using distancing harm.**

Associated Contexts **Actualize-tao**, TE: realize tao in action; power, virtue; ability to follow the course traced by the ongoing process of the cosmos; keyword. The ideogram: to go, straight, and heart. Linked with acquire, TE: acquiring that which makes a being become what it is meant to be. **Adjust**, HSIU: regulate, repair, clean up, renovate.

Before(hand)/earlier, HSIEN: come before in time; first, at first; formerly, past, previous; begin, go ahead of. **Heavy**, NAN: arduous, grievous, difficult; hardship, distress; harass; contrasts with versatile, I, deal lightly with. The ideogram: domestic bird with clipped tail and drying sticky earth. **And-also**, ERH: joins and contrasts two terms. **After(wards)/later**, HOU: come after in time, subsequent; put oneself after; the second; attendant, heirs, successors, posterity. **Versatility**, I: sudden and unpredictable change; mental mobility and openness; easy and light, not difficult and heavy; occurs in name of the I CHING.

Use(-of), YI: make use of, by means of, owing to; employ, make functional. **Distance**, YÜAN: far off, remote; keep at a distance; alienated. The ideogram: go and a long way. **Harm**, HAI: damage, injure, offend; suffer; hurtful, hindrance; fearful, anxious.

● *Symbol Tradition*

> **Below mountain possessing marsh. Diminishing.**
> **A chün tzu uses curbing anger to block the appetites.**

Associated Contexts **Below**, HSIA: anything below, in all senses; lower, inner; lower trigram; opposite of above, SHANG. **Mountain**, SHAN: limit, boundary; the Symbol of the trigram Bound, KEN. The ideogram: three peaks, a mountain range. **Marsh**, TSE: open surface of a flat body of water and the vapors rising from it; fertilize, enrich; kindness, favor; the Symbol of the trigram Open, TUI.

Chün tzu: ideal of a person who uses divination to order his/her life in accordance with tao rather than wilful intention; keyword. **Curb**, CH'ENG: reprimand, reprove, repress; warn, caution; corrective punishment. The ideogram: heart and action, the heart acting on itself. **Anger**, FEN: resentment; cross, wrathful; irritated at, indignant. The ideogram: heart and divide, the heart dividing people. **Block**, CHIH: obstruct, stop up, close, restrain, fill up. **Appetites**, YÜ: drives, instinctive craving; wishes, passions, desires, aspirations; long for, seek ardently; covet.

● *Image Tradition*

> **Diminishing. [I]**
> **Below Diminishing, above augmenting.**
> **One's tao moving above.**
> **Diminishing and-also possessing conformity.**
>
> **Spring significant. [II]**
> **Without fault, permitting Trial.**
> **Harvesting: possessing directed going.**
> **Asking-why: having availing-of.**
> **Two platters permit availing-of presenting.**
>
> **Two platters corresponding possess the season. [III]**
> **Diminishing solid, augmenting supple, possessing the season.**
> **Diminishing augmenting, overfilling emptiness.**
> **Associating-with the season, accompanying the movement.**

Associated Contexts **[I] Above**, SHANG: anything above, in all senses; higher, upper, outer; upper trigram; opposite of below, HSIA.

One's/one, CH'I: third person pronoun; also: it/its, he/his, she/hers, they/theirs. **Tao:** way or path; ongoing process of being and the course it traces for each specific person or thing; keyword. The ideogram: go and head, leading and the path it creates. **Move**, HSING: move or move something; motivate, emotionally moving; walk, act, do. The ideogram: stepping left then right.

[III] Correspond(-to), YING: be in agreement or harmony; resonate together, invoke and fulfill each other; answer to, suitable; relation between the lines (1:4, 2:5, 3:6) when they form the pair opened and whole, supple and solid. The ideogram: heart and obey. **Season**, SHIH: quality of the time; the right time, opportune, in harmony; planning in accord with the time; seasons of the year. The ideogram: sun and temple, time as sacred.

Solid, KANG: quality of the whole lines; firm, strong, unyielding, persisting. **Supple**, JOU: quality of the opened lines; flexible, pliant, tender, adaptable.

Overfill, YING: at the point of overflowing; more than wanted, stretch beyond; replenished, full; arrogant. The ideogram: vessel and too much. **Empty**, HSÜ: no images or concepts; vacant, unsubstantial; empty yet fertile space.

Associate(-with), YÜ: consort with, combine; companions; group, band, company; agree with, comply, help. The ideogram: pair of hands reaching downward meets a pair of hands reaching upward, helpful association. **Accompany**, HSIEH: take or go along with; jointly, all at once.

● *Transforming Lines*

Initial nine

a) **Climaxing affairs, swiftly going.**
Without fault.
Discussing Diminishing it.

b) **Climaxing affairs, swiftly going.**
Honoring uniting purposes indeed.

Associated Contexts a) **Climax**, YI: come to a high point and stop, bring to an end; use up, lay aside; decline, reject. **Affairs**, SHIH: all kinds of personal activity; matters at hand; business, occupation; manage a business, case in court. **Swiftly**, CH'UAN: quickly; hurry, hasten. **Go**, WANG, and come, LAI, describe the stream of time as it flows from future through present to past; go, WANG, indicates what is departing from present to past; proceed, move on; keyword.

Discuss, CHO: deliberate; hear opinions; reach and act on a decision. The ideogram: wine and ladle, pouring out wine to open discussion. **It/them/have(-it)/'s**, CHIH: expresses possession, directly or as an object pronoun.

b) **Honor**, SHANG: esteem, give high rank to; eminent; put one thing on top of another. **Unite**, HO: join, match, correspond, agree, collect, reply; unison, harmony; also: close, shut the mouth. The ideogram: mouth and assemble. **Purpose**, CHIH: focus of mind and heart; will, inclination, resolve. The ideogram: heart and scholar, high inner resolve, or heart and go, inner determination.

Nine at-second

a) **Harvesting Trial.**
Chastising: pitfall.
Nowhere Diminishing, augmenting it.

b) **Nine at-second, Harvesting Trial.**
Centering using activating purposes indeed.

Associated Contexts a) **Harvesting Trial**, LI CHEN: advantageous divination; putting the action in question to the test is beneficial.

Chastise, CHENG: punish, subjugate, discipline; reduce to order; punishing expedition. The ideogram: step and correct, a rectifying move.
Pitfall, HSIUNG: leads away from the experience of meaning; stuck and exposed to danger, unable to take in the situation; flow of life and spirit is blocked; unfortunate, baleful; keyword.

Nothing/nowhere, FU: strong negative; not a single thing/place.
It/them/have(-it)/'s, CHIH: expresses possession, directly or as an object pronoun.

b) **Center**, CHUNG: inner, central; put in the center; middle, stable point enabling you to face inner and outer changes; middle line of trigram. The ideogram: field divided in two equal parts. Image of Hexagram 61.
Activate, WEI: act or cause to act; do, make, manage; make active; attend to, help; because of. **Purpose**, CHIH: focus of mind and heart; will, inclination, resolve. The ideogram: heart and scholar, high inner resolve, or heart and go, inner determination.

Six at-third

a) **Three people moving.**
By-consequence Diminishing the-one person.
The-one person moving.
By-consequence acquiring one's friend.

b) **The-one person moving.**
Three by-consequence doubting indeed.

Associated Contexts a) **Three**, SAN: number three, third time or place; active phases of a cycle; superlative; beginning of repetition. **People, person**, JEN: humans individually and collectively; an individual; humankind. Image of Hexagrams 13 and 37.

By-consequence(-of), TSE: very strong connection; reason, cause, result; rule, law, pattern, standard; therefore. **One, the-one**, YI: single unit; number one; undivided, simple, whole; any one of; first, the first.

Acquire, TE: obtain the desired object; wish for, desire covetously; gains, possessions. The ideogram: go and obstacle, going through obstacles to the goal. **One's/one**, CH'I: third person pronoun; also: it/its, he/his, she/hers, they/theirs. **Friend**, YU: companion, associate; of the same mind; attached, in pairs. The ideogram: two hands joined.

b) **Doubt**, YI: suspect, distrust; dubious; surmise, conjecture.

Six at-fourth

a) **Diminishing one's affliction.**
Commissioning swiftly possesses rejoicing.
Without fault.

b) **Diminishing one's affliction.**
Truly permitting rejoicing indeed.

Associated Contexts a) **One's/one**, CH'I: third person pronoun; also: he/his, she/hers, they/theirs, it/its. **Afflict**, CHI: sickness, disorder, defect, calamity; injurious; pressure and consequent anger, hate or dislike. The ideogram: sickness and dart, a sudden affliction.

Commission, CHIH: employ for a task; command, order; messenger, agent. The ideogram: person and office. **Swiftly**, CH'UAN: quickly; hurry, hasten. **Rejoice(-in)**, HSI: feel and give joy; delight, exult; cheerful, merry. The ideogram: joy (music) and mouth, expressing joy.

b) **Truly**, YI: statement is true and precise.

Six at-fifth

a) **Maybe augmenting's ten: partnering's tortoise.**
Nowhere a controlling contradiction.
Spring significant.

b) **Six at-fifth, Spring significant.**
Originating-from shielding above indeed.

Associated Contexts a) **Maybe**, HUO: possible but not certain, perhaps. **Ten**, SHIH: goal and end of reckoning; whole, complete, all; entire, perfected, the full amount; reach everywhere, receive everything. The ideogram: East–West line crosses North–South line, a grid that contains all. **Partner**, P'ENG: associate for mutual benefit; two equal or similar things; companions, friends, peers; join in; commercial ventures. The ideogram: linked strings of cowries or coins. **Tortoise**, KUEI: turtles; armored animals, shells and shields; long-living; oracle-consulting by tortoise shell; image of the macrocosm: heaven and earth, between them the soft flesh of humans.

Nothing/nowhere, FU: strong negative; not a single thing/place. **Control**, K'O: command; check, impede, prevail, obstruct, repress; adequate, able. The ideogram: roof beams support a house, controlling the structure. **Contradict**, WEI: oppose, disregard, disobey; seditious, perverse.

b) **Origin**, TZU: source, beginning, ground; cause, reason, motive; line of descent; path to the origin; yourself, intrinsic. **Shield**, YU: protect; defended by spirits; heavenly kindness and protection. The ideogram: numinous and right hand, spirit power.

Nine above

a) **Nowhere Diminishing, augmenting it.**
Without fault.
Trial: significant.
Harvesting: possessing directed going.
Acquiring a servant, without dwelling.

b) **Nowhere Diminishing, augmenting it.**
The great acquiring purpose indeed.

Associated Contexts a) **Nothing/nowhere**, FU: strong negative; not a single thing/place. **It/them/have(-it)/'s**, CHIH: expresses possession, directly or as an object pronoun.

Acquire, TE: obtain the desired object; wish for, desire covetously; gains, possessions. The ideogram: go and obstacle, going through obstacles to the goal. **Servant**, CH'EN: attendant, minister, vassal; courtier who can speak to the sovereign; wait on, serve in office. The ideogram: person bowing low. **Without**, WU: devoid of; -less as suffix. **Dwell**, CHI: home, house, household, family; domestic, within doors; live in. The ideogram: roof and pig or dog, the most valued domestic animals. Image of Hexagram 37.

b) **Great**, TA: big, noble, important, very; orient the will toward a self-imposed goal, impose direction; ability to lead or guide your life; contrasts with small, HSIAO, flexible adaptation to what crosses your path; keyword. Image of Hexagrams 14, 26, 28, 34. **Purpose**, CHIH: focus of mind and heart; will, inclination, resolve. The ideogram: heart and scholar, high inner resolve, or heart and go, inner determination.

AUGMENTING ▮ YI

This hexagram describes your situation in terms of increase and advance. It emphasizes that expanding the quantity and quality of your involvement is the adequate way to handle it. To be in accord with the time, your are told to: **augment!**

● *Image of the Situation*

> **Augmenting, Harvesting: possessing directed going.**
> **Harvesting: wading the Great River.**

Associated Contexts **Augment**, YI: increase, advance, promote, benefit, strengthen; pour in more; full, superabundant; restorative. The ideogram: water and vessel, pouring in more. **Harvest**, LI: advantageous, profitable; acute, insightful; benefit, nourish; third stage of the Time Cycle. **Possessing directed going**, YU YU WANG: imposing a direction on the flow of time from present to past; have a specific goal or purpose.

Wading the Great River, SHE TA CH'UAN: consciously moving into the flow of time; enter the stream of life with a goal or purpose; embark on a significant enterprise.

● *Outer and Inner Aspects*

☴ **Ground**: Wind and wood subtly enter from the ground, penetrating and pervading. **Ground** is the center of the yang hemicycle, spreading pervasive action.

Connection to the outer: penetrating and bringing together, the Woody Moment culminating. **Ground** pervades, matches and couples, seeding a new generation.

☳ **Shake**: Thunder rises from below, shaking and stirring things up. **Shake** begins the yang hemicycle by germinating new action.

Connection to the outer: sprouting energies thrusting from below, the Woody Moment beginning. **Shake** stirs things up to issue-forth.

Germinating inner energy continually **augments** and expands outer pervading and growth.

- *Counter Indications*

Nuclear trigrams **Bound**, KEN, and **Field**, K'UN, result in Counter Hexagram 23, **Stripping**, PO. Increase and expansion through **augmenting** are contrasted with **stripping** and eliminating things.

- *Sequence*

> **Diminishing and-also not climaxing necessarily Augments.**
> **Anterior acquiescence has the use-of Augmenting.**

Associated Contexts **Diminish**, SUN: lessen, make smaller; take away from; lose, damage, spoil, wound; bad luck; blame, criticize; offer up, give away. The ideogram: hand and ceremonial vessel, offering sacrifice. Image of Hexagram 41. **And-also**, ERH: joins and contrasts two terms. **Not**, PU: simple negative. **Climax**, YI: come to a high point and stop, bring to an end; use up, lay aside; decline, reject. **Necessarily**, PI: unavoidably, indispensably, certainly.

Anterior ... the use-of: activating this hexagram depends on understanding and accepting the previous statement.

- *Contrasted Definitions*

> **Diminishing, Augmenting.**
> **Increasing, decreasing's beginning indeed.**

Associated Contexts **Increase**, SHENG: grow or make larger; flourishing, exuberant, full, abundant; heaped up; excellent, fine. **Decrease**, SHUAI: grow or make smaller; fade, decline, decay, diminish, cut off; grow old; adversity, misfortune. **'s/have(-it)/it/them**, CHIH: expresses possession, directly or as an object pronoun. **Begin**, SHIH: commence, start, open; earliest, first; beginning of a time-span, ended by completion, CHUNG. The ideogram: woman and eminent, beginning new life. **Indeed**, YEH: intensifier; indicates comment on previous statement.

● *Attached Evidences*

> **Augmenting: actualizing-tao's enriching indeed.**
> **Augmenting: long-living enriching and-also not setting-up.**
> **Augmenting: using the rising Harvest.**

Associated Contexts **Actualize-tao,** TE: realize tao in action; power, virtue; ability to follow the course traced by the ongoing process of the cosmos; keyword. The ideogram: to go, straight, and heart. Linked with acquire, TE: acquiring that which makes a being become what it is meant to be. **Enrich,** YÜ: make richer (excluding land); material, mental or spiritual wealth; bequeath; generous, abundant. The ideogram: garments, portable riches.

Long-living, CHANG: enduring, constant; senior, superior, greater; increase, prosper; respect, elevate. **Set-up,** SHE: establish, institute; arrange, set in order; spread a net. The ideogram: words and impel, establish with words.

Use(-of), YI: make use of, by means of, owing to; employ, make functional. **Rise,** HSING: get up, grow, lift; begin, give rise to, construct; be promoted; flourishing, fashionable. The ideogram: lift, two hands and unite, lift with both hands.

● *Symbol Tradition*

> **Wind, thunder. Augmenting.**
> **A chün tzu uses visualizing improvement, by-consequence shifting.**
> **[A chün tzu uses] possessing excess, by-consequence amending.**

Associated Contexts **Wind,** FENG: moving air, breeze, gust; weather and its influence on mood and humor; fashion, usage; wind and wood are the Symbols of the trigram Ground, SUN. **Thunder,** LEI: rising, arousing power; the Symbol of the trigram Shake, CHEN.

Chün tzu: ideal of a person who uses divination to order his/her life in accordance with tao rather than wilful intention; keyword. **Visualize,** CHIEN: seeing in all its aspects: vision, being visible, forming mental images; visit, call on, consult. The ideogram: eye above person, active and receptive sight. **Improve,** SHAN: make better, reform, perfect, repair; virtuous, wise; mild, docile; clever, skillful, handy. The ideogram: mouth and sheep, gentle speech. **By-consequence(-of),** TSE: very strong connection; reason, cause, result; rule, law, pattern, standard; therefore. **Shift**, CH'IEN: move, change, transpose; improve, ascend, be promoted; deport, dismiss, remove.

Possess, YU: in possession of, have, own; opposite of lack, WU. **Exceed**, KU: go beyond, pass by, pass over; excessive, transgress; error, fault. Image of Hexagrams 28 and 62. **Amend**, KAI: correct, reform, make new, alter, mend. The ideogram: self and strike, fighting your own errors.

- *Image Tradition*

> **Above diminishing, below Augmenting. [I]**
> **The commoners stimulated without delimiting.**
> **Above origin, below the below.**
> **One's tao, the great shining.**
>
> **Harvesting: possessing directed going. [II]**
> **Centering correcting possessing reward.**
> **Harvesting: wading the Great River.**
> **Woody tao, thereupon moving.**
>
> **Augmenting stirring-up and-also Ground. [III]**
> **Sun advancing without delimiting.**
> **Heaven spreading-out, earth giving-birth.**
> **One's Augmenting without sides.**
> **Total Augmenting's tao.**
> **Associating-with the season, accompanying the movement.**

Associated Contexts **[I] Above**, SHANG: anything above, in all senses; higher, upper, outer; upper trigram; opposite of below, HSIA. **Below**, HSIA: anything below, in all senses; lower, inner; lower trigram; opposite of above, SHANG.

Commoners, MIN: class of workers the state draws on to sustain the social hierarchy; undeveloped potential outside the organized personality. **Stimulate**, SHUO: rouse to action and good feeling; free from constraint, stir up, urge on; persuade, cheer, delight; set out in words; the Action of the trigram Open, TUI. The ideogram: words and exchange. **Without**, WU: devoid of; -less as suffix. **Delimit**, CHIANG: define frontiers, draw limits; boundary, border.

Origin, TZU: source, beginning, ground; cause, reason, motive; line of descent; path to the origin; yourself, intrinsic.

One's/one, CH'I: third person pronoun; also: it/its, he/his, she/hers, they/theirs. **Tao:** way or path; ongoing process of being and the course it traces for each specific person or thing; keyword. The ideogram: go and head, leading and the path it creates. **Great**, TA: big, noble, important, very; orient the will toward a self-imposed goal, impose direction; ability to lead or guide your life; contrasts with small, HSIAO, flexible adaptation to what crosses your path; keyword. Image of Hexagrams 14, 26, 28, 34. **Shine**, KUANG: illuminate; give off brilliant, bright light; honor, glory, éclat; result of action, contrasts with brightness, MING, light of heavenly bodies. The ideogram: fire above person, lifting the light.

[II] Centering correcting, CHUNG CHENG: central and correct; make rectifying one-sidedness and error your central concern; reaching a stable center in yourself can correct the situation. **Reward**, CH'ING: gift given from gratitude or benevolence; favor from heaven; congratulate with gifts. The ideogram: heart, follow and deer (wealth), the heart expressed through gifts.

Wood/tree, MU: all things woody or wooden, alive or constructed from wood; associated with the Woody Moment; wood and wind are the Symbols of the trigram Ground, SUN. The ideogram: a tree with roots and branches. **Thereupon**, NAI: on that ground, because of. **Move**, HSING: move or move something; motivate, emotionally moving; walk, act, do. The ideogram: stepping left then right.

[III] Stir-up, TUNG: excite, influence, move, affect; work, take action; come out of the egg or the bud; the Action of the trigram Shake, CHEN. The ideogram: strength and heavy, move weighty things. **Ground**, SUN: base on which things rest; support, foundation; mild, subtly penetrating; nourishing. The ideogram: stand and things arranged on it, the subtle influence of the ground. Image of Hexagram 57.

Sun/day, JIH: actual sun and the time of a sun-cycle, a day. **Advance**, CHIN: exert yourself, make progress, climb; be promoted; further the development of, augment; adopt a religion or conviction; offer, introduce.

Heaven, T'IEN: highest; sky, firmament, heavens; power above the human as opposed to earth, TI, below; the Symbol of the trigram Force, CH'IEN. The ideogram: great and the one above. **Spread-out**, SHIH: expand, diffuse, distribute, arrange, exhibit; add to, aid. The ideogram: flag and indeed, claiming new country. **Earth**, TI: ground on which the human world rests; basis of all things, nourishes all things; the Symbol of the trigram Field, K'UN. **Birth/give-birth-to**, SHENG: produce, beget, grow, bear, arise; life, vitality. The ideogram: earth and sprout.

Sides (on-all-sides), FANG: limits, boundaries; square, surface of the earth extending to the four cardinal points; everywhere. **Total**, FAN: all, everything; world, humankind.

Associate(-with), YÜ: consort with, combine; companions; group, band, company; agree with, comply, help. The ideogram: pair of hands reaching downward meets a pair of hands reaching upward, helpful association. **Season**, SHIH: quality of the time; the right time, opportune, in harmony; planning in accord with the time; seasons of the year. The ideogram: sun and temple, time as sacred. **Accompany**, HSIEH: take or go along with; jointly, all at once.

- *Transforming Lines*

   Initial nine

   a) **Harvesting: availing-of activating the great, arousing.
   Spring significant, without fault.**

   b) **Spring significant, without fault.
   The below, not munificent affairs indeed.**

Associated Contexts a) **Avail-of**, YUNG: take advantage of; benefit from, profit by; use for a specific purpose; apply to advantage. The ideogram: to divine and center, applying divination to central concerns. **Activate**, WEI: act or cause to act; do, make, manage; make active; attend to, help; because of. **Arouse**, TSO: stir up, stimulate, rouse from inactivity; generate; appear, arise. The ideogram: person and beginning.

   Spring, YÜAN: source, origin, head; great, excellent; arise, begin, generating power; first stage of the Time Cycle. **Significant**, CHI: leads to the experience of meaning; favorable, propitious, advantageous, appropriate; keyword. The ideogram: scholar and mouth, wise words of a sage. **Without fault**, WU CHIU: no error or harm in the situation.

b) **Munificence**, HOU: liberal, kind, generous; create abundance; thick, large. The ideogram: gift of a superior to an inferior. **Affairs**, SHIH: all kinds of personal activity; matters at hand; business, occupation; manage a business, case in court.

Six at-second

a) Maybe Augmenting's ten: partnering's tortoise.
Nowhere a controlling contradiction.
Perpetual Trial significant.
Kinghood availing-of presenting
                                     tending-towards the supreme, significant.

b) Maybe Augmenting it.
Originating-from outside, coming indeed.

Associated Contexts a) **Maybe,** HUO: possible but not certain, perhaps. **Ten,** SHIH: goal and end of reckoning; whole, complete, all; entire, perfected, the full amount; reach everywhere, receive everything. The ideogram: East–West line crosses North–South line, a grid that contains all. **Partner,** P'ENG: associate for mutual benefit; two equal or similar things; companions, friends, peers; join in; commercial ventures. The ideogram: linked strings of cowries or coins. **Tortoise,** KUEI: turtles; armored animals, shells and shields; long-living; oracle-consulting by tortoise shell; image of the macrocosm: heaven and earth, between them the soft flesh of humans.

Nothing/nowhere, FU: strong negative; not a single thing/place. **Control,** K'O: command; check, impede, prevail, obstruct, repress; adequate, able. The ideogram: roof beams support a house, controlling the structure. **Contradict,** WEI: oppose, disregard, disobey; seditious, perverse.

Perpetual, YUNG: continuing; everlasting, ever-flowing. The ideogram: flowing water. **Trial,** CHEN: test by ordeal; inquiry by divination and its result; righteous, firm; separating wheat from chaff; the kernel, the proven core; fourth stage of the Time Cycle. The ideogram: pearl and divination. **Significant,** CHI: leads to the experience of meaning; favorable, propitious, advantageous, appropriate; keyword. The ideogram: scholar and mouth, wise words of a sage.

King(hood), WANG: effective ruler, by authority of the Emperor, from whom others derive their power. **Avail-of,** YUNG: take advantage of; benefit from, profit by; use for a specific purpose; apply to advantage. The ideogram: to divine and center, applying divination to central concerns. **Present(-to),** HSIANG: present in sacrifice, offer with thanks, give to the gods or a superior; confer dignity on. **Tend-towards,** YÜ: move toward but not reach, in the direction of; contrasts with reach(-to), HU, actually arriving. **Supreme**, TI: highest, above all on earth; sovereign lord, source of power; emperor.

b) **It/them/have(-it)/'s**, CHIH: expresses possession, directly or as an object pronoun.

    Outside, WAI: outer, exterior, external; people working in places other than their home; unfamiliar, foreign; the upper trigram, as opposed to inside, NEI, the lower. **Come**, LAI, and go, WANG, describe the stream of time as it flows from future through present to past; come, LAI, indicates what is approaching; move toward, arrive at; keyword.

    Six at-third

    a) **Augmenting's availing-of pitfall affairs.**
      Without fault.
      Possessing conformity, center moving.
      Notifying the prince, availing-of the scepter.

    b) **Augmenting availing-of pitfall affairs.**
      Firmly possessing it indeed.

Associated Contexts a) **Avail-of**, YUNG: take advantage of; benefit from, profit by; use for a specific purpose; apply to advantage. The ideogram: to divine and center, applying divination to central concerns. **Pitfall**, HSIUNG: leads away from the experience of meaning; stuck and exposed to danger, unable to take in the situation; flow of life and spirit is blocked; unfortunate, baleful; keyword. **Affairs**, SHIH: all kinds of personal activity; matters at hand; business, occupation; manage a business, case in court.

    Without fault, WU CHIU: no error or harm in the situation.

    Possessing conformity, YU FU: inner and outer are in accord; confidence of the spirits has been captured; sincere, truthful; proper to take action. **Center**, CHUNG: inner, central; put in the center; middle, stable point enabling you to face inner and outer changes; middle line of trigram. The ideogram: field divided in two equal parts. Image of Hexagram 61.

    Notify, KAO: proclaim, order, decree; advise, inform, tell. The ideogram: mouth and ox head, imposing speech. **Prince**, KUNG: nobles acting as ministers of state in the capital; governing from the center rather than active in daily life; contrasts with feudatory, HOU, governors of the provinces. **Scepter**, KUEI: sign of rank that gives you freedom to report to the prince.

b) **Firm**, KU: constant, fixed, steady; chronic, recurrent. The ideogram: old and enclosure, long preserved. **It/them/have(-it)/'s**, CHIH: expresses possession, directly or as an object pronoun.

Six at-fourth

a) **Center moving.**
  Notifying the prince, adhering.
  Harvesting: availing-of activating depending-on shifting the city.

b) **Notifying the prince, adhering.**
  Using Augmenting purpose indeed.

Associated Contexts a) **Center**, CHUNG: inner, central; put in the center; middle, stable point enabling you to face inner and outer changes; middle line of trigram. The ideogram: field divided in two equal parts. Image of Hexagram 61.

  Notify, KAO: proclaim, order, decree; advise, inform, tell. The ideogram: mouth and ox head, imposing speech. **Prince**, KUNG: nobles acting as ministers of state in the capital; governing from the center rather than active in daily life; contrasts with feudatory, HOU, governors of the provinces. **Adhere(-to)**, TS'UNG: follow a way, hold to a doctrine, school, or person; hear and comply with, agree to; forced to follow, follower. The ideogram: two men walking, one following the other.

  Avail-of, YUNG: take advantage of; benefit from, profit by; use for a specific purpose; apply to advantage. The ideogram: to divine and center, applying divination to central concerns. **Activate**, WEI: act or cause to act; do, make, manage; make active; attend to, help; because of. **Depend-on**, YI: rely on, trust; conform to; image, illustration. **City**, KUO: area of only human constructions; political unit, polis. First of the territorial zones: city, suburbs, countryside, forests.

b) **Purpose**, CHIH: focus of mind and heart; will, inclination, resolve. The ideogram: heart and scholar, high inner resolve, or heart and go, inner determination.

Nine at-fifth

a) **Possessing conformity, a benevolent heart.**
  No question, Spring significant.
  Possessing conformity, benevolence: my actualizing-tao.

b) **Possessing conformity, a benevolent heart.**
  Actually no questioning it.
  Benevolence: my actualizing-tao.
  The great acquiring purpose indeed.

Associated Contexts a) **Possessing conformity**, YU FU: inner and outer are in accord; confidence of the spirits has been captured; sincere, truthful; proper to take action. **Benevolence**, HUI: regard for others, humanity; fulfill social duties; unselfish, kind, merciful. **Heart**, HSIN: heart as center of being; seat of mind's images and affections; moral nature; source of desires, intentions, will.

  No, WU: simple negative; un-, dis-. **Question**, WEN: ask, inquire about, examine; clear up doubts; convict and sentence. **Spring**, YÜAN: source, origin, head; great, excellent; arise, begin, generating power; first stage of the Time Cycle. **Significant**, CHI: leads to the experience of meaning; favorable, propitious, advantageous, appropriate; keyword. The ideogram: scholar and mouth, wise words of a sage.

  My/me/I, WO: first person pronoun; indicates an unusually strong emphasis on your own subjective experience.

b) **Actually**, YI: truly, really, at present. The ideogram: a dart and done, strong intention fully expressed. **It/them/have(-it)/'s**, CHIH: expresses possession, directly or as an object pronoun.

  Acquire, TE: obtain the desired object; wish for, desire covetously; gains, possessions. The ideogram: go and obstacle, going through obstacles to the goal. **Purpose**, CHIH: focus of mind and heart; will, inclination, resolve. The ideogram: heart and scholar, high inner resolve, or heart and go, inner determination.

  Nine above

  a) **Absolutely-no Augmenting it.**
    Maybe smiting it.
    Establishing the heart, no persevering.
    Pitfall.

  b) **Absolutely-no Augmenting it.**
    One-sided evidence indeed.
    Maybe smiting it.
    Originating-from outside, coming indeed.

Associated Contexts a) **Absolutely-no(thing)**, MO: complete elimination; not any, by no means. **It/them/have(-it)/'s**, CHIH: expresses possession, directly or as an object pronoun.

Maybe, HUO: possible but not certain, perhaps. **Smite**, CHI: hit, beat, attack; hurl against, rush a position; rouse to action. The ideogram: hand and hit, fist punching.

Establish, LI: set up, institute, order, arrange; stand erect; settled principles. **Heart**, HSIN: heart as center of being; seat of mind's images and affections; moral nature; source of desires, intentions, will. **No**, WU: simple negative; un-, dis-. **Persevere**, HENG: continue in the same way or spirit; constant, perpetual, regular; self-renewing; extend everywhere. Image of Hexagram 32.

Pitfall, HSIUNG: leads away from the experience of meaning; stuck and exposed to danger, unable to take in the situation; flow of life and spirit is blocked; unfortunate, baleful; keyword.

b) **One-sided**, P'IEN: excessive, partial, selfish; long for, bent on; lit.: inclined to one side. **Evidence**, TZ'U: verbal proof; instructions, orders, arguments; apology.

Outside, WAI: outer, exterior, external; people working in places other than their home; unfamiliar, foreign; the upper trigram, as opposed to inside, NEI, the lower. **Come**, LAI, and go, WANG, describe the stream of time as it flows from future through present to past; come, LAI, indicates what is approaching; move toward, arrive at; keyword.

PARTING ▪ *KUAI*

This hexagram describes your situation in terms of separation and diverging directions. It emphasizes that resolutely dividing your energies is the adequate way to handle it. To be in accord with the time, you are told to: **part**!

● *Image of the Situation*

> **Parting, displaying tending-towards kingly chambers.**
> **Conforming, crying-out, possessing adversity.**
> **Notifying originates-from the capital.**
> **Not Harvesting: approaching arms.**
> **Harvesting: possessing directed going.**

Associated Contexts **Part**, KUAI: separate, fork, cut off, decide; pull or flow in different directions; certain, settled; prompt, decisive, stern. **Display**, YANG: spread, extend, scatter, divulge; publish abroad, make famous. The ideogram: hand and expand, spreading a message. **Tend-towards**, YÜ: move toward but not reach, in the direction of; contrasts with reach(-to), HU, actually arriving. **King(hood)**, WANG: effective ruler, by authority of the Emperor, from whom others derive their power. **Chambers**, T'ING: family room, courtyard, hall; domestic. The ideogram: shelter and hall, a secure place.

Conforming, FU: accord between inner and outer in a particular moment; sincere, truthful, verified, reliable, in accord with the spirits; capture; prisoners, spoils; contrasts with trustworthy, HSIN, consistent over time. The ideogram: bird's claw enclosing young animals, possessive grip. Image of Hexagram 61. **Cry-out/outcry**, HAO: call out, proclaim; signal, order, command; mark, label, sign. **Possess**, YU: in possession of, have, own; opposite of lack, WU. **Adversity**, LI: danger; threatening, malevolent demon. This has two aspects: grind, sharpen, improve, perfect, stimulate; and: poisonous, sinister, cruel, contrary. It indicates a spirit or ghost that seeks revenge by inflicting suffering upon the living. Pacifying or exorcizing such a spirit can have a healing effect. The ideogram: sheltering cliff and stinging insect.

Notify, KAO: proclaim, order, decree; advise, inform, tell. The ideogram: mouth and ox head, imposing speech. **Origin**, TZU: source, beginning, ground; cause, reason, motive; line of descent; path to the origin; yourself, intrinsic. **Capital**, YI: populous fortified city, center and symbol of the domain it rules. The ideogram: enclosure and official seal.

Not, PU: simple negative. **Harvest**, LI: advantageous, profitable; acute, insightful; benefit, nourish; third stage of the Time Cycle. **Approach**, CHI: come near to, advance toward; about to do; soon. **Arms**, JUNG: weapons; armed people, soldiers; military, violent. The ideogram: spear and armor, offensive and defensive weapons.

Possessing directed going, YU YU WANG: imposing a direction on the flow of time from present to past; have a specific goal or purpose.

- *Outer and Inner Aspects*

☱ **Open**: vapor rising from the marsh's open surface stimulates and fertilizes; stimulating words cheer and inspire. **Open** begins the yin hemicycle by initiating the formative process.

Connection to the outer: liquifying, casting, skinning off the mold, the Metallic Moment beginning. **Open** stimulates, cheers and reveals innate form.

☰ **Force**: The force of heaven struggles on, persistent and unwearied; heavenly bodies persist in their orbits. **Force** is the center of the yin hemicycle, completing the formative process.

Connection to the inner: struggling forces are bound together in dynamic tension, the Metallic Moment culminating. **Force** brings elements to grips, creating enduring relations.

Inner struggle is broken up by outer stimulation, **parting** the grappling powers.

- *Counter Indications*

The doubled Nuclear trigram **Force**, CH'IEN, results in Counter Hexagram 1, **Force**, CH'IEN. **Parting** the energies active in a situation is contrasted with the homogenous drive of **force**.

● *Sequence*

> **Augmenting and-also not climaxing necessarily breaks-up.**
> **Anterior acquiescence has the use-of Parting.**
> **Parting implies breaking-up indeed.**

Associated Contexts **Augment**, YI: increase, advance, promote, benefit, strengthen; pour in more; full, superabundant; restorative. The ideogram: water and vessel, pouring in more. Image of Hexagram 42. **And-also**, ERH: joins and contrasts two terms. **Climax,** YI: come to a high point and stop, bring to an end; use up, lay aside; decline, reject. **Necessarily**, PI: unavoidably, indispensably, certainly. **Break-up**, CHÜEH: streams diverging; break through an obstacle and scatter; separate, break into parts; cut or bite through; decide, pass sentence. The ideogram: water and parting.

    Anterior ... the use-of: activating this hexagram depends on understanding and accepting the previous statement.

    Imply, CHE: further signify; additional meaning. **Indeed**, YEH: intensifier; indicates comment on previous statement.

● *Contrasted Definitions*

> **Coupling: meeting indeed.**
> **Supple meeting solid indeed.**
> **Parting: breaking-up indeed.**
> **Solid breaking-up supple indeed.**

Associated Contexts **Couple**, KOU: driven encounter, at once transitory and enduring, that is the reflection of primal yin and yang; meet, encounter, copulate; mating animals; magnetism, gravity; to be gripped by impersonal forces. Image of Hexagram 44. **Meet**, YÜ: come on unexpectedly, encounter; occur, happen; pleasant meeting, lucky coincidence; agree.

    Supple, JOU: quality of the opened lines; flexible, pliant, tender, adaptable. **Solid**, KANG: quality of the whole lines; firm, strong, unyielding, persisting.

● *Symbol Tradition*

> Above marsh with-respect-to heaven. Parting.
> A chün tzu uses spreading-out benefits to extend-to the below.
> [A chün tzu uses] residing-in actualizing-tao,
> > by-consequence keeping-aloof.

Associated Contexts **Above**, SHANG: anything above, in all senses; higher, upper, outer; upper trigram; opposite of below, HSIA. **Marsh**, TSE: open surface of a flat body of water and the vapors rising from it; fertilize, enrich; kindness, favor; the Symbol of the trigram Open, TUI. **With-respect-to**, YÜ: relates to, refers to; hold a position in. **Heaven**, T'IEN: highest; sky, firmament, heavens; power above the human as opposed to earth, TI, below; the Symbol of the trigram Force, CH'IEN. The ideogram: great and the one above.

    Chün tzu: ideal of a person who uses divination to order his/her life in accordance with tao rather than wilful intention; keyword. **Use(-of)**, YI: make use of, by means of, owing to; employ, make functional. **Spread-out**, SHIH: expand, diffuse, distribute, arrange, exhibit; add to, aid. The ideogram: flag and indeed, claiming new country. **Benefits**, LU: pay, salary, income; have the use of; goods received, revenues; official recognition. **Extend(-to)**, CHI: reach to, draw out, prolong; continuous, enduring. **Below**, HSIA: anything below, in all senses; lower, inner; lower trigram; opposite of above, SHANG.

    Reside(-in), CHÜ: dwell, live in, stay; sit down, fill an office; settled parts of a country. The ideogram: body and seat. **Actualize-tao**, TE: realize tao in action; power, virtue; ability to follow the course traced by the ongoing process of the cosmos; keyword. The ideogram: to go, straight, and heart. Linked with acquire, TE: acquiring that which makes a being become what it is meant to be. **By-consequence(-of)**, TSE: very strong connection; reason, cause, result; rule, law, pattern, standard; therefore. **Keep-aloof**, CHI: keep at a distance; avoid, fear, shun; antipathy. The ideogram: heart and self, keeping to yourself.

● *Image Tradition*

> Parting. Breaking-up indeed. [I]
> Solid breaking-up supple indeed.
> Persisting and-also stimulating.
> Breaking-up and-also harmonizing.

Displaying tending-towards kingly chambers. [II]
Supple riding five solids indeed.
Conforming, crying-out, possessing adversity.
One's exposure thereupon shining indeed.

Notifying originates-from the capital. [III]
Not Harvesting: approaching arms.
The place to honor thereupon exhausted indeed.
Harvesting: possessing directed going.
Solid long-living, thereupon completing indeed.

Associated Contexts [I] **Persist**, CHIEN: strong, robust, dynamic, tenacious; continuous; unwearied heavenly bodies in their orbits; the Action of the trigram Force, CH'IEN. **Stimulate**, SHUO: rouse to action and good feeling; free from constraint, stir up, urge on; persuade, cheer, delight; set out in words; the Action of the trigram Open, TUI. The ideogram: words and exchange.

Harmony, HO: concord, union; conciliate; at peace, mild; fit, tune, adjust.

[II] **Ride**, CH'ENG: ride an animal or a chariot; have the upper hand, seize the right time; control strong power; overcome the nature of the other; supple opened line above a solid whole line. **Five**, WU: number for active groups: Five Moments, Directions, colors, smells, tastes, tones, feelings; fifth.

One's/one, CH'I: third person pronoun; also: it/its, he/his, she/hers, they/theirs. **Expose**, WEI: exposed to danger, precipitous, unsteady; too high, not upright; uneasy. The ideogram: overhanging rock, person and limit, exposure in an extreme position. **Thereupon**, NAI: on that ground, because of. **Shine**, KUANG: illuminate; give off brilliant, bright light; honor, glory, éclat; result of action, contrasts with brightness, MING, light of heavenly bodies. The ideogram: fire above person, lifting the light.

[III] **Place**, SO: where something belongs or comes from; residence, dwelling; habitual focus or object. **Honor**, SHANG: esteem, give high rank to; eminent; put one thing on top of another. **Exhaust**, CH'IUNG: bring to an end; limit, extremity; destitute; investigate exhaustively; end without a new beginning. The ideogram: cave and naked person, bent with disease or old age.

Long-living, CHANG: enduring, constant; senior, superior, greater; increase, prosper; respect, elevate. **Complete**, CHUNG: end of a cycle that begins the next; last, whole, all; contrasts with exhaust, CH'IUNG, final end. The ideogram: silk cocoons, follow and ice, winter linking one year with the next.

● *Transforming Lines*

Initial nine

a) **Invigorating tending-towards the preceding foot.**
Going not mastering, activating faulty.

b) **Not mastering and-also going.**
Fault indeed.

Associated Contexts a) **Invigorate**, CHUANG: inspirit, animate; strong, robust; full grown, flourishing, abundant; attain manhood (at 30); damage through unrestrained strength. The ideogram: strength and scholar, intellectual impact. Image of Hexagram 34. **Precede**, CH'IEN: come before in time and thus in value; anterior, former, ancient; lead forward. **Foot**, CHIH: literal foot; foundation, base.

Go, WANG, and come, LAI, describe the stream of time as it flows from future through present to past; go, WANG, indicates what is departing from present to past; proceed, move on; keyword. **Master**, SHENG: have the upper hand, conquer; worthy of, able to; control, check, command. **Activate**, WEI: act or cause to act; do, make, manage; make active; attend to, help; because of. **Fault**, CHIU: unworthy conduct that leads to harm, illness, misfortune. The ideogram: person and differ, differ from what you should be.

Nine at-second

a) **Awe, an outcry.**
Absolutely-no night-time, possessing arms.
No cares.

b) **Possessing arms, no cares.**
Acquiring centering tao indeed.

Associated Contexts a) **Awe**, T'I: alarmed and cautious; respect, regard, fear; stand in awe of. The ideogram: heart and versatile, the heart aware of sudden change.

Absolutely-no(thing), MO: complete elimination; not any, by no means. **Night-time**, YEH: dark half of 24 hour cycle.

No, WU: simple negative; un-, dis-. **Care**, HSÜ: fear, doubt, concern; heartfelt attachment; relieve, soothe, aid; sympathy, compassion, consolation. The ideogram: heart and blood, the heart's blood affected.

b) **Acquire**, TE: obtain the desired object; wish for, desire covetously; gains, possessions. The ideogram: go and obstacle, going through obstacles to the goal. **Center**, CHUNG: inner, central; put in the center; middle, stable point enabling you to face inner and outer changes; middle line of trigram. The ideogram: field divided in two equal parts. Image of Hexagram 61. **Tao:** way or path; ongoing process of being and the course it traces for each specific person or thing; keyword. The ideogram: go and head, leading and the path it creates.

Nine at-third

a) **Invigorating tending-towards the cheek-bones:**
    Possessing a pitfall.
    A chün tzu: Parting, Parting.
    Solitary going, meeting rain.
    Like soaking, possessing indignation.
    Without fault.

b) **A chün tzu: Parting, Parting.**
    Completing without fault indeed.

Associated Contexts a) **Invigorate**, CHUANG: inspirit, animate; strong, robust; full grown, flourishing, abundant; attain manhood (at 30); damage through unrestrained strength. The ideogram: strength and scholar, intellectual impact. Image of Hexagram 34. **Cheek-bones**, CH'ÜAN: facial feature denoting character; high cheek-bones indicate cruelty.

Pitfall, HSIUNG: leads away from the experience of meaning; stuck and exposed to danger, unable to take in the situation; flow of life and spirit is blocked; unfortunate, baleful; keyword.

Parting, KUAI: The doubled character intensifies this quality. **Solitary**, TI: alone; single; isolated, abandoned. **Go**, WANG, and come, LAI, describe the stream of time as it flows from future through present to past; go, WANG, indicates what is departing from present to past; proceed, move on; keyword. **Rain**, YÜ: all precipitation; sudden showers, fast and furious; associated with the trigram Gorge, K'AN, and the Streaming Moment.

Like, JO: same as; just as, similar to. **Soak**, JU: immerse, steep; damp, wet; stain, pollute, blemish; urinate on. **Indignation**, WEN: irritated, wrathful; feeling of injustice, rage; hateful.

Without fault, WU CHIU: no error or harm in the situation.

Nine at-fourth

a) The sacrum without flesh.
One moves the resting-place moreover.
Hauling-along the goat, repenting extinguished.
Hearing words, not trustworthy.

b) One moves the resting-place moreover.
Situation not appropriate indeed.
Hearing words, not trustworthy.
Understanding not brightened indeed.

Associated Contexts a) **Sacrum**, T'UN: lower back where it joins legs; buttocks, seat, lower spine. **Without**, WU: devoid of; -less as suffix. **Flesh**, FU: muscles, organs, skin, in contrast to bones.

Move, HSING: move or move something; motivate, emotionally moving; walk, act, do. The ideogram: stepping left then right. **Rest(ing-place)**, TZ'U: camp, inn, shed; halting-place, breathing-spell; put in consecutive order. The ideogram: two and breath, pausing to breathe. **Moreover**, CH'IEH: further, and also.

Haul-along, CH'IEN: haul or pull, drag behind; pull an animal on a rope; pull toward. The ideogram: ox and halter. **Goat**, YANG: sheep and goats; direct thought and action. **Repenting extinguished**, HUI WANG: previous troubles and consequent remorse will disappear.

Hear, WEN: perceive sound; learn by report; news, fame. The ideogram: ear and door. **Word**, YEN: speech, spoken words, sayings; talk, discuss, address. The ideogram: mouth and rising vapor, words as speech. **Trustworthy**, HSIN: truthful, faithful, consistent over time; integrity; confide in, follow; credentials; contrasts with conforming, FU, connection in a specific moment. The ideogram: person and word, true speech.

b) **Situation**, WEI: place or seat according to rank; post, position, command; right, proper; established, arranged. The ideogram: person and stand, servants in their places. **Appropriate**, TANG: suitable; opportune, convenient; adequate, competent; equal to; whole lines in uneven places and opened lines in even places.

Understand, TS'UNG: perceive quickly, astute, sharp; discriminate intelligently. The ideogram: ear and quick. **Brightness**, MING: light-giving aspect of burning, heavenly bodies and consciousness; with fire, the Symbol of the trigram Radiance, LI.

Nine at-fifth

a) **Reeds, highlands: Parting, Parting.**
   Center moving, without fault.

b) **Center moving, without fault.**
   Center not-yet shining indeed.

Associated Contexts a) **Reeds**, KUAN: marsh and swamp plants, rushes. **Highlands**, LU: high, dry land as distinct from swamps; plateau. **Parting**, KUAI: the doubled character intensifies this quality.

   Center, CHUNG: inner, central; put in the center; middle, stable point enabling you to face inner and outer changes; middle line of trigram. The ideogram: field divided in two equal parts. Image of Hexagram 61. **Move**, HSING: move or move something; motivate, emotionally moving; walk, act, do. The ideogram: stepping left then right. **Without fault**, WU CHIU: no error or harm in the situation.

b) **Not-yet**, WEI: temporal negative; something will but has not yet occurred; contrary of already, CHI. Image of Hexagram 64. **Shine**, KUANG: illuminate; give off brilliant, bright light; honor, glory, éclat; result of action, contrasts with brightness, MING, light of heavenly bodies. The ideogram: fire above person, lifting the light.

Six above

a) **Without crying-out.**
   Completing: possessing a pitfall.

b) **Without crying-out's pitfall.**
   Completing not permitting long-living indeed.

Associated Contexts a) **Without,** WU: devoid of; -less as suffix. **Pitfall,** HSIUNG: leads away from the experience of meaning; stuck and exposed to danger, unable to take in the situation; flow of life and spirit is blocked; unfortunate, baleful; keyword.

b) **'s/have(-it)/it/them,** CHIH: expresses possession, directly or as an object pronoun.

Not permitting, PU K'O: not possible; contradicts an inherent principle. The ideogram: mouth and breath, silent consent.

44

COUPLING ▪ *KOU*

This hexagram describes your situation in terms of the encounter of primal energies. It emphasizes that seeing-through your personal situation as the connection of objective forces is the adequate way to handle it. To be in accord with the time, you are told to: **couple!**

● *Image of the Situation*

> **Coupling, womanhood invigorating.**
> **No availing-of grasping womanhood.**

Associated Contexts **Couple**, KOU: intense, driven encounter, at once transitory and enduring, that is the reflection of primal yin and yang; meet, encounter, copulate; mating animals; magnetism, gravity; to be gripped by impersonal forces. **Woman(hood)**, NÜ: a woman; what is inherently female. **Invigorate**, CHUANG: inspirit, animate; strong, robust; full grown, flourishing, abundant; attain manhood (at 30); damage through unrestrained strength. The ideogram: strength and scholar, intellectual impact. Image of Hexagram 34.

No, WU: simple negative; un-, dis-. **Avail-of**, YUNG: take advantage of; benefit from, profit by; use for a specific purpose; apply to advantage. The ideogram: to divine and center, applying divination to central concerns. **Grasp**, CH'Ü: lay hold of, take and use, seize, appropriate; grasp the meaning, understand. The ideogram: ear and hand, hear and grasp.

● *Outer and Inner Aspects*

☰ **Force**: The force of heaven struggles on, persistent and unwearied; heavenly bodies persist in their orbits. **Force** is the center of the yin hemicycle, completing the formative process.

Connection to the outer: struggling forces are bound together in dynamic tension, the Metallic Moment culminating. **Force** brings elements to grips, creating enduring relations.

☴ **Ground**: Wind and wood subtly enter from the ground, penetrating and pervading. **Ground** is the center of the yang hemicycle, spreading pervasive action.

Connection to the inner: penetrating and bringing together, the Woody Moment culminating. **Ground** pervades, matches and couples, seeding a new generation.

Primal forces **couple** in the inner world, seeding enduring new forms. These trigrams form the vertical axis of yin and yang.

● *Counter Indications*

The doubled Nuclear trigram **Force**, CH'IEN, results in Counter Hexagram 1, **Force**, CH'IEN. The intermittent intensity of **coupling** is contrasted with the steady persistence of **force**.

● *Sequence*

> **Breaking-up necessarily possesses meeting.**
> **Anterior acquiescence has the use-of Coupling.**
> **Coupling implies meeting indeed.**

Associated Contexts **Break-up**, CHÜEH: streams diverging; break through an obstacle and scatter; separate, break into parts; cut or bite through; decide, pass sentence. The ideogram: water and parting. **Necessarily**, PI: unavoidably, indispensably, certainly. **Possess**, YU: in possession of, have, own; opposite of lack, WU. **Meet**, YÜ: come on unexpectedly, encounter; occur, happen; pleasant meeting, lucky coincidence; agree.

Anterior ... the use-of: activating this hexagram depends on understanding and accepting the previous statement.

Imply, CHE: further signify; additional meaning. **Indeed**, YEH: intensifier; indicates comment on previous statement.

● *Contrasted Definitions*

> **Coupling: meeting indeed.**
> **Supple meeting solid indeed.**
> **Parting: breaking-up indeed.**
> **Solid breaking-up supple indeed.**

Associated Contexts **Supple**, JOU: quality of the opened lines; flexible, pliant, tender, adaptable. **Solid**, KANG: quality of the whole lines; firm, strong, unyielding, persisting. **Part**, KUAI: separate, fork, cut off, decide; pull or flow in different directions; certain, settled; prompt, decisive, stern. Image of Hexagram 43.

- *Symbol Tradition*

> **Below heaven possessing wind. Coupling.**
> **The crown-prince uses spreading-out fate to command the four sides.**

Associated Contexts **Below**, HSIA: anything below, in all senses; lower, inner; lower trigram; opposite of above, SHANG. **Heaven**, T'IEN: highest; sky, firmament, heavens; power above the human as opposed to earth, TI, below; the Symbol of the trigram Force, CH'IEN. The ideogram: great and the one above. **Wind**, FENG: moving air, breeze, gust; weather and its influence on mood and humor; fashion, usage; wind and wood are the Symbols of the trigram Ground, SUN.

Crown-prince, HOU: successor to the sovereign. The ideogram: one, mouth and shelter, one with the sovereign's orders. **Use(-of)**, YI: make use of, by means of, owing to; employ, make functional. **Spread-out**, SHIH: expand, diffuse, distribute, arrange, exhibit; add to, aid. The ideogram: flag and indeed, claiming new country. **Fate**, MING: individual destiny; birth and death as limits of life; issue orders with authority; consult the gods. The ideogram: mouth and order, words with heavenly authority. **Command**, KAO: give orders; insist on, express wishes; official seal. The ideogram: words and announce, verbal commands. **Four sides**, SSU FANG: the cardinal points; the limits or boundaries of the earth; everywhere, all around.

- *Image Tradition*

> **Coupling. Meeting indeed. [I]**
> **Supple meeting solid indeed.**
> **No availing-of grasping womanhood.**
> **Not permitting associating-with long-living indeed.**
>
> **Heaven, Earth: mutually meeting. [II]**
> **The kinds: beings conjoining composition indeed.**

Solid meeting centering correctness. [III]
Below Heaven, the great moving indeed.
Actually Coupling's season righteously great in-fact.

Associated Contexts [I] **Not permitting**, PU K'O: not possible; contradicts an inherent principle. The ideogram: mouth and breath, silent consent. **Associate(-with)**, YÜ: consort with, combine; companions; group, band, company; agree with, comply, help. The ideogram: pair of hands reaching downward meets a pair of hands reaching upward, helpful association. **Long-living**, CHANG: enduring, constant; senior, superior, greater; increase, prosper; respect, elevate.

[II] **Heaven**, T'IEN: highest; sky, firmament, heavens; power above the human as opposed to earth, TI, below; the Symbol of the trigram Force, CH'IEN. The ideogram: great and the one above. **Earth**, TI: ground on which the human world rests; basis of all things, nourishes all things; the Symbol of the trigram Field, K'UN. **Mutual**, HSIANG: reciprocal assistance, encourage, help; bring together, blend with; examine, inspect; by turns.

   Kinds, P'IN: species and their essential qualities; sorts, classes; classify, select. **Being(s)**, WU: creature, thing, any single being; matter, substance, essence; nature of things. **Conjoin**, HSIEN: come into contact with, influence; reach, join together; put together as parts of a previously separated whole; come into conjunction, as the celestial bodies; totally, completely; lit.: broken piece of pottery, the halves of which join to identify partners. Image of Hexagram 31. **Composition**, CHANG: a well-composed whole and its structure; beautiful creations; elegant, clear, brilliant; contrasts with pattern, WEN, beauty of intrinsic design.

[III] **Centering correcting**, CHUNG CHENG: central and correct; make rectifying one-sidedness and error your central concern; reaching a stable center in yourself can correct the situation.

   Below Heaven, T'IEN HSIA: the human world, between heaven and earth. **Great**, TA: big, noble, important, very; orient the will toward a self-imposed goal, impose direction; ability to lead or guide your life; contrasts with small, HSIAO, flexible adaptation to what crosses your path; keyword. Image of Hexagrams 14, 26, 28, 34. **Move**, HSIANG: move or move something; motivate, emotionally moving; walk, act, do. The ideogram: stepping left then right.

Actually ... in-fact, YI TSAI: stresses the importance of a statement. The ideogram: a dart and done, strong intention fully expressed. **'s/have(-it)/it/them,** CHIH: expresses possession, directly or as an object pronoun. **Season,** SHIH: quality of the time; the right time, opportune, in harmony; planning in accord with the time; seasons of the year. The ideogram: sun and temple, time as sacred. **Righteous,** YI: proper and just, meets the standards; things in their proper place; the heart that rules itself; upright, moral rule; contrasts with Harvest, LI, advantage or profit.

● *Transforming Lines*

Initial six

a) **Attaching tending-towards a metallic chock.**
Trial: significant.
Possessing directed going.
Visualizing: pitfall.
Ruining the pig, conforming: hoof dragging.

b) **Attaching tending-towards a metallic chock.**
Supple tao hauling-along indeed.

Associated Contexts a) **Attach,** HSI: fasten to, bind, tie; retain, continue; keep in mind, emotionally attached. **Tend-towards,** YÜ: move toward but not reach, in the direction of; contrasts with reach(-to), HU, actually arriving. **Metallic,** CHIN: smelting and casting; all things pertaining to metal, particularly gold; autumn, West, sunset; one of the Five Moments. **Chock,** NI: block used to stop a cart wheel; inquire, investigate.

Trial, CHEN: test by ordeal; inquiry by divination and its result; righteous, firm; separating wheat from chaff; the kernel, the proven core; fourth stage of the Time Cycle. The ideogram: pearl and divination. **Significant,** CHI: leads to the experience of meaning; favorable, propitious, advantageous, appropriate; keyword. The ideogram: scholar and mouth, wise words of a sage.

Possessing directed going, YU YU WANG: imposing a direction on the flow of time from present to past; have a specific goal or purpose.

Visualize, CHIEN: seeing in all its aspects: vision, being visible, forming mental images; visit, call on, consult. The ideogram: eye above person, active and receptive sight. **Pitfall,** HSIUNG: leads away from the experience of meaning; stuck and exposed to danger, unable to take in the situation; flow of life and spirit is blocked; unfortunate, baleful; keyword.

Ruin, LEI: destroy, break, overturn; debilitated, meager, emaciated; entangled. **Pig**, SHIH: all swine; sign of wealth and good fortune; associated with the Streaming Moment. **Conforming**, FU: accord between inner and outer in a particular moment; sincere, truthful, verified, reliable, in accord with the spirits; capture; prisoners, spoils; contrasts with trustworthy, HSIN, consistent over time. The ideogram: bird's claw enclosing young animals, possessive grip. Image of Hexagram 61. **Hoof**, TI: pig's trotters and horse's hooves. **Drag**, CHU: pull along a hurt or malfunctioning foot; limping, lame. The ideogram: foot and worm, an infected foot.

b) **Tao**: way or path; ongoing process of being and the course it traces for each specific person or thing; keyword. The ideogram: go and head, leading and the path it creates. **Haul-along**, CH'IEN: haul or pull, drag behind; pull an animal on a rope; pull toward. The ideogram: ox and halter.

Nine at-second

 a) **Enwrapping possessing fish.**
 Without fault.
 Not Harvesting: guesting.

 b) **Enwrapping possessing fish.**
 Righteously not extending-to guesting indeed.

Associated Contexts a) **Enwrap**, PAO: envelop, hold, contain; patient; take on responsibility, engaged. The ideogram: enfold and self, a fetus in the womb. **Fish**, YÜ: scaly, aquatic beings hidden in the water; symbol of abundance; connected with the Streaming Moment.
 Without fault, WU CHIU: no error or harm in the situation.
 Not, PU: simple negative. **Harvest**, LI: advantageous, profitable; acute, insightful; benefit, nourish; third stage of the Time Cycle. **Guest**, PIN: entertain a guest; visit someone, enjoy hospitality; receive a stranger.

b) **Extend(-to)**, CHI: reach to, draw out, prolong; continuous, enduring.

Nine at-third

 a) **The sacrum without flesh.**
 One moves the resting-place moreover.
 Adversity.
 Without the great: fault.

b) **One moves the resting-place moreover.**
Moving, not-yet hauling-along indeed.

Associated Contexts a) **Sacrum**, T'UN: lower back where it joins
legs; buttocks, seat, lower spine. **Without**, WU: devoid of; -less as suffix.
Flesh, FU: muscles, organs, skin, in contrast to bones.

One's/one, CH'I: third person pronoun; also: it/its, he/his, she/hers,
they/theirs. **Rest(ing-place)**, TZ'U: camp, inn, shed; halting-place,
breathing-spell; put in consecutive order. The ideogram: two and breath,
pausing to breath. **Moreover**, CH'IEH: further, and also.

Adversity, LI: danger; threatening, malevolent demon. This has two
aspects: grind, sharpen, improve, perfect, stimulate; and: poisonous,
sinister, cruel, contrary. It indicates a spirit or ghost that seeks revenge
by inflicting suffering upon the living. Pacifying or exorcizing such a
spirit can have a healing effect. The ideogram: sheltering cliff and
stinging insect.

Fault, CHIU: unworthy conduct that leads to harm, illness,
misfortune. The ideogram: person and differ, differ from what you should
be.

b) **Not-yet**, WEI: temporal negative; something will but has not yet
occurred; contrary of already, CHI. Image of Hexagram 64. **Haul-along**,
CH'IEN: haul or pull, drag behind; pull an animal on a rope; pull toward.
The ideogram: ox and halter.

Nine at-fourth

a) **Enwrapping without fish.**
Rising-up: pitfall.

b) **Without fish's pitfall.**
Distancing the commoners indeed.

Associated Contexts a) **Enwrap**, PAO: envelop, hold, contain;
patient; take on responsibility, engaged. The ideogram: enfold and self, a
fetus in the womb. **Without**, WU: devoid of; -less as suffix. **Fish**, YÜ:
scaly, aquatic beings hidden in the water; symbol of abundance; connected
with the Streaming Moment.

Rise-up, CH'I: stand up, lift; undertake, begin, originate. **Pitfall**,
HSIUNG: leads away from the experience of meaning; stuck and exposed
to danger, unable to take in the situation; flow of life and spirit is blocked;
unfortunate, baleful; keyword.

b) **Distance**, YÜAN: far off, remote; keep at a distance; alienated. The ideogram: go and a long way. **Commoners**, MIN: class of workers the state draws on to sustain the social hierarchy; undeveloped potential outside the organized personality.

Nine at-fifth

a) **Using osier, enwrapping melons.**
   Containing composition.
   Possessing tumbling, originating-from heaven.

b) **Nine at-fifth, containing composition.**
   Centering correctness indeed.
   Possessing tumbling, originating-from heaven.
   Purpose, not stowing-away fate indeed.

Associated Contexts a) **Osier**, CH'I: willow branches used to make baskets. **Enwrap**, PAO: envelop, hold, contain; patient; take on responsibility, engaged. The ideogram: enfold and self, a fetus in the womb. **Melon**, KUA: general term for melon, gourd, squash, cucumber; symbol of Heaven[and]Earth, the cosmos.

   Contain, HAN: retain, embody, cherish; withhold, tolerate; lit.: contain in the mouth, put a coin in a corpse's mouth.

   Tumble, YÜN: fall with a crash, fall from the sky; roll down. **Origin**, TZU: source, beginning, ground; cause, reason, motive; line of descent; path to the origin; yourself, intrinsic. **Heaven**, T'IEN: highest; sky, firmament, heavens; power above the human as opposed to earth, TI, below; the Symbol of the trigram Force, CH'IEN. The ideogram: great and the one above.

b) **Purpose**, CHIH: focus of mind and heart; will, inclination, resolve. The ideogram: heart and scholar, high inner resolve, or heart and go, inner determination. **Not**, PU: simple negative. **Stow(-away)**, SHE: set aside, put away, store; halt, rest in; temporary lodgings, breathing-spell.

Nine above

a) **Coupling: one's horns.**
   Abashment.
   Without fault.

b) **Coupling: one's horns.**
Exhausting abashment above indeed.

Associated Contexts a) **One's/one**, CH'I: third person pronoun; also: it/its, he/his, she/hers, they/theirs. **Horns,** CHIO: strength and power; gore; dispute, test your strength; headland.

Abashment, LIN: distress, shame, regret, humiliation; aware of having lost the right track; leads to repenting, HUI, correcting the direction of mind and life.

Without fault, WU CHIU: no error or harm in the situation.

b) **Exhaust,** CH'IUNG: bring to an end; limit, extremity; destitute; investigate exhaustively; end without a new beginning. The ideogram: cave and naked person, bent with disease or old age. **Above,** SHANG: anything above, in all senses; higher, upper, outer; upper trigram; opposite of below, HSIA.

CLUSTERING ▪ *TS'UI*

This hexagram describes your situation in terms of collecting and assembling. It emphasizes that bringing people and things together through a common feeling or goal is the adequate way to handle it. To be in accord with the time, you are told to: **cluster!**

● *Image of the Situation*

> **Clustering, Growing.**
> **The king imagines possessing a temple.**
> **Harvesting: visualizing Great People. Growing.**
> **Harvesting Trial. Availing-of the great:**
> > **sacrificial-victims significant.**
> **Harvesting: possessing directed going.**

Associated Contexts **Cluster**, TS'UI: call or pack together; tight groups of people, animals, things; collect, gather, assemble, concentrate; bunch, crowd, collection; lit.: dense, tussocky grass. **Grow**, HENG: success through a sacrifice; pervade, persevere; bring to full growth; enjoy; vigorous, effective; second stage of the Time Cycle.

King(hood), WANG: effective ruler, by authority of the Emperor, from whom others derive their power. **Imagine**, CHIA: create in the mind; fantasize, suppose, pretend, imitate; fiction; illusory, unreal; costume. The ideogram: person and borrow. **Possess**, YU: in possession of, have, own; opposite of lack, WU. **Temple**, MIAO: building used to honor gods and ancestors.

Harvest, LI: advantageous, profitable; acute, insightful; benefit, nourish; third stage of the Time Cycle. **Visualize**, CHIEN: seeing in all its aspects: vision, being visible, forming mental images; visit, call on, consult. The ideogram: eye above person, active and receptive sight. **Great People**, TA JEN: important, noble, influential; those who impose a ruling principle on their lives; effect of the great within an individual; keyword.

Harvesting Trial, LI CHEN: advantageous divination; putting the action in question to the test is beneficial. **Avail-of**, YUNG: take advantage of; benefit from, profit by; use for a specific purpose; apply to advantage. The ideogram: to divine and center, applying divination to central concerns. **Great**, TA: big, noble, important, very; orient the will toward a self-imposed goal, impose direction; ability to lead or guide your life; contrasts with small, HSIAO, flexible adaptation to what crosses your path; keyword. Image of Hexagrams 14, 26, 28, 34. **Sacrificial-victims**, SHENG: the six sacrificial animals: horse, ox, lamb, cock, dog and pig. **Significant**, CHI: leads to the experience of meaning; favorable, propitious, advantageous, appropriate; keyword. The ideogram: scholar and mouth, wise words of a sage.

Possessing directed going, YU YU WANG: imposing a direction on the flow of time from present to past; have a specific goal or purpose.

- *Outer and Inner Aspects*

☱ **Open**: vapor rising from the marsh's open surface stimulates and fertilizes; stimulating words cheer and inspire. **Open** begins the yin hemicycle by initiating the formative process.

Connection to the outer: liquifying, casting, skinning off the mold, the Metallic Moment beginning. **Open** stimulates, cheers and reveals innate form.

☷ **Field**: The field of earth yields and sustains, serving in order to produce. **Field** is the equalizing point between yin and yang where things labor and serve.

Connection to the inner: the common labor of sowing and hoarding, the Earthy Moment. **Field** produces concrete results through serving.

An inner willingness to yield and serve **clusters** and stimulates, revealing the forms that bring people together.

- *Counter Indications*

Nuclear trigrams **Ground**, SUN, and **Bound**, KEN, result in Counter Hexagram 53, **Infiltrating**, CHIEN. **Clustering** and holding things together are contrasted with gradual outward penetration through **infiltrating**.

● *Sequence*

> **Beings mutually meeting and-also afterwards assembling.**
> **Anterior acquiescence has the use-of Clustering.**
> **Clustering implies assembling indeed.**

Associated Contexts **Being(s)**, WU: creature, thing, any single being; matter, substance, essence; nature of things. **Mutual**, HSIANG: reciprocal assistance, encourage, help; bring together, blend with; examine, inspect; by turns. **Meet**, YÜ: come on unexpectedly, encounter; occur, happen; pleasant meeting, lucky coincidence; agree. **And-also**, ERH: joins and contrasts two terms. **After(wards)/later**, HOU: come after in time, subsequent; put oneself after; the second; attendants, heirs, successors, posterity. **Assemble**, CHÜ: gather, bring together, collect; call to assembly; dwell together, converge; meeting, reunion, collection; meeting place, dwelling place. The ideogram: three (= many) people.

  Anterior ... the use-of: activating this hexagram depends on understanding and accepting the previous statement.

  Imply, CHE: further signify; additional meaning. **Indeed**, YEH: intensifier; indicates comment on previous statement.

● *Contrasted Definitions*

> **Clustering: assembling and-also**
> **Ascending: not coming indeed.**

Associated Contexts **Ascend**, SHENG: go up; climb step by step; rise in office; advance through effort; accumulate; bring out and fulfill; lit.: a measure for fermented liquor, ascension as distillation. Image of Hexagram 46. **Not**, PU: simple negative. **Come**, LAI, and go, WANG, describe the stream of time as it flows from future to present; come, LAI, indicates what is approaching; keyword.

● *Symbol Tradition*

> **Above marsh with-respect-to earth. Clustering.**
> **A chün tzu uses eliminating arms to implement.**
> **[A chün tzu uses] warning, not precautions.**

Associated Contexts **Above,** SHANG: anything above, in all senses; higher, upper, outer; upper trigram; opposite of below, HSIA. **Marsh,** TSE: open surface of a flat body of water and the vapors rising from it; fertilize, enrich; kindness, favor; the Symbol of the trigram Open, TUI. **With-respect-to,** YÜ: relates to, refers to; hold a position in. **Earth,** TI: ground on which the human world rests; basis of all things, nourishes all things; the Symbol of the trigram Field, K'UN.

Chün tzu: ideal of a person who uses divination to order his/her life in accordance with tao rather than wilful intention; keyword. **Use(-of),** YI: make use of, by means of, owing to; employ, make functional. **Eliminate,** CH'U: root out, remove, do away with, take off, keep out; vacate, exchange. **Arms,** JUNG: weapons; armed people, soldiers; military, violent. The ideogram: spear and armor, offensive and defensive weapons. **Implements,** CH'I: utensils, tools; molded or carved objects; use a person or thing suitably; capacity, talent, intelligence. **Warn,** CHIEH: alert, alarm, put on guard; caution, inform; guard against, refrain from (as in a diet). The ideogram: spear held in both hands, warning enemies and alerting friends. **Precaution,** YÜ: provide against, preventive measures; anxious, vigilant, ready; preoccupied with, think about, expect; mishap, accident.

● *Image Tradition*

> **Clustering, assembling indeed. [I]**
> **Yielding uses stimulating.**
> **Solid centering and-also corresponding.**
> **Anterior assembling indeed.**
>
> **The king imagines possessing a temple. [II]**
> **Involving reverence presenting indeed.**
> **Harvesting: visualizing Great People Growing.**
> **Assembling uses correcting indeed.**
>
> **Availing-of the great: sacrificial-victims significant. [III]**
> **Harvesting: possessing directed going.**
> **Yielding-to heavenly fate indeed.**
> **Actually viewing one's place to assemble.**
> **And-also actually Heaven[and]Earth,**
> > **the myriad beings's motives, permitting visualizing.**

Associated Contexts **[I] Yield(-to),** SHUN: give way and bear produce; comply, agree, follow, obey; unresisting, docile, flexible; nourish, provide; the Action of the trigram Field, K'UN. The ideogram: head and current, water flowing from the head of a river, yielding to the banks. **Stimulate,** SHOU: rouse to action and good feeling; free from constraint, stir up, urge on; persuade, cheer, delight; set out in words; the Action of the trigram Open, TUI. The ideogram: words and exchange.

Solid, KANG: quality of the whole lines; firm, strong, unyielding, persisting. **Center,** CHUNG: inner, central; put in the center; middle, stable point enabling you to face inner and outer changes; middle line of trigram. The ideogram: field divided in two equal parts. Image of Hexagram 61. **Correspond(-to),** YING: be in agreement or harmony; resonate together, invoke and fulfill each other; answer to, suitable; relation between the lines (1:4, 2:5, 3:6) when they form the pair opened and whole, supple and solid. The ideogram: heart and obey.

Anterior, KU: come before as cause; formerly, ancient; reason, purpose, intention; grievance, quarrel, dissatisfaction, sorrow, mourning resulting from previous causes and intentions; situation leading to a divination.

[II] Involve, CHIH: include, entangle, implicate; induce, cause. The ideogram: person walking, induced to follow. **Reverence,** HSIAO: filial duty, respect and obedience owed to elders; loyalty, dignity, confidence, self-respect; brave in battle; period of mourning for deceased parents. **Present(-to),** HSIANG: present in sacrifice, offer with thanks, give to the gods or a superior; confer dignity on.

Correct, CHENG: rectify deviation or one-sidedness; proper, straight, exact, regular; constant, rule, model. The ideogram: stop and one, hold to one thing.

[III] Heaven, T'IEN: highest; sky, firmament, heavens; power above the human as opposed to earth, TI, below; the Symbol of the trigram Force, CH'IEN. The ideogram: great and the one above. **Fate,** MING: individual destiny; birth and death as limits of life; issue orders with authority; consult the gods. The ideogram: mouth and order, words with heavenly authority.

Actually, YI: truly, really, at present. The ideogram: a dart and done, strong intention fully expressed. **View,** KUAN: contemplate, observe from a distance; look at carefully, gaze at; also: a monastery, an observatory; scry, divine through liquid in a cup. The ideogram: see and waterbird, observe through air or water. Image of Hexagram 20. **One's/one**, CH'I: third person pronoun; also: it/its, he/his, she/hers, they/theirs. **Place**, SO: where something belongs or comes from; residence, dwelling; habitual focus or object.

Heaven[and]Earth, T'IEN TI: dynamic relation between the primal powers and the world it produces; cosmos, natural or human world; keyword. **Myriad**, WAN: countless; many, everyone; lit.: ten thousand. The ideogram: swarm of insects. **'s/have(it)/it/them**, CHIH: expresses possession, directly or as an object pronoun. **Motive**, CH'ING: true nature; feelings, desires, passions. The ideogram: heart and green, germinated in the heart. **Permit**, K'O: possible because in harmony with an inherent principle. The ideogram: mouth and breath, silent consent.

● *Transforming Lines*

Initial six

a) **Possessing conformity, not completing.**
Thereupon disarraying, thereupon Clustering.
Like an outcry, the-one handful activates laughing.
No cares.
Going without fault.

b) **Thereupon disarraying, thereupon Clustering.**
One's purpose disarrayed indeed.

Associated Contexts a) **Possessing conformity**, YU FU: inner and outer are in accord; confidence of the spirits has been captured; sincere, truthful; proper to take action. **Complete**, CHUNG: end of a cycle that begins the next; last, whole, all; contrasts with exhaust, CH'IUNG, final end. The ideogram: silk cocoons, follow and ice, winter linking one year with the next.

Thereupon, NAI: on that ground, because of. **Disarray**, LUAN: throw into disorder, mislay, confuse; out of place; discord, insurrection, anarchy. **Like**, JO: same as; just as, similar to.

Cry-out/outcry, HAO: call out, proclaim; signal, order, command; mark, label, sign. **One, the-one**, YI: single unit; number one; undivided, simple, whole; any one of; first, the first. **Handful**, WU: as much as the hand can hold; a little; grasp, hold. **Activate**, WEI: act or cause to act; do, make, manage; make active; attend to, help; because of. **Laugh**, HSIAO:

manifest joy or mirth; giggle, laugh at, ridicule; pleased, merry; associated with the Fiery Moment.

No, WU: simple negative; un-, dis-. **Care**, HSÜ: fear, doubt, concern; heartfelt attachment; relieve, soothe, aid; sympathy, compassion, consolation. The ideogram: heart and blood, the heart's blood affected.

Go, WANG, and come, LAI, describe the stream of time as it flows from future through present to past; go, WANG, indicates what is departing from present to past; proceed, move on; keyword. **Without fault**, WU CHIU: no error or harm in the situation.

b) **Purpose**, CHIH: focus of mind and heart; will, inclination, resolve. The ideogram: heart and scholar, high inner resolve, or heart and go, inner determination.

Six at-second

a) **Protracting significant, without fault.**
Conforming, thereupon Harvesting availing-of dedicating.

b) **Protracting significant, without fault.**
Centering, not-yet transforming indeed.

Associated Contexts a) **Protract**, YIN: draw out, prolong; carried on; lead on, to bring forward; lit.: drawing a bow. **Without fault**, WU CHIU: no error or harm in the situation.

Conforming, FU: accord between inner and outer in a particular moment; sincere, truthful, verified, reliable, in accord with the spirits; capture; prisoners, spoils; contrasts with trustworthy, HSIN, consistent over time. The ideogram: bird's claw enclosing young animals, possessive grip. Image of Hexagram 61. **Thereupon**, NAI: on that ground, because of. **Dedicate**, YO: offering at the spring equinox, when stores are low; offer a sacrifice with limited resources. The ideogram: spring and thin.

b) **Not-yet**, WEI: temporal negative; something will but has not yet occurred; contrary of already, CHI. Image of Hexagram 64. **Transform**, PIEN: abrupt, radical, fundamental mutation from one state of being to another; transformation of lines in hexagrams; contrasts with change, HUA, gradual metamorphosis.

Six at-third

a) **Clustering thus, lamenting thus.**
   Without direction: Harvesting.
   Going without fault.
   The small abashed.

b) **Going without fault.**
   Ground above indeed.

Associated Contexts a) **Thus ... thus**, JU ... JU: when there is one thing, then there must be the second thing. **Lament**, CHÜEH: express intense regret or sorrow; mourn over; painful recollections.

Without direction: Harvesting, WU YU LI: no plan or direction is advantageous; in order to take advantage of the situation, do not impose a direction on events.

Go, WANG, and come, LAI, describe the stream of time as it flows from future through present to past; go, WANG, indicates what is departing from present to past; proceed, move on; keyword. **Without fault**, WU CHIU: no error or harm in the situation.

Small, HSIAO: little, common, unimportant; adapting to what crosses your path; ability to move in harmony with the vicissitudes of life; contrasts with great, TA, self-imposed theme or goal; keyword. Image of Hexagrams 9 and 62. **Abashment**, LIN: distress, shame, regret, humiliation; aware of having lost the right track; leads to repenting, HUI, correcting the direction of mind and life.

b) **Ground**, SUN: base on which things rest; support, foundation; mild, subtly penetrating; nourishing. The ideogram: stand and things arranged on it, the subtle influence of the ground. Image of Hexagram 57.

Nine at-fourth

a) **The great significant, without fault.**

b) **The great significant, without fault.**
   Situation not appropriate indeed.

Associated Contexts a) **Without fault**, WU CHIU: no error or harm in the situation.

b) **Situation**, WEI: place or seat according to rank; post, position, command; right, proper; established, arranged. The ideogram: person and stand, servants in their places. **Appropriate**, TANG: suitable; opportune, convenient; adequate, competent; equal to; whole lines in uneven places and opened lines in even places.

Nine at-fifth

a) **Clustering: possessing the situation.**
Without fault: in-no-way conforming.
Spring, perpetual Trial.
Repenting extinguished.

b) **Clustering: possessing the situation.**
Purpose not-yet shining indeed.

Associated Contexts a) **Situation**, WEI: place or seat according to rank; post, position, command; right, proper; established, arranged. The ideogram: person and stand, servants in their places.

Without fault, WU CHIU: no error or harm in the situation. **In-no-way**, FEI: strong negative; not so. The ideogram: a box filled with opposition. **Conforming**, FU: accord between inner and outer in a particular moment; sincere, truthful, verified, reliable, in accord with the spirits; capture; prisoners, spoils; contrasts with trustworthy, HSIN, consistent over time. The ideogram: bird's claw enclosing young animals, possessive grip. Image of Hexagram 61.

Spring, YÜAN: source, origin, head; great, excellent; arise, begin, generating power; first stage of the Time Cycle. **Perpetual**, YUNG: continuing; everlasting, ever-flowing. The ideogram: flowing water. **Trial**, CHEN: test by ordeal; inquiry by divination and its result; righteous, firm; separating wheat from chaff; the kernel, the proven core; fourth stage of the Time Cycle. The ideogram: pearl and divination.

Repenting extinguished, HUI WANG: previous troubles and consequent remorse will disappear.

b) **Purpose**, CHIH: focus of mind and heart; will, inclination, resolve. The ideogram: heart and scholar, high inner resolve, or heart and go, inner determination. **Not-yet**, WEI: temporal negative; something will but has not yet occurred; contrary of already, CHI. Image of Hexagram 64. **Shine**, KUANG: illuminate; give off brilliant, bright light; honor, glory, éclat; result of action, contrasts with brightness, MING, light of heavenly bodies. The ideogram: fire above person, lifting the light.

Six above

a) **Paying-tribute: sighs, tears, snot.
Without fault.**

b) **Paying-tribute: sighs, tears, snot.
The above not-yet quiet indeed.**

Associated Contexts a) **Pay-tribute**, CHI: compulsory payments; present property to a superior. **Sigh**, TZU: lament, express grief, sorrow or yearning. **Tears**, T'I: weep, cry; water from the eyes. **Snot**, YI: mucus from the nose; snivel, whine.

Without fault, WU CHIU: no error or harm in the situation.

b) **Not-yet**, WEI: temporal negative; something will but has not yet occurred; contrary of already, CHI. Image of Hexagram 64. **Quiet**, AN: peaceful, still, settled; calm, tranquilize. The ideogram: woman under a roof, a tranquil home.

46

ASCENDING ∎ *SHENG*

This hexagram describes your situation in terms of rising to a higher level. It emphasizes that setting a higher goal and working toward it step by step is the adequate way to handle it. To be in accord with the time, you are told to: **ascend**!

● *Image of the Situation*

Ascending, Spring Growing.
Availing-of visualizing Great People.
No cares.
The South, chastising significant.

Associated Contexts **Ascend,** SHENG: go up; climb step by step; rise in office; advance through effort; accumulate; bring out and fulfill; lit.: a measure for fermented liquor, ascension as distillation. **Spring,** YÜAN: source, origin, head; great, excellent; arise, begin, generating power; first stage of the Time Cycle. **Grow,** HENG: success through a sacrifice; pervade, persevere; bring to full growth; enjoy; vigorous, effective; second stage of the Time Cycle.

Avail-of, YUNG: take advantage of; benefit from, profit by; use for a specific purpose; apply to advantage. The ideogram: to divine and center, applying divination to central concerns. **Visualize,** CHIEN: seeing in all its aspects: vision, being visible, forming mental images; visit, call on, consult. The ideogram: eye above person, active and receptive sight. **Great People,** TA JEN: important, noble, influential; those who impose a ruling principle on their lives; effect of the great within an individual; keyword.

No, WU: simple negative; un-, dis-. **Care,** HSÜ: fear, doubt, concern; heartfelt attachment; relieve, soothe, aid; sympathy, compassion, consolation. The ideogram: heart and blood, the heart's blood affected.

South, NAN: corresponds to summer, Growing, and the Fiery Moment; end of the yang hemicycle; reference point of compass; rulers face South, thus true principles and correct decisions. **Chastise,** CHENG: punish, subjugate, discipline; reduce to order; punishing expedition. The ideogram: step and correct, a rectifying move. **Significant,** CHI: leads to the experience of meaning; favorable, propitious, advantageous, appropriate; keyword. The ideogram: scholar and mouth, wise words of a sage.

- ## *Outer and Inner Aspects*

☷ **Field:** The field of earth yields and sustains, serving in order to produce. **Field** is the equalizing point between yin and yang where things labor and serve.

Connection to the outer: the common labor of sowing and hoarding, the Earthy Moment. **Field** produces concrete results through serving.

☴ **Ground:** Wind and wood subtly enter from the ground, penetrating and pervading. **Ground** is the center of the yang hemicycle, spreading pervasive action.

Connection to the inner: penetrating and bringing together, the Woody Moment culminating. **Ground** pervades, matches and couples, seeding a new generation.

Subtle penetration and coupling within slowly **ascends** to a higher field of activity.

- ## *Counter Indications*

Nuclear trigrams **Shake,** CHEN, and **Open,** TUI, result in Counter Hexagram 54, **Converting Maidenhood,** KUEI MEI. The effort needed to **ascend** is contrasted with the passive position of the **maiden converted** into a wife.

- ## *Sequence*

> **Assembling and-also the above implies designating's Ascending.**
> **Anterior acquiescence has the use-of Ascending.**

Associated Contexts **Assemble,** CHÜ: gather, bring together, collect; call to assembly; dwell together, converge; meeting, reunion, collection; meeting place, dwelling place. The ideogram: three (= many) people. **And-also,** ERH: joins and contrasts two terms. **Above,** SHANG:

anything above, in all senses; higher, upper, outer; upper trigram; opposite of below, HSIA. **Imply**, CHE. further signify; additional meaning. **Designate**, WEI: represent in words, assign a name or meaning; report on, talk about. The ideogram: words and belly, describing the essential. **'s/have(-it)/it/them**, CHIH: expresses possession, directly or as an object pronoun.

Anterior ... the use-of: activating this hexagram depends on understanding and accepting the previous statement.

- *Contrasted Definitions*

> **Clustering: assembling and-also**
> **Ascending: not coming indeed.**

Associated Contexts **Cluster**, TS'UI: call or pack together; tight groups of people, animals, things; collect, gather, assemble, concentrate; bunch, crowd, collection; lit.: dense, tussocky grass. Image of Hexagram 45.

Not, PU: simple negative. **Come**, LAI, and go, WANG, describe the stream of time as it flows from future through present to past; come, LAI, indicates what is approaching; move toward, arrive at; keyword. **Indeed**, YEH: intensifier; indicates comment on previous statement.

- *Symbol Tradition*

> **Earth center giving-birth-to wood. Ascending.**
> **A chün tzu uses yielding to actualize-tao.**
> **[A chün tzu uses] amassing the small to use the high great.**

Associated Contexts **Earth**, TI: ground on which the human world rests; basis of all things, nourishes all things; the Symbol of the trigram Field, K'UN. **Center**, CHUNG: inner, central; put in the center; middle, stable point enabling you to face inner and outer changes; middle line of trigram. The ideogram: field divided in two equal parts. Image of Hexagram 61. **Birth/give-birth-to**, SHENG: produce, beget, grow, bear, arise; life, vitality. The ideogram: earth and sprout. **Wood/tree**, MU: all things woody or wooden, alive or constructed from wood; associated with the Woody Moment; wood and wind are the Symbols of the trigram Ground, SUN. The ideogram: a tree with roots and branches.

Chün tzu: ideal of a person who uses divination to order his/her life in accordance with tao rather than wilful intention; keyword. **Use(-of)**, YI: make use of, by means of, owing to; employ, make functional. **Yield(-to)**, SHUN: give way and bear produce; comply, agree, follow, obey; unresisting, docile, flexible; nourish, provide; the Action of the trigram Field, K'UN. The ideogram: head and current, water flowing from the head of a river, yielding to the banks. **Actualize-tao**, TE: realize tao in action; power, virtue; ability to follow the course traced by the ongoing process of the cosmos; keyword. The ideogram: to go, straight, and heart. Linked with acquire, TE: acquiring that which makes a being become what it is meant to be.

Amass, CHI: hoard, accumulate, pile up, store up, add up, increase. **Small**, HSIAO: little, common, unimportant; adapting to what crosses your path; ability to move in harmony with the vicissitudes of life; contrasts with great, TA, self-imposed theme or goal; keyword. Image of Hexagrams 9 and 62. **High(-ness)**, KAO: high, elevated, lofty, eminent; excellent, advanced. **Great**, TA: big, noble, important, very; orient the will toward a self-imposed goal, impose direction; ability to lead or guide your life; contrasts with small, HSIAO, flexible adaptation to what crosses your path; keyword. Image of Hexagrams 14, 26, 28, 34.

- *Image Tradition*

> **Supple using the season, Ascending. [I]**
> **Ground and-also yielding.**
> **Solid centering and-also corresponding.**
> **That uses great Growing to avail-of visualizing Great People.**
>
> **No cares. [II]**
> **Possessing reward indeed.**
> **The South, chastising significant.**
> **Purpose moving indeed.**

Associated Contexts **[I] Supple**, JOU: quality of the opened lines; flexible, pliant, tender, adaptable. **Season**, SHIH: quality of the time; the right time, opportune, in harmony; planning in accord with the time; seasons of the year. The ideogram: sun and temple, time as sacred.

Ground, SUN: base on which things rest; support, foundation; mild, subtly penetrating; nourishing. The ideogram: stand and things arranged on it, the subtle influence of the ground. Image of Hexagram 57.

Solid, KANG: quality of the whole lines; firm, strong, unyielding, persisting. **Correspond(-to)**, YING: be in agreement or harmony; resonate together, invoke and fulfill each other; answer to, suitable; relation between the lines (1:4, 2:5, 3:6) when they form the pair opened and whole, supple and solid. The ideogram: heart and obey.

That uses, SHIH YI: involves and is involved by.

[II] Possess, YU: in possession of, have, own; opposite of lack, WU. **Reward**, CH'ING: gift given from gratitude or benevolence; favor from heaven; congratulate with gifts. The ideogram: heart, follow and deer (wealth), the heart expressed through gifts.

Purpose, CHIH: focus of mind and heart; will, inclination, resolve. The ideogram: heart and scholar, high inner resolve, or heart and go, inner determination. **Move**, HSING: move or move something; motivate, emotionally moving; walk, act, do. The ideogram: stepping left then right.

● *Transforming Lines*

Initial six

a) **Sincere Ascending, the great significant.**

b) **Sincere Ascending, the great significant.**
Uniting purposes above indeed.

Associated Contexts a) **Sincere**, YÜN: true, honest, loyal; according to the facts; have confidence in, permit, assent. The ideogram: vapor rising, words directed upwards.

b) **Unite**, HO: join, match, correspond, agree, collect, reply; unison, harmony; also: close, shut the mouth. The ideogram: mouth and assemble.

Nine at-second

a) **Conforming, thereupon Harvesting availing-of dedicating.**
Without fault.

b) **Nine at-second's conforming.**
   Possessing rejoicing indeed.

Associated Contexts *a)* **Conforming**, FU: accord between inner and outer in a particular moment; sincere, truthful, verified, reliable, in accord with the spirits; capture; prisoners, spoils; contrasts with trustworthy, HSIN, consistent over time. The ideogram: bird's claw enclosing young animals, possessive grip. Image of Hexagram 61. **Thereupon**, NAI: on that ground, because of. **Harvest**, LI: advantageous, profitable; acute, insightful; benefit, nourish; third stage of the Time Cycle. **Dedicate**, YO: offering at the spring equinox, when stores were low; offer a sacrifice with limited resources. The ideogram: spring and thin.
   Without fault, WU CHIU: no error or harm in the situation.

b) **Rejoice(-in)**, HSI: feel and give joy; delight, exult; cheerful, merry. The ideogram: joy (music) and mouth, expressing joy.

Nine at-third

a) **Ascending: an empty capital.**

b) **Ascending: an empty capital.**
   Without a place to doubt indeed.

Associated Contexts *a)* **Empty**, HSÜ: no images or concepts; vacant, unsubstantial; empty yet fertile space. **Capital**, YI: populous fortified city, center and symbol of the domain it rules. The ideogram: enclosure and official seal.

b) **Without**, WU: devoid of; -less as suffix. **Place**, SO: where something belongs or comes from; residence, dwelling; habitual focus or object. **Doubt**, YI: suspect, distrust; dubious; surmise, conjecture.

Six at-fourth

a) **Kinghood availing-of Growing**
                        tending-towards the twin-peaked mountain.
   Significant.
   Without fault.

b) **Kinghood availing-of Growing**
                 tending-towards the twin-peaked mountain.
   Yielding affairs indeed.

Associated Contexts a) **King(hood)**, WANG: effective ruler, by authority of the Emperor, from whom others derive their power. **Tend-towards,** YÜ: move toward but not reach, in the direction of; contrasts with reach(-to), HU, actually arriving. **Twin-peaked,** CH'I: mountain with two peaks; forked road; diverge, ambiguous. The ideogram: mountain and branched. **Mountain,** SHAN: limit, boundary; the Symbol of the trigram Bound, KEN. The ideogram: three peaks, a mountain range. **Twin-peaked Mountain,** CH'I SHAN, was the ancestral shrine of the Chou Dynasty.

   Without fault, WU CHIU: no error or harm in the situation.

b) **Affairs,** SHIH: all kinds of personal activity; matters at hand; business, occupation; manage a business, case in court.

   Six at-fifth

a) **Trial: significant, Ascending steps.**

b) **Trial: significant, Ascending steps.**
   The great acquiring the purpose indeed.

Associated Contexts a) **Trial,** CHEN: test by ordeal; inquiry by divination and its result; righteous, firm; separating wheat from chaff; the kernel, the proven core; fourth stage of the Time Cycle. The ideogram: pearl and divination. **Steps,** CHIEH: stairs leading to a gate or hall; grade, degree, rank; emulate, rise.

b) **Acquire,** TE: obtain the desired object; wish for, desire covetously; gains, possessions. The ideogram: go and obstacle, going through obstacles to the goal.

   Six above

a) **Dim Ascending.**
   Harvesting: tending-towards not pausing's Trial.

b) **Dim Ascending located above.**
Dissolving, not affluence indeed.

Associated Contexts a) **Dim**, MING: dark, obscure; misinformed, immature; cavern, the underworld. The ideogram: 16th day of moon-month, when the moon begins to dim.

Harvest, LI: advantageous, profitable; acute, insightful; benefit, nourish; third stage of the Time Cycle. **Tend-towards**, YÜ: move toward but not reach, in the direction of; contrasts with reach(-to), HU, actually arriving. **Pause**, HSI: stop and rest, repose; breathe, a breathing-spell; suspended. **Trial**, CHEN: test by ordeal; inquiry by divination and its result; righteous, firm; separating wheat from chaff; the kernel, the proven core; fourth stage of the Time Cycle. The ideogram: pearl and divination.

b) **Locate(-in)**, TSAI: live in, dwell, reside; belong to, involved with, depend on; within. The ideogram: earth and persevere, place on the earth.

Dissolve, HSIAO: liquify, melt, thaw; diminish, disperse; eliminate, exhaust. The ideogram: water dissolving differences. **Affluence**, FU: rich, abundant; wealth; enrich, provide for; flow toward, accrue.

CONFINING ∎ *K'UN*

This hexagram describes your situation in terms of restriction and distress. It emphasizes that turning inward through accepting enclosure is the adequate way to handle it. To be in accord with the time, you are told to: **confine!**

● *Image of the Situation*

> **Confining, Growing.**
> **Trial: Great People significant. Without fault.**
> **Possessing words not trustworthy.**

Associated Contexts **Confine**, K'UN: enclose, restrict, limit; oppressed; impoverish, distress; afflicted, exhausted, disheartened, weary. The ideogram: an enclosed tree. **Grow**, HENG: success through a sacrifice; pervade, persevere; bring to full growth; enjoy; vigorous, effective; second stage of the Time Cycle.

   Trial, CHEN: test by ordeal; inquiry by divination and its result; righteous, firm; separating wheat from chaff; the kernel, the proven core; fourth stage of the Time Cycle. The ideogram: pearl and divination. **Great People**, TA JEN: important, noble, influential; those who impose a ruling principle on their lives; effect of the great within an individual; keyword. **Significant**, CHI: leads to the experience of meaning; favorable, propitious, advantageous, appropriate; keyword. The ideogram: scholar and mouth, wise words of a sage.

   Without fault, WU CHIU: no error or harm in the situation.

   Possess, YU: in possession of, have, own; opposite of lack, WU. **Word**, YEN: speech, spoken words, sayings; talk, discuss, address. The ideogram: mouth and rising vapor, words as speech. **Not**, PU: simple negative. **Trustworthy**, HSIN: truthful, faithful, consistent over time; integrity; confide in, follow; credentials; contrasts with conforming, FU, connection in a specific moment. The ideogram: person and word, true speech.

● *Outer and Inner Aspects*

☱ **Open**: vapor rising from the marsh's open surface stimulates and fertilizes; stimulating words cheer and inspire. **Open** begins the yin hemicycle by initiating the formative process.

　　Connection to the outer: liquifying, casting, skinning off the mold, the Metallic Moment beginning. **Open** stimulates, cheers and reveals innate form.

☵ **Gorge**: Stream ventures and falls into the gorge, flowing on through toil and danger. **Gorge** ends the yin hemicycle by leveling and dissolving forms.

　　Connection to the inner: flooding and leveling dissolve direction and shape, the Streaming Moment. **Gorge** ventures, falls, toils and flows on.

Drawn in by the falling stream, outer stimulation and cheer are **confined** to creating inner forms.

● *Counter Indications*

Nuclear trigrams **Ground**, SUN, and **Radiance**, LI, result in Counter Hexagram 37, **Dwelling People**, CHIA JEN. Confining isolation is contrasted with the cooperation of **people** working together in their **dwelling**.

● *Sequence*

Ascending and-also not climaxing necessarily Confines.
Anterior acquiescence has the use-of Confining.

Associated Contexts **Ascend**, SHENG: go up; climb step by step; rise in office; advance through effort; accumulate; bring out and fulfill; lit.: a measure for fermented liquor, ascension as distillation. Image of Hexagram 46. **And-also**, ERH: joins and contrasts two terms. **Climax**, YI: come to a high point and stop, bring to an end; use up, lay aside; decline, reject. **Necessarily**, PI: unavoidably, indispensably, certainly.
　　Anterior ... the use-of: activating this hexagram depends on understanding and accepting the previous statement.

- *Contrasted Definitions*

> The Well: interpenetrating and-also
> Confining: mutual meeting indeed.

Associated Contexts **Well**, CHING: water well at the center of the fields; rise and flow of water in a well, rise and surge from an inner source; life-water, nucleus of life; found a capital city. The ideogram: two vertical lines crossing two horizontal ones, eight fields with a well at the center. Image of Hexagram 48. **Interpenetrate**, T'UNG: mutually penetrate; permeate, flow through, reach everywhere; see clearly, communicate with.

  Mutual, HSIANG: reciprocal assistance, encourage, help; bring together, blend with; examine, inspect; by turns. **Meet**, YÜ: come on unexpectedly, encounter; occur, happen; pleasant meeting, lucky coincidence; agree. **Indeed**, YEH: intensifier; indicates comment on previous statement.

- *Attached Evidences*

> Confining: actualizing-tao's marking-off indeed.
> Confining: exhausting and-also interpenetrating.
> Confining: using few grudges.

Associated Contexts **Actualize-tao** TE: realize tao in action; power, virtue; ability to follow the course traced by the ongoing process of the cosmos; keyword. The ideogram: to go, straight, and heart. Linked with acquire, TE: acquiring that which makes a being become what it is meant to be. **'s/have(-it)/it/them**, CHIH: expresses possession, directly or as an object pronoun. **Mark-off**, PIEN: distinguish by dividing; mark off a plot of land; frame which divides a bed from its stand; discuss and dispute. The ideogram: knife and acrid, biting division.

  Exhaust, CH'IUNG: bring to an end; limit, extremity; destitute; investigate exhaustively; end without a new beginning. The ideogram: cave and naked person, bent with disease or old age.

  Use(-of), YI: make use of, by means of, owing to; employ, make functional. **Few**, KUA: small number; seldom, rarely; unusual, solitary. **Grudges**, YÜAN: bitter feelings, ill-will; hate, abhor; murmur against. The ideogram: heart and overturn, upset emotion.

● *Symbol Tradition*

Marsh without stream. Confining.
A chün tzu uses involving fate to release purpose.

Associated Contexts **Marsh**, TSE: open surface of a flat body of water and the vapors rising from it; fertilize, enrich; kindness, favor; the Symbol of the trigram Open, TUI. **Without**, WU: devoid of; -less as suffix. **Stream**, SHUI: flowing water; fluid, dissolving; river, tide, flood; the Symbol of the trigram Gorge, K'AN. The ideogram: rippling water.

Chün tzu: ideal of a person who uses divination to order his/her life in accordance with tao rather than wilful intention; keyword. **Involve**, CHIH: include, entangle, implicate; induce, cause. The ideogram: person walking, induced to follow. **Fate**, MING: individual destiny; birth and death as limits of life; issue orders with authority; consult the gods. The ideogram: mouth and order, words with heavenly authority. **Release**, SUI: loose, let go, free; unhindered, in accord; follow, spread out, progress; penetrate, invade. The ideogram: go and follow your wishes, unimpeded movement. **Purpose**, CHIH: focus of mind and heart; will, inclination, resolve. The ideogram: heart and scholar, high inner resolve, or heart and go, inner determination.

● *Image Tradition*

Confining. [I]
Solid enshrouded indeed.
Venturing uses stimulating.
Confining and-also not letting-go one's place: Growing.

Reaching-to one's very chün tzu. [II]
Trial: Great People significant.
Using solid centering indeed.
Possessing words not trustworthy.
Honoring the mouth thereupon exhausted indeed.

Associated Contexts **[I] Solid**, KANG: quality of the whole lines; firm, strong, unyielding, persisting. **Enshroud**, YEN: screen, shade from view, hide, cover. The ideogram: hand and cover.

Venture, HSIEN: risk without reserve; key point, point of danger;

difficulty, obstruction that must be confronted; water falling and filling the holes on its way; the Action of the trigram Gorge, K'AN. The ideogram: mound and all or whole, everything engaged at one point. **Stimulate**, SHUO: rouse to action and good feeling; free from constraint, stir up, urge on; persuade, cheer, delight; set out in words; the Action of the trigram Open, TUI. The ideogram: words and exchange.

Let-go, SHIH: lose, omit, miss, fail, let slip; out of control. The ideogram: drop from the hand. **One's/one**, CH'I: third person pronoun; also: it/its, he/his, she/hers, they/theirs. **Place**, SO: where something belongs or comes from; residence, dwelling; habitual focus or object.

Reach(-to), HU: arrive at a goal; reach toward and achieve; connect; contrasts with tend-towards, YU. **Verily, very**, WEI: the epitome of; in truth, the only; very important.

[II] **Center**, CHUNG: inner, central; put in the center; middle, stable point enabling you to face inner and outer changes; middle line of trigram. The ideogram: field divided in two equal parts. Image of Hexagram 61.

Honor, SHANG: esteem, give high rank to; eminent; put one thing on top of another. **Mouth**, K'OU: literal mouth, words going out and food coming in; entrance, hole. **Thereupon**, NAI: on that ground, because of.

- *Transforming Lines*

Initial six

  a) The sacrum Confined, tending-towards stump wood.
  Entering tending-towards a shady gully.
  Three year's-time not encountering.

  b) Entering tending-towards a shady gully.
  Shady, not bright indeed.

Associated Contexts a) **Sacrum**, T'UN: lower back where it joins legs; buttocks, seat, lower spine. **Tend-towards**, YÜ: move toward but not reach, in the direction of; contrasts with reach(-to), HU, actually arriving. **Stump**, CHU: trunk, bole, stalk; wooden post; keep down, degrade. **Wood/tree**, MU: all things woody or wooden, alive or constructed from wood; associated with the Woody Moment; wood and wind are the Symbols of the trigram Ground, SUN. The ideogram: a tree with roots and branches.

Enter, JU: penetrate, go into, enter on, progress; put into, encroach on; the Action of the trigram Ground, SUN, contrary of issue-forth, CH'U. **Shade**, YU: hidden from view; retired, solitary, secret; dark, obscure, occult, mysterious; ignorant. The ideogram: small within hill, a cave or grotto. **Gully**, KU: valley, ravine, river bed, gap. The ideogram: divide and river, a river bed separating hills.

Three, SAN: number three, third time or place; active phases of a cycle; superlative; beginning of repetition. **Year's-time**, SUI: actual length of time in a year; contrasts with years-revolved, NIEN, number of years elapsed. **Encounter**, TI: see face to face; admitted to an audience; visit, interview.

b) **Brightness**, MING: light-giving aspect of burning, heavenly bodies and consciousness; with fire, the Symbol of the trigram Radiance, LI.

Nine at-second

a) **Confined, tending-towards liquor taken-in.**
Scarlet sashes on-all-sides coming.
Harvesting: availing-of presenting oblations.
Chastising: pitfall, without fault.

b) **Confined, tending-towards liquor taken-in.**
Center possessing reward indeed.

Associated Contexts a) **Tend-towards**, YÜ: move toward but not reach, in the direction of; contrasts with reach(-to), HU, actually arriving. **Liquor**, CHIU: alcoholic beverages, distilled spirits; spirit which perfects the good and evil in human nature. The ideogram: liquid above fermenting must, separating the spirits. **Take-in**, SHIH: eat, ingest, swallow, devour; incorporate.

Scarlet, CHU: vivid red signifying honor, luck, marriage, riches, literary accomplishment; culmination of the Woody Moment. **Sash**, FU: ceremonial belt of official which holds seal of office. **Sides (on-all-sides)**, FANG: limits, boundaries; square, surface of the earth extending to the four cardinal points; everywhere. **Come**, LAI, and go, WANG, describe the stream of time as it flows from future through present to past; come, LAI, indicates what is approaching; move toward, arrive at; keyword.

Harvest, LI: advantageous, profitable; acute, insightful; benefit, nourish; third stage of the Time Cycle. **Avail-of**, YUNG: take advantage of; benefit from, profit by; use for a specific purpose; apply to advantage.

The ideogram: to divine and center, applying divination to central concerns. **Present(-to)**, HSIANG: present in sacrifice, offer with thanks, give to the gods or a superior; confer dignity on. **Oblations**, SSU: sacrifices offered situation; flow of life and spirit is blocked; unfortunate, baleful; keyword.

Chastise, CHENG: punish, subjugate, discipline; reduce to order; punishing expedition. The ideogram: step and correct, a rectifying move. **Pitfall**, HSIUNG: leads away from the experience of meaning; stuck and exposed to danger, unable to take in the situation; flow of life and spirit is blocked; unfortunate, baleful; keyword.

b) **Reward**, CH'ING: gift given from gratitude or benevolence; favor from heaven; congratulate with gifts. The ideogram: heart, follow and deer (wealth), the heart expressed through gifts.

Six at-third

a) **Confined, tending-towards petrification.**
Seizing tending-towards star thistles.
Entering tending-towards one's house.
                           Not visualizing one's consort.
Pitfall.

b) **Seizing tending-towards star thistles.**
Riding a solid indeed.
Entering tending-towards one's house.
                           Not visualizing one's consort.
Not auspicious indeed.

Associated Contexts a) **Tend-towards**, YÜ: move toward but not reach, in the direction of; contrasts with reach(-to), HU, actually arriving. **Petrify**, SHIH: become stone or stony; rocks, stony land; objects made of stone; firm, decided; a barren womb.

Seize, CHÜ: grasp, lay hands on; lean on, rely on; maintain, become concrete; testimony, evidence. **Star thistles**, CHI LI: spiny weeds that entangle the feet; caltrops, metal snares.

Enter, JU: penetrate, go into, enter on, progress; put into, encroach on; the Action of the trigram Ground, SUN, contrary of issue-forth, CH'U. **House**, KUNG: residence, mansion; surround; fence, walls, roof. **Visualize**, CHIEN: seeing in all its aspects: vision, being visible, forming mental images; visit, call on, consult. The ideogram: eye above person, active and receptive sight. **Consort**, CH'I: single official partner; legal status of married woman (first wife); contrasts with function of wife, FU, head of household, and concubine, CH'IEH, secondary wives.

    Pitfall, HSIUNG: leads away from the experience of meaning; stuck and exposed to danger, unable to take in the situation; flow of life and spirit is blocked; unfortunate, baleful; keyword.

b) **Ride**, CH'ENG: ride an animal or a chariot; have the upper hand, seize the right time; control strong power; overcome the nature of the other; supple opened line above a solid whole line. **Auspicious**, HSIANG: omen of good luck and prosperity; sign, auspices.

    Nine at-fourth

    a) **Coming, ambling, ambling.**
      Confined, tending-towards a metallic chariot.
      Abashment.
      Possessing completion.

    b) **Coming, ambling, ambling.**
      Purpose located below indeed.
      Although not an appropriate situation,
                         possessing associating indeed.

Associated Contexts a) **Come**, LAI, and go, WANG, describe the stream of time as it flows from future through present to past; come, LAI, indicates what is approaching; move toward, arrive at; keyword. **Amble**, HSÜ: walk quietly and carefully; leisurely, tardy, slow; composed, dignified. The doubled character intensifies this quality.

    Tend-towards, YÜ: move toward but not reach, in the direction of; contrasts with reach(-to), HU, actually arriving. **Metallic**, CHIN: smelting and casting; all things pertaining to metal, particularly gold; autumn, West, sunset; one of the Five Moments. **Chariot**, CH'E: wheeled travelling vehicle; contrasts with cart, YÜ, which carries.

    Abashment, LIN: distress, shame, regret, humiliation; aware of having lost the right track; leads to repenting, HUI, correcting the direction of mind and life.

    Complete, CHUNG: end of a cycle that begins the next; last, whole, all; contrasts with exhaust, CH'IUNG, final end. The ideogram: silk cocoons, follow and ice, winter linking one year with the next.

b) **Locate(-in)**, TSAI: live in, dwell, reside; belong to, involved with, depend on; within. The ideogram: earth and persevere, place on the earth. **Below**, HSIA: anything below, in all senses; lower, inner; lower trigram; opposite of above, SHANG.

Although, SUI: even though, supposing that, if, even if. **Appropriate**, TANG: suitable; opportune, convenient; adequate, competent; equal to; whole lines in uneven places and opened lines in even places. **Situation**, WEI: place or seat according to rank; post, position, command; right, proper; established, arranged. The ideogram: person and stand, servants in their places. **Associate(-with)**, YÜ: consort with, combine; companions; group, band, company; agree with, comply, help. The ideogram: pair of hands reaching downward meets a pair of hands reaching upward, helpful association.

Nine at-fifth

a) **Nose-cutting, foot-cutting.**
Confined, tending-towards a crimson sash.
Thereupon ambling possesses stimulating.
Harvesting: availing-of offering oblations.

b) **Nose-cutting, foot-cutting.**
Purpose not-yet acquired indeed.
Thereupon ambling possesses stimulating.
Using centering straightening indeed.
Harvesting: availing-of offering oblations.
Acquiescing-in blessing indeed.

Associated Contexts a) **Nose-cutting**, YI: punish through loss of public face or honor. **Foot-cutting**, YÜEH: crippling punishment for serious crimes.

Tend-towards, YÜ: move toward but not reach, in the direction of; contrasts with reach(-to), HU, actually arriving. **Crimson**, CH'IH: color associated with the Fiery Moment, South and Actualized Yang; fire, burning; dark complexion; color of new-born child; drunk, angry; polished metal; strip, naked, barren; also: sign of official rank. **Sash**, FU: ceremonial belt of official which holds seal of office.

Amble, HSÜ: walk quietly and carefully; leisurely, tardy, slow; composed, dignified.

Harvest, LI: advantageous, profitable; acute, insightful; benefit, nourish; third stage of the Time Cycle. **Avail-of**, YUNG: take advantage of; benefit from, profit by; use for a specific purpose; apply to advantage. The ideogram: to divine and center, applying divination to central concerns. **Offer**, CHI: gifts to gods and spirits. The ideogram: hand, meat and worship. **Oblations**, SSU: sacrifices offered to the gods and the dead.

b) **Not-yet**, WEI: temporal negative; something will but has not yet occurred; contrary of already, CHI. Image of Hexagram 64. **Acquire**, TE: obtain the desired object; wish for, desire covetously; gains, possessions. The ideogram: go and obstacle, going through obstacles to the goal.

   Straighten, CHIH: correct the crooked, reform, repay injustice; proceed directly; sincere, upright, just; blunt, outspoken.

   Acquiesce(-in), SHOU: accept, make peace with, agree to; at rest, satisfied; patient. **Bless**, FU: heavenly gifts; make happy; spiritual power and goodwill. The ideogram: spirit and plenty, heavenly gifts in abundance.

   Six above

   a) **Confined, tending-towards trailing creepers.**
   Tending-towards the unsteady[and]unsettled.
   Spoken-thus: stirring-up repenting possesses repenting.
   Chastising significant.

   b) **Confined, tending-towards trailing creepers.**
   Not-yet appropriate indeed.
   Stirring-up repenting possesses repenting.
   Significance moving indeed.

Associated Contexts a) **Tend-towards**, YÜ: move toward but not reach, in the direction of; contrasts with reach(-to), HU, actually arriving. **Trailing creeper**, KO LEI: lush, fast-growing hanging plants; spread rapidly and widely; numerous progeny.

   Unsteady[and]unsettled, NIEH WU: badly based; unquiet, hazardous; uneasy, anxious; dizzy, giddy as on a high place.

   Spoken-thus, YÜEH: designated, termed, called. The ideogram: open mouth and tongue. **Stir-up**, TUNG: excite, influence, move, affect; work, take action; come out of the egg or the bud; the Action of the trigram Shake, CHEN. The ideogram: strength and heavy, move weighty things. **Repent**, HUI: dissatisfaction with past conduct causing a change of heart; proceeds from abashment, LIN, shame and confusion at having lost the right way.

Chastise, CHENG: punish, subjugate, discipline; reduce to order; punishing expedition. The ideogram: step and correct, a rectifying move.

b) **Not-yet**, WEI: temporal negative; something will but has not yet occurred; contrary of already, CHI. Image of Hexagram 64. **Appropriate**, TANG: suitable; opportune, convenient; adequate, competent; equal to; whole lines in uneven places and opened lines in even places.

Move, HSING: move or move something; motivate, emotionally moving; walk, act, do. The ideogram: stepping left then right.

THE WELL/WELLING ▪ *CHING*

This hexagram describes your situation in terms of the lifewater coming from the depths that everyone may draw on. It emphasizes that maintaining access to this central source is the adequate way to handle it. To be in accord with the time, you are told to: go to the **well**!

● *Image of the Situation*

> **The Well: amending the capital, not amending the Well.**
> **Without losing, without acquiring.**
> **Going, coming: Welling, Welling.**
> **Muddy culmination: truly not-yet the well-rope Well.**
> **Ruining one's pitcher:**
> **Pitfall.**

Associated Contexts **Well**, CHING: water well at the center of the fields; rise and flow of water in a well, rise and surge from an inner source; life-water, nucleus of life; found a capital city. The ideogram: two vertical lines crossing two horizontal ones, eight fields with a well at the center. **Amend**, KAI: correct, reform, make new, alter, mend. The ideogram: self and strike, fighting your own errors. **Capital**, YI: populous fortified city, center and symbol of the domain it rules. The ideogram: enclosure and official seal. **Not**, PU: simple negative.

Without, WU: devoid of; -less as suffix. **Lose**, SANG: fail to obtain, cease, become obscure; forgotten, destroyed; lament, mourn; funeral. The ideogram: weep and the dead. **Acquire**, TE: obtain the desired object; wish for, desire covetously; gains, possessions. The ideogram: go and obstacle, going through obstacles to the goal.

Come, LAI, and **Go**, WANG, describe the stream of time as it flows from future through present to past. Come, LAI, indicates what is approaching; move toward, arrive at; go, WANG, indicates what is departing; proceed, move on; keywords. **Welling,** CHING: the doubled character intensifies this quality.

Mud, HSI: ground left wet by water, muddy shores; danger; shed tears; nearly. **Culminate**, CHIH: bring to the highest degree; arrive at the end or summit; superlative. **Truly**, YI: statement is true and precise. **Not-yet**, WEI: temporal negative; something will but has not yet occurred; contrary of already, CHI. Image of Hexagram 64. **Well-rope**, YÜ: rope used to draw water.

Ruin, LEI: destroy, break, overturn; debilitated, meager, emaciated; entangled. **One's/one,** CH'I: third person pronoun; also: it/its, he/his, she/hers, they/theirs. **Pitcher**, P'ING: clay jug or vase.

Pitfall, HSIUNG: leads away from the experience of meaning; stuck and exposed to danger, unable to take in the situation; flow of life and spirit is blocked; unfortunate, baleful; keyword.

● *Outer and Inner Aspects*

☵ **Gorge**: Stream ventures and falls into the gorge, flowing on through toil and danger. **Gorge** ends the yin hemicycle by leveling and dissolving forms.

Connection to the outer: flooding and leveling dissolve direction and shape, the Streaming Moment. **Gorge** ventures, falls, toils and flows on.

☴ **Ground**: Wind and wood subtly enter from the ground, penetrating and pervading. **Ground** is the center of the yang hemicycle, spreading pervasive action.

Connection to the inner: penetrating and bringing together, the Woody Moment culminating. **Ground** pervades, matches and couples, seeding a new generation.

Outer venturing and falling reach an inner ground where nourishment **wells** up from the depths.

● *Counter Indications*

Nuclear trigrams **Radiance**, LI, and **Open**, TUI, result in Counter Hexagram 38, **Polarizing**, K'UEI. The **well**'s inner center which is open to all is contrasted with the outer opposition of **polarizing**.

● *Sequence*

> **Confining reaching-to the above**
> **implies necessarily reversing the below.**
> **Anterior acquiescence has the use-of The Well.**

Associated Contexts **Confine**, K'UN: enclose, restrict, limit; oppressed; impoverish, distress; afflicted, exhausted, disheartened, weary. The ideogram: an enclosed tree. Image of Hexagram 47. **Reach(-to)**, HU: arrive at a goal; reach towards and achieve; connect; contrasts with tend-towards, YU. **Above**, SHANG: anything above, in all senses; higher, upper, outer; upper trigram; opposite of below, HSIA. **Imply**, CHE: further signify; additional meaning. **Necessarily**, PI: unavoidably, indispensably, certainly. **Reverse**, FAN: turn and move in the opposite direction; turn around or upside down (180 degrees); change to the opposite position; contrary. **Below**, HSIA: anything below, in all senses; lower, inner; lower trigram; opposite of above, SHANG.

Anterior ... the use-of: activating this hexagram depends on understanding and accepting the previous statement.

● *Contrasted Definitions*

> **The Well: interpenetrating and-also**
> **Confining: mutual meeting indeed.**

Associated Contexts **Interpenetrate**, T'UNG: mutually penetrate; permeate, flow through, reach everywhere; see clearly, communicate with.

Mutual, HSIANG: reciprocal assistance, encourage, help; bring together, blend with; examine, inspect; by turns. **Meet**, YÜ: come on unexpectedly, encounter; occur, happen; pleasant meeting, lucky coincidence; agree. **Indeed**, YEH: intensifier; indicates comment on previous statement.

● *Attached Evidences*

> **The Well: actualizing-tao's earth indeed.**
> **The Well: residing-in one's place and-also shifting.**
> **The Well: using differentiating righteousness.**

Associated Contexts **Actualize-tao**, TE: realize tao in action; power, virtue; ability to follow the course traced by the ongoing process of the cosmos; keyword. The ideogram: to go, straight, and heart. Linked with acquire, TE: acquiring that which makes a being become what it is meant to be. **'s/have(-it)/it/them**, CHIH: expresses possession, directly or as an object pronoun. **Earth**, TI: ground on which the human world rests; basis of all things, nourishes all things; the Symbol of the trigram Field, K'UN.

Reside(-in), CHU: dwell, live in, stay; sit down, fill an office; settled parts of a country. The ideogram: body and seat. **Place**, SO: where something belongs or comes from; residence, dwelling; habitual focus or object. **And-also**, ERH: joins and contrasts two terms. **Shift**, CH'IEN: move, change, transpose; improve, ascend, be promoted; deport, dismiss, remove.

Use(-of), YI: make use of, by means of, owing to; employ, make functional. **Differentiate**, PIEN: argue, dispute, criticize; sophisticated, artful. The ideogram: words and sharp or pungent. **Righteous**, YI: proper and just, meets the standards; things in their proper place; the heart that rules itself; upright, moral rule; contrasts with Harvest, LI, advantage or profit.

- *Symbol Tradition*

Above wood possessing stream. The Well.
A chün tzu uses toiling commoners to encourage mutualizing.

Associated Contexts **Wood/tree**, MU: all things woody or wooden, alive or constructed from wood; associated with Woody Moment; wood and wind are the Symbols of the trigram Ground, SUN. The ideogram: a tree with roots and branches. **Possess**, YU: in possession of, have, own; opposite of lack, WU. **Stream**, SHUI: flowing water; fluid, dissolving; river, tide, flood; the Symbol of the trigram Gorge, K'AN. The ideogram: rippling water.

Chün tzu: ideal of a person who uses divination to order his/her life in accordance with tao rather than wilful intention; keyword. **Toil**, LAO: labor, take pains, exert yourself; burdened, careworn; worthy actions. The ideogram: strength and fire, producing heat. **Commoners**, MIN: class of workers the state draws on to sustain the social hierarchy; undeveloped potential outside the organized personality. **Encourage**, CH'ÜAN: exhort, stimulate, influence; admonish.

- *Image Tradition*

> Ground reaching-to stream and-also stream above. The Well. [I]
> The Well nourishing and-also not exhausted indeed.
>
> Amending the capital, not amending the Well. [II]
> Thereupon using solid centering indeed.
>
> Muddy culmination: truly not-yet the well-rope Well. [III]
> Not-yet possessing achievement indeed.
> Ruining one's pitcher.
> That uses a pitfall indeed.

Associated Contexts **[I] Ground**, SUN: base on which things rest; support, foundation; mild, subtly penetrating; nourishing. The ideogram: stand and things arranged on it, the subtle influence of the ground. Image of Hexagram 57.

Nourish, YANG: feed, sustain, support; provide, care for; bring up, improve, grow, develop. **Exhaust**, CH'IUNG: bring to an end; limit, extremity; destitute; investigate exhaustively; end without a new beginning. The ideogram: cave and naked person, bent with disease or old age.

[II] Thereupon, NAI: on that ground, because of. **Solid**, KANG: quality of the whole lines; firm, strong, unyielding, persisting. **Center**, CHUNG: inner, central; put in the center; middle, stable point enabling you to face inner and outer changes; middle line of trigram. The ideogram: field divided in two equal parts. Image of Hexagram 61.

[III] Achieve, KUNG: work done, results; real accomplishment, praise, worth, merit. The ideogram: workman's square and forearm, combining craft and strength.

That uses, SHIH YI: involves and is involved by.

- *Transforming Lines*

Initial six

a) The Well: a bog, not taking-in.
   The ancient Well without wildfowl.

b) **The Well: a bog, not taking-in.**
The below indeed.
The ancient Well without wildfowl.
The season stowed-away indeed.

Associated Contexts a) **Bog**, NI: wet spongy soil; mire, slush, quicksand; unable to move. **Take-in**, SHIH: eat, ingest, swallow, devour; incorporate.

Ancient, CHIU: of old, long before; worn out, spoiled; defunct. **Wildfowl**, CH'IN: all wild and game birds; untamed.

b) **Season**, SHIH: quality of the time; the right time, opportune, in harmony; planning in accord with the time; seasons of the year. The ideogram: sun and temple, time as sacred. **Stow(-away)**, SHE: set aside, put away, store; halt, rest in; temporary lodgings, breathing-spell.

Nine at-second

a) **The Well: a gully, shooting bass.**
The jug cracked, leaking.

b) **The Well: a gully, shooting bass.**
Without associating indeed.

Associated Contexts a) **Gully**, KU: valley, ravine, river bed, gap. The ideogram: divide and river, a river bed separating hills. **Shoot**, SHE: shoot with a bow, point at and hit; project from, spurt, issue forth; glance at; scheme for. The ideogram: arrow and body. **Bass**, FU: freshwater fish, said to go in pairs and be faithful.

Jug, WENG: earthen jar; jug used to draw water. **Cracked**, PI: broken, ruined, tattered; unfit, unworthy. The ideogram: strike and break. **Leak**, LOU: seep, drip, ooze out; reveal; forget, let slip.

b) **Associate(-with)**, YÜ: consort with, combine; companions; group, band, company; agree with, comply, help. The ideogram: pair of hands reaching downward meets a pair of hands reaching upward, helpful association.

Nine at-third

a) The Well: oozing, not taking-in.
  Activating my heart aching.
  Permitting availing-of drawing-water:
  Kingly brightness.
  Together-with acquiescing-in one's blessing.

b) The Well: oozing, not taking-in.
  Moving: aching indeed.
  Seeking kingly brightness:
  Acquiescing-in blessing indeed.

Associated Contexts *a)* **Ooze**, TIEH: exude moisture; mud, slime; turbid, tainted. **Take-in**, SHIH: eat, ingest, swallow, devour; incorporate.

Activate, WEI: act or cause to act; do, make, manage; make active; attend to, help; because of. **My/me/I**, WO: first person pronoun; indicates an unusually strong emphasis on your own subjective experience. **Heart**, HSIN: heart as center of being; seat of mind's images and affections; moral nature; source of desires, intentions, will. **Ache**, TS'E: acute pain or grief; pity, sympathy, sorrow, grief.

Permit, K'O: possible because in harmony with an inherent principle. The ideogram: mouth and breath, silent consent. **Avail-of**, YUNG: take advantage of; benefit from, profit by; use for a specific purpose; apply to advantage. The ideogram: to divine and center, applying divination to central concerns. **Draw-water**, CHI: draw water from a well; draw forth, lead; take in a doctrine or example. The ideogram: water and reach to.

King(hood), WANG: effective ruler, by authority of the Emperor, from whom others derive their power. **Brightness**, MING: light-giving aspect of burning, heavenly bodies and consciousness; with fire, the Symbol of the trigram Radiance, LI.

Together-with, PING: also, both, at the same time. The ideogram: two people standing together. **Acquiesce(-in)**, SHOU: accept, make peace with, agree to; at rest, satisfied; patient. **Bless**, FU: heavenly gifts; make happy; spiritual power and goodwill. The ideogram: spirit and plenty, heavenly gifts in abundance.

b) **Move**, HSING: move or move something; motivate, emotionally moving; walk, act, do. The ideogram: stepping left then right.

  Seek, CH'IU: search for, aim at, wish for, desire; implore, supplicate; covetous.

Six at-fourth

a) The Well: lining, without fault.

b) The Well: lining, without fault.
   Adjusting the Well indeed.

Associated Contexts a) **Line,** TS'OU: line or repair a well. **Without fault,** WU CHIU: no error or harm in the situation.

b) **Adjust,** HSIU: regulate, repair, clean up, renovate.

Nine at-fifth

a) The Well: limpid, cold springwater taken-in.

b) Cold springwater's taking-in.
     Centering correcting indeed.

Associated Contexts a) **Limpid,** LIEH: pure, clear, clean liquid; wash clean. **Cold,** HAN: chilled, wintry; destitute, poor; shiver; fear; associated with the Streaming Moment. The ideogram: person huddled in straw under a roof. **Springwater,** CH'ÜAN: headwaters of a river; pure water. The ideogram: water and white, pure water at the source. **Take-in,** SHIH: eat, ingest, swallow, devour; incorporate.

b) **Centering correcting,** CHUNG CHENG: central and correct; make rectifying one-sidedness and error your central concern; reaching a stable center in yourself can correct the situation.

Six above

a) The Well: collecting, no cover.
     Possessing conformity, Spring significant.

b) Spring significant located-in the above.
     The great accomplishing indeed.

Associated Contexts a) **Collect,** SHOU: gather, harvest; receive what is due; involve, snare, bind, restrain. **No,** WU: simple negative; un-, dis-. **Cover,** MU: canvas covering; tent, booth, screen, tarpaulin.

Possessing conformity, YU FU: inner and outer are in accord; confidence of the spirits has been captured; sincere, truthful; proper to take action. **Spring**, YÜAN: source, origin, head; great, excellent; arise, begin, generating power; first stage of the Time Cycle. **Significant**, CHI: leads to the experience of meaning; favorable, propitious, advantageous, appropriate; keyword. The ideogram: scholar and mouth, wise words of a sage.

b) **Locate(-in)**, TSAI: live in, dwell, reside; belong to, involved with, depend on; within. The ideogram: earth and persevere, place on the earth.

Great, TA: big, noble, important, very; orient the will toward a self-imposed goal, impose direction; ability to lead or guide your life; contrasts with small, HSIAO, flexible adaptation to what crosses your path; keyword. Image of Hexagrams 14, 26, 28, 34. **Accomplish**, CH'ENG: complete, finish, bring about; perfect, full, whole; play your part, do your duty; mature. The ideogram: weapon and man, able to bear arms thus, fully developed.

49

SKINNING ▪ KO

This hexagram describes your situation in terms of stripping away a protective cover. It emphasizes that radically changing and renewing the way you present yourself is the adequate way to handle it. To be in accord with the time, you are told to: **skin!**

- ## Image of the Situation

> **Skinning: before-zenith sun, thereupon conforming.**
> **Spring Growing Harvesting Trial.**
> **Repenting extinguished.**

Associated Contexts **Skin, KO:** take off the covering, skin or hide; change, renew, molt; remove, peel off; revolt, overthrow, degrade from office; leather armor, protection. **Before-zenith sun,** SSU JIH: double hour from 9 to 11 a.m., month of June, both symbolized by the serpent; about to, on the point of. **Thereupon,** NAI: on that ground, because of. **Conforming,** FU: accord between inner and outer in a particular moment; sincere, truthful, verified, reliable, in accord with the spirits; capture; prisoners, spoils; contrasts with trustworthy, HSIN, consistent over time. The ideogram: bird's claw enclosing young animals, possessive grip. Image of Hexagram 61.

    Spring Growing Harvesting Trial: Spring, YÜAN; **Grow,** HENG; **Harvest,** LI; and **Trial,** CHEN, are the four stages of the Time Cycle, the model for all dynamic processes. They indicate that your question is connected to the cycle as a whole rather than a part of it, and that the origin (Spring) of a favorable result (Harvesting Trial) is an offering to the spirits (Growing).

    Repenting extinguished, HUI WANG: previous troubles and consequent remorse will disappear.

- ## Outer and Inner Aspects

☱ **Open:** vapor rising from the marsh's open surface stimulates and fertilizes; stimulating words cheer and inspire. **Open** begins the yin hemicycle by initiating the formative process.

Connection to the outer: liquifying, casting, skinning off the mold, the Metallic Moment beginning. **Open** stimulates, cheers and reveals innate form.

☲ **Radiance**: Fire and brightness radiate light and warmth, attached to their support; congregating people see and become aware. **Radiance** ends the yang hemicycle, consuming action in awareness.
Connection to the inner: light, heat, consciousness bring continual change, the Fiery Moment. **Radiance** spreads outward, congregating, becoming aware and changing.

Changing inner awareness **skins** away obsolete outer forms, releasing a stimulating new potential.

● *Counter Indications*

Nuclear trigrams **Force**, CH'IEN, and **Ground**, SUN, result in Counter Hexagram 44, **Coupling**, KOU. Individual renewal through **skinning** is contrasted with meeting and **coupling** with another person.

● *Sequence*

> **The Well tao not permitting not Skinning.**
> **Anterior acquiescence has the use-of Skinning.**

Associated Contexts **Well**, CHING: water well at the center of the fields; rise and flow of water in a well, rise and surge from an inner source; life-water, nucleus of life; found a capital city. The ideogram: two vertical lines crossing two horizontal ones, eight fields with a well at the center. Image of Hexagram 48. **Tao**: way or path; ongoing process of being and the course it traces for each specific person or thing; keyword. The ideogram: go and head, leading and the path it creates. **Not permitting**, PU K'O: not possible; contradicts an inherent principle. The ideogram: mouth and breath, silent consent. **Not**, PU: simple negative.
Anterior ... the use-of: activating this hexagram depends on understanding and accepting the previous statement.

● *Contrasted Definitions*

Skinning: departing anteriority indeed.
The Vessel: grasping renewal indeed.

Associated Contexts **Depart**, CH'Ü: leave, quit, remove; repudiate, reject, dismiss. **Anterior**, KU: come before as cause; formerly, ancient; reason, purpose, intention; grievance, quarrel, dissatisfaction, sorrow, mourning resulting from previous causes and intentions; situation leading to a divination. **Indeed**, YEH: intensifier; indicates comment on previous statement.

Vessel/holding, TING: bronze cauldron with three feet and two ears, sacred vessel used to cook food for sacrifice to gods and ancestors; founding symbol of family or dynasty; melting pot, receptacle; hold, contain, transform; establish, secure; precious, respectable. Image of Hexagram 50. **Grasp**, CH'Ü: lay hold of, take and use, seize, appropriate; grasp the meaning, understand. The ideogram: ear and hand, hear and grasp. **Renew**, HSIN: restore, improve, make or get better; new, fresh; the best, the latest.

● *Symbol Tradition*

Marsh center possessing fire. Skinning.
A chün tzu uses regulating time-reckoning to brighten the seasons.

Associated Contexts **Marsh**, TSE: open surface of a flat body of water and the vapors rising from it; fertilize, enrich; kindness, favor; the Symbol of the trigram Open, TUI. **Center**, CHUNG: inner, central; put in the center; middle, stable point enabling you to face inner and outer changes; middle line of trigram. The ideogram: field divided in two equal parts. Image of Hexagram 61. **Possess**, YU: in possession of, have, own; opposite of lack, WU. **Fire**, HUO: warming and consuming aspect of burning; fire and brightness are the Symbols of the trigram Radiance, LI.

Chün tzu: ideal of a person who uses divination to order his/her life in accordance with tao rather than wilful intention; keyword. **Use(-of)**, YI: make use of, by means of, owing to; employ, make functional. **Regulate**, CHIH: govern well, ensure prosperity; remedy disorder, heal; someone fit to govern land, house and heart. **Time-reckoning**, LI: fix times, seasons, calender; reckon the course of heavenly bodies, astronomical events.

Brightness, MING: light-giving aspect of burning, heavenly bodies and consciousness; with fire, the Symbol of the trigram Radiance, LI. **Season**, SHIH: quality of the time; the right time, opportune, in harmony; planning in accord with the time; seasons of the year. The ideogram: sun and temple, time as sacred.

• *Image Tradition*

> **Skinning. Stream, fire, mutually pausing. [I]**
> **Two women concording, residing.**
> **Their purposes not mutually acquired. Spoken-thus: Skinning.**
>
> **Before-zenith sun, thereupon conforming. [II]**
> **Skinning and-also trusting it.**
>
> **Pattern brightening uses stimulating. [III]**
> **Great Growing uses correcting.**
> **Skinning and-also appropriate.**
> **One's repenting thereupon extinguished.**
>
> **Heaven[and]Earth Skinning and-also**
> **the four seasons accomplishing. [IV]**
> **Majestically martial, Skinning fate.**
> **Yielding reaching-to heaven and-also**
> **corresponding reaching-to the people.**
> **Actually Skinning's season great in-fact.**

Associated Contexts **[I] Stream**, SHUI: flowing water; fluid, dissolving; river, tide, flood; the Symbol of the trigram Gorge, K'AN. The ideogram: rippling water. **Mutual**, HSIANG: reciprocal assistance, encourage, help; bring together, blend with; examine, inspect; by turns. **Pause**, HSI: stop and rest, repose; breathe, a breathing-spell; suspended.

Two, ERH: pair, even numbers, binary, duplicate. **Woman(hood)**, NÜ: a woman; what is inherently female. **Concord**, T'UNG: harmonize, unite, equalize, assemble; agree, share in; together, at once, same time and place. The ideogram: cover and mouth, silent understanding and perfect fit. Image of Hexagram 13. **Reside(-in)**, CHÜ: dwell, live in, stay; sit down, fill an office; settled parts of a country. The ideogram: body and seat.

Their/they, one's/one, CH'I: third person pronoun; also: it/its, he/his, she/hers. **Purpose**, CHIH: focus of mind and heart; will, inclination, resolve. The ideogram: heart and scholar, high inner resolve, or heart and go, inner determination. **Acquire**, TE: obtain the desired object; wish for, desire covetously; gains, possessions. The ideogram: go and obstacle, going through obstacles to the goal. **Spoken-thus**, YÜEH: designated, termed, called. The ideogram: open mouth and tongue.

[II] **And-also**, ERH: joins and contrasts two terms. **Trust(worthy)**, HSIN: truthful, faithful, consistent over time; integrity; confide in, follow; credentials; contrasts with conforming, FU, connection in a specific moment. The ideogram: person and word, true speech. **It/them/have(-it)/'s**, CHIH: expresses possession, directly or as an object pronoun.

[III] **Pattern**, WEN: intrinsic or natural design and its beauty; stylish, elegant; noble; contrasts with composition, CHANG, a conscious creation. **Stimulate**, SHUO: rouse to action and good feeling; free from constraint, stir up, urge on; persuade, cheer, delight; set out in words; the Action of the trigram Open, TUI. The ideogram: words and exchange.

Great, TA: big, noble, important, very; orient the will toward a self-imposed goal, impose direction; ability to lead or guide your life; contrasts with small, HSIAO, flexible adaptation to what crosses your path; keyword. Image of Hexagrams 14, 26, 28, 34. **Grow**, HENG: success through a sacrifice; pervade, persevere; bring to full growth; enjoy; vigorous, effective; second stage of the Time Cycle. **Correct**, CHENG: rectify deviation or one-sidedness; proper, straight, exact, regular; constant, rule, model. The ideogram: stop and one, hold to one thing.

Appropriate, TANG: suitable; opportune, convenient; adequate, competent; equal to; whole lines in uneven places and opened lines in even places.

Repent, HUI: dissatisfaction with past conduct causing a change of heart; proceeds from abashment, LIN, shame and confusion at having lost the right way. **Extinguish**, WANG: ruin, destroy; gone, dead, lost without trace; extinct, forgotten, out of mind. The ideogram: person concealed by a wall, out of sight.

[IV] **Heaven[and]Earth**, T'IEN TI: dynamic relation between the primal powers and the world it produces; cosmos, natural or human world; keyword. **Four seasons**, SSU SHIH: the four dynamic qualities of time that make up the year and the Time Cycle; the right time, in accord with the time; time as sacred; all-encompassing. **Accomplish**, CH'ENG: complete, finish, bring about; perfect, full, whole; play your part, do your duty; mature. The ideogram: weapon and man, able to bear arms, thus fully developed.

Majestic, T'ANG: grand, awesome; extending everywhere; repel injustice, correct grievances; lit.: large river and its periodic floods. **Martial**, WU: military, warlike; strong, stern; power to make war. The ideogram: fight and stop, force deterring aggression. **Fate**, MING: individual destiny; birth and death as limits of life; issue orders with authority; consult the gods. The ideogram: mouth and order, words with heavenly authority.

Yield(-to), SHUN: give way and bear produce; comply, agree, follow, obey; unresisting, docile, flexible; nourish, provide; the Action of the trigram Field, K'UN. The ideogram: head and current, water flowing from the head of a river, yielding to the banks. **Reach(-to)**, HU: arrive at a goal; reach toward and achieve; connect; contrasts with tend-towards, YU. **Heaven**, T'IEN: highest; sky, firmament, heavens; power above the human as opposed to earth, TI, below; the Symbol of the trigram Force, CH'IEN. The ideogram: great and the one above. **Correspond(-to)**, YING: be in agreement or harmony; resonate together, invoke and fulfill each other; answer to, suitable; relation between the lines (1:4, 2:5, 3:6) when they form the pair opened and whole, supple and solid. The ideogram: heart and obey. **People, person**, JEN: humans individually and collectively; an individual; humankind. Image of Hexagrams 13 and 37.

Actually ... in-fact, YI TSAI: stresses the importance of a statement. The ideogram: a dart and done, strong intention fully expressed. **'s/have(-it)/it/them**, CHIH: expresses possession, directly or as an object pronoun.

- *Transforming Lines*

  Initial nine

  a) **Thonging avails-of yellow cattle's Skin.**

  b) **Thonging avails-of yellow cattle.**
  Not permitted to use possessing activating indeed.

Associated Contexts a) **Thong**, KUNG: bind with thongs, secure; well-guarded, strong, stiffened. **Avail-of**, YUNG: take advantage of; benefit from, profit by; use for a specific purpose; apply to advantage. The ideogram: to divine and center, applying divination to central concerns. **Yellow**, HUANG: color of the productive middle; associated with the Earthy Moment between the yang and yin hemicycles; color of soil in central China; emblematic and imperial color of China since the Yellow Emperor (2500 BCE). **Cattle**, NIU: ox, bull, cow, calf; kine; power and strength of work animals.

b) **Activate**, WEI: act or cause to act; do, make, manage; make active; attend to, help; because of.

Six at-second

a) **Before-zenith sun, thereupon Skinning it.**
   Chastising significant, without fault.

b) **Before-zenith sun Skinning it.**
   Moving possessing excellence indeed.

Associated Contexts a) **Chastise**, CHENG: punish, subjugate, discipline; reduce to order; punishing expedition. The ideogram: step and correct, a rectifying move. **Significant**, CHI: leads to the experience of meaning; favorable, propitious, advantageous, appropriate; keyword. The ideogram: scholar and mouth, wise words of a sage. **Without fault**, WU CHIU: no error or harm in the situation.

b) **Move**, HSING: move or move something; motivate, emotionally moving; walk, act, do. The ideogram: stepping left then right. **Excellence**,CHIA: superior quality; fine, delicious, glorious; happy, pleased; rejoice in, praise. The ideogram: increasing goodness, pleasure and happiness.

Nine at-third

a) **Chastising: pitfall, Trial: adversity.**
   Skinning words three-times drawing-near:
   Possessing conformity.

b) **Skinning words three-times drawing-near.**
   Furthermore actually wherefore having-them.

Associated Contexts a) **Chastise**, CHENG: punish, subjugate, discipline; reduce to order; punishing expedition. The ideogram: step and correct, a rectifying move. **Pitfall**, HSIUNG: leads away from the experience of meaning; stuck and exposed to danger, unable to take in the situation; flow of life and spirit is blocked; unfortunate, baleful; keyword. **Trial**, CHEN: test by ordeal; inquiry by divination and its result; righteous, firm; separating wheat from chaff; the kernel, the proven core; fourth stage of the Time Cycle. The ideogram: pearl and divination. **Adversity**, LI: danger; threatening, malevolent demon. This has two aspects: grind, sharpen, improve, perfect, stimulate; and: poisonous, sinister, cruel, contrary. It indicates a spirit or ghost that seeks revenge by inflicting suffering upon the living. Pacifying or exorcizing such a spirit can have a healing effect. The ideogram: sheltering cliff and stinging insect.

Word, YEN: speech, spoken words, sayings; talk, discuss, address. The ideogram: mouth and rising vapor, words as speech. **Three-times**, SAN: serial repetition. **Draw-near**, CHIU: approach, encounter, come near; follow; approach completion; composed, finished; able, willing; in a little while.

Possessing conformity, YU FU: inner and outer are in accord; confidence of the spirits has been captured; sincere, truthful; proper to take action.

b) **Furthermore**, YU: in addition to; higher degree of. **Actually**, YI: truly, really, at present. The ideogram: a dart and done, strong intention fully expressed. **Wherefore**, HO: interrogative: why? for what reason? what is? and affirmation: therefore, for that reason. **Have(-them)/it/'s**, CHIH: expresses possession, directly or as an object pronoun.

Nine at-fourth

a) **Repenting extinguished, possessing conformity.**
    Amending fate significant.

b) **Amending fate's significance.**
    Trustworthy purpose indeed.

Associated Contexts. *a)* **Possessing conformity**, YU FU: inner and outer are in accord; confidence of the spirits has been captured; sincere, truthful; proper to take action.

Amend, KAI: correct, reform, make new, alter, mend. The ideogram: self and strike, fighting your own errors. **Significant**, CHI: leads to the experience of meaning; favorable, propitious, advantageous, appropriate;

keyword. The ideogram: scholar and mouth, wise words of a sage.

Nine at-fifth

a) **Great People: tiger transforming.**
   Not-yet an augury, possessing conformity.

b) **Great People: tiger transforming.**
   One's pattern luminous indeed.

Associated Contexts a) **Great People**, TA JEN: important, noble, influential; those who impose a ruling principle on their lives; effect of the great within an individual; keyword. **Tiger**, HU: fierce king of animals; extreme yang; opposed to and protects against demoniacs on North–South axis of Universal Compass. **Transform**, PIEN: abrupt, radical, fundamental mutation from one state of being to another; transformation of lines in hexagrams; contrasts with change, HUA, gradual metamorphosis.

   Not-yet, WEI: temporal negative; something will but has not yet occurred; contrary of already, CHI. Image of Hexagram 64. **Augury**, CHAN: sign, omen; divine by casting lots, sortilege; look at as a sign or augury. **Possessing conformity**, YU FU: inner and outer are in accord; confidence of the spirits has been captured; sincere, truthful; proper to take action.

b) **Luminous**, PING: bright, fire-like, light-giving; alert, intelligent.

Six above

a) **A chün tzu: leopard transforming.**
   Small People: Skinning the visage.
   Chastising: pitfall.
   Residing-in Trial significant.

b) **A chün tzu: leopard transforming.**
   One's pattern beautiful indeed.
   Small People: Skinning the visage.
   Yielding uses adhering-to the chief indeed.

Associated Contexts a) **Leopard**, PAO: spotted wild cats, beautiful and independent; mark of high-ranking officers. **Transform**, PIEN: abrupt, radical, fundamental mutation from one state of being to another; transformation of lines in hexagrams; contrasts with change, HUA, gradual metamorphosis.

Small People, HSIAO JEN: lowly, common, humble; those who adjust to circumstances with the flexibility of the small; effect of the small within an individual; keyword. **Visage**, MIEN: face, countenance; honor, character, reputation; front, surface; face to face.

Chastise, CHENG: punish, subjugate, discipline; reduce to order; punishing expedition. The ideogram: step and correct, a rectifying move. **Pitfall**, HSIUNG: leads away from the experience of meaning; stuck and exposed to danger, unable to take in the situation; flow of life and spirit is blocked; unfortunate, baleful; keyword.

Reside(-in), CHÜ: dwell, live in, stay; sit down, fill an office; settled parts of a country. The ideogram: body and seat. **Trial**, CHEN: test by ordeal; inquiry by divination and its result; righteous, firm; separating wheat from chaff; the kernel, the proven core; fourth stage of the Time Cycle. The ideogram: pearl and divination. **Significant**, CHI: leads to the experience of meaning; favorable, propitious, advantageous, appropriate; keyword . The ideogram: scholar and mouth, wise words of a sage.

b) **Beautiful**, WEI: elegant, classic, fine; luxuriant, lush.

Adhere(-to), TS'UNG: follow a way, hold to a doctrine, school, or person; hear and comply with, agree to; forced to follow, follower. The ideogram: two men walking, one following the other. **Chief**, CHÜN: effective ruler; preside over, take the lead; influence others; term of respect. The ideogram: mouth and director, giving orders.

50

THE VESSEL/HOLDING ▪ *TING*

This hexagram describes your situation in terms of the imaginative capacity of a sacred vessel. It emphasizes that securing and imaginatively transforming the material at hand is the adequate way to handle it. To be in accord with the time, you are told to: **hold** and transform things in the **vessel**!

● *Image of the Situation*

> **The Vessel, Spring significant.**
> **Growing.**

Associated Contexts **Vessel/holding**, TING: bronze cauldron with three feet and two ears, sacred vessel used to cook food for sacrifice to gods and ancestors; founding symbol of family or dynasty; melting pot, receptacle; hold, contain, transform; establish, secure; precious, respectable. **Spring**, YÜAN: source, origin, head; great, excellent; arise, begin, generating power; first stage of the Time Cycle. **Significant**, CHI: leads to the experience of meaning; favorable, propitious, advantageous, appropriate; keyword. The ideogram: scholar and mouth, wise words of a sage.

> **Grow**, HENG: success through a sacrifice; pervade, persevere; bring to full growth; enjoy; vigorous, effective; second stage of the Time Cycle.

● *Outer and Inner Aspects*

☲ **Radiance**: Fire and brightness radiate light and warmth, attached to their support; congregating people see and become aware. **Radiance** ends the yang hemicycle, consuming action in awareness.

> Connection to the outer: light, heat, consciousness bring continual change, the Fiery Moment. **Radiance** spreads outward, congregating, becoming aware and changing.

☵ **Ground**: Wind and wood subtly enter from the ground, penetrating and pervading. **Ground** is the center of the yang hemicycle, spreading pervasive action.

Connection to the inner: penetrating and bringing together, the Woody Moment culminating. **Ground** pervades, matches and couples, seeding a new generation.

Inner substance feeds a spreading outer light, cooking and transforming what is **held** in the **vessel**.

● *Counter Indications*

Nuclear trigrams **Open**, TUI, and **Force**, CH'IEN, result in Counter Hexagram 43, **Parting**, KUAI. **Holding** and containing things in the **vessel** is contrasted with **parting** energy into diverging streams.

● *Sequence*

> **Skinning beings implies absolutely-nothing like a Vessel.**
> **Anterior acquiescence has the use-of the Vessel.**

Associated Contexts **Skin**, KO: take off the covering, skin or hide; change, renew, molt; remove, peel off; revolt, overthrow, degrade from office; leather armor, protection. Image of Hexagram 49. **Being(s)**, WU: creature, thing, any single being; matter, substance, essence; nature of things. **Imply**, CHE: further signify; additional meaning. **Absolutely-no(thing)**, MO: complete elimination; not any, by no means. **Like**, JO: same as; just as, similar to.

Anterior ... the use-of: activating this hexagram depends on understanding and accepting the previous statement.

● *Contrasted Definitions*

> **Skinning: departing anteriority indeed.**
> **The Vessel: grasping renewal indeed.**

Associated Contexts **Depart**, CH'Ü: leave, quit, remove; repudiate, reject, dismiss. **Anterior**, KU: come before as cause; formerly, ancient; reason, purpose, intention; grievance, quarrel, dissatisfaction, sorrow, mourning resulting from previous causes and intentions; situation leading to a divination. **Indeed**, YEH: intensifier; indicates comment on previous statement.

Grasp, CH'Ü: lay hold of, take and use, seize, appropriate; grasp the meaning, understand. The ideogram: ear and hand, hear and grasp. **Renew**, HSIN: restore, improve, make or get better; new, fresh; the best, the latest.

- *Symbol Tradition*

> **Above wood possessing fire. The Vessel.**
> **A chün tzu uses correcting the situation to solidify fate.**

Associated Contexts **Above**, SHANG: anything above, in all senses; higher, upper, outer; upper trigram; opposite of below, HSIA. **Wood/tree**, MU: all things woody or wooden, alive or constructed from wood; associated with the Woody Moment; wood and wind are the Symbols of the trigram Ground, SUN. The ideogram: a tree with roots and branches. **Possess**, YU: in possession of, have, own; opposite of lack, WU. **Fire**, HUO: warming and consuming aspect of burning; fire and brightness are the Symbols of the trigram Radiance, LI.

Chün tzu: ideal of a person who uses divination to order his/her life in accordance with tao rather than wilful intention; keyword. **Use(-of)**, YI: make use of, by means of, owing to; employ, make functional. **Correct**, CHENG: rectify deviation or one-sidedness; proper, straight, exact, regular; constant, rule, model. The ideogram: stop and one, hold to one thing. **Situation**, WEI: place or seat according to rank; post, position, command; right, proper; established, arranged. The ideogram: person and stand, servants in their places. **Solidify**, NING: congeal, freeze, curdle, stiffen; coagulate, make solid or firm. **Fate**, MING: individual destiny; birth and death as limits of life; issue orders with authority; consult the gods. The ideogram: mouth and order, words with heavenly authority.

- *Image Tradition*

> **The Vessel. A symbol indeed. [I]**
> **Using wood: Ground, fire.**
> **Growing: cooking indeed.**

The all-wise person Growing
                         uses presenting-to the Supreme Above. [II]
And-also great Growing uses nourishing all-wise eminences.
Ground and-also the ear[and]eye: understanding brightened.

Supple advancing and-also moving above. [III]
Acquiring the center and-also corresponding reaching the solid.
That uses Spring Growing.

Associated Contexts [I] **Symbol**, HSIANG: image invested with intrinsic power to connect visible and invisible; magic spell; figure, form, shape, likeness; pattern, model; create an image, imitate; act, play; writing.

Wood/tree, MU: all things woody or wooden, alive or constructed from wood; associated with the Woody Moment; wood and wind are the Symbols of the trigram Ground, SUN. The ideogram: a tree with roots and branches. **Ground**, SUN: base on which things rest; support, foundation; mild, subtly penetrating; nourishing. The ideogram: stand and things arranged on it, the subtle influence of the ground. Image of Hexagram 57.

Cook, JEN: cook very thoroughly; transform completely. The ideogram: food and full or complete.

[II] **All-wise**, SHENG: intuitive universal wisdom; mythical sages; holy, sacred; mark of highest distinction. The ideogram: ear and inform, one who knows all from a single sound. **People**, **person**, JEN: humans individually and collectively; an individual; humankind. Image of Hexagrams 13 and 37. **Present(-to)**, HSIANG: present in sacrifice, offer with thanks, give to the gods or a superior; confer dignity on. **Supreme Above**, SHANG TI: highest power in universe, lord of all.

And-also, ERH: joins and contrasts two terms. **Great**, TA: big, noble, important, very; orient the will toward a self-imposed goal, impose direction; ability to lead or guide your life; contrasts with small, HSIAO, flexible adaptation to what crosses your path; keyword. Image of Hexagrams 14, 26, 28, 34. **Nourish**, YANG: feed, sustain, support; provide, care for; bring up, improve, grow, develop. **Eminent**, HSIEN: moral and intellectual power; worthy, excellent, virtuous; sage second to the all-wise, SHENG.

Ear[and]eye, ERH MU, organs of perception and awareness; see and understand; observe. **Understand**, TSUNG: perceive quickly, astute, sharp; discriminate intelligently. The ideogram: ear and quick. **Brightness**, MING: light-giving aspect of burning, heavenly bodies and consciousness; with fire, the Symbol of the trigram Radiance, LI.

[III] **Supple**, JOU: quality of the opened lines; flexible, pliant, tender, adaptable. **Advance**, CHIN: exert yourself, make progress, climb; be promoted; further the development of, augment; adopt a religion or conviction; offer, introduce. **Move**, HSING: move or move something; motivate, emotionally moving; walk, act, do. The ideogram: stepping left then right.

Acquire, TE: obtain the desired object; wish for, desire covetously; gains, possessions. The ideogram: go and obstacle, going through obstacles to the goal. **Center**, CHUNG: inner, central; put in the center; middle, stable point enabling you to face inner and outer changes; middle line of trigram. The ideogram: field divided in two equal parts. Image of Hexagram 61. **Correspond(-to)**, YING: be in agreement or harmony; resonate together, invoke and fulfill each other; answer to, suitable; relation between the lines (1:4, 2:5, 3:6) when they form the pair opened and whole, supple and solid. The ideogram: heart and obey. **Reach(-to)**, HU: arrive at a goal; reach toward and achieve; connect; contrasts with tend-towards, YU. **Solid**, KANG: quality of the whole lines; firm, strong, unyielding, persisting.

That uses, SHIH YI: involves and is involved by.

- *Transforming Lines*

  Initial six

  a) **The Vessel: toppling the foot.**
  Harvesting: issuing-forth-from obstruction.
  Acquiring a concubine, using one's sonhood.
  Without fault.

  b) **The Vessel: toppling the foot.**
  Not-yet rebelling indeed.
  Harvesting: issuing-forth-from obstruction.
  Using adhering-to valuing indeed.

Associated Contexts a) **Topple**, TIEN: fall over because top-heavy; overthrow, subvert; top, summit. **Foot**, CHIH: literal foot; foundation, base.

Harvest, LI: advantageous, profitable; acute, insightful; benefit, nourish; third stage of the Time Cycle. **Issue-forth(-from)**, CH'U: emerge from, come out of, proceed from, spring from; the Action of the trigram

Shake, CHEN; contrary of enter, JU. The ideogram: stem with branches and leaves emerging. **Obstruct**, P'I: closed, stopped; bar the way; obstacle; unfortunate, wicked; refuse, disapprove, deny. The ideogram: mouth and not, blocked communication. Image of Hexagram 12.

Concubine, CH'IEH: secondary wife taken without ceremony to ensure a male descendant; handmaid. **One's/one**, CH'I: third person pronoun; also: it/its, he/his, she/hers, they/theirs. **Son(hood)**, TZU: living up to ideal of ancestors as highest human development; act with concern and reverence; male child; offspring, posterity; seed, kernel, egg; sage, teacher; nadir, deepest point, midnight, mid-winter.

Without fault, WU CHIU: no error or harm in the situation.

b) **Not-yet**, WEI: temporal negative; something will but has not yet occurred; contrary of already, CHI. Image of Hexagram 64. **Rebel**, PEI: go against nature or usage; insubordinate; perverse, unreasonable.

Adhere(-to), TS'UNG: follow a way, hold to a doctrine, school, or person; hear and comply with, agree to; forced to follow, follower. The ideogram: two men walking, one following the other. **Value**, KUEI: regard as valuable, give worth and dignity to; precious, high priced; honorable, exalted, illustrious. The ideogram: cowries (coins) and basket.

Nine at-second

a) The Vessel possesses substance.
   My companion possesses affliction.
   Not me able to approach. Significant.

b) The Vessel possesses substance.
   Considering places it indeed.
   My companion possesses affliction.
   Completing without surpassing indeed.

Associated Contexts a) **Substance**, SHIH: real, solid, full; results, fruits, possessions; essence; honest, sincere. The ideogram: string of coins under a roof, riches in the house.

My/me/I, WO: first person pronoun; indicates an unusually strong emphasis on your own subjective experience. **Companion**, CH'IU: equal, spouse; unite, join in marriage. Also: opponent, rival, enemy; contradict, hate. **Afflict**, CHI: sickness, disorder, defect, calamity; injurious; pressure and consequent anger, hate or dislike. The ideogram: sickness and dart, a sudden affliction.

Not, PU: simple negative. **Able**, NENG: enable; ability, power, skill, art; competent, talented; duty, function, capacity. The ideogram: an animal with strong hooves and bones, able to carry and defend. **Approach**, CHI: come near to, advance toward; about to do; soon.

b) **Consider**, SHEN: act carefully, seriously; cautious, attentive, circumspect; still, quiet, sincere. The ideogram: heart and true. **Place**, SO: where something belongs or comes from; residence, dwelling; habitual focus or object. **It/them/have(-it)/'s**, CHIH: expresses possession, directly or as an object pronoun.

Complete, CHUNG: end of a cycle that begins the next; last, whole, all; contrasts with exhaust, CH'IUNG, final end. The ideogram: silk cocoons, follow and ice, winter linking one year with the next. **Without**, WU: devoid of; -less as suffix. **Surpass**, YU: exceed; beyond measure, excessive; extraordinary; transgress, blame.

Nine at-third

a) **The Vessel: the ears skinned.**
  Its movement clogged.
  Pheasant juice not taken-in.
  On-all-sides rain lessens repenting.
  Completing significant.

b) **The Vessel: the ears skinned.**
  Letting-go its righteousness indeed.

Associated Contexts. a) **Ear**, ERH: organ of hearing; handle, sides. **Its/it**, CH'I: third person pronoun; also: one/one's, he/his, she/hers, they/theirs. **Clog**, SAI: stop up, fill up, close, obstruct, hinder, prevent; unintelligent, dull, hard to understand.

Pheasant, CHIH: clever, beautiful bird associated with the trigram Radiance, LI; also: embrasures on ramparts and forts; arrange, put in order. **Juice**, KAO: active principle, essence; oil, grease, ointment; fertilizing, rich; genius. **Not**, PU: simple negative. **Take-in**, SHIH: eat, ingest, swallow, devour; incorporate.

Sides (on-all-sides), FANG: limits, boundaries; square, surface of the earth extending to the four cardinal points; everywhere. **Rain**, YÜ: all precipitation; sudden showers, fast and furious; associated with the trigram Gorge, K'AN, and the Streaming Moment. **Lessen**, K'UEI: diminish, injure, wane; lack, defect, failure. **Repent**, HUI: dissatisfaction with past conduct causing a change of heart; proceeds from abashment, LIN, shame and confusion at having lost the right way.

Complete, CHUNG: end of a cycle that begins the next; last, whole, all; contrasts with exhaust, CH'IUNG, final end. The ideogram: silk cocoons, follow and ice, winter linking one year with the next.

b) **Let-go**, SHIH: lose, omit, miss, fail, let slip; out of control. The ideogram: drop from the hand. **Righteous**, YI: proper and just, meets the standards; things in their proper place; the heart that rules itself; upright, moral rule; contrasts with Harvest, LI, advantage or profit.

Nine at-fourth

a) The Vessel: a severed stand.
Overthrowing a princely stew.
Its form soiled. Pitfall.

b) Overthrowing a princely stew.
Wherefore trustworthy thus indeed?

Associated Contexts a) **Sever**, CHE: break off, separate, sunder, cut in two; discriminate, judge the true and false. **Stand**, TSU: base, foot, leg; rest on, support; stance. The ideogram: foot and calf resting.

Overthrow, FU: subvert, upset, defeat, throw down; unstable, move back and forth. **Prince**, KUNG: nobles acting as ministers of state in the capital; governing from the center rather than active in daily life; contrasts with feudatory, HOU, governors of the provinces. **Stew**, SU: cooked or boiled rice and meat; mixed contents of a pot.

Its/it, CH'I: third person pronoun; also: one/one's, he/his, she/hers, they/theirs. **Form**, HSING: shape; body, bodily; material appearance. **Soil**, WU: covered thick; dirty, stain; moisten, enrich. **Pitfall**, HSIUNG: leads away from the experience of meaning; stuck and exposed to danger, unable to take in the situation; flow of life and spirit is blocked; unfortunate, baleful; keyword.

b) **Wherefore**, HO: interrogative: why? for what reason? what is? and affirmation: therefore, for that reason. **Trustworthy**, HSIN: truthful, faithful, consistent over time; integrity; confide in, follow; credentials; contrasts with conforming, FU, connection in a specific moment. The ideogram: person and word, true speech. **Thus**, JU: as, in this way.

Six at-fifth

a) **The Vessel: yellow ears, metallic rings.**
  Harvesting Trial.

b) **The Vessel: yellow ears.**
  Centering uses activating substance indeed.

Associated Contexts a) **Yellow,** HUANG: color of the productive middle; associated with the Earthy Moment between the yang and yin hemicycles; color of soil in central China; emblematic and imperial color of China since the Yellow Emperor (2500 BCE). **Ear,** ERH: organ of hearing; handle, sides. **Metallic,** CHIN: smelting and casting; all things pertaining to metal, particularly gold; autumn, West, sunset; one of the Five Moments. **Rings,** HSÜAN: handles or ears for carrying a tripod.

  Harvesting Trial, LI CHEN: advantageous divination; putting the action in question to the test is beneficial.

b) **Activate,** WEI: act or cause to act; do, make, manage; make active; attend to, help; because of. **Substance,** SHIH: real, solid, full; results, fruits, possessions; essence; honest, sincere. The ideogram: string of coins under a roof, riches in the house.

Nine above

a) **The Vessel: jade rings.**
  The great significant.
  Without not Harvesting.

b) **Jade rings located above.**
  Solid[and]Supple articulating indeed.

Associated Contexts a) **Jade,** YÜ: all gemstones; precious beauty; delightful, happy; perfect, clear. **Rings,** HSÜAN: handles or ears for carrying a tripod.

  Without not Harvesting, WU PU LI: nothing for which this will not be beneficial; advantageous potential, borderline where the balance is swinging from not Harvesting to actually Harvesting.

b) **Locate(-in),** TSAI: live in, dwell, reside; belong to, involved with, depend on; within. The ideogram: earth and persevere, place on the earth.

  Solid[and]Supple, KANG JOU: field of creative tension between the whole and opened lines and their qualities; field of psychic movement. **Articulate**, CHIEH: separate and distinguish, as well as join, different things; express thought through speech; joint, section, chapter, interval, unit of time; zodiacal sign; moderate, regulate; lit.: nodes on bamboo stalks. Image of Hexagram 60.

51

SHAKE ▪ *CHEN*

This hexagram describes your situation in terms of a disturbing and inspiring shock. It emphasizes that rousing things to new activity, the action of **Shake**, is the adequate way to handle it. To be in accord with the time, you are told to: **stir** things **up**!

● *Image of the Situation*

> **Shake, Growing.**
> **Shake coming: frightening, frightening.**
> **Laughing words, shrieking, shrieking.**
> **Shake scaring a hundred miles.**
> **Not losing the ladle, the libation.**

Associated Contexts **Shake**, CHEN: arouse, excite, inspire; thunder rising from below; awe, alarm, trembling; fertilizing intrusion. The ideogram: excite and rain. **Shake** is the thunder trigram doubled and includes that trigram's attributes: *Symbol:* **Thunder**, LEI: rising, arousing power. *Actions:* **Stir-up**, TUNG: excite, influence, move, affect; work, take action; come out of the egg or the bud. The ideogram: strength and heavy, able to move weighty things. **Grow**, HENG: success through a sacrifice; pervade, persevere; bring to full growth; enjoy; vigorous, effective; second stage of the Time Cycle.

Come, LAI, and go, WANG, describe the stream of time as it flows from future through present to past; come, LAI, indicates what is approaching; move toward, arrive at; keyword. **Fright**, HSI: frighten or be frightened; alarm, terror; awestruck. The doubled character intensifies this quality.

Laugh, HSIAO: manifest joy or mirth; giggle, laugh at, ridicule; pleased, merry; associated with the Fiery Moment. **Word**, YEN: speech, spoken words, sayings; talk, discuss, address. The ideogram: mouth and rising vapor, words as speech. **Shriek**, YA: shout, yell; warning cry of animals; sounds of someone learning to speak; confused noise, exclamations. The doubled character intensifies this quality.

Scare, CHING: create and spread fear, terrify; apprehensive, alarmed, perturbed. The ideogram: horse and strike, havoc created by a terrified horse. **Hundred**, PO: numerous, many, all; a whole class or type. **Mile**, LI: measure of distance, about 1800 feet; village; street, square.

Not, PU: simple negative. **Lose**, SANG: fail to obtain, cease, become obscure; forgotten, destroyed; lament, mourn; funeral. The ideogram: weep and the dead. **Ladle**, PI: ceremonial spoon used to pour libations. **Libation**, CH'ANG: sacrifical liquor, poured out to draw the gods near.

- *Outer and Inner Aspects*

☷ **Shake**: Thunder rises from below, shaking and stirring things up. **Shake** begins the yang hemicycle by germinating new action.

Connection to both inner and outer: sprouting energies thrusting from below, the Woody Moment beginning. **Shake** stirs things up to issue-forth.

- *Counter Indications*

Nuclear trigrams **Gorge**, K'AN, and **Bound**, KEN, result in Counter Hexagram 39, **Limping**, CHIEN. The dynamic thrust of **shake** is contrasted with the hampered moving of **limping**.

- *Sequence*

A lord's implementing implies absolutely-nothing
like the long-living son.
Anterior acquiescence has the use-of Shake.
Shake implies stirring-up indeed.

Associated Contexts **Lord**, CHU: ruler, master, chief; authority. The ideogram: lamp and flame, giving light. **'s/have(-it)/it/them**, CHIH: expresses possession, directly or as an object pronoun. **Implements**, CH'I: utensils, tools; molded or carved objects; use a person or thing suitably; capacity, talent, intelligence. **Imply**, CHE: further signify; additional meaning. **Absolutely-no(thing)**, MO: complete elimination; not any, by no means. **Like**, JO: same as; just as, similar to. **Long-living**, CHANG: enduring, constant; senior, superior, greater; increase, prosper; respect, elevate. **Son(hood)**, TZU: living up to ideal of ancestors as highest human development; act with concern and reverence; male child; offspring, posterity; seed, kernel, egg; sage, teacher; nadir, deepest point, midnight, mid-winter.

Anterior ... the use-of: activating this hexagram depends on understanding and accepting the previous statement.

Indeed, YEH: intensifier; indicates comment on previous statement.

- ## Contrasted Definitions

    Shake: rising-up indeed.
    Bound: stopping indeed.

Associated Contexts **Rise-up**, CH'I: stand up, lift; undertake, begin, originate.

Bound, KEN: limit, boundary; encounter an obstacle, stop; still, quiet, motionless; confine, enclose, mark off; turn around to look behind; hard, adamant, obstinate; perverse. The ideogram: eye and person turning round to compare and group what is behind. Image of Hexagram 52. **Stop**, CHIH: bring or come to a standstill; the Action of the trigram Bound, KEN. The ideogram: a foot stops walking.

- ## Symbol Tradition

    Reiterated thunder. Shake.
    A chün tzu uses anxious fearing to adjust inspecting.

Associated Contexts **Reiterate**, CHIEN: repeat, duplicate; successive. **Chün tzu**: ideal of a person who uses divination to order his/her life in accordance with tao rather than wilful intention; keyword. **Use(-of)**, YI: make use of, by means of, owing to; employ, make functional. **Anxious**, K'UNG: apprehensive, alarmed, agitated; suspicious of. The ideogram: heart and sick, agitated within. **Fear**, CHÜ: afraid, intimidated, apprehensive; stand in awe of. **Adjust**, HSIU: regulate, repair, clean up, renovate. **Inspect**, HSING: examine on all sides, careful inquiry; watchful.

● *Image Tradition*

Shake, Growing. [I]
Shake coming: frightening, frightening.
Anxiety involving blessing indeed.

Laughing words, shrieking, shrieking. [II]
Afterwards possessing by-consequence indeed.

Shake scaring a hundred miles. [III]
Scaring the distant and-also fearing the nearby indeed.

Issuing-forth permits using guarding
     the ancestral temple, field-altar, offertory-millet. [IV]
Using activating the offering lord indeed.

Associated Contexts **[I] Involve**, CHIH: include, entangle, implicate; induce, cause. The ideogram: person walking, induced to follow. **Bless**, FU: heavenly gifts; make happy; spiritual power and goodwill. The ideogram: spirit and plenty, heavenly gifts in abundance.

[II] After(wards)/later, HOU: come after in time, subsequent; put oneself after; the second; attendants, heirs, successors, posterity. **Possess**, YU: in possession of, have, own; opposite of lack, WU. **By-consequence(-of)**, TSE: very strong connection; reason, cause, result; rule, law, pattern, standard; therefore.

[III] Distance, YÜAN: far off, remote; keep at a distance; alienated. The ideogram: go and a long way. **And-also**, ERH: joins and contrasts two terms. **Nearby**, ERH: near, close; close relation.

[IV] Permit, K'O: possible because in harmony with an inherent principle. The ideogram: mouth and breath, silent consent. **Guard**, SHOU: keep in custody; protect, ward off harm, attend to, supervise. **Ancestry**, TSUNG: clan, kin, origin; those who bear the same surname; ancestral hall and tablets; honor, revere; a doctrine; contrasts with predecessor, K'AO, individual ancestors. **Temple**, MIAO: building used to honor gods and ancestors. **Field-altar**, SHE: altar and sacrifices to spirits of place; village, with a common god and field-altar. **Offertory-millet**, CHI: grain presented to the god of agriculture; presence of the god in the grain.

Activate, WEI: act or cause to act; do, make, manage; make active; attend to, help; because of. **Offer**, CHI: gifts to gods and spirits. The ideogram: hand, meat and worship.

- *Transforming Lines*

  Initial nine

  a) Shake coming: frightening, frightening.
  After laughing words, shrieking, shrieking.
  Significant.

  b) Shake coming: frightening, frightening.
  Anxiety involving blessing indeed.
  Laughing words, shrieking, shrieking.
  Afterwards possessing by-consequence indeed.

Associated Contexts a) **Significant**, CHI: leads to the experience of meaning; favorable, propitious, advantageous, appropriate; keyword. The ideogram: scholar and mouth, wise words of a sage.

  Six at-second

  a) Shake coming: adversity.
  A hundred-thousand lost coins.
  Climbing tending-towards the ninth mound.
  No pursuit.
  The seventh day: acquiring.

  b) Shake coming: adversity.
  Riding a solid indeed.

Associated Contexts a) **Adversity**, LI: danger; threatening, malevolent demon. This has two aspects: grind, sharpen, improve, perfect, stimulate; and: poisonous, sinister, cruel, contrary. It indicates a spirit or ghost that seeks revenge by inflicting suffering upon the living. Pacifying or exorcizing such a spirit can have a healing effect. The ideogram: sheltering cliff and stinging insect.

Hundred-thousand, YI: ten myriads (groups of ten thousand); huge quantity, number beyond imagination. **Coins**, PEI: cowrie shells used for money; adorned with shell; money, riches; precious, valuable.

Climb, CHI: ascend, scale; climb steep cliffs; rise as clouds. **Tend-towards**, YÜ: move toward but not reach, in the direction of; contrasts with reach(-to), HU, actually arriving. **Nine**, CHIU: number of a transforming whole line; superlative: best, perfect; ninth. **Mound**, LING: grave-mound, barrow; small hill.

No, WU: simple negative; un-, dis-. **Pursue**, CHU: chase, follow closely, press hard; expel, drive out. The ideogram: pig (wealth) and go, chasing fortune.

Seven, CH'I: number seven, seventh; seven planets; seventh day when moon changes from crescent to waxing; the Tangram game makes pictures of all phenomena from seven basic shapes. **Day/sun**, JIH: actual sun and the time of a sun-cycle, a day. **Acquire**, TE: obtain the desired object; wish for, desire covetously; gains, possessions. The ideogram: go and obstacle, going through obstacles to the goal.

b) **Ride**, CH'ENG: ride an animal or a chariot; have the upper hand, seize the right time; control strong power; overcome the nature of the other; supple opened line above a solid whole line. **Solid**, KANG: quality of the whole lines; firm, strong, unyielding, persisting.

Six at-third

a) **Shake: reviving, reviving.**
   Shake moving without blunder.

b) **Shake: reviving, reviving.**
   Situation not appropriate indeed.

Associated Contexts a) **Revive**, SU: regain vital energy, courage or strength; bring to life, cheer up; relief; lit.: herb whose smell revives weary spirits. The doubled character intensifies this quality.

Move, HSING: move or move something; motivate, emotionally moving; walk, act, do. The ideogram: stepping left then right. **Without**, WU: devoid of; -less as suffix. **Blunder**, SHENG: mistake due to ignorance or fault; contrasts with calamity, TSAI, disaster from without. The ideogram: eye and grow, a film clouding sight.

b) **Situation**, WEI: place or seat according to rank; post, position, command; right, proper; established, arranged. The ideogram: person and stand, servants in their places. **Appropriate**, TANG: suitable; opportune, convenient; adequate, competent; equal to; whole lines in uneven places and opened lines in even places.

Nine at-fourth

a) **Shake: releasing the bog.**

b) **Shake: releasing the bog.**
   Not-yet shining indeed.

Associated Contexts a) **Release**, SUI: loose, let go, free; unhindered, in accord; follow, spread out, progress; penetrate, invade. The ideogram: go and follow your wishes, unimpeded movement. **Bog**, NI: wet spongy soil; mire, slush, quicksand; unable to move.

b) **Not-yet**, WEI: temporal negative; something will but has not yet occurred; contrary of already, CHI. Image of Hexagram 64. **Shine**, KUANG: illuminate; give off brilliant, bright light; honor, glory, éclat; result of action, contrasts with brightness, MING, light of heavenly bodies. The ideogram: fire above person, lifting the light.

Six at-fifth

a) **Shake going, coming adversity.**
   Intention without losing possesses affairs.

b) **Shake going, coming adversity.**
   Exposed moving indeed.
   One's affairs located-in the center.
   The great without losing indeed.

Associated Contexts a) **Come**, LAI, and **Go**, WANG, describe the stream of time as it flows from future through present to past. Come, LAI, indicates what is approaching; move toward, arrive at; go, WANG, indicates what is departing; proceed, move on; keywords. **Adversity**, LI: danger; threatening, malevolent demon. This has two aspects: grind, sharpen, improve, perfect, stimulate; and: poisonous, sinister, cruel, contrary. It indicates a spirit or ghost that seeks revenge by inflicting suffering upon the living. Pacifying or exorcizing such a spirit can have a healing effect. The ideogram: sheltering cliff and stinging insect.

Intention, YI: thought, meaning, idea, will, motive; what gives words their significance. The ideogram: heart and sound, heartfelt expression. **Without**, WU: devoid of; -less as suffix. **Affairs**, SHIH: all kinds of personal activity; matters at hand; business, occupation; manage a business, case in court.

b) **Expose**, WEI: exposed to danger, precipitous, unsteady; too high, not upright; uneasy. The ideogram: overhanging rock, person and limit, exposure in an extreme position. **Move**, HSING: move or move something; motivate, emotionally moving; walk, act, do. The ideogram: stepping left then right.

One's, **one**, CH'I: third person pronoun; also: he/his, she/hers, they/theirs, it/its. **Locate(-in)**, TSAI: live in, dwell, reside; belong to, involved with, depend on; within. The ideogram: earth and persevere, place on the earth. **Center**, CHUNG: inner, central; put in the center; middle, stable point enabling you to face inner and outer changes; middle line of trigram. The ideogram: field divided in two equal parts. Image of Hexagram 61.

Great, TA: big, noble, important, very; orient the will toward a self-imposed goal, impose direction; ability to lead or guide your life; contrasts with small, HSIAO, flexible adaptation to what crosses your path; keyword. Image of Hexagrams 14, 26, 28, 34.

Six above

a) **Shake: twining, twining.**
   Observing: terrorizing, terrorizing.
   Chastising: pitfall.
   Shake: not tending-towards one's body,
                                tending-towards one's neighbor.
   Without fault.
   Matrimonial allying possesses words.

b) **Shake: twining, twining.**
   Center not-yet acquired indeed.
   Although a pitfall, without fault.
   Dreading the neighbor, a warning indeed.

Associated Contexts a) **Twine**, SO: string or rope of many strands twisted together; tie up, bind together; reins; ruling ideas, obligations; demand, search for, inquire; scatter, loosen, destroy authority. The doubled character intensifies this quality.

Observe, SHIH: see and inspect carefully; gain knowledge of; compare and imitate. The ideogram: see and omen, taking account of what you see. **Terrorize**, CH'IO: look around in great alarm; frightened and trying to escape. The ideogram: eyes of bird trapped by a hand. The doubled character intensifies this quality.

Chastise, CHENG: punish, subjugate, discipline; reduce to order; punishing expedition. The ideogram: step and correct, a rectifying move. **Pitfall**, HSIUNG: leads away from the experience of meaning; stuck and exposed to danger, unable to take in the situation; flow of life and spirit is blocked; unfortunate, baleful; keyword.

Tend-towards, YÜ: move toward but not reach, in the direction of; contrasts with reach(-to), HU, actually arriving. **One's/one**, CH'I: third person pronoun; also: it/its, he/his, she/hers, they/theirs. **Body**, KUNG: physical being, power and self expression; contrasts with individuality, SHEN, the total personality. **Neighbor**, LIN: person living nearby; extended family; assist, support.

Without fault, WU CHIU: no error or harm in the situation.

Matrimonial allying, HUN KOU: legal institution of marriage; make alliances through marriage rather than force.

b) **Center**, CHUNG: inner, central; put in the center; middle, stable point enabling you to face inner and outer changes; middle line of trigram. The ideogram: field divided in two equal parts. Image of Hexagram 61. **Not-yet**, WEI: temporal negative; something will but has not yet occurred; contrary of already, CHI. Image of Hexagram 64. **Acquire**, TE: obtain the desired object; wish for, desire covetously; gains, possessions. The ideogram: go and obstacle, going through obstacles to the goal.

Although, SUI: even though, supposing that, if, even if.

Dread, WEI: stand in awe of, respect, venerate; a just fear. **Warn**, CHIEH: alert, alarm, put on guard; caution, inform; guard against, refrain from (as in a diet). The ideogram: spear held in both hands, warning enemies and alerting friends.

52

B O U N D ▪ *K E N*

This hexagram describes your situation in terms of confronting a boundary or obstacle. It emphasizes that stopping and acknowledging the limit, the action of **Bound**, is the adequate way to handle it. To be in accord with the time, you are told to: **stop!**

● *Image of the Situation*

> **Bound: one's back.**
> **Not catching one's individuality.**
> **Moving one's chambers.**
> **Not visualizing one's people.**
> **Without fault.**

Associated Contexts **Bound**, KEN: limit, boundary; encounter an obstacle, stop; still, quiet, motionless; confine, enclose, mark off; turn around to look behind; hard, adamant, obstinate; perverse. The ideogram: eye and person turning round to compare and group what is behind. **Bound** is the mountain trigram doubled and includes that trigram's attributes: *Symbol:* **Mountain**, SHAN: limit, boundary. The ideogram: three peaks, a mountain range. *Action:* **Stop**, CHIH: bring or come to a standstill. The ideogram: a foot stops walking. **One's/one**, CH'I: third person pronoun; also: it/its, he/his, she/hers, they/theirs. **Back**, PEI: spine; opposite of front; behind, rear, hidden; turn the back on; north side; oppose, disobey, transgress. The ideogram: body and north, where the face is south.

    Not, PU: simple negative. **Catch**, HUO: take in hunt; catch a thief; obtain, seize; hit the mark, opportune moment; prisoner, spoils, prey; slave, servant. **Individuality**, SHEN: total person: psyche, body and lifespan; character, virtue, duty; contrasts with body, KUNG, physical being.

    Move, HSING: move or move something; motivate, emotionally moving; walk, act, do. The ideogram: stepping left then right. **Chambers**, T'ING: family room, courtyard, hall; domestic. The ideogram: shelter and hall, a secure place.

Visualize, CHIEN: seeing in all its aspects: vision, being visible, forming mental images; visit, call on, consult. The ideogram: eye above person, active and receptive sight. **People, person**, JEN: humans individually and collectively; an individual; humankind. Image of Hexagrams 13 and 37.

Without fault, WU CHIU: no error or harm in the situation.

- *Outer and Inner Aspects*

☶ **Bound**: Mountains bound, limit and set a place off, stopping forward movement. **Bound** completes a full yin-yang cycle.

Connection to both inner and outer: accomplishing words, which express things fully. **Bound** articulates what is complete and suggests what is beginning.

- *Counter Indications*

Nuclear trigrams **Shake**, CHEN, and **Gorge**, K'AN, result in Counter Hexagram 40, **Taking-apart**, HSIEH. Stopping and accepting a limit or **bound** is contrasted with **taking** an obstacle **apart** to eliminate it.

- *Sequence*

> **Beings not permitted to use completing stirring-up.**
> **Stopping it.**
> **Anterior acquiescence has the use-of Bound.**
> **Bounding implies stopping indeed.**

Associated Contexts **Beings not permitted to use ...** : no one is allowed to make use of; nothing can exist by means of. **Complete**, CHUNG: end of a cycle that begins the next; last, whole, all; contrasts with exhaust, CH'IUNG, final end. The ideogram: silk cocoons, follow and ice, winter linking one year with the next. **Stir-up**, TUNG: excite, influence, move, affect; work, take action; come out of the egg or the bud; the Action of the trigram Shake, CHEN. The ideogram: strength and heavy, move weighty things.

It/them/have(-it)/'s, CHIH: expresses possession, directly or as an object pronoun.

Anterior ... the use-of: activating this hexagram depends on understanding and accepting the previous statement.

Imply, CHE: further signify; additional meaning. **Indeed,** YEH: intensifier; indicates comment on previous statement.

● *Contrasted Definitions*

> **Shake: rising-up indeed.**
> **Bound: stopping indeed.**

Associated Contexts **Shake,** CHEN: arouse, excite, inspire; thunder rising from below; awe, alarm, trembling; fertilizing intrusion. The ideogram: excite and rain. Image of Hexagram 51. **Rise-up,** CH'I: stand up, lift; undertake, begin, originate.

● *Symbol Tradition*

> **Joined mountains. Bound.**
> **A chün tzu uses pondering not to issue-forth-from one's situation.**

Associated Contexts **Join,** CHIEN: add or bring together; unite, absorb; attend to many things. The ideogram: hand grasps two grain stalks, two things at once.

Chün tzu: ideal of a person who uses divination to order his/her life in accordance with tao rather than wilful intention; keyword. **Use(-of),** YI: make use of, by means of, owing to; employ, make functional. **Ponder,** SSU: reflect, consider, remember; deep thought; desire, wish. The ideogram: heart and field, the heart's concerns. **Issue-forth(-from),** CH'U: emerge from, come out of, proceed from, spring from; the Action of the trigram Shake, CHEN; contrary of enter, JU. The ideogram: stem with branches and leaves emerging. **One's/one,** CH'I: third person pronoun; also: it/its, she/hers, he/his, they/theirs. **Situation,** WEI: place or seat according to rank; post, position, command; right, proper; established, arranged. The ideogram: person and stand, servants in their places.

● *Image Tradition*

> Bound: stopping indeed. [I]
> The season stopping, by-consequence stopping.
> The season moving, by-consequence moving.
> Stirring-up, stilling, not letting-go one's season.
> One's tao: shining brightness.
> Bound: one's stopping.
> Stopping: one's place indeed.
>
> Above[and]Below, antagonistic correspondence. [II]
> Not mutually associating indeed.
> That uses not catching one's individuality.
> Moving one's chambers.
> Not visualizing one's people.
> Without fault indeed.

Associated Contexts **[I] Season,** SHIH: quality of the time; the right time, opportune, in harmony; planning in accord with the time; seasons of the year. The ideogram: sun and temple, time as sacred. **By-consequence(-of),** TSE: very strong connection; reason, cause, result; rule, law, pattern, standard; therefore.

Still, CHING: quiet, at rest; imperturbable. **Let-go,** SHIH: lose, omit, miss, fail, let slip; out of control. The ideogram: drop from the hand.

Tao: way or path; ongoing process of being and the course it traces for each specific person or thing; keyword. The ideogram: go and head, leading and the path it creates. **Shine,** KUANG: illuminate; give off brilliant, bright light; honor, glory, éclat; result of action, contrasts with brightness, MING, light of heavenly bodies. The ideogram: fire above person, lifting the light. **Brightness,** MING: light-giving aspect of burning, heavenly bodies and consciousness; with fire, the Symbol of the trigram Radiance, LI.

Place, SO: where something belongs or comes from; residence, dwelling; habitual focus or object.

[II] Above[and]Below, SHANG HSIA: realm of dynamic interaction between the upper and the lower; the vertical dimension. **Antagonistic,** TI: opposed and equal; competitor, enemy; a contest between equals. **Correspond(-to),** YING: be in agreement or harmony; resonate together, invoke and fulfill each other; answer to, suitable; relation between the lines (1:4, 2:5, 3:6) when they form the pair opened and whole, supple and solid. The ideogram: heart and obey.

Mutual, HSIANG: reciprocal assistance, encourage, help; bring together, blend with; examine, inspect; by turns. **Associate(-with)**, YÜ: consort with, combine; companions; group, band, company; agree with, comply, help. The ideogram: pair of hands reaching downward meets a pair of hands reaching upward, helpful association.

That uses, SHIH YI: involves and is involved by.

● *Transforming Lines*

Initial six

a) **Bound: one's feet.**
   Without fault.
   Harvesting: perpetual Trial.

b) **Bound: one's feet.**
   Not-yet letting-go correcting indeed.

Associated Contexts a) **Foot**, CHIH: literal foot; foundation, base.

Harvest, LI: advantageous, profitable; acute, insightful; benefit, nourish; third stage of the Time Cycle. **Perpetual**, YUNG: continuing; everlasting, ever-flowing. The ideogram: flowing water. **Trial**, CHEN: test by ordeal; inquiry by divination and its result; righteous, firm; separating wheat from chaff; the kernel, the proven core; fourth stage of the Time Cycle. The ideogram: pearl and divination.

b) **Not-yet**, WEI: temporal negative; something will but has not yet occurred; contrary of already, CHI. Image of Hexagram 64. **Correct,** CHENG: rectify deviation or one-sidedness; proper, straight, exact, regular; constant, rule, model. The ideogram: stop and one, hold to one thing.

Six at-second

a) **Bound: one's calves.**
   Not rescuing one's following.
   One's heart not keen.

b) **Not rescuing one's following.**
   Not-yet withdrawing-from hearkening indeed.

Associated Contexts a) **Calf**, FEI: muscle of lower leg; rely on; prop, rest.

Rescue, CHENG: aid, deliver from trouble; pull out, raise up, lift. The ideogram: hand and aid, a helping hand. **Follow**, SUI: come or go after; pursue, impelled to move; come after in inevitable sequence; move in the same direction, comply with what is ahead; follow a way or religion; according to, next, subsequent. The ideogram: go and fall, unavoidable movement. Image of Hexagram 17.

Heart, HSIN: heart as center of being; seat of mind's images and affections; moral nature; source of desires, intentions, will. **Keen**, K'UAI: sharp, eager, prompt, cheerful; spirited.

b) **Not-yet**, WEI: temporal negative; something will but has not yet occurred; contrary of already, CHI. Image of Hexagram 64. **Withdraw(-from)**, T'UI: draw back, retreat, recede; decline, refuse. **Hearken**, T'ING: listen to, obey, accept, acknowledge; examine, judge, decide. The ideogram: ear and actualizing-tao, hear and obey.

Nine at-third

a) **Bound: one's limit.**
  Assigned-to one's loins:
  Adversity smothers the heart.

b) **Bound: one's limit.**
  Exposure smothers the heart indeed

Associated Contexts a) **Limit**, HSIEN: boundary, frontier, threshold; restriction, impediment; set a limit. distinguish, separate.

Assign-to, LIEH: place according to rank; arrange in order; distinguish, separate. **Loins**, YIN: hips, pelvis, lumbar region; kidneys; respect, honor; work toward a distant aim; money belt.

Adversity, LI: danger; threatening, malevolent demon. This has two aspects: grind, sharpen, improve, perfect, stimulate; and: poisonous, sinister, cruel, contrary. It indicates a spirit or ghost that seeks revenge by inflicting suffering upon the living. Pacifying or exorcizing such a spirit can have a healing effect. The ideogram: sheltering cliff and stinging insect. **Smother**, HSÜN: suffocate, smoke out; fog, steam, miasma, vapor; broil, parch; offend; evening mists. **Heart**, HSIN: heart as center of being; seat of mind's images and affections; moral nature; source of desires, intentions, will.

b) **Expose**, WEI: exposed to danger, precipitous, unsteady; too high, not upright; uneasy. The ideogram: overhanging rock, person and limit, exposure in an extreme position.

Six at-fourth

a) **Bound: one's individuality.**
   Without fault.

b) **Bound: one's individuality.**
   Stopping connoting the body indeed.

Associated Contexts b) **Connote**, CHU: imply the meaning; signify. The ideogram: words and imply. **Body**, KUNG: physical being, power and self expression; contrasts with individuality, SHEN, the total personality.

Six at-fifth

a) **Bound: one's jawbones.**
   Words possessing sequence.
   Repenting extinguished.

b) **Bound: one's jawbones.**
   Using centering correcting indeed.

Associated Contexts a) **Jawbones/brace**, FU: support, consolidate, reinforce, strengthen, stiffen, prop up, fix; rigid, steady, firm; help, rescue; support the mouth that speaks. The ideogram: cart and great.

   Word, YEN: speech, spoken words, sayings; talk, discuss, address. The ideogram: mouth and rising vapor, words as speech. **Possess**, YU: in possession of, have, own; opposite of lack, WU. **Sequence**, HSÜ: order, precedence, series; follow in order.

   Repenting extinguished, HUI WANG: previous troubles and consequent remorse will disappear.

b) **Centering correcting**, CHUNG CHENG: central and correct; make rectifying one-sidedness and error your central concern; reaching a stable center in yourself can correct the situation.

Nine above

a) **Magnanimous Bounding, significant.**

b) **Magnanimous Bounding's significance.**
    Using munificence to complete indeed.

Associated Contexts a) **Magnanimous**, TUN: generous; honest, substantial, important, wealthy; honor, increase; firm, solid. The ideogram: strike and accept, warrior magnanimous in attack and defense. **Significant**, CHI: leads to the experience of meaning; favorable, propitious, advantageous, appropriate; keyword. The ideogram: scholar and mouth, wise words of a sage.

b) **Munificence**, HOU: liberal, kind, generous; create abundance; thick, large. The ideogram: gift of a superior to an inferior.

53

I N F I L T R A T I N G ▪ *CHIEN*

This hexagram describes your situation in terms of gradually achieving a goal. It emphasizes that advancing through diffuse but steady penetration is the adequate way to handle it. To be in accord with the time, you are told to: **infiltrate!**

● *Image of the Situation*

> **Infiltrating, womanhood converting significant.**
> **Harvesting Trial.**

Associated Contexts **Infiltrate**, CHIEN: advance by degrees; penetrate slowly and surely, as water; stealthily; permeate throughout; influence, affect. The ideogram: water and cut. **Woman(hood)**, NÜ: a woman; what is inherently female. **Convert**, KUEI: change to another form, persuade; return to yourself or the place where you belong; restore, revert, become loyal; turn into; give a young girl in marriage. The ideogram: arrive and wife, become mistress of a household. Image of Hexagram 54. **Significant**, CHI: leads to the experience of meaning; favorable, propitious, advantageous, appropriate; keyword. The ideogram: scholar and mouth, wise words of a sage.

Harvesting Trial, LI CHEN: advantageous divination; putting the action in question to the test is beneficial.

● *Outer and Inner Aspects*

☴ **Ground**: Wind and wood subtly enter from the ground, penetrating and pervading. **Ground** is the center of the yang hemicycle, spreading pervasive action.

Connection to the outer: penetrating and bringing together, the Woody Moment culminating. **Ground** pervades, matches and couples, seeding a new generation.

☶ **Bound**: Mountains bound, limit and set a place off, stopping forward movement. **Bound** completes a full yin-yang cycle.

Connection to the inner: accomplishing words, which express things. **Bound** articulates what is complete to suggest what is beginning.

Inner accomplishing provides the basis for **infiltrating** the outer ground.

● *Counter Indications*

Nuclear trigrams **Radiance**, LI, and **Gorge**, K'AN, result in Counter Hexagram 64, **Not-yet Fording**, WEI CHI. Smooth and constant **infiltrating** is contrasted with **not-yet** beginning to **ford** the stream of events.

● *Sequence*

Beings not permitted to use completing stopping.
Anterior acquiescence has the use-of Infiltrating.
Infiltrating implies advancing indeed.

Associated Contexts **Beings not permitted to use ...** : no one is allowed to make use of; nothing can exist by means of. **Complete**, CHUNG: end of a cycle that begins the next; last, whole, all; contrasts with exhaust, CH'IUNG, final end. The ideogram: silk cocoons, follow and ice, winter linking one year with the next. **Stop**, CHIH: bring or come to a standstill; the Action of the trigram Bound, KEN. The ideogram: a foot stops walking.
    Anterior ... the use-of: activating this hexagram depends on understanding and accepting the previous statement.
    Imply, CHE: further signify; additional meaning. **Advance**, CHIN: exert yourself, make progress, climb; be promoted; further the development of, augment; adopt a religion or conviction; offer, introduce. **Indeed**, YEH: intensifier; indicates comment on previous statement.

● *Contrasted Definitions*

Infiltrating: womanhood converting
                                awaits manhood moving indeed.
Converting Maidenhood: womanhood's completion indeed.

Associated Contexts **Await**, TAI: expect, wait for, welcome (friendly or hostile), provide against. **Man(hood)**, NAN: a man; what is inherently male. The ideogram: fields and strength, hard labor in the fields. **Move**, HSING: move or move something; motivate, emotionally moving; walk, act, do. The ideogram: stepping left then right.

 Maiden(hood), MEI: girl not yet nubile, virgin; younger sister; daughter of a secondary wife. The ideogram: woman and not-yet. **Converting Maidenhood** is the Image of Hexagram 54. **'s/have(-it)/ it/them,** CHIH: expresses possession, directly or as an object pronoun.

- *Symbol Tradition*

 Above mountain possessing wood. Infiltrating.
 A chün tzu uses residing-in eminent actualizing-tao
         to improve the vulgar.

Associated Contexts **Above**, SHANG: anything above, in all senses; higher, upper, outer; upper trigram; opposite of below, HSIA. **Mountain**, SHAN: limit, boundary; the Symbol of the trigram Bound, KEN. The ideogram: three peaks, a mountain range. **Possess**, YU: in possession of, have, own; opposite of lack, WU. **Wood/tree**, MU: all things woody or wooden, alive or constructed from wood; associated with the Woody Moment; wood and wind are the Symbols of the trigram Ground, SUN. The ideogram: a tree with roots and branches.

 Chün tzu: ideal of a person who uses divination to order his/her life in accordance with tao rather than willful intention; keyword. **Use(-of)**, YI: make use of, by means of, owing to; employ, make functional. **Reside(-in)**, CHÜ: dwell, live in, stay; sit down, fill an office; settled parts of a country. The ideogram: body and seat. **Eminent**, HSIEN: moral and intellectual power; worthy, excellent, virtuous; sage second to the all-wise, SHENG. **Actualize-tao**, TE: realize tao in action; power, virtue; ability to follow the course traced by the ongoing process of the cosmos; keyword. The ideogram: to go, straight, and heart. Linked with acquire, TE: acquiring that which makes a being become what it is meant to be. **Improve**, SHAN: make better, reform, perfect, repair; virtuous, wise; mild, docile; clever, skilful, handy. The ideogram: mouth and sheep, gentle speech. **Vulgar**, SU: common people and their desires; inelegant, low; grovelling; the pressure of everyday life.

• *Image Tradition*

Infiltrating's advancing indeed. [I]
Womanhood converting significant.
Advancing acquiring the situation.
Going possessing achievement indeed.

Advancing uses correcting. [II]
Permitting using correcting the fiefdoms indeed.
One's situation: solid acquiring the center indeed.

Stopping and-also Ground. [III]
Stirring-up not exhausted indeed.

Associated Contexts **[I] Acquire**, TE: obtain the desired object; wish for, desire covetously; gains, possessions. The ideogram: go and obstacle, going through obstacles to the goal. **Situation**, WEI: place or seat according to rank; post, position, command; right, proper; established, arranged. The ideogram: person and stand, servants in their places.

Go, WANG, and come, LAI, describe the stream of time as it flows from future through present to past; go, WANG, indicates what is departing from present to past; proceed, move on; keyword. **Achieve**, KUNG: work done, results; real accomplishment, praise, worth, merit. The ideogram: workman's square and forearm, combining craft and strength.

[II] Correct, CHENG: rectify deviation or one-sidedness; proper, straight, exact, regular; constant, rule, model. The ideogram: stop and one, hold to one thing.

Permit, K'O: possible because in harmony with an inherent principle. The ideogram: mouth and breath, silent consent. **Fiefdom**, PANG: region governed by a feudatory, an order of nobility.

One's/one, CH'I: third person pronoun; also: it/its, he/his, she/hers, they/theirs. **Solid**, KANG: quality of the whole lines; firm, strong, unyielding, persisting. **Center**, CHUNG: inner, central; put in the center; middle, stable point enabling you to face inner and outer changes; middle line of trigram. The ideogram: field divided in two equal parts. Image of Hexagram 61.

[III] And-also, ERH: joins and contrasts two terms. **Ground**, SUN: base on which things rest; support, foundation; mild, subtly penetrating; nourishing. The ideogram: stand and things arranged on it, the subtle influence of the ground. Image of Hexagram 57.

Stir-up, TUNG: excite, influence, move, affect; work, take action; come out of the egg or the bud; the Action of the trigram Shake, CHEN. The ideogram: strength and heavy, move weighty things. **Not**, PU: simple negative. **Exhaust**, CH'IUNG: bring to an end; limit, extremity; destitute; investigate exhaustively; end without a new beginning. The ideogram: cave and naked person, bent with disease or old age.

● *Transforming Lines*

Initial six

a) **The wild-swan Infiltrating tending-towards the barrier.**
The small son, adversity possessing words.
Lacking fault.

b) **The small son's adversity.**
Righteous, without fault indeed.

Associated Contexts a) **Wild-swan**, HUNG: large white water bird, symbol of the soul and its spiritual aspirations; wild swan and wild goose as emblems of the messenger and of conjugal fidelity; vast, profound, far-reaching, great; valued, learned. **Tend-towards**, YÜ: move toward but not reach, in the direction of; contrasts with reach(-to), HU, actually arriving. **Barrier**, KAN: boundary, limit; fend off, protect; stream, parapet, river bank; shield, defensive armor; the Ten Heavenly Barriers are part of the calendar system.

Small, HSIAO: little, common, unimportant; adapting to what crosses your path; ability to move in harmony with the vicissitudes of life; contrasts with great, TA, self-imposed theme or goal; keyword. Image of Hexagrams 9 and 62. **Son(hood)**, TZU: living up to ideal of ancestors as highest human development; act with concern and reverence; male child; offspring, posterity; seed, kernel, egg; sage, teacher; nadir, deepest point, midnight, mid-winter. **Adversity**, LI: danger; threatening, malevolent demon. This has two aspects: grind, sharpen, improve, perfect, stimulate;

and: poisonous, sinister, cruel, contrary. It indicates a spirit or ghost that seeks revenge by inflicting suffering upon the living. Pacifying or exorcizing such a spirit can have a healing effect. The ideogram: sheltering cliff and stinging insect. **Word**, YEN: speech, spoken words, sayings; talk, discuss, address. The ideogram: mouth and rising vapor, words as speech.

Lacking, WU: strong negative; does not possess. **Fault**, CHIU: unworthy conduct that leads to harm, illness, misfortune. The ideogram: person and differ, differ from what you should be.

b) **Righteous**, YI: proper and just, meets the standards; things in their proper place; the heart that rules itself; upright, moral rule; contrasts with Harvest, LI, advantage or profit.

Without fault, WU CHIU: no error or harm in the situation.

Six at-second

a) The wild-swan Infiltrating tending-towards the stone.
Drinking[and]taking-in: feasting, feasting.
Significant.

b) Drinking[and]taking-in: feasting, feasting.
Not sheer satiation indeed.

Associated Contexts a) **Wild-swan**, HUNG: large white water bird, symbol of the soul and its spiritual aspirations; wild swan and wild goose as emblems of the messenger and of conjugal fidelity; vast, profound, far-reaching, great; valued, learned. **Tend-towards**, YÜ: move toward but not reach, in the direction of; contrasts with reach(-to), HU, actually arriving. **Stone**, P'AN: large conspicuous rock, foundation stone; stable, immovable.

Drinking[and]taking-in, YIN SHIH: comprehensive term for eating, drinking and breathing; a meal, eating together. **Feast**, K'AN: take part in or give a feast; rejoice, give pleasure; pleased, contented. The doubled character intensifies this quality.

b) **Sheer**, SU: plain, unadorned; original color or state; clean, pure. The ideogram: white silk, symbol of mourning. **Satiation**, PAO: full, replete, satisfied; swollen, sated; gratified, flattered.

Nine at-third

a) **The wild-swan Infiltrating tending-towards the highlands.**
The husband chastised, not returning.
The wife pregnant, not nurturing.
Pitfall.
Harvesting: resisting outlawry.

b) **The husband chastised, not returning.**
Radiance flocking demons indeed.
The wife pregnant, not nurturing.
Letting-go her tao indeed.
Harvesting: availing-of resisting outlawry.
Yielding mutualizes protection indeed.

Associated Contexts a) **Wild-swan**, HUNG: large white water bird, symbol of the soul and its spiritual aspirations; wild swan and wild goose as emblems of the messenger and of conjugal fidelity; vast, profound, far-reaching, great; valued, learned. **Tend-towards**, YÜ: move toward but not reach, in the direction of; contrasts with reach(-to), HU, actually arriving. **Highlands**, LU: high, dry land as distinct from swamps; plateau.

Husband, FU: household manager; administer with thrift and prudence; responsible for; sustain with your earnings; old enough to assume responsibility; married man. **Chastise**, CHENG: punish, subjugate, discipline; reduce to order; punishing expedition. The ideogram: step and correct, a rectifying move. **Return**, FU: go back, turn back to the starting point; recur, reappear, come again; restore, recover, retrace; an earlier time or place. The ideogram: step and retrace a path. Image of Hexagram 24.

Wife, FU: responsible position of married woman within the household; contrasts with consort, CH'I, her legal position and concubine, CH'IEH, secondary wives. The ideogram: woman, hand and broom, household duties. **Pregnant**, JEN: carrying a child. **Nurture**, YÜ: bring up, support, rear, raise; increase.

Pitfall, HSIUNG: leads away from the experience of meaning; stuck and exposed to danger, unable to take in the situation; flow of life and spirit is blocked; unfortunate, baleful; keyword.

Harvest, LI: advantageous, profitable; acute, insightful; benefit, nourish; third stage of the Time Cycle. **Resist**, YÜ: withstand, oppose; bring to an end; prevent. The ideogram: rule and worship, imposing ethical or religious limits. **Outlawry**, K'OU: break the laws; violent people, outcasts, bandits.

b) **Radiance**, LI: glowing light, spreading in all directions; light-giving, discriminating, articulating; divide and arrange in order; the power of consciousness. The ideogram: bird and weird, the magical fire-bird with brilliant plumage. Image of Hexagram 30. **Flock**, CH'UN: herd, group; people of same kind, friends, equals; all, entire; move in unison, flock together. The ideogram: chief and sheep, flock around a leader. **Demon(iac)**, CH'OU: possessed by a malignant genius; ugly, physically or morally deformed; vile, disgraceful, shameful; drunken. The ideogram: fermenting liquor and soul. Demoniac and tiger are opposed on the Universal Compass North–South axis; the tiger (Extreme Yang) scares away and protects against demoniacs (Extreme Yin).

Let-go, SHIH: lose, omit, miss, fail, let slip; out of control. The ideogram: drop from the hand. **Her/she**, CH'I: third person pronoun; also: one/one's, it/its, he/his, they/their. **Tao**: way or path; ongoing process of being and the course it traces for each specific person or thing; keyword. The ideogram: go and head, leading and the path it creates.

Avail-of, YUNG: take advantage of; benefit from, profit by; use for a specific purpose; apply to advantage. The ideogram: to divine and center, applying divination to central concerns.

Yield(-to), SHUN: give way and bear produce; comply, agree, follow, obey; unresisting, docile, flexible; nourish, provide; the Action of the trigram Field, K'UN. The ideogram: head and current, water flowing from the head of a river, yielding to the banks. **Mutual**, HSIANG: reciprocal assistance, encourage, help; bring together, blend with; examine, inspect; by turns. **Protect**, PAO: guard, defend, keep safe; secure.

Six at-fourth

a) The wild-swan Infiltrating tending-towards the trees.
  Maybe acquiring one's rafter.
  Without fault.

b) Maybe acquiring one's rafter.
  Yielding using Ground indeed.

Associated Contexts a) **Wild-swan**, HUNG: large white water bird, symbol of the soul and its spiritual aspirations; wild swan and wild goose as emblems of the messenger and of conjugal fidelity; vast, profound, far-reaching, great; valued, learned. **Tend-towards**, YÜ: move toward but not reach, in the direction of; contrasts with reach(-to), HU, actually arriving.

Maybe, HUO: possible but not certain, perhaps. **Rafter**, CHÜEH: roof beams; flat branches.

Without fault, WU CHIU: no error or harm in the situation.

b) **Yield(-to)**, SHUN: give way and bear produce; comply, agree, follow, obey; unresisting, docile, flexible; nourish, provide; the Action of the trigram Field, K'UN. The ideogram: head and current, water flowing from the head of a river, yielding to the banks.

Nine at-fifth

a) The wild-swan Infiltrating tending-towards the mound.
The wife, three year's-time not pregnant.
Completing: absolutely-nothing has mastering.
Significant.

b) Completing: absolutely-nothing has mastering, significant.
Acquiring the place desired indeed.

Associated Contexts a) **Wild-swan**, HUNG: large white water bird, symbol of the soul and its spiritual aspirations; wild swan and wild goose as emblems of the messenger and of conjugal fidelity; vast, profound, far-reaching, great; valued, learned. **Tend-towards**, YÜ: move toward but not reach, in the direction of; contrasts with reach(-to), HU, actually arriving. **Mound**, LING: grave-mound, barrow; small hill.

Wife, FU: responsible position of married woman within the household; contrasts with consort, CH'I, her legal position and concubine, CH'IEH, secondary wives. The ideogram: woman, hand and broom, household duties. **Three**, SAN: number three, third time or place; active phases of a cycle; superlative; beginning of repetition. **Year's-time**, SUI: actual length of time in a year; contrasts with years-revolved, NIEN, number of years elapsed. **Pregnant**, JEN: carrying a child.

Absolutely-no(thing), MO: complete elimination; not any, by no means. **Master**, SHENG: have the upper hand, conquer; worthy of, able to; control, check, command.

b) **Place**, SO: where something belongs or comes from; residence, dwelling; habitual focus or object. **Desire**, YÜAN: wish, hope or long for; covet; desired object.

Nine above

a) **The wild-swan Infiltrating tending-towards the highlands.
Its feathers permit availing-of activating fundamentals.
Significant.**

b) **Its feathers permit availing-of
activating fundamentals, significant.
Not permitting disarray indeed.**

Associated Contexts a) **Wild-swan**, HUNG: large white water bird, symbol of the soul and its spiritual aspirations; wild swan and wild goose as emblems of the messenger and of conjugal fidelity; vast, profound, far-reaching, great; valued, learned. **Tend-towards**, YÜ: move toward but not reach, in the direction of; contrasts with reach(-to), HU, actually arriving. **Highlands**, LU: high, dry land as distinct from swamps; plateau.

Its/it, CH'I: third person pronoun; also: one/one's, he/his, she/hers, they/theirs. **Feathers**, YU: wings, plumes; feathered; quick, flying. **Avail-of**, YUNG: take advantage of; benefit from, profit by; use for a specific purpose; apply to advantage. The ideogram: to divine and center, applying divination to central concerns. **Activate**, WEI: act or cause to act; do, make, manage; make active; attend to, help; because of. **Fundamentals**, YI: primary natural powers; origins, essentials; good and do good; correct, proper, just; rule, rite, decorum; paired, matched. The ideogram: person and righteous.

b) **Not permitting**, PU K'O: not possible; contradicts an inherent principle. The ideogram: mouth and breath, silent consent. **Disarray**, LUAN: throw into disorder, mislay, confuse; out of place; discord, insurrection, anarchy.

CONVERTING MAIDENHOOD ▪
KUEI MEI

This hexagram describes your situation in terms of the changing status of someone who cannot control their circumstances. It emphasizes that finding a real field of activity through accepting this imposition is the adequate way to handle it. To be in accord with the time, you are told to: **convert** the **maiden**!

- *Image of the Situation*

> **Converting Maidenhood, chastising: pitfall.**
> **Without direction: Harvesting.**

Associated Contexts **Convert**, KUEI: change to another form, persuade; return to yourself or the place where you belong; restore, revert, become loyal; turn into; give a young girl in marriage. The ideogram: arrive and wife, become mistress of a household. **Maiden(hood)**, MEI: girl not yet nubile; younger sister, daughter of a secondary wife. The ideogram: woman and not-yet. **Chastise**, CHENG: punish, subjugate, discipline; reduce to order; punishing expedition. The ideogram: step and correct, a rectifying move. **Pitfall**, HSIUNG: leads away from the experience of meaning; stuck and exposed to danger, unable to take in the situation; flow of life and spirit is blocked; unfortunate, baleful; keyword.

    Without direction: Harvesting, WU YU LI: no plan or direction is advantageous; in order to take advantage of the situation, do not impose a direction on events.

- *Outer and Inner Aspects*

☳ **Shake**: Thunder rises from below, shaking and stirring things up. **Shake** begins the yang hemicycle by germinating new action.
    Connection to the outer: sprouting energies thrusting from below, the Woody Moment beginning. **Shake** stirs things up to issue-forth.

☱ **Open**: vapor rising from the marsh's open surface stimulates and fertilizes; stimulating words cheer and inspire. **Open** begins the yin hemicycle by initiating the formative process.

Connection to the inner: liquifying, casting, skinning off the mold, the Metallic Moment beginning. **Open** stimulates, cheers and reveals innate form.

Rousing energy from without **converts** the **maiden**'s potential to stimulate, inspire and give form. These trigrams emphasize the Pivoting Phase, initiating new action.

● *Counter Indications*

Nuclear trigrams **Gorge**, K'AN, and **Radiance**, LI, result in Counter Hexagram 63, **Already Fording**, CHI CHI. The **maiden** who stands on the threshold of **converting** is contrasted with **already fording** the stream of events.

● *Sequence*

Advancing necessarily possessing a place to Convert.
Anterior acquiescence has the use-of Converting Maidenhood.

Associated Contexts **Advance**, CHIN: exert yourself, make progress, climb; be promoted; further the development of, augment; adopt a religion or conviction; offer, introduce. **Necessarily**, PI: unavoidably, indispensably, certainly. **Possess**, YU: in possession of, have, own; opposite of lack, WU. **Place**, SO: where something belongs or comes from; residence, dwelling; habitual focus or object.
　　Anterior ... the use-of: activating this hexagram depends on understanding and accepting the previous statement.

● *Contrasted Definitions*

Infiltrating: womanhood converting
　　　　　　　　　　　　awaits manhood moving indeed.
Converting Maidenhood: womanhood's completion indeed.

Associated Contexts **Infiltrate**, CHIEN: advance by degrees; penetrate slowly and surely, as water; stealthily; permeate throughout; influence, affect. The ideogram: water and cut. Image of Hexagram 53.

Woman(hood), NÜ: a woman; what is inherently female. **Await**, TAI: expect, wait for, welcome (friendly or hostile), provide against. **Man(hood)**, NAN: a man; what is inherently male. The ideogram: fields and strength, hard labor in the fields. **Move**, HSING: move or move something; motivate, emotionally moving; walk, act, do. The ideogram: stepping left then right. **Indeed**, YEH: intensifier; indicates comment on previous statement.

's/have(-it)/it/them, CHIH: expresses possession, directly or as an object pronoun. **Complete**, CHUNG: end of a cycle that begins the next; last, whole, all; contrasts with exhaust, CH'IUNG, final end. The ideogram: silk cocoons, follow and ice, winter linking one year with the next.

• *Symbol Tradition*

> **Above marsh possessing thunder. Converting Maidenhood.**
> **A chün tzu uses perpetually completing to know the cracked.**

Associated Contexts **Above**, SHANG: anything above, in all senses; higher, upper, outer; upper trigram; opposite of below, HSIA. **Marsh**, TSE: open surface of a flat body of water and the vapors rising from it; fertilize, enrich; kindness, favor; the Symbol of the trigram Open, TUI. **Thunder**, LEI: rising, arousing power; the Symbol of the trigram Shake, CHEN.

Chün tzu: ideal of a person who uses divination to order his/her life in accordance with tao rather than wilful intention; keyword. **Use(-of)**, YI: make use of, by means of, owing to; employ, make functional. **Perpetual**, YUNG: continuing; everlasting, ever-flowing. The ideogram: flowing water. **Know**, CHIH: understand, perceive, remember; informed, aware, wise. The ideogram: arrow and mouth, words focused and swift. **Cracked**, PI: broken, ruined, tattered; unfit, unworthy. The ideogram: strike and break.

• *Image Tradition*

> **Converting Maidenhood. [I]**
> **Heaven[and]Earth's great righteousness indeed.**
> **Heaven[and]Earth not mingling**
> **and-also the myriad beings not rising.**
> **Converting Maidenhood.**

A person's completion beginning indeed. [II]
Stimulating uses stirring-up.
A place to Convert Maidenhood indeed.
Chastising: pitfall.
Situation not appropriate indeed.

Without direction: Harvesting. [III]
Supple riding solid indeed.

Associated Contexts **[I] Heaven[and]Earth,** T'IEN TI: dynamic relation between the primal powers and the world it produces; cosmos, natural or human world; keyword. **Great,** TA: big, noble, important, very; orient the will toward a self-imposed goal, impose direction; ability to lead or guide your life; contrasts with small, HSIAO, flexible adaptation to what crosses your path; keyword. Image of Hexagrams 14, 26, 28, 34. **Righteous,** YI: proper and just, meets the standards; things in their proper place; the heart that rules itself; upright, moral rule; contrasts with Harvest, LI, advantage or profit.

Not, PU: simple negative. **Mingle,** CHIAO: blend with, communicate, join, exchange; trade, business; copulation; friendship. **And-also,** ERH: joins and contrasts two terms. **Myriad,** WAN: countless; many, everyone; lit.: ten thousand. The ideogram: swarm of insects. **Being(s),** WU: creature, thing, any single being; matter, substance, essence; nature of things. **Rise,** HSING: get up, grow, lift; begin, give rise to, construct; be promoted; flourishing, fashionable. The ideogram: lift, two hands and unite, lift with both hands.

[II] People, person, JEN: humans individually and collectively; an individual; humankind. Image of Hexagrams 13 and 37. **Begin,** SHIH: commence, start, open; earliest, first; beginning of a time-span, ended by completion, CHUNG. The ideogram: woman and eminent, beginning new life.

Stimulate, SHUO: rouse to action and good feeling; free from constraint, stir up, urge on; persuade, cheer, delight; set out in words; the Action of the trigram Open, TUI. The ideogram: words and exchange. **Stir-up,** TUNG: excite, influence, move, affect; work, take action; come out of the egg or the bud; the Action of the trigram Shake, CHEN. The ideogram: strength and heavy, move weighty things.

Situation, WEI: place or seat according to rank; post, position, command; right, proper; established, arranged. The ideogram: person and stand, servants in their places. **Appropriate**, TANG: suitable; opportune, convenient; adequate, competent; equal to; whole lines in uneven places and opened lines in even places.

[III] Supple, JOU: quality of the opened lines; flexible, pliant, tender, adaptable. **Ride**, CH'ENG: ride an animal or a chariot; have the upper hand, seize the right time; control strong power; overcome the nature of the other; supple opened line above a solid whole line. **Solid**, KANG: quality of the whole lines; firm, strong, unyielding, persisting.

- *Transforming Lines*

    Initial nine

    a) **Converting Maidenhood using the junior-sister.**
    Halting enabling treading.
    Chastising significant.

    b) **Converting Maidenhood using the junior-sister.**
    Using persevering indeed.
    Halting enabling treading, significant.
    Mutualizing receiving indeed.

Associated Contexts a) **Junior-sister**, TI: younger woman in family or clan; younger sister, under authority of the first wife.
    Halt, P'O: limp; lame, crippled; indecorous. **Able**, NENG: enable; ability, power, skill, art; competent, talented; duty, function, capacity. The ideogram: an animal with strong hooves and bones, able to carry and defend. **Tread**, LÜ: step, path, track; footsteps; walk a path or way; course of the stars; act, practise; conduct; salary, means of subsistence. The ideogram: body and repeating steps, following a trail. Image of Hexagram 10.
    Significant, CHI: leads to the experience of meaning; favorable, propitious, advantageous, appropriate; keyword. The ideogram: scholar and mouth, wise words of a sage.

b) **Persevere**, HENG: continue in the same way or spirit; constant, perpetual, regular; self-renewing; extend everywhere. Image of Hexagram 32.

Mutual, HSIANG: reciprocal assistance, encourage, help; bring together, blend with; examine, inspect; by turns. **Receive,** CH'ENG: receive gifts or commands from superiors or customers; take in hand; catch falling water. The ideogram: accepting a seal of office.

Nine at-second

a) Squinting enabling observing.
   Harvesting: shade people's Trial.

b) Harvesting: shade people's Trial.
   Not-yet transforming the rules indeed.

Associated Contexts a) **Squint**, MIAO: look at with one eye, glance at; obstructed vision. **Able**, NENG: enable; ability, power, skill, art; competent, talented; duty, function, capacity. The ideogram: an animal with strong hooves and bones, able to carry and defend. **Observe**, SHIH: see and inspect carefully; gain knowledge of; compare and imitate. The ideogram: see and omen, taking account of what you see.

   Harvest, LI: advantageous, profitable; acute, insightful; benefit, nourish; third stage of the Time Cycle. **Shade**, YU: hidden from view; retired, solitary, secret; dark, obscure, occult, mysterious; ignorant. The ideogram: small within hill, a cave or grotto. **Trial**, CHEN: test by ordeal; inquiry by divination and its result; righteous, firm; separating wheat from chaff; the kernel, the proven core; fourth stage of the Time Cycle. The ideogram: pearl and divination.

b) **Not-yet**, WEI: temporal negative; something will but has not yet occurred; contrary of already, CHI. Image of Hexagram 64. **Transform,** PIEN: abrupt, radical, fundamental mutation from one state of being to another; transformation of lines in hexagrams; contrasts with change, HUA, gradual metamorphosis. **Rules,** CH'ANG: unchanging principles; regular, constant, habitual; maintain laws and customs.

Six at-third

a) Converting Maidenhood: using hair-growing.
   Reversing Converting: using the junior-sister.

b) **Converting Maidenhood: using hair-growing.**
    Not-yet appropriate indeed.

Associated Contexts a) **Hair-growing**, HSÜ: beard, hair; patience symbolized as waiting for hair to grow; hold back, wait for; slow; necessary.
    Reverse, FAN: turn and move in the opposite direction; turn around or upside down (180 degrees); change to the opposite position; contrary. **Junior-sister**, TI: younger woman in family or clan; younger sister, under authority of the first wife.

b) **Not-yet**, WEI: temporal negative; something will but has not yet occurred; contrary of already, CHI. Image of Hexagram 64.

Nine at-fourth

a) **Converting Maidenhood overrunning the term.**
    Procrastinating Converting possesses the season.

b) **Overrunning the term's purpose.**
    Possessing awaiting and-also moving indeed.

Associated Contexts a) **Overrun**, CH'IEN: pass the limit; mistake, transgression, disease. **Term**, CH'I: set time, fixed period, agreed date; seasons; person a hundred years old.
    Procrastinate, CH'IH: delay, act at leisure, retard; slow, late. **Season**, SHIH: quality of the time; the right time, opportune, in harmony; planning in accord with the time; seasons of the year. The ideogram: sun and temple, time as sacred.

b) **Purpose**, CHIH: focus of mind and heart; will, inclination, resolve. The ideogram: heart and scholar, high inner resolve, or heart and go, inner determination.

Six at-fifth

a) **The supreme burgeoning Converting Maidenhood.**
    One's chief's sleeves:
    One's junior-sister's sleeves not thus fine.
    The moon almost facing, significant.

b) **The supreme burgeoning Converting Maidenhood.**
One's junior-sister's sleeves not thus fine.
One's situation located-in the center.
Using valuing movement indeed.

Associated Contexts a) **Supreme**, TI: highest, above all on earth; sovereign lord, source of power; emperor. **Burgeon**, YI: beginning of growth after seedburst, CHIA, early spring; associated with the Woody Moment. **Supreme Burgeoning**, TI YI, refers to the great Shang emperor (1191–1151 BCE) who took a wife from the family of King Wen's father in order to assure an heir. This ennobled the line from which the Chou Dynasty came. It is an omen of great happiness and good fortune in the future.

One's/one, CH'I: third person pronoun; also: it/its, he/his, she/hers, they/theirs. **Chief**, CHÜN: effective ruler; preside over, take the lead; influence others; term of respect. The ideogram: mouth and director, giving orders. **Sleeve**, MEI: displays signs showing quality and rank of the wearer; symbol of self; womb symbol.

Junior-sister, TI: younger woman in family or clan; younger sister, under authority of the first wife. **Thus**, JU: as, in this way. **Fine**, LIANG: excellent, refined, valuable; gentle, considerate, kind; natural.

Moon, YÜEH: actual moon and moon-month; yin, the sun being yang. **Almost**, CHI: nearly, about to; subtle, almost imperceptible; the first sign. **Face**, WANG: full moon; moon directly facing the sun; 15th day of the moon-month; look at hopefully. **Significant**, CHI: leads to the experience of meaning; favorable, propitious, advantageous, appropriate; keyword. The ideogram: scholar and mouth, wise words of a sage.

b) **Locate(-in)**, TSAI: live in, dwell, reside; belong to, involved with, depend on; within. The ideogram: earth and persevere, place on the earth. **Center**, CHUNG: inner, central; put in the center; middle, stable point enabling you to face inner and outer changes; middle line of trigram. The ideogram: field divided in two equal parts. Image of Hexagram 61.

Value, KUEI: regard as valuable, give worth and dignity to; precious, high priced; honorable, exalted, illustrious. The ideogram: cowries (coins) and basket.

Six above

a) **A woman receiving a basket without substance.**
A notable disembowelling a goat without blood.
Without direction: Harvesting.

b) **Six above, without substance.**
Receiving an empty basket indeed.

Associated Contexts **a) Receive**, CH'ENG: receive gifts or commands from superiors or customers; take in hand; catch falling water. The ideogram: accepting a seal of office. **Basket**, K'UANG: open basket; put in baskets; bottom of a bed. **Without**, WU: devoid of; -less as suffix. **Substance**, SHIH: real, solid, full; results, fruits, possessions; essence; honest, sincere. The ideogram: string of coins under a roof, riches in the house.

Notable, SHIH: learned, upright, important man; scholar, gentleman. **Disembowel**, K'UEI: cut open and clean; prepare for sacrifice; stab. **Goat**, YANG: sheep and goats; direct thought and action. **Blood**, HSÜEH: yin fluid that maintains life; money, property.

b) **Empty**, HSÜ: no images or concepts; vacant, unsubstantial; empty yet fertile space.

55
ABOUNDING ▪ FENG

This hexagram describes your situation in terms of profusion and abundance reaching culmination. It emphasizes that exuberantly increasing things to their fullest is the adequate way to handle it. To be in accord with the time, you are told to: **abound!**

- ## Image of the Situation

  Abounding, Growing.
  The king imagining it.
  No grief. Properly sun centering.

  Associated Contexts **Abound**, FENG: abundant, plentiful, copious; grow wealthy; at the point of overflowing; exuberant, fertile, prolific; rich in talents, property, friends; fullness, culmination; ripe, sumptuous, fat. **Grow**, HENG: success through a sacrifice; pervade, persevere; bring to full growth; enjoy; vigorous, effective; second stage of the Time Cycle.

  King(hood), WANG: effective ruler, by authority of the Emperor, from whom others derive their power. **Imagine**, CHIA: create in the mind; fantasize, suppose, pretend, imitate; fiction; illusory, unreal; costume. The ideogram: person and borrow. **It/them/have(-it)/'s**, CHIH: expresses possession, directly or as an object pronoun.

  No, WU: simple negative; un-, dis-. **Grieve(-over)**, YU: sorrow, melancholy; mourn; anxious, careworn; hidden sorrow. The ideogram: heart, head, and limp, heart-sick and anxious. **Proper**, YI: reasonable of itself; fit and right, harmonious; ought, should. **Sun/day**, JIH: actual sun and the time of a sun-cycle, a day. **Center**, CHUNG: inner, central; put in the center; middle, stable point enabling you to face inner and outer changes; middle line of trigram. The ideogram: field divided in two equal parts. Image of Hexagram 61.

- ## Outer and Inner Aspects

  ☳ **Shake**: Thunder rises from below, shaking and stirring things up. **Shake** begins the yang hemicycle by germinating new action.

  Connection to the outer: sprouting energies thrusting from below, the Woody Moment beginning. **Shake** stirs things up to issue-forth.

☲ **Radiance**: Fire and brightness radiate light and warmth, attached to their support; congregating people see and become aware. **Radiance** ends the yang hemicycle, consuming action in awareness.

Connection to the inner: light, heat, consciousness bring continual change, the Fiery Moment. **Radiance** spreads outward, congregating, becoming aware and changing.

Inner brightness and warmth permeate the outer world, stirring up **abounding**. These trigrams begin and end the yang hemicycle, emphasizing the fruits of action.

- *Counter Indications*

Nuclear trigrams **Open**, TUI, and **Ground**, SUN, result in Counter Hexagram 28, **Great Exceeding**, TA KUO. **Abounding** generosity for all is contrasted with the **excessive** concern with a single **great** idea.

- *Sequence*

> **Acquiring one's place to Convert implies necessarily the great.**
> **Anterior acquiescence has the use-of Abounding.**
> **Abounding implies the great indeed.**

Associated Contexts **Acquire**, TE: obtain the desired object; wish for, desire covetously; gains, possessions. The ideogram: go and obstacle, going through obstacles to the goal. **One's/one**, CH'I: third person pronoun; also: it/its, he/his, she/hers, they/theirs. **Place**, SO: where something belongs or comes from; residence, dwelling; habitual focus or object. **Convert**, KUEI: change to another form, persuade; return to yourself or the place where you belong; restore, revert, become loyal; turn into; give a young girl in marriage. The ideogram: arrive and wife, become mistress of a household. Image of Hexagram 54. **Imply**, CHE: further signify; additional meaning. **Necessarily**, PI: unavoidably, indispensably, certainly. **Great**, TA: big, noble, important, very; orient the will toward a self-imposed goal, impose direction; ability to lead or guide your life; contrasts with small, HSIAO, flexible adaptation to what crosses your path; keyword. Image of Hexagrams 14, 26, 28, 34.

Anterior ... the use-of: activating this hexagram depends on understanding and accepting the previous statement.

Indeed, YEH: intensifier; indicates comment on previous statement.

● *Contrasted Definitions*

Abounding: numerous anteriority indeed.
Connecting the few: Sojourning indeed.

Associated Contexts **Numerous**, TO: great number, many; often. **Anterior**, KU: come before as cause; formerly, ancient; reason, purpose, intention; grievance, quarrel, dissatisfaction, sorrow, mourning resulting from previous causes and intentions; situation leading to a divination.

Connect, CH'IN: attach to, approach, come near; cherish, help, favor; intimate; relatives, kin. **Few**, KUA: small number; seldom, rarely; unusual, solitary. **Sojourn**, LÜ: travel, stay in places other than your home; itinerant troops, temporary residents; visitor, guest, lodger. The ideogram: banner and people around it, loyal to a symbol rather than their temporary residence. Image of Hexagram 56.

● *Symbol Tradition*

Thunder, lightning, altogether culminating. Abounding.
A chün tzu uses severing litigating to involve punishing.

Associated Contexts **Thunder**, LEI: rising, arousing power; the Symbol of the trigram Shake, CHEN. **Lightning**, TIEN: lightning flash, electric discharge; sudden clarity; look attentively. **Altogether**, CHIEH: all, the whole; the same sort, all alike; entirely. **Culminate**, CHIH: bring to the highest degree; arrive at the end or summit; superlative.

Chün tzu: ideal of a person who uses divination to order his/her life in accordance with tao rather than wilful intention; keyword. **Use(-of)**, YI: make use of, by means of, owing to; employ, make functional. **Sever**, CHE: break off, separate, sunder, cut in two; discriminate, judge the true and false. **Litigate**, YÜ: legal proceedings; take a case to court. The ideogram: two dogs and words, barking arguments at each other. **Involve**, CHIH: include, entangle, implicate; induce, cause. The ideogram: person walking, induced to follow. **Punish**, HSING: legal punishment; physical penalties for severe criminal offenses; whip, torture, behead.

● *Image Tradition*

Abounding, the great indeed. [I]
Brightness using stirring-up. Anterior Abounding.

The king imagining it. [II]
Honoring the great indeed.
No grief, properly sun centering.
Properly illuminating Below Heaven indeed.

Sun centering, by-consequence going-down. [III]
Moon overfilling, by-consequence taking-in.
Heaven[and]Earth overfilling emptiness.
Associating-with the season: dissolving pause.
And-also even-more with-respect-to the people reached.
Even-more with-respect-to the Souls[and]Spirits reached.

Associated Contexts **[I] Brightness,** MING: light-giving aspect of burning, heavenly bodies and consciousness; with fire, the Symbol of the trigram Radiance, LI. **Stir-up,** TUNG: excite, influence, move, affect; work, take action; come out of the egg or the bud; the Action of the trigram Shake, CHEN. The ideogram: strength and heavy, move weighty things.

[II] Honor, SHANG: esteem, give high rank to; eminent; put one thing on top of another.

Illuminate, CHAO: shine light on; enlighten, reflect: care for, supervise. The ideogram: fire and brightness. **Below Heaven,** T'IEN HSIA: the human world, between heaven and earth.

[III] By-consequence(-of), TSE: very strong connection; reason, cause, result; rule, law, pattern, standard; therefore. **Go-down,** TSE: sun setting, afternoon; waning moon; decline.

Moon, YÜEH actual moon and moon-month; yin, the sun being yang. **Overfill,** YING: at the point of overflowing; more than wanted, stretch beyond; replenished, full; arrogant. The ideogram: vessel and too much. **Take-in,** SHIH: eat, ingest, swallow, devour; incorporate.

Heaven[and]Earth, T'IEN TI: dynamic relation between the primal powers and the world it produces; cosmos, natural or human world; keyword. **Empty,** HSÜ: no images or concepts; vacant, unsubstantial; empty yet fertile space.

Associate(-with), YÜ: consort with, combine; companions; group, band, company; agree with, comply, help. The ideogram: pair of hands reaching downward meets a pair of hands reaching upward, helpful association. **Season**, SHIH: quality of the time; the right time, opportune, in harmony; planning in accord with the time; seasons of the year. The ideogram: sun and temple, time as sacred. **Dissolving pause**, HSIAO HSI: yin or structure dissolves so that yang or action may emerge; transitional phase of Universal Compass.

And-also, ERH: joins and contrasts two terms. **Even-more**, K'UANG: even more so, all the more. **With-respect-to**, YÜ: relates to, refers to; hold a position in. **People, person**, JEN: humans individually and collectively; an individual; humankind. Image of Hexagrams 13 and 37. **Reach(-to)**, HU: arrive at a goal; reach toward and achieve; connect; contrasts with tend-towards, YU.

Souls[and]Spirits, KUEI SHEN: the whole range of imaginary beings both inside and outside the individual; spiritual powers, gods, demons, ghosts, powers, faculties.

● *Transforming Lines*

Initial nine

a) **Meeting one's equal lord.**
   Although a decade, without fault.
   Going possesses honor.

b) **Although a decade, without fault.**
   Exceeding a decade, calamity indeed.

Associated Contexts a) **Meet**, YÜ: come on unexpectedly, encounter; occur, happen; pleasant meeting, lucky coincidence; agree. **Equal**, P'EI: on the same level; pair, husband or wife; together. **Lord**, CHU: ruler, master, chief; authority. The ideogram: lamp and flame, giving light.

Although, SUI: even though, supposing that, if, even if. **Decade**, HSÜN: ten days or years; complete time period. **Without fault**, WU CHIU: no error or harm in the situation.

Go, WANG, and come, LAI, describe the stream of time as it flows from future through present to past; go, WANG, indicates what is departing from present to past; proceed, move on; keyword. **Possess**, YU: in possession of, have, own; opposite of lack, WU.

b) **Exceed**, KU: go beyond, pass by, pass over; excessive, transgress; error, fault. Image of Hexagrams 28 and 62. **Calamity**, TSAI: disaster from outside; flood, plague, drought, blight, ruin; contrasts with blunder, SHENG, indicating personal fault. The ideogram: water and fire, elemental powers.

Six at-second

a) **Abounding: one's screen.**
Sun centering: visualizing a bin.
Going acquiring doubt, affliction.
Possessing conformity, like shooting-forth.
Significant.

b) **Possessing conformity, like shooting-forth.**
Trustworthiness using shooting-forth purpose indeed.

Associated Contexts a) **Screen**, P'U: curtain, veil, awning, hanging mat; hide, protect; lit.: luxuriant plant growth.

Visualize, CHIEN: seeing in all its aspects: vision, being visible, forming mental images; visit, call on, consult. The ideogram: eye above person, active and receptive sight. **Bin**, TOU: measure and container for grain; gauge, hold, contain.

Go, WANG, and come, LAI, describe the stream of time as it flows from future through present to past; go, WANG, indicates what is departing from present to past; proceed, move on; keyword. **Doubt**, YI: suspect, distrust; dubious; surmise, conjecture. **Afflict**, CHI: sickness, disorder, defect, calamity; injurious; pressure and consequent anger, hate or dislike. The ideogram: sickness and dart, a sudden affliction.

Possessing conformity, YU FU: inner and outer are in accord; confidence of the spirits has been captured; sincere, truthful; proper to take action. **Like**, JO: same as; just as, similar to. **Shoot-forth**, FA: expand, send out; shoot an arrow; ferment, rise; be displayed. The ideogram: stance, bow and arrow, shooting from a solid base.

Significant, CHI: leads to the experience of meaning; favorable, propitious, advantageous, appropriate; keyword. The ideogram: scholar and mouth, wise words of a sage.

b) **Trustworthy**, HSIN: truthful, faithful, consistent over time; integrity; confide in, follow; credentials; contrasts with conforming, FU, connection in a specific moment. The ideogram: person and word, true speech.

Purpose, CHIH: focus of mind and heart; will, inclination, resolve. The ideogram: heart and scholar, high inner resolve, or heart and go, inner determination.

Nine at-third

a) **Abounding: one's profusion.**
Sun centering: visualizing froth.
Severing one's right arm.
Without fault.

b) **Abounding: one's profusion.**
Not permitting Great Affairs indeed.
Severing one's right arm.
Completing, not permitting availing-of indeed.

Associated Contexts a) **Profusion,** P'EI: spread and flow in many directions, like rain or rivers; enlarge; irrigate; luxuriant water plants.

Visualize, CHIEN: seeing in all its aspects: vision, being visible, forming mental images; visit, call on, consult. The ideogram: eye above person, active and receptive sight. **Froth,** MO: spume, foam, bubbles; perspire, drool.

Sever, CHE: break off, separate, sunder, cut in two; discriminate, judge the true and false. **Right,** YU: right side, right hand; noble, honorable; make things right. **Arm,** KUNG: the arms as the body's instruments; staunch supporter; officer, minister of state.

Without fault, WU CHIU: no error or harm in the situation.

b) **Not permitting,** PU K'O: not possible; contradicts an inherent principle. The ideogram: mouth and breath, silent consent.

Complete, CHUNG: end of a cycle that begins the next; last, whole, all; contrasts with exhaust, CH'IUNG, final end. The ideogram: silk cocoons, follow and ice, winter linking one year with the next. **Avail-of,** YUNG: take advantage of; benefit from, profit by; use for a specific purpose; apply to advantage. The ideogram: to divine and center, applying divination to central concerns.

Nine at-fourth

a) **Abounding: one's screen.**
Sun centering: visualizing a bin.
Meeting one's hiding lord.
Significant.

b) **Abounding: one's screen.**
   Situation not appropriate indeed.
   Sun centering: visualizing a bin.
   Shade, not brightening indeed.
   Meeting one's hiding lord.
   Significant movement indeed.

Associated Contexts a) **Screen**, P'U: curtain, veil, awning, hanging mat; hide, protect; lit.: luxuriant plant growth.

Visualize, CHIEN: seeing in all its aspects: vision, being visible, forming mental images; visit, call on, consult. The ideogram: eye above person, active and receptive sight. **Bin**, TOU: measure and container for grain; gauge, hold, contain.

Meet, YÜ: come on unexpectedly, encounter; occur, happen; pleasant meeting, lucky coincidence; agree. **Hide**, YI: keep out of sight; remote, distant from the center; equalize by lowering; squat, level, make ordinary; pacified, colorless; cut, wound, destroy, exterminate. Image of Hexagram 36. **Lord**, CHU: ruler, master, chief; authority. The ideogram: lamp and flame, giving light.

Significant, CHI: leads to the experience of meaning; favorable, propitious, advantageous, appropriate; keyword. The ideogram: scholar and mouth, wise words of a sage.

b) **Situation**, WEI: place or seat according to rank; post, position, command; right, proper; established, arranged. The ideogram: person and stand, servants in their places. **Not**, PU: simple negative. **Appropriate**, TANG: suitable; opportune, convenient; adequate, competent; equal to; whole lines in uneven places and opened lines in even places.

Shade, YU: hidden from view; retired, solitary, secret; dark, obscure, occult, mysterious; ignorant. The ideogram: small within hill, a cave or grotto.

Move, HSING: move or move something; motivate, emotionally moving; walk, act, do. The ideogram: stepping left then right.

Six at-fifth

a) **Coming composition.**
   Possessing reward, praise, significant.

b) Six at-fifth's significance.
Possessing reward indeed.

Associated Contexts a) **Come,** LAI, and go, WANG, describe the stream of time as it flows from future through present to past. Come, LAI, indicates what is approaching; move toward, arrive at; keyword. **Composition,** CHANG: a well-composed whole and its structure; beautiful creations; elegant, clear, brilliant; contrasts with pattern, WEN, beauty of intrinsic design.

Possess, YU: in possession of, have, own; opposite of lack, WU. **Reward,** CH'ING: gift given from gratitude or benevolence; favor from heaven; congratulate with gifts. The ideogram: heart, follow and deer (wealth), the heart expressed through gifts. **Praise,** YÜ: admire and approve; magnify, eulogize; flatter. The ideogram: words and give, offering words. **Significant,** CHI: leads to the experience of meaning; favorable, propitious, advantageous, appropriate; keyword. The ideogram: scholar and mouth, wise words of a sage.

Six above

a) Abounding: one's roof.
   Screening one's dwelling.
   Peeping-through one's door.
   Living-alone, one without people.
   Three year's-time not encountering.
   Pitfall.

b) Abounding: one's roof.
   The heavenly border, hovering indeed.
   Peeping-through one's door.
   Living-alone, one without people.
   Originating-from concealing indeed.

Associated Contexts a) **Roof,** WU: cover, shelter; house, room, cabin, tent; stop or remain at.

Screen, P'U: curtain, veil, awning, hanging mat; hide, protect; lit.: luxuriant plant growth. **Dwell,** CHI: home, house, household, family; domestic, within doors; live in. The ideogram: roof and pig or dog, the most valued domestic animals. Image of Hexagram 37.

Peep-through, K'UEI: observe from hiding; stealthily, furtive. **Door**, HU: inner door, chamber door; a household; contrasts with gate, MEN, the outer door.

Live-alone, CH'Ü: lonely, solitary; quiet, still; deserted. **Without**, WU: devoid of; -less as suffix.

Three, SAN: number three, third time or place; active phases of a cycle; superlative; beginning of repetition. **Year's-time**, SUI: actual length of time in a year; contrasts with years-revolved, NIEN, number of years elapsed. **Not**, PU: simple negative. **Encounter**, TI: see face to face; admitted to an audience; visit, interview.

Pitfall, HSIUNG: leads away from the experience of meaning; stuck and exposed to danger, unable to take in the situation; flow of life and spirit is blocked; unfortunate, baleful; keyword.

b) **Heaven**, T'IEN: highest; sky, firmament, heavens; power above the human as opposed to earth, TI, below; the Symbol of the trigram Force, CH'IEN. The ideogram: great and the one above. **Border**, CHI: limit, frontier, line which joins and divides. The ideogram: place and sacrifice, border between human and spirit. **Hover**, HSIANG: glide; rise, soar, roam.

Origin, TZU: source, beginning, ground; cause, reason, motive; line of descent; path to the origin; yourself, intrinsic. **Conceal**, TS'ANG: hide from view; store up, put aside, accumulate; stores, property; internal organs.

56

SOJOURNING ▪ *LÜ*

This hexagram describes your situation in terms of wandering journeys and living in exile. It emphasizes that mingling with others as a stranger whose identity comes from a distant center is the adequate way to handle it. To be in accord with the time, you are told to: **sojourn!**

● *Image of the Situation*

> **Sojourning, the small: Growing.**
> **Sojourning, Trial: significant.**

Associated Contexts **Sojourn**, LÜ: travel; stay in places other than your home; itinerant troops, temporary residents; visitor, guest, lodger. The ideogram: banner and people around it, loyal to a symbol rather than their temporary residence. **Small**, HSIAO: little, common, unimportant; adapting to what crosses your path; ability to move in harmony with the vicissitudes of life; contrasts with great, TA, self-imposed theme or goal; keyword. Image of Hexagrams 9 and 62. **Grow**, HENG: success through a sacrifice; pervade, persevere; bring to full growth; enjoy; vigorous, effective; second stage of the Time Cycle.

  Trial, CHEN: test by ordeal; inquiry by divination and its result; righteous, firm; separating wheat from chaff; the kernel, the proven core; fourth stage of the Time Cycle. The ideogram: pearl and divination. **Significant**, CHI: leads to the experience of meaning; favorable, propitious, advantageous, appropriate; keyword. The ideogram: scholar and mouth, wise words of a sage.

● *Outer and Inner Aspects*

☲ **Radiance**: Fire and brightness radiate light and warmth, attached to their support; congregating people see and become aware. **Radiance** ends the yang hemicycle, consuming action in awareness.

  Connection to the outer: the Fiery Moment; light, heat and consciousness bring continual change. **Radiance** spreads outward, congregating, generating insight and changing.

⚏ **Bound**: Mountains bound, limit and set a place off, stopping forward movement. **Bound** completes a full yin-yang cycle. Connection to the inner: accomplishing words express limits. **Bound** articulates what is complete to suggest what is beginning.

Articulating inner limits provides a stable base for **sojourning**'s continually changing awareness,

● *Counter Indications*

Nuclear trigrams **Open**, TUI, and **Ground**, SUN, result in Counter Hexagram 28, **Great Exceeding**. **Sojourning**'s cautious observance of the immediate is contrasted with **greatly exceeding** ordinary limits.

● *Sequence*

> **Exhausting the great implies necessarily letting-go one's residing.**
> **Anterior acquiescence has the use-of Sojourning.**

Associated Contexts **Exhaust**, CH'IUNG: bring to an end; limit, extremity; destitute; investigate exhaustively; end without a new beginning. The ideogram: cave and naked person, bent with disease or old age. **Great**, TA: big, noble, important, very; orient the will toward a self-imposed goal, impose direction; ability to lead or guide your life; contrasts with small, HSIAO, flexible adaptation to what crosses your path; keyword. Image of Hexagrams 14, 26, 28, 34. **Imply**, CHE: further signify; additional meaning. **Necessarily**, PI: unavoidably, indispensably, certainly. **Let-go**, SHIH: lose, omit, miss, fail, let slip; out of control. The ideogram: drop from the hand. **One's/one**, CH'I: third person pronoun; also: it/its, he/his, she/hers, they/theirs. **Reside(-in)**, CHÜ: dwell, live in, stay; sit down, fill an office; settled parts of a country. The ideogram: body and seat.

> **Anterior ... the use-of**: activating this hexagram depends on understanding and accepting the previous statement.

● *Contrasted Definitions*

> **Abounding: numerous anteriority indeed.**
> **Connecting the few: Sojourning indeed.**

Associated Contexts **Abound**, FENG: abundant, plentiful, copious; grow wealthy; at the point of overflowing; exuberant, fertile, prolific; rich in talents, property, friends; fullness, culmination; ripe, sumptuous, fat. Image of Hexagram 55. **Numerous**, TO: great number, many; often. **Anterior**, KU: come before as cause; formerly, ancient; reason, purpose, intention; grievance, quarrel, dissatisfaction, sorrow, mourning resulting from previous causes and intentions; situation leading to a divination. **Indeed**, YEH: intensifier; indicates comment on previous statement.

   Connect, CH'IN: attach to, approach, come near; cherish, help, favor; intimate; relatives, kin. **Few**, KUA: small number; seldom, rarely; unusual, solitary.

- *Symbol Tradition*

> **Above mountain possessing fire. Sojourning.**
> **A chün tzu uses brightening consideration**
> **to avail-of punishing and-also not to detain litigating.**

Associated Contexts **Above**, SHANG: anything above, in all senses; higher, upper, outer; upper trigram; opposite of below, HSIA. **Mountain**, SHAN: limit, boundary; the Symbol of the trigram Bound, KEN. The ideogram: three peaks, a mountain range. **Possess**, YU: in possession of, have, own; opposite of lack, WU. **Fire**, HUO: warming and consuming aspect of burning; fire and brightness are the Symbols of the trigram Radiance, LI.

   Chün tzu: ideal of a person who uses divination to order his/her life in accordance with tao rather than wilful intention; keyword. **Use(-of)**, YI: make use of, by means of, owing to; employ, make functional. **Brightness**, MING: light-giving aspect of burning, heavenly bodies and consciousness; with fire, the Symbol of the trigram Radiance, LI. **Consider**, SHEN: act carefully, seriously; cautious, attentive, circumspect; still, quiet, sincere. The ideogram: heart and true. **Avail-of**, YUNG: take advantage of; benefit from, profit by; use for a specific purpose; apply to advantage. The ideogram: to divine and center, applying divination to central concerns. **Punish**, HSING: legal punishment; physical penalties for severe criminal offenses; whip, torture, behead. **And-also**, ERH: joins and contrasts two terms. **Not**, PU: simple negative. **Detain**, LIU: hold back or on to; delay, remain; slow. **Litigate**, YÜ: legal proceedings; take a case to court. The ideogram: two dogs and words, barking arguments at each other.

598

- *Image Tradition*

Sojourning. [I]
The small Growing.
Supple acquiring the center reaching-to the outside
and-also yielding reaching-to the solid.

Stopping and-also congregating reaching-to brightness. [II]
That uses the small Growing.
Sojourning, Trial: significant indeed.
Actually Sojourning's season righteously great in-fact.

Associated Contexts **[I] Supple**, JOU: quality of the opened lines; flexible, pliant, tender, adaptable. **Acquire**, TE: obtain the desired object; wish for, desire covetously; gains, possessions. The ideogram: go and obstacle, going through obstacles to the goal. **Center**, CHUNG: inner, central; put in the center; middle, stable point enabling you to face inner and outer changes; middle line of trigram. The ideogram: field divided in two equal parts. Image of Hexagram 61. **Reach(-to)**, HU: arrive at a goal; reach towards and achieve; connect; contrasts with tend-towards, YU. **Outside**, WAI: outer, exterior, external; people working in places other than their home; unfamiliar, foreign; the upper trigram, as opposed to inside, NEI, the lower. **Yield(-to)**, SHUN: give way and bear produce; comply, agree, follow, obey; unresisting, docile, flexible; nourish, provide; the Action of the trigram Field, K'UN. The ideogram: head and current, water flowing from the head of a river, yielding to the banks. **Solid**, KANG: quality of the whole lines; firm, strong, unyielding, persisting.

[II] Stop, CHIH: bring or come to a standstill; the Action of the trigram Bound, KEN. The ideogram: a foot stops walking. **Congregate**, LI: cling together; depend on, attached to, rely on; couple, pair, herd; the Action of the trigram Radiance, LI. The ideogram: deer flocking together.

That uses, SHIH YI: involves and is involved by.

Actually ... in-fact, YI TSAI: stresses the importance of a statement. The ideogram: a dart and done, strong intention fully expressed. **'s/have(-it)/it/them**, CHIH: expresses possession, directly or as an object pronoun. **Season**, SHIH: quality of the time; the right time, opportune, in harmony; planning in accord with the time; seasons of the year. The ideogram: sun and temple, time as sacred. **Righteous**, YI: proper and just, meets the standards; things in their proper place; the heart that rules itself; upright, moral rule; contrasts with Harvest, LI, advantage or profit.

● *Transforming Lines*

Initial six

a) **Sojourning: fragmenting, fragmenting.**
   Splitting-off one's place, grasping calamity.

b) **Sojourning: fragmenting, fragmenting.**
   Purpose exhausted, calamity indeed.

Associated Contexts a) **Fragment**, SO: break into small pieces, broken parts; minute, fine; petty, trivial; annoying; lit.: splinters of precious stones. The ideogram: small and cowrie shells, the tinkling of small coins. The doubled character intensifies this quality.
   Split-off, SSU: lop off, split with an ax, rive; white (color eliminated). The ideogram: ax and possessive, splitting what belongs together. **Place,** SO: where something belongs or comes from; residence, dwelling; habitual focus or object. **Grasp**, CH'Ü: lay hold of, take and use, seize, appropriate; grasp the meaning, understand. The ideogram: ear and hand, hear and grasp. **Calamity**, TSAI: disaster from outside; flood, plague, drought, blight, ruin; contrasts with blunder, SHENG, indicating personal fault. The ideogram: water and fire, elemental powers.

b) **Purpose**, CHIH: focus of mind and heart; will, inclination, resolve. The ideogram: heart and scholar, high inner resolve, or heart and go, inner determination.

Six at-second

a) **Sojourning, approaching a resting-place.**
   Cherishing one's own.
   Acquiring a youthful vassal: Trial.

b) **Acquiring a youthful vassal: Trial.**
   Completing without surpassing indeed.

Associated Contexts a) **Approach**, CHI: come near to, advance toward; about to do; soon. **Rest(ing-place)**, TZ'U: camp, inn, shed; halting-place, breathing-spell; put in consecutive order. The ideogram: two and breath, pausing to breathe.

Cherish, HUAI: dwell on, think of; carry in the heart or womb; cling to. The ideogram: heart and hide, cherish in the heart. **Own**, TZU: possession and the things possessed; avail of, depend on; property, riches.

Youthful, T'UNG: young person between eight and fifteen; young animals and plants. **Vassal**, P'U: servant, menial, retainer; helper in heavy work; palace officers, chamberlains; follow, serve, belong to.

b) **Complete**, CHUNG: end of a cycle that begins the next; last, whole, all; contrasts with exhaust, CH'IUNG, final end. The ideogram: silk cocoons, follow and ice, winter linking one year with the next. **Without**, WU: devoid of; -less as suffix. **Surpass**, YU: exceed; beyond measure, excessive; extraordinary; transgress, blame.

Nine at-third

a) **Sojourning, burning one's resting-place.**
Losing one's youthful vassal.
Trial: adversity.

b) **Sojourning, burning one's resting-place.**
Actually truly using injuring.
Using Sojourning to associate-with the below.
One's righteousness lost indeed.

Associated Contexts a) **Burn**, FEN: set fire to, destroy completely. **Rest(ing-place)**, TZ'U: camp, inn, shed; halting-place, breathing-spell; put in consecutive order. The ideogram: two and breath, pausing to breathe.

Lose, SANG: fail to obtain, cease, become obscure; forgotten, destroyed; lament, mourn; funeral. The ideogram: weep and the dead. **Youthful**, T'UNG: young person between eight and fifteen; young animals and plants. **Vassal**, P'U: servant, menial, retainer; helper in heavy work; palace officers, chamberlains; follow, serve, belong to.

Adversity, LI: danger; threatening, malevolent demon. This has two aspects: grind, sharpen, improve, perfect, stimulate; and: poisonous, sinister, cruel, contrary. It indicates a spirit or ghost that seeks revenge by inflicting suffering upon the living. Pacifying or exorcizing such a spirit can have a healing effect. The ideogram: sheltering cliff and stinging insect.

b) **Actually**, YI: truly, really, at present. The ideogram: a dart and done, strong intention fully expressed. **Truly**, YI: statement is true and precise. **Injure**, SHANG: hurt, wound, grieve, distress; mourn, sad at heart, humiliated.

Associate(-with), YÜ: consort with, combine; companions; group, band, company; agree with, comply, help. The ideogram: pair of hands reaching downward meets a pair of hands reaching upward, helpful association. **Below**, HSIA: anything below, in all senses; lower, inner; lower trigram; opposite of above, SHANG.

Nine at-fourth

a) **Sojourning, tending-towards abiding.**
Acquiring one's own emblem-ax.
My heart not keen.

b) **Sojourning, tending-towards abiding.**
Not-yet acquiring the situation indeed.
Acquiring one's own emblem-ax.
The heart not-yet keen indeed.

Associated Contents a) **Tend-towards**, YÜ: move toward but not reach, in the direction of; contrasts with reach(-to), HU, actually arriving. **Abide**, CH'U: rest in, dwell; stop yourself; arrive at a place or condition; distinguish, decide; do what is proper. The ideogram: tiger, stop and seat, powerful movement coming to rest.

Own, TZU: possession and the things possessed; avail of, depend on; property, riches. **Emblem-ax**, FU: moon-shaped ax, symbol of power to govern.

My/me/I, WO: first person pronoun; indicates an unusually strong emphasis on your own subjective experience. **Heart**, HSIN: heart as center of being; seat of mind's images and affections; moral nature; source of desires, intentions, will. **Keen**, K'UAI: sharp, eager, prompt, cheerful; spirited.

b) **Not-yet**, WEI: temporal negative; something will but has not yet occurred; contrary of already, CHI. Image of Hexagram 64. **Situation**, WEI: place or seat according to rank; post, position, command; right, proper; established, arranged. The ideogram: person and stand, servants in their places.

Six at-fifth

a) **Shooting a pheasant.**
The-one arrow extinguishing.
Completing uses praising fate.

b) **Completing uses praising fate.**
Overtaking the above indeed.

Associated Contexts *a)* **Shoot**, SHE: shoot with a bow, point at and hit; project from, spurt, issue forth; glance at; scheme for. The ideogram: arrow and body. **Pheasant**, CHIH: clever, beautiful bird associated with Radiance, LI; also: embrasures on ramparts and forts; arrange, put in order.

One, the-one, YI: single unit; number one; undivided, simple, whole; any one of; first, the first. **Arrow**, SHIH: arrow, javelin, dart; swift, direct as an arrow; marshal together. **Extinguish**, WANG: ruin, destroy; gone, dead, lost without trace; extinct, forgotten, out of mind. The ideogram: person concealed by a wall, out of sight.

Complete, CHUNG: end of a cycle that begins the next; last, whole, all; contrasts with exhaust, CH'IUNG, final end. The ideogram: silk cocoons, follow and ice, winter linking one year with the next. **Praise**, YÜ: admire and approve; magnify, eulogize; flatter. The ideogram: words and give, offering words. **Fate**, MING: individual destiny; birth and death as limits of life; issue orders with authority; consult the gods. The ideogram: mouth and order, words with heavenly authority.

b) **Overtake**, TI: come up to, reach; arrest, seize; until; also: harmonious, peaceful. The ideogram: go, hand and reach, reaching to seize satisfaction.

Nine above

a) **A bird burning its nest.**
Sojourning people beforehand laughing,
                                        afterwards crying-out sobbing.
Losing the cattle, tending-towards versatility.
Pitfall.

b) Using Sojourning to locate-in the above.
One's righteousness burning indeed.
Losing the cattle, tending-towards versatility.
Completing absolutely-nothing: having hearing indeed.

Associated Contexts a) **Bird,** NIAO: all feathered animals; associated with the Fiery Moment. **Burn,** FEN: set fire to, destroy completely. **Its/it,** CH'I: third person pronoun; also: one/one's, he/his, she/hers, they/theirs. **Nest,** CH'AO: nest in a tree; haunt, retreat; make a nest.

People, person, JEN: humans individually and collectively; an individual; humankind. Image of Hexagrams 13 and 37. **Before(hand)/earlier,** HSIEN: come before in time; first, at first; formerly, past, previous; begin, go ahead of. **Laugh,** HSIAO: manifest joy or mirth; giggle, laugh at, ridicule; pleased, merry; associated with the Fiery Moment. **After(wards)/later,** HOU: come after in time, subsequent; put oneself after; the second; attendants, heirs, successors, posterity. **Cry-out/outcry,** HAO: call out, proclaim; signal, order, command; mark, label, sign. **Sob,** T'AO: cry, weep aloud; wailing children. The ideogram: mouth and omen, ominous sounds.

Lose, SANG: fail to obtain, cease, become obscure; forgotten, destroyed; lament, mourn; funeral. The ideogram: weep and the dead. **Cattle,** NIU: ox, bull, cow, calf; kine; power and strength of work animals. **Tend-towards,** YÜ: move toward but not reach, in the direction of; contrasts with reach(-to), HU, actually arriving. **Versatility,** I: sudden and unpredictable change; mental mobility and openness; easy and light, not difficult and heavy; occurs in name of the I CHING.

Pitfall, HSIUNG: leads away from the experience of meaning; stuck and exposed to danger, unable to take in the situation; flow of life and spirit is blocked; unfortunate, baleful; keyword.

b) **Locate(-in),** TSAI: live in, dwell, reside; belong to, involved with, depend on; within. The ideogram: earth and persevere, place on the earth.

Complete, CHUNG: end of a cycle that begins the next; last, whole, all; contrasts with exhaust, CH'IUNG, final end. The ideogram: silk cocoons, follow and ice, winter linking one year with the next. **Absolutely-no(thing),** MO: complete elimination; not any, by no means. **Hear,** WEN: perceive sound; learn by report; news, fame. The ideogram: ear and door.

GROUND ▪ *SUN*

This hexagram describes your situation in terms of providing an underlying support. It emphasizes that subtly penetrating and nourishing things from below, the action of **Ground**, is the adequate way to handle it. To be in accord with the time, you are told to: **enter** the situation from **below**!

● *Image of the Situation*

> **Ground, the small: Growing.**
> **Harvesting: possessing directed going.**
> **Harvesting: visualizing Great People.**

Associated Contexts **Ground**, SUN: base on which things rest; support, foundation; mild, subtly penetrating; nourishing. The ideogram: stand and things arranged on it, the subtle influence of the ground. **Ground** is the wood and wind trigram doubled and includes that trigram's attributes: *Symbols:* **Wood/tree,** MU: all things woody or wooden, alive or constructed from wood; associated with the Woody Moment. The ideogram: a tree with roots and branches. **Wind,** FENG: moving air, breeze, gust; weather and its influence on mood and humor; fashion, usage. *Action:* **Enter,** JU: penetrate, go into, enter on, progress; put into, encroach on; contrary of issue-forth, CH'U. **Small,** HSIAO: little, common, unimportant; adapting to what crosses your path; ability to move in harmony with the vicissitudes of life; contrasts with great, TA, self-imposed theme or goal; keyword. Image of Hexagrams 9 and 62. **Grow,** HENG: success through a sacrifice; pervade, persevere; bring to full growth; enjoy; vigorous, effective; second stage of the Time Cycle.

   Harvest, LI: advantageous, profitable; acute, insightful; benefit, nourish; third stage of the Time Cycle. **Possessing directed going,** YU YU WANG: imposing a direction on the flow of time from present to past; have a specific goal or purpose.

   Visualize, CHIEN: seeing in all its aspects: vision, being visible, forming mental images; visit, call on, consult. The ideogram: eye above person, active and receptive sight. **Great People,** TA JEN: important, noble, influential; those who impose a ruling principle on their lives; effect of the great within an individual; keyword.

• *Outer and Inner Aspects*

☴ **Ground**: Wind and wood subtly enter from the ground, penetrating and pervading. **Ground** is the center of the yang hemicycle, spreading pervasive action.

Connection to both inner and outer: penetrating and bringing together, the Woody Moment culminating. **Ground** pervades, matches and couples, seeding a new generation.

• *Counter Indications*

Nuclear trigrams **Radiance**, LI, and **Open**, TUI, result in Counter Hexagram 38, **Polarizing,** KUEI. The gentle union of inner and outer in **ground** is contrasted with the tense opposition of **polarizing**.

• *Sequence*

Sojourning and-also lacking a place to tolerate.
Anterior acquiescence has the use-of Ground.
Ground implies entering indeed.

Associated Contexts **Sojourn,** LU: travel, stay in places other than your home; itinerant troops, temporary residents; visitor, guest, lodger. The ideogram: banner and people around it, loyal to a symbol rather than their temporary residence. Image of Hexagram 56. **And-also,** ERH: joins and contrasts two terms. **Lacking,** WU: strong negative; does not possess. **Place,** SO: where something belongs or comes from; residence, dwelling; habitual focus or object. **Tolerate,** JUNG: allow, contain, endure, bear with; accept graciously. The ideogram: full stream bed, tolerating and containing.

Anterior ... the use-of: activating this hexagram depends on understanding and accepting the previous statement.

Imply, CHE: further signify; additional meaning. **Indeed,** YEH: intensifier; indicates comment on previous statement.

• *Contrasted Definitions*

Open: visualizing and-also
Ground: hiding-away indeed.

Associated Contexts **Open**, TUI: an open surface, promoting interaction and interpenetration; responsive, free, unhindered, pleasing; opening, passage; the mouth; exchange, barter; straight, direct; meet, gather; place where water accumulates. The ideogram: person, mouth and vapor, speaking with others. Image of Hexagram 58.

Hide-away, FU: conceal, place in ambush; secretly, silently; prostrate, fall on your face; humble. The ideogram: man and dog, man crouching.

- *Attached Evidences*

> **Ground: actualizing-tao's paring indeed.**
> **Ground: evaluating and-also occulting.**
> **Ground: using moving the counterpoise.**

Associated Contexts **Actualize-tao**, TE: realize tao in action; power, virtue; ability to follow the course traced by the ongoing process of the cosmos; keyword. The ideogram: to go, straight, and heart. Linked with acquire, TE: acquiring that which makes a being become what it is meant to be. **'s/have(-it)/it/them**, CHIH: expresses possession, directly or as an object pronoun. **Pare**, CHIH: cut away; form, tailor, carve; invent; limit, prevent. The ideogram: knife and incomplete.

Evaluate, CH'ENG: assess, appraise; weigh, estimate, reckon; designate, name. The ideogram: weigh and grain, attributing value. **Occult**, YIN: screen, obscure, keep from view, keep back; private; retired, not in office.

Use(-of), YI: make use of, by means of, owing to; employ, make functional. **Move**, HSING: move or move something; motivate, emotionally moving; walk, act, do. The ideogram: stepping left then right. **Counterpoise**, CH'UAN: balance, equalize, plan; act as the position demands, expedient; influential; lit.: balance on a sliding scale.

- *Symbol Tradition*

> **Following winds. Ground.**
> **A chün tzu uses distributing fate to move affairs.**

Associated Contexts **Follow**, SUI: come or go after; pursue, impelled to move; come after in inevitable sequence; move in the same direction, comply with what is ahead; follow a way or religion; according to, next, subsequent. The ideogram: go and fall, unavoidable movement. Image of Hexagram 17.

Chün tzu: ideal of a person who uses divination to order his/her life in accordance with tao rather than wilful intention; keyword. **Distribute**, SHEN: give out, spread, scatter, allot, diffuse. **Fate**, MING: individual destiny; birth and death as limits of life; issue orders with authority; consult the gods. The ideogram: mouth and order, words with heavenly authority. **Affairs**, SHIH: all kinds of personal activity; matters at hand; business, occupation; manage a business, case in court.

- *Image Tradition*

> **Redoubling Ground uses distributing fate.**
> **Solid Ground reaching-to centering correcting**
> **and-also purpose moving.**
> **Supple altogether yielding reaching the solid.**
> **That uses the small Growing.**
> **Harvesting: possessing directed going.**
> **Harvesting: visualizing Great People.**

Associated Contexts **Redouble**, CH'UNG: repeat, reiterate, add to; build up by layers.

Solid, KANG: quality of the whole lines; firm, strong, unyielding, persisting. **Reach(-to)**, HU: arrive at a goal; reach toward and achieve; connect; contrasts with tend-towards, YU. **Centering correcting**, CHUNG CHENG: central and correct; make rectifying one-sidedness and error your central concern; reaching a stable center in yourself can correct the situation. **Purpose**, CHIH: focus of mind and heart; will, inclination, resolve. The ideogram: heart and scholar, high inner resolve, or heart and go, inner determination.

Supple, JOU: quality of the opened lines; flexible, pliant, tender, adaptable. **Altogether**, CHIEH: all, the whole; the same sort, all alike; entirely. **Yield(-to)**, SHUN: give way and bear produce; comply, agree, follow, obey; unresisting, docile, flexible; nourish, provide; the Action of the trigram Field, K'UN. The ideogram: head and current, water flowing from the head of a river, yielding to the banks.

That uses, SHIH YI: involves and is involved by.

- *Transforming Lines*

  Initial six

  a) Advancing, withdrawing.
     Martial people's Harvesting Trial.

  b) Advancing, withdrawing.
     Purpose doubted indeed.
     Martial people's Harvesting Trial:
     Purpose regulated indeed.

Associated Contexts a) **Advance**, CHIN: exert yourself, make progress, climb; be promoted; further the development of, augment; adopt a religion or conviction; offer, introduce. **Withdraw(-from)**, T'UI: draw back, retreat, recede; decline, refuse.

    Martial, WU: military, warlike; strong, stern; power to make war. The ideogram: fight and stop, force deterring aggression. **People, person**, JEN: humans individually and collectively; an individual; humankind. Image of Hexagrams 13 and 37. **Harvesting Trial**, LI CHEN: advantageous divination; fruit of an action is a test or trial.

b) **Doubt**, YI: suspect, distrust; dubious; surmise, conjecture.

    Regulate, CHIH: govern well, ensure prosperity; remedy disorder, heal; someone fit to govern land, house and heart.

  Nine at-second

  a) Ground located below the bed.
     Availing-of chroniclers, shamans.
     The mottled like significant.
     Without fault.

  b) The mottled like has significance.
     Acquiring the center indeed.

Associated Contexts a) **Locate(-in)**, TSAI: live in, dwell, reside; belong to, involved with, depend on; within. The ideogram: earth and persevere, place on the earth. **Below**, HSIA: anything below, in all senses; lower, inner; lower trigram; opposite of above, SHANG. **Bed**, CH'UANG: sleeping place; couch, sofa, lounge; bench around a well.

Avail-of, YUNG: take advantage of; benefit from, profit by; use for a specific purpose; apply to advantage. The ideogram: to divine and center, applying divination to central concerns. **Chronicles**, SHIH: histories, records, annals; authoritative record; narrator of events, annalist. **Shaman**, WU: medium of the gods; sorcerer, enchantress; perform magic; wizard, witch.

Mottled, FEN: variegated, spotted; mixed, assorted, confused; cloudy, perplexed. **Like**, JO: same as; just as, similar to. **Significant**, CHI: leads to the experience of meaning; favorable, propitious, advantageous, appropriate; keyword. The ideogram: scholar and mouth, wise words of a sage.

Without fault, WU CHIU: no error or harm in the situation.

b) **Have(-it)/it/them/'s**, CHIH: expresses possession, directly or as an object pronoun. **Acquire**, TE: obtain the desired object; wish for, desire covetously; gains, possessions. The ideogram: go and obstacle, going through obstacles to the goal. **Center**, CHUNG: inner, central; put in the center; middle, stable point enabling you to face inner and outer changes; middle line of trigram. The ideogram: field divided in two equal parts. Image of Hexagram 61.

Nine at-third

a) **Imminent Ground, abashment.**

b) **Imminent Ground's abashment**
   Purpose exhausted indeed.

Associated Contexts *a)* **Imminent**, P'IN: on the brink of; pressing, urgent. **Abashment**, LIN: distress, shame, regret, humiliation; aware of having lost the right track; leads to repenting, HUI, correcting the direction of mind and life.

b) **Exhaust**, CH'IUNG: bring to an end; limit, extremity; destitute; investigate exhaustively; end without a new beginning. The ideogram: cave and naked person, bent with disease or old age.

Six at-fourth

a) **Repenting extinguished.**
   The fields, catching three kinds.

b) **The fields, catching three kinds.**
   Possessing achievement indeed.

Associated Contexts a) **Repenting extinguished**, HUI WANG: previous troubles and consequent remorse will disappear.

Fields, T'IEN: cultivated land, plantation; also: hunting, game in the fields cannot escape the hunt. The ideogram: square divided into four sections, delineating fields. **Catch**, HUO: take in hunt; catch a thief; obtain, seize; hit the mark, opportune moment; prisoner, spoils, prey; slave, servant. **Three**, SAN: number three, third time or place; active phases of a cycle; superlative; beginning of repetition. **Kinds**, P'IN: species and their essential qualities; sorts, classes; classify, select.

b) **Possess**, YU: in possession of, have, own; opposite of lack, WU. **Achieve**, KUNG: work done, results; real accomplishment, praise, worth, merit. The ideogram: workman's square and forearm, combining craft and strength.

Nine at-fifth

a) Trial: significant, repenting extinguished.
   Without not Harvesting.
   Without initially possessing completion.
   Before husking, three days.
   After husking, three days.
   Significant.

b) Nine at-fifth's significance.
   Situation correctly centered indeed.

Associated Contexts a) **Trial**, CHEN: test by ordeal; inquiry by divination and its result; righteous, firm; separating wheat from chaff; the kernel, the proven core; fourth stage of the Time Cycle. The ideogram: pearl and divination. **Significant**, CHI: leads to the experience of meaning; favorable, propitious, advantageous, appropriate; keyword. The ideogram: scholar and mouth, wise words of a sage. **Repenting extinguished**, HUI WANG: previous troubles and consequent remorse will disappear.

Without not Harvesting, WU PU LI: nothing for which this will not be beneficial; advantageous potential, borderline where the balance is swinging from not Harvesting to actually Harvesting.

Without, WU: devoid of; −less as suffix. **Initial**, CH'U: first step or part; beginning, incipient; bottom line of hexagram. The ideogram: knife and garment, cutting out the pattern. **Possess**, YU: in possession of, have,

own; opposite of lack, WU. **Complete**, CHUNG: end of a cycle that begins the next; last, whole, all; contrasts with exhaust, CH'IUNG, final end. The ideogram: silk cocoons, follow and ice, winter linking one year with the next.

Before(hand)/earlier, HSIEN: come before in time; first, at first; formerly, past, previous; begin, go ahead of. **Husking**, KENG: fruit and grain husks bursting in autumn; seventh of the Ten Heavenly Barriers in calender system; bestow, reward; blade or sword; associated with the Metallic Moment. The ideogram: receiving things in the hand. **Three**, SAN: number three, third time or place; active phases of a cycle; superlative; beginning of repetition. **Day/sun**, JIH: actual sun and the time of a sun-cycle, a day.

After(wards)/later, HOU: come after in time, subsequent; put oneself after; the second; attendants, heirs, successors, posterity.

b) **Situation**, WEI: place or seat according to rank; post, position, command; right, proper; established, arranged. The ideogram: person and stand, servants in their places. **Correct**, CHENG: rectify deviation or one-sidedness; proper, straight, exact, regular; constant, rule, model. The ideogram: stop and one, hold to one thing. **Center**, CHUNG: inner, central; put in the center; middle, stable point enabling you to face inner and outer changes; middle line of trigram. The ideogram: field divided in two equal parts. Image of Hexagram 61.

Nine above

a) **Ground located below the bed.**
   Losing one's own emblem-ax.
   Trial: pitfall.

b) **Ground located below the bed.**
   Above exhaustion indeed.
   Losing one's own emblem-ax.
   Correcting reaching a pitfall indeed.

Associated Contexts a) **Locate(-in)**, TSAI: live in, dwell, reside; belong to, involved with, depend on; within. The ideogram: earth and persevere, place on the earth. **Below**, HSIA: anything below, in all senses; lower, inner; lower trigram; opposite of above, SHANG. **Bed**, CH'UANG: sleeping place; couch, sofa, lounge; bench around a well.

Lose, SANG: fail to obtain, cease, become obscure; forgotten, destroyed; lament, mourn; funeral. The ideogram: weep and the dead. **One's/one**, CH'I: third person pronoun; also: it/its, he/his, she/hers, they/theirs. **Own**, TZU: possession and the things possessed; avail of, depend on; property, riches. **Emblem-ax**, FU: moon-shaped ax, symbol of power to govern.

Trial, CHEN: test by ordeal; inquiry by divination and its result; righteous, firm; separating wheat from chaff; the kernel, the proven core; fourth stage of the Time Cycle. The ideogram: pearl and divination. **Pitfall**, HSIUNG: leads away from the experience of meaning; stuck and exposed to danger, unable to take in the situation; flow of life and spirit is blocked; unfortunate, baleful; keyword.

b) **Above**, SHANG: anything above, in all senses; higher, upper, outer; upper trigram; opposite of below, HSIA. **Exhaust**, CH'IUNG: bring to an end; limit, extremity; destitute; investigate exhaustively; end without a new beginning. The ideogram: cave and naked person, bent with disease or old age.

Correct, CHENG: rectify deviation or one-sidedness; proper, straight, exact, regular; constant, rule, model. The ideogram: stop and one, hold to one thing.

58

OPEN ▪ *TUI*

This hexagram describes your situation in terms of interaction and exchange. It emphasizes that stimulating things through cheering and persuasive speech, the action of **Open**, is the adequate way to handle it. To be in accord with the time, you are told to: **stimulate!**

• *Image of the Situation*

**Open, Growing,
Harvesting Trial.**

Associated Contexts **Open**, TUI: an open surface, promoting interaction and interpenetration; responsive, free, unhindered, pleasing; opening, passage; the mouth; exchange, barter; straight, direct; meet, gather; place where water accumulates. The ideogram: person, mouth and vapor, speaking with others. **Open** is the marsh trigram doubled and includes that trigram's attributes: *Symbol:* **Marsh**, TSE: open surface of a flat body of water and the vapors rising from it; fertilize, enrich; kindness, favor. *Action:* **Stimulate**, SHUO: rouse to action and good feeling; stir up, urge on; persuade; set out in words; free from constraint, cheer, delight. The ideogram: words and exchange. **Grow**, HENG: success through a sacrifice; pervade, persevere; bring to full growth; enjoy; vigorous, effective; second stage of the Time Cycle.

Harvesting Trial, LI CHEN: advantageous divination; putting the action in question to the test is beneficial.

• *Outer and Inner Aspects*

☱ **Open**: vapor rising from the marsh's open surface stimulates and fertilizes; stimulating words cheer and inspire. **Open** begins the yin hemicycle by initiating the formative process.

Connection to the outer: liquifying, casting, skinning off the mold, the Metallic Moment beginning. **Open** stimulates, cheers and reveals innate form.

- *Counter Indications*

Nuclear trigrams **Ground**, SUN, and **Radiance**, LI, result in Counter Hexagram 37, **Dwelling People**, CHIA JEN. **Open** exchange and contact with others is contrasted with the closed circle of **people** in their **dwelling**.

- *Sequence*

> **Entering and-also afterwards stimulating it.**
> **Anterior acquiescence has the use-of Open.**
> **Open implies stimulating indeed.**

Associated Contexts **Enter**, JU: penetrate, go into, enter on, progress; put into, encroach on; the Action of the trigram Ground, SUN, contrary of issue-forth, CH'U. **And-also**, ERH: joins and contrasts two terms. **After(wards)/later**, HOU: come after in time, subsequent; put oneself after; the second; attendants, heirs, successors, posterity. **It/them/have(-it)/'s**, CHIH: expresses possession, directly or as an object pronoun.

   Anterior ... the use-of: activating this hexagram depends on understanding and accepting the previous statement.

   Imply, CHE: further signify; additional meaning. **Indeed**, YEH: intensifier; indicates comment on previous statement.

- *Contrasted Definitions*

> **Open: visualizing and-also**
> **Ground: hiding-away indeed.**

Associated Contexts **Visualize**, CHIEN: seeing in all its aspects: vision, being visible, forming mental images; visit, call on, consult. The ideogram: eye above person, active and receptive sight.

   Ground, SUN: base on which things rest; support, foundation; mild, subtly penetrating; nourishing. The ideogram: stand and things arranged on it, the subtle influence of the ground. Image of Hexagram 57. **Hide-away**, FU: conceal, place in ambush; secretly, silently; prostrate, fall on your face; humble. The ideogram: man and dog, man crouching.

- *Symbol Tradition*

> **Congregating marshes. Open.**
> **A chün tzu uses partnering friends to explicate repeating.**

Associated Contexts **Congregate**, LI: cling together; depend on, attached to, rely on; couple, pair, herd; the Action of the trigram Radiance, LI. The ideogram: deer flocking together.

Chün tzu: ideal of a person who uses divination to order his/her life in accordance with tao rather than wilful intention; keyword. **Use(-of)**, YI: make use of, by means of, owing to; employ, make functional. **Partner**, P'ENG: associate for mutual benefit; two equal or similar things; companions, friends, peers; join in; commercial ventures. The ideogram: linked strings of cowries or coins. **Friend**, YU: companion, associate; of the same mind; attached, in pairs. The ideogram: two hands joined. **Explicate**, CHIANG: explain, unfold, narrate; converse, speak; investigate, plan, discuss. The ideogram: speech and crossing beams, speech blending harmoniously. **Repeat**, HSI: series of similar acts; practise, rehearse; familiar with, skilled. The ideogram: two wings and a cap, thought carried by repeated movements.

- *Image Tradition*

> **Open stimulating indeed. [I]**
> **Solid centering and-also supple outside.**
> **Stimulating uses Harvesting Trial.**
> **That uses yielding reaching-to heaven and-also**
> **corresponding reaching-to the people.**
>
> **Stimulating using beforehand the commoners: [II]**
> **The commoners forget their toiling.**
> **Stimulating using opposing heaviness:**
> **The commoners forget their dying.**
> **Stimulating's great:**
> **Actually the commoners encouraged in-fact.**

Associated Contexts **Solid**, KANG: quality of the whole lines; firm, strong, unyielding, persisting. **Center**, CHUNG: inner, central; put in the center; middle, stable point enabling you to face inner and outer changes;

middle line of trigram. The ideogram: field divided in two equal parts. Image of Hexagram 61. **Supple,** JOU: quality of the opened lines; flexible, pliant, tender, adaptable. **Outside,** WAI: outer, exterior, external; people working in places other than their home; unfamiliar, foreign; the upper trigram, as opposed to inside, NEI, the lower.

That uses, SHIH YI: involves and is involved by. **Yield(-to),** SHUN: give way and bear produce; comply, agree, follow, obey; unresisting, docile, flexible; nourish, provide; the Action of the trigram Field, K'UN. The ideogram: head and current, water flowing from the head of a river, yielding to the banks. **Reach(-to),** HU: arrive at a goal; reach toward and achieve; connect; contrasts with tend-towards, YU. **Heaven,** T'IEN: highest; sky, firmament, heavens; power above the human as opposed to earth, TI, below; the Symbol of the trigram Force, CH'IEN. The ideogram: great and the one above. **Correspond(-to),** YING: be in agreement or harmony; resonate together, invoke and fulfill each other; answer to, suitable; relation between the lines (1:4, 2:5, 3:6) when they form the pair opened and whole, supple and solid. The ideogram: heart and obey. **People, person,** JEN: humans individually and collectively; an individual; humankind. Image of Hexagrams 13 and 37.

[II] **Before(hand)/earlier,** HSIEN: come before in time; first, at first; formerly, past, previous; begin, go ahead of. **Commoners,** MIN: class of workers the state draws on to sustain the social hierarchy; undeveloped potential outside the organized personality.

Forget, WANG: escape the mind; leave undone, disregard, neglect. The ideogram: heart and lost. **Their/they,** CH'I: third person pronoun; also: one/one's, it/its, he/his, she/hers. **Toil,** LAO: labor, take pains, exert yourself; burdened, careworn; worthy actions. The ideogram: strength and fire, producing heat.

Oppose, FAN: resist; violate, offend, attack; possessed by an evil spirit; criminal. The ideogram: violate and dog, brutal offense. **Heavy,** NAN: arduous, grievous, difficult; hardship, distress; harass; contrasts with versatile, I, deal lightly with. The ideogram: domestic bird with clipped tail and drying sticky earth.

Die, SSU: sudden or untimely death; run out of energy; immobile, fixed.

Great, TA: big, noble, important, very; orient the will toward a self-imposed goal, impose direction; ability to lead or guide your life; contrasts with small, HSIAO: flexible adaptation to what crosses your path; keyword. Image of Hexagrams 14, 26, 28, 34.

Actually ... in-fact, YI TSAI: stresses the importance of a statement. The ideogram: a dart and done, strong intention fully expressed. **Encourage**, CH'ÜAN: exhort, stimulate, influence; admonish.

- *Transforming Lines*

Initial nine

a) **Harmonious Opening, significant.**

b) **Harmonious Opening's significance.**
Movement not-yet doubted indeed.

Associated Contexts a) **Harmony**, HO: concord, union; conciliate; at peace, mild; fit, tune, adjust. **Significant**, CHI: leads to the experience of meaning; favorable, propitious, advantageous, appropriate; keyword. The ideogram: scholar and mouth, wise words of a sage.

b) **Move**, HSING: move or move something; motivate, emotionally moving; walk, act, do. The ideogram: stepping left then right. **Not-yet**, WEI: temporal negative; something will but has not yet occurred; contrary of already, CHI. Image of Hexagram 64. **Doubt**, YI: suspect, distrust; dubious; surmise, conjecture.

Nine at-second

a) **Conforming Opening, significant.**
Repenting extinguished.

b) **Conforming Opening's significance.**
Trustworthy purpose indeed.

Associated Contexts a) **Conforming**, FU: accord between inner and outer in a particular moment; sincere, truthful, verified, reliable, in accord with the spirits; capture; prisoners, spoils; contrasts with trustworthy, HSIN, consistent over time. The ideogram: bird's claw enclosing young animals, possessive grip. Image of Hexagram 61. **Significant**, CHI: leads to the experience of meaning; favorable, propitious, advantageous, appropriate; keyword. The ideogram: scholar and mouth, wise words of a sage.
Repenting extinguished, HUI WANG: previous troubles and consequent remorse will disappear.

b) **Trustworthy**, HSIN: truthful, faithful, consistent over time; integrity; confide in, follow; credentials; contrasts with conforming, FU, connection in a specific moment. The ideogram: person and word, true speech. **Purpose**, CHIH: focus of mind and heart; will, inclination, resolve. The ideogram: heart and scholar, high inner resolve, or heart and go, inner determination.

Six at-third

a) **Coming Opening, pitfall.**

b) **Coming Opening's pitfall.**
Situation not appropriate indeed.

Associated Contexts a) **Come**, LAI, and go, WANG, describe the stream of time as it flows from future through present to past; come, LAI, indicates what is approaching; move toward, arrive at; keyword. **Pitfall**, HSIUNG: leads away from the experience of meaning; stuck and exposed to danger, unable to take in the situation; flow of life and spirit is blocked; unfortunate, baleful; keyword.

b) **Situation**, WEI: place or seat according to rank; post, position, command; right, proper; established, arranged. The ideogram: person and stand, servants in their places. **Not**, PU: simple negative. **Appropriate**, TANG: suitable; opportune, convenient; adequate, competent; equal to; whole lines in uneven places and opened lines in even places.

Nine at-fourth

a) **Bargaining Opening, not-yet soothing.**
Chain-mail afflicting: possessing rejoicing.

b) **Nine at-fourth's rejoicing.**
Possessing reward indeed.

Associated Contexts a) **Bargain**, SHANG: argue over prices; consult, deliberate, do business; dealers, traveling merchants; hour before sunrise and sunset. The ideogram: stutter and sentences, repetitive speaking. **Not-yet**, WEI: temporal negative; something will but has not yet occurred; contrary of already, CHI. Image of Hexagram 64. **Soothe**, NING: calm, pacify; create peace of mind; tranquil, quiet. The ideogram: shelter above heart, dish and breath, physical and spiritual comfort.

Chain-mail, CHIEH: chain-armor; tortoise or crab shell; protective covering; border, limit; protection, support. **Afflict,** CHI: sickness, disorder, defect, calamity; injurious; pressure and consequent anger, hate or dislike. The ideogram: sickness and dart, a sudden affliction. **Possess,** YU: in possession of, have, own; opposite of lack, WU. **Rejoice(-in),** HSI: feel and give joy; delight, exult; cheerful, merry. The ideogram: joy (music) and mouth, expressing joy.

b) **Reward,** CH'ING: gift given from gratitude or benevolence; favor from heaven; congratulate with gifts. The ideogram: heart, follow and deer (wealth), the heart expressed through gifts.

Nine at-fifth

a) Conforming tending-towards stripping.
Possessing adversity.

b) Conforming tending-towards stripping.
Situation correcting appropriate indeed.

Associated Contexts a) **Conforming,** FU: accord between inner and outer in a particular moment; sincere, truthful, verified, reliable, in accord with the spirits; capture; prisoners, spoils; contrasts with trustworthy, HSIN, consistent over time. The ideogram: bird's claw enclosing young animals, possessive grip. Image of Hexagram 61. **Tend-towards,** YÜ: move toward but not reach, in the direction of; contrasts with reach(-to), HU, actually arriving. **Strip,** PO: flay, peel, skin; remove, uncover, degrade; split, slice; reduce to essentials; slaughter an animal. The ideogram: knife and carve, trenchant action. Image of Hexagram 23.

Possess, YU: in possession of, have, own; opposite of lack, WU. **Adversity,** LI: danger; threatening, malevolent demon. This has two aspects: grind, sharpen, improve, perfect, stimulate; and: poisonous, sinister, cruel, contrary. It indicates a spirit or ghost that seeks revenge by inflicting suffering upon the living. Pacifying or exorcizing such a spirit can have a healing effect. The ideogram: sheltering cliff and stinging insect.

b) **Situation,** WEI: place or seat according to rank; post, position, command; right, proper; established, arranged. The ideogram: person and stand, servants in their places. **Correct,** CHENG: rectify deviation or one-sidedness; proper, straight, exact, regular; constant, rule, model. The ideogram: stop and one, hold to one thing. **Appropriate,** TANG: suitable;

opportune, convenient; adequate, competent; equal to; whole lines in uneven places and opened lines in even places.

Six above

a) **Protracting Opening.**

b) **Six above, protracting Opening.**
    Not-yet shining indeed.

Associated Contexts a) **Protract**, YIN: draw out, prolong; carried on; lead on, to bring forward; lit.: drawing a bow.

b) **Not-yet,** WEI: temporal negative; something will but has not yet occurred; contrary of already, CHI. Image of Hexagram 64. **Shine**, KUANG: illuminate; give off brilliant, bright light; honor, glory, éclat; result of action, contrasts with brightness, MING, light of heavenly bodies. The ideogram: fire above person, lifting the light.

DISPERSING ▪ *HUAN*

This hexagram describes your situation in terms of confronting obstacles, illusions and misunderstandings. It emphasizes that clearing away what is blocking the light is the adequate way to handle it. To be in accord with the time, you are told to: **disperse** what obstructs awareness!

● *Image of the Situation*

Dispersing, Growing.
The king imagines possessing a temple.
Harvesting: wading the Great River.
Harvesting Trial.

Associated Contexts **Disperse**, HUAN: scatter clouds or crowds; break up obstacles; dispel illusions, fears and suspicions; clear up misunderstandings; dissolve, evaporate, disintegrate, fade, vanish; fog lifting or clearing away. **Grow**, HENG: success through a sacrifice; pervade, persevere; bring to full growth; enjoy; vigorous, effective; second stage of the Time Cycle.

King(hood), WANG: effective ruler, by authority of the Emperor, from whom others derive their power. **Imagine**, CHIA: create in the mind; fantasize, suppose, pretend, imitate; fiction; illusory, unreal; costume. The ideogram: person and borrow. **Possess**, YU: in possession of, have, own; opposite of lack, WU. **Temple**, MIAO: building used to honor gods and ancestors.

Harvest, LI: advantageous, profitable; acute, insightful; benefit, nourish; third stage of the Time Cycle. **Wading the Great River**, SHE TA CH'UAN: consciously moving into the flow of time; enter the stream of life with a goal or purpose; embark on a significant enterprise.

Harvesting Trial, LI CHEN: advantageous divination; putting the action in question to the test is beneficial.

● *Outer and Inner Aspects*

☴ **Ground**: Wind and wood subtly enter from the ground, penetrating and pervading. **Ground** is the center of the yang hemicycle, spreading pervasive action.

Connection to the outer: penetrating and bringing together, the Woody Moment culminating. **Ground** pervades, matches and couples, seeding a new generation.

☵ **Gorge**: Stream ventures and falls into the gorge, flowing on through toil and danger. **Gorge** ends the yin hemicycle by leveling and dissolving forms.

Connection to the inner: flooding and leveling dissolve direction and shape, the Streaming Moment. **Gorge** ventures, falls, toils and flows on.

The inner stream subtly penetrates the outer world, dissolving forms and **dispersing** obstacles.

- *Counter Indications*

Nuclear trigrams **Bound**, KEN, and **Shake**, CHEN, result in Counter Hexagram 27, **Jaws/Swallowing**, YI. The outward movement of **dispersing** and clearing away obstacles is contrasted with taking things in through **swallowing**.

- *Sequence*

> **Stimulating and-also afterwards scattering it.**
> **Anterior acquiescence has the use-of Dispersing.**
> **Dispersing implies Radiance indeed.**

Associated Contexts **Stimulate**, SHUO: rouse to action and good feeling; free from constraint, stir up, urge on; persuade, cheer, delight; set out in words; the Action of the trigram Open, TUI. The ideogram: words and exchange. **And-also**, ERH: joins and contrasts two terms. **After(wards)/later**, HOU: come after in time, subsequent; put oneself after; the second; attendants, heirs, successors, posterity. **Scatter,** SAN: disperse in small pieces; separate, divide, distribute. The ideogram: strike and crumble. **It/them/have(-it)/it/'s**, CHIH: expresses possession, directly or as an object pronoun.

Anterior ... the use-of: activating this hexagram depends on understanding and accepting the previous statement.

Imply, CHE: further signify; additional meaning. **Radiance**, LI: glowing light, spreading in all directions; light-giving, discriminating, articulating; divide and arrange in order; the power of consciousness. The ideogram: bird and weird, the magical fire-bird with brilliant plumage. Image of Hexagram 30. **Indeed**, YEH: intensifier; indicates comment on previous statement.

- *Contrasted Definitions*

> **Dispersing: Radiance indeed.**
> **Articulating: stopping indeed.**

Associated Contexts **Articulate**, CHIEH: separate and distinguish, as well as join, different things; express thought through speech; joint, section, chapter, interval, unit of time; zodiacal sign; moderate, regulate; lit.: nodes on bamboo stalks. Image of Hexagram 60. **Stop**, CHIH: bring or come to a standstill; the Action of the trigram Bound, KEN. The ideogram: a foot stops walking.

- *Symbol Tradition*

> **Wind moves above stream. Dispersing.**
> **The Earlier Kings used presenting tending-towards**
> **the supreme to establish the temples.**

Associated Contexts **Wind**, FENG: moving air, breeze, gust; weather and its influence on mood and humor; fashion, usage; wind and wood are the Symbols of the trigram Ground, SUN. **Move**, HSING: move or move something; motivate, emotionally moving; walk, act, do. The ideogram: stepping left then right. **Above**, SHANG: anything above, in all senses; higher, upper, outer; upper trigram; opposite of below, HSIA. **Stream**, SHUI: flowing water; fluid, dissolving; river, tide, flood; the Symbol of the trigram Gorge, K'AN. The ideogram: rippling water.

Earlier Kings, HSIEN WANG: ideal rulers of old; the golden age, primal time, power in harmony with nature; model for the chün tzu. **Use(-of)**, YI: make use of, by means of, owing to; employ, make functional. **Present(-to)**, HSIANG: present in sacrifice, offer with thanks, give to the gods or a superior; confer dignity on. **Tend-towards**, YÜ: move toward but not reach, in the direction of; contrasts with reach(-to),

HU, actually arriving. **Supreme**, TI: highest, above all on earth; sovereign lord, source of power; emperor. **Establish**, LI: set up, institute, order, arrange; stand erect; settled principles.

●　*Image Tradition*

> **Dispersing, Growing. [I]**
> **Solid coming and-also not exhausted.**
> **Supple acquiring the situation reaching-to the outside**
> 　　　　　　　　　　　　　　**and-also concording above.**
>
> **The king imagines possessing a temple. [II]**
> **Kinghood thereupon located-in the center indeed.**
>
> **Harvesting: wading the Great River. [III]**
> **Riding wood possesses achievement indeed.**

Associated Contexts **[I] Solid**, KANG: quality of the whole lines; firm, strong, unyielding, persisting. **Come**, LAI, and go, WANG, describe the stream of time as it flows from future through present to past; come, LAI, indicates what is approaching; move toward, arrive at; keyword. **Not**, PU: simple negative. **Exhaust**, CH'IUNG: bring to an end; limit, extremity; destitute; investigate exhaustively; end without a new beginning. The ideogram: cave and naked person, bent with disease or old age.

Supple, JOU: quality of the opened lines; flexible, pliant, tender, adaptable. **Acquire**, TE: obtain the desired object; wish for, desire covetously; gains, possessions. The ideogram: go and obstacle, going through obstacles to the goal. **Situation**, WEI: place or seat according to rank; post, position, command; right, proper; established, arranged. The ideogram: person and stand, servants in their places. **Reach(-to)**, HU: arrive at a goal; reach toward and achieve; connect; contrasts with tend-towards, YU. **Outside**, WAI: outer, exterior, external; people working in places other than their home; unfamiliar, foreign; the upper trigram, as opposed to inside, NEI, the lower. **Concord**, T'UNG: harmonize, unite, equalize, assemble; agree, share in; together, at once, same time and place. The ideogram: cover and mouth, silent understanding and perfect fit. Image of Hexagram 13.

[II] Thereupon, NAI: on that ground, because of. **Locate(-in)**, TSAI: live in, dwell, reside; belong to, involved with, depend on; within. The ideogram: earth and persevere, place on the earth. **Center**, CHUNG: inner, central; put in the center; middle, stable point enabling you to face inner and outer changes; middle line of trigram. The ideogram: field divided in two equal parts. Image of Hexagram 61.

[III] Ride, CH'ENG: ride an animal or a chariot; have the upper hand, seize the right time; control strong power; overcome the nature of the other; supple opened line above a solid whole line. **Wood/tree**, MU: all things woody or wooden, alive or constructed from wood; associated with the Woody Moment; wood and wind are the Symbols of the trigram Ground, SUN. The ideogram: a tree with roots and branches. **Achieve**, KUNG: work done, results; real accomplishment, praise, worth, merit. The ideogram: workman's square and forearm, combining craft and strength.

● *Transforming Lines*

    Initial six

    a) **Availing-of a rescuing horse, invigorating significant.**

    b) **Initial six's significance.**
       Yielding indeed.

Associated Contexts a) **Avail-of**, YUNG: take advantage of; benefit from, profit by; use for a specific purpose; apply to advantage. The ideogram: to divine and center, applying divination to central concerns. **Rescue**, CHENG: aid, deliver from trouble; pull out, raise up, lift. The ideogram: hand and aid, a helping hand. **Horse**, MA: symbol of spirited strength in the natural world, counterpart of dragon, LUNG; associated with the trigram Force, CH'IEN, heaven, T'IEN, and high noon. **Invigorate**, CHUANG: inspirit, animate; strong, robust; full grown, flourishing, abundant; attain manhood (at 30); damage through unrestrained strength. The ideogram: strength and scholar, intellectual impact. Image of Hexagram 34. **Significant**, CHI: leads to the experience of meaning; favorable, propitious, advantageous, appropriate; keyword. The ideogram: scholar and mouth, wise words of a sage.

b) **Yield(-to)**, SHUN: give way and bear produce; comply, agree, follow, obey; unresisting, docile, flexible; nourish, provide; the Action of the trigram Field, K'UN. The ideogram: head and current, water flowing from the head of a river, yielding to the banks.

Nine at-second

a) **Dispersing: fleeing one's bench.**
 Repenting extinguished.

b) **Dispersing: fleeing one's bench.**
 Acquiring desire indeed.

Associated Contexts a) **Flee**, PEN: run away quickly; urgent, hurry; bustle, confusion; marry without rites. The ideogram: three oxen and fright, a stampede. **One's/one**, CH'I: third person pronoun; also: it/its, he/his, she/hers, they/theirs. **Bench**, CHI: low table used to lean on; side-table; stool or support.

Repenting extinguished, HUI WANG: previous troubles and consequent remorse will disappear.

b) **Desire**, YÜAN: wish, hope or long for; covet; desired object.

Six at-third

a) **Dispersing one's body.**
 Without repenting.

b) **Dispersing one's body.**
 Purpose located outside indeed.

Associated Contexts a) **One's/one**, CH'I: third person pronoun; also: it/its, he/his, she/hers, they/theirs. **Body**, KUNG: physical being, power and self expression; contrasts with individuality, SHEN, the total personality.

Without repenting, WU HUI: devoid of the sort of trouble that leads to sorrow, regret and the necessity to change your attitude.

b) **Purpose**, CHIH: focus of mind and heart; will, inclination, resolve. The ideogram: heart and scholar, high inner resolve, or heart and go, inner determination.

Six at-fourth

a) **Dispersing one's flock, Spring significant.**
Dispersing possessing the hill-top.
In-no-way hiding, a place to ponder.

b) **Dispersing one's flock, Spring significant.**
Shining great indeed.

Associated Contexts a) **One's/one**, CH'I: third person pronoun; also: it/its, he/his, she/hers, they/theirs. **Flock**, CH'ÜN: herd, group; people of same kind, friends, equals; all, entire; move in unison, flock together. The ideogram: chief and sheep, flock around a leader. **Spring**, YÜAN: source, origin, head; great, excellent; arise, begin, generating power; first stage of the Time Cycle. **Significant**, CHI: leads to the experience of meaning; favorable, propitious, advantageous, appropriate; keyword. The ideogram: scholar and mouth, wise words of a sage.

Hill-top, CH'IU: hill with hollow top used for worship and as grave-site; knoll, hillock.

In-no-way, FEI: strong negative; not so. The ideogram: a box filled with opposition. **Hide**, YI: keep out of sight; remote, distant from the center; equalize by lowering; squat, level, make ordinary; pacified, colorless; cut, wound, destroy, exterminate. Image of Hexagram 36. **Place**, SO: where something belongs or comes from; residence, dwelling; habitual focus or object. **Ponder**, SSU: reflect, consider, remember; deep thought; desire, wish. The ideogram: heart and field, the heart's concerns.

b) **Shine**, KUANG: illuminate; give off brilliant, bright light; honor, glory, éclat; result of action, contrasts with brightness, MING, light of heavenly bodies. The ideogram: fire above person, lifting the light. **Great**, TA: big, noble, important, very; orient the will toward a self-imposed goal, impose direction; ability to lead or guide your life; contrasts with small, HSIAO, flexible adaptation to what crosses your path; keyword. Image of Hexagrams 14, 26, 28, 34.

Nine at-fifth

a) **Dispersing sweat, one's great crying-out.**
Dispersing.
Kinghood residing, without fault.

b) **Kinghood residing, without fault.**
Correcting the situation indeed.

Associated Contexts a) **Sweat**, HAN: perspiration; labor, trouble.
Dispersing sweat, HUAN HAN, also denotes an imperial edict. **One's/one**,
CH'I: third person pronoun; also it/its, he/his, she/hers, they/theirs.
Great, TA: big, noble, important, very; orient the will toward a self-
imposed goal, impose direction; ability to lead or guide your life; contrasts
with small, HSIAO, flexible adaptation to what crosses your path;
keyword. Image of Hexagrams 14, 26, 28, 34. **Cry-out/outcry**, HAO: call
out, proclaim; signal, order, command; mark, label, sign.

Reside(-in), CHÜ: dwell, live in, stay; sit down, fill an office; settled
parts of a country. The ideogram: body and seat. **Without fault**, WU
CHIU: no error or harm in the situation.

b) **Correct**, CHENG: rectify deviation or one-sidedness; proper, straight,
exact, regular; constant, rule, model. The ideogram: stop and one, hold to
one thing.

Nine above

a) **Dispersing one's blood.**
Departing far-away, issuing-forth.
Without fault.

b) **Dispersing one's blood.**
Distancing harm indeed.

Associated Contexts a) **One's/one**, CH'I: third person pronoun;
also: it/its, he/his, she/hers, they/theirs. **Blood**, HSÜEH: yin fluid that
maintains life; money, property.

Depart, CH'Ü: leave, quit, remove; repudiate, reject, dismiss. **Far-
away**, TI: far, remote; send away, exile. **Issue-forth(-from)**, CH'U: emerge
from, come out of, proceed from, spring from; the Action of the trigram
Shake, CHEN; contrary of enter, JU. The ideogram: stem with branches
and leaves emerging.

Without fault, WU CHIU: no error or harm in the situation.

b) **Distance**, YÜAN: far off, remote; keep at a distance; alienated. The
ideogram: go and a long way. **Harm**, HAI: damage, injure, offend; suffer;
hurtful, hindrance; fearful, anxious.

60

ARTICULATING ▮ *CHIEH*

This hexagram describes your situation in terms of confused relations. It emphasizes that making limits and connections clear, particularly through speech, is the adequate way to handle it. To be in accord with the time, you are told to: **articulate!**

- *Image of the Situation*

    Articulating, Growing.
    Bitter Articulating not permitting Trial.

    Associated Contexts **Articulate**, CHIEH: separate and distinguish, as well as join different things; express thought through speech; joint, section, chapter, interval, unit of time; regulations, limits; zodiacal sign; lit.: nodes on bamboo stalks. **Grow**, HENG: success through a sacrifice; pervade, persevere; bring to full growth; enjoy; vigorous, effective; second stage of the Time Cycle.

    Bitter, K'U: taste corresponding to the Fiery Moment; unpleasant, troublesome, painful affliction; take pains; urgent, pressing; dislike, grieve, mortify. **Not permitting**, PU K'O: not possible; contradicts an inherent principle. The ideogram: mouth and breath, silent consent. **Trial**, CHEN: test by ordeal; inquiry by divination and its result; righteous, firm; separating wheat from chaff; the kernel, the proven core; fourth stage of the Time Cycle. The ideogram: pearl and divination.

- *Outer and Inner Aspects*

    ☵ **Gorge**: Stream ventures and falls into the gorge, flowing on through toil and danger. **Gorge** ends the yin hemicycle by leveling and dissolving forms.

    Connection to the outer: flooding and leveling dissolve direction and shape, the Streaming Moment. **Gorge** ventures, falls, toils and flows on.

    ☱ **Open**: vapor rising from the marsh's open surface stimulates and fertilizes; stimulating words cheer and inspire. **Open** begins the yin hemicycle by initiating the formative process.

Connection to the inner: liquifying, casting, skinning off the mold, the Metallic Moment beginning. **Open** stimulates, cheers and reveals innate form.

Stimulating words from within **articulate** and transform the undifferentiated stream of events.

- *Counter Indications*

Nuclear trigrams **Bound**, KEN, and **Shake**, CHEN, result in Counter Hexagram 27, **Jaws/Swallowing**, YI. Discriminating and **articulating** things is contrasted with indiscriminately **swallowing** and taking them in.

- *Sequence*

> **Beings not permitted to use completing Radiance.**
> **Anterior acquiescence has the use-of Articulating.**

Associated Contexts **Beings not permitted to use ...** : no one is allowed to make use of; nothing can exist by means of. **Complete**, CHUNG: end of a cycle that begins the next; last, whole, all; contrasts with exhaust, CH'IUNG, final end. The ideogram: silk cocoons, follow and ice, winter linking one year with the next. **Radiance**, LI: glowing light, spreading in all directions; light-giving, discriminating, articulating; divide and arrange in order; the power of consciousness. The ideogram: bird and weird, the magical fire-bird with brilliant plumage. Image of Hexagram 30.
    Anterior ... the use-of: activating this hexagram depends on understanding and accepting the previous statement.

- *Contrasted Definitions*

> **Dispersing: Radiance indeed.**
> **Articulating: stopping indeed.**

Associated Contexts **Disperse**, HUAN: scatter clouds or crowds; break up obstacles; dispel illusions, fears and suspicions; clear up misunderstandings; dissolve, evaporate, disintegrate, fade, vanish; fog

lifting or clearing away. Image of Hexagram 59. **Indeed,** YEH: intensifier; indicates comment on previous statement.

Stop, CHIH: bring or come to a standstill; the Action of the trigram Bound, KEN. The ideogram: a foot stops walking.

- *Symbol Tradition*

> **Above marsh possessing stream. Articulating.**
> **A chün tzu uses paring to reckon the measures.**
> **[A chün tzu uses] deliberating actualizing-tao to move.**

Associated Contexts **Above,** SHANG: anything above, in all senses; higher, upper, outer; upper trigram; opposite of below, HSIA. **Marsh,** TSE: open surface of a flat body of water and the vapors rising from it; fertilize, enrich; kindness, favor; the Symbol of the trigram Open, TUI. **Possess,** YU: in possession of, have, own; opposite of lack, WU. **Stream,** SHUI: flowing water; fluid, dissolving; river, tide, flood; the Symbol of the trigram Gorge, K'AN. The ideogram: rippling water.

Chün tzu: ideal of a person who uses divination to order his/her life in accordance with tao rather than wilful intention; keyword. **Use(-of),** YI: make use of, by means of, owing to; employ, make functional. **Pare,** CHIH: cut away; form, tailor, carve; invent; limit, prevent. The ideogram: knife and incomplete. **Reckon,** SHU: count, find the number; give out; sum up, discriminate; also: account, bill, list; fate, destiny; many cares, dilemma. **Measures,** TU: rule, regulation, limit, test; interval in music; capacity, endurance.

Deliberate, YI: consult, discuss, criticize; weigh the options and find the best course; arrange, select; laws, rules. The ideogram: words and right. **Actualize-tao,** TE: realize tao in action; power, virtue; ability to follow the course traced by the ongoing process of the cosmos; keyword. The ideogram: to go, straight, and heart. Linked with acquire, TE, acquiring that which makes a being become what it is meant to be. **Move,** HSING: move or move something; motivate, emotionally moving; walk, act, do. The ideogram: stepping left then right.

● *Image Tradition*

Articulating, Growing. [I]
Solid[and]Supple apportioning and-also solid acquiring the center.
Bitter Articulating not permitting Trial.
One's tao exhausted indeed.

Stimulating uses movement venturing. [II]
Appropriate situating uses Articulating.
Centering correcting uses interpenetrating.
Heaven, Earth: Articulating and-also
                          the four seasons accomplishing.

Articulating used to pare the measures: [III]
Not injuring property.
Not harming the commoners.

Associated Contexts **[I] Solid[and]Supple,** KANG JOU: field of creative tension between the whole and opened lines and their qualities; field of psychic movement. **Apportion,** FEN: divide for distribution; sort out; allot to. **And-also,** ERH: joins and contrasts two terms. **Solid,** KANG: quality of the whole lines; firm, strong, unyielding, persisting. **Acquire,** TE: obtain the desired object; wish for, desire covetously; gains, possessions. The ideogram: go and obstacle, going through obstacles to the goal. **Center,** CHUNG: inner, central; put in the center; middle, stable point enabling you to face inner and outer changes; middle line of trigram. The ideogram: field divided in two equal parts. Image of Hexagram 61.

One's/one, CH'I: third person pronoun; also: it/its, he/his, she/hers, they/theirs. **Tao:** way or path; ongoing process of being and the course it traces for each specific person or thing; keyword. The ideogram: go and head, leading and the path it creates. **Exhaust,** CH'IUNG: bring to an end; limit, extremity; destitute; investigate exhaustively; end without a new beginning. The ideogram: cave and naked person, bent with disease or old age.

[II] Stimulate, SHUO: rouse to action and good feeling; free from constraint, stir up, urge on; persuade, cheer, delight; set out in words; the Action of the trigram Open, TUI. The ideogram: words and exchange. **Venture,** HSIEN: risk without reserve; key point, point of danger; difficulty, obstruction that must be confronted; water falling and filling

the holes on its way; the Action of the trigram Gorge, K'AN. The ideogram: mound and all or whole, everything engaged at one point.

Appropriate, TANG: suitable; opportune, convenient; adequate, competent; equal to; whole lines in uneven places and opened lines in even places. **Situation**, WEI: place or seat according to rank; post, position, command; right, proper; established, arranged. The ideogram: person and stand, servants in their places.

Centering correcting, CHUNG CHENG: central and correct; make rectifying one-sidedness and error your central concern; reaching a stable center in yourself can correct the situation. **Interpenetrate**, T'UNG: mutually penetrate; permeate, flow through, reach everywhere; see clearly, communicate with.

Heaven, T'IEN: highest; sky, firmament, heavens; power above the human as opposed to earth, TI, below; the Symbol of the trigram Force, CH'IEN. The ideogram: great and the one above. **Earth**, TI: ground on which the human world rests; basis of all things, nourishes all things; the Symbol of the trigram Field, K'UN. **Four seasons**, SSU SHIH: the four dynamic qualities of time that make up the year and the Time Cycle; the right time, in accord with the time; time as sacred; all-encompassing. **Accomplish**, CH'ENG: complete, finish, bring about; perfect, full, whole; play your part, do your duty; mature. The ideogram: weapon and man, able to bear arms, thus fully developed.

[III] Not, PU: simple negative. **Injure**, SHANG: hurt, wound, grieve, distress; mourn, sad at heart, humiliated. **Property**, TS'AI: possessions, goods, substance, wealth. The ideogram: pearl and value.

Harm, HAI: damage, injure, offend; suffer; hurtful, hindrance; fearful, anxious. **Commoners**, MIN: class of workers the state draws on to sustain the social hierarchy; undeveloped potential outside the organized personality.

● *Transforming Lines*

Initial nine

a) **Not issuing-forth-from the door chambers.**
Without fault.

b) **Not issuing-forth-from the door chambers.**
Knowing interpenetrating clogging indeed.

Associated Contexts a) **Issue-forth(-from)**, CH'U: emerge from, come out of, proceed from, spring from; the Action of the trigram Shake, CHEN; contrary of enter, JU. The ideogram: stem with branches and leaves emerging. **Door**, HU: inner door, chamber door; a household; contrasts with gate, MEN, the outer door. **Chambers**, T'ING: family room, courtyard, hall; domestic. The ideogram: shelter and hall, a secure place.

    Without fault, WU CHIU: no error or harm in the situation.

b) **Know**, CHIH: understand, perceive, remember; informed, aware, wise. The ideogram: arrow and mouth, words focused and swift. **Clog**, SAI: stop up, fill up, close, obstruct, hinder, prevent; unintelligent, dull, hard to understand.

Nine at-second

a) Not issuing-forth-from the gate chambers.
    Pitfall.

b) Not issuing-forth-from the gate chambers, pitfall.
    Letting-go the season end indeed.

Associated Contexts a) **Issue-forth(-from)**, CH'U: emerge from, come out of, proceed from, spring from; the Action of the trigram Shake, CHEN; contrary of enter, JU. The ideogram: stem with branches and leaves emerging. **Gate,** MEN: outer door, between courtyard and street; a text or master as gate to a school of thought. **Chambers**, T'ING: family room, courtyard, hall; domestic. The ideogram: shelter and hall, a secure place.

    Pitfall, HSIUNG: leads away from the experience of meaning; stuck and exposed to danger, unable to take in the situation; flow of life and spirit is blocked; unfortunate, baleful; keyword.

b) **Let-go**, SHIH: lose, omit, miss, fail, let slip; out of control. The ideogram: drop from the hand. **End**, CHI: last or highest point; final, extreme; on the verge; ridgepole of a house.

Six at-third

a) **Not the Articulating like, by-consequence the lamenting like.**
    Without fault.

b) **Not Articulating's lamenting.**
   Furthermore whose fault indeed?

Associated Contexts a) **Like**, JO: same as; just as, similar to. **By-consequence(-of)**, TSE: very strong connection; reason, cause, result; rule, law, pattern, standard; therefore. **Lament**, CHÜEH: express intense regret or sorrow; mourn over; painful recollections.
   Without fault, WU CHIU: no error or harm in the situation.

b) **'s/have(it)/it/them**, CHIH: expresses possession, directly or as an object pronoun.
   Furthermore, YU: in addition to; higher degree of. **Whose**, SHUI: relative and interrogative pronoun; also: whose? **Fault**, CHIU: unworthy conduct that leads to harm, illness, misfortune. The ideogram: person and differ, differ from what you should be.

Six at-fourth

a) **Quiet Articulating Growing.**

b) **Quiet Articulating's Growing.**
   Receiving tao above indeed.

Associated Contexts a) **Quiet**, AN: peaceful, still, settled; calm, tranquilize. The ideogram: woman under a roof, a tranquil home.

b) **'s/have(it)/it/them**, CHIH: expresses possession, directly or as an object pronoun.
   Receive, CH'ENG: receive gifts or commands from superiors or customers; take in hand; catch falling water. The ideogram: accepting a seal of office.

Nine at-fifth

a) **Sweet Articulating significant.**
   Going possesses honor.

b) **Sweet Articulating's significance.**
   Residing-in the situation: centering indeed.

Associated Contexts a) **Sweet**, KAN: taste corresponding to the Earthy Moment; agreeable, happy, delightful, refreshing; grateful. **Significant**, CHI: leads to the experience of meaning; favorable, propitious, advantageous, appropriate; keyword. The ideogram: scholar and mouth, wise words of a sage.

Go, WANG, and come, LAI, describe the stream of time as it flows from future through present to past; go, WANG, indicates what is departing from present to past; proceed, move on; keyword. **Honor,** SHANG: esteem, give high rank to; eminent; put one thing on top of another.

b) **'s/have(it)/it/them**, CHIH: expresses possession, directly or as an object pronoun.

Reside(-in), CHÜ: dwell, live in, stay; sit down, fill an office; settled parts of a country. The ideogram: body and seat.

Six above

a) **Bitter Articulating, Trial: pitfall.**
   Repenting extinguished.

b) **Bitter Articulating, Trial: pitfall.**
   One's tao exhausted indeed.

Associated Contexts a) **Pitfall**, HSIUNG: leads away from the experience of meaning; stuck and exposed to danger, unable to take in the situation; flow of life and spirit is blocked; unfortunate, baleful; keyword.

Repenting extinguished, HUI WANG: previous troubles and consequent remorse will disappear.

61

CENTERING CONFORMING ▪
CHUNG FU

This hexagram describes your situation in terms of the relation between your inner core and the circumstances of your life. It emphasizes that bringing your central concerns and your life situation into a sincere and reliable accord is the adequate way to handle it. To be in accord with the time, you are told to: **center conforming**!

- *Image of the Situation*

> **Centering Conforming, hog fish significant.**
> **Harvesting: wading the Great River.**
> **Harvesting Trial.**

Associated Contexts **Center**, CHUNG: inner, central; calm, stable; put in the center; stable point which enables you to face inner and outer changes; middle line of trigram. The ideogram: field divided in two equal parts. **Conforming**, FU: accord between inner and outer in a particular moment; sincere, truthful, verified, reliable, in accord with the spirits; capture; prisoners, spoils; contrasts with trustworthy, HSIN, consistent over time. The ideogram: bird's claw enclosing young animals, possessive grip. **Hog fish**, T'UN YÜ: aquatic mammals; porpoise, dolphin; intelligent aquatic animals whose development parallels the human; sign of abundance and good luck. **Significant**, CHI: leads to the experience of meaning; favorable, propitious, advantageous, appropriate; keyword. The ideogram: scholar and mouth, wise words of a sage.

    Harvest, LI: advantageous, profitable; acute, insightful; benefit, nourish; third stage of the Time Cycle. **Wading the Great River**, SHE TA CH'UAN: consciously moving into the flow of time; enter the stream of life with a goal or purpose; embark on a significant enterprise.

    Harvesting Trial, LI CHEN: advantageous divination; putting the action in question to the test is beneficial.

- *Outer and Inner Aspects*

☴ **Ground**: Wind and wood subtly enter from the ground, penetrating and pervading. **Ground** is the center of the yang hemicycle, spreading pervasive action.

Connection to the outer: penetrating and bringing together, the Woody Moment culminating. **Ground** pervades, matches and couples, seeding a new generation.

☱ **Open**: vapor rising from the marsh's open surface stimulates and fertilizes; stimulating words cheer and inspire. **Open** begins the yin hemicycle by initiating the formative process.

Connection to the inner: liquifying, casting, skinning off the mold, the Metallic Moment beginning. **Open** stimulates, cheers and reveals innate form.

The open **center** stimulates **conforming** by penetrating and coupling the outer and the inner.

- *Counter Indications*

Nuclear trigrams **Bound**, KEN, and **Shake**, CHEN, result in Counter Hexagram 27, **Jaws/Swallowing**, YI. Creating **conforming** between the **center** and the outer situation is contrasted with **swallowing** outer things to take them in.

- *Sequence*

Articulating and-also trusting it.
Anterior acquiescence has the use-of Centering Conforming.

Associated Contexts **Articulate**, CHIEH: separate and distinguish, as well as join, different things; express thought through speech; joint, section, chapter, interval, unit of time; zodiacal sign; moderate, regulate; lit.: nodes on bamboo stalks. Image of Hexagram 60. **And-also**, ERH: joins and contrasts two terms. **Trust(worthy)**, HSIN: truthful, faithful, consistent over time; integrity; confide in, follow; credentials; contrasts with conforming, FU, connection in a specific moment. The ideogram: person and word, true speech. **It/them/have(-it)/'s**, CHIH: expresses possession, directly or as an object pronoun.

Anterior ... the use-of: activating this hexagram depends on understanding and accepting the previous statement.

- *Contrasted Definitions*

Small Exceeding: Excess indeed.
Centering Conforming: trustworthiness indeed.

Associated Contexts **Small**, HSIAO: little, common, unimportant; adapting to what crosses your path; ability to move in harmony with the vicissitudes of life; contrasts with great, TA, self-imposed theme or goal; keyword. **Exceed**, KU: go beyond, pass by, pass over; excessive, transgress; error, fault. **Small Exceeding** is the Image of Hexagram 62. **Indeed**, YEH: intensifier; indicates comment on previous statement.

- *Symbol Tradition*

Above marsh possessing wind. Centering Conforming.
A chün tzu uses deliberating litigating to delay dying.

Associated Contexts **Above**, SHANG: anything above, in all senses; higher, upper, outer; upper trigram; opposite of below, HSIA. **Marsh**, TSE: open surface of a flat body of water and the vapors rising from it; fertilize, enrich; kindness, favor; the Symbol of the trigram Open, TUI. **Possess**, YU: in possession of, have, own; opposite of lack, WU. **Wind**, FENG: moving air, breeze, gust; weather and its influence on mood and humor; fashion, usage; wind and wood are the Symbols of the trigram Ground, SUN.

Chün tzu: ideal of a person who uses divination to order his/her life in accordance with tao rather than wilful intention; keyword. **Use(-of)**, YI: make use of, by means of, owing to; employ, make functional. **Deliberate**, YI: consult, discuss, criticize; weigh the options and find the best course; arrange, select; laws, rules. The ideogram: words and right. **Litigate**, YÜ: legal proceedings; take a case to court. The ideogram: two dogs and words, barking arguments at each other. **Delay**, HUAN: retard, put off; let things take their course, tie loosely; gradually, leisurely; lax, tardy, negligent. **Die**, SSU: sudden or untimely death; run out of energy; immobile, fixed.

● *Image Tradition*

> **Centering Conforming. [I]**
> **Supple located inside and-also solid acquiring the center.**
> **Stimulating and-also Ground: Conforming.**
> **Thereupon changing the fiefdoms indeed.**
>
> **Hog fish significant. [II]**
> **Trustworthiness extending-to hog fish indeed.**
> **Harvesting: wading the Great River.**
> **Riding a wooden dug-out, emptiness indeed.**
>
> **Centering Conforming uses Harvesting Trial. [III]**
> **Thereupon corresponding reaching-to heaven indeed.**

Associated Contexts **[I] Supple**, JOU: quality of the opened lines; flexible, pliant, tender, adaptable. **Locate(-in)**, TSAI: live in, dwell, reside; belong to, involved with, depend on; within. The ideogram: earth and persevere, place on the earth. **Inside**, NEI: within, inner, interior; inside of the house and those who work there, particularly women; the lower trigram, as opposed to outside, WAI, the upper. The ideogram: border and enter, cross a border. **Solid**, KANG: quality of the whole lines; firm, strong, unyielding, persisting. **Acquire**, TE: obtain the desired object; wish for, desire covetously; gains, possessions. The ideogram: go and obstacle, going through obstacles to the goal.

Stimulate, SHUO: rouse to action and good feeling; free from constraint, stir up, urge on; persuade, cheer, delight; set out in words; the Action of the trigram Open, TUI. The ideogram: words and exchange. **Ground**, SUN: base on which things rest; support, foundation; mild, subtly penetrating; nourishing. The ideogram: stand and things arranged on it, the subtle influence of the ground. Image of Hexagram 57.

Thereupon, NAI: on that ground, because of. **Change**, HUA: gradual, continuous metamorphosis; influence someone; contrasts with transform, PIEN, sudden mutation. The ideogram: person alive and dead, the life-process. **Fiefdom**, PANG: region governed by a feudatory, an order of nobility.

[II] Extend(-to), CHI: reach to, draw out, prolong; continuous, enduring.

Ride, CH'ENG: ride an animal or a chariot; have the upper hand, seize the right time; control strong power; overcome the nature of the other;

supple opened line above a solid whole line. **Wood/tree**, MU: all things woody or wooden, alive or constructed from wood; associated with the Woody Moment; wood and wind are the Symbols of the trigram Ground, SUN. The ideogram: a tree with roots and branches. **Dug-out**, CHOU: hollowed log, canoe; boat, ride or transport by boat. **Empty**, HSÜ: no images or concepts; vacant, unsubstantial; empty yet fertile space.

[III] **Correspond(-to)**, YING: be in agreement or harmony; resonate together, invoke and fulfill each other; answer to, suitable; relation between the lines (1:4, 2:5, 3:6) when they form the pair opened and whole, supple and solid. The ideogram: heart and obey. **Reach(-to)**, HU: arrive at a goal; reach toward and achieve; connect; contrasts with tend-towards, YU. **Heaven**, T'IEN: highest; sky, firmament, heavens; power above the human as opposed to earth, TI, below; the Symbol of the trigram Force, CH'IEN. The ideogram: great and the one above.

- *Tranforming Lines*

    Initial nine

    a) **Precaution significant.**
    Possessing this, not a swallow.

    b) **The initial nine, precaution significant.**
    Purpose not-yet transformed indeed.

Associated Contexts a) **Precaution**, YÜ: provide against, preventive measures; anxious, vigilant, ready; preoccupied with, think about, expect; mishap, accident.
    This, T'A: specifically this thing. The ideogram: person and indeed. **Not**, PU: simple negative. **Swallow**, YEN: house swallow, martin, swift; retired from official life; easy, peaceful, private; give a feast; relation between elder and younger brother.

b) **Purpose**, CHIH: focus of mind and heart; will, inclination, resolve. The ideogram: heart and scholar, high inner resolve, or heart and go, inner determination. **Not-yet**, WEI: temporal negative; something will but has not yet occurred; contrary of already, CHI. Image of Hexagram 64. **Transform**, PIEN: abrupt, radical, fundamental mutation from one state of being to another; transformation of lines in hexagrams; contrasts with change, HUA, gradual metamorphosis.

Nine at-second

a) **Calling crane located-in yin.
One's sonhood harmonizing it.
I possess a loved wine-cup.
Myself associating, simply spilling it.**

b) **One's sonhood harmonizing it.
Centering the heart desiring indeed.**

Associated Contexts a) **Call**, MING: bird and animal cries, through which they recognize each other; distinctive sound, song, statement. The ideogram: bird and mouth, a distinguishing call. **Crane**, HAO: large wading birds; sign of long life, wisdom and bliss; messenger to the immortals; relation between father and son. **Yin**: Struction; consolidating, shadowy aspect of phenomena: conserves, substantializes, creates structures; spacial extension; limited, bound, given specific being; build, make something concrete.

One's/one, CH'I: third person pronoun; also: it/its, he/his, she/hers, they/theirs. **Son(hood)**, TZU: living up to ideal of ancestors as highest human development; act with concern and reverence; male child; offspring, posterity; seed, kernel, egg; sage, teacher; nadir, deepest point, midnight, mid-winter. **Harmony**, HO: concord, union; conciliate; at peace, mild; fit, tune, adjust.

I/me/my, WO: first person pronoun; indicates an unusually strong emphasis on your own subjective experience. **Love**, HAO: affection; fond of, take pleasure in; fine, graceful. **Wine-cup**, CHIO: libation cup originally in the form of a bird; all small birds; rank of nobility, confer rank on someone.

Myself, WU: first person intensifier; the particular person I am. **Associate(-with)**, YÜ: consort with, combine; companions; group, band, company; agree with, comply, help. The ideogram: pair of hands reaching downward meets a pair of hands reaching upward, helpful association. **Simply**, ERH: just so, only. **Spill**, MI: pour out; disperse, spread; waste, overturn; fleeing soldiers; showy, extravagant.

b) **Heart**, HSIN: heart as center of being; seat of mind's images and affections; moral nature; source of desires, intentions, will. **Desire**, YÜAN: wish, hope or long for; covet; desired object.

Six at-third

a) Acquiring antagonism.
Maybe drumbeating, maybe desisting.
Maybe weeping, maybe singing.

b) Maybe drumbeating, maybe desisting.
Situation not appropriate indeed.

Associated Contexts a) **Antagonistic**, TI: opposed and equal; competitor, enemy; a contest between equals.

Maybe, HUO: possible but not certain, perhaps. **Drumbeating**, KU: skin or earthenware drums; play a drum; excite, arouse, encourage; joyous, happy. **Desist**, PA: cease, leave off, discontinue, finish; enough.

Weep, CH'I: lament wordlessly; grieved, heart-broken. **Sing**, KO: chant, sing elegies, sad or mournful songs; associated with the Earthy Moment, turning from yang to yin.

b) **Situation**, WEI: place or seat according to rank; post, position, command; right, proper; established, arranged. The ideogram: person and stand, servants in their places. **Not**, PU: simple negative. **Appropriate**, TANG: suitable; opportune, convenient; adequate, competent; equal to; whole lines in uneven places and opened lines in even places.

Six at-fourth

a) The moon almost facing.
The horse team extinguished.
Without fault.

b) The horse team extinguished.
Cutting-off the above, sorting indeed.

Associated Contexts a) **Moon**, YÜEH: actual moon and moon-month; yin, the sun being yang. **Almost**, CHI: nearly, about to; subtle, almost imperceptible; the first sign. **Face**, WANG: full moon; moon directly facing the sun; 15th day of the moon-month; look at hopefully.

Horse, MA: symbol of spirited strength in the natural world, counterpart of dragon, LUNG; associated with the trigram Force, CH'IEN, heaven, T'IEN, and high noon. **Team**, P'I: pair, matched horses; fellow, mate; united. **Extinguish**, WANG: ruin, destroy; gone, dead, lost without trace; extinct, forgotten, out of mind. The ideogram: person concealed by a wall, out of sight.

Without fault, WU CHIU: no error or harm in the situation.

b) **Cut-off**, CHÜEH: cut short, interrupt, disconnect, break off, sever; destroy, renounce; alienated. The ideogram: silk, knife and knot, cutting through. **Sort**, LEI: group according to kind, class with; like nature or purpose; species, class, genus.

Nine at-fifth

a) **Possessing conformity, binding thus.**
   Without fault.

b) **Possessing conformity, binding thus.**
   Situation correcting appropriate indeed.

Associated Contexts a) **Possessing conformity**, YU FU: inner and outer are in accord; confidence of the spirits has been captured; sincere, truthful; proper to take action. **Bind**, LÜAN: tie, connect, take hold of; bent, contracted. The ideogram: hand and connect, binding things. **Thus,** JU: as, in this way.
   Without fault, WU CHIU: no error or harm in the situation.

b) **Situation**, WEI: place or seat according to rank; post, position, command; right, proper; established, arranged. The ideogram: person and stand, servants in their places. **Correct**, CHENG: rectify deviation or one-sidedness; proper, straight, exact, regular; constant, rule, model. The ideogram: stop and one, hold to one thing. **Appropriate**, TANG: suitable; opportune, convenient; adequate, competent; equal to; whole lines in uneven places and opened lines in even places.

Nine above

a) **A soaring sound mounting, tending-towards heaven.**
   Trial: pitfall.

b) **A soaring sound mounting, tending-towards heaven.**
   Wherefore permitting long-living indeed?

Associated Contexts a) **Soar**, HAN: fly high; rising sun, the firebird with red plumage; trunk or stem of a plant; vertical support. The ideogram: feathers and dawn. **Sound**, YIN: any sound, particularly music; pronunciation of words. The ideogram: words and hold in the mouth,

vocal sound. **Mount**, TENG: ascend, step up; ripen, complete. **Tend-towards**, YÜ: move toward but not reach, in the direction of; contrasts with reach(-to), HU, actually arriving.

Trial, CHEN: test by ordeal; inquiry by divination and its result; righteous, firm; separating wheat from chaff; the kernel, the proven core; fourth stage of the Time Cycle. The ideogram: pearl and divination. **Pitfall**, HSIUNG: leads away from the experience of meaning; stuck and exposed to danger, unable to take in the situation; flow of life and spirit is blocked; unfortunate, baleful; keyword.

b) **Wherefore**, HO: interrogative: why? for what reason? what is? and affirmation: therefore, for that reason. **Permit**, K'O: possible because in harmony with an inherent principle. The ideogram: mouth and breath, silent consent. **Long-living**, CHANG: enduring, constant; senior, superior, greater; increase, prosper; respect, elevate.

62

SMALL EXCEEDING ▪

HSIAO KUO

This hexagram describes your situation in terms of an overwhelming variety of encounters and details. It emphasizes that an excessive concern with adapting yourself to these inner and outer events is the adequate way to handle it. To be in accord with the time, you are told to: be **excessively small!**

● *Image of the Situation*

> **Small Exceeding, Growing.**
> **Harvesting Trial.**
> **Permitting Small Affairs. Not permitting Great Affairs.**
> **Flying bird: abandoning's sound.**
> **Above not proper, below proper.**
> **The great significant.**

Associated Contexts **Small**, HSIAO: little, common, unimportant; adapting to what crosses your path; ability to move in harmonious relation to the vicissitudes of life; contrasts with great, TA, self-imposed theme or goal; keyword. **Exceed**, KU: go beyond, pass by, pass over; excessive, transgress; error, fault. **Grow**, HENG: success through a sacrifice; pervade, persevere; bring to full growth; enjoy; vigorous, effective; second stage of the Time Cycle.

Harvesting Trial, LI CHEN: advantageous divination; putting the action in question to the test is beneficial.

Permit, K'O: possible because in harmony with an inherent principle. The ideogram: mouth and breath, silent consent. **Affairs**, SHIH: all kinds of personal activity; matters at hand; business, occupation; manage a business, case in court. **Not permitting**, PU K'O: not possible; contradicts an inherent principle. **Great**, TA: big, noble, important, very; orient the will toward a self-imposed goal, impose direction; ability to lead or guide your life; contrasts with small, HSIAO, flexible adaptation to what crosses your path; keyword. Image of Hexagrams 14, 26, 28, 34.

Fly, FEI: spread your wings, fly away; let free; swift. **Bird**, NIAO: all feathered animals; associated with the Fiery Moment. **Abandon**, YI: leave behind, forget; die; lose through unawareness. The ideogram: go and value, value is gone. **'s/have(-it)/it/them**, CHIH: expresses possession, directly or as an object pronoun. **Sound**, YIN: any sound, particularly music; pronunciation of words. The ideogram: words and hold in the mouth, vocal sound.

Above, SHANG: anything above, in all senses; higher, upper, outer; upper trigram; opposite of below, HSIA. **Not**, PU: simple negative. **Proper**, YI: reasonable of itself; fit and right, harmonious; ought, should. **Below**, HSIA: anything below, in all senses; lower, inner; lower trigram; opposite of above, SHANG.

Significant, CHI: leads to the experience of meaning; favorable, propitious, advantageous, appropriate; keyword. The ideogram: scholar and mouth, wise words of a sage.

- *Outer and Inner Aspects*

⚏ **Shake**: Thunder rises from below, shaking and stirring things up. **Shake** begins the yang hemicycle by germinating new action.

Connection to the outer: sprouting energies thrusting from below, the Woody Moment beginning. **Shake** stirs things up to issue-forth.

⚏ **Bound**: Mountains bound, limit and set a place off, stopping forward movement. **Bound** completes a full yin-yang cycle.

Connection to the inner: accomplishing words, which express things. **Bound** articulates what is complete to suggest what is beginning.

Previous accomplishment limits outer stirring-up through an **exceeding** concern with the **small**.

- *Counter Indications*

Nuclear trigrams **Open**, TUI, and **Ground**, SUN, result in Counter Hexagram 28, **Great Exceeding**, TA KUO. An **excessive** concern with adapting through the **small** is contrasted with an **excessive** concern with imposing a **great** idea on things.

- *Sequence*

> Possessing one's trustworthiness implies necessarily moving it.
> Anterior acquiescence has the use-of Small Exceeding.

Associated Contexts **Possess**, YU: in possession of, have, own; opposite of lack, WU. **One's/one**, CH'I: third person pronoun; also: it/its, he/his, she/hers, they/theirs. **Trustworthy**, HSIN: truthful, faithful, consistent over time; integrity; confide in, follow; credentials; contrasts with conforming, FU, connection in a specific moment. The ideogram: person and word, true speech. **Imply**, CHE: further signify; additional meaning. **Necessarily**, PI: unavoidably, indispensably, certainly. **Move**, HSING: move or move something; motivate, emotionally moving; walk, act, do. The ideogram: stepping left then right.

    Anterior ... the use-of: activating this hexagram depends on understanding and accepting the previous statement.

- *Contrasted Definitions*

> Small Exceeding: Excess indeed.
> Centering Conforming: trustworthiness indeed.

Associated Contexts **Indeed**, YEH: intensifier; indicates comment on previous statement.

    Center, CHUNG: inner, central; put in the center; middle, stable point enabling you to face inner and outer changes; middle line of trigram. The ideogram: field divided in two equal parts. **Conforming**, FU: accord between inner and outer in a particular moment; sincere, truthful, verified, reliable, in accord with the spirits; capture; prisoners, spoils; contrasts with trustworthy, HSIN, consistent over time. The ideogram: bird's claw enclosing young animals, possessive grip. **Centering Conforming** is the Image of Hexagram 61.

- *Symbol Tradition*

> Above mountain possessing thunder. Small Exceeding.
> A chün tzu uses moving Exceeding to reach-to courtesy.
> [A chün tzu uses] losing Exceeding to reach-to mourning.
> [A chün tzu uses] availing-of Exceeding to reach-to parsimony.

Associated Contexts **Mountain**, SHAN: limit, boundary; the Symbol of the trigram Bound, KEN. The ideogram: three peaks, a mountain range. **Thunder**, LEI: rising, arousing power; the Symbol of the trigram Shake, CHEN.

Chün tzu: ideal of a person who uses divination to order his/her life in accordance with tao rather than wilful intention; keyword. **Use(-of)**, YI: make use of, by means of, owing to; employ, make functional. **Reach(-to)**, HU: arrive at a goal; reach towards and achieve; connect; contrasts with tend-towards, YU. **Courtesy**, KUNG: display respect, treat courteously, show reverence; affable, decorous, modest, polite; obsequious.

Lose, SANG: fail to obtain, cease, become obscure; forgotten, destroyed; lament, mourn; funeral. The ideogram: weep and the dead. **Mourn**, AI: grieve, lament over something gone; distress, sorrow; compassion. The ideogram: mouth and clothes, display of feelings.

Avail-of, YUNG: take advantage of; benefit from, profit by; use for a specific purpose; apply to advantage. The ideogram: to divine and center, applying divination to central concerns. **Parsimonious**, CHIEN: thrifty; moderate, temperate; stingy, scanty.

- *Image Tradition*

> **Small Exceeding. [I]**
> **Small implies Exceeding and-also Growing indeed.**
> **Exceeding uses Harvesting Trial.**
> **Associating-with the season moving indeed.**
>
> **Supple acquiring the center. [II]**
> **That uses Small Affairs, significant indeed.**
> **Solid letting-go the situation and-also not centering.**
> **That uses not permitting Great Affairs indeed.**
>
> **Possessing the flying bird's symbol in-truth. [III]**
> **Flying bird: abandoning's sound.**
> **Above not proper, below proper.**
> **The great significant.**
> **Countering above and-also yielding below indeed.**

Associated Contexts [I] **And-also**, ERH: joins and contrasts two terms.

Associate(-with), YÜ: consort with, combine; companions; group, band, company; agree with, comply, help. The ideogram: pair of hands reaching downward meets a pair of hands reaching upward, helpful association. **Season**, SHIH: quality of the time; the right time, opportune, in harmony; planning in accord with the time; seasons of the year. The ideogram: sun and temple, time as sacred.

[II] Supple, JOU: quality of the opened lines; flexible, pliant, tender, adaptable. **Acquire**, TE: obtain the desired object; wish for, desire covetously; gains, possessions. The ideogram: go and obstacle, going through obstacles to the goal.

That uses, SHIH YI: involves and is involved by.

Solid, KANG: quality of the whole lines; firm, strong, unyielding, persisting. **Let-go**, SHIH: lose, omit, miss, fail, let slip; out of control. The ideogram: drop from the hand. **Situation**, WEI: place or seat according to rank; post, position, command; right, proper; established, arranged. The ideogram: person and stand, servants in their places. **Not**, PU: simple negative.

[III] Symbol, HSIANG: image invested with intrinsic power to connect visible and invisible; magic spell; figure, form, shape, likeness; pattern, model; create an image, imitate; act, play; writing. **In-truth**, YEN: statement is complete and correct.

Counter, NI: oppose, resist, seek out; contrary, rebellious, refractory. The ideogram: go and rise against, active revolt. **Yield(-to)**, SHUN: give way and bear produce; comply, agree, follow, obey; unresisting, docile, flexible; nourish, provide; the Action of the trigram Field, K'UN. The ideogram: head and current, water flowing from the head of a river, yielding to the banks.

● *Transforming Lines*

Initial six

a) **Flying bird: using a pitfall.**

b) **Flying bird: using a pitfall.**
Wherefore not permitted thus indeed.

Associated Contexts a) **Pitfall,** HSIUNG: leads away from the experience of meaning; stuck and exposed to danger, unable to take in the situation; flow of life and spirit is blocked; unfortunate, baleful; keyword.

b) **Wherefore,** HO: interrogative: why? for what reason? what is? and affirmation: therefore, for that reason. **Thus,** JU: as, in this way.

Six at-second

a) **Exceeding one's grandfather.**
Meeting one's grandmother.
Not extending-to one's chief.
Meeting one's servant.
Without fault.

b) **Not extending-to one's chief.**
A servant not permitted Exceeding indeed.

Associated Contexts a) **Grandfather,** TSU: second ancestor generation; deceased grandfather, honored more than actual father. **Meet,** YÜ: come on unexpectedly, encounter; occur, happen; pleasant meeting, lucky coincidence; agree.
Grandmother, PI: second ancestor generation; deceased grandmother, venerated as source of her many descendants.
Extend(-to), CHI: reach to, draw out, prolong; continuous, enduring.
Chief, CHÜN: effective ruler; preside over, take the lead; influence others; term of respect. The ideogram: mouth and director, giving orders.
Servant, CH'EN: attendant, minister, vassal; courtier who can speak to the sovereign; wait on, serve in office. The ideogram: person bowing low.
Without fault, WU CHIU: no error or harm in the situation.

Nine at-third

a) **Nowhere Exceeding defending-against it.**
Adhering, maybe killing it.
Pitfall.

b) **Adhering, maybe killing it.**
Wherefore a pitfall thus indeed.

Associated Contexts a) **Nothing/nowhere,** FU: strong negative; not a single thing/place. **Defend-against,** FANG: keep off, protect from, guard against; erect a protective barrier. The ideogram: open space and earthen ramparts.

Adhere(-to), TS'UNG: follow a way, hold to a doctrine, school, or person; hear and comply with, agree to; forced to follow, follower. The ideogram: two men walking, one following the other. **Maybe**, HUO: possible but not certain, perhaps. **Kill**, CH'IANG: put to death; violent assault; maltreat, misuse; kill an important person.

Pitfall, HSIUNG: leads away from the experience of meaning; stuck and exposed to danger, unable to take in the situation; flow of life and spirit is blocked; unfortunate, baleful; keyword.

b) **Wherefore**, HO: interrogative: why? for what reason? what is? and affirmation: therefore, for that reason. **Thus**, JU: as, in this way.

Nine at-fourth

a) **Without fault.**
   Nowhere Exceeding meeting it.
   Going adversity necessarily warning.
   No availing-of perpetual Trial.

b) **Nowhere Exceeding meeting it.**
   Situation not appropriate indeed.
   Going adversity necessarily warning.
   Completing not permitting long-living indeed.

Associated Contexts a) **Without fault**, WU CHIU: no error or harm in the situation.

Nothing/nowhere, FU: strong negative; not a single thing/place. **Meet**, YÜ: come on unexpectedly, encounter; occur, happen; pleasant meeting, lucky coincidence; agree.

Go, WANG, and come, LAI, describe the stream of time as it flows from future through present to past; go, WANG, indicates what is departing from present to past; proceed, move on; keyword. **Adversity**, LI: danger; threatening, malevolent demon. This has two aspects: grind, sharpen, improve, perfect, stimulate; and: poisonous, sinister, cruel, contrary. It indicates a spirit or ghost that seeks revenge by inflicting suffering upon the living. Pacifying or exorcizing such a spirit can have a healing effect. The ideogram: sheltering cliff and stinging insect. **Warn**, CHIEH: alert, alarm, put on guard; caution, inform; guard against, refrain from (as in a diet). The ideogram: spear held in both hands, warning enemies and alerting friends.

No, WU: simple negative; un-, dis-. **Perpetual**, YUNG: continuing; everlasting, ever-flowing. The ideogram: flowing water. **Trial**, CHEN: test by ordeal; inquiry by divination and its result; righteous, firm; separating wheat from chaff; the kernel, the proven core; fourth stage of the Time Cycle. The ideogram: pearl and divination.

b) **Appropriate**, TANG: suitable; opportune, convenient; adequate, competent; equal to; whole lines in uneven places and opened lines in even places.

Complete, CHUNG: end of a cycle that begins the next; last, whole, all; contrasts with exhaust, CH'IUNG, final end. The ideogram: silk cocoons, follow and ice, winter linking one year with the next. **Long-living**, CHANG: enduring, constant; senior, superior, greater; increase, prosper; respect, elevate.

Six at-fifth

a) Shrouding clouds, not raining.
　Originating-from my Western suburbs.
　A prince, a string-arrow grasping another located-in a cave.

b) Shrouding clouds, not raining.
　Above climaxing indeed.

Associated Contexts a) **Shroud**, MI: dense, close together, thick, tight; hidden, secret; retired, intimate. **Clouds**, YÜN: fog, mist, water vapor; connects to the Streaming Moment and Stream, the Symbol of the trigram Gorge, K'AN. **Rain**, YÜ: all precipitation; sudden showers, fast and furious; associated with the trigram Gorge, K'AN, and the Streaming Moment.

Origin, TZU: source, beginning, ground; cause, reason, motive; line of descent; path to the origin; yourself, intrinsic. **My/me/I**, WO: first person pronoun; indicates an unusually strong emphasis on your own subjective experience. **West**, HSI: corresponds to autumn, Harvest and the Streaming Moment; begins the yin hemicycle of the Universal Compass. **Suburbs**, CHIAO: area adjoining a city where human constructions and nature interpenetrate; second of the territorial zones: city, suburbs, countryside, forests.

Prince, KUNG: nobles acting as ministers of state in the capital; governing from the center rather than active in daily life; contrasts with feudatory, HOU, governors of the provinces. **String-arrow**, YI: arrow with string attached used to retrieve what is shot; seize, appropriate; arrest a criminal. **Grasp**, CH'Ü: lay hold of, take and use, seize, appropriate; grasp the meaning, understand. The ideogram: ear and hand, hear and grasp. **Another**, PEI: yet one more; the other party; exclude, leave out. **Locate(-in)**, TSAI: live in, dwell, reside; belong to, involved with, depend on; within. The ideogram: earth and persevere, place on the earth. **Cave**, HSÜEH: hole used for dwelling; cavern, den, pit; open grave.

b) **Climax**, YI: come to a high point and stop, bring to an end; use up, lay aside; decline, reject.

Six above

a) **Nowhere meeting, Exceeding it.**
Flying bird radiating it.
Pitfall.
That designates Calamity[and]Blunder.

b) **Nowhere meeting, Exceeding it.**
Climaxing overbearing indeed.

Associated Contexts a) **Nothing/nowhere**, FU: strong negative; not a single thing/place. **Meet**, YÜ: come on unexpectedly, encounter; occur; happen; pleasant meeting, lucky coincidence; agree.

Radiance, LI: glowing light, spreading in all directions; light-giving, discriminating, articulating; divide and arrange in order; the power of consciousness. The ideogram: bird and weird, the magical fire-bird with brilliant plumage. Image of Hexagram 30.

Pitfall, HSIUNG: leads away from the experience of meaning; stuck and exposed to danger, unable to take in the situation; flow of life and spirit is blocked; unfortunate, baleful; keyword.

That, SHIH: preceding statement. **Designate**, WEI: represent in words, assign a name or meaning; report on, talk about. The ideogram: words and belly, describing the essential. **Calamity[and]Blunder**, TSAI SHENG: disaster from without and within; natural disaster combined with misfortune due to ignorance or fault; ruin, defeat, rout, collapse.

b) **Climax**, YI: come to a high point and stop, bring to an end; use up, lay aside; decline, reject. **Overbearing**, K'ANG: excessive, overpowering authority; disparage; rigid, unbending; excessive display of force.

63

ALREADY FORDING ▮
CHI CHI

This hexagram describes your situation in terms of an important move from one position to another. It emphasizes that actively proceeding with the crossing is the adequate way to handle it. To be in accord with the time, you are told to: **already ford** the stream of events!

● *Image of the Situation*

> **Already Fording. Growing: the small.**
> **Harvesting Trial.**
> **Initially significant.**
> **Completing: disarraying.**

Associated Contexts **Already**, CHI: completed, done, has occurred; past tense, contrary of not-yet, WEI. **Ford**, CHI: cross a river at a ford or shallow place; overcome an obstacle, embark on a course of action; help, relieve; cease. The ideogram: water and level, running smooth over a flat bottom. **Grow**, HENG: success through a sacrifice; pervade, persevere; bring to full growth; enjoy; vigorous, effective; second stage of the Time Cycle. **Small**, HSIAO: little, common, unimportant; adapting to what crosses your path; ability to move in harmony with the vicissitudes of life; contrasts with great, TA, self-imposed theme or goal; keyword. Image of Hexagrams 9 and 62.

    Harvesting Trial, LI CHEN: advantageous divination; putting the action in question to the test is beneficial.

    Initial, CH'U: first step or part; beginning, incipient; bottom line of hexagram. The ideogram: knife and garment, cutting out the pattern. **Significant**, CHI: leads to the experience of meaning; favorable, propitious, advantageous, appropriate; keyword. The ideogram: scholar and mouth, wise words of a sage.

    Complete, CHUNG: end of a cycle that begins the next; last, whole, all; contrasts with exhaust, CH'IUNG, final end. The ideogram: silk cocoons, follow and ice, winter linking one year with the next. **Disarray**, LUAN: throw into disorder, mislay, confuse; out of place; discord, insurrection, anarchy.

- *Outer and Inner Aspects*

☵ **Gorge**: Stream ventures and falls into the gorge, flowing on through toil and danger. **Gorge** ends the yin hemicycle by leveling and dissolving forms.

Connection to the outer: flooding and leveling dissolve direction and shape, the Streaming Moment. **Gorge** ventures, falls, toils and flows on.

☲ **Radiance**: Fire and brightness radiate light and warmth, attached to their support; congregating people see and become aware. **Radiance** ends the yang hemicycle, consuming action in awareness.

Connection to the inner: light, heat, consciousness bring continual change, the Fiery Moment. **Radiance** spreads outward, congregating, becoming aware and changing.

Inner brightness has joined with outer venturing, **already fording** the stream of events.

- *Counter Indications*

Nuclear trigrams **Radiance**, LI, and **Gorge**, K'AN, result in Counter Hexagram 64, **Not-yet Fording**, WEI CHI. The necessity to expend energy in **already fording** is contrasted with building up potential by **not-yet fording** the stream of events.

- *Sequence*

Possessing Exceeding being implies necessarily Fording.
Anterior acquiescence has the use-of Already Fording.

Associated Contexts **Possess**, YU: in possession of, have, own; opposite of lack, WU. **Exceed**, KU: go beyond, pass by, pass over; excessive, transgress; error, fault. Image of Hexagrams 28 and 62. **Being(s)**, WU: creature, thing, any single being; matter, substance, essence; nature of things. **Imply**, CHE: further signify; additional meaning. **Necessarily**, PI: unavoidably, indispensably, certainly.

Anterior ... the use-of: activating this hexagram depends on understanding and accepting the previous statement.

Contrasted Definitions

> **Already Fording: setting-right indeed.**
> **Not-yet Fording: manhood exhausted indeed.**

Associated Contexts **Set-right**, TING: settle, fix, put in place; at rest, repose. **Indeed**, YEH: intensifier; indicates comment on previous statement.

Not-yet, WEI: temporal negative; something will but has not yet occurred; contrary of already, CHI. **Not-yet Fording** is the Image of Hexagram 64. **Man(hood)**, NAN: a man; what is inherently male. The ideogram: fields and strength, hard labor in the fields. **Exhaust,**, CH'IUNG: bring to an end; limit, extremity; destitute; investigate exhaustively; end without a new beginning. The ideogram: cave and naked person, bent with disease or old age.

Symbol Tradition

> **Stream located above fire. Already Fording.**
> **A chün tzu uses pondering distress and-also**
> > **providing-for defending-against it.**

Associated Contexts **Stream**, SHUI: flowing water; fluid, dissolving; river, tide, flood; the Symbol of the trigram Gorge, K'AN. The ideogram: rippling water. **Locate(-in)**, TSAI: live in, dwell, reside; belong to, involved with, depend on; within. The ideogram: earth and persevere, place on the earth. **Above**, SHANG: anything above, in all senses; higher, upper, outer; upper trigram; opposite of below, HSIA. **Fire**, HUO: warming and consuming aspect of burning; fire and brightness are the Symbols of the trigram Radiance, LI.

Chün tzu: ideal of a person who uses divination to order his/her life in accordance with tao rather than wilful intention; keyword. **Use(-of)**, YI: make use of, by means of, owing to; employ, make functional. **Ponder**, SSU: reflect, consider, remember; deep thought; desire, wish. The ideogram: heart and field, the heart's concerns. **Distress**, HUAN: tribulation, grief, affliction. The ideogram: heart and clamor, the heart distressed. **And-also**, ERH: joins and contrasts two terms. **Provide-for/provision**, YÜ: ready, prepared for; pre-arrange, take precaution, think beforehand; satisfied, contented, at ease. The ideogram: sonhood and elephant, careful, reverent and very strong. Image of Hexagram 16. **Defend-against**, FANG: keep off, protect from, guard against; erect a protective barrier. The ideogram: open space and earthen ramparts. **It/them/have(-it)/'s** CHIH: expresses possession, directly or as an object pronoun.

● *Image Tradition*

> **Already Fording, Growing. [I]**
> **The small implies Growing indeed.**
> **Harvesting Trial.**
> **Solid[and]Supple correcting and-also**
> **the situation appropriate indeed.**
>
> **Initially significant. [II]**
> **Supple acquiring the center indeed.**
> **Completing, stopping by-consequence disarraying.**
> **One's tao exhausted indeed.**

Associated Contexts **[I] Solid[and]Supple**, KANG JOU: field of creative tension between the whole and opened lines and their qualities; field of psychic movement. **Correct**, CHENG: rectify deviation or one-sidedness; proper, straight, exact, regular; constant, rule, model. The ideogram: stop and one, hold to one thing. **Situation**, WEI: place or seat according to rank; post, position, command; right, proper; established, arranged. The ideogram: person and stand, servants in their places. **Appropriate**, TANG: suitable; opportune, convenient; adequate, competent; equal to; whole lines in uneven places and opened lines in even places.

[II] **Supple**, JOU: quality of the opened lines; flexible, pliant, tender, adaptable. **Acquire**, TE: obtain the desired object; wish for, desire covetously; gains, possessions. The ideogram: go and obstacle, going through obstacles to the goal. **Center**, CHUNG: inner, central; put in the center; middle, stable point enabling you to face inner and outer changes; middle line of trigram. The ideogram: field divided in two equal parts. Image of Hexagram 61.

Stop, CHIH: bring or come to a standstill; the Action of the trigram Bound, KEN. The ideogram: a foot stops walking. **By-consequence(-of)**, TSE: very strong connection; reason, cause, result; rule, law, pattern, standard; therefore.

One's/one, CH'I: third person pronoun; also: it/its, he/his, she/hers, they/theirs. **Tao**: way or path; ongoing process of being and the course it traces for each specific person or thing; keyword. The ideogram: go and head, leading and the path it creates.

● *Transforming Lines*

Initial nine

a) **Pulling-back one's wheels.**
Soaking one's tail.
Without fault.

b) **Pulling-back one's wheels.**
Righteous, without fault indeed.

Associated Contexts a) **Pull-back**, YI: pull or drag something toward you; drag behind, take by the hand; leave traces. **Wheel**, LUN: disk, circle, round; revolution, circuit; rotate, roll, by turns.
Soak, JU: immerse, steep; damp, wet; stain, pollute, blemish; urinate on. **Tail**, WEI: animal's tail; last, extreme; remnants, unimportant.
Without fault, WU CHIU: no error or harm in the situation.

b) **Righteous**, YI: proper and just, meets the standards; things in their proper place; the heart that rules itself; upright, moral rule; contrasts with Harvest, LI, advantage or profit.

Six at-second

a) **A wife losing her veil.**
No pursuit.
The seventh day: acquiring.

b) **The seventh day: acquiring.**
Using centering tao indeed.

Associated Contexts a) **Wife**, FU: responsible position of married woman within the household; contrasts with consort, CH'I, her legal position and concubine, CH'IEH, secondary wives. The ideogram: woman, hand and broom, household duties. **Lose**, SANG: fail to obtain, cease, become obscure; forgotten, destroyed; lament, mourn; funeral. The ideogram: weep and the dead. **Her/she**, CH'I: third person pronoun; also: one/one's, it/its, he/his, they/their. **Veil**, FU: screen on person or carriage; hair ornaments; lit.: luxuriant, tangled vegetation that conceals the path.

No, WU: simple negative; un-, dis-. **Pursue**, CHU: chase, follow closely, press hard; expel, drive out. The ideogram: pig (wealth) and go, chasing fortune.

Seven, CH'I: number seven, seventh; seven planets; seventh day when moon changes from crescent to waxing; the Tangram game makes pictures of all phenomena from seven basic shapes. **Day/sun**, JIH: actual sun and the time of a sun-cycle, a day.

Nine at-third

a) **The high ancestor subjugating souls on-all-sides.**
   Three years-revolved controlling it.
   Small People, no availing-of.

b) **Three years-revolved controlling it.**
   Weariness indeed.

Associated Contexts a) **High(-ness)**, KAO: high, elevated, lofty, eminent; excellent, advanced. **Ancestry**, TSUNG: clan, kin, origin; those who bear the same surname; ancestral hall and tablets; honor, revere; a doctrine; contrasts with predecessor, K'AO: individual ancestors. **High Ancestor**, KAO TSUNG, is the ceremonial title of a great Shang emperor (1364–1324 BCE) seen as a model of the just warrior and glorious ruler. His spirit is felt to protect his descendants. **Subjugate**, FA: chastise rebels, make dependent; cut down, subject to rule. The ideogram: man and lance, armed soldiers. **Soul**, KUEI: power that creates individual existence; union of volatile-soul, HUN, spiritual and intellectual power, and dense-soul, P'O: bodily strength and movement. The HUN rises after death, the P'O remains with the body and may communicate with the living. **Sides (on-all-sides)**, FANG: limits, boundaries; square, surface of the earth extending to the four cardinal points; everywhere.

Three, SAN: number three, third time or place; active phases of a cycle; superlative; beginning of repetition. **Years-revolved**, NIEN: number of years elapsed; a person's age; contrasts with year's-time, SUI, length of time in a year. **Control**, K'O: command; check, impede, prevail, obstruct, repress; adequate, able. The ideogram: roof beams support a house, controlling the structure.

Small People, HSIAO JEN: lowly, common, humble; those who adjust

to circumstances with the flexibility of the small; effect of the small within an individual; keyword. **No**, WU: simple negative; un-, dis-. **Avail-of**, YUNG: take advantage of; benefit from, profit by; use for a specific purpose; apply to advantage. The ideogram: to divine and center, applying divination to central concerns.

b) **Weariness**, PAI: fatigue; debilitated, exhausted, distressed; weak.

Six at-fourth

a) **A token: possessing clothes in-tatters.**
Completing the day, a warning.

b) **Completing the day, a warning.**
Possessing a place to doubt indeed.

Associated Contexts a) **Token**, HSÜ: halves of a torn piece of silk which identify the bearers when joined. **Clothes**, YI: upper body garments; dress; cover, husk. **In-tatters**, JU: worn-out garments, used for padding or stopping leaks.

   Day/sun, JIH: actual sun and the time of a sun-cycle, a day. **Warn**, CHIEH: alert, alarm, put on guard; caution, inform; guard against, refrain from (as in a diet). The ideogram: spear held in both hands, warning enemies and alerting friends.

b) **Place**, SO: where something belongs or comes from; residence, dwelling; habitual focus or object. **Doubt**, YI: suspect, distrust; dubious; surmise, conjecture.

Nine at-fifth

a) **The Eastern neighbor slaughters cattle.**
Not thus the Western neighbor's dedicated offering.
The substance: acquiescing-in one's blessing.

b) **The Eastern neighbor slaughters cattle.**
Not thus the Western neighbor's season indeed.
The substance: acquiescing-in one's blessing.
Significant, the great coming indeed.

Associated Contexts a) **East**, TUNG: corresponds to Spring, YÜAN, and the Woody Moment, stirs-up and germinates new life-cycle; place of honor and the person in it. **Neighbor**, LIN: person living nearby; extended family; assist, support. **Slaughter**, SHA: kill, murder, execute; hunt game; mow grass. **Cattle**, NIU: ox, bull, cow, calf; kine; power and strength of work animals.

Not, PU: simple negative. **Thus**, JU: as, in this way. **West**, HSI: corresponds to autumn, Harvest and the Streaming Moment; begins the yin hemicycle of the Universal Compass. **Dedicate**, YO: offering at the spring equinox, when stores were low; offer a sacrifice with limited resources. The ideogram: spring and thin. **Offer**, CHI: gifts to gods and spirits. The ideogram: hand, meat and worship.

Substance, SHIH: real, solid, full; results, fruits, possessions; essence; honest, sincere. The ideogram: string of coins under a roof, riches in the house. **Acquiesce(-in)**, SHOU: accept, make peace with, agree to; at rest, satisfied; patient. **Bless**, FU: heavenly gifts; make happy; spiritual power and goodwill. The ideogram: spirit and plenty, heavenly gifts in abundance.

b) **Season**, SHIH: quality of the time; the right time, opportune, in harmony; planning in accord with the time; seasons of the year. The ideogram: sun and temple, time as sacred.

Great, TA: big, noble, important, very; orient the will toward a self-imposed goal, impose direction; ability to lead or guide your life; contrasts with small, HSIAO, flexible adaptation to what crosses your path; keyword. Image of Hexagrams 14, 26, 28, 34. **Come**, LAI, and go, WANG, describe the stream of time as it flows from future through present to past; come, LAI, indicates what is approaching; move toward, arrive at; keyword.

Six above

a) **Soaking one's head.**
   Adversity.

b) **Soaking one's head, adversity.**
   Wherefore permitting lasting indeed?

Associated Contexts a) **Soak**, JU: damp, wet; immerse, steep; stain, pollute, blemish; urinate on. **Head**, SHOU: literal head; leader, foremost; subject headings; beginning, model; superior, upper, front.

Adversity, LI: danger; threatening, malevolent demon. This has two aspects: grind, sharpen, improve, perfect, stimulate; and: poisonous,

sinister, cruel, contrary. It indicates a spirit or ghost that seeks revenge by inflicting suffering upon the living. Pacifying or exorcizing such a spirit can have a healing effect. The ideogram: sheltering cliff and stinging insect.

b) **Wherefore**, HO: interrogative: why? for what reason? what is? and affirmation: therefore, for that reason. **Permit**, K'O: possible because in harmony with an inherent principle. The ideogram: mouth and breath, silent consent. **Last**, CHIU: long, protracted; enduring.

NOT-YET FORDING ▮ *WEI CHI*

This hexagram describes your situation in terms of being on the edge of an important change of situation. It emphasizes that waiting and accumulating energy to begin the upcoming move is the adequate way to handle it. To be in accord with the time, you are told to: **not-yet ford** the stream of events!

● *Image of the Situation*

> **Not-yet Fording, Growing.**
> **The small fox, a muddy Ford.**
> **Soaking one's tail:**
> **Without direction: Harvesting.**

Associated Contexts **Not-yet**, WEI: temporal negative; incomplete, has not yet occurred; contrary of already, CHI. **Ford**, CHI: cross a river at a ford or shallow place; overcome an obstacle, embark on a course of action; help, relieve; cease. The ideogram: water and level, running smooth over a flat bottom. **Grow**, HENG: success through a sacrifice; pervade, persevere; bring to full growth; enjoy; vigorous, effective; second stage of the Time Cycle.

Small, HSIAO: little, common, unimportant; adapting to what crosses your path; ability to move in harmony with the vicissitudes of life; contrasts with great, TA, self-imposed theme or goal; keyword. Image of Hexagrams 9 and 62. **Fox**, HU: crafty, shape-changing animal; used by spirits, often female; ambivalent night-spirit that can create havoc and bestow abundance. **Mud**, HSI: ground left wet by water, muddy shores; danger; shed tears; nearly. **Soak**, JU: immerse, steep; damp, wet; stain, pollute, blemish; urinate on. **One's/one**, CH'I: third person pronoun; also: it/its, he/his, she/hers, they/theirs. **Tail**, WEI: animal's tail; last, extreme; remnants, unimportant.

Without direction: Harvesting, WU YU LI: no plan or direction is advantageous; in order to take advantage of the situation, do not impose a direction on events.

Outer and Inner Aspects

☲ **Radiance**: Fire and brightness radiate light and warmth, attached to their support; congregating people see and become aware. **Radiance** ends the yang hemicycle, consuming action in awareness.

Connection to the outer: light, heat, consciousness bring continual change, the Fiery Moment. **Radiance** spreads outward, congregating, becoming aware and changing.

☵ **Gorge**: Stream ventures and falls into the gorge, flowing on through toil and danger. **Gorge** ends the yin hemicycle by leveling and dissolving forms.

Connection to the inner: flooding and leveling dissolve direction and shape, the Streaming Moment. **Gorge** ventures, falls, toils and flows on.

Inner venturing blocks outer congregating, **not-yet** accumulating the energy necessary to **ford** the stream of events.

Counter Indications

Nuclear trigrams **Gorge**, K'AN, and **Radiance**, LI, result in Counter Hexagram 63, **Already Fording**, CHI CHI. Accumulating energy for an important move by **not-yet fording** is contrasted with being **already** engaged in **fording** the stream of events.

Sequence

> **Beings not permitted exhaustion indeed.**
> **Anterior acquiescence has the use-of Not-yet Fording**
> **completed in-truth.**

Associated Contexts **Being(s)**, WU: creature, thing, any single being; matter, substance, essence; nature of things. **Not permitting**, PU K'O: not possible; contradicts an inherent principle. The ideogram: mouth and breath, silent consent. **Exhaust**, CH'IUNG: bring to an end; limit, extremity; destitute; investigate exhaustively; end without a new beginning. The ideogram: cave and naked person, bent with disease or old age. **Indeed**, YEH: intensifier; indicates comment on previous statement.

Anterior ... the use-of: activating this hexagram depends on understanding and accepting the previous statement. **Complete**, CHUNG: end of a cycle that begins the next; last, whole, all; contrasts with exhaust, CH'IUNG, final end. The ideogram: silk cocoons, follow and ice, winter linking one year with the next. **In-truth**, YEN: statement is complete and correct.

● *Contrasted Definitions*

> **Already Fording: setting-right indeed.**
> **Not-yet Fording: manhood exhausted indeed.**

Associated Contexts **Already**, CHI: completed, done, has occurred; past tense, contrary of not-yet, WEI. **Already Fording** is the Image of Hexagram 63. **Set-right**, TING: settle, fix, put in place; at rest, repose.

Man(hood), NAN: a man; what is inherently male. The ideogram: fields and strength, hard labor in the fields.

● *Symbol Tradition*

> **Fire located above stream. Not-yet Fording.**
> **A chün tzu uses considering**
> > **to mark-off the beings residing on-all-sides.**

Associated Contexts **Fire**, HUO: warming and consuming aspect of burning; fire and brightness are the Symbols of the trigram Radiance, LI. **Locate(-in)**, TSAI: live in, dwell, reside; belong to, involved with, depend on; within. The ideogram: earth and persevere, place on the earth. **Above**, SHANG: anything above, in all senses; higher, upper, outer; upper trigram; opposite of below, HSIA. **Stream**, SHUI: flowing water; fluid, dissolving; river, tide, flood; the Symbol of the trigram Gorge, K'AN. The ideogram: rippling water.

Chün tzu: ideal of a person who uses divination to order his/her life in accordance with tao rather than wilful intention; keyword. **Use(-of)**, YI: make use of, by means of, owing to; employ, make functional. **Consider**, SHEN: act carefully, seriously; cautious, attentive, circumspect; still, quiet, sincere. The ideogram: heart and true. **Mark-off**, PIEN: distinguish by dividing; mark off a plot of land; frame which divides a bed from its stand; discuss and dispute. The ideogram: knife and acrid, biting division. **Reside(-in)**, CHÜ: dwell, live in, stay; sit down, fill an office; settled parts

of a country. The ideogram: body and seat. **Sides(on-all-sides)**, FANG: limits, boundaries; square, surface of the earth extending to the four cardinal points; everywhere.

● *Image Tradition*

Not-yet Fording, Growing. [I]
Supple acquiring the center indeed.

The small fox, a muddy Ford. [II]
Not-yet issuing-forth-from the center indeed.
Soaking one's tail:
Without direction: Harvesting.
Not continuing, completing indeed.

Although not an appropriate situation. [III]
Solid[and]Supple corresponding indeed.

Associated Contexts **[I] Supple**, JOU: quality of the opened lines; flexible, pliant, tender, adaptable. **Acquire**, TE: obtain the desired object; wish for, desire covetously; gains, possessions. The ideogram: go and obstacle, going through obstacles to the goal. **Center**, CHUNG: inner, central; put in the center; middle, stable point enabling you to face inner and outer changes; middle line of trigram. The ideogram: field divided in two equal parts. Image of Hexagram 61.

[II] Issue-forth(-from), CH'U: emerge from, come out of, proceed from, spring from; the Action of the trigram Shake, CHEN; contrary of enter, JU. The ideogram: stem with branches and leaves emerging.

 Not, PU: simple negative. **Continue**, HSÜ: carry on what another began; succeed to, join on, attach to; keep up, follow.

[III] Although, SUI: even though, supposing that, if, even if. **Appropriate**, TANG: suitable; opportune, convenient; adequate, competent; equal to; whole lines in uneven places and opened lines in even places. **Situation**, WEI: place or seat according to rank; post, position, command; right, proper; established, arranged. The ideogram: person and stand, servants in their places.

 Solid[and]Supple, KANG JOU: field of creative tension between the whole and opened lines and their qualities; field of psychic movement.

Correspond(-to), YING: be in agreement or harmony; resonate together, invoke and fulfill each other; answer to, suitable; relation between the lines (1:4, 2:5, 3:6) when they form the pair opened and whole, supple and solid. The ideogram: heart and obey.

• *Transforming Lines*

Initial six

a) **Soaking one's tail.**
   Abashment.

b) **Soaking one's tail.**
   Truly not knowing the end indeed.

Associated Contexts a) **Abashment**, LIN: distress, shame, regret, humiliation; aware of having lost the right track; leads to repenting, HUI, correcting the direction of mind and life.

b) **Truly**, YI: statement is true and precise. **Know**, CHIH: understand, perceive, remember; informed, aware, wise. The ideogram: arrow and mouth, words focused and swift. **End**, CHI: last or highest point; final, extreme; on the verge; ridgepole of a house.

Nine at-second

a) **Pulling-back one's wheels.**
   Trial: significant.

b) **Nine at-second, Trial: significant.**
   Centering using moving correcting indeed.

Associated Contexts a) **Pull-back**, YI: pull or drag something towards you; drag behind, take by the hand; leave traces. **Wheel**, LUN: disk, circle, round; revolution, circuit; rotate, roll, by turns.
   Trial, CHEN: test by ordeal; inquiry by divination and its result; righteous, firm; separating wheat from chaff; the kernel, the proven core; fourth stage of the Time Cycle. The ideogram: pearl and divination. **Significant**, CHI: leads to the experience of meaning; favorable, propitious, advantageous, appropriate; keyword. The ideogram: scholar and mouth, wise words of a sage.

b) **Move**, HSING: move or move something; motivate, emotionally moving; walk, act, do. The ideogram: stepping left then right. **Correct**, CHENG: rectify deviation or one-sidedness; proper, straight, exact, regular; constant, rule, model. The ideogram: stop and one, hold to one thing.

Six at-third

a) Not-yet Fording, chastising: pitfall.
   Harvesting: wading the Great River.

b) Not-yet Fording, chastising: pitfall.
   Situation not appropriate indeed.

Associated Contexts a) **Chastise**, CHENG: punish, subjugate, discipline; reduce to order; punishing expedition. The ideogram: step and correct, a rectifying move. **Pitfall**, HSIUNG: leads away from the experience of meaning; stuck and exposed to danger, unable to take in the situation; flow of life and spirit is blocked; unfortunate, baleful; keyword.

   Harvest, LI: advantageous, profitable; acute, insightful; benefit, nourish; third stage of the Time Cycle. **Wading the Great River**, SHE TA CH'UAN: consciously moving into the flow of time; enter the stream of life with a goal or purpose; embark on a significant enterprise.

Nine at-fourth

a) Trial: significant, repenting extinguished.
   Shake avails-of subjugating souls on-all-sides.
   Three years-revolved, possessing donating
                          tending-towards the great city.

b) Trial: significant, repenting extinguished.
   Purpose moving indeed.

Associated Contexts a) **Trial**, CHEN: test by ordeal; inquiry by divination and its result; righteous, firm; separating wheat from chaff; the kernel, the proven core; fourth stage of the Time Cycle. The ideogram: pearl and divination. **Significant**, CHI: leads to the experience of meaning; favorable, propitious, advantageous, appropriate; keyword. The ideogram: scholar and mouth, wise words of a sage. **Repenting extinguished**, HUI WANG: previous troubles and consequent remorse will disappear.

Shake, CHEN: arouse, excite, inspire; thunder rising from below; awe, alarm, trembling; fertilizing intrusion. The ideogram: excite and rain. Image of Hexagram 51. **Avail-of,** YUNG: take advantage of; benefit from, profit by; use for a specific purpose; apply to advantage. The ideogram: to divine and center, applying divination to central concerns. **Subjugate,** FA: chastise rebels, make dependent; cut down, subject to rule. The ideogram: man and lance, armed soldiers. **Soul,** KUEI: power that creates individual existence; union of volatile-soul, HUN, spiritual and intellectual power, and dense-soul, P'O, bodily strength and movement. The HUN rises after death, the P'O remains with the body and may communicate with the living.

Three, SAN: number three, third time or place; active phases of a cycle; superlative; beginning of repetition. **Years-revolved,** NIEN: number of years elapsed; a person's age; contrasts with year's-time, SUI, length of time in a year. **Possess,** YU: in possession of, have, own; opposite of lack, WU. **Donate,** SHANG: bestow, confer, grant; rewards, gifts; celebrate, take pleasure in. **Tend-towards,** YÜ: move toward but not reach, in the direction of; contrasts with reach(-to), HU, actually arriving. **Great,** TA: big, noble, important, very; orient the will toward a self-imposed goal, impose direction; ability to lead or guide your life; contrasts with small, HSIAO, flexible adaptation to what crosses your path; keyword. Image of Hexagrams 14, 26, 28, 34. **City,** KUO: area of only human constructions; political unit, polis. First of the territorial zones: city, suburbs, countryside, forests.

b) **Purpose,** CHIH: focus of mind and heart; will, inclination, resolve. The ideogram: heart and scholar, high inner resolve, or heart and go, inner determination. **Move,** HSING: move or move something; motivate, emotionally moving; walk, act, do. The ideogram: stepping left then right.

Six at-fifth

a) **Trial: significant, without repenting.**
   A chün tzu's shining.
   Possessing conformity, significant.

b) **A chün tzu's shining.**
   One's brilliance significant indeed.

Associated Contexts a) **Trial**, CHEN: test by ordeal; inquiry by divination and its result; righteous, firm; separating wheat from chaff; the kernel, the proven core; fourth stage of the Time Cycle. The ideogram: pearl and divination. **Significant**, CHI: leads to the experience of meaning; favorable, propitious, advantageous, appropriate; keyword. The ideogram: scholar and mouth, wise words of a sage. **Without repenting**, WU HUI: devoid of the sort of trouble that leads to sorrow, regret and the necessity to change your attitude.

's/have(-it)/it/them, CHIH: expresses possession, directly or as an object pronoun. **Shine**, KUANG: illuminate; give off brilliant, bright light; honor, glory, éclat; result of action, contrasts with brightness, MING, light of heavenly bodies. The ideogram: fire above person, lifting the light.

Possessing conformity, YU FU: inner and outer are in accord; confidence of the spirits has been captured; sincere, truthful; proper to take action.

b) **One's/one**, CH'I: third person pronoun; also: it/its, he/his, she/hers, they/theirs. **Brilliance**, HUI: sunlight, sunshine, sunbeam; bright, splendid.

Nine above

a) **Possessing conformity: tending-towards drinking liquor.**
Without fault.
Soaking one's head.
Possessing conformity: letting-go that.

b) **Drinking liquor, soaking the head.**
Truly not knowing articulating indeed.

Associated Contexts a) **Possessing conformity**, YU FU: inner and outer are in accord; confidence of the spirits has been captured; sincere, truthful; proper to take action. **Tend-towards**, YÜ: move toward but not reach, in the direction of; contrasts with reach(-to), HU, actually arriving. **Drink**, YIN: take in liquid or air; quench thirst, give liquid to; inhale, suck in. **Liquor**, CHIU: alcoholic beverages, distilled spirits; spirit which perfects the good and evil in human nature. The ideogram: liquid above fermenting must, separating the spirits.

Without fault, WU CHIU: no error or harm in the situation. **Head**, SHOU: literal head; leader, foremost; subject headings; beginning, model; superior, upper, front.

Let-go, SHIH: lose, omit, miss, fail, let slip; out of control. The ideogram: drop from the hand. **That**, SHIH: preceding statement.

b) **Truly**, YI: statement is true and precise. **Know**, CHIH: understand, perceive, remember; informed, aware, wise. The ideogram: arrow and mouth, words focused and swift. **Articulate**, CHIEH: separate and distinguish, as well as join, different things; express thought through speech; joint, section, chapter, interval, unit of time; zodiacal sign; moderate, regulate; lit.: nodes on bamboo stalks. Image of Hexagram 60.

PART THREE

周易

CONCORDANCE

CONCORDANCE

A concordance is a tool which has been used to deepen the understanding of some of the world's most important books. The present one-to-one translation of the *I Ching* makes a Concordance to it possible for the first time in a Western language. It is an invaluable tool to more fully understand the divinatory context of words and phrases. It also enables you to locate a passage or a hexagram from the memory of a specific word.

Entries in the Concordance are alphabetical, according to the English core words marked in bold in the hexagrams which translate the Chinese terms. Each sentence in which the term appears is reprinted, along with its hexagram number and location. If, for instance, you remember only a word from an answer given to you by the oracle and want to find the relevant hexagram again, you can consult the list of phrases in which the word appears. By looking further at other uses of your word, you will acquire a deeper sense of its significance and its relation to the *I Ching* as a whole.

CONCORDANCE TO THE DIVINATORY TEXTS

ABBREVIATIONS

Im	*Image of the Situation*
S	*Sequence*
CD	*Contrasted Definitions*
AE	*Attached Evidences*
ST	*Symbol Tradition*
ImT	*Image Tradition*
1 - 6a/b	*Transforming Lines*

Abandon, YI: leave behind, forget; die; lose through unawareness. The ideogram: go and value, value is gone.

> **11.**2a Not putting-off abandoning.
> **62.**Im/ImT Flying bird: abandoning's sound.

Abashment, LIN: distress, shame, regret, humiliation; aware of having lost the right track; leads to repenting, HUI, correcting the direction of mind and life.

> **3.**3a Going abashed.
> **3.**3b Going abashment exhausted indeed.
> **4.**1a Using going abashed.
> **4.**4a/b Confining Enveloping. Abashment.
> **11.**6a Trial: abashment.
> **13.**2a Abashment.
> **13.**2b Abashment: tao indeed.
> **18.**4a Going: visualizing abashment.
> **20.**1a Chün tzu: abashment.
> **21.**3a The small abashed.
> **22.**5a Abashment. Completing significant.
> **28.**4a Possessing more: abashment.
> **31.**3a Going abashed.
> **32.**3a Trial: abashment.
> **35.**6a Trial: abashment.
> **37.**3a Completing abashed.
> **40.**3a Trial: abashment.
> **44.**6a Abashment.
> **44.**6b Exhausting abashment above indeed.
> **45.**3a The small abashed.
> **47.**4a Abashment.
> **57.**3a/b Imminent Ground, abashment.
> **64.**1a Abashment.

Abide, CH'U: rest in, dwell; stop yourself; arrive at a place or condition; distinguish, decide; do

what is proper. The ideogram: tiger, stop and seat, powerful movement coming to rest.

> **9.**10 Treading: not abiding indeed.
> **9.**6a/b Already rain, already abiding.
> **31.**3b Truly not abiding indeed.
> **56.**4a/b Sojourning, tending-towards abiding.

Able, NENG: enable; ability, power, skill, art; competent, talented; duty, function, capacity. The ideogram: an animal with strong hooves and bones, able to carry and defend.

> **7.**ImT Able to use the crowds correcting:
> **9.**3b Not able correcting the home indeed.
> **10.**3a/b Squinting enabling observing.
> **10.**3a/b Halting enabling Treading.
> **13.**ImT Verily a chün tzu activating enables interpenetrating Below Heaven's purpose.
> **16.**S Possessing the Great and-also enabling Humbling necessarily Provides-for.
> **26.**ImT Ability stopping persisting.
> **32.**ImT Sun[and]Moon acquiring heaven and-also enabling lasting illumination.
> **32.**ImT The four seasons transforming changes and-also enabling lasting accomplishment.
> **32.**2b Ability lasting, centering indeed.
> **34.**6a/b Not enabling withdrawing, not enabling releasing.
> **36.**ImT Inside heaviness and-also enabling correcting one's purpose.
> **39.**ImT Visualizing venturing and-also enabling stopping.
> **50.**2a Not me able to approach. Significant.
> **54.**1a/b Halting enabling treading.
> **54.**2a Squinting enabling observing.

Abound, FENG: abundant, plentiful, copious; grow wealthy; at the point of overflowing; exuberant, fertile, prolific; rich in talents, property, friends; fullness, culmination; ripe, sumptuous, fat.

> Image of Hexagram 55 and occurs throughout its texts.
> **55/56.**CD Abounding: numerous anteriority indeed.

Above, SHANG: anything above, in all senses;

higher, upper, outer; upper trigram; opposite of below, HSIA. See also: **Above[and]Below** and **Supreme Above**

This term occurs in the Symbol Tradition and the Image Tradition of most hexagrams describing the upper trigram and lines. It also occurs at:

6.2b Below origin, above Arguing

6.3b Adhering-to the above significant indeed.

8.4b Using adhering-to the above indeed.

8.5b Commissioning centering above indeed.

9.4b Uniting purposes above indeed.

10.6b Spring significant located above.

14.6b Great Possessing the above: significant.

16.ST Exalting worship's Supreme Above.

16.6b Dim Providing-for located above.

17.6b Exhausting the above indeed.

22.2b Associating-with the above, rising indeed.

22.6b Acquiring purpose above indeed.

24.S Above Stripping exhausted, below reversing.

26.3b Uniting purposes above indeed.

27.4b Spreading-out shining above indeed.

27.5b Yielding uses adhering-to the above indeed.

29/30.CD Above Radiance and-also below Gorge indeed.

29.6b Six above, letting-go tao.

32.6b Rousing Persevering located-in the above.

35.3b Moving above indeed.

40.6a A prince avails-of shooting a hawk, tending-towards the high rampart's above.

41.5b Originating-from shielding above indeed.

44.6b Exhausting abashment above indeed.

45.3b Ground above indeed.

45.6b The above not-yet quiet indeed.

46.S Assembling and-also the above implies designating's Ascending.

46.1b Uniting purposes above indeed.

46.6b Dim Ascending located-in the above.

48.S Confining reaching-to the above implies necessarily reversing the below.

48.6b Spring significant located-in the above.

50.6b Jade rings located above.

54.6b Six above, without substance.

56.5b Overtaking the above indeed.

56.6b Using Sojourning to locate-in the above.

57.6b Above exhaustion indeed.

58.6b Six above, protracting Opening.

60.4b Receiving tao above indeed.

61.4b Cutting-off the above, sorting indeed.

62. Im Above not proper, below proper.

62.5b Above climaxing indeed.

Above[and]Below, SHANG HSIA: realm of dynamic interaction between the upper and the lower; the vertical dimension.

4.6b Above[and]Below yielding indeed.

8.ImT Above[and]Below corresponding indeed.

9.ImT Supple acquiring the situation and-also Above[and]Below corresponding-to it.

10.ST A chün tzu uses differentiating Above[and]Below.

11. ImT Above[and]Below mingling and-also one's purpose concording indeed.

12. ImT Above[and]Below not mingling and-also Below Heaven without fiefdoms indeed

14. ImT And-also Above[and]Below corresponding-to it.

23.3b Letting-go Above[and]Below indeed.

31.S Therefore afterwards possessing Above[and]Below.

31.S Possessing Above[and]Below:

52. ImT Above[and]Below, antagonistic correspondence.

Absence, WANG: emptiness, vacancy; lit.: a net, open spaces between threads; used as a negative. The ideogram: net and lost, empty spaces divide what is kept from what is lost.

34.3a A chün tzu avails-of absence.

34.3b A chün tzu: absence indeed.

35.1a Absence: conforming.

Absolutely-no(thing), MO: complete elimination; not any, by no means.

22.3b Completing absolutely-nothing: having a mound indeed.

33.2a Absolutely-nothing has mastering stimulating.

42.6a/b Absolutely-no Augmenting it.

43.2a Absolutely-no night-time, possessing arms.

50.S Skinning beings implies absolutely-nothing like a Vessel.

51.S A lord's implementing implies absolutely-nothing like the long-living son.

53.5a/b Completing: absolutely-nothing has mastering.

56.6b Completing absolutely-nothing: having hearing indeed.

Abyss, YÜAN: deep hole or gulf, where backwaters eddy and accumulate; whirlpool; deep water.

1.4a/b Maybe capering located-in the abyss.

6.ImT Entering tending-towards the abyss indeed.

Accompany, HSIEH: take or go along with; jointly, all at once.

41/42.ImT Associating-with the season, accompanying the movement.

Accomplish, CH'ENG: complete, finish, bring about; perfect, full, whole; play your part, do your duty; mature. The ideogram: weapon and man, able to bear arms, thus fully developed.

1.ImT The six situations: the season accomplishing.

2.3a Without accomplishing possessing completion.

6.ImT Arguing not permitting accomplishment indeed.

6.3a Without accomplishment.

11.ST The crown-prince uses property to accomplish Heaven[and]Earth's tao.

16.6a Accomplishment: possessing denial.

22.ImT Using changes accomplishing Below Heaven.

30.ImT Thereupon changes accomplishing Below Heaven.

32.ImT The four seasons transforming changes and-also enabling lasting accomplishment.

32.ImT The all-wise person lasting with-respect-to his tao and-also Below Heaven the changes accomplishing.

48.6b The great accomplishing indeed.

49.ImT Heaven[and]Earth Skinning and-also the four seasons accomplishing.

60.ImT Heaven, Earth: Articulating and-also the four seasons accomplishing.

Accumulate, CH'U: retain, hoard, gather, herd together; control, restrain; domesticate, tame, train; raise, feed, sustain, bring up. The ideogram: field and black, fertile black soil good for pastures, accumulated through retaining silt.

Image of Hexagrams 9 and 26 and occurs throughout their texts.

7.ST A chün tzu uses tolerating commoners to accumulate crowds.

10.S Beings Accumulating, therefore afterwards possessing

10.CD Small Accumulating: few indeed.

25.CD Great Accumulating: the season indeed.

27.S Beings accumulating therefore afterwards permitting nourishing.

30.Im Growing. Accumulating female cattle. Significant.

30.ImT That uses accumulating female cattle, significant indeed.

33.3a/b Accumulating servants, concubines, significant.

Ache, TS'E: acute pain or grief; pity, sympathy, sorrow, grief.

48.3a Activating my heart aching.

48.3b Moving: aching indeed.

Achieve, KUNG: work done, results; real accomplishment, praise, worth, merit. The ideogram: workman's square and forearm, combining craft and strength.

4.ImT The all-wise achieving indeed.

5.ImT Going possesses achievement indeed.

7.3b The great without achievement indeed.

7.6b Using correcting achieving indeed.

17.1a/b Issuing-forth-from the gate, mingling possesses achievement.

17.4b Brightening achieving indeed.

29.ImT Going possesses achievement indeed.

29.3b Completing without achieving indeed.

32.6b The great without achievement indeed.

39/40.ImT Going possesses achievement indeed.

48.ImT Not-yet possessing achievement indeed.

53.ImT Going possessing achievement indeed.

57.4b Possessing achievement indeed.

59. ImT Riding wood possesses achievement indeed.

• **Acquiesce(-in)**, SHOU: accept, make peace with, agree to; at rest, satisfied; patient.

3-64.S Anterior acquiescence has the use of

6.6b Using Arguing acquiesces-in submitting.

31.ST A chün tzu uses emptiness to acquiesce people.

35.1b Not-yet acquiescing-in fate indeed.

35.2a/b Acquiescing-in closely-woven chain-mail: blessing.

47.5b Acquiescing-in blessing indeed.

48.3a Together-with acquiescing-in one's blessing.

48.3b Acquiescing-in blessing indeed.

63.5a/b The substance: acquiescing-in one's blessing.

• **Acquire**, TE: obtain the desired object; wish for, desire covetously; gains, possessions. The ideogram: go and obstacle, going through obstacles to the goal.

2.Im Beforehand delusion, afterwards acquiring.

2.Im/ImT Western South: acquiring partnering.

2.ImT Afterwards yielding acquiring rules.

3.1b The great acquiring the commoners indeed.

6.ImT Solid coming and-also acquiring the center indeed.

9.ImT Supple acquiring the situation and-also Above[and]Below corresponding-to it.

11.2a Acquiring honor, tending-towards centering moving.

11.2b Enwrapping wasteland, acquiring honor,

12.2b Centering the heart acquiring indeed.

13. ImT Supple acquiring the situation.

13. ImT Acquiring centering and-also corresponding reaching-to Force.

13.6b Purpose not-yet acquired indeed.

14. ImT Supple acquiring the dignifying situation, the great centering.

15.6b Purpose not-yet acquired indeed.

16.4a The great possesses acquiring.

16.4b Antecedent Provision, the great possesses acquiring.

17.3a Following possessing seeking, acquiring.

18.2b Acquiring centering tao indeed.

18.4b Going, not-yet acquiring indeed.

21. ImT Supple acquiring the center and-also moving above.

21.4a Acquiring a metallic arrow.

21.5a Gnawing parched meat. Acquiring yellow metal.

21.5b Acquiring the appropriate indeed.

22.6b Acquiring purpose above indeed.

23.6a/b A chün tzu acquiring a cart.

25.1b Acquiring purpose indeed.

25.3a Moving people's acquiring:

25.3b Moving people acquiring cattle.

28.2a A venerable husband acquiring his woman consort.

28.5a A venerable wife acquiring her notable husband.

29.2a/b Seeking, the small acquiring.

29.6a Three year's-time, not acquiring. Pitfall.

30.2b Acquiring centering tao indeed.

32. ImT Sun[and]Moon acquiring heaven and-also enabling lasting illumination.

32.4b Quietly acquiring the wildfowl indeed.

35.5a/b Letting-go, acquiring, no cares.

36.3a Acquiring its great, the head.

36.3b Thereupon acquiring the great indeed.

38. ImT Acquiring the center and-also corresponding reaching the solid.

39. ImT Going acquires the center indeed.

40. ImT Going acquiring crowds indeed.

40. ImT Thereupon acquiring the center indeed.

40.2a Acquiring a yellow arrow.

40.2b Acquiring centering tao indeed.

41.3a By-consequence acquiring his friend.

41.6a Acquiring a servant, without dwelling.

41.6b The great acquiring purpose indeed.

42.5b The great acquiring purpose indeed.

43.2b Acquiring centering tao indeed.

46.5b The great acquiring the purpose indeed.

47.5b Purpose not-yet acquired indeed.

48. Im Without losing, without acquiring.

49. ImT Their purposes not mutually acquired.

50. ImT Acquiring the center and-also corresponding reaching the solid.

50.1a Acquiring a concubine, using one's sonhood.

51.2a The seventh day: acquiring.

51.6b Center not-yet acquired indeed.

53. ImT Advancing acquiring the situation.

53. ImT One's situation: solid acquiring the center indeed.

53.4a/b Maybe acquiring one's rafter.

53.5b Acquiring the place desired indeed.

55.S Acquiring one's place to Convert implies necessarily the great.

55.2a Going acquiring doubt, affliction.

56. ImT Supple acquiring the center reaching-to the outside and-also yielding reaching-to the solid.

56.2a/b Acquiring a youthful vassal: Trial.

56.4a Acquiring one's own emblem-ax.

56.4b Not-yet acquiring the situation indeed.

56.4b Acquiring one's own emblem-ax.

57.2b Acquiring the center indeed.

59. ImT Supple acquiring the situation reaching-to the outside and-also concording above.

59.2b Acquiring desire indeed.

60. ImT Solid[and]Supple apportioning and-also solid acquiring the center.

61. ImT Supple located inside and-also solid acquiring the center.

61.3a Acquiring antagonism.

62. ImT Supple acquiring the center.

63. ImT Supple acquiring the center indeed.

63.2a/b The seventh day: acquiring.

64. ImT Supple acquiring the center indeed.

Activate, WEI: act or cause to act; do, make, manage; make active; attend to, help; because of.

1.7b Heavenly actualizing-tao not permitting activating the head indeed.

4.6a Not Harvesting: activating outlawry.

10.3a/b Martial people activating: tending-towards a Great Chief.

13. ImT Verily a chün tzu activating enables interpenetrating Below Heaven's purpose.

25. ImT Solid originating-from the outside coming and-also activating a lord with-respect-to the inside.

41.2b Centering using activating purposes indeed.

42.1a Harvesting: availing-of activating the great, arousing.

42.4a Harvesting: availing-of activating depending-on shifting the city.

43.1a Going not mastering, activating faulty.

45.1a Like an outcry, the-one handful activates laughing.

48.3a Activating my heart aching.

49.1b Not permitted to use possessing activating indeed.

50.5b Centering uses activating substance indeed.

51. ImT Using activating the offering lord indeed.

53.6a Its feathers permit availing-of activating fundamentals.

53.6b Its feathers permit availing-of activating

Actualize-tao, TE: realize tao in action; power, virtue; ability to follow the course traced by the ongoing process of the cosmos; keyword. The ideogram: to go, straight, and heart. Linked with acquire, TE: acquiring that which makes a being become what it is meant to be.

1.2b Actualizing-tao spreading-out throughout indeed.

1.7b Heavenly actualizing-tao not permitting activating the head indeed.

2.ST A chün tzu uses munificent actualizing-tao to carry the beings.

2.ImT Actualizing-tao uniting without delimiting.

4.ST A chün tzu uses fruiting movement to nurture actualizing-tao.

6.3a/b Taking-in ancient actualizing-tao.

9.ST A chün tzu uses highlighting the pattern to actualize-tao.

9.6a Honoring actualizing-tao carrying.

9.6b Actualizing-tao amassing carrying indeed.

10.AE Treading: actualizing-tao's foundation indeed.

12.ST A chün tzu uses parsimonious actualizing-tao to cast-out heaviness.

14. ImT One's actualizing-tao: solid persisting and-also pattern brightening.

15.AE Humbling: actualizing-tao's handle indeed.

16.ST The Earlier Kings used arousing delight to extol actualizing-tao.

18.ST A chün tzu uses rousing the commoners to nurture actualizing-tao.

18.5b Receiving uses actualizing-tao indeed.

24.AE Returning: actualizing-tao's root indeed.

26.ST [A chün tzu] uses accumulating one's actualizing-tao.

26.ImT A day renewing one's actualizing-tao.

29.ST A chün tzu uses rules actualizing-tao to move.

32.AE Persevering: actualizing-tao's firmness indeed.

32.AE Persevering: using the-one actualizing-tao.

32.3a/b Not Persevering one's actualizing-tao.

32.5a Persevering one's actualizing-tao: Trial.

35.ST A chün tzu uses originating enlightening to brighten actualizing-tao.

39.ST A chün tzu uses reversing individuality to renovate actualizing-tao.

41.AE Diminishing: actualizing-tao's adjustment indeed.

42.AE Augmenting: actualizing-tao's enriching indeed.

42.5a Possessing conformity, benevolence: my actualizing-tao.

42.5b Benevolence: my actualizing-tao.

43.ST [A chün tzu uses] residing-in actualizing-tao, by-consequence keeping-aloof.

46.ST A chün tzu uses yielding to actualize-tao.

47.AE Confining: actualizing-tao's marking-off indeed.

48.AE The Well: actualizing-tao's earth indeed.

53.ST A chün tzu uses residing-in eminent actualizing-tao to improve the vulgar.

57.AE Ground: actualizing-tao's paring indeed.

60.ST [A chün tzu uses] deliberating actualizing-tao to move.

Actually, YI: truly, really, at present. The ideogram: a dart and done, strong intention fully expressed.

5.ImT Actually one's righteousness, not confining exhaustion.

7.ImT Actually permitting using kinghood.

7.ImT Actually significant, furthermore wherefore faulty?

20.ImT And-also actually Below Heaven submitting.

23.S Actually involving embellishing, therefore afterwards Growing by-consequence used-up.

25.S Actually Returning, by-consequence not Embroiling.

25.ImT Actually wherefore having-it?

31/32.ImT And-also actually Heaven[and]Earth, the myriad beings's motives permitting visualizing.

34.ImT Actually the correcting Great and-also Heaven[and]Earth's motives permitting visualizing.

37.ImT Actually correcting Dwelling and-also Below Heaven set-right.

42.5b Actually no questioning it.

45.ImT Actually viewing one's place to assemble.

45.ImT And-also actually Heaven[and]Earth, the myriad beings's motives, permitting visualizing.

49.3b Furthermore actually wherefore having-them.

56.3b Actually truly using injuring.

Actually … in-fact, YI TSAI: stresses the importance of a statement. The ideogram: a dart and done, strong intention fully expressed.

16.ImT Actually Provision's season righteously great in-fact.

17.ImT Actually Following the season's righteous great in-fact.

25.ImT Actually moving in-fact.

27.ImT Actually Jaws's season great in-fact.

28.ImT Actually Great Exceeding's season great in-fact.

29.ImT Actually venturing's season availing-of the great in-fact.

33.ImT Actually Retiring's season righteously great in-fact.

38.ImT Actually Polarizing's season availing-of the great in-fact.

39.ImT Actually knowing in-fact.

39.ImT Actually Limping's season availing-of the great in-fact.

40.ImT Actually Taking-apart's season great in-fact.

44.ImT Actually Coupling's season righteously great in-fact.

49.ImT Actually Skinning's season great in-fact.

56. ImT Actually Sojourning's season righteously great in-fact.

58. ImT Actually the commoners encouraged in-fact.

Add, ERH: join to something previous; reiterate, repeat; second, double; assistant.

29.4a/b A cup, liquor, a platter added.

Adhere(-to), TS'UNG: follow a way, hold to a doctrine, school, or person; hear and comply with, agree to; forced to follow, follower. The ideogram: two men walking, one following the other.

2.3a/b Maybe adhering-to kingly affairs:

3.3b Using adhering-to wildfowl indeed.

6.3a Maybe adhering-to kingly affairs:

6.3b Adhering-to the above significant indeed.

7.ImT Using the latter poisons Below Heaven and-also the commoners adhering-to it.

8.ImT Yielding adhering-to the below indeed.

8.4b Using adhering-to the above indeed.

17.1b Adhering-to correcting significant indeed.

17.6a Thereupon adhering holding-fast-to it.

24.4b Using adhering-to tao indeed.

27.5b Yielding uses adhering-to the above indeed.

31.4a Partnering adheres-to simply pondering.

32.5b Adhering-to the-one and-also completing indeed.

32.5b Adhering-to the wife: pitfall indeed.

39.6b Using adhering-to valuing indeed.

42.4a/b Notifying the prince, adhering.

49.6b Yielding uses adhering-to the chief indeed.

50.1b Using adhering-to valuing indeed.

62.3a/b Adhering, maybe killing it.

Adjoin, FU: next to, lean on; join; near, approaching.

23.ST Mountain adjoining with-respect-to earth. Stripping.

Adjust, HSIU: regulate, repair, clean up, renovate.

24.1b Using adjusting individuality indeed.

41.AE Diminishing: actualizing-tao's adjustment indeed.

48.4b Adjusting the Well indeed.

51.ST A chün tzu uses anxious fearing to adjust inspecting.

Admonish, CHIEH: make someone obey; rule of conduct, precept, warning. The ideogram: words and warning.

8.5a/b Capital people not admonished.

Adorn, PI: embellish, ornament, deck out, beautify; variegated (flowers); elegant, brilliant; also: energetic, passionate, eager, intrepid; capable of great effort; brave. The ideogram: cowrie shells (money) and flowers, linking ornaments and value.

Image of Hexagram 22 and occurs throughout its texts.

Advance, CHIN: exert yourself, make progress, climb; be promoted; further the development of, augment; adopt a religion or conviction; offer, introduce.

1.4b Advancing, without fault indeed.

5/6.CD Attending: not advancing indeed.

20.3a/b Viewing my birth, advancing, withdrawing.

35.S Prospering implies advancing indeed.

35. ImT Prospering. Advancing indeed.

35. ImT Supple advancing and-also moving above.

36.S Advancing necessarily possessing a place: injuring.

38. ImT Supple advancing and-also moving above.

42. ImT Sun advancing without delimiting.

50. ImT Supple advancing and-also moving above.

53.S Infiltrating implies advancing indeed.

53. ImT Infiltrating's advancing indeed.

53. ImT Advancing acquiring the situation.

53. ImT Advancing uses correcting.

54.S Advancing necessarily possessing a place to Convert.

57.1a/b Advancing, withdrawing.

Adversity, LI: danger; threatening, malevolent demon. This has two aspects: grind, sharpen, improve, perfect, stimulate; and: poisonous, sinister, cruel, contrary. It indicates a spirit or ghost that seeks revenge by inflicting suffering upon the living. Pacifying or exorcizing such a spirit can have a healing effect. The ideogram: sheltering cliff and stinging insect.

1.3a Nightfall, awe, like adversity.

6.3a Adversity, completing significant.

9.6a The wife, Trial: adversity.

10.5a/b Parting Treading. Trial: adversity.

18.1a Adversity, completing significant.

21.5a Trial: adversity.

21.5b Trial: adversity, without fault.

24.3a/b Imminent Returning. Adversity.

26.1a Possessing adversity.

27.6a/b Antecedent Jaws. Adversity significant.

33.1a Retiring tail, adversity.

33.1b Retiring tail's adversity.

33.3a Tied Retiring. Possessing afflicting adversity.

33.3b Tied Retiring's adversity.

34.3a Trial: adversity.

35.4a Trial: adversity.

35.4b Bushy-tailed rodents, Trial: adversity.

35.6a Adversity significant, without fault.

37.3a Repenting, adversity significant.

38.4a Adversity, without fault.

43.Im/ImT Conforming, crying-out, possessing adversity.

44.3a Adversity.

49.3a Chastising: pitfall, Trial: adversity.

51.2a/b Shake coming: adversity.

51.5a/b Shake going, coming adversity.

52.3a Adversity smothers the heart.

53.1a The small son, adversity possessing words.

53.1b The small son's adversity.

56.3a Trial: adversity.

58.5a Possessing adversity.

62.4a/b Going adversity necessarily warning.

63.6a Adversity.

63.6b Soaking one's head, adversity.

Affairs, SHIH: all kinds of personal activity; matters at hand; business, occupation; manage a business, case in court.

2.3a/b Maybe adhering-to kingly affairs:

6.ST A chün tzu uses arousing affairs to plan beginning.

6.1a/b Not a perpetual place, affairs.

6.3a Maybe adhering-to kingly affairs:

18.S Using rejoicing Following people implies necessarily possessing affairs.

18.S Corrupting implies affairs indeed.

18.ImT Going possesses affairs indeed.

18.6a/b Not affairs, kingly feudatories.

18.6a Honoring highness: one's affair.

19.S Possessing affairs and-also afterwards permitting the great.

29.ST [A chün tzu uses] repeating to teach affairs.

33.3b Not permitting Great Affairs indeed.

38.Im Polarizing, Small Affairs significant.

38.ImT That uses Small Affairs significant.

38.ImT Heaven, Earth, Polarizing and-also one's affairs concording indeed.

38.ImT The myriad beings Polarizing and-also their affairs sorted indeed.

41.1a/b Climaxing affairs, swiftly going.

42.1b The below, not munificent affairs indeed.

42.3a/b Augmenting's availing-of pitfall affairs.

46.4b Yielding affairs indeed.

51.5a Intention without losing possesses affairs.

51.5b One's affairs located-in the center.

55.3b Not permitting Great Affairs indeed.

57.ST A chün tzu uses distributing fate to move affairs.

62.Im Permitting Small Affairs. Not permitting Great Affairs.

62.ImT That uses Small Affairs, significant indeed.

62.ImT That uses not permitting Great Affairs indeed.

Affection, AI: love, show affection; benevolent feelings; kindness, regard.

37.5b Mingling mutual affection indeed.

Afflict, CHI: sickness, disorder, defect, calamity; injurious; pressure and consequent anger, hate or dislike. The ideogram: sickness and dart, a sudden affliction.

16.5a Trial: affliction.

16.5b Six at-fifth, Trial: affliction.

24.Im Issuing-forth, entering, without affliction.

24.ImT That uses issuing-forth, entering, without affliction.

25.5a Without Embroiling's affliction.

33.3a Tied Retiring. Possessing afflicting adversity.

33.3b Possessing afflicting weariness indeed.

36.3a Not permitting affliction: Trial.

41.4a/b Diminishing one's affliction.

50.2a/b My companion possesses affliction.

55.2a Going acquiring doubt, affliction.

58.4a Chain-mail afflicting: possessing rejoicing.

Affluence, FU: rich, abundant; wealth; enrich, provide for; flow toward, accrue.

9.5a Affluence: using one's neighbor.

9.5b Not solitary affluence indeed.

11.4a Not affluence: using one's neighbor.

11.4b Fluttering, fluttering: not affluence.

15.5a Not affluence: using one's neighbor.

25.2b Not-yet affluence indeed.

37.4a/b Affluence Dwelling, the great significant.

46.6b Dissolving, not affluence indeed.

● **Afoot**, T'U: travel on foot; footman, foot-soldier; follower, disciple; ruffian, bond-servant.

22.1a/b Stowing-away the chariot and-also afoot.

● **After(wards)/later**, HOU: come after in time, subsequent; put oneself after; the second; attendants, heirs, successors, posterity. See also: **Therefore ... afterwards**

This term occurs throughout the hexagram texts.

● **Age (the)**, SHIH: an age, an epoch, a generation; the world, mankind; the time, as "in the time of."

28.ST [A chün tzu uses] retiring-from the age without melancholy.

● **Agencies**, CH'I: fluid energy, configurative power, vital force; interacts with essence, CHING, to produce things and beings. The ideogram: vapor and rice, heat and moisture producing substance.

31.ImT The two agencies influencing correspondence use mutual associating.

● **Ail**, CHIU: chronic disease; disheartened, distressed by.

10.ImT Treading the supreme situation and-also not ailing.

● **All**, see: **Sides, on-all-sides**

● **All-wise**, SHENG: intuitive universal wisdom; mythical sages; holy, sacred; mark of highest distinction. The ideogram: ear and inform, one who knows all from a single sound.

4.ImT The all-wise achieving indeed.

16.ImT The all-wise person uses yielding stirring-up.

20.ImT The all-wise person uses spirit tao to set-up teaching.

27.ImT The all-wise person nourishes eminence used to extend-to the myriad commoners.

31.ImT The all-wise person influencing the people at-heart and-also Below Heaven harmony evening.

32.ImT The all-wise person lasting with-respect-to his tao and-also Below Heaven the changes accomplishing.

50.ImT The all-wise person Growing uses presenting-to the Supreme Above.

50.ImT And-also great Growing uses nourishing all-wise eminences.

● **Ally**, see: **Matrimonial allying**

● **Almost**, CHI: nearly, about to; subtle, almost imperceptible; the first sign.

3.3a A chün tzu almost not thus stowing-away.

9.6a The moon almost facing.

54.5a The moon almost facing, significant.

61.4a The moon almost facing.

● **Alone**, KU: solitary; without a protector; fatherless, orphan-like; as a title: the only, unequalled. See also: **Living-alone**

38.4a/6a Polarizing alone.

● **Already**, CHI: completed, done, has occurred; past tense, contrary of not-yet, WEI.

Image of Hexagram 63 and occurs throughout its texts.

9.6a/b Already rain, already abiding.

19.3a/b Already grieving-over it:

29.5a Merely already evened.

● **Although**, SUI: even though, supposing that, if, even if.

3.1b Although a stone pillar, purpose moving correctly indeed.

5.2b Although the small possesses words, using completing significant indeed.

5.6b Although not an appropriate situation, not-yet the great let-go indeed.

6.1b Although the small possesses words, one's differentiation brightening indeed.

21.ImT Although not an appropriate situation, Harvesting:

31.2b Although a pitfall, residing significant.

47.4b Although not an appropriate situation, possessing associating indeed.

51.6b Although a pitfall, without fault.

55.1a/b Although a decade, without fault.

64.ImT Although not an appropriate situation.

● **Altogether**, CHIEH: all, the whole; the same sort, all alike; entirely.

11.4b Altogether letting-go substance indeed.

32.ImT Solid[and]Supple altogether corresponding. Persevering.

40.ImT Thunder[and]Rain arousing and-also the hundred fruits, grasses, trees, altogether seedburst boundary.

55.ST Thunder, lightning, altogether culminating.

57. ImT Supple altogether yielding reaching the solid.

Amass, CHI: hoard, accumulate, pile up, store up, add up, increase.

9.6b Actualizing-tao amassing carrying indeed.

14.2b Amassing centering, not destroying indeed.

46.ST [A chün tzu uses] amassing the small to use the high great.

Amble, HSÜ: walk quietly and carefully; leisurely, tardy, slow; composed, dignified.

47.4a/b Coming, ambling, ambling.

47.5a/b Thereupon ambling possesses stimulating.

Amend, KAI: correct, reform, make new, alter, mend. The ideogram: self and strike, fighting your own errors.

42.ST [A chün tzu uses] possessing excess, by-consequence amending.

48. Im/ImT Amending the capital, not amending the Well.

49.4a/b Amending fate significant.

Ancestry, TSUNG: clan, kin, origin; those who bear the same surname; ancestral hall and tablets; honor, revere; a doctrine; contrasts with predecessor, K'AO, individual ancestors.

13.2a/b Concording People tending-towards ancestry.

38.5a/b Your ancestor gnawing flesh.

51. ImT Issuing-forth permits using guarding the ancestral temple, field-altar, offertory-millet.

63.3a The high ancestor subjugating souls on-all-sides.

Ancient, CHIU: of old, long before; worn out, spoiled; defunct.

6.3a Taking-in ancient actualizing-tao. Trial.

6.3b Taking-in ancient actualizing-tao.

48.1a/b The ancient Well without wildfowl.

And-also, ERH: joins and contrasts two terms. This term occurs throughout the hexagram texts.

Anger, FEN: resentment; cross, wrathful; irritated at, indignant. The ideogram: heart and divide, the heart dividing people.

41.ST A chün tzu uses curbing anger to block the appetites.

Another, PEI: yet one more; the other party; exclude, leave out.

62.5a A prince, a string-arrow grasping another located-in a cave.

Antagonistic, TI: opposed and equal; competitor, enemy; a contest between equals.

13.3b Antagonistic solid indeed.

52. ImT Above[and]Below, antagonistic correspondence.

61.3a Acquiring antagonism.

Antecedent, YU: come before as origin and cause; through, by, from; depend on; permit, enter by way of.

16.4a Antecedent Provision.

16.4b Antecedent Provision, the great possesses acquiring.

27.6a/b Antecedent Jaws. Adversity significant.

Anterior, KU: come before as cause; formerly, ancient; reason, purpose, intention; grievance, quarrel, dissatisfaction, sorrow, mourning resulting from previous causes and intentions; situation leading to a divination.

16. ImT Anterior Heaven[and]Earth thus having-it.

16. ImT Anterior Sun[and]Moon not exceeding.

17/18.CD Following: without anteriority indeed.

22. ImT Anterior Growth.

22. ImT The anterior small, Harvesting: possessing directed going.

30. ImT Anterior Growing.

34. ImT Solid uses stirring-up. Anterior Invigorating.

39.2a In-no-way body's anteriority.

45. ImT Anterior assembling indeed.

49/50.CD Skinning: departing anteriority indeed.

55/56.CD Abounding: numerous anteriority indeed.

55. ImT Brightness using stirring-up. Anterior Abounding.

Anterior ... the use-of: activating this hexagram depends on understanding and accepting the previous statement.

This phrase occurs in the Sequence of Hexagrams **3-64.**

Anxious, K'UNG: apprehensive, alarmed, agitated; suspicious of. The ideogram: heart and sick, agitated within.

51.ST A chün tzu uses anxious fearing to adjust inspecting.

51. ImT/1b Anxiety involving blessing indeed.

Appetites, YÜ: drives, instinctive craving; wishes, passions, desires, aspirations; long for, seek ardently; covet.

27.4a His appetites: pursuing, pursuing.

41.ST A chün tzu uses curbing anger to block the appetites.

Apportion, FEN: divide for distribution; sort out; allot to.

21. ImT Solid[and]Supple apportioning.

22. ImT Above apportioning solid and-also patterning supple.

60. ImT Solid[and]Supple apportioning and-also solid acquiring the center.

Apprehensive, CH'OU: anticipating adversity, afraid of what approaches; chagrined, grieved. The ideogram: heart and autumn, dreading the coming winter.

35.2a Prospering thus, apprehensive thus.

Approach, CHI: come near to, advance toward; about to do; soon.

3.3a/b Approaching stag, lacking precaution.

6.4a/b Returning, approaching fate.

43. Im/ImT Not Harvesting: approaching arms.

50.2a Not me able to approach. Significant.

56.2a Sojourning, approaching a resting-place.

Appropriate, TANG: suitable; opportune, convenient; adequate, competent; equal to; whole lines in uneven places and opened lines in even places.

This term occurs in the Image Tradition and in the Transforming Lines b) of most hexagrams.

Apron, SHANG: ceremonial garment; skirt, clothes; curtains of a carriage. The ideogram: garment and manifest, clothing as display.

2.5a/b A yellow apron. Spring significant.

Argue, SUNG: dispute, plead in court, contend before a ruler, demand justice; wrangles, quarrels, litigation. The ideogram: words and public, public disputation.

Image of Hexagram 6 and occurs throughout its texts.

Arm, KUNG: the arms as the body's instruments; staunch supporter; officer, minister of state.

55.3a/b Severing one's right arm.

Arms, JUNG: weapons; armed people, soldiers; military, violent. The ideogram: spear and armor, offensive and defensive weapons.

13.3a/b Hiding-away arms, tending-towards the thickets.

40.3b Originating-from my involving arms.

43. Im/ImT Not Harvesting: approaching arms.

43.2a Absolutely-no night-time, possessing arms.

43.2b Possessing arms, no cares.

45.ST A chün tzu uses eliminating arms to implement.

Arouse, TSO: stir up, stimulate, rouse from inactivity; generate; appear, arise. The ideogram: person and beginning. See also: **Rouse**

6.ST A chün tzu uses arousing affairs to plan beginning.

16.ST The Earlier Kings used arousing delight to extol actualizing tao.

30.ST Brightness doubled arousing Radiance.

40.ST Thunder, Rain, arousing. Taking-apart.

40. ImT Heaven[and]Earth Taking-apart and-also Thunder[and]Rain arousing.

40. ImT Thunder[and]Rain arousing and-also the hundred fruits, grasses, trees, altogether seedburst boundary.

42.1a Harvesting: availing-of activating the great, arousing.

Array, PAN: classify and display; arrange according to rank; assign to a group, as soldiers to their units. The ideogram: knife between two gems, separating values.

3.2a/4a/6a Riding a horse, arraying thus.

Arrest, TS'UI: stop, drive back, repress; force obedience, overpower, impel; scorn; destroy, break.

35.1a/b Prospering thus, arresting thus.

Arrow, SHIH: arrow, javelin, dart; swift, direct as an arrow; marshal together. See also: **String-arrow**

21.4a Acquiring a metallic arrow.

40.2a Acquiring a yellow arrow.

56.5a The-one arrow extinguishing.

Articulate, CHIEH: separate and distinguish, as well as join, different things; express thought through speech; joint, section, chapter, interval,unit of time; zodiacal sign; moderate, regulate; lit.: nodes on bamboo stalks.

Image of Hexagram 60 and occurs throughout its texts.

4.2b Solid[and]Supple articulating indeed.

27.ST [A chün tzu uses] articulating to drink[and]take-in.

37.3b Letting-go Dwelling articulating indeed.

39.5b Using centering articulating indeed.

50.6b Solid[and]Supple articulating indeed.

59.CD Articulating: stopping indeed.

61.S Articulating and-also trusting it.

64.6b Truly not knowing articulating indeed.

• **Ascend**, SHENG: go up; climb step by step; rise in office; advance through effort; accumulate; bring out and fulfill; lit.: a measure for fermented liquor, ascension as distillation.

Image of Hexagram 46 and occurs throughout its texts.

13.3a Ascending one's high mound.

29.ImT Heaven venturing, not permitting ascending indeed.

45.CD Ascending: not coming indeed.

47.S Ascending and-also not climaxing necessarily Confines.

• **Ask-why**, HO: interjection: why? how? why not?; interrupt with questions; intimidate, heckle. The ideogram: speak and beg, demanding an answer.

41.Im/ImT Asking-why having availing-of.

• **Assail**, T'U: rush against; abrupt attack; suddenly stricken; insolent, offensive.

30.4a/b Assailing thus, its coming thus.

• **Assemble**, CHÜ: gather, bring together, collect; call to assembly; dwell together, converge; meeting, reunion, collection; meeting place, dwelling place. The ideogram: three (= many) people.

45.S Beings mutually meeting and-also afterwards assembling.

45.S Clustering implies assembling indeed.

45/46.CD Clustering: assembling and-also Ascending: not coming indeed.

45.ImT Clustering, assembling indeed.

45.ImT Anterior assembling indeed.

45.ImT Assembling uses correcting indeed.

45.ImT Actually viewing one's place to assemble.

46.S Assembling and-also the above implies designating's Ascending.

• **Assign-to**, LIEH: place according to rank; arrange in order; distinguish, separate.

52.3a Assigned-to one's loins:

• **Associate(-with)**, YÜ: consort with, combine; companions; group, band, company; agree with,

comply, help. The ideogram: pair of hands reaching downward meets a pair of hands reaching upward, helpful association.

2.ImT Thereupon associating sorting movement.

6.ST Heaven associating-with stream, contradicting movements.

10.3b Not the stand to use associating-with moving indeed.

13.ST Heaven associating-with fire.

14.S Associating-with People Concording implies beings necessarily converting in-truth.

17.2b Nowhere joining associating indeed.

19/20.CD Maybe associating-with, maybe seeking.

22.2b Associating-with the above, rising indeed.

23.2b Not-yet possessing associating indeed.

25.ST Below heaven thunder moving. Beings associating

28.2b Exceeding uses mutual associating indeed.

31.ImT The two agencies influencing correspondence use mutual associating.

32.ImT Thunder, wind, mutually associating.

33.ImT Associating-with the season moving indeed.

41/42.ImT Associating-with the season, accompanying the movement.

44.ImT Not permitting associating-with long-living indeed.

47.4b Although not an appropriate situation, possessing associating indeed.

48.2b Without associating indeed.

52.ImT Not mutually associating indeed.

55.ImT Associating-with the season: dissolving pause.

56.3b Using Sojourning to associate-with the below.

61.2a Myself associating, simply spilling it.

62.ImT Associating-with the season moving indeed.

Attach, HSI: fasten to, bind, tie; retain, continue; keep in mind, emotionally attached.

12.5a Attaching tending-towards bushy mulberry-trees.

25.3a Maybe attaching's cattle.

44.1a/b Attaching tending-towards a metallic chock.

Attack, KUNG: fight with; aggression; go to work, apply to; rouse by criticizing, put in order; stimulate vital power; urgent desire. The ideogram: toil and strike.

> **13.**4a Nothing controlling attacking.

Attend, HSÜ: take care of, look out for, care or service of; turn your mind to; needs; obstinate, fixed on; wait, await, wait on; hesitate, doubt. The ideogram: rain and stopped, compelled to wait, or rain and origin, providing what is needed.

> Image of Hexagram 5 and occurs throughout its texts..
>
> **6.**CD Attending: not advancing indeed.

Augment, YI: increase, advance, promote, benefit, strengthen; pour in more; full, superabundant; restorative. The ideogram: water and vessel, pouring in more.

> Image of Hexagram 42 and occurs throughout its texts.
>
> **15.**ST A chün tzu uses reducing the numerous to augment the few.
>
> **15.**ImT Heavenly tao lessening overfilling and-also augmenting Humbling.
>
> **41.**CD Diminishing, Augmenting.
>
> **41.**ImT Below Diminishing, above augmenting.
>
> **41.**ImT Diminishing solid, augmenting supple, possessing the season.
>
> **41.**ImT Diminishing augmenting, overfilling emptiness.
>
> **41.**2a Nowhere Diminishing, augmenting it.
>
> **41.**5a Maybe augmenting's ten: partnering's tortoise.
>
> **41.**6a/b Nowhere Diminishing, augmenting it.
>
> **43.**S Augmenting and-also not climaxing necessarily breaks-up.

Augury, CHAN: sign, omen; divine by casting lots, sortilege; look at as a sign or augury.

> **49.**5a Not-yet an augury, possessing conformity.

Auspicious, HSIANG: omen of good luck and prosperity; sign, auspices.

> **10.**6a Observing Treading, predecessors auspicious.
>
> **47.**3b Not auspicious indeed.

Avail-of, YUNG: take advantage of; benefit from, profit by; use for a specific purpose; apply to advantage. The ideogram: to divine and center, applying divination to central concerns.

This term occurs throughout the hexagram texts.

Await, TAI: expect, wait for, welcome (friendly or hostile), provide against.

> **16.**AE Used to await violent visitors.
>
> **39.**1b Proper to await indeed.
>
> **53/54.**CD Infiltrating: womanhood converting awaits manhood moving indeed.
>
> **54.**4b Possessing awaiting and-also moving indeed.

Awe, T'I: alarmed and cautious; respect, regard, fear; stand in awe of. The ideogram: heart and versatile, the heart aware of sudden change.

> **1.**3a Nightfall, awe, like adversity.
>
> **6.**Im Arguing, possessing conformity. Blocking awe.
>
> **6.**ImT Blocking awe, centering significant.
>
> **9.**4a Blood departing, awe issuing-forth.
>
> **9.**4b Possessing conformity, awe issuing-forth.
>
> **43.**2a Awe, an outcry.

Ax, see: **Emblem-ax**

Axle-strap, FU: fastens the body of a cart to axle and wheels.

> **26.**2a/b Carting, stimulating the axle-strap.
>
> **34.**4a Invigorating tending-towards the Great: a cart's axle-straps.

Back, PEI: spine; opposite of front; behind, rear, hidden; turn the back on; north side; oppose, disobey, transgress. The ideogram: body and north, where the face is south.

> **52.**Im Bound: one's back.

Bag, NANG: sack, purse; put in a bag; property, salary.

> **2.**4a/b Bundled-in the bag.

Bar, PI: close a door, stop up a hole; obstruct, exclude, screen. The ideogram: door and hand, closing the door.

> **24.**ST The Earlier Kings used culminating sun to bar the passages.

Bargain, SHANG: argue over prices; consult, deliberate, do business; dealers, travelling merchants; hour before sunrise and sunset. The ideogram: stutter and sentences, repetitive speaking.

> **24.**ST Bargaining sojourners [used culminating sun] not to move.
>
> **58.**4a Bargaining Opening, not-yet soothing.

Barrier, KAN: boundary, limit; fend off, protect; stream, parapet, river bank; shield, defensive armor; the Ten Heavenly Barriers are part of the calendar system.

53.1a The wild-swan Infiltrating tending-towards the barrier.

● **Basket**, K'UANG: open basket; put in baskets; bottom of a bed.

54.6a A woman receiving a basket without substance.

54.6b Receiving an empty basket indeed.

● **Bass**, FU: freshwater fish, said to go in pairs and be faithful.

48.2a/b The Well: a gully, shooting bass.

● **Bear**, FU: carry on your back; take on a responsibility; rely on, depend on; loaded down; burden, duty; math term for minus.

38.6a Visualizing pigs bearing mire.

40.3a/b Bearing, moreover riding.

● **Beater**, CH'Ü: servants who drive animals toward hunters; order people to their places; drive on, whip up, animate, exhort.

8.5a The king avails-of three beaters.

● **Beautiful**, WEI: elegant, classic, fine; luxuriant, lush.

49.6b One's pattern beautiful indeed.

● **Bed**, CH'UANG: sleeping place; couch, sofa, lounge; bench around a well.

23.1a/b Stripping the bed, using the stand.

23.2a/b Stripping the bed, using marking-off.

23.4a/b Stripping the bed, using flesh.

57.2a,6a/b Ground located below the bed.

● **Before(hand)/earlier**, HSIEN: come before in time; first, at first; formerly, past, previous; begin, go ahead of.

This term occurs throughout the hexagram texts.

● **Before-zenith sun**, SSU JIH: double hour from 9 to 11 a.m., month of June, both symbolized by the serpent; about to, on the point of.

49.Im/ImT Before-zenith sun, thereupon conforming.

49.2a Before-zenith sun, thereupon Skinning it.

49.2b Before-zenith sun Skinning it.

● **Begin**, SHIH: commence, start, open; earliest, first; beginning of a time-span, ended by completion, CHUNG. The ideogram: woman and eminent, beginning new life.

1.ImT The myriad beings's own beginning.

1.ImT Great brightening completing beginning.

2.1b Yin begins solidifying indeed.

3.S Sprouting implies beings's beginning giving-birth indeed.

3.ImT Solid[and]Supple beginning mingling and-also heaviness giving-birth indeed.

6.ST A chün tzu uses arousing affairs to plan beginning.

18.ImT Completing, by-consequence possessing the beginning.

32.ImT Completing by-consequence possessing the beginning indeed.

32.1b Beginning seeking depth indeed.

41/42.CD Increasing, decreasing's beginning indeed.

54.ImT A person's completion beginning indeed.

Being(s), WU: creature, thing, any single being; ●
matter, substance, essence; nature of things. See also: **Beings not permitted to use**

1.ImT The myriad beings's own beginning.

1.ImT The kinds: being diffusing forms.

1.ImT Heads issuing-forth-from the multitudinous beings.

2.ST A chün tzu uses munificent actualizing-tao to carry the beings.

2.ImT The myriad beings's own birth.

2.ImT Field: munificence carrying the beings.

2.ImT The kinds: being conjoining Growing.

3.S Therefore afterwards the myriad beings giving-birth in-truth.

3.S Overfilling Heaven[and]Earth's interspace implies verily the myriad beings.

3.S Sprouting implies beings's beginning giving-birth indeed.

4.S Beings giving-birth necessarily Enveloping.

4.S Being's immaturity indeed.

5.S Being immature not permitting not nourishing indeed.

10.S Beings Accumulating, therefore afterwards possessing codes.

11.ImT By-consequence-of that Heaven[and]Earth mingling and-also the myriad beings interpenetrating indeed.

12.ImT By-consequence-of that Heaven[and]Earth not mingling and-also the myriad beings not interpenetrating indeed.

13.ST A chün tzu uses sorting the clans to mark-off the beings.

14.S Associating-with People Concording implies beings necessarily converting in-truth.

15.ST [A chün tzu uses] evaluating beings to even spreading-out.

20.S Being great therefore afterwards permitting Viewing.

21. ImT Jaws center possesses being.

24.AE Returning: the small and-also marking-off with-respect-to beings.

25.ST Below heaven thunder moving. Beings associating Without Embroiling.

25.ST The Earlier Kings used luxuriance suiting the season to nurture the myriad beings.

27.S Beings accumulating therefore afterwards permitting nourishing.

27. ImT Heaven[and]Earth nourishes the myriad beings.

31.S Therefore afterwards possessing the myriad beings.

31.S Possessing the myriad beings:

31. ImT Heaven[and]Earth influencing and-also the myriad beings changing give-birth.

31/32. ImT And-also actually Heaven[and]Earth, the myriad beings's motives permitting visualizing.

37.ST A chün tzu uses words to possess beings and-also movement to possess perseverance.

37.5a Beings: care significant.

38. ImT The myriad beings Polarizing and-also their affairs sorted indeed.

44. ImT The kinds: beings conjoining composition indeed.

45.S Beings mutually meeting and-also afterwards assembling.

45. ImT And-also actually Heaven[and]Earth, the myriad beings's motives, permitting visualizing.

50.S Skinning beings implies absolutely-nothing like a Vessel.

54. ImT Heaven[and]Earth not mingling and-also the myriad beings not rising.

63.S Possessing Exceeding being implies necessarily Fording.

64.S Beings not permitted exhaustion indeed.

64.ST A chün tzu uses considering to mark-off the beings residing on-all-sides.

Beings not permitted to use: no one is allowed to make use of; nothing can exist by means of.

This phrase occurs in the Sequence of Hexagrams **12, 13, 22, 24, 29, 33, 34, 35, 40, 52, 53, 60.**

Belly, See: **Left belly**

Below, HSIA: anything below, in all senses; lower, inner; lower trigram; opposite of above, SHANG. See also: **Above[and]Below**, and **Below Heaven**

This term occurs in the Symbol Tradition and the Image Tradition of most hexagrams describing the lower trigram and lines. It also occurs at:

1.1b Yang located below indeed.

3.1b Using valuing the mean below.

6.2b Below origin, above Arguing.

15. ImT Heavenly tao fording below and-also shining brightness.

17.3b Below, purpose stowed-away indeed.

23.1b Below using submerging indeed.

24.S Above Stripping exhausted, below reversing.

24.2b Using humanity below indeed.

28.1b Supple located below indeed.

28.4b Not sagging, reaching-to the below indeed.

29/30.CD Above Radiance and-also below Gorge indeed.

31.3b A place to hold-on-to the below indeed.

42.1b The below, not munificent affairs indeed.

47.4b Purpose located below indeed.

48.S Confining reaching-to the above implies necessarily reversing the below.

48.1b The below indeed.

56.3b Using Sojourning to associate-with the below.

57.2a,6a/b Ground located below the bed.

62. Im Above not proper, below proper.

Below Heaven, T'IEN HSIA: the human world, between heaven and earth.

7.ImT Using the latter poisons Below Heaven and-also the commoners adhering-to it.

12. ImT Above[and]Below not mingling and-also Below Heaven without fiefdoms indeed.

13. ImT Verily a chün tzu activating enables interpenetrating Below Heaven's purpose.

17. ImT And-also Below Heaven Following the season.

18. ImT And-also Below Heaven regulated indeed.

20. ImT Centering correcting uses Viewing Below Heaven.

20.ImT And-also actually Below Heaven submitting.

22.ImT Using changes accomplishing Below Heaven.

30.ImT Thereupon changes accomplishing Below Heaven.

31.ImT The all-wise person influencing the people at-heart and-also Below Heaven harmony evening.

32.ImT The all-wise person lasting with-respect-to his tao and-also Below Heaven the changes accomplishing.

37.ImT Actually correcting Dwelling and-also Below Heaven set-right.

44.ImT Below Heaven, the great moving indeed.

55.ImT Properly illuminating Below Heaven indeed.

Belt, see: **Pouched belt**

Bench, CHI: low table used to lean on; side-table; stool or support.

59.2a/b Dispersing: fleeing one's bench.

Benefits, LU: pay, salary, income; have the use of; goods received, revenues; offical recognition.

12.ST [A chün tzu uses] not permitting splendor to use benefits.

43.ST A chün tzu uses spreading-out benefits to extend-to the below.

Benevolence, HUI: regard for others, humanity; fulfill social duties; unselfish, kind, merciful.

42.5a/b Possessing conformity, a benevolent heart.

42.5a Possessing conformity, benevolence: my actualizing-tao.

42.5b Benevolence: my actualizing-tao.

Bestow, HSI: grant, confer upon; reward, gift. The ideogram: metal used in coins and insignia.

6.6a Maybe bestowing's pouched belt.

7.2a/b The king three-times bestowing fate.

35.Im/ImT The calm feudatory avails-of bestowing horses to multiply the multitudes.

Big-toe, see: **Thumb**

Bin, TOU: measure and container for grain;gauge, hold, contain.

55.2a,4a/b Sun centering: visualizing a bin.

Bind, LÜAN: tie, connect, take hold of; bent, contracted. The ideogram: hand and connect, binding things.

9.5a/b Possessing conformity, binding thus.

61.5a/b Possessing conformity, binding thus.

Bird, NIAO: all feathered animals; associated with the Fiery Moment.

56.6a A bird burning its nest.

62.Im Flying bird: abandoning's sound.

62.ImT Possessing the flying bird's symbol in-truth.

62.ImT Flying bird: abandoning's sound.

62.1a/b Flying bird: using a pitfall.

62.6a Flying bird radiating it.

Birth/give-birth-to, SHENG: produce, beget, grow, bear, arise; life, vitality. The ideogram: earth and sprout.

2.ImT The myriad beings's own birth.

3.S Therefore afterwards the myriad beings giving-birth in-truth.

3.S Sprouting implies beings' beginning giving-birth indeed.

3.ImT Solid[and]Supple beginning mingling and-also heaviness giving-birth indeed.

4.S Beings giving-birth necessarily Enveloping.

20.3a/b Viewing my birth, advancing, withdrawing.

20.5a/b Viewing my birth.

20.6a/b Viewing one's birth.

28.2a A withered willow giving-birth-to a sprig.

28.5a/b A withered willow giving-birth-to flowers.

31.ImT Heaven[and]Earth influencing and-also the myriad beings changing give-birth.

42.ImT Heaven spreading-out, earth giving-birth.

46.ST Earth center giving-birth-to wood.

Bite, HO: close the jaws, bite through, crush between the teeth. The ideogram: mouth and cover, jaws fit together as a lid fits a vessel.

Image of Hexagram 21 and occurs throughout its texts.

Bitter, K'U: taste corresponding to the Fiery Moment; unpleasant, troublesome, painful affliction; take pains; urgent, pressing; dislike, grieve, mortify.

60.Im/ImT Bitter Articulating not permitting Trial.

60.6a/b Bitter Articulating, Trial: pitfall.

Bless, FU: heavenly gifts; make happy; spiritual power and goodwill. The ideogram: spirit and plenty, heavenly gifts in abundance.

11.3a Tending-towards taking-in possesses blessing.

15. ImT Souls[and]Spirits harming overfilling and-also blessing Humbling.

35.2a/b Acquiescing-in closely-woven chain-mail: blessing.

47.5b Acquiescing-in blessing indeed.

48.3a Together-with acquiescing-in one's blessing.

48.3b Acquiescing-in blessing indeed.

51. ImT,1b Anxiety involving blessing indeed.

63.5a/b The substance: acquiescing-in one's blessing.

Block, CHIH: obstruct, stop up, close, restrain, fill up.

6.Im Arguing, possessing conformity. Blocking awe.

6.ImT Blocking awe, centering significant.

41.ST A chün tzu uses curbing anger to block the appetites.

Blood, HSÜEH: yin fluid that maintains life; money, property.

2.6a Their blood: indigo, yellow.

3.6a/b Weeping blood, coursing thus.

5.4a/b Attending tending-towards blood.

9.4a Blood departing, awe issuing-forth.

54.6a A notable disembowelling a goat without blood.

59.6a/b Dispersing one's blood.

Blunder, SHENG: mistake due to ignorance or fault; contrasts with calamity, TSAI, disaster from without. The ideogram: eye and grow, a film clouding sight. See also: **Calamity[and]Blunder**

6.2a Without blunder.

25. Im/ImT One in-no-way correcting: possessing blunder.

25.6a Without Embroiling. Moving possessing blunder.

51.3a Shake moving without blunder.

Body, KUNG: physical being, power and self expression; contrasts with individuality, SHEN, the total personality.

4.3a Not possessing the body.

39.2a In-no-way body's anteriority.

51.6a Shake: not tending-towards one's body, tending-towards one's neighbor.

52.4b Stopping connoting the body indeed.

59.3a/b Dispersing one's body.

Bog, NI: wet spongy soil; mire, slush, quicksand; unable to move.

5.3a/b Attending tending-towards bogs.

48.1a/b The Well: a bog, not taking-in.

51.4a/b Shake: releasing the bog.

Bonds, YO: cords, ropes; contracts, treaties, legal and moral obligations; moderate, restrain, restrict.

29.4a Letting-in bonds originating-from the window.

Border, CHI: limit, frontier, line which joins and divides. The ideogram: place and sacrifice, border between human and spirit.

11.3b Heaven[and]Earth, the border indeed.

29.4b Solid[and]Supple, the border indeed.

40.1b Solid[and]Supple's border.

55.6b The heavenly border, hovering indeed.

Bound, KEN: limit, boundary; encounter an obstacle, stop; still, quiet, motionless; confine, enclose, mark off; turn around to look behind; hard, adamant, obstinate; perverse. The ideogram: eye and person turning round to compare and group what is behind.

Image of Hexagram 52 and occurs throughout its texts.

Boundary, CHI: border, limit, frontier; confine.

40. ImT Thunder[and]Rain arousing and-also the hundred fruits, grasses, trees, altogether seedburst boundary.

Bow, HU: wooden bow; curved flag pole; curved, arched.

38.6a Beforehand stretching's bow.

38.6a Afterwards stimulating's bow.

Brace/jawbones, FU: support, consolidate, reinforce, strengthen, stiffen, prop up, fix; steady, firm, rigid; help, rescue; support the speaking mouth. The ideogram: cart and great.

8.ImT Grouping bracing indeed.

11.ST [The crown-prince uses] bracing to mutualize Heaven[and]Earth's propriety.

28.3b Not permitted to use possessing bracing indeed.

31.6a/b Conjoining one's jawbones, cheeks, tongue.

52.5a/b Bound: one's jawbones.

Break-up, CHÜEH: streams diverging; break through an obstacle and scatter; separate, break into parts; cut or bite through; decide, pass sentence. The ideogram: water and parting.

34.4a/b The hedge broken-up, not ruined.

43.S Augmenting and-also not climaxing necessarily breaks-up.

43.S Parting implies breaking-up indeed.

43/44.CD Parting: breaking-up indeed.

43/44.CD Solid breaking-up supple indeed.

43. ImT Parting. Breaking-up indeed.

43. ImT Solid breaking-up supple indeed.

43. ImT Breaking-up and-also harmonizing.

44.S Breaking-up necessarily possesses meeting.

Brightness, MING: light-giving aspect of burning, heavenly bodies and consciousness; with fire, a Symbol of the trigram Radiance, LI.
Image of Hexagram 36 and occurs throughout its texts.

1.ImT Great brightening completing beginning.

3.4b Brightness indeed.

6.1b Although the small possesses words, one's differentiation brightening indeed.

10. ImT Shining brightness indeed.

10.3b Not the stand to use possessing brightness indeed.

13. ImT Pattern brightening uses persisting.

14. ImT One's actualizing-tao: solid persisting and-also pattern brightening.

14.4b Brightness differentiating clearly indeed.

15. ImT Heavenly tao fording below and-also shining brightness.

17.4a Possessing conformity, locating-in tao uses brightening.

17.4b Brightening achieving indeed.

21.ST The Earlier Kings used brightening flogging to enforce the laws.

21. ImT Stirring-up and-also brightening.

21.6b Understanding not brightened indeed.

22.ST A chün tzu uses brightening the multitudinous standards without daring to sever litigating.

22. ImT Pattern brightening, stopping:

30.ST Brightness doubled arousing Radiance.

30.ST Great People use consecutive brightening to illuminate tending-towards the four sides.

30. ImT Redoubling brightness uses congregating to reach-to correcting.

35.CD Brightness Hiding: proscribed indeed.

35.ST Brightness issuing-forth above earth.

35.ST A chün tzu uses originating enlightening to brighten actualizing-tao.

35. ImT Brightness issuing-forth above earth.

35. ImT Yielding and-also congregating reaching-to great brightening.

38. ImT Stimulating and-also congregating reaching-to brightness.

43.4b Understanding not brightened indeed.

47.1b Shady, not bright indeed.

48.3a Kingly brightness.

48.3b Seeking kingly brightness:

49.ST A chün tzu uses regulating time-reckoning to brighten the seasons.

49. ImT Pattern brightening uses stimulating.

50. ImT Ground and-also the ear[and]eye: understanding brightened.

52. ImT One's tao: shining brightness.

55. ImT Brightness using stirring-up.

55.4b Shade, not brightening indeed.

56.ST A chün tzu uses brightening consideration to avail-of punishing and-also not to detain litigating.

56. ImT Stopping and-also congregating reaching-to brightness.

Brilliance, HUI: sunlight, sunshine, sunbeam; bright, splendid.

64.5b One's brilliance significant indeed.

Buckle, JAO: distort, wrench out of shape, collapse, break; weak; flexible, lithe.

28.3a/b The ridgepole buckling. Pitfall.

Bulwark, CH'ENG: city wall, citadel, place walled for defense.

11.6a/b The bulwark returned tending-towards the moat.

Bundle-in, KUA: enclose, envelop, tie up; embrace, include.

2.4a Bundled-in the bag.

2.4b Bundled-in the bag, without fault.

Burgeon, YI: beginning of growth after seedburst, CHIA; early spring; associated with the Woody Moment.

11.5a The supreme burgeoning, converting maidenhood.

54.5a/b The supreme burgeoning Converting Maidenhood.

Burn, FEN: set fire to, destroy completely.

30.4a Burning thus. Dying thus. Thrown-out thus.

56.3a/b Sojourning, burning one's resting-place.

56.6a A bird burning its nest.

56.6b One's righteousness burning indeed.

Bushy, PAO: luxuriant growth, dense thicket; conceal, screen; sleeping mats; wrap as a gift. The ideogram: wrap and bushes.

12.5a Attaching tending-towards bushy mulberry-trees.

Bushy-tailed rodent, SHIH SHU: animals who destroy stored grain; mean, thieving people; timid, skulking, mournful, brooding.

35.4a Prospering, thus bushy-tailed rodents.

35.4b Bushy-tailed rodents, Trial: adversity.

Butt, CHU: push or strike with the horns; attack, oppose, offend; stirred up, excited; obnoxious; associated with Woody Moment.

34.3a,6a The he goat butts a hedge.

By-consequence(-of), TSE: very strong connection; reason, cause, result; rule, law, pattern, standard; therefore.

This term occurs throughout the hexagram texts.

Calamity, TSAI: disaster from outside; flood, plague, drought, blight, ruin; contrasts with blunder, SHENG, indicating personal fault. The ideogram: water and fire, elemental powers.

5.3b Calamity located outside indeed.

23.4b Slicing close-to calamity indeed.

25/26.CD Without Embroiling: calamity indeed.

25.3a Without Embroiling's calamity.

25.3a Capital people's calamity.

25.3b Capital people, calamity indeed.

25.6b Exhaustion's calamity indeed.

26.1b Not opposing calamity indeed.

33.1b Not going, wherefore calamity indeed.

55.1b Exceeding a decade, calamity indeed.

56.1a Splitting-off one's place, grasping calamity.

56.1b Purpose exhausted, calamity indeed.

Calamity[and]Blunder, TSAI SHENG: disaster from without and within; natural disaster combined with misfortune due to ignorance or fault; ruin, defeat, rout, collapse.

24.6a Possessing Calamity[and]Blunder.

62.6a That designates Calamity[and]Blunder.

Calf, FEI: muscle of lower leg; rely on; prop, rest.

31.2a Conjoining one's calves.

52.2a Bound: one's calves.

Call, MING: bird and animal cries, through which they recognize each other; distinctive sound, song, statement. The ideogram: bird and mouth, a distinguishing call.

15.2a/b,6a/b Calling Humbling.

16.1a Calling Provision.

16.1b Initial six, calling Provision.

61.2a Calling crane located-in yin.

Calm, K'ANG: confident strength and poise; stability, peace, ease; joy, delight.

35. Im/ImT The calm feudatory avails-of bestowing horses to multiply the multitudes.

Canons, CHING: standards, laws; regular, regulate; the Five Classics. The ideogram: warp-threads in a loom.

3.ST A chün tzu uses the canons to coordinate.

27.2a Rejecting the canons, tending-towards the hill-top.

27.5a Rejecting the canons.

Caper, YO: play, frolic, dance and leap for joy, frisk, gambol. The ideogram: foot and feather, light-footed.

1.4a/b Maybe capering located-in the abyss.

Capital, YI: populous fortified city, center and symbol of the domain it rules. The ideogram: enclosure and official seal.

6.2a Converting and-also escaping one's capital.

8.5a/b Capital people not admonished.

11.6a Originating-from the capital, notifying fate.

15.6a Chastising the capital city.

15.6b Chastising the capital city indeed.

25.3a Capital people's calamity.

25.3b Capital people, calamity indeed.

35.6a/b Holding-fast avails-of subjugating the capital.

43. Im/ImT Notifying originates-from the capital.

46.3a/b Ascending: an empty capital.

48. Im/ImT Amending the capital, not amending the Well.

Care, HSÜ: fear, doubt, concern; heartfelt attachment; relieve, soothe, aid; sympathy, compassion, consolation. The ideogram: heart and blood, the heart's blood affected.

11.3a No cares: one's conforming.

35.5a/b Letting-go, acquiring, no cares.

37.5a Beings: care significant.

43.2a No cares.

43.2b Possessing arms, no cares.

45.1a No cares.

46. Im/ImT No cares.

Carry, TSAI: bear, carry with you; contain, sustain; load a ship or cart, cargo; fill in, complete.

2.ST A chün tzu uses munificent actualizing-tao to carry the beings.

2.ImT Field: munificence carrying the beings.

9.6a Honoring actualizing-tao carrying.

9.6b Actualizing-tao amassing carrying indeed.

14.2a/b The great chariot used to carry.

23.6b Commoners: the place to carry indeed.

38.6a Carrying souls, the-one chariot.

Cart, YÜ: carrying capacity of a vehicle; contain, hold, sustain.

7.3a/b Legions maybe carting corpses.

7.5a/b The junior son carting corpses.

9.3a Carting stimulating the spokes.

23.6a/b A chün tzu acquiring a cart.

26.2a/b Carting, stimulating the axle-strap.

26.3a An enclosed cart, escorting.

34.4a Invigorating tending-towards the Great: a cart's axle-straps.

38.3a/b Visualizing the cart pulled-back.

Cast-out, P'I: expel, repress, exclude, punish; exclusionary laws and their enforcement. The ideogram: punish, authority and mouth, give orders to expel.

12.ST A chün tzu uses parsimonious actualizing-tao to cast-out heaviness.

30.1b Using casting-out fault indeed.

38.1b Using casting-out fault indeed.

Catch, HUO: take in hunt; catch a thief; obtain, seize; hit the mark, opportune moment; prisoner, spoils, prey; slave, servant.

17.4a/b Following possessing catching.

30.6a Severing the head. Catching in-no-way its demons.

36.4a Catching Brightness Hiding's heart.

36.4b Catching the heart, intention indeed.

40.2a The fields, catching three foxes.

40.6a Without not Harvesting: catching it.

52. Im/ImT Not catching one's individuality.

57.4a/b The fields, catching three kinds.

Cattle, NIU: ox, bull, cow, calf; kine; power and strength of work animals.

25.3a Maybe attaching's cattle.

25.3b Moving people acquiring cattle.

26.4a Youthful cattle's stable.

30. Im/ImT Accumulating female cattle. Significant.

33.2a Holding-on-to it: availing-of yellow cattle's skin.

33.2b Holding-on avails-of yellow cattle.

38.3a One's cattle hampered.

49.1a Thonging avails-of yellow cattle's Skin.

49.1b Thonging avails-of yellow cattle.

56.6a/b Losing the cattle, tending-towards versatility.

63.5a/b The Eastern neighbor slaughters cattle.

Cave, HSÜEH: hole used for dwelling; cavern, den, pit; open grave.

5.4a Issuing-forth originates-from the cave.

5.6a Entering tending-towards the cave.

62.5a A prince, a string-arrow grasping another located-in a cave.

Center, CHUNG: inner, central; put in the center; middle, stable point enabling you to face inner and outer changes; middle line of trigram. The ideogram: field divided in two equal parts. See also: **Centering correcting**

This term occurs in many hexagrams at the second and/or fifth Transforming Line. It also occurs at:

Image of Hexagram 61 and occurs throughout its texts.

3.ImT Stirring-up reaching-to venturing center.

3.3a Namely, entering tending-towards the forest center.

4.ImT Season centering indeed.

4.ImT Using solid centering indeed.

5.ImT Using correcting centering indeed.

6.Im Centering significant.

6.ImT Blocking awe, centering significant.

6.ImT Solid coming and-also acquiring the center indeed.

7.ST Earth center possessing stream.

7.ImT Solid centering and-also corresponding.

8.ImT Using solid centering indeed.

9.ImT Solid centering and-also purpose moving.

11.4b Centering the heart desiring indeed.

13. ImT Acquiring centering and-also corresponding reaching-to Force.

14. ImT Supple acquiring the dignifying situation, the great centering.

15.ST Earth center possessing mountain.

17.ST Marsh center possessing thunder.

19. ImT Solid centering and-also corresponding.

21. ImT Jaws center possesses being.

21. ImT Supple acquiring the center and-also moving above.

24.ST Thunder located-in earth center. Returning.

24.4a/b Centering movement, solitary Returning.

25. ImT Solid centering and-also corresponding.

26.ST Heaven located-in mountain center.

28. ImT Solid Exceeding and-also centering.

29. ImT Holding-fast the heart's Growing, thereupon using solid centering indeed.

36.ST/ImT Brightness entering earth center.

38. ImT Acquiring the center and-also corresponding reaching the solid.

39. ImT Going acquires the center indeed.

40. ImT Thereupon acquiring the center indeed.

42.3a Possessing conformity, center moving.

42.4a Center moving.

45. ImT Solid centering and-also corresponding.

46.ST Earth center giving-birth-to wood. Ascending.

46. ImT Solid centering and-also corresponding.

47. ImT Using solid centering indeed.

48. ImT Thereupon using solid centering indeed.

49.ST Marsh center possessing fire. Skinning.

50. ImT Acquiring the center and-also corresponding reaching the solid.

51.6b Center not-yet acquired indeed.

53. ImT One's situation: solid acquiring the center indeed.

55. Im/ImT No grief. Properly sun centering.

55. ImT Sun centering, by-consequence going-down.

55.3a Sun centering: visualizing froth.

55.4a/b Sun centering: visualizing a bin.

56. ImT Supple acquiring the center reaching-to the outside and-also yielding reaching-to the solid.

58. ImT Solid centering and-also supple outside.

59. ImT Kinghood thereupon located-in the center indeed.

60. ImT Solid[and]Supple apportioning and-also solid acquiring the center.

62.CD Centering Conforming: trustworthiness indeed.

62. ImT Supple acquiring the center.

62. ImT Solid letting-go the situation and-also not centering.

63. ImT Supple acquiring the center indeed.

64. ImT Supple acquiring the center indeed.

64. ImT Not-yet issuing-forth-from the center indeed.

Centering correcting, CHUNG CHENG: central and correct; make rectifying one-sidedness and error your central concern; reaching a stable center in yourself can correct the situation.

5.5b Using centering correcting indeed.

6.ImT Honoring centering correcting indeed.

6.5b Using centering correcting indeed.

10. ImT Solid centering correctly.

13. ImT Centering correcting and-also corresponding.

16.2b Using centering correcting indeed.

20. ImT Centering correcting uses Viewing Below Heaven.

30. ImT Supple congregating reaches-to centering correcting.

35.2b Using centering correcting indeed.

42. ImT Centering correcting possessing reward.

44. ImT Solid meeting centering correctness.

44.5b Centering correctness indeed.

48.5b Centering correcting indeed.

52.5b Using centering correcting indeed.

57. ImT Solid Ground reaching-to centering correcting and-also purpose moving.

60. ImT Centering correcting uses interpenetrating.

Chain-mail, CHIEH: chain-armor; tortoise or crab shell; protective covering; border, limit; protection, support.

16.2a Chain-mail tending-towards petrification:

35.2a/b Acquiescing-in closely-woven chain-mail: blessing.

58.4a Chain-mail afflicting: possessing rejoicing.

Chambers, T'ING: family room, courtyard, hall; domestic. The ideogram: shelter and hall, a secure place.

36.4a Tending-towards issuing-forth-from the gate chambers.

43. Im/ImT Displaying tending-towards kingly chambers.

52. Im/ImT Moving one's chambers.

60.1a/b Not issuing-forth-from the door chambers.

60.2a Not issuing-forth-from the gate chambers.

60.2b Not issuing-forth-from the gate chambers, pitfall.

Change, HUA: gradual, continuous meta-morphosis; influence someone; contrasts with transform, PIEN, sudden mutation. The ideogram: person alive and dead, the life-process.

1.ImT Force: tao transforming changes.

20. ImT Viewing below and-also changing indeed.

22. ImT Using changes accomplishing Below Heaven.

30. ImT Thereupon changes accomplishing Below Heaven.

31. ImT Heaven[and]Earth influencing and-also the myriad beings changing give-birth.

32. ImT The four seasons transforming changes and-also enabling lasting accomplishment.

32. ImT The all-wise person lasting with-respect-to his tao and-also Below Heaven the changes accomplishing.

61. ImT Thereupon changing the fiefdoms indeed.

Channel, HO: bed of river or stream; running water.

11.2a Availing-of crossing the channel.

Chariot, CH'E: wheeled travelling vehicle; contrasts with cart, YÜ, which carries.

14.2a/b The great chariot used to carry.

22.1a/b Stowing-away the chariot and-also afoot.

38.6a Carrying souls, the-one chariot.

47.4a Confined, tending-towards a metallic chariot.

Chastise, CHENG: punish, subjugate, discipline; reduce to order; punishing expedition. The ideogram: step and correct, a rectifying move.

9.6a/b A chün tzu chastising: pitfall.

11.1a Chastising significant.

11.1b Eradicating thatch-grass, chastising significant.

15.5b Chastising, not submitting indeed.

15.6a Chastising the capital city.

15.6b Chastising the capital city indeed.

24.6a Culminating tending-towards ten years-revolved not controlling chastisement.

27.2a Jaws chastising: pitfall.

27.2b Six at-second, chastising: pitfall.

30.6a/b Kinghood availing-of issuing-forth chastising.

34.1a Chastising: pitfall, possessing conformity.

41.2a Chastising: pitfall.

46. Im/ImT The South, chastising significant.

47.2a Chastising: pitfall, without fault.

47.6a Chastising significant.

49.2a Chastising significant, without fault.

49.3a Chastising: pitfall, Trial: adversity.

49.6a Chastising: pitfall.

51.6a Chastising: pitfall.

53.3a/b The husband chastised, not returning.

54. Im/ImT Chastising: pitfall.

54.1a Chastising significant.

64.3a/b Not-yet Fording, chastising: pitfall.

Cheek-bones, CH'UAN: facial feature denoting character; high cheek-bones indicate cruelty.

43.3a Invigorating tending-towards the cheek-bones:

Cheeks, CHIA: sides of the face; speak, articulate.

31.6a/b Conjoining one's jawbones, cheeks, tongue.

Cherish, HUAI: dwell on, think of; carry in the heart or womb; cling to. The ideogram: heart and hide, cherish in the heart.

7.2b Cherishing the myriad fiefdoms indeed.

56.2a Cherishing one's own.

Chief, CHÜN: effective ruler; preside over, take the lead; influence others; term of respect. The ideogram: mouth and director, giving orders. See also: **Chief[and]Servant**

7.6a/b The Great Chief possesses fate.

10.3a/b Martial people activating: tending-towards a Great Chief.

12.1b Purpose located-in a chief indeed.

19.5a/b A Great Chief's propriety.

24.6a Using one's city chief: pitfall.

24.6b Reversing the chief: tao indeed.

37. ImT Dwelling People possess an intimidating chief in-truth.

49.6b Yielding uses adhering-to the chief indeed.

54.5a One's chief's sleeves:

62.2a/b Not extending-to one's chief.

Chief[and]Servant, CHÜN CH'EN: cooperative relation between those who give orders and those who carry them out. See also: **Servant**
31.S Therefore afterwards possessing Chief[and]Servant.
31.S Possessing Chief[and]Servant:

Chock, NI: block used to stop a cart wheel; inquire, investigate.
44.1a/b Attaching tending-towards a metallic chock.

Chroniclers, SHIH: histories, records, annals; authoritative record; narrator of events, annalist.
57.2a Availing-of chroniclers, shamans.

Chün tzu: ideal of a person who uses divination to order his/her life in accordance with tao rather than wilful intention; keyword.
This term occurs in the Symbol Tradition of all hexagrams except **8, 11, 16, 20, 21, 23, 24, 30, 44, 59**. It also occurs at:
1.3a A chün tzu completing the day: Force, Force.
2.Im A chün tzu possesses directed going.
2.ImT A chün tzu directing moving.
3.3a A chün tzu almost not thus stowing-away.
3.3b A chün tzu stowing it:
9.6a/b A chün tzu chastising: pitfall.
11. ImT Inside chün tzu and-also outside Small People.
11. ImT A chün tzu: tao long-living.
12. Im/ImT Not Harvesting: chün tzu, Trial.
12. ImT Inside Small People and-also outside chün tzu.
12. ImT A chün tzu: tao dissolving indeed.
13. Im Harvesting: chün tzu, Trial.
13. ImT A chün tzu, correcting indeed.
13. ImT Verily a chün tzu activating enables interpenetrating Below Heaven's purpose.
15. Im A chün tzu possesses completing.
15. ImT A chün tzu's completing indeed.
15.1a/b Humbling, Humbling: chün tzu.
15.3a/b Toiling Humbling: chün tzu.
20.1a Chün tzu: abashment
20.5a/6a A chün tzu: without fault.
23. ImT A chün tzu honors the dissolving pause to overfill emptiness.
23.6a/b A chün tzu acquiring a cart.
33.4a A chün tzu significant.
33.4b A chün tzu lovingly Retiring.
34.3a A chün tzu avails-of absence.

34.3b A chün tzu: absence indeed.
36.1a/b A chün tzu tending-towards moving:
40.5a A chün tzu holding-fast possesses Taking-apart.
40.5b A chün tzu possessing Taking-apart.
43.3a/b A chün tzu: Parting, Parting.
47. ImT Reaching-to one's very chün tzu.
49.6a/b A chün tzu: leopard transforming.
64.5a/b A chün tzu's shining.

City, KUO: area of only human constructions; political unit, polis. First of the territorial zones: city, suburbs, countryside, forests.
1.ImT Myriad cities, conjoining, soothing.
7.6a Disclosing the city, receiving a dwelling.
8.ST The Earlier Kings used installing myriad cities to connect the connoted feudatories.
15.6a Chastising the capital city.
15.6b Chastising the capital city indeed.
20.4a/b Viewing the city's shining.
24.6a Using one's city chief: pitfall.
29. ImT The kingly prince sets-up venturing used to guard his city.
36.6b Illuminating the four cities indeed.
42.4a Harvesting: availing-of activating depending-on shifting the city.
64.4a Three years-revolved, possessing donating tending-towards the great city.

Clan, TSU: extended family with same ancestor and surname; kin, relatives; tribe, class, kind. The ideogram: flag and spear, a rallying point.
13.ST A chün tzu uses sorting the clans to mark-off the beings.

Clapper, T'O: board used by watchmen to strike the hours.
16.AE Redoubling gates, smiting clappers.

Classification, HUI: class, collection, series; same kind; put or group together.
11.1a Using one's classification.
12.1a Using one's classification.

Clear, TZU: cultivate wild or overgrown land; reclaim.
25.2a Not clearing the plow-land.

Clearly, CHE: make clear, illuminate; shine, emit light; starlight.
14.4b Brightness differentiating clearly indeed.

Climax, YI: come to a high point and stop, bring to an end; use up, lay aside; decline, reject.
22.S Beings not permitted to use unconsidered uniting and-also climaxing.
26.1a Harvesting: climaxing.

26.1b Possessing adversity, Harvesting: climaxing.
32. ImT Persevering lasting and-also not climaxing indeed.
41.1a/b Climaxing affairs, swiftly going.
42.S Diminishing and-also not climaxing necessarily Augments.
43.S Augmenting and-also not climaxing necessarily breaks-up.
47.S Ascending and-also not climaxing necessarily Confines.
62.5b Above climaxing indeed.
62.6b Climaxing overbearing indeed.

Climb, CHI: ascend, scale; climb steep cliffs; rise as clouds.
51.2a Climbing tending-towards the ninth mound.

Clog, SAI: stop up, fill up, close, obstruct, hinder, prevent; unintelligent, dull, hard to understand.
50.3a Its movement clogged.
60.1b Knowing interpenetrating clogging indeed.

Close-to, CHIN: near in time or place, next to; approach; recently, lately; familiar.
23.4b Slicing close-to calamity indeed.

Closely-woven, TZU: compact, close textured, dense, solid, impenetrable. The ideogram: herbs and silk, dense fabric or foliage.
35.2a/b Acquiescing-in closely-woven chain-mail: blessing.

Clothes, YI: upper body garments; dress; cover, husk.
63.4a A token: possessing clothes in-tatters.

Clouds, YÜN: fog, mist, water vapor; connects to the Streaming Moment and Stream, the Symbol of the trigram Gorge, K'AN.
1.ImT Clouds moving, rain spreading-out.
3.ST Clouds, Thunder, Sprouting.
5.ST Above clouds with-respect-to heaven.
9.Im/ImT Shrouding clouds, not raining.
62.5a/b Shrouding clouds, not raining.

Cluster, TS'UI: call or pack together; tight groups of people, animals, things; collect, gather, assemble, concentrate; bunch, crowd, collection; lit.: dense, tussocky grass.
Image of Hexagram 45 and occurs throughout its texts.

Codes, LI: rites, rules, ritual; usage, manners; worship, ceremony, observance. The ideogram: worship and sacrificial vase, handling a sacred vessel.

10.S Beings Accumulating, therefore afterwards possessing codes.
15.AE Humbling: using paring the codes.
31.S Therefore afterwards the codes righteously possessing a place to polish.
34.ST A chün tzu uses no codes whatever, nowhere treading.

Coins, PEI: cowrie shells used for money; adorned with shell; money, riches; precious, valuable.
51.2a A hundred-thousand lost coins.

Cold, HAN: chilled, wintry; destitute, poor; shiver; fear; associated with the Streaming Moment. The ideogram: person huddled in straw under a roof.
48.5a The Well: limpid, cold springwater taken-in.
48.5b Cold springwater's taking-in.

Collect, SHOU: gather, harvest; receive what is due; involve, snare, bind, restrain.
48.6a The Well: collecting, no cover.

Come, LAI, and go, WANG, describe the stream of time as it flows from future through present to past; come, LAI, indicates what is approaching; move toward, arrive at; keyword.
5.6a Three people coming.
5.6b Not urging's visitors coming.
6.ImT Solid coming and-also acquiring the center indeed.
8.Im/ImT Not soothing, on-all-sides coming.
8.1a Completing coming possesses more significance.
11. Im The small going, the great coming.
11. ImT The small going, the great coming: significance Growing.
12. Im/ImT The great going, the small coming.
17. ImT Solid coming and-also supple below.
22. ImT Supple coming and-also patterning solid.
24. Im/ImT Partnering coming, without fault.
24. Im/ImT The seventh day coming: Returning.
25. ImT Solid originating-from the outside coming and-also activating a lord with-respect-to the inside.
29.3a/b Coming's Gorge, the Gorge.
30.4a/b Assailing thus, its coming thus.
31.4a/b Wavering, wavering: going, coming.
39.1a/b Going Limping, coming praise.

39.3a/b Going Limping, coming reversing.
39.4a/b Going Limping, coming continuity.
39.5a/b The great Limping, partnering coming.
39.6a/b Going Limping, coming ripening.
40. Im/ImT One's coming return significant.
42.2b/6b Originating-from outside, coming indeed.
45/46.CD Ascending: not coming indeed.
47.2a Scarlet sashes on-all-sides coming.
47.4a/b Coming, ambling, ambling.
48. Im Going, coming: Welling, Welling.
51. Im/ImT Shake coming: frightening, frightening.
51.1a/b Shake coming: frightening, frightening.
51.2a/b Shake coming: adversity.
51.5a/b Shake going, coming adversity.
55.5a Coming composition.
58.3a/b Coming Opening, pitfall.
59. ImT Solid coming and-also not exhausted.
63.5b Significant, the great coming indeed.

- **Command**, KAO: give orders; insist on, express wishes; official seal. The ideogram: words and announce, verbal commands.
  44.ST The crown-prince uses spreading-out fate to command the four sides.

- **Commission**, SHIH: employ for a task; command, order; messenger, agent. The ideogram: person and office.
  7.5b Commissioning not appropriate indeed.
  8.5b Commissioning centering above indeed.
  41.4a Commissioning swiftly possesses rejoicing.

- **Commoners**, MIN: class of workers the state draws on to sustain the social hierarchy; undeveloped potential outside the organized personality.
  3.1b The great acquiring the commoners indeed.
  7.ST A chün tzu uses tolerating commoners to accumulate crowds.
  7.ImT Using the latter poisons Below Heaven and-also the commoners adhering-to it.
  10.ST [A chün tzu uses] setting-right the commoners, the purpose.
  11.ST [The crown-prince] uses the left to right the commoners.
  15.3b The myriad commoners submitting indeed.

16. ImT By-consequence punishing flogging purifies and-also the commoners submit.
18.ST A chün tzu uses rousing the commoners to nurture actualizing-tao.
19.ST [A chün tzu uses] tolerating to protect the commoners without delimiting.
20.ST The earlier kings used inspecting on-all-sides, Viewing the commoners to set-up teaching.
20.5b Viewing the commoners indeed.
23.6b Commoners: the place to carry indeed.
27. ImT The all-wise person nourishes eminence used to extend-to the myriad commoners.
42. ImT The commoners stimulated without delimiting.
44.4b Distancing the commoners indeed.
48.ST A chün tzu uses toiling commoners to encourage mutualizing.
58. ImT Stimulating using beforehand the commoners:
58. ImT The commoners forget their toiling.
58. ImT The commoners forget their dying.
58. ImT Actually the commoners encouraged in-fact.
60. ImT Not harming the commoners.

Companion, CH'IU: equal, spouse; unite, join in marriage. Also: opponent, rival, enemy; contradict, hate.
  50.2a/b My companion possesses affliction.

Complete, CHUNG: end of a cycle that begins the next; last, whole, all; contrasts with exhaust, CH'IUNG, final end. The ideogram: silk cocoons, follow and ice, winter linking one year with the next.
  1.ImT Great brightening completing beginning.
  1.3a A chün tzu completing the day: Force, Force.
  1.3b Completing the day: Force, Force.
  2.ImT Thereupon completing possesses reward.
  2.3a Without accomplishing possessing completion.
  2.7b Using the great to complete indeed.
  5.2a Completing significant.
  5.2b Although the small possesses words, using completing significant indeed.
  5.6a/b Respecting them: completing significant.

6.Im/ImT Completing: pitfall.
6.1a The small possesses words, completing significant.
6.3a Adversity, completing significant.
6.6a Completing dawn three-times depriving it.
8.1a Completing coming possesses more significance.
8.6b Without a place to complete indeed.
10.4a/b Pleading, pleading: completing significant.
12.S Beings not permitted to use completing interpenetrating.
12.6b Obstruction completed, by-consequence subverting.
13.S Beings not permitted to use completing Obstructing.
15. Im A chün tzu possesses completing.
15. ImT A chün tzu's completing indeed.
15.3a Possessing completing significant.
16.2a Not completing the day.
16.2b Not completing the day, Trial: significant.
18. ImT Completing, by-consequence possessing the beginning.
18.1a Adversity, completing significant.
18.3b Completing without fault indeed.
22.3b Completing absolutely-nothing: having a mound indeed.
22.4b Completing without surpassing indeed.
22.5a Abashment. Completing significant.
23.5b Completing without surpassing indeed.
23.6b Completing, not permitting availing-of indeed.
24.S Beings not permitted to use completing using-up.
24.6a Completing possesses great destroying.
29.S Beings not permitted to use completing Exceeding.
29.3b Completing without achieving indeed.
29.4a Completing, without fault.
32. ImT Completing by-consequence possessing the beginning indeed.
32.5b Adhering-to the-one and-also completing indeed.
34.S Beings not permitted to use completing Retiring.
35.S Beings not permitted to use completing Invigorating.
37.3a Completing abashed.

37.6a Completing significant.
38.3a/b Without initially possessing completion.
39.2b Completing without surpassing indeed.
40.S Beings not permitted to use completing heaviness.
43. ImT Solid long-living, thereupon completing indeed.
43.3b Completing without fault indeed.
43.6a Completing: possessing a pitfall.
43.6b Completing not permitting long-living indeed.
45.1a Possessing conformity, not completing.
47.4a Possessing completion.
50.2b Completing without surpassing indeed.
50.3a Completing significant.
52.S Beings not permitted to use completing stirring-up.
52.6b Using munificence to complete indeed.
53.S Beings not permitted to use completing stopping.
53/54.CD Converting Maidenhood: womanhood's completion indeed.
53.5a Completing: absolutely-nothing has mastering.
53.5b Completing: absolutely-nothing has mastering, significant.
54.ST A chün tzu uses perpetually completing to know the cracked.
54. ImT A person's completion beginning indeed.
55.3b Completing, not permitting availing-of indeed.
56.2b Completing without surpassing indeed.
56.5a/b Completing uses praising fate.
56.6b Completing absolutely-nothing: having hearing indeed.
57.5a Without initially possessing completion.
60.S Beings not permitted to use completing Radiance.
62.4b Completing not permitting long-living indeed.
63. Im Completing: disarraying.
63. ImT Completing, stopping by-consequence disarraying.
63.4a/b Completing the day, a warning.
64.S Anterior acquiescence has the use-of Not-yet Fording completed in-truth.
64. ImT Not continuing, completing indeed.

Complexion, SE: appearance, expression; color, hue; air, manner, deportment; beautiful.

    21/22.CD Adorning: without complexion indeed.

Composition, CHANG: a well-composed whole and its structure; beautiful creations; elegant, clear, brilliant; contrasts with pattern, WEN, beauty of intrinsic design.

    2.3a/b Containing composition permitting Trial.

    21. ImT Thunder, lightning, uniting and-also composing.

    44. ImT The kinds: beings conjoining composition indeed.

    44.5a Containing composition.

    44.5b Nine at-fifth, containing composition.

    55.5a Coming composition.

Conceal, TS'ANG: hide from view; store up, put aside, accumulate; stores, property; internal organs.

    55.6b Originating-from concealing indeed.

Concord, T'UNG: harmonize, unite, equalize, assemble; agree, share in; together, at once, same time and place. The ideogram: cover and mouth, silent understanding and perfect fit.

    Image of Hexagram 13 and occurs throughout its texts.

    11. ImT Above[and]Below mingling and-also one's purpose concording indeed.

    14.S Associating-with People Concording implies beings necessarily converting in-truth.

    14.CD Concording People: connecting indeed.

    38.ST A chün tzu uses concording and-also dividing.

    38. ImT Two women concording: residing.

    38. ImT Their purposes not concording: moving.

    38. ImT Heaven, Earth, Polarizing and-also one's affairs concording indeed.

    49. ImT Two women concording, residing.

    59. ImT Supple acquiring the situation reaching-to the outside and-also concording above.

Concubine, CH'IEH: secondary wife taken without ceremony to ensure a male descendant; handmaid.

    33.3a/b Accumulating servants, concubines, significant.

50.1a Acquiring a concubine, using one's sonhood.

Conduct, SHUAI: lead; leader, chief, commander; follow, follower.

    7.5a/b The long-living son conducting Legions.

Confine, K'UN: enclose, restrict, limit; oppressed; impoverish, distress; afflicted, exhausted, disheartened, weary. The ideogram: an enclosed tree.

    Image of Hexagram 47 and occurs throughout its texts.

    4.4a/b Confining Enveloping. Abashment.

    5.ImT Actually one's righteousness, not confining exhaustion.

    13.4b By-consequence confining and-also reversing by-consequence indeed.

    48.S Confining reaching-to the above implies necessarily reversing the below.

    48.CD Confining: mutual meeting indeed.

Conforming, FU: accord between inner and outer in a particular moment; sincere, truthful, verified, reliable, in accord with the spirits; capture; prisoners, spoils; contrasts with trustworthy, HSIN, consistent in time. The ideogram: bird's claw enclosing young animals, possessive grip.

See also: **Possessing conformity**

    Image of Hexagram 61 and occurs throughout its texts.

    11.3a No cares: one's conforming.

    11.4a/b Not warning: using conforming.

    14.5a Your conforming: mingling thus, impressing thus.

    14.5b Your conforming, mingling thus.

    17.5a/b Conformity tending-towards excellence. Significant.

    34.1b One's conforming exhausted indeed.

    35.1a Absence: conforming.

    38.4a Mingling conforming.

    38.4b Mingling conforming, without fault.

    40.4a Partnering culminating, splitting-off conforming.

    43. Im/ImT Conforming, crying-out, possessing adversity.

    44.1a Ruining the pig, conforming: hoof dragging.

    45.2a Conforming, thereupon Harvesting availing-of dedicating.

    45.5a Without fault: in-no-way conforming.

46.2a Conforming, thereupon Harvesting availing-of dedicating.
46.2b Nine at-second's conforming.
49. Im Skinning: before-zenith sun, thereupon conforming.
49. ImT Before-zenith sun, thereupon conforming.
58.2a/b Conforming Opening, significant.
58.5a/b Conforming tending-towards stripping.
62.CD Centering Conforming: trustworthiness indeed.

Congregate, LI: cling together; depend on, attached to, rely on; couple, pair, herd; the Action of the trigram Radiance, LI. The ideogram: deer flocking together.
30.S Falling necessarily possesses a place to congregate.
30.S Radiance implies congregating indeed.
30. ImT Radiance. Congregating indeed.
30. ImT Sun[and]Moon congregating reach-to heaven.
30. ImT The hundred grains, grasses, trees congregating reach-to earth.
30. ImT Redoubling brightness uses congregating to reach-to correcting.
30. ImT Supple congregating reach-to centering correcting.
35. ImT Yielding and-also congregating reaching-to great brightening.
38. ImT Stimulating and-also congregating reaching-to brightness.
56. ImT Stopping and-also congregating reaching-to brightness.
58.ST Congregating marshes.

Conjoin, HSIEN: come into contact with, influence; reach, join together; put together as parts of a previously separated whole; come into conjunction, as the celestial bodies; totally, completely; lit.: broken piece of pottery, the halves of which join to identify partners.
Image of Hexagram 31 and occurs throughout its texts.
1.ImT Myriad cities, conjoining, soothing.
2.ImT The kinds: being conjoining Growing.
19.1a/b Conjunction Nearing, Trial: significant.
19.2a/b Conjunction Nearing: significant.
32.CD Conjoining: urging indeed.

44. ImT The kinds: beings conjoining composition indeed.

Connect, CH'IN: attach to, approach, come near; cherish, help, favor; intimate; relatives, kin.
5/6.CD Arguing: not connecting indeed.
8.ST The Earlier Kings used installing myriad cities to connect the connoted feudatories.
13/14.CD Concording People: connecting indeed.
55/56.CD Connecting the few: Sojourning indeed.

Connote, CHU: imply the meaning; signify. The ideogram: words and imply.
8.ST The Earlier Kings used installing myriad cities to connect the connoted feudatories.
16.AE Surely, grasping connotes Providing-for.
52.4b Stopping connoting the body indeed.

Consecutive, CHI: follow after, continue; take another's place; line of succession, adopt an heir. The ideogram: silk thread and continuous.
30.ST Great People use consecutive brightening to illuminate tending-towards the four sides.

Consider, SHEN: act carefully, seriously; cautious, attentive, circumspect; still, quiet, sincere. The ideogram: heart and true.
2.4b Consideration not harmful indeed.
5.3b Respectful consideration, not destroying indeed.
27.ST A chün tzu uses considering words to inform.
50.2b Considering places it indeed.
56.ST A chün tzu uses brightening consideration to avail-of punishing and-also not to detain litigating.
64.ST A chün tzu uses considering to mark-off the beings residing on-all-sides.

Consort, CH'I: single official partner; legal status of married woman (first wife); contrasts with function of wife, FU, head of household, and concubine, CH'IEH, secondary wives.
9.3a/b Husband, consort, reversing eyes.
28.2a A venerable husband acquiring his woman consort.
28.2b A venerable husband, a woman consort.
47.3a/b Entering tending-towards one's house. Not visualizing one's consort.

Conspicuous, CHU: manifest, obvious, clear.

3/4.CD Enveloping: motley and-also conspicuous.

Contain, HAN: retain, embody, cherish; withold, tolerate; lit.: contain in the mouth, put a coin in a corpse's mouth.

2.ImT Containing generosity, the shining great.

2.3a/b Containing composition permitting Trial.

44.5a Containing composition.

44.5b Nine at-fifth, containing composition.

Continue, HSÜ: carry on what another began; succeed to, join on, attach to; keep up, follow.

64. ImT Not continuing, completing indeed.

Continuity, LIEN: connected, continuous, attached, annexed, consistent; follow, reach, stick to, join; series.

39.4a/b Going Limping, coming continuity.

Contradict, WEI: oppose, disregard, disobey; seditious, perverse.

6.ST Heaven associating-with stream, contradicting movements.

15.4b Not contradicting by-consequence indeed.

41.5a Nowhere a controlling contradiction.

42.2a Nowhere a controlling contradiction.

Control, K'O: command; check, impede, prevail, obstruct, repress; adequate, able. The ideogram: roof beams support a house, controlling the structure.

4.2a/b The son controlling the dwelling.

6.2a/b,4a Not controlling Arguing.

13.4a Nothing controlling attacking.

13.4b Righteously nothing controlling indeed.

13.5a/b Great legions controlling mutual meeting.

13.5b Words mutualize controlling indeed.

14.3a Small People nowhere controlling.

24.6a Culminating tending-towards ten years-revolved not controlling chastisement.

41.5a Nowhere a controlling contradiction.

42.2a Nowhere a controlling contradiction.

63.3a/b Three years-revolved controlling it.

Convert, KUEI: change to another form, persuade; return to yourself or the place where you belong; restore, revert, become loyal; turn into; give a young girl in marriage. The ideogram: arrive and wife, become mistress of a household.

Image of Hexagram 54 and occurs throughout its texts.

6.2a Converting and-also escaping one's capital.

6.2b Converting escaping, skulking indeed.

11.5a The supreme burgeoning, converting maidenhood.

14.S Associating-with People Concording implies beings necessarily converting in-truth.

53. Im Infiltrating, womanhood converting significant.

53.CD Infiltrating: womanhood converting awaits manhood moving indeed.

53.CD Converting Maidenhood: womanhood's completion indeed.

53. ImT Womanhood converting significant.

55.S Acquiring one's place to Convert implies necessarily the great.

Cook, JEN: cook very thoroughly; transform completely. The ideogram: food and full or complete.

50. ImT Growing: cooking indeed.

Coordinate, LUN: classify, bind, adjust; weave together; lit.: unravel and twist silk together into threads.

3.ST A chün tzu uses the canons to coordinate.

Corpse, SHIH: dead human body; effigy, statue; inefficient, useless; impersonate.

7.3a/b Legions maybe carting corpses.

7.5a/b The junior son carting corpses.

Correct, CHENG: rectify deviation or one-sidedness; proper, straight, exact, regular; constant, rule, model. The ideogram: stop and one, hold to one thing. See also: **Centering correcting**

1.ImT Each-one correcting innate fate.

3.1b Although a stone pillar, purpose moving correctly indeed.

4.ImT Enveloping used to nourish correcting:

4.1b Using correcting laws indeed.

5.ImT Using correcting centering indeed.

7.ImT Trial: correcting indeed.

7.ImT Able to use the crowds correcting:

7.6b Using correcting accomplishing indeed.

8.5b Situation correctly centered indeed.

9.3b Not able correcting the home indeed.

10.5b Situation correcting appropriate indeed.

12.5b Situation correcting appropriate indeed.

13. ImT A chün tzu, correcting indeed.

17.1b Adhering-to correcting significant indeed.

17.5b Situation correctly centering indeed.

19. ImT Great Growing uses correcting.

19.1b Purpose moving, correcting indeed.

25. Im One in-no-way correcting: possessing blunder.

25. ImT Great Growing using correcting.

25. ImT One in-no-way correcting: possessing blunder.

26. ImT The great correcting indeed.

27/28.CD Jaws: nourishing correcting indeed.

27. ImT Nourishing correcting, by-consequence significant indeed.

30. ImT Redoubling brightness uses congregating to reach-to correcting.

30.6b Using correcting the fiefdoms indeed.

33.5b Using correcting the purpose indeed.

34. ImT The Great implies correcting indeed.

34. ImT Actually the correcting Great and-also Heaven[and]Earth's motives permitting visualizing.

35.1b Solitary moving correcting indeed.

36. ImT Inside heaviness and-also enabling correcting one's purpose.

37. ImT The woman correcting the situation reaching-to the inside.

37. ImT The man correcting the situation reaching-to the outside.

37. ImT Man[and]Woman correcting.

37. ImT And-also Dwelling tao correcting.

37. ImT Actually correcting Dwelling and-also Below Heaven set-right.

39. ImT Using correcting the fiefdoms indeed.

45. ImT Assembling uses correcting indeed.

49. ImT Great Growing uses correcting.

50.ST A chün tzu uses correcting the situation to solidify fate.

52.1b Not-yet letting-go correcting indeed.

53. ImT Advancing uses correcting.

53. ImT Permitting using correcting the fiefdoms indeed.

57.5b Situation correctly centered indeed.

57.6b Correcting: reaching a pitfall indeed.

58.5b Situation correcting appropriate indeed.

59.5b Correcting the situation indeed.

61.5b Situation correcting appropriate indeed.

63. ImT Solid[and]Supple correcting and-also the situation appropriate indeed.

64.2b Centering using moving correcting indeed.

Correspond(-to), UING: be in agreement or harmony; resonate together, invoke and fulfill each other; answer to, suitable; relation between the lines (1:4, 2:5, 3:6) when they form the pair opened and whole, supple and solid. The ideogram: heart and obey.

This term occurs in the Image Tradition of most hexagrams.

Corrupt, KU: rotting, poisonous; intestinal worms, venomous insects; evil magic; disorder, error; pervert by seduction, flattery; unquiet ghost. The ideogram: dish and worms, putrefaction and poisonous decay.

Image of Hexagram 18 and occurs throughout its texts.

Counter, NI: oppose, resist, seek out; contrary, rebellious, refractory. The ideogram: go and rise against, active revolt.

8.5b Stowing-away countering, grasping yielding.

62. ImT Countering above and-also yielding below indeed.

Counterpoise, CH'ÜAN: balance, equalize, plan; act as the position demands, expedient; influential; lit.: balance on a sliding scale.

57.AE Ground: using moving the counterpoise.

Countryside, YEH: cultivated fields and grassland, where nature and human construction interact; third of the territorial zones: city, suburbs, countryside, forests.

2.6a/b Dragons struggling tending-towards the countryside.

13. Im/ImT Concording People, tending-towards the countryside.

Couple, KOU: driven encounter, at once transitory and enduring, that is the reflection of primal yin and yang; meet, encounter, copulate; mating animals; magnetism, gravity; to be gripped by impersonal forces.

Image of Hexagram 44 and occurs throughout its texts.

Course, LIEN: move, flow like ripples spreading on water; unceasing.

3.6a/b Weeping blood, coursing thus.

Courtesy, KUNG: display respect, treat courteously, show reverence; affable, decorous, modest, polite; obsequious.

62.ST A chün tzu uses moving Exceeding to reach-to courtesy.

Cover, MU: canvas covering; tent, booth, screen, tarpaulin.

48.6a The Well: collecting, no cover.

Cracked, PI: broken, ruined, tattered; unfit, unworthy. The ideogram: strike and break.

48.2a The jug cracked, leaking.

54.ST A chün tzu uses perpetually completing to know the cracked.

Crane, HAO: large wading birds; sign of long life, wisdom and bliss; messenger to the immortals; relation between father and son.

Create, TSAO: make, construct, build, form, establish.

1.5b Great People creating indeed.

3.ImT Heaven creating grass, duskiness.

Creeper, see: **Trailing creeper**

Crimson, CH'IH: color associated with the Fiery Moment, South and Actualized Yang; fire, burning; dark complexion; color of new-born child; drunk, angry; polished metal; strip, naked, barren; also: sign of official rank. See also: **Scarlet**

47.5a Confined, tending-towards a crimson sash.

Crop, HUO: grain gathered in autumn; reap, harvest.

25.2a/b Not tilling the crop.

Cross, P'ING: cross a river without a boat; cross a dry or frozen river. The ideogram: horse and ice.

11.2a Availing-of crossing the channel.

Crowds, CHUNG: many people, large group; majority; in common.

7.S Arguing necessarily possesses crowds rising-up.

7.S Legions imply crowds indeed.

7.ST A chün tzu uses tolerating commoners to accumulate crowds.

7.ImT Legions: crowds indeed.

7.ImT Able to use the crowds correcting:

8.S Crowds necessarily possess a place to Group.

13/14.CD Great Possessing: crowds indeed.

35.3a Crowds, sincerity, repenting extinguished.

35.3b Crowds: sincerity's purpose.

36.ST A chün tzu uses supervising the crowds to avail-of darkening and-also Brightening.

40. ImT Going acquiring crowds indeed.

Crown, LUNG: place above all others; peak; high, surpassing.

28.4a/b The ridgepole crowning.

Crown-prince, HOU: successor to the sovereign. The ideogram: one, mouth and shelter, one with the sovereign's orders.

11.ST The crown-prince uses property to accomplish Heaven[and]Earth's tao.

11.ST [The crown-prince uses] bracing to mutualize Heaven[and]Earth's propriety.

11.ST [The crown-prince] uses the left to right the commoners.

24.ST The crown-prince [used culminating sun] not to inspect on-all-sides.

44.ST The crown-prince uses spreading-out fate to command the four sides.

Cry-out/outcry, HAO: call out, proclaim; signal, order, command; mark, label, sign.

13.5a Concording People beforehand crying-out sobbing and-also afterwards laughing.

43. Im/ImT Conforming, crying-out, possessing adversity.

43.2a Awe, an outcry.

43.6a Without crying-out.

43.6b Without crying-out's pitfall.

45.1a Like an outcry, the-one handful activates laughing.

56.6a Sojourning people beforehand laughing, afterwards crying-out sobbing.

59.5a Dispersing sweat, one's great crying-out.

Culminate, CHIH: bring to the highest degree; arrive at the end or summit; superlative. See also: **Culminating sun**

2.ImT Culminating Field, Spring in-fact.

2.1a Treading frost, hardening ice culminating.

2.1b Culminating hardening the ice indeed.

5.3a Involving outlawry culminating.

6.2b Distress culminating, reaping indeed.

10.AE Treading: harmonizing and-also culminating.

19. Im/ImT Culminating tending-towards the eighth moon: possessing a pitfall.

19.4a Culminating Nearing.

19.4b Culminating Nearing, without fault.

24.6a Culminating tending-towards ten years-revolved not controlling chastisement.

29.ST Streams reiterating culminating.

40.3a Involving outlawry culminating.

40.4a Partnering culminating, splitting-off conforming.

48. Im/ImT Muddy culmination: Truly not-yet the well-rope Well.

55.ST Thunder, lightning, altogether culminating.

Culminating sun, CHIH JIH acme of any time period; midday, summer solstice; midpoint of life.

24.ST The Earlier Kings used culminating sun to bar the passages.

24.ST Bargaining sojourners [used culminating sun] not to move.

24.ST The crown-prince [used culminating sun] not to inspect on-all-sides.

Cultivate, CHOU: till fields or gardens; continue successively, like annual plowing. The ideogram: fields and long life.

12.4a Cultivating radiant satisfaction.

Cup, TSUN: quantity a libation vessel contains; glass, decanter, bottle. See also: **Wine-cup**

29.4a/b A cup, liquor, a platter added.

Curb, CH'ENG: reprimand, reprove, repress; warn, caution; corrective punishment. The ideogram: heart and action, the heart acting on itself.

41.ST A chün tzu uses curbing anger to block the appetites.

Cut-off, CHÜEH: cut short, interrupt, disconnect, break off, sever; destroy, renounce; alienated. The ideogram: silk, knife and knot, cutting through. See also: **Foot-cutting** and **Nose-cutting**

61.4b Cutting-off the above, sorting indeed.

Dare, KAN: have the courage to, try, permit yourself: bold, intrepid; rash, offensive.

22.ST A chün tzu uses brightening the multitudinous standards without daring to sever litigating.

Darken, HUI: make or become dark; last day of the moon; obscure, night, mist.

17.ST A chün tzu uses turning-to darkening to enter a reposing pause.

36.ST A chün tzu uses supervising the crowds to avail-of darkening and-also Brightening.

36. ImT Darkening one's Brightness indeed.

36.6a Not Brightening, darkening.

Dawn, CHAO: early morning, before daybreak; opposite of nightfall, HSI.

6.6a Completing dawn three-times depriving it.

Day/sun, JIH: actual sun and the time of a sun-cycle, a day. See also: **Sun[and]Moon**

1.3a A chün tzu completing the day: Force, Force.

1.3b Completing the day: Force, Force.

16.2a Not completing the day.

16.2b Not completing the day, Trial: significant.

18. Im/ImT Before seedburst three days, after seedburst three days.

24. Im/ImT The seventh day coming: Returning.

26. ImT A day renewing one's actualizing-tao.

36.1a Three days, not taking-in.

51.2a The seventh day: acquiring.

57.5a Before husking, three days.

57.5a After husking, three days.

63.2a/b The seventh day: acquiring.

63.4a/b Completing the day, a warning.

Daybreak, SU: first light, after dawn; early morning; early, careful attention.

40. Im Daybreak significant.

40. ImT Possessing directed going, daybreak significant.

Day-time, CHOU: daylight half of 24-hour cycle.

35. Im Day-time sun three-times reflected.

35/36.CD Prospering: day-time indeed.

35. ImT Day-time sun three-times reflected indeed.

Decade, HSÜN: ten days or years; complete time period.

55.1a/b Although a decade, without fault.

55.1b Exceeding a decade, calamity indeed.

Decrease, SHUAI: grow or make smaller; fade, decline, decay, diminish, cut off; grow old; adversity, misfortune.

41/42.CD Increasing, decreasing's beginning indeed.

Dedicate, YO: offering at the spring equinox, when stores are low; offer a sacrifice with limited resources. The ideogram: spring and thin.

45.2a Conforming, thereupon Harvesting availing-of dedicating.

46.2a Conforming, thereupon Harvesting availing-of dedicating.

63.5a Not thus the Western neighbor's dedicated offering.

Defend-against, FANG: keep off, protect from, guard against; erect a protective barrier. The ideogram: open space and earthen ramparts.

62.3a Nowhere Exceeding defending-against it.

63.ST A chün tzu uses pondering distress and-also providing-for defending-against it.

Delay, HUAN: retard, put off; let things take their course, tie loosely; gradually, leisurely; lax, tardy, negligent.

39/40.CD Taking-apart: delay indeed.

40.S Taking-apart implies delay indeed.

41.S Delaying necessarily possesses a place to let-go.

61.ST A chün tzu uses deliberating litigating to delay dying.

Deliberate, YI: consult, discuss, criticize; weigh the options and find the best course; arrange, select; laws, rules. The ideogram: words and right.

60.ST [A chün tzu uses] deliberating actualizing-tao to move.

61.ST A chün tzu uses deliberating litigating to delay dying.

Delight, LO: take joy or pleasure in; pleasant, relaxed; also: music as harmony, elegance and pleasure.

5.ST A chün tzu uses drinking[and]taking-in to repose delighting.

7/8.CD Grouping: delighting.

16.ST The Earlier Kings used arousing delight to extol actualizing-tao.

Delimit, CHIANG: define frontiers, draw limits; boundary, border. See also: **Limit**

2.ImT Actualizing-tao uniting without delimiting.

2.ImT Moving, the earth without delimiting.

2.ImT Corresponding earth without delimiting.

19.ST [A chün tzu uses] tolerating to protect the commoners without delimiting.

42. ImT The commoners stimulated without delimiting.

42. ImT Sun advancing without delimiting.

Delude, MI: confused, stupefied, infatuated; blinded by vice; bewitch, fascinate, deceive.

2.Im Beforehand delusion, afterwards acquiring.

2.ImT Beforehand delusion letting-go tao.

24.6a/b Deluding Returning. Pitfall.

Demon(iac), CH'OU: possessed by a malignant genius; ugly, physically or morally deformed; vile, disgraceful, shameful; drunken. The ideogram: fermenting liquor and soul. Demoniac and tiger are opposed on the Universal Compass North–South axis; the tiger (Extreme Yang) scares away and protects against demoniacs (Extreme Yin).

20.2b Truly permitting the demoniac indeed.

28.5b Truly permitting the demoniac indeed.

30.6a Severing the head. Catching in-no-way its demons.

40.3b Truly permitting the demoniac indeed.

53.3b Radiance flocking demons indeed.

Demonstrate, HUI: show, signal, point out. The ideogram: hand and act, giving signals.

15.4a/b Without not Harvesting, demonstrating Humbling.

Dense, TS'UNG: close-set, bushy, crowded; a grove.

29.6a Dismissing tending-towards dense jujube-trees.

Deny, YÜ: retract, repudiate; deterioration, regress.

6.4a/b Denying quiet Trial.

16.6a Accomplishment: possessing denial.

17.1a/b An office: possessing denial.

Depart, CH'Ü: leave, quit, remove; repudiate, reject, dismiss.

9.4a Blood departing, awe issuing-forth.

49/50.CD Skinning: departing anteriority indeed.

59.6a Departing far-away, issuing-forth.

Depend-on, YI: rely on, trust; conform to; image, illustration.

42.4a Harvesting: availing-of activating depending-on shifting the city.

Deprive, CH'IH: strip (of rank), take away; undress; put an end to.

6.6a Completing dawn three-times depriving it.

Depth, SHEN: deep water; profound, abstruse; ardent, strong, intense, inner; sound the depths.

32.1b Beginning seeking depth indeed.

Designate, WEI: represent in words, assign a name or meaning; report on, talk about. The ideogram: words and belly, describing the essential.

19.5b Moving the center's designating indeed.

37. ImT Father[and]Mother's designating indeed.

37.6b Reversing individuality's designating indeed.

46.S Assembling and-also the above implies designating's Ascending.

62.6a That designates Calamity[and]Blunder.

Desire, YÜAN: wish, hope or long for; covet; desired object.

10.1b Solitarily moving desire indeed.

11.4b Centering the heart desiring indeed.

11.5b Center uses moving desire indeed.

53.5b Acquiring the place desired indeed.

59.2b Acquiring desire indeed.

61.2b Centering the heart desiring indeed.

Desist, PA: cease, leave off, discontinue, finish; enough.

61.3a/b Maybe drumbeating, maybe desisting.

Destroy, PAI: ruin, defeat, violate, subvert, break.

5.3b Respectful consideration, not destroying indeed.

14.2b Amassing centering, not destroying indeed.

24.6a Completing possesses great destroying.

Detain, LIU: hold back or on to; delay, remain; slow.

56.ST A chün tzu uses brightening consideration to avail-of punishing and-also not to detain litigating.

Die, SSU: sudden or untimely death; run out of energy; immobile, fixed.

16.5a/b Persevering, not dying.

30.4a Burning thus. Dying thus. Thrown-out thus.

58. ImT The commoners forget their dying.

61.ST A chün tzu uses deliberating litigating to delay dying.

Differentiate, PIEN: argue, dispute, criticize; sophisticated, artful. The ideogram: words and sharp or pungent.

6.1b Although the small possesses words, one's differentiation brightening indeed.

10.ST A chün tzu uses differentiating Above[and]Below.

14.4b Brightness differentiating clearly indeed.

48.AE The Well: using differentiating righteousness.

Diffuse, LIU: flow out, spread, permeate.

1.ImT The kinds: being diffusing forms.

15. ImT Earthly tao transforming overfilling and-also diffusing Humbling.

29. ImT Stream diffusing and-also not overfilling.

Dignify, TSUN: honor, make eminent; noble, respected. The ideogram: presenting wine to a guest.

14. ImT Supple acquiring the dignifying situation, the great centering.

15.AE/ImT Humbling: dignifying and-also shining.

Dim, MING: dark, obscure; misinformed, immature, cavern, the underworld. The ideogram: 16th day of moon-month, when the moon begins to dim.

16.6a Dim Providing-for.

16.6b Dim Providing-for located above.

46.6a Dim Ascending.

46.6b Dim Ascending located above.

Diminish, SUN: lessen, make smaller; take away from; lose, damage, spoil, wound; bad luck; blame, criticize; offer up, give away. The ideogram: hand and ceremonial vessel, offering sacrifice.

Image of Hexagram 41 and occurs throughout its texts.

42.S Diminishing and-also not climaxing necessarily Augments.

42.CD Diminishing, Augmenting.

42. ImT Above diminishing, below Augmenting.

Direct, YU: move toward a specific place or goal; have a focus. The ideogram: person moving through or over water, direction without visible landmarks. See also: **Possessing directed going** and **Without direction: Harvesting**

2.ImT A chün tzu directing moving.

37.2a Without direction, releasing.

Disarray, LUAN: throw into disorder, mislay, confuse; out of place; discord, insurrection, anarchy.

7.6b Necessarily disarraying the fiefdoms indeed.

10.2b Centering, not originating-from disarray indeed.

11.6b One's fate disarrayed indeed.

12.2b Not disarraying the flock indeed.

45.1a/b Thereupon disarraying, thereupon Clustering.

45.1b One's purpose disarrayed indeed.

53.6b Not permitting disarray indeed.

63. Im Completing: disarraying.

63. ImT Completing, stopping by-consequence disarraying.

Discard, MIEH: disregard, ignore; petty, worthless, insignificant; trash.

23.1a,2a Discarding the Trial: pitfall.

Disclose, K'AI: open, reveal, unfold, display; enact rites, clear land; final phase of both hemicycles in the Universal Compass. The ideogram: house doors bursting open.

7.6a Disclosing the city, receiving a dwelling.

Discuss, CHO: deliberate; hear opinions; reach and act on a decision. The ideogram: wine and ladle, pouring out wine to open discussion.

41.1a Discussing Diminishing it.

Disembowel, K'UEI: cut open and clean; prepare for sacrifice; stab.

54.6a A notable disembowelling a goat without blood.

Dismiss, CHIH: put aside; judge and find wanting.

29.6a Dismissing tending-towards dense jujube-trees.

Disperse, HUAN: scatter clouds or crowds; break up obstacles; dispel illusions, fears and suspicions; clear up misunderstandings; dissolve, evaporate, disintegrate, fade, vanish; fog lifting or clearing away.

Image of Hexagram 59 and occurs throughout its texts.

Display, YANG: spread, extend, scatter, divulge; publish abroad, make famous. The ideogram: hand and expand, spreading a message.

14.ST A chün tzu uses terminating hate to display improvement.

43. Im Parting, displaying tending-towards kingly chambers.

43. ImT Displaying tending-towards kingly chambers.

Dissolve, HSIAO: liquify, melt, thaw; diminish, disperse; eliminate, exhaust. The ideogram: water dissolving differences.

11. ImT Small People: tao dissolving indeed.

12. ImT A chün tzu: tao dissolving indeed.

19. ImT Dissolving, not lasting indeed.

46.6b Dissolving, not affluence indeed.

Dissolving pause, HSIAO HSI: yin or structure dissolves so that yang or action may emerge; transitional phase of the Universal Compass.

23. ImT A chün tzu honors the dissolving pause to overfill emptiness.

55. ImT Associating-with the season: dissolving pause.

Distance, YÜAN: far off, remote; keep at a distance; alienated. The ideogram: go and a long way.

4.4b Solitariness distancing substance indeed.

24.1a/b Not distancing Returning.

33.ST A chün tzu uses distancing Small People.

41.AE Diminishing: using distancing harm.

44.4b Distancing the commoners indeed.

51. ImT Scaring the distant and-also fearing the nearby indeed.

59.6b Distancing harm indeed.

Distress, HUAN: tribulation, grief, affliction. The ideogram: heart and clamor, the heart distressed.

6.2b Distress culminating, reaping indeed.

63.ST A chün tzu uses pondering distress and-also providing-for defending-against it.

Distribute, SHEN: give out, spread, scatter, allot, diffuse.

57.ST A chün tzu uses distributing fate to move affairs.

57. ImT Redoubling Ground uses distributing fate.

Dive, CH'ÊN: jump into deep water; deepen; serious, abstruse.

32.1a Diving Persevering, Trial: pitfall.

32.1b Diving Persevering's pitfall.

Divide, YI: separate, break apart, sever; oppose; different, foreign, strange, unusual, rare.

38.ST A chün tzu uses concording and-also dividing.

Docile, HSÜN: amiable, mild, yielding; tame; gradually attained.

2.1b Docilely involving one's tao:

Donate, SHANG: bestow, confer, grant; rewards, gifts; celebrate, take pleasure in.

64.4a Three years-revolved, possessing donating tending-towards the great city.

Door, HU: inner door, chamber door; a household; contrasts with gate, MEN, the outer door.

6.2a People, three hundred doors.

55.6a/b Peeping-through one's door.

60.1a/b Not issuing-forth-from the door chambers.

Doubled, LIANG: twice, both, again, dual, a pair.

30.ST Brightness doubled arousing Radiance.

Doubt, YI: suspect, distrust; dubious; surmise, conjecture.
  9.6b Possessing a place to doubt indeed.
  16.4a No doubting.
  22.4b Six at-fourth. Appropriate situation to doubt indeed.
  33.6b Without a place to doubt indeed.
  38.6b The flock, doubt extinguished indeed.
  41.3b Three by-consequence doubting indeed.
  46.3b Without a place to doubt indeed.
  55.2a Going acquiring doubt, affliction.
  57.1b Purpose doubted indeed.
  58.1b Movement not-yet doubted indeed.
  63.4b Possessing a place to doubt indeed.

Drag, CHU: pull along a hurt or malfunctioning foot; limping, lame. The ideogram: foot and worm, an infected foot.
  44.1a Ruining the pig, conforming: hoof dragging.

Dragon, LUNG: powerful spirit-energy emerging from waters below; mythical shape-changer with supreme power; connected with heaven, T'IEN, and the trigram Force, CH'IEN.
  1.ImT The season riding six dragons used going-to-meet heaven.
  1.1a/b Immersed dragon, no availing-of.
  1.2a/b Visualizing dragon located-in the fields.
  1.5a/b Flying dragon located-in heaven.
  1.6a/b Overbearing dragon possesses repenting.
  1.7a Visualizing flocking dragons without a head.
  2.6a/b Dragons struggling tending-towards the countryside.

Draw-near, CHIU: approach, encounter, come near; follow; approach completion; composed, finished; able, willing; in a little while.
  49.3a/b Skinning words three-times drawing-near:

Draw-water, CHI: draw water from a well; draw forth, lead; take in a doctrine or example. The ideogram: water and reach to.
  48.3a Permitting availing-of drawing-water:

Dread, WEI: stand in awe of, respect, venerate; ajust fear.
  51.6b Dreading the neighbor, a warning indeed.

Drench, CH'IN: soak, penetrate, immerse, steep in; imbued with.
  19. ImT Solid drenched and-also long-living.

33. ImT Drenched and-also long-living indeed.

Drink, YIN: take in liquid or air; quench thirst, give liquid to; inhale, suck in.
  64.6a Possessing conformity: tending-towards drinking liquor.
  64.6b Drinking liquor, soaking the head.

Drink[and]take-in, YIN SHIH: comprehensive term for eating, drinking and breathing; a meal, eating together.
  5.S Attending implies drinking[and]taking-in's tao indeed.
  5.ST A chün tzu uses drinking[and]taking-in to repose delighting.
  6.S Drinking[and]taking-in necessarily possesses Arguing.
  27.ST [A chün tzu uses] articulating to drink[and]take-in.
  53.2a/b Drinking[and]taking-in: feasting, feasting.

Droop, CH'UI: hang down, let fall; bow; condescend to inferiors; almost, near; suspended; hand down from past to future.
  36.1a Drooping one's wings.

Drudgery, CHIEN: difficult, hard, repetitive work; hard to cultivate; distressing, sorrowful. The ideogram: sticky earth and a person looking around, hard work in comparison to others.
  11.3a Drudgery, Trial: without fault.
  14.1a Drudgery by-consequence without fault.
  21.4a Harvesting: drudgery, Trial.
  21.4b Harvesting: drudgery, Trial significant.
  26.3a Harvesting: drudgery, Trial.
  34.6a/b Drudgery by-consequence significant.
  36. Im/ImT Harvesting: drudgery, Trial.

Drumbeating, KU: skin or earthenware drums; play a drum; excite, arouse, encourage; joyous, happy.
  30.3a Not drumbeating a jar and-also singing.
  61.3a/b Maybe drumbeating, maybe desisting.

Dug-out, CHOU: hollowed log, canoe; boat, ride or transport by boat.
  61. ImT Riding a wooden dug-out, emptiness indeed.

Duskiness, MAI: obscure, indistinct; insufficient light; times of day when it is not fully light. The ideogram: day and not-yet.
  3.ImT Heaven creating grass, duskiness.

Dwell, CHI: home, house, household, family; domestic, within doors; live in. The ideogram:

roof and pig or dog, the most valued domestic animals.

Image of Hexagram 37 and occurs throughout its texts.

4.2a/b The son controlling the dwelling.

7.6a Disclosing the city, receiving a dwelling.

26. Im/ImT Not dwelling, taking-in. Significant.

38.S Dwelling tao exhausted, necessarily returning.

38.CD Dwelling People: inside indeed.

41.6a Acquiring a servant, without dwelling.

55.6a Screening one's dwelling.

Each-one, KO: every, all, wherever; each separate thing.

1.ImT Each-one correcting innate fate.

Ear, ERH: organ of hearing; handle, sides.

21.6a/b Wherefore locking-up submerging the ears?

50. ImT Ground and-also the ear[and]eye: understanding brightened.

50.3a/b The Vessel: the ears skinned.

50.5a The Vessel: yellow ears, metallic rings.

50.5b The Vessel: yellow ears.

Earlier Kings, HSIEN WANG: ideal rulers of old; the golden age, primal time, power in harmony with nature; model for the chün tzu.

This term occurs in the Symbol Tradition of Hexagrams **8, 16, 20, 21, 24, 25, 59.**

Earth, TI: ground on which the human world rests; basis of all things, nourishes all things; the Symbol of the trigram Field, K'UN. See also: **Heaven[and]Earth**

2.ST Earth potency: Field.

2.ImT The female horse: earth sorting.

2.ImT Moving, the earth without delimiting.

2.ImT Corresponding earth without delimiting.

2.2b Earthly tao shining indeed.

7.ST Earth center possessing stream.

8.ST Above earth possessing stream.

12.ST Heaven, earth, not mingling.

15.ST Earth center possessing mountain.

15. ImT Earth tao lowly and-also moving above.

15. ImT Earthly tao transforming overfilling and-also diffusing Humbling.

16.ST Thunder issuing-forth-from earth impetuously.

19.ST Above marsh possessing earth.

20.ST Wind moving above earth.

23.ST Mountain adjoining with-respect-to earth.

24.ST Thunder located-in earth center.

29. ImT Earth venturing, mountains, rivers, hill-tops, mounds indeed.

30. ImT The hundred grains, grasses, trees congregating reaching-to earth.

35.ST/ImT Brightness issuing-forth above earth.

36.ST/ImT Brightness entering earth center.

36.6a/b Afterwards entering tending-towards earth.

38. ImT Heaven, Earth, Polarizing and-also one's affairs concording indeed.

42. ImT Heaven spreading-out, earth giving-birth.

44. ImT Heaven, Earth: mutually meeting.

45.ST Above marsh with-respect-to earth.

46.ST Earth center giving-birth-to wood.

48.AE The Well: actualizing-tao's earth indeed.

60. ImT Heaven, Earth: Articulating and-also the four seasons accomplishing.

East, TUNG: corresponds to Spring, YÜAN, and the Woody Moment, stirs-up and germinates new life-cycle; place of honor and the person in it.

63.5a/b The Eastern neighbor slaughters cattle.

Eastern North: border, limit, completion; boundary between cycles: Mountain; accomplishing words, summing up before new germination; dark, cold, lonely winter night.

2.Im/ImT Eastern North: losing partnering.

39. Im/ImT Not Harvesting: Eastern North.

Eight, PA: number of highly valued essentials: eight trigrams, eight immortals, eight compass points; eighth.

19. Im/ImT Culminating tending-towards the eighth moon: possessing a pitfall.

Eliminate, CH'U: root out, remove, do awaywith, take off, keep out; vacate, exchange.

45.ST A chün tzu uses eliminating arms to implement.

Embarrassed, HSIU: conscious of guilt or fault; unworthy; ashamed, confused; shy, blushing. The ideogram: sheep, sheepish feeling.

12.3a/b Enwrapping embarrassing.

32.3a Maybe receiving's embarrassing.

Embellish, SHIH: ornament, paint, brighten, patch up the appearance; apply cosmetics; pretend, make believe.

22.S Adorning implies embellishing indeed.

23.S Actually involving embellishing, therefore afterwards Growing by-consequence used-up.

Emblem-ax, FU: moon-shaped ax, symbol of power to govern.

56.4a/b Acquiring one's own emblem-ax.

57.6a/b Losing one's own emblem-ax.

Embroil, WANG: caught up in, entangled, involved; disorder, incoherence; foolish, wild, reckless; false, brutish behaviour; vain, idle, futile. Image of Hexagram 25 and occurs throughout its texts.

26.S Possessing Without Embroiling therefore afterwards permitting Accumulating.

Eminent, HSIEN: moral and intellectual power; worthy, excellent, virtuous; sage second to the all-wise, SHENG.

8.4b Outside Grouping with-respect-to eminence.

26. ImT Above solid and-also honoring eminence.

26. ImT Nourishing eminence indeed.

27. ImT The all-wise person nourishes eminence used to extend-to the myriad commoners.

50. ImT And-also great Growing uses nourishing all-wise eminences.

53.ST A chün tzu uses residing-in eminent actualizing-tao to improve the vulgar.

Empty, HSÜ: no images or concepts; vacant, unsubstantial; empty yet fertile space.

23. ImT A chün tzu honors the dissolving pause to overfill emptiness.

31.ST A chün tzu uses emptiness to acquiesce people.

41. ImT Diminishing augmenting, overfilling emptiness.

46.3a/b Ascending: an empty capital.

54.6b Receiving an empty basket indeed.

55. ImT Heaven[and]Earth overfilling emptiness.

61. ImT Riding a wooden dug-out, emptiness indeed.

Enable, see: **Able**

Enclose, HSIEN: put inside a fence or barrier; restrain, obstruct, forbid; pen, corral.

26.3a Spoken-thus: an enclosed cart, escorting.

37.1a/b Enclosing: possessing Dwelling.

Encounter, TI: see face to face; admitted to an audience; visit, interview.

47.1a Three year's-time not encountering.

55.6a Three year's-time not encountering.

Encourage, CH'ÜAN: exhort, stimulate, influence; admonish.

48.ST A chün tzu uses toiling commoners to encourage mutualizing.

58. ImT Actually the commoners encouraged in-fact.

Encroach, CH'IN: invade, usurp, appropriate; advance stealthily, enter secretly; possessed by a spirit.

15.5a/b Harvesting: availing-of encroaching subjugating.

End, CHI: last or highest point; final, extreme; on the verge; ridgepole of a house.

60.2b Letting-go the season end indeed.

64.1b Truly not knowing the end indeed.

Enforce, LAI: compel obedience; have charge of; imposed by highest authority; arrest, deliver for punishment.

21.ST The Earlier Kings used brightening flogging to enforce the laws.

Enlighten, CHAO: cast light on, display, show; instruct, give knowlege; manifest, bright, splendid. The ideogram: sun and call, bring into the light.

35.ST A chün tzu uses originating enlightening to brighten actualizing-tao.

Enrich, YÜ: make richer (excluding land); material, mental or spiritual wealth; bequeath; generous, abundant. The ideogram: garments, portable riches.

18.4a/b Enriching the father's Corrupting.

35.1a/b Enriching, without fault.

42.AE Augmenting: actualizing-tao's enriching indeed.

42.AE Augmenting: long-living enriching and-also not setting-up.

Enshroud, YEN: screen, shade from view, hide, cover. The ideogram: hand and cover. See also: **Shroud**

47. ImT Solid enshrouded indeed.

Enter, JU: penetrate, go into, enter on, progress;

put into, encroach on; the Action of the trigram Ground, SUN, contrary of issue-forth, CH'U.

3.3a Namely, entering tending-towards the forest center.

5.6a Entering tending-towards the cave.

6.ImT Entering tending-towards the abyss indeed.

17.ST A chün tzu uses turning-to darkening to enter a reposing pause.

24. Im Issuing-forth, entering, without affliction.

24. ImT That uses issuing-forth, entering, without affliction.

29.1a Entering tending-towards the Gorge, the recess.

29.1b Repeating Gorge, entering Gorge.

29.3a Entering tending-towards the Gorge, the recess.

36.ST/ImT Brightness entering earth center.

36.4a/b Entering tending-towards the left belly.

36.6a/b Afterwards entering tending-towards earth.

47.1a/b Entering tending-towards a shady gully.

47.3a/b Entering tending-towards one's house.

57.S Ground implies entering indeed.

58.S Entering and-also afterwards stimulating it.

Envelop, MENG: cover, pull over, hide, conceal; lid or cover; clouded awareness, dull; ignorance, immaturity; unseen beginnings. The ideogram: plant and covered, hidden growth.

Image of Hexagram 4 and occurs throughout its texts.

3.CD Enveloping: motley and-also conspicuous.

36. ImT Using the enveloped great: heaviness.

Enwrap, PAO: envelop, hold, contain; patient; take on responsibility, engaged. The ideogram: enfold and self, a fetus in the womb.

4.2a Enwrapping Enveloping.

11.2a Enwrapping wasteland.

11.2b Enwrapping wasteland, acquiring honor, tending-towards centering moving.

12.2a Enwrapping receiving.

12.3a/b Enwrapping embarrassing.

44.2a/b Enwrapping possessing fish.

44.4a Enwrapping without fish.

44.5a Using osier, enwrapping melons.

Equal, P'EI: on the same level; pair, husband or wife; together.

16.ST Using equaling the grandfather predecessors.

55.1a Meeting one's equal lord.

Eradicate, PA: pull up, root out, extirpate; extricate from difficulties; elevate, promote.

11.1a Eradicating thatch-grass intertwisted.

11.1b Eradicating thatch-grass, chastising significant.

12.1a Eradicating thatch-grass intertwisted.

12.1b Eradicating thatch-grass, Trial: significant.

Escape, P'U: flee, run away, turn tail; deserter, fugitive. The ideogram: go and first, precipitous flight.

6.2a Converting and-also escaping one's capital.

6.2b Converting escaping, skulking indeed.

Escort, WEI: accompany, protect, guard, defend, honor; restrain; military outpost.

26.3a Spoken-thus: an enclosed cart, escorting.

Establish, LI: set up, institute, order, arrange; stand erect; settled principles.

28.ST A chün tzu uses solitary establishing not to fear.

32.ST A chün tzu uses establishing, not versatility on-all-sides.

42.6a Establishing the heart, no persevering.

59.ST The earlier kings used presenting tending-towards the supreme to establish the temples.

Evade, MIEN: avoid, escape from, get away; be free of, dispense with; remove from office. The ideogram: a hare, known for its evasive skill.

40. ImT Stirring-up and-also evading reaching-to venturing.

Evaluate, CH'ENG: assess, appraise; weigh, estimate, reckon; designate, name. The ideogram: weigh and grain, attributing value.

15.ST [A chün tzu uses] evaluating beings to even spreading-out.

57.AE Ground: evaluating and-also occulting.

Even, P'ING: level, make even or equal; uniform, peaceful, tranquil; restore quiet, harmonize.

11.3a Without evening, not unevening.

15.ST [A chün tzu uses] evaluating beings to even spreading-out.

20.6b Purpose not-yet evened indeed.

29.5a Merely already evened.

31. ImT The all-wise person influencing the people at-heart and-also Below Heaven harmony evening.

Even-more, K'UANG: even more so, all the more.

16. ImT And-also even-more installing feudatories to move legions reached.

55. ImT And-also even-more with-respect-to the people reached.

55. ImT Even-more with-respect-to the Souls[and]Spirits reached.

Evidence, TZ'U: verbal proof; instructions, orders, arguments; apology.

42.6b One-sided evidence indeed.

Exalting worship, YIN CHIEN: superlative of worship; glorify; intensify feelings of praise and awe.

16.ST Exalting worship's Supreme Above.

Exceed, KU: go beyond, pass by, pass over; excessive, transgress; error, fault.

Image of Hexagrams 28 and 62 and occurs throughout their texts.

16. ImT Anterior Sun[and]Moon not exceeding.

27.CD Great Exceeding: toppling indeed.

29.S Beings not permitted to use completing Exceeding.

40.ST A chün tzu uses forgiving excess to pardon offenses.

42.ST [A chün tzu uses] possessing excess, by-consequence amending.

55.1b Exceeding a decade, calamity indeed.

61.CD Small Exceeding: Excess indeed.

63.S Possessing Exceeding being implies necessarily Fording.

Excellence, CHIA: superior quality; fine, delicious, glorious; happy, pleased; rejoice in, praise. The ideogram: increasing goodness, pleasure and happiness.

17.5a Conformity tending-towards excellence. Significant.

17.5b Conformity tending-towards excellence significant.

30.6a Possessing excellence.

33.5a/b Excellence Retiring, Trial: significant.

49.2b Moving possessing excellence indeed.

Exhaust, CH'IUNG: bring to an end; limit, extremity; destitute; investigate exhaustively; end without a new beginning. Contrasts with complete, CHUNG, end of a cycle.The ideogram: cave and naked person, bent with disease or old age.

2.6b Their tao exhausted indeed.

3.3b Going abashment exhausted indeed.

5.ImT Actually one's righteousness, not confining exhaustion.

8.ImT One's tao exhausted indeed.

16.1b Purpose exhausted, pitfall indeed.

17.6b Exhausting the above indeed.

19.ST A chün tzu uses teaching to ponder without exhausting.

24.S Above Stripping exhausted, below reversing.

25.6b Exhaustion's calamity indeed.

34.1b One's conforming exhausted indeed.

38.S Dwelling tao exhausted, necessarily returning.

39. ImT One's tao exhausted indeed.

43. ImT The place to honor thereupon exhausted indeed.

44.6b Exhausting abashment above indeed.

47.AE Confining: exhausting and-also interpenetrating.

47. ImT Honoring the mouth thereupon exhausted indeed.

48. ImT The Well nourishing and-also not exhausted indeed.

53. ImT Stirring-up not exhausted indeed.

56.S Exhausting the great implies necessarily letting-go one's residing.

56.1b Purpose exhausted, calamity indeed.

57.3b Purpose exhausted indeed.

57.6b Above exhaustion indeed.

59. ImT Solid coming and-also not exhausted.

60. ImT,6b One's tao exhausted indeed.

63/64.CD Not-yet Fording: manhood exhausted indeed.

63. ImT One's tao exhausted indeed.

64.S Beings not permitted exhaustion indeed.

Explicate, CHIANG: explain, unfold, narrate; converse, speak; investigate, plan, discuss. The ideogram: speech and crossing beams, speech blending harmoniously.

58.ST A chün tzu uses partnering friends to explicate repeating.

Expose, WEI: exposed to danger, precipitous, unsteady; too high, not upright; uneasy. The ideogram: overhanging rock, person and limit, exposure in an extreme position.

43. ImT One's exposure thereupon shining indeed.

51.5b Exposed moving indeed.

52.3b Exposure smothers the heart indeed.

Extend(-to), CHI: reach to, draw out, prolong; continuous, enduring.

27.ImT The all-wise person nourishes eminence used to extend-to the myriad commoners.

43.ST A chün tzu uses spreading-out benefits to extend-to the below.

44.2b Righteously not extending-to guesting indeed.

61.ImT Trustworthiness extending-to hog fish indeed.

62.2a/b Not extending-to one's chief.

Extinguish, WANG: ruin, destroy; gone, dead, lost without trace; extinct, forgotten, out of mind. The ideogram: person concealed by a wall, out of sight. See also: **Repenting extinguished**

11.2a Partnering extinguished.

12.5a Its extinction, its extinction.

16.5b Center not-yet extinguished indeed.

38.6b The flock, doubt extinguished indeed.

56.5a The-one arrow extinguishing.

61.4a/b The horse team extinguished.

Extol, CH'UNG: praise, honor, magnify, revere; eminent, lofty; worthy of worship.

16.ST The Earlier Kings used arousing delight to extol actualizing-tao.

Eye, MU: eye and its functions: look, see, glance, observe.

9.3a/b Husband, consort, reversing eyes.

50.ImT Ground and-also the ear[and]eye: understanding brightened.

Face, WANG: full moon; moon directly facing the sun; 15th day of the moon-month; look at hopefully.

9.6a The moon almost facing.

54.5a The moon almost facing, significant.

61.4a The moon almost facing.

Fade, JO: lose strength or freshness, wither, wane; fragile, feeble, weak; decayed, ruined; infirm purpose.

28.ImT Roots, tips, fading indeed.

Fall, HSIEN: fall down or into, sink, drop, descend; falling water; the Action of the trigram Gorge, K'AN.

5.ImT Solid persisting and-also not falling.

29.S Gorge implies falling indeed.

30.S Falling necessarily possesses a place to congregate.

Far-away, TI: far, remote; send away, exile.

59.6a Departing far-away, issuing-forth.

Fate, MING: individual destiny; birth and death as limits of life; issue orders with authority; consult the gods. The ideogram: mouth and order, words with heavenly authority.

1.ImT Each-one correcting innate fate.

6.4a/b Returning, approaching fate.

7.2a/b The king three-times bestowing fate.

7.6a/b The Great Chief possesses fate.

11.6a Originating-from the capital, notifying fate.

11.6b One's fate disarrayed indeed.

12.4a/b Possessing fate, without fault.

14.ST [A chün tzu uses] yielding-to heaven to relinquish fate.

19.2b Not-yet yielding-to fate indeed.

25.ImT Heaven's fate indeed.

25.ImT Heavenly fate not shielding.

35.1b Not-yet acquiescing-in fate indeed.

44.ST The crown-prince uses spreading-out fate to command the four sides.

44.5b Purpose, not stowing-away fate indeed.

45.ImT Yielding-to heavenly fate indeed.

47.ST A chün tzu uses involving fate to release purpose.

49.ImT Majestically martial, Skinning fate.

49.4a/b Amending fate significant.

50.ST A chün tzu uses correcting the situation to solidify fate.

56.5a/b Completing uses praising fate.

57.ST A chün tzu uses distributing fate to move affairs.

57.ImT Redoubling Ground uses distributing fate.

Father(hood), FU: ruler of the family; act as a father, paternal, patriarchal; authoritative rule. The ideogram: hand and rod, the chastising father. See also: **Father[and]Mother** and **Father[and]Son**

18.1a/b,3a/b Managing the father's Corrupting.

18.4a/b Enriching the father's Corrupting.

18.5a Managing the father's Corrupting.

18.5b Managing the father availing-of praise.

37.ImT The father, a father.

Father[and]Mother, FU MU: cooperative relation between man and woman in ruling and caring for a family.

37.ImT Father[and]Mother's designating indeed.

Father[and]Son, FU TZU: proper relation

between generations serving and living up to the ideal of the ancestors, carrying on a tradition.

31.S Therefore afterwards possessing Father[and]Son.

31.S Possessing Father[and]Son:

Fault, CHIU: unworthy conduct that leads to harm, illness, misfortune. The ideogram: person and differ, differ from what you should be. See also: **Without fault**

7.ImT Actually significant, furthermore wherefore faulty?

9.1a Wherefore one's fault? Significant.

13.1b Furthermore whose fault indeed?

14.1a In-no-way faulty.

17.4a Wherefore faulty?

18.3a Without the great: fault.

19.3b Fault not long-living indeed.

28.6b Not permitting fault indeed.

30.1b Using casting-out fault indeed.

34.6b Fault not long-living indeed.

38.1b Using casting-out fault indeed.

38.5a Going wherefore faulty?

40.3b Furthermore whose fault indeed.

43.1a Going not mastering, activating faulty.

43.1b Fault indeed.

44.3a Without the great: fault.

53.1a Lacking fault.

60.3b Furthermore whose fault indeed?

Favor, CH'UNG: receive or confer gifts, obtain grace, win favor; dote on a woman; gifted for.

7.2b Receiving heavenly favor indeed.

23.5a/b Using housing people, favor.

Fear, CHÜ: afraid, intimidated, apprehensive; stand in awe of.

28.ST A chün tzu uses solitary establishing not to fear.

51.ST A chün tzu uses anxious fearing to adjust inspecting.

51. ImT Scaring the distant and-also fearing the nearby indeed.

Feast, K'AN: take part in or give a feast; rejoice, give pleasure; pleased, contented.

53.2a/b Drinking[and]taking-in: feasting, feasting.

Feathers, YU: wings, plumes; feathered; quick, flying.

53.6a Its feathers permit availing-of activating fundamentals.

53.6b Its feathers permit availing-of activating fundamentals, significant.

Feed, K'UEI: prepare and present food; provisions.

37.2a Locating the center, feeding.

Female, P'IN: female sexual organs, particularly of farm animals; concave, hollow. The ideogram: cattle and ladle, a hollow, reproductive organ.

2.Im Field: Spring Growing Harvesting, female horse's Trial.

2.ImT The female horse: earth sorting.

30. Im Growing. Accumulating female cattle.

30. ImT That uses accumulating female cattle, significant indeed.

Fetter, CHIH: tie, manacle; restrain and hinder movement, clog wheels; impede.

4.1a Availing-of stimulating fettering shackles.

Feudatory, HOU: nobles entrusted with governing the provinces; active in daily life rather than governing from the center; contrasts with prince, KUNG, executives at the court.

3.Im Harvesting: installing feudatories.

3.ImT Proper to instal feudatories and-also not to soothe.

3.1a Harvesting: installing feudatories.

8.ST The Earlier Kings used installing myriad cities to connect the connoted feudatories.

16. Im Providing-for, Harvesting: installing feudatories to move legions:

16. ImT And-also even-more installing feudatories to move legions reached.

18.6a/b Not affairs, kingly feudatories.

35. Im Prospering, the calm feudatory avails-of bestowing horses to multiply the multitudes.

35. ImT That uses the calm feudatory availing-of bestowing horses to multiply the multitudes.

Few, KUA: small number; seldom, rarely; unusual, solitary.

9/10.CD Small Accumulating: few indeed.

15.ST A chün tzu uses reducing the numerous to augment the few.

47.AE Confining: using few grudges.

55/56.CD Connecting the few: Sojourning indeed.

Fiefdom, PANG: region governed by a feudatory, an order of nobility.

7.2b Cherishing the myriad fiefdoms indeed.

7.6b Necessarily disarraying the fiefdoms indeed.

12. ImT Above[and]Below not mingling and-
also Below Heaven without fiefdoms
indeed.

30.6b Using correcting the fiefdoms indeed.

39. ImT Using correcting the fiefdoms indeed.

53. ImT Permitting using correcting the
fiefdoms indeed.

61. ImT Thereupon changing the fiefdoms
indeed.

Field, K'UN: surface of the world; concrete
extension; basis of all existence, where Force or
heaven exerts its power; all-involving service;
earth; moon, wife, mother; courtiers, servants.
The ideogram: terrestrial globe and stretch out,
stability and extension.

Image of Hexagram 2 and occurs throughout
its texts.

1.CD Field: supple.

Field-altar, SHE: altar and sacrifices to spirits of
place; village, with a common god and field-altar.

51. ImT Issuing-forth permits using guarding
the ancestral temple, field-altar, offertory-
millet.

Fields, T'IEN: cultivated land, plantation; also:
hunting, game in the fields cannot escape the
hunt. The ideogram: square divided into four
sections, delineating fields.

1.2a/b Visualizing dragon located-in the fields.

7.5a The fields possess wild-fowl.

32.4a The fields without wildfowl.

40.2a The fields, catching three foxes.

57.4a/b The fields, catching three kinds.

Fine, LIANG: excellent, refined, valuable; gentle,
considerate, kind; natural.

26.3a A fine horse, pursuing.

54.5a/b One's junior-sister's sleeves not thus
fine.

Fire, HUO: warming and consuming aspect of
burning; fire and brightness are the Symbols of
the trigram Radiance, LI.

13.ST Heaven associating-with fire.

14.ST Fire located above heaven.

22.ST Below mountain possessing fire.

37.ST Wind originating-from fire issuing-
forth.

38.ST Fire above, marsh below.

38. ImT Fire stirring-up and-also above.

49.ST Marsh center possessing fire.

49. ImT Skinning. Stream, fire, mutually
pausing.

50.ST Above wood possessing fire.

50. ImT Using wood: Ground, fire.

56.ST Above mountain possessing fire.

63.ST Stream located above fire.

64.ST Fire located above stream.

Firm, FU: constant, fixed, steady; chronic,
recurrent. The ideogram: old and enclosure, long
preserved.

25.4b Firmly possessing it indeed.

32.AE Persevering: actualizing-tao's firmness
indeed.

33.2b Firm purpose indeed.

42.3b Firmly possessing it indeed.

Fish, YÜ: scaly, aquatic beings hidden in the
water; symbol of abundance; connected with the
Streaming Moment. See also: **Hog Fish**

23.5a Threading fish.

44.2a/b Enwrapping possessing fish.

44.4a Enwrapping without fish.

44.4b Without fish's pitfall.

Five, WU: number for active groups: Five
Moments, Directions, colors, smells, tastes,
tones, feelings; fifth.

This term occurs at the fifth Transforming
Line of each hexagram. It also occurs at:

43. ImT Supple riding five solids indeed.

Flee, PEN: run away quickly; urgent, hurry;
bustle, confusion; marry without rites. The
ideogram: three oxen and fright, a stampede.

59.2a/b Dispersing: fleeing one's bench.

Flesh, FU: muscles, organs, skin, in contrast to
bones.

21.2a/b Gnawing flesh, submerging the nose.

23.4a/b Stripping the bed, using flesh.

38.5a/b Your ancestor gnawing flesh.

43.4a The sacrum without flesh.

44.3a The sacrum without flesh.

Flock, CH'ÜN: herd, group; people of same kind,
friends, equals; all, entire; move in unison, flock
together. The ideogram: chief and sheep, flock
around a leader.

1.7a Visualizing flocking dragons without a
head.

12.2b Not disarraying the flock indeed.

38.6b The flock, doubt extinguished indeed.

53.3b Radiance flocking demons indeed.

59.4a/b Dispersing one's flock, Spring
significant.

Flog, FA: punish with blows, beat, whip; used to
find out the truth.

16. ImT By-consequence punishing flogging
purifies and-also the commoners submit.

21.ST The Earlier Kings used brightening flogging to enforce the laws.

Flower, HUA: beauty, abundance; variegated, elegant, blooming, garden-like; symbol of culture and literature.

28.5a/b A withered willow giving-birth-to flowers.

Flutter, P'IEN: fly or run about; bustle, fussy. The ideogram: young bird leaving the nest.

11.4a Fluttering, fluttering.

11.4b Fluttering, fluttering: not affluence.

Fly, FEI: spread your wings, fly away; let free; swift.

1.5a/b Flying dragon located-in heaven.

36.1a Brightness Hiding tending-towards flying.

62. Im Flying bird: abandoning's sound.

62. ImT Possessing the flying bird's symbol in-truth.

62. ImT Flying bird: abandoning's sound.

62.1a/b Flying bird: using a pitfall.

62.6a Flying bird radiating it.

Follow, SUI: come or go after; pursue, impelled to move; come after in inevitable sequence; move in the same direction, comply with what is ahead; follow a way or religion; according to, next, subsequent. The ideogram: go and fall, unavoidable movement.

Image of Hexagram 17 and occurs throughout its texts.

18.S Using rejoicing Following people implies necessarily possessing affairs.

18.CD Following: without anteriority indeed.

31.3a Holding-on-to one's following.

31.3b Purpose located-in following people.

52.2a/b Not rescuing one's following.

57.ST Following winds. Ground.

Foot, CHIH: literal foot; foundation, base.

21.1a/b Shoes locked-up, submerging the feet.

22.1a Adorning one's feet.

34.1a/b Invigorating tending-towards the feet.

43.1a Invigorating tending-towards the preceding foot.

50.1a/b The Vessel: toppling the foot.

52.1a/b Bound: one's feet.

Foot-cutting, YÜEH: crippling punishment for serious crimes.

47.5a/b Nose-cutting, foot-cutting.

Force, CH'IEN: spirit power, creative and destructive; unceasing forward motion; dynamic, enduring, untiring; firm, stable; heaven,sovereign, father; also: dry up, parched, exhausted, cleared away. The ideogram: sprouts or vapors rising from the ground and sunlight, both fecundating moisture and scorching drought. See also: **Parch**

Image of Hexagram 1 and occurs throughout its texts.

2.CD Force: solid.

10. ImT Stimulating and-also corresponding reaching-to Force.

13. ImT Acquiring centering and-also corresponding reaching-to Force.

13. ImT Force moving indeed.

Ford, CHI: cross a river at a ford or shallow place; overcome an obstacle, embark on a course of action; help, relieve; cease. The ideogram: water and level, running smooth over a flat bottom.

Image of Hexagrams 63 and 64 and occurs throughout their texts.

15. ImT Heavenly tao fording below and-also shining brightness.

Forest, LIN: area with no mark of human construction; woods, wild luxuriance; wilderness; last of the territorial zones: city, suburbs, countryside, forests.

3.3a Namely, entering tending-towards the forest center.

Forget, WANG: escape the mind; leave undone, disregard, neglect. The ideogram: heart and lost.

58. ImT The commoners forget their toiling.

58. ImT The commoners forget their dying.

Forgive, SHE: excuse, pass over, set aside, reprieve.

40.ST A chün tzu uses forgiving excess to pardon offenses.

Form, HSING: shape; body, bodily; material appearance.

1.ImT The kinds: being diffusing forms.

50.4a Its form soiled. Pitfall.

Foundation, CHI: base of wall or building; basis, starting point; found, establish.

10.AE Treading: actualizing-tao's foundation indeed.

Four, SSU: number four, fourth; everywhere, allaround; the earth with four sides, FANG. See also: **Four seasons** and **Four sides**

This term occurs at the fourth Transforming Line of each hexagram. It occurs also at:

36.6b Illuminating the four cities indeed.

Four seasons, SSU SHIH: the four dynamic qualities of time that make up the year and the Time Cycle; the right time, in accord with the time; time as sacred; all-encompassing.

16. ImT And-also the four seasons not straying.

20. ImT And-also the four seasons not straying.

32. ImT The four seasons transforming changes and-also enabling lasting accomplishment.

49. ImT Heaven[and]Earth Skinning and-also the four seasons accomplishing.

60. ImT Heaven, Earth: Articulating and-also the four seasons accomplishing.

Four sides, SSU FANG: the cardinal points; the limits or boundaries of the earth; everywhere, all around. See also: **Sides**

30.ST Great People use consecutive brightening to illuminate tending-towards the four sides.

44.ST The crown-prince uses spreading-out fate to command the four sides.

Fox, HU: crafty, shape-changing animal; used by spirits, often female; ambivalent night-spirit that can create havoc and bestow abundance.

40.2a The fields, catching three foxes.

64. Im/ImT The small fox, a muddy Ford.

Fragment, SO: break into small pieces, broken parts; minute, fine; petty, trivial; annoying; lit.: splinters of precious stones. The ideogram: small and cowrie shells, the tinkling of small coins.

56.1a/b Sojourning: fragmenting, fragmenting.

Friend, YU: companion, associate; of the same mind; attached, in pairs. The ideogram: two hands joined.

41.3a By-consequence acquiring one's friend.

58.ST A chün tzu uses partnering friends to explicate repeating.

Fright, HSI: frighten or be frightened; alarm, terror; awestruck.

51. Im/ImT,1a/b Shake coming: frightening, frightening.

Frost, SHUANG: frozen dew, hoar-frost, rime; crystallized; severe, frigid.

2.1a Treading frost, hardening ice culminating.

2.1b Treading frost hardening the ice:

Froth, MO: spume, foam, bubbles; perspire, drool.

55.3a Sun centering: visualizing froth.

Fruit, KUO: plants' annual produce; tree fruits; come to fruition, fruits of actions; produce, results, effects; reliable; conclude, surpass. The ideogram: tree topped by a round fruit.

4.ST A chün tzu uses fruiting movement to nurture actualizing-tao.

23.6a The ripe fruit not taken-in.

40. ImT Thunder[and]Rain arousing and-also the hundred fruits, grasses, trees, altogether seedburst boundary.

Full, MAN: as much as possible; replete, bulging, stuffed, abounding; complete; proud.

3.ImT Thunder[and]Rain's stirring-up, fullness overfilling.

Fundamentals, YI: primary natural powers; origins, essentials; good and do good; correct, proper, just; rule, rite, decorum; paired, matched. The ideogram: person and righteous.

53.6a Its feathers permit availing-of activating fundamentals.

53.6b Its feathers permit availing-of activating fundamentals, significant.

Furthermore, YU: in addition to; higher degree of.

7.ImT Actually significant, furthermore wherefore faulty?

13.1b Furthermore whose fault indeed?

40.3b Furthermore whose fault indeed?

49.3b Furthermore actually wherefore having-them.

60.3b Furthermore whose fault indeed?

Garden, YÜAN: enclosed garden; park, yard; imperial tombs.

22.5a Adorning tending-towards a hill-top garden.

Gate, MEN: outer door, between court-yard and street; a text or master as gate to a school of thought.

13.1a Concording People tending-towards the gate.

13.1b Issuing-forth-from the gate Concording People.

16.AE Redoubling gates, smiting clappers.

17.1a/b Issuing-forth-from the gate, mingling possesses achievement.

36.4a Tending-towards issuing-forth-from the gate chambers.

60.2a Not issuing-forth-from the gate chambers.

60.2b Not issuing-forth-from the gate chambers, pitfall.

- **Geld**, FEN: castrate a pig; deprive, take out.
  26.5a A gelded pig's tusks.
- **Generous**, HUNG: liberal, large; vast, expanded; give or share willingly, munificent; develop fully.
  2.ImT Containing generosity, the shining great.
- **Giggle**, HSI: laugh or titter uncontrollably; merriment, delight, surprise; foolish.
  37.3a/b The wife, the son, giggling, giggling:
- **Give-birth-to**, see: **Birth**
- **Glare**, TAN: stare intensely; obstruct, prevent. The ideogram: look and hesitate, staring without acting.
  27.4a Tiger observing: glaring, glaring.
- **Gnaw**, SHIH: bite away, chew; bite persistently and remove; snap at, nibble; reach the essential by removing the unnecessary. The ideogram: mouth and divination, revealing the essential.
  Image of Hexagram 21 and occurs throughout its texts.
  38.5a/b Your ancestor gnawing flesh.
- **Go**, WANG, and come, LAI, describe the stream of time as it flows from future through present to past; go, WANG, indicates what is departing from present to past; proceed, move on; keyword. See also: **Go-to-meet**; **Let-go**; **Possessing directed going**
  3.3a Going abashed.
  3.3b Going abashment exhausted indeed.
  3.4a Going significant.
  3.4b Seeking and-also going.
  4.1a Using going abashed.
  5.ImT Going possesses achievement indeed.
  9.ImT Honoring going indeed.
  10.1a/b Sheer Treading going.
  11. Im/ImT The small going, the great coming.
  11.3a/b Without going, not returning.
  12. Im/ImT The great going, the small coming.
  18. ImT Going possesses affairs indeed.
  18.4a Going: visualizing abashment.
  18.4b Going, not-yet acquiring indeed.
  25. ImT Without Embroiling's going.
  25.1a Without Embroiling. Going significant.
  25.1b Without Embroiling's going.
  26.ST A chün tzu uses the numerous recorded preceding words going to move.

29. ImT Movement possesses honor. Going possesses achievement indeed.
31.3a Going abashed.
31.4a/b Wavering, wavering: going, coming.
33.1b Not going, wherefore calamity indeed.
34.4b Honoring going indeed.
35.5a Going significant, without not Harvesting.
35.5b Going possessing reward indeed.
38.5a Going wherefore faulty?
38.5b Going possessing reward indeed.
38.6a Going meeting rain, by-consequence significant.
39. ImT Going acquires the center indeed.
39. ImT Going possesses achievement indeed.
39.1a/b Going Limping, coming praise.
39.3a/b Going Limping, coming reversing.
39.4a/b Going Limping, coming continuity.
39.6a/b Going Limping, coming ripening.
40. Im Without a place to go:
40. ImT Going acquiring crowds indeed.
40. ImT Going possesses achievement indeed.
41.1a/b Climaxing affairs, swiftly going.
43.1a Going not mastering, activating faulty.
43.1b Not mastering and-also going.
43.3a Solitary going, meeting rain.
45.1a,3a/b Going without fault.
48. Im Going, coming: Welling, Welling.
51.5a/b Shake going, coming adversity.
53. ImT Going possessing achievement indeed.
55.1a Going possesses honor.
55.2a Going acquiring doubt, affliction.
60.5a Going possesses honor.
62.4a/b Going adversity necessarily warning.

Goat, YANG: sheep and goats; direct thought and action.
  34.3a The he goat butts a hedge.
  34.5a/b Losing the goat, tending-towards versatility.
  34.6a The he goat butts a hedge.
  43.4a Hauling-along the goat, repenting extinguished.
  54.6a A notable disembowelling a goat without blood.
Go-down, TSE: sun setting, afternoon; waning moon; decline.
  30.3a/b Sun going-down's Radiance.
  55. ImT Sun centering, by-consequence going-down.

Go-to-meet, YA: advance to encounter and receive; invoke; anticipate, face, provide for; govern; drive or tame a horse; extending everywhere, as the imperial power.

    1.ImT The season riding six dragons used going-to-meet heaven.

Gorge, K'AN: dangerous place; hole, cavity, hollow; pit, snare, trap, grave, precipice; critical time, test; risky. The ideogram: earth and pit.

    Image of Hexagram 29 and occurs throughout its texts.

Grains, KU: cereal crops, corn; substantial, well-off; income; bless with plenty.

    30. ImT The hundred grains, grasses, trees congregating reaching-to earth.

Grandfather, TSU: second ancestor generation; deceased grandfather, honored more than actual father.

    16.ST Using equaling the grandfather predecessors.

    62.2a Exceeding one's grandfather.

Grandmother, PI: second ancestor generation; deceased grandmother, venerated as source of her many descendants.

    62.2a Meeting one's grandmother.

Grapple, CHÜ: grasp and detain; restrain, attach to, hook.

    17.6a/b Grappling, tying-to it.

Grasp, CH'Ü: lay hold of, take and use, seize, appropriate; grasp the meaning, understand. The ideogram: ear and hand, hear and grasp.

    4.3a/b No availing-of grasping womanhood.

    8.5b Stowing-away countering, grasping yielding.

    16.AE Surely, grasping connotes Providing-for.

    31. Im/ImT Grasping womanhood significant.

    44. Im/ImT No availing-of grasping womanhood.

    49/50.CD The Vessel: grasping renewal indeed.

    56.1a Splitting-off one's place, grasping calamity.

    62.5a A prince, a string-arrow grasping another located-in a cave.

Grass, TS'AO: all grassy plants and herbs; young, tender plants; rough draft; hastily. See also: **Thatch-grass**

    3.ImT Heaven creating grass, duskiness.

    30. ImT The hundred grains, grasses, trees congregating reaching-to earth.

    40. ImT Thunder[and]Rain arousing and-also the hundred fruits, grasses, trees, altogether seedburst boundary.

Great, TA: big, noble, important, very; orient the will toward a self-imposed goal, impose direction; ability to lead or guide your life; contrasts with small, HSIAO, flexible adaptation to what crosses your path; keyword. See also: **Great People, Wading the Great River**

    Image of Hexagrams 14, 26, 28, 34 and occurs throughout their texts.

    1.ImT The great Force, Spring in-fact.

    1.ImT Great brightening completing beginning.

    1.ImT Protection uniting the great harmony.

    2.ImT Containing generosity, the shining great.

    2.2a Straightening on-all-sides, great.

    2.3b Knowing the shining great indeed.

    2.7b Using the great to complete indeed.

    3.ImT Great Growing: Trial.

    3.1b The great acquiring the commoners indeed.

    3.5a The great, Trial: pitfall.

    5.6b Although not an appropriate situation, not-yet the great let-go indeed.

    7.3b The great without achievement indeed.

    7.6a/b The Great Chief possesses fate.

    10.3a/b Martial people activating: tending-towards a Great Chief.

    10.6b The great possesses reward indeed.

    11. Im/ImT The small going, the great coming.

    11.2b Using the shining great indeed.

    12. Im/ImT The great going, the small coming.

    13.CD Great Possessing: crowds indeed.

    13.5a/b Great legions controlling mutual meeting.

    16.S Possessing the Great and-also enabling Humbling necessarily Provides-for.

    16. ImT Actually Provision's season righteously great in-fact.

    16.4a The great possesses acquiring.

    16.4b Antecedent Provision, the great possesses acquiring.

    16.4b Purpose: the great moving indeed.

    17. ImT Great Growing, Trial: without fault.

17. ImT Actually Following the season's righteous great in-fact.

18.3a Without the great: fault.

19.S Possessing affairs and-also afterwards permitting the great.

19.S Nearing implies the great indeed.

19. ImT Great Growing uses correcting.

19.5a/b A Great Chief's propriety.

20.S Being great therefore afterwards permitting Viewing.

20. ImT The great: Viewing located above.

24.6a Completing possesses great destroying.

25.CD Great Accumulating: the season indeed.

25. ImT Great Growing using correcting.

27.CD Great Exceeding: toppling indeed.

27. ImT Actually Jaws's season great in-fact.

27.3b Tao, the great rebelling indeed.

27.6b The great possessing reward indeed.

29. ImT Actually venturing's season availing-of the great in-fact.

29.5b Centering, not-yet great indeed.

30.3a By-consequence great old-age's lamenting. Pitfall.

31.4b Not-yet the shining great indeed.

32.6b The great without accomplishment indeed.

33.CD Great Invigorating: by-consequence stopping.

33. ImT Actually Retiring's season righteously great in-fact.

33.3b Not permitting Great Affairs indeed.

35. ImT Yielding and-also congregating reaching-to great brightening.

36. ImT Using the enveloped great: heaviness.

36.3a Acquiring its great, the head.

36.3b Thereupon acquiring the great indeed.

37. ImT Heaven[and]Earth's great righteousness indeed.

37.4a/b Affluence Dwelling, the great significant.

38. ImT Actually Polarizing's season availing-of the great in-fact.

39. ImT Actually Limping's season availing-of the great in-fact.

39.5a/b The great Limping, partnering coming.

40. ImT Actually Taking-apart's season great in-fact.

41.6b The great acquiring purpose indeed.

42. ImT One's tao, the great shining.

42.1a Harvesting: availing-of activating the great, arousing.

42.5b The great acquiring purpose indeed.

44. ImT Below Heaven, the great moving indeed.

44. ImT Actually Coupling's season righteously great in-fact.

44.3a Without the great: fault.

45. Im/ImT Availing-of the great: sacrificial-victims significant.

45.4a/b The great significant, without fault.

46.ST [A chün tzu uses] amassing the small to use the high great.

46. ImT That uses great Growing to avail-of visualizing Great People.

46.1a/b Sincere Ascending, the great significant.

46.5b The great acquiring the purpose indeed.

48.6b The great accomplishing indeed.

49. ImT Great Growing uses correcting.

49. ImT Actually Skinning's season great in-fact.

50. ImT And-also great Growing uses nourishing all-wise eminences.

50.6a The great significant.

51.5b The great without losing indeed.

54. ImT Heaven[and]Earth's great righteousness indeed.

55.S Acquiring one's place to Convert implies necessarily the great.

55.S Abounding implies the great indeed.

55. ImT Abounding, the great indeed.

55. ImT Honoring the great indeed.

55.3b Not permitting Great Affairs indeed.

56.S Exhausting the great implies necessarily letting-go one's residing.

56. ImT Actually Sojourning's season righteously great in-fact.

58. ImT Stimulating's great.

59.4b Shining great indeed.

59.5a Dispersing sweat, one's great crying-out.

62. Im Permitting Small Affairs. Not permitting Great Affairs.

62. Im The great significant.

62. ImT That uses not permitting Great Affairs indeed.

62. ImT The great significant.

63.5b Significant, the great coming indeed.

64.4a Three years-revolved, possessing donating tending-towards the great city.

Great People, TA JEN: important, noble, influential; those who impose a ruling principle on their lives; effect of the great within an individual; keyword.

1.2a,5a Harvesting: visualizing Great People.
1.5b Great People creating indeed.
6.Im/ImT Harvesting: visualizing Great People.
12.2a/b Great People Obstructed. Growing.
12.5a/b Great People significant.
30.ST Great People use consecutive brightening to illuminate tending-towards the four sides.
39. Im/ImT,6a/b Harvesting: visualizing Great People.
45. Im/ImT Harvesting: visualizing Great People. Growing.
46. Im Availing-of visualizing Great People.
46. ImT That uses great Growing to avail-of visualizing Great People.
47. Im/ImT Trial: Great People significant.
49.5a/b Great People: tiger transforming.
57. Im/ImT Harvesting: visualizing Great People.

Grieve(-over), YU: sorrow, melancholy; mourn; anxious, careworn; hidden sorrow. The ideogram: heart, head, and limp, heart-sick and anxious.

7/8.CD Legions: grieving.
19.3a/b Already grieving-over it:
55. Im/ImT No grief. Properly sun centering.

Ground, SUN: base on which things rest; support, foundation; mild, subtly penetrating; nourishing. The ideogram: stand and things arranged on it, the subtle influence of the ground.

Image of Hexagram 57 and occurs throughout its texts.

4.5b Yielding uses Ground indeed.
9.ImT Persisting and-also Ground.
18. ImT Ground and-also stopping. Corrupting.
20. ImT Yielding and-also Ground.
28. ImT Ground and-also stimulating movement.
32. ImT Ground and-also stirring-up.
37.2b Yielding uses Ground indeed.
42. ImT Augmenting stirring-up and-also Ground.
45.3b Ground above indeed.

46. ImT Ground and-also yielding.
48. ImT Ground reaching-to stream and-also stream above.
50. ImT Using wood: Ground, fire.
50. ImT Ground and-also the ear[and]eye: understanding brightened.
53. ImT Stopping and-also Ground.
53.4b Yielding using Ground indeed.
58.CD Ground: hiding-away indeed.
61. ImT Stimulating and-also Ground: Conforming.

Group, PI: compare and select, order things and put them in classes; find what you belong with; sort, examine correspondences; choose and harmonize; unite. The ideogram: person who stops walking, looking around to examine and compare.

Image of Hexagram 8 and occurs throughout its texts.

7.CD Grouping: delighting.
9.S Grouping necessarily possesses a place to Accumulate.

Grow, HENG: success through a sacrifice; pervade, persevere; bring to full growth; enjoy; vigorous, effective; second stage of the Time Cycle. See also: **Hair-grow** and **Spring Growing Harvesting Trial**

2.ImT The kinds: being conjoining Growing.
3.ImT Great Growing: Trial.
4.Im/ImT Enveloping, Growing.
4.ImT Using Growing movement.
5.Im/ImT Shining Growing, Trial: significant.
9.Im Small Accumulating, Growing.
9.ImT Thereupon Growing.
10. Im/ImT Not snapping-at people. Growing.
11. Im Significance Growing.
11. ImT The small going, the great coming: significance Growing.
12.1a Trial: significant. Growing.
12.2a/b Great People Obstructed. Growing.
13. Im/ImT Concording People, tending-towards the countryside. Growing.
14. Im Great Possessing, Spring Growing.
14. ImT That uses Spring Growing.
14.3a/b A prince availing-of Growing, tending-towards heavenly sonhood.
15. Im/ImT Humbling, Growing.
17. ImT Great Growing, Trial: without fault.

17.6a The king availing-of Growing tending-
towards the Western mountain.

18.Im/ImT Corrupting, Spring Growing.

19.ImT Great Growing uses correcting.

21.Im Gnawing Bite, Growing.

21.ImT Gnawing Bite and-also Growing.

22.Im/ImT Adorning, Growing.

22.ImT Anterior Growth.

23.S Actually involving embellishing, therefore
afterwards Growing by-consequence
used-up.

24.Im/ImT Returning, Growing.

25.ImT Great Growing using correcting.

26.6a Growing.

28.Im Growing.

28.ImT Thereupon Growing.

29.Im Holding-fast the heart Growing.

29.ImT Holding-fast the heart's Growing,
thereupon using solid centering indeed.

30.Im Growing. Accumulating female cattle.
Significant.

30.ImT Anterior Growing.

31.Im Conjoining, Growing.

31.ImT That uses Growth Harvesting Trial,
grasping womanhood significant.

32.Im Persevering, Growing.

32.ImT Persevering Growing, without fault.

33.Im/ImT Retiring, Growing.

33.ImT Retiring and-also Growing indeed.

45.Im Clustering, Growing.

45.Im/ImT Harvesting: visualizing Great
People. Growing.

46.Im Ascending, Spring Growing.

46.ImT That uses great Growing to avail-of
visualizing Great People.

46.4a/b Kinghood availing-of Growing,
tending-towards the twin-peaked
mountain.

47.Im Confining, Growing.

47.ImT Confining and-also not letting-go
one's place: Growing.

49.ImT Great Growing uses correcting.

50.Im Growing.

50.ImT Growing, cooking indeed.

50.ImT The all-wise person Growing uses
presenting-to the Supreme Above.

50.ImT And-also great Growing uses
nourishing all-wise eminences.

50.ImT That uses Spring Growing.

51.Im/ImT Shake, Growing.

55.Im Abounding, Growing.

56.Im Sojourning, the small: Growing.

56.ImT The small Growing.

56.ImT That uses the small Growing.

57.Im Ground, the small: Growing.

57.ImT That uses the small Growing.

58.Im Open, Growing,

59.Im/ImT Dispersing, Growing.

60.Im/ImT Articulating, Growing.

60.4a/b Quiet Articulating Growing.

62.Im Small Exceeding, Growing.

62.ImT Small implies Exceeding and-also
Growing indeed.

63.Im Already Fording. Growing: the small.

63.ImT Already Fording, Growing.

63.ImT The small implies Growing indeed.

64.Im/ImT Not-yet Fording, Growing.

Grudges, YÜAN: bitter feelings, ill-will; hate,
abhor; murmur against. The ideogram: heart and
overturn, upset emotion.

47.AE Confining: using few grudges.

Guard, SHOU: keep in custody; protect, ward off
harm, attend to, supervise.

29.ImT The kingly prince sets-up venturing
used to guard his city.

51.ImT Issuing-forth permits using guarding
the ancestral temple, field-altar, offertory-
millet.

Guest, PIN: entertain a guest; visit someone,
enjoy hospitality; receive a stranger.

20.4a Harvesting: availing-of guesting
tending-towards kinghood.

20.4b Honoring guesting indeed.

44.2a Not Harvesting: guesting.

44.2b Righteously not extending-to guesting
indeed.

Gully, KU: valley, ravine, river bed, gap. The
ideogram: divide and river, a river bed separating
hills.

47.1a/b Entering tending-towards a shady
gully.

48.2a/b The Well: a gully, shooting bass.

Gush, T'O: water surging in streams; falling
tears; heavy rain.

30.5a Issuing-forth tears like gushing. Sadness
like lamenting.

Hair-growing, HSÜ: beard, hair; patience
symbolized as waiting for hair to grow; hold back,
wait for; slow; necessary.

5.ImT Attending: hair-growing indeed.
22.2a/b Adorning: one's hair-growing.
54.3a/b Converting Maidenhood using hair-growing.

● **Halt**, P'O: limp; lame, crippled; indecorous.
10.3a/b Halting enabling Treading.
54.1a Halting enabling treading.
54.1b Halting enabling treading, significant.

● **Hamper**, CH'E: hinder, obstruct, hold or pull back; embarrass; select. The ideogram: hand and limit, grasp and control.
38.3a One's cattle hampered.

● **Handful**, WU: as much as the hand can hold; a little; grasp, hold.
45.1a Like an outcry, the-one handful activates laughing.

● **Handle**, PING: haft; control of, power to.
15.AE Humbling: actualizing-tao's handle indeed.

● **Hand-washing**, KUAN: wash the hands before a sacramental act; ablutions, a basin.
20. Im/ImT Viewing: hand-washing and-also not worshipping.

● **Harden**, CHIEN: make or become hard; establish, strengthen; durable, resolute.
2.1a Treading frost, hardening ice culminating.
2.1b Treading frost hardening the ice:
2.1b Culminating hardening the ice indeed.

● **Harm**, HAI: damage, injure, offend; suffer; hurtful, hindrance; fearful, anxious.
2.4b Consideration not harmful indeed.
14.1a Without mingling harm.
14.1b Without mingling harm indeed.
14.3b Small People harmful indeed.
15. ImT Souls[and]Spirits harming overfilling and-also blessing Humbling.
31.2b Yielding, not harming indeed.
31.4b Not-yet influencing harming indeed.
41.AE Diminishing: using distancing harm.
59.6b Distancing harm indeed.
60. ImT Not harming the commoners.

● **Harmony**, HO: concord, union; conciliate; at peace, mild; fit, tune, adjust.
1.ImT Protection uniting the great harmony.
10.AE Treading: harmonizing and-also culminating.
10.AE Treading: using harmonizing movement.

31. ImT The all-wise person influencing the people at-heart and-also Below Heaven harmony evening.
43. ImT Breaking-up and-also harmonizing.
58.1a/b Harmonious Opening: significant.
61.2a/b One's sonhood harmonizing it.

● **Harvest**, LI: advantageous, profitable; acute, insightful; benefit, nourish; third stage of the Time Cycle. See also: **Harvesting Trial**. Harvesting introduces or is connected with several other phrases. See: **Spring Growing Harvesting Trial**; **Without direction: Harvesting**; **Without not Harvesting**
1.2a,5a Harvesting: visualizing Great People.
2.Im A lord Harvesting.
3.Im/1a Harvesting: installing feudatories.
4.1a/b Harvesting: availing-of punishing people.
4.3a Without direction: Harvesting.
4.6a Not Harvesting: activating outlawry.
4.6a Harvesting: resisting outlawry.
4.6b Harvesting: availing-of resisting outlawry.
5.Im/ImT Harvesting: wading the Great River.
5.1a Harvesting: availing-of persevering.
5.1b Harvesting: availing-of persevering, without fault.
6.Im/ImT Harvesting: visualizing Great People.
6.Im/ImT Not Harvesting: wading the Great River.
7.5a Harvesting: holding-on-to words.
13. Im/ImT Harvesting: wading the Great River.
15.1a Availing-of wading the Great River. Significant.
15.5a/b Harvesting: availing-of encroaching subjugating.
15.6a Harvesting: availing-of moving legions.
16. Im Providing-for, Harvesting: installing feudatories to move legions.
18. Im/ImT Harvesting: wading the Great River.
19.3a Without direction: Harvesting.
20.4a Harvesting: availing-of guesting tending-towards kinghood.
21. Im Harvesting: availing-of litigating.
21. ImT Although not an appropriate situation, Harvesting: availing-of litigating indeed.

22. Im The small, Harvesting: possessing directed going.

22. ImT The anterior small, Harvesting: possessing directed going.

23. Im Stripping not Harvesting: possessing directed going.

23. ImT Not Harvesting: possessing directed going.

24. Im/ImT Harvesting: possessing directed going.

25. Im/ImT Not Harvesting: possessing directed going.

25.2a By-consequence, Harvesting: possessing directed going.

25.6a Without direction: Harvesting.

26. Im/ImT Harvesting: wading the Great River.

26.1a Harvesting: climaxing.

26.1b Possessing adversity, Harvesting: climaxing.

26.3a/b Harvesting: possessing directed going.

27.3a Without direction: Harvesting.

27.6a Harvesting: wading the Great River.

28. Im/ImT Harvesting: possessing directed going.

32. Im/ImT Harvesting: possessing directed going.

32. Ia Without direction: Harvesting.

34.6a Without direction: Harvesting.

39. Im Limping, Harvesting: Western South.

39. Im Not Harvesting: Eastern North.

39. Im Harvesting: visualizing Great People.

39. ImT Limping, Harvesting: Western South.

39. ImT Not Harvesting: Eastern North.

39. ImT,6a/b Harvesting: visualizing Great People.

40. Im/ImT Taking-apart. Harvesting: Western South.

41. Im/ImT Harvesting: possessing directed going.

41.6a Harvesting: possessing directed going.

42. Im Augmenting, Harvesting: possessing directed going.

42. Im/ImT Harvesting: wading the Great River.

42. ImT Harvesting: possessing directed going.

42.AE Augmenting: using the rising Harvest.

42.1a Harvesting: availing-of activating the great, arousing.

42.4a Harvesting: availing-of activating depending-on shifting the city.

43. Im/ImT Not Harvesting: approaching arms.

43. Im/ImT Harvesting: possessing directed going.

44.2a Not Harvesting: guesting.

45. Im Harvesting: visualizing Great People.

45. Im/ImT Harvesting: possessing directed going.

45. ImT Harvesting: visualizing Great People,

45.2a Conforming, thereupon Harvesting availing-of dedicating.

45.3a Without direction: Harvesting.

46.2a Conforming, thereupon Harvesting availing-of dedicating.

47.2a Harvesting: availing-of presenting oblations.

47.5a/b Harvesting: availing-of offering oblations.

50.1a/b Harvesting: issuing-forth-from obstruction.

53.3a Harvesting: resisting outlawry.

53.3b Harvesting: availing-of resisting outlawry.

54. Im/ImT,6a Without direction: Harvesting.

57. Im/ImT Harvesting: visualizing Great People.

59. Im/ImT Harvesting: wading the Great River.

61. Im/ImT Harvesting: wading the Great River.

64. Im/ImT Without direction: Harvesting.

64.3a Harvesting: wading the Great River.

Harvesting Trial, LI CHEN: advantageous divination; putting the action in question to the test is beneficial.

1.ImT Thereupon Harvesting Trial.

2.ImT Supple yielding, Harvesting Trial.

2.7a Harvesting: perpetual Trial.

3.1a Harvesting: residing-in Trial.

4.Im Harvesting Trial.

12. Im/ImT Not Harvesting: chün tzu, Trial.

13. Im Harvesting: chün tzu, Trial.

17.3a Harvesting: residing-in Trial.

20.2a Harvesting: woman Trial.

21.4a Harvesting: drudgery, Trial.

21.4b Harvesting: drudgery, Trial significant.

26. Im Harvesting Trial.

26.3a Harvesting: drudgery, Trial.
30. Im Radiance, Harvesting Trial.
31. Im Harvesting Trial.
31. ImT That uses Growth Harvesting Trial, grasping womanhood significant.
32. Im/ImT Harvesting Trial.
33. Im/ImT The small: Harvesting Trial.
34. Im/ImT Great Invigorating, Harvesting Trial.
36. Im Brightness Hiding, Harvesting: drudgery, Trial.
36. ImT Harvesting: drudgery, Trial.
36.5a Harvesting Trial.
37. Im Dwelling People, Harvesting: woman Trial.
41.2a Harvesting Trial.
41.2b Nine at-second, Harvesting Trial.
45. Im Harvesting Trial.
46.6a Harvesting: tending-towards not pausing's Trial.
50.5a Harvesting Trial.
52.1a Harvesting: perpetual Trial.
53. Im Harvesting Trial.
54.2a/b Harvesting: shade people's Trial.
57.1a/b Martial people's Harvesting Trial.
58. Im Harvesting Trial.
58. ImT Stimulating uses Harvesting Trial.
59. Im Harvesting Trial.
61. Im Harvesting Trial.
61. ImT Centering Conforming uses Harvesting Trial.
62. Im Harvesting Trial.
62. ImT Exceeding uses Harvesting Trial.
63. Im/ImT Harvesting Trial.

Hate, WU: dislike, dread; averse to, ashamed of; repulsive, vicious, vile, ugly, wicked. The ideogram: twisted bowels and heart, heart entangled in emotion.
14.ST A chün tzu terminating hate to display improvement.
15. ImT People tao hating overfilling and-also loving Humbling.
33.ST [A chün tzu uses] not hating and-also intimidating.
38.1a/b Visualizing hateful people.

Haul-along, CH'IEN: haul or pull, drag behind; pull an animal on a rope; pull toward. The ideogram: ox and halter.
9.2a Hauling-along, returning. Significant.

9.2b Hauling-along, returning, locating-in the center.
43.4a Hauling-along the goat, repenting extinguished.
44.1b Supple tao hauling-along indeed.
44.3b Moving, not-yet hauling-along indeed.

Have(-it)/'s/it/them, CHIH: expresses possession, directly or as an object pronoun. This term occurs throughout the hexagram texts.

Hawk, SHUN: bird of prey used in hunting; falcon, kestrel.
40.6a A prince avails-of shooting a hawk, tending-towards the high rampart's above.
40.6b A prince avails-of shooting a hawk.

Head, SHOU: literal head; leader, foremost; subject headings; beginning, model; superior, upper, front.
1.ImT Heads issuing-forth-from the multitudinous beings.
1.7a Visualizing flocking dragons without a head.
1.7b Heavenly actualizing-tao not permitting activating the head indeed.
8.6a/b Without a head, Grouping it.
30.6a Severing the head.
36.3a Acquiring its great, the head.
63.6a Soaking one's head.
63.6b Soaking one's head, adversity.
64.6a Soaking one's head.
64.6b Drinking liquor, soaking the head.

Hear, WEN: perceive sound; learn by report; news, fame. The ideogram: ear and door.
43.4a Hearing words, not trustworthy.
56.6b Completing absolutely-nothing: having hearing indeed.

Hearken, T'ING: listen to, obey, accept, acknowledge; examine, judge, decide. The ideogram: ear and actualizing-tao, hear and obey.
5.4b Yielding uses hearkening indeed.
52.2b Not-yet withdrawing-from hearkening indeed.

Heart, HSIN: heart as center of being; seat of mind's images and affections; moral nature; source of desires, intentions, will.
11.4b Centering the heart desiring indeed.
15.2b Centering the heart acquiring indeed.
24. ImT Reaching-to Returning one's visualizing Heaven[and]Earth's heart.
29. Im Holding-fast the heart Growing.

29. ImT Holding-fast the heart's Growing, thereupon using solid centering indeed.

31. ImT The all-wise person influencing the people at-heart and-also Below Heaven harmony evening.

36.4a Catching Brightness Hiding's heart.

36.4b Catching the heart, intention indeed.

42.5a/b Possessing conformity, a benevolent heart.

42.6a Establishing the heart, no persevering.

48.3a Activating my heart aching.

52.2a One's heart not keen.

52.3a Adversity smothers the heart.

52.3b Exposure smothers the heart indeed.

56.4a My heart not keen.

56.4b The heart not-yet keen indeed.

61.2b Centering the heart desiring indeed.

Heaven, T'IEN: highest; sky, firmament, heavens; power above the human as opposed to earth, TI, below; the Symbol of the trigram Force, CH'IEN. The ideogram: great and the one above. See also: **Below Heaven** and **Heaven[and]Earth**

1.ST Heaven moves persistingly.

1.ImT Thereupon primary heaven.

1.ImT The season riding six dragons used going-to-meet heaven.

1.5a/b Flying dragon located-in heaven.

1.7b Heavenly actualizing-tao not permitting activating the head indeed.

2.ImT Thereupon yielding receiving heaven.

3.ImT Heaven creating grass, duskiness.

5.ST Above clouds with-respect-to heaven.

5.ImT Situation reaching-to the heavenly situation.

6.ST Heaven associating-with stream, contradicting movements.

7.2b Receiving heavenly favor indeed.

9.ST Wind moving above heaven.

10.ST Heaven above, marsh below.

12.ST Heaven, earth, not mingling.

13.ST Heaven associating-with fire.

14.ST Fire located above heaven.

14.ST [A chün tzu uses] yielding-to heaven to relinquish fate.

14. ImT Corresponding reaching-to heaven and-also the season moving.

14.3a/b A prince availing-of Growing, tending-towards heavenly sonhood.

14.6a Originating-from heaven shielding it.

14.6b Originating-from heaven shielding indeed.

15. ImT Heavenly tao lessening overfilling and-also augmenting Humbling.

18. ImT Heaven moving indeed.

19. ImT Heavenly tao indeed.

20. ImT Viewing heaven's spirit tao.

22. ImT Heavenly pattern indeed.

22. ImT Viewing reaching-to the heavenly pattern.

23. ImT Heaven moving indeed.

24. ImT Heaven moving indeed.

25. ImT Heaven's fate indeed.

25. ImT Heavenly fate not shielding.

26.ST Heaven located-in mountain center.

26. ImT Corresponding reaching-to heaven indeed.

26.6a/b Wherefore heaven's highway?

29. ImT Heaven venturing, not permitting ascending indeed.

30. ImT Sun[and]Moon congregating reaching-to heaven.

32. ImT Sun[and]Moon acquiring heaven and-also enabling lasting illumination.

33.ST Below heaven possessing mountain.

34.ST Thunder located above heaven.

36.6a/b Initially mounting tending-towards heaven.

38. ImT Heaven, Earth, Polarizing and-also one's affairs concording indeed.

42. ImT Heaven spreading-out, earth giving-birth.

43.ST Above marsh with-respect-to heaven.

44.ST Below heaven possessing wind.

44. ImT Heaven, Earth: mutually meeting.

44.5a/b Possessing tumbling, originating-from heaven.

45. ImT Yielding-to heaven: fate indeed.

49. ImT Yielding reaching-to heaven and-also corresponding reaching-to the people.

55.6b Heaven bordering, hovering indeed.

58. ImT That uses yielding reaching-to heaven and-also corresponding reaching-to the people.

60. ImT Heaven, Earth: Articulating and-also the four seasons accomplishing.

61. ImT Thereupon corresponding reaching-to heaven indeed.

61.6a/b A soaring sound mounting, tending-towards heaven.

Heaven[and]Earth, T'IEN TI: dynamic relation between the primal powers and the world it produces; cosmos, natural or human world; keyword.

3.S Possessing Heaven[and]Earth.

3.S Overfilling Heaven[and]Earth's interspace implies verily the myriad beings.

11.ST Heaven[and]Earth mingling.

11.ST The crown-prince uses property to accomplish Heaven[and]Earth's tao.

11.ST [The crown-prince uses] bracing to mutualize Heaven[and]Earth's propriety.

11. ImT By-consequence-of that Heaven[and]Earth mingling and-also the myriad beings interpenetrating indeed.

11.3b Heaven[and]Earth, the border indeed.

12. ImT By-consequence-of that Heaven[and]Earth not mingling and-also the myriad beings not interpenetrating indeed.

16. ImT Anterior Heaven[and]Earth thus having-it.

16. ImT Heaven[and]Earth uses yielding stirring-up.

24. ImT Reaching-to Returning one's visualizing Heaven[and]Earth's heart.

27. ImT Heaven[and]Earth nourishes the myriad beings.

31.S Possessing Heaven[and]Earth:

31. ImT Heaven[and]Earth influencing and-also the myriad beings changing give-birth.

31. ImT And-also actually Heaven[and]Earth, the myriad beings's motives permitting visualizing.

32. ImT Heaven[and]Earth's tao.

32. ImT And-also actually Heaven[and]Earth, the myriad beings's motives permitting visualizing.

34. ImT Actually the correcting Great and-also Heaven[and]Earth's motives permitting visualizing.

37. ImT Heaven[and]Earth's great righteousness indeed.

40. ImT Heaven[and]Earth Taking-apart and-also Thunder[and]Rain arousing.

45. ImT And-also actually Heaven[and]Earth, the myriad beings's motives, permitting visualizing.

49. ImT Heaven[and]Earth Skinning and-also the four seasons accomplishing.

54. ImT Heaven[and]Earth's great righteousness indeed.

54. ImT Heaven[and]Earth not mingling and-also the myriad beings not rising.

55. ImT Heaven[and]Earth overfilling emptiness.

Heavy, NAN: arduous, grievous, difficult; hardship, distress; harass; contrasts with versatile, I, deal lightly with. The ideogram: domestic bird with clipped tail and drying sticky earth.

3.ImT Solid[and]Supple beginning mingling and-also heaviness giving-birth indeed.

3.2b Six at-second's heaviness.

5.1b Not opposing heavy moving indeed.

12.ST A chün tzu uses parsimonious actualizing-tao to cast-out heaviness.

36. ImT Using the enveloped great: heaviness.

36. ImT Inside heaviness and-also enabling correcting one's purpose.

39.S Turning-away necessarily possesses heaviness.

39.S Limping implies heaviness indeed.

39/40.CD Limping: heaviness indeed.

39. ImT Limping. Heaviness indeed.

40.S Beings not permitted to use completing heaviness.

41.AE Diminishing: beforehand heaviness and-also afterwards versatility.

58. ImT Stimulating using opposing heaviness:

Hedge, FAN: row of bushes, fence, boundary; protect, fend off, enclose.

34.3a,6a The he goat butts a hedge.

34.4a/b The hedge broken-up, not ruined.

He goat, TI YANG: ram or buck; three-year-old male at peak of strength. See also: **Goat**

34.3a,6a The he goat butts a hedge.

Her/she, CH'I: third person pronoun; also: one/one's, it/its, he/his, they/their.

This term occurs throughout the hexagram texts.

Herd, MU: tend cattle; watch over, superintend; ruler, teacher.

15.1b Lowliness uses originating-from herding indeed.

Hide, YI: keep out of sight; remote, distant from the center; equalize by lowering; squat, level, make ordinary; pacified, colorless; cut, wound, destroy, exterminate.

Image of Hexagram 36 and occurs throughout its texts.

35.CD Brightness Hiding: proscribed indeed.
55.4a/b Meeting one's hiding lord.
59.4a In-no-way hiding, a place to ponder.
Hide-away, FU: conceal, place in ambush; secretly, silently; prostrate, fall on your face; humble. The ideogram: man and dog, man crouching.
   13.3a/b Hiding-away arms, tending-towards the thickets.
57/58.CD Ground: hiding-away indeed.
High(-ness), KAO: high, elevated, lofty, eminent; excellent, advanced.
   13.3a Ascending one's high mound.
   18.6a Honoring highness: one's affair.
   40.6a A prince avails-of shooting a hawk, tending-towards the high rampart's above.
   46.ST [A chün tzu uses] amassing the small to use the high great.
   63.3a The high ancestor subjugating souls on-all-sides.
Highlands, LU: high, dry land as distinct from swamps; plateau.
   43.5a Reeds, highlands: Parting, Parting.
   53.3a,6a The wild-swan Infiltrating tending-towards the highlands.
Highlight, YI: emphasize what is inherently good; concentrate, focus on; virtuous, worthy; an accomplished, graceful woman.
   9.ST A chün tzu uses highlighting the pattern to actualize-tao.
Highway, CH'Ü: main road, thoroughfare; where many ways meet.
   26.6a/b Wherefore heaven's highway?
Hill-top, CH'IU: hill with hollow top used for worship and as grave-site; knoll, hillock.
   22.5a Adorning tending-towards a hill-top garden.
   27.2a Rejecting the canons, tending-towards the hill-top.
   29. ImT Earth venturing, mountains, rivers, hill-tops, mounds indeed.
   59.4a Dispersing possessing the hill-top.
His/he, CH'I: third person pronoun; also: one/one's, it/its, she/hers, they/theirs.
   This term occurs throughout the hexagram texts.
Hoary, PO: silvery grey hair; old and venerable, aging.
   22.4a Adorning thus, hoary thus.

Hog fish, T'UN YÜ: aquatic mammals; porpoise, dolphin; intelligent aquatic animals whose development parallels the human; sign of abundance and good luck.
   61. Im Centering Conforming, hog fish significant.
   61. ImT Hog fish significant.
   61. ImT Trustworthiness extending-to hog fish indeed.
Hold-fast(-to), WEI: hold together; tie to, connect; reins, net.
   17.6a Thereupon adhering holding-fast-to it.
   29. Im/ImT Holding-fast the heart Growing.
   35.6a/b Holding-fast avails-of subjugating the capital.
   40.5a A chün tzu holding-fast possesses Taking-apart.
Hold-on(-to), CHIH: lay hold of, seize, take in hand; keep, maintain, look after. The ideogram: criminal and seize.
   7.5a Harvesting: holding-on-to words.
   31.3a Holding-on-to one's following.
   31.3b A place to hold-on-to the below indeed.
   33.2a Holding-on-to it: availing-of yellow cattle's skin.
   33.2b Holding-on avails-of yellow cattle.
Home, SHIH: place of rest, dwelling, family; the grave.
   9.3b Not able correcting the home indeed.
Honor, SHANG: esteem, give high rank to; eminent; put one thing on top of another.
   6.ImT Honoring centering correcting indeed.
   9.ImT Honoring going indeed.
   9.6a Honoring actualizing-tao carrying.
   11.2a Acquiring honor, tending-towards centering moving.
   11.2b Enwrapping wasteland, acquiring honor, tending-towards centering moving.
   18.6a Honoring highness: one's affair.
   20.4b Honoring guesting indeed.
   23. ImT A chün tzu honors the dissolving pause to overfill emptiness.
   26. ImT Above solid and-also honoring eminence.
   29. Im Movement possesses honor.
   29. ImT Movement possesses honor.
   34.4b Honoring going indeed.
   41.1b Honoring uniting purposes indeed.
   43. ImT The place to honor thereupon exhausted indeed.

47. ImT Honoring the mouth thereupon exhausted indeed.
55. ImT Honoring the great indeed.
55.1a Going possesses honor.
60.5a Going possesses honor.
Hoof, TI: pig's trotters and horse's hooves.
　44.1a Ruining the pig, conforming: hoof dragging.
Horns, CHIO: strength and power; gore; dispute, test your strength; headland.
　34.3a Ruining his horns.
　35.6a Prospering: one's horns.
　44.6a/b Coupling: one's horns.
Horse, MA: symbol of spirited strength in the natural world, counterpart of dragon, LUNG; associated with the trigram Force, CH'IEN, heaven, T'IEN, and high noon.
　2.Im Field: Spring Growing Harvesting, female horse's Trial.
　2.ImT The female horse: earth sorting.
　3.2a,4a,6a Riding a horse, arraying thus.
　22.4a A white horse, soaring thus.
　26.3a A fine horse, pursuing.
　35. Im Prospering, the calm feudatory avails-of bestowing horses to multiply the multitudes.
　35. ImT That uses the calm feudatory availing-of bestowing horses to multiply the multitudes.
　36.2a Availing-of a rescuing horse, invigorating significant.
　38.1a Losing the horse, no pursuit, originating-from returning.
　59.1a Availing-of a rescuing horse, invigorating significant.
　61.4a/b The horse team extinguished.
Hound, SHOU: hunt with dogs; annual winter hunt; pursue closely, press hard; burn dry fields to drive game; inspect the frontiers.
　36.3a Brightness Hiding tending-towards the South, hounding.
　36.3b The South: hounding's purpose.
House, KUNG: residence, mansion; surround; fence, walls, roof.
　23.5a/b Using housing people, favor.
　47.3a/b Entering tending-towards one's house.
Hover, HSIANG: glide; rise, soar, roam.
　55.6b Heaven bordering, hovering indeed.
Humanity, JEN: fellow-feeling, regard for others;

benevolence, fulfil social duties; unselfish, kind, merciful.
　24.2b Using humanity below indeed.
Humble, CH'IEN: think and speak of yourself in a modest way; respectful, unassuming, retiring, unobtrusive; yielding, compliant, reverent, lowly. The ideogram: words and unite, keeping words close to underlying facts.
　Image of Hexagram 15 and occurs throughout its texts.
　16.S Possessing the Great and-also enabling Humbling necessarily Provides-for.
　16.CD Humbling: levity indeed.
Hundred, PO: numerous, many, all; a whole class or type.
　6.2a People, three hundred doors.
　30. ImT The hundred grains, grasses, trees congregating reaching-to earth.
　40. ImT Thunder[and]Rain arousing and-also the hundred fruits, grasses, trees, altogether seedburst boundary.
　51. Im/ImT Shake scaring a hundred miles.
Hundred-thousand, YI: ten myriads (groups of ten thousand); huge quantity, number beyond imagination.
　51.2a A hundred-thousand lost coins.
Husband, FU: household manager; administer with thrift and prudence; responsible for; sustain with one's earnings; old enough to assume responsibility; married man.
　4.3a Visualizing a metallic husband.
　8.Im/ImT Afterwards, husbanding: pitfall.
　9.3a/b Husband, consort, reversing eyes.
　17.2a Letting-go the respectable husband.
　17.3a/b Tied-to the respectable husband.
　28.2a A venerable husband acquiring his woman consort.
　28.2b A venerable husband, a woman consort.
　28.5a A venerable wife acquiring her notable husband.
　28.5b A venerable wife, a notable husband.
　32.5a The husband, the son: pitfall.
　32.5b The husband, the son: paring righteously.
　37. ImT The husband, a husband. The wife, a wife.
　38.4a Meeting Spring, husbanding.
　53.3a/b The husband chastised, not returning.
Husband[and]Wife, FU FU: the cooperative

effort of man and woman in establishing and maintaining a home.

31.S Therefore afterwards possessing Husband[and]Wife.

31.S Possessing Husband[and]Wife:

32.S Husband[and]Wife's tao.

Husking, KENG: fruit and grain husks bursting in autumn; seventh of the Ten Heavenly Barriers in calender system; bestow, reward; blade or sword; associated with the Metallic Moment. The ideogram: receiving things in the hand.

57.5a Before husking, three days.

57.5a After husking, three days.

Hut, LU: thatched hut, cottage, roadside lodge, hovel; house as personal shelter.

23.6a/b Small People Stripping the hut.

I/me/my, WO: first person pronoun; indicates an unusually strong emphasis on your own subjective experience.

4.Im/ImT In-no-way me seeking youthful Enveloping.

4.ImT Youthful Enveloping seeking me.

5.3b Originating-from my involving outlawry.

9.Im/ImT Originating-from my Western suburbs.

20.3a/b Viewing my birth, advancing, withdrawing.

20.5a/b Viewing my birth.

27.1a/b Viewing my pendent Jaws.

40.3b Originating-from my involving arms.

42.5a Possessing conformity, benevolence: my actualizing-tao.

42.5b Benevolence: my actualizing-tao.

48.3a Activating my heart aching.

50.2a Not me able to approach. Significant.

50.2a/b My companion possesses affliction.

56.4a My heart not keen.

61.2a I possess a loved wine-cup.

62.5a Originating-from my Western suburbs.

Ice, PING: frozen water; icy, freezing; clear, pure.

2.1a Treading frost, hardening ice culminating.

2.1b Treading frost hardening the ice:

2.1b Culminating hardening the ice indeed.

Illuminate, CHAO: shine light on; enlighten, reflect: care for, supervise. The ideogram: fire and brightness.

30.ST Great People use consecutive brightening to illuminate tending-towards the four sides.

32. ImT Sun[and]Moon acquiring heaven and-also enabling lasting illumination.

36.6b Illuminating the four cities indeed.

55. ImT Properly illuminating Below Heaven indeed.

Imagine, CHIA: create in the mind; fantasize, suppose, pretend, imitate; fiction, illusory, unreal; costume. The ideogram: person and borrow.

37.5a/b The king imagines possessing a Dwelling.

45. Im/ImT The king imagines possessing a temple.

55. Im/ImT The king imagining it.

59. Im/ImT The king imagines possessing a temple.

Immature, CHIH: small, tender, young, delicate; undeveloped; conceited, haughty; late grain.

4.S Being's immaturity indeed.

5.S Being immature not permitting not nourishing indeed.

Immerse, CH'IEN: submerge, hide in water; make away with; secret, reserved; carefully.

1.1a/b Immersed dragon, no availing-of.

Imminent, P'IN: on the brink of; pressing, urgent.

24.3a Imminent Returning.

24.3b Imminent Returning's adversity.

57.3a/b Imminent Ground, abashment.

Impetuous, FEN: sudden energy; lively, spirited, impulsive; excite, arouse; press on.

16.ST Thunder issuing-forth-from earth impetuously.

Implements, CH'I: utensils, tools; molded or carved objects; use a person or thing suitably; capacity, talent, intelligence.

45.ST A chün tzu uses eliminating arms to implement.

51.S A lord's implementing implies absolutely-nothing like the long-living son.

Imply, CHE: further signify; additional meaning. This term occurs in the Sequence of most hexagrams. It also occurs at:

28. ImT Great implies Exceeding indeed.

34. ImT Great Invigorating. The Great implies Invigorating indeed.

34. ImT The Great implies correcting indeed.

62. ImT Small implies Exceeding and-also Growing indeed.

63. ImT The small implies Growing indeed.

Impress, WEI: impose on, intimidate; august, solemn; pomp, majesty.

14.5a Your conforming: mingling thus, impressing thus.

14.5b Impressing thus, having significance.

37.6a Possessing conformity, impressing thus.

37.6b Impressing thus, having significance.

Improve, SHAN: make better, reform, perfect, repair; virtuous, wise; mild, docile; clever, skillful, handy. The ideogram: mouth and sheep, gentle speech.

  14.ST A chün tzu uses terminating hate to display improvement.

  42.ST A chün tzu uses visualizing improvement, by-consequence shifting.

  53.ST A chün tzu uses residing-in eminent actualizing-tao to improve the vulgar.

Increase, SHENG: grow or make larger; flourishing, exuberant, full, abundant; heaped up; excellent, fine.

  41/42.CD Increasing, decreasing's beginning indeed.

Indeed, YEH: intensifier; indicates comment on previous statement.

  This term occurs throughout the hexagram texts. It characterizes the Image Tradition and the Transforming Lines b).

Indignation, WEN: irritated, wrathful; feeling of injustice, rage; hateful.

  43.3a Like soaking, possessing indignation.

Indigo, HSÜAN: color associated with the Metallic Moment; deep blue-black, color of the sky's depths; profound, subtle, deep; veneration of the gods and spirits.

  2.6a Their blood: indigo, yellow.

Individuality, SHEN: total person: psyche, body and lifespan; character, virtue, duty; contrasts with body, KUNG, physical being.

  24.1b Using adjusting individuality indeed.

  37.6b Reversing individuality's designating indeed.

  39.ST A chün tzu uses reversing individuality to renovate actualizing-tao.

  52. Im Not catching one's individuality.

  52. ImT That uses not catching one's individuality.

  52.4a/b Bound: one's individuality.

Indolence, TAI: idle, inattentive, careless; self-indulgent; disdainful, contemptuous.

  15/16.CD Provision: indolence indeed.

In-fact, TSAI: in actual fact, currently. See also: **Actually ... in-fact**

1.ImT The great Force, Spring in-fact.

2.ImT Culminating Field, Spring in-fact.

Infiltrate, CHIEN: advance by degrees; penetrate slowly and surely, as water; stealthily; permeate throughout; influence, affect. The ideogram: water and cut.

  Image of Hexagram 53 and occurs throughout its texts.

Influence, KAN: excite, act on, touch; affect someone's feelings, move the heart. The ideogram: heart and all, pervasive influence.

  31. ImT Conjoining. Influencing indeed.

  31. ImT The two agencies influencing correspondence use mutual associating.

  31. ImT Heaven[and]Earth influencing and-also the myriad beings changing give-birth.

  31. ImT The all-wise person influencing the people at-heart and-also Below Heaven harmony evening.

  31. ImT Viewing one's place to influence.

  31.4b Not-yet influencing harming indeed.

Inform, YÜ: tell, warn; talk with, converse, exchange ideas.

  27.ST A chün tzu uses considering words to inform.

Initial, CH'U: first step or part; beginning, incipient; bottom line of hexagram. The ideogram: knife and garment, cutting out the pattern.

  This term frequently occurs in the first Transforming Line b).

  4.Im/ImT The initial oracle-consulting notifying.

  36.6a/b Initially mounting tending-towards heaven.

  38.3a/b Without initially possessing completion.

  57.5a Without initially possessing completion.

  63. Im/ImT Initially significant.

Injure, SHANG: hurt, wound, grieve, distress; mourn, sad at heart, humiliated.

  8.3b Reaching-to not truly injuring.

  36.S Advancing necessarily possessing a place: injuring.

  36.S Hiding implies injury.

  37.S Injury with-respect-to the outside implies necessarily reversing with-respect-to Dwelling.

  56.3b Actually truly using injuring.

  60. ImT Not injuring property.

Innate, HSING: inborn character; spirit, quality, ability; naturally, without constraint. The ideogram: heart and produce, spontaneous feeling.

  1.ImT Each-one correcting innate fate.

In-no-way, FEI: strong negative; not so. The ideogram: a box filled with opposition.

  3.2a In-no-way outlawry, matrimonial allying.

  4.Im/ImT In-no-way me seeking youthful Enveloping.

  8.3a/b Grouping's in-no-way people.

  12. Im/ImT Obstructing it, in-no-way people.

  14.1a In-no-way faulty.

  14.4a In-no-way one's preponderance.

  14.4b In-no-way one's preponderance. Without fault.

  22.4a/b In-no-way outlawry, matrimonial allying.

  25. Im/ImT One in-no-way correcting: possessing blunder.

  30.6a Severing the head. Catching in-no-way its demons.

  38.6a In-no-way outlawry, matrimonial allying.

  39.2a In-no-way body's anteriority.

  45.5a Without fault: in-no-way conforming.

  59.4a In-no-way hiding, a place to ponder.

In-no-way people, FEI FEN: there are no people, no people are involved; also: worthless people; barbarians, rebels, foreign slaves, captives.

  8.3a/b Grouping's in-no-way people.

  12. Im/ImT Obstructing it, in-no-way people.

Inside, NEI: within, inner, interior; inside of the house and those who work there, particularly women; the lower trigram, as opposed to outside, WAI, the upper. The ideogram: border and enter, cross a border.

  8.2a/b Grouping's origin inside.

  11. ImT Inside yang and-also outside yin.

  11. ImT Inside persisting and-also outside yielding.

  11. ImT Inside chün tzu and-also outside Small People.

  12. ImT Inside yin and-also outside yang.

  12. ImT Inside supple and-also outside solid.

  12. ImT Inside Small People and-also outside chün tzu.

  19.6b Purpose located inside indeed.

  25. ImT Solid originating-from the outside coming and-also activating a lord with-respect-to the inside.

  36. ImT Inside pattern Brightening and-also outside supple yielding.

  36. ImT Inside heaviness and-also enabling correcting one's purpose.

37/38.CD Dwelling People: inside indeed.

  37. ImT The woman correcting the situation reaching-to the inside.

  39.3b Inside rejoicing-in it indeed.

  39.6b Purpose located inside indeed.

  61. ImT Supple located inside and-also solid acquiring the center.

Inspect, HSING: examine on all sides, careful inquiry; watchful.

  20.ST The Earlier Kings used inspecting on-all-sides, Viewing the commoners to set-up teaching.

  24.ST The crown-prince [used culminating sun] not to inspect on-all-sides.

  51.ST A chün tzu uses anxious fearing to adjust inspecting.

Install, CHIEN: set up, establish; confirm a position or law.

  3.Im/ImT,1a Harvesting: installing feudatories.

  8.ST The Earlier Kings used installing myriad cities to connect the connoted feudatories.

  16. Im Providing-for, Harvesting: installing feudatories to move legions.

  16. ImT And-also even-more installing feudatories to move legions reached.

In-tatters, JU: worn-out garments, used for padding or stopping leaks.

  63.4a A token: possessing clothes in-tatters.

Intention, YI: thought, meaning, idea, will, motive; what gives words their significance. The ideogram: heart and sound, heartfelt expression.

  18.1b Intention receiving the predecessors indeed.

  36.4b Catching the heart, intention indeed.

  51.5a Intention without losing possesses affairs.

Interpenetrate, T'UNG: mutually penetrate; permeate, flow through, reach everywhere; see clearly, communicate with.

  11.S Pervading implies interpenetrating indeed.

  11. ImT By-consequence-of that Heaven[and]Earth mingling and-also the myriad beings interpenetrating indeed.

12.S Beings not permitted to use completing interpenetrating.

12. ImT By-consequence-of that Heaven[and]Earth not mingling and-also the myriad beings not interpenetrating indeed.

13. ImT Verily a chün tzu activating enables interpenetrating Below Heaven's purpose.

38. ImT Man, Woman, Polarizing and-also their purposes interpenetrating indeed.

47/48.CD The Well: interpenetrating and-also Confining: mutual meeting indeed.

47.AE Confining: exhausting and-also interpenetrating.

60. ImT Centering correcting uses interpenetrating.

60.1b Knowing interpenetrating clogging indeed.

Interspace, HSIEN: space between, interval, crevice; vacant, empty.

3.S Overfilling Heaven[and]Earth's interspace implies verily the myriad beings.

Intertwist, JU: interlaced; entangled roots.

11.1a Eradicating thatch-grass intertwisted.

12.1a Eradicating thatch-grass intertwisted.

Intimidate, YEN: inspire with fear or awe; severe, rigid, strict, austere, demanding; a severe father; tight, a closed door.

33.ST [A chün tzu uses] not hating and-also intimidating.

37. ImT Dwelling People possess an intimidating chief in-truth.

In-truth, YEN: statement is complete and correct.

3.S Therefore afterwards the myriad beings giving-birth in-truth.

14.S Associating-with People Concording implies beings necessarily converting in-truth.

37. ImT Dwelling People possess an intimidating chief in-truth.

62. ImT Possessing the flying bird's symbol in-truth.

64.S Anterior acquiescence has the use-of Not-yet Fording completed in-truth.

Invigorate, CHUANG: inspirit, animate; strong, robust; full grown, flourishing, abundant; attain manhood (at 30); damage through unrestrained strength. The ideogram: strength and scholar, intellectual impact.

Image of Hexagram 34 and occurs throughout its texts.

33.CD Great Invigorating: by-consequence stopping.

35.S Beings not permitted to use completing Invigorating.

36.2a Availing-of a rescuing horse, invigorating significant.

43.1a Invigorating tending-towards the preceding foot.

43.3a Invigorating tending-towards the cheek-bones:

44. Im Coupling, womanhood invigorating.

59.1a Availing-of a rescuing horse, invigorating significant.

Involve, CHIH: include, entangle, implicate; induce, cause. The ideogram: person walking, induced to follow.

2.1b Docilely involving one's tao:

5.3a Involving outlawry culminating.

5.3b Originating-from my involving outlawry.

23.S Actually involving embellishing, therefore afterwards Growing by-consequence used-up.

40.3a Involving outlawry culminating.

40.3b Originating-from my involving arms.

45. ImT Involving reverence presenting indeed.

47.ST A chün tzu uses involving fate to release purpose.

51. ImT,1b Anxiety involving blessing indeed.

55.ST A chün tzu uses severing litigating to involve punishing.

Issue-forth(-from), CH'U: emerge from, come out of, proceed from, spring from; the Action of the trigram Shake, CHEN; contrary of enter, JU. The ideogram: stem with branches and leaves emerging.

1.ImT Heads issuing-forth-from the multitudinous beings.

4.ST Below the mountain issuing-forth springwater.

5.4a Issuing-forth originates-from the cave.

7.1a/b Legions issuing-forth using ordinance.

9.4a Blood departing, awe issuing-forth.

9.4b Possessing conformity, awe issuing-forth.

13.1b Issuing-forth-from the gate Concording People.

16.ST Thunder issuing-forth-from earth impetuously.

17.1a/b Issuing-forth-from the gate, mingling possesses achievement.

24. Im Issuing-forth, entering, without affliction.

24. ImT That uses issuing-forth, entering, without affliction.

29.2b Not-yet issuing-forth-from the center indeed.

30.5a Issuing-forth tears like gushing.

30.6a/b Kinghood availing-of issuing-forth chastising.

35.ST,ImT Brightness issuing-forth above earth.

36.4a Tending-towards issuing-forth-from the gate chambers.

37.ST Wind originating-from fire issuing-forth.

50.1a/b Harvesting: issuing-forth-from obstruction.

51. ImT Issuing-forth permits using guarding the ancestral temple, field-altar, offertory-millet.

52.ST A chün tzu uses pondering not to issue-forth-from his situation.

59.6a Departing far-away, issuing-forth.

60.1a/b Not issuing-forth-from the door chambers.

60.2a Not issuing-forth-from the gate chambers.

60.2b Not issuing-forth-from the gate chambers, pitfall.

64. ImT Not-yet issuing-forth-from the center indeed.

Its/it, CH'I: third person pronoun; also: one/one's, he/his, she/hers, they/theirs.

This term occurs throughout the hexagram texts.

It, see: **Have(-it)**

Jade, YÜ: all gemstones; precious beauty; delightful, happy; perfect, clear.

50.6a The Vessel: jade rings.

50.6b Jade rings located above.

Jar, FOU: earthenware vessels; wine-jars and drums. The ideogram: jar containing liquor.

8.1a Possessing conformity, overfilling the jar.

29.4a Availing-of a jar.

30.3a Not drumbeating a jar and-also singing.

Jawbones, see: **Brace**

Jaws/swallow, YI: mouth, jaws, cheeks, chin; take in, ingest; feed, nourish, sustain, rear; furnish

what is necessary. The ideogram: open jaws. Image of Hexagram 27 and occurs throughout its texts.

21. ImT Jaws center possesses being. Spoken-thus: Gnawing Bite.

Join, CHIEN: add or bring together; unite; absorb; attend to many things. The ideogram: hand grasps two grain stalks, two things at once. See also: **Conjoin**

17.2b Nowhere joining associating indeed.

52.ST Joined mountains. Bound.

Join-together, HO: unite for a purpose; assemble friends for a specific aim.

16.4a Partners join-together suddenly.

Jug, WENG: earthen jar; jug used to draw water.

48.2a The jug cracked, leaking.

Juice, KAO: active principle, essence; oil, grease, ointment; fertilizing, rich; genius.

3.5a/b Sprouting: one's juice.

50.3a Pheasant juice not taken-in.

Jujube-tree, CHI: thorny bush or tree; sign of a court of justice or site of official literary examinations.

29.6a Dismissing tending-towards dense jujube-trees.

Junior, TI: younger relatives who owe respect to their elders.

7.5a/b The junior son carting corpses.

37. ImT The senior, a senior. The junior, a junior.

Junior-sister, TI: younger woman in family or clan; younger sister, under authority of the first wife.

54.1a/b Converting Maidenhood using the junior-sister.

54.3a Reversing Converting using the junior-sister.

54.5a/b One's junior-sister's sleeves not thus fine.

Keen, K'UAI: sharp, eager, prompt, cheerful; spirited.

52.2a One's heart not keen.

56.4a My heart not keen.

56.4b The heart not-yet keen indeed.

Keep-aloof, CHI: keep at a distance; avoid, fear, shun; antipathy. The ideogram: heart and self, keeping to yourself.

43.ST [A chün tzu uses] residing-in actualizing-tao, by-consequence keeping-aloof.

Kill, CH'IANG: put to death; violent assault; maltreat, misuse; kill an important person.

62.3a/b Adhering, maybe killing it.

Kinds, P'IN: species and their essential qualities; sorts, classes; classify, select.

1.ImT The kinds: being diffusing forms.

2.ImT The kinds: being conjoining Growing.

44. ImT The kinds: beings conjoining composition indeed.

57.4a/b The fields, catching three kinds.

King(hood), WANG: effective ruler, by authority of the Emperor, from whom others derive their power. See also: **Earlier Kings**

2.3a/b Maybe adhering-to kingly affairs:

6.3a Maybe adhering-to kingly affairs:

7.ImT Actually permitting using kinghood.

7.2a/b The king three-times bestowing fate.

8.5a The king avails-of three beaters.

17.6a The king availing-of Growing tending-towards the Western mountain.

18.6a/b Not affairs, kingly feudatories.

20.4a Harvesting: availing-of guesting tending-towards kinghood.

29. ImT The kingly prince sets-up venturing used to guard his city.

30.5b Radiance: the kingly prince indeed.

30.6a/b Kinghood availing-of issuing-forth chastising.

35.2a Tending-towards one's kingly mother.

36. ImT The pattern king uses it.

37.5a/b The king imagines possessing a Dwelling.

39.2a/b A king, a servant: Limping, Limping.

42.2a Kinghood availing-of presenting tending-towards the supreme, significant.

43. Im Parting, displaying tending-towards kingly chambers.

43. ImT Displaying tending-towards kingly chambers.

45. Im/ImT The king imagines possessing a temple.

46.4a/b Kinghood availing-of Growing, tending-towards the twin-peaked mountain.

48.3a Kingly brightness.

48.3b Seeking kingly brightness:

55. Im/ImT The king imagining it.

59. Im/ImT The king imagines possessing a temple.

59. ImT Kinghood thereupon located-in the center indeed.

59.5a/b Kinghood residing, without fault.

Know, CHIH: understand, perceive, remember; informed, aware, wise. The ideogram: arrow and mouth, words focused and swift.

2.3b Knowing the shining great indeed.

19.5a Knowledge Nearing.

24.AE Returning: using originating knowledge.

39. ImT Actually knowing in-fact.

54.ST A chün tzu uses perpetually completing to know the cracked.

60.1b Knowing interpenetrating clogging indeed.

64.1b Truly not knowing the end indeed.

64.6b Truly not knowing articulating indeed.

Lacking, WU: strong negative; does not possess.

3.3a Approaching stag, lacking precaution.

53.1a Lacking fault.

57.S Sojourning and-also lacking a place to tolerate.

Ladle, PI: ceremonial spoon used to pour libations.

51. Im Not losing the ladle, the libation.

Lament, CHÜEH: express intense regret or sorrow; mourn over; painful recollections.

30.3a By-consequence great old-age's lamenting.

30.5a Issuing-forth tears like gushing. Sadness like lamenting.

45.3a Clustering thus, lamenting thus.

60.3a Not the Articulating like, by-consequence the lamenting like.

60.3b Not Articulating's lamenting.

Last, CHIU: long, protracted; enduring.

1.6b Overfilling, not permitting lasting indeed.

19. ImT Dissolving, not lasting indeed.

28.5b Wherefore permitting lasting indeed?

30.3b Wherefore permitting lasting indeed?

31/32.CD Persevering: lasting indeed.

32.S Not permitting using not lasting indeed.

32.S Persevering implies lasting indeed.

32. ImT Persevering. Lasting indeed.

32. ImT Lasting with-respect-to one's tao indeed.

32. ImT Persevering lasting and-also not climaxing indeed.

32. ImT Sun[and]Moon acquiring heaven and-also enabling lasting illumination.

32. ImT The four seasons transforming changes and-also enabling lasting accomplishment.

32. ImT The all-wise person lasting with-respect-to his tao and-also Below Heaven the changes accomplishing.

32.2b Ability lasting, centering indeed.

32.4b No lasting whatever: one's situation.

33.S Beings not permitted to use lasting residing-in their place.

63.6b Wherefore permitting lasting indeed?

Latter, TZ'U: what was last spoken of.

7.ImT Using the latter poisons Below Heaven and-also the commoners adhering-to it.

Laugh, HSIAO: manifest joy or mirth; giggle, laugh at, ridicule; pleased, merry; associated with the Fiery Moment.

13.5a Concording People beforehand crying-out sobbing and-also afterwards laughing.

45.1a Like an outcry, the-one handful activates laughing.

51. Im/ImT Laughing words, shrieking, shrieking.

51.1a After laughing words, shrieking, shrieking.

51.1b Laughing words, shrieking, shrieking.

56.6a Sojourning people beforehand laughing, afterwards crying-out sobbing.

Laws, FA: rules, statutes, model, method.

4.1b Using correcting laws indeed.

21.ST The Earlier Kings used brightening flogging to enforce the laws.

Leak, LOU: seep, drip, ooze out; reveal; forget, let slip.

48.2a The jug cracked, leaking.

Left, TSO: left side, left hand; secondary; deputy, assistant; inferior.

7.4a Legions: the left resting.

7.4b The left resting, without fault.

11.ST [The crown-prince] uses the left to right the commoners.

36.2a Brightness Hiding. Hiding tending-towards the left thigh.

Left belly, TSO FU: body cavity holding heart and spleen, considered the seat of emotion.

36.4a/b Entering tending-towards the left belly.

Legions/leading, SHIH: troops; an organized

unit, a metropolis; leader, general, model, master; organize, make functional; take as a model, imitate. The ideogram: heap and whole, organize confusion into functional units.

Image of Hexagram 7 and occurs throughout its texts.

8.CD Legions: grieving.

11.6a No availing-of legions.

13.5a/b Great legions controlling mutual meeting.

15.6a Harvesting: availing-of moving legions.

15.6b Permitting availing-of moving legions.

16. Im Providing-for, Harvesting: installing feudatories to move legions.

16. ImT And-also even-more installing feudatories to move legions reached.

24.6a Availing-of moving legions:

Leopard, PAO: spotted wild cats, beautiful and independent; mark of high-ranking officers.

49.6a/b A chün tzu: leopard transforming.

Lessen, K'UEI: diminish, injure, wane; lack, defect, failure.

15. ImT Heavenly tao lessening overfilling and-also augmenting Humbling.

50.3a On-all-sides rain lessens repenting.

Let-go, SHIH: lose, omit, miss, fail, let slip; out of control. The ideogram: drop from the hand.

2.ImT Beforehand delusion letting-go tao.

3/4.CD Sprouting: visualizing and-also not letting-go one's residing.

5.1b Not-yet letting-go rules indeed.

5.6b Although not an appropriate situation, not-yet the great let-go indeed.

6.4b Not letting-go indeed.

7.1b Letting-go ordinance: pitfall indeed.

7.4b Not-yet letting-go the rules indeed.

8.2b Not originating letting-go indeed.

8.5a Letting-go the preceding wildfowl.

8.5b Letting-go the preceding wildfowl indeed.

9.2b Truly not originating-from letting-go indeed.

11.4b Altogether letting-go substance indeed.

17.1b Not letting-go indeed.

17.2a Letting-go the respectable husband.

17.3a Letting-go the small son.

20.3b Not-yet letting-go tao indeed.

23.3b Letting-go Above[and]Below indeed.

27.2b Movement letting-go sorting indeed.

29.ImT Movement venturing and-also not letting-go one's trustworthiness.

29.1b Letting-go tao: pitfall indeed.

29.6b Six above, letting-go tao.

35.5a/b Letting-go, acquiring, no cares.

36.6b Letting-go by-consequence indeed.

37.3b Not-yet letting-go indeed.

37.3b Letting-go Dwelling articulating indeed.

38.2b Not-yet letting-go tao indeed.

41.S Delaying necessarily possesses a place to let-go.

47.ImT Confining and-also not letting-go one's place: Growing.

50.3b Letting-go its righteousness indeed.

52.ImT Stirring-up, stilling, not letting-go one's season.

52.1b Not-yet letting-go correcting indeed.

53.3b Letting-go her tao indeed.

56.S Exhausting the great implies necessarily letting-go one's residing.

60.2b Letting-go the season ending indeed.

62.ImT Solid letting-go the situation and-also not centering.

64.6a Possessing conformity: letting-go that.

Let-in, NA: allow to enter; take in, grow smaller; insert; collect. The ideogram: silk and enter, shrinking silk threads.

4.2a Letting-in the wife. Significant.

29.4a Letting-in bonds originating-from the window.

Levity, CH'ING: frivolous, think lightly of, unimportant; alert, agile; gentle. The ideogram: cart and stream, empty cart floating downstream.

15.CD Humbling: levity indeed.

Libation, CH'ANG: sacrifical liquor, poured out to draw the gods near.

51.Im Not losing the ladle, the libation.

Lightning, TIEN: lighting flash, electric discharge; sudden clarity; look attentively.

21.ST Thunder, lightning. Gnawing Bite.

21.ImT Thunder, lightning, uniting and-also composing.

55.ST Thunder, lightning, altogether culminating.

Like, JO: same as; just as, similar to.

1.3a Nightfall, awe, like adversity.

20.Im/ImT Possessing conformity, like a presence.

30.5a Issuing-forth tears like gushing. Sadness like lamenting.

43.3a Like soaking, possessing indignation.

45.1a Like an outcry, the-one handful activates laughing.

50.S Skinning beings implies absolutely-nothing like a Vessel.

51.S A lord's implementing implies absolutely-nothing like the long-living son.

55.2a/b Possessing conformity, like shooting-forth.

57.2a The mottled like significant.

57.2b The mottled like has significance

60.3a Not the Articulating like, by-consequence the lamenting like.

Limit, HSIEN: boundary, frontier, threshold; restriction, impediment; set a limit, distinguish, separate. See also: **Delimit**

52.3a/b Bound: one's limit.

Limp, CHIEN: walk lamely, proceed haltingly; weak-legged, afflicted, crooked; feeble; weak; unfortunate, difficult. The ideogram: foot and cold, impeded circulation in the feet.

Image of Hexagram 39 and occurs throughout its texts.

Limpid, LIEH: pure, clear, clean liquid; wash clean.

48.5a The Well: limpid, cold springwater taken-in.

Lining, TS'OU: line or repair a well.

48.4a/b The Well: lining, without fault.

Liquor, CHIU: alcoholic beverages, distilled spirits; spirit which perfects the good and evil in human nature. The ideogram: liquid above fermenting must, separating the spirits.

5.5a Attending tending-towards liquor taken-in.

5.5b Liquor taken-in, Trial: significant.

29.4a/b A cup, liquor, a platter added.

47.2a/b Confined, tending-towards liquor taken-in.

64.6a Possessing conformity: tending-towards drinking liquor.

64.6b Drinking liquor, soaking the head.

Litigate, YÜ: legal proceedings; take a case to court. The ideogram: two dogs and words, barking arguments at each other.

21.Im Harvesting: availing-of litigating.

21.ImT Although not an appropriate situation, Harvesting: availing-of litigating indeed.

22.ST A chün tzu uses brightening the multitudinous standards without daring to sever litigating.

55.ST A chün tzu uses severing litigating to involve punishing.

56.ST A chün tzu uses brightening consideration to avail-of punishing and-also not to detain litigating.

61.ST A chün tzu uses deliberating litigating to delay dying.

Little, CHIEN: small, narrow, insignificant, petty; diminish, contract.

22.5a Rolled plain-silk: little, little.

Live-alone, CH'Ü: lonely, solitary; quiet, still; deserted.

55.6a/b Living-alone, one without people.

Locate(-in), TSAI: live in, dwell, reside; belong to, involved with, depend on; within. The ideogram: earth and persevere, place on the earth.

1.1b Yang located below indeed.

1.2a/b Visualizing dragon located-in the fields.

1.4a/b Maybe capering located-in the abyss.

1.5a/b Flying dragon located-in heaven.

2.5b Pattern located-in the center indeed.

5.ImT Venturing located-in precedence indeed.

5.2b Overflowing located-in the center indeed.

5.3b Calamity located outside indeed.

7.2a Locating Legions, centering significant.

7.2b Locating Legions, centering significant.

9.2b Hauling-along, returning, locating-in the center.

10.6b Spring significant located above.

11.1b Purpose located outside indeed.

12.1b Purpose located-in a chief indeed.

14.ST Fire located above heaven.

16.6b Dim Providing-for located above.

17.4a Possessing conformity, locating-in tao uses brightening.

17.4b Possessing conformity located-in tao.

19.6b Purpose located inside indeed.

20. ImT The great: Viewing located above.

24.ST Thunder located-in earth center.

26.ST Heaven located-in mountain center.

28.1b Supple located below indeed.

31.1b Purpose located outside indeed.

31.3b Purpose located-in following people.

32.6b Rousing Persevering located-in the above.

34.ST Thunder located above heaven.

37.2a Locating the center, feeding.

37.4b Yielding located-in the situation indeed.

39. ImT Venturing located-in precedence indeed.

39.6b Purpose located inside indeed.

46.6b Dim Ascending located above.

47.4b Purpose located below indeed.

48.6b Spring significant located-in the above.

50.6b Jade rings located above.

51.5b One's affairs located-in the center.

54.5b One's situation located-in the center.

56.6b Using Sojourning to locate-in the above.

57.2a,6a/b Ground located below the bed.

59. ImT Kinghood thereupon located-in the center indeed.

59.3b Purpose located outside indeed.

61. ImT Supple located inside and-also solid acquiring the center.

61.2a Calling crane located-in yin.

62.5a A prince, a string-arrow grasping another located-in a cave.

63.ST Stream located above fire.

64.ST Fire located above stream.

Lock-up, CHIAO: imprison, lock up the feet; prison, pen.

21.1a/b Shoes locked-up, submerging the feet.

21.6a/b Wherefore locking-up submerging the ears?

Loins, YIN: hips, pelvis, lumbar region; kidneys; respect, honor; work toward a distant aim; money belt.

52.3a Assigned-to one's loins.

Long-living, CHANG: enduring, constant; senior, superior, greater; increase, prosper; respect, elevate.

3.6b Wherefore permitting long-living indeed?

6.1b Arguing not permitting long-living indeed.

7.5a/b The long-living son conducting Legions.

11. ImT A chün tzu: tao long-living.

12. ImT Small People: tao long-living.

12.6b Wherefore permitting long-living indeed?

16.6b Wherefore permitting long-living indeed?

19. ImT Solid drenched and-also long-living.

19.3b Fault not long-living indeed.

23. ImT Small People long-living indeed.

24. ImT Solid long-living indeed.

33. ImT Drenched and-also long-living indeed.

34.6b Fault not long-living indeed.

42.AE Augmenting: long-living enriching and-also not setting-up.

43. ImT Solid long-living, thereupon completing indeed.

43.6b Completing not permitting long-living indeed.

44. ImT Not permitting associating-with long-living indeed.

51.S A lord's implementing implies absolutely-nothing like the long-living son.

61.6b Wherefore permitting long-living indeed?

62.4b Completing not permitting long-living indeed.

Lord, CHU: ruler, master, chief; authority. The ideogram: lamp and flame, giving light.

2.Im A lord Harvesting.

25. ImT Solid originating-from the outside coming and-also activating a lord with-respect-to the inside.

36.1a A lord: the people possessing words.

38.2a/b Meeting a lord, tending-towards the street.

51.S A lord's implementing implies absolutely-nothing like the long-living son.

51. ImT Using activating the offering lord indeed.

55.1a Meeting one's equal lord.

55.4a/b Meeting one's hiding lord.

Lose, SANG: fail to obtain, cease, become obscure; forgotten, destroyed; lament, mourn; funeral. The ideogram: weep and the dead.

2.Im/ImT Eastern North: losing partnering.

34.5a/b Losing the goat, tending-towards versatility.

38.1a Losing the horse, no pursuit, originating-from returning.

48. Im Without losing, without acquiring.

51. Im Not losing the ladle, the libation.

51.2a A hundred-thousand lost coins.

51.5a Intention without losing possesses affairs.

51.5b The great without losing indeed.

56.3a Losing one's youthful vassal.

56.3b One's righteousness lost indeed.

56.6a/b Losing the cattle, tending-towards versatility.

57.6a/b Losing one's own emblem-ax.

62.ST [A chün tzu uses] losing Exceeding to reach-to mourning.

63.2a A wife losing her veil.

Love, HAO: affection; fond of, take pleasure in; fine, graceful.

15. ImT People tao hating overfilling and-also loving Humbling.

33.4a Loving Retiring.

33.4b A chün tzu lovingly Retiring.

61.2a I possess a loved wine-cup.

Lowly, PEI: speak and think of yourself humbly; modest, yielding; base, mean, contemptible.

15. ImT Earth tao lowly and-also moving above.

15. ImT Lowliness and-also not permitting passing-beyond.

15.1b Lowliness uses originating-from herding indeed.

Luminous, PING: bright, fire-like, light-giving; alert, intelligent.

49.5b One's pattern luminous indeed.

Luxuriance, MAO: thriving, flourishing, vigorous; highly developed, elegant. The ideogram: plants and flourish.

25.ST The Earlier Kings used luxuriance suiting the season to nurture the myriad beings.

Magnanimous, TUN: generous; honest, substantial, important, wealthy; honor, increase; firm, solid. The ideogram: strike and accept, warrior magnanimous in attack and defense.

19.6a Magnanimity Nearing.

19.6b Magnanimity Nearing's significance.

24.5a Magnanimous Returning.

24.5b Magnanimous Returning, without repenting.

52.6a/b Magnanimous Bounding significant.

Maiden(hood), MEI: girl not yet nubile, virgin; younger sister; daughter of a secondary wife. The ideogram: woman and not-yet.

Image of Hexagram 54 and occurs throughout its texts.

11.5a The supreme burgeoning, converting maidenhood.

53.CD Converting Maidenhood: womanhood's completion indeed.

Majestic, T'ANG: grand, awesome; extending everywhere; repel injustice, correct grievances; lit.: large river and its periodic floods.

    49. ImT Majestically martial, Skinning fate.

Manage, KAN: cope with, deal with, able; undertake, attend to business; trunk, stem, spine, skeleton.

    18.1a/b Managing the father's Corrupting.

    18.2a/b Managing the mother's Corrupting.

    18.3a/b Managing the father's Corrupting.

    18.5a Managing the father's Corrupting.

    18.5b Managing the father availing-of praise.

Man(hood), NAN: a man; what is inherently male. The ideogram: fields and strength, hard labor in the fields.

    31. ImT Below manhood, womanhood.

    37. ImT The man correcting the situation reaching-to the outside.

    38. ImT Man, Woman, Polarizing and-also their purposes interpenetrating indeed.

    53/54.CD Infiltrating: womanhood converting awaits manhood moving indeed.

    63/64.CD Not-yet Fording: manhood exhausted indeed.

Man[and]Woman, NAN NÜ: creative relation between what is inherently male and what is inherently female.

    31.S Therefore afterwards possessing Man[and]Woman.

    31.S Possessing Man[and]Woman:

    37. ImT Man[and]Woman correcting.

Manifest, HSIEN: apparent, conspicuous; illustrious; make clear.

    8.5a Manifest Grouping.

    8.5b Manifest Grouping's significance.

Mark-off, PEIN: distinguish by dividing; mark off a plot of land; frame which divides a bed from its stand; discuss and dispute. The ideogram: knife and acrid, biting division.

    13.ST A chün tzu uses sorting the clans to mark-off the beings.

    23.2a/b Stripping the bed, using marking-off.

    24.AE Returning: the small and-also marking-off with-respect-to beings.

    47.AE Confining: actualizing-tao's marking-off indeed.

    64.ST A chün tzu uses considering to mark-off the beings residing on-all-sides.

Marsh, TSE: open surface of a flat body of water and the vapors rising from it; fertilize, enrich;

kindness, favor; the Symbol of the trigram Open, TUI.

    10.ST Heaven above, marsh below.

    17.ST Marsh center possessing thunder.

    19.ST Above marsh possessing earth.

    28.ST Marsh submerging wood.

    31.ST Above mountain possessing marsh.

    38.ST Fire above, marsh below.

    38. ImT Marsh stirring-up and-also below.

    41.ST Below mountain possessing marsh.

    43.ST Above marsh with-respect-to heaven.

    45.ST Above marsh with-respect-to earth.

    47.ST Marsh without stream.

    49.ST Marsh center possessing fire.

    54.ST Above marsh possessing thunder.

    58.ST Congregating marshes.

    60.ST Above marsh possessing stream.

    61.ST Above marsh possessing wind.

Martial, WU: military, warlike; strong, stern; power to make war. The ideogram: fight and stop, force deterring aggression.

    10.3a Martial people activating: tending-towards a Great Chief.

    10.3b Martial people activating: tending-towards a Great Chief.

    49. ImT Majestically martial, Skinning fate.

    57.1a/b Martial people's Harvesting Trial.

Master, SHENG: have the upper hand, conquer; worthy of, able to; control, check, command.

    33.2a Absolutely-nothing has mastering stimulating.

    43.1a Going not mastering, activating faulty.

    43.1b Not mastering and-also going.

    53.5a Completing: absolutely-nothing has mastering.

    53.5b Completing: absolutely-nothing has mastering, significant.

Matrimonial allying, HUN KOU: legal institution of marriage; make alliances through marriage rather than force.

    3.2a In-no-way outlawry, matrimonial allying.

    3.4a Seeking matrimonial allying.

    22.4a/b In-no-way outlawry, matrimonial allying.

    38.6a In-no-way outlawry, matrimonial allying.

    51.6a Matrimonial allying possesses words.

Maybe, HUO: possible but not certain, perhaps.

    1.4a/b Maybe capering located-in the abyss.

2.3a/b Maybe adhering-to kingly affairs:

6.3a Maybe adhering-to kingly affairs:

6.6a Maybe bestowing's pouched belt.

7.3a/b Legions maybe carting corpses.

19/20.CD Maybe associating-with, maybe seeking.

25.3a Maybe attaching's cattle.

32.3a Maybe receiving's embarrassing.

41.5a Maybe augmenting's ten: partnering's tortoise.

42.2a Maybe Augmenting's ten: partnering's tortoise.

42.2b Maybe Augmenting it.

42.6a/b Maybe smiting it.

53.4a/b Maybe acquiring one's rafter.

61.3a Maybe drumbeating, maybe desisting.

61.3a Maybe weeping, maybe singing.

61.3b Maybe drumbeating, maybe desisting.

62.3a/b Adhering, maybe killing it.

Me, see: **I/me/my**

Mean, CHIEN: low, poor, cheap; depreciate, undervalue; opposite of value, KUEI.

3.1b Using valuing the mean below.

Measures, TU: rule, regulation, limit, test; interval in music; capacity, endurance.

60.ST A chün tzu uses paring to reckon the measures.

60. ImT Articulating used to pare the measures.

Meat, JU: flesh of animals, pulp of fruit.

21.3a Gnawing seasoned meat. Meeting poison.

21.5a Gnawing parched meat. Acquiring yellow metal.

Meat-bones, TZU: meat with bones; bones left after a meal.

21.4a Gnawing parched meat-bones.

Medicinal-herbs, YAO: plants used as remedies; medical as opposed to other ways of healing.

25.5a No medicinal-herbs, possessing rejoicing.

25.5b Without Embroiling's medicinal-herbs.

Meet, YÜ: come on unexpectedly, encounter; occur, happen; pleasant meeting, lucky coincidence; agree. See also: **Going-to-meet**

13.5a/b Great legions controlling mutual meeting.

21.3a Gnawing seasoned meat. Meeting poison.

21.3b Meeting poison.

38.2a/b Meeting a lord, tending-towards the street.

38.3b Meeting a solid indeed.

38.4a Meeting Spring, husbanding.

38.6a Going meeting rain, by-consequence significant.

38.6b Meeting rain's significance.

43/44.CD Coupling: meeting indeed.

43/44.CD Supple meeting solid indeed.

43.3a Solitary going, meeting rain.

44.S Breaking-up necessarily possesses meeting.

44.S Coupling implies meeting indeed.

44. ImT Coupling. Meeting indeed.

44. ImT Supple meeting solid indeed.

44. ImT Heaven, Earth: mutually meeting.

44. ImT Solid meeting centering correctness.

45.S Beings mutually meeting and-also afterwards assembling.

47/48.CD Confining: mutual meeting indeed.

55.1a Meeting one's equal lord.

55.4a/b Meeting one's hiding lord.

62.2a Meeting one's grandmother.

62.2a Meeting one's servant.

62.4a/b Nowhere Exceeding meeting it.

62.6a/b Nowhere meeting Exceeding it.

Melancholy, MEN: sad, unhappy, chagrined, heavy-hearted. The ideogram: gate and heart, the heart confined.

28.ST [A chün tzu uses] retiring-from the age without melancholy.

Melon, KUA: general term for melon, gourd, squash, cucumber; symbol of Heaven[and]Earth, the cosmos.

44.5a Using osier, enwrapping melons.

Merely, CHIH: nothing more than.

24.1a Without merely repenting.

29.5a Merely already evened.

Metallic, CHIN: smelting and casting; all things pertaining to metal, particularly gold; autumn, West, sunset; one of the Five Moments.

4.3a Visualizing a metallic husband.

21.4a Acquiring a metallic arrow.

21.5a Gnawing parched meat. Acquiring yellow metal.

44.1a/b Attaching tending-towards a metallic chock.

47.4a Confined, tending-towards a metallic chariot.

50.5a The Vessel: yellow ears, metallic rings.

Mile, LI: measure of distance, about 1800 feet; village; street, square.

    51. Im/ImT Shake scaring a hundred miles.

Mingle, CHIAO: blend with, communicate, join, exchange; trade, business; copulation; friendship.

    3.ImT Solid[and]Supple beginning mingling and-also heaviness giving-birth indeed.

    11.ST Heaven[and]Earth mingling.

    11. ImT By-consequence-of that Heaven[and]Earth mingling and-also the myriad beings interpenetrating indeed.

    11. ImT Above[and]Below mingling and-also one's purpose concording indeed.

    12.ST Heaven, earth, not mingling.

    12. ImT By-consequence-of that Heaven[and]Earth not mingling and-also the myriad beings not interpenetrating indeed.

    12. ImT Above[and]Below not mingling and-also Below Heaven without fiefdoms indeed.

    14.1a Without mingling harm.

    14.1b Without mingling harm indeed.

    14.5a Your conforming: mingling thus, impressing thus. Significant.

    14.5b Your conforming, mingling thus.

    17.1a/b Issuing-forth-from the gate, mingling possesses achievement.

    37.5b Mingling mutual affection indeed.

    38.4a Mingling conformity.

    38.4b Mingling conforming, without fault.

    54. ImT Heaven[and]Earth not mingling and-also the myriad beings not rising.

Mire, T'U: mud, dirt, filth; besmear, blot out; stupid, pig-headed. The ideogram: earth and water.

    38.6a Visualizing pigs bearing mire.

Moat, HUANG: ditch around city or fort.

    11.6a/b The bulwark returned tending-towards the moat.

Moon, YÜEH: actual moon and moon-month; yin, the sun being yang. See also: **Sun[and]Moon**

    9.6a The moon almost facing.

    19. Im/ImT Culminating tending-towards the eighth moon: possessing a pitfall.

    54.5a The moon almost facing, significant.

    55. ImT Moon overfilling, by-consequence taking-in.

    61.4a The moon almost facing.

More, T'O: another; add to. See also: **Even-more, Furthermore**

8.1a Completing coming possesses more significance.

    8.1b Possessing more significance indeed.

    28.4a Possessing more: abashment.

Moreover, CH'IEH: further, and also.

    29.3a Venturing moreover reclining.

    38.3a One's person stricken, moreover nose-cut.

    40.3a/b Bearing, moreover riding.

    43.4a/b One moves the resting-place moreover.

    44.3a/b One moves the resting-place moreover.

Mother(hood), MU: child-bearing and nourishing. The ideogram: two breasts. See also: **Father[and]Mother** and **Grandmother**

    18.2a/b Managing the mother's Corrupting.

    35.2a Tending-towards one's kingly mother.

Motive, CH'ING: true nature; feelings, desires, passions. The ideogram: heart and green, germinated in the heart.

    31. ImT And-also actually Heaven[and]Earth, the myriad beings's motives permitting visualizing.

    32. ImT And-also actually Heaven[and]Earth, the myriad beings's motives permitting visualizing.

    34. ImT Actually the correcting Great and-also Heaven[and]Earth's motives permitting visualizing.

    45. ImT And-also actually Heaven[and]Earth, the myriad beings's motives, permitting visualizing.

Motley, TSA: mingled, variegated, mixed; disorder.

    3/4.CD Enveloping: motley and-also conspicuous.

    32.AE Persevering: motley and-also not restricting.

Mottled, FEN: variegated, spotted; mixed, assorted, confused; cloudy, perplexed.

    57.2a The mottled like significant.

    57.2b The mottled like has significance.

Mound, LING: grave-mound, barrow; small hill.

    13.3a Ascending one's high mound.

    22.3b Completing absolutely-nothing: having a mound indeed.

    29. ImT Earth venturing, mountains, rivers, hill-tops, mounds indeed.

    51.2a Climbing tending-towards the ninth mound.

53.5a The wild-swan Infiltrating tending-towards the mound.

Mount, TENG: ascend, step up; ripen, complete.
 36.6a/b Initially mounting tending-towards heaven.
 61.6a/b A soaring sound mounting, tending-towards heaven.

Mountain, SHAN: limit, boundary; the Symbol of the trigram Bound, KEN. The ideogram: three peaks, a mountain range.
 4.ST Below the mountain issuing-forth springwater.
 4.ImT Enveloping. Below mountain possessing venturing.
 15.ST Earth center possessing mountain.
 17.6a The king availing-of Growing tending-towards the Western mountain.
 18.ST Below mountain possessing wind.
 22.ST Below mountain possessing fire.
 23.ST Mountain adjoining with-respect-to earth.
 26.ST Heaven located-in mountain center.
 27.ST Below mountain possessing thunder.
 29. ImT Earth venturing, mountains, rivers, hill-tops, mounds indeed.
 31.ST Above mountain possessing marsh.
 33.ST Below heaven possessing mountain.
 39.ST Above mountain possessing stream.
 41.ST Below mountain possessing marsh.
 46.4a/b Kinghood availing-of Growing, tending-towards the twin-peaked mountain.
 52.ST Joined mountains.
 53.ST Above mountain possessing wood.
 56.ST Above mountain possessing fire.
 62.ST Above mountain possessing thunder.

Mourn, AI: grieve, lament over something gone; distress, sorrow; compassion. The ideogram: mouth and clothes, display of feelings.
 62.ST [A chün tzu uses] losing Exceeding to reach-to mourning.

Mouth, K'OU: literal mouth, words going out and food coming in; entrance, hole.
 27. Im/ImT Originating-from seeking mouth substance.
 31.6b The spouting mouth stimulating indeed.
 47. ImT Honoring the mouth thereupon exhausted indeed.

Move, HSING: move or move something; motivate, emotionally moving; walk, act, do. The ideogram: stepping left then right.

This term occurs throughout the hexagram texts.

Mud, HSI: ground left wet by water, muddy shores; danger; shed tears; nearly.
 48. Im/ImT Muddy culmination: Truly not-yet the well-rope Well.
 64. Im/ImT The small fox, a muddy Ford.

Mulberry-tree, SANG: literal tree and silk production; tranquility; retired, rural place.
 12.5a Attaching tending-towards bushy mulberry-trees.

Multiply, FAN: augment, enhance, increase; thriving, plentiful.
 35. Im Prospering, the calm feudatory avails-of bestowing horses to multiply the multitudes.
 35. ImT That uses the calm feudatory availing-of bestowing horses to multiply the multitudes.

Multitude, SHU: the people; mass, herd; all, the whole.
 1.ImT Heads issuing-forth-from the multitudinous beings.
 22.ST A chün tzu uses brightening the multitudinous standards without daring to sever litigating.
 35. Im Prospering, the calm feudatory avails-of bestowing horses to multiply the multitudes.
 35. ImT That uses the calm feudatory availing-of bestowing horses to multiply the multitudes.

Munificence, HOU: liberal, kind, generous; create abundance; thick, large. The ideogram: gift of a superior to an inferior.
 2.ST A chün tzu uses munificent actualizing-tao to carry the beings.
 2.ImT Field: munificence carrying the beings.
 23.ST Using munificence above to quiet the position below.
 42.1b The below, not munificent affairs indeed.
 52.6b Using munificence, completing indeed.

Mutual, HSIANG: reciprocal assistance, encourage, help; bring together, blend with; examine, inspect; by turns.
 11.ST [The crown-prince uses] bracing to mutualize Heaven[and]Earth's propriety.
 13.5a/b Great legions controlling mutual meeting.

13.5b Words mutualize controlling indeed.

28.2b Exceeding uses mutual associating indeed.

31. ImT The two agencies influencing correspondence use mutual associating.

32. ImT Thunder, wind, mutually associating.

37.5b Mingling mutual affection indeed.

44. ImT Heaven, Earth: mutually meeting.

45.S Beings mutually meeting and-also afterwards assembling.

47/48.CD Confining: mutual meeting indeed.

48.ST A chün tzu uses toiling commoners to encourage mutualizing.

49. ImT Skinning. Stream, fire, mutually pausing.

49. ImT Their purposes not mutually acquired.

52. ImT Not mutually associating indeed.

53.3b Yielding mutualizes protection indeed.

54.1b Mutualizing receiving indeed.

My, see: **I/me/my**. See also: **Myself**

Myriad, WAN: countless; many, everyone; lit.: ten thousand. The ideogram: swarm of insects.

1.ImT The myriad beings's own beginning.

1.ImT Myriad cities, conjoining, soothing.

2.ImT The myriad beings's own birth.

3.S Therefore afterwards the myriad beings giving-birth in-truth.

3.S Overfilling Heaven[and]Earth's interspace implies verily the myriad beings.

7.2b Cherishing the myriad fiefdoms indeed.

8.ST The Earlier Kings used installing myriad cities to connect the connoted feudatories.

11. ImT By-consequence-of that Heaven[and]Earth mingling and-also the myriad beings interpenetrating indeed.

12. ImT By-consequence-of that Heaven[and]Earth not mingling and-also the myriad beings not interpenetrating indeed.

15.3b The myriad commoners submitting indeed.

25.ST The Earlier Kings used luxuriance suiting the season to nurture the myriad beings.

27. ImT Heaven[and]Earth nourishes the myriad beings.

27. ImT The all-wise person nourishes eminence used to extend-to the myriad commoners.

31.S Therefore afterwards possessing the myriad beings.

31.S Possessing the myriad beings:

31. ImT Heaven[and]Earth influencing and-also the myriad beings's changing give-birth.

31. ImT And-also actually Heaven[and]Earth, the myriad beings's motives permitting visualizing.

32. ImT And-also actually Heaven[and]Earth, the myriad beings's motives permitting visualizing.

38. ImT The myriad beings Polarizing and-also their affairs sorted indeed.

45. ImT And-also actually Heaven[and]Earth, the myriad beings's motives, permitting visualizing.

54. ImT Heaven[and]Earth not mingling and-also the myriad beings not rising.

Myself, WU: first person intensifier; the particular person I am.

61.2a Myself associating, simply spilling it.

Namely, WEI: precisely, only that.

3.3a Namely, entering tending-towards the forest center.

Near, LIN: approach or be approached: behold with care, look on sympathetically; condescend; bless or curse by coming nearer; a superior visits an inferior.

Image of Hexagram 19 and occurs throughout its texts.

Nearby, ERH: near, close; close relation.

51. ImT Scaring the distant and-also fearing the nearby indeed.

Necessarily, PI: unavoidably, indispensably, certainly.

4.S Beings giving-birth necessarily Enveloping.

6.S Drinking[and]taking-in necessarily possesses Arguing.

7.S Arguing necessarily possesses crowds rising-up.

7.6b Necessarily disarraying the fiefdoms indeed.

8.S Crowds necessarily possess a place to Group.

9.S Grouping necessarily possesses a place to Accumulate.

14.S Associating-with People Concording implies beings necessarily converting in-truth.

16.S Possessing the Great and-also enabling Humbling necessarily Provides-for.

17.S Providing-for necessarily possesses Following.

18.S Using rejoicing Following people implies necessarily possessing affairs.

30.S Falling necessarily possesses a place to congregate.

36.S Advancing necessarily possessing a place: injuring.

37.S Injury with-respect-to the outside implies necessarily reversing with-respect-to Dwelling.

38.S Dwelling tao exhausted, necessarily returning.

39.S Turning-away necessarily possesses heaviness.

41.S Delaying necessarily possesses a place to let-go.

42.S Diminishing and-also not climaxing necessarily Augments.

43.S Augmenting and-also not climaxing necessarily breaks-up.

44.S Breaking-up necessarily possesses meeting.

47.S Ascending and-also not climaxing necessarily Confines.

48.S Confining reaching-to the above implies necessarily reversing the below.

54.S Advancing necessarily possessing a place to Convert.

55.S Acquiring one's place to Convert implies necessarily the great.

56.S Exhausting the great implies necessarily letting-go one's residing.

62.S Possessing one's trustworthiness implies necessarily moving it.

62.4a/b Going adversity necessarily warning.

63.S Possessing Exceeding being implies necessarily Fording.

Neck, MEI: muscular base of neck, shoulders and arms; source of strength in arms and shoulders; persist.

31.5a/b Conjoining one's neck.

Neighbor, LIN: person living nearby; extended family; assist, support.

9.5a Affluence: using one's neighbor.

11.4a Not affluence: using one's neighbor.

15.5a Not affluence: using one's neighbor.

51.6a Shake: not tending-towards one's body, tending-towards one's neighbor.

51.6b Dreading the neighbor, a warning indeed.

63.5a/b The Eastern neighbor slaughters cattle.

63.5a Not thus the Western neighbor's dedicated offering.

63.5b Not thus the Western neighbor's season indeed.

Nest, CH'AO: nest in a tree; haunt, retreat; make a nest.

56.6a A bird burning its nest.

Nightfall, HSI: day's end, dusk; late; last day of month or year.

1.3a Nightfall, awe, like adversity.

Night-time, YEH: dark half of 24 hour cycle.

43.2a Absolutely-no night-time, possessing arms.

Nine, CHIU: number of a transforming whole line; superlative: best, perfect; ninth.

1.7b Availing-of nines.

14.1b Great Possessing, the initial nine.

32.2b Nine at-second, repenting extinguished.

34.2b Nine at-second, Trial: significant.

40.2b Nine at-second, Trial: significant.

41.2b Nine at-second, Harvesting Trial.

44.5b Nine at-fifth, containing composition.

46.2b Nine at-second's conforming.

51.2a Climbing tending-towards the ninth mound.

57.5b Nine at-fifth's significance.

58.4b Nine at-fourth's rejoicing.

61.1b The initial nine, precaution significant.

64.2b Nine at-second, Trial: significant.

No, WU: simple negative; un-, dis-.
This term occurs throughout the hexagram texts.

North, see: **Eastern North**

Nose, PI: literal nose; the first, original.

21.2a/b Gnawing flesh, submerging the nose.

Nose-cutting, YI: punish through loss of public face or honor; contrasts with foot-cutting, YEH, crippling punishment for serious crime.

38.3a One's person stricken, moreover nose-cut.

47.5a/b Nose-cutting, foot-cutting.

Not, PU: simple negative.
This term occurs throughout the hexagram texts.

Not permitting, PU K'O: not possible; contradicts an inherent principle. The ideogram: mouth and breath, silent consent. See also: **Permit**

1.6b Overfilling, not permitting lasting indeed.

1.7b Heavenly actualizing-tao not permitting activating the head indeed.

5.S Being immature not permitting not nourishing indeed.

6.ImT Arguing not permitting accomplishment indeed.

6.1b Arguing not permitting long-living indeed.

12.ST [A chün tzu uses] not permitting splendor to use benefits.

15.S Possessing the Great implies not permitting using overfilling.

15. ImT Lowliness and-also not permitting passing-beyond.

18.2a Not permitting Trial.

23.6b Completing, not permitting availing-of indeed.

25.5b Not permitting testing indeed.

27.5a Not permitting wading the Great River.

28.S Not nourishing, by-consequence not permitting stirring-up.

28.3b Not permitted to use possessing bracing indeed.

28.6b Not permitting fault indeed.

29. ImT Heaven venturing, not permitting ascending indeed.

32.S Not permitting using not lasting indeed.

33.3b Not permitting Great Affairs indeed.

36.3a Not permitting affliction: Trial.

36.5b Brightness not permitted to pause indeed.

43.6b Completing not permitting long-living indeed.

44. ImT Not permitting associating-with long-living indeed.

49.S The Well tao not permitting not Skinning.

49.1b Not permitted to use possessing activating indeed.

53.6b Not permitting disarray indeed.

55.3b Not permitting Great Affairs indeed.

55.3b Completing, not permitting availing-of indeed.

60. Im/ImT Bitter Articulating not permitting Trial.

62. Im Permitting Small Affairs. Not permitting Great Affairs.

62. ImT That uses not permitting Great Affairs indeed.

62.1b Wherefore not permitted thus indeed.

62.2b A servant not permitted Exceeding indeed.

62.4b Completing not permitting long-living indeed.

64.S Beings not permitted exhaustion indeed.

Notable, SHIH: learned, upright, important man; scholar, gentleman.

28.5a A venerable wife acquiring her notable husband.

28.5b A venerable wife, a notable husband.

54.6a A notable disembowelling a goat without blood.

Nothing/nowhere, FU: strong negative; not a single thing/place. See also: **Absolutely-nothing**

13.4a Nothing controlling attacking.

13.4b Righteously nothing controlling indeed.

14.3a Small People nowhere controlling.

17.2b Nowhere joining associating indeed.

22.1b Righteously nothing to ride indeed.

34.ST A chün tzu uses no codes whatever, nowhere treading.

41.2a Nowhere Diminishing, augmenting it.

41.5a Nowhere a controlling contradiction.

41.6a/b Nowhere Diminishing, augmenting it.

42.2a Nowhere a controlling contradiction.

62.3a Nowhere Exceeding defending-against it.

62.4a/b Nowhere Exceeding meeting it.

62.6a/b Nowhere meeting Exceeding it.

Notify, KAO: proclaim, order, decree; advise, inform, tell. The ideogram: mouth and ox head, imposing speech.

4.Im/ImT The initial oracle-consulting notifying.

4.Im/ImT Obscuring, by-consequence not notifying.

11.6a Originating-from the capital, notifying fate.

42.3a Notifying the prince, availing-of the scepter.

42.4a/b Notifying the prince, adhering.

43. Im/ImT Notifying originates-from the capital.

Not-yet, WEI: temporal negative; something will but has not yet occurred; contrary of already, CHI.

Image of Hexagram 64 and occurs throughout its texts.

3.5b Spreading-out not-yet shining indeed.

5.1b Not-yet letting-go rules indeed.

5.6b Although not an appropriate situation, not-yet the great let-go indeed.

7.4b Not-yet letting-go the rules indeed.

9.ImT Spreading-out, not-yet moving indeed.

13.6b Purpose not-yet acquired indeed.

15.6b Purpose not-yet acquired indeed.

16.5b Center not-yet extinguished indeed.

18.4b Going, not-yet acquiring indeed.

19.2b Not-yet yielding-to fate indeed.

20.3b Not-yet letting-go tao indeed.

20.6b Purpose not-yet evened indeed.

21.4b Not-yet shining indeed.

23.2b Not-yet possessing associating indeed.

25.2b Not-yet affluence indeed.

29.2b Not-yet issuing-forth-from the center indeed.

29.5b Centering, not-yet great indeed.

31.4b Not-yet influencing harming indeed.

31.4b Not-yet the shining great indeed.

35.1b Not-yet acquiescing-in fate indeed.

35.6b Tao not-yet shining indeed.

37.1b Purpose not-yet transformed indeed.

37.3b Not-yet letting-go indeed.

38.2b Not-yet letting-go tao indeed.

40.4b Not-yet an appropriate situation indeed.

43.5b Center not-yet shining indeed.

44.3b Moving, not-yet hauling-along indeed.

45.2b Centering, not-yet transforming indeed.

45.5b Purpose not-yet shining indeed.

45.6b The above not-yet quiet indeed.

47.5b Purpose not-yet acquired indeed.

47.6b Not-yet appropriate indeed.

48. Im/ImT Muddy culmination: Truly not-yet the well-rope Well.

48. ImT Not-yet possessing achievement indeed.

49.5a Not-yet an augury, possessing conformity.

50.1b Not-yet rebelling indeed.

51.4b Not-yet shining indeed.

51.6b Center not-yet acquired indeed.

52.1b Not-yet letting-go correcting indeed.

52.2b Not-yet withdrawing-from hearkening indeed.

54.2b Not-yet transforming the rules indeed.

54.3b Not-yet appropriate indeed.

56.4b Not-yet acquiring the situation indeed.

56.4b The heart not-yet keen indeed.

58.1b Movement not-yet doubted indeed.

58.4a Bargaining Opening, not-yet soothing.

58.6b Not-yet shining indeed.

61.1b Purpose not-yet transformed indeed.

63.CD Not-yet Fording: manhood exhausted indeed.

Nourish, YANG: feed, sustain, support; provide, care for; bring up, improve, grow, develop.

4.ImT Enveloping used to nourish correcting:

5.S Being immature not permitting not nourishing indeed.

26. ImT Nourishing eminence indeed.

27.S Beings accumulating therefore afterwards permitting nourishing.

27.S Jaws imply nourishing indeed.

27.CD Jaws: nourishing correcting indeed.

27. ImT Nourishing correcting, by-consequence significant indeed.

27. ImT Viewing one's place to nourish indeed.

27. ImT Viewing one's origin: nourishing indeed.

27. ImT Heaven[and]Earth nourishes the myriad beings.

27. ImT The all-wise person nourishes eminence used to extend-to the myriad commoners.

28.S Not nourishing, by-consequence not permitting stirring-up.

28.CD Jaws: nourishing correcting indeed.

48. ImT The Well nourishing and-also not exhausted indeed.

50. ImT And-also great Growing uses nourishing all-wise eminences.

No ... whatever, FEI: strongest negative; not at all!

32.4b No lasting whatever: one's situation.

34.ST A chün tzu uses no codes whatever, nowhere treading.

Nowhere, see: **Nothing**

Numerous, TO: great number, many; often.

15.ST A chün tzu uses reducing the numerous to augment the few.

26.ST A chün tzu uses the numerous recorded preceding words going to move.

55/56.CD Abounding: numerous anteriority indeed.

Nurse, TZU: love, care for and shelter; act as a mother. The ideogram: child and shelter.

3.2a Woman[and]Son, Trial: not nursing.

3.2a/b Ten years-revolved, thereupon nursing.

Nurture, YÜ: bring up, support, rear, raise; increase.

4.ST A chün tzu uses fruiting movement to nurture actualizing-tao.

18.ST A chün tzu uses rousing the commoners to nurture actualizing-tao.

25.ST The Earlier Kings used luxuriance suiting the season to nurture the myriad beings.

53.3a/b The wife pregnant, not nurturing.

Oblations, SSU: sacrifices offered to the gods and the dead.

47.2a Harvesting: availing-of presenting oblations.

47.5a/b Harvesting: availing-of offering oblations.

Obscure, TU: confuse, muddy, agitate; muddled, cloudy, turbid; agitated water; annoy through repetition.

4.Im/ImT Twice, three-times: obscuring.

4.Im/ImT Obscuring, by-consequence not notifying.

4.ImT Obscuring Enveloping indeed.

Observe, SHIH: see and inspect carefully; gain knowledge of; compare and imitate. The ideogram: see and omen, taking account of what you see.

10.3a/b Squinting enabling observing.

10.6a Observing Treading, predecessors auspicious.

27.4a Tiger observing: glaring, glaring.

51.6a Observing: terrorizing, terrorizing.

54.2a Squinting enabling observing.

Obstruct, P'I: closed, stopped; bar the way; obstacle; unfortunate, wicked; refuse, disapprove, deny. The ideogram: mouth and not, blocked communication.

Image of Hexagram 12 and occurs throughout its texts.

7.1a Obstructing virtue: pitfall.

11.CD Obstructing, Pervading: reversing one's sorting indeed.

13.S Beings not permitted to use completing Obstructing.

33.4a Small People obstructing.

33.4b Small People obstructing indeed.

50.1a/b Harvesting: issuing-forth-from obstruction.

Occult, YIN: screen, obscure, keep from view, keep back; private; retired, not in office.

57.AE Ground: evaluating and-also occulting.

Offense, TSUI: crime, sin, fault; violate laws or rules; incur blame, incriminated. The ideogram: net and wrong, entangled in guilt.

40.ST A chün tzu uses forgiving excess to pardon offenses.

Offer, CHI: present gifts to gods and spirits. The ideogram: hand, meat and worship.

47.5a/b Harvesting: availing-of offering oblations.

51. ImT Using activating the offering lord indeed.

63.5a Not thus the Western neighbor's dedicated offering.

Offertory-millet, CHI: grain presented to the god of agriculture; presence of the god in the grain.

51. ImT Issuing-forth permits using guarding the ancestral temple, field-altar, offertory-millet.

Office, KUAN: government officials, magistrates, dignitaries.

17.1a An office: possessing denial. Trial: significant.

17.1b An office: possessing denial.

Old-age, TIEH: seventy or older; aged, no longer active.

30.3a By-consequence great old-age's lamenting. Pitfall.

On-all-sides, see: **Sides**

One's/one, CH'I: third person pronoun; also: it/its, he/his, she/hers, they/theirs.

This term occurs throughout the hexagram texts.

One, the-one, YI: single unit; number one; undivided, simple, whole; any one of; first, the first.

32.AE Persevering: using the-one actualizing-tao.

32.5b Adhering-to the-one and-also completing indeed.

38.6a Carrying souls, the-one chariot.

41.3a By-consequence Diminishing the-one person.

41.3a/b The-one person moving.

45.1a Like an outcry, the-one handful activates laughing.

56.5a The-one arrow extinguishing.

One-sided, P'IEN: excessive, partial, selfish; long for, bent on; lit.: inclined to one side.

  42.6b One-sided evidence indeed.

Ooze, TIEH: exude moisture; mud; slime; turbid, tainted.

  48.3a/b The Well: oozing, not taking-in.

Open, TUI: an open surface, promoting interaction and interpenetration; responsive, free, unhindered, pleasing; opening, passage; the mouth; exchange, barter; straight, direct; meet, gather; place where water accumulates. The ideogram: person, mouth and vapor, speaking with others.

  Image of Hexagram 58 and occurs throughout its texts.

Oppose, FAN: resist; violate, offend, attack; possessed by an evil spirit; criminal. The ideogram: violate and dog, brutal offense.

  5.1b Not opposing heavy moving indeed.

  26.1b Not opposing calamity indeed.

  58. ImT Stimulating using opposing heaviness:

Oracle-consulting, SHIH: yarrow stalk divination; find your allotted destiny.

  4.Im/ImT The initial oracle-consulting notifying.

  8.Im/ImT Retracing the oracle-consulting: Spring, perpetual Trial.

Ordinance, LÜ: law, fixed regulation; regulate by law, divide into right and wrong. The ideogram: writing and move, codes that govern action.

  7.1a/b Legions issuing-forth using ordinance.

  7.1b Letting-go ordinance: pitfall indeed.

Origin, TZU: source, beginning, ground; cause, reason, motive; line of descent; path to the origin; yourself, intrinsic.

  1.ST A chün tzu uses originating strength not to pause.

  5.3b Originating-from my involving outlawry.

  5.4a Issuing-forth originates-from the cave.

  6.2b Below origin, above Arguing.

  8.2a/b Grouping's origin inside.

  8.2b Not originating letting-go indeed.

  9.Im/ImT Originating-from my Western suburbs.

  9.1a/b Returning originating-from tao.

  9.2b Truly not originating-from letting-go indeed.

10.2b Centering, not originating-from disarray indeed.

11.6a Originating-from the capital, notifying fate.

14.6a Originating-from heaven shielding it.

14.6b Originating-from heaven shielding indeed.

15.1b Lowliness uses originating-from herding indeed.

24.AE Returning: using originating knowledge.

24.5b Centering originating-from the predecessor indeed.

25. ImT Solid originating-from the outside coming and-also activating a lord with-respect-to the inside.

27. Im/ImT Originating-from seeking mouth substance.

27. ImT Viewing one's origin: nourishing indeed.

29.4a Letting-in bonds originating-from the window.

35.ST A chün tzu uses originating enlightening to brighten actualizing-tao.

37.ST Wind originating-from fire issuing-forth.

38.1a Losing the horse, no pursuit, originating-from returning.

40.3b Originating-from my involving arms.

41.5b Originating-from shielding above indeed.

42. ImT Above origin, below the below.

42.2b,6b Originating-from outside, coming indeed.

43. Im/ImT Notifying originates-from the capital.

44.5a/b Possessing tumbling, originating-from heaven.

55.6b Originating-from concealing indeed.

62.5a Originating-from my Western suburbs.

Osier, CH'I: willow branches used to make baskets.

  44.5a Using osier, enwrapping melons.

Outcry, see: **Cry-out**

Outlawry, K'OU: break the laws; violent people, outcasts, bandits.

  3.2a In-no-way outlawry, matrimonial allying.

  4.6a Not Harvesting: activating outlawry.

4.6a Harvesting: resisting outlawry.
4.6b Harvesting: availing-of resisting outlawry.
5.3a Involving outlawry culminating.
5.3b Originating-from my involving outlawry.
22.4a/b In-no-way outlawry, matrimonial
  allying.
38.6a In-no-way outlawry, matrimonial
  allying.
40.3a Involving outlawry culminating.
53.3a Harvesting: resisting outlawry.
53.3b Harvesting: availing-of resisting
  outlawry.

Outside, WAI: outer, exterior, external; people
working in places other than their home;
unfamiliar, foreign; the upper trigram, as opposed
to inside, NEI, the lower.
  5.3b Calamity located outside indeed.
  8.4a Outside Grouping it.
  8.4b Outside Grouping with-respect-to
  eminence.
  11. ImT Inside yang and-also outside yin.
  11. ImT Inside persisting and-also outside
  yielding.
  11. ImT Inside chün tzu and-also outside
  Small People.
  11.1b Purpose located outside indeed.
  12. ImT Inside yin and-also outside yang.
  12. ImT Inside supple and-also outside solid.
  12. ImT Inside Small People and-also outside
  chün tzu.
  25. ImT Solid originating-from the outside
  coming and-also activating a lord with-
  respect-to the inside.
  31.1b Purpose located outside indeed.
  36. ImT Inside pattern Brightening and-also
  outside supple yielding.
  37.S Injury with-respect-to the outside implies
  necessarily reversing with-respect-to
  Dwelling.
  37/38.CD Polarizing: outside indeed.
  37. ImT The man correcting the situation
  reaching-to the outside.
  42.2b,6b Originating-from outside, coming
  indeed.
  56. ImT Supple acquiring the center reaching-
  to the outside and-also yielding reaching-to
  the solid.
  58. ImT Solid centering and-also supple
  outside.

  59. ImT Supple acquiring the situation
  reaching-to the outside and-also concording
  above.
  59.3b Purpose located outside indeed.
Overbearing, K'ANG: excessive, overpowering
authority; disparage; rigid, unbending; excessive
display of force.
  1.6a/b Overbearing dragon possesses
  repenting.
  62.6b Climaxing overbearing indeed.
Overfill, YING: at the point of overflowing; more
than wanted, stretch beyond; replenished, full;
arrogant. The ideogram: vessel and too much.
  1.6b Overfilling, not permitting lasting
  indeed.
  3.S Overfilling Heaven[and]Earth's interspace
  implies verily the myriad beings.
  3.S Sprouting implies overfilling indeed.
  3.ImT Thunder[and]Rain's stirring-up,
  fullness overfilling.
  8.1a Possessing conformity, overfilling the jar.
  15.S Possessing the Great implies not
  permitting using overfilling.
  15. ImT Earthly tao transforming overfilling
  and-also diffusing Humbling.
  15. ImT Heavenly tao lessening overfilling
  and-also augmenting Humbling.
  15. ImT Souls[and]Spirits harming overfilling
  and-also blessing Humbling.
  15. ImT People tao hating overfilling and-also
  loving Humbling.
  23. ImT A chün tzu honors the dissolving
  pause to overfill emptiness.
  29. ImT Stream diffusing and-also not
  overfilling.
  29.5a/b Gorge not overfilled.
  41. ImT Diminishing augmenting, overfilling
  emptiness.
  55. ImT Moon overfilling, by-consequence
  taking-in.
  55. ImT Heaven[and]Earth overfilling
  emptiness.
Overflow, YEN: flow over the top; inundate,
spread out; abundant, rich.
  5.2b Overflowing located-in the center indeed.
Overrun, CH'IEN: pass the limit; mistake,
transgression, disease.
  54.4a Converting Maidenhood overrunning
  the term

54.4b Overrunning the term's purpose.

Overtake, TI: come up to, reach; arrest, seize; until; also: harmonious, peaceful. The ideogram: go, hand and reach, reaching to seize satisfaction.

56.5b Overtaking the above indeed.

Overthrow, FU: subvert, upset, defeat, throw down; unstable, move back and forth.

50.4a/b Overthrowing a princely stew.

Own, TZU: possession and the things possessed; avail of, depend on; property, riches.

1.ImT The myriad beings's own beginning.

2.ImT The myriad beings's own birth.

56.2a Cherishing one's own.

56.4a/b Acquiring one's own emblem-ax.

57.6a/b Losing one's own emblem-ax.

Parch, KAN: dry up; dried, exhausted, dessicated; cleaned away, gone. See also: **Force**

21.4a Gnawing parched meat-bones.

21.5a Gnawing parched meat. Acquiring yellow metal.

Pardon, YU: forgive, indulge, relax; lenient.

40.ST A chün tzu uses forgiving excess to pardon offenses.

Pare, CHIH: cut away; form, tailor, carve; invent; limit, prevent. The ideogram: knife and incomplete.

15.AE Humbling: using paring the codes.

32.5b The husband, the son: paring righteously.

57.AE Ground: actualizing-tao's paring indeed.

60.ST A chün tzu uses paring to reckon the measures.

60.ImT Articulating used to pare the measures.

Parsimonious, CHIEN: thrifty; moderate, temperate; stingy, scanty.

12.ST A chün tzu uses parsimonious actualizing-tao to cast-out heaviness.

62.ST [A chün tzu uses] availing-of Exceeding to reach-to parsimony.

Part, KUAI: separate, fork, cut off, decide; pull or flow in different directions; certain, settled; prompt, decisive, stern.

Image of Hexagram 43 and occurs throughout its texts.

10.5a/b Parting Treading. Trial: adversity.

44.CD Parting: breaking-up indeed.

Partner, P'ENG: associate for mutual benefit; two

equal or similar things; companions, friends, peers; join in; commercial ventures. The ideogram: linked strings of cowries or coins.

2.Im/ImT Western South: acquiring partnering.

2.Im/ImT Eastern North: losing partnering.

11.2a Partnering extinguished.

16.4a Partners join-together suddenly.

24.Im/ImT Partnering coming, without fault.

31.4a Partnering adheres-to simply pondering.

39.5a/b The great Limping, partnering coming.

40.4a Partnering culminating, splitting-off conforming.

41.5a Maybe augmenting's ten: partnering's tortoise.

42.2a Maybe Augmenting's ten: partnering's tortoise.

58.ST A chün tzu uses partnering friends to explicate repeating.

Passage, KUAN: market gate, customs house, frontier post; limit, crisis, important point.

24.ST The Earlier Kings used culminating sun to bar the passages.

Pass-beyond, YÜ: go beyond set time or limits; get over a wall or obstacle; pass to the other side.

15.ImT Lowliness and-also not permitting passing-beyond.

Pattern, WEN: intrinsic or natural design and its beauty; stylish, elegant; noble; contrasts with composition, CHANG, a conscious creation.

2.5b Pattern located-in the center indeed.

9.ST A chün tzu uses highlighting the pattern to actualize-tao.

13.ImT Pattern brightening uses persisting.

14.ImT One's actualizing-tao: solid persisting and-also pattern brightening.

22.ImT Supple coming and-also patterning solid.

22.ImT Above apportioning solid and-also patterning supple.

22.ImT Heavenly pattern indeed.

22.ImT Pattern brightening, stopping:

22.ImT People pattern indeed.

22.ImT Viewing reaching-to the heavenly pattern.

22.ImT Viewing reaching-to the people pattern.

36.ImT Inside pattern Brightening and-also outside supple yielding.

36. ImT The pattern king uses it.
49. ImT Pattern brightening uses stimulating.
49.5b One's pattern luminous indeed.
49.6b One's pattern beautiful indeed.

● **Pause**, HSI: stop and rest, repose; breathe, a breathing-spell; suspended. See also: **Dissolving Pause**

1.ST A chün tzu uses originating strength not to pause.
17.ST A chün tzu uses turning-to darkening to enter a reposing pause.
36.5b Brightness not permitted to pause indeed.
46.6a Harvesting: tending-towards not pausing's Trial.
49. ImT Skinning. Stream, fire, mutually pausing.

● **Pay-tribute**, CHI: compulsory payments; present property to a superior.

45.6a/b Paying-tribute: sighs, tears, snot.

● **Peak**, TING: top, summit, crown; carry on the head; superior. See also: **Twin-peaked**

28.6a Exceeding wading submerges the peak. Pitfall.

● **Peep-through**, K'UEI: observe from hiding; stealthily, furtive.

20.2a Peeping-through Viewing.
20.2b Peeping-through Viewing: woman Trial.
55.6a/b Peeping-through one's door.

● **Pendent**, TO: hanging; flowering branch, date or grape clusters.

27.1a/b Viewing my pendent Jaws.

● **People, person**, JEN: humans individually and collectively; an individual; humankind. See also: **Great People** and **Small People**

Image of Hexagrams 13 and 37 and occurs throughout their texts.

4.1a/b Harvesting: availing-of punishing people.
5.6a Three people coming.
6.2a People, three hundred doors.
7.Im Respectable people significant.
8.3a/b Grouping's in-no-way people.
8.5a Capital people not admonished. Significant.
8.5b Capital people not admonished.
10. Im/ImT Not snapping-at people. Growing.
10.2a/b Shade people, Trial: significant.
10.3a/b Snapping-at people: pitfall.

10.3a/b Martial people activating: tending-towards a Great Chief.
12. Im/ImT Obstructing it, in-no-way people.
14.S Associating-with People Concording implies beings necessarily converting in-truth.
14.CD Concording People: connecting indeed.
15. ImT People tao hating overfilling and-also loving Humbling.
16. ImT The all-wise person uses yielding stirring-up.
18.S Using rejoicing Following people implies necessarily possessing affairs.
20. ImT The all-wise person uses spirit tao to set-up teaching.
22. ImT People pattern indeed.
22. ImT Viewing reaching-to the people pattern.
23.5a/b Using housing people, favor.
25.3a Moving people's acquiring:
25.3a Capital people's calamity.
25.3b Moving people acquiring cattle.
25.3b Capital people, calamity indeed.
27. ImT The all-wise person nourishes eminence used to extend-to the myriad commoners.
31.ST A chün tzu uses emptiness to acquiesce people.
31. ImT The all-wise person influencing the people at-heart and-also Below Heaven harmony evening.
31.3b Purpose located-in following people.
32. ImT The all-wise person lasting with-respect-to his tao and-also Below Heaven the changes accomplishing.
32.5a Wife people: significant.
32.5b Wife people, Trial: significant.
36.1a A lord: the people possessing words.
38.CD Dwelling People: inside indeed.
38.1a/b Visualizing hateful people.
38.3a One's person stricken, moreover nose-cut.
41.3a Three people moving.
41.3a By-consequence Diminishing the-one person.
41.3a/b The-one person moving.
49. ImT Yielding reaching-to heaven and-also corresponding reaching-to the people.

50. ImT The all-wise person Growing uses presenting-to the Supreme Above.

52. Im/ImT Not visualizing one's people.

54. ImT A person's completion beginning indeed.

54.2a/b Harvesting: shade people's Trial.

55. ImT And-also even-more with-respect-to the people reached.

55.6a/b Living-alone, one without people.

56.6a Sojourning people beforehand laughing, afterwards crying-out sobbing.

57.1a/b Martial people's Harvesting Trial.

58. ImT That uses yielding reaching-to heaven and-also corresponding reaching-to the people.

Permit, K'O: possible because in harmony with an inherent principle. The ideogram: mouth and breath, silent consent. See also: **Beings not permitted to use**

2.3a/b Containing composition permitting Trial.

3.6b Wherefore permitting long-living indeed?

7.ImT Actually permitting using kinghood.

12.6b Wherefore permitting long-living indeed?

15.6b Permitting availing-of moving legions.

16.6b Wherefore permitting long-living indeed?

18.6b Purpose permitted by-consequence indeed.

19.S Possessing affairs and-also afterwards permitting the great.

20.S Being great therefore afterwards permitting Viewing.

20.2b Truly permitting the demoniac indeed.

21.S Permitting Viewing and-also afterwards possessing a place to unite.

25.4a Permitting Trial.

25.4b Permitting Trial, without fault.

26.S Possessing Without Embroiling therefore afterwards permitting Accumulating.

27.S Beings accumulating therefore afterwards permitting nourishing.

28.5b Wherefore permitting lasting indeed?

28.5b Truly permitting the demoniac indeed.

30.3b Wherefore permitting lasting indeed?

31. ImT And-also actually Heaven[and]Earth, the myriad beings's motives permitting visualizing.

32. ImT And-also actually Heaven[and]Earth, the myriad beings's motives permitting visualizing.

34. ImT Actually the correcting Great and-also Heaven[and]Earth's motives permitting visualizing.

40.3b Truly permitting the demoniac indeed.

41. Im/ImT Without fault, permitting Trial.

41. Im/ImT Two platters permit availing-of presenting.

41.4b Truly permitting rejoicing indeed.

45. ImT And-also actually Heaven[and]Earth, the myriad beings's motives, permitting visualizing.

48.3a Permitting availing-of drawing-water.

51. ImT Issuing-forth permits using guarding the ancestral temple, field-altar, offertory-millet.

53. ImT Permitting using correcting the fiefdoms indeed.

53.6a Its feathers permit availing-of activating fundamentals.

53.6b Its feathers permit availing-of activating fundamentals, significant.

61.6b Wherefore permitting long-living indeed?

62. Im Permitting Small Affairs. Not permitting Great Affairs.

63.6b Wherefore permitting lasting indeed?

Perpetual, YUNG: continuing; everlasting, ever-flowing. The ideogram: flowing water.

2.7a Harvesting: perpetual Trial.

2.7b Availing-of the sixes, perpetual Trial.

6.1a/b Not a perpetual place, affairs.

8.Im/ImT Retracing the oracle-consulting: Spring, perpetual Trial.

22.3a Perpetual Trial significant.

22.3b Perpetual Trial's significance.

42.2a Perpetual Trial significant.

45.5a Spring, perpetual Trial.

52.1a Harvesting: perpetual Trial.

54.ST A chün tzu uses perpetually completing to know the cracked.

62.4a No availing-of perpetual Trial.

Persevere, HENG: continue in the same way or spirit; constant, perpetual, regular; self-renewing; extend everywhere.

Image of Hexagram 32 and occurs throughout its texts.

5.1a Harvesting: availing-of persevering.

5.1b Harvesting: availing-of persevering, without fault.

16.5a/b Persevering, not dying.

31.CD Persevering: lasting indeed.

37.ST A chün tzu uses words to possess beings and-also movement to possess perseverance.

42.6a Establishing the heart, no persevering.

54.1b Using persevering indeed.

Persist, CHIEN: strong, robust, dynamic, tenacious; continuous; unwearied heavenly bodies in their orbits; the Action of the trigram Force, CH'IEN.

1.ST Heaven moves persistingly.

5.ImT Solid persisting and-also not falling.

6.ImT Venturing and-also persisting.

9.ImT Persisting and-also Ground.

11.ImT Inside persisting and-also outside yielding.

13.ImT Pattern brightening uses persisting.

14.ImT One's actualizing-tao: solid persisting and-also pattern brightening.

25.ImT Stirring-up and-also persisting.

26.ImT Solid persisting: staunch substance, resplendent shining.

26.ImT Ability stopping persisting.

43.ImT Persisting and-also stimulating.

Pervade, T'AI: spread and reach everywhere, permeate, diffuse; communicate; extensive, abundant, prosperous; smooth, slippery; extreme, extravagant, prodigal. The ideogram: person in water, connected to the universal medium.

Image of Hexagram 11 and occurs throughout its texts.

Petrify, SHIH: become stone or stony; rocks, stony land; objects made of stone; firm, decided; a barren womb.

16.2a Chain-mail tending-towards petrification:

47.3a Confined, tending-towards petrification.

Pheasant, CHIH: clever, beautiful bird associated with the trigram Radiance, LI; also: embrasures on ramparts and forts; arrange, put in order.

50.3a Pheasant juice not taken-in.

56.5a Shooting a pheasant.

Pig, SHIH: all swine; sign of wealth and good fortune; associated with the Streaming Moment.

26.5a A gelded pig's tusks.

38.6a Visualizing pigs bearing mire.

44.1a Ruining the pig, conforming: hoof dragging.

Pillar, HUAN: post or tablet marking a grave.

3.1a Stone pillar.

3.1b Although a stone pillar, purpose moving correctly indeed.

Pitcher, P'ING: clay jug or vase.

48.Im/ImT Ruining one's pitcher.

Pitfall, HSIUNG: leads away from the experience of meaning; stuck and exposed to danger, unable to take in the situation; flow of life and spirit is blocked; unfortunate, baleful; keyword.

3.5a The great, Trial: pitfall.

6.Im Centering significant. Completing: pitfall.

6.ImT Completing: pitfall.

7.1a Obstructing virtue: pitfall.

7.1b Letting-go ordinance: pitfall indeed.

7.3a Pitfall.

7.5a Trial: pitfall.

8.Im/ImT Afterwards, husbanding: pitfall.

8.6a Pitfall.

9.6a/b A chün tzu chastising: pitfall.

10.3a/b Snapping-at people: pitfall.

16.1a Pitfall.

16.1b Purpose exhausted, pitfall indeed.

17.4a Following possessing catching. Trial: pitfall.

17.4b One's righteousness: pitfall indeed.

19.Im/ImT Culminating tending-towards the eighth moon: possessing a pitfall.

21.6a Pitfall.

23.1a,2a Discarding the Trial: pitfall.

23.4a Pitfall.

24.6a/b Deluding Returning. Pitfall.

24.6a Using one's city chief: pitfall.

27.1a Pitfall.

27.2a Jaws chastising: pitfall.

27.2b Six at-second, chastising: pitfall.

27.3a Rejecting Jaws. Trial: pitfall.

28.3a/b The ridgepole buckling. Pitfall.

28.6a Exceeding wading submerges the peak. Pitfall.

28.6b Exceeding wading's pitfall.

29.1a Pitfall.

29.1b Letting-go tao: pitfall indeed.

29.6a Three year's-time, not acquiring. Pitfall.

29.6b Pitfall: three year's-time indeed.

30.3a By-consequence great old-age's lamenting. Pitfall.

31.2a Pitfall. Residing significant.

31.2b Although a pitfall, residing significant.

32.1a Diving Persevering, Trial: pitfall.
32.1b Diving Persevering's pitfall.
32.5a The husband, the son: pitfall.
32.5b Adhering-to the wife: pitfall indeed.
32.6a Rousing Persevering: pitfall.
34.1a Chastising: pitfall, possessing
conformity.
41.2a Chastising: pitfall.
42.3a/b Augmenting's availing-of pitfall
affairs.
42.6a Pitfall.
43.3a Possessing a pitfall.
43.6a Completing: possessing a pitfall.
43.6b Without crying-out's pitfall.
44.1a Visualizing: pitfall.
44.4a Rising-up: pitfall.
44.4b Without fish's pitfall.
47.2a Chastising: pitfall, without fault.
47.3a Pitfall.
48. Im Ruining one's pitcher: Pitfall.
48. ImT That uses a pitfall indeed.
49.3a Chastising: pitfall, Trial: adversity.
49.6a Chastising: pitfall.
50.4a Its form soiled. Pitfall.
51.6a Chastising: pitfall.
51.6b Although a pitfall, without fault.
53.3a Pitfall.
54. Im Converting Maidenhood, chastising:
pitfall.
54. ImT Chastising: pitfall.
55.6a Pitfall.
56.6a Pitfall.
57.6a Trial: pitfall.
57.6b Correcting: reaching a pitfall indeed.
58.3a/b Coming Opening: pitfall.
60.2a Pitfall.
60.2b Not issuing-forth-from the gate
chambers, pitfall.
60.6a/b Bitter Articulating, Trial: pitfall.
61.6a Trial: pitfall.
62.1a/b Flying bird: using a pitfall.
62.3a Pitfall.
62.3b Wherefore a pitfall thus indeed.
62.6a Pitfall.
64.3a/b Not-yet Fording, chastising: pitfall.

Place, SO: where something belongs or comes
from; residence, dwelling; habitual focus or
object. See also: **Resting-place**
6.1a/b Not a perpetual place, affairs.

8.S Crowds necessarily possess a place to
Group.
8.6b Without a place to complete indeed.
9.S Grouping necessarily possesses a place to
Accumulate.
9.6b Possessing a place to doubt indeed.
21.S Permitting Viewing and-also afterwards
possessing a place to unite.
23.6b Commoners: the place to carry indeed.
27. ImT Viewing one's place to nourish indeed.
30.S Falling necessarily possesses a place to
congregate.
30.4b Without a place to tolerate indeed.
31.S Therefore afterwards the codes
righteously possessing a place to polish.
31. ImT Viewing one's place to influence.
31.3b A place to hold-on-to the below indeed.
32. ImT Viewing one's place to Persevere.
32.3b Without a place to tolerate indeed.
33.S Beings not permitted to use lasting
residing-in their place.
33.6b Without a place to doubt indeed.
36.S Advancing necessarily possessing a place:
injuring.
40. Im Without a place to go:
41.S Delaying necessarily possesses a place to
let-go.
43. ImT The place to honor thereupon
exhausted indeed.
45. ImT Actually viewing one's place to
assemble.
46.3b Without a place to doubt indeed.
47. ImT Confining and-also not letting-go
one's place: Growing.
48.AE The Well: residing-in one's place and-
also shifting.
50.2b Considering places it indeed.
52. ImT Stopping: one's place indeed.
53.5b Acquiring the place desired indeed.
54.S Advancing necessarily possessing a place
to Convert.
54. ImT A place to Convert Maidenhood
indeed.
55.S Acquiring one's place to Convert implies
necessarily the great.
56.1a Splitting-off one's place, grasping
calamity.
57.S Sojourning and-also lacking a place to
tolerate.
59.4a In-no-way hiding, a place to ponder.

63.4b Possessing a place to doubt indeed.

Plain-silk, PAI: unbleached, undyed silk.

22.5a Rolled plain-silk: little, little.

Plan, MOU: plot, ponder, deliberate; project, device, stratagem.

6.ST A chün tzu uses arousing affairs to plan beginning.

Platter, KUEI: wood or bamboo plate; sacrificial utensil.

29.4a/b A cup, liquor, a platter added.

41. Im/ImT Two platters permit availing-of presenting.

41. ImT Two platters corresponding possess the season.

Plead, SU: defend or prosecute a case in court; enter a plea; statement of grievance.

10.4a/b Pleading, pleading: completing significant.

Plow-land, YÜ: newly opened fields, after two or three years plowing.

25.2a Not tilling the crop. Not clearing the plow-land.

Poison, TU: noxious, malignant, hurtful, destructive; despise.

7.ImT Using the latter poisons Below Heaven and-also the commoners adhering-to it.

21.3a Gnawing seasoned meat. Meeting poison.

21.3b Meeting poison.

Polarize, K'UEI: separate, oppose; contrary, mutually exclusive; distant from, absent, remote; animosity, anger; astronomical or polar opposition: the ends of an axis, 180 degrees apart.

Image of Hexagram 38 and occurs throughout its texts.

37.CD Polarizing: outside indeed.

Polish, TS'O: file away imperfections; wash or plate with gold; confused, in disorder, mixed. The ideogram: metal and old, clearing away accumulated disorder.

30.1a Treading, polishing therefore.

30.1b Treading, polishing it respectfully.

31.S Therefore afterwards the codes righteously possessing a place to polish.

Ponder, SSU: reflect, consider, remember; deep thought; desire, wish. The ideogram: heart and field, the heart's concerns.

19.ST A chün tzu uses teaching to ponder without exhausting.

31.4a Partnering adheres-to simply pondering.

52.ST A chün tzu uses pondering not to issue-forth-from his situation.

59.4a In-no-way hiding, a place to ponder.

63.ST A chün tzu uses pondering distress and-also providing-for defending-against it.

Position, CHAI: dwelling site, good situation in life; consolidate, reside, fill an office.

23.ST Using munificence above to quiet the position below.

Possess, YU: in possession of, have, own; opposite of lack, WU. See also: **Possessing conformity** and **Possessing directed going**

This term occurs throughout the hexagram texts and in the Image of Hexagram 14.

Possessing conformity, YU FU: inner and outer are in accord; confidence of the spirits has been captured; sincere, truthful; proper to take action.

5.Im/ImT Attending, possessing conformity.

6.Im/ImT Arguing, possessing conformity.

8.1a Possessing conformity, Grouping it.

8.1a Possessing conformity, overfilling the jar.

9.4a Possessing conformity.

9.4b Possessing conformity, awe issuing-forth.

9.5a/b Possessing conformity, binding thus.

17.4a Possessing conformity, locating-in tao uses brightening.

17.4b Possessing conformity located-in tao.

20. Im/ImT Possessing conformity, like a presence.

29. Im Possessing conformity.

34.1a Chastising: pitfall, possessing conformity.

37.6a Possessing conformity, impressing thus.

40.5a Possessing conformity, tending-towards Small People.

41. Im Diminishing, possessing conformity.

41. ImT Diminishing and-also possessing conformity.

42.3a Possessing conformity, center moving.

42.5a/b Possessing conformity, a benevolent heart.

42.5a Possessing conformity, benevolence: my actualizing-tao.

45.1a Possessing conformity, not completing.

48.6a Possessing conformity, Spring significant.

49.3a Possessing conformity.

49.4a Repenting extinguished, possessing conformity.

49.5a Not-yet an augury, possessing conformity.

55.2a/b Possessing conformity, like shooting-forth.

61.5a/b Possessing conformity, binding thus.

64.5a Possessing conformity significant.

64.6a Possessing conformity: tending-towards drinking liquor.

64.6a Possessing conformity: letting-go that.

Possessing directed going, YU YU WANG: imposing a direction on the flow of time from present to past; have a specific goal or purpose.

2.Im A chün tzu possesses directed going.

3.Im No availing-of possessing directed going.

14.2a Possessing directed going. Without fault.

22. Im The small, Harvesting: possessing directed going.

22. ImT The anterior small, Harvesting: possessing directed going.

23. Im Stripping not Harvesting: possessing directed going.

23. ImT Not Harvesting: possessing directed going.

24. Im/ImT Harvesting: possessing directed going.

25. Im/ImT Not Harvesting: possessing directed going.

25.2a By-consequence, Harvesting: possessing directed going.

26.3a/b Harvesting: possessing directed going.

28. Im/ImT Harvesting: possessing directed going.

32. Im/ImT Harvesting: possessing directed going.

33.1a No availing-of possessing directed going.

36.1a Possessing directed going.

40. Im Possessing directed going:

40. ImT Possessing directed going, daybreak significant.

41. Im/ImT Harvesting: possessing directed going.

41.6a Harvesting: possessing directed going.

42. Im Augmenting, Harvesting: possessing directed going.

42. ImT Harvesting: possessing directed going.

43. Im/ImT Harvesting: possessing directed going.

44.1a Possessing directed going.

45. Im/ImT Harvesting: possessing directed going.

57. Im/ImT Harvesting: possessing directed going.

Potency, SHIH: power, influence, strength; authority, dignity; virility. The ideogram: strength and skill.

2.ST Earth potency: Field.

Pouched belt, P'AN TAI: sash that serves as a purse; money-belt.

6.6a Maybe bestowing's pouched belt.

Praise, YÜ: admire and approve; magnify, eulogize; flatter. The ideogram: words and give, offering words.

2.4a Without fault, without praise.

18.5a Availing-of praise.

18.5b Managing the father availing-of praise.

28.5a Without fault, without praise.

39.1a/b Going Limping, coming praise.

55.5a Possessing reward, praise significant.

56.5a/b Completing uses praising fate.

Precaution, YÜ: provide against, preventive measures; anxious, vigilant, ready; preoccupied with, think about, expect; mishap, accident.

3.3a Approaching stag, lacking precaution.

3.3b Approaching stag, without precaution.

45.ST [A chün tzu uses] warning, not precautions.

61.1a Precaution significant.

61.1b The initial nine, precaution significant.

Precede, CH'IEN: come before in time and thus in value; anterior, former, ancient; lead forward.

5.ImT Venturing located-in precedence indeed.

8.5a Letting-go the preceding wildfowl.

8.5b Letting-go the preceding wildfowl indeed.

26.ST A chün tzu uses the numerous recorded preceding words going to move.

39. ImT Venturing located-in precedence indeed.

43.1a Invigorating tending-towards the preceding foot.

Predecessor, K'AO: deceased ancestor, especially the grandfather; the ancients; aged, long-lived; consult, verify. The ideogram: old and ingenious, the old wise man.

10.6a Observing Treading, predecessors auspicious.

16.ST Using equaling the grandfather predecessors.

18.1a Predecessors without fault.

18.1b Intention receiving the predecessors indeed.

24.5b Centering originating-from the predecessor indeed.

Pregnant, JEN: carrying a child.

53.3a/b The wife pregnant, not nurturing.

53.5a The wife, three year's-time not pregnant.

Prepare, PEI: make ready, provide for; sufficient.

14.5b Versatility and-also without preparing indeed.

Preponderance, P'ENG: forceful, dominant; overbearing, encroaching. The ideogram: drum beats, dominating sound.

14.4a In-no-way one's preponderance.

14.4b In-no-way one's preponderance. Without fault.

Presence, YUNG: noble bearing; prestige, dignity; imposing; haughty, conceited; lit.: a large head.

20. Im/ImT Possessing conformity, like a presence.

Present(-to), HSIANG: present in sacrifice, offer with thanks, give to the gods or a superior; confer dignity on.

41. Im/ImT Two platters permit availing-of presenting.

42.2a Kinghood availing-of presenting tending-towards the supreme, significant.

45. ImT Involving reverence presenting indeed.

47.2a Harvesting: availing-of presenting oblations.

50. ImT The all-wise person Growing uses presenting-to the Supreme Above.

59.ST The Earlier Kings used presenting tending-towards the supreme to establish the temples.

Primary, T'UNG: origin, beginning; first of a class; clue, hint; whole, general.

1.ImT Thereupon primary heaven.

Prince, KUNG: nobles acting as ministers of state in the capital; governing from the center rather than active in daily life; contrasts with feudatory, HOU, governors of the provinces. See also: **Crown-prince**

14.3a/b A prince availing-of Growing, tending-towards heavenly sonhood.

29. ImT The kingly prince sets-up venturing used to guard his city.

30.5b Radiance: the kingly prince indeed.

40.6a A prince avails-of shooting a hawk, tending-towards the high rampart's above.

40.6b A prince avails-of shooting a hawk.

42.3a Notifying the prince, availing-of the scepter.

42.4a/b Notifying the prince, adhering.

50.4a/b Overthrowing a princely stew.

62.5a A prince, a string-arrow grasping another located-in

Procrastinate, CH'IH: delay, act at leisure, retard; slow, late.

16.3a Procrastinating possesses repenting.

54.4a Procrastinating Converting possesses the season.

Profusion, P'EI: spread and flow in many directions, like rain or rivers; enlarge; irrigate; luxuriant water plants.

55.3a/b Abounding: one's profusion.

Proper, YI: reasonable of itself; fit and right, harmonious; ought, should.

3.ImT Proper to instal feudatories and-also not to soothe.

11.ST [The crown-prince uses] bracing to mutualize Heaven[and]Earth's propriety.

19.5a/b A Great Chief's propriety.

39.1b Proper to await indeed.

55. Im/ImT No grief. Properly sun centering.

55. ImT Properly illuminating Below Heaven indeed.

62. Im/ImT Above not proper, below proper.

Property, TS'AI: possessions, goods, substance, wealth. The ideogram: pearl and value.

11.ST The crown-prince uses property to accomplish Heaven[and]Earth's tao.

60. ImT Not injuring property.

Propriety, see: **Proper**

Proscribe, CHU: exclude, reject by proclamation; denounce, forbid; reprove, seek as a criminal; condemn to death; clear away.

35/36.CD Brightness Hiding: proscribed indeed.

Prospering, CHIN: grow and flourish as young plants in the sun; increase, progress, permeate, impregnate; attached to. The ideogram: sun and reaching, the daylight world.

Image of Hexagram 35 and occurs throughout its texts.

Protect, PAO: guard, defend, keep safe; secure.
1.ImT Protection uniting the great harmony.
19.ST [A chün tzu uses] tolerating to protect the commoners without delimiting.
53.3b Yielding mutualizes protection indeed.

Protract, YIN: draw out, prolong; carried on; lead on, to bring forward; lit.: drawing a bow.
45.2a/b Protracting significant, without fault.
58.6a Protracting Opening.
58.6b Six above, protracting Opening.

Provide-for/provision, YÜ: ready, prepared for; pre-arrange, take precaution, think beforehand; satisfied, contented, at ease. The ideogram: sonhood and elephant, careful, reverent and very strong.
Image of Hexagram 16 and occurs throughout its texts.
15.CD Provision: indolence indeed.
17.S Providing-for necessarily possesses Following.
63.ST A chün tzu uses pondering distress and-also providing-for defending-against it.

Psyche, LING: life force, vital energy; spirit of a being; magical action or influence.
27.1a Stowing-away simply the psyche tortoise.

Pull-back, YI: pull or drag something towards you; drag behind, take by the hand; leave traces.
38.3a/b Visualizing the cart pulled-back.
63.1a/b Pulling-back one's wheels.
64.2a Pulling-back one's wheels.

Punish, HSING: legal punishment; physical penalties for severe criminal offenses; whip, torture, behead.
4.1a/b Harvesting: availing-of punishing people.
16. ImT By-consequence punishing flogging purifies and-also the commoners submit.
55.ST A chün tzu uses severing litigating to involve punishing.
56.ST A chün tzu uses brightening consideration to avail-of punishing and-also not to detain litigating.

Purify, CH'ING: clean a water course; limpid, unsullied; right principles.
16. ImT By-consequence punishing flogging purifies and-also the commoners submit.

Purpose, CHIH: focus of mind and heart; will, inclination, resolve. The ideogram: heart and scholar, high inner resolve, or heart and go, inner determination.

3.1b Although a stone pillar, purpose moving correctly indeed.
4.ImT Purpose corresponding indeed.
9.ImT Solid centering and-also purpose moving.
9.4b Uniting purposes above indeed.
10.ST [A chün tzu uses] setting-right the commoners, the purpose.
10.3b Purpose solid indeed.
10.4b Purpose moving indeed.
11. ImT Above[and]Below mingling and-also one's purpose concording indeed.
11.1b Purpose located outside indeed.
12.1b Purpose located-in a chief indeed.
12.4b Purpose moving indeed.
13. ImT Verily a chün tzu activating enables interpenetrating Below Heaven's purpose.
13.6b Purpose not-yet acquired indeed.
14.5b Trustworthiness uses shooting-forth purpose indeed.
15.6b Purpose not-yet acquired indeed.
16. ImT Providing-for. Solid corresponding and-also purpose moving.
16.1b Purpose exhausted, pitfall indeed.
16.4b Purpose: the great moving indeed.
17.3b Below, purpose stowed-away indeed.
18.6b Purpose permitted by-consequence indeed.
19.1b Purpose moving, correcting indeed.
19.6b Purpose located inside indeed.
20.6b Purpose not-yet evened indeed.
22.6b Acquiring purpose above indeed.
25.1b Acquiring purpose indeed.
26.3b Uniting purposes above indeed.
31.1b Purpose located outside indeed.
31.3b Purpose located-in following people.
31.5b Purpose, the tips indeed.
33.2b Firm purpose indeed.
33.5b Using correcting the purpose indeed.
35.3b Crowds: sincerity's purpose.
36. ImT Inside heaviness and-also enabling correcting one's purpose.
36.3b The South: hounding's purpose.
37.1b Purpose not-yet transformed indeed.
38. ImT Their purposes not concording: moving.
38. ImT Man, Woman, Polarizing and-also their purposes interpenetrating indeed.
38.4b Purpose moving indeed.
39.6b Purpose located inside indeed.

41.1b Honoring uniting purposes indeed.
41.2b Centering using activating purposes indeed.
41.6b The great acquiring purpose indeed.
42.4b Using Augmenting purpose indeed.
42.5b The great acquiring purpose indeed.
44.5b Purpose, not stowing-away fate indeed.
45.1b One's purpose disarrayed indeed.
45.5b Purpose not-yet shining indeed.
46.ImT Purpose moving indeed.
46.1b Uniting purposes above indeed.
46.5b The great acquiring the purpose indeed.
47.ST A chün tzu uses involving fate to release purpose.
47.4b Purpose located below indeed.
47.5b Purpose not-yet acquired indeed.
49.ImT Their purposes not mutually acquired.
49.4b Trustworthy purpose indeed.
54.4b Overrunning the term's purpose.
55.2b Trustworthiness using shooting-forth purpose indeed.
56.1b Purpose exhausted, calamity indeed.
57.ImT Solid Ground reaching-to centering correcting and-also purpose moving.
57.1b Purpose doubted indeed.
57.1b Purpose regulated indeed.
57.3b Purpose exhausted indeed.
58.2b Trustworthy purpose indeed.
59.3b Purpose located outside indeed.
61.1b Purpose not-yet transformed indeed.
64.4b Purpose moving indeed.

Pursue, CHU: chase, follow closely, press hard; expel, drive out. The ideogram: pig (wealth) and go, chasing fortune.
26.3a A fine horse, pursuing.
27.4a His appetites: pursuing, pursuing.
38.1a Losing the horse, no pursuit, originating-from returning.
51.2a No pursuit.
63.2a No pursuit.

Put-off, HSIA: delay; put at a distance; far away, remote in time.
11.2a Not putting-off abandoning.

Question, WEN: ask, inquire about, examine; clear up doubts; convict and sentence.
42.5a No question, Spring significant.
42.5b Actually no questioning it.

Quiet, AN: peaceful, still, settled; calm, tranquilize. The ideogram: woman under a roof, a tranquil home.
2.Im/ImT Quiet Trial significant.
6.4a Denying quiet Trial. Significant.
6.4b Denying quiet Trial.
11.S Therefore afterwards quieting.
13.3b Quieting movement indeed.
23.ST Using munificence above to quiet the position below.
32.4b Quietly acquiring the wildfowl indeed.
45.6b The above not-yet quiet indeed.
60.4a/b Quiet Articulating Growing.

Quit, CHAN: stop, change because unsuccessful; unable to advance.
3.2a Sprouting thus, quitting thus.

Radiance, LI: glowing light, spreading in all directions; light-giving, discriminating, articulating; divide and arrange in order; the power of consciousness. The ideogram: bird and weird, the magical fire-bird with brilliant plumage.
Image of Hexagram 30 and occurs throughout its texts.
12.4a Cultivating radiant satisfaction.
29.CD Above Radiance and-also below Gorge indeed.
53.3b Radiance flocking demons indeed.
59.S Dispersing implies Radiance indeed.
59/60.CD Dispersing: radiance indeed.
60.S Beings not permitted to use completing Radiance.
62.6a Flying bird radiating it.

Rafter, CHÜEH: roof beams; flat branches.
53.4a/b Maybe acquiring one's rafter.

Rain, YÜ: all precipitation; sudden showers, fast and furious; associated with the trigram Gorge, K'AN, and the Streaming Moment. See also:
Thunder[and]Rain
1.ImT Clouds moving, rain spreading-out.
9.Im/ImT Shrouding clouds, not raining.
9.6a/b Already rain, already abiding.
38.6a Going meeting rain, by-consequence significant.
38.6b Meeting rain's significance.
40.ST Thunder, Rain, arousing.
43.3a Solitary going, meeting rain.
50.3a On-all-sides rain lessens repenting.
62.5a/b Shrouding clouds, not raining.

Rampart, YUNG: defensive wall; bulwark, redoubt.

13.4a/b Riding one's rampart.

40.6a A prince avails-of shooting a hawk, tending-towards the high rampart's above.

Reach(-to), HU: arrive at a goal; reach toward and achieve; connect; contrasts with tend-towards, YU.

This term occurs throughout the hexagram texts.

Reap, TO: harvest, collect, gather up, pick; arrange. The ideogram: hand and join, taking in both hands.

6.2b Distress culminating, reaping indeed.

Rebel, PEI: go against nature or usage; insubordinate; perverse, unreasonable.

27.3b Tao, the great rebelling indeed.

40.6b Using Taking-apart rebelling indeed.

50.1b Not-yet rebelling indeed.

Receive, CH'ENG: receive gifts or commands from superiors or customers; take in hand; catch falling water. The ideogram: accepting a seal of office.

2.ImT Thereupon yielding receiving heaven.

7.2b Receiving heavenly favor indeed.

7.6a Disclosing the city, receiving a dwelling.

12.2a Enwrapping receiving.

18.1b Intention receiving the predecessors indeed.

18.5b Receiving uses actualizing-tao indeed.

32.3a Maybe receiving's embarrassing.

54.1b Mutualizing receiving indeed.

54.6a A woman receiving a basket without substance.

54.6b Receiving an empty basket indeed.

60.4b Receiving tao above indeed.

Recess, TAN: pit within a large cave, entered from the side.

29.1a,3a Entering tending-towards the Gorge, the recess.

Reckon, SHU: count, find the number; give out; sum up, discriminate; also: account, bill, list; fate, destiny; many cares, dilemma. See also: **Time-reckoning**

60.ST A chün tzu uses paring to reckon the measures.

Recline, CHEN: lean back or on; soften, relax; head rest, back support; stake to tie cattle.

29.3a Venturing moreover reclining.

Record, SHIH: write down, inscribe; memorize; learn; recognize; annals, monuments.

26.ST A chün tzu uses the numerous recorded preceding words going to move.

Recur, HSÜAN: return to the same point; orbit, revolve; spiral.

10.6a One's recurring Spring significant.

Redouble, CH'UNG: repeat, reiterate, add to; build up by layers.

16.AE Redoubling gates, smiting clappers.

29. ImT Redoubling venturing indeed.

30. ImT Redoubling brightness uses congregating to reach-to correcting.

57. ImT Redoubling Ground uses distributing fate.

Reduce, P'OU: diminish in number; collect in fewer, larger groups.

15.ST A chün tzu uses reducing the numerous to augment the few.

Reeds, KUAN: marsh and swamp plants, rushes.

43.5a Reeds, highlands: Parting, Parting.

Reflect, CHIEH: receive and pass on; follow in office; inherit, as father and son; associate with. The ideogram: hand and concubine, passed on through natural, not legal, ways.

35. Im Day-time sun three-times reflected.

35. ImT Day-time sun three-times reflected indeed.

Regulate, CHIH: govern well, ensure prosperity; remedy disorder, heal; someone fit to govern land, house and heart.

18. ImT And-also Below Heaven regulated indeed.

49.ST A chün tzu uses regulating time-reckoning to brighten the seasons.

57.1b Purpose regulated indeed.

Reiterate, CHIEN: repeat, duplicate; successive.

29.ST Streams reiterating culminating. Repeating Gorge.

51.ST Reiterated thunder.

Reject, FU: push away, expel, brush off; oppose, contradict; perverse, proud. The ideogram: hand and do not, pushing something away.

27.2a Rejecting the canons, tending-towards the hill-top.

27.3a Rejecting Jaws. Trial: pitfall.

27.5a Rejecting the canons.

Rejoice(-in), HSI: feel and give joy; delight, exult; cheerful, merry. The ideogram: joy (music) and mouth, expressing joy.

12.6a Beforehand Obstruction, afterwards rejoicing.

18.S Using rejoicing Following people implies necessarily possessing affairs.

22.5b Possessing rejoicing indeed.

25.5a No medicinal-herbs, possessing rejoicing.

26.4b Possessing rejoicing indeed.

39.3b Inside rejoicing-in it indeed.

41.4a Commissioning swiftly possesses rejoicing.

41.4b Truly permitting rejoicing indeed.

46.2b Possessing rejoicing indeed.

58.4a Chain-mail afflicting: possessing rejoicing.

58.4b Nine at-fourth's rejoicing.

Release, SUI: loose, let go, free; unhindered, in accord; follow, spread out, progress; penetrate, invade. The ideogram: go and follow your wishes, unimpeded movement.

34.6a/b Not enabling withdrawing, not enabling releasing.

37.2a Without direction, releasing.

47.ST A chün tzu uses involving fate to release purpose.

51.4a/b Shake: releasing the bog.

Relinquish, HSIU: let go of, stop temporarily, rest; resign, release; act gently; enjoy; relaxed. The ideogram: person leaning on a tree.

12.5a Relinquishing Obstruction.

14.ST [A chün tzu uses] yielding-to heaven to relinquish fate.

24.2a Relinquishing Returning.

24.2b Relinquishing Returning's significance.

Renew, HSIN: restore, improve, make or get better; new, fresh; the best, the latest.

26. ImT A day renewing one's actualizing-tao.

49/50.CD The Vessel: grasping renewal indeed.

Renovate, HSIU: repair, mend, clean, adorn; adjust, regulate; cultivate, practice, acquire skills.

39.ST A chün tzu uses reversing individuality to renovate actualizing-tao.

Repeat, HSI: series of similar acts; practice, rehearse; familiar with, skilled. The ideogram: two wings and a cap, thought carried by repeated movements.

2.2a/b Not repeating: without not Harvesting.

29. Im Repeating Gorge.

29.ST Streams reiterating culminating. Repeating Gorge.

29.ST [A chün tzu uses] repeating to teach affairs.

29. ImT,1a Repeating Gorge.

29.1b Repeating Gorge, entering Gorge.

58.ST A chün tzu uses partnering friends to explicate repeating.

Repent, HUI: dissatisfaction with past conduct causing a change of heart; proceeds from abashment, LIN, shame and confusion at having lost the right way. See also: **Repenting extinguished** and **Without repenting**

1.6a/b Overbearing dragon possesses repenting.

16.3a Skeptical Providing-for, repenting.

16.3a Procrastinating possesses repenting.

16.3b Skeptical Providing-for possesses repenting.

18.3a The small possesses repenting.

37.3a Repenting, adversity significant.

47.6a/b Stirring-up repenting possesses repenting.

50.3a On-all-sides rain lessens repenting.

Repenting extinguished, HUI WANG: previous troubles and consequent remorse will disappear.

31.4a/b Trial: significant, repenting extinguished.

32.2a Repenting extinguished.

32.2b Nine at-second, repenting extinguished.

34.4a Repenting extinguished.

35.3a Crowds, sincerity, repenting extinguished.

35.5a Repenting extinguished.

37.1a Repenting extinguished.

38.1a,5a Repenting extinguished.

43.4a Hauling-along the goat, repenting extinguished.

45.5a Repenting extinguished.

49. Im Repenting extinguished.

49. ImT One's repenting thereupon extinguished.

49.4a Repenting extinguished, possessing conformity.

52.5a Repenting extinguished.

57.4a Repenting extinguished.

57.5a Trial: significant, repenting extinguished.

58.2a Repenting extinguished.

59.2a Repenting extinguished.

60.6a Repenting extinguished.

64.4a/b Trial: significant, repenting
extinguished.

Repose, YEN: rest, leisure, peace of mind;
banquet, feast. The ideogram: shelter and rest, a
wayside inn.

5.ST A chün tzu uses drinking[and]taking-in
to repose delighting.

17.ST A chün tzu uses turning-to darkening
to enter a reposing pause.

Rescue, CHENG: aid, deliver from trouble; pull
out, raise up, lift. The ideogram: hand and aid, a
helping hand.

36.2a Availing-of a rescuing horse,
invigorating significant.

52.2a/b Not rescuing one's following.

59.1a Availing-of a rescuing horse,
invigorating significant.

Reside(-in), CHÜ: dwell, live in, stay; sit down,
fill an office; settled parts of a country. The
ideogram: body and seat.

3/4.CD Sprouting: visualizing and-also not
letting-go one's residing.

3.1a Harvesting: residing-in Trial.

17.3a Harvesting: residing-in Trial.

27.5a/b Residing-in Trial significant.

31.2a Pitfall. Residing significant.

31.2b Although a pitfall, residing significant.

33.S Beings not permitted to use lasting
residing-in their place.

38. ImT Two women concording: residing.

43.ST [A chün tzu uses] residing-in
actualizing-tao, by-consequence keeping-
aloof.

48.AE The Well: residing-in one's place and-
also shifting.

49. ImT Two women concording, residing.

49.6a Residing-in Trial significant.

53.ST A chün tzu uses residing-in eminent
actualizing-tao to improve the vulgar.

56.S Exhausting the great implies necessarily
letting-go one's residing.

59.5a/b Kinghood residing, without fault.

60.5b Residing-in the situation: centering
indeed.

64.ST A chün tzu uses considering to mark-
off the beings residing on-all-sides.

Resist, YÜ: withstand, oppose; bring to an end;
prevent. The ideogram: rule and worship,
imposing ethical or religious limits.

4.6a Harvesting: resisting outlawry.

4.6b Harvesting: availing-of resisting outlawry.

53.3a Harvesting: resisting outlawry.

53.3b Harvesting: availing-of resisting
outlawry.

Respect(ful), CHING: reverent, attentive; stand
in awe of, honor; inner respect; contrasts with
courtesy, KUNG, good manners. The ideogram:
teacher's rod taming speech and attitude. See
also: **With-respect-to**

5.3b Respectful consideration, not destroying
indeed.

5.6a/b Respecting them, completing
significant.

6.6b Truly not standing respectfully indeed.

30.1a Respecting it.

30.1b Treading, polishing it respectfully.

Respectable, CHANG: worthy of respect;
standard by which others are measured.

7.Im Respectable people significant.

17.2a Letting-go the respectable husband.

17.3a/b Tied-to the respectable husband.

Resplendent, HUI: glorious, sun-like, refulgent;
brighten.

26. ImT Solid persisting: staunch substance,
resplendent shining.

Rest(ing-place), TZ'U: camp, inn, shed; halting-
place, breathing-spell; put in consecutive order.
The ideogram: two and breath, pausing to breathe.

7.4a Legions: the left resting.

7.4b The left resting, without fault.

43.4a/b One moves the resting-place
moreover.

44.3a/b One moves the resting-place
moreover.

56.2a Sojourning: approaching a resting-place.

56.3a/b Sojourning: burning one's resting-
place.

Restrict, YEN: keep in order, maintain discipline;
subjugate, repress; narrow, obedient.

32.AE Persevering: motley and-also not
restricting.

Retire(-from), TUN: withdraw; run away, flee;
conceal yourself, become obscure, invisible;
secluded, non-social. The ideogram: walk and
swine (wealth and luck), satisfaction through
walking away.

Image of Hexagram 33 and occurs throughout
its texts.

28.ST [A chün tzu uses] retiring-from the age
without melancholy.

34.S Beings not permitted to use completing Retiring.

Retrace, YÜAN: repeat, another; trace to the source. The ideogram: pure water at its source.

  8.Im/ImT Retracing the oracle-consulting: Spring, perpetual Trial.

Return, FU: go back, turn back to the starting point; recur, reappear, come again; restore, recover, retrace; an earlier time or place. The ideogram: step and retrace a path.

  Image of Hexagram 24 and occurs throughout its texts.

  1.3b Reversing returning tao indeed.

  6.4a/b Returning, approaching fate.

  9.1a/b Returning originating-from tao.

  9.2a Hauling-along, returning. Significant.

  9.2b Hauling-along, returning, locating-in the center.

  11.3a/b Without going, not returning.

  11.6a/b The bulwark returned tending-towards the moat.

  23.CD Returning: reversing indeed.

  25.S Actually Returning, by-consequence not Embroiling.

  38.S Dwelling tao exhausted, necessarily returning.

  38.1a Losing the horse, no pursuit, originating-from returning.

  40. Im/ImT One's coming return significant.

  53.3a/b The husband chastised, not returning.

Reverence, HSIAO: filial duty, respect and obedience owed to elders; loyalty, dignity, confidence, self-respect; brave in battle; period of mourning for deceased parents.

  45. ImT Involving reverence presenting indeed.

Reverse, FAN: turn and move in the opposite direction; turn around or upside down (180 degrees); change to the opposite position; contrary.

  1.3b Reversing returning tao indeed.

  3.2b Reversing rules indeed.

  9.3a/b Husband, consort, reversing eyes.

  11/12.CD Obstructing, Pervading: reversing one's sorting indeed.

  13.4b By-consequence confining and-also reversing by-consequence indeed.

  23/24.CD Returning: reversing indeed.

  24. Im Reversing Returning one's tao.

  24.S Above Stripping exhausted, below reversing.

24. ImT Returning, Growing. Solid reversing.

24. ImT Reversing Returning one's tao.

24.6b Reversing the chief: tao indeed.

37.S Injury with-respect-to the outside implies necessarily reversing with-respect-to Dwelling.

37.6b Reversing individuality's designating indeed.

39.ST A chün tzu uses reversing individuality to renovate actualizing-tao.

39.3a/b Going Limping, coming reversing.

48.S Confining reaching-to the above implies necessarily reversing the below.

54.3a Reversing Converting using the junior-sister.

Revive, SU: regain vital energy, courage or strength; bring to life, cheer up; relief; lit.: herb whose smell revives weary spirits.

  51.3a/b Shake: reviving, reviving.

Reward, CH'ING: gift given from gratitude or benevolence; favor from heaven; congratulate with gifts. The ideogram: heart, follow and deer (wealth), the heart expressed through gifts.

  2.ImT Thereupon completing possesses reward.

  10.6b The great possesses reward indeed.

  26.5b Possessing reward indeed.

  27.6b The great possessing reward indeed.

  35.5b Going possessing reward indeed.

  38.5b Going possessing reward indeed.

  42. ImT Centering correcting possessing reward.

  46. ImT Possessing reward indeed.

  47.2b Center possessing reward indeed.

  55.5a Possessing reward, praise significant.

  55.5b Possessing reward indeed.

  58.4b Possessing reward indeed.

Rich, FEI: fertile, abundant, fat; manure, fertilizer. See also: **Enrich**

  33.6a/b Rich Retiring, without not Harvesting.

Ride, CH'ENG: ride an animal or a chariot; have the upper hand, seize the right time; control strong power; overcome the nature of the other; supple opened line above a solid whole line.

  1.ImT The season riding six dragons used going-to-meet heaven.

  3.2a,4a,6a Riding a horse, arraying thus.

  3.2b Riding a solid indeed.

  13.4a/b Riding one's rampart.

16.5b Riding a solid indeed.
21.2b Riding a solid indeed.
22.1b Righteously nothing to ride indeed.
40.3a/b Bearing, moreover riding.
43. ImT Supple riding five solids indeed.
47.3b Riding a solid indeed.
51.2b Riding a solid indeed.
54. ImT Supple riding solid indeed.
59. ImT Riding wood possesses achievement indeed.
61. ImT Riding a wooden dug-out, emptiness indeed.

Ridgepole, TUNG: highest and key beam in a house; summit, crest.
28. Im Great Exceeding, the ridgepole sagging.
28. ImT The ridgepole sagging.
28.3a/b The ridgepole buckling. Pitfall.
28.4a/b The ridgepole crowning. Significant.

Right, YU: right side, right hand; noble, honorable; make things right. See also: **Set-right**
11.ST [The crown-prince] uses the left to right the commoners.
55.3a/b Severing one's right arm.

Righteous, YI: proper and just, meets the standards; things in their proper place; the heart that rules itself; upright, moral rule; contrasts with Harvest, LI, advantage or profit.
5.ImT Actually one's righteousness, not confining exhaustion.
9.1b One's righteousness significant indeed.
13.4b Righteously nothing controlling indeed.
16. ImT Actually Provision's season righteously great in-fact.
17. ImT Actually Following the season's righteous great in-fact.
17.4b One's righteousness: pitfall indeed.
19/20.CD Nearing Viewing's righteousness.
22.1b Righteously nothing to ride indeed.
24.3b Righteous, without fault indeed.
31.S Therefore afterwards the codes righteously possessing a place to polish.
32.5b The husband, the son: paring righteously.
33. ImT Actually Retiring's season righteously great in-fact.
36.1b Righteously not taking-in indeed.
37. ImT Heaven[and]Earth's great righteousness indeed.
40.1b Righteous, without fault indeed.

44. ImT Actually Coupling's season righteously great in-fact.
44.2b Righteously not extending-to guesting indeed.
48.AE The Well: using differentiating righteousness.
50.3b Letting-go its righteousness indeed.
53.1b Righteous, without fault indeed.
54. ImT Heaven[and]Earth's great righteousness indeed.
56. ImT Actually Sojourning's season righteously great in-fact.
56.3b One's righteousness lost indeed.
56.6b One's righteousness burning indeed.
63.1b Righteous, without fault indeed.

Rings, HSÜAN: handles or ears for carrying a tripod.
50.5a The Vessel: yellow ears, metallic rings.
50.6a The Vessel: jade rings.
50.6b Jade rings located above.

Ripe, SHIH: mature, full-grown; great, eminent.
23.6a The ripe fruit not taken-in.
39.6a/b Going Limping, coming ripening.

Rise, HSING: get up, grow, lift; begin, give rise to, construct; be promoted; flourishing, fashionable. The ideogram: lift, two hands and unite, lift with both hands.
13.3a/b Three year's-time not rising.
22.2b Associating-with the above, rising indeed.
42.AE Augmenting: using the rising Harvest.
54. ImT Heaven[and]Earth not mingling and-also the myriad beings not rising.

Rise-up, CH'I: stand up, lift; undertake, begin, originate.
7.S Arguing necessarily possesses crowds rising-up.
44.4a Rising-up: pitfall.
51/52.CD Shake: rising-up indeed.

River, CH'UAN: water flowing between banks; current, channel; associated with the Streaming Moment and the trigram Gorge, K'AN. See also: **Wading the Great River**
29. ImT Earth venturing, mountains, rivers, hill-tops, mounds indeed.

Rodent, see: **Bushy-tailed rodent**

Roll, SHU: gather into a bundle, bind together; restrain.
22.5a Rolled plain-silk: little, little.

Roof, WU: cover, shelter; house, room, cabin,

tent; stop or remain at.

55.6a/b Abounding: one's roof.

Root, PEN: origin, cause, source of nourishment; essential. The ideogram: tree with roots in earth.

    24.AE Returning: actualizing-tao's root indeed.

    28. ImT Roots, tips, fading indeed.

Rope, see: **Stranded ropes** and **Well-rope**

Rotten, LAN: corrupt, putrid, antiquated, worn out, dirty; a running sore; boil over.

    23/24.CD Stripping: rotten indeed.

Rouse, CHEN: stir up, excite, stimulate; issue forth; put in order. The ideogram: hand and shake, shaking things up. See also: **Arouse**

    18.ST A chün tzu uses rousing the commoners to nurture actualizing-tao.

    32.6a Rousing Persevering: pitfall.

    32.6b Rousing Persevering located-in the above.

Ruin, LEI: destroy, break, overturn; debilitated, meager, emaciated; entangled.

    34.3a Ruining his horns.

    34.4a/b The hedge broken-up, not ruined.

    44.1a Ruining the pig, conforming: hoof dragging.

    48. Im/ImT Ruining one's pitcher:

Rules, CH'ANG: unchanging principles; regular, constant, habitual; maintain laws and customs.

    2.ImT Afterwards yielding acquiring rules.

    3.2b Reversing rules indeed.

    5.1b Not-yet letting-go rules indeed.

    7.4b Not-yet letting-go the rules indeed.

    29.ST A chün tzu uses rules actualizing-tao to move.

    54.2b Not-yet transforming the rules indeed.

Ruminate, HSIANG: ponder and discuss; examine minutely, learn fully, watch over, pay attention to. The ideogram: word and sheep, ruminating on words.

    34.6b Not ruminating indeed.

Sacrifice, CHIEH: make offerings to gods and the dead; depend on, call on, borrow; lit.: straw mat used to hold offerings.

    28.1a/b A sacrifice availing-of white thatch-grass.

Sacrificial-victims, SHENG: the six sacrificial animals: horse, ox, lamb, cock, dog and pig.

    45. Im/ImT Availing-of the great: sacrificial-victims significant.

Sacrum, T'UN: lower back where it joins legs; buttocks, seat, lower spine.

    43.4a The sacrum without flesh.

    44.3a The sacrum without flesh.

    47.1a The sacrum Confined, tending-towards stump wood.

Sad, CH'I: unhappy, low in spirits, distressed; mourn, sorrow over; commiserate with.

    30.5a Issuing-forth tears like gushing. Sadness like lamenting.

Sag, NAO: yield, bend, distort, twist; disturbed, confused.

    28. Im Great Exceeding, the ridgepole sagging.

    28. ImT The ridgepole sagging.

    28.4b Not sagging, reaching-to the below indeed.

Sands, SHA: beach, sandbanks, shingle; gravel, pebbles; granulated. The ideogram: water and few, areas laid bare by receding water.

    5.2a/b Attending tending-towards sands.

Sash, FU: ceremonial belt of official which holds seal of office.

    47.2a Scarlet sashes on-all-sides coming.

    47.5a Confined, tending-towards a crimson sash.

Satiation, PAO: full, replete, satisfied; swollen, sated; gratified, flattered.

    53.2b Not sheer satiation indeed.

Satisfaction, CHIH: fulfilment, gratification, happy in realizing your aim; take pleasure in, fulfil a need.

    11.5a/b Using satisfaction, Spring significant.

    12.4a Cultivating radiant satisfaction.

Scare, CHING: create and spread fear, terrify; apprehensive, alarmed, perturbed. The ideogram: horse and strike, havoc created by a terrified horse.

    51. Im/ImT Shake scaring a hundred miles.

    51. ImT Scaring the distant and-also fearing the nearby indeed.

Scarlet, CHU: vivid red signifying honor, luck, marriage, riches, literary accomplishment; culmination of the Woody Moment.

    47.2a Scarlet sashes on-all-sides coming.

Scatter, SAN: disperse in small pieces; separate, divide, distribute. The ideogram: strike and crumble.

    59.S Stimulating and-also afterwards scattering it.

Scepter, KUEI: sign of rank that gives you freedom to report to the prince.

42.3a Notifying the prince, availing-of the scepter.

Scold, HO: rebuke, blame, demand and enforce obedience; severe, stern.

37.3a/b Dwelling People, scolding, scolding:

Screen, P'U: curtain, veil, awning, hanging mat; hide, protect; lit.: luxuriant plant growth.

55.2a,4a/b Abounding: one's screen.

55.6a Screening one's dwelling.

Scrutinize, CH'A: investigate, observe carefully, learn the particulars, get at the truth. The ideogram: sacrifice as central to understanding.

22. ImT Using scrutinizing the seasons transforming.

Season, SHIH: quality of the time; the right time, opportune, in harmony; planning in accord with the time; seasons of the year. The ideogram: sun and temple, time as sacred.

1.ImT The six situations: the season accomplishing.

1.ImT The season riding six dragons used going-to-meet heaven.

4.ImT Season centering indeed.

14. ImT Corresponding reaching-to heaven and-also the season moving.

16. ImT And-also the four seasons not straying.

16. ImT Actually Provision's season righteously great in-fact.

17. ImT And-also Below Heaven Following the season.

17. ImT Actually Following the season's righteous great in-fact.

20. ImT And-also the four seasons not straying.

22. ImT Using scrutinizing the seasons transforming.

25/26.CD Great Accumulating: the season indeed.

25.ST The Earlier Kings used luxuriance suiting the season to nurture the myriad beings.

27. ImT Actually Jaws's season great in-fact.

28. ImT Actually Great Exceeding's season great in-fact.

29. ImT Actually venturing's season availing-of the great in-fact.

32. ImT The four seasons transforming changes and-also enabling lasting accomplishment.

33. ImT Associating-with the season moving indeed.

33. ImT Actually Retiring's season righteously great in-fact.

38. ImT Actually Polarizing's season availing-of the great in-fact.

39. ImT Actually Limping's season availing-of the great in-fact.

40. ImT Actually Taking-apart's season great in-fact.

41. ImT Two platters corresponding possess the season.

41. ImT Diminishing solid, augmenting supple, possessing the season.

41. ImT Associating-with the season, accompanying the movement.

42. ImT Associating-with the season, accompanying the movement.

44. ImT Actually Coupling's season righteously great in-fact.

46. ImT Supple using the season, Ascending.

48.1b The season stowed-away indeed.

49.ST A chün tzu uses regulating time-reckoning to brighten the seasons.

49. ImT Heaven[and]Earth Skinning and-also the four seasons accomplishing.

49. ImT Actually Skinning's season great in-fact.

52. ImT The season stopping, by-consequence stopping.

52. ImT The season moving, by-consequence moving.

52. ImT Stirring-up, stilling, not letting-go one's season.

54.4a Procrastinating Converting possesses the season.

55. ImT Associating-with the season: dissolving pause.

56. ImT Actually Sojourning's season righteously great in-fact.

60. ImT Heaven, Earth: Articulating and-also the four seasons accomplishing.

60.2b Letting-go the season ending indeed.

62. ImT Associating-with the season moving indeed.

63.5b Not thus the Western neighbor's season indeed.

Seasoned, HSI: dried meat, prepared for a journey.

21.3a Gnawing seasoned meat. Meeting poison.

- **Second,** see: **Twice** and **Two**
- **Seedburst,** CHIA: seeds bursting forth in spring; first of the Ten Heavenly Barriers in calendar system; begin, first, number one; associated with the Woody Moment.
  - **18.**Im/ImT Before seedburst three days, after seedburst three days.
  - **40.**ImT Thunder[and]Rain arousing and-also the hundred fruits, grasses, trees, altogether seedburst boundary.
- **Seek,** CH'IU: search for, aim at, wish for, desire; implore, supplicate; covetous.
  - **3.**4a Seeking matrimonial allying.
  - **3.**4b Seeking and-also going.
  - **4.**Im/ImT In-no-way me seeking youthful Enveloping.
  - **4.**Im/ImT Youthful Enveloping seeking me.
  - **17.**3a Following possessing seeking, acquiring.
  - **19/20.**CD Maybe associating-with, maybe seeking.
  - **27.**Im/ImT Originating-from seeking mouth substance.
  - **29.**2a/b Seeking, the small acquiring.
  - **32.**1b Beginning seeking depth indeed.
  - **48.**3b Seeking kingly brightness.
- **Seize,** CHÜ: grasp, lay hands on; lean on, rely on; maintain, become concrete; testimony, evidence.
  - **47.**3a/b Seizing tending-towards star thistles.
- **Senior,** HSIUNG: elder; recognized as one to whom respect is due.
  - **37.**ImT The senior, a senior. The junior, a junior.
- **Sequence,** HSÜ: order, precedence, series; follow in order. The name of a section of each hexagram. It also occurs at:
  - **52.**5a Words possessing sequence.
- **Servant,** CH'EN: attendant, minister, vassal; courtier who can speak to the sovereign; wait on, serve in office. The ideogram: person bowing low. See also: **Chief[and]Servant**
  - **33.**3a/b Accumulating servants, concubines, significant.
  - **39.**2a/b A king, a servant: Limping, Limping.
  - **41.**6a Acquiring a servant, without dwelling.
  - **62.**2a Meeting one's servant.
  - **62.**2b A servant not permitted Exceeding indeed.
- **Set-right,** TING: settle, fix, put in place; at rest, repose.

  - **10.**ST [A chün tzu uses] setting-right the commoners, the purpose.
  - **37.**ImT Actually correcting Dwelling and-also Below Heaven set-right.
  - **63/64.**CD Already Fording: setting-right indeed.
- **Set-up,** SHE: establish, institute; arrange, set in order; spread a net. The ideogram: words and impel, establish with words.
  - **20.**ST The Earlier Kings used inspecting on-all-sides, Viewing the commoners to set-up teaching.
  - **20.**ImT The all-wise person uses spirit tao to set-up teaching.
  - **29.**ImT The kingly prince sets-up venturing used to guard his city.
  - **42.**AE Augmenting: long-living enriching and-also not setting-up.
- **Seven,** CH'I: number seven, seventh; seven planets; seventh day when moon changes from crescent to waxing; the Tangram game makes pictures of all phenomena from seven basic shapes.
  - **24.**Im/ImT The seventh day coming: Returning.
  - **51.**2a The seventh day: acquiring.
  - **63.**2a/b The seventh day: acquiring.
- **Sever,** CHE: break off, separate, sunder, cut in two; discriminate, judge the true and false.
  - **22.**ST A chün tzu uses brightening the multitudinous standards without daring to sever litigating.
  - **30.**6a Severing the head. Catching in-no-way its demons.
  - **50.**4a The Vessel: a severed stand.
  - **55.**ST A chün tzu uses severing litigating to involve punishing.
  - **55.**3a/b Severing one's right arm.
- **Shackles,** KU: chains used to secure prisoners; restrain freedom of action; self-restraint, good principles.
  - **4.**1a Availing-of stimulating fettering shackles.
- **Shade,** YU: hidden from view; retired, solitary, secret; dark, obscure, occult, mysterious; ignorant. The ideogram: small within hill, a cave or grotto.
  - **10.**2a/b Shade people, Trial: significant.
  - **47.**1a/b Entering tending-towards a shady gully.
  - **47.**1b Shady, not bright indeed.
  - **54.**2a/b Harvesting: shade people's Trial.

55.4b Shade, not brightening indeed.

Shake, CHEN: arouse, excite, inspire; thunder rising from below; awe, alarm, trembling; fertilizing intrusion. The ideogram: excite and rain.

> Image of Hexagram 51 and occurs throughout its texts.
>
> **52.**CD Shake: rising-up indeed.
> **64.**4a Shake avails-of subjugating souls on-all-sides.

Shaman, WU: medium of the gods; sorcerer, enchantress; perform magic; wizard, witch.

> **57.**2a Availing-of chroniclers, shamans.

Sheer, SU: plain, unadorned; original color or state; clean, pure. The ideogram: white silk, symbol of mourning.

> **10.**1a/b Sheer Treading going.
> **53.**2b Not sheer satiation indeed.

Shield, YU: protect; defended by spirits; heavenly kindness and protection. The ideogram: numinous and right hand, spirit power.

> **14.**6a Originating-from heaven shielding it.
> **14.**6b Originating-from heaven shielding indeed.
> **25.**ImT Heavenly fate not shielding.
> **41.**5b Originating-from shielding above indeed.

Shift, CH'IEN: move, change, transpose; improve, ascend, be promoted; deport, dismiss, remove.

> **42.**ST A chün tzu uses visualizing improvement, by-consequence shifting.
> **42.**4a Harvesting: availing-of activating depending-on shifting the city.
> **48.**AE The Well: residing-in one's place and-also shifting.

Shine, KUANG: illuminate; give off brilliant, bright light; honor, glory, éclat; result of action, contrasts with brightness, MING, light of heavenly bodies. The ideogram: fire above person, lifting the light.

> **2.**ImT Containing generosity, the shining great.
> **2.**2b Earthly tao shining indeed.
> **2.**3b Knowing the shining great indeed.
> **3.**5b Spreading-out not-yet shining indeed.
> **5.**Im/ImT Shining Growing, Trial: significant.
> **10.**ImT Shining brightness indeed.
> **11.**2b Using the shining great indeed.

15.AE Humbling: dignifying and-also shining.

15. ImT Heavenly tao fording below and-also shining brightness.

15. ImT Humbling dignifying and-also shining.

20.4a/b Viewing the city's shining.

21.4b Not-yet shining indeed.

26. ImT Solid persisting: staunch substance, resplendent shining.

27.4b Spreading-out shining above indeed.

31.4b Not-yet the shining great indeed.

35.6b Tao not-yet shining indeed.

42. ImT One's tao, the great shining.

43. ImT One's exposure thereupon shining indeed.

43.5b Center not-yet shining indeed.

45.5b Purpose not-yet shining indeed.

51.4b Not-yet shining indeed.

52. ImT One's tao: shining brightness.

58.6b Not-yet shining indeed.

59.4b Shining great indeed.

64.5a/b A chün tzu's shining.

Shoes, CHÜ: footwear, sandals.

> **21.**1a/b Shoes locked-up, submerging the feet.

Shoot, SHE: shoot with a bow, point at and hit; project from, spurt, issue forth; glance at; scheme for. The ideogram: arrow and body.

> **40.**6a A prince avails-of shooting a hawk, tending-towards the high rampart's above.
> **40.**6b A prince avails-of shooting a hawk.
> **48.**2a/b The Well: a gully, shooting bass.
> **56.**5a Shooting a pheasant.

Shoot-forth, FA: expand, send out; shoot an arrow; ferment, rise; be displayed. The ideogram: stance, bow and arrow, shooting from a solid base.

> **4.**1a Shooting-forth Enveloping.
> **14.**5b Trustworthiness uses shooting-forth purpose indeed.
> **55.**2a/b Possessing conformity, like shooting-forth.
> **55.**2b Trustworthiness using shooting-forth purpose indeed.

Shriek, YA: shout, yell; warning cry of animals; sounds of someone learning to speak; confused noise, exclamations.

> **51.**Im/ImT,1b Laughing words, shrieking, shrieking.

51.1a After laughing words, shrieking,
shrieking.

Shroud, MI: dense, close together, thick,
tight; hidden, secret; retired, intimate. See
also: **Enshroud**

9.Im/ImT Shrouding clouds, not raining.
62.5a/b Shrouding clouds, not raining.

Sides (on-all-sides), FANG: limits, boundaries;
square, surface of the earth extending to the four
cardinal points; everywhere. See also: **Four sides**

2.2a Straightening on-all-sides, great.
2.2b Straightening used on-all-sides indeed.
8.Im/ImT Not soothing, on-all-sides coming.
20.ST The Earlier Kings used inspecting on-
all-sides, Viewing the commoners to set-up
teaching.
24.ST The crown-prince [used culminating
sun] not to inspect on-all-sides.
32.ST A chün tzu uses establishing, not
versatility on-all-sides.
42.ImT One's Augmenting without sides.
47.2a Scarlet sashes on-all-sides coming.
50.3a On-all-sides rain lessens repenting.
63.3a The high ancestor subjugating souls on-
all-sides.
64.ST A chün tzu uses considering to mark-
off the beings residing on-all-sides.
64.4a Shake avails-of subjugating souls on-all-
sides.

Sigh, TZU: lament, express grief, sorrow or
yearning.

45.6a/b Paying-tribute: sighs, tears, snot.

Significant, CHI: leads to the experience of
meaning; favorable, propitious, advantageous,
appropriate; keyword. The ideogram: scholar and
mouth, wise words of a sage.

1.7a Significant.
2.Im/ImT Quiet Trial significant.
2.5a/b A yellow apron. Spring significant.
3.4a Going significant.
3.5a The small, Trial: significant.
4.2a Enwrapping Enveloping. Significant.
4.2a Letting-in the wife. Significant.
4.5a/b Youthful Enveloping. Significant.
5.Im/ImT Shining Growing, Trial:
significant.
5.2a Completing significant.
5.2b Although the small possesses words,
using completing significant indeed.
5.5a Trial: significant.

5.5b Liquor taken-in, Trial: significant.
5.6a/b Respecting them: completing
significant.
6.Im Centering significant. Completing:
pitfall.
6.ImT Blocking awe, centering significant.
6.1a The small possesses words, completing
significant.
6.3a Adversity, completing significant.
6.3b Adhering-to the above significant indeed.
6.4a Denying quiet Trial. Significant.
6.5a/b Arguing. Spring significant.
7.Im Respectable people significant.
7.ImT Actually significant, furthermore
wherefore faulty?
7.2a/b Locating Legions, centering significant.
8.Im Grouping, significant.
8.ImT Grouping significant indeed.
8.1a Completing coming possesses more
significance.
8.1b Possessing more significance indeed.
8.2a,4a Trial: significant.
8.5a Capital people not admonished.
Significant.
8.5b Manifest Grouping's significance.
9.1a Wherefore one's fault? Significant.
9.1b One's righteousness significant indeed.
9.2a Hauling-along, returning. Significant.
10.2a/b Shade people, Trial: significant.
10.4a/b Pleading, pleading: completing
significant.
10.6a One's recurring Spring significant.
10.6b Spring significant located above.
11.Im Significance Growing.
11.ImT The small going, the great coming:
significance Growing.
11.1a Chastising significant.
11.1b Eradicating thatch-grass, chastising
significant.
11.5a/b Using satisfaction, Spring significant.
12.1a Trial: significant. Growing.
12.1b Eradicating thatch-grass, Trial:
significant.
12.2a Small People significant.
12.5a/b Great People significant.
13.4a Significant.
13.4b One's significance.
14.5a Your conforming: mingling thus,
impressing thus. Significant.
14.5b Impressing thus, having significance.

14.6a Significant, without not Harvesting.
14.6b Great Possessing the above: significant.
15.1a Availing-of wading the Great River. Significant.
15.2a/b Calling Humbling. Trial: significant.
15.3a Possessing completing significant.
16.2a Trial: significant.
16.2b Not completing the day, Trial: significant.
17.1a An office: possessing denial. Trial: significant.
17.1b Adhering-to correcting significant indeed.
17.5a/b Conformity tending-towards excellence. Significant.
18.1a Adversity, completing significant.
19.1a/b Conjunction Nearing, Trial: significant.
19.2a/b Conjunction Nearing: significant.
19.5a Significant.
19.6a Significant. Without fault.
19.6b Magnanimity Nearing's significance.
21.4a Significant.
21.4b Harvesting: drudgery, Trial significant.
22.3a/b Perpetual Trial significant.
22.5a Abashment. Completing significant.
22.5b Six at-fifth's significance.
24.1a Spring significant.
24.2a Significant.
24.2b Relinquishing Returning's significance.
25.1a Without Embroiling. Going significant.
26.1m/ImT Not dwelling, taking-in. Significant.
26.4a Spring significant.
26.4b Six at-fourth, Spring significant.
26.5a Significant.
26.5b Six at-fifth's significance.
27. Im/ImT Jaws, Trial: significant.
27. ImT Nourishing correcting, by-consequence significant indeed.
27.4a/b Toppling Jaws. Significant.
27.5a/b Residing-in Trial significant.
27.6a/b Antecedent Jaws. Adversity significant.
28.4a/b The ridgepole crowning. Significant.
30. Im Growing. Accumulating female cattle. Significant.
30. ImT That uses accumulating female cattle, significant indeed.
30.2a/b Yellow Radiance. Spring significant.

30.5a Significant.
30.5b Six at-fifth's significance.
31. Im Grasping womanhood significant.
31. ImT That uses Growth Harvesting Trial, grasping womanhood significant.
31.2a Pitfall. Residing significant.
31.2b Although a pitfall, residing significant.
31.4a/b Trial: significant, repenting extinguished.
32.5a Wife people: significant.
32.5b Wife people, Trial: significant.
33.3a/b Accumulating servants, concubines, significant.
33.4a A chün tzu significant.
33.5a/b Excellence Retiring, Trial: significant.
34.2a Trial: significant.
34.2b Nine at-second, Trial: significant.
34.4a Trial: significant.
34.6a/b Drudgery by-consequence significant.
35.1a,2a Trial: significant.
35.5a Going significant, without not Harvesting.
35.6a Adversity significant, without fault.
36.2a Availing-of a rescuing horse, invigorating significant.
36.2b Six at-second's significance.
37.2a Trial: significant.
37.2b Six at-second's significance.
37.3a Repenting, adversity significant.
37.4a/b Affluence Dwelling, the great significant.
37.5a Beings: care significant.
37.6a Completing significant.
37.6b Impressing thus, having significance.
38. Im Polarizing, Small Affairs significant.
38. ImT That uses Small Affairs significant.
38.6a Going meeting rain, by-consequence significant.
38.6b Meeting rain's significance.
39. Im Trial: significant.
39. ImT Appropriate situation, Trial: significant.
39.6a Significant.
40. Im/ImT One's coming return significant.
40. Im Daybreak significant.
40. ImT Possessing directed going, daybreak significant.
40.2a Trial: significant.
40.2b Nine at-second, Trial: significant.
40.5a Significant.

41. Im/ImT,5a Spring significant.
41.5b Six at-fifth, Spring significant.
41.6a Trial: significant.
42.1a/b Spring significant, without fault.
42.2a Perpetual Trial significant.
42.2a Kinghood availing-of presenting tending-towards the supreme, significant.
42.5a No question, Spring significant.
44.1a Trial: significant.
45. Im/ImT Availing-of the great: sacrificial-victims significant.
45.2a/b Protracting significant, without fault.
45.4a/b The great significant, without fault.
46. Im/ImT The South, chastising significant.
46.1a/b Sincere Ascending, the great significant.
46.4a Significant.
46.5a/b Trial: significant, Ascending steps.
47. Im/ImT Trial: Great People significant.
47.6a Chastising significant.
47.6b Significance moving indeed.
48.6a Possessing conformity, Spring significant.
48.6b Spring significant located-in the above.
49.2a Chastising significant, without fault.
49.4a/b Amending fate significant.
49.6a Residing-in Trial significant.
50. Im The Vessel, Spring significant.
50.2a Not me able to approach. Significant.
50.3a Completing significant.
50.6a The great significant.
51.1a Significant.
52.6a/b Magnanimous Bounding significant.
53. Im Infiltrating, womanhood converting significant.
53. ImT Womanhood converting significant.
53.2a,5a Significant.
53.5b Completing: absolutely-nothing has mastering, significant.
53.6a Significant.
53.6b Its feathers permit availing-of activating fundamentals, significant.
54.1a Chastising significant.
54.1b Halting enabling treading, significant.
54.5a The moon almost facing, significant.
55.2a,4a Significant.
55.4b Significant movement indeed.
55.5a Possessing reward, praise significant.
55.5b Six at-fifth's significance.
56. Im Sojourning, Trial: significant.

56. ImT Sojourning, Trial: significant indeed.
57.2a The mottled like significant.
57.2b The mottled like has significance.
57.5a Trial: significant, repenting extinguished.
57.5a Significant.
57.5b Nine at-fifth's significance.
58.1a/b Harmonious Opening: significant.
58.2a/b Conforming Opening: significant.
59.1a Availing-of a rescuing horse, invigorating significant.
59.1b Initial six's significance.
59.4a/b Dispersing one's flock, Spring significant.
60.5a/b Sweet Articulating significant.
61. Im/ImT Hog fish significant.
61.1a Precaution significant.
61.1b The initial nine, precaution significant.
62. Im The great significant.
62. ImT That uses Small Affairs, significant indeed.
62. ImT The great significant.
63. Im/ImT Initially significant.
63.5b Significant, the great coming indeed.
64.2a Trial: significant.
64.2b Nine at-second, Trial: significant.
64.4a/b Trial: significant, repenting extinguished.
64.5a Trial: significant, without repenting.
64.5a Possessing conformity significant.
64.5b One's brilliance significant indeed.

Simply, ERH: just so, only.
   27.1a Stowing-away simply the psyche tortoise.
   31.4a Partnering adheres-to simply pondering.
   61.2a Myself associating, simply spilling it.

Sincere, YÜN: true, honest, loyal; according to the facts; have confidence in, permit, assent. The ideogram: vapor rising, words directed upward.
   35.3a Crowds, sincerity, repenting extinguished.
   35.3b Crowds: sincerity's purpose.
   46.1a/b Sincere Ascending, the great significant.

Sing, KO: chant, sing elegies, sad or mournful songs; associated with the Earthy Moment, turning from yang to yin.
   30.3a Not drumbeating a jar and-also singing.
   61.3a Maybe weeping, maybe singing.

Situation, WEI: place or seat according to rank;

post, position, command; right, proper; established, arranged. The ideogram: person and stand, servants in their places.

1.ImT The six situations: the season accomplishing.

5.ImT Situation reaching-to the heavenly situation.

5.6b Although not an appropriate situation, not-yet the great let-go indeed.

8.5b Situation correctly centered indeed.

9.ImT Supple acquiring the situation and-also Above[and]Below corresponding-to it.

10. ImT Treading the supreme situation and-also not ailing.

10.3b Situation not appropriate indeed.

10.5b Situation correcting appropriate indeed.

12.3b Situation not appropriate indeed.

12.5b Situation correcting appropriate indeed.

13. ImT Supple acquiring the situation.

14. ImT Supple acquiring the dignifying situation, the great centering.

16.3b Situation not appropriate indeed.

17.5b Situation correctly centering indeed.

19.3b Situation not appropriate indeed.

19.4b Situation appropriate indeed.

21. ImT Although not an appropriate situation, Harvesting: availing-of litigating indeed.

21.3b Situation not appropriate indeed.

22.4b Six at-fourth. Appropriate situation to doubt indeed.

32.4b No lasting whatever: one's situation.

33. ImT Solid: appropriate situation and-also corresponding.

34.5b Situation not appropriate indeed.

35.4b Situation not appropriate indeed.

37. ImT The woman correcting the situation reaching-to the inside.

37. ImT The man correcting the situation reaching-to the outside.

37.4b Yielding located-in the situation indeed.

38.3b Situation not appropriate indeed.

39. ImT Appropriate situation, Trial: significant.

39.4b Appropriate situation, substance indeed.

40.4b Not-yet an appropriate situation indeed.

43.4b Situation not appropriate indeed.

45.4b Situation not appropriate indeed.

45.5a/b Clustering: possessing the situation.

47.4b Although not an appropriate situation, possessing associating indeed.

50.ST A chün tzu uses correcting the situation to solidify fate.

51.3b Situation not appropriate indeed.

52.ST A chün tzu uses pondering not to issue-forth-from his situation.

53. ImT Advancing acquiring the situation.

53. ImT One's situation: solid acquiring the center indeed.

54. ImT Situation not appropriate indeed.

54.5b One's situation located-in the center.

55.4b Situation not appropriate indeed.

56.4b Not-yet acquiring the situation indeed.

57.5b Situation correctly centered indeed.

58.3b Situation not appropriate indeed.

58.5b Situation correcting appropriate indeed.

59. ImT Supple acquiring the situation reaching-to the outside and-also concording above.

59.5b Correcting the situation indeed.

60. ImT Appropriate situating uses Articulating.

60.5b Residing-in the situation: centering indeed.

61.3b Situation not appropriate indeed.

61.5b Situation correcting appropriate indeed.

62. ImT Solid letting-go the situation and-also not centering.

62.4b Situation not appropriate indeed.

63. ImT Solid[and]Supple correcting and-also the situation appropriate indeed.

64. ImT Although not an appropriate situation.

64.3b Situation not appropriate indeed.

Six, LU: transforming opened line; six lines or places of a hexagram; sixth.

1.ImT The six situations: the season accomplishing.

1.ImT The season riding six dragons used going-to-meet

2.7b Availing-of the sixes, perpetual Trial.

Skeptical, YÜ: doubtful, cynical; wonder at, wide-eyed suprise.

16.3a Skeptical Providing-for, repenting.

16.3b Skeptical Providing-for possesses repenting.

Skin, KO: take off the covering, skin or hide; change, renew, molt; remove, peel off; revolt, overthrow, degrade from office; leather armor, protection.

Image of Hexagram 49 and occurs throughout its texts.

33.2a Holding-on-to it: availing-of yellow cattle's skin.

50.S Skinning beings implies absolutely-nothing like a Vessel.

50.CD Skinning: departing anteriority indeed.

50.3a/b The Vessel: the ears skinned.

Skulk, TS'UAN: sneak away and hide; furtive, stealthy; seduce into evil. The ideogram: cave and rat, rat lurking in its hole.

6.2b Converting escaping, skulking indeed.

Slaughter, SHA: kill, murder, execute; hunt game; mow grass.

63.5a/b The Eastern neighbor slaughters cattle.

Sleeve, MEI: displays signs showing quality and rank of the wearer; symbol of self; womb symbol.

54.5a One's chief's sleeves:

54.5a/b One's junior-sister's sleeves not thus fine.

Slice, CH'IEH: cut, carve, mince; urge, press; a resumé.

23.4b Slicing close-to calamity indeed.

Small, HSIAO: little, common, unimportant; adapting to what crosses your path; ability to move in harmony with the vicissitudes of life; contrasts with great, TA, self-imposed theme or goal; keyword. See also: **Small People**

Image of Hexagrams 9 and 62 and occurs throughout their texts.

3.5a The small, Trial: significant.

5.2a The small possesses words.

5.2b Although the small possesses words, using completing significant indeed.

6.1a The small possesses words, completing significant.

6.1b Although the small possesses words, one's differentiation brightening indeed.

10.CD Small Accumulating: few indeed.

11. Im The small going, the great coming.

11. ImT The small going, the great coming: significance Growing.

12. Im/ImT The great going, the small coming.

17.2a/b Tied-to the small son.

17.3a Letting-go the small son.

18.3a The small possesses repenting.

21.3a The small abashed.

22. Im The small, Harvesting: possessing directed going.

22. ImT The anterior small, Harvesting: possessing directed going.

24.AE Returning: the small and-also marking-off with-respect-to beings.

29.2a/b Seeking, the small acquiring.

33. Im/ImT The small: Harvesting Trial.

38. Im Polarizing, Small Affairs significant.

38. ImT That uses Small Affairs concording indeed.

45.3a The small abashed.

46.ST [A chün tzu uses] amassing the small to use the high great.

53.1a The small son, adversity possessing words.

53.1b The small son's adversity.

56. Im Sojourning, the small: Growing.

56. ImT The small Growing.

56. ImT That uses the small Growing.

57. Im Ground, the small: Growing.

57. ImT That uses the small Growing.

61.CD Small Exceeding: Excess indeed.

63. Im Already Fording. Growing: the small.

63. ImT The small implies Growing indeed.

64. Im/ImT The small fox, a muddy Ford.

Small People, HSIAO JEN: lowly, common, humble; those who adjust to circumstances with the flexibility of the small; effect of the small within an individual; keyword.

7.6a/b Small People, no availing-of.

11. ImT Inside chün tzu and-also outside Small People.

11. ImT Small People: tao dissolving indeed.

12. ImT Inside Small People and-also outside chün tzu.

12. ImT Small People: tao long-living.

12.2a Small People significant.

14.3a Small People nowhere controlling.

14.3b Small People harmful indeed.

20.1a Small People: without fault.

20.1b Small People: tao indeed.

23. ImT Small People long-living indeed.

23.6a/b Small People Stripping the hut.

33.ST A chün tzu uses distancing Small People.

33.4a Small People obstructing.

33.4b Small People obstructing indeed.

34.3a/b Small People avail-of Invigorating.

40.5a Possessing conformity, tending-towards Small People.

40.5b Small People withdrawing indeed.

49.6a/b Small People: Skinning the visage.

63.3a Small People, no availing-of.

Smite, CHI: hit, beat, attack; hurl against, rush a position; rouse to action. The ideogram: hand and hit, fist punching.

4.6a Smiting Enveloping.

16.AE Redoubling gates, smiting clappers.

42.6a/b Maybe smiting it.

Smooth, T'AN: plain, leveled; even, make smooth; tranquil, composed, at ease.

10.2a Treading tao, smoothing, smoothing.

Smother, HSÜN: suffocate, smoke out; fog, steam, miasma, vapor; broil, parch; offend; evening mists.

52.3a Adversity smothers the heart.

52.3b Exposure smothers the heart indeed.

Snap-at, TIEH: bite, seize with the teeth, maul; sneering laughter, rebuke. The ideogram: mouth and reach.

10. Im/ImT Not snapping-at people. Growing.

10.3a/b Snapping-at people: pitfall.

Snot, YI: mucus from the nose; snivel, whine.

45.6a/b Paying-tribute: sighs, tears, snot.

Soak, JU: immerse, steep; damp, wet; stain, pollute, blemish; urinate on.

22.3a Adorning thus, soaking thus.

43.3a Like soaking, possessing indignation.

63.1a Soaking one's tail.

63.6a Soaking one's head.

63.6b Soaking one's head, adversity.

64. Im/ImT,1a/b Soaking one's tail:

64.6a Soaking one's head.

64.6b Drinking liquor, soaking the head.

Soar, HAN: fly high; rising sun, the firebird with red plumage; trunk or stem of a plant; vertical support. The ideogram: feathers and dawn.

22.4a A white horse, soaring thus.

61.6a/b A soaring sound mounting, tending-towards heaven.

Sob, T'AO: cry, weep aloud; wailing children. The ideogram: mouth and omen, ominous sounds.

13.5a Concording People beforehand crying-out sobbing and-also afterwards laughing.

56.6a Sojourning people beforehand laughing, afterwards crying-out sobbing.

Soil, WU: covered thick; dirty, stain; moisten, enrich.

50.4a Its form soiled. Pitfall.

Sojourn, LU: travel, stay in places other than your home; itinerant troops, temporary residents; visitor, guest, lodger. The ideogram: banner and people around it, loyal to a symbol rather than their temporary residence.

Image of Hexagram 56 and occurs throughout its texts.

24.ST Bargaining sojourners [used culminating sun] not to move.

55.CD Connecting the few: Sojourning indeed.

57.S Sojourning and-also lacking a place to tolerate.

Solid, KANG: quality of the whole lines; firm, strong, unyielding, persisting. See also: **Solid[and]Supple**

This term occurs throughout the hexagram texts in the Image Tradition and in the Transforming Lines b). It also occurs at:

1/2.CD Force: solid.

43/44.CD Supple meeting solid indeed.

43/44.CD Solid breaking-up supple indeed.

Solid[and]Supple, KANG JOU: field of creative tension between the whole and opened lines and their qualities; field of psychic movement.

3.ImT Solid[and]Supple beginning mingling and-also heaviness giving-birth indeed.

4.2b Solid[and]Supple articulating indeed.

21. ImT Solid[and]Supple apportioning.

29.4b Solid[and]Supple, the border indeed.

32. ImT Solid[and]Supple altogether corresponding. Persevering.

40.1b Solid[and]Supple's border.

50.6b Solid[and]Supple articulating indeed.

60. ImT Solid[and]Supple apportioning and-also solid acquiring the center.

63. ImT Solid[and]Supple correcting and-also the situation appropriate indeed.

64. ImT Solid[and]Supple corresponding indeed.

Solidify, NING: congeal, freeze, curdle, stiffen; coagulate, make solid or firm.

2.1b Yin begins solidifying indeed.

50.ST A chün tzu uses correcting the situation to solidify fate.

Solitary, TI: alone, single; isolated, abandoned.

4.4b Solitariness distancing substance indeed.

9.5b Not solitary affluence indeed.

10.1b Solitarily moving desire indeed.

24.4a/b Centering movement, solitary Returning.

28.ST A chün tzu uses solitary establishing not to fear.

35.1b Solitary moving correcting indeed.

43.3a Solitary going, meeting rain.

Son(hood), TZU: living up to ideal of ancestors as highest human development; act with concern and reverence; male child; offspring, posterity; seed, kernel, egg; sage, teacher; nadir, deepest point, midnight, mid-winter. See also: **Father[and]Son** and **Woman[and]Son**

4.2a/b The son controlling the dwelling.

7.5a/b The long-living son conducting Legions.

7.5a/b The junior son carting corpses.

14.3a/b A prince availing-of Growing, tending-towards heavenly sonhood.

17.2a/b Tied-to the small son.

17.3a Letting-go the small son.

18.1a Possessing sonhood.

32.5a The husband, the son: pitfall.

32.5b The husband, the son: paring righteously.

36. ImT The winnowing son uses it.

36.5a The winnowing son's Brightness Hiding.

36.5b The winnowing son's Trial.

37. ImT The father, a father. The son, a son.

37.3a/b The wife, the son, giggling, giggling:

50.1a Acquiring a concubine, using one's sonhood.

51.S A lord's implementing implies absolutely-nothing like the long-living son.

53.1a The small son, adversity possessing words.

53.1b The small son's adversity.

61.2a/b One's sonhood harmonizing it.

Soothe, NING: calm, pacify; create peace of mind; tranquil, quiet. The ideogram: shelter above heart, dish and breath, physical and spiritual comfort.

1.ImT Myriad cities, conjoining, soothing.

3.ImT Proper to instal feudatories and-also not to soothe.

8.Im/ImT Not soothing, on-all-sides coming.

58.4a Bargaining Opening, not-yet soothing.

Sort, LEI: group according to kind, class with; like nature or purpose; species, class, genus.

2.ImT The female horse: earth sorting.

2.ImT Thereupon associating sorting movement.

11/12.CD Obstructing, Pervading: reversing one's sorting indeed.

13.ST A chün tzu uses sorting the clans to mark-off the beings.

27.2b Movement letting-go sorting indeed.

38. ImT The myriad beings Polarizing and-also their affairs sorted indeed.

61.4b Cutting-off the above, sorting indeed.

Soul, KUEI: power that creates individual existence; union of volatile-soul, HUN, spiritual and intellectual power, and dense-soul, P'O, bodily strength and movement. The HUN rises after death, the P'O remains with the body and may communicate with the living.

38.6a Carrying souls, the-one chariot.

63.3a The high ancestor subjugating souls on-all-sides.

64.4a Shake avails-of subjugating souls on-all-sides.

Souls[and]Spirits, KUEI SHEN: the whole range of imaginal beings both inside and outside the individual; spiritual powers, gods, demons, ghosts, powers, faculties.

15. ImT Souls[and]Spirits harming overfilling and-also blessing Humbling.

55. ImT Even-more with-respect-to the Souls[and]Spirits reached.

Sound, YIN: any sound, particularly music; pronunciation of words. The ideogram: words and hold in the mouth, vocal sound.

61.6a/b A soaring sound mounting, tending-towards heaven.

62. Im/ImT Flying bird: abandoning's sound.

South, NAN: corresponds to summer, Growing, and the Fiery Moment; end of the yang hemicycle; reference point of compass; rulers face South, thus true principles and correct decisions. See also: **Western South**

36.3a Brightness Hiding tending-towards the South, hounding.

36.3b The South: hounding's purpose.

46. Im/ImT The South, chastising significant.

Spill, MI: pour out; disperse, spread; waste, overturn; fleeing soldiers; showy, extravagant.

61.2a Myself associating, simply spilling it.

Spirit(s), SHEN: independent spiritual powers that confer intensity on heart and mind by acting on the soul, KUEI; gods, daimones. See also: **Souls[and]Spirits**

20. ImT Viewing heaven's spirit tao.

20. ImT The all-wise person uses spirit tao to set-up teaching.

Splendor, JUNG: glory, elegance, honor, beauty; flowering; elaborate carved corners of a temple roof.

12.ST [A chün tzu uses] not permitting splendor to use benefits.

Split-off, SSU: lop off, split with an ax, rive; white (color eliminated). The ideogram: ax and possessive, splitting what belongs together.

40.4a Partnering culminating, splitting-off conforming.

56.1a Splitting-off one's place, grasping calamity.

Spoken-thus, YÜEH: designated, termed, called. The ideogram: open mouth and tongue.

9.ImT Spoken-thus: Small Accumulating.

13. ImT Spoken-thus: Concording People.

13. ImT Concording People: spoken-thus.

14. ImT Spoken-thus: Great Possessing.

21. ImT Jaws center possesses being. Spoken-thus: Gnawing Bite.

26.3a Spoken-thus: an enclosed cart, escorting.

47.6a Spoken-thus: stirring-up repenting possesses repenting.

49. ImT Their purposes not mutually acquired. Spoken-thus: Skinning.

Spokes, FU: braces that connect hub and rim of wheel; tributaries.

9.3a Carting stimulating the spokes.

Spout, T'ENG: spurt, burst forth; open mouth, loud talk.

31.6b The spouting mouth stimulating indeed.

Spread-out, SHIH: expand, diffuse, distribute, arrange, exhibit; add to, aid. The ideogram: flag and indeed, claiming new country.

1.ImT Clouds moving, rain spreading-out.

1.2b Actualizing-tao spreading-out throughout indeed.

3.5b Spreading-out not-yet shining indeed.

9.ImT Spreading-out, not-yet moving indeed.

15.ST [A chün tzu uses] evaluating beings to even spreading-out.

27.4b Spreading-out shining above indeed.

42. ImT Heaven spreading-out, earth giving-birth.

43.ST A chün tzu uses spreading-out benefits to extend-to the below.

44.ST The crown-prince uses spreading-out fate to command the four sides.

Sprig, T'I: tender new shoot of a tree, twig, new branch.

28.2a A withered willow giving-birth-to a sprig.

Spring, YÜAN: source, origin, head; great, excellent; arise, begin, generating power; first stage of the Time Cycle.

1.ImT The great Force, Spring in-fact.

2.ImT Culminating Field, Spring in-fact.

2.5a/b A yellow apron. Spring significant.

6.5a/b Arguing. Spring significant.

8.Im/ImT Retracing the oracle-consulting: Spring, perpetual Trial.

10.6a One's recurring Spring significant.

10.6b Spring significant located above.

11.5a/b Using satisfaction, Spring significant.

14. Im Great Possessing, Spring Growing.

14. ImT That uses Spring Growing.

18. Im/ImT Corrupting, Spring Growing.

24.1a Spring significant.

26.4a Spring significant.

26.4b Six at-fourth, Spring significant.

30.2a/b Yellow Radiance. Spring significant.

38.4a Meeting Spring, husbanding.

41. Im/ImT,5a Spring significant.

41.5b Six at-fifth, Spring significant.

42.1a/b Spring significant, without fault.

42.5a No question, Spring significant.

45.5a Spring, perpetual Trial.

46. Im Ascending, Spring Growing.

48.6a Possessing conformity, Spring significant.

48.6b Spring significant located-in the above.

50. Im The Vessel, Spring significant.

50. ImT That uses Spring Growing.

59.4a/b Dispersing one's flock, Spring significant.

Spring Growing Harvesting Trial: Spring, YÜAN; **Grow,** HENG; **Harvest,** LI; and **Trial,** CHEN, are the four stages of the Time Cycle, the model for all dynamic processes. They indicate that your question is connected to the cycle as a whole rather than a part of it, and that the origin (Spring) of a favorable result (Harvesting Trial) is an offering to the spirits (Growing).

1.Im Force: Spring Growing Harvesting Trial.

2.Im Field: Spring Growing Harvesting, female horse's Trial.

3.Im Spring Growing Harvesting Trial.

17. Im Spring Growing Harvesting Trial.

19. Im Nearing, Spring Growing Harvesting Trial.

25. Im Spring Growing Harvesting Trial.

49. Im Spring Growing Harvesting Trial.

Springwater, CH'ÜAN: headwaters of a river; pure water. The ideogram: water and white, pure water at the source.

4.ST Below the mountain issuing-forth springwater.

48.5a The Well: limpid, cold springwater taken-in.

48.5b Cold springwater's taking-in.

Sprout, CHUN: begin or cause to grow; assemble, accumulate, bring under control; hoard possessions; gather soldiers in a military camp; difficult, arduous. The ideogram: sprout piercing hard soil.

Image of Hexagram 3 and occurs throughout its texts.

Squint, MIAO: look at with one eye, glance at; obstructed vision.

10.3a/b Squinting enabling observing.

54.2a Squinting enabling observing.

Stability, CH'IH: firm, prepared for; careful, respectful.

17/18.CD Corrupting: by-consequence stability indeed.

Stable, KU: shed or pen for cattle and horses.

26.4a Youthful cattle's stable.

Stag, LU: mature male deer with horns.

3.3a/b Approaching stag, lacking precaution.

Stand, TSU: base, foot, leg; rest on, support; stance. The ideogram: foot and calf resting.

6.6b Truly not standing respectfully indeed.

10.3b Not the stand to use possessing brightness indeed.

10.3b Not the stand to use associating-with moving indeed.

23.1a/b Stripping the bed, using the stand.

27.1b Truly not the stand to value indeed.

50.4a The Vessel: a severed stand.

Standard, CHENG: measure, test, limit, rule; musical interval; subjugate, regulate; capacity, endurance.

22.ST A chün tzu uses brightening the multitudinous standards without daring to sever litigating.

Star thistles, CHI LI: spiny weeds that entangle the feet; caltrops, metal snares.

47.3a/b Seizing tending-towards star thistles.

Staunch, TU: firm, solid, reliable; pure; consolidate, establish; sincere, honest.

26. ImT Solid persisting: staunch substance, resplendent shining.

Steps, CHIEH: stairs leading to a gate or hall; grade, degree, rank; emulate, rise.

46.5a/b Trial: significant, Ascending steps.

Stew, SU: cooked or boiled rice and meat; mixed contents of a pot.

50.4a/b Overthrowing a princely stew.

Still, CHING: quiet, at rest; imperturbable.

52. ImT Stirring-up, stilling, not letting-go one's season.

Stimulate, SHUO: rouse to action and good feeling; free from constraint, stir up, urge on; persuade, cheer, delight; set out in words; the Action of the trigram Open, TUI. The ideogram: words and exchange.

4.1a Availing-of stimulating fettering shackles.

9.3a Carting stimulating the spokes.

10. ImT Stimulating and-also corresponding reaching-to Force.

17. ImT Stirring-up and-also stimulating.

19. ImT Stimulating and-also yielding.

26.2a/b Carting, stimulating the axle-strap.

28. ImT Ground and-also stimulating movement.

31. ImT Stopping and-also stimulating.

31.6b The spouting mouth stimulating indeed.

33.2a Absolutely-nothing has mastering stimulating.

38. ImT Stimulating and-also congregating reaching-to brightness.

38.6a Afterwards stimulating's bow.

42. ImT The commoners stimulated without delimiting.

43. ImT Persisting and-also stimulating.

45. ImT Yielding uses stimulating.

47. ImT Venturing uses stimulating.

47.5a/b Thereupon ambling possesses stimulating.

49. ImT Pattern brightening uses stimulating.

54. ImT Stimulating uses stirring-up.

58.S Entering and-also afterwards stimulating it.

58.S Open implies stimulating indeed.

58. ImT Open stimulating indeed.

58. ImT Stimulating uses Harvesting Trial.

58. ImT Stimulating using beforehand the commoners:

58. ImT Stimulating using opposing heaviness:
58. ImT Stimulating's great.
59.S Stimulating and-also afterwards
scattering it.
60. ImT Stimulating uses movement venturing.
61. ImT Stimulating and-also Ground:
Conforming.

Stir-up, TUNG: excite, influence, move, affect;
work, take action; come out of the egg or
the bud; the Action of the trigram Shake,
CHEN. The ideogram: strength and heavy, move
weighty things.

2.2b Six at-second's stirring-up.
3.ImT Stirring-up reaching-to venturing
center.
3.ImT Thunder[and]Rain's stirring-up,
fullness overfilling.
16. ImT Yielding uses stirring-up. Provision.
16. ImT Providing-for: yielding uses stirring-
up.
16. ImT Heaven[and]Earth uses yielding
stirring-up.
16. ImT The all-wise person uses yielding
stirring-up.
17. ImT Stirring-up and-also stimulating.
Following.
21. ImT Stirring-up and-also brightening.
24. ImT Stirring-up and-also using yielding
movement.
25. ImT Stirring-up and-also persisting.
28.S Not nourishing, by-consequence not
permitting stirring-up.
32. ImT Ground and-also stirring-up.
34. ImT Solid uses stirring-up. Anterior
Invigorating.
38. ImT Fire stirring-up and-also above.
38. ImT Marsh stirring-up and-also below.
40. ImT Taking-apart. Venturing uses stirring-
up.
40. ImT Stirring-up and-also evading
reaching-to venturing. Taking-apart.
42. ImT Augmenting stirring-up and-also
Ground.
47.6a/b Stirring-up repenting possesses
repenting.
51.S Shake implies stirring-up indeed.
52.S Beings not permitted to use completing
stirring-up.
52. ImT Stirring-up, stilling, not letting-go
one's season.

53. ImT Stirring-up not exhausted indeed.
54. ImT Stimulating uses stirring-up.
55. ImT Brightness using stirring-up. Anterior
Abounding.

Stone, P'AN: large conspicuous rock, foundation
stone; stable, immovable.

3.1a Stone pillar.
3.1b Although a stone pillar, purpose moving
correctly indeed.
53.2a The wild-swan Infiltrating tending-
towards the stone.

Stop, CHIH: bring or come to a standstill; the
Action of the trigram Bound, KEN. The
ideogram: a foot stops walking.

4.ImT Venturing and-also stopping.
Enveloping.
18. ImT Ground and-also stopping.
Corrupting.
22. ImT Pattern brightening, stopping:
23. ImT Yielding and-also stopping it.
26. ImT Ability stopping persisting.
31. ImT Stopping and-also stimulating.
33/34.CD Great Invigorating: by-consequence
stopping.
39. ImT Visualizing venturing and-also
enabling stopping.
51/52.CD Bound: stopping indeed.
52.S Stopping it.
52.S Bounding implies stopping indeed.
52. ImT Bound: stopping indeed.
52. ImT The season stopping, by-consequence
stopping.
52. ImT Bound: one's stopping.
52. ImT Stopping: one's place indeed.
52.4b Stopping connoting the body indeed.
53.S Beings not permitted to use completing
stopping.
53. ImT Stopping and-also Ground.
56. ImT Stopping and-also congregating
reaching-to brightness.
59/60.CD Articulating: stopping indeed.
63. ImT Completing, stopping by-consequence
disarraying.

Stow(-away), SHE: set aside, put away, store;
halt, rest in; temporary lodgings, breathing-spell.

3.3a A chün tzu almost not thus stowing-
away.
3.3b A chün tzu stowing it:
8.5b Stowing-away countering, grasping
yielding.

17.3b Below, purpose stowed-away indeed.

22.1a/b Stowing-away the chariot and-also afoot.

27.1a Stowing-away simply the psyche tortoise.

44.5b Purpose, not stowing-away fate indeed.

48.1b The season stowed-away indeed.

Straighten, CHIH: correct the crooked, reform, repay injustice; proceed directly; sincere, upright, just; blunt, outspoken.

2.2a Straightening on-all-sides, great.

2.2b Straightening used on-all-sides indeed.

13.5b Using centering straightening indeed.

47.5b Using centering straightening indeed.

Stranded ropes, HUI MO: three stranded ropes; royal garments; beautiful, honorable.

29.6a Tying availing-of stranded ropes.

Stray, T'E: wander blindly; deviate, err, alter, doubt; excess.

16.ImT And-also the four seasons not straying.

20.ImT And-also the four seasons not straying.

Stream, SHUI: flowing water; fluid, dissolving; river, tide, flood; the Symbol of the trigram Gorge, K'AN. The ideogram: rippling water.

6.ST Heaven associating-with stream, contradicting movements.

7.ST Earth center possessing stream.

8.ST Above earth possessing stream.

29.ST Streams reiterating culminating. Repeating Gorge.

29.ImT Stream diffusing and-also not overfilling.

39.ST Above mountain possessing stream.

47.ST Marsh without stream.

48.ST Above wood possessing stream.

48.ImT Ground reaching-to stream and-also stream above. The Well.

49.ImT Skinning. Stream, fire, mutually pausing.

59.ST Wind moves above stream.

60.ST Above marsh possessing stream.

63.ST Stream located above fire.

64.ST Fire located above stream.

Street, HSIANG: public space between dwellings, public square; side-street, alley, lane. The ideogram: place and public.

38.2a/b Meeting a lord, tending-towards the street.

Strengthen, CH'IANG: invigorate, test; compel, rely on force; determined, sturdy; overcome a desire.

1.ST A chün tzu uses originating strength not to pause.

Stretch, CHANG: draw a bow taut; open, extend, spread, display; make much of.

38.6a Beforehand stretching's bow.

Stricken, YAO: afflicted by fate; untimely, premature death; tender, delicate, young; pleasing. The ideogram: great with a broken point, interrupted growth.

38.3a One's person stricken, moreover nose-cut.

String-arrow, YI: arrow with string attached used to retrieve what is shot; seize, appropriate; arrest a criminal.

62.5a A prince, a string-arrow grasping another located-in a cave.

Strip, PO: flay, peel, skin; remove, uncover, degrade; split, slice; reduce to essentials; slaughter an animal. The ideogram: knife and carve, trenchant action.

Image of Hexagram 23 and occurs throughout its texts.

24.S Above Stripping exhausted, below reversing.

24.CD Stripping: rotten indeed.

58.5a/b Conforming tending-towards stripping.

Struggle, CHAN: fight with, combat; make war, join battle; hostilities; alarmed, terrified.

2.6a/b Dragons struggling tending-towards the countryside.

Stump, CHU: trunk, bole, stalk; wooden post; keep down, degrade.

47.1a The sacrum Confined, tending-towards stump wood.

Subjugate, FA: chastise rebels, make dependent; cut down, subject to rule. The ideogram: man and lance, armed soldiers.

15.5a/b Harvesting: availing-of encroaching subjugating.

35.6a/b Holding-fast avails-of subjugating the capital.

63.3a The high ancestor subjugating souls on-all-sides.

64.4a Shake avails-of subjugating souls on-all-sides.

Submerge, MIEH: plunge under water, put out a

fire; exterminate, finish, cut off. The ideogram: water and destroy.

 21.1a/b Shoes locked-up, submerging the feet.
 21.2a/b Gnawing flesh, submerging the nose.
 21.6a/b Wherefore locking-up submerging the ears?
 23.1b Below using submerging indeed.
 28.ST Marsh submerging wood.
 28.6a Exceeding wading submerges the peak. Pitfall.

Submit, FU: yield to, serve; undergo.

 6.6b Using Arguing acquiesces-in submitting.
 15.3b The myriad commoners submitting indeed.
 15.5b Chastising, not submitting indeed.
 16. ImT By-consequence punishing flogging purifies and-also the commoners submit.
 20. ImT And-also actually Below Heaven submitting.

Substance, SHIH: real, solid, full; results, fruits, possessions; essence; honest, sincere. The ideogram: string of coins under a roof, riches in the house.

 4.4b Solitariness distancing substance indeed.
 11.4b Altogether letting-go substance indeed.
 26. ImT Solid persisting: staunch substance, resplendent shining.
 27. Im/ImT Originating-from seeking mouth substance.
 39.4b Appropriate situation, substance indeed.
 50.2a/b The Vessel possesses substance.
 50.5b Centering uses activating substance indeed.
 54.6a A woman receiving a basket without substance.
 54.6b Six above, without substance.
 63.5a/b The substance: acquiescing-in one's blessing.

Suburbs, CHIAO: area adjoining a city where human constructions and nature interpenetrate; second of the territorial zones: city, suburbs, countryside, forests.

 5.1a/b Attending tending-towards the suburbs.
 9.Im/ImT Originating-from my Western suburbs.
 13.6a/b Concording People tending-towards the suburbs. Without repenting.
 62.5a Originating-from my Western suburbs.

Subvert, CHING: undermine, overturn,

overthrow; falling; pour out, empty; waste, squander. The ideogram: man, head and ladle, emptying out old ideas.

 12.6a Subverting Obstruction.
 12.6b Obstruction completed, by-consequence subverting.

Suddenly, TSAN: quick, prompt, abrupt action; collect together. The ideogram: clasp used to gather the hair.

 16.4a Partners join-together suddenly.

Suiting, TUI: correspond to, agree with, consistent; pair; parallel sentences in poetic language.

 25.ST The Earlier Kings used luxuriance suiting the season to nurture the myriad beings.

Sun/day, JIH: actual sun and the time of a sun-cycle, a day. See also: **Before-zenith sun** and **Day**

 24.ST The earlier kings used culminating sun to bar the passages.
 24.ST Bargaining sojourners [used culminating sun] not to move.
 24.ST The crown-prince [used culminating sun] not to inspect on-all-sides.
 30.3a/b Sun going-down's Radiance.
 35. Im Day-time sun three-times reflected.
 35. ImT Day-time sun three-times reflected indeed.
 42. ImT Sun advancing without delimiting.
 55. Im/ImT No grief. Properly sun centering.
 55. ImT Sun centering, by-consequence going-down.
 55.2a,4a/b Sun centering: visualizing a bin.
 55.3a Sun centering: visualizing froth.

Sun[and]Moon, JIH YÜEH: the two dimensions of calendar time that define any specific moment; time as interlocking cycles.

 16. ImT Anterior Sun[and]Moon not exceeding.
 30. ImT Sun[and]Moon congregating reaching-to heaven.
 32. ImT Sun[and]Moon acquiring heaven and-also enabling lasting illumination.

Supervise, LI: oversee, inspect, administer; visit subordinates; headquarters.

 36.ST A chün tzu uses supervising the crowds to avail-of darkening and-also Brightening.

Supple, JOU: quality of the opened lines; flexible, pliant, tender, adaptable. See also: **Solid[and]Supple**

This term occurs throughout the hexagram texts in the Image Tradition and in the Transforming Lines b).

Supreme, TI: highest, above all on earth; sovereign lord, source of power; emperor.

10.ImT Treading the supreme situation and-also not ailing.

11.5a The supreme burgeoning, converting maidenhood.

42.2a Kinghood availing-of presenting tending-towards the supreme, significant.

54.5a/b The supreme burgeoning Converting Maidenhood.

59.ST The Earlier Kings used presenting tending-towards the supreme to establish the temples.

Supreme Above, SHANG TI: highest power in universe, lord of all.

16.ST Exalting worship's Supreme Above.

50.ImT The all-wise person Growing uses presenting-to the Supreme Above.

Surely, KAI: preceding statement is undoubtedly true.

16.AE Surely, grasping connotes Providing-for.

Surpass, YU: exceed; beyond measure, excessive; extraordinary; transgress, blame.

22.4b Completing without surpassing indeed.

23.5b Completing without surpassing indeed.

26.2b Centering without surpassing indeed.

39.2b Completing without surpassing indeed.

50.2b Completing without surpassing indeed.

56.2b Completing without surpassing indeed.

Swallow, YEN: house swallow, martin, swift; retired from official life; easy, peaceful, private; give a feast; relation between elder and younger brother.

61.1a Possessing this, not a swallow.

Swallowing, see: **Jaws**

Sweat, HAN: perspiration; labor, trouble. Dispersing sweat, HUAN HAN, denotes an imperial edict.

59.5a Dispersing sweat, one's great crying-out.

Sweet, KAN: taste corresponding to the Earthy Moment; agreeable, happy, delightful, refreshing; grateful.

19.3a/b Sweetness Nearing.

60.5a/b Sweet Articulating significant.

Swiftly, CH'UAN: quickly; hurry, hasten.

41.1a/b Climaxing affairs, swiftly going.

41.4a Commissioning swiftly possesses rejoicing.

Symbol, HSIANG: image invested with intrinsic power to connect visible and invisible; magic spell; figure, form, shape, likeness; pattern, model; create an image, imitate; act, play; writing.

23.ImT Viewing symbols indeed.

50.ImT The Vessel. A symbol indeed.

62.ImT Possessing the flying bird's symbol in-truth.

Tail, WEI: animal's tail; last, extreme; remnants, unimportant. See also: **Bushy-tailed rodent**

10.Im,3a,4a Treading a tiger tail.

10.ImT That uses Treading a tiger tail.

33.1a/b Retiring tail, adversity.

63.1a Soaking one's tail.

64.Im/ImT,1a/b Soaking one's tail:

Take-apart, HSIEH: loosen, disjoin, untie, sever, scatter; analyse, explain, understand; release, dispel sorrow; eliminate effects, solve problems; resolution, deliverance. The ideogram: horns and knife, cutting into forward thrust.

Image of Hexagram 40 and occurs throughout its texts.

39.CD Taking-apart: delay indeed.

Take-in, SHIH: eat, ingest, swallow, devour; incorporate. See also: **Drink[and]take-in**

5.5a Attending tending-towards liquor taken-in.

5.5b Liquor taken-in, Trial: significant.

6.3a Taking-in ancient actualizing-tao. Trial.

6.3b Taking-in ancient actualizing-tao.

11.3a Tending-towards taking-in possesses blessing.

21/22.CD Gnawing Bite: taking-in indeed.

23.6a The ripe fruit not taken-in.

26.Im/ImT Not dwelling, taking-in. Significant.

36.1a Three days, not taking-in.

36.1b Righteously not taking-in indeed.

47.2a/b Confined, tending-towards liquor taken-in.

48.1a/b The Well: a bog, not taking-in.

48.3a/b The Well: oozing, not taking-in.

48.5a The Well: limpid, cold springwater taken-in.

48.5b Cold springwater's taking-in.

50.3a Pheasant juice not taken-in.

55. ImT Moon overfilling, by-consequence taking-in.

Tao: way or path; ongoing process of being and the course it traces for each specific person or thing; keyword. The ideogram: go and head, leading and the path it creates. See also: **Actualize-tao**

1.ImT Force: tao transforming changes.
1.3b Reversing returning tao indeed.
2.ImT Beforehand delusion letting-go tao.
2.1b Docilely involving one's tao:
2.2b Earthly tao shining indeed.
2.6b One's tao exhausted indeed.
5.S Attending implies drinking[and]taking-in's tao indeed.
8.ImT One's tao exhausted indeed.
9.1a/b Returning originating-from tao.
10.2a Treading tao, smoothing, smoothing.
11.ST The crown-prince uses property to accomplish Heaven[and]Earth's tao.
11. ImT A chün tzu: tao long-living.
11. ImT Small People: tao dissolving indeed.
12. ImT Small People: tao long-living.
12. ImT A chün tzu: tao dissolving indeed.
13.2b Abashment: tao indeed.
15. ImT Heavenly tao fording below and-also shining brightness.
15. ImT Earth tao lowly and-also moving above.
15. ImT Heavenly tao lessening overfilling and-also increasing Humbling.
15. ImT Earthly tao transforming overfilling and-also diffusing Humbling.
15. ImT People tao hating overfilling and-also loving Humbling.
17.4a Possessing conformity, locating-in tao uses brightening.
17.4b Possessing conformity located-in tao.
18.2b Acquiring centering tao indeed.
19. ImT Heavenly tao indeed.
20. ImT Viewing heaven's spirit tao.
20. ImT The all-wise person uses spirit tao to set-up teaching.
20.1b Small People: tao indeed.
20.3b Not-yet letting-go tao indeed.
24. Im/ImT Reversing Returning one's tao.
24.4b Using adhering-to tao indeed.
24.6b Reversing the chief: tao indeed.
26.6b Tao: the great moving indeed.
27.3b Tao, the great rebelling indeed.

29.1b Letting-go tao: pitfall indeed.
29.6b Six above, letting-go tao.
30.2b Acquiring centering tao indeed.
32.S Husband[and]Wife's tao.
32. ImT Lasting with-respect-to one's tao indeed.
32. ImT Heaven[and]Earth's tao.
32. ImT The all-wise person lasting with-respect-to his tao and-also Below Heaven the changes accomplishing.
35.6b Tao not-yet shining indeed.
37. ImT And-also Dwelling tao correcting.
38.S Dwelling tao exhausted, necessarily returning.
38.2b Not-yet letting-go tao indeed.
39. ImT One's tao exhausted indeed.
40.2b Acquiring centering tao indeed.
41. ImT One's tao moving above.
42. ImT One's tao, the great shining.
42. ImT Woody tao, thereupon moving.
42. ImT Total Augmenting's tao.
43.2b Acquiring centering tao indeed.
44.1b Supple tao hauling-along indeed.
49.S The Well tao not permitting not Skinning.
52. ImT One's tao: shining brightness.
53.3b Letting-go her tao indeed.
60. ImT,6b One's tao exhausted indeed.
60.4b Receiving tao above indeed.
63. ImT One's tao exhausted indeed.
63.2b Using centering tao indeed.

Tatters, see: **In-tatters**
Teach, CHIAO: instruct, show; precept, doctrine.
19.ST A chün tzu uses teaching to ponder without exhausting.
20.ST The Earlier Kings used inspecting on-all-sides, Viewing the commoners to set-up teaching.
20. ImT The all-wise person uses spirit tao to set-up teaching.
29.ST [A chün tzu uses] repeating to teach affairs.
Team, P'I: pair, matched horses; fellow, mate; united.
61.4a/b The horse team extinguished.
Tears, T'I: weep, cry; water from the eyes.
30.5a Issuing-forth tears like gushing. Sadness like lamenting.
45.6a/b Paying-tribute: sighs, tears, snot.
Temple, MIAO: building used to honor gods and ancestors.

45. Im/ImT The king imagines possessing a temple.

51. ImT Issuing-forth permits using guarding the ancestral temple, field-altar, offertory-millet.

59. Im/ImT The king imagines possessing a temple.

59.ST The Earlier Kings used presenting tending-towards the supreme to establish the temples.

Ten, SHIH: goal and end of reckoning; whole, complete, all; entire, perfected, the full amount; reach everywhere, receive everything. The ideogram: East–West line crosses North–South line, a grid that contains all.

    3.2a/b Ten years-revolved, thereupon nursing.

    24.6a Culminating tending-towards ten years-revolved not controlling chastisement.

    27.3a/b Ten years-revolved, no availing-of.

    41.5a Maybe augmenting's ten: partnering's tortoise.

    42.2a Maybe Augmenting's ten: partnering's tortoise.

Tend-towards, YÜ: move toward but not reach, in the direction of; contrasts with reach(-to), HU, actually arriving.

    This term occurs throughout the hexagram texts.

Term, CH'I: set time, fixed period, agreed date; seasons; person a hundred years old.

    54.4a Converting Maidenhood overrunning the term.

    54.4b Overrunning the term's purpose.

Terminate, O: cut off, check, extinguish, bring to a standstill. The ideogram: go and why, no reason to move.

    14.ST A chün tzu uses terminating hate to display improvement.

Terrorize, CH'IO: look around in great alarm; frightened and trying to escape. The ideogram: eyes of bird trapped by a hand.

    51.6a Observing: terrorizing, terrorizing.

Test, SHIH: compare, try, experiment; tempt.

    25.5b Not permitting testing indeed.

That, SHIH: preceding statement.

    11. ImT By-consequence-of that Heaven[and]Earth mingling and-also the myriad beings interpenetrating indeed.

    12. ImT By-consequence-of that Heaven[and]Earth not mingling and-also the myriad beings not interpenetrating indeed.

    62.6a That designates Calamity[and]Blunder.

    64.6a Possessing conformity: letting-go that.

That uses, SHIH YI: involves and is involved by.

    10. ImT That uses Treading a tiger tail.

    14. ImT That uses Spring Growing.

    24. ImT That uses issuing-forth, entering, without affliction.

    30. ImT That uses accumulating female cattle, significant indeed.

    31. ImT That uses Growth Harvesting Trial, grasping womanhood significant.

    35. ImT That uses the calm feudatory availing-of bestowing horses to multiply the multitudes.

    38. ImT That uses Small Affairs, concording indeed.

    46. ImT That uses great Growing to avail-of visualizing Great People.

    48. ImT That uses a pitfall indeed.

    50. ImT That uses Spring Growing.

    52. ImT That uses not catching one's individuality.

    56. ImT That uses the small Growing.

    57. ImT That uses the small Growing.

    58. ImT That uses yielding reaching-to heaven and-also corresponding reaching-to the people.

    62. ImT That uses Small Affairs, significant indeed.

    62. ImT That uses not permitting Great Affairs indeed.

Thatch-grass, MAO: thick grass used for the roofs of humble houses.

    11.1a Eradicating thatch-grass intertwisted.

    11.1b Eradicating thatch-grass, chastising significant.

    12.1a Eradicating thatch-grass intertwisted.

    12.1b Eradicating thatch-grass, Trial: significant.

    28.1a/b A sacrifice availing-of white thatch-grass.

Their/they, CH'I: third person pronoun; also: one/one's, it/its, he/his, she/hers.

    This term occurs throughout the hexagram texts.

Them, see: **have(-it)**

Therefore, JAN: follows logically, thus.

    30.1a Treading, polishing therefore.

Therefore afterwards, JAN HOU: logical consequence of, necessarily follows in time.

3.S Therefore afterwards the myriad beings giving-birth in-truth.

10.S Beings Accumulating, therefore afterwards possessing codes.

11.S Therefore afterwards quieting.

20.S Being great therefore afterwards permitting Viewing.

23.S Actually involving embellishing, therefore afterwards Growing by-consequence used-up.

26.S Possessing Without Embroiling therefore afterwards permitting Accumulating.

27.S Beings accumulating therefore afterwards permitting nourishing.

31.S Therefore afterwards possessing the myriad beings.

31.S Therefore afterwards possessing Man[and]Woman.

31.S Therefore afterwards possessing Husband[and]Wife.

31.S Therefore afterwards possessing Father[and]Son.

31.S Therefore afterwards possessing Chief[and]Servant.

31.S Therefore afterwards possessing Above[and]Below.

31.S Therefore afterwards the codes righteously possessing a place to polish.

Thereupon, NAI: on that ground, because of.

1.ImT Thereupon primary heaven.

1.ImT Thereupon Harvesting Trial.

2.ImT Thereupon yielding receiving heaven.

2.ImT Thereupon associating sorting movement.

2.ImT Thereupon completing possesses reward.

3.2a/b Ten years-revolved, thereupon nursing.

9.ImT Thereupon Growing.

17.6a Thereupon adhering holding-fast-to it.

28.ImT Thereupon Growing.

29.ImT Holding-fast the heart's Growing, thereupon using solid centering indeed.

30.ImT Thereupon changes accomplishing Below Heaven.

36.3b Thereupon acquiring the great indeed.

40.ImT Thereupon acquiring the center indeed.

42.ImT Woody tao, thereupon moving.

43.ImT One's exposure thereupon shining indeed.

43.ImT The place to honor thereupon exhausted indeed.

43.ImT Solid long-living, thereupon completing indeed.

45.1a/b Thereupon disarraying, thereupon Clustering.

45.2a Conforming, thereupon Harvesting availing-of dedicating.

46.2a Conforming, thereupon Harvesting availing-of dedicating.

47.ImT Honoring the mouth thereupon exhausted indeed.

47.5a/b Thereupon ambling possesses stimulating.

48.ImT Thereupon using solid centering indeed.

49.Im/ImT Before-zenith sun, thereupon conforming.

49.ImT One's repenting thereupon extinguished.

49.2a Before-zenith sun, thereupon Skinning it.

59.ImT Kinghood thereupon located-in the center indeed.

61.ImT Thereupon changing the fiefdoms indeed.

61.ImT Thereupon corresponding reaching-to heaven indeed.

Thicket, MANG: underbrush, tangled vegetation, thick grass, jungle; rustic, rude, socially inept.

13.3a/b Hiding-away arms, tending-towards the thickets.

Thigh, KU: upper leg that provides power for walking; strands of a rope.

31.3a/b Conjoining one's thighs.

36.2a Brightness Hiding. Hiding tending-towards the left thigh.

This, T'A: specifically this thing. The ideogram: person and indeed.

61.1a Possessing this, not a swallow.

Thistle, see: **Star thistle**

Thong, KUNG: bind with thongs, secure; well-guarded, strong, stiffened.

49.1a Thonging avails-of yellow cattle's Skin.

49.1b Thonging avails-of yellow cattle.

Thread, KUAN: string together; string of a thousand coins.

23.5a Threading fish.

Three, SAN: number three, third time or place; active phases of a cycle; superlative; beginning of repetition. See also: **Twice, three-times**

5.6a Three people coming.

6.2a People, three hundred doors.

6.6a Completing dawn three-times
depriving it.

7.2a/b The king three-times bestowing fate.

8.5a The king avails-of three beaters.

13.3a/b Three year's-time not rising.

18. Im/ImT Before seedburst three days, after
seedburst three days.

29.6a Three year's-time, not acquiring. Pitfall.

29.6b Pitfall: three year's-time indeed.

35. Im Day-time sun three-times reflected.

35. ImT Day-time sun three-times reflected
indeed.

36.1a Three days, not taking-in.

40.2a The fields, catching three foxes.

41.3a Three people moving.

41.3b Three by-consequence doubting indeed.

47.1a Three year's-time not encountering.

49.3a/b Skinning words three-times
drawing-near:

53.5a The wife, three year's-time not
pregnant.

55.6a Three year's-time not encountering.

57.4a/b The fields, catching three kinds.

57.5a Before husking, three days.

57.5a After husking, three days.

63.3a/b Three years-revolved controlling it.

64.4a Three years-revolved, possessing
donating tending-towards the great city.

Throughout, P'U: universal, all; great, pervading
light. The ideogram: sun and equal, equal to
the sun.

1.2b Actualizing-tao spreading-out
throughout indeed.

Throw-out, CH'I: reject, discard, abandon, push
aside, break off: renounce, forget.

30.4a Burning thus. Dying thus. Thrown-out
thus.

Thumb/big-toe, MU: in lower trigram: big-toe;
in upper trigram: thumb; the big-toe enables the
foot to walk, as the thumb enables the hand
to grasp.

31.1a/b Conjoining one's big-toes.

40.4a/b Taking-apart and-also the thumbs.

Thunder, LEI: rising, arousing power; the
Symbol of the trigram Shake, CHEN.

3.ST Clouds, Thunder, Sprouting.

16.ST Thunder issuing-forth-from earth
impetuously.

17.ST Marsh center possessing thunder.

21.ST Thunder, lightning.

21. ImT Thunder, lightning, uniting and-also
composing.

24.ST Thunder located-in earth center.

25.ST Below heaven thunder moving.

27.ST Below mountain possessing thunder.

32.ST Thunder, wind, Persevering.

32. ImT Thunder, wind, mutually associating.

34.ST Thunder located above heaven.

40.ST Thunder, Rain, arousing.

42.ST Wind, thunder.

51.ST Reiterated thunder.

54.ST Above marsh possessing thunder.

55.ST Thunder, lightning, altogether
culminating.

62.ST Above mountain possessing thunder.

Thunder[and]Rain, LEI YÜ: fertilizing shock of
storms; associated with the trigrams Shake,
CHEN, and Gorge, K'AN.

3.ImT Thunder[and]Rain's stirring-up,
fullness overfilling.

40. ImT Heaven[and]Earth Taking-apart and-
also Thunder[and]Rain arousing.

40. ImT Thunder[and]Rain arousing and-also
the hundred fruits, grasses, trees, altogether
seedburst boundary.

Thus, JU: as, in this way. See also: **Spoken-thus**
and **Thus ... thus**

3.2a,4a,6a Riding a horse, arraying thus.

3.3a A chün tzu almost not thus stowing-
away.

3.6a/b Weeping blood, coursing thus.

9.5a/b Possessing conformity, binding thus.

14.5b Your conforming, mingling thus.

14.5b Impressing thus, having significance.

16. ImT Anterior Heaven[and]Earth thus
having-it.

22.4a A white horse, soaring thus.

35.4a Prospering, thus bushy-tailed rodents.

37.6a Possessing conformity, impressing thus.

37.6b Impressing thus, having significance.

50.4b Wherefore trustworthy thus indeed?

54.5a/b One's junior-sister's sleeves not
thus fine.

61.5a/b Possessing conformity, binding thus.

62.1b Wherefore not permitted thus indeed.

62.3b Wherefore a pitfall thus indeed.

63.5a Not thus the Western neighbor's dedicated offering.

63.5b Not thus the Western neighbor's season indeed.

Thus ... thus, JU ... JU: when there is one thing, then there must be the second thing.

3.2a Sprouting thus, quitting thus.

14.5a Your conforming: mingling thus, impressing thus. Significant.

22.3a Adorning thus, soaking thus.

22.4a Adorning thus, hoary thus.

30.4a Assailing thus, its coming thus.

30.4a Burning thus. Dying thus. Thrown-out thus.

30.4b Assailing thus, its coming thus.

35.1a/b Prospering thus, arresting thus.

35.2a Prospering thus, apprehensive thus.

45.3a Clustering thus, lamenting thus.

Tie(-to), HSI: connect, attach to, bind; devoted to; relatives. The ideogram: person and connect, ties between humans.

17.2a/b Tied-to the small son.

17.3a/b Tied-to the respectable husband.

17.6a/b Grappling, tying-to it.

29.6a Tying availing-of stranded ropes.

33.3a Tied Retiring. Possessing afflicting adversity.

33.3b Tied Retiring's adversity.

Tiger, HU: fierce king of animals; extreme yang; opposed to and protects against demoniacs on North–South axis of Universal Compass.

10. Im,3a,4a Treading a tiger tail.

10. ImT That uses Treading a tiger tail.

27.4a Tiger observing: glaring, glaring.

49.5a/b Great People: tiger transforming.

Till, KENG: plow; labor at, cultivate.

25.2a/b Not tilling the crop.

Time-reckoning, LI: fix times, seasons, calendar; reckon the course of heavenly bodies, astronomical events.

49.ST A chün tzu uses regulating time-reckoning to brighten the seasons.

Tips, MO: growing ends, outermost twigs; last, most distant.

28. ImT Roots, tips, fading indeed.

31.5b Purpose, the tips indeed.

Together-with, PING: also, both, at the same time. The ideogram: two people standing together.

48.3a Together-with acquiescing-in one's blessing.

Toil, LAO: labor, take pains, exert yourself; burdened, careworn; worthy actions. The ideogram: strength and fire, producing heat.

15.3a/b Toiling Humbling: chün tzu.

48.ST A chün tzu uses toiling commoners to encourage mutualizing.

58. ImT The commoners forget their toiling.

Token, HSÜ: halves of a torn piece of silk which identify the bearers when joined.

63.4a A token: possessing clothes in-tatters.

Tolerate, JUNG: allow, contain, endure, bear with; accept graciously. The ideogram: full stream bed, tolerating and containing.

7.ST A chün tzu uses tolerating commoners to accumulate crowds.

19.ST [A chün tzu uses] tolerating to protect the commoners without delimiting.

30.4b Without a place to tolerate indeed.

32.3b Without a place to tolerate indeed.

57.S Sojourning and-also lacking a place to tolerate.

Tongue, SHE: tongue in the mouth; clapper in a bell, valve in a pump, hook of a clasp; talkative, wordy.

31.6a/b Conjoining one's jawbones, cheeks, tongue.

Topple, TIEN: fall over because top-heavy; overthrow, subvert; top, summit.

27.CD Great Exceeding: toppling indeed.

27.2a Toppling Jaws.

27.4a/b Toppling Jaws. Significant.

28.CD Great Exceeding: toppling indeed.

50.1a/b The Vessel: toppling the foot.

Tortoise, KUEI: turtles; armored animals, shells and shields; long-living; oracle-consulting by tortoise shell; image of the macrocosm: heaven and earth, between them the soft flesh of humans.

27.1a Stowing-away simply the psyche tortoise.

41.5a Maybe augmenting's ten: partnering's tortoise.

42.2a Maybe Augmenting's ten: partnering's tortoise.

Total, FAN: all, everything; world, humankind.

42. ImT Total Augmenting's tao.

Trailing creeper, KO LEI: lush, fast-growing hanging plants; spread rapidly and widely; numerous progeny.

47.6a/b Confined, tending-towards trailing creepers.

Transform, PIEN: abrupt, radical, fundamental mutation from one state of being to another; transformation of lines in hexagrams; contrasts with change, HUA, gradual metamorphosis.

1.ImT Force: tao transforming changes.
15. ImT Earthly tao transforming overfilling and-also diffusing Humbling.
22. ImT Using scrutinizing the seasons transforming.
23. ImT Supple transforming solid indeed.
32. ImT The four seasons transforming changes and-also enabling lasting accomplishment.
37.1b Purpose not-yet transformed indeed.
45.2b Centering, not-yet transforming indeed.
49.5a/b Great People: tiger transforming.
49.6a/b A chün tzu: leopard transforming.
54.2b Not-yet transforming the rules indeed.
61.1b Purpose not-yet transformed indeed.

Tread, LÜ: step, path, track; footsteps; walk a path or way; course of the stars; act, practise; conduct; salary, means of subsistence. The ideogram: body and repeating steps, following a trail.

Image of Hexagram 10 and occurs throughout its texts.

2.1a Treading frost, hardening ice culminating.
2.1b Treading frost hardening the ice:
9.CD Treading: not abiding indeed.
11.S Treading and-also Pervading.
30.1a Treading, polishing therefore.
30.1b Treading, polishing it respectfully.
34.ST A chün tzu uses no codes whatever, nowhere treading.
54.1a Halting enabling treading.
54.1b Halting enabling treading, significant.

Tree, see: **Wood**

Trial, CHEN: test by ordeal; inquiry by divination and its result; righteous, firm; separating wheat from chaff; the kernel, the proven core; fourth stage of the Time Cycle. The ideogram: pearl and divination. See also: **Spring Growing Harvesting Trial** and **Harvesting Trial**

2.Im/ImT Quiet Trial significant.
2.3a/b Containing composition permitting Trial.
2.7b Availing-of the sixes, perpetual Trial.
3.ImT Great Growing: Trial.
3.2a Woman[and]Son, Trial: not nursing.

3.5a The small, Trial: significant.
3.5a The great, Trial: pitfall.
5.Im/ImT Shining Growing, Trial: significant.
5.5a Trial: significant.
5.5b Liquor taken-in, Trial: significant.
6.3a Taking-in ancient actualizing-tao. Trial.
6.4a Denying quiet Trial. Significant.
6.4b Denying quiet Trial.
7.Im Legions: Trial.
7.ImT Trial: correcting indeed.
7.5a Trial: pitfall.
8.Im/ImT Retracing the oracle-consulting: Spring, perpetual Trial.
8.2a,4a Trial: significant.
9.6a The wife, Trial: adversity.
10.2a/b Shade people, Trial: significant.
10.5a/b Parting Treading. Trial: adversity.
11.3a Drudgery, Trial: without fault.
11.6a Trial: abashment.
12.1a Trial: significant. Growing.
12.1b Eradicating thatch-grass, Trial: significant.
15.2a/b Calling Humbling. Trial: significant.
16.2a Trial: significant.
16.2b Not completing the day, Trial: significant.
16.5a Trial: affliction.
16.5b Six at-fifth, Trial: affliction.
17. ImT Great Growing, Trial: without fault.
17.1a An office: possessing denial. Trial: significant.
17.4a Following possessing catching. Trial: pitfall.
18.2a Not permitting Trial.
19.1a/b Conjunction Nearing, Trial: significant.
20.2b Peeping-through Viewing: woman Trial.
21.5a Trial: adversity.
21.5b Trial: adversity, without fault.
22.3a/b Perpetual Trial significant.
23.1a,2a Discarding the Trial: pitfall.
25.4a Permitting Trial.
25.4b Permitting Trial, without fault.
27. Im/ImT Jaws, Trial: significant.
27.3a Rejecting Jaws. Trial: pitfall.
27.5a/b Residing-in Trial significant.
31.4a/b Trial: significant, repenting extinguished.

32.1a Diving Persevering, Trial: pitfall.
32.3a Trial: abashment.
32.5a Persevering one's actualizing-tao: Trial.
32.5b Wife people, Trial: significant.
33.5a/b Excellence Retiring, Trial: significant.
34.2a Trial: significant.
34.2b Nine at-second, Trial: significant.
34.3a Trial: adversity.
34.4a Trial: significant.
35.1a,2a Trial: significant.
35.4a Trial: adversity.
35.4b Bushy-tailed rodents, Trial: adversity.
35.6a Trial: abashment.
36.3a Not permitting affliction: Trial.
36.5b The winnowing son's Trial.
37.2a Trial: significant.
39. Im Trial: significant.
39. ImT Appropriate situation, Trial: significant.
40.2a Trial: significant.
40.2b Nine at-second, Trial: significant.
40.3a Trial: abashment.
41. Im/ImT Without fault, permitting Trial.
41.6a Trial: significant.
42.2a Perpetual Trial significant.
44.1a Trial: significant.
45.5a Spring, perpetual Trial.
46.5a/b Trial: significant, Ascending steps.
46.6a Harvesting: tending-towards not pausing's Trial.
47. Im/ImT Trial: Great People significant.
49.3a Chastising: pitfall, Trial: adversity.
49.6a Residing-in Trial significant.
56. Im Sojourning, Trial: significant.
56. ImT Sojourning, Trial: significant indeed.
56.2a/b Acquiring a youthful vassal: Trial.
56.3a Trial: adversity.
57.5a Trial: significant, repenting extinguished.
57.6a Trial: pitfall.
60. Im/ImT Bitter Articulating not permitting Trial.
60.6a/b Bitter Articulating, Trial: pitfall.
61.6a Trial: pitfall.
62.4a No availing-of perpetual Trial.
64.2a Trial: significant.
64.2b Nine at-second, Trial: significant.
64.4a/b Trial: significant, repenting extinguished.
64.5a Trial: significant, without repenting.

Truly, YI: statement is true and precise.
6.6b Truly not standing respectfully indeed.
8.3b Reaching-to not truly injuring.
9.2b Truly not originating-from letting-go indeed.
20.2b Truly permitting the demoniac indeed.
27.1b Truly not the stand to value indeed.
28.5b Truly permitting the demoniac indeed.
31.3b Truly not abiding indeed.
40.3b Truly permitting the demoniac indeed.
41.4b Truly permitting rejoicing indeed.
48. Im/ImT Muddy culmination: Truly not-yet the well-rope Well.
56.3b Actually truly using injuring.
64.1b Truly not knowing the end indeed.
64.6b Truly not knowing articulating indeed.

Trustworthy, HSIN: truthful, faithful, consistent over time; integrity; confide in, follow; credentials; contrasts with conforming, FU, connection in a specific moment. The ideogram: person and word, true speech.
14.5b Trustworthiness uses shooting-forth purpose indeed.
29. ImT Movement venturing and-also not letting-go one's trustworthiness.
43.4a/b Hearing words, not trustworthy.
47. Im/ImT Possessing words not trustworthy.
49. ImT Skinning and-also trusting it.
49.4b Trustworthy purpose indeed.
50.4b Wherefore trustworthy thus indeed?
55.2b Trustworthiness using shooting-forth purpose indeed.
58.2b Trustworthy purpose indeed.
61.S Articulating and-also trusting it.
61/62.CD Centering Conforming: trustworthiness indeed.
61. ImT Trustworthiness extending-to hog fish indeed.
62.S Possessing one's trustworthiness implies necessarily moving it.

Tumble, YÜN: fall with a crash, fall from the sky; roll down.
44.5a/b Possessing tumbling, originating-from heaven.

Turn-away, KUAI: turn your back on something and focus on its opposite; contradict, cross purposes; cunning, crafty; perverse; contrasts with return, FU, going back to the start.
38.S Dwelling tao exhausted, necessarily turning-away.

38.S Polarizing implies turning-away indeed.

39.S Turning-away necessarily possesses heaviness.

Turn-to, HSIANG: direct your mind towards, seek.

17.ST A chün tzu uses turning-to darkening to enter a reposing pause.

Tusk, YA: teeth of animals; toothlike, jagged, gnaw; ivory; a tax collector.

26.5a A gelded pig's tusks.

Twice, three-times, TSAI SAN: serial repetition.

4.Im/ImT Twice, three-times: obscuring.

Twine, SO: string or rope of many strands twisted together; tie up, bind together; reins; ruling ideas, obligations; demand, search for, inquire; scatter, loosen, destroy authority.

51.6a/b Shake: twining, twining.

Twin-peaked, CH'I: mountain with two peaks; forked road; diverge, ambiguous. The ideogram: mountain and branched. Twin-peaked Mountain, CH'I SHAN, is the ancestral shrine of the Chou Dynasty.

46.4a/b Kinghood availing-of Growing, tending-towards the twin-peaked mountain.

Two, ERH: pair, even numbers, binary, duplicate. See also: **Twice, three-times**

31. ImT The two agencies influencing correspondence use mutual associating.

38. ImT Two women concording: residing.

41. Im/ImT Two platters permit availing-of presenting.

41. ImT Two platters corresponding possess the season.

49. ImT Two women concording, residing.

Unconsidered, KOU: offhand, impromptu, improvised; careless, improper; illicit.

22.S Beings not permitted to use unconsidered uniting and-also climaxing.

Understand, TS'UNG: perceive quickly, astute, sharp; discriminate intelligently. The ideogram: ear and quick.

21.6b Understanding not brightened indeed.

43.4b Understanding not brightened indeed.

50. ImT Ground and-also the ear[and]eye: understanding brightened.

Uneven, PEI: any difference in level; inclined, falling down, tipped over, dilapidated; also: rising; bank, shore, dam, dikes.

11.3a Without evening, not unevening.

Unite, HO: join, match, correspond, agree, collect, reply; unison, harmony; also: close, shut the mouth. The ideogram: mouth and assemble.

1.ImT Protection uniting the great harmony.

2.ImT Actualizing-tao uniting without delimiting.

9.4b Uniting purposes above indeed.

21.S Permitting Viewing and-also afterwards possessing a place to unite.

21.S Gnawing Bite implies uniting indeed.

21. ImT Thunder, lightning, uniting and-also composing.

22.S Beings not permitted to use unconsidered uniting and-also climaxing.

26.3b Uniting purposes above indeed.

41.1b Honoring uniting purposes indeed.

46.1b Uniting purposes above indeed.

Unsteady[and]unsettled, NIEH WU: badly based; unquiet, hazardous; uneasy, anxious; dizzy, giddy as on a high place.

47.6a Tending-towards the unsteady[and]unsettled.

Urge, SU: strong specific desire; quick, hurried; call, invite.

5.6a Possessing not urging's visitors.

5.6b Not urging's visitors coming.

31/32.CD Conjoining: urging indeed.

Use(-of), YI: make use of, by means of, owing to; employ, make functional.

This term occurs throughout the hexagram texts.

Use-up, CHIN: exhaust, use all; ended, an empty vessel.

23.S Actually involving embellishing, therefore afterwards Growing by-consequence used-up.

24.S Beings not permitted to use completing using-up.

Value, KUEI: regard as valuable, give worth and dignity to; precious, high priced; honorable, exalted, illustrious. The ideogram: cowries (coins) and basket.

3.1b Using valuing the mean below.

27.1b Truly not the stand to value indeed.

39.6b Using adhering-to valuing indeed.

50.1b Using adhering-to valuing indeed.

54.5b Using valuing movement indeed.

Vassal, P'U: servant, menial, retainer; helper in

heavy work; palace officers, chamberlains; follow, serve, belong to.

56.2a/b Acquiring a youthful vassal: Trial.

56.3a Losing one's youthful vassal.

Veil, FU: screen on person or carriage; hair ornaments; lit.: luxuriant, tangled vegetation that conceals the path.

63.2a A wife losing her veil.

Venerable, LAO: term of respect due to old age.

28.2a A venerable husband acquiring his woman consort.

28.2b A venerable husband, a woman consort.

28.5a A venerable wife acquiring her notable husband.

28.5b A venerable wife, a notable husband.

Venture, HSIEN: risk without reserve; key point, point of danger; difficulty, obstruction that must be confronted; water falling and filling the holes on its way; the Action of the trigram Gorge, K'AN. The ideogram: mound and all or whole, everything engaged at one point.

3.ImT Stirring-up reaching-to venturing center.

4.ImT Enveloping. Below mountain possessing venturing.

4.ImT Venturing and-also stopping.

5.ImT Venturing located-in precedence indeed.

6.ImT Arguing. Solid above, venture below.

6.ImT Venturing and-also persisting.

7.ImT Movement venturing and-also yielding.

29. ImT Redoubling venturing indeed.

29. ImT Movement venturing and-also not letting-go one's trustworthiness.

29. ImT Heaven venturing, not permitting ascending indeed.

29. ImT Earth venturing, mountains, rivers, hill-tops, mounds indeed.

29. ImT The kingly prince sets-up venturing used to guard his city.

29. ImT Actually venturing's season availing-of the great in-fact.

29.2a Gorge possessing venturing.

29.3a Venturing moreover reclining.

39. ImT Venturing located-in precedence indeed.

39. ImT Visualizing venturing and-also enabling stopping.

40. ImT Taking-apart. Venturing uses stirring-up.

40. ImT Stirring-up and-also evading reaching-to venturing.

47. ImT Venturing uses stimulating.

60. ImT Stimulating uses movement venturing.

Verily, WEI: the epitome of; in truth, the only; very important.

3.S Overfilling Heaven[and]Earth's interspace implies verily the myriad beings.

13. ImT Verily a chün tzu activating enables interpenetrating Below Heaven's purpose.

47. ImT Reaching-to one's very chün tzu.

Versatility, I: sudden and unpredictable change; mental mobility and openness; easy and light, not difficult and heavy; occurs in name of the I CHING.

14.5b Versatility and-also without preparing indeed.

32.ST A chün tzu uses establishing, not versatility on-all-sides.

34.5a/b Losing the goat, tending-towards versatility.

41.AE Diminishing: beforehand heaviness and-also afterwards versatility.

56.6a/b Losing the cattle, tending-towards versatility.

Vessel/holding, TING: bronze cauldron with three feet and two ears, sacred vessel used to cook food for sacrifice to gods and ancestors; founding symbol of family or dynasty; melting pot, receptacle; hold, contain, transform; establish, secure; precious, respectable.

Image of Hexagram 50 and occurs throughout its texts.

View, KUAN: contemplate, observe from a distance; look at carefully, gaze at; also: a monastery, an observatory; scry, divine through liquid in a cup. The ideogram: see and waterbird, observe through air or water.

Image of Hexagram 20 and occurs throughout its texts.

19/20.CD Nearing Viewing's righteousness.

21.S Permitting Viewing and-also afterwards possessing a place to unite.

22. ImT Viewing reaching-to the heavenly pattern.

22. ImT Viewing reaching-to the people pattern.

23. ImT Viewing symbols indeed.

27. Im/ImT Viewing Jaws.

27. ImT Viewing one's place to nourish indeed.

27. ImT Viewing one's origin: nourishing indeed.

27.1a/b Viewing my pendent Jaws.

31. ImT Viewing one's place to influence.

32. ImT Viewing one's place to Persevere.

45. ImT Actually viewing one's place to assemble.

● **Violent**, PAO: fierce, oppressive, cruel; strike hard.

16.AE Used to await violent visitors.

● **Virtue**, TSANG: essential force or quality; generous, good, dexterous.

7.1a Obstructing virtue: pitfall.

● **Visage**, MIEN: face, countenance; honor, character, reputation; front, surface; face to face.

49.6a/b Small People: Skinning the visage.

● **Visitor**, K'O: guest, stranger, foreign, from afar; squatter.

5.6a Possessing not urging's visitors.

5.6b Not urging's visitors coming.

16.AE Used to await violent visitors.

● **Visualize**, CHIEN: seeing in all its aspects: vision, being visible, forming mental images; visit, call on, consult. The ideogram: eye above person, active and receptive sight.

1.2a,5a Harvesting: visualizing Great People.

1.2a/b Visualizing dragon located-in the fields.

1.7a Visualizing flocking dragons without a head.

3/4.CD Sprouting: visualizing and-also not letting-go one's residing.

4.3a Visualizing a metallic husband.

6.Im/ImT Harvesting: visualizing Great People.

18.4a Going: visualizing abashment.

24. ImT Reaching-to Returning one's visualizing Heaven[and]Earth's heart.

31. ImT And-also actually Heaven[and]Earth, the myriad beings's motives permitting visualizing.

32. ImT And-also actually Heaven[and]Earth, the myriad beings's motives permitting visualizing.

34. ImT Actually the correcting Great and-also Heaven[and]Earth's motives permitting visualizing.

38.1a/b Visualizing hateful people.

38.3a/b Visualizing the cart pulled-back.

38.6a Visualizing pigs bearing mire.

39. Im/ImT,6a/b Harvesting: visualizing Great People.

39. ImT Visualizing venturing and-also enabling stopping.

42.ST A chün tzu uses visualizing improvement, by-consequence shifting.

45. Im/ImT Harvesting: visualizing Great People. Growing.

45. ImT And-also actually Heaven[and]Earth, the myriad beings's motives, permitting visualizing.

46. Im Availing-of visualizing Great People.

46. ImT That uses great Growing to avail-of visualizing Great People.

47.3a/b Entering tending-towards one's house. Not visualizing one's consort.

52. Im/ImT Not visualizing one's people.

55.2a,4a/b Sun centering: visualizing a bin.

55.3a Sun centering: visualizing froth.

57. Im/ImT Harvesting: visualizing Great People.

57/58.CD Open: visualizing

● **Vulgar**, SU: common people and their desires; inelegant, low; grovelling; the pressure of everyday life.

53.ST A chün tzu uses residing-in eminent actualizing-tao to improve the vulgar.

● **Wade**, SHE: walk in or through the water; spend time on something; contrasts with ford, CHI, to cross. The ideogram: step and water. See also: **Wading the Great River**

28.6a Exceeding wading submerges the peak. Pitfall.

28.6b Exceeding wading's pitfall.

● **Wading the Great River**, SHE TA CH'UAN consciously moving into the flow of time; enter the stream of life with a goal or purpose; embark on a significant enterprise.

5.Im/ImT Harvesting: wading the Great River.

6.Im/ImT Not Harvesting: wading the Great River.

13. Im/ImT Harvesting: wading the Great River.

15.1a Availing-of wading the Great River. Significant.

18. Im/ImT Harvesting: wading the Great River.

26.Im/ImT Harvesting: wading the Great River.

27.5a Not permitting wading the Great River.

27.6a Harvesting: wading the Great River.

42.Im/ImT Harvesting: wading the Great River.

59.Im/ImT Harvesting: wading the Great River.

61.Im/ImT Harvesting: wading the Great River.

64.3a Harvesting: wading the Great River.

Warn, CHIEH: alert, alarm, put on guard; caution, inform; guard against, refrain from (as in a diet). The ideogram: spear held in both hands, warning enemies and alerting friends.

11.4a/b Not warning: using conforming.

45.ST [A chün tzu uses] warning, not precautions.

51.6b Dreading the neighbor, a warning indeed.

62.4a/b Going adversity necessarily warning.

63.4a/b Completing the day, a warning.

Wasteland, HUANG: wild, barren, deserted, unproductive; jungle, moor, heath; reckless, neglectful.

11.2a Enwrapping wasteland.

11.2b Enwrapping wasteland, acquiring honor, tending-towards centering moving.

Waver, CH'UNG: irresolute, hesitating; unsettled, disturbed; fluctuate, sway to and fro.

31.4a/b Wavering, wavering: going, coming.

Weariness, PAI: fatigue; debilitated, exhausted, distressed; weak.

33.3b Possessing afflicting weariness indeed.

63.3b Weariness indeed.

Weep, CH'I: lament wordlessly; grieved, heart-broken.

3.6a/b Weeping blood, coursing thus.

61.3a Maybe weeping, maybe singing.

Well, CHING: water well at the center of the fields; rise and flow of water in a well, rise and surge from an inner source; life-water, nucleus of life; found a capital city. The ideogram: two vertical lines crossing two horizontal ones, eight fields with a well at the center.

Image of Hexagram 48 and occurs throughout its texts.

47.CD The Well: interpenetrating

49.S The Well tao not permitting not Skinning.

Well-rope, YÜ: rope used to draw water.

48.Im/ImT Muddy culmination: Truly not-yet the well-rope Well.

West, HSI: corresponds to autumn, Harvest and Streaming Moment; begins the yin hemicycle of the Universal Compass. See also: **Western South**

9.Im/ImT Originating-from my Western suburbs.

17.6a The king availing-of Growing tending-towards the Western mountain.

62.5a Originating-from my Western suburbs.

63.5a Not thus the Western neighbor's dedicated offering.

63.5b Not thus the Western neighbor's season indeed.

Western South: neutral Earthy Moment between the yang and yin hemicycles; bring forth concrete results, ripe fruits of late summer.

2.Im/ImT Western South: acquiring partnering.

39.Im/ImT Limping, Harvesting: Western South.

40.Im/ImT Taking-apart. Harvesting: Western South.

Wheel, LUN: disk, circle, round; revolution, circuit; rotate, roll, by turns.

63.1a/b Pulling-back one's wheels.

64.2a Pulling-back one's wheels.

Wherefore, HO: interrogative: why? for what reason? what is? and affirmation: therefore, for that reason.

3.6b Wherefore permitting long-living indeed?

7.ImT Actually significant, furthermore wherefore faulty?

9.1a Wherefore one's fault? Significant.

12.6b Wherefore permitting long-living indeed?

16.6b Wherefore permitting long-living indeed?

17.4a Wherefore faulty?

21.6a/b Wherefore locking-up submerging the ears?

25.ImT Actually wherefore having-it?

26.6a/b Wherefore heaven's highway?

28.5b Wherefore permitting lasting indeed?

30.3b Wherefore permitting lasting indeed?

33.1b Not going, wherefore calamity indeed.

38.5a Going wherefore faulty?

49.3b Furthermore actually wherefore having-them.

50.4b Wherefore trustworthy thus indeed?

61.6b Wherefore permitting long-living indeed?

62.1b Wherefore not permitted thus indeed.

62.3b Wherefore a pitfall thus indeed.

63.6b Wherefore permitting lasting indeed?

White, PO: associated with autumn, Harvest and the Metallic Moment; clear, immaculate; plain, pure, essential; explicit; color of death and mourning.

22.4a A white horse, soaring thus.

22.6a White Adorning.

22.6b White Adorning, without fault.

28.1a/b A sacrifice availing-of white thatch-grass.

Whose, SHUI: relative and interrogative pronoun; also: whose?

13.1b Furthermore whose fault indeed?

40.3b Furthermore whose fault indeed.

60.3b Furthermore whose fault indeed?

Wife, FU: responsible position of married woman within the household; contrasts with consort, CH'I, her legal position and concubine, CH'IEH, secondary wives. The ideogram: woman, hand and broom, household duties. See also: **Husband[and]Wife**

4.2a Letting-in the wife. Significant.

9.6a The wife, Trial: adversity.

28.5a A venerable wife acquiring her notable husband.

28.5b A venerable wife, a notable husband.

32.5a Wife people: significant.

32.5b Wife people, Trial: significant.

32.5b Adhering-to the wife: pitfall indeed.

37. ImT The husband, a husband. The wife, a wife.

37.3a/b The wife, the son, giggling, giggling:

53.3a/b The wife pregnant, not nurturing.

53.5a The wife, three year's-time not pregnant.

63.2a A wife losing her veil.

Wildfowl, CH'IN: all wild and game birds; untamed.

3.3b Using adhering-to wildfowl indeed.

8.5a Letting-go the preceding wildfowl.

8.5b Letting-go the preceding wildfowl indeed.

32.4a The fields without wildfowl.

32.4b Quietly acquiring the wildfowl indeed.

48.1a/b The ancient Well without wildfowl.

Wild-swan, HUNG: large white water bird, symbol of the soul and its spiritual aspirations; wild swan and wild goose as emblems of the messenger and of conjugal fidelity; vast, profound, far-reaching, great; valued, learned.

53.1a The wild-swan Infiltrating tending-towards the barrier.

53.2a The wild-swan Infiltrating tending-towards the stone.

53.3a,6a The wild-swan Infiltrating tending-towards the highlands.

53.4a The wild-swan Infiltrating tending-towards the trees.

53.5a The wild-swan Infiltrating tending-towards the mound.

Willow, YANG: all thriving, fast growing trees; willow, poplar, tamarisk, aspen. The ideogram: tree and expand.

28.2a A withered willow giving-birth-to a sprig.

28.5a/b A withered willow giving-birth-to flowers.

Wind, FENG: moving air, breeze, gust; weather and its influence on mood and humor; fashion, usage; wind and wood are the Symbols of the trigram Ground, SUN.

9.ST Wind moving above heaven.

18.ST Below mountain possessing wind.

20.ST Wind moving above earth.

32.ST Thunder, wind, Persevering.

32. ImT Thunder, wind, mutually associating.

37.ST Wind originating-from fire issuing-forth.

42.ST Wind, thunder. Augmenting.

44.ST Below heaven possessing wind.

50.ST Above wind possessing fire.

57.ST Following winds.

59.ST Wind moves above stream.

61.ST Above marsh possessing wind.

Window, YU: opening in wall or roof to let in light; open, instruct, enlighten.

29.4a Letting-in bonds originating-from the window.

Wine-cup, CHIO: libation cup originally in the form of a bird; all small birds; rank of nobility, confer rank on someone.

61.2a I possess a loved wine-cup.

Wings, YI: birds' wings; sails, flanks, side-rooms; brood over, shelter and defend.

36.1a Drooping one's wings.

● **Winnow**, CHI: separate grain from chaff by tossing it in the wind; separate the valuable from the worthless, good from bad; sieve, winnowing-basket; fan out.

36. ImT The winnowing son uses it.

36.5a The winnowing son's Brightness Hiding.

36.5b The winnowing son's Trial.

● **Withdraw(-from)**, T'UI: draw back, retreat, recede; decline, refuse.

20.3a/b Viewing my birth, advancing, withdrawing.

33.S Retiring implies withdrawing indeed.

33/34.CD Retiring: by-consequence withdrawing indeed.

34.6a/b Not enabling withdrawing, not enabling releasing.

40.5b Small People withdrawing indeed.

52.2b Not-yet withdrawing-from hearkening indeed.

57.1a/b Advancing, withdrawing.

● **Withered**, K'U: dry up; dry wood, dried up bogs; decayed, rotten. The ideogram: tree and old.

28.2a A withered willow giving-birth-to a sprig.

28.5a/b A withered willow giving-birth-to flowers.

● **Without**, WU: devoid of; -less as suffix. See also: **Without direction: Harvesting; Without fault; Without not Harvesting** and **Without repenting**

Image of Hexagram 25 and occurs throughout its texts.

1.7a Visualizing flocking dragons without a head.

2.ImT Actualizing-tao uniting without delimiting.

2.ImT Moving, the earth without delimiting.

2.ImT Corresponding earth without limits.

2.3a Without accomplishing possessing completion.

2.4a Without fault, without praise.

3.3b Approaching stag, without precaution.

6.2a Without blunder.

6.3a Without accomplishment.

7.3b The great without achievement indeed.

8.6a/b Without a head, Grouping it.

8.6b Without a place to complete indeed.

11.3a Without evening, not unevening.

11.3a/b Without going, not returning.

12. ImT Above[and]Below not mingling and-also Below Heaven without fiefdoms indeed.

14.1a Without mingling harm.

14.1b Without mingling harm indeed.

14.5b Versatility and-also without preparing indeed.

17/18.CD Following: without anteriority indeed.

18.3a Without the great: fault.

19.ST A chün tzu uses teaching to ponder without exhausting.

19.ST [A chün tzu uses] tolerating to protect the commoners without delimiting.

21/22.CD Adorning: without complexion indeed.

22.ST A chün tzu uses brightening the multitudinous standards without daring to sever litigating.

22.4b Completing without surpassing indeed.

23.5b Completing without surpassing indeed.

24. Im Issuing-forth, entering, without affliction.

24. ImT That uses issuing-forth, entering, without affliction.

26.S Possessing Without Embroiling therefore afterwards permitting Accumulating.

26.CD Without Embroiling: calamity indeed.

26.2b Centering without surpassing indeed.

28.ST [A chün tzu uses] retiring-from the age without melancholy.

28.5a Without fault, without praise.

29.3b Completing without achieving indeed.

30.4b Without a place to tolerate indeed.

32.3b Without a place to tolerate indeed.

32.4a The fields without wildfowl.

32.6b The great without accomplishment indeed.

33.6b Without a place to doubt indeed.

37.2a Without direction, releasing.

38.3a/b Without initially possessing completion.

39.2b Completing without surpassing indeed.

40. Im Without a place to go:

41.6a Acquiring a servant, without dwelling.

42. ImT The commoners stimulated without delimiting.

42. ImT Sun advancing without limit.

42. ImT One's Augmenting without sides.

43.4a The sacrum without flesh.
43.6a Without crying-out.
43.6b Without crying-out's pitfall.
44.3a The sacrum without flesh.
44.3a Without the great: fault.
44.4a Enwrapping without fish.
44.4b Without fish's pitfall.
46.3b Without a place to doubt indeed.
47.ST Marsh without stream.
48. Im Without losing, without acquiring.
48.1a/b The ancient Well without wildfowl.
48.2b Without associating indeed.
50.2b Completing without surpassing indeed.
51.3a Shake moving without blunder.
51.5a Intention without losing possesses affairs.
51.5b The great without losing indeed.
54.6a A woman receiving a basket without substance.
54.6a A notable disembowelling a goat without blood.
54.6b Six above, without substance.
55.6a/b Living-alone, one without people.
56.2b Completing without surpassing indeed.

● **Without direction: Harvesting,** WU YU LI: no plan or direction is advantageous; in order to take advantage of the situation, do not impose a direction on events.
4.3a Without direction: Harvesting.
19.3a Without direction: Harvesting.
25.6a Without direction: Harvesting.
27.3a Without direction: Harvesting.
32.1a Without direction: Harvesting.
34.6a Without direction: Harvesting.
45.3a Without direction: Harvesting.
54. Im/ImT,6a Without direction: Harvesting.
64. Im/ImT Without direction: Harvesting.

● **Without fault,** WU CHIU: no error or harm in the situation.
1.3a,4a Without fault.
1.4b Advancing, without fault indeed.
2.4a Without fault, without praise.
2.4b Bundled-in the bag, without fault.
5.1a Without fault.
5.1b Harvesting: availing-of persevering, without fault.
7.Im,2a,4a,5a Without fault.
7.4b The left resting, without fault.
8.Im/ImT,1a Without fault.
9.4a Without fault.

10.1a Without fault.
11.3a Drudgery, Trial: without fault.
12.4a/b Possessing fate, without fault.
13.1a Without fault.
14.1a Drudgery by-consequence without fault.
14.2a Possessing directed going. Without fault.
14.4a Without fault.
14.4b In-no-way one's preponderance. Without fault.
16.6a Without fault.
17. Im Without fault.
17. ImT Great Growing, Trial: without fault.
18.1a Predecessors without fault.
18.3b Completing without fault indeed.
19.3a,4a Without fault.
19.4b Culminating Nearing, without fault.
19.6a Significant. Without fault.
20.1a Small People: without fault.
20.5a,6a A chün tzu: without fault.
21.1a,2a,3a,5a,6a Without fault.
21.5b Trial: adversity, without fault.
22.6b White Adorning, without fault.
23.3a/b Stripping it, without fault.
24. Im/ImT Partnering coming, without fault.
24.3a Without fault.
24.3b Righteous, without fault indeed.
25.4a Without fault.
25.4b Permitting Trial, without fault.
27.4a Without fault.
28.1a,6a Without fault.
28.5a Without fault, without praise.
29.4a Completing, without fault.
29.5a Without fault.
30.1a,6a Without fault.
32. Im Without fault.
32. ImT Persevering Growing, without fault.
35.1a/b Enriching, without fault.
35.6a Adversity significant, without fault.
38.1a,2a Without fault.
38.4a Adversity, without fault.
38.4b Mingling conforming, without fault.
40.1a Without fault.
40.1b Righteous, without fault indeed.
41. Im/ImT Without fault, permitting Trial.
41.1a,4a,6a Without fault.
42.1a/b Spring significant, without fault.
42.3a Without fault.
43.3a Without fault.
43.3b Completing without fault indeed.

43.5a Center moving, without fault.
43.5a/b Center moving, without fault.
44.2a,6a Without fault.
45.1a,3a/b Going without fault.
45.2a/b Protracting significant, without fault.
45.4a/b The great significant, without fault.
45.5a Without fault: in-no-way conforming.
45.6a Without fault.
46.2a,4a Without fault.
47. Im Without fault.
47.2a Chastising: pitfall, without fault.
48.4a/b The Well: lining, without fault.
49.2a Chastising significant, without fault.
50.1a Without fault.
51.6a Without fault.
51.6b Although a pitfall, without fault.
52. Im,1a,4a Without fault.
52. ImT Without fault indeed.
53.1b Righteous, without fault indeed.
53.4a Without fault.
55.1a/b Although a decade, without fault.
55.3a Without fault.
57.2a Without fault.
59.5a/b Kinghood residing, without fault.
59.6a Without fault.
60.1a,3a Without fault.
61.4a,5a Without fault.
62.2a,4a Without fault.
63.1a Without fault.
63.1b Righteous, without fault indeed.
64.6a Without fault.

● **Without not Harvesting**, WU PU LI: nothing for which this will not be beneficial; advantageous potential, borderline where the balance is swinging from not Harvesting to actually Harvesting.
2.2a/b Not repeating: without not Harvesting.
3.4a Without not Harvesting.
14.6a Significant, without not Harvesting.
15.4a/b Without not Harvesting, demonstrating Humbling.
15.5a Without not Harvesting.
19.2a/b Without not Harvesting.
23.5a Without not Harvesting.
28.2a Without not Harvesting.
33.6a/b Rich Retiring, without not Harvesting.
35.5a Going significant, without not Harvesting.
40.6a Without not Harvesting: catching it.

50.6a Without not Harvesting.
57.5a Without not Harvesting.

Without repenting, WU HUI: devoid of the sort ●
of trouble that leads to sorrow, regret and the
necessity to change your attitude.
13.6a/b Concording People tending-towards the suburbs. Without repenting.
24.1a Without merely repenting.
24.5a Without repenting.
24.5b Magnanimous Returning, without repenting.
31.5a Without repenting.
34.5a Without repenting.
59.3a Without repenting.
64.5a Trial: significant, without repenting.

With-respect-to, YÜ: relates to, refers to; hold a ●
position in.
5.ST Above clouds with-respect-to heaven.
8.4b Outside Grouping with-respect-to eminence.
23.ST Mountain adjoining with-respect-to earth.
24.AE Returning: the small and-also marking-off with-respect-to beings.
25. ImT Solid originating-from the outside coming and-also activating a lord with-respect-to the inside.
32. ImT Lasting with-respect-to one's tao indeed.
32. ImT The all-wise person lasting with-respect-to his tao and-also Below Heaven the changes accomplishing.
37.S Injury with-respect-to the outside implies necessarily reversing with-respect-to Dwelling.
43.ST Above marsh with-respect-to heaven.
45.ST Above marsh with-respect-to earth.
55. ImT And-also even-more with-respect-to the people reached.
55. ImT Even-more with-respect-to the Souls[and]Spirits reached.

Woman(hood), NÜ: a woman; what is inherently ●
female. See also: **Man[and]Woman** and
Woman[and]Son
4.3a/b No availing-of grasping womanhood.
20.2a Harvesting: woman Trial.
20.2b Peeping-through Viewing: woman Trial.
28.2a A venerable husband acquiring his woman consort.

28.2b A venerable husband, a woman consort.

31.Im Grasping womanhood significant.

31.ImT Below manhood, womanhood.

31.ImT That uses Growth Harvesting Trial, grasping womanhood significant.

37.Im Dwelling People, Harvesting: woman Trial.

37.ImT The woman correcting the situation reaching-to the inside.

38.ImT Man, Woman, Polarizing and-also their purposes interpenetrating indeed.

44.Im Coupling, womanhood invigorating.

44.Im/ImT No availing-of grasping womanhood.

53.Im Infiltrating, womanhood converting significant.

53/54.CD Infiltrating: womanhood converting awaits manhood moving indeed.

53/54.CD Converting Maidenhood: womanhood's completion indeed.

53.ImT Womanhood converting significant.

54.6a A woman receiving a basket without substance.

Woman[and]Son, NÜ TZU: particular relation between a woman and her child.

3.2a Woman[and]Son, Trial: not nursing.

Wood/tree, MU: all things woody or wooden, alive or constructed from wood; associated with the Woody Moment; wood and wind are the Symbols of the trigram Ground, SUN. The ideogram: a tree with roots and branches.

28.ST Marsh submerging wood.

30.ImT The hundred grains, grasses, trees congregating reaching-to earth.

40.ImT Thunder[and]Rain arousing and-also the hundred fruits, grasses, trees, altogether seedburst boundary.

42.ImT Woody tao, thereupon moving.

46.ST Earth center giving-birth-to wood.

47.1a The sacrum Confined, tending-towards stump wood.

48.ST Above wood possessing stream.

50.ImT Using wood: Ground, fire.

53.ST Above mountain possessing wood.

53.4a The wild-swan Infiltrating tending-towards the trees.

59.ImT Riding wood possesses achievement indeed.

61.ImT Riding a wooden dug-out, emptiness indeed.

Word, YEN: speech, spoken words, sayings; talk, discuss, address. The ideogram: mouth and rising vapor, words as speech.

5.2a The small possesses words.

5.2b Although the small possesses words, using completing significant indeed.

6.1a The small possesses words, completing significant.

6.1b Although the small possesses words, one's differentiation brightening indeed.

7.5a Harvesting: holding-on-to words.

13.5b Words mutualize controlling indeed.

26.ST A chün tzu uses the numerous recorded preceding words going to move.

27.ST A chün tzu uses considering words to inform.

36.1a A lord: the people possessing words.

37.ST A chün tzu uses words to possess beings and-also movement to possess perseverance.

43.4a/b Hearing words, not trustworthy.

47.Im/ImT Possessing words not trustworthy.

49.3a/b Skinning words three-times drawing-near:

51.Im/ImT Laughing words, shrieking, shrieking.

51.1a After laughing words, shrieking, shrieking.

51.1b Laughing words, shrieking, shrieking.

51.6a Matrimonial allying possesses words.

52.5a Words possessing sequence.

53.1a The small son, adversity possessing words.

Worship, CHIEN: honor the gods and ancestors; make sacrifice; recommend or introduce yourself. The ideogram: leading animals to green pastures.

16.ST Exalting worship's Supreme Above.

20.Im/ImT Viewing: hand-washing and-also not worshipping.

Yang: Action; dynamic and light aspect of phenomena: arouses, transforms, dissolves existing structures; linear thrust; stimulus, drive, focus; direct or orient something.

1.1b Yang located below indeed.

11.ImT Inside yang and-also outside yin.

12.ImT Inside yin and-also outside yang.

Years-revolved, NIEN: number of years elapsed; a person's age; contrasts with year's-time, SUI, length of time in a year.

3.2a/b Ten years-revolved, thereupon nursing.

24.6a Culminating tending-towards ten years-revolved not controlling chastisement.

27.3a/b Ten years-revolved, no availing-of.

63.3a/b Three years-revolved controlling it.

64.4a Three years-revolved, possessing donating tending-towards the great city.

Year's-time, SUI: actual length of time in a year; contrasts with years-revolved, NIEN, number of years elapsed.

13.3a/b Three year's-time not rising.

29.6a Three year's-time, not acquiring. Pitfall.

29.6b Pitfall: three year's-time indeed.

47.1a Three year's-time not encountering.

53.5a The wife, three year's-time not pregnant.

55.6a Three year's-time not encountering.

Yellow, HUANG: color of the productive middle; associated with the Earthy Moment between the yang and yin hemicycles; color of soil in central China; emblematic and imperial color of China since the Yellow Emperor (2500 BCE).

2.5a/b A yellow apron. Spring significant.

2.6a Their blood: indigo, yellow.

21.5a Gnawing parched meat. Acquiring yellow metal.

30.2a/b Yellow Radiance. Spring significant.

33.2a Holding-on-to it: availing-of yellow cattle's skin.

33.2b Holding-on avails-of yellow cattle.

40.2a Acquiring a yellow arrow.

49.1a Thonging avails-of yellow cattle's Skin.

49.1b Thonging avails-of yellow cattle.

50.5a The Vessel: yellow ears, metallic rings.

50.5b The Vessel: yellow ears.

Yield(-to), SHUN: give way and bear produce; comply, agree, follow, obey; unresisting, docile, flexible; nourish, provide; the Action of the trigram Field, K'UN. The ideogram: head and current, water flowing from the head of a river, yielding to the banks.

2.ImT Thereupon yielding receiving heaven.

2.ImT Supple yielding, Harvesting Trial.

2.ImT Afterwards yielding acquiring rules.

4.3b Movement not yielding indeed.

4.5b Yielding uses Ground indeed.

4.6b Above[and]Below yielding indeed.

5.4b Yielding uses hearkening indeed.

7.ImT Movement venturing and-also yielding.

8.ImT Yielding adhering-to the below indeed.

8.5b Stowing-away countering, grasping yielding.

11. ImT Inside persisting and-also outside yielding.

14.ST [A chün tzu uses] yielding-to heaven to relinquish fate.

16. ImT Yielding uses stirring-up. Provision.

16. ImT Providing-for: yielding uses stirring-up.

16. ImT Heaven[and]Earth uses yielding stirring-up.

16. ImT The all-wise person uses yielding stirring-up.

19. ImT Stimulating and-also yielding.

19.2b Not-yet yielding-to fate indeed.

20. ImT Yielding and-also Ground.

23. ImT Yielding and-also stopping it.

24. ImT Stirring-up and-also using yielding movement.

27.5b Yielding uses adhering-to the above indeed.

31.2b Yielding, not harming indeed.

35. ImT Yielding and-also congregating reaching-to great brightening.

36. ImT Inside pattern Brightening and-also outside supple yielding.

36.2b Yielding used by-consequence indeed.

37.2b Yielding uses Ground indeed.

37.4b Yielding located-in the situation indeed.

45. ImT Yielding uses stimulating.

45. ImT Yielding-to heaven: fate indeed.

46.ST A chün tzu uses yielding to actualize-tao.

46. ImT Ground and-also yielding.

46.4b Yielding affairs indeed.

49. ImT Yielding reaching-to heaven and-also corresponding reaching-to the people.

49.6b Yielding uses adhering-to the chief indeed.

53.3b Yielding mutualizes protection indeed.

53.4b Yielding using Ground indeed.

56. ImT Supple acquiring the center reaching-to the outside and-also yielding reaching-to the solid.

56. ImT Supple acquiring the center reaching-to the outside and-also yielding reaching-to the solid.

57. ImT Supple altogether yielding reaching the solid.

58. ImT That uses yielding reaching-to heaven and-also corresponding reaching-to the people.

59.1b Yielding indeed.

62. ImT Countering above and-also yielding below indeed.

Yin: Struction; consolidating, shadowy aspect of phenomena: conserves, substantializes, creates structures; spacial extension; limited, bound, given specific being; build, make something concrete.

2.1b Yin begins solidifying indeed.

11. ImT Inside yang and-also outside yin.

12. ImT Inside yin and-also outside yang.

61.2a Calling crane located-in yin.

Your, CHÜEH: intensifying personal pronoun, specifically you! your!; intensify, concentrate, tense, contract; lit.: muscle spasms.

14.5a Your conforming: mingling thus, impressing thus. Significant.

14.5b Your conforming, mingling thus.

38.5a/b Your ancestor gnawing flesh.

Youthful, T'UNG: young person between eight and fifteen; young animals and plants.

4.Im/ImT In-no-way me seeking youthful Enveloping.

4.Im/ImT Youthful Enveloping seeking me.

4.5a/b Youthful Enveloping. Significant.

20.1a Youthful Viewing.

20.1b Initial six, youthful Viewing.

26.4a Youthful cattle's stable.

56.2a/b Acquiring a youthful vassal: Trial.

56.3a Losing one's youthful vassal.

■

FURTHER READING

The following list suggests themes and books that may help you understand the *I Ching* as an oracle, its origins, and its background old and new. It is not exhaustive, nor is there any reference to works in Chinese or, for the most part, in languages other than English.

● *Related I Ching Publications*

There is a two-cassette audio presentation of lectures, practical advice, procedures and consultations from the *Eranos I Ching Seminars* available from Spring Audio (PO Box 365, Gracie Station, NY, NY, 10028). Order through your local bookstore, Eranos Foundation, or Spring Audio.

The 1992 *Eranos Yearbook* is a collection of articles by scholars, writers and artists on the *I Ching*, divination, depth psychology and the ethic of the imagination. They are available through the Foundation, Spring Publications or your local bookstore.

● *Basic Commentary*

The work of Hellmut Wilhelm, son of the translator Richard Wilhelm, is a fundamental source of insight into the philosophy and use of the *I Ching*.

● HELLMUT WILHELM, *Change: Eight Lectures on the I Ching*, trans. Cary F. Baynes, (Princeton: Princeton University Press, Bollingen Series lxii, 1960).

HELLMUT WILHELM, *Heaven, Earth and Man in the Book of Changes*, Seven Eranos Lectures, (Seattle and London: University of Washington Press, 1977).

HELLMUT WILHELM, *"On Sacrifice in the I Ching,"* (Spring *1972*, 74-89.)

He also assembled a bibliography of sources on the *I Ching* until 1975:

HELLMUT WILHELM, *The Book of Changes in the Western Tradition: A Selective Bibliography*, Parerga 2, (Seattle: Institute for Comparative and Foreign Area Studies, University of Washington, 1975).

In the last 50 years, a school of thought has developed that sees the *I Ching* primarily as a sociological and historical document. Though it ignores the imaginative and spiritual significance of the book, it provides interesting information on the book's various levels and layers, the culture surrounding its origins, and old meanings for many of the divinatory terms. This critical approach employs Western analytical methods. It originated in China largely in reaction to the moralistic imperial stance taken by official philosophers. A primary source, with an interesting Foreword by an exponent of a different school of thought, is:

JULIAN K. SCHUTSKII, *Researches on the I Ching*, (Princeton: Princeton University Press, 1979).

Perhaps the best current example of such scholarship in English is a translation and commentary on the oldest known manuscript of the *I Ching* (from the tombs at *Mawangdui*, dated to c. 168 BCE). It is very technical and includes an extensive multi-lingual bibliography.

RICHARD ALAN KUNST, *The Original Yijing: A Text, Phonetic Transcription and Indexes with Sample Glosses*, (Ann Arbor: University Microfilms, 1985).

A non-technical bibliography (English only) and assemblage of information "perspectives" of varied quality is contained in:

EDWARD A. HACKER, *The I Ching Handbook: A Practical Guide to Personal and Logical Perspectives from the Ancient Chinese Book of Changes*, (Brookline MA: Paradigm Publications, 1993).

The Great Treatise or Commentary on the Attached Evidences

The *Hzi t'zu chuan* or *Ta chuan*, the "Great Treatise" attached to the *I Ching*, was "for 2000 years one of the most influential statements in Chinese tradition on knowing how the cosmos worked and how humans might relate to it" (Peterson). An excellent description, analysis and partial new translation, which relates divination with the *I* to various magical traditions, is:

WILLARD PETERSON, "*Making Connections: 'Commentary on the Attached Verbalizations' of the Book of Changes*," (Harvard Journal of Asiatic Studies, 42/1, June 1982, 67–112.)

For Chinese ideas on how the *I Ching* works, see:

WILLARD PETERSON, "Some Connective Concepts in China," *Eranos 57/1988*.

This treatise is translated in the central part of the Wilhelm/Baynes translation and in:

GERALD SWANSON, *The Great Treatise: Commentary Tradition to the Book of Changes*, (Ann Arbor: University Microfilms, 1974).

A very interesting modern translation can be found in an Appendix to:

WU JING-NUAN, *Yijing*, (Washington, D.C.: Taoist Study Series, distributed by University of Hawaii Press, 1991).

Divination

An overview:

GEORGE KERLIN PARK, "Divination," *Encyclopedia Britannica*, 15th ed., Macropedia, v. 5, 916–20.

MICHAEL LOEWE AND CARMEN BLACKER, eds, *Oracles and Divination*, (Boulder CO: Shambala, 1981).

The best examination of divination in classical Mediterranean culture has never been translated into English:

A. BOUCHÉ-LECLERQ, *L'histoire de la divination dans l'antiquité*, 4 vol., (Paris, 1879, rpt. Aalen: Scientia Verlag, 1978).

See also:

H. W. PARKE, *Greek Oracles*, (London, 1967).

A very interesting look at the shift in divinatory methods which produced the *I Ching*, also not translated, is:

H. W. PARKE, "De la tortue a l'achillée," in *Divination et Rationalité*, ed. Jean-Paul Vernant, (Paris: Editions du Seuil, 1974).

LEON VANDERMEERSCH, "The Origin of Milfoil Divination and the Primitive I Ching," unpublished paper presented at the Workshop on Divination and Portent Interpretation, University of California, Berkeley, June 20–July 1, 1983; published in French in *Hexagrammes* 4/1989, (Paris).

See also:

NGO VAN XUYET, *Divination, magie et politique dans la Chine ancienne*, (Paris: Presses Universitaires de France, 1976).

The closest living analogy to the divinatory process of the *I Ching* is African Ifa divination, probably developed from the Arabic geomantic system that shadowed European high culture for centuries. See:

PHILLIP PEEK, ed., *African Divination Systems: Ways of Knowing*, (Bloomington: Indiana University Press, 1991).

WILLIAM BASCOM, *Ifa Divination*, (Bloomington: Indiana University Press, 1969).

JUDITH GLEASON, with Awotunde Aworinde and John Olaniyi Ogundipe, *A Recitation of Ifa, Oracle of the Yoruba*, (New York: Grossman, 1973).

JEAN SERVIER, "Une ouverture sur le monde: magie et religion en Afrique du Nord. Un technique divinatoire: la geomancie," *Eranos 46/1977*, English translation, *Eranos 62/1993*.

Works from a classical Jungian perspective are:

C. G. JUNG, *Synchronicity: An Acausal Connecting Principle*, trans. R. F. C. Hull, (Princeton: Princeton University Press, Bollingen Series xx, 1960).

C. G. JUNG, Foreword to *The I Ching or Book of Changes. The Richard Wilhelm Translation rendered into English by Cary F. Baynes*, 3rd ed., (Princeton: Princeton University Press, Bollingen Series xix, 1967), reproduced in *CW 11*.

MARIE-LOUISE VON FRANZ, *On Divination and Sychronicity: the Psychology of Meaningful Chance*, (Toronto: Inner City Books, 1980).

An examination of how the "magic spells" used in divination became the "magic of philosophy" is:

● PEDRO LAIN ENTRALGO, *The Therapy of the Word in Classical Antiquity*, eds and trans L. J. Rather and John M. Sharp, (New Haven: Yale University Press, 1970).

One of the most interesting new developments in the practice of divination, linking it directly to "soul-making," imagination and psychology is:

● RACHEL POLLACK, *Seventy-Eight Degrees of Wisdom: a Book of Tarot*, parts 1 & 2, (London: Aquarian Press, 1980-83).

RACHEL POLLACK, *Tarot: Meditations and Readings*, (London: Aquarian Press, 1986).

RACHEL POLLACK, *Shining Woman Tarot Guide*, (London: Aquarian Press, 1992).

A wider context for practice of divination can be found in:

● STEPHEN KARCHER, "Oracle's Contexts: Gods, Dreams, Shadow, Language," *Spring 53/1992*.

STEPHEN KARCHER, "Making Spirits Bright: Divination and the Demonic Image," *Eranos 61/1992*.

STEPHEN KARCHER, *"Which Way I Fly is Hell:* Divination and the Shadow of the West," *Spring 55/1994*.

● ## *Correlative Systems and the Universal Compass*

The most extensive and detailed examination of the fundamental ideas and categories involved in the "correlative systems" of traditional Chinese science is:

● JOSEPH NEEDHAM, *Science and Civilization in China, Volume 2*, (Cambridge: Cambridge University Press, 1956).

The source for most of these systems, the report of the discussions held under Imperial auspices in 79 CE, is translated and examined in:

● TJAN TJOE SOM, *PO HU TUNG: The Comprehensive Discussions in the White Tiger Hall*, 2 vol., (Leiden: E.J. Brill, 1952).

A rare but extremely valuable discussion of divinatory and cosmological systems and their social and ideological function is:

● STEPHAN D. R. FEUCHTWANG, *An Anthropological Analysis of Chinese Geomancy*, (Vientiane, Laos: Editions Vithagna, 1974).

A technical, difficult but remarkable analysis of the systems in Chinese medicine is:

● MANFRED PORKERT, *The Theoretical Foundations of Chinese Medicine: Systems of Correspondence*, (Cambridge MA: MIT Press, 1974).

On the origin, development and decline of traditional Chinese cosmology, see:

● SARAH ALLEN, *The Shape of the Turtle: Myth, Art and Cosmos in Early China*, (New York: State University of New York Press, 1991).

JOHN B. HENDERSON, *The Development and Decline of Chinese Cosmology*, (New York: Columbia University Press, 1984).

A simple, concise encyclopedia of motifs in the "hidden symbolic language" of Chinese myth is:

WOLFRAM EBERHARD, *A Dictionary of Chinese Symbols*, trans. G. L. Campbell, (London and New York: Routledge/Methuen, 1986).

Psychology

The following form an introduction to the kind of depth psychology used to understand the imaginative impact of the *I Ching*, its symbols and its process of transformation.

An overview:

C. G. JUNG, *Man and his Symbols*, (New York: Bantam Books, 1st ed. 1964, many reprints).

C. G. JUNG, *Modern Man in Search of a Soul*, (New York: Harcourt Brace, 1st ed. 1955, many reprints).

From the *Collected Works:*

C.G. JUNG, *Collected Works*, trans. R. F. C. Hull, 20 vols and supplements, (Princeton: Princeton University Press, Bollingen Series xx, 1950–76).

CW 8: The Structure and Dynamics of the Psyche

CW 9i: The Archetypes and the Collective Unconscious

CW 11: Psychology and Religion East and West

The clearest synopsis of Jung's approach to psyche, archetype and the transformative nature of symbols is:

JOLANDE JACOBI, *Complex/Archetype/Symbol*, (Princeton: Princeton University Press, 1974).

On the inner search, soul-making, personifying, pathologizing, and the imaginal ego, see:

JAMES HILLMAN, *Insearch*, (Dallas TX: Spring Publications, 1967).

JAMES HILLMAN, *Re-visioning Psychology*, (New York: Harper and Row, 1975).

Chinese History, Traditional Culture and the Warring States Period

An interesting and dramatic account of traditional China is:

MARCEL GRANET, *Chinese Civilization*, (London: Routledge and Kegan Paul, 1930), translation of *La civilisation chinoise*, (Paris, 1929).

What is possibly the best single volume on Chinese thought written in this century remains untranslated:

● MARCEL GRANET, *La pensée chinoise*, (Paris, 1934).

An excellent source on ancient China is:

● HENRI MASPERO, *China in Antiquity*, trans. Frank A. Kierman of *La Chine antique* (Paris, 1965), (University of Massachusetts Press, 1978).

See also:

● HERRLEE G. CREEL, *The Birth of China*, (New York: Ungar Press, 1937).

● A. C. GRAHAM, *Disputers of the Tao: Philosophical Argument in Ancient China*, (LaSalle, IL: Open Court, 1985).

● DAVID KEIGHTLY, *Sources of Shang History*, (Berkeley: University of California Press, 1978).

● DAVID ROY and TSUEN-HSUIN TSIEN, eds, *Ancient China: Studies in Early Civilization*, (Hong Kong: Chinese University Press, 1978).

● BENJAMIN SCHWARTZ, *The World of Thought in Ancient China*, (Cambridge MA and London: Harvard University Press, 1985).

● ## *Philosophy, Religion, Literature*

A detailed overview:

● FUNG YULAN, *A History of Chinese Philosophy*, trans. Derk Bodde, 2 vols., (Princeton: Princeton University Press, 1952–3).

Excerpts from the "Taoist oriented *summa* of Chinese philosophy of the early Han" (c. 145 BCE), with a consideration of the key ideas of resonance and interconnection, is:

● CHARLES LE BLANC, *Huai Nan Tzu: Philosophical Synthesis in Early Han Thought*, (Hong Kong: Hong Kong University Press, 1985).

The beautiful and classic study of the tao in its literary origin is:

● ARTHUR WALEY, *The Way and its Power: A Study of the Tao Tê Ching and its Place in Chinese Thought*, (1934, rpt. New York: Grove Press, 1958).

An interesting and insightful description of the Five Classics, the central works of later culture, is found in:

● BURTON WATSON, *Early Chinese Literature*, (New York: Columbia University Press, 1962).

Diverse perspectives on the "way" and its many permutations in religious practices come from:

● HOLMES WELCH and ANNA SEIDEL, eds, *Facets of Taoism: Essays in Chinese Religion*, (New Haven: Yale University Press, 1979).

Discussions and documents from the Confucian and neo-Confucian school are found in:

* WM. THEODORE DU BARY, *Neo-Confucian Orthodoxy and the Learning of the Mind-Heart*, (New York: Columbia University Press, 1981).

* WING-TSIT CHAN (trans.), *Reflections on Things at Hand: The Neo-Confucian Anthology Compiled by Chu Hsi and Lü Tzu-Ch'ien*, (New York: Columbia University Press, 1967).

I Ching: History and Key Commentators

An excellent overview of various historical views on divination, preparatory to an equally interesting consideration of a key Sung Dynasty figure, is:

* J. A. ADLER, *Divination and Philosophy: Chu Hsi's Understanding of the I Ching*, (Ann Arbor: University Microfilms, 1984),

For "historicist" speculations on the first assembling of the book in the late Chou period and the sort of diviners who used it, see:

* EDWARD LOUIS SHAUGHNESSY, *The Composition of the Zhouyi*, (Ann Arbor: University Microfilms, 1983).

On the two fundamental schools of interpretation, *hsiang-shu* or "image-number," first associated with the *fang shih* or traveling magicians and diviners, and *i-li* or "moral-principle," first associated with the scholar-philosopher *Wang Pi* (226–273 CE), see:

* KENNETH J. DE WOSKIN, ed. and trans., *Doctors, Diviners and Magicians of Ancient China: Biographies of Fang Shih*, (New York: Columbia University Press, 1983).

* T'ANG YUNG-T'UNG, "Wang Pi's New Interpretation of the *I-Ching* and *Lun-yü*", trans. Walter Liebenthal, *Harvard Journal of Asiatic Studies*, 10/2 (1947).

* HOWARD GOODMAN, *Exegetes and Exegeses of the Book of Changes in the 3rd Century AD: Historical and Scholastic Contexts for Wang Pi*, (Ann Arbor: University Microfilms, 1985).

* RICHARD JOHN LYNN, *The Classic of Changes (as interpreted by Wang Bi)*, (New York: Columbia University Press, 1994).

On the pivotal Sung Dynasty re-interpretation of the *I Ching* (c.1100 CE), which altered the course of Chinese culture, see Adler, cited above, and:

* KIDDER SMITH JR, PETER K. BOL, JOSEPH A. ADLER and DON WYATT, *Sung Dynasty Uses of the I Ching*, (Princeton: Princeton University Press, 1990).

An extremely interesting look at a later interpreter whose perspective adds much to the modern psychological sense of the *I Ching* is:

* LARRY SCHULTZ, *Lai Chih-te (1525–1604) and the Phenomenology of the Classic of Change*, (Ann Arbor: University Microfilms, 1982).

An extensive examination of the mathematical aspects of *I Ching* divination is:

* LEO REISINGER, *Das I Ging: Eine formalwissenschaftliche Untersuchung des chinesichen Orakels*, (Acta Ethnologica et Linguistica 25/1972, Vienna).

A reconstruction of ancient practices involved in oracle consultation can be found in:

SHIH-CHUAN CHEN, "How to Form a Hexagram and Consult the I Ching," (*Journal of the American Oriental Society* 92, April-June 1972).

Translations

New *I Ching* translations are proliferating. Most do not go to the Chinese, but re-interpret existing standard translations. Others are versions of the oldest layers, the "original" *I Ching*, cut off from its later development. The first complete translation in English, still very interesting in its literal fidelity, was:

JAMES LEGGE, trans., edited and with an Introduction by Ch'u Chai and Winberg Chai, (New York: Bantam Books, 1964). This edition reproduces the version that appeared in the series *Sacred Books of the East* (1896).

The "landmark" translation into English, the first to take the book seriously as a spiritual document is:

RICHARD WILHELM AND CARY F. BAYNES, trans., *The I Ching or Book of Changes. The Richard Wilhelm Translation rendered into English by Cary F. Baynes*, 3rd ed., (Princeton: Princeton University Press, Bollingen Series xix, 1967).

However, Wilhelm's German translation (Jena, 1927), which Cary Baynes translated into English (1st ed. New York, 1950), consistently used an orthodox Neo-Confucian perspective. Other interpretations, equally stringent, can be found in Thomas Cleary's translations, published by Shambala Press:

THOMAS CLEARY, *The Taoist I Ching*, (1986).

THOMAS CLEARY, *The Buddhist I Ching*, (1987).

THOMAS CLEARY, *I Ching Mandalas*, (1992).

An extremely interesting version of the "original *I Ching*" is:

WU JING-NUAN, *Yijing*, (Washington, D.C.: Taoist Study Series, distributed by University of Hawaii Press, 1991).

Eranos

The Eranos Foundation has sponsored Conferences and published Yearbooks since 1933. Many of these papers have been gathered around key themes and translated in the series *Papers from the Eranos Yearbooks*, edited by Joseph Campbell and published by Princeton University Press as *Bollingen Series xxx*. For a better insight into what the Foundation is and does, see:

HENRY CORBIN, "The Time of Eranos," trans. Willard Trask, in *Man and Time: Papers from the Eranos Yearbooks*, vol.3.

MIRCEA ELIADE, "Encounters at Ascona," trans. Willard Trask in *Spiritual Disciplines: Papers from the Eranos Yearbooks*, vol. 4.

RUDOLF RITSEMA, "The Origins and Opus of Eranos," *Eranos 56/1987.*

RUDOLF RITSEMA, "Encompassing Versatility: Keystone of the Eranos Project," *Eranos 57/1988.*

UPPER TRIGRAMS

		FORCE	FIELD	SHAKE	GORGE
LOWER TRIGRAMS	**FORCE**	1	11	34	5
	FIELD	12	2	16	8
	SHAKE	25	24	51	3
	GORGE	6	7	40	29
	BOUND	33	15	62	39
	GROUND	44	46	32	48
	RADIANCE	13	36	55	63
	OPEN	10	19	54	60

● *A Key
to the
Hexagrams*

*To find the
hexagram that the
Oracle has given
you as an answer to
your question, locate
the lower trigram
on the left and the
upper trigram on
the top of the chart
above. Then turn to
the hexagram text
that the number
indicates.*

UPPER TRIGRAMS

	BOUND	GROUND	RADIANCE	OPEN	
	26	9	14	43	FORCE
	23	20	35	45	FIELD
	27	42	21	17	SHAKE
	4	59	64	47	GORGE
	52	53	56	31	BOUND
	18	57	50	28	GROUND
	22	37	30	49	RADIANCE
	41	61	38	58	OPEN

LOWER TRIGRAMS

THE ERANOS *I CHING PROJECT*

The purpose of the Eranos *I Ching Project* and the Round Table Sessions was to recover oracular language and the use of divination as a connection between the individual and the unseen – the world of images described in myth and dream, shamanic journey and mystery cult. It grew out of Eranos' long-term engagement with the fields of depth psychology, myth and the history of religions, an activity inspired in its beginnings by C. G. Jung's sense of the objective psyche.

The Eranos *I Ching Project* has three main aspects:

– this new translation of the *I Ching*'s divinatory texts which preserves the multivalence and depth of the oracular language;

– introductory sessions on the use of these divinatory images;

– an exploration of the areas in Western imagination and culture these images activate and renew.